Praise for *Industrial Policy for the United States*

A strong, vibrant manufacturing sector is critical to the future prosperity of the United States and its workers. The authors provide enormous background, case studies, and analysis about how to implement strong trade and industrial policies to restore America's leadership in innovation and manufacturing – and the good jobs that come with it. Even the most controversial policy recommendations are worthy of review and consideration, no matter your position on trade policies. This should be required reading for any policymaker working to increase America's productive capacity and strengthen our supply chains.

Rep. Earl Blumenauer (D-OR)
Ranking Member Subcommittee on
Trade House Ways and Means Committee

Industrial Policy for the United States is truly impressive. While readers may disagree with some of its recommendations, almost all will find its documentation of the practice over the last three centuries a source of valuable historical perspective. And its assessments of past successes and failures – overseas and in the US – will be helpful to policymakers in a world where industrial policy is likely to become de rigueur.

Willy Shih
Robert & Jane Cizik Baker Foundation
Professor of Management Practice
Harvard Business School

Industrial Policy for the United States is an indispensable guide for CEOs – multinationals to small and medium-sized manufacturers – for understanding and taking full advantage of America's return to industrial policy. Equally valuable, it is also a guide to what US business should ask of our government to help them succeed against Chinese and other foreign competition. The book convincingly rebuts the "leave everything to the market" argument against industrial policy and quantifies the horrific damage done to our businesses, workers, and national security during our decades-long pursuit of the free trade mirage. It explains, in theory and through country and industry case studies, why government support of US innovation and manufacturing, the strategic use of tariffs to ensure that things are made as well as invented here, and ending the overvaluation of the dollar are all necessary for sustained success. Its comprehensive, well-thought-out, and coherent set of policy recommendations should be required reading for every policymaker in Washington.

Dan DiMicco
Former Chairman and CEO Nucor

There has been a global trend of policymakers drifting away from laissez faire and free trade, because of various reasons. And that story has not been explained rigorously enough by most books and research papers that exist today. This in-depth treatise on industrial policy fills in this huge gap in a scintillating manner with references and explanations from across the world. The book provides the reader with the intellectual ammunition needed to contrast and compare various policy pathways and their potential impact on industries.

Badri Narayanan
Former Head of Trade and Commerce NITI
Aayog Lead Trade Advisor to PM Narendra Modi

State ownership and control of industry have failed, as has leaving everything to the market. Instead, governments need judicious and evidence-based industrial policies. This book makes a brilliant case for the same, combining strategic guidance by the state with the innovative potential of competitive enterprise. Everyone who cares about our economic future should read this.

Geoffrey M. Hodgson
Emeritus Professor of Economics Loughborough
University Editor in Chief Journal of Institutional Economics

If America and its democratic allies are to recover the economic and strategic bulk lost over the last four decades, elected officials and policymakers will need a plan. No longer can they blindly put their hopes in the abstractions of free-market ideology. They must have industrial policy tethered to the reality of strategic competition. Our strategic rivals are embracing industrial policy to our detriment; we must respond. This excellent book lights the way ahead.

Andrew Hastie
Member of Parliament and Shadow
Minister for Defence Commonwealth of Australia

A well-written, well-reasoned, and remarkably thorough case for a much more vigorous and targeted industrial policy. It correctly argues that markets alone will not optimize output from the most valuable industries because of significant market failures. Its detailed, well-articulated proposal for a specific "industrial policy for the United States" should give free-market acolytes pause and progressives ammunition in the battle for an industrial revival.

Jeffrey Fuhrer
Nonresident Fellow Brookings Institution
Foundation Fellow Eastern Bank Foundation

So much economic analysis and controversy misses the real heart of our current crisis – America's *industries*, especially manufacturing, and why they keep losing ground to foreign competitors. This book finally gives a complete picture of what went wrong and what we can do about it. I especially appreciated the discussion of how the development and deployment of innovations depend on not only the private sector, but also on crucial, underappreciated programs like the Manufacturing Extension Partnership and Manufacturing USA. If American industry is to convincingly recover its formerly world-leading position, this country will need to support every step of the innovation pipeline, not just pure science and defense-oriented technologies, across the entire industrial spectrum.

Carroll Thomas Former Director Manufacturing
Extension Partnership

The fight to control tomorrow's strategic industries will not be determined by market forces but by industrial policy. This superb and timely book explains why and how America must act if it is to be a major player in the world's industrial future.

Stewart Paterson
Author China, Trade and Power:
Why the West's Economic Engagement Has Failed

Without a doubt this is the most definitive analysis of industrial policy ever written. For anyone interested in industrial policy and its implications for the economy, this is the perfect source and a real triumph!

Barry Bluestone
Professor Emeritus of Public Policy
and Urban Affairs Russell B. and Andree B. Stearns
Trustee Professor of Political Economy
Northeastern University

Research, discussion, and policy initiatives advocating industrial policy for the US are spreading in the wake of the failure of neoliberal doctrines to deliver inclusive growth and technological leadership. Fasteau and Fletcher's seminal contribution advances this agenda and paves the way for a proactive commonsensical set of industrial policies.

John Komlos
Professor Emeritus of Economics
and Economic History University of Munich

This book illuminates the path through the complexities and escalating costs of industry and advanced manufacturing, where current US policy is insufficient. Presenting a detailed plan and advocating for a whole-of-government industrial policy, it offers essential guidance for students and policymakers to navigate and shape the future of American industry.

David Bourne
Principal Scientist, Robotics Carnegie Mellon
Associate Director Manufacturing Futures Institute

Fasteau and Fletcher have assembled an extraordinarily comprehensive work on industrial history and strategy. It should be a must-read for policymakers. It is an impressive and insightful exploration and analysis of not just America's industrial past, present, and future, but of how its competencies compare to the rest of the world. Moreover, the authors have compiled such a tremendous amount of data in making their case that this book will serve as an essential go-to reference book for years to come.

Ira Moskowitz
CEO Advanced Robotics for Manufacturing
Institute Former Vice President General Manager
of US Operations Analog Devices Inc.

The authors demolish the illusion that our post–WWII economic dominance was the result of the private sector on its own developing and commercializing technologies from the underlying science. They address the need for a multipronged growth policy targeting a portfolio of high technologies with a market focus. They rightly advocate investment in R&D, capital formation, labor upskilling, and technological infrastructure, and address the quasi-public-good nature of much of this investment, necessitating a combined government–industry approach. Although recent legislation offers hope for such reforms, the jury is still out, making this book very timely.

Gregory Tassey
Economic Policy Research
Center University of Washington

This book explores the profound effects of America's failure to embark on sound industrial policies and how these could evolve. Importantly, it makes a real contribution in pulling together the economic side of industrial policy: the need to pull together manufacturing promotion, trade, and exchange rate policies.

William Bonvillian
Lecturer Massachusetts Institute of Technology
Former Senior Policy Advisor US Senate

This book turns an opinion not widely held not so long ago into a statement of the obvious through the logic inherent in the wealth of facts it deploys. Its powerful argument for America to adopt a coherent industrial policy is driven home by cataloguing the deleterious impact unbridled globalized free trade has had on the US economy and chronicling the successes (and failures) in this field of America's competitors. Fasteau and Fletcher have managed to cram more common sense into one book than any author since Tom Paine.

Nicholas Comfort
Author Surrender: How British Industry
Gave Up the Ghost, 1952–2012

A major cause of the declining wages of non-elite workers over the past decades has been the deindustrialization of America. In this remarkable volume Fasteau and Fletcher present a powerful case for coherent industrial policy that can reverse this disturbing trend. They discuss in detail both successful and unsuccessful past experiences of governments implementing industrial policy worldwide, and how industrial policy should be implemented in practice. Anybody who worries about where America is heading needs to read this book.

Peter Turchin
Author End Times: Elites, Counter-elites, and
the Path of Political Disintegration

As questions about technological competitiveness and the accelerating loss of good jobs press themselves ever more intensely to the front of public debate, industrial policy looms as a nearly inescapable imperative for US policy makers. This extremely timely book is the most thorough historical and comparative examination of industrial policy practice and variants across the advanced political economies. No informed discussion of our industrial options in the US moving forward should proceed without familiarity with the arguments in this book.

Gary Herrigel
Paul Klapper Professor College
and Division of Social Science Department
of Political Science University of Chicago

Industrial Policy for the United States

The U.S. is losing the international competition for good jobs and high-value industries because Washington largely believes trade should be free, the dollar should float, and innovation comes from the private sector. In this book, the authors make the bold case that such laissez-faire ideas have failed and that a robust industrial policy is the best way for America to remain prosperous and secure. Trump and Biden have enacted some elements, yet America now needs something systematic and comprehensive, including tariffs, a competitive exchange rate, and federal support for commercialization—not just invention—of new technologies.

Timely, meticulously researched, and bipartisan, this impressive analysis replaces misunderstandings about industrial policy with lucid explanations of its underlying economic theory, the tools that implement it, and its successes (and failures) in America and abroad. It examines key industries of the past and future – steel, automobiles, television, semiconductors, space, aviation, robotics, and nanotechnology, while offering an actionable policy roadmap.

A work of rigor and ambition, *Industrial Policy for the United States* is essential reading.

Marc Fasteau is a vice-chair of the Coalition of a Prosperous America. Before founding an insurance company acquired by Progressive, he was a partner at Dillon Read & Co., a New York investment bank. Earlier in his career he served on the professional staffs of the US Senate majority leader, the Joint Economic Committee and the House Banking and Currency Committee. He is a graduate of Harvard College and Harvard Law School, where he was on the Harvard Law Review.

Ian Fletcher is on the Advisory Board of the Coalition for a Prosperous America. He is the author of *Free Trade Doesn't Work* and coauthor of *The Conservative Case against Free Trade*. He was a senior economist at the Coalition and previously a research fellow at the US Business and Industry Council. He was educated at Columbia and the University of Chicago.

Industrial Policy for the United States

Winning the Competition for Good
Jobs and High-Value Industries

Marc Fasteau
Ian Fletcher

CAMBRIDGE
UNIVERSITY PRESS

Shaftesbury Road, Cambridge CB2 8EA, United Kingdom

One Liberty Plaza, 20th Floor, New York, NY 10006, USA

477 Williamstown Road, Port Melbourne, VIC 3207, Australia

314–321, 3rd Floor, Plot 3, Splendor Forum, Jasola District Centre,
New Delhi – 110025, India

103 Penang Road, #05–06/07, Visioncrest Commercial, Singapore 238467

Cambridge University Press is part of Cambridge University Press & Assessment,
a department of the University of Cambridge.

We share the University's mission to contribute to society through the pursuit of
education, learning and research at the highest international levels of excellence.

www.cambridge.org
Information on this title: www.cambridge.org/9781009243070

DOI: 10.1017/9781009243087

First published 2024

Printed in Mexico by Litográfica Ingramex, S.A. de C.V.

A catalogue record for this publication is available from the British Library

A Cataloging-in-Publication data record for this book is available from the Library
of Congress

ISBN 978-1-009-24307-0 Hardback
ISBN 978-1-009-24305-6 Paperback

For Anne
For Abby

The general reader will have to make up his mind whether he wants simple answers to his questions or *useful* ones – in this as in other economic matters he cannot have both.

Joseph Schumpeter, 1930

CONTENTS

FIGURES

TABLES

Preface

This book advocates for a coherent and comprehensive industrial policy for the United States, so it must deal with the dominant view of most US economists, policymakers, journalists, and citizens that industrial policy has not worked and cannot work. Americans have been inculcated to believe that government intervention in industries should be limited to funding basic research and correcting a few market failures, that trade can and should be free, and that exchange rates should be left to the market.

For this book to help change this paradigm, it must explain what industrial policy is, explicitly address the arguments against it, and make the arguments in its favor. It therefore addresses industrial policy's underlying economic theory, its policy tools, and how these tools have been successfully and unsuccessfully deployed in other countries, in the US, and in several key industries.

Our argument identifies three pillars of industrial policy:

1. Supporting innovation, commercialization, and retention in the US of what we call "advantageous" industries
2. Designing and implementing trade policies to support and, when necessary, protect these industries from imports and to pressure foreign governments to reduce the obstacles they place on US exports of the products of these industries
3. Managing the dollar's exchange rate to the level that balances US trade and countering the efforts of other governments to manipulate their currencies to make their goods cheaper in our markets and ours more expensive in theirs

We explain how deeply entwined these pillars are and how they must be coordinated to avoid working at cross-purposes and sapping the efficacy of multibillion-dollar US innovation and manufacturing programs.

This is virgin territory. To our knowledge, no US university has a degree-granting program in industrial policy – either by this or another name – covering this ground. With very few exceptions, these three phenomena are studied in silos. Because we are starting almost from scratch, our argument must be fully elaborated to be persuasive.

We also believe that sound industrial policy must be highly specific to industries and the domestic and international context in which they compete. This requires an understanding of its general principles *and* a granular feel for how varied and tailored to specific circumstances the application of these principles must be. The latter can be conveyed only through the particularities of national histories and industry case studies.

So this is a big book, because industrial policy for the US is a big subject. We have tried to make it both technically sound *and* accessible to readers without expertise in economics. Given its length and scope, we expect that some readers will choose certain chapters over others, hopefully while noting and taking comfort that the topics of the other chapters are covered in depth.

To help navigate the book, here is its structure with its underlying logic:

The Introduction describes the economic crisis that motivated us to write this book and summarizes the industrial policy we propose to resolve it.

Part I The Underlying Economics

Chapter 1, "Why the Free Market Can't Do Everything," explains why free markets on their own cannot deliver prosperity and why purely free-market thinking cannot design industrial policies that can.

Chapter 2, "The Dynamics of Advantageous Industries," spells out our concept of "advantageous" industries and the economics that derives from it.

Chapter 3, "The Industrial Policy Tool Kit," describes the tools governments worldwide have used to implement industrial policy based on this alternative view of economics.

Chapter 4, "Trade, Currencies, and Industrial Policy," explains how international trade, including comparative advantage and foreign exchange rates, fits into our economic theory and policy proposals.

Part II Country Case Studies

These studies:

1. Exemplify the principles, practices, successes, and pitfalls of industrial policy more completely than the history of US industrial policy alone
2. Rebut critics who argue that industrial policy has never truly succeeded or, where its success is undeniable, that it is due to a culture or political structure so different from ours that the US should not even bother to try
3. Show that industrial policy has driven rapid, high-quality economic development using the same basic principles in many countries with widely differing cultures and governments
4. Illustrate the many ways industrial policy must address a nation's stage of economic development, its political structure, the sophistication of its industries, and the trade and exchange-rate policies of other countries
5. Show that industrial policy failures are not due to unknowable causes but to readily comprehensible and thus avoidable errors in understanding and applying its strategies and tools

Each country chapter serves this expository purpose in a different way:

Chapter 5, "Japan: The First Asian Miracle," describes an extreme and clear case of successful, proactive industrial policy, and the first that attracted American attention. The chapter introduces the all-important Asian economic model and how industrial policy plays out over time at national scale.

Chapter 6, "Korea: Development despite Turbulence," discusses that country's industrial policy, derived from Japan's, showing how industrial policy has been transmitted around the world as a *practitioners' tradition* rather than a theoretical doctrine. This chapter is more historical, concrete, and industry-specific than Japan's.

Chapter 7, "China: Pursuing Economic Hegemony through Mercantilism," explores how that country's extremely proactive, systematic, and aggressive industrial policy – drawn from those of Japan and Korea – ups the ante to a full-blown economic challenge to the US. Geopolitics and national security enter the narrative here.

Chapter 8, "Germany: The Art of Relationship Capitalism," extends our model beyond East Asia and introduces the idea of *indirect* multilevel industrial policies, in sharp contrast to the explicit, centralized East Asian approach.

Chapter 9, "France: The Triumph and Failures of the State," comes next because that country's record of both success and failure, despite having all the ingredients for success, is instructive.

Chapter 10, "Britain: No Theory and Little Execution," is the first example of a systematically *un*successful industrial policy, chosen because its familiarity to Americans makes its travails easier to grasp.

Chapter 11, "India: Dysfunctional Socialism, Directionless Capitalism," is another failure case and a Third World example to show that our theory applies to radically different societies and levels of development. It is also a revealing comparator to China.

Chapter 12, "Argentina: A Dual Cautionary Tale," because that country's decades of catastrophic industrial policy failures give a readily understood picture of what *not* to do and of how repeated lurches toward laissez faire also failed.

The country case studies precede America's own industrial-policy history to make clear the powerful effects that foreign industrial policies have had on the US economy and the challenges they will pose to the US going forward. Summaries of the strengths and weaknesses of these nations' industrial policies are included for the benefit of readers who may not wish to read all these chapters.

Part III The Forgotten History

Chapter 13, "The Renaissance Origins of Industrial Policy," because the centuries-long, multi-continental record of industrial policy's success bolsters its credibility today.

Chapter 14, "US Industrial Policy 1750–1865: Developing a New Nation," shows how, contrary to prevailing myth, the US was founded as protectionist nation and used industrial policy to develop economically.

Chapter 15, "US Industrial Policy 1866–1939: The High Point of Protectionism," describes the forgotten hand of industrial policy in well-known events from the Civil War to the Great Depression.

Chapter 16, "US Industrial Policy 1940–1973: The Golden Age of the US Economy," explains how the US abandoned its successful heritage of protectionism and, due to the Cold War, undertook massive governmental support for technology development.

Chapter 17, "US Industrial Policy 1974–2007: Doubling Down on Free Markets," describes how the US largely misdiagnosed its growing economic problems and, instead of returning to sound trade and industrial policies, chose increasingly extreme free-market strategies.

Chapter 18, "US Industrial Policy 2008–Present: The End of the Old Order," tells how Obama tried but failed to fix these problems by doubling down on free-market policies, and how Trump challenged this consensus, breaking new ground that Biden built on.

Part IV Innovation as a System

These chapters make two important points. First, they show that the US *already* has quite a lot of effective industrial policy, even if not recognized as such, supporting our thesis that the US can design and execute coherent industrial policy. Second, they highlight deficiencies of America's current innovation system that need fixing. The detail in these chapters is needed to make clear the scope, diversity, and mechanisms of existing programs. They show how innovation is not a one-size-fits-all process, but requires institutions tailored to the needs of specific industries and contexts.

Chapter 19, "Governmentally Supported Innovations," provides striking counterexamples against the widely held belief that almost all innovation comes from the private sector.

Chapter 20, "Federal Science and Technology Programs," describes the most established, least controversial, most widely understood federal programs supporting innovation.

Chapter 21, "Federal Proactive Innovation Programs," turns to lesser known, more controversial institutions that exemplify what the authors would like to see happen, as opposed to what already exists.

Chapter 22, "Industrial Policy for Advanced Manufacturing," looks at advanced manufacturing to elucidate the key battlefield where innovation rivalry will play out.

Chapter 23, "Micro-governance of Industrial Policy," examines the organization and management of day-to-day operations of industrial policy agencies for innovation and its commercialization.

Chapter 24, "The Crisis of the American Patent System," describes the decline of our patent system that will be a major negative for US industrial policy unless reversed. It is also a revealing case study of special interests' corruption of obscure and technical but extremely important policies.

Part V Industry Case Studies

Chapter 25, "Automobiles: Decline and a Chance at Revival," introduces the reader to what failed US industrial policy looks like on a multi-decade, industry-specific level.

Chapter 26, "Semiconductors, Aviation, and Space: The Military Developmental State," covers military industrial policies in the three industries in which the post–World War II US has had the most success at industrial policy.

Chapter 27, "Robotics: A Global Industrial Policy Competition," describes the superior scale and sophistication of foreign industrial policy in an industry that is already important and will only become more so.

Chapter 28, "Nanotechnology: Is America Losing the Future?," shows how much technological "wide open space" there is for new industries and industrial policies.

Part VI Cluster Case Studies

Chapter 29, "The Massachusetts Life Sciences Cluster," features a state-level industrial policy success story and a good illustration of how to tailor policies to the characteristics and needs of the industry being supported.

Chapter 30, "The Upstate New York Semiconductor Cluster," shows how state-level policies require many different players and, ultimately, support from Washington.

Recommendations

Recommendations answers the question, "Assuming our argument is valid, what specifically should the government do now?" Some recommendations will lose relevance as circumstances change. But even these will remain valuable as illustrations of the policy implications of our proposed economics.

INTRODUCTION

The US has been losing the international competition for high-value industries and the good jobs, wealth, tax revenues, and national defense capabilities they provide.

From 1998 to 2010, 6 million US manufacturing jobs disappeared.[1] Many – 3.5 million between 1991 and 2019 alone – are estimated to have been lost due to imports.[2] Real wages for nonsupervisory workers have stagnated for 40 years in part because of such job losses.[3] Consumers have benefited from the imports, but not enough to outweigh the lost industries and jobs.

The lost industries are not all low-tech. The US runs an annual $200 billion-plus deficit in Advanced Technology Products made by the very industries in which *we* were the innovators and first movers.[4] Competitor nations have turned American scientific and technological advances into new products they make and industries they dominate.

Our trade deficit in goods is the broadest measure of our deindustrialization. In 2023, it exceeded $1 *trillion*, about 4 percent of GDP.[5] Because these deficits go back decades, other nations have accumulated $18 trillion of US assets net of American overseas assets, making us the world's largest net debtor.[6] Foreign-owned stocks, corporate bonds, and government bonds are now a massive claim on our future private-sector earnings and tax revenues.[7] GDP has been estimated to be as much as 20 percent less than if our trade had been balanced over the past five decades.[8]

America's trade surplus in services – $288 billion in 2023 – is not large enough to compensate for our deficit in goods.[9] Manufacturing has become a sick sector. In 2022, the share of manufactured goods sold in the US that is made there fell to 66 percent, a record low.[10] Labor productivity in manufacturing has been declining.[11] Arguments that manufacturing is healthy turn on measurement errors.[12]

Key military components now come from abroad, some from China and other adversaries, leaving the US exposed to supply cutoffs, sabotage, and spyware.[13] The COVID-19 pandemic revealed the vulnerability of America's medical and other important supply chains.

A comprehensive and coherent industrial policy is required to solve these manifold, interrelated problems.

The US government has recently taken important first steps in this direction. It has imposed policies to revive manufacturing in semiconductors, clean energy, and EVs, and to bolster R&D and its commercialization in these and other key industries. Similar reforms should now be made across a much wider range of industries.

Crucially, for these reforms to be succeed, our trade policy must be replaced with one that comprehensively and systematically supports them. America's free trade policy, forged in a long-vanished era of global economic dominance, has failed in both theory and practice. Innovative economic modeling has shown how well-designed tariffs, to give only one example of industrial policy, could give us better jobs, higher incomes, and GDP growth.[14]

What Is Industrial Policy?

Industrial policy is the deliberate governmental support of *industries*, with such support falling into two categories. First are broad policies that assist all industries, such as exchange rate management and tax breaks for R&D. Second are policies that target *particular* industries or technologies, such as tariffs, subsidies, government procurement, export controls, and technological research done or funded by government.

Until very recently, industrial policy has been dismissed in the US as a recipe for ill-advised, inefficient interventions in free markets, both domestically and abroad. Domestically, it has been associated with failing industries, such as steel in the 1980s, lobbying for bailouts.[15] It has been associated with companies, such as Lockheed in the 1970s and Chrysler in the 1980s, that appeared to fail the test of market competition and needed government help to survive.[16] And it has been associated with purported boondoggles such as synthetic fuels and the breeder reactor.[17]

Abroad, industrial policy has been associated with governments propping up failing state-owned companies while mismanaging them. It has been blamed for commercially unviable lunges for technological sophistication such as the Anglo-French Concorde and the European computer industry. It has been blamed for expensive, failed attempts to transplant modern industry to developing nations.

But systematic, proactive industrial policy is in fact the norm for the rich, technologically advanced nations America competes with, especially in East Asia and Continental Europe. There it is not only believed in as theory – it is what governments actually do.[18] Sometimes their policies are overt and sometimes they are obscured, but they definitely exist.

When properly implemented, these policies have worked. The most obvious evidence is that some high-wage nations, such as Germany and Japan, that employ them have done better at holding onto valuable industries and their jobs than the US (see Chapters 5 and 8).[19] Meanwhile, China and other low-wage nations have used industrial policies to establish strong new positions in key industries (see Chapter 7).

Because these foreign successes have come, in part, from targeting industries and taking them away from the US, these policies require an American response.

The ongoing success in the US of a few high-value, high-wage industries, such as aircraft manufacturing (see Chapters 15 and 26), that *have* benefited from effective industrial policy shows that our government can design and implement it, and that the payoff is large. The recent emergence in the US of private-sector space launch, deliberately nurtured by industrial policy, shows that America can still create major new industries in this way (see Chapter 26).

Comprehensive, proactive industrial policy has substantial domestic precedents. During World War II, we implemented industrial policies that reached into every sector of our economy. The Cold War was fought using industrial policies to support science, technology, and the military industrial base. Further back in American history, it is possible to trace more than 200 years of diverse, changing, but often highly effective industrial policies (see Chapters 14–16).

Industrial policy is not a conservative versus liberal question, as it has credible arguments and a policy heritage in both parties.[20] In 2019, Senator Marco Rubio (R-FL) issued a report calling for proactive industrial policies to counter Beijing's Made-in-China 2025 industrial policy initiative.[21] That same year, Senator Elizabeth Warren (D-MA) issued a manifesto, "A Plan for Economic Patriotism," calling for industrial policies and the centralization of economic policy in a new Department of Economic Development.[22]

America's Neglect of Industrial Policy

America already has many de facto industrial policies. These include federal science funding, tax credits for R&D, subsidized loans for everything from exports to housing to college, and occasional bailouts for sectors and firms. In addition, states and localities spend $90 billion annually in grants, rebates, and foregone taxes as incentives for firms to remain or locate in their jurisdictions.[23]

The US also has industry-specific industrial policies for defense, pharmaceuticals, space, green energy, agriculture, and – new with the Biden administration – computer chips, batteries, and EVs. However, almost all of these policies aim at noneconomic objectives, with economic benefits not the primary motivation in their formulation or adoption. Industrial policy programs such as Manufacturing USA and the Manufacturing Extension Partnership whose purpose *is* deliberately economic are effective, but far too small (see Chapters 21 and 22).

Since World War II, the US has not recognized, let alone acted upon, the fact that its industries' problems require a coherent, integrated, and continuing response at the highest levels of government. Instead, it has done three things. First, it has responded in a reactive and short-term fashion, imposing industrial policies only under the pressure of crisis and pulling back when crisis has passed (see Chapters 16 and 17). Second, it has coordinated only weakly, if at all, the relevant policies – for example, tariff policy, exchange rate management, the tax code, scientific research, governmental technology development, and workforce training. Third, while engaging in quite a lot of de facto industrial policy, it has until Biden denied engaging in industrial policy at all. The failure to acknowledge such measures *as* industrial policy has contributed to America's continuing misunderstanding of what it is and what it can accomplish.

In the decades after World War II, the US outperformed other major economies in every important industry, in large part because it was not ravaged by war. So, as the concrete of its postwar policies, assumptions, and institutions set, it did not seem to *need* much deliberate industrial policy. The conviction developed that the US was so strong economically that, in pursuit of geopolitical goals such as shoring up Cold War alliances, it could afford to allow its allies to chip away portions of American industry. And over subsequent decades, they did.

The US put its faith in the international institutional architecture it created. The Bretton Woods currency system, the International Monetary Fund, the World Bank, and the General Agreement on Tariffs and Trade were believed to reduce the risk of another war, cement the Free World against the Communist Bloc, and contribute to the prosperity of all participating nations. As America was the leading producer of advanced manufactured goods, its leaders thought the country had everything to gain and nothing to lose from progressively freer trade. So, they embraced an economic ideology that assumed the sufficiency of free markets, the win-win character of international trade, the willingness of other nations to abide by free trade rules, and, later, the declining importance of manufacturing.

The evidence that this ideology and its implementing policies have failed has now been accumulating for decades.

The China Threat

Industrial policy is back on the agenda in large part because of China, the first combined military and economic threat America has faced in more than 200 years. Beijing engages in extremely proactive, systematic, and aggressive industrial policy (see Chapter 7) and its economy, second in size only to that of the US, was until recently growing more than 6 percent per year.[24]

China's success is prima facie evidence that industrial policy can work and that near total reliance on free markets is not the only, or even the best, path to economic development. Its success has discredited the idea that the world will inevitably see the benefits of, and converge on, America's market-oriented economic ideology.[25]

China has also dispelled the idea that trade is always a win-win game, because it has become clear that much of its growth has come at the expense of the US. An increasing number of Chinese industries are in acute rivalry with high-value American industries, and China's gains are our losses.

The US cannot remain a military superpower without being an industrial superpower. The supply chains for advanced American weapons now have large, dangerous gaps. Some are the result of Beijing's deliberate targeting of key technologies with the aim of not only taking over their production but also making the US dependent on Chinese output.[26]

The Return of Industrial Policy

Over the past 15 years, industrial policy has been slowly filtering back into America's policy space.[27] Although not so characterized at the time, the 2008–10 federal rescue of the auto industry was a classic act of industrial policy. It was a success, though more needs to be done if the industry is to remain healthy (see Chapter 25).[28]

In 2021 and 2022, Biden proposed and Congress enacted the Bipartisan Infrastructure Act (BIA), the CHIPS and Science Act (CHIPS), and the Inflation Reduction Act (IRA). These ambitious new programs, combined with their *explicitly pro–industrial policy* rationales, were a big step forward.

The $550 billion BIA authorized upgrades to the nation's infrastructure.[29] The CHIPS Act authorized $170 billion for government-wide R&D and $52 billion in subsidies for semiconductor R&D and manufacturing, plus tax credits and other incentives (see Chapter 18).[30] The IRA authorized $370 billion in incentives to shift industry and consumers to clean energy.[31]

Economic nationalism is returning to the US. The IRA includes buy American requirements with only limited exemptions. The CHIPS Acts incentivizes US and foreign firms to build advanced chip factories *in the* US and prohibits participating firms from producing advanced semiconductors in China and other "countries of concern" for 10 years.[32]

In a significant departure from past practice, the BIA, the IRA, and CHIPS explicitly endorsed and embodied a number of core industrial policy principles. First, that economic and technological leadership and secure supply chains in civilian industries, not just defense industries, are critical to national security. Second, that making things, not just inventing them, is required for prosperity. Third, that large-scale government investment is needed to foster commercialization of new technologies and support US manufacturing in high technology and other economically important industries.

But much remains to be done. Trade policy should be reconfigured to support US industrial policy and counter other countries' efforts to thwart it (see Chapter 4). More funding should be allocated to flagship manufacturing programs, while others need refinement (see Chapters 21 and 22). Because the overvalued dollar is the single greatest headwind to reshoring industries, reducing imports, and making US exports more competitive, capital controls should be used to manage its value down to the level that balances America's trade (see Chapter 4).

Finally, to prevent backsliding, the theoretical foundations of opposition to industrial policy should be skeptically reexamined. They should be replaced with a version of economics that takes into account important realities ignored by American mainstream economics and that can therefore guide sound industrial policy.

Mainstream Economics Doesn't Understand Industrial Policy

Mainstream US economists have opposed industrial policy for decades.[33] During the Japanese challenge to American manufacturing in the 1970s and 1980s, interest in industrial policy surged. But, as Paul Krugman, who played a significant role in the Democratic Party's decision *not* to embrace it in the early 1980s, later correctly wrote:[34]

> Economists have been extremely negative about the idea of industrial policy even in principle. The general presumption of most economic theory is that the best industrial policy is to let the market work – that

decentralized incentives of the marketplace will push resources to the places with the highest expected return, and that no second-guessing of market decisions is necessary or desirable.[35]

The US will not be able to successfully implement a systematic industrial policy until this thinking is refuted and replaced by economic theory that shows how industrial policy can succeed. America also needs such a theory to understand the strategies other nations are using against us and effectively parry them.

Theories matter. Despite the dominance of purely practical considerations and interest group politics in the short run, nations' long-term, big-picture economic decisions generally depend upon them. These theories can be explicitly articulated or so widely accepted that they are not even noticed. As John Maynard Keynes once wrote:

> The ideas of economists and political philosophers, both when they are right and when they are wrong, are more powerful than is commonly understood. Indeed, the world is ruled by little else. Practical men, who believe themselves to be quite exempt from any intellectual influences, are usually the slaves of some defunct economist . . . But, soon or late, it is ideas, not vested interests, which are dangerous for good or evil.[36]

The 2008 financial crisis dented the credibility of mainstream economics, most of whose practitioners failed to anticipate it or propose measures to avoid it. Public skepticism should expand from financial economics to other branches of the discipline that are getting things wrong – to the economics of trade, the economics of growth, and the economics of technology – as these are the keys to understanding and designing industrial policy.

A major problem with mainstream economics, once one gets past recitations of free-market theology and looks at the actual scholarship, is that it is only good at understanding things that are well suited to mathematical modeling, such as price setting in freely competitive markets.[37] It has weak insight into organization, management, corporate strategy, R&D, engineering, workforce development, the origins of technology, product design, policy-making by governments, and the strategies nations use to compete. None of these reduce to equations well, but they are central to how modern firms, governments, and thus economies function. Even some fields that *do* mathematize well, such as finance and international trade, are prone to oversimplifications that lead to false conclusions.[38]

An Alternative but Credible Economics

This book takes current mainstream economics as its starting point and analyzes why it does not accurately describe how the world works. Our analysis nevertheless relies on many of its well-accepted ideas.[39] In fact, many of our *un*conventional ideas are not explicitly deemed false by mainstream economics. Rather, they are poorly integrated into the overall picture, swept to the corners of public discourse, abandoned but never refuted. One scholar has described them as "an underground river, springing to the surface only every few decades," often under the pressure of crisis.[40] Above all, their implications are rejected, ignored, or downplayed.

Mainstream economics, in a nutshell, holds that free markets are always, or with only a few exceptions, best. It concedes the appropriateness of nonmarket provision of public goods like pure science and national security, and social insurance programs like Medicare and Social Security. It accepts the efficacy of Keynesian countercyclical spending. But it holds that the *productive core* of the economy, where innovation, growth, and wealth are generated, is, and to be effective must be, a free market.

In contrast, the economics of this book holds that economic success requires, right at the very core of the economy, not only a) letting free markets work, but also b) *systematically exploiting gaps in free-market logic.*[41] And because such exploitation, by definition, involves things markets *can't* do, government intervention is generally the only way to accomplish this.

This view is actually closer to how real-world businesses are run. Businesses necessarily make money by exploiting market imperfections because where markets are perfect, competition squeezes profits toward zero.[42] Everybody wants perfect markets when they are the buyer but imperfect markets when they are the seller. The consumer-side view of economics and the producer-side view thus differ, and one way to understand the approach of this book is to grasp that mainstream economics is biased to contemplate almost entirely the former, while this book gives them more equal consideration.[43]

A concise definition of industrial policy, as the term is used in this book, may be helpful: *Industrial policy is government interventions in the economy based on the following propositions.*

1. Economic activities differ in value.
2. A laissez faire policy will not maximize a nation's capture of the most valuable economic activities.
3. Government interventions can enable the capture of more.

Using government policies to overcome, and in many situations take advantage of, market shortcomings is how industrial policy can attract, grow, and retain high value – or, in the terminology we will introduce, "advantageous" – economic activities and the industries that host them.

What America Needs

The US does not need, and politically would not accept, a large new government agency with authority over all of its industrial policies.[44] But it does need a reasonably coherent *set of policies* involving all relevant government agencies and coordinated at the highest levels of government. Its main elements (detailed in Recommendations) should be:

1. Expansion of domestic programs designed to support manufacturing, especially in the creation and commercialization of innovation.
2. Controls on international capital flows to drive the dollar down to a value that produces balanced trade – that is, an average of surpluses and deficits close to zero.
3. Tariffs (and occasionally quotas and related policies) to protect specific industries of high economic value, especially in advanced manufacturing.
4. Tariffs (and ditto) to protect industries important for military reasons, for public health, or because they are strategic chokepoints for the whole economy, such as semiconductors.
5. Policies to deny economic and geopolitical adversaries key technologies developed by the US and its allies.

Industrial policy is often characterized as requiring that the government, rather than the marketplace, "pick winners," a practice criticized as both inefficient and unfair. But for a developed nation like the US, almost all sound industrial policy would *not* involve picking winners, as it would not directly choose which firms make a profit. And in the few unavoidable cases, not picking winners would just allow a foreign government to move leadership in the sector to one of its own companies.

Concerns that an American industrial policy would be distorted and made ineffective by corruption and capture by special interests are legitimate. But these problems are likely to be no worse than in other major areas of economic policy. As elsewhere, rent-seeking will generate opposition because it is a known problem and a resented behavior.

What This Book Does Not Discuss

Economies include both traded sectors (cars, petroleum, movies) and non-traded sectors (restaurants, home-building, most healthcare services).[45] The latter are a big proportion of GDP, and living standards are a function of an economy's productivity in all sectors, traded and non-traded. But because America does not generally need to respond to foreign threats in non-traded sectors, this book does not give them much space.[46]

This book addresses the economics of both developed and developing nations. Although the lessons derived from the latter are not *directly* applicable to the US, America is in a state of economic rivalry with some developing nations and therefore, to marshal an effective response, needs to understand how they compete with us. Understanding the economics of developing nations also illuminates industrial policy realities, choices, and pitfalls that all nations face.

Around the world, much industrial policy has been about establishing basic "market-enabling" facilities, such as national road networks and banking systems, as these rarely develop without at least the passive support of the state.[47] We do not discuss these subjects much, despite their importance, because they have little relevance to contemporary US problems.

One problem whose causes and costs we describe, but for which we do not propose remedies, is the financialization of the US economy – that is, the "tail" of the financial side of the economy wagging the "dog" of the real side. Short-termism and the doctrine of shareholder primacy continue to work against long-term capital investment and innovation, creating a powerful headwind against effective industrial policy. The specifics of how to return the financial sector to its critical but limited role of supporting the real economy are beyond our scope, but we flag the problem because of its many interactions with industrial policy.

We also give little attention to education and workforce training, because they are thoroughly and competently discussed elsewhere.

The Preface includes a description of the book's structure and organizational logic that is intended as a navigational aid to the reader.

Part I
The Underlying Economics

Part I presents the underlying economics of the industrial policies advocated in this book. Its more general, theoretical analysis provides a framework for understanding the more specific, descriptive material that follows. Chapter 1 explains why free markets on their own cannot deliver prosperity. Chapter 2 explains the idea of "advantageous" industries and the economics they imply. Chapter 3 describes the tools governments have successfully used to implement industrial policy. Chapter 4 explains how international trade, including comparative advantage and foreign exchange rates, fits into the economics of industrial policy and this book's policy proposals.

1 WHY THE FREE MARKET CAN'T DO EVERYTHING

The free market cannot optimize everything that generates economic value. Industrial policy is an extended series of responses to this fact.[1]

The shortcomings of free markets are a vast topic, with many of them having little relevance to industrial policy. Those important for our purposes here are:[2]

1. Externalities
2. Time horizons
3. Systemic effects
4. Fundamental innovations
5. Dynamic efficiency
6. Increasing returns

Because each of the above creates at least the *possibility* of the free market producing a suboptimal outcome, it creates, in principle, the possibility that government intervention could produce something better.[3]

Let us examine these shortcomings in turn, and the policies used in attempts to overcome them. This discussion is simplified and abstract, but we will spend the rest of this book filling in the concrete details.

Externalities

An externality occurs whenever an economic activity "leaks" costs or benefits elsewhere, without the entity performing the activity incurring the cost or benefit itself. Some externalities are negative, such as pollution, which harms the environment without this cost being borne by the firm doing the harm. The classic governmental responses are emissions regulations and fines for polluters.

Other externalities are positive, such as when a firm develops a new technology that will create value all over the economy, beyond the reach of its own profits.[4] When its innovation cannot be protected by patents or trade secrets, a firm may not be able to capture all of its value and thus may choose to underinvest in developing the technology.[5] Governmental responses include tax credits for, and direct investments in, R&D (see Chapters 19–23).

Another example is training personnel who may then go to work for other companies – a disincentive to invest in training. Governmental responses include free public schools and subsidies for worker training.

The concept of *inappropriability* embraces everything firms do that generates economic value they cannot fully capture. Inappropriability also occurs, for example, when a firm invests in upgrading its supplier companies, which will then be able to sell to anyone, not just the company paying for the upgrades. Governments have responded by funding technology extension services to help small and medium enterprises upgrade themselves (see Chapter 22).

Time Horizons

Short-term investing can accomplish many important economic tasks, but some of the most crucial investments must be long term. And there is nothing in capitalism guaranteeing that capitalists will have sufficiently long time horizons.[6] But without long-term investments, whose payoff may not come for years or even decades, businesses often won't develop the next generation of technology, instead sticking with variations on what already exists. Companies with short time horizons will cede market after market to rivals with longer time horizons. Entire industries can be outcompeted by foreign rivals with time horizons artificially lengthened by their home country's industrial policies.

Short-term thinking may be economically rational for the firms engaging in it, and even more so for managers compensated for short-term results. But society, as opposed to any one firm, goes on forever, so it has good reason to prefer long time horizons. Thus, governments try to lengthen firms' time horizons with tools such as low-cost, "patient" capital (see Chapter 3). This capital is often generated by the many, often hidden, policies used to force or incentivize people and firms to save more. Governments also offer tax credits for, and incentivize banks to lend preferentially to, projects expected to have long-term payoffs for the economy as a whole, and directly fund high-risk technological research whose potential payoff is too far in the future to interest private firms.

Systemic Effects

Systemic effects are aspects of the economy that are not optimizable at the level of individual actors like people and firms. Most things *are* optimizable at this level, which is why market economies work in the first place. But a market economy, by definition, is *not* centrally planned, so it will have a hard time achieving outcomes that don't emerge naturally from the actions of its individual profit-seeking players. Even if every player does what's best for itself, the result will not always be optimal for the economy as a whole.

For example, "quality of demand" refers to the fact that companies selling anything from jewelry to jet engines to exceptionally sophisticated customers will be driven by their demands to excel.[7] Competitive pressure to respond to these demands will drive them to *upgrade* their capabilities, since they can no longer maximize profits by standing pat. But no individual customer will see a financial reward commensurate with the benefits that the quality of their demand confers on the whole economy. As a result, markets alone will not always induce an optimal quality of demand. Therefore, governments have deliberately pushed their nation's industries to upgrade more aggressively than immediate profitability would have caused (see Chapter 6). Quality of supply has an analogous logic.

Another systemic issue concerns the benefits of geographical clusters of related firms such as Silicon Valley, which are often extraordinarily successful. Once a cluster exists, the market will automatically prompt firms to locate in it. However, it is very hard for an individual firm, unless it is extremely large, to create a cluster on its own. The *coordination problem* is usually not solvable by a single firm. Therefore, governments try to create and nurture clusters (see Chapters 29 and 30).

Market Shortcomings: Fundamental Innovations

Per capita economic growth requires that an economy produce more goods and services on Tuesday than it did on Monday because something changed that made its workers more productive.[8] Adding capital investment is the obvious candidate, but how should the money be invested? Simply buying every mechanic in a factory a second wrench won't make that factory more productive.[9] The mechanics need something they *don't* already have, something that will enable them to produce more output with the same amount of labor: a *better* wrench, or perhaps some automation. In other words, technology.

Technological advance in developing nations can mean adoption of technologies already existing elsewhere. But in developed nations that already use existing technologies to their full potential, new technologies must be created.[10] In these economies, *innovation* is required for productivity growth.[11]

Unfortunately, free-market economics, despite its enthusiastic rhetoric about innovation, has a very incomplete explanation for why and how technology advances. It is on reasonably solid ground explaining incremental advances by the private sector. The market will pay to develop technologies that are readily monetizable. But many technologies must pass through long stages of risky and expensive development before they earn a profit. Because the market can't optimize their creation, it has not, in recent decades, produced many of the most economically important technologies. Since World War II, the great majority have originated elsewhere: in government labs, especially military ones, in publicly supported nonprofits such as universities, and in government-sanctioned monopolies such as AT&T. The internet, for example, was created to enable government scientists to share data, not to make money. Jet engines were first developed for the Air Force (see Chapters 19 and 26).

Market Shortcoming: Static versus Dynamic Efficiency

With respect to economic growth, each nation faces not one question but two:

1. What is the most productive thing to do today, given the current state of its productive resources?
2. How can it transition to better productive resources tomorrow?

Markets are generally good at achieving the former, so-called static efficiency. But they are less good at the latter, "dynamic" efficiency. This is clearest in developing nations: Growth is about turning Burkina Faso into South Korea, not about being the most efficient possible Burkina Faso forever. But it is also true for developed nations.

Why? Because static and dynamic efficiency are not only different, but can conflict. It can sometimes be rational to do things that are *inefficient* in the short run because there is a long-run payoff. For example, a nation can protect infant industries – forcing its consumers to buy more expensive domestically produced goods for a time – to get lucrative new industries started. This difficult but fruitful trade-off between static and dynamic efficiency is central to many aspects of industrial policy.

Market Shortcoming: Increasing Returns

Increasing returns mean that when a firm spends more money on inputs, the value of its outputs goes up even faster. For example, if baking a loaf of bread requires a $1,000 oven and $1 worth of dough, then baking one loaf will cost $1,001 per loaf. But if one bakes two loaves, the cost will be

$501 per loaf – and if one bakes enough loaves, it will eventually get close to $1. Because the cost per loaf continually falls, the value of additional bread obtained for each additional dollar continually rises.

In industries where increasing returns are present, the market will not be completely free. This is clearest in the extreme case, increasing returns that go on forever, costs dropping ad infinitum with each additional unit. (A search engine like Google is probably the closest thing to this in the real world.)[12] The most efficient outcome is one producer for the entire world, because two producers would each produce half as much and therefore have higher costs. An initially free market will tend to deliver this one-producer outcome because whichever producer has slightly higher volume will have slightly lower costs per unit, be more competitive, gain volume at the expense of its rivals, lower its costs more, and inexorably drive them out of business. But then the free market will come to an end, because there will be a monopoly. Any new firm entering the industry, unless it can do so with the same production volume as the incumbent, will not be competitive, so the monopoly will persist.

Most increasing returns are not this extreme, but the more they are present in an industry, the less free the market will be. There will be "imperfect" competition: not one single producer but only a few, so that each firm will be big enough for its actions to affect the entire market. In other words, an *oligopoly*. Increasing returns tend to make the industries in which they occur oligopolistic – a fact with great significance for industrial policy, as we will see in the next section.

Advantageous Economic Activities

Increasing returns are the first of a set of characteristics of what this book will refer to as "advantageous" economic activities.[13] These characteristics tend to coincide, reinforce each other, and build up *cumulative causation* (when something happens because multiple causes build up over time). To wit:

- Increasing returns
- Pricing power
- Technological dynamism
- Dynamic rent-seeking
- Synergies

Economic activities with these characteristics tend to produce dynamic efficiency, causing an economy to repeatedly gain in productivity and thus grow. The more a nation's economy consists of such activities, the more prosperous it will be today and the better its growth prospects will be for tomorrow. *Industrial policy, at root, is about increasing the quantity of such activities in an economy.*

Pricing power occurs whenever a firm can choose to charge more and sell less, or charge less and sell more – as opposed to just having to accept the market price. The latter happens when there are many small competitors: Each will be able to sell at will at the market price, but not at all if it charges a penny more. Pricing power requires that some factor be present that reduces competition, so pricing power tends to accompany increasing returns.

Pricing power means that sellers get a higher price. It can come from being the only coffee shop on the block, but the kind relevant to industrial policy comes from producing *things that are hard to produce*, such as jet engines or smartphones. When only a small number of highly skilled firms can produce a product, an oligopoly will develop – whose members will have pricing power. In fact, whenever know-how is the major production cost, there will necessarily be increasing returns, because once that know-how has been paid for, each additional unit of product amortizes its cost over more output.

Technological dynamism: "Hard to produce" usually means sophisticated technology. But what was once cutting-edge usually becomes commonplace and easy to produce over time. So, what producers want is ongoing technological change, so that they can stay forever near the leading edge, employing the difficult, relatively new technology that confers pricing power.

One way to accomplish this is to produce the technological change oneself. Enter R&D. Pursuing profits in this way is called "**dynamic rent-seeking.**" (The term "rent," in the peculiar usage of economics, means profits exceeding what a free market would grant.) Dynamic rent-seeking is based on continually innovating and upgrading to keep earning the rent. Its opposite is static rent-seeking, which means seeking some privilege, such as a legal monopoly, that enables charging a premium without doing anything productive to earn it. Static rent-seeking does an economy no good, but dynamic rent-seeking increases productivity and thus produces growth.

Synergies: Some economic activities, when they first emerge or later improve their productivity, enable other activities to emerge or improve *their* productivity. For example, cheap mass-produced steel, whose first major market was railroad rails, made skyscrapers possible. Vacuum tube production originally flowered to build radios, then enabled televisions. Computer chips were invented when computers were room-sized, but eventually became sufficiently small, powerful, and cheap to enable smartphones. Smartphones, in turn, enabled ride-hailing services. Jet engines developed for military aircraft enabled passenger jets, mass tourism, and ultimately Disney World.

When synergies are present, advances in one part of the economy tend to push forward other parts. This is important for long-term growth because there is a limit to how much any one industry can grow, simply because there is a limit to how much of any one product consumers want. When are synergies absent?

Consider single-export economies, producing, say, bananas or petroleum. A nation may be poor if it produces only bananas, or rich if it produces only petroleum, but either way, market forces alone are unlikely to set it on a path to producing anything else.

Advantageous Industries Produce Growth

Advantageous economic activities are *activities*, not industries, but all economic activities take place in industries. Some industries are "tightly packaged" – that is, one must perform all their activities to perform any. Others are loosely packaged: Some activities can be delegated to other firms, or geographically scattered so a country can host some but not others.

Advantageous industries tend to have six key characteristics:

1. High income elasticity of demand
2. Susceptibility to repeated improvement
3. Competition *not* on pure price
4. Capacity to absorb investment
5. Path dependence
6. Human capital accumulation

Advantageous industries generally produce products for which **income elasticity of demand** is high. For example, people spend significantly more money on cars as their incomes go up, but only a little more on milk. Therefore demand for products like cars can rise with the overall income growth of an economy. As a result, productivity gains in making such products do not just drive down their price, as output can rise along with those gains. Productivity gains are thus shared between producers, in the form of higher profits and wages, and consumers, in the form of lower prices. Contrarily, with products of relatively inelastic demand, such as commodity foodstuffs, productivity gains usually go mostly to consumers, not producers.[14]

Advantageous industries tend to produce goods **susceptible to repeated improvement,** like computers or airplanes, while disadvantageous industries produce goods whose character is basically fixed, like fruit or T-shirts. When a product exhibits meaningful variety, producers can establish mini-oligopolies in specific niches, enabling dynamic rent-seeking. Product variety also increases opportunities for innovation, both because inventing new varieties is itself an innovation, and because innovation can now advance on multiple fronts.

Advantageous industries tend **not to compete on pure price.** (Price is obviously a factor with anything sold for money, but it is *relatively* less important here.) They compete instead on quality, technology, reliability, reputation, marketing, service, variety, style, rapid innovation, understanding of buyer needs, vendor financing, managerial sophistication, and customer relationships.[15] Importantly, these forms of competition make cheap foreign labor much less relevant, allowing advantageous traded industries to maintain their workers' incomes despite foreign competition.

Advantageous industries tend to have a high **capacity to absorb investment**. Buying another $1,000,000 worth of tractors for a coffee plantation that already has them won't increase its productivity very much. But a television factory will likely be able to repay investment in better machinery with higher productivity. Even better, advantageous industries tend to activate a virtuous cycle in which innovation absorbs capital and repays it by raising profitability, generating more capital and repeating the cycle. Economy-wide growth often involves a multi-industry virtuous cycle, in which the upgrading of one industry causes others to upgrade and so on.

Advantageous industries tend to exhibit **path dependence**. That is, having advantageous industries makes it easier for a nation to acquire other advantageous industries.[16] For example, nations that produced radios were better equipped to produce televisions. As a result, economic growth is path dependent: What nations can produce tomorrow largely depends on what they produce today. This is why much industrial policy, historically, has centered on policies, from infant-industry protection to cash subsidies, designed to break into industries expected to lead somewhere. Historically, this usually meant getting out of agriculture and raw materials and into manufacturing (especially of products sophisticated at the time), although a *small* segment of advanced service industries has been entering the advantageous category since the late 1970s.

Advantageous industries tend to experience **human capital accumulation,** because they use technology their workers must have training to operate. This creates a premium on a skilled, not just cheap, workforce. Human capital embodied in the workers themselves encourages better treatment of labor, for the same reason factory owners do not let valuable machinery rust away. Advantageous industries thus make at least *possible* the "countervailing powers," such as the bargaining power of unions, that spread the profits of industry beyond its owners. (Such leverage is not guaranteed, but workers can't bargain for a share of profits that aren't there.) Rising worker incomes also provide the purchasing power to sustain growth, and as incomes rise, consumers generally demand better products, driving the industries of the nation – which will depend at least in part upon domestic demand – to upgrade.

Advantageous versus disadvantageous is not binary, but a sliding scale from very advantageous to very disadvantageous, with most industries falling somewhere in between. It is also not guaranteed that any given advantageous industry will have all six listed qualities. But these qualities are interlinked, mutually dependent, and tend to appear as a package. For example, technological advance is linked to expanding production because it is much easier to invest in new technology when one is adding new machinery to expand production. And expanding production is linked to elastic demand, or else nobody would buy the output.

Note, finally, that our treatment here is highly abstract and elides many industry-specific details. Exceptions will not be hard to find. But it is certainly true enough of the time to be a useful guide to policy.

The ideas of increasing returns and oligopoly industries have been around for a long time. But mainstream economics does not generally follow the train of thought just discussed, largely because its logic interferes with the idea of general equilibrium, the keystone of the notion that free markets are best.[17] This is because in the presence of increasing returns, there is not one possible equilibrium but many, depending on contingent events.

The main academic home of these concepts is thus not economics departments but business schools. For example, here is Michael Porter of Harvard Business School, who refers to our "advantageous" industries as "structurally attractive":

> [I]ndustries important to a high standard of living are often those that are structurally attractive. Structurally attractive industries, with sustainable entry barriers in such areas as technology, specialized skills, channel access, and brand reputation, often involve high labor productivity and will earn more attractive returns to capital. Standard of living will depend importantly on the capacity of a nation's firms to successfully penetrate structurally attractive industries.[18]

Disadvantageous Industries

In *dis*advantageous industries, some or all of the positive dynamics just explained are absent – or worse, run in reverse. Such industries not only tend to have low wages and profits today, but also tend not to lead to better industries tomorrow. For centuries, "disadvantageous" has meant commodity agriculture, natural-resource extraction, and services such as domestic servants and retail. And since the late 1960s, low-skilled manufacturing has been inexorably joining this category.

Agriculture and natural resources generally exhibit diminishing, not increasing, returns, as once the best land and most accessible resource deposits have been exploited, increasing production means turning to inferior land and deposits.[19] Such industries rarely have pricing power, as they generally produce undifferentiated commodities. (Commodity booms come but they also go.) Because price and income elasticity of demand for their products are low, productivity growth tends to flow to consumers as lower prices, rather than to producers as profits and wages. American farmers, for example, use advanced technologies ranging from genetically engineered seeds to satellite positioning systems for their tractors, but struggle to stay solvent.[20]

Industries such as retail and restaurants have less scope for productivity improvement than manufacturing. A 1950s diner is not that different from one today, while a 1950s auto assembly line would be totally uncompetitive. Technological innovations in disadvantageous industries tend to come from *other* industries: Farmers themselves don't invent satellite-navigating tractors or genetically engineered corn. As a result, innovations tend to increase the productivity of all producers at once, driving down the price of the product: The producer of the innovation, not its end user, earns the premium. Agricultural prices also tend to be volatile: Soybean or banana prices can vary by 50 percent from year to year, but not car prices.

Disadvantageous industries generally lack synergies. When the Santa Clara Valley in California (better known today as Silicon Valley) specialized in plum production before World War II, this brought about a prune industry and fruit canning, but little more. When it became a center for aerospace and defense electronics, this led to transistors, then integrated circuits, then computer hardware, computer software, and, contemporaneously, a venture capital industry feeding on and nurturing these industries and others. Their output is worth many, many times what the region's fruit production once was.

The presence of advantageous industries in an economy generally improves wages in even that economy's disadvantageous industries. For example, growth of manufacturing in a developing nation raises the incomes of farm workers by tightening the labor supply. Rising manufacturing wages generate higher prices for farm goods that must be consumed locally because of transport costs and perishability. Advantageous industries can also set a "wage floor," preventing the unemployed from crowding into disadvantageous industries and dragging down productivity due to these industries' diminishing returns.[21]

Underdeveloped nations are poor because their economies are predominantly composed of disadvantageous industries and they can't find a way out of them. Developed nations are not wealthier because they engage in the same economic activities as developing nations, only with greater productivity. They engage in fundamentally different activities because they host fundamentally different industries. Commodity agriculture, for example, exists in developed nations, but is a small percentage of GDP and employment.

Nations that used to be poor and agricultural, such as South Korea in 1960, didn't become rich by finding ways to produce rice and fish (South Korea's main industries then) with 20 times the productivity. They used proactive industrial policies to break into industries, like steel and cars, where 20 times the per-worker productivity of a small-scale fisherman or peasant farmer is the norm.

Note, finally, that having a lot of advantageous industries is not the same thing as merely being *rich*, as small-population states with large natural resources, such as Argentina in 1900 (beef; see Chapter 12) or Kuwait in 1980 (oil), can have high per capita incomes. But the resource-based model doesn't scale. There has never been a large nation that was rich purely on the strength of natural resources because no nation has ever had enough resources. As Chinese economist Justin Yifu Lin, the World Bank's former chief economist, puts it, "except for a few oil-exporting countries, no countries have ever gotten rich without industrialization first."[22] But advantageous industries, on the other hand, can scale. And when their ability to scale is exhausted and their products commoditized, they lead to new industries and scaling can begin anew.

2 THE DYNAMICS OF ADVANTAGEOUS INDUSTRIES

The core justification for industrial policy is that the market alone will not give a nation the greatest possible amount of advantageous economic activities because the industries that host them are shot through with *non-free-market dynamics*:[1]

- **Increasing returns** industries are protected from entry by the superior scale of incumbents, so the market, on its own, tends to keep newcomers out. As a result, nations can benefit from subsidizing entry into these industries. And nations already hosting them must sometimes protect themselves against rivals employing such policies.
- **Pricing power** exists precisely when markets are *not* perfectly free, so getting it requires penetrating oligopolistic, increasing-returns industries, which in turn entails overcoming the incumbent advantages just mentioned.
- **Fundamental technological advances** often do not come from the private sector operating under free-market conditions. They come from public-sector research, from the private sector enjoying public-sector help, or from government-sanctioned monopolies and oligopolies.[2]
- **Synergies** do not generally give the parties creating them profits commensurate with the value they generate across the entire economy. As a result, the market underprices industries that have synergies and won't create the optimal amount of them on its own.
- The private sector often has **short time horizons,** not the multi-decade time horizons needed to lift a nation from poverty to prosperity – or to keep it prosperous if it already is.

For these reasons, markets are less effective for entering and retaining advantageous industries than the combination of markets and effective industrial policy.

As a nation develops, more of its economic activities can be left to markets, which is why industrial policy matters more in developing nations. But even developed nations never reach a state where markets alone are sufficient. And in an international environment where their rivals are using proactive industrial policies, relying on markets alone can result in a loss of existing advantageous industries and a failure to acquire those of the future.

The Quality Index of Economic Activities

The Quality Index of Economic Activities is a tool for comparing the advantageousness of industries.[3] Figure 2.1 is an adaptation of a diagram by Norwegian economist Erik Reinert.[4]

This diagram is a simplification. For a start, industries subdivide into niches not shown. Also, it is from 2007. But the anachronism is revealing, because the reality that industries change in advantageousness over time should inform policy, and by looking at a historic chart, we can analyze subsequent changes.

At the top are the most advantageous industries, made up of firms that held oligopoly positions derived from control of new innovations. Here were ultra-high-end industries such as advanced electronics, computer software, biopharmaceuticals, and sophisticated professional services.

These industries were based on new knowledge with a high market value, fast growth in output, rapid technological progress, and high R&D. Their employees embodied scarce skills and commanded high wages. Early entrants benefited from fast productivity gains and large increasing returns as they assimilated the new technology and scaled up production.

Investments often had to take place in large indivisible units, such as huge individual plants, creating barriers to entry.[5] Some industries benefited from network effects, installed-base effects, and other dynamics that helped entrench them against competitors. They had opportunities for both product (new things) and process (new ways of making existing things) innovation.

Just below these industries appear lesser high-return, high-tech industries. These enjoyed massive output, and their know-how and factories had now largely been paid for, resulting in healthy current profits. But much output was now for replacement sales, so output growth had slowed and increasing returns had plateaued. But they still gained from increasing returns among their suppliers, which reduced their input costs, and from increasing manufacturing automation as production methods stabilized.

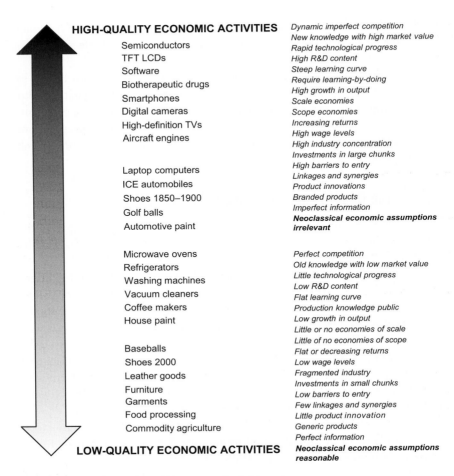

HIGH-QUALITY ECONOMIC ACTIVITIES

Semiconductors
TFT LCDs
Software
Biotherapeutic drugs
Smartphones
Digital cameras
High-definition TVs
Aircraft engines

Laptop computers
ICE automobiles
Shoes 1850–1900
Golf balls
Automotive paint

Microwave ovens
Refrigerators
Washing machines
Vacuum cleaners
Coffee makers
House paint

Baseballs
Shoes 2000
Leather goods
Furniture
Garments
Food processing
Commodity agriculture

LOW-QUALITY ECONOMIC ACTIVITIES

Dynamic imperfect competition
New knowledge with high market value
Rapid technological progress
High R&D content
Steep learning curve
Require learning-by-doing
High growth in output
Scale economies
Scope economies
Increasing returns
High wage levels
High industry concentration
Investments in large chunks
High barriers to entry
Linkages and synergies
Product innovations
Branded products
Imperfect information
Neoclassical economic assumptions irrelevant

Perfect competition
Old knowledge with low market value
Little technological progress
Low R&D content
Flat learning curve
Production knowledge public
Low growth in output
Little or no economies of scale
Little of no economies of scope
Flat or decreasing returns
Low wage levels
Fragmented industry
Investments in small chunks
Low barriers to entry
Few linkages and synergies
Little product innovation
Generic products
Perfect information
Neoclassical economic assumptions reasonable

Figure 2.1 Quality Index of Economic Activities, circa 2007

Midway down the diagram are industries where most of the big gains had already been exhausted, such as gasoline cars, microwave ovens, refrigerators, washing machines, vacuum cleaners, coffee makers, and other appliances. Many of these products were technologically stagnant for extended periods, though they benefited from ongoing process innovations that produced quality gains and lower unit costs. This class of industrial activity was large and employed many people worldwide.

At the bottom of the chart are industries that were mostly in their diminishing-returns era (and may not have had any other), such as garments, shoes, leather products, and most furniture. These were large industries globally, so they remained economically significant even though their rents per worker were far lower than in the industries above them. They now yielded low or no productivity gains. Wages and profits were low, despite large demand, because of fierce global competition. Commodity agriculture was also in this category, because (as noted in Chapter 1), inelastic demand caused technological progress to be captured by consumers, not by producers.

How Advantageousness Changes

The advantageousness of industries changes as technology advances. Yesterday's high technology becomes commoditized, loses patent and trade-secret protection, and diffuses around the world. Therefore, a technologically static industry's advantageousness will generally decline over time, though barriers to industry entry can slow this process.

Most industries must thus constantly upgrade to hold onto their advantageousness. (Different economic activities within an industry can, of course, evolve at different rates.) Thus, in traded industries nations must generally move forward to stay in place. This is mostly a healthy process, because it forces developed nations to upgrade and allows developing nations to enter segments advanced nations have left. But it also means that developed nations can lose advantageous industries they already have.

Industries that have lost advantageousness in recent years include laptops, where the limits of consumer performance requirements have been reached, resulting in price competition between similar models. (This is not yet true of some of their key components, such as microprocessors.) Decades ago, products such as refrigerators, washing machines, and bread-making machines were highly advantageous, but then they declined.

Conversely, some industries have recently seen their advantageousness *increase* thanks to new waves of innovation. The most obvious example is automobiles, where advances in battery technology enabled electric cars and AI will enable self-driving vehicles (see Chapter 25).

Other products have held their position, at least for premium models, through incremental innovations: Televisions, for example, acquired Bluetooth, ultra-high-definition, curved screens, and intelligent TV. Refrigerators over several decades got separate cooling chambers, automatic defrosting, in-door ice and water dispensers, see-through doors, TV screens, and internet connections.

Other industries held (and some continue to hold) advantageousness because their internal structures create barriers to entry. These include large integrated systems such as aircraft, other major aerospace systems, weapons systems, flight simulators, factory automation equipment, Formula I race cars, and offshore drilling platforms. These are design-intensive, small-volume, high-priced sectors. Their products are generally made of complex, often custom-tailored components, which are themselves high in value and produced in relatively small volumes.

Component suppliers tended to be located near the master integrators to work closely together on the design and integration issues inevitable with complex, continually evolving products.

Other industries that have held advantageousness center on product design and continuous processing, rather than unit manufacturing: nongeneric pharmaceuticals, oil refining, chemicals, biotechnology, and advanced materials. In these industries, the physical manufacturing step is often a relatively small fraction of the cost of the product. For many, accumulated intellectual property in the form of patents and trade secrets creates barriers to entry.

Some industries that are not truly advantageous behave like advantageous industries. High style has some of the characteristics of high technology. Proximity-sensitive manufacturing, such as architectural components and custom kitchen cabinets, lacks most attributes of advantageous industries, but makes up for this by being sheltered from foreign, sometimes even national, competition by transport costs and the need for onsite inspection and installation. Similarly sheltered are industries like processing of local agricultural products that are perishable, delicate to transport, or must be consumed shortly after production. Similar factors apply to industries, such as heavy construction materials, where transport costs are high relative to price.

Advantageousness Is Not Just about High Technology

"Advantageous" does not merely collapse in practice into "high tech," and industrial policies solely focused on pursuing more-advanced technology have a poor track record all over the world. Consider the technological triumph, but commercial failure, of the Concorde (see Chapter 19).

A high-tech-only policy will not meet the employment needs of a large country. Everybody can't work at Apple. There are not enough jobs in these industries, and most people are too old or uneducable to be trained for them, or don't live where these jobs are. There are also many lower-tech, less advantageous industries that society needs just to function, so no economy can consist only of the most advantageous industries. Advantageous industries also depend upon less advantageous supporting industries.

Many mid-range industries have *some* increasing returns, pricing power, technological dynamism, and synergies. This category includes utilities, infrastructure, construction, transport, healthcare, energy production, and government. Together, these industries represent a large portion of GDP and employment. Many cannot be performed remotely, protecting them from foreign competition and making them viable sources of large numbers of at least medium-wage jobs. But precisely because these industries bulk so large in GDP and employment, it is important to ensure that they make full use of available technology to become as advantageous as possible.

Productivity gains come not from inventing new technologies per se but from deploying them, and many jobs created by new technologies are outside the sector producing the technology. For example, it was estimated in 2017 that the personal computer had enabled the creation of 16 million net new jobs in the US since 1980.[6] The number of people employed actually building computers in the US in 2021? 158,000.[7] Therefore, in addition to technology-creating industries, a nation also needs industries capable of absorbing technology. Some industries are thus particularly important because they serve as matrices for the deployment of technologies developed elsewhere. Without a thriving manufacturing sector in this country, for example, productivity gains from emerging robotic manufacturing technologies will accrue to other nations. And America loses many potentially high-productivity jobs when advanced products designed here are manufactured elsewhere.

Forces Driving Industry Evolution

Technologically dynamic industries tend to be located in the most advanced economies. But as productivity plateaus and their technology becomes commonplace, they tend to migrate to less advanced economies with lower labor costs. Sometimes a new general-purpose technology, such as digitization, reshuffles a whole range of industries at once. The rise of microelectronics, for example, made the existing versions of many mechanical and electromechanical industries, from watches to machine tools, obsolete. It made the electronic versions of these products more innovative, and thus the industries producing them more advantageous, in a process that has continued because digital technology has continued to advance.

Robotics and AI are currently on the cusp of changing almost every industry. The impact may be even more profound on currently disadvantageous industries, because automation is already deployed closer to the limits of its potential in advantageous ones. Car plants, for example, have had a significant robotic presence for decades now, T-shirt factories almost none.

AI is likely to create opportunities for developed nations in currently disadvantageous traded industries. For example, robotic T-shirt factories would throw a lot of people out of work in Honduras but not in the US – so roboticization would be a pure economic gain for America. And if those factories are going to be robotic, they're more likely to be built here, closer to markets and where labor skilled in robotics is more available.

Evolving technology is not, however, the only reason industries migrate. Migration has also been driven by advances in transportation, communications, business software, and other things that made it easier for firms to use cheaper foreign labor. The container ship was a key enabler.[8] Government policies have also had their effects, including foreign currency manipulation and the failure of the US government to manage the dollar (see Chapter 4). Trade agreements have facilitated offshoring by guaranteeing access to the US market and protecting American firms' investments in facilities abroad. And foreign governments have deployed subsidies and other tactics in pursuit of advantageous industries.

Where Does Productivity Grow?

There are only a limited number of major sectors where large, ongoing productivity gains are possible: manufacturing and a few others, such as IT. This is where R&D pays off in productivity, which is why manufacturing accounts for nearly 60 percent of US R&D.[9]

Productivity growth in these sectors is the main ultimate source of economy-wide income growth.[10] Between 1950 and 2020, labor productivity in US manufacturing increased by a factor of nine, while productivity in the economy as a whole merely tripled.[11] Average wages in an economy are determined, other things being equal, by average productivity, so as productivity in manufacturing and other advantageous sectors rises, it pulls up the economy's average despite stagnant productivity in many sectors.

Rising productivity in manufacturing also pulls up wages, due to a phenomenon economists call Baumol's Cost Disease that might better be called Baumol's Prosperity Sharing. Consider: Barbers earn nearly nine times as much in Germany as in the Philippines.[12] But do they use more capital or better technology in Germany? Not significantly. The main difference is that wages *generally* are higher in Germany, so barbers have to be paid more or nobody would be one. But how did wages get to be higher there? *Somebody's* productivity must have gone way up, and it wasn't the productivity of barbers, which hasn't changed much in millennia. Nor has the productivity of many other local service jobs, such as retailing, dining, or teaching. (In America, these sectors make up two-thirds of all jobs.)[13]

As previously noted, a restaurant today and one from 1950 are not all that different. But a steel mill or a telephone switchboard are unrecognizably so: Productivity at the mill, in man-hours per ton, is about eight times higher, and the switchboard has all but disappeared.[14] But because of productivity growth in industries like steel and telecommunications, more people can afford to eat in restaurants than in 1950. Non-oil-rich nations are rich today because they experienced wave after wave of productivity surges in successive advantageous industries over many decades. This allowed technology, skills, deployed capital, and wealth to relentlessly accumulate.

This sharing of the fruits of productivity gains is not automatic and depends on other factors affecting labor's bargaining power, but the fruits must be there to be fought over. One implication is that everyone in the economy, not just workers in advantageous industries, has a stake in their health.

The Misunderstood Value of Manufacturing

Not all advantageous industries are in manufacturing. But manufacturing is their quintessential home: overwhelmingly so historically, although in developed nations today generally only in *advanced* manufacturing. Manufacturing is the major focus of this book for this reason and because, as a tradable sector, it is one in which the US needs policy responses to other nations. As the largest sector in which the US has been falling short of its potential in recent decades, it is an appropriate focus of reform efforts.[15] It is also the sector where the correction of mistaken ideas is most likely to enable significant new and better policies.

The significance of manufacturing for the US economy is often misunderstood. A major cause is literally accurate but misinterpreted statistics, such as the fact that manufacturing is "only" 11 percent of GDP and 8 percent of employment.[16] This confusion is due to the distinction between *value added* and *gross output*. Every industry not selling directly to consumers receives inputs from and supplies outputs to other industries. Therefore, statistics must avoid double-counting output both when industry X produces it and then again when industry Y takes it in, does something with it, and spits it out the other end. The concept of "value added" solves this problem by subtracting from each industry's output the value of the inputs that went into it, thus measuring only the value that it creates rather than merely passes on.

This bookkeeping is necessary for the sum of all individual industries to equal the whole economy's value added (GDP). But it also invites underestimation of the importance of manufacturing. Measured by gross output – that is, *without* subtracting inputs – manufacturing in 2015 was not 12 percent, but 35 percent, of GDP, and the source of not 9 percent, but 21 percent, of all jobs.[17] These larger numbers include the additional GDP that manufacturing contributes by creating demand for services and non-manufactured goods.

"Upstream" inputs to American manufacturing range from iron mining to accounting; as of 2014, their fractions of manufacturing's inputs were:[18]

Agriculture, Mining, Utilities, Construction	14%
Other Manufacturing	13%
Wholesale & Retail Trade	9%
Transportation	6%
Financial & Real Estate Services	10%
Information Technology & Business Services	23%
Other Services, Government	4%
Imported Inputs	22%

Together, they accounted for 15.4 million domestic jobs.[19] Every manufacturing job thus supported 1.4 jobs *outside* manufacturing, the highest multiplier of any major sector.[20] Almost a quarter of the jobs in the computer systems design and related services industry, for example, were attributable to manufacturing.[21]

"Downstream" activities, which accounted for 23.5 million jobs, included everything from retail stores to auto repair – that is, anything that added value between the factory and the final consumer. In 2014, their fractions of this value-added were:[22]

Transport	4%
Wholesaling	33%
Retailing	47%
Services	17%

The key difference between upstream and downstream activities, of course, is that America loses the former when goods are imported, but not the latter.

Manufacturing R&D benefits not only manufacturing, but also technology-intensive service sectors whose ongoing growth depends upon advances in hardware.[23] For example, smartphone-based delivery apps only became possible once smartphones became physically manufacturable, roughly a decade after the software in question had become possible.

There is a strong link between the location of production and the location of innovation. When production leaves, research and development, product design, and testing often follow.[24] Innovation and production are embedded in an "industrial commons" of specialized suppliers, key service companies, shared engineering skills, and manufacturing competencies.[25] Capturing and retaining manufacturing is thus vital to maintaining the entire commons (see Chapters 21 and 22).

The Costly Decline of Manufacturing

From 1953 to 2015, manufacturing's share of American employment dropped from 32 to 9 percent, and its share of GDP from 28 to 12 percent.[26] While part of this decline was beneficial, part was not.

The economically beneficial portion consisted simply in the fact that other sectors grew faster. Since the early 1950s, services such as healthcare, education, and business services have exploded in dollar value. But their growth largely just reflected higher inflation in services, which depend on direct human labor, than in manufacturing, which continually grows more automated.[27] When adjusted for the inflation difference, the implied share of total *value* of manufactured goods in the economy (as opposed to their *price*) has not dropped significantly.[28]

The US has shed many manufacturing industries that are no longer viable in any developed nation because their production cost is mainly low-skilled labor. This has brought Americans cheaper goods at the price of lost jobs. According to mainstream trade theory, this *necessarily* resulted in a net gain in well-being, as the cost savings were necessarily worth more than the jobs. But this "law" holds true if and only if most workers displaced from these industries find better alternatives – an assumption that history and recent research have challenged (see Chapter 4).[29]

The US has also lost manufacturing jobs in advantageous industries it should have held on to.[30] We run a trade deficit in Advanced Technology Products of more than $200 billion.[31] There was nothing inevitable about this. Some developed nations that have hung on to these industries better, such as Japan and Germany, have manufacturing wages comparable to ours.[32] Direct labor cost in manufacturing averages only about 20 percent of output value – ranging from 11 percent for motor vehicles to 44 percent for apparel and leather goods – so high-wage countries can be competitive in many products.[33]

Statistics that appear to show that American manufacturing is robust are misleading. As economist Susan Houseman noted in 2016,

> A small industry – computers, semiconductors and related products, which account for only 13 percent of value-added in manufacturing – drives the apparent robust output and productivity growth in the sector. Performance in most manufacturing industries has been very weak. Excluding output from the computer and semiconductor industry, the amount produced in American factories is barely higher than in the late 1990s ... The extraordinary output and productivity growth in computers and semiconductors reflects the way statistical agencies account for improvements in the products produced in this industry.[34]

This last sentence refers to the fact that standard statistics mistakenly count cost savings from offshoring as increases in domestic productivity – but one example of needed reforms to government statistics.[35]

3 THE INDUSTRIAL POLICY TOOL KIT

We have examined why some economic activities are more "advantageous" than others – that is, more conducive to economic growth – and why the free market (let alone the actual, unfree market) will not maximize a nation's amount of them. This chapter discusses how effective industrial policy can nurture these activities with policies at the local, regional, national, and supranational levels.

Effective industrial policy begins with basic sound government and economics. Nations need, if not the rule of law, at least the rule of reasonably rational, consistent, and predictable rulers. Even one-party tyrannies like China can be consistent, or consistent enough. Businesses do not require fairness per se, but they do need to know that if they make an investment, they will be allowed to keep enough profit for the investment to be worth making.

Sound economics does not require pure capitalism, but it does require some form of private property. It does not require absolutely free markets, but it does require that markets be manipulated only in rational ways for productive ends. It does not require an economy run solely for profit, but it does require acceptance of the profit motive. These requirements ultimately entail the three-way mixed economy of all economically successful nations, including the US: part public, part free-market private, part regulated private.

Sound economics also generally means a stable macro-economy – that is, no wild inflation or volatile interest rates.[1] It means reasonable rates of taxation – that is, comparable to competing nations, but not zero because no government can function without revenue and therefore no country has to compete with a tax-free alternative.[2] It means infrastructure sufficient for the level of development the nation aspires to, and an education system teaching skills to match.

The poorest countries often lack basic institutions and infrastructure, such as banks and roads, and much industrial policy there has been about creating these things. Such policies are obviously important for them, but will not be our focus here because these early stages of economic development have little relevance to current US policy. We only note in passing that in the early nineteenth century, when the US was itself a developing country, it was precisely fights over federally sponsored banks and roads that convulsed our politics (see Chapter 14).[3]

The key points in this chapter are: A wide array of tools is used in industrial policy; these tools are omnipresent, including in the most market-oriented countries, and while they sometimes fail, well-designed and implemented industrial policies can be very effective.[4] Note that these policies are rarely beneficial in isolation: What pushes an economy into ever-more-advantageous activities and industries is the *cumulative* effect of multiple policies implemented in a coordinated way.

The Tools of Industrial Policy

Below is a list of the major industrial policy tools. These is *tools*, not blanket policy choices: Some will be useful to some nations at some times, and none will be useful to all nations at all times.

- Infant-Industry Protection
- Local-Content Rules
- Stage-Differential Tariffs
- Import Substitution
- Selective Importation
- Export Subsidies and Targets
- Incentives for Foreign Firms
- Export Processing Zones
- Regulatory Competition
- Credit Allocation
- Forced Savings Policies
- Sovereign Wealth Funds
- Government Procurement
- State Entrepreneurship
- National Champions
- Imposing Competitive Industry Structure
- Fostering Clusters
- Supporting the Industrial Commons
- Supporting Private Research
- Supporting Public Research

- Intellectual Property Policy
- Standards Setting
- Technology Mapping
- Technology Denial
- Combining Policies
- Picking Winners

Infant-Industry Protection means protecting a nation's emerging industries from foreign competition so that domestic sales will support the growth of the nation's own industry, not that of other countries. This policy comes in many varieties, of which only a few are described here.

A tariff will, despite a nation's initially uncompetitive cost basis, allow the industry to build up sales volume and production skills. The goal is to drive its costs down and its quality up, eventually making it competitive with imports. Infant-industry protection imposes the short-term cost of forcing consumers to buy more expensive and/or lower-quality domestically produced goods. Whether the long-term benefits exceed these costs depends on whether the policy succeeds in hoisting the nation into more-advantageous industries.

Infant-industry protection will only work if the country gets a lot of other things right. It will need a domestic market large enough to support the industry, so this policy is less useful in small nations. Small countries like Singapore that have had very aggressive industrial policies overall have there-fore tended *not* to be protectionist, while large countries, like China and the US pre–World War II, have been (see Chapters 7, 14, and 15).[5] If domestic sales alone will be useful but not enough, protectionism must be combined with efforts to penetrate foreign markets.

Infant-industry protection cannot guarantee success on its own, as advantageous industries are difficult to master quite apart from foreign compe-tition. There is a risk of launching infant industries that remain eternally dependent on tariff protection to survive. There is a risk of cutting the economy off from state-of-the-art goods and services by making low-cost, high-quality imports too expensive, undermining the competitiveness of industries that use the protected product. Consider Brazil's luckless computer industry, finally abandoned in 1992 after handicapping other Brazilian industries with expen-sive, mediocre product for years.[6]

Infant-industry protection will only work when government protects the right industries – that is, those in which the nation can eventually become competitive. Getting this right depends upon key supporting choices and actions:

1. Predicting the evolution of technology – for example, don't master mechan-ical clock making just before the industry goes digital.

2. Predicting the future evolution of world markets – that is, don't target a product if there will be a glut of it in 10 years.
3. Knowing which supporting industries will be needed and ensuring their development.
4. Educating a workforce with the right skills, both blue and white collar.

Because these choices require predicting the future, success requires an accurate assessment of the nation's potential: neither underestimating, unnecessarily limiting growth, nor overestimating, resulting in waste and ultimate failure. Larger issues of political consensus and national will enter the equation here. For example, a country where all political parties buy into the chosen industrial policy, avoiding flip-flops as parties rotate in power, is more likely to succeed. (Britain from 1945 to 1979 suffered from this problem, as discussed in Chapter 10.)

If protected firms just pocket the profits, instead of investing them in upgrading their capabilities, protecting industries will merely enrich their owners. Therefore, measures to pressure firms to upgrade are generally required. This requires a state that can put the interests of the economy as a whole ahead of those of particular sectors or businesses. This comes more easily to authoritarian governments, like present-day China or pre-democracy Taiwan and Korea, to highly technocratic regimes such as Japan, and to social-democratic governments like those in Europe.[7] These regimes are ideologically and institutionally equipped to resist the demands of business when necessary. Conversely, governments highly vulnerable to business lobbying (the US) or dominated by entrenched oligarchies (Latin America, Southeast Asia) find this harder.

Local-Content Rules are a type of protectionism. These mandate that 50 percent, say, of a complex product such as a car must be made in-country. Their advantage over a tariff on the entire product is that they can be adjusted over time to move more steps of the production process onshore as the nation's producers develop the ability to handle them.

The OECD estimated in 2018 that since the 2008 financial crisis, 145 new local-content measures had been introduced worldwide.[8] Argentina, Brazil, China, India, Indonesia, Russia, and Saudi Arabia were major users. Indonesia, for example, required 40 percent local content in smartphones, while Canada had rules for wind turbines.

Historically, local-content rules were often attached to incentives for foreign direct investment (FDI) to create jobs. More recently, their purpose often has often included forcing transmission of technological know-how to local firms.

The danger of local-content rules is that by driving up the cost of the finished product or compromising its quality, they can undermine its competitiveness both as an export and against imports. This is likely to happen if the nation hasn't yet developed a sufficiently sophisticated supplier base. This problem illustrates how industrial policy, generally, needs to be pushed *hard enough but not too hard*, or its short-term costs swamp its long-term benefits.

Even the US imposes local-content rules, though it has until recently done so very mildly. For example, the automobile section of the 2018 United States–Mexico–Canada Agreement (USMCA) requires a certain percentage of a car to come from the US, Mexico, or Canada to qualify for the lower USMCA tariff. The Bipartisan Infrastructure Act of 2021 and the Inflation Reduction Act of 2022 contained local-content provisions for electric cars to incentivize part sourcing and car assembly in the US. The CHIPS and Science Act of 2022 required that companies funded by its $50 billion Chips for America Fund manufacture their chips and related equipment here.

Stage-Differential Tariffs place, for example, a higher tariff on cotton made into thread than on raw cotton, and a higher tariff still on cloth woven from thread. Such duties, proposed by Treasury Secretary Alexander Hamilton in 1791, had been used by European nations for at least 200 years before that (see Chapter 13). Their purpose is to push the economy out of raw materials production and into the more advantageous manufacturing-oriented steps of supply chains. For example, China in 2019 had duties of 5.5 percent on raw lithium oxide, a component of lithium-ion batteries, 12 percent on battery parts, and 14 percent on completed batteries.[9]

A parallel policy, sometimes used by nations producing raw materials, is taxing *exports* of raw materials to encourage their processing at home. These are known as Differential Export Taxes, and the WTO has estimated that more than half its members imposed them between 2003 and 2009.[10]

Import Substitution is another protectionist policy, common, for example, in Latin America during the second half of the twentieth century. This aims to replace items currently imported with domestic production. Although the policy was progressively abandoned in Latin America, particularly during the 1990s, China has since adopted it at massive scale. In 2006, Beijing introduced its National Medium-and Long-Term Plan for the Development of Science and Technology (2006–20). This sought to reduce China's reliance on products containing foreign technology from 60 percent in 2006 to 30 percent by 2020 (see Chapter 7).[11]

The advantage of targeting currently imported goods is that these are often products on the next rung up of industrial sophistication, and the market already exists. The disadvantages are a) The policy focuses industry on serving the domestic market, which may not make demands as rigorous as overseas customers, and b) Some goods will not be manufacturable domestically at acceptable cost within an acceptable timeframe.

Selective Importation is the deliberate importation of product components and foreign capital goods, typically production machinery, by nations pursuing export-led growth. This policy often allows tariff-free importation of machinery and technology while forbidding or heavily taxing imports of consumer and luxury goods.

As of 2019, in Korea, all imports of equipment for manufacturing computer chips were duty-free, but only 45 percent of computer chips themselves were.[12] Japan's Mitsubishi, when trying unsuccessfully to break into passenger jets, opted to import the Pratt and Whitney PW1000G engine from the US, rather than developing its own.[13] After World War II, the Japanese government compiled a list – periodically updated to reflect the country's rising living standards – of consumer goods deemed luxurious.[14]

Such restrictions conserve foreign exchange, often scarce in developing nations, for investments that upgrade the nation's productive capacities. They also increase the national savings rate by tilting expenditures away from consumption, resulting in more investment capital.

Today, China stands out regarding such policies in the sheer size of the consumer market thereby stifled. A combination of import tariffs, value-added taxes, and consumption taxes means that the effective tax rate can easily reach 30–50 percent for items such as jewelry, luxury leather goods, automobiles, and cosmetics. A thriving industry of overseas shopping or *daigou* has developed alongside rampant smuggling and counterfeiting.

Export Subsidies and Targets are most effective when used together, and are often combined with infant industry protection.

The *subsidy* component is about helping newcomer firms succeed in difficult industries. For example, a government may cause a state-owned bank to lend money cheaply to a manufacturer wishing to import machine tools for an export-oriented assembly line. The *target* component is about making the subsidy conditional on achieving a specified quantity of export sales, because a subsidy without conditions easily becomes a handout. If the required exports do not occur, the subsidy ends.

This policy keeps protectionism from creating a "lazy" industry content with the easy profits from its domestic market (see Chapter 11). Export sales are a simple test, and easy to enforce because foreign cash is hard to fake. In combination with tariffs or other protection, the policy generates the invigorating pressure of foreign competition *without* risking losing the industry to imports. Domestic firms are forced to become competitive in the global market, where the best in the world compete, setting the standard for technology, quality, and cost.

For governments eager to climb the ladder of ever-more-advantageous industries, the short-term profitability of firms is often secondary to acquiring technical know-how. Therefore, firms may receive government subsidies even after they have achieved profitability in their initial niches, so that they may continue up the learning curve. Generalized, this process is known as "export-led industrialization," as export demand pulls the whole economy forward, industry by industry, including their supply chains.[15]

Japan, Korea, and China, among others, have for decades grown industries by subsidizing exports while protecting their domestic markets. Korea, for example, used to maintain very low real interest rates on bank loans to targeted sectors, under such names as the Machine Industry Promotion Fund, the Term Loan Fund, the Medium Industry Fund, and the Export Industry Equipment Fund (see Chapter 6).[16] Less successfully, India is trying to do the same today. The names of its programs speak for themselves: the Remission of Duties and Taxes on Exported Products Scheme, the Export Oriented Units Scheme, the Export Promotion Capital Goods Scheme, and the Duty-Free Imports for Exporters Program (see Chapter 11).[17]

China has used, and still uses, subsidize-and-target policies at epic scale: Between 2000 and 2006, 140,000 manufacturing exporters benefited from subsidies with Export Share Requirements (ESRs).[18] The government makes subsidized loans, even outright grants, to fund firms' modernization and enable them to export. It offers tax breaks conditional on a certain share of output being exported – usually 50 percent. Further exemptions, from local taxes, for example, may follow at an even higher export intensity. A telltale sign of this policy is that many Chinese companies export all or almost all of their output, something rarely seen elsewhere (see Chapter 7).

Export subsidies can not only nurture infant industries, but also allow mature industries to underprice and decimate foreign competitors. Most such subsidies violate WTO rules, but since *any* policy that reduces the cost of producing a product can serve, this restriction only tells against the most explicit subsidies.

Incentives for Foreign Firms are inducements to locate in a country and export. These include low corporate taxes, investment subsidies, preferential import tariffs for inputs, special export zones, and streamlining of bureaucracy. Some national and local governments have even offered free land or buildings.

Foreign firms are valued for their capital, technology, and international distribution networks. Measures to court them also include investments in infrastructure and education in the targeted sectors, such as electronics in Southeast Asia and automobiles in Mexico and Brazil. Ireland since the 1950s has implemented a very favorable corporate tax regime. America's federal government has not offered such incentives, but individual states have, for example to German, Japanese, and Korean automakers, especially in the South.

While foreign investments bring benefits, the fact that their offshore owners can withdraw them risks the host country getting trapped in a competition to offer the lowest taxes, lowest wages, highest subsidies, and laxest regulation. During economic downturns, foreign owners often close their offshore plants first, something the UK has experienced multiple times (see Chapter 10).

To avoid such problems, nations accepting foreign investment must transition over time to competing on attributes other than price. For example, they can foster the accumulation of specialized skills by local workers and advanced capabilities by local supply chains, creating advantages that are difficult to duplicate elsewhere.

Nations with internal markets large enough to create leverage, like Japan in past decades and China today, have required foreign firms wishing to sell there to form joint ventures with local companies to force the transfer of product and production know-how. (This violates WTO rules, so it tends to be implemented informally, rather than by law or written agreement.) China today also offers, both formally and informally, better access to its domestic market for companies that export from China.

Export Processing Zones (EPZs) are geographic regions, also known as Free Trade Zones, or in China Special Economic Zones, with special laws and policies designed to make them attractive for foreign industrial investment. Provisions include tariff exemptions on inputs imported for export production and liberalized rules on foreign ownership. By 2006, 130 countries had more than 3,500 such zones, with 66 million workers.[19] Some EPZs are single factories, while others, such as the Chinese SEZs, are entire major cities. The SEZs have been key drivers of China's growth. In 2015, they accounted for 60 percent of its exports, 22 percent of GDP, and 45 percent of FDI (see Chapter 7).[20]

A less successful example is Mexico's *maquiladora* plants along its US border. These were set up starting in 1965, when Mexico was still a closed economy with very limited imports and exports. Mexico allowed duty-free entry to materials and equipment, plus 100 percent foreign ownership, conditional on exporting 100 percent of production. By 2000, these plants employed 1.3 million people, and by 2013, they produced 65 percent of Mexico's manufactured exports.[21] But due to Mexico's lack of a full array of complementary policies, they have *not* been launchpads for an economy-wide rise in productivity. The country has mostly remained stuck in mid-range processing and assembly activities, and its per capita GDP has not significantly converged with that of the US.[22]

Regulatory Competition means lowering regulatory costs or expanding the range of permitted activities to compete with established business centers. A more sophisticated practice is establishing effective legal governance frameworks to enable emerging industries to achieve sustained growth, rather than the boom, corruption, and bust that tends to accompany the absence of regulation.

In manufacturing, regulatory competition often involves environmental protections or worker health and safety rules. A lax regulatory regime, both in legal standards and in actual enforcement, is common in developing nations.

In services, strategies include low transparency and reporting requirements, compliance with which can be expensive. The downside is a greater risk of dubious practices and disreputable players. Thus, Singapore and Hong Kong have taken market share from the traditional money management centers of London, New York, and Tokyo. Online gambling is another industry currently in search of the friendliest regulatory environment, and as of 2024, AI regulation is up in the air, with the EU having just enacted rules.

Credit Allocation means directing capital to uses believed to be more conducive to the long-term growth of the economy than those the market would choose on its own. The global omnipresence of financial institutions with the words "industrial," "development," and the name of the country in their names testifies to how widespread the policy is.

In China, the state-controlled banking system is used to finance whatever industries the Communist Party wishes to prioritize.

In Germany, KfW (Reconstruction Credit Institution) has played a crucial role in post–World War II industrial development, providing long-term financing for expansion, innovation, and exports. Today, its Mittelstandbank focuses on small and medium enterprises (SMEs) (see Chapter 8).

Oséo was a French public institution that financed innovative SMEs through loan guarantees, subsidies, and grants. In 2010, it supplied 22 percent of public funding for private-sector R&D.[23] It has since been merged into Bpifrance, which aims to be a "one-stop shop" to bolster France's entrepreneurship ecosystem, providing equity investments, loan guarantees, export credit, private equity investments, and working capital (see Chapter 9).[24]

The EU's 2007–13 Competitiveness and Innovation Framework Programme was designed, among other things, to increase SME access to finance by offering loan guarantees.[25] At that time, the EU's Risk-Sharing Finance Facility supported high-risk, high-reward ventures through loans, guarantees, and equity investments.[26]

In many countries, industrial conglomerates have grown up around financial institutions owned by the conglomerates themselves. Such combinations, often buttressed by cross-shareholdings and shared directors, have been and remain a major factor in the growth of Japan, South Korea, Brazil, and

Indonesia, among others. These conglomerates have all been actively or passively supported by their respective governments.[27]

The US itself engages in credit allocation. The federal government subsidizes loans for housing (Fannie Mae, Freddie Mac, the mortgage interest deduction), small businesses (the Small Business Administration), universities (federal student loan programs), and exports (the Export–Import Bank). It de facto subsidizes financial speculation by bailing out the financial sector and creating the expectation of future bailouts (see Chapter 18). This highlights the importance of de facto industrial policy – that is, what a nation actually encourages, quite apart from what it may like to think it does.

Forced Savings Policies aim to increase investment capital available to industry. Government encourages or forces people and firms to save money, especially in designated financial institutions and instruments. Policies include restricting opportunities to spend money (import restrictions on luxury goods, curtailed shopping days and hours, limits on nonbusiness foreign travel, restrictions on currency convertibility), limiting opportunities to invest abroad (prohibitions on foreign banking or securities accounts), and incentivizing people to want large savings (a sparse social safety net and prohibiting home mortgages).

Singapore, for example, forces people to save a quota of their income for retirement and doesn't pay significant unemployment benefits.

In China, the state-owned banking system keeps returns on savings low to keep capital cheap and forces citizens to accept these low returns by limiting overseas investment. In recent years, Beijing has managed to squeeze private consumption down to 38 percent of national income, which has allowed savings, and thus investment, to reach 43 percent.[28]

The corresponding figures for the US are 68 and 18 percent.[29] But developed nations *need* less savings, as they already have enough capital stock to generate a high per capita GDP and have plenty of liquid investment capital. As nations develop, less can be gained from maximizing the sheer quantity of investable capital and more from making better choices about how to use it.[30] Developing nations often prefer forced domestic savings to foreign capital because they fear losing control, a fear exacerbated for some by memories of colonialism.

Forced savings policies go hand in hand with trade surpluses and currency manipulation because someone other than the squeezed domestic consumer has to buy the output resulting from the increased capital investment. They are thus a hidden but significant cause of international economic conflict. (See Chapter 4.)

Sovereign Wealth Funds (SWFs) are large pools of capital owned and controlled by governments for funding investments and covering long-term liabilities such as pensions.

The SWF Institute in 2023 estimated the total size of the top 100 funds at $11.5 trillion.[31] (Global financial assets are $530 trillion.)[32] In some nations, SWF money derives from overseas assets accumulated as a byproduct of currency manipulation. In others, it comes from petroleum exports.

Countries invest SWF funds abroad because of limited domestic investment opportunities and because investing abroad reduces the currency appreciation that would otherwise undermine their export competitiveness. The latter problem is known as the "Dutch disease," after the harm done to Dutch manufacturing by the appreciation of the guilder after a huge natural gas field went into production in 1963.

Sovereign wealth money is often used to support national champion companies. For example, Singapore's fund, Temasek, has successfully promoted state-owned champions across a wide range of industries, including shipping, airlines, telecommunications, shipbuilding, and financial services, many of which have become dominant regional players.[33]

In recent years, China has become the most aggressive country in using sovereign wealth to promote exports. The most visible example is China State Construction and Engineering Corporation (CSCEC). A state-owned and state-financed company, it has become one of the largest construction firms in the world. It is at the forefront of China's Belt and Road infrastructure initiative to open up Eurasian markets for Chinese exports.

CSCEC epitomizes how state capital is used to promote national economic *and geopolitical* interests. It is one of many firms under the ownership of the State-owned Assets Supervision and Administration Commission (SASAC). SASAC is now the single largest economic entity in the world, with the 96 companies under its control having combined assets of $10 trillion in 2020.[34] (The value of all American firms listed on US stock exchanges is about $53 trillion.)[35]

Government Procurement is the purchase of goods and services by government to create demand that would not otherwise exist. Government purchases are a significant percentage of GDP in most nations, so this tactic can be potent. Typical areas include health, education, public works, energy supply, public transport, military hardware, and telecommunications.

In developing nations, the government is often the only entity large and sophisticated enough to buy products at scale sufficient to create the markets needed to launch domestic producers. It can also promote new technologies ahead of private-sector demand: In China, government fleet purchases jump-started the electric vehicle market.

Since World War II, the US government has played a significant role as a *lead buyer* of technologies and services ahead of private-sector demand. The early stages of most of America's high-technology industries of today were created by federal investments in basic and applied research followed by large-scale government procurement. For example, the military was a major early buyer of transistors, integrated circuits, and jet aircraft (see Chapters 19 and 26).

State Entrepreneurship is the state itself acting as a risk-taking investor. This is not socialism, with its renunciation of the profit motive, but the state as a capitalist.

In 1968, for example, the Korean government founded a state-owned steel manufacturer, Pohang Iron and Steel, with the help of US and Japanese investments and technology. Seoul showered the firm with subsidies, and it eventually replaced 109 inefficient older steelmakers in the country. It has since become a world leader, and its price and quality have been an advantage for Korean carmakers – an important spillover to another advantageous industry. Pohang was eventually taken private (with foreigners buying 50 percent) in 1998 (see Chapter 6).

Dutch State Mines (DSM) was established in 1902 to mine Dutch coal because the nation's existing coal industry was foreign owned. After the European coal crisis of 1958–9, in which overproduction produced falling prices and mine closures, DSM systematically phased out coal production and transitioned to distributing Holland's recently discovered natural gas and developing its petrochemical industry. In the 1990s, it transitioned again, out of commodity chemicals and into fine chemicals, materials, biotechnology, and food ingredients. Privatized in 1989–96, it is today an innovative, diversified global company employing 23,000.[36]

India's state-owned pharmaceutical firms have had government support since the 1950s. Their science base has been supported by government research institutes. An intellectual property regime that did not recognize foreign patents allowed them to manufacture drugs designed and tested elsewhere. Protected from imports and subsidized, they were able to invest in R&D and accumulate production skills. Today, India is the world's largest (though sometimes unsafe) supplier of generic medicines, accounting for roughly 20 percent of global output (see Chapter 11).[37]

The Brazilian government founded Embraer in 1969 as part of a strategy to develop the country's aircraft industry, and today it is the world's largest builder of regional jets.[38] Public procurement, government-established engineering schools, research and training centers, as well as financial support from the Brazilian development bank, BNDES, allowed it to survive in a highly competitive and capital-intensive industry. Today, it is a private company, but with the government retaining a "golden share" conferring veto power over key decisions.[39]

National Champions are particular firms supported by government to be industry leaders. In many advantageous industries, due to scale economies, only firms as large as the global leaders can be competitive. So, firms in such industries are encouraged by their governments to merge to attain this scale and avoid the fierce domestic competition in which no one firm is profitable enough to afford the required ongoing investments.

A national champion policy can work, but has pitfalls. At worst, it has produced bloated failures soldered together from incompatible companies.[40] Examples include the nationalized automaker British Leyland, whose final rump successor went bankrupt in 2005 after decades of decline, and the still-existing French computer firm Machines Bull, which, like Britain's now-defunct ICL and Italy's Olivetti, struggled to compete with IBM in the 1960s and '70s.

The governments responsible for these computer firms were not wrong to imagine that the industry was advantageous, or that state action could build a viable position in it. After all, the globally dominant US industry was nurtured on government support (see Chapters 19, 26, and 30). But they failed to understand that in a "winner take all" industry such as computers, their only options were a) sufficient investment to achieve global dominance, b) nibbling around the edges of the industry selling add-ons and exploiting niches ignored by IBM, or c) very expensive failure. The successful non-IBM US computer makers of the day chose option b), but because the French, British, and Italians did not choose b) and could not afford a), they ended up with c).

However, designating national champions has been a successful strategy in some nations. Saudi Basic Industries Corporation is one of the world's largest and most profitable chemical firms. Dubai's DP World is among the world's biggest operators of ports and cargo terminals. Firms as diverse as Hyundai, Samsung, Siemens, Embraer, Volkswagen, and LG have been supported as national champions at various times in their histories. In large passenger aircraft, a multination, half-century effort has created Airbus, the European *multinational* champion that has taken roughly half the global market.[41]

Many Chinese national champions are among China's largest firms, and several are state-owned enterprises (SOEs). In 1998, Premier Zhu Rongji began reforming the SOE sector, including a major push to turn the largest into champions that could dominate the domestic market, compete on the global stage, and be instruments of China's national interests abroad. American companies competing against these firms are, to say the least, not on a level playing field. China's strategy emphasizes maximizing assets, rather than profits, and the ability of these firms to ignore the profit imperatives under which US companies operate is a significant advantage.

Imposing Competitive Industry Structure means driving excellence by enhancing competition.

Korea, during the 1961–87 heyday of its active industrial policies, usually made sure there were at least three or four *chaebol* conglomerates competing in each sector.[42] Taiwan fostered hundreds of small firms in electronics so that a few large ones could emerge from the pack. Singapore, Malaysia, and China have all ensured that multiple foreign multinationals competed against each other on their soil.

As discussed in Chapter 1, intense price competition is generally a characteristic of *dis*advantageous industries, where producers of an unchanging, undifferentiated product, such as plain T-shirts, are forced to compete on mere price. And yet fierce competition *within advantageous industries* is beneficial, because in technologically dynamic industries, firms can respond by innovating, not just cutting prices.

The US has traditionally used antitrust law to ensure competition in industries where competition is feasible, and utility regulation to restrain natural monopolies where it is not. Since 1980, changed doctrine (following Robert Bork) and less enforcement has led to greater concentration in industry after industry, and some public utility regulation has been eliminated outright.

Concentration caused by abusive, anticompetitive conduct is very different from that caused by scale economies and technological dynamism. For the latter, forcing breakups is not beneficial. Such cases fall into two categories:

1. Industries requiring such vast capital and expertise that only a few firms are viable. Here, policy should try to ensure that competition happens through innovation and productivity, not anticompetitive behavior.
2. Network and other systems where fragmentation is inefficient, such as the old AT&T. Here, policy should aim at fair treatment of customers, suppliers, and other firms, using tools such as rate regulation, interoperability mandates, and standards setting.

Antitrust policy is complicated by the fact that many industries are global. A concentrated domestic market may thus be irrelevant, and membership in a global oligarchy that extracts rent from nations outside it may be in the national interest.

Economies as large as the US, the EU, and China can usually have both firms of global scale *and* competitive internal markets, as they can support multiple competitors in almost every advantageous industry. And many of their single-firm industries will face strong international competition, as with Boeing and Airbus.

Fostering Clusters means supporting and creating geographic industry clusters, which are often extraordinarily successful. Governments try to sustain and improve existing clusters, nurture nascent ones to fruition, and create new ones from scratch.

A cluster contains firms and supporting institutions such as government agencies, universities, and nonprofits. Clusters tend to include multiple stages in industries' supply chains: Some firms assemble final products, while others make components or provide specialized services such as contract research.

Clusters work for several reasons. Transaction costs are lower with local suppliers. Clusters facilitate complex communication between firms at different stages in supply chains, easing innovations requiring coordination across these stages.

Clusters tend to develop support firms, such as specialized law firms, consultants, and venture capitalists. Companies can share infrastructure, such as specialized training or testing facilities, which no one firm could support. The top people in an industry are attracted to a region where they will not be dependent on one potential employer. Firms are attracted to the deep talent pool.

Clusters accumulate social capital as a result of repeated interactions, personal relationships, and shared educational paths. Accumulated trust increases willingness to take risks. Clusters expose employees to other firms, helping prevent companies from getting stuck in ruts, and foster cross-fertilization of ideas. If someone with an innovative idea is stymied at their current employer, it is easy to move to another.

Clusters encourage rivalry because they make each firm's successes more visible to the others. They tend to spawn new firms. Clusters thus help avoid the economic brittleness that can result when a single firm, which can decline or go bankrupt, is the dominant employer in a region. When one firm declines, others can pick up the slack. And if an industry's products or technology change, the ascendant firms are more likely to be local.

Not that clusters are a panacea: The world's leading aerospace cluster, in greater Los Angeles, unraveled after the end of the Cold War, and the concentration of America's auto industry in Detroit helped create inbred thinking (see Chapter 25). Still, ascendant SpaceX is located in LA today because the aerospace cluster was there previously.

It is much easier for governments to support existing clusters than to create new ones. A cluster requires a critical mass of many firms, skilled employees, and supporting institutions, so creating one from nothing requires huge investments, on multiple fronts, often for decades. (See Chapters 29 and 30.)

To support existing clusters, governments use most of the policies mentioned in this chapter. To create new ones, they do the same with an emphasis on seeding *new* firms, institutions, and programs, often growing these out of existing entities. Thus, 2022's Chips and Science Act included $500 million to help create new technology clusters in regions currently lacking them.[43]

Supporting the Industrial Commons refers to the networks of suppliers and know-how that industries rely on.

Industries are often critically dependent upon resources shared with and supported by *other* industries. For example, in the words of Gary Pisano and Willy Shih of Harvard Business School,

> Software knowledge and skills, for instance, are vital to an extremely wide range of industries (machine tools, medical devices, earth-moving equipment, automobiles, aircraft, computers, consumer electronics, defense). Similarly, capabilities related to thin-film deposition processes are crucial to sophisticated optics; to such electronic products as semiconductors and disk drives; and to industrial tools, packaging, solar panels, and advanced displays. The knowledge, skills, and equipment related to the development and production of advanced materials are a commons for such diverse industries as aerospace, automobiles, medical devices, and consumer products. Biotechnology is a commons not just for drugs but also for agriculture and the emerging alternative-fuels industry.[44]

These relationships mean that the thriving of one industry can depend on the health of quite different industries, and a lack of local capability in key supporting industries can make it impossible to produce or innovate certain products in a country or region. When one industry moves offshore, it can damage others, and once a tipping point is passed, a cascading collapse of interdependent industries can follow. It can be difficult and costly to rebuild the lost capabilities – often requiring strategic, expensive, and sustained government support. For example, the US lost the ability to manufacture the most advanced computer chips, so the CHIPS Act in 2022 committed $52 billion to get it back.

Other products whose US production is threatened or already lost include LEDs for lighting, advanced LCD displays, advanced carbon fiber components, many key starting materials and active ingredients for drugs, integrated-circuit packaging (though the firm American Semiconductor is trying to bring it back using new technology), fine chemicals, forging and casting, advanced ceramics, and consumer-grade advanced composites.[45] Many capabilities were lost gradually: Foreign producers first entered the US market with lower-end products, or took over the simpler steps of their manufacture, such as labor-intensive final assembly. They then used that base to develop more advanced capabilities.

Policies to support the industrial commons also include almost all the policies discussed in this chapter, but with this objective.

Supporting Private Research: As noted in Chapter 1, there are often positive spillovers to the wider economy from the research of private firms, so governments subsidize it.[46]

The federal R&D tax credit was created in 1981 and extended 16 times before being made permanent in 2015. It offers a credit of 20 percent of qualified expenditures over a base calculated from prior years to avoid incentivizing research that would have happened anyway. Studies show that it succeeds at increasing R&D.[47] Other nations have similar policies, but while the US once had the world's most generous version, by 2022 it ranked 35th.[48]

Some governments have agencies that perform industrial research on a cost-sharing basis with private firms. Germany's Fraunhofer Society is one example (see Chapters 8 and 23), as are parts of Japan's National Institute of Advanced Industrial Science and Technology.[49] The Industrial Technology Research Institute of Taiwan has played a major role in transforming Taiwan's economy over the past 50 years (see Chapter 23). America has the excellent but far too small Manufacturing USA (see Chapter 21).

Other governmental support for private research targets the notorious "valley of death" between pure science and the commercialization of technology, where many promising technologies perish. For example, Cyclotron Road at Lawrence Berkeley National Laboratory, a Department of Energy facility in California, provides fellowships to PhD-level researchers working to advance their ideas from concept to initial product (see Chapter 21).

To have economic impact, knowledge must not only be created, but also transmitted to firms and deployed at scale. The federal Manufacturing Extension Partnership (MEP) focuses on this for smaller firms that lack the resources to stay abreast of and implement technological advances on their own. It has 51 centers nationwide, with 1,450 manufacturing specialists at more than 400 service locations.[50] It operates on a cost-sharing basis between its industry clients, local governments, the federal government, and the states. As of 2022, every federal dollar it spent generated $40.50 in new private investment, and every $1,353 of federal money created or saved one manufacturing job (see Chapter 22).[51]

Supporting Public Research means governments directly funding research in basic science and hard-to-commercialize technologies.

Basic science is usually impossible for any firm to keep to itself, so it is rarely funded by for-profit entities. In the past, it was sometimes funded by state-sanctioned monopolies, such as AT&T, and by oligopolistic private companies, such as GE and Westinghouse, as they had sufficient commercial scope to anticipate profitably harvesting its benefits. (See Chapter 21 for how this system broke down.) Federally funded R&D – the spending that generates fundamental technological breakthroughs – peaked at 1.9 percent of GDP in 1962, fell to 0.7 percent by 2020, and as of 2024, is only beginning a possible turnaround.[52]

Hard-to-commercialize technologies usually fall into two categories: *fundamental* technologies and *infratechnologies.*

Fundamental technologies are the most basic innovations, such as jet engines and the internet. Since World War II, they have rarely come from the private sector on its own (see Chapter 19). The federal government currently spends more than $140 billion a year researching them, through NASA, the National Institutes of Health, the Defense Advanced Research Projects Agency, and others (see Chapters 20 and 26).[53]

Infratechnologies are the often-hidden but crucial technologies used, inter alia, for communication, measurement, standardization, testing, and cataloguing. Here are examples from the emerging field of biological nanotechnology (see Chapter 28):

- Methods for detecting nanomaterials in biological matrices, environments, and workplaces
- Methods for standardizing particle sizes and size distribution
- Standardized tools for assessing nanomaterial shape, structure, and surface area
- Inventories of engineered nanomaterials and their uses
- Methods to quantify and characterize exposure to nanomaterials in biological matrices[54]

Infratechnologies include the protocols, such as Wi-Fi, that enable devices to interact. Because these are generally most useful when freely available, it makes sense for them to be provided by the public or nonprofit sectors, rather than being owned or controlled by a for-profit firm.

In the US, the underappreciated National Institute of Standards and Technologies (NIST) is the agency focused on Infratechnologies (see Chapter 20).

Intellectual Property (IP) Policy – The governance of proprietary know-how such as patents, trade secrets, trademarks, and copyrights.

Patents provide a period of market exclusivity in exchange for public disclosure of their contents, thereby rewarding innovation without blocking related innovations. They are national, so global markets require patenting in many countries. They are not self-enforcing and require expensive lawsuits to defend. America's patent system is currently in a state of crisis (see Chapter 24).

Trade secrets are confidential information with commercial value, and stealing them is illegal under the domestic laws of all major nations. Trademarks distinguish the products of one firm from another; Chinese counterfeit consumer goods and machine parts are the best-known problem area here. Copyrights protect the creative industries: publishing and media more generally, plus computer software.

The 1994 Agreement on Trade-Related Aspects of Intellectual Property Rights (TRIPS), which all WTO member states have signed, commits nations to protecting the patents, trade secrets, trademarks, and copyrights of other member states. The exact same rules do not apply to all countries, and the differences have been the subject of intense negotiations between developing and developed nations.

The US is a major exporter of IP, with a $75 billion surplus in 2022, so IP violations are a major problem for America.[55] Movies, designs for consumer goods, computer chip designs, cellular telephony software, and other major technology systems have all been stolen. The nonprofit Commission on the Theft of American Intellectual Property has estimated the value of theft of American IP at 1–3 percent of US GDP.[56]

Nations needing foreign IP enter into license agreements if they are honest, or reverse engineer or steal it if they are not. China is the worst offender; it is no accident that IP theft was the major stated justification for the Trump administration's first round of tariffs against that nation in 2017. Ironically, China is now *strengthening* its domestic patent system as it transitions from being a net consumer of IP to being a significant producer in its own right.

Nations also design IP-acquisition policies not involving theft. For example, IP rules, together with other regulations, were used in several countries, the outstanding example being India, to support development of a generic drug industry – though doing so has become more difficult since the TRIPS Agreement.[57] Other lawful tactics include governments' organizing cartels of domestic buyers of foreign IP to drive the price down, as Japan has done (see Chapter 5).

Standards Setting covers the rules, such as car safety standards and cell phone protocols, required for technologies to function, interface with other technologies, and be accepted in the marketplace.

Standards setting is often done by governments, as opposed to the private sector, for good reasons. The private sector, where each firm pushes its own standard, may not be able to agree, resulting in a fragmented industry with incompatible products. Allowing one firm to impose its proprietary standard on a whole industry can sometimes work, as with IBM from the 1960s to the early 1980s, but raises antitrust concerns.

Standards setting can also serve as a form of protectionism. As an obscure, WTO-compliant policy, it can strengthen a national champion due to its familiarity with the idiosyncratic national standard.

Standards setting has also been used to force up quality of demand, compel replacement sales by making older models obsolete, and push the local industry to the technological frontier. Japan's rigorous annual auto inspection, the *shaken*, incentivizes drivers to drive a relatively new car. (It also makes Japan a huge exporter of used cars, making it harder for other countries to compete with Japan at the lower end of the car market.)

During China's 2004–9 migration from 2G to 3G, the country's largest mobile operator, China Mobile, was required to use the TD-SCDMA standard.[58] It was inferior to available global standards but chosen because it was indigenously developed (more precisely, adapted from a German standard). This put China Mobile at a disadvantage relative to other operators in the short run, as they were allowed to use more efficient foreign standards. However, the Chinese telecom equipment industry gained huge expertise by developing and deploying the system, building up firms such as Huawei and ZTE. This broke foreign control over China's mobile industry and freed China from paying huge foreign licensing fees. When 4G arrived, China was able to promote a standard, LTE-TDD, that it had developed itself. And when the world migrated to 5G, China was a major export player.

Going forward, China aspires, as shown by its China Standards 2035 plan, to set not just domestic but *global* standards for emerging technologies such as artificial intelligence and the Internet of Things (IOT) – which would be a major step toward global Chinese technological dominance (see Chapter 7).

Technology Mapping means understanding dependencies between technological capabilities, so as to know in what order they must mastered to achieve a targeted end product, and to block rivals attempting the same thing. During the Reagan administration, pathbreaking work on technology mapping was done in Project Socrates, a CIA-Defense Intelligence Agency project that should be revived.[59] In 2023, NSF's new Directorate for Technology, Innovation and Partnerships announced funding of $30 million to develop a new program, Assessing and Predicting Technology Outcomes (APTO).[60] Its purpose is to understand America's competitive position in the technology focus areas designated in 2022's CHIPS Act.

Technology Denial means efforts to deny rival nations access to key technologies. It goes back centuries: in the eighteenth century, China banned export of its porcelain technology, Britain of its textile technology. During the Cold War, the US and its allies established the Coordinating Committee for Multilateral Export Control to block Soviet access to military and dual-use civilian-military technologies. In 2019, Japan even blocked chip exports to

South Korea in a political spat unrelated to trade. The CHIPS Act prohibits funded companies from making advanced integrated circuits in China and other "countries of concern" for 10 years after a grant. Following the Act, the Commerce Department tightened export controls to deny China and other hostile nations advanced semiconductor and semiconductor-manufacturing technology (see Chapter 18).

Combining Policies is important because industrial policy tools rarely succeed in isolation. (A common way to mistakenly dismiss the entire concept of industrial policy is to examine the track record of one specific tool, such as cash subsidies, on its own.) Instead, the tools discussed above, when successful, are almost always employed in strategic combination. There is no universally applicable protocol for how to combine them, because the right strategy will be specific to each industry and its national and international context.

Modern economies are complex and have many "pressure points" where industrial policies can be applied. This chapter has focused on the more obvious tools, but there are many others. Intricacies of the tax code and accounting rules, tacit understandings between government officials and industry associations, deliberate gaps between what laws say and what actually gets enforced: All can serve as tools of industrial policy, though they often leave only faint paper trails, especially for outsiders. Obscurity doesn't mean these policies don't exist – but it does mean that legalistic efforts, such as those of the WTO, to outlaw them are futile.

Picking Winners: The net result of applying the policies discussed in this chapter is that many governments have favored particular firms at particular times, so that government, not the marketplace, picked which grew and made a profit. *Pace* abstract arguments that it is impossible to thereby outperform the market, *some* governments have succeeded at this *some* of the time (see Chapters 5–9).

Many governments have also failed, as the outcome depends on the quality of the policies imposed. Above all, failure has been the rule in nations that have lacked a) systemic understanding of what industrial policy should aim at and how, and b) institutions to efficiently impose policies once devised (see Chapters 10–12).

Opponents of industrial policy often point to its documented failures, which are real, as evidence that the very concept is doomed. But in the private sector, the failure of some firms is not taken as proof that capitalism is unworkable. Similarly, arguments against full-blown central planning, in which government controls *all* economic decisions, are misapplied against rational industrial policy, which takes a market framework as given and intervenes only strategically.

Another understandable objection to industrial policy is political capture, the corruption of decision-making by industry for its own interests. But industrial policy is no different from any other area of government in this regard. Those on the receiving end of policy will *always* try to bend it to their own benefit, and much of our political system revolves around countering such efforts. For example, because rent-seeking is well known and resented, attempts at it will generate political pushback. (See Chapter 15 for how this worked during America's own tariff era.)

Sound industrial policy programs have processes to mitigate corruption, such as transparency rules, conflict-of-interest laws, and requirements that officials making scientific decisions have corresponding scientific credentials. Metrics such as numbers of jobs created and sales figures for startups nurtured enable monitoring and culling of ineffective policies. Clawback provisions recover grants from firms when goals for which subsidies are provided are not met. (See Chapter 29 for one successful program with such provisions.)

In a developed nation like the US, picking winners will very rarely be appropriate, as the sophistication of our private sector, unlike in developing nations, makes it quite capable of picking most winners on its own. Most of the industrial policies America will need will therefore not involve favoring the profitability of any one enterprise. Picking *technologies* and favoring advantageous *sectors* is not picking winners, because these policies do not direct profit to any particular company. Nor is it picking winners to level the playing field with tariffs. There is a "market layer" between these governmental decisions and private sector bottom lines.

However, it will sometimes be necessary for the US government to pick winners to create or sustain national champions. It would not be rational for America to neglect Boeing or Intel, its de facto national champions in large commercial aircraft and semiconductors. And it was appropriate for the CHIPS Act of 2022 to subsidize Intel's and TSMC's creation of onshore capacity to manufacture the most advanced computer chips. The appropriate quid pro quo for such support is that the recipient firms continually develop and manufacture risky, difficult technologies with long time horizons *in the US*.

Also, where the risk is too high, the rewards too uncertain, and the time to market too long for private capital, it will sometimes be necessary for government to pick winners to help small companies developing breakthrough technologies get through the "Valley of Death" to initial commercialization (see Chapter 21). In such cases, a public version of the portfolio strategy of private-sector VCs will be appropriate, supporting multiple firms taking different approaches with the understanding that most will fail – but that the successes will be valuable enough to outweigh them. The alternative is to allow these technologies to languish in the lab and watch other nations commercialize them.

Large-scale public support for particular companies may also be necessary when the need for rapid large-scale production is urgent and the technology is still experimental, as with the COVID vaccines.

Similarly, when the 2008–10 financial crisis disrupted private financial markets, the solar and wind power industries merited the public help they received to keep financing large-scale installations.

4 TRADE, CURRENCIES, AND INDUSTRIAL POLICY

Bringing trade into the industrial policy picture ends the possibility of a purely free-market policy because so few of America's trading partners play by free-market rules. Trading with them thus necessarily entails the distorting effects of *their* policies on *our* markets. If China sells subsidized widgets in the US, their price here will not be a free-market price. As a result, whether widgets are produced in the US, and at what profit and with what wages, will no longer be determined by the market, but by the size of China's subsidy. Americans will not be able to rely upon the market efficiently allocating the location of production between the two nations, or allocating the labor and capital to each industry that is optimal – either for the US or for the world at large.[1]

Under these conditions, any attempt by the US to embrace a free-market policy will just result in the size and product mix of our tradable sectors being determined by the industrial policies of other nations. The US today is in the position small nations have always been in and that America itself was in through the early nineteenth century: needing to design its economic policies around those of other countries. It follows that some degree of *mercantilism* – that is, state intervention in trade to defend our national economic interests – is now forced upon us. Whether to intervene is no longer a choice: The unavoidable question is what kind of intervention is best.

The overarching theme of this book is that while free markets are a vital part of a successful economy, it is also necessary to a) take advantage of and respond proactively to their inherent shortcomings, and b) counter the efforts of other nations to intervene in markets to our disadvantage. As explained in this chapter, mainstream trade theory is essentially a perfect-markets theory and falls apart when one examines the shortcomings of international markets and how they can be deliberately exploited.

The Opportunities and Threats of Trade

Trade enables every nation to plug into a global economy that has greater technological sophistication and production scale than it has. This is true for all nations, but especially for small ones, as they lack the ability to produce most goods domestically, either efficiently or at all. Their internal markets are too small to support production facilities at viable scale, and domestic sales alone will not provide enough profits to plow back into R&D to keep these industries up to date.

But by exporting, even small nations can achieve production scale sufficient to be cost-competitive in scale-economy, advantageous, industries – with all the benefits of such industries discussed in Chapter 2. They can specialize in narrow but lucrative niches. Taiwan, for example, in 2012 made 89 percent of the world's laptops with a domestic market of only 1 percent of the world's total.[2] These niches can be not only end products, but also components or steps in supply chains.

Imports play a key role too. Few nations can produce all the goods their citizens want. Import competition disciplines domestic producers against inefficiency, presses them to improve, and disrupts crony capitalists. Nations can "import" quality-of-demand and quality-of-supply (explained in Chapter 1) by serving demanding foreign customers and buying from the best foreign suppliers. And imports can provide components and raw materials for a nation's exports.

But trade *also* confronts every nation seeking to acquire more-advantageous industries with the fact that nations that already have them will often have entrenched positions that are hard to overcome by market means alone (see Chapter 2). Incumbents already producing at high volumes will have lower per-unit costs than newcomers. Supply chains with interlocking dependencies and established business relationships can be hard to shift. Specialized expertise – especially learning-by-doing, which requires actual production – can be difficult to acquire.

As a result, new entrants must use proactive industrial policies to break in. Nations already hosting advantageous industries must then defend themselves against these efforts to take them away. So effective industrial policy for the US will require some protectionist measures. But because a group of interrelated mainstream theories opposes almost all protectionism, choosing sound policies requires understanding these theories and why they are misleading half-truths.

The Theory of Comparative Advantage

The foundation of mainstream free trade economics is the venerable theory of comparative advantage, invented by British economist David Ricardo in 1817.[3] While there are other arguments for free trade, they rely upon Ricardian logic to argue that its benefits exceed its costs, so criticisms of Ricardo tell against them also.

To understand the theory, begin with a simpler but related concept: *absolute* advantage. Absolute advantage simply says that if a foreign nation is a more efficient producer of some product than America is, then free trade will cause America to import it, to the benefit of both nations. We get the product for less, the foreigners get a market, and production comes from the most efficient producer, maximizing world output.

Unfortunately, absolute advantage fails to explain observed trading patterns, because the US imports many products of which *it* is the most efficient producer. *Comparative* advantage, on the other hand, not only predicts that less efficient producers will sometimes wind up producing the product (observably true) but also argues that this is good for both the exporting and the importing nation (the controversy). This is why trade must be analyzed in terms of comparative, not absolute, advantage.

At bottom, the theory of comparative advantage simply says this: *Nations trade for the same reasons people do.* And the theory can be made comprehensible with one simple question: *Why don't lawyers do the work of their paralegals?*

Lawyers can, after all, perform all the tasks their paralegals perform, indeed presumably more efficiently, as they have more training. And yet paralegals perform these tasks anyway. Per the analogy to trade, lawyers have "absolute advantage" producing legal services – yet nobody finds it strange that they "import" such services from less efficient "producers." Why? *Because they have better things to do with their time.* By having paralegals do some work, lawyers free themselves for tasks with a higher bill rate that paralegals cannot perform.

This logic is the key to the whole theory. Comparative advantage says that it is better for America to import certain things in order to free up our workforce to produce more-valuable things instead. America has "better things to do with its time" than produce the things it imports. And, as with lawyers and paralegals, it doesn't matter whether America or its trading partner is more efficient at producing these things. The logic holds either way.

This logic doesn't apply only to our time – that is, our person-hours of labor – either. It also applies to our land, capital, technology, and every other factor of production. So, if we could produce something more valuable with the factors we currently use to produce something, then we should, according to the theory, import the less valuable product, free up those factors, and make that more valuable thing instead.

According to the theory, under free trade this reallocation of production will happen automatically. Our *relatively* less productive industries will shrink, and our *relatively* more productive ones will expand. We will lose jobs in the former and gain them in the latter. It is always a matter of relative, not absolute, productivity: Is our productivity advantage in shoes bigger than our advantage in airplanes, or smaller? Because we may be a more efficient producer of both.

On this basis, production of every product will (supposedly) migrate to the nation that can produce it at the lowest "opportunity cost" – the nation that *wastes the least opportunity* to produce more-valuable things instead. The implication is that whenever nations have different *relative* efficiencies at producing this product versus that one, gains from trade for both nations *must* occur.

Only mutually beneficial exchanges will ever take place.[4] Rich nations won't be bled dry by the cheap labor of poor nations, and poor nations won't be crushed by the industrial sophistication of rich ones. Every nation, considered as a whole, will always be better off under free trade. Certain groups within any given nation may be worse off, but the benefit to other people in the same country will always exceed their losses. Even if protectionist foreign nations refuse to buy a nation's exports, it is still better off importing *their* goods, and the foreigners have only harmed themselves by depriving themselves of imports they could have had.

The implication is that any policy other than free trade will just trap nations producing less-valuable things than they could have. When a nation is not competitive in an industry and therefore imports these goods, this *must* benefit it, as it must be allocating its factors to producing more-valuable things instead. If wages, which are paid in domestic currency, don't accurately reflect productivity differences between nations, exchange rates will adjust until they do.

It follows that trade conflicts between nations are always misguided and due either to a failure to understand why free trade is always best, or to interest group politics. Nations should indeed welcome job losses due to trade, because these mean that their labor has been freed up for better uses. And nations should accept whatever industries they end up with, because the free market has necessarily assigned them those that are best for them – that is, their optimal trade-off of producing some goods versus others.

Or so the theory says.

Flaws in the Theory of Comparative Advantage

The problem with the theory of comparative advantage, and thus mainstream trade economics as a whole, is that it ignores a number of key realities by tacitly assuming them away. As a result, the theory does not accurately describe reality and should not be relied upon to set policy. The theory's flaws are discussed herein separately for clarity, though they often come into play simultaneously, compounding its inadequacy.

Ignored Reality #1: Free trade can deplete wealth in the long run

When a nation runs a trade deficit, it must pay for its trade by assuming debt or selling assets. Although chronic deficits are thus bad for the importing nation in the long run, mainstream economics views the trade-off of short-term versus long-term prosperity as arbitrary: It has no principle favoring the long term. The country would be better off imposing trade restrictions to push back against this dynamic.

Ignored Reality #2: There are externalities

As noted in Chapter 1, an externality occurs whenever the price of a product does not reflect its full cost or value to the larger economy. For example, a negative externality makes goods from a nation with lax pollution standards too cheap. Conversely, a positive externality occurs when an industry generates technological spillovers for the rest of the economy – so if free trade wipes it out, the importing nation loses these benefits. The lesson here is not to let industries important for America's future, the "advantageous" industries discussed in Chapters 2 and 3, or the industries they depend on, be destroyed by imports. (For obvious reasons, such industries are often deliberately targeted by the industrial policies of foreign nations.)

Ignored Reality #3: Trade can increase inequality

The benefits of trade promised by the theory are only promised to the economy as a whole, not to every group within it. So even if the economy as a whole expands, some people may lose income. Surprisingly, "some" people may even mean *most* people.

Suppose, for example, that freer trade means that a nation starts exporting more airplanes and importing more clothes than before. Because it expands an industry in which it is relatively more productive and contracts one in which it is less so, the economy as a whole becomes more productive and GDP goes up. Good. But suppose that, per dollar of output, airplane production requires more white-collar workers and fewer blue-collar workers than clothing. Then the more the economy shifts to producing airplanes, the lower will be the demand for blue-collar labor. But *most* workers are blue-collar workers – so freer trade has lowered wages for most workers.[5]

Naturally, this scenario is not the only one that can happen. The outcome will depend on how job opportunities in other industries are changing at the time. But there is no *guarantee* of a happy outcome for income distribution. This is one reason why, in advanced nations, freer trade has contributed to rising inequality. This is not a trivial problem: Harvard economist Dani Rodrik has estimated that freeing up trade reshuffles five dollars of income between different groups of people domestically for every one dollar of gain it brings to the economy as a whole.[6]

Ignored Reality #4: Factors of production do not move easily between industries

The theory depends for its validity on factors of production moving from less-valuable to more-valuable uses within each nation. But it tacitly assumes that these moves take place easily and without significant costs. If they don't, imports will not push an economy into better industries better suited to its comparative advantage but just kill off existing industries without replacing them.

Although this lack-of-mobility problem applies to all factors of production, it is most serious for labor, because unemployment of people, as opposed to that of materials or machines, is a social ill. When workers cannot move easily between industries (usually because they don't have the right skills or don't live in the right place) shifts in an economy's comparative advantage will not move them into more-productive industries, but into unemployment. Or into low-productivity, low-wage, non-tradable service industries – where wages are then dragged down by this influx of workers. Studies show this has indeed happened in the US.[7]

Studies also show that it has often taken years, if ever, for displaced American manufacturing workers to find jobs with comparable pay.[8] Geographic labor mobility is finite for good reasons: People have roots where their family and friends, their economic and social support, live. After a factory shuts down, the local real estate market often collapses, so they can't sell their homes for enough money to buy another where the jobs are.

Capital can also be hard to reallocate. It is generally lost in an industry put out of business: There are massive write-downs. When a factory closes, there is usually no way to extract the capital put into it. The machinery can perhaps be sold, more likely auctioned off – if the entire US industry has not yet been destroyed – or sometimes sold at a huge discount to the very foreign competitors that drove it out of business.[9] The land generally becomes unsaleable, because nobody wants it, and reverts to the county after tax liens reach a certain point.

Ignored Reality #5: Factors of production are internationally mobile

The theory is about the best uses to which nations can put their factors of production. But it rests on the assumption that market forces will merely redeploy factors *within* each nation's economy – not drive them right out of the nation in question. Unfortunately, if their most productive use is in another country, free trade can drive them there. This result will benefit the world economy and the nation they move to, but not necessarily the nation they left.

When a productive asset – for example, a factory – is shut down in one nation and its replacement opened in another, these two actions amount, from an economic point of view, to this asset moving from the former to the latter, even if the factory is not literally crated up. Losing an industry in this way will only be good for a nation when the savings from importing what it formerly produced outweigh the cost of losing that industry. And this will generally be true only when the nation has good alternative uses for the people who lost their jobs and for the idled capital assets. As noted, this is not guaranteed, but contingent on the state of the rest of the economy.

Capital mobility replaces comparative advantage, which applies when capital is forced to choose between alternative uses within a single economy, with its aforementioned cousin absolute advantage. And absolute advantage doesn't even *claim* to guarantee that the results will be good for both trading partners.

Absolute advantage is really the natural order of things in capitalism, and comparative advantage is a special case caused by the existence of national borders that factors of production can't freely cross. The division of the world into nation-states forces national economies to interact by means of trade, exchanging goods and services *made from* those factors – which places comparative advantage in control. Without national borders, nations would simply be *regions* of a single economy, which is why absolute advantage governs economic relations within nations. In 1950, Michigan had absolute advantage in automobiles and Alabama in cotton. But by 2000, automobile plants were closing in Michigan and opening in Alabama. This change benefited Alabama, but it did not benefit Michigan. It only would have if Michigan had moved into a higher-value industry than automobiles, but it did not.

Immobility of capital does not have to be perfect to put comparative advantage in control, but it has to be significant and as it melts away, the theory's guarantee of win-win trade relations melts with it. Ricardo actually knew this, but argued that capital would not migrate much because investments overseas would be perceived as insecure by capitalists due to differences in legal systems, customs, culture, language, et cetera.[10] Today, trade agreements, despite their name, are first and foremost *investment* agreements, designed to protect capital from expropriation by foreign governments, and international capital flows are now measured in the trillions.

The mobility problem also applies to technological know-how and other intellectual property. In 1975, the average S&P 500 company had 83 percent tangible assets and 17 percent intangibles, but by 2020, the figures were 10 and 90 percent.[11] It *may* be a good move for a nation to sell a rival nation IP, but there is no guarantee this won't result in losing the industry the IP supports, which may be worth more, long term, than what the IP sold for. The free market is not guaranteed to give the right answer, even in theory, let alone in the actual unfree market distorted by mercantilist trading strategies.

Ignored Reality #6: Trade can change productivity abroad

America's trade with a foreign nation will affect that nation's industries, making some expand and others contract. Those that trade causes to expand will generally increase in productivity, and it would be nice to assume that this productivity growth can only be good for us.[12] Foreigners will just become more efficient at supplying the things we want, right? Unfortunately, wrong. Productivity growth in our trade counterparties can be either good or bad for us, depending on how it affects which industries we and they have comparative advantage in.[13]

Contrary to a common misunderstanding, the theory of comparative advantage doesn't even claim to say anything about who benefits from *changes* in productivity. It only says that for any given set of productivities, free trade is best. Who benefits from changes is simply a different question. The theory definitely does *not* say that a rising tide lifts all boats – that is, that productivity gains anywhere must benefit everyone (or every nation considered as a whole) everywhere.[14]

Suppose, for example, that another country acquires comparative advantage in an industry where we previously had it. This shift will mean that the other country gains some production in this industry and we lose some, forcing us to reallocate our factors of production to other industries.[15] Now *if* we have growing industries, with higher productivity, suited to the displaced factors of production, we will indeed be able to reallocate them to a higher-productivity industry than the one we lost. Then all will be well.[16] But as noted earlier, this is not automatic.

Foreign productivity growth can thus sometimes leave us worse off. We can be pushed out of more productive industries and into less productive ones. Granted, there will be the countervailing benefit that we can now import more cheaply the products we formerly produced, but there is no guarantee this will outweigh the cost of losing these industries. We will also face the long-term cost of losing every new industry they would have led to. (Recall path dependence from Chapter 1.)

When Nobelist Paul Samuelson reminded economists in a 2004 article that foreign productivity growth can cost Americans, he shocked many of his colleagues. But he went unrefuted, because the logic here (unlike some parts of this book) is wholly within the mathematics accepted by mainstream economics, though widely ignored.[17]

Ignored Reality #7: Static efficiency is not dynamic efficiency

As noted in #6, trade doesn't just move goods around the world. It also changes the economies that produce them. In such changes lies most of what determines national prosperity in the long run. Prosperity, that is, is *not* mainly a matter of squeezing every last drop of efficiency from the factors of production a nation has right now, by importing and exporting according to its immediate comparative advantage. Prosperity is mainly a matter of developing *better* comparative advantage – that is, comparative advantage in more advantageous industries – over time.[18]

As a result, Ricardian thinking, even if true (and it has all the other flaws here recounted) misses the question that really matters: *What changes over time does trade cause?* The theory says nothing about the impact of trade on acquiring better industries.

We encountered this problem before, in Chapter 1, when we phrased it in terms of the free market maximizing only static efficiency (what's most productive right now), not dynamic efficiency (productivity growth over time). And we saw in #4, #5, and #6 that there is no guarantee that free trade will assign any particular nation the most advantageous industries it is capable of, or even preserve those it already has.

Free trade thus has very ambiguous implications for dynamic efficiency: It can do good when static efficiency happens to coincide with dynamic efficiency, but harm when it does not. Sometimes it will nourish advantageous industries; other times it will kill them or the industries that would have led to them.

Ignored Reality #8: There are scale economies

As we saw in Chapters 1 and 2, advantageous industries are scale-economy industries. Unfortunately, the theory of comparative advantage takes no notice of scale economies, so it cannot generate recommendations reflecting their consequences.[19]

What happens if we modify the theory to fix this?

Because cost-per-unit in scale-economy industries goes *down* as output goes *up*, whichever national industry is producing the most will be, other things being equal, the global low-cost producer. And whichever nation reaches large production volume *first* will thereby acquire a cost advantage that will lock other nations out.[20] And when there is not a monopoly, there will be an oligopoly, with all the consequences previously examined.

The name for these entrenched, oligopolistic, scale-economy industries, in the trade theory that does recognize them, such as the work of Ralph Gomory and William Baumol, is "retainable" industries.[21] Once the market has dealt out a certain distribution of such industries among nations, that distribution will tend to *stick*. Contrarily, in the Ricardian model, historical accidents of which nation reaches high-volume production first can happen, but don't matter because their consequences get washed away afterward by competitive forces. Ricardo didn't allow for scale economies, and in their absence, a head start doesn't lead to entrenchment.[22]

It also follows from not accounting for scale economies that for Ricardo, there are no advantageous or disadvantageous industries. As we saw in Chapter 1, scale economies are not 100 percent of what makes industries advantageous, because there are other factors, such as technological dynamism, pricing power, and synergies. But scale economies are a big enough factor that ignoring them blinds Ricardian theory, as it doesn't recognize these other factors either. And as a result of this blindness, his theory assumes two things:

1. An industry's value is simply a matter of its current productivity.
2. The free market smoothly shuffles industries around the world to their most productive locations without significant frictional costs.

As a result of these two assumptions, Ricardo concludes that today's market prices tell us accurately what industries are worth, and therefore should not be overridden by government policy. It is best for every nation to allow industries to move to wherever the free market, acting according to comparative advantage, puts them.

But when scale economies and the other factors that make certain industries advantageous are brought into the picture, both assumptions are revealed to be false, because:

1. Advantageous industries are worth more than their current productivity and profitability – the factors that determine market prices – indicate.
2. Industries don't get smoothly shuffled around the world, due to the retainability of advantageous industries.

The net result of these dynamics is that the free market can deal out a distribution of industries between nations that is *not* best for any given nation or for the world as a whole. *And the free market on its own won't automatically correct this maldistribution.*

We already saw in Chapter 2 why free market policies, even ignoring trade, won't reliably give a nation the most advantageous industries it could have had: Advantageous economic activities and industries are shot through with non-free-market dynamics. Trade intensifies this reality. First, it tends to reinforce whatever industries a nation is *already* competitive in, because other nations will lock it out of everything else.[23] Second, because of trade, other nations employing proactive industrial policies can threaten the advantageous industries it already has.

Win-Win versus Win-Lose Trade

Ricardian theory holds that free trade always produces a net economic benefit for every nation. So trade is always "win-win." It follows that economic rivalry between nations is an illusion.

However, as we have seen in the ignored realities above, gains for one nation sometimes entail losses for another. As a result, win-lose situations sometimes exist, and rivalry is real.

Trade is *sometimes* win-win, but sometimes win-lose. Trade where a nation improves, or at least does not harm, its own productive capacities, while obtaining cheaper products from abroad, is win-win. Trade where one nation improves its productive capacities at the expense of another is win-lose.

It follows that many of the trade conflicts that have roiled the world for centuries and continue today have been fights over real substance, rather than the results of special interest pleading or failed economic analysis that Ricardianism views them as.

The Governance of International Economic Rivalry

The idea that trade is fundamentally a harmony of economic interests was the foundation for institutions such as the WTO, and to a lesser extent its predecessor, the 1947–95 General Agreement on Tariffs and Trade (GATT).

The creators of GATT understood that political interests in each member nation would rarely be perfectly aligned with the interests of that nation's economy as a whole. They therefore accepted that a certain amount of horse trading was necessary to create the GATT system. They also understood that nations can get locked into "prisoner's dilemma" trade conflicts with other nations, where the only way out is an agreement by *every* nation not to impose trade restrictions on others, with an impartial umpire to settle disputes.

The WTO built on GATT, starting with the dispute adjudication procedures that had evolved there. The WTO does not punish violations of its trade rules itself. Instead, it adjudicates victim nations' complaints, granting permission to impose tariffs on the violating country as a remedy. But this weak framework is only effective against nations that lack a serious commitment to violating free trade. It also has little effect against nontariff barriers and tends to push violations into the gray area of hidden policies. Many foreign mercantilist strategies are too indirect, tacit, or covert to be within the reach of precise definition and thus legalistic remedies.

The WTO enforcement mechanism is expensive and biased against claimants. Injured companies, even those big enough to hypothetically afford it, cannot sue directly, but must convince their governments to take their cases. Prompt action by these governments, given limited personnel and conflicting political interests, is not guaranteed. The process is often too slow to save firms from bankruptcy.

The WTO's creators did not understand that mercantilism, the systematic pursuit of advantageous industries at the expense of other nations, is a viable economic strategy and therefore would be widely employed.[24] The WTO's unstated assumption was that free trade is optimal for all nations at all times, that nations would inexorably come to understand this, and therefore that they would not be strongly committed to trade barriers.

The WTO does not have the coercive power to restrain large, rich, technically competent nations, especially authoritarian ones under one-party rule. Only an organization with the wisdom of Solomon and an authority over its members comparable to that of a strong national government over its subdivisions, capable of reaching deep into their internal economic arrangements, could have secured genuine free trade. The major trading powers, including the US, would never have agreed to cede so much sovereignty, nor was such an impartial judge possible.

Only the US and a few other Anglosphere nations actually believe in free trade. Other nations have played along because they see the WTO as a convenient tool for gaining better access to foreign markets in exchange for promised access to their own that they can de facto limit as required by their mercantilist economic strategies. A more accurate theory of international trade would have predicted this outcome from first principles, and should therefore be the basis of reforms of trade's legal infrastructure. The bottom line: The US will need to rely more directly on its own sovereign powers to protect its economic interests, because no international organization will ever be able to do so adequately.

The Arithmetic of Trade Deficits

Let us now turn to the financial side of trade economics, which abstracts differences between industries and analyzes the simple fact that imports must be paid for with money. We must nail down a surprisingly controversial fact, one regularly denied in the attempt to persuade Americans that there is no trade crisis, namely *trade deficits are real money, and they matter*.

The fundamental logic of trade deficits is the following:

Step 1. *Nations engage in trade*. So Americans sell things (goods and services) to people in other nations and buy things in return.

Step 2. *One cannot get things for free*. So Americans have to give foreigners something in return.

Step 3. *There are only three things we can give in return*:
   a. things we produce today
   b. things we produced yesterday
   c. things we will produce tomorrow
   Here are examples of a, b, and c:
   a. is when we sell foreigners jet airplanes
   b. is when we sell foreigners American office buildings
   c. is when we go into debt to foreigners[25]

When America runs a trade deficit, b) and c) happen. Because we are not requiting the value of our imports with the value of our exports, we must make up the difference by either selling assets or assuming debt. If either is happening, America is either gradually being sold off to foreigners or gradually sinking into debt to them. We become poorer by definition: We own less and owe more.

Trade deficits also destroy jobs at the time that they occur. When we export jets – scenario a) – we must employ people to produce them and can afford to because selling the jets brings in money to pay their salaries. But in scenario b), those office buildings have already been built, so no jobs are created today by selling them.[26] And in scenario c), no jobs are created today because the goods are promised for the future. While jobs will be created *then* to produce these goods, the wages of these future jobs will be paid by us, not by foreigners. Because the foreigners already gave us their goods, back when we bought from them on credit, they won't owe us anything later.

How Trade Deficits Are Misunderstood

There are three main mistaken views about trade deficits.

The first is that they are merely an "arbitrary" accounting construct. But they represent real changes in production, consumption, and wealth. They are no more arbitrary than any other dollar measure of the economy.

The second is that they don't matter because the US is getting valuable goods in exchange for low-cost loans that don't have to be paid off for a long time and can be serviced with money whose value erodes with inflation. Meanwhile, the complexity of modern finance creates the *illusion* of getting something for nothing for a long time, as it seems that we can borrow or sell assets without consequences indefinitely.

But the second argument only considers the direct cost of the debt we assume. It says nothing about losses of jobs or industries. Furthermore, going into debt does not result only in passive investments by the creditor. It also means that the creditor country (read "China") has a large stash of dollars it can use to outbid American and other firms for control of intellectual property, startups, and established companies in advantageous and otherwise important industries.

The third view is that trade deficits are America's own fault, because we supposedly don't save enough.[27] (The savings rate relevant here is not the personal savings rate but the economy-wide savings rate, which includes saving by firms and government.) But this analysis misunderstands the *arithmetic* relationship between trade deficits and savings rates as a *causal* relationship. Our savings are simply the economy-wide excess of production over consumption, because if we don't consume what we produce, saving it is the only other thing we can do with it. And a trade deficit is simply the opposite. If we wish to consume more than we produce, there are only two ways to get the goods: either draw down supplies saved up in the past or import them.

As a result, trade deficits do not "cause" a low savings rate or vice versa; they are simply the same numbers showing up on opposite sides of the national ledger. Neither our trade deficit nor our savings rate is intrinsically a lever that moves the other, or a valid excuse for it. Trade balances between nations are not "caused by differences in savings rates," but by the interaction of *all* the relevant variables: supply and demand for goods, supply and demand for savings, in both nations – and thus by *all* the policies, ranging from barriers to trade to incentives for capital accumulation, that affect all these things.

But doesn't the free market guarantee beneficial, win-win outcomes? Aren't trade deficits under free-market conditions therefore guaranteed to be beneficial, or at least harmless? Unfortunately, per Ignored Reality #1 above, free-market economics takes no position on short-term versus long-term well-being.[28] So America can "efficiently" become poorer, getting what we want now at the cost of getting less later. This problem is more severe in trade than in domestic economics, because short-termism can result in the loss of industries, jobs, and wealth to other countries, not just slower growth here. When no foreigners are involved, each debtor creates a creditor within the same society, keeping the economy as a whole in balance whatever other problems it may cause. But when foreign countries are involved, a nation as a whole can become poorer.

How the Overvalued Dollar Drives Trade Deficits

The largest cause of America's trade deficits in recent decades has been dollar overvaluation, due to both currency manipulation and private sector capital flows. The mechanism of the former, in the paradigmatic case of China, is as follows:

1. China offers US consumers (businesses, government, and households) goods at prices below US suppliers.
2. US consumers buy Chinese, instead of American, goods. (Note that US consumers are *not* spending more and saving less. If anything, they are spending *less*.)
3. China requires its exporters to turn in the dollars they receive to its central bank in exchange for renminbi at an artificially low exchange rate – that is, more renminbi per dollar than the free market rate.[29]
4. Instead of selling these dollars back into the international market in exchange for renminbi, China's central bank uses them to buy US government securities and other dollar-denominated assets.
5. This "sterilization" prevents China's failure to import as much from the US as it exports to the US from pushing up the renminbi–dollar exchange rate.
6. Because the renminbi does not rise, the US–China trade balance does not adjust, because Chinese exports do not become more expensive in the US and US exports cheaper in China.
7. China now owns more dollar-denominated assets than before step 1 (as of June 2022, approximately $1.4 trillion).[30]
8. Because these assets are now owned by a foreign entity, the net debt (what we owe minus what we are owed) Americans owe foreigners has increased, and US national savings have declined by an amount equal to the increase in foreign holdings.

The key mechanism of the trade deficit is thus *the failure of exchange rates to adjust* to balance trade as mainstream theory assumes they will. The usual way of describing this sequence of events is to say that China manipulates its currency, but one can just as accurately say that China forces its exports to be requited not with goods, but with assets and debt.

Beijing has occasionally paused such tactics when other factors have intervened, such as capital flight caused by the risks of keeping one's wealth where it is only as secure as one's political connections. These factors sometimes drive China's currency down to levels that the government desires, so Beijing's routine denials of currency manipulation are sometimes technically accurate. But it is the overall multiyear pattern that counts.

The vast majority, in value terms, of trade surpluses around the world accrue to countries that manipulate, or have manipulated, their currencies. These include Japan, Switzerland, Taiwan, and Korea. Germany shares the euro with many other nations, giving it a currency that is too cheap, as its price reflects their inferior export competitiveness. It is no accident that Germany runs huge trade surpluses, or that many eurozone countries run corresponding deficits. (See Chapter 8 for more about Germany's export machine.)

The IMF's Articles of Agreement prohibit its members from manipulating their exchange rates, but the Fund has no real enforcement mechanism.[31]

Note that the dollar would be mispriced even without foreign government interventions. The US has large net inflows of foreign *private* capital because it has the largest, safest, most liquid capital markets, open to the world and protected by the rule of law. It has also generally had the best economy, the most profitable investment opportunities, and the greatest openness of those opportunities to outsiders. It also issues the world's dominant reserve currency, which gives nations reason to hold significant dollar reserves. This net demand for dollars and dollar-denominated assets drives up the dollar the same way as Step 4 above does.

As a result of both deliberate manipulation and this structural mispricing, the dollar has been estimated to be 16 percent above the level that would balance America's trade.[32] It has been estimated that each 10 percent rise of the dollar increases the trade deficit by about 1.2 percent of GDP.[33]

Exchange Rate Management

Under the 1944–71 Bretton Woods system of fixed exchange rates, governments committed to keeping their currencies within very narrow ranges by buying and selling their own currency, with restrictions on international capital flows to prevent other factors from interfering. If the system existed today, it would block Step 4 above.[34] (See Chapter 16 for the details of its creation and eventual collapse.)

Absent such general agreements, how can governments fight currency manipulation and misalignment? When one government buys another nation's currency to drive it up, the victim can buy the aggressor's currency to drive it back down. This is affordable, despite the huge quantities of money required, because the purchasing nation ends up with an asset of equal worth: the currency of the offender. This tactic is known as countervailing currency intervention or CCI.

Capital flow management is another option. Capital controls would prohibit, limit, or tax the sale of American assets to foreigners and the assumption by Americans of debt to foreigners. One such mechanism, the Market Access Charge (MAC), was proposed by Senators Tammy Baldwin (D-WI) and Josh Hawley (R-MO) in the 2019 Senate bill The Competitive Dollar for Jobs and Prosperity Act.[35] This would have directed the Federal Reserve to impose a variable tax on foreign purchases of dollar-denominated assets to lower their net yield, making them less attractive to foreign buyers and thereby reducing inflows of foreign capital until the dollar reached a trade-balancing price.

A 2021 study estimated that a 5 percent MAC would lower the dollar enough to balance trade over five years, increase GDP by $1.6 trillion, and create 3.9 million jobs. It projected $300 billion per year in additional tax revenue, which could be rebated to taxpayers or used to fund federal programs. The MAC would raise interest rates by an inconsequential 0.12 percent and inflation by only 0.22 percent.[36] (The estimated inflationary impact is so small because imports are only 15 percent of the economy and pass-through of higher import costs is partial due to contraction of foreign profit margins.) If foreign nations retaliated by imposing capital controls of their own, this would make the policy more effective, not less so.

The MAC has precedents. From 1963 to 1974, the US had the Interest Equalization Tax, which could go as high as 15 percent, in order to control America's capital *out*flows. This propped up the dollar, then under *downward* pressure, to defend its Bretton Woods peg.

Value-Added Tax and Fiscal Devaluation

Value-added tax (VAT) is levied by almost all other countries. It is paid by the seller at each step in the supply chain as a percentage of the price. Because each seller is reimbursed for VAT paid in the previous step, the seller pays tax only on the value the seller adds. As with a sales tax, the consumer ultimately bears the cost. VAT averages 15.5 percent worldwide, 21.5 percent in the EU.[37]

Governments rebate VAT on exports because collecting it would subject foreigners to double taxation, given their own country's VAT, thereby putting exports at a disadvantage. Conversely, governments levy VAT on imports because not doing so would create an unfair advantage for imports. This all makes sense according to the logic of VAT and is WTO-compliant. But it means that when a country *with* VAT trades with one without, an export advantage is created for the former and a disadvantage for the latter. This is a significant problem for the US.

Prevailing analyses dismiss this problem because they consider only the VAT itself, ignoring the changes it entails in the overall tax burden on exports. This is because VAT is levied as an alternative to or to reduce taxes that are *not* refunded upon export, such as corporate income, payroll, and property taxes. A German car imported into the US has its 19 percent VAT refunded on export, while an American car exported to Germany is burdened with all US taxes embedded into its price during its production, because these are not refunded. Assuming roughly equal total taxation in Germany and the US, the size of the American car manufacturers' disadvantage is approximately the 19 percent.[38]

Governments sometimes deliberately pursue the advantage VAT differentials can confer by shifting a greater fraction of their total tax levy onto VAT and off of taxes not refunded on export. This creates an effect similar to a currency devaluation, so it is called "fiscal devaluation." France, for example, employed this tactic in 2012, Germany in 2006, Sweden in 1993, and Denmark in 1988.[39] For similar reasons, nations often increase their VAT following tariff reductions and commensurately reduce non-border-refundable taxes.

A Better Trade Strategy

The implication for trade policy of all the dynamics reviewed in this chapter is that *fairly open trade, most of the time, is a good thing.* No valid analysis supports autarky, knee-jerk protectionism, or crude protectionism that aims at nothing more than the short-term retention of existing jobs. But 100 percent free trade with 100 percent of the world 100 percent of the time – even if this were possible – is not optimal. Free trade, like free markets in other areas of the economy, should be just one strand of policy, employed as a strategic choice, not a blanket ideological commitment.

So, what trade strategy for America is implied by the foregoing? In a nutshell, three things:

First, America should manage its currency, using capital controls such as the MAC, CCI, and other tools to achieve a dollar price that balances its trade.

Second, America should insist upon genuine tariff reciprocity, rather than allowing foreign nations to impose higher tariffs than it imposes on them. Either foreign "bound tariff rates" must come down or ours must go up to match. Unconditional most-favored-nation (MFN) treatment, in which the US does not discriminate between nations that offer the US favorable treatment and those that do not, should end.

Third, America should try to defend, establish, or reestablish strong positions in advantageous industries by means of industrial policy, which should sometimes include protectionism. Because the US is closer to being competitive in more-advanced industries, even a flat tariff (the same on every product) will be biased toward bringing the right industries to the US.[40] And a strategically discriminating tariff could be even more potent.

Innovative modeling by economists Jeff Ferry and Andrew Heritage of the bipartisan Coalition for a Prosperous America projected that an additional tariff of 35 percent on manufactured goods and 15 percent on agricultural and primary products would generate a 6 percent increase in GDP, an 18 percent increase in household income, a 16 percent increase in investment, and 2.1 million more manufacturing jobs.[41] A 10 percent flat tariff also showed positive results.[42]

Effective future trade and industrial policy for the US will necessarily require policies that violate today's WTO rules. Consequently, designing policy to conform to America's existing dysfunctional treaty commitments would be putting the cart before the horse. Our approach in this book is therefore to propose an industrial policy based on the assumption that a different international legal structure will eventually be adopted and that in the meantime, US policy should not be constrained by the one that now exists. Tacitly accepting this reasoning, the Trump and Biden administrations have, in fact, already imposed WTO-noncompliant policies (see Chapter 18).

Part II
Country Case Studies

The economics of this book, set forth in the first four chapters, shows that economic development is path-dependent, that what industries a nation can have tomorrow largely depends on what industries it has today, and that industrial policy interventions by governments can push economies onto different paths, some better than others. This path dependence makes economic history radically more important for understanding how economies develop than mainstream economics assumes. That is why the following country studies are in this book. They exemplify the principles, practices, successes, and pitfalls of industrial policy in nations that differ widely in their level of economic development, political structure, and technological sophistication.

China, Japan, Korea, and Germany are industrial policy success stories with some policies that America could fruitfully imitate. India, Britain, and Argentina are examples of failure, of what not to do. France illustrates both. The success cases show that industrial policy has driven rapid, high-quality economic development using the same basic principles in countries with widely differing cultures and governments. The failure cases show that industrial policies do not fail for reasons that are mysterious, innate to the very concept, or impossible to avoid. Instead, we shall see that they fail for reasons that are consistent with our analytical approach, readily comprehensible, and thus potentially avoidable.

5 JAPAN
The First Asian Miracle

Japan's industrial policies took its economy from the devastation of World War II to being the second largest in the world.[1] Their remarkable success triggered a revival of American interest in industrial policy in the late 1970s.[2]

Japan has employed two kinds. The first is catch-up industrial policy (CUIP), which is appropriate for nations that have not yet developed their economies for the global technological frontier. Japan practiced CUIP from roughly 1870 to 1990. The second is mature-economy industrial policy (MEIP), which Japan has practiced since.

Thanks to good MEIP, Japan remains one of the world's richest nations, albeit with the slower growth of every developed nation. In recent years, other countries, notably China and South Korea, by using similar industrial policies, have chipped away at Japan's positions in key industries such as automobiles and semiconductors. But Japan remains a significant rival to the US in many advantageous industries, running a trade surplus with the US of around $60 billion per year and exporting to America roughly twice what it imports.[3]

Japan remains a global leader in advanced manufacturing. For example, it has a world market share of at least 60 percent in 70 different advanced materials, with exports equal in value to its better-known car exports.[4] It has a larger share of global semiconductor production (13 percent) than the US (10 percent), despite an economy less than half the size.[5] It is the world's largest net exporter of cars and third-largest exporter of ships.[6]

Japan is also a leader in some key nonmanufacturing industries of the future. For example, it has led the world in commercial adoption of artificial intelligence, aided by government programs such as Society 5.0.[7] In 2018, it was ranked second in the world (ahead of the US) for the quality of its policy environment for cloud computing.[8]

Industrial Policy Successes

For 40 years after World War II, Tokyo had a good batting average at CUIP, above all in choosing which industries to focus on. It became internationally competitive in most that it targeted, and almost all had major positive spillovers to other industries.

To be sure, good industrial policy was not the only reason for Japan's success. Sound macroeconomic policy, good education, smart corporate management, American assistance in the early years, and a strong world economy during the peak years of Japan's growth all helped.

Japan's CUIP was most successful when targeting manufacturing industries with tangible products based on technologies amenable to dissection and reverse engineering. These included steel, autos, consumer electronics, and semiconductors. These were industries in which pure scale economies (e.g., as opposed to network effects) were the major factor in creating an entrenched position, and where product quality was a matter of straightforward metrics.

In less tangible areas, such as software, where Japan had little experience and could not easily learn by reverse engineering, it was less successful. Japan failed to dominate aerospace because it was well supported by industrial policy in its competitors, for military reasons in the US and for military and economic reasons in the EU. In semiconductors, the US pushed back with aggressive trade and industrial policies of its own when Japan's challenge became acute, and successfully headed it off (see Chapter 26).

Japan has had very different policies, and very different results, in its non-tradable sectors. For example, for both political reasons (its small-business lobby) and social ones (preserving urban neighborhoods), it generally did not allow big-box retailers, with their efficient chain store logistics, until the 1990s, when it did so under American pressure. Similar efficiency-neglecting values and politics have governed several other sectors, including agriculture. Thus, in 1992, it was estimated that Japan's automobile, electronics, and steel industries had productivity averaging 130 percent of US levels, while its retail sector was at only 50 percent.[9]

National Ideology

Japan's industrial policy successes have been rooted in its national ideology. Its citizens have thought (and still think) about their economy very differently than Americans.

They believe it is the state's responsibility to proactively position the nation in the global economy. They have had little interest in the ideal of a self-regulating economy with only minimal state involvement. They also have not viewed the state and the private sector as being locked in a zero-sum rivalry for control. Rather, they should, in their view, work *together* for the good of the nation.[10]

That they generally have is shown by the fact that Japan has one of the lowest levels of wealth inequality among major developed nations.[11] It is also one of the world's most cohesive societies: not just in rhetoric but in practice. Japanese culture places the group's interest front and center, facilitating the adoption of policies that subordinate individual gains and short-term profits to long-term economic growth.

Japan's leaders have viewed the market as just one tool, albeit an important one, in their toolbox, *not* as an ideological value in its own right. Despite decades of disingenuous claims by Tokyo about becoming a market-centered economy, this attitude endures. Japan has, however, relied *more* on market forces since the late 1990s – which makes sense for a now-developed nation. But it remains a mixed economy with a collectivist orientation closer to the "coordinated market economies" of Germany and France than to the US.

By American standards, Japan also has considerable blurring between the public and private sectors (also found in other non-Anglosphere countries). This is the origin of the term "Japan, Inc.," coined during the 1980s by Westerners experiencing governmental orchestration of Japan's corporate sector.

Long-Term Economic Objectives

During Japan's CUIP era, the ruling technocrats consistently chose dynamic over static efficiency (see Chapter 2). They were more concerned with the long-term development of specific industries and capabilities than with short-term efficiency or maximizing profits.[12] They explicitly regarded some industries as more valuable than others and did not believe that the free market would automatically develop them in Japan.[13] They did not believe in submitting to comparative advantage as a given, but instead that protectionism and subsidies could *create* comparative advantage in the industries they wanted. As Myohei Shinohara, for nearly 25 years a member of the Industrial Structure Council of Japan's powerful Ministry of International Trade and Industry (MITI), explained:

> The two basic criteria to which the industrial structure policies adopted by MITI conformed ... were an "income elasticity criterion" and a "comparative technical progress criterion." ... Such a dynamic

factor was completely detached from the premises behind the traditional theory of division of labor, which assumes away not only any dynamic intertemporal shift in comparative advantage but also the selective growth capability of the industries concerned.[14]

Japan's policymakers were also skeptical about the American emphasis on price competition. In targeted industries, they revived pre–World War II institutions such as industrial groups (*zaibatsu* before the war, *keiretsu* after), and enacted laws and policies (cartels, subsidies) to reduce price competition while *increasing* competition on cost, quality, product features, technological sophistication, and aftermarket services.

Japan did not allow, and even today does not fully allow, its financial sector to pursue the highest returns. Instead, it was structured to direct artificially cheap capital to industries expected to have the highest long-term value for the whole economy. The powerful Ministry of Finance (MOF) played the key role in this capital allocation, while MITI was central in technology and corporate management. MOF and MITI were and are rivals, though MITI is now the Ministry of Economy, Trade, and Industry (METI) and both have less power than in their heyday.

Pre–World War II History

Because Japan is near much-larger China, it has had centuries of experience at selectively adopting foreign cultural advances. Much of Japan's culture, from written characters to architecture to religion, consists of adaptations of originals from China. And because Japan was for centuries divided into relatively autonomous domains under a common shogun, economic rivalry between these domains caused Japan to develop proto-mercantilist ideas even before it came into contact with Western mercantilism.[15] The individual person and private profit, the cores of liberal economics, were never much valued in Japanese culture, religion, or political thought.[16]

Japan's exposure to the West began in 1543 with shipwrecked Portuguese sailors and Catholic missionaries. In 1639, after Japanese Christians revolted, all Westerners except the Dutch, who had sided with the regime, were expelled. The Dutch were confined to one small island in Nagasaki harbor and used as a source of *rangaku*, or Western scientific and technological learning. Japan's diligent study of this material over the next two centuries helps explain why it was later so successful at mastering Western technologies.

After American warships under Commodore Perry appeared in Tokyo Bay in 1853 demanding trading rights, Japan's leadership grasped that the country's self-isolation was no longer tenable and that it would need to develop a modern military and its industrial underpinnings to avoid being reduced to a colony. The Meiji Restoration of 1868, a coup d'état followed by a short civil war framed as the restoration of a figurehead emperor, put in power an oligarchy determined to implement this agenda.

The state thus took the initiative to spark Japan's industrial revolution. It undertook foreign missions to discover the best models for modernization: the British Navy, the Belgian central bank, and a constitution modeled on Germany – whose oligarchical, militaristic regime, similarly bent on national industrialization, held obvious appeal (see Chapter 8). The US, protectionist at the time, contributed Hamiltonian ideas, notably in the person of E. Peshine Smith, an American economist who moved to Japan and became in 1871 the first foreigner to hold a position in its government.[17]

The Meiji government (1868–1912) proactively established and nurtured infrastructure and basic industries. This included railroads, communications, universities, banking, a postal system, and a postal savings system. As far back as the 1890s, Japan's leaders favored *ichigo yunyu, ni go kokusan*: importing the first product and making later ones domestically. But government soon discovered that outright state ownership was inefficient and often led to corruption.[18] So it learned to instead *partner* with industry, consisting primarily of merchant family firms such as Mitsui and Sumitomo, precursors of the *zaibatsu*.[19] Other than a short time in the 1920s, when laissez-faire thinking emerged briefly during the Taishō period of partial democratization, the Japanese have thought of active government intervention in the economy as normal and indispensable.[20]

Much of Japan's economic thinking derived from the German historical school, viewed as an alternative to the classical liberal version of capitalism. Friedrich List's 1841 book *The National System of Political Economy* was translated into Japanese at least three times.[21] Like List, Japan's rulers saw production as the foundation of national power and collective national goals as paramount (see Chapter 8).

Japan emerged as a first-class military power after victory in the First Sino-Japanese War (1894–5) and the Russo-Japanese War (1904–5). By the 1920s, it was becoming a force in world trade in some industries, notably textiles, producing trade conflicts with Britain and the US.

World War II and Its Aftermath

The roots of Japan's post–World War II industrial policies lie in the 1930s, as its military government assumed greater control of the economy as a result of its conquest of Manchuria in 1931, which placed vast resources under direct military control, and in preparation for an anticipated wider war. The state shifted business financing from stock issuance to bank credit so that its control of the banks would give it more leverage over industry.[22] Its objectives were to free firms from the need to maximize shareholder returns, let the state channel capital to military industries, and compel firms to play their appointed economic roles in the growing empire.[23] The Bank of Japan Act of 1942, modeled on Nazi Germany's central bank law of 1939, gave the government additional power over the financial system. Other laws, such as the Important Industries Control Law of 1931 and the Important Industries Association Ordinance of 1941, directed the targeting of specific sectors.[24]

Postwar policy continued, albeit sometimes in different forms, in much of this wartime system. Japan was far behind the US economically and technologically, but it was a nearly developed nation rebuilding from war, not an undeveloped country creating a modern economy from scratch. The country had been technologically advanced enough to fight the world's greatest military powers. Thanks to decades of policy, it had a high literacy rate and a well-educated population. It had a disciplined society and a citizenry accustomed to hard work. It had a strong sense of national unity, respect for authority, and a long bureaucratic tradition. It had learned development strategy not only on its own soil but also in developing its empire in Korea, Manchuria, and Taiwan. It had experience with adversarial trade relations.[25]

During the first two years of the Occupation, the US encouraged strong unions and viewed leftist political parties as a useful counter to Japan's historic right-wing militarism. But the real foundations of postwar Japan were laid after the Occupation authorities' "Reverse Course" policies began in 1947–8. Spurred by the tightening hold of the Soviet Union on Eastern Europe and the advances of the Chinese communists, tens of thousands of known and suspected communists were removed from the government, political parties, and unions. Previously purged rightists were rehabilitated.

The US began pushing Japan to reindustrialize and provided Marshall Plan–type financial assistance and experts to advise its government and corporations.[26] General Douglas MacArthur halted efforts to break up the *zaibatsu* that had underpinned Japan's war effort.[27] The Dodge Plan of 1948 extinguished rampant inflation through tighter monetary and fiscal policy, enabling revival of a functioning market economy. And the country was reopened to trade with the yen fixed at 360 to the dollar under Bretton Woods.

The postwar US was at its economic peak and not inclined to view Japan as an economic threat or counter its mercantilist strategies. Above all, Washington wanted a strong democratic, capitalist ally against the USSR and Communist China.

In 1955, Japan's two largest conservative parties merged to create the Liberal Democratic Party (LDP) and defeat the Socialist Party in the 1955 elections. Except for 1993–4 and 2009–12, when LDP factions formed parties of their own, the LDP has been in power ever since. Rather than strong individual leaders, Japan has had collective leadership in which policy is set by the "iron triangle" of big business, the bureaucracy, and the LDP.

Industrial Policy Tools

Japan created MITI in 1949 along with other institutions and laws that would become key instruments of its industrial policy. Exports were the top priority as the country aimed to shift over time from labor-intensive, to capital-intensive, and finally to knowledge-intensive industries.

These institutions were:[28]

1. MITI, which developed and implemented industrial policy at the level of specific industries, technologies, and management practices.
2. The Ministry of Finance (MOF), which controlled the financial system, enabling it to divert capital from short-term profits to long-term strategic investments.
3. The Development Bank of Japan (DBJ), a government bank that invested small amounts in targeted industries and thus *signaled* to private banks which industries the government was implicitly guaranteeing.
4. A second, quasi-hidden Fiscal Investment and Loan Program (FILP) budget in addition to the main government budget. Through the 1970s, this allowed the MOF to loan money from postal savings accounts and public pensions to strategic industries.[29]

For its first two to three decades, the FILP budget was made annually by MITI and MOF bureaucrats with little input from elected officials. It ranged from 3.3 percent of GDP in 1956 to a high of 6.3 percent in 1972, a third to half the size of the regular government budget.[30]

The private financial system was manipulated to provide cheap capital for favored industries, partly by pushing up the personal savings rate. Consumer credit was not allowed to develop until the 1980s and 1990s, forcing citizens to save for homes and other large purchases. State-funded pensions were kept spartan so people would save more for retirement. Housing construction was limited (a policy since relaxed) to limit the flow of investment into residential real estate, as opposed to industry.[31] Until 1988, interest on savings up to $24,000 was tax-exempt.

Japan deliberately, in this era and later, set out to minimize the appearance of its own success, correctly reasoning that this would reduce America's inclination to regard it as a rival. In the words of formerly Tokyo-based Irish journalist Eamonn Fingleton: "To that end Japanese officials organised cast-of-thousands pantomimes aimed at convincing visiting foreigners that Japan was a Third World country and thus posed no threat to the advanced industries on which the West's economic success was based."[32] Such practices continue to this day in other forms, with the acquiescence of a substantial number of American Japan "experts," journalists, and government officials.

Controlling Trade

After World War II, the state controlled the flow of foreign exchange. The Foreign Exchange Control Law of 1933 remained on the books, reinforced by the Foreign Exchange and Foreign Trade Control Law of 1949 and the Foreign Investment Law of 1950. These laws, used to manage the balance of payments, also protected industries from import competition independently of tariffs by limiting what imports foreign currency could be spent on.[33] (They remained in force far longer than Occupation forces had intended, revised only in the 1960s and 1970s.)

By giving some industries and firms, but not others, money to import technology, the state tilted investment and production toward them.[34] Foreign direct investment was welcomed only in nonstrategic industries, such as simple consumer products like razors and breakfast cereals, and in strategic industries, such as computers, where it was the only way to acquire advanced technologies.

The US and other nations were not completely blind to Japan's mercantilist trade policies. Hence there was significant opposition in 1954–5, in foreign countries and in Congress, to letting Japan join the GATT. Opponents included the old guard of President Eisenhower's own Republican Party, but they were overruled for Cold War reasons (see Chapter 16).

Japan's Corporate Networks

A key private institution that helped Japan implement industrial policy was (and is) the industrial groups known as *keiretsu*.[35] There are three types: distribution, supply-chain, and horizontal.

Distribution keiretsu are created by large final-product manufacturers to control their distribution systems from production, through wholesaling and other distribution, to the prices in retail outlets that sell only their products.

Supply-chain keiretsu are centered around a major manufacturer that dominates its subcontractors and provides them with financing, technology, management advice, et cetera. These have been especially important for lean manufacturing, just-in-time (JIT) parts delivery, zero-defects efforts, and keeping foreign firms out of supply chains. All major auto and electronics firms have had supply-chain keiretsu that included only domestic firms – though since about 2000, they have admitted more foreign suppliers.

The horizontal groups, the most important for industrial policy, are corporate "families" in which member firms own shares in the others, with preferential buyer-supplier and financing ties. The six major ones have been Sumitomo, Mitsui, Mitsubishi, Fuyo, Daiichi Kangyo, and Sanwa, each centered on a bank. (The first four have roots in prewar *zaibatsu*.) Their member firms have interlocking directorates and hold regular monthly meetings of top executives. They have trading companies that deal in a wide range of products and materials and act as intermediaries, providing services such as logistics, market information, financing, and international resource exploration.

Keiretsu make it easier for member firms to have long time horizons. In the US, shareholders buy and sell stocks based on profit expectations. But in Japan, shareholders, until quite recently, didn't generally choose firms at all. Instead, *firms chose their own key shareholders*: the other companies in their keiretsu. Their main considerations were profit patience and strategic synergies inside the group. Since group members never sold each other's shares, 60–80 percent were never traded and Tokyo's stock exchange was largely a sideshow with respect to the real management of corporate Japan. True power rested with the groups' main banks, under MOF direction to favor long-term success, not with a board of directors elected by shareholders.[36] (This changed significantly, but not completely, in the 1990s.)

These close interfirm ties would mostly have been illegal in America under antitrust law. They helped firms survive in times of trouble and protected the lifetime employment commitments major firms made to core employees. The lockup of shares also meant that foreign firms could not acquire Japanese companies as a market-entry strategy. And government could indirectly and privately "advise" firms not to source parts from abroad or distribute imports at retail.

These discreet tactics became increasingly important as Japan was pressured to phase out openly protectionist measures such as tariffs. It agreed in 1964 to adopt advanced-nation status under GATT and joined the Organisation for Economic Co-operation and Development (OECD). These commitments required Tokyo, on paper, to open to foreign trade and investment. As a result, the government encouraged the remnants of the zaibatsu to reemerge as the horizontal keiretsu to provide unofficial protection.[37]

Governance of Industrial Policies

Japan, unlike several nations (see Chapters 10, 11, and 12) that have failed at industrial policy, had institutions to actually *impose* the plans it devised. They were backed up by a political power structure that was able, when needed, to put the economic interest of the nation as a whole ahead of the profit demands of business.

For example, government bodies enforced performance standards on the firms they assisted or regulated. Even better, Japan had a *flexible* system of mostly indirect governance, by way of the keiretsu, keeping government out of the weeds of day-to-day corporate affairs and leaving most decisions to those with on-the-ground expertise.

In addition to the keiretsu, Japan used cartels to manage industries, press firms to compete on variables other than price, and avoid firms going bankrupt in recessions. To stop cartelization from degrading into lazy, static oligopoly, the government imposed export requirements and made firms compete for subsidized capital.[38]

Government rarely had the ability to dictate to firms outright. Instead, there was negotiation and compromise, with firms sometimes rejecting its guidance. For example, in the auto and computer industries, firms overruled MITI's plans to consolidate the industries. MITI once tried, unsuccessfully, to keep Honda from entering the auto business – one of its more notorious mistakes. There were many, but its successes far outweighed them.

At the apex of the system, stable and trusted pilot institutions, insulated from interest group pressures, provided consistent guidance. Even when there was a change in the elected government, companies knew that fundamental policies would not change. Japan's electorate and the Diet it elected trusted the technocrats to direct precious taxpayer money to the right industries. Bureaucratic institutions perceived as legitimate, fair, and working in the national interest, not that of vested interests, were the key. This social consensus was easier to maintain when the economic pie was growing rapidly, and weakened after the slowdown in the 1990s, but it has not disappeared.

Why Japan's Catch-Up Policies Succeeded

Although Japan was not practicing pure capitalism in the sense most Americans would understand it, its policies were nonetheless generally structured in *market-conforming* ways. The state accepted the basic capitalist framework of private property, profit motive, and free markets, then set out to manipulate key parameters of the system.

Market interventions were based on a correct understanding of advantageous economic activities and industries. Interventions were based on a correct understanding of technological sequencing – that is, what capabilities were prerequisites for each successive step up the technology ladder. Japan correctly worked from the bottom up, starting, for example, with vacuum tubes and transistors before moving on to more sophisticated semiconductors.

Japan in this era was often dismissed as a mere imitator. But successful imitation of such products, at globally competitive quality and price, was a feat few other nations achieved. Its manufacturing success was due in large part to mundane but cumulatively important improvements such as reducing factory waste, decreasing inventories, and minimizing dust in semiconductor plants.[39] After decades when "made in Japan" was synonymous with junk, its manufacturers became famous for quality.

Japan's domestic market (117 million people in 1980) was large enough for its firms to build scale at home before entering foreign markets. They generally entered foreign markets gradually, after a dominant design had stabilized and after they had assembled the assets – manufacturing processes, facilities, inventory control, marketing, and distribution – to beat the incumbents.[40]

Japan maintained domestic competition in tradable sectors and required these firms to become internationally competitive. MITI almost always promoted several firms in an industry, and cooperative R&D projects usually had two or more companies working on each problem. When government encouraged cooperation in R&D or collusion in pricing, it deliberately stimulated competition in other dimensions.

Government understood the need for corporate buy-in to the industrial policy process. This started with having businesspeople involved in policymaking. It also generally required firms to have skin in the game – that is, invest some of their own money in subsidized projects and provide their own scientists for shared R&D efforts. It made future aid contingent on success in the current project.

Japan's major corporations have not historically been principally motivated by profit, aiming instead at global market share. The high fixed costs of their lifetime employment commitments to core employees were one motivation. Another was their long-term relationships with keiretsu suppliers, which also became de facto fixed costs because they could not cut off a sibling firm. A greater market share meant that firms would become stronger global competitors, which the government wanted. It was assumed that profits would follow – as they generally did, but as a secondary effect of a strategy whose priorities were elsewhere.

Many of Japan's top internationally competitive firms, even in their 1980s heyday, had profit rates unacceptable to US financial markets. This did not make them less formidable as competitors, but more so, as American firms ceded market after market as insufficiently lucrative. It was not until the 2000s, when foreigners started to become major shareholders, that firms began giving higher priority to profits.[41]

Outwitting the American Giant

Japan's industry-targeting policies could not have succeeded without open access to the US market. Luckily for Japan, its strategies dovetailed well with the blind spots of America's government and corporate sector.

As the Cold War began, the US opened its markets to imports and directed transfers of technology to a number of countries to prop them up economically and enlist them as allies against the Soviets (see Chapter 16). Japan's trade barriers, its dumping, and the rest of its export machine were tolerated. There was no credible threat that Japan would change sides and ally itself with the Soviet Union or Maoist China, both with highly alien ideologies and long-standing geopolitical conflicts with Japan. But there was, until the early 1960s, legitimate concern that Japan might drift leftward politically and become an unreliable ally.[42]

When, in the late 1970s, Japan became an obvious economic rival, American officialdom had very little understanding of its strategies or how to respond. America's own mercantilist, protectionist heritage (see Chapters 14 and 15) had been forgotten. America's own strategies had been very different anyway, due to its different economic circumstances. Washington did not grasp that Japan's mercantilist behavior was a rational, systematic strategy, or that it could harm the US. America thus retaliated against only the most blatant cases of economic aggression, usually ineffectually and often years too late, well after Japan's manufacturers had established strong competitive positions.

Corporate America also underestimated Japan. It licensed foundational technologies too cheaply, costing it dearly when Japanese products based on these licenses flooded US markets. The US government was sometimes complicit: For antitrust reasons, Washington pressured IBM to unbundle its hardware and software and compelled AT&T to license its transistor technology. Corporate America let its product quality slip and disdained some market niches as insufficiently profitable, letting Japan gain footholds from which it later expanded.

The US allowed the yen to remain at 360 to the dollar from 1949 to 1971, an undervaluation that increased over time as Japan's productivity grew. In 1971, Nixon knocked the yen off its peg by ending Bretton Woods, and, in a rare post–World War II case of effective US tariff strategy, instituted a 10 percent surcharge on dutiable imports from all countries. Regrettably, his concern with currency was not followed up by Ford or Carter.

In 1981, Reagan put in automobile quotas, the Voluntary Restraint Agreement (VRA) (see Chapter 25). In response, Japanese firms set up assembly plants and parts suppliers in the US. But instead of halting Japanese penetration of the US market, the VRA ultimately *expanded* Japan's industrial and political presence in the US. The Japanese got two senators and a congressman from each state where they put a car plant. And because the VRA limited the number, rather than the total value, of imported cars, Japan moved upmarket and exported more expensive models.

Reagan also imposed Japan-oriented VRAs or other measures on motorcycles (1983), machine tools (1986), semiconductors (1986), and steel (1987). His administration conducted negotiations to hold Japan to its commitments regarding opening its home markets. For example, negotiations began in earnest in 1983 on opening financial services, as Japan had gained access to America's market in 1978 but had not reciprocated.

The Reagan administration also started the Sematech consortium as a riposte to Japan's threat to the semiconductor industry (see Chapter 26). And the 1985 Plaza Accord addressed the overvaluation of the dollar, reducing America's trade deficit with Japan for several years (see Chapter 17).

During the 1980s, Japan was exceptionally adroit at running influence operations in Washington, through think tanks and the press.[43] Truthful critics were demonized as "protectionists," "Japan bashers," and "racists."

The George H. W. Bush administration tried to pressure Japan to more fully open its auto and auto parts market, but with little effect.

In 1994, Bill Clinton announced that he would use Section 301 of the 1974 Trade Act to impose punitive tariffs if Japan did not open up its markets for automobiles and parts. The US initiated a WTO case shortly thereafter and Japan countersued. The issue was eventually resolved by Japanese promises to allow more dealer networks for foreign cars and more parts imports. But the actual result was that US auto exports to Japan *declined*. Parts exports rose, but most were from Japanese-owned plants in the US.[44] Other US responses are discussed below and in Chapters 17, 18, and 26.

Industry Case Studies

We look next at how industrial policy played out in key Japanese industries.

Steel

Japan built an internationally competitive steel industry despite having no initial comparative advantage. It had, in fact, a huge *dis*advantage because it had to import every raw material save coal.

The effort began with protectionism. Until the late 1960s, the various measures were the equivalent of a 30 percent tariff.[45] But raw materials and production equipment were generally exempt from import duties and from limits on access to foreign exchange.

Government provided financial assistance for steelmakers to invest in up-to-date production technologies and new, large, modern plants. All the steel firms were in or allied with keiretsu, so they also had deep private-sector pockets backing them. Assured demand from brother firms de-risked the required large, "lumpy" investments. In the early years, steel-consuming keiretsu firms accepted the higher cost and lower quality of domestic steel as the price of building up the industry.

Steel is a capital-intensive, high-fixed-cost industry with a long time lag between decisions to add capacity and commencement of production. Having stimulated demand, the government also had to ensure that the firms didn't all pile in to the point of overcapacity, creating a boom–bust cycle and bankrupting its carefully nurtured companies. So it managed price competition and apportioned big capital investments. It encouraged mergers to gain scale and compete with the international giants, but it did *not* consolidate the industry to the point of blunting competition.

As in other industries, financial aid had strings attached: MITI allocated money to the firms it believed were strongest and best able to use it. Money was available only for investments in newer, more efficient technologies, not for expansion using legacy technologies, a mistake of American steelmakers in the 1950s and '60s. Firms had to show high productivity in their existing plants to get permission to invest in new capacity.[46]

MITI allowed increased tax depreciation on the equipment it wanted companies to invest in and tax exemptions for the cash reserves that buffered firms against price fluctuations. The Export–Import Bank and the Overseas Economic Cooperation Fund provided long-term state financing to help firms make long-term export contracts. Government also helped the firms make strategic overseas investments in raw materials extraction, providing tax incentives and insurance against losses.[47]

MITI helped the steel companies adopt a key innovation, basic oxygen furnace (BOF) technology.[48] In 1955, when two steelmakers asked for foreign exchange permission to import the technology from its Austrian creators, MITI, concerned that competition among buyers would result in a higher price, selected one to be the general licensee and required that it sublicense to other steelmakers on the same terms.[49] As a result, BOF cost Japanese makers 0.36 cents per ton in royalties, whereas American steelmakers paid 15–25 cents.[50]

Over time, as a result of these policies and good corporate management, Japanese steel met the test of international competition. By 1960, it had become the country's largest export.[51] The industry earned a relatively low return on investment, even compared to others in Japan, but Japan's industrial strategy was not about maximizing profits.[52] The steel industry gained a large global market share and built a strong foundation for advantageous steel-consuming industries such as automobiles, shipbuilding, and machine tools.

Automobiles

As with steel, Japan used protectionism, subsidies, bars to foreign direct investment, and other policies to develop an internationally competitive auto industry from a weak starting position.[53]

Right after World War II, the keiretsu system was not yet up and running, and private banks were unwilling to loan money to Japan's fledgling carmakers. Therefore, their first loans came from the state-owned Reconstruction Finance Bank, which also guaranteed their other debts to encourage private banks to lend to them.[54] In 1949, when Toyota was on the brink of bankruptcy and private banks rejected its entreaties, the central bank bailed it out.[55] All told, from 1951 to 1956, government-related loans made up 19 percent of the industry's capital.[56]

The US military's demand for vehicles during the 1950–3 Korean War helped kick-start the industry (and many others in Japan).[57] In 1951, the tariff on cars was set at 40 percent and in 1955, different rates on large (lower) and small cars (higher) were imposed. Auto exports, like all exports, also benefited from a provision, created in 1953, providing a tax deduction of up to 8 percent of export income.

The 1956 Extraordinary Measures Law for the Promotion of the Machinery Industries targeted autos and auto parts.[58] MITI required that foreign licensing agreements include increasing local content over time. To encourage foreign firms to grant licenses for parts then being imported, MITI guaranteed the remittance of royalties, but required that 90 percent of the parts be made in Japan within five years.[59] Another law guaranteed profit repatriation only if the facilities "contributed significantly to the development of the domestic industry."[60] There were also FILP loans, special depreciation allowances, exemptions from import duties on production machinery, access to foreign exchange to import technology, and diverse other subsidies.

As Japan's car industry became more competitive, tariffs were lowered, starting in 1962 for trucks and 1968 for cars. Inbound foreign investment in autos was liberalized in 1973. Tariffs were completely lifted in 1978 – by which time they were irrelevant because Japan's car industry was so strong and Japan's nontariff trade barriers had been perfected.[61] The industry's breakthrough to world-class status in the late 1970s is recounted in Chapter 25.

Protectionism and other industrial policies were not the sole cause of Japan's success in autos. Good corporate decisions had a huge impact, especially the industry's focus, ahead of its foreign competitors, on lean manufacturing, JIT delivery, and smart management of technology. Eiji Toyoda of Toyota was an industrial genius. Japanese producers set a new standard for quality that the entire global industry eventually had to meet. Lean production, which started at Toyota, eventually became generalized to industries all over the world. Toyota, the leading firm, was in fact known as the company that *refused* to listen to MITI and never coordinated with it. (Runner-up Nissan was the cooperative company.) But state industrial policy was still a necessary enabler that tilted an otherwise unfriendly environment toward Japan's carmakers, especially during their vulnerable early years.[62]

Color Television

In the 1950s, Japan imposed tariffs of 14–21 percent on imported TVs.[63] Foreign firms also had to set up their own retail networks because until the early 1990s, shops only carried TVs made by their keiretsu.[64] (Unsurprisingly, government approval was required for foreign ownership of more than 50 percent of 10 or more retail outlets.[65]) These impediments induced foreign firms to license their technology to Japanese producers rather than entering the market themselves.

All of Japan's electronics industries were backed by the 1957 Extraordinary Measures Law for the Promotion of the Electronics Industries, plus follow-on legislation in 1971 and 1978.[66] Among other things, these laws gave MITI the authority to create specific support packages for different segments of the industry. In 1956, the largest TV manufacturers formed a cartel known as the Home Electronic Appliance Market Stabilization Council.

MITI helped Japanese producers set domestic prices artificially high to subsidize below-cost exports.[67] Managers of the firms met regularly under MITI supervision to fix domestic and export prices.[68] Japan's Fair Trade Commission, charged with preventing price fixing as an antitrust violation, knew this was going on but did nothing. When US producers complained in the late 1960s, Japanese consumers became aware they were paying inflated prices and boycotted domestic televisions. MITI responded by giving "administrative guidance" to the industry to cut prices – which it did, though not as low as its export prices.[69] Dumping in the US inexorably pushed American makers out of the industry, increasing Japanese firms' market share and thus scale economies, which then made them even more competitive.[70]

Having destroyed the American TV industry, Japan enjoyed an entrenched, lucrative position until the introduction of flat-panel screens in the late 1990s. It used TVs as a base to enter related products such as tape recorders, stereos, the Walkman, VCRs, video cameras, DVDs, fax machines, copiers, and printers. Demand for components of these devices also helped kick-start Japan's semiconductor industry.

Again, good industrial policy was not the only reason for the industry's success. Japanese makers were more aggressive than their American counterparts in driving costs down, especially by deploying new technologies such as solid-state electronics and single circuit boards.[71] Their products were more reliable. But these strategies did not develop in a vacuum, but in the cheap-capital, long-time-horizons hothouse of keiretsu corporate governance, protectionism, and government support.

The US Fails to Counter

The color TV industry is a good case study of America's historically poor defenses against predatory foreign industrial policies.[72] Tokyo took full advantage of Washington's failure to understand the sophisticated techno-mercantilist game it was playing, successfully pitting American manufacturers against Treasury Department free traders and American retailers against American manufacturers.

In 1971, the US Tariff Commission, based on a Treasury finding, ruled that Japan was dumping – that is, selling below the price in its home market – *three years* after the industry filed a complaint. Dumping is illegal and subject to trade retaliation under the Tariff Act of 1930. But Treasury let the importers' lawyers game the process and no significant penalties were imposed.

American firms, hemorrhaging money, tried other tactics, including an antitrust suit in 1974.[73] Shortly thereafter, in response to growing pressure, the Japanese did appear to raise their US prices. But in reality, they continued to sell at lower prices by giving illegal kickbacks to US retailers.[74]

US producers initiated other legal actions. Zenith, the leading firm, charged that Japanese TV exporters were benefiting from the rebate of a national commodity tax and asked Treasury to impose a countervailing duty. Treasury sat on this request for four years, finally rejecting it in 1976. Zenith then appealed to the US Customs Court, which ruled in its favor in 1977.[75] Around this time, the Justice Department started investigating customs fraud and the kickbacks.

Finally, in May 1977, President Carter announced an orderly marketing agreement with Japan to limit Japanese TV exports to the US.[76] But this was a decade too late, as the industry was already mortally wounded. Years of dumping had starved it of the profits needed to invest in new products and better manufacturing. It never recovered: The last American company to make TVs in the US closed its assembly line in 1993.[77] By that time, two-thirds of the color TVs sold in the US were made here but all, except for Zenith, by European or Japanese firms.[78]

Semiconductors Part I

Even industrial policy skeptics have conceded that it was important in nurturing Japan's semiconductor and computer industries.[79] Indeed, semiconductors nicely illustrate the intricacy, orchestration of multiple tools, and sheer cunning of Japanese industrial policy.

The industry was a natural target for MITI. It had continuous, incremental, but predictable technological change: think Moore's law. It had huge scale economies. Global sales were booming with no end in sight. It was well suited to Japan's strengths: large companies with skilled human resources, sophisticated organizational capacities, and financial stamina, competing via reverse engineering and high-quality, low-cost manufacturing.

As semiconductors, starting with transistors, started replacing vacuum tubes in the early 1960s, Japanese producers were far behind.[80] Without policy intervention, American firms would have dominated even the Japanese market. In response, Japan used tariffs, quotas, and limits on foreign investment. Financial assistance took the form of low-interest loans, subsidies, accelerated depreciation, and grants for collaborative R&D.

Because of the exceptionally knowledge-intensive character of the industry, Tokyo had to do two things: first, induce American firms to transfer their technology to Japanese companies, ideally at artificially low prices; and second, keep the Americans out of the Japanese market, despite US government pressure, until Japanese firms were competitive.

When, in 1960, the then leading firm Texas Instruments (TI) applied for Japanese recognition of its US patents and, in 1964, for permission to open a wholly owned subsidiary, MITI initially refused to even acknowledge its applications.[81] This bought domestic firms time to learn the technology and build scale. At the time, Japanese firms had to charge three times the US price for chips because their "yields" (percentage of usable chips per wafer) were under 10 percent, compared to 25 percent in the US.[82] If TI's patents had been recognized, they would have had to pay TI royalties on top of the 6–7 percent they were already paying Western Electric and Fairchild for underlying technologies.[83]

But MITI also knew Japanese firms would ultimately need TI's patents to produce legally and export to nations that recognized them. So MITI told TI in 1966 that, as a condition to allowing a 50–50 joint venture with a Japanese firm, it would have to license its patents to other Japanese companies. Furthermore, the venture would be limited to no more than 10 percent of Japan's production for three years. TI complained to the US government and the Commerce Department complained to MITI that these restrictions were contrary to Japan's IMF and OECD obligations regarding free international capital flows. Tokyo replied that the treaties allowed such restrictions when foreign currency reserves were low, which was nominally true despite the dubious logic of using the argument to justify restricting *inbound* capital flows.[84] The pro–free trade Treasury Department accepted this legal argument, and the US, failing to grasp Japan's overall strategy, backed off.

Events then forced Tokyo's hand. Japan's consumer electronics producers, its primary users of semiconductors, pressured MITI to compromise. TI had threatened a lawsuit in the US against firms importing goods that infringed on its patents, and this was hurting exports.[85] In exchange for MITI allowing TI to open a subsidiary in Japan, TI acceded to MITI's conditions, including that its undertaking be a joint venture with Sony, as MITI wanted to avoid setting the precedent of a wholly owned foreign firm.[86] But the venture was a sham that lasted only three years before Sony, never involved in its management, sold its stock.

MITI's ability to compel this phony partnership without pushback from Washington meant that Motorola and Fairchild, the other key American players, were also forced into joint ventures. But no major Japanese firms were willing to collaborate with them, as they knew MITI would be heavily funding the industry and would favor domestic companies over ventures including foreigners.[87] MITI ultimately arranged for Motorola to tie up with Alps Electronics and Fairchild with TDK – but these were both makers of products like cassette tapes and inexperienced in ICs. Both ventures collapsed as intended, and tying up Motorola and Fairchild for a few crucial years minimized their impact on the Japanese chip market.

As of 1971, Japanese chipmakers still needed to sell their chips at 20 percent below production cost to compete.[88] Thus, as late as 1972, all the semiconductor divisions of Japan's main producers were in the red.[89] But they could absorb years of losses because their keiretsu did not require immediate profitability and had profits from other divisions to keep them solvent.[90]

Tokyo indirectly subsidized long-term semiconductor research. Between 1961 and 1995, Nippon Telephone and Telegraph (NTT) spent $25 billion on research, much of it on semiconductors.[91] Purchases from its family of supplier firms, including NEC, Fujitsu, and Hitachi, nurtured their capabilities, with the cost ultimately funded by overpriced telephone service.[92] These suppliers conducted research with NTT's laboratories, modeled after AT&T's legendary Bell Labs. (NTT researchers frequently visited AT&T, and in 1966, a formal agreement between the two firms facilitated regular visits.[93])

America Fights Back in Semiconductors

After penetrating markets for relatively simple semiconductors, such as for calculators and watches, Japan's chipmakers mastered metal-on-silicon (MOS) memory technology, which set them on a path to dominate that sector when it later exploded. Japan's chip industry dumped memory chips in the mid-1980s, pushing out American producers.[94] In the words of *MIT Technology Review*, "By all appearances, the US semiconductor industry was on the ropes in the mid-1980s. After a multiyear effort to become a force in semiconductor memory chips, Japan now led the industry – both in market share and in the quality of its products."[95] Then, because awareness of the military importance of chips and of Japan's emergence as a rival economy had grown, America's government and firms fought back.

American chipmakers filed a dumping claim in 1985 that resulted in a 5–0 ruling in their favor by the US International Trade Commission. The negotiations that followed led in 1986 to an "arrangement" between the two governments to monitor prices against dumping and allow the US up to 20 percent of Japan's market, double what it had.[96] (The Japanese firms all announced production cuts on the same day, making clear their orchestration by MITI.)[97] While this agreement did not meet all its objectives, it did stabilize the US share of the global dynamic random-access memory (DRAM) market, reverse the plunge of the US share of other memory chips, and increase the US share in Japan.[98]

That same year, the US set up Sematech, a vast cooperative R&D endeavor that did much to restore the fortunes of the American industry and is recounted in Chapter 26.

Although Japan was not ultimately able to dominate the world semiconductor market, it did establish a lucrative and enduring position. As of 2020, it had a larger share of global semiconductor production (13 percent) than the US (10 percent).[99] Not least because of the human resources and organizational skills accumulated in semiconductors, its success spilled over into many other industries, including computers, consumer electronics, telecommunications, numerically controlled machine tools, avionics, robotics, AI, and semiconductor manufacturing equipment. As of 2015, Japan's global 30 percent share in this last industry was second only to that of the US.[100]

Computer Hardware

It is unlikely that Japan would have developed a mainframe computer industry without strong state support. It used five major policies:

1. Protectionism
2. Financial aid
3. Government procurement
4. State-sponsored cooperative R&D projects
5. A quasi-public computer rental company, the Japan Electronic Computer Company (JECC)

As a result of these policies and others, the foreign share of Japan's market (imports plus IBM's Japanese production) fell from 93 percent in 1958 to 43 percent in 1969, 34 percent in 1977, and 23 percent in 1986.[101]

Tokyo raised computer tariffs from 15 to 25 percent in the early 1960s and attached a lot of strings to IBM's producing in Japan.[102] MITI forced it to license key patents to 15 Japanese firms, forming a de facto buyers' cartel to cut a better deal.[103] America's second tier of computer makers was also managed: Sperry Rand (UNIVAC) was forced into a joint venture with Oki Electric, TRW with Mitsubishi, and GE with Toshiba.

In 1961, MITI helped create a joint venture among seven state-selected computer makers, JECC, to rent out domestic computers, and from 1961 to 1981, the state awarded it $2 billion in low-interest loans.[104] By using its monopoly of computer leasing to avoid price discounting, JECC shifted competition to quality, technology, marketing, and support services.[105] JECC was, in fact, so effective that Japan adopted a similar system for other products such as robotics.

Startled by IBM's 1964 triumph with its pathbreaking System/360, MITI rapidly allocated $770,000 (2023 dollars) to help firms learn about the then new use of ICs in computers.[106] To move the industry into ever more sophisticated segments, it then created and subsidized cooperative R&D projects. A MITI lab member later admitted that "frankly [much of the project's aim is] to avoid patents that cover procedures developed in the US."[107]

Japan's efforts were facilitated, starting in 1969, by the Justice Department's pressure on IBM, because of antitrust concerns, to "unbundle" its product – that is, sell its software and hardware separately. Compliance required disclosing technical information needed for outsiders to write software for IBM machines, which helped the Japanese reverse engineer IBM's hardware and "borrow" and tweak its software, enough to create their own royalty-free systems.

Japan supported several domestic players, unlike failed attempts in the UK (ICL), Germany (Siemens), France (Bull), and Italy (Olivetti) to create single national champions. Policymakers chose to support large, diversified keiretsu firms over smaller consumer electronics companies that wanted in because they believed the former had the scale and deep pockets to compete.[108]

In the 1960s and 1970s, sometimes MITI paid for an entire cooperative computer R&D project, but often it paid only half. The 1962–4 FONTAC Project, focused on building a prototype to counter IBM's second-generation computer, helped jump-start the entire industry.[109] From 1961 to 1969, subsidies and tax benefits amounted to 46 percent of what the firms invested.[110] Counting low-interest loans, this figure becomes 188 percent (!) and the corresponding figures for 1970–5 are 57 and 169 percent, and for 1976–80, 25 and 93 percent.[111]

Japanese mainframe makers needed ever-more-advanced chips to stay competitive with IBM, the global standard-setter at the time. Thus, MITI started its 1976–9 very-large-scale integration (VLSI) project. Government provided $150 million and the firms $60 million.[112] Critical topics were each attacked by three parallel groups using different approaches to increase the chance of success. This project eventually made possible computers that exceeded IBM's top-of-the-line machines in price and performance.[113]

Today, Fujitsu is one of the three main players (with IBM and Unisys) in the global mainframe market, and the smaller Hitachi also has a global presence.

Computer Software

Japan's inability to catch up in computer software illustrates the limits of its industrial policy capabilities.

Software research was supported in MITI's various computer projects, but MITI did not seriously shift its attention to the field until the mid-1980s, when the FBI caught Japanese firms stealing IBM's software. After Japanese firms could no longer copy IBM software with impunity, MITI organized several projects to help firms shift to non-IBM standards. Its Sigma Project (1985–90), based on UNIX, did not catch on.[114] A new Japanese system called TRON – its derivatives popular in devices such as cameras and cars but never a success as a desktop OS – was developed by the private sector starting in 1984.[115]

Struggling to blunt America's overwhelming advantage, MITI in 1983 proposed a law that would protect software copyrights for only 15 years instead of the international standard of 50 years.[116] The proposal would also have authorized MITI to require any firm operating in Japan to license its software to a Japanese company. However, with the US government and American firms now alert to Japan's aggressive policies, MITI was forced to abandon the plan.[117]

During the 1980s, a decade that set the future direction of the computer industry down to the present day, Japan's firms made several strategic mistakes. Fujitsu and Hitachi both modified IBM's operating system so that it was not compatible with IBM's machines – or with each other's. To protect themselves from competition, they bundled their hardware and software to lock users into their standard.[118] But this approach, which had once served even IBM well, was becoming obsolete as the industry shifted to PCs, a shift Japan (like IBM itself) failed to foresee.

Japan's biggest failure in computers was its 1982–92 Fifth Generation Computing Systems project, funded at $400 million.[119] This project was taken seriously enough abroad to induce America's similar Strategic Computing Initiative and the European Strategic Programme on Research in Information Technology. It aimed to leapfrog existing technologies by using massively parallel processing to achieve true artificial intelligence. It was visionary, but failed because it was 40 years ahead of the required processing power.

By the mid-1990s, Japan's government and computer firms had given up on becoming competitive in operating systems. But Japanese companies remained strong in the software embedded in manufactured goods such as consumer electronics, robots, autos, and machine tools.[120] For example, as of 2019, Renesas Electronics was the world's largest maker of computer chips, including their software, for cars.[121]

Aviation

In aviation, Japan's industrial policy succeeded *despite* its failures. Its attempt to break into large passenger aircraft failed, but led to lucrative success building some of their key components.

Like Germany, Japan had produced sophisticated aircraft during World War II. Also like Germany, it was banned from producing planes by its occupation authorities, in Japan's case until 1952, causing it to fall behind during the crucial transition from propellers to jets. Germany has since clawed its way back into the industry as a major supplier to French-led Airbus. Japan's experience, despite disappointments, has been similar.

In 2020, Mitsubishi Heavy Industries finally cancelled its 90-passenger SpaceJet after investing $10 billion over 18 years. The plane had been unable to obtain FAA certification due to poor design and technology, dooming its prospects globally.

However, 35 percent of the airframe of Boeing's 787 is today made in Japan.[122] This includes the wings and the wing box, the all-important hard-to-make component that connects the wings under the fuselage, thereby determining what wings the plane can have, which determines its load capacity and performance, which fix its economics. In addition to manufacturing them, Japanese firms designed 70 percent of their parts.[123] Much of the 787's avionics is also made in Japan. Boeing is currently retreating from this outsourcing strategy, which has worked out badly (see Chapter 18), but is stuck with it for models already in production.

Japan systematically mastered the technologies required for success in aviation. The transfer of US fighter jet technology was crucial, starting in the 1950s with assembly of F-86s from kits, followed by licensed production of the

F-104, F-4, and F-15J. With each successive plane, Japanese manufacturers built more of the aircraft. For the F-15J in 1981, more than 100 US firms partnered with Japanese counterparts to transfer technology: Bendix transferred engine parts to Ishikawajima–Harima Heavy Industries, Honeywell transferred flight computers to Japan Aviation Electronics, TRW transferred fuel pumps to Mitsubishi Heavy Industries, and McDonnell Douglas transferred landing gear to Shinko Electric.[124]

Japan's relative failures in computer hardware, computer software, and aviation are revealing. Unlike steel, these industries were not well suited to mastery by using cheap capital to apply the most advanced available technology, bought at a concessionary price, on a scale equal to or larger than the incumbents. Unlike automobiles, Japan did not have a lead in a potent new production philosophy. And unlike color TVs, Japan did not face a technologically sluggish American industry whose government failed to defend it in time. In computer hardware, Japan faced pushback in trade policy and proactive industrial policy from the US. In aviation, it faced an industry with the long-term, technologically progressive, deep-pocketed backing of the Pentagon (see Chapter 26). In software, Japan had no special advantage or good policy tools for desktop systems or the internet, itself a fruit of American industrial policy (see Chapter 19).

Japan after 1990

The myth of an unstoppable Japan that flared in the US in from roughly 1978 to 1990 never made sense, as it was based on extrapolating Japan's then intimidating catch-up growth rates into a future in which Japan would be at the global technological frontier and thus constrained to grow at the lower rate of all developed nations.[125]

But despite much US commentary about "lost decades" starting around 1990, Japan's economy has not unraveled. Growth in aggregate GDP, where Japan has lagged, is an inappropriate metric because Japan has a declining and aging population that has caused its working-age (15–64) population to fall 14 percent from its 1995 peak.[126] Japan has also been reducing its average hours worked per year to a level now lower than the US, a noneconomic lifestyle choice.[127] A better metric is GDP per person of working age, where Japan has basically matched US performance since 1990.[128]

Not that Japan hasn't made major mistakes. The 1985 Plaza Accord hurt Japan's export-oriented economy, so Tokyo responded by keeping interest rates too low for too long. This produced a speculative bubble in real estate and stocks that lasted until 1990. The Development Bank of Japan then raised interest rates too high too fast, popping the bubble, and followed this with insufficient fiscal stimulus.

After 1990, as Japan transitioned from CUIP to MEIP and its corporate sector became more sophisticated, there was less need for government planning as firms could now successfully make more big decisions on their own. The economy now tended to draw capital to high-value uses of its own accord, reducing the need for government efforts to allocate it. Government's role thus shifted toward controlling firms *indirectly* by managing the incentives they faced.

Thus MITI went into decline. In 2001, it was merged with other agencies to create METI.[129] Although METI has less power than MITI once had, its overall objectives remain similar: industry management, trade management, and long-term economic planning. The MOF has also lost power.[130] By 2000, to prop up a declining stock market, Japan had stopped discouraging foreign purchases of stocks. As a result, foreign shareholdings increased from 4 percent in 1990 to 32 percent in 2015, which then forced firms to give more priority to short-term profitability.[131] This caused a decline of the horizontal keiretsu and other less formal corporate alliances.[132]

Since then, Japan's large firms have been changing, although slowly. Despite the expectations of 20 years ago, the keiretsu networks and main-bank relationships have persisted, though they have had to adapt.[133] The governance and behavior of Japanese companies have diversified.[134] For example, in 2016, Toyota set up the Toyota Research Institute with its headquarters in Silicon Valley and a non-Japanese CEO. This is a dramatic change from the days when Japanese firms consistently kept critical R&D in Japan.

Japan, like the US, is now confronting an increasingly problematic China. It passed the Economic Security Promotion Act in May 2022, whose objectives are creating resilient supply chains, protecting critical infrastructure, reinforcing Japan's technology base, and developing a new class of secret patents for militarily and economically strategic areas.[135] The Act empowers METI and other ministries to respond to security risks with protectionist measures and financial incentives for the private sector to diversify their suppliers and investments away from China. This is clearly a return to a more proactive, interventionist industrial policy, and indeed, some corporate leaders have expressed concerns about a possible slide back toward more government control of Japan's economy.

Strengths

- High social solidarity that enabled government to prioritize long-term interests of the whole economy over short-term consumption and profit demands of private businesses.

- Long history and strong consensus in favor of strategic direction of the economy by government, resulting in consistent policies implemented by competent, meritocratically selected technocrats insulated from politics.
- Commitment to an economically sound concept of industrial policy – that is, the pursuit of ever-more-advantageous industries unconstrained by commitments to free markets, socialism, or other ideologies per se.
- Policymaking that was coordinated, adjusted over time, and able to deploy the full array of industrial policy tools.
- Accurate understanding of technological sequencing and of which industries drive growth in others.
- Skill at managing the rivalrous, mercantilist realities of global trade.
- Requiring firms to become internationally competitive as a condition of government support.
- Effective use of keiretsus as tools to discourage outsourcing, prevent foreign takeovers, guarantee markets, provide internal financing for long-term projects, and impose informal, unwritten protectionism.

Weaknesses

- Lack of a good model for industrial policy in industries unsuited to "copy, improve, scale, export, jump to next rung of the existing technology ladder, and repeat."
- Failed, overambitious technology bets such as the Fifth-Generation Computing System and the Mitsubishi SpaceJet.
- Lack of a strong startup and venture capital ecosystem, leading to relatively weak performance in industries where innovation is best realized by these means.
- Lack of a superpower national security posture to motivate pursuit of breakthrough innovations and related basic science research.

6 KOREA
Development despite Turbulence

South Korea's (hereinafter "Korea") per capita GDP growth from 1961 to 2021 averaged 5.9 percent, the second highest in the world after China.[1] Adjusted for purchasing power, per capita GDP passed Japan in 2018 and reached 68 percent of the US in 2021.[2] Korea is home to world-class companies such as Samsung (consumer electronics and memory chips), Hyundai (cars, ships, and more), and POSCO (steel). It has enjoyed a notably flat (though recently sharpening) income distribution, with a 2016 Gini coefficient was 0.31, versus 0.41 in the US.[3] Korea succeeded despite an unpredictable, existential military threat, economic volatility, and internal political turbulence. It survived assassinations, dissident movements that filled the streets with protestors, brutal crackdowns on political opposition, and labor militancy.

Korea's growth was achieved through proactive, dynamically managed, export-focused industrial policy.[4] Its leaders understood and harnessed, but did not bow to, market forces. They made policy adjustments on the fly as conditions changed and measures were seen to succeed or fail. And they were backed by an effective bureaucracy with strong leadership continuity. Korea poured subsidized capital into increasingly large firms capable of delivering growth through exports. It steadily increased its capital stock, technological sophistication, and penetration of foreign markets. Policymakers promoted scalable and productivity-enhancing industries that reinforced each other and used technologies and addressed markets already proven abroad. They unabashedly picked winners and showered subsidies on individual firms and entire industries. The state worked closely with business to build up first light, then heavy, and, finally, high-tech manufacturing.

Korea's industrial policies developed over time from experiment, experience, and many failures. Policy goals and the structure of the planning bureaucracy were repeatedly changed to accommodate new realities. The country's leaders had enormous ambition and Japan as a model, but no specific template for policy.[5] The system suffered from both hard and soft corruption, with cronyism and kickbacks in return for favorable loans and other preferential treatment.[6] But corruption did not derail its essential dynamics. Even recipients of corruptly won government favors were held to their commitments to master technologies, expand production, and export.[7] When initiatives to localize manufacturing or enhance competitiveness failed, the authorities changed course even when it meant hurting incumbent firms.

Because of rapid capacity growth fueled by subsidized capital, Korea's export-oriented economy faced frequent crises caused by fluctuations in global markets. In response, the government developed stabilization tools that kept critical companies alive, allowing growth to resume when markets recovered. After the 1961–87 peak of its activist industrial policy, Korea reduced its degree of intervention, but it has never embraced American-style laissez-faire. Instead, its industrial policy has evolved to one suited to its now developed economy, with initiatives focused on maintaining its high-value manufacturing and growing its now innovation-driven, knowledge-based economy.

Inauspicious Beginnings

From 1910 to 1945, Korea was a Japanese colony. Through heavy-handed, state-driven development, Japan brutally restructured its agrarian economy to support the export first of rice, then of processed foods, minerals, iron, steel, even ships, to Japan and its empire.[8] Korean manufacturing began in this period.

The Korean War (1950–3) was fought between the communist North and the new South Korean state established in 1948. It ended with only an armistice: To this day there is no peace treaty. At its end, South Korea's per capita GDP was less than 1 percent of America's. Most Koreans were illiterate.[9] The country's only major export was tungsten.[10] Most fuel to power factories, cotton to make textiles, and iron ore to make steel had to be imported. Even with American aid, South Korea struggled to maintain its balance of payments, let alone industrialize.

Land reform in 1950 required that holdings over three hectares be sold to the government, with compensation paid in government bonds. The state then resold the land to tenant farmers, with 70 percent of farm households receiving land.[11] Peasants working their own land tend to be more productive, creating an initial growth spurt that builds support for further reforms. The

wealth of large landowners is difficult to commandeer for industrial development, and rural unrest can threaten political stability.[12] Thus, Asian nations
that have not had effective land reform, such as Thailand and the Philippines,
have not achieved the rapid development of those – Japan, Korea, Taiwan, and,
in a brutal communist fashion, China – that have.

Korea's capital stock in the 1950s was far too small to fund meaningful
economic development. Most capital came from American aid, which peaked at
22 percent of GDP in 1957. At the time, US officials were not interested in
promoting advanced industries in Korea, believing this futile.[13] They preferred
industries within the country's existing comparative advantage, such as food
processing, textile mills, tungsten mining, and other natural resource processing. American assistance paid for raw materials and infrastructure, while the
American defense umbrella spared Korea from having to spend all its money on
defense.

Syngman Rhee, president from 1948 to 1960, sought to build an
economy strong enough to withstand the North Korean threat and not depend
on American economic aid. His administration established the beginnings of
a planning apparatus, drawing on the colonial-era Chosen (Japanese for Korea)
Bank, which was renamed the Korea Development Bank (KDB) in 1954. The
KDB was placed under the direct control of the Ministry of Finance instead of
the central bank, setting the precedent for other special banks independent of
the latter's control. By the end of 1955, KDB accounted for more than 40 percent of total bank lending.[14] Rhee also created the Ministry of Reconstruction,
which became a nexus of technocratic competence, more isolated from political
interference than the rest of the otherwise corrupt administrative state.[15]

The Rhee government tried a classic import substitution approach (see
Chapter 3), raising tariffs to an average of 40 percent by the mid-1950s. But its
strategy was clumsy and its implementation was weak. Politicians from Rhee's
Liberal Party kept a strong hold on policymaking, leaving development technocrats with little real power. Party members are estimated to have held direct
interests in more than half the private projects receiving US aid, with the profits
funding political kickbacks.[16]

With infant industry protection and low-quality state coordination,
there was some growth. Following the 1957 lowering of tariffs on capital goods
and raw materials, companies in the "three white industries" (sugar refineries,
flour mills, and textile mills) became highly profitable. But this produced
a capitalist class dependent on government favors and with little
accountability.[17] And Korea's currency was overvalued, making an export-led
strategy almost impossible.[18]

Beyond these low-skilled light industries serving the small domestic
market, Rhee's attempts at industrial development failed. These industries were

not internationally competitive. The textile mills built capacity beyond what the domestic market demanded, but failed to penetrate overseas markets due to the currency, low product quality, and poor distribution. They were banned from exporting to the US so long as they relied on US aid for their cotton. Manufacturers of more advanced goods, such as the first factory of what later became Goldstar's electronics division, were uncompetitive even in Korea.

Park Chung Hee Takes Control

By 1960, many factions of society were openly expressing frustration with corruption, failed economic reforms, vote rigging, and poor living standards. Rhee resigned in April 1960 and, after an election, was succeeded by a center-left government. This government devalued the currency and tried to rein in disorder, but had limited success and was widely seen as corrupt. The public backlash grew.

In May 1961, claiming that only the military could prevent further chaos, Major General Park Chung Hee staged a coup. His junta, the Supreme Council for National Reconstruction (SCNR), then suspended the National Assembly. He pledged to fight communism, strengthen relations with the US, end corruption, work toward the reunification of North and South, and return Korea to democratic rule within two years.[19]

From 1961 to 1963, the SCNR dramatically restructured Korean politics. Thousands of politicians, businessmen, bureaucrats, and military officers were investigated for corruption. Some 74 senior politicians, 40 generals, and 1,863 government employees were removed from their positions. Thirteen major business leaders were arrested. These purges secured the power of the junta and began destroying the Rhee era's payoff-based political machine.[20] Military men were appointed to top administrative positions.

But Park soon realized that a modern economy needed the technical expertise, managerial skills, and overseas information networks of the business leaders he had jailed. Those charged with illicit wealth accumulation, war profiteering, and other corruption were therefore let off with reduced financial penalties – to be paid toward "national reconstruction." Park nationalized banking: Shares in banks were among the assets that business leaders were forced to give up.[21] Thus began a new state–business relationship, with the state able to both financially support and discipline business leaders to induce them to serve its economic strategy.

Taking Charge of the Economy

Under the previous government, reform-minded bureaucrats, inspired by Japanese thinking, had drafted an outline for an economic planning apparatus with real power. They submitted their plan to the junta only a week after it took power, and in time, much of it was adopted. A new "super ministry," the Economic Planning Board (EPB), was created and given wide-ranging powers to coordinate other ministries.[22]

As the SCNR struggled to win public support, measures to overcome poverty and promote social welfare initially took higher priority than industrialization.[23] Price guarantees for farmers and new infrastructure lifted agricultural productivity and reduced dependence on foreign aid. Although organized labor was weak, Park at first saw labor–management cooperation as a key to rapid economic development, or at least as a way to get workers on his side.[24]

In 1962, Park pushed through a new constitution that gave the executive branch far greater powers. After narrowly winning an election in October 1963, he began to consolidate authority in the Office of the President, building a new power and patronage network.[25] He gave many former leaders of the SCNR high positions in the newly formed Democratic Republic Party (DRP), through which he subsequently governed.

Export-oriented industrialization (EOI) was *not* Park's initial strategy. From 1961 to 1963, he continued a modestly improved version of the import substitution industrialization (ISI) of the 1950s. However, importing the needed equipment and raw materials at a time when US aid was dropping caused trade deficits that threatened to pull down the won, making needed imports unaffordable.[26] By 1964, import substitution was visibly stalling out as a growth strategy, textile exports were beginning to look promising, and the US was demanding stabilization of the trade deficit. So Park turned to EOI *as a tactical move to deal with immediate pressures.*

In part to obtain more development funding, Park committed in 1965 to assisting the US in Vietnam, ultimately sending more than 300,000 soldiers. The US paid the cost, with Korean firms providing goods and services including military uniforms, building materials, construction services, and transportation. Through 1973, America's war effort brought in $2 billion, and the goodwill of US policymakers helped Korea obtain better access to US markets and remain under America's defense umbrella.[27]

After a narrow election victory in 1971, Park's solution to continued unrest was to declare a national emergency and pass the Special Law Regarding National Security. This marked his definitive shift away from democracy. In 1972, he imposed another new constitution, creating a near-dictatorial system that eliminated direct popular elections and term limits for the presidency and essentially gave himself the power to appoint one-third of the National Assembly.[28]

For support, Park relied on a power base consisting of the military, Korea's own CIA, big business, and the technocrats, in roughly that order. The regime held together through the 1970s as Park pushed his aggressive industrialization programs, but fell apart in 1979. As his rule grew more dictatorial, Park proved unable to mediate conflicts and maintain the balance of power within his administration. Amid popular protests that both US and Korean intelligence feared might lead to a full-blown insurrection, he was assassinated in October by Kim Chae-gyu, head of the KCIA, who was later executed.

Rapid Catch-Up Development

Park's administrations aimed at the sort of catch-up industrialization previously achieved by Japan. The end point of this strategy was developed nation status, an extraordinarily ambitious goal for a country as poor as Korea. The strategy required a series of risky, high-stakes bets on key export industries and rapid policy pivots. Huge successes and costly failures were both common.

Success with this strategy required an effective bureaucracy orchestrating policy without rival power centers undermining its efforts.[29] The planning apparatus that took shape after Park's 1963 consolidation of power transformed the state's capacity to execute industrial policy. Planning, capital, state authority, and nuts-and-bolts execution were all needed, and the EPB played a role in all four.

To make the EPB efficient and effective, it was tied directly to the executive, with weekly briefings providing direct communication with Park himself. From 1963, it was led by the deputy prime minister. Planning and control offices in other agencies were established to track them and improve their effectiveness. Hiring and promotion for EPB bureaucrats was merit-based.[30] After 1963, Park was able to insulate it almost entirely from electoral and party politics, directing priorities himself.[31] Although the regime worked *with* the financial and business communities, they were too weak to derail or pervert his program. Park's vision of a strong, industrialized Korea dominated, with the state strong-arming uncooperative companies.

The EPB's powers and capabilities were gradually expanded to include coordinating foreign capital inflows, promoting technical cooperation with foreign companies, and collecting and synthesizing industrial statistics. It rapidly implemented Park's frequent directives to explore new policy directions, delegating planning of specific projects to other ministries and then adjusting the plans and budgets they submitted. Policy priorities were spelled out in Annual and Five-Year Economic Development Plans covering economy-wide priorities, from which flowed detailed industry-specific plans and targets.

Five-Year Plans and Working with Business

The first Five-Year Plan (1962–6) largely reflected the factional politics of the SCNR and political pressures on the EPB from both the government and US aid administrators. Some factions pushed for unworkable production quotas, expanded from those of the previous administration in a sort of one-upmanship, while other factions focused on tearing down the mechanisms that had enriched members of the Rhee government.[32] Meanwhile, the US pushed for balanced budgets and balanced trade, rather than economic development, and was reducing its aid.

The EPB changed leadership seven times from its founding in 1961 to 1964, but then stabilized. Pressure from disparate elements of the SCNR and uncooperative legacy bureaucracies subsided. It was then that planning became truly deliberate and purposeful.[33] Execution of the 1967, 1972, and 1977 Five-Year Plans was much smoother than that of the first.

Although bureaucrats and business leaders often had considerable discretion in execution, the Plans were top-down, with the key decisions almost always made in Seoul. There was little public accountability. Park himself took an active role in pushing specific priorities and in ensuring the smooth running of the bureaucracy.[34]

In 1961, business leaders worked with Park to build a forum for government-business collaboration, the Korean Businessmen's Association.[35] Park used it to articulate his goals; business used it to lobby for government support. A system of industry associations predating Park became part of this mechanism. These associations were made the exclusive representatives of their industries and were delegated tasks ranging from setting import rules to allocating state funding.[36]

Business leaders were closely involved in formulating and implementing policy, helping choose target industries and set production quotas. But government was always the senior partner. Starting in 1965, Park personally participated in monthly National Export Promotion Meetings. He discussed challenges faced by specific businesses and industries and issued directives to help them on the spot.[37] Using customs data and intelligence about overseas markets and rivals, the government and the private sector measured progress against annual plans and made midcourse corrections.

In the late 1960s and early 1970s, Park pivoted to the Heavy and Chemical Industry (HCI) drive, a massive bet on steel, electronics, shipbuilding, petrochemicals, machine tools, and automobiles targeting goals he had had since the beginning of his rule. The planning infrastructure was again expanded and reformed. New policy research institutes were formed to coordinate development efforts and respond to crises, including the Korea Development

Institute (KDI) and the Korea Institute for Industrial Economics and Technology (KIET).

The Japanese Connection

Park had received a colonial Japanese education, culminating in two years at the Imperial Military Academy outside Tokyo. Having been exposed to Japanese economic and political ideas and having seen Japan's economic success, he looked to the country, despite its brutal history in Korea, as a source of policy inspiration, capital, and technology.[38]

After 20 years without formal diplomatic relations, Park normalized relations in 1965. This precipitated mass demonstrations in Korea, but paved the way for a fruitful economic relationship.[39] Japan gave loans, grants, and commercial credits to Korea worth approximately $5 billion in 2024 dollars. Often ambiguously described as war reparations, these payments were used for highways, dams, telephone lines, power lines, dredging, and other purposes. Approximately $1 billion was used to start the key Pohang Iron and Steel Company discussed later in this chapter.[40]

Japan's support for Korean industrialization was driven by self-interest. A prosperous Korea would help secure Japan against North Korea, China, and the Soviet Union. Japan also wanted industries in Korea that would *complement* its own pursuit of advantageous industries.[41] It no longer wanted certain low-wage, polluting industries at home, preferring instead to have them overseas, but nearby and under some measure of its control.[42]

Japanese officials became involved in Korean development planning in the 1970s. Japanese firms happily sold Korea capital equipment for light industries. But they were more hesitant about large-scale joint projects in heavy industries. They were concerned about feasibility and feared that the Koreans would later compete with them – as in fact they did. However, Seoul worked with the government in Tokyo to pressure major firms with the threat of working with other nations such as Germany.[43]

Aggressive Pursuit of Export Growth

Korea's focus on exports had the usual benefits that accrue to a small country from such a strategy:

1. Exports generated foreign exchange that resource-poor Korea needed to pay for key imports, starting with oil.
2. Businesses were required to meet export quotas to keep their government support, pressuring them to meet international standards of quality and cost.

3. International markets could support large-scale, technologically sophisticated manufacturing that the small domestic market could not.

Exporters received tax breaks, preferential bank lending, government
grants, and access to foreign exchange.[44] Manufacturers also received de facto
subsidies from the tariff-inflated prices of the domestic market and from the
weak won. Permission to import inputs for manufactured goods was linked to
a firm's export performance, so even companies with no prior interest in
exporting were incentivized to export.

These policies worked. From 1961 to 1965, manufactured exports,
including processed foods and minerals, went from 14% to 61% of total
exports.[45] Absolute volumes were still small, and in some areas would grow
by 100 fold in the coming decades, but Korea was learning to compete in the
demanding but lucrative US and European markets. Exports rose from
$30 million in 1960 to $180 million in 1965, $5 billion in 1975, and
$30 billion in 1985. They grew as a percentage of GDP from 2.6% in 1960 to
11.4% in 1970, 28.4% in 1980, 25% in 1990, 34% in 2000, and 47% in
2010.[46] But throughout the Park era, imports rose just as quickly, so trade
deficits persisted.[47]

With the Third and Fourth Plans (1972–81), import substitution ree-
merged. But this time, the industries launched did not confine their ultimate
ambitions to the domestic market. Korean industry had developed to the point
where many of its imported inputs were products of advantageous industries
that the country was now technologically sophisticated enough to develop and
then export from. The US was the largest buyer of Korea's exports, but imports
came primarily from Japan. Korean products from TVs to VCRs to computerized lathes relied heavily on Japanese components. Often a third to half of their
export value went to paying for them.[48] But this was all according to plan:
Korea was exporting more and more high-end products, gaining market knowledge, and building more advanced industries.

Protectionism and industry subsidies always come with the risk that
the beneficiaries may pocket the profits instead of doing the hard work of
moving up the technology ladder. Korea dealt with this risk by tying support
to measurable results – in mastery of technologies, output growth, and, above
all, in exports. When existing targets were achieved, it set new, higher ones.[49]
When a policy failed, stronger supports or different strategies were tried. When
firms did not become competitive, they were allowed to go bankrupt and
required to sell their assets to more promising contenders. New companies
were allowed to enter a market if the incumbents were not delivering. For
example, in 1965, the government was working with Sinjin Automotive to
build up the auto parts industry. But the firm focused on assembly of imported

semi-knocked-down kits, not on developing an indigenous supply chain. So new competitors were allowed into the industry in 1967.[50]

Because Korea relied so heavily on imports and exports, good exchange rate policy was essential to keeping its plans on track. When the won was weak relative to the dollar and the yen, exports became more competitive, but imported inputs became more expensive. Park's policy from 1965 to 1979 was to keep the won weak and pegged to the dollar, adjusting the peg periodically to compensate for Korea's chronically high inflation.[51] Starting in 1971, after the Bretton Woods system broke down, the won got progressively cheaper against the yen, helping Korea in the many industries in which it was now competing with Japan.[52]

The Chaebols

Korean planners were able to formulate and execute their aggressive policies in large part because of their tight relationship with the business community. Park's policies, especially during the HCI drive, fostered large business conglomerates that came to be known as *chaebols*. Small firms were seen as relatively unimportant because they could not manufacture at the scale required for heavy industrial exports.

Though many business groups predated the Park administration, the chaebols took their enduring form during the 1960s and 1970s. These large, diversified business groups were each controlled by a single family through a central holding company or organizing firm, with close supply chain and financing relationships.[53] After substantial turnover from 1950 to 1975, the list of the largest stabilized.[54] In 1975, these were Samsung, Lucky (including Goldstar and rebranded LG in 1995), Hyundai, Hanjin, Hyosung, SsangYong, and Daewoo. All except Daewoo are major players today, and Daewoo's huge shipbuilding division survives as Hanwha Oceans.

The size and diversification of the chaebols were crucial. Their size enabled the economies of scale required to be globally competitive in advantageous industries. Their diverse lines of business helped them weather the risks of entering new areas. Risky new endeavors could be put into the hands of proven leaders with established business networks. It was also easier for the government to coordinate plans with a small number of large players. But it worked to keep competition between them fierce, and, to protect its financial leverage over them, forbade them from holding more than a nominal percent of bank shares.[55]

Over time, government stepped back from directly dictating the chaebols' decisions, in part because they were successful but also because the government was less able to control them. By the end of the Park era, the largest had become a nexus of power that challenged the state's dominance over the economy.[56] Increasingly sophisticated companies needed a more sophisticated, indirect style of guidance and support than the old carrot-and-stick.

Mobilizing Capital

Korea's rapid growth in the 1960s and 1970s required ever more capital. Having nationalized the banks, government was well positioned to control capital investment, but the low domestic savings rate meant that the banks had little to work with. In 1961, Korea's savings rate was only 2 percent of its then tiny per capita GDP ($94 in 2022 dollars), and investment only 12 percent, with the gap mostly funded by the US. Especially in the mid-1960s, with foreign aid dropping from its high of 22.5 percent of GDP in 1957 to below 5 percent by 1965, the banking system could not provide enough capital.[57]

Policies were imposed to increase savings. Corporate savings were increased by keeping wages low (partly by suppressing organized labor) so that wage growth lagged productivity growth. (With productivity booming, wages grew substantially anyway.) Household savings were encouraged by high interest rates, doubled in 1965. To suppress individual consumption, many consumer and luxury goods, which were mostly imported, were made unaffordable through tariffs and quotas, or simply prohibited. There were nationwide savings drives and citizens were encouraged to view saving as a patriotic duty.[58] Awards were given to bankers who increased consumer savings. To further encourage households to save and to reserve scarce capital for industry, home mortgages were unavailable until the 1990s.

The savings rate rose, at first driven by households, from 2 percent in 1961 to 8 percent in 1963, 11 percent in 1966, and 18 percent in 1969.[59] Then, as the chaebols raked in profits from exports in the 1970s, corporate savings exploded. Total savings reached 20 percent of GDP in 1973, 25 percent in 1977, and 30 percent in 1984.[60] Because this flow of capital was all under government direction in one way or another, it became the state's single most powerful tool to both support and control industry.

But even these policies did not yield enough capital for the government's ambitious plans.[61] Seoul thus turned to foreign governments and private banks in the 1960s and 1970s. Through the 1966 Foreign Capital Inflow Act, building on earlier 1960 and 1962 legislation, it guaranteed public and private borrowing abroad. This gave Korean businesses access to foreign capital, often at lower interest rates than domestic banks, albeit at the price of putting the government on the hook for massive amounts of private debt. External debt grew from 4 percent of GDP in 1961 to nearly 56 percent in 1985.[62] Despite the risks of borrowing from foreigners in their currencies, Korea preferred foreign debt to direct foreign investment because the latter would have surrendered more managerial control.

In the 1960s, special-purpose public banks, organized under a special act rather than the normal Banking Act, supplemented KDB, investing in industry and infrastructure.[63] The Bank of Korea directly controlled a large fraction of the country's capital and kept them well capitalized.[64] In 1973, the Ministry of Finance created the National Investment Fund (NIF) to channel money toward the HCI drive. Nonbank financial institutions such as pension funds and insurance companies were required to purchase NIF bonds. Later legislation dedicated 8 percent of wage income to a pension fund, much of which was then invested in the NIF.[65] State ownership of banks was reduced by the mid-1980s, but state direction of capital continued.

Managing Recurring Crises

Large subsidies to industry produced rapid growth. From 1974 to 1978, the average number of affiliates of the 11 largest chaebols grew from 12 to 28.[66] But growth meant companies often carried enormous debt, while high fixed costs made companies exceptionally vulnerable to slumps in global demand. Many industries suffered from excess capacity and insolvencies when demand fell or foreign competitors bested them.

This volatility was less dangerous to the overall economy for most of the 1960s, as the chaebols were small enough that they could be allowed to fail or shrink if management made poor decisions. However, when the 1969 global recession hit them hard, it put the whole system at risk. The Park administration therefore came up with a new policy tool: industrial rationalization. Failing companies were given enough financial support to preserve their productive assets, but their owners forfeited their equity.[67] This preserved hard-won industrial capacity while avoiding the perverse incentives of bailing out bad management.

To get firms to take the large risks of penetrating new industries and climbing the technology ladder, the government had to protect them from failing. Repeatedly bailing them out and doubling down on the most successful unavoidably gave them access to the vast resources of the state and disadvantaged their competitors. This situation was ripe for corruption. Kickbacks to government officials and party members – both legal, in the form of campaign contributions, and illegal – became commonplace again. But pressure to keep corruption from interfering with growth came from the very top. Park's political coalition depended upon economic growth both for popular support and to fund its political activities. Thus, companies that were poor exporters were almost always eventually cut off even if they had friends in high places.

In 1972, companies had again overextended themselves and faced slumping demand. To avoid another crisis, the regime sharply reduced interest rates.[68] Further centralizing economic controls in 1973, Park gave his appointed economic secretary the authority to bypass and sometimes to dictate to the EPB and the Ministry of Finance regarding investment in heavy industries.[69] Preferential "policy loans" remained below market rates. Indeed, they were lower than inflation during most of the HCI period, so their real interest rate was generally negative, especially for export loans.[70]

The Erosion of Military Rule

In 1979, massive new plants in heavy industry were starting up in the middle of a global recession. The debt-to-equity ratio of Korea's manufacturing sector had reached an astonishing 488 percent.[71] Crisis loomed yet again. There were riots, concentrated in Pusan and Masan, centers of textile production and heavy industry, over inflation, harsh labor policies, and other grievances.[72] Simply extending loans and reshuffling business groups between chaebols was not going to be enough this time. So Seoul imposed a new stabilization program with tighter monetary policy, reduced subsidies for chaebol borrowing, lower tariffs, and some import liberalization.

The unrest continued and US military intelligence became concerned about the possibility of a full-blown insurrection. Then Park's assassination in October threw the country into even deeper crisis. Two months later, his prime minister, Choi Kyu-ha, was elected president unopposed under the indirect 1972 constitution. Shortly afterwards, General Chun Doo-hwan seized power in a bloody coup, leaving Choi as president in name only. Mass protests broke out, culminating in the Gwangju Uprising of May 1980, which was brutally put down. Chun declared martial law and Choi resigned, leaving Chun to run unopposed in a new election.

Chun never achieved Park's legitimacy. His harsh crackdowns created many enemies. His economic challenges were different from those of the Park era. Korea now had large, established exporters. Hyundai was building cars with more than 90 percent Korean content. The managements of the chaebols and even of some smaller firms were increasingly able to ramp up new technologies on their own. Because proactive industrial policy was seen as connected to military rule, the latter's declining legitimacy reduced the legitimacy of the former, a process encouraged by the increasing number of American-educated academicians and government officials trained in contrary economic doctrines.[73]

Many industries built in the HCI drive were now financially self-supporting, so Chun could cut back their loans, reducing overinvestment.

Meanwhile, it was becoming increasingly unworkable to impose central planning on industry.[74] Policy therefore needed to evolve away from direct manipulation to indirect measures designed to *incentivize and enable* firms to succeed in increasingly advanced industries. But less state control also meant that the imperfect but real discipline that had once come with the heavy hand of the state declined. Thus, the attempted industrial rationalizations Chun imposed in 1981 did little more than bail out many chaebols, creating massive moral hazards.[75]

In the late 1980s, Korea saw its first trade surpluses. This was partly due to the strengthening of the yen after the Plaza Accord of 1985 and the decline of oil prices, but also reflected the growing strength of Korea's export machine. The Chun regime was successful in some of its reforms. In addition to tighter monetary policy, tariffs (which pushed up domestic prices) were cut from 36 percent in 1978 to 28 percent in 1988. Inflation finally fell from 13.3 percent in 1978 to 2.8 percent in 1987.[76]

From 1981 to 1983, major commercial banks were privatized – with the government supposedly retaining substantial supervision – in the hope that market forces would discipline lending. But the financial system had been designed to operate under direct government control and lacked the regulatory structures needed to restrain it under private management. Firms within chaebols were allowed to backstop each other's debt and banks rolled over loans that could not be repaid, lending even more money to help firms survive and repay later.[77]

In 1981, the government tried again to rein in chaebol management and regain more control by creating the Fair Trade Commission within the EPB. Cross-shareholding was penalized and the practice of debt guarantees by sibling companies was limited.[78] The chaebols were required to divest businesses outside their core area if they wanted to invest in a new area. But these new controls were insufficient to prevent yet another crisis. By 1985, the overleveraged chaebols faced another liquidity crunch and required restructuring.[79]

By the late 1980s, the chaebols were pushing into new industries on their own terms. They claimed that government agencies such as the Ministry of Trade and Industry did not understand the technical details, which was increasingly true.[80] While the state remained involved in pushing key national projects, such as the first exportable wholly Korean-made car, the chaebols were generally now given freer rein to set their own priorities.

Democracy and Liberalization

Chun had promised to serve just a single six-year term. Under heavy pressure, including street protests by more than a million students and others, he allowed direct popular elections in 1987. He did not run, but picked another general, Roh Tae-woo, to succeed him.

Roh was elected and served from 1988 to 1993. His industrial policies were similar to his predecessor's. He kept up efforts to get the chaebols back under control, promoting their specialization by swapping ownership of incongruous businesses between them and encouraging them to focus on four or five main areas. He did not reverse the liberalization of the financial sector, but instead imposed new rules and taxes designed to limit the chaebols' real estate speculation, both to avoid financial bubbles and to keep them focused on manufacturing.[81] New financial regulation helped prevent pseudonymous transactions, improving transparency and making it easier to root out corruption. Meanwhile, after decades of labor suppression, workers began winning wage and hours concessions. Their rising wages then created pressure for Korea to keep moving up the value chain.

The next president was Kim Young-sam (1993–8), a longtime leader of democratic opposition to the military regime. He had even weaker tools to keep the chaebols in check because elected politicians now increasingly relied on them for campaign donations.[82] So his government continued to bail them out. For example, when they faced financial difficulties in early 1993, the Bank of Korea sharply cut interest rates to reduce their debt service.[83] Instead of the state being a senior partner imposing strategic direction, the chaebols were now using it as a guarantor for risky bets with little relation to national strategy. For example, in 1994, Samsung used its political connections to get approval to enter the auto industry despite this being outside its existing core businesses – a bet that failed massively.[84]

Prioritizing heavily leveraged growth over profits had once aided rapid industrialization, but as the economy matured, fundamental change was needed to shift the economy to a less extreme business cycle with manageable expansions and contractions. Kim started this pivot but did not finish it. He presided over the first stages of disassembling the planning apparatus: The EPB was abolished in 1994 and the last Five-Year Plan ended in 1996. But his reforms were insufficient. Liberalization moves often meant giving even *more* leeway to the chaebols. For example, banking deregulation allowed them to found dozens of merchant banks in 1994–6, and interest rate deregulation, combined with opening capital markets to foreign investors, gave them access to even more funding.[85] Their average debt-to-equity ratio rose from an already high 250–300 percent in 1985–95 to almost 400 percent in 1997.[86] Much of the new debt came from foreign sources and was denominated in dollars.[87]

Financial Crisis and Recovery

By 1995, Korea was emerging as a developed country, joining the WTO that year and the OECD the next. Business was booming: The top five chaebols grew by an average of 22 percent per year from 1990 to 1995.[88] Then, in 1996, a slump in global demand coincided with a fall in the Japanese yen that reduced Korea's price advantage.[89] Problems escalated in July 1997 with the onset of the Asian Financial Crisis. In chain-reaction response to the collapse of Thailand's currency, overburdened corporate and governmental borrowers in Thailand, Malaysia, Indonesia, and the Philippines defaulted. This hit Korean banks hard, as they had offset many of their dollar-denominated liabilities with loans to these nations. (It did not help that after being so tightly regulated for so long, they had little experience with unsecured loans.)

The won started to fall as foreign currency reserves plummeted from $22.3 billion in October 1997 to $7.3 billion in November.[90] As the won fell, the interest and principal repayment burdens of dollar-denominated debts rose. Seoul worked with the IMF to secure an aid package, hoping to calm foreign investors and stop the rise in interest rates that was hurting both consumers and the corporate sector. On December 3, 1997, the IMF approved a $58 billion package.[91]

The imposition of the reforms it required in return was felt as a national humiliation. These included, inter alia, that the government restructure insolvent financial institutions, sharply raise interest rates, impose tighter monetary policy, and generate a budget surplus in 1998.[92] At the nadir of the crisis, in December 1997, the leader of the opposition party, Kim Dae-Jung, won the national elections. He had at first opposed the bailout, but then recognized its necessity and implemented its reforms.

A cap was finally imposed on chaebol borrowing, limiting their debt to 200 percent of equity.[93] Financial markets were almost completely opened to foreigners, even the banking sector, which had previously been walled off to maintain it as a tool for industrial policy. Caps on foreign ownership of Korean companies were lifted and the bond markets were opened. In a major departure from past bailouts, the chaebols were largely left to make their own settlements with creditors. More than 20 went bankrupt.[94] Daewoo, the second largest, collapsed under $80 billion in debt.[95]

These reforms did much to eliminate the vestiges of the old industrial policy regime and shift Korea toward more of a free-market economy. When the dust settled, foreigners held a large part of Korean banks and publicly traded Korean companies. Average tariffs were lowered from 13.4 percent in 1997 to 5.9 percent in 1999.[96]

It seemed to many observers that the country was abandoning state direction of its economy. But the state was still unwilling to let large businesses with valuable productive capacities disappear if their failures were purely financial. Thus, the viable parts of Daewoo were restructured, and Kia was saved by the government before being sold to Hyundai.[97] As the economy stabilized, the economic and political power of the chaebols recovered. But policymakers had learned some lessons. Restrictions were reimposed on chaebol ownership of banks, and the Fair Trade Commission reported in 2018 that cross-shareholding had been reduced by over 99 percent.[98] In the years after the crisis, regulators continued capital controls, partly to avoid instability and partly to minimize appreciation of the now-floating exchange rate.[99]

We look next at how some important Korean industries – ordered roughly by chronology and sophistication – were developed.

Textiles

Commodity textiles are a labor-intensive light industry requiring relatively little technological sophistication, and thus can serve as a bridge from a preindustrial economy to an industrialized one. As in many other countries, textiles in Korea spearheaded early industrialization.

After the Korean War, up to 10 percent of foreign aid was spent on equipment and raw materials for spinning and weaving.[100] But textile makers soon struggled with excess capacity and weak export sales. They lacked overseas sales networks and, with their out-of-date equipment, could not meet international quality standards.[101]

A 1961 drop in the won from 65 to the dollar to 130 raised the cost of imported cotton but failed to boost textile exports. Learning from this failure, the government sharply increased its export subsidies and export-contingent subsidized loans for capital investments in manufacturing. The textile industry took better advantage of these policies than other industries.[102] Its exports grew *fortyfold* from 1961 to 1965, rising from 25 percent of manufactured exports to 41 percent, with growth in subsidies keeping pace.[103]

Seeing success, the government doubled down and textile exports grew even further.[104] The industry then used foreign loans to finance productivity-improving investments. It started producing synthetic fibers, reducing its dependence on imported cotton. (Producers of synthetic fibers received tariff protection and special subsidies for capital investment.)[105] By the late 1960s, Korean textile firms were competitive with Japan, the global leader.[106]

Production grew 20 percent per year through the 1970s, with rapid increases in profits and penetration of foreign markets. By 1980, Korea's textile exports exceeded those of Japan, which was moving on to more advanced industries. But the industry, despite high profitability, was already showing signs of being past its prime. Firms were harvesting profits rather than reinvesting. They were operating equipment past its point of obsolescence. Quality improvements slowed.[107] As wages rose and other low-wage countries, especially China, entered the industry, opportunities for automation were not great enough for Korea to remain competitive by using more technology.

Textiles were no longer a strategically useful industry, so, while government continued to support it as an existing generator of wealth, it no longer underwrote expansion. Today, Korean firms remain successful (with offshored production), but the industry has never returned to its prior importance in Korea's economy.

There is no natural progression from light industries such as textiles to heavy industries such as steel, shipbuilding, and automobiles. But because these industries offer a higher value-added per man-hour, Korea needed to penetrate them to keep incomes and GDP growing. The more complex value chains of these industries required not just more sophisticated companies, but more sophisticated industrial policies.[108] So there were several policy shifts. The first was to much larger loans. But this meant the recipient firms could not fail without damaging the broader economy. Therefore, the government had to be much more judicious about who received loans, and more creative in handling the inevitable defaults. The second shift was to more knowledge transfer from abroad, which the EPB, and even Park himself, worked to facilitate. Sometimes foreign technicians and managers were brought to Korea to provide training; other times Koreans were sent abroad to learn how to manage the new, complex production facilities.

Steel

Steel is a critical upstream industry for automobiles, shipbuilding, and many other advantageous industries. Modern steel production had existed in Korea since the Japanese built two mills there in 1941 to support their military needs.[109] In the 1950s, several Korean companies, such as Hyundai Steel, emerged, but with limited capacity and largely obsolete equipment.[110] In 1962, Korea produced only 141,000 tons of steel, importing an additional 179,000.

In 1961, the government tried to increase domestic steel production through joint ventures with foreign firms, but its insistence on large-scale production alienated potential partners. A World Bank study concluded that a full-scale integrated steel plant in Korea would not be feasible.[111] President Park, however, was persistent, and ultimately obtained financing as part of Japan's 1968–9 "reparations" payments.[112] Pohang Iron and Steel Company (POSCO) was created as a state-owned enterprise unaffiliated with any existing company. Park Tae-Joon, a retired general, was chosen to run it.

The Iron and Steel Industry Promotion Law of 1970 was modeled on Japanese industry-support laws.[113] The government spent $320 million in 2022 dollars for supporting facilities, building new infrastructure, and providing subsidized electricity, rail, water, gas, and port access.[114] POSCO provided and coordinated the construction labor. Foreign firms, above all Japan's Nippon Steel, provided credit, design, engineering, and training in areas such as process design, inventory management, scheduling, and maintenance. The Koreans had their Japanese plant designs vetted by other international partners.[115] Some 597 POSCO engineers and managers were sent to Japan and Austria for training.

In 1973, the plant opened two months ahead of schedule, and by the next year, POSCO was able to run it at 114 percent of its rated capacity of 1.03 million tons per year.[116] The firm was immediately successful at producing cost-competitive steel. Even accounting for its subsidies, its productivity was comparable to the world's best, the Japanese.[117] Despite strong domestic demand, POSCO at first exported 40 percent of its output, then set a target of 30 percent for the next decade. Export subsidies made this profitable, but the firm also sought foreign markets because their demand profile was different and thus allowed POSCO to more fully utilize its high-end capacity.[118]

Improving production further required new technologies, substantial investment, and learning. From Phase I (completed 1973) to Phase II (1976), POSCO introduced continuous casting and a cold-strip mill. From 1973 to 1978, its focus was on increasing output, but then shifted to improving quality. By 1985, 7 percent of production was specialty steels – mostly for international customers – that required better quality control and more sophisticated process engineering.[119] Both capital goods and consumables, such as spare parts, were increasingly purchased from domestic suppliers, with both topping 50 percent by the late 1980s.[120]

Domestic demand was heavily subsidized by the HCI push. Steel was an essential input for many of the industries HCI targeted, so POSCO was a do-or-die operation for the entire economy – and for the regime's survival. Pressure to perform was intensified when it was made clear that a planned *second* government-subsidized integrated steel complex might be handed to a different firm. (POSCO won the contract and the new complex was the largest steel plant in the world until a Chinese one surpassed it in the 2000s.)

In 1993, the partly privatized POSCO was listed on the New York and London Stock Exchanges, allowing it to use its excellent credit to raise more capital. In 2000, its privatization was completed. Korea today is the world's sixth largest steel producer, and POSCO is the world's sixth largest steel company.

Shipbuilding

Modern shipbuilding in Korea started with a Mitsubishi yard in 1937.[121] After World War II, this became the state-run Korean Shipbuilding and Engineering Corporation (KSEC), the country's most advanced shipbuilder. Despite state backing, its expansion was held back by limited technical capability – it was only in the late 1960s that steel rather than wooden vessels made up more than half its output – and the lack of high-quality domestic steel.[122]

The first Five-Year Plan (1962–6) expanded KSEC's facilities, tripling its capital and allowing it to build ships of up to 13,000 tons. A three-year Ship Quality Improvement Plan focused on replacing outdated engines and dismantling old ships. The Shipbuilding Industry Promotion Act of 1967 provided funds to optimize production methods and modernize shipbuilding technologies.[123]

From 1961 to 1971, ship production increased ninefold. Then, after the opening of Pohang Steel in 1973, President Park set the goal of becoming a major exporter of ships, with aggressive targets for the coming decade.[124] The chaebols entered the industry and policy shifted to supporting them, even to the exclusion of established firms such as KSEC. Hyundai Heavy Industries (HHI) built a huge shipyard (costing $2.2 billion in 2022 dollars), and Daewoo built two more. HHI (as a subcontractor for Japan's Kawasaki, which had a backlog) learned by building copies of ships built by Scot Lithgow, a British firm. Seventy engineers were sent to Scotland to learn how to lay out a shipyard, and Lithgow engineers reviewed the parts and the assembly process during construction.

Aiming to build out the shipbuilding ecosystem, government actively worked to secure funding, subsidize infrastructure, and provide financial guarantees to foreign buyers. In 1974, the government formed Samsung Heavy Industries in order to increase competition. From 1972 to 1976, shipbuilders successfully executed a government-ordained 14-fold capacity increase.[125] Then, because of production delays and a severe drop in global demand, especially for oil tankers, several major HHI deliveries were rejected. In response, in 1976, Hyundai Merchant Marine (HMM) was created to provide shipping services to Hyundai's trading company with HHI ships, providing a backstop when other sales fell through.[126] The government launched the Planned Shipbuilding program that same year, laying out an annual tonnage to be built for each type of ship and lending money to Korean shipping firms to buy ships when foreign demand dropped.[127]

Once Korean industry had acquired the necessary technical skills, import substitution was used to build out supplier industries, reduce input costs, and cut production delays. Korean-made engines from the Hyundai Engine Division (founded 1975) and in-house ship design at HHI (1978) initially troubled foreign buyers, who did not trust the untested Koreans, so HHI sold its first such ships to Hyundai Merchant Marine Company (HMMC).[128] After several successful deliveries, the concerns of overseas customers subsided, and Korean shipbuilding became profitable as global demand recovered by the end of the 1970s.[129]

Heavily subsidized investment led to overcapacity coinciding with a demand slump in the early 1980s. The key shipbuilding firms survived only because of bailouts. After demand and profitability returned, Korea's share of the global market grew from 4 percent in 1980 to 22 percent in 1986. Not all companies succeeded: KSEC, once the national champion, went bankrupt in 1987, with the government brokering a merger with Hanjin Group's operations.[130]

Daewoo became the top shipbuilder in the world by 1993, and remained profitable even when the larger Daewoo Group ran into the financial trouble that led to its bankruptcy in 1999. (Renamed, it remains a major player today, alongside Samsung and Hyundai.) In 2000, Korea overtook Japan to become the world's largest shipbuilder until surpassed by China in 2010. By this time, Korean firms were building high-value-added specialty vessels, such as offshore drilling platforms and liquid natural gas tankers, and competing successfully on engineering and design, not just lower prices.

Automobiles

Automobile manufacturing is more complex than textiles, steel, or even shipbuilding. But the industry is well worth acquiring. It is not only advantageous itself, but also has huge spillover effects on other advantageous industries from glass to machine tools. It is thus a good tool for building a broader industrial base. Many developing countries tried to establish an auto industry in the 1960s and 1970s, but Korea is one of the few that became internationally competitive.

The policy push started under Park with the Automotive Industry Five-Year Plan of 1962, which prohibited car imports but reduced tariffs on their components.[131] Saenara Motor Company (a major funder of Park's 1963 election campaign) was designated to build cars from kits supplied by Nissan.[132] However, after building a mere 2,700 rebranded Nissan Bluebirds, the government was forced to cut off its access to imported kits because of strains on foreign currency reserves.

In 1964, the new Promotion Plan for the Automobile Industry designated Shinjin Automotive the national champion. It took over Saenara's factories and used Toyota kits. Government pressed it to increase its local content, but Shinjin pushed back, arguing that the Korean market was too small to support local component production.[133] The government responded by allowing new entrants into the industry. Hyundai (in 1967) and Asia Motors (in 1968) then created car-making businesses, working with Ford and Fiat respectively.[134]

In 1970, the state mandated construction of a factory to build engines, the most critical imported component, granting Shinjin a monopoly. The firm worked with GM in a joint venture tilted heavily in GM's favor.[135] This venture, named General Motors Korea, also did auto assembly and temporarily became the dominant player in the market.

During the HCI drive, Park shifted gears again, now pushing hard for a small, Korean-designed "citizen car." Hyundai, already formulating ambitious plans, was showered with support because it promised to build a fully domestic supply chain, abandoning its partnership with Ford. In 1975, the Hyundai Pony was launched, with 90 percent local content. Its Japanese engine was its only major imported part, though many design elements had been copied from Ford.

The government delegated some policymaking to the Korea Auto Industry Co-op, a private organization that was given power over import restrictions, and, as intended, only parts that could not be produced domestically were allowed to be imported. The parts industry grew rapidly from 1975 to 1979, with the Co-op growing from 100 to 327 members.[136]

After the global recession of the early 1980s, government started pushing the now maturing industry toward exports. The Hyundai Excel was introduced specifically for export in 1985, meeting stringent foreign safety, emission, and quality standards. In 1986, more than 168,000 were sold in the US. While cars made for the domestic market by this point used almost entirely Korean parts, to meet regulatory and quality demands the cars destined for export continued to use some imported parts.[137]

With success, the industry saw heavy investment, including new chaebol entrants – SsangYong in 1988 and Samsung in 1994. These ambitions collapsed with the Asian Financial Crisis in 1997: Only Hyundai survived unscathed. Kia was taken over by it, while the other firms were sold, in whole or in part, to foreign companies: Daewoo to its partner GM and Samsung to Renault.

Production continued to grow, from 2.3 million in 1999 to 4.2 million in 2011, with most being exported.[138] Korea today has the world's fifth largest automotive industry and Hyundai-Kia is the third largest producer. Auto manufacturing anchors a large, complex, and profitable cluster. By 2021, the industry generated 10 percent of Korea's GDP and had $42.6 billion in exports.[139] It has driven demand and improved technology in steel, plastics, chemicals, glass, shipbuilding, and shipping. In a clear sign of the sophistication of Korea's auto-design skills, GM today has its third-biggest design center in Incheon.

Electronics

Electronics is well suited to the advanced stages of economic development. Demand elasticity is high, the rewards for innovation and improved product performance are large, and huge scale economies can be achieved across a wide range of product lines. It has a clear internal developmental ladder: A nation can begin with simple assembly operations and work its way up through progressively more advanced components to the very top.

Starting in the late 1950s, Korea, slowly and then rapidly, climbed this ladder, reaching maturity in the 1990s. As more of the supply chain was brought in-country, a greater fraction of its value-added was captured, with positive spillover effects for industries such as plastics (for consumer electronics) and chemicals (for industrial processes).

Radio exports had already reached 24,000 units when the Park government added electronics to its growing export drive in 1965.[140] Working with overseas experts, an aggressive road map was set for transitioning from labor-intensive assembly to the manufacturing of components and integrated circuits.[141] In 1966, the Korea Institute of Science and Technology (KIST) was created to advise on the electronics industrial policies of the Second Five Year Plan (1967–71) and the Electronics Industry Promotion Act of 1969.

The Ministry of Commerce and Industry was given the power to promote specific electronic products with the best potential for upgrading skills, improving quality, raising productivity, expanding manufacturing scale, achieving standardization, and promoting firm specialization.[142] Companies were asked to submit business plans for developing and producing products from a government-provided list, then provided state financing. The 1977–81 Five-Year Plan explained the overall strategy:

> The electronics industry will change structurally from assembly-type production to one which mainly produces the basic components and parts. In the meantime, product quality will be improved. The electronics industry will be promoted as a major export industry through the development of new technology products and the expansion of overseas sales activities ... 57 items including semiconductors, computers, and related items have been selected as strategic products.[143]

By 1969, Goldstar had a domestic market share of 40 percent in consumer electronics, but Samsung (the largest chaebol at the time) had already entered the industry.[144] With government support, Samsung, Hyundai, and many smaller entrants began aggressive expansion attempts, Samsung forming joint ventures with Japanese companies such as Sanyo.

The National Investment Fund was a major source of investment. The government's foreign investment promotion efforts helped bring in an additional $1 billion from 1962 to 1982, primarily from the US and Japan.[145] Samsung capitalized on this more effectively than the others. Manufacturing its own transistors, LEDs, and semiconductor components, its black-and-white TVs went from 50 percent to more than 90 percent local content through the 1970s.[146] Meanwhile, it brought to market the first Korean color TV (supported by KIST), the first Korean microwave oven (by reverse engineering foreign products), and the first Korean VCR. This string of successes spurred aggressive investment by Goldstar and other competitors.

The chaebols and smaller manufacturers continued to ride successive technology booms in the electronics industry, from components to consumer devices, from the 1980s to the present. Today, Korea makes some of the world's most advanced consumer devices such as smartphones. By 2021, electronics exports included $129 billion in semiconductors, $25 billion in displays, $14 billion in mobile phones, and $13 billion in solid-state drives.[147]

Semiconductors

Samsung believed as early as the 1980s that making chips was essential to its long-term competitiveness. But the EPB believed success impossible because Korea had too small a domestic market.[148] Samsung ignored it and forged ahead on its own, releasing a 64K memory chip in 1984. Hyundai and Goldstar followed shortly thereafter, with Hyundai's semiconductor division eventually spun out as a separate company, SK Hynix.

Once it became clear that chipmaking was feasible in Korea, the government joined forces with the chaebols. Tariff breaks on capital equipment and tax breaks for R&D accelerated investment. As part of a governmentally planned effort, Hyundai, Goldstar, and Samsung committed to building new factories for very large-scale integration (VLSI) memory chips. They were backed by loans (some government-subsidized) from Korean banks and worked with an expanding network of government-funded research institutes and universities.[149]

By 1989, Korea had out-invested and outcompeted other nations to become the world's largest producer of memory chips, with 90 percent of its production exported.[150] It has maintained this lead: In 2021, its global market share was 59 percent, with the US at number two and Japan at number three.[151]

Since 2021, government and the industry have coordinated a 10-year, $450 billion push into new areas of R&D and manufacturing, bankrolled by the companies and backed by large government incentives. Samsung plans to invest $152 billion in its advanced logic business by 2030, and SK Hynix plans to spend $97 billion to expand existing facilities and $106 billion to build new plants. (Government will provide 40–50 percent tax credits for investments in

R&D and 10–20 percent for new facilities.)[152] As of 2024, Samsung and Taiwan Semiconductor were the only firms in the world making the most advanced, 3nm, semiconductors (see Chapter 30).

Nuclear Power

Nuclear power is one of the most advanced technologies, requiring highly trained scientists and technicians, extreme quality control across a complex supply chain, and enormous capital. Very few countries can design and construct a nuclear power plant on their own. For a resource-poor country like Korea, it is an attractive technology, offering stable, green power and allowing large reductions in fossil fuel imports. In addition, building nuclear plants for other nations, either directly via licensed designs, or by supplying key components, is lucrative.

Korea joined the International Atomic Energy Agency in 1957 and established the Korea Atomic Energy Research Institute (KAERI) in 1959.[153] In 1962, using a design from General Dynamics, KAERI successfully built a research reactor. General Park shifted the focus to nuclear weapons when, beginning in the Nixon administration, America's commitment to Korea's defense appeared to be at risk. But the US and Canada (Korea's other main partner in nuclear technology) pressured Korea to give up its weapons program and ratify the Nuclear Non-proliferation Treaty, which it did in 1975.[154]

Korea subsequently acquired nuclear power plants built by firms from the US, Canada, and France. Then, in 1984, KAERI began a long-term project to design its own reactor with a foreign partner as a first step toward a domestic design capability and supply chain. The American firm Combustion Engineering was chosen in 1986, and a team of Korean engineers and researchers, modeled on CE's own organization, was set up. In 1987, the Korean team traveled to Connecticut to learn directly from CE's staff.

In 1989, a nuclear design center was built in Korea. Starting that year, a 1,000-megawatt plant based on a joint KAERI–CE design was built, with commercial operation starting in 1995.[155] A total of twelve of these OPR-1000 units were ultimately built in Korea. In 1992, Korea Electric Power Corporation (KEPCO) began designing the next-generation 1,400-megawatt APR-1400.

By producing many identical plants in succession, KEPCO achieved remarkably low construction costs. By 2021, Korea had 24 operating reactors, the most for any country its size, generating roughly 30 percent of its electricity.[156] KEPCO maintained a monopoly on Korean power generation and plant construction, combining significant vertical integration with major contracts to private industry for components (e.g., Doosan Group) and testing (e.g., Saehan Group).[157]

The next step was exports. After a personal appeal by President Lee Myung-bak, in 2009, a consortium led by KEPCO won a bid to build four APR-1400s in the United Arab Emirates (UAE). The Korean bid was $18.6 billion, half the price offered by rival state-owned French firm Areva. Korea looked well positioned to take a huge share of the global reactor market.[158]

Then the 2011 Fukushima disaster turned global sentiment against the industry. Japan took all its reactors offline and planned to phase out the industry, as did Germany. Global reactor orders, which had been on the upswing, tailed off.

New regulatory watchdogs and whistleblower protection laws revealed safety and corruption issues in Korea's nuclear plant construction, operations, and supply chains, including the UAE project. Some 0.7 percent of materials test reports and 2.3 percent of equipment qualification documents were found to have been falsified.[159] A similar number could not be verified. Investigation revealed that KEPCO had excessively pressured its suppliers to keep prices low and localize production. Weak regulatory bodies and poor corporate governance had resulted in failure to maintain quality control.[160] The courts ultimately ordered a total of 253 years of jail time for 68 people.

The government began a major overhaul of the corporate structure and regulation of the industry. Its future became a major political issue. When center-left Moon Jae-in was elected president in 2017, he promised to begin a gradual phaseout. While Seoul continued to press for sales abroad, Korea had not sold another reactor since the UAE, and observers were writing the industry's obituary as the greatest industrial policy failure in Korean history.

But Moon soon faced pushback from the public and heavy industries that relied on cheap, abundant energy. And foreign regulators seemed satisfied with Korea's reforms. In 2017, the APR-1400 received approval from the European Utility Requirements organization, and in 2019, from the US Nuclear Regulatory Commission.[161] The first three UAE reactors were completed in 2020–2, with the first two coming online.[162]

KEPCO, Doosan, and other Korean firms are also engaged in ambitious projects with US partners to develop small modular reactors, touted as the technology's next big advance. Domestically, Korea tilted back toward nuclear power, restarting work on two reactors under construction and making plans to extend the lives of its existing plants.[163] President Yoon Suk Yeol was aggressively pronuclear (including for export), though domestic political opposition remained.

Korean Industrial Policy Today

Beyond broad strategies on exchange rates, trade, and foreign investment, Korea's twenty-first-century industrial policy is largely focused on promoting high-tech manufacturing and related services such as IT.

Korea's economy today is much more market-oriented than in the heyday of its interventionist industrial policies. The government no longer subsidizes corporate borrowing, banks are no longer state-run, and the won is not pegged to the dollar. The chaebols continue to dominate, but their structure and role have evolved. While Korea was ranked the most restrictive country in the OECD for foreign investment in 2013, by 2020 it was only sixth.[164]

Barriers for cross-border flows of goods are low on paper, and Korea mostly eschews open violations of WTO rules, triggering only occasional disputes.[165] Although the 2007 US–Korea Free Trade Agreement (KORUS) was touted in the US as a means to balance trade, the US trade deficit with Korea more than doubled between 2012, when KORUS came into effect, and 2022.[166]

In fact, Korea has never truly embraced free trade. After some tariff cuts right after the Asian Financial Crisis, tariffs were quickly raised back to an average of 9.6 percent in 2000. (They did not drop below 6 percent again until 2015.) Many products remain subject to nontariff trade barriers, including registration, import approvals, and idiosyncratic safety standards. Trade deals such as the 2018 update to KORUS attempted to remedy some of these issues, but succeeded only on paper.[167] The Ministry of Trade, Industry, and Energy sets an annual trade plan, including designating certain imports as requiring approval.[168] Seoul continues to manage the won.[169]

A few imports such as luxury cars are popular, but most foreign consumer products have poor penetration. For example, Kia and its parent, Hyundai, together retain nearly 90 percent of the car market.[170] (Testimony before the US Congress in 2008 revealed "safety" standards being wielded as a tool against imported cars, even tax audits being used to discourage buying foreign cars.)[171] In smartphones, it was only in 2021, with LG exiting the business, that Apple achieved a market share over 20 percent, with Samsung still dominating the market.[172] Recent years have, however, seen more low-end manufactured imports and some shifts in consumer preferences toward foreign goods, to the dismay of policymakers.

Foreign investors now hold a substantial fraction of Korean equities. A mid-2000s initiative to make Korea a major financial hub, with a market-based rather than a bank-based financial system, was abandoned, largely due to a reluctance to allow foreign firms to dominate financial services.[173] The chaebols continue to prize their access to foreign financing, but remain wary of foreign ownership and protective of their managerial prerogatives. Policymakers still see the chaebols as policy tools, and even though they can no longer control them outright, still strive to avoid foreign domination of their decision-making. In early 2023, the Korean government unveiled new plans to make it more attractive for foreigners to invest in Korean financial markets, but its commitment to Korean *control* did not appear to be wavering.[174]

Strengths

- National will to succeed, despite initial poverty, that led to extremely ambitious, successful bids to break into the most advantageous industries.
- Commitment to an economically sound concept of industrial policy – that is, pursuit of ever-more-advantageous industries.
- Policymaking that was pragmatic, coordinated, adjusted over time, able to embrace any effective method, adapt to new industries, and learn from mistakes.
- An accurate understanding of technological sequencing and of which industries would generate growth in others.
- Meritocratically selected technocrats insulated from political pressures that would derail policy.
- General Park Chung-Hee's vision and leadership during the formative period (1961–79) of the country's industrial policy.
- In targeted industries, Korea's general support of several companies, using competition and export targets to avoid stagnant monopolies.
- Effective use of chaebols as tools for development, to discourage outsourcing, prevent foreign takeovers, provide guaranteed markets, provide internal financing for long-term projects, and impose informal, unwritten protectionism.
- When a chaebol or one of its constituent companies failed for financial reasons, management and shareholders lost but productive assets were transferred to viable competitors.
- Good management of volatility and recurring crises.

Weaknesses

- Chaotic, sometimes brutal politics.
- Incrementally growing capture of system by big business, leading to abuse of government support.
- Inability to prevent (as opposed to survive) economic volatility.

7 CHINA
Pursuing Economic Hegemony through Mercantilism

China's economy is a unique combination of cheap, well-trained, disciplined workers, modern technology, generously funded R&D, and a production scale that in many industries is the largest in the world.[1] Its share of global manufacturing value-added grew from 6 percent in 2000 to 28 percent by 2018 – more than twice its share of global GDP – and it has today 136 million manufacturing workers, versus 12 million in the US.[2]

China is not only a threat to America's positions in key industries and technologies, but also a geopolitical rival and promoter of an authoritarian challenge to liberal democracy worldwide. It is more dangerous than the USSR because it is more competently governed, vastly wealthier, and ideologically pragmatic. It has a global presence through its trade and construction programs. It will soon be a technological peer of the US, and has four times the population.

Beijing today has the world's most intensive all-of-government industrial policy, based on a full-spectrum theory about how nations develop and compete. This theory has no ideological commitment to either the private or the public sector per se: Both are viewed as tools to be used pragmatically – though they must always support the power and legitimacy of the Chinese Communist Party (CCP).

China's policies proactively shape the country's comparative advantage. Its relentless aim has been to move up the technology and manufacturing ladder to ever-more-advantageous industries. Crudely put, its method has been to shower new, high-technology sectors with state resources and protection, while lower-return, aging, and nonessential industries are left to fend for themselves in the market or relegated to supplying cheap inputs to favored industries.

Since rapprochement in 1971, the US has been China's key enabler, absorbing its trade surpluses, granting it Permanent Normal Trade Relations in

2000, allowing it to join the WTO in 2001, and failing to counter its currency manipulation, intellectual property theft, and other illegal practices. It has also given Beijing access to its capital markets, and by the end of 2020, US investors held at least $1.2 trillion of Chinese corporate securities.[3]

The US has paid a large price for this indulgence. As of 2022, China accounted for about a quarter ($366 billion) of America's gross bilateral trade deficits.[4] Job losses directly attributable to China from 2001 to 2011 were about 1 million, with another 1–1.4 million from multiplier effects.[5] As of 2021, the affected regions had not recovered.[6]

The History

For most of recorded history, China, civilized but autocratic, was the world's largest economy.[7] But until about 1980, its modern history was one of turmoil and weakness. It cut itself off from the rest of the world just as the West began the Scientific and Industrial Revolutions that underpinned the West's nineteenth-century explosion of technology and economic growth. Among the costs to China was the loss of territorial sovereignty, epitomized by the "unequal treaties" of the 1840s that gave several European nations, the US, and Japan extraterritorial control of Shanghai's and Hong Kong's economies. Since that time, China has lived through 150 years of colonization, revolution, invasion, occupation, civil war, and economically destructive policy experiments, most famously the Maoist variety of Marxism.

In 1911, a revolution ended the decaying Qing dynasty and installed Sun Yat-sen's Chinese Republic. But this regime proved unequal to the task of reforming the country, which disintegrated into warlord-ruled fiefdoms. Nationalist General Chiang Kai-shek nominally reunified China in 1928, but spent most of the next 20 years waging civil war or under Japanese occupation. Japan's defeat in World War II ended the occupation, but the Communists won the civil war in 1949 and the Nationalists fled to Taiwan.

Mao believed in a socialist economy, but even Chiang distrusted capitalists and believed in a strong state role and government control of key industries. Mao rejected the USSR's model of a total command economy and allowed some entrepreneurship – albeit by socialist not-for-profit collectives, rather than individuals. His failure to understand basic economics led to the disastrous 1958–62 Great Leap Forward, in which the rural economy was brutally milked for resources in a failed attempt at rapid industrialization. Thirty million people died from famine as farmers were given irrational tasks such as manufacturing iron in primitive backyard furnaces instead of growing rice.

Beginning in 1978, when Deng Xiaoping assumed power, a historic turnaround has been produced, thanks to selectively using *aspects* of capitalism and China's innate advantages. Chinese culture regards strong, centralized economic and political leadership as legitimate, and it has a large, industrious, inexpensive workforce and a vast potential market to attract foreign investment.

Creating Comparative Advantage

Beijing's openly stated aim is to restore China's historic preeminence among nations, and it has designed and implemented elaborate plans to get there.[8] None of its industrial policies are novel, especially in East Asia, and many were previously deployed in Japan, South Korea, Taiwan, and Singapore. But China has been exceptionally aggressive in how it has applied them, in how many agencies of government have been involved, and in how quickly and radically they have been changed as its economy has evolved. And unlike its East Asian predecessors, China has not transitioned to even modestly democratic governance as it has become wealthier.

For important industries, Beijing proactively manipulates every possible variable – financial resources, investment decisions, R&D levels, senior management, protection against foreign competitors, domestic regulations, inbound foreign direct investment (FDI), and outbound FDI. As economic goals have been reached and new ones have become possible, China's policies have changed, though its overall goals have not.

The CCP thinks of industrial policy as an intricate, long-term orchestration of its largest corporations, often deliberately striving to weaken foreign competitors in a dance of moves and countermoves managed by the state. The National Development and Reform Commission (NDRC) does China's overall economic planning, while other agencies, such as the Ministry of Industry and Information Technology (MIIT), are more micro-oriented and industry-specific.

The state does not hesitate to wield its authority over private firms. For example, it forced the merger of small, weak, domestic home appliance makers to create a few large, globally competitive producers. Firms over a certain size are required to have a CCP official in a senior position. There is lots of red tape for most businesses, but for the top firms in each prefecture, local officials make sure the business environment is efficient and that their needs are met.[9] They do this in part because the CCP promotes them based on the economic performance of the regions they govern.[10]

Industrial policy in China is always partly political – that is, about balancing the interests of powerful factions. Overall, the CCP is split between elitist and populist factions, the elitists being familial descendants of the original 1949 revolutionaries, the populists having risen to power through the military, business, or other paths. The elitists are more oriented to the state companies, and this split created something akin to checks and balances until Xi Jinping (an elitist) short-circuited the system by declining to step down in 2022.[11]

Problems with China's Economic Model

China still has vast, grinding rural poverty, even if one ignores the fact that its own government occasionally admits that its national economic statistics are inaccurate.[12] The country has far more corruption, especially in the state sector, than market economies. Both the private and state sectors are corrupt, but there are more *forms* of corruption in the state sector, such as officials shaking down firms that need licenses, directing university research toward crony companies, and misdirecting public procurement. Private corruption is the same as in many other countries: violating building codes, selling fraudulent products, overstating earnings or assets to qualify for loans or boost stock prices, insider trading, et cetera.

China has a huge excess of debt and ghost cities of empty apartment towers. It has wasted large amounts of its scarce capital, especially in heavy industry, where subsidized financing and unrealistic growth targets have created excess capacity – whose production then destroys industries worldwide when dumped abroad below cost.

The CCP believes that, over time, it can tame environmental destruction, corruption, resource misallocation, and cronyism. It sees corruption as a curable addiction, not an inherent feature of the system, and believes that exposing state-owned enterprises (SOEs) to market forces will contain their cronyism. It sees environmental degradation as controllable through investment in cleaner technologies and punishment of offenders. And it believes that unsubsidized interest rates and continued expansion of the private sector will reduce wasteful investment.

This optimism may be overconfident, a classic hazard of competent authoritarian regimes on the rise, especially for one that believes it can correct these ills while retaining a CCP monopoly on political power that places it quite literally above the law. Many of its cadres still resist the creativity and efficiency of the market and underestimate what superior corporate management can do. The Party sometimes rotates its officials through corporate leadership roles for which they are unqualified. It understands that non-state enterprises use capital more efficiently, as shown by their higher return on assets, but fears the growth of private economic power.

The CCP cracks down when private firms challenge state companies or threaten Party "discipline" – that is, control. This is why Xi Jinping cracked down on Big Tech and other sectors in 2020. But he remains well aware that China needs private companies to keep innovating and perform other tasks for which the state is unsuited. And some of his crackdowns were simply rational policy, for example against diploma mills and overleveraged real estate firms.

The CCP and state bureaucrats do not deserve all the credit for China's accomplishments. China's private companies made the products, solved the technical problems, took the risks, moved quickly, and priced aggressively. Although entrepreneurs had to fight for acceptance, China remains a highly entrepreneurial, risk-taking culture. Its people are hardworking. Yet the example of other nations that also have entrepreneurs and toiling workers, but have not matched China's growth, makes it clear that these private-sector accomplishments depended upon a context created by government.

Gaming the Trading System

China's extreme mercantilism stressed the international system of trade and investment governance to its breaking point. In 2016, it began to crack with the Trump administration's turn to tariffs and the milder but still real cutbacks of trade openness to China by Europe, Japan, and other nations.

The WTO was never designed to constrain a technically competent authoritarian state ruling nearly a fifth of the world's population. Its rules-based architecture presumed that the rule of law, including trade law, would be followed by its members, so it was intrinsically vulnerable to a government determined to combine nominal compliance with actual defiance.

When China began the process of joining the WTO in 1987, other nations realized that existing General Agreement on Tariffs and Trade (GATT) rules were insufficient, so special negotiations with Beijing were undertaken. By the time it was allowed to join in 2001, a detailed special set of rules, applicable only to China and designed to conform its policies to WTO rules, had been agreed upon.

However, these rules are regularly flouted in practice.[13] WTO enforcement relies on aggrieved companies complaining to their own governments, which then file cases with the WTO. But firms are often kept silent by Beijing's threats to retaliate by, for example, suspending licenses for current operations, initiating investigations into product standards or antitrust violations, or granting new privileges to competitors. The US and EU often push back diplomatically and China commonly withdraws the most offending measures, but with compromises that tend to leave more discretionary, case-by-case violations in place.

China's SOEs pose a special problem. WTO rules for SOEs were written for SOEs that operate independently, as is common outside China. But China's are tied to and at least partly controlled by a single agency, the State-owned Assets Supervision and Administration Commission (SASAC). With $10 trillion in assets, it is the world's single largest economic entity, and its 96 companies are directed to support one another, have below-market financing from state-owned banks, and are insulated from the financial markets' profit discipline.[14] China promised in 2001 to sign a WTO agreement on government procurement (which, if interpreted to treat SOEs as governmental entities, would affect their purchases and sales), but 22 years later, Beijing is still "negotiating" the terms.

China's industrial policies have unfolded in three phases: the first from 1980 through the mid-2000s, the second from then to the present, and the third consisting of Beijing's plans for the future.

Phase One: 1980–Mid-2000s

In 1978, Chinese industry was wholly in the public sector, stagnant, and riddled with inefficient, poorly performing SOEs. Many enterprises, often village- or province-owned, were basically warehouses for marginal workers. Then Deng Xiaoping began a series of pro-market reforms. At the time, China's per capita GDP was $156 in today's dollars and its economy was 6 *percent* the size of the US, despite having more than four times the population.[15]

Deng's first big changes were:

1. Introducing market forces by decollectivizing agriculture and allowing privately owned businesses
2. Allowing SOEs to sell production exceeding their quotas and permitting individuals and private groups to manage them under contract
3. Allowing primitive capital markets to appear (but still controlling important features, including interest rates)
4. Managing the yuan, including formal and informal pegs to the dollar, devaluing it, and keeping it undervalued
5. Opening up to foreign investment

The first objective of these reforms was to give profit incentives to peasant farmers, entrepreneurs, and managers of village enterprises. Farmers were allowed to own their own land and sell for profit any production over the amount contracted to the government. China also began to invite multinationals to manufacture and export from Chinese plants.

Results came fast. In 1978, trade was only 10 percent of GDP,[16] and the country accounted for a mere 0.8 percent of world exports.[17] But by 1985, these numbers were 21 and 1.4 percent, respectively. Chinese exports at this time were mainly labor-intensive products such as apparel, toys, furniture, and other light manufactures.

Increasing and Upgrading Industrial Production

The reformers' first priority was improving the performance of the 150,000 state- and village-owned enterprises. This meant closing some, consolidating others, and replacing hidebound communist management committees with strong, dynamic, individual CEOs.

The big SOEs in steel, shipbuilding, petroleum, and other heavy industries were forced to compete, in some cases with each other. But Beijing still made sure (as it still does) that the SOEs, profitable or not, would always be able to carry out their designated economic roles. For example, oil companies were often required to sell their products at below-market prices to subsidize other industries. The central bank kept interest rates well below market levels to keep their cost of capital low. One result is that the four major state-owned banks, which made these loans, to this day carry record levels of nonperforming loans, often labeled as something else.

China gradually allowed foreign firms into *some* of its markets to upgrade the capabilities of domestic enterprises. Beijing quickly opened many mid- and low-tech manufacturing industries. It needed foreign technology, management skills, and smart capital, all of which were in short supply. Foreign companies thus opened Chinese plants in industries ranging from hand tools to diesel engines to commodity chemicals. China's leaders assumed, correctly, that indigenous firms would learn from the foreigners, improve their performance over time, and eventually become viable competitors domestically and as exporters. Foreign firms investing in China freely brought their technology, which, while not cutting-edge and no threat to their operations back home, was still superior to what China had.

China also encouraged the growth of indigenous private firms. But these were not allowed to operate as freely as private companies in the West. Close relationships with CCP and government officials at the provincial and local levels were (and are) required for financing, operating licenses, access to SOE customers, use of land, tax subsidies, and other things. Symbiotic relationships are the rule: Local and provincial officials need successful private-sector firms to prove their value to the CCP hierarchy, and the CCP needs entrepreneurs to grow the tax base and to help sustain the party's legitimacy by joining it.

Accessing Global Markets through the WTO

For Beijing, joining the WTO was never about embracing free trade, in which it never believed. It always planned to limit real market access for foreigners. It used every known trick, from tariffs to technical standards, to keep foreigners out of sectors in which it did not want imports or foreign investment. Nontariff barriers included "voluntary" local-content rules and elaborate requirements for getting onto approved vendor lists, designed to add so much time, expense, and risk that importers gave up.

America's political and economic leadership believed that China's entry into the WTO in 2001 would not only expand trade and investment but also stimulate liberal political reforms.[18] Sandy Berger, Bill Clinton's national security advisor, said, "Approval of PNTR and accession to the WTO will make China more likely to emerge as a more open, stable, cooperative nation that plays by the rules of the international system and provides greater freedom to its people."[19] Mike Moore, the WTO's director-general, said "China's decision to join ... will entrench market-based reform and strengthen the rule of law."[20] These political judgments must in retrospect rank as among the most naive of all time.

Official Washington believed that China would comply with its WTO obligations. The multinationals thought that, with China's WTO market-opening commitments, they would conquer its markets. Smaller corporations (albeit large enough to offshore production) believed that they could compete with Chinese exports only if they could manufacture there themselves.

China's WTO entry negotiations were complex. It was given extra time to implement particularly sensitive changes, such as allowing 100 percent foreign ownership of firms. China insisted on being designated a developing economy, which allowed it higher import tariffs, industry subsidies, and many other practices denied developed nations. (It is still designated as such at the WTO.) In return, developed nations insisted that it be designated a nonmarket economy, which made it easier for US and EU firms to bring antidumping actions against it.

China used (and kept using until the Trump and Biden administrations) America's preoccupation with formal rules and multilateralism against it. Beijing committed to revising more than 7,000 tariffs, cutting them from 17 percent to 9 percent on average and phasing out quantitative restrictions. It has largely met these commitments on paper: Its average tariff dropped from 14.1 percent in 2001 to 2.5 percent by 2020, a figure comparable to other major economies.[21] It has continued to impose some tariffs, but in general, they are not the big problem.

Foreign Investment to Obtain Technology and Build Exports

China's first major export industries came from Hong Kong and Taiwanese investors. Western manufacturers soon followed. China's central, provincial, and local governments built the infrastructure, cut the deals, and even ensured much of the labor supply. For Beijing, FDI, both greenfield and brownfield, fell into four categories:

1. Consumer goods and general manufacturing, which were mostly open because they were not regarded as economically strategic or politically sensitive. Here 100 percent foreign ownership was allowed.
2. Advanced capital goods and high technology. China wanted the multinationals, especially for capital goods domestic companies could not produce, but only on its own terms. Foreigners could own up to 50 percent, with an SOE owning the rest, often as a joint venture.
3. Services such as banking, insurance, credit card payment systems, and telecom. Beijing viewed foreign ownership in these sectors as a threat to its control of its economy and society, so foreign ownership was either prohibited or marginalized by regulations.
4. Strategic mid-tech industrial sectors, such as steel, petroleum, mining, and chemicals. These were reserved for the big SOEs.

Foreigners were required to partner with an SOE to limit competition and promote technology transfer. Mandatory partnering also allowed the state to follow foreign firms closely and keep them under tight control. Generally, the foreign partners carried out the bulk of the R&D, while the Chinese side focused on the manufacturing.[22]

Old-line CCP officials opposed the private sector, largely because it offered them no sinecures, but more forward-thinking cadres managed to keep the door open. By 2018, 88 percent of exports were from the private sector or foreign multinationals.[23]

Controlling Wages

After 1980, more than 100 million rural workers left farms and failing rural SOEs to work in urban factories, a surge that lowered and still suppresses manufacturing wages. Wage growth since 1980 has averaged 8 percent per year, but even today, manufacturing wages are about a quarter of America's.[24] China will not be losing its labor cost advantage over developed nations anytime soon, though its advantage over other developing nations is diminishing. The wage differential gets smaller higher up the skill scale, but is still substantial even for skilled professionals. As of 2021, Chinese manufacturing enjoyed a total cost advantage over the US averaging 35 percent, broken down in Figure 7.1.[25]

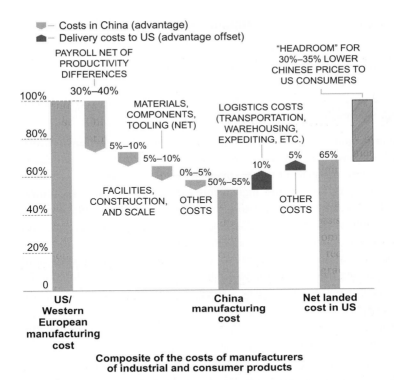

Figure 7.1 China's cost advantages versus the United States

Foxconn, the Shenzhen-based assembler of iPhones, illustrates the aggressive labor practices made possible by workers desperate for employment and the absence of unions. The firm extends working hours at will, without regulatory restraint or worker recourse, depending on changing production needs. In 2007, for example, Apple decided to change a product's screen just weeks before launch. Workers were awakened at midnight, when the new screens arrived at the vast, one-square-mile campus (which includes offices and dormitories as well as production facilities) and were set to work installing them to keep the launch on schedule.

Currency Manipulation

In 1981, China started moving its currency down in steps from the artificially high rates of its socialist era, and in 1994 it suddenly devalued the yuan from 5.9 to the dollar to 8.3 (see Figure 7.2). It maintained this rate until 2005 by intervening in currency markets to keep the dollars received for China's exports off the foreign exchange markets, thereby preventing the increase that

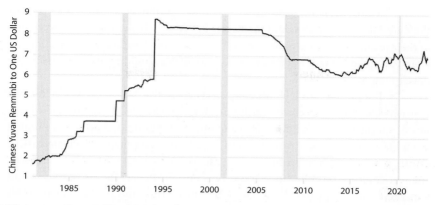

Figure 7.2 Renminbi per dollar[26]

its productivity gains of 8 percent per year would otherwise have produced (see Chapter 4 for more about the mechanism).[27]

The underpriced yuan made exports more competitive, and Beijing accepted the trade-off of higher import prices because raising the cost of imported consumer goods helped suppress domestic consumption. This suppression drove the high savings rate needed to finance a high level of investment without borrowing abroad. Keeping domestic interest rates low then required restricting outbound capital flows to prevent capital from seeking higher returns abroad.

China saw currency and capital-flow volatility damage other Asian economies in the 1990s, culminating in the Asian Financial Crisis of 1997. It therefore sought larger foreign currency reserves as a cushion against liquidity crises, to pay for imports and, later, to fund its international lending and investing. Large foreign currency reserves meant that its borrowers, including governments, would not be dependent for liquidity on foreign countries, their banks, or the IMF.

The End of Phase One

By the mid-2000s, China's productivity, competitive position, and international economic leverage had improved substantially. This created new opportunities, but also new conflicts with the US, Europe, and Japan, whose multinationals were operating profitably in China but whose domestic industries were now threatened by Chinese competition.

China had begun to run large trade surpluses in manufactured goods. From its WTO entry in 2001 to 2005, imports grew 27 percent annually. But exports grew at 29 percent. A huge fraction of China's imports were components for products to be assembled and reexported. Japan, among others, was thereby able to launder a lot of its own trade surpluses through China.

Many foreign corporations' Chinese output was now a key part of their global supply chains, and their sales in China generated a large percentage of their profits. China was also becoming a major buyer of food, ore, and energy from Australia, Brazil, Southeast Asia, and Africa, building its leverage in the developing world.

But all was not well. Beijing was surprised at how slowly, if at all, the gap was closing between the multinationals and the SOEs in complex businesses. In the mid-2000s, foreign companies still dominated products ranging from elevators to excavators to high-speed rail equipment to jet aircraft to semiconductors. They accounted for nearly all China's high-tech exports, such as computers, cell phones, and telecom hardware. In autos, China had arranged joint ventures between SOE auto firms and Volkswagen, GM, Toyota, and others, expecting that the SOEs would readily absorb their technology and then displace them. Instead, these joint ventures grew to dominate the market while the indigenous industry remained second tier and niche oriented.

These realities meant China needed a new set of industrial policies. Beijing needed to keep foreign firms from controlling its most sophisticated markets *without* denying itself the high-end capital goods and technology they provided. At the same time, it needed to accelerate the development of indigenous firms in these sectors. And the CCP needed to maintain its rule in economic affairs and preserve enough state-controlled sinecures to keep its cadres happy.

Phase Two: Mid-2000s–Present

In response to these problems, the industrial policies that emerged in the ensuing years had the following core elements:

State-Owned Enterprises

SOEs continued to control major heavy industries such as steel, construction, and mining, plus sensitive areas such as communications, petroleum, and finance. These sectors provided basic business infrastructure, housing, healthcare, and other social goods (including jobs in depressed areas), so they were considered critical to nonmarket objectives such as national security and avoidance of political unrest.

More emphasis was placed on consolidating competing SOEs in capital goods industries such as rail equipment and aircraft, where China needed to catch up. China began to demand that the multinationals' most advanced technology be transferred to their Chinese partners, which were often now actual or potential competitors.

But the rise of China's private sector was inexorable. By 2005, private firms were investing twice as much in manufacturing as the SOEs, and by 2017, four times.[28] In 2005, the private and SOE shares of exports were equal, but by 2017, the private share was three times larger.[29] Private companies' average return on assets was also more than twice that of the SOEs, indicating more efficient use of capital.[30] And they made up 75 percent of China's 4,000 publicly listed companies.[31]

In digital and telecom high technology, the slow-moving SOEs have found it hard to compete, and China's progress has been led by private companies. But Beijing is experienced at cajoling and coercing private companies into roles compatible with the SOEs remaining in control of major industries. For example, it forced several private airlines to merge with state airlines. It believes that it can determine the optimal structure for any industry and impose it at will.

While SOEs today account for a declining share of capital investment and GDP, they still represent more than 60 percent of all earnings of listed firms and about 40 percent of GDP, simply because they are so large.[32] Seventeen of China's largest 20 industrial and financial corporations by revenue are state-owned.[33] Roughly 40 percent operate at a loss and are kept afloat by government policy, though the major ones do much better.[34]

Foreign High-Tech and Capital Goods

Local-content requirements for foreign high-tech and capital goods companies were raised, forcing them and their suppliers to bring more production to China. Foreign multinationals' continued access to the Chinese market was increasingly conditioned on their agreement – disingenuously labeled as voluntary to skirt WTO rules – to transfer technology. One result was a steadily increasing trade surplus in capital goods with the US since 2006.[35]

Because China could not do without companies such as IBM, Ericsson, Oracle, GE, Siemens, Westinghouse-Toshiba,[36] and Areva (a French nuclear fuel cycle firm),[37] it set out to control them. Antimonopoly actions were disproportionately directed against them, not to protect competition but to pressure them. Most big capital-goods projects involved a state-owned buyer or contractor such as China Railways or Aviation Industry Corporation of China (the national champion created to someday compete with Boeing and Airbus), giving Beijing a great deal of influence over technologies used, who could bid, and who won.

China also used a novel patent regime against the foreign multinationals. In 2018, despite massive cheating, the country was still paying $36 billion annually in royalties and licensing fees to foreign entities. (The reverse flow was $6 billion.)[38] Multinationals were filing patent lawsuits in third countries where China was trying to sell products that used pirated technology. To get around expensive patents,

China adopted the concept of "utility patents," which enabled small changes in a product's design to escape a patent.

Unique technical standards were used as a protectionist tool. China first did this in 2004 for wireless devices. It required manufacturers to make their devices compatible with China's indigenous WAPI standard instead of the globally established Wi-Fi. Western producers fought back, saying this rule forced disclosure of proprietary designs and encryption technology. When the International Organization for Standardization rejected WAPI as inferior, Beijing labeled it a Western conspiracy. Nevertheless, to sell in China, producers must now comply with both standards. In theory and per WTO rules, this is not a trade barrier, but in practice, it is because most products produced elsewhere do not meet the standard.

But all remains negotiable, Beijing insists. The rules are flexible. Translation: It will give better terms to companies with the best technology.

Local Content Requirements

"Voluntary" local-content requirements were used as a Sinification strategy. Consider Germany's Siemens's experience in high-speed rail. To bid on a $1 billion contract for a Beijing–Tianjin project of 60 train sets, it was obliged to form a joint venture (owning 49 percent) with China National Railway (CNR). Siemens provided the designs and trained CNR's engineers. The first 3 train sets were built in Germany, the next 57 in Tangshan. This strategy advanced CNR enough technically that it was subsequently awarded a $5.7 billion Beijing–Shanghai project based on Siemens's designs, with Siemens as a subcontractor for only $1 billion in components.[39] Multinationals, in particular Japan's Kawasaki, France's Alstom, Germany's Siemens, and Canada's Bombardier, once controlled two-thirds of China's high-speed rail market. From 2009 to 2011, 63 percent of that market was open to foreign-based firms, a window that shrank to 17 percent by 2017–19. (The corresponding rate for Europe in 2021 was 79 percent.)[40] China Railway Rolling Stock Corporation (CRRC), the product of megamergers of China's SOE rail equipment producers, now owns the Chinese market and is the world's largest rail equipment exporter.

Wind turbines are another example. From 1996 to 2005, foreign firms held 75 percent of China's market. Then the government, to reduce dependence on fossil fuels, decided to grow the industry dramatically by offering buyer subsidies and other incentives. It increased the local content requirement from 40 percent to 70 percent and hiked tariffs on components. As the market exploded, foreign manufacturers were unable to expand quickly enough, but their Chinese competitors, who had been licensing technology from Europe, took up the slack rapidly and cheaply. By 2009, Chinese firms, led by private Goldwind and state-owned Sinovel, controlled more than two-thirds of the market. (The 70 percent local content requirement was later dropped, but only after sufficient component production had moved to China.)[41]

Beijing is a master of using timing and sequencing to pretend to open its markets while in fact controlling them. China, not surprisingly, views these policies differently than do the US, EU, and Japan, all of whom regard them as sophisticated forms of state-assisted technology theft. The United States Trade Representative (USTR) estimated in 2018 that China's intellectual property theft costs America $225–600 billion a year.[42] Whether China will continue to succeed with these strategies will depend, in large part, on how the rest of the world's leading multinationals and their governments reshape their own strategies and industrial policies to push back.

Developing Indigenous Technology

Development of indigenous technology was accelerated. In 2006, the National Medium- and Long-Term Plan for the Development of Science and Technology: 2006–2020 targeted eight fields: biotechnology, information technology, advanced materials, energy, marine, lasers, aerospace, and agriculture. The Plan focused on building up SOEs as China's best hope for innovation in major infrastructure sectors. It included big-ticket projects such as clean coal power generation, long-haul commercial aircraft, and new generations of nuclear reactors to avoid buying expensive French and Japanese models.

The Plan called for China to increase R&D spending from 1.3 percent of GDP in 2006 to 2.5 percent by 2020. (The actual figure attained in 2020 was 2.4 percent, vs. the US at 3.5 percent.)[43] But, in the words of one 2023 study, "China's gross innovation capabilities (e.g., R&D expenditures, venture capital [VC] investments, advanced-industry output, patent output, etc.) are now almost 40 percent greater than those of the United States."[44] China's government funds an estimated 69 percent of its R&D, compared to US government's 28 percent.[45] (See Chapters 19 to 24 about America's innovation system and its problems.)

Beijing was enamored with America's old AT&T model for technology, which combined development and deployment in a single national champion. This strategy reflects certain core beliefs: that putting scientists, engineers, and managers under one roof will outperform more distributed, competitive models; that China's scale was its principal advantage; and that the CCP's interests were best served by central control. But Beijing had more policy levers than the US had in AT&T's day. It owned all the land, so it could set its price, even to zero. It controlled the big banks, hence the interest rate SOEs had to pay. It controlled national laboratories and universities, hence scientific resources. And it controlled the tax collection agency, hence who paid what. Intramural politics in Beijing was (and is) largely about which SOEs got the best deals on all these fronts.

The success of this model has varied by industry. Notable winners are CRRC, Shanghai Zhenhua Heavy Industries (ZPMC), and China Mobile. CRRC and ZPMC, which makes port machinery, are global market leaders, and China is now world class in wireless networks. The big failures have been in semiconductors and internal combustion engine cars, although China is now sprinting ahead in electric vehicles (EVs), albeit with a private firm in the lead.[46]

Acquisition of technology-rich foreign companies was another strategy for building indigenous technological know-how, and was especially encouraged when the buyer was an SOE. This SOE favoritism contrasted with the government's often less enthusiastic guidance regarding private firms' foreign acquisitions and its foot-dragging on needed capital-export permissions, citing money wasted on hasty deals in the past.

Industrial Espionage

State-sponsored espionage to gain advantage in technology-intensive international industries is nothing new: French intelligence was caught spying on Boeing in the 1990s.[47] But Beijing escalated such espionage by orders of magnitude, both in its encouragement of private efforts and in its willingness to deploy state intelligence services. The latter are used for direct information gathering and for threats and bribes against private actors to get them to disclose information.

Huawei is a paradigmatic, although not unique malefactor.[48] It stole Motorola's wireless technology and Cisco's router source code. It violated SolarEdge's patents for inverters, PanOptis's for smartphone software, and the MPEG Consortium's for video compression.[49] A 2019 indictment in federal court revealed that the firm had a company-wide program to pay bonuses to employees for stealing secrets.[50]

China's stealing sometimes blends seamlessly with programs that have a legitimate side, such as the Thousand Talents Program (TTP) that recruited (mainly ethnic Chinese) scientists abroad to work in China. Thus, scientist Hongjin Tan, a Chinese citizen and US permanent resident, went to prison in 2020 for stealing more than $1 billion in battery trade secrets from his former employer in Oklahoma.[51] TTP was terminated in 2018 due to US pressure, but reemerged two years later under a new name, Qiming.[52]

Half the FBI's 5,000 active counterintelligence cases involve China. In 2019, a third of American CFOs reported that Chinese entities had stolen their firms' intellectual property over the previous decade.[53] Highly regarded Harvard chemistry professor Charles Lieber was found guilty in 2020 of concealing his involvement with the Wuhan University of Technology.[54] Although other nations report similar problems, the US, as a more open and diverse society than other high-tech hubs like Japan, is exceptionally vulnerable.

The naivete of China's American victims has played into Beijing's hands. For example, when GM complained to its Chinese partner, SAIC, about theft of its designs by the Chinese firm Chery, it was surprised to learn that SAIC *owned* 20 percent of the latter.[55] And China has not only stolen industrial secrets: In 2017, its military hacked the Equifax credit-reporting firm, taking sensitive personal information on 150 million Americans.[56] In the social media age, the possibilities for exploiting this information are infinite.

Engaging the World Economy on Its Own Terms

After 2005, China gradually managed the yuan up, relaxing *some* capital controls but not allowing full convertibility. Official reasons included cooling the economy and reducing the cost of imports and foreign asset purchases. There is evidence for additional motivations. Beijing feared that China's growing trade surpluses and foreign currency reserves were on the verge of triggering foreign pushback. With domestic goods prices, asset prices, physical capital investment rates, exports, and other indicators rising, it feared that hot money would sense a coming yuan upward revaluation and attempt large-scale inflows, stressing China's capital controls.

The yuan rose against the dollar, but as of late 2023, by only 20 percent, far less than fundamentals such as productivity growth and inflation differentials would imply. It is still undervalued on a purchasing power parity basis – that is, by comparing the price of identical goods in the two nations. As of June 2023, China's currency was estimated by the bipartisan Coalition for a Prosperous America's Currency Misalignment Monitor to be 23 percent undervalued against the dollar.[57]

China will not be opening its capital markets to free flows any time soon. Beijing relaxes its rules from time to time, but never scraps them entirely. For example, in 2015, wealthy Chinese private capital was fleeing the country, in part due to uncertainty stemming from Xi Jinping's crackdown on "corruption" (especially against his political enemies). This capital flight forced China's central bank to intervene to keep the value of the yuan *up*.

Consumption is still suppressed: It rose from its trough of 49 percent of GDP in 2010 to 55 percent by 2020, but this is still very low by international standards. China's economy is still investment driven.[58] Gross investment in hard assets such as factories and infrastructure as a percentage of GDP has been on a steadily rising trend from 1962 (when the Great Leap Forward ended) through 2016, and now stands at 43 percent.[59] Developed nations are generally around 20 percent. However, per capita, China still has only about 10 percent of their accumulated capital, so it needs to keep accumulating.[60]

As China's domestic economy has developed, it has become less dependent on exports, which peaked at 36 percent of GDP in 2006 and fell to 19 percent by 2020.[61] Measured by share of global export markets, by 2017 China had reached parity with the US in many key industries. The startling chart in Figure 7.3 is from Made in China 2025 and the Future of American Industry, a report released by Senator Marco Rubio (R-FL), and demonstrates this trend.[62]

Between 2010 and 2020, China's corporate sector burgeoned. In 2010, only 46 firms were in the Global Fortune 500, versus 71 for Japan and 139 for the US. Five years later, China had 98, with Japan at 54 and the US at 128. By 2020, China was number one at 124. But in revenue, US firms still led at $9.8 trillion versus China's $8.3 trillion and Japan's $3.1 trillion.[63] During this period, much of China's economy was thriving. In the digital sector, private companies like Tencent and Alibaba were succeeding without subsidies. Chinese-branded EVs were gaining global market share, even though the US imposed a 27.5 percent tariff on Chinese cars in 2018.[64] Then an economic slowdown in 2023 stalled much of China's economic engine; this was compounded when the government intentionally deflated a giant real estate bubble. The number of Chinese companies on the Fortune Global 500 dropped for the first time in 15 years.[65]

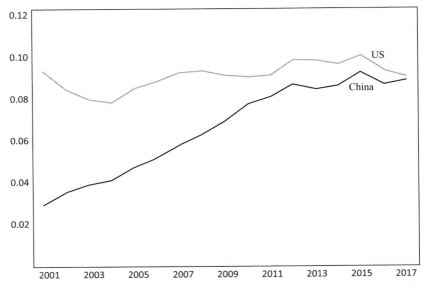

Figure 7.3 Share of global export market in 32 high-unit-value capital goods[66]

Phase Three: The Future

Today, the economy is mainly driven by services, manufacturing, and agriculture, with strength in finance, energy, and materials. But it still lags in sophistication and competitiveness in key research-intensive industries such as semiconductors, aerospace, computers, electronics, and pharmaceuticals.

For reasons ranging from technological shortfalls to the aggressive defense of product positions by foreign multinationals, China has been unable to match some elite competitors. These include Boeing and Airbus in commercial aircraft, GE Power and Siemens in gas turbines, BAE Systems and Honeywell in avionics, Samsung and Kioxia in memory chips, TSMC and Intel in microprocessors, Omron and Bosch in auto electronics, Yamazaki Mazak and Trumpf in machine tools, Seagate and Toshiba in hard drives, Mitsubishi and Carrier in refrigeration compressors, Berry Packaging and Amcor in food packaging, and ABB and Fanuc in robotics.

These big-system and upstream-component industries are less vulnerable to market-share shifts because their competitive advantages are deeply rooted in complex science, accumulated engineering prowess, multidisciplinary design, and inside knowledge of customers' business processes that take decades to develop. Their products cannot readily be reverse engineered or their production relocated using China's standard "carrots" of cheap labor and subsidies and "sticks" of tariffs and controlled market access.

China is today therefore ramping up industrial policies better suited to these industries and the advantageous industries of the future. The flagship program here is Made in China 2025, announced in 2015, which sets forth Beijing's plan to become the world's leading manufacturer and innovator by 2049. It aims to create 40 national innovation centers in 10 sectors, including smart transportation, information technology, artificial intelligence, industrial robots, and aerospace. The long-run objective is to make China technologically independent. Figure 7.4 shows the program's goals for taking market share from imports.

This program has gotten the US government's attention: In the alarmed words of Senator Rubio, "If MIC2025 is successful by these terms, what the 'China shock' did to domestic US production of electronics, furniture, plastics, metals, and vehicle parts could threaten to repeat itself in capital goods like machinery, automobiles, high-end computers, rail, and aerospace products."

While the Chinese government no longer talks publicly about Made in China 2025, it is clearly still the plan.[67] For example, in 2021, the Chinese government allocated more than $28 billion in subsidies to large Chinese firms centered on the technologies targeted by Made in China 2025.[68]

Share of Chinese Market Served by Domestic Companies		
	2020	**2025**
High-tech ship components	60%	80%
New energy vehicles	70	80
Renewable energy equipment	50	80
Industrial robots	50	70
High performance medical products	50	70
Large farm tractors and harvesters	30	60
Mobile phone chips	35	45
Large-body aircraft	5	10

Figure 7.4 "Made in China 2025" market-share goals for eight product areas

To succeed in these areas, China is increasing its R&D. Much of its spending has been pedestrian, even wasted, in part because funds are misallocated to serve political agendas and because Beijing over-incentivizes the mere filing of patents. By more rigorous metrics, such as number of journal articles and patents used by others, or royalties and licensing fees, American R&D is more productive. But China's research is improving fast and its researchers are gaining international respect. Its university R&D is now highly regarded in fields such as telecommunications, nanotechnology, and mining.

China is proactively developing a world-class innovation ecosystem. Its models for entrepreneurship are Silicon Valley and Israel. The country is relatively new to venture capital, but its state-linked funds are making sizeable investments in startups. In 2022, China claimed to add 74 new "unicorns."[69] In total, China had 283, bested by the US at 704 and followed by India at 83.[70] Two of the world's five largest technology clusters are in China.[71] There are three main areas of interest:

Internet-based services such as search, fintech, virtual private network (VPN) apps, cryptocurrencies, payment systems, and cloud computing. Policies here are straightforward: promote indigenous firms by limiting the services the American incumbents can offer. Many internationally successful American firms, including Amazon, eBay, Yahoo, Uber, and Google, have been squeezed out of the country after making major investments.[72] Those that remain are kept on a short leash: Apple, for example, was obliged to remove a VPN app (which undermines censorship) from its online store and to store data in China, where its law and judges rule. The firm is also being required to build R&D centers in China with local partners. But, as always, companies with strong technology platforms have leverage. China's censorship of Google's search engine drove the company out in 2010 and Google Cloud does not operate there, but the firm was later partly allowed back in with its superior deep-learning tool TensorFlow (now outmoded).

Artificial Intelligence, currently exploding in economic and military importance. Beijing says that it wants to be the global leader by 2030 and claims (perhaps falsely) that it will spend up to $80 billion to get there. It is moving fast and China is ranked among the top three countries for the vibrancy of its AI sector. Beijing pursues a two-front campaign, throwing money at domestic players (in the form of low interest loans, R&D subsidies, and seed capital) and investing in American startups.

Private companies lead China's AI effort. Big, established internet companies such as Baidu, Tencent, and Alibaba provide the big data for analysis and are willing to invest substantial sums. Computer scientists trained at China's top universities, and returning Chinese nationals with American PhDs, bring skills. Wealthy Chinese individuals and American and Japanese venture capitalists supply capital. The state is playing as well: In 2017, Baidu launched an AI lab in Beijing with the National Development and Reform Commission. (Such blurring of lines between private tech companies, financial sources, and the state makes it difficult to classify many Chinese players.)

America's deep, rich AI environment is China's other main source of research. Baidu, Tencent, Alibaba, and Didi Chuxing (China's Uber) all have AI labs in the US, and are making similar investments in Tel Aviv, Moscow, and other AI-intensive locations. American startups, many otherwise going unfunded, are attracted to Chinese venture capitalists' large risk appetite and fast decision-making. The gaps in America's own innovation system are playing into China's hands. For example, in 2016, Haiyin Capital invested $1.2 million for a minority stake in Neurala, a Boston-based AI company. Neurala's early work was with NASA and the US Air Force, but it could not secure later-stage American funding.

Hardware components, especially telecom networks and semiconductors. In telecoms, Huawei and ZTE are world class. Including other manufacturers, China in 2019 had 38 percent of the global market.[73] But China still cannot compete head-to-head in semiconductors with the Taiwanese and Korean chip companies in the first tier, or even with the American, Japanese, Singaporean, and German firms in the second. It still depends on foreign manufacturing equipment.[74] Chinese chip companies are not expected to catch up for years.[75]

In 2017, Congress restricted DOD networks from using Huawei or ZTE telecom equipment over espionage concerns. Washington subsequently tightened restrictions against these and other Chinese telecom equipment makers. It stopped buying from Huawei and removed equipment already installed in federal agencies.[76] In 2019, the FCC designated Huawei and ZTE national security threats and the Commerce Department put Huawei on the "entities list." In 2022, the FTC banned the sale of Huawei and ZTE equipment in the US and restricted the use of some Chinese-made video surveillance systems.[77] And in 2023, the US declined to issue further licenses to export goods to Huawei. These measures and those imposed by the UK and Australia significantly cut Huawei's sales.[78]

In 2014, Beijing issued its Guidelines to Promote National Integrated Circuit Industry Development, which targeted "establishing a world-leading semiconductor industry in all areas of the integrated circuit supply chain by 2030."[79] To achieve this, it launched the China Integrated Circuit Investment Industry Fund with an estimated capitalization of $150 billion, in 2019 set up a second fund of $29 billion, and in 2022 was reportedly assembling an additional $143 billion.[80] But the leading edge of the industry moves so rapidly that the state has difficulty keeping up with where to target its money, and the fund was later put on hold. Nominally the hold was due to COVID, but audits that showed a lot of money being misspent, some corruptly, were an important factor.[81]

China has tried to buy American chipmakers, but all attempts have been blocked by the Committee on Foreign Investment in the US (CFIUS). However, there are other ways to acquire US technology, such as cross-border partnerships, often with American companies under profit pressure due to Chinese competition. Thus XMC, a rapidly growing Chinese memory chip designer and manufacturer, partnered with Spansion, part of $2 billion Cypress Semiconductor, and Advanced Micro Devices licensed its technology to a joint venture in Tianjin. But China's overall flow of FDI into the US declined sharply after 2016 due to political tensions.[82]

Strengths

- A unified national government with strong policy traction over the country.
- Commitment to an economically sound concept of industrial policy – that is, the pursuit of ever-more-advantageous industries at largest feasible scale.
- Pragmatic, coordinated policymaking deploying the full range of industrial policy tools and adjusting effectively as China moves up the technological ladder.
- A good understanding of technological sequencing and of which industries would generate growth in others.
- Ability to raise investment capital through a wide range of forced savings policies.
- Meritocratically selected technocrats who do not allow political pressures or outright corruption to derail rational policymaking.

- Ability of the state to discipline the private sector, including the banks and financial markets, requiring it to succeed at state goals in return for support.
- Successful harnessing of the entrepreneurial, hardworking culture of China's people.
- Ability to reverse-engineer, improve, and then efficiently manufacture technologies developed in the West on an unprecedentedly large scale.

Weaknesses

- Hyperaggressive mercantilism, including industrial espionage on an unprecedented scale, that has alienated much of the rest of the world and caused growing pushback.
- Corruption, especially in the state-owned sector.
- Tendency to overinvest scarce capital in some targeted sectors such as real estate, infrastructure, and heavy industry.
- A significant number of SOEs that are still unprofitable, inefficient CCP patronage sinks.
- Continued heavy reliance on overseas markets – especially the US – to absorb the overproduction of its industries.
- Reluctance, driven by CCP fear of political blowback, to increase domestic consumption and decrease national investment as other nations raise barriers to subsidized or dumped Chinese exports.
- The danger that extreme concentration of political power in a single leader will create a cult of personality and a climate of fear that will stifle open discussion, especially of failed policies, degrading the quality of decision-making and administration.

8 GERMANY
The Art of Relationship Capitalism

In so-called liberal market economies (LMEs) such as the US, Canada, Australia, and the UK, the private sector functions almost entirely through the market mechanism. But in "coordinated market economies" (CMEs) such as Germany, Austria, Sweden, and Switzerland, it *also* functions through non-market mechanisms that run *in parallel to* the market.[1] German industrial policy must be understood in this context.

Germany's monetary, trade, fiscal, and competition policies are today connected with and constrained by EU rules, but it has nonetheless been able to maintain a distinctive approach. Like many of its neighbors, it has subsidized green energy for environmental reasons and declining sectors such as steel and coal for social ones. The state has owned utilities like rail and electricity. It has openly supported its automotive industry (successfully) and undertaken large, state-owned, high-tech ventures (unsuccessfully). Today, under French leadership, it shares Airbus with several other European nations.

But these interventions are not the core of German industrial policy. Instead, that core is the sophisticated use of *indirect* measures to create an economic and regulatory environment favorable to the development and retention of advantageous industries. Institutions and practices fill the gaps and correct the counterproductive dynamics of a system based solely on markets. The system faces serious challenges today, but still holds valuable lessons for the US.

Germans call their economic strategy "ordoliberalism." The federal and state (*Länder*) governments commit *rhetorically* to a relatively noninterventionist, free-market approach. In theory, government confines itself to setting rules and voluntary norms to ensure smoothly running markets without favoring particular economic activities or sectors.[2] In practice, however, its relatively subtle and indirect interventions have profound effects. Policy is devised and administered by a multilayered system including local, regional, national, and EU authorities. Private firms, industry associations, labor unions, and civil society organizations are also deeply involved.[3]

The "social market economy" is another term Germans use. The social bargain referred to brings workers, by way of their unions, into the division of corporate profits in exchange for their cooperation in optimizing productivity. The state, as ultimate arbiter, is the third party to this arrangement, sometimes called "tripartism." A core segment of skilled workers in high-value internationally traded manufacturing industries is treated by firms as a critical business asset. These workers receive lifelong training and education, and their employment is viewed as a commitment transcending market volatility and business cycles. Their skills are honed by a vast, sophisticated apprenticeship system.

The German economic system efficiently incorporates new product and process technologies into well-established, high-skill, high-quality industries such as automobiles, mechanical engineering, and machine tools, in firms of all sizes. The *Mittelstand*, a class of small and medium-sized, generally family-owned firms with exceptional global reach, extends productivity growth throughout the country and down into the lower levels of supply chains.[4]

Germany's effective governmental support for manufacturing has resulted in less deindustrialization than in the US. Manufacturing is still 19 percent of GDP, versus 11 percent.[5] Manufacturing's strength – and the quantity and quality of its exports – have sustained high-paying jobs. Since 2006, Germany has had the highest per capita GDP, at purchasing-power parity to adjust for differing costs among nations, of any large country except the US.[6]

Germany is highly exposed to global economic forces, as exports in 2022 were 51 percent of GDP (vs. 12 percent in the US).[7] In 2022, its share of world exports was 6.5 percent, surpassed only by China's 11.7 and America's 9.5, despite having only a quarter of America's population and *one seventeenth* of China's.[8] It is even a successful exporter to China, especially in capital goods for manufacturing such as robots and automated assembly equipment.

The complex collaborations facilitated by the German system are excellent for managing adaptive change and gradual innovation, but less effective at accommodating disruptive change and fostering radical innovation. Thus Germany succeeds most often in mature technologies and underperforms in the most advanced sectors such as biotech and semiconductors.[9]

Germany's economic success is increasingly at risk because of the maturing of its major manufacturing industries, a decline in the quality and technology gap between its manufacturers and foreign competitors, and its overconcentration in legacy mechanical engineering technologies such as the internal combustion engine.[10] (Other than BMW, its legendary auto industry is behind in the transition to EVs.)[11] Berlin has also made major policy blunders, notably overreliance on Russian gas resulting from geopolitical wishful thinking and an unwise decision to phase out nuclear power.

A Relationship-Oriented Financial System

Although Germany's financial system has been changing due to globalization and European integration, it has resisted financialization.[12] In contrast with the US and other LMEs, that system is well aligned with key elements of the country's industrial policy and reinforces the competitive advantages of the country's exporters.

The German financial system is more oriented to longer-term financial *relationships* than to the shorter-term *transactions* that dominate in LMEs. Large firms generally rely on banks – which tend not to prioritize short-term returns – for capital. Stock ownership is concentrated, with each stockholder owning enough of a firm to be motivated and able to intervene in its corporate strategies. Mittelstand firms' nonfamily capital comes most often from local and state banks.[13] On average, they are financed more than half with retained earnings and a third with debt.[14]

Equity markets have grown in the past 20 years in absolute terms and as a percentage of GDP, but still play a relatively minor role. Listing stocks on German exchanges is expensive and difficult, especially for small and medium-sized enterprises.[15] German multinationals list in New York and London, but also depend on bank loans. To ease the way for IPOs, a new submarket was created within the Frankfurt stock exchange in 1997, but it did not survive the dot-com crash and closed in 2003.[16]

A robust network of public-sector and cooperative banks serves as an even more conservative and long term-oriented adjunct to the private banks. The *Landesbanken*, the state banks of the *Länder*, serve institutional clients and have preferential credit programs focused on their regional economies.[17] Local public-sector savings banks (*Sparkassen*) lend to the Mittelstand and other businesses.[18] Municipalities are their "responsible public bodies," but they are managed by licensed bankers and independent in their day-to-day operations.[19] A high percentage of the loans of the national public development bank *KfW* go to SMEs. KfW is the world's largest development bank outside China, with €554 billion in assets. Owned 80 percent by the federal government and 20 percent by the states, it raises money primarily from sales of bonds and commercial paper.[20]

Interfirm Relations

Relations between firms, and between firms, unions, and government, are more collaborative than in the US. Compared to America's reliance on laws and formal regulations, Germany has far more voluntary regulatory arrangements between these players. Government regulations are usually promulgated after consultations with employer federations and unions that are more extensive, formalized, and influential than in most other countries. The announcement of prospective regulations often leads to voluntary industry-wide rules that exert extralegal but very real pressure on companies.

Industry associations play an important role. Chambers of Commerce and Industry are established by law and firms are required to join one and pay dues.[21] Industry associations, another type of group, lobby the government on issues like taxes, regulation, and trade. (The BDI is the confederation of these associations.) Employers' Associations, a third type, lobby on labor law and social policy and engage in collective labor bargaining for some of their members.

Technology transfer generally takes place by means of common industry standards ("norms") and shared practices, both organized by the industry associations. This collaborative approach fits well with an innovation system that focuses on incremental, as opposed to breakthrough, innovation. The BDI estimates the benefit of these standards and norms at €17 billion per year.[22] They are effective: Automation is deployed extensively, with 45 percent more robots per worker than in the US.[23]

Cooperative relations between firms also help make Germany's regional clusters work. Through these clusters, Mittelstand firms are brought into the supply chains of multinationals that have the scale to compete internationally.

The National Innovation System

Germany allocates most of its R&D funding to applied – as opposed to basic – research, relentlessly optimizing and refining existing technologies. It is Europe's most research-intensive major economy: R&D was 2.5 percent of GDP during the 2000s – well above the EU and OECD averages, and in 2017, Germany set a target of 3.5 percent by 2025.[24] By 2022, public (government + nonprofit + higher education) R&D totaled €39.6 billion, and business R&D €81.8 billion.[25] The federal government makes substantial R&D grants to business, and firms are also eligible for the EU's €100 billion Horizon Europe R&D funding program.

Most German universities are public.[26] Those specializing in the practical and industrial applications of science are the second most popular option for postsecondary education. Over the past decade, they have evolved from vocational centers to full-fledged schools of applied science able to grant PhDs. Many offer internships at private firms where student projects are overseen by professors with industry experience.[27]

Nonprofit research associations include the Max Planck Society for basic research in the natural and social sciences, the Helmholtz Association for basic research in the natural and life sciences, and the Gottfried-Wilhelm-Leibniz-Association for applied research in natural and social sciences. All operate in cooperation with industry.[28] The Fraunhofer Society (see Chapter 23 for details), funded by both government and private-industry clients, performs applied industrial research on a contract basis.

As noted, Germany is comparatively weak in new fields such as semiconductors, biotechnology, and AI.[29] In 2022, the EU ranked it thirteenth among its 27 member states for adoption of digital technology (Finland was first). Its workforce had digital skills below the EU average, and Germany also lagged at integration of digital technology into business.[30] It lacks a startup ecosystem comparable to the US, Israel, or even neighboring Sweden.[31] Foreign venture capital, mainly from the US, exceeds domestic by a factor of three (€5.0 billion vs. €1.7 billion in 2019).[32] Germany lacks personnel in some key new technologies and has weak support for university spin-offs in new industries and radical innovations.

Skills, Education, and Training

Germany has an exceptionally skilled labor force thanks to good primary and secondary education and its apprenticeship system, which combines academic and on-the-job training and enrolls half the country's youth.[33] Because of apprenticeships, youth unemployment is lower in Germany than in other large Western European countries.[34]

In Germany, as in other European countries, the vocational pathway is the norm, although this is beginning to change. Employers select apprentices for employment, usually for two to three years, at a reduced wage while continuing their schooling. Upon graduation, their skills are formally certified. They can then be employed in other firms or industries, but often get jobs where they apprenticed.[35]

Apprenticeships are the start of lifelong learning, with training programs partly funded by government and industry associations. Employers, unions, and educational institutions work together with government support to anticipate changes in skill needs.[36] Training and skills upgrading fall within the ambit of union codetermination, discussed in the next section.[37]

The apprenticeship system was adopted in its current form in 1969, codifying a national framework for the various training paths. Reforms in the 1980s made its curriculum less narrowly occupational and more inclusive of general skills. Today, it is facing challenges. Matching students' preferences with employers' skill needs has become more difficult, as has finding willing employers. A declining share of youth wish to enter the system: University or equivalent education for 25–34-year-olds in Germany has risen from 22 percent in 2000 to 36 percent in 2021. (The corresponding figures for the US are 38 and 51 percent.)[38]

Labor–Management Relations

Unions play a much larger role in Germany than in the US. As of 2018, 17 percent of German workers were unionized, versus 10 percent in the US.[39] More importantly, thanks to sector-wide agreements, 54 percent were covered by collective bargaining agreements, versus only 12 percent in the US.[40]

It is common for the regional affiliate of a sectoral employers' association to negotiate with the unions in its region.[41] The agreement is then used as a model for other regions. This bargaining format reduces the opportunity – and thus the pressure – for firms to cut wages to gain an edge over their (local) competitors. It also makes them less antagonistic toward unions generally.

German unions rarely abuse their power. They understand that cooperation with management maintains the cycle of productivity → profits → higher wages → cooperation → productivity. They thus differ from their more politicized, conflict-oriented, and militant French and Italian counterparts, which view employers as social adversaries, and from British and American unions, which play a much smaller role in shaping their employers' business strategies.

Other key labor institutions are codetermination and works councils. The former is workers' right to participate in management, including representation on companies' supervisory boards, the upper level of Germany's two-tier corporate board system. The latter, composed of worker representatives elected to four-year terms, exist in both unionized and nonunion firms. Working conditions, work organization, employee benefits, large-scale dismissals, and even changes in firm ownership are within their purview. The leading union IG Metall reports that wages are 8 percent higher at firms with such councils than at otherwise comparable firms.[42] In cases of irresolvable conflict, recourse is to an internal arbitration board made up of representatives of both sides and an agreed-upon neutral chairperson.[43] As a last resort, government labor courts can force a settlement.

German unions today are facing the same challenges from globalization as those in other developed nations. Wage, benefit, and working hours concessions have been made, including at some highly profitable firms.[44] From 1998 to 2016, the percentage of workers under collective bargaining fell from 76 to 59 percent in Western Germany, and from 63 to 47 percent in former East Germany.[45]

The labor regime is constantly being fine-tuned. For example, while firm-level exceptions to labor laws have increased in recent years, weakening state control, a national minimum wage was instituted for the first time in 2015 and the labor minister's power to extend collective bargaining agreements to non-covered workers was enhanced, strengthening the hand of the state.

The Mittelstand

The Mittelstand are sophisticated small and medium-sized firms with fewer than 500 employees and annual revenues under €50 million. In 2017, they accounted for a quarter of Germany's manufacturing output and exported an average of 20 percent of their production.[46]

The Mittelstand is a major foundation of Germany's manufacturing export strength.[47] Many such firms play hidden but crucial roles in sophisticated global industries. One 2007 study found that roughly 1,130 such small and medium-sized companies held the number one or number two global position for their products, or the number one position in the European market.[48] The existence of these high-quality local suppliers, often forming industry clusters that cannot easily be replicated elsewhere, has helped anchor larger firms in Germany.

Mittelstand firms are characterized by a mutually reinforcing set of values, attitudes, and strategies. They usually combine family ownership and long-term business relationships with craft-rooted, skills-based, quality-oriented production.[49] They never outsource their core competencies, and dominate their markets through constant incremental improvement rather than price competition.[50] The federal and regional governments make special efforts to help them develop and apply new technologies and increase their exports. Examples include the Industrie 4.0 program discussed later in this chapter.

These firms have deep roots in their local communities and a strong sense of social responsibility. They create quality jobs outside the big urban centers, as they tend to be located in small towns and rural areas.[51] Their workers identify with them and are highly motivated. Worker turnover is low, about 3 percent per year, compared with 18 percent in Germany as a whole and 21 percent in the US. This increases their return on investments in skills upgrading.[52] Most such firms also offer incentives to employees to contribute new ideas and have relatively flat management hierarchies, allowing employees a substantial a role in decision-making.[53]

To avoid the liquidity problems that could force a sale to outsiders when the controlling shareholder dies, Germany gives inherited businesses preferential tax treatment. In 2009, this preference was expanded, granting an 85 percent reduction in inheritance taxes when heirs maintain employment and manage the family firm for five years.[54]

Regional, Entrepreneurship, and Technology Policies

Entrepreneurship is not Germany's strength. As of 2022, Berlin ranked slightly below Paris (and far below London and several cities in China and the US) as a startup hub.[55] Policymakers are aware of and have tried to fix this problem.[56] The EXIST program, established in 1998 and cofinanced by the EU's European Social Fund, supports startup networks at universities and other research institutions. In 2010, it added funding for entrepreneurial education centers to infuse startup culture into universities.[57] Its 2019 funding was €129 million.[58]

Established in 2005, the High-Tech Gründerfonds (HTGF), a public–private venture capital fund, is Germany's largest investor in technology startups. The principal government participant is the Ministry for Economic Affairs and Climate Action (BMWK); private funding comes from 45 companies in a wide range of industries.[59] HTGF has supported more than 700 startups in such fields as healthcare, automation, media, chemistry, and the internet, with over successful 160 exits.[60] As of May 2023, it managed €1.4 billion, with total public and private-sector follow-on investments in its portfolio companies of €4.5 billion.[61]

Germany's main government program for industry clusters is its Leading-Edge Cluster Competition, operating since 2007, which has successfully induced firms to increase R&D.[62] Winning cluster proposals from firms agreeing to invest in prioritized fields receive matching public funds. For example, the Cool Silicon cluster in Saxony was chosen (as one of five clusters) and funded from 2009 to 2014 with €40 million from the Federal Ministry for Education and Research plus €30 million from Saxony's Ministry of Science and the Fine Arts.[63] In 2019, Germany launched its Clusters4Future Initiative, and in 2021, the program, through a public competition, identified and funded its first seven "next generation networks," a/k/a clusters. By 2024, 14 such networks had received federal funding and had progressed to implementation. These clusters are funded for three years, with up to three renewals subject to review and approval.[64]

The History

Until 1871, there was no unified German state, only a collection of principalities, cities, bishoprics, and duchies that joined in a loose confederation in the early nineteenth century. Germany's pre-industrialization economic policies thus evolved among competing sovereignties. The economic administration of states and their subunits was carried out through a set of public policies known as *cameralism*, a variety of the Europe-wide mercantilism we will discuss in Chapter 13.

Beginning in the 1820s, policies were influenced by economist Friedrich List, who played a leading entrepreneurial role in developing Germany's railways and offered an explicitly nationalistic perspective on economic development.[65] He advocated a common external tariff for the German states, plus investment in research, education, and infrastructure. His views were informed by exile in the US from 1825 to 1833, where he became acquainted with Alexander Hamilton's tariff-based development strategy (see Chapter 14). List was the single largest intellectual influence behind the creation of the customs union between Prussia and allied German states in 1834.[66] His 1841 book *The National System of Political Economy* had an immense international influence, especially in Japan, and through the Japanese model all over East Asia.[67]

Following the victory of a Prussian-led alliance in a war against France, the German Empire (*Reich*) was founded in 1871. Its constitution combined an authoritarian monarchy with major democratic elements, including universal male suffrage for electing the *Reichstag* (Parliament). Once united, Germany attempted to combine the best practices that had developed in its different regions. The training system that exists to this day came from the Baden region, generalized to the rest of the country starting in 1897.[68] An interventionist Prussian model of state-led industrialization had channeled resources into industries critical for security and defense, and this approach was instrumental to developing heavy industry of the Ruhr region. A more liberal southwest German model emphasizing interconnected medium-sized manufacturing firms laid the foundation for regional clusters with skilled personnel and high-quality products.[69]

Although a fairly liberal, free-market perspective was adopted immediately after unification, the global recession of 1873–7 turned the government permanently toward protectionism.[70] In the words of one historian, "The adoption of protectionism in 1879 has been considered so important that its institution has been called the 'second founding of the Reich,' a refoundation on a conservative-nationalist, not liberal basis."[71] A political coalition, "the marriage of iron and rye," united the powerful Prussian *Junker* aristocracy, with its large agricultural estates, with heavy industry in support of tariffs. Germans would henceforth look to the state, as well as the market, to guide economic development.

Germany's economic strategy was implemented with disciplined bureaucratic competence. Government supported key heavy industries such as iron, coal, and chemicals, both for military reasons and because they were the high-tech, large-scale, advantageous industries of the day. State intervention kept the growth of industrial output stable, avoiding the boom–bust cycles prevailing in the US in this era.[72] The country thrived economically.

Employers' associations were first formed to fight unions, and strikes were brutal, with violence on both sides. Organized labor was integrated into the political system in stages, beginning with formation of the German Workers' Association in 1863 and the Social Democratic Workers' Party (SDAP/SPD) in 1869.[73] From 1878 to 1890, Chancellor Otto von Bismarck implemented an antisocialist campaign, including a ban on the SDP's meetings, associations, and newspapers.[74] Simultaneously, to mollify the workers, he *also* created the world's first comprehensive welfare state. When the SPD was re-legalized in 1890, it became a powerful political force, but no longer aspired to overthrow capitalism by revolution. Workers' committees were given legal rights to consult with management, first in the Bavarian mining industry in 1900, then in other industries and parts of the country.

In pursuit of scale economies, the government encouraged mergers and supported industry's preexisting inclination to form cartels. Industry-wide production quotas and coordination of prices followed, with the aim of safe-guarding profitability, enabling orderly investment in capital-intensive indus-tries, enforcing quality standards, and increasing the certainty of business planning.[75] Cartelization strengthened the financial–industrial nexus, with a few large private banks providing long-term credit to industrial enterprises and gaining a say in their operations and strategic planning.[76] A strong focus on penetrating export markets prevented cartelization from degenerating into rent-seeking and technological stagnation.[77]

The Rise of Science-Based Industry

Germany's national innovation system, the first in the world to be deliberately designed, took shape in the decades after unification. Its focus was advanced manufacturing, including chemicals, electrical goods, machine tools, and optics. Leading firms from this era that remain prominent today include Siemens (electrical goods), Merck (pharmaceuticals), and Zeiss (optics, includ-ing those used to manufacture the world's most advanced computer chips).

Germany pioneered collaboration between corporate research and public universities.[78] From the start, there was a focus on both theoretical science, at which Germany then excelled, and its applications, unhindered by the cultural and institutional split between theory and practice in nations such as the UK. German universities were centers of technological research long before their counterparts in Britain and the US.[79]

Between 1868 and 1910, the Prussian and then the German government redirected half of its R&D spending from military to industrial research.[80] Research institutes, such as the Imperial Institute of Physics and Technology focused on precision engineering, were founded.[81] Associations were formed to foster the creation of technical knowledge, chief among them the Kaiser Wilhelm Society (today's Max Planck Society), funded from private and public contributions.

Between 1871 and 1914, enrollment at universities and technical colleges quadrupled. Between 1900 and 1910, Germany produced 30,000 engineers, exceeding the US total of 21,000 and many times more than Britain, where laissez-faire militated against state responsibility for education and industry preferred on-the-job training.[82] Between 1901 and 1933, the country produced 32 Nobel laureates in science, compared to France with 15, the UK with 15, and the US with 8.[83] By 1913, German firms held a third of all foreign patents granted in America.[84]

Germany imported innovations from abroad, enhanced them, and grew them into major industries. For example, the Bessemer process that turned steel into a mass commodity was invented in England in 1856, but Germany used that process to become Europe's largest steel producer. The first synthetic dye was created by an Englishman in 1856, but Germans developed the industry.

Benefiting from sustained public and private investments in research, these dyes were the foundation for Germany's later success in chemicals generally and then in pharmaceuticals. Steel and other metalworking were part of an expanding military–industrial complex that produced technologically advanced armaments.[85] By 1913, the German chemical industry accounted for a quarter of global production and 27 percent of global exports.[86] Firms such as Bayer, BASF, Agfa, Hoechst, Cassella, and Kalle formed alliances for research, production, and marketing. Their sophisticated professional management, in an era when most large companies were still controlled by family dynasties, earned them the descriptor "the world's first truly managerial industrial enterprises."[87]

The World Wars

By 1913, Germany produced 29 percent of global machinery exports, compared to Great Britain with 28 percent and the US with 27.[88] It had surpassed Britain in industrial production and almost caught up in foreign trade.[89]

During World War I, the War Raw Materials Department used public–private research projects to develop synthetic raw materials to replace embargoed imports. In strategic industries such as iron, steel, coal, and electricity, the government merged companies and took a direct role in management. The wartime economy was never truly efficient, but its push for productivity increases and technological progress paved the way for postwar recovery and growth.[90] For example, industry-wide technical standards were first systematically set by the Standards Association of German Industry, established in 1917.[91] Wartime Germany pioneered state intervention in labor disputes, ranging from mediation and arbitration to preventing work stoppages by force. In December 1916, the Auxiliary Service Law was passed, requiring so-called patriotic labor service. To mollify labor, the law established workers' committees in all firms involved in the war effort with more than 50 employees. Although primarily consultative, these committees laid the foundation for later codetermination.

In 1918, the regime collapsed, and in its place, the Social Democrats led a coalition that established the Weimar Republic. This fragile government was under constant fire from radicals on both right and left, but during its 14-year existence, it promoted consolidation and modernization in all major industries. Its 1923 Cartel Act allowed businesses to collaborate far more closely than the antitrust policies of other major capitalist economies.[92] In the name of industrial democracy, the Works Council Act of 1920 required such councils in firms with more than 20 employees. This and other legislation firmly inserted workers into management.

German industry wanted to shift to an American-style mass production, mass consumption economy, and US direct investments in Germany pressured German industry to upgrade.[93] But modernization was difficult, as it meant abandoning established structures and processes, investing a lot more capital, and getting workers to adapt. Germany, being poorer, also lacked the large middle-class market that, for example, had made automobiles a viable mass production industry in the US. Nonetheless, by the end of the 1920s, many German industries had reestablished their strong prewar positions in international markets.[94]

The Great Depression ended this recovery. American loans that had financed Germany's war reparations to France, which repaid France's debts to Britain, which repaid Britain's debts to the US, dried up. Unemployment reached 34 percent in 1933, and the Nazis took power.

Despite their "National Socialist" name and sometimes anti-capitalist rhetoric, the Nazis did not impose socialism. Property rights continued for the non-persecuted, and Germany remained a basically capitalist economy, albeit permeated by ever more state controls. The regime used price and wage regulations, strategic investments, profit guarantees, and related policies to control the private sector.[95] The result, until the war, was a hybrid economy of markets, cartels, and direct interventions.

To prepare for the war Hitler had already planned, an economic planning system was established in 1936, starting with the first Four-Year Plan. Government manipulated everything it could: prices, wages, capital flows, banking, stocks, imports, and exports. At great cost, it pushed for domestic substitutes for imported raw materials such as rubber.[96] Foreign trade was managed with currency controls, tariffs, quotas, and barter treaties. The government took nearly total control of existing cartels and, especially in strategic industries such as steel and chemicals, forced nonmember firms to join them.[97]

During World War II, Germany imposed its economic system on the countries it occupied, aiming to make them suppliers of raw materials and the locations of lesser industry while Germany took the most valuable industry for itself. (The accompanying brutalities included slave labor.) After Germany's defeat at Stalingrad, the regime, realizing it might lose, centralized control even *further* to dedicate an even larger fraction of output to military production. Surprisingly, however, later statistics revealed that the democratic UK had managed to mobilize a higher percentage of its economy for the war effort.[98]

Some armament-related technologies, such as the aircraft industry, flourished during the war.[99] The push for *Wunderwaffen* (miracle weapons), while not militarily effective, led to technological breakthroughs such as the first jet fighter (the Me-262) and the first ballistic missile (the V-2), which laid the foundations for the postwar arms, aircraft, and aerospace industries of the US and USSR.

Occupation and Rebuilding

After Germany's surrender, the Allies, aiming to deindustrialize Germany so that it could never again became a major military power, implemented the Potsdam Agreement. It terms included dismantling manufacturing facilities with military applications; limiting production of coal, iron, and steel; disassembling factories and exporting them as reparations; decentralizing and decartelizing German industry; and seizing German patents, copyrights, and trademarks. The economy was to be reorganized around agriculture and light industry.

But American occupation leaders soon realized that a stable, functioning, *industrial* economy was needed not only to feed, house, and employ the Germans, but also to rebuild the rest of Western Europe and resist Soviet communism. The result was a massive assistance program, the European Recovery Program, better known as the Marshall Plan. It began mainly by providing necessities such as food and fuel, but over time, it was increasingly used to buy industrial raw materials.[100] German firms used its funds to modernize business procedures and implement best practices from the US.[101] American experts gave technical assistance. Plan funds were also used for capital investments in public utilities and the transportation, iron, and steel industries.[102]

In 1948, a harsh but effective currency reform (debts and savings written down by 90 percent) reestablished the mark on a solid foundation. The new government used industrial policy from the start. Targeted industry subsidies, export incentives and tax exemptions played major roles in enabling the *Wirtschaftswunder* ("economic miracle") of the 1950s and 1960s. Between 1949 and 1957, the tax exemptions alone cost 30 billion marks – 2 percent of GDP.[103] KfW, founded in 1948 to help administer the Marshall Plan, was reorganized in the 1950s as a state-owned development bank. It channeled credit to SMMs and sectors deemed essential to reconstruction such as housing, coal mining, electricity, and steel. (1.1 billion marks went to raw materials, cement, chemicals, and engineering.)[104]

In 1959, the SDP accepted capitalism in the form of the social market economy. The center-right Christian Democrats (CDU/CSU) gave up toying with Christian socialism and embraced similar economic principles with a more conservative slant. Despite corporate opposition, the unions and their allies in the SPD and the CDU/CSU passed the Co-determination Act in 1951. This gave worker representatives half the seats on coal and steel firms' supervisory boards, the upper level of Germany's two-tier corporate board system. Among other things, this helped workers monitor their employers' compliance with investment and work organization commitments. In 1952, a similar policy was extended to companies in all sectors with more than 500 employees.[105]

1949–1973: The Social Market Economy

1949 to 1973 was the golden age of Germany's social market economy, with rapid growth shared by all social strata. During the 1950s, Germany's share of the exports of the industrial nations almost tripled.[106]

Unemployment fell to 1 percent in 1960. Exports' share of GDP doubled from 10 percent in 1950 to more than 20 in the early 1970s.[107] GDP growth during the 1950s averaged 8.2 percent, compared to 4.6 percent in France, 3.3 percent in the US, and 2.8 percent in the UK.[108] Labor productivity grew at 7.3 percent annually during the 1950s and 5.2 percent in the 1960s.[109] Granted, Germany, rebuilding from war, was experiencing catch-up growth, but this performance was still impressive.

Manufacturing employment peaked at almost 50 percent in the early 1960s, then fell steadily during the 1970s, stabilizing just below 40 percent – still higher than peer nations.[110] The sector, driven by strong export demand, productivity increases, and union wage restraint, was a growth locomotive for the entire economy.[111] Macroeconomic policies were managed to support manufacturing exports. As one commentator explains,

> Export success was not merely an expression of the immediate strengths of the economy, it was also a function of policy. Far from adopting a Keynesian approach, the government curtailed the growth of domestic demand by running state budget surpluses and by enforcing tight credit leading to high interest rates. It thereby forced a search for overseas sales, while facilitating this by limiting upward pressure on prices.[112]

Support for the Mittelstand included cheap credit, tax breaks, and other financial support.[113]

State ownership of and direct subsidies to industry peaked in this era. one historian notes that,

> Volkswagen was owned by the German state, and, even when the company was privatized in 1957, the government retained the largest share, enough to prevent a foreign sale. The state prohibited foreign companies from purchasing German auto companies ... Strategic industries obtained financial aid and protection from competition. They acquired dispensation from labor laws and the usual debt liability. Serious subsidy of industry began in the late 1960s, in the wake of the approval of the Kennedy Round tariff reductions of the GATT negotiations, completed in 1967. Domestic subsidies and tax allowances substituted for tariffs. The results were stunning: Germany exported 11.5 percent of the autos it produced in 1960, and 46.1 in 1974; it exported 20.3 percent of its machines in 1950, and 43.5 in 1974.[114]

By the 1960s, the state owned 40 percent of coal and iron, 62 percent of electric power, 62 percent of banking, and 72 percent of aluminum.[115] For coal and steel, long-term investment plans were negotiated between industry, unions, and government. Outside these sectors, government ownership was lower, falling from 12 percent of equity in 1960 to 4 percent by 1992.[116]

Trade policy combined support for the lowering of tariffs abroad with promotion of exports by means of preferential loans, tax rebates, and credit risk insurance.[117] Partly in response to tariff reductions due to increasing European integration and successive GATT rounds (see Chapter 16), in 1968 Germany enacted an 11 percent value-added tax (19 percent today) to protect its export competitiveness (see Chapter 4 for the mechanism). The decades-long under-valuation of the mark under Bretton Woods also helped. The end of Bretton Woods in 1971 was followed by its rise, but German firms adapted through productivity increases and product improvements. Wage discipline by the key unions in the export sector, above all IG Metall, kept inflation in check. This enabled low interest rates, which held the mark down by avoiding an influx of foreign capital.

1974–1989: Picking Winners and Bailing Out Losers

The 1973 oil shock ended the era of easy postwar growth for all the developed Western economies. Growth based on rebuilding from World War II and then catching up to the technological frontier, defined at the time by the US, had been exhausted. East Asia, with Japan in the lead, was beginning to apply competitive pressure.

Germany's export position remained favorable, with the export share of GDP reaching 30 percent in the late 1980s and an ongoing trade surplus.[118] Manufacturing retained a large share of GDP and employment compared to other Western economies. Germany successfully offshored its most labor-intensive tradable industries, such as commodity textiles, while keeping the highest-value parts of their supply chains.[119]

Nevertheless, during the 1970s, growth was less than what Germans had grown accustomed to. Wage growth declined as wages failed to keep pace with still-growing productivity.[120] The country's share of world trade in manufactures slowly declined from 15.1 percent in 1970–3 to 13.8 percent in 1989.[121] Unemployment and inflation increased. Recognition grew that familiar Keynesian macroeconomic measures could not resolve the stagnation or the resulting union discontent. The government responded with two initiatives.

First, it reorganized to give responsibility for supporting R&D to the new Ministry for Research and Technology.[122] This ministry funded all aspects of technology development, with foci including transportation systems, civil aviation, information technology, maritime technology, new materials, com-puter-aided design, biotechnology, space, and nuclear power. But attempts to pick specific winning products led to huge failures, including the fast-breeder nuclear reactor, Siemens's large-capacity computer, and the Transrapid maglev railway. But these failures were acknowledged and prompted a shift toward strengthening the innovation system as a whole rather than placing bets on specific products.

Second, the government intervened in the declining steel and coal industries. The state facilitated their consolidation, funded skills training for laid-off workers, and subsidized deployment of new technologies. Between 1983 and 1985, it spent $1 billion directly subsidizing steel.[123] As a result, Germany's rustbelt declined with less social and economic disruption than in the US and UK.[124]

1990–2005: Opening to the East

Integrating the former East Germany involved massive deindustrialization in the East, high unemployment there, and the migration of more than 4 million people to the West. The federal and state governments spent more than $230 billion in 2023 dollars reconstructing its economy and infrastructure.[125] Attempts were made to revive existing industries and create new firms, but the introduction of Western institutions such as the apprenticeship system could not on their own fix the low productivity, obsolete technologies, and inefficient management of ex-communist companies.[126] Existing industry clusters were supported through infrastructure investments, fiscal incentives, and temporary subsidies.[127] This successfully induced cluster dynamics in a variety of industries, though the process took longer than expected. The East's per capita GDP rose slowly: from 43 percent of the West's in 1991 to 68 percent by 2005 and 82 percent by 2018.[128]

The opening of Eastern Europe created considerable temptation for German firms to offshore work, but Germany handled offshoring better than the US, partly because CMEs place greater value on retaining the high-value parts of their supply chains.[129] Unions recognized and accommodated businesses' need to adapt.[130] Thus, German firms' costs were lowered by *selective* offshoring. Writing in 2015, one analyst analyzed both the pressures that drove firms to offshoring and the factors that limited it:

> This threat has only been heightened as more countries become integrated into the EU, first with Spain in the 1980s and now with Eastern Europe beginning in the 1990s ... German auto producers can reduce unit labor costs by about 70 percent in several Central European countries through direct investment. Despite growth in both final assembly and parts manufacturing in areas outside of Germany, employment in the auto industry continues to grow in Germany, albeit at a modest pace. German producers are not nearly as concerned with labor costs as the US given their product model and institutional setting ... German producers still see many advantages to producing at home, and ... the massive offshoring seen in the US simply has not occurred in

Germany ... In Germany, industrial relations, the strength of labor, product strategies and company culture all discourage offshoring.[131]

German manufacturers have since increasingly used foreign direct investment (FDI) to move production closer to major markets, reduce production costs, step over trade barriers, and tap R&D knowledge pools.[132] But by 2021, thanks in part to supply-chain concerns and deteriorating relations with China, more than half of German companies surveyed said they were looking into *reshoring*.[133]

Between 1995 and 2005, GDP grew only about 1 percent per year, less than the other European economies or the US.[134] To restore growth, Germany embraced policies focused on export competitiveness.[135] The 1999 adoption of the euro helped by giving Germany an undervalued currency, and from 2000 to 2008, exports rose 76 percent.[136] To lower unemployment, policies were imposed to make low-wage workers more attractive to employers and unemployment less attractive to workers – but this did *not* amount to a full turn to market-driven labor relations.[137] For the well-paid, high-skill segment of the workforce, the pact of trading wage restraint for employment security held. Codetermination remained important, with additional laws and regulations implemented in the 2000s.

2006–2018: Upgrading Technology Support

To strengthen manufacturing R&D, Germany in 2006 launched its High-Tech Strategy (HTS) program. In 2010, it broadened and updated this plan, now dubbed HTS 2020, to deepen scientific and engineering collaboration among universities, other R&D organizations, and industry. In 2018, it doubled down again with HTS 2025, with funding reaching €15.8 billion and a goal of making R&D 3.5 percent of GDP by 2025.[138]

The Industrie 4.0 program (4IR) (see Chapter 22 for details about the Fourth Industrial Revolution concept) launched in 2011 is at the core of HTS.[139] It supports research into cyber-physical systems, networking high-tech businesses, and digital standardization within and across industries, and has funding of €40 million per year.[140]

4IR has had programs for the Mittelstand since the mid-2010s. These include "SMM 4.0 – Digital Production and Work Processes," whose innovation centers provide SMMs with information, advice, physical demonstrations, and testing facilities. There is also a program that demonstrates to SMMs how they can use 4IR technologies.[141] These programs appear to be working: Mittelstand exports have been rising in the sectors targeted.[142]

Germany thus became one of the early adopters and leading implementers of smart manufacturing technologies.[143] As of 2023, China, Germany, and Japan led in the adoption of smart factories, followed by South Korea, the US, and France.[144] In 2023, two German firms, Bosch and Siemens, ranked first and second in the top 10 as suppliers of such plants.[145]

2019–Present: Euro-Neo-Mercantilism?

China's aggressive industrial policy is pushing Germany back toward a more explicit mercantilism. In 2019, the BDI cataloged China's unfair business practices, including industrial tariffs, nontariff trade barriers, investment controls, forced joint ventures, forced technology transfers, intellectual property theft, ineffective legal remedies, corporate subsidies, state interference in markets, and takeovers of German high-tech firms.[146]

Important companies, including the vehicle parts supplier Grammer and the robotics firms KUKA, have been acquired by Chinese entities.[147] In both cases, the purchasers reneged on commitments to maintain the independence of German management and took direct control. Thus, in 2018, Germany imposed stricter limits on the acquisition by non-EU investors of shares in German companies in "security relevant" fields such as telecommunications, software, IT security, energy, and defense. And it introduced similar EU-wide legislation, which went into effect in 2020.[148] Berlin has also been pressing for relaxation of EU rules that constrain its authority to allow inter-corporate alliances, favor particular sectors with state support, and apply competition rules to the American digital giants.[149]

In 2019, Peter Altmaier, Minister for Economic Affairs and Energy, announced National Industry Strategy 2030.[150] By its own account, the strategy was motivated by a) China's growing technological sophistication, b) the danger of China acquiring monopoly positions in key industries, and c) the risk of Germany's export markets, above all the US, turning protectionist.[151] If fully implemented, NIS2030 would constitute a much more explicit mercantilism than the soft version Germany currently practices. In the words of one scholar, it envisioned "an activist state nurturing infant industries, choosing winners, protecting high-tech sectors, and promoting national and regional value chains."[152]

Openly repudiating Germany's ordoliberal commitment to sector neutrality, NIS2030 specifically targeted particular sectors including AI, digitization, the internet, telecommunications, autonomous driving, and biotech. Legacy industries deemed worthy of financial support and trade protection included steel, copper, aluminum, chemicals, mechanical engineering, plant construction, automobiles, optics, medical devices, greentech, armaments, aerospace, and additive manufacturing. NIS2030 privileged manufacturing more broadly: One of its stated goals was for the sector to rise from 23 to

25 percent of GDP. In a shift back to national champions, it identified firms whose survival was in the national political and economic interest. This included Siemens, the big automakers, and major chemical, electrical, and mechanical engineering companies.[153] It proposed a state investment fund to take stakes in technologically important companies to protect them from foreign takeovers.

NIS2030 attracted both support and opposition from industry, with the usual complaints about government meddling and the folly of picking winners. Although the plan was only conceptual, some elements are already being implemented. In 2022, Berlin blocked Chinese acquisitions of two key microchip companies, and tightened federal scrutiny is causing a steady decrease in Chinese direct investment.[154] In 2023, Berlin released its official China strategy focused on untangling from China-dependent supply chains, protecting German and EU technology, and cooperating with friendly nations to achieve these goals.[155]

NIS2030 envisioned Germany as a model for an aggressive and far-reaching EU-wide industrial policy that would privilege inside-the-EU supply chains. It proposed that Germany and the EU together create "European champions" with scale sufficient to compete with their US and Chinese counterparts. In this vein, in 2019, the Ministry for Economic Affairs and Energy and France's Ministry of the Economy and Finance issued a joint "Manifesto for a European Industrial Policy." And in 2023, EU Commissioner for Internal Market Thierry Breton called for a comprehensive European industrial policy aiming at "a Europe that sets its own rules of the game and proactively reaffirms its role and interests in the new geopolitical landscape."[156]

In 2023, Brussels approved an EU-wide Chips Act, promising $47 billion to increase semiconductor production and aiming to raise the EU's lagging share of global output from 10 to 20 percent by 2030.[157] The EU has since further embraced proactive trade and investment strategy with its Foreign Subsidies Regulation, its Foreign Direct Investment Screening Framework, and its International Procurement Instrument.[158] In 2023, it announced political agreement on an Anti-Coercion Instrument to defend EU firms globally against economic coercion by third countries (read "China"), including countermeasures such as tariffs, restrictions on trade in services, and FDI restrictions.[159] It is too early to know how far either the EU or Germany will go in this new direction, but Berlin has clearly decided that mercantilism-light no longer suffices.[160]

Strengths

- Institutions for managing complex cooperation between government, workers, management, industry associations, and universities.

- A wide and sophisticated array of regional and national programs supporting R&D and its commercialization.
- Well-resourced universities focusing on applied science and its translation into commercially successful products.
- A nominally WTO-compliant trade policy that protects advantageous industries through informal, unwritten norms and VAT.
- A labor movement that bargains for a share of the profits while supporting the profitability of the enterprise, and management that values skilled workers.
- Well-designed systems of apprenticeships and technical education.
- A *Mittelstand* of family-owned, exceptionally sophisticated and well-run medium-sized firms.
- A multilayered public–private financial system that supports all levels of industry and is resistant to financialization.
- A de facto undervalued currency due to the euro.

Weaknesses

- An innovation system that rarely produces breakthrough products.
- Overconcentration in the industries of yesterday.
- A small, weak startup culture and venture capital system.
- Irrational macroeconomic decisions like abandoning nuclear power and overreliance on Russian natural gas.
- Sharp decline from the country's once world-leading position in pure science.
- Until recently, excessive accommodation of China's aggressive FDI and excessive dependence on its market.

9 FRANCE

The Triumph and Failures of the State

If ever industrial policy and a Western country were made for each other, that country is France. It has a centralized government friendly to technocracy, an electorate and business class willing to let it supervise industry, elite higher education whose graduates freely move between senior positions in government and industry, and a longing for its own distinct version of national greatness – all the ingredients for a successful industrial policy. But its record has been mixed.

The greatest success of French industrial policy has simply been in creating a modern industrial country. In 1945, France was only semi-industrialized, with 37 percent of its workforce still in agriculture, versus 8.5 percent in the UK.[1] Then, between 1950 and 1973, its GDP grew 5.4 percent per year, and per capita GDP rose from 51 percent of the US to 82 percent.[2] It took 50 years from 1900 for French GDP to double, but only 15 more for it to double again.[3]

In subsequent decades, French industrial policy has been less success-ful. When appropriate policies have been applied to ends susceptible to state intervention, results have been favorable. Thus, French successes in high-value industries range from nuclear power to pharmaceuticals to airliners. France's failures, by contrast, have generally been due to politicians bypassing the professional planners to launch or defend industries in which the country had, for varying reasons, little chance, such as computers, steel, and mass-market shoes.

The state has historically been France's main vehicle for large-scale enterprise. In 1945, it did not have the comprehensive set of capitalist institu-tions and practices that had driven the commercial success of first Britain and then the US, so government had to fill the gap. The institutional matrix then established has, with changes, endured to the present day. Even administrations ostensibly more oriented to market economics have made only minor revisions.

France continues to strive for more balance between small-town, agricultural life and urban, industrial life than most of its peers. It has a work-to-live ethos, not the live-to-work ethos of the US or Japan. Even today, with unionization down to 10 percent of the labor force, attempts to ease restrictions on the working week or raise the retirement age (now 55 for favored groups) provoke strikes and civil unrest.[4] A suspicion of private profit, long ingrained in the nation's psyche, endures.

Industrial policy priorities have varied over time, reflecting tensions between attempting to develop all industries simultaneously and focusing on those deemed strategic, between choosing national champions and encouraging competition within sectors, between regional interests and the national interest, and between modernization and "national solidarity." This phrase de facto means "featherbedding favored sections of the working class."

For decades after the war, and even to an extent today, French industry has seen government intervention to protect jobs as natural and appropriate whenever high costs and low productivity have gotten it into trouble. Recently, France has begun, somewhat reluctantly, to embrace freer markets, freer trade, and international competitiveness. A sizable part of the public now accepts that closure may be inevitable for plants whose prospects are hopeless.

The French state still energetically promotes the nation's commercial interests abroad – in particular, those embodied in its national champions. Its practices have ranged from manipulating the exchange rate (outlawed by the EEC and IMF and impossible since the euro began in 1999) to the rarely punished bribery of foreign, and even French, officials.[5] Paris still tries to ensure that most of the products French people buy are French, though over the decades this has become more difficult. The COVID crisis, where the Finance Ministry tried to save every threatened firm from bankruptcy, showed the enduring strength of its interventionist instinct.

The History

France's statist economic philosophy traces back to Louis XIV's finance minister Jean Baptiste Colbert (1619–83), a practitioner of the Europe-wide mercantilism discussed in Chapter 13. From then onward, in the words of one historian:

> The essential French view [was] that the effective conduct of a nation's economic life must depend on the concentration of power in the hands of a small number of exceptionally able people, exercising foresight and judgement of a kind not possessed by the average successful man

of business ... The instinct to intervene in the management of the economy has never been curbed; the only problem, as the French have seen it, is how to make this interference more intelligent and coherent.[6]

Unlike some nations, France has not always engaged in a single-minded attempt to develop the most advanced industries of the era. Instead, it has sometimes tried to preserve a comfortable, stable, traditional, agriculture-heavy economy whose performance was neither terrible nor internationally competitive. Well into the twentieth century, there were serious people in France who did not believe in modern industry *at all*, and much of the country accepted industrialization only grudgingly. This attitude was helped by the Gallic talent for driving up the value of agricultural products with triumphs of quality and marketing like $150 bottles of champagne.

Thus, industrialization started later and proceeded more slowly in France than in Britain, the first industrializer. France entered the Industrial Revolution at scale only after its defeat by Prussia in 1871. But it did so in its own way. Rather than aim for mass production at low prices, French industry, starting with its staple of textiles, pursued quality products, designed with flair, for niche markets. Over time, France also capitalized on homegrown innovations such as photography, the automobile, the removable pneumatic tire, and cinema.[7] The country was, for example, in 1903 the number one producer of cars, then a handcrafted luxury, though this leadership position did not long survive the introduction of Ford's Model T.

Between World War I and World War II, France lacked the large-scale corporate capitalism of Germany or the US. Businesses were almost all small or medium-sized family-owned firms. Their owners tended to be conservative and risk-averse, thanks in part to laws that treated bankruptcy as a near-criminal failure to honor obligations, rather than a regrettable inevitability in a world of shifting commercial fortunes. Domestically, markets were small and fragmented, limiting production runs and economies of scale, and highways were poor. The modern, at the time mainly American, concept of mass production and mass consumer markets, supplied by large, efficient plants and low-cost distribution, had made limited headway. Goods were generally either luxury items, at which France still excels, made by craft methods, or low-quality, not globally competitive, products for the home market.

The French economy during the first half of the twentieth century was inward-looking and protectionist (especially after the Great Depression hit), with both agriculture and industry sheltered from imports. Even product markets that were open to the world in theory were largely closed in practice by a tangled and inefficient distribution system. Many government interventions held the economy back, but few were designed to push it forward: "plenty of brakes but not much of a motor."[8] France's industrial backwardness spared it the worst effects of the Depression, but also limited the pressure on its manufacturing to reform.[9]

World War II

Because economies are not frictionless, they can – despite market pressures and incentives – get stuck in suboptimal ruts for lengthy periods until some disruptor comes along. For France, that disruptor was World War II.

While war raged, little could be done as Albert Speer's united European war economy systematically milked the country. By 1944, the index of French industrial production had tumbled from 100 in 1939 to 44.[10] But even then, some in France were preparing for recovery. The collaborationist Vichy regime made comprehensive plans to assert central direction over the French economy when the war ended. In 1943, inspired by the USSR and to a lesser extent the New Deal, the left-dominated National Council of the Resistance endorsed structural reforms intended to immunize France against another capitalist crisis like the Depression.[11] General Charles de Gaulle's provisional government of 1944–5 quietly used the Vichy plans as a base for its own eventual reconstruction strategy.

After the war, on essentially all points of the French political spectrum, there was a revulsion at the state of the nation that had enabled Germany to defeat it so quickly. The political details were complex, and many did not concern economics, but there was a near-universal sense that the old France had to go. Its old economic ideology was criticized not only for poor industrial performance but also for all the usual things people criticize about capitalism. As one historian has put it,

> Liberal capitalism also stood condemned for its disorganization and wastefulness, its partiality for *les gros* [almost literally, the fat cats], the bitter character of its industrial relations, its celebration of selfishness, and its flaccid performance. Vichy and the Resistance articulated reforms that, despite obvious differences, had much in common. Both sought a nationalist revival, social reconciliation, moral rehabilitation, a planned and more just economy, and a dynamic state.[12]

Some, of course, interpreted these issues as simply reason to turn left, and the socialist and communist parties were strong at this point. But they were not strong enough to impose their views. The French were unhappy with the distribution of private property, but not interested in abolishing it.

The obvious nonsocialist alternative model for an economy was not Germany, which had discredited itself as an evil enemy and lost the war. It was not Britain, which although victorious and an ally, had many of the same economic shortcomings as France and was fast becoming a financial ward of the US. It was the US itself, with its dazzlingly, even intimidatingly successful economy.

But the model for France was not the US in the "free markets are everything" sense in which contemporary Americans have been taught to conceive of their economy. Even if the US had been a pure free-market economy, France's political culture would not have been comfortable entrusting the economic fate of the nation to "uncontrolled" market forces, seen as both unethical and disturbingly "Anglo-Saxon." Instead, French economic reformers saw the essence of the US economy not as free markets but as *the link between efficient mass production and mass consumption.* In other words, the French chose to imitate the concrete US economy that actually existed – not the popular, abstract, and mistaken theory of how it worked. And because capitalism in France had not delivered a mass-production, mass-consumption economy on its own, state intervention was deemed necessary to achieve one.

Planning after World War II: Monnet

Postwar state direction or *dirigisme* began with the Monnet Plan of 1946, which established comprehensive industrial planning. Jean Monnet was an international businessman who enjoyed the confidence of FDR and Churchill and would later be known as the "Father of Europe" for his role in founding what became the EU.

De Gaulle put him in charge of creating the machinery for France's industrial recovery. Monnet built on the preparatory work done during the war.[13] His first Plan de modernisation et d'équipement, for 1946–50, became the cornerstone of France's subsequent growth. It aimed at not merely getting French industrial production back to prewar levels, but at increasing it by 50 percent. Its wider aim was to modernize the economy sufficiently to make France internationally competitive.

Monnet created the Commissariat Général du Plan (CGP), an independent body reporting directly to the prime minister, with himself as its first commissioner. Initially staffed by just 50 civil servants, it carried out the bulk of its work through Modernization Commissions. In 1946, there were 10 with 494 total members, and by 1963, there were 32 with 1,950 members. Over time, vertical commissions dealing with specific industry sectors were joined by horizontal commissions handling the likes of regional policy, manpower, and R&D.[14]

Targets for economic growth set by the CGP implied, in the words of one British economist,

> [A] relationship between public authority and private enterprise which is quite different from the tradition of the Anglo-American world. It belongs to the very stuff of the French tradition . . . ; [N]o other nation has so self-consciously fought to make a coherent system out of the devices which have been adopted more or less haphazardly elsewhere.[15]

This coherence, across the board, is what made French industrial policy effective. Capitalist central planning was underway.

Despite the overall statism, there were also green shoots of private enterprise in this era, with the stagnant old-fashioned family firm ceasing to be the norm and the legal framework for businesses becoming less restrictive. Business began to regain influence over policy after the Communists was expelled from the government in 1947, and private-sector business formation picked up beginning in 1949.[16] However, the industrial planning regime did not set as high technological standards for the private sector as for state-owned firms, clearly taking private companies less seriously as instruments of growth.[17]

While organized labor was initially given considerable input, "Once the concessions were extracted from industry, French political elites quickly and firmly pushed labor out of the coalition," making French industrial policy "an affair between the state and large firms," per one unhappy leftist commentator.[18] Two of the three main trade union groups withdrew from preparation of Monnet's Second Plan and did not return to the planning process until they helped socialist François Mitterrand gain power in 1981. By 1963, only 281 of the 2,138 members of the Commissions de Modernisation were trade unionists, compared with 1,267 employers and 781 civil servants.[19]

The university-level École Nationale d'Administration (ENA) was founded in 1945 to centralize recruitment to the civil service and provide future French administrations with the skills and attitudes appropriate to the task of directing the economy.[20] The leadership of both France's public and private sectors, at the highest levels, has for decades consisted largely of its alumni. (It was nominally replaced in 2022 by a new Institut National du Service Public.)

Nationalization and Modernization

Despite hostility toward industrial planning from an old guard of businessmen, France's new leaders rapidly extended state control over key sectors and established institutions to expand the state's ability to administer the economy. Gas, electricity, and coal were nationalized, as were Air France, pillars of French manufacturing such as carmaker Renault, and most large insurance firms.

Nationalization of the Banque de France, begun in 1936, was completed, and state control over the allocation of capital was extended by nationalizing several private banks, reducing the number of banks from 200 in 1946 to 69 by 1972.[21] The state established tight controls over more than half the country's total bank credit through the Banque de France and the state investment agency Caisse des Dépôts et de Consignations.[22]

Contra Marxism (a real force in France at the time), the planners, unlike in Britain, understood that *owning* the means of production is not what really counts. Controlling them is. So, even industries not nationalized were brought under state regulation. By the time François Mitterrand's leftist administration imposed further large-scale nationalizations in the early 1980s, the state already had most industries under its thumb.

The planners initially focused on industries believed strategic for their ability to kick-start the rest of the economy into recovery. These were steel, cement, coal, chemicals, tractors, fertilizers, transport, energy (mainly hydro-electricity), and automobiles. The first four were needed to rebuild and modernize other industries, the next two to modernize agriculture, and the last to earn foreign exchange to buy imports essential to reconstruction. Stimulating these would then, it was reasoned, drive demand in other industries, while planning would prevent supply bottlenecks.[23]

Reconstruction efforts were significantly helped by the US waiving $2 billon of France's World War I debts and by its contribution, between 1946 and 1953, of $58 billion in 2023 dollars of Marshall Plan aid. (At its height, Marshall aid was a quarter of government revenues.) In 1948, American aid accounted for 93 percent of publicly funded industrial investment – above all in the heavily nationalized sectors of electricity, gas, coal, railways, iron, and steel.[24] The agency set up in 1948 to apportion this aid, the Fonds de modernisation et d'équipement, became the main purveyor of financial assistance to industry. With the French savings rate inadequate (though it would soon grow), the planners used Marshall Plan and other funds for investment, which by 1949 comprised 20.5 percent of GNP, versus 13 percent in 1938.[25]

Results came quickly. By 1947, production was back to the level of 1938 and by 1953, had matched the prewar record set in 1929.[26] Throughout the 1950s, the economy grew an average of 4.6 percent annually.[27] The relatively small size of the domestic market, particularly right after the war, made it vital that firms buy French to induce positive feedback loops where development in one sector spurred another. Policies thus led, for example, to the electrical equipment industry – a beneficiary of purchasing by the national electric utility – being effectively controlled by the state.[28] State-owned industries were used as a yardstick to judge the performance of private firms, helping the state push the latter to up their technology and productivity game. And state ownership gave government a seat at the table on the same side as management, which was useful for managing the labor movement.

Planning Takes Hold

For the first 15 postwar years, France remained protectionist, with tariffs, quotas, import licensing, tariffs, nontariff barriers, and tight controls over access to foreign exchange. And by 1949, after 11 devaluations since 1928, it had a competitively priced currency.[29]

But for planning to work, there had to be not only control over imports but growth in exports – and as late as 1950, France's proportion of exports to GDP was lower than in 1929.[30] To promote exports, the public Banque Française du Commerce Extérieur was established to offer below-market loans to exporters. This was joined in 1946 by the Compagnie Française d'Assurance pour le Commerce Extérieur, a private but state-backed company to insure exporters against risks.

After Monnet left in 1952, French state intervention reached its apotheosis, as planners sought to ensure demand and supply matched in every sector.[31] They developed an intricate network of commitments from private firms: to invest in specified projects, to manufacture in a particular region, to adopt particular production techniques. In return, firms got favors from the state: generally cheap loans, from which 80 percent of business borrowers would benefit by the early 1960s.[32]

Crucially, these commitments were enforced and thus generally adhered to. The day-to-day role of a CGP official toward the industry he supervised became part management consultant, part banker, part bully – all to constantly pressure it to move in the direction desired by the planners.[33] It took until the early 1960s for most industrialists to truly get the message, but the desired shift to the mass-production, mass-consumption model eventually took hold.[34]

Industrial policy was informed by consensus with inputs from stake-holders passing through the CGP, which served as strategic lead and final arbiter. Planners continued to distinguish between economically strategic industries, the fulfillment of whose targets was essential to the overall success of the economy, and those that could be allowed to lag. This list of strategic industries changed as the economy evolved.

The Second Plan

The Second Plan (1953–7) aimed for a 25 percent increase in GDP – which was more than achieved.[35] While continuing to prioritize heavy industry, it set detailed targets across every sphere of manufacturing and broadened its scope to include housing construction, urban development, and scientific research.[36]

Planning became steadily more concerned with the relationships between different economic activities: specifically, to identify *bottlenecks* caused by an inadequate growth in supply, and *multipliers*, where an increase in demand at one point in the system would lead to growth at other points.[37]

Socialist prime minister Pierre Mendès-France agreed in 1954 to a "super-budget" that the planners could spend on industrial policy independent of normal parliamentary budgeting.[38] This was a sign of the depth of France's commitment to technocratic, as opposed to democratic or capitalist management of its economy, and of its belief that unelected bureaucrats could best discern and advance its economic interests.

The mid-1950s were the golden age of French industrial planning, as the needs of the economy closely matched the available policy tools and political pressures pushed planners toward appropriate goals that they could actually achieve. Despite political instability due to France's decolonization wars in Algeria and Vietnam, the most rapid productivity growth occurred during this period: 8 percent annually between 1955 and 1958, faster than any other European country.[39]

In this era, French industry first began mass-producing popular, good-quality consumer goods: the Renault Dauphine, the first popular French car not to resemble a tin box, and the Moulinex coffee grinder both made their debuts in 1956. It was also at this time (1952–3 and 1957) that France signaled its caution about the first tentative global steps to liberalize trade by opting out of certain provisions of the GATT under the pretext of combating inflation.[40]

The Third Plan

With incomes rising and pulling in discretionary purchases from abroad, the Third Plan (1957–61) concentrated on import substitution, not previously a major goal, to correct the balance of payments. Detailed growth projections, sector by sector, were coordinated with an overall program for resource allocation, with a goal of 20 percent GDP growth by 1961 – which was achieved.

The Third Plan was overshadowed by the launch of the European Economic Community (EEC) in 1957, consisting of France, Belgium, Italy, Luxembourg, Holland, and West Germany. Building on the European Coal and Steel Community founded in 1951, the EEC aimed to incrementally achieve free trade between its six members behind a common external tariff. There was near unanimity among the French that the EEC was essential to preventing Germany from ever starting another war, but France disliked the lowering of trade barriers because it would lose considerable policy autonomy. The country's planners suggested that the EEC as a whole should engage in coordinated industrial planning, but Germany, still hoping for economic dominance in Europe, rejected the idea.[41]

The Fourth Republic collapsed in 1958 and de Gaulle emerged from retirement to become president under a new constitution that concentrated economic power in the presidency. Planners now found themselves following orders, not making decisions.[42] Ministers made politically motivated appointments to the CGP, politically embarrassing projections disappeared from successive plans, and the modernization commissions were increasingly ignored.[43] The planners' golden age of autonomous power was over.

An increasingly sophisticated capitalist class had become reluctant to accept administrative tutelage. However, this attitude was offset by a growing interpenetration between big business and the bureaucracy, to a degree unimaginable in the US: By 1973, 43 percent of the heads of the largest companies were former civil servants.[44] And planning did not cease: While politicians, rather than planners, were now setting the agenda, that agenda was still tightly adhered to.

In the early years of de Gaulle's presidency, France was forced to accept *some* trade liberalization due to the 1960–1 Dillon Round of GATT and its EEC commitment to begin lowering trade barriers in 1962.[45] This liberalization, accepted only grudgingly, benefited the French economy because existing policy was too protectionist and the lowering was not excessive.

Corporate Consolidation

Trade liberalization created an actual and perceived need for French corporations large and powerful enough to compete internationally.

The prewar weakness of French industry had been partly due to its fragmentation, which left its firms smaller than their foreign rivals. To remedy this, French governments, especially after 1965, did all they could to build national champions, either by encouraging mergers or by focusing subsidies and other favors on a particular company.[46] Previously independent firms were melded by bureaucrats into giants such as Saint-Gobain-Pont-à-Mousson (building materials), Creusot-Loire (engineering, later steel), Dassault (aircraft), and Compagnie Générale D'électricité (electrical goods).

This policy had some successes: in 1958, only 1 of the world's largest 100 companies was French, but by 1970, 9 were.[47] Unfortunately, the policy also handed a blank check to a number of basket cases. A firm cannot simply expand its way out of trouble, and merging troubled firms with sound ones risks the health of the latter, especially when political imperatives to avoid layoffs interfere with the process of consolidation. Partly because of these problems, by the mid-to-late 1970s, the concept of a comprehensive array of national champions was scaled back to seeking dominance in a few niches.

From the late 1960s, ministers also began trying to foster competition by helping more than one company per sector. Thus, while some industries retained a single champion, in others the government, up to around 2000, backed two. In petroleum, there was Elf-Aquitaine and the firm successively known as Total SA, CFP, and Total CFP. In automobiles, there was Peugeot and Renault, and in telecom equipment, Alcatel and Thomson-CSF.

But France, in truth, has never really seen the point of competition.[48] As Prime Minister Raymond Barre explained in 1977, such antitrust machinery as it possesses is not supposed to "call in question the policy of industrial concentration that has been pursued for many years by successive governments." Since the European Single Market took effect in 1993, however, meaningful sanctions on monopolies have reluctantly been applied.

Today, French multinationals, few still state-owned but all kept under state influence, operate worldwide: AXA (insurance), Bouygues (construction and telecoms), Électricité de France (electricity, including exports of nuclear-generated electricity), Engie (environmental and utilities), LafargeHolcim (building materials), Orange (telephones), Renault (autos), Saint-Gobain (glass), Sanofi (pharmaceuticals), Thales (electrical and defense hardware), Total (petroleum), Veolia (waste, water, and energy), Vinci (construction), Vivendi (entertainment), and others.

Inbound Investment

Prior to the mid-1960s, France had encouraged foreign investment, at that time mainly coming from the US, because it was thought better for US companies to invest in France than elsewhere in Europe. But the warmth faded when de Gaulle fell out politically with Washington. Tighter controls were introduced, with France in vain urging the EEC to follow suit. In 1962, the Finance Ministry stated: "All potential investments are scrutinized carefully to ensure that they contribute substantially to French technology or business know-how, or provide aid to important but expensive lines of research ... We just object to anything that looks like speculation, a simple takeover, or an investment which France can perfectly well handle itself."[49]

A policy review in 1965 – the year of greatest Franco-American hostility, with 47 out of 138 applications rejected – set out criteria for "good" and "bad" foreign investments and raised concerns that excessive penetration would eliminate French firms or reduce them to satellites.[50] By the early 1970s, the concern was that entire sectors could fall under foreign ownership. British investments in food were rated "excessive," and paint and retail clothing were thought to be at risk.[51]

Concern about takeovers by foreign firms eager for a foothold in Europe had been an issue since the start of the EEC. France characteristically ignored the EEC's removal of restrictions, continuing until 1980 to make inward investments subject to government approval. Even after that, a two-month review period was required while a "French solution" was canvassed. One tool was delay, especially for US firms. (One French textile company went bankrupt while waiting.)

Hostility toward inward investment had its price, as foreign investors could locate elsewhere in the EEC and still export to France. Rebuffed by France, GM sited one new plant in Belgium instead. Ford pointedly built a factory just across the German border.[52] De Gaulle's successor, George Pompidou, brought a more welcoming attitude, his government proactively wooing Ford after its previous rejection, but takeovers by US firms remained a sore point.[53]

This preoccupation with creating or saving jobs at home has also led to governments at times preventing French companies from investing abroad, either by blocking the finance or simply by exerting pressure from on high, for fear that jobs would be exported. As late as 2004, by which point French firms could boast 19,000 subsidiaries worldwide, employing 3.5 million people, some commentators still argued that these jobs should have been in France.[54]

France's "Third Industrial Revolution"

In June 1966, de Gaulle withdrew France from the command structure of NATO. The resulting push for France to develop its own sophisticated armaments led to defense accounting for 70 percent of French sales in aerospace, 65 percent in electronics, 50 percent in shipbuilding, and 50 percent in nuclear power.[55] De Gaulle initiated a space program, with a launch base at Kourou in French Guiana – which two generations later became a viable commercial enterprise for launching satellites.

De Gaulle was also fixated on matching the US in nonmilitary technology. The result was, in the words of one observer, that,

> During the Gaullist period, as responses to the American challenge, government backed new ventures in high-technology industries. The so-called *grands projets* were designed to give France national independence in technologies associated with aircraft, space, nuclear weapons, nuclear energy, oil drilling and refining, computers, and electronics. In the 1970s the high-technology industries that had been promoted in the 1960s were able to achieve noticeable success in world markets, even challenging American leadership in military and civilian aeronautics, helicopter production, and nuclear engineering.[56]

France's "Third Industrial Revolution" was thus underway just as, from the end of the Fifth Plan in 1970, the planning process became less rigid.

The oil price shock of 1973 showed France's industrial planners at their best. Within weeks, the world's most ambitious nuclear power program was launched. Électricité de France was encouraged to open six new reactors a year and the nuclear engineering industry was reorganized. The pressure vessels were provided by Framatome, a joint venture between France's Atomic Energy Commission and the firm Schneider (French despite its name), while the generators were built by Alstom.[57] By 1984, the industry would employ 150,000 people and 80 percent of France's electricity would be nuclear. (One byproduct is that the country now has the one of the lowest per capita carbon footprints and some of the cleanest air in Western Europe.) Since then, with most Western countries scrapping or pausing their nuclear power programs, the French industry has become a world leader, focusing on exports.[58] China, Russia, South Korea, and France are today the only significant exporters of nuclear power plants.

Driven by an assertive industrial policy, between 1960 and 1973 French GDP growth averaged 5.8 percent. Of the major industrial nations, only Japan and Spain grew faster.[59] And in 1962, for the first time in over a century, per capita GDP overtook Britain.[60] Convinced of its natural role as a world leader, France even touted its economic planning as a middle way between supposed American laissez-faire and Soviet central planning.

Failure in Computers: 1966–2014

France also had major industrial policy failures. The Plan Calcul, launched in 1966 to make France independent in the design and manufacture of scientific computers, was in part a response to GE's attempted acquisition of Machines Bull, France's leading computer company, and in part a response to America's refusal to sell France the high-performance models it needed for nuclear weapons research.[61] Ministers vetoed the GE deal in 1964, then allowed it on worse terms after realizing that reorganizing Bull under French ownership would not create a viable national champion.[62]

To reestablish a French presence in the industry, the government created an enterprise, CII, owned partly by the state and partly by Thomson and CGE, then supported it with research grants and public procurement.[63] But CII struggled, and in 1975 was merged with Bull to form CII-HB. A plan for integrated circuits was initiated in 1976, five French firms receiving subsidies and procurement support. Technology-sharing agreements were signed with leading US companies and the electronic components industry was restructured around Thomson and Matra.[64]

By 1985, Groupe Bull was one of Europe's largest computer companies, but struggled to win the orders outside France it needed to become viable. Bull was nationalized in 1982, reprivatized in 1994, and in 2014 taken over by Atos, one of the new generation of French multinationals. In the meantime, it had expanded into defense, finance, healthcare, manufacturing, and telecom to more than 100 countries. But it never became the mainframe computing giant de Gaulle had hoped for, and the PC revolution passed it by. Jean Monnet's planners probably would never have backed such a politically motivated project.

1973–1981: Decade of Crisis

The Sixth Plan was on course to meet its target of 7.5 percent annual growth in industrial production (entailing GDP growth of 5.8–6.0 percent) until the oil crisis of 1973 quadrupled the price of oil. At this point, what the French call *Les Trente Glorieuses* ("the thirty glorious years") came to an abrupt end. A decade of crisis and upheaval began.

Stiffer competition in trade was emerging, especially from the newly industrializing nations of East Asia. From 1974 to 1982, despite heavy government support, French shipbuilding lost 25,000 jobs, steelmaking 80,000, and textiles 175,000.[65] Traditional manufacturing thus joined agriculture in slow, featherbedded decline.

Pompidou, in office from 1969, moved the center of economic planning from the presidential Élysée Palace to the Industry Ministry and set up agencies to tackle regional economic problems. France's steel, textile, footwear, and leather goods industries were all being exposed as uncompetitive, so, under the Sixth Plan (1970–5), *plans sectoriels* were developed for each. A system of "warning lights" was introduced to alert the government when goals being missed. Clearly, the planners had lost the initiative and were being forced into reactive mode.[66]

Overall, the *plans sectoriels* were not a success, as they focused on two all-but-impossible tasks.[67] Some aimed to revitalize labor-intensive industries, such as footwear, that had become uneconomic, outside specialty segments, in all developed nations. Others aimed to fix industries, such as steel, that were still viable there but whose capital-intensiveness, combined with overoptimistic expansion and the difficulty of closing old plants, had induced worldwide overcapacity.

By 1974, France was producing 27 million tons of steel a year, but with too many workers and producers saddled with debt.[68] French industries using bulk steel were declining and those that survived were finding alternative materials. With overcapacity at 40 percent by 1977, the industry lost $3.5 billion in three years.[69] In 1978, government took on half the industry's medium- and long-term debt, converting some into equity to become its principal shareholder.[70] Because almost every European steelmaker had similar problems, the European Commission declared a "manifest crisis" in steel. The Commission then used its powers to curb capacity and promote efficiency, after which the industry was returned to the private sector.[71] This rare assertion of industrial policy from Brussels had some medium-term benefits, but did not keep the problem from recurring later.

1973–1981: Decade of Transition

The economies of all developed nations were transitioning at this time toward industries less tractable to the old planning techniques. The top-down planning that had been so successful was proving "a clumsy instrument when it came to anticipating and organising the production and distribution of consumer goods and semi-durables."[72] Employment in service industries, similarly unworkable under central control, reached 50 percent of France's total in this era.

As some of the national champions of the 1960s began to falter, misgivings emerged as to whether size was the true determinant of international competitiveness. The loss-makers among them were a heavy drain on the public purse, forcing them into conflict with every other spending priority and creating pressures to become profitable or close. They were increasingly no longer expected to dominate all parts of their markets, but particular niches.

Pompidou's successor, Valéry Giscard d'Estaing, who took office in 1974, flirted with what was supposedly a market-oriented industrial policy, his economy minister declaring: "I want to remove the administration from day-to-day management of the economy . . . Industrial policy means nothing. It is not up to the state to choose the way to the future, it is up to the leaders of business."[73] Giscard slashed the Modernization Commissions from 2,900 people to 650, downgraded the CGP to think-tank status, and established, in its place, the highly political Central Planning Council in the presidential office.[74]

Giscard thus *sounded* less enamored of state direction and *grands projets*. But in practice, he drove advances in nuclear power and telecom, plus preparations for the TGV high-speed rail network, all de facto *grands projets*. Despite his free-market rhetoric, his government rescued niche industries such as machine tools, footwear, leather goods, watches, and clocks.[75] It maintained 150 programs of aid to industry, primarily to keep the usual declining sectors afloat.[76] It channeled 2.7 percent of GDP to industrial subsidies: Steel got $625 million, aeronautics $625 million, computers $208 million, and shipbuilding $313 million.[77]

Giscard's prime minister, Raymond Barre, set out to improve companies' managerial capabilities, balance sheets, and autonomy so that they, rather than the state, could shoulder prime responsibility for countering foreign competition. Conveniently for politicians who took the credit when times were good, this meant firms now took the blame for failures. Fearful of challenging the social consensus, government indulged organized labor by declining to reform excessively expensive social benefits and an inflexible system of labor-market regulation that made it almost impossible to lay off workers.[78]

On the trade front, in 1978, the government declared that Japan would be restricted to 3 percent of the auto market and blocked car shipments at customs until Tokyo got the message.[79]

The years after 1973 did see some new industries emerge and grow: Employment rose to 300,000 in electronics, 150,000 in nuclear and electrical engineering, and 100,000 in aerospace.[80] These jobs were the fruits of the industrial policies of the previous decade. And in 1981, one of the most successful *grands projets*, the TGV, opened its first route, generating exports sales as several foreign countries adopted its technology.

Giscard's channeling of resources into exports heavily reliant on state-to-state sales (arms, aircraft, and turnkey plants) and into massive capital projects (France's telephone system, nuclear plants, and TGV) improved France's infrastructure and export performance. But it left the consumer goods sector vulnerable to import penetration, so in this era, Germany and Japan increasingly took French markets for cars, electronics, and consumer durables.[81]

Airbus

Aircraft manufacturing has probably been the single biggest sectoral success of French industrial policy. France began to carve out a position in civil and military aircraft in the 1950s with the Caravelle airliner and the Mystère jet fighter. In 1967, it set out to collaborate with Britain and West Germany on airliners, forming a consortium that morphed in 1970 into Airbus. (Britain pulled out in 1969, rejoining later as a junior partner.) Airbus's first product – the A300, the first twin-engine, wide-body airliner – attracted no orders for its first two years and without government support the venture would have collapsed. But by 1978, a steady stream of orders was flowing and the project was vindicated.

By the mid-1980s, France was second only to the US as an aircraft producer. Airbus has since gone from strength to strength and now, as part of EADS, is under French control with German participation. Its only failure has been the A380, the world's largest airliner, which attracted few buyers and was taken out of production in 2021. Airbus's export sales have received strong financial and diplomatic backing. In 2004, the US filed a complaint against the EU at the WTO, accusing it of illegally subsidizing Airbus. The EU launched a countercomplaint, alleging American support for Boeing through military contracts, state-level tax concessions, and other means. (The dispute dragged on until 2021, when the Biden administration and EU leaders negotiated a settlement).

By the mid-1980s, France's aerospace sector was dominated by three companies: SNIAS (civil aircraft, helicopters, missiles, space launchers, and satellites), Dassault-Breguet (military aircraft), and SNECMA (aircraft engines). Other players included Matra (missiles and satellites), Turbomeca (helicopter engines), and Messier-Hispano (aircraft engines). And in 1984, Arianespace began the world's first commercial space launch operation, quickly capturing a large share of the market.

The main industrial policy instruments in the aerospace sector have been procurement by the state and Air France (effectively the same thing), subsidized research, subsidized exports, and "industrial diplomacy," including outright bribes on a scale and degree of brazenness not generally matched by France's Western competitors.

1981–1984: The Last Hurrah of the Left

A second oil price shock in 1979 reinforced the effects of the first, making further structural adjustment essential. But the elections of May–June 1981 that swept socialist Francois Mitterrand to power made this impossible. Backed by organized labor and the still-significant Communist Party (reentering government for the first time in 30 years), Mitterrand was committed to reflation, job creation, and the expansion of industry across the board, largely under direct state ownership.

It was to be the last hurrah of the economic left in France. The problem was not only Mitterrand's attempt to reverse economic liberalization, but the multitude of different voices now involved in what had always been a top-down policy. Mitterrand's parliamentary majority was divided between Marxists who wanted a completely socialized economy, leftists who wanted worker control, and center-left elements who merely wanted conventional left-wing goals such as greater equality.[82]

Several ministries now contended to set industrial policy and professional planners were kept even further from the process. The real decisions were taken by the Finance Ministry, which controlled the purse strings.[83] Mitterrand's recipe for tackling stagflation and unemployment was ambitious. Gambling on a rapid global recovery, he set out to create 500,000 jobs in two years, most of them in the public sector, and to lower the retirement age.[84] The workweek was cut to 39 hours and workers were guaranteed five weeks' paid holiday.[85]

Mitterrand's presidency up to 1984 indeed marked a watershed, but not as he had intended. Hitherto, the avowed aims of France's main political parties with regard to the capitalist system had been to terminate it (communists), reform it (socialists), or tame and reorganize it (Gaullists). All aspired to dictate guidelines for corporate management.[86] Only the Gaullist option survived his term, and that in sharply modified form.

Mitterrand initially reasserted the policy of national champions, through a combination of nationalization, semi-forced mergers, and subsidies to rustbelt industries. This challenged one of the fundamentals of postwar French industrial policy: that some industries had better futures and should therefore receive the greatest support. His stated premise, in the words of his industry minister Pierre Dreyfus, was that "there are no doomed industries, only outmoded technologies."[87] Conveniently, stimulating all industries put off the politically sensitive selection of some for abandonment.[88]

Individual companies were asked to merge, increase spending on R&D, increase production and employment, increase the export share of production, or modify specific product lines. In return, government agreed to help finance their investments, increase public training of skilled labor, buy more of their products, and stimulate private-sector purchases.[89]

But as it became evident that certain economic activities were indeed no longer viable in France, emphasis shifted to a policy of supporting *filières*, or vertical streams of production. There was an electronics *filière* (the most developed), a metallurgical *filière*, an agrochemical *filière*, and so on. The *filière* approach was to some extent a repackaging of the old policy of sheltering French industries, as, for example, it rejected the increasingly obvious reality that consumer electronics would be produced mainly in East Asia.

Mitterrand's nationalization program of 1981–2 reads like a *Who's Who* of the French economy: Usinor (steel), Sacilor (steel), CII-HB (computers), Thomson-Brandt (electronics), CGE (electricals), Rhône-Poulenc (chemicals), Saint-Gobain (building and packaging materials), Suez (mainly banking, also gas, water, and media), Paribas (banking), Rothschild (banking), and 35 other banks.[90] The state ended up owning 13 of France's largest firms outright, with its holdings in the industrial and energy sectors accounting for 24 percent of employees, 32 percent of sales, 30 percent of exports, and 60 percent of investment.[91]

But before long, the government was discovering that there are problems with nationalizing companies to achieve quick results. Large businesses can expand only so fast. The investment used to expand them starves smaller firms of capital. Companies cannot adopt every social goal without harming their global competitiveness. And restructuring for efficiency is harder for nationalized firms, not easier, because of political pressures to avoid layoffs.[92]

The French planning process declined from the high standard of previous decades. The newly nationalized giants were no longer given carefully structured long-range objectives, but relatively crude specifications of what they were to accomplish and what state support they would get over three to five years. And they were subject to day-to-day interference from ministers. In many cases, Mitterrand's nationalizations did not even change much, as they simply formalized state control over private industry that was already far greater than in other Western countries.[93]

Having come to power with many of France's key industries – steel, textiles, machine tools, coal, shipbuilding, furniture, toys, and parts of chemicals – in chronic decline, Mitterrand's ministers devised plans for their revival.[94] Even coal, where production had halved in a decade, took on new workers, though the decline in demand for coal only accelerated. More successfully, the chemicals sector was restructured into three massive, initially state-owned firms: CDF-Chimie and Elf-Aquitaine for heavy chemicals, and Rhône-Poulenc for specialty products.[95]

The most ambitious new investment – $23 billion over five years – went into electronics, hailed by Mitterrand as "our weapon of the future." A target of 80,000 new jobs was set. France was strong in this sector in some areas already subject to active industrial policy, such as telecommunications and heavy equipment for defense and broadcasting. But it was weak in others, such as office equipment, robotics, and scientific instruments. Four giant state-owned firms were created: Thomson, CIT-Alcatel, Matra, and Groupe Bull. Four sponsoring ministries backed them, using state procurement and R&D funding as the main tools.

The Great U-Turn

At first, Mitterrand's Keynesian demand stimulation worked: The rise in unemployment slowed, and France's 2 percent growth outpaced most other European countries. But the resulting boom pulled in imports and, with the global economy too weak to take increased French exports, France developed a large trade deficit. In October 1981, the franc was devalued, with West Germany insisting on French budget cuts as the price of accepting a revaluation of the franc within the European Monetary System (EMS) of managed exchange rates.[96] June 1982 marked the end of fiscal expansion and austerity now supposedly set in. But the vast sums spent on nationalized industry to insulate it against the vagaries of "business confidence" continued.[97]

Losses had soared, but propping up steel, coal, and shipbuilding was proving financially unsustainable and in breach of tightening EC antisubsidy rules.[98]

Mitterrand's agenda finally collapsed in May 1984 and the entire package of neo-socialist policies was abandoned. The communists bolted the government, and their credibility and mass support never recovered. The new premier, Laurent Fabius, wanted state-owned industries to at least break even, and to show he meant business, the massive steel firm Creusot-Loire was allowed to go under – the largest bankruptcy in French history. (Its viable parts were spun off after management rejected a rescue plan that would have handed control to the banks.)[99] Shipbuilding capacity was sharply reduced, coal production cut by 30 percent in four years, and one in three steelmaking jobs eliminated.[100] Even relatively new steel plants were closed if they were poorly sited, technologically backward, or produced outmoded products.

The age of blanket support was clearly over. From this point forward, almost half of state support for industry was concentrated on five large enterprises: CGE, Thomson-CSF, Groupe Bull, Dassault, and the Franco-Belgian heavy engineering company Empain-Schneider.[101] All were in sectors believed, with varying degrees of rationality, to have viable futures. France's scope for industrial policy continued to narrow. Closer European integration, increasingly deregulated international finance, and growing commitments to open markets under the GATT/WTO all reduced its freedom of action. As did, from 1983, a commitment to hold the franc steady against the mark, anchor of the EMS.

From this point on, although France did not turn to "American-style" laissez-faire, it did accept that it would have to compromise with rather than defy the economic forces of the outside world. Nevertheless, Paris has still, according to economic historian Jean-Pierre Dormois, "sought to evade, rather than confront, the challenges of the global economy."[102] It has only grudgingly accepted that entrepreneurship is necessary and valuable rather than a necessary evil tolerated for jobs and tax revenues.[103] The mentality that industry exists as a sort of social program, rather than to make things people want at a price they are willing to pay, still lives. The same goes for the crude economic nationalism that fetishizes economic sovereignty but lacks any strategy for using it in the national economic interest.

1984–1999: Compromise with the Market

Elections in 1986 left the socialist Mitterrand with a right-wing (by French standards) premier, Jacques Chirac. This arrangement worked surprisingly well, Mitterrand having tired of economic radicalism. Chirac immediately embarked on a program of deregulation, with growth recovering to 3.1 percent by 1989.[104]

While this government could not be described as internationalist (few French administrations have been), it did show a greater openness in commercial dealings with the outside world. The last restrictions on banking were lifted, which brought a proliferation of lenders offering credit to business and weakened the power of the Treasury as a tool of industrial policy. Government returned several nationalized banks to the private sector. And starting in the mid-1980s, Britain deregulated its financial markets, increasing liquidity throughout the EU.

The EEC's Single European Act of 1986 paved the way for the Single Market in 1992, which swept away the remaining, mainly nontariff, barriers to trade between EU members. To prepare for the 2002 creation of the euro, currencies were coordinated and eventually locked into the Exchange Rate Mechanism (ERM). This took even more power away from the French Treasury, as monetary policy and some financial policy were now decided in Brussels. But within the diminished range now possible, France continued to pursue its economic interests, to the point of ignoring EU policy and even legislation when necessary.

Many large French firms were restructured behind the shield of government ownership, then sold to French shareholders embedded in networks of cross-shareholdings that prevented foreigners from buying controlling interests.[105] More important French companies thus remained in French hands than would have under free-market conditions, an arrangement lasting until roughly 2000.

Neither did France passively agree to greater global economic integration, especially on terms it had not designed. In 1992, over the issue of farm subsidies, Jacques Delors, the French president of the European Commission, did his best to abort the Uruguay Round of GATT talks that led to the creation of the WTO. He tried to sink a deal between Washington and the British trade commissioner, using the customary argument that French agriculture was uniquely threatened and that Gallic culture was being left at the mercy of "Anglo-Saxon" influence.[106]

France was now fighting a rearguard action against what it called "social dumping" – that is, multinationals moving production to countries with lesser social obligations on business. Paris worked with Germany and the Benelux countries to promote a "European social model" under which each would undertake to set similar standards, but some EEC members, notably Britain under Thatcher, refused to cooperate. And after the fall of the Berlin Wall in 1989, firms were leaving France for the lower-wage economies of former communist countries of Eastern Europe.

Chirac became president in his own right in 1995, setting in train even more vigorous deregulation and privatization. Automaker Renault was privatized in 1996 (government keeping 46 percent and thereafter gradually reducing its stake) and also the Elf oil company, in which the government retained a "golden share" until Elf merged with Franco-Belgian TotalFina in 2000.

Though privatization was not carried out to attract FDI, in some cases it opened the door for mergers with foreign firms. Steel was privatized, then the resulting firm merged with Luxembourgish and Spanish producers to form Arcelor. These sales brought the government between 70 and 100 billion francs.[107] Even sacred cows like naval shipbuilders were privatized, though in practice this often meant shuffling activities between companies in which the state had either a controlling interest or a "golden share" conferring veto power over key corporate decisions.

2000–2007: Stagnation and Response

In 2000, France had one of the EU's highest unemployment rates.[108] (Its competitiveness had not been helped by the adoption of a 35-hour workweek that year.) One French economic historian put it thus:

> In 2000, as in 1900, a number of privileged activities benefited from government protection and support, including agriculture and a host of public services; today's prevalent egalitarianism ... remains suspicious of the market economy, but taxpayers are increasingly unwilling to bear the cost of a redistributive machinery which has become harder and harder to maintain ... High unemployment and gradual demotion in terms of per capita income have been the price France has had to pay for its this procrastination. The French, once among the keenest supporters of European integration, are now the slowest nation but one when it comes to aligning legislation on European directives.[109]

Doubts also emerged whether France's supposedly stellar commitment to R&D was doing much for its manufacturing outside elite industries.

In response to the national concern about underperformance, Prime Minister Jean-Pierre Raffarin set up a task force under Jean-Louis Beffa, chief executive of Saint-Gobain. The resulting report, *Pour Une Nouvelle Politique Industrielle (For a New Industrial Policy)*, presented in 2005, pulled no punches.[110] French manufacturing, it concluded, was "starting to lose ground," due primarily to focusing on activities not based on R&D.

Beffa recommended creating Industrial Innovation Stimulation Programs (PMIIs in French) with 5–15-year timeframes. These would identify and pursue industrial opportunities involving major technological innovations and new, growing European or global markets. They would foster partnerships between companies large and small and governmental, university, and private labs. The partnerships would be given subsidies and below-market-rate loans (at the pre-competitive stages of development allowed by EU rules). They would be administered by an Industrial Innovation Agency (IIA), which would match private-sector investments from a budget of €2 billion a year by 2007.[111] Once in place, the IIA did spread state-funded R&D to more sectors and push large firms to innovate, but it soon became evident it would concentrate on developing national champions in areas such as nanotechnology, biotech, and renewables, only indirectly encouraging startups and university spin-offs.

Meanwhile, responding to public outrage at an attempt by PepsiCo to take over the yogurt maker Danone, President Jacques Chirac in 2005 endorsed what became known as the Loi Danone that protected 11 strategic sectors of French industry from foreign takeovers. Nevertheless, France finally accepted that its steel industry was no longer a strategic asset by allowing the Luxembourg company that already owned Arcelor to be taken over by India's Mittal.

2008–2016: Crisis and Reform

The 2008 global financial crisis struck with the center-right Nicolas Sarkozy newly installed as president. Casting himself as a reformer championing a clean break with the existing ruling elite, he advocated cutting taxes, slimming down the public sector, and reviving the work ethic. Yet *The Economist* also quoted him as saying, with satisfaction, "The main feature of this crisis is the return of the state, the end of the ideology of public powerlessness." And soon after, he approved a $7.6 billion loan to Renault and PSA Peugeot Citroen to keep their French plants open.

France's unique response to the downturn was the creation of a Strategic Investment Fund and the unveiling in 2009 of the *Grand Emprunt* ("big loan") – $53 billion of state support for forward-looking strategic investments. Higher education and training were to receive $16.5 billion; industrial, health, and biotech research $12 billion; industry, especially aviation, space, autos, rail, and shipbuilding $9.8 billion; digital infrastructure $6.8 billion; and sustainable development $7.5 billion.[112] The rest would go for state investments in digital, biotech, nanotech, and carbon reduction. This increased the impact of the IIA and strengthened the link between innovation and creation of saleable products.

Socialist François Hollande became president in 2012 facing yet another auto industry crisis, and responded with $9 billion in guarantees to PSA Peugeot Citroën to avert layoffs.[113] Despite his Mitterrand-era socialist rhetoric, he recognized new thinking was needed and commissioned a report from Louis Gallois, the former head of several major state-owned companies.[114] The report concluded that France needed a "competitiveness shock" to prompt rollback of its excessive regulation, above all in the labor market, and a sharp reduction in social welfare spending.[115] Its 22 proposals included more worker training, government-funded research, incentives for private investment, and corporate tax cuts. The government incurred considerable public outcry by implementing most of them *except* for the cuts to social spending.

2017–2022: Innovation and Europeanization

By the time centrist outsider Emmanuel Macron took office in 2017, France was boasting that it had the third largest number (12) of companies and research centers in the Clarivate Analytics Top 100 Global Innovators.[116] Firms included Arkema (advanced materials), Safran (aerospace components), Thales (defense systems), Saint-Gobain (construction and other materials), Alstom (railroad equipment), Total (petroleum), and Valeo (auto parts). There was even a breakthrough in consumer electronics, where France had struggled for decades: At the 2018 Consumer Electronics Show in Las Vegas, 361 French firms were represented, versus 1,329 from China and just 73 from Britain.[117]

Through his La French Tech initiative, announced in 2019, Macron intensified the strategies he inherited. This program further incentivized start-ups, streamlined the legal framework for growing a business, and enhanced France's R&D tax credits to make them, according to the OECD, the most attractive in Europe.[118] By 2020, 12 percent of French private-sector jobs were under foreign control, and by 2022, France was hosting 16,900 foreign-owned businesses.

Around this time, France began advocating an EU-wide industrial strategy, though this met opposition from the more laissez-faire member states. This would have allowed, for example, the creation of European champions such as the proposed Alstom-Siemens Franco-German merger of 2018. That merger was blocked by the European Commission, and in response, Paris and Berlin began a push to change EU competition rules.[119]

As in Germany, the press of Chinese mercantilism has caused an increase in French support for an EU industrial strategy. Serious official discussions in Brussels began in 2019 and the European Commission has since made specific plans in the areas of high technology and the environment.[120]

More recently, France and other EU countries have elevated the issue of "European strategic autonomy." This concept was initially pushed by France with respect to national security, but the COVID crisis revealed vulnerabilities in pharmaceuticals and other essential goods, expanding its scope to include virtually all aspects of EU public policy, and specifically, mitigating dependence on China.[121]

Strengths

- History and ideology supportive of proactive government direction of the economy.
- Sound underlying idea of achieving economic development by imitating the most developed nation.
- During period of greatest success, planners isolated from political pressures.
- Coordinated, coherent use of the full panoply of industrial policy tools.
- Close relationships between highly competent elite graduates in senior government and private-sector leadership positions.
- Ability to learn, albeit with a delay, from mistakes and to abandon outdated policies.
- Generally effective resistance to financialization of the economy. (See Chapter 18.)

Weaknesses

- Choice of industries for support sometimes made on economically irrational grounds: politics, prestige, preservation of doomed jobs.
- Historically, top-down planning led to ineffective research and commercialization support for startups and small companies.
- Absence of a startup culture, venture capital firms, and effective support of university spin-offs.
- At times, overreliance on nationalization per se as a solution to market, technological, and management problems.
- Inflexible labor laws that discourage new investment and impede necessary downsizing, plus adversarial labor–management relations that make technological upgrading difficult.
- Slow, inefficient, ineffective responses to global overcapacity in declining industries like steel and coal.
- A cultural mentality often hostile to basic realities of capitalism.

10 BRITAIN
No Theory and Little Execution

British manufacturing has shrunk relentlessly since 1945, and the country today accounts for less than 2 percent of the world's manufactured exports.[1] But as late as 1950, the UK was second only to the US as a technology and manufacturing power, accounting for 25.4 percent of this same figure.[2] Its auto, aircraft, and shipbuilding industries were the world's second largest. The country pioneered radar, computers, nuclear power, television, jet airliners, and more.

Since then, important industries have either vanished or sharply declined. Aerospace barely retains the capacity to develop an airframe, and merchant shipbuilding is all but gone. The auto industry nearly collapsed amid shop-floor anarchy before stabilizing under foreign ownership as the world's eleventh largest. Computer maker ICL long ago vanished into Japanese ownership. Britain's new generation of nuclear power stations will be built by French firms. Manufacturing of consumer electronics has effectively ceased. And except for pharmaceuticals, British technological innovations have mostly been commercialized by others.

These facts explain why Britain has become an exemplar of ineffective industrial policy. It was inevitable that its share of world manufacturing output would fall as it grew more slowly than nations experiencing catch-up growth. But its decline did not have to be so precipitous. Its European peers have done better at retaining advantageous industries and their jobs. As Britain's *Financial Times* noted in 2022, "On present trends, the average Slovenian household will be better off than its British counterpart by 2024, and the average Polish family will move ahead before the end of the decade."[3]

A Self-Inflicted Decline

Some Americans have blamed British decline on socialism and the failure, until Margaret Thatcher in 1979, to subdue the trade unions and pursue free markets. The reality is far more complex.

Several European countries with economies that are more socialist than Britain's outperformed it. And Britain's private sector has plenty to answer for. Unimaginative, hidebound management tolerated poor quality, amateurish salesmanship, outdated production technology, underinvestment, and archaic working practices for decades. It was slow to embrace new markets. British culture's obsession with social class inflamed union militancy and produced an elite that looked down on manufacturing. The educational system failed to teach skills essential to industry, from basic shop skills to modern management practices. (Britain today has a decent, albeit small, apprenticeship system, but it arrived decades too late to save manufacturing.)

Despite the nominal commitment, for decades, to socialist planning, the reality was an *absence* of real strategic direction. Governments had no coherent economic theory as to how proactive industrial policy could deliver better results than laissez-faire. They lacked a framework for translating economic theory into policy. And they largely lacked institutions and mechanisms for implementing the policies they did arrive at.

Britain's leadership failed to coordinate among government, business, finance, and labor. That leadership believed it was not the job of government officials (outside a few niches) to be involved with industry, or even to know much about it. Industry was regarded as something that should be left in the hands of blunt-spoken men from the north of England. Until 1970, there was no government department with the word "industry" in its name. And until 1975, the all-important Treasury, keeper of the purse strings, had minimal policy responsibility for, or even understanding of, manufacturing.[4]

Government was thus oblivious to important emerging trends in industry and forced into reactive mode with minimal understanding. A cadre of industry experts exists today, but it emerged only decades later and its expertise is still often ignored. Government often only became aware that British firms were in trouble when complaints came in about unfair foreign competition, dumping, and the labeling of foreign products as British-made.[5] As late as 1961, Britain was directly spending more than $760 million a year on its agriculture but less than $140 million on industry, a derisory sum compared to its peers.[6]

No frameworks for even a partial industrial policy were developed in the immediate postwar years, with the first attempts made from 1962 to 1970 and from 1972 to 1979. Even these regimes were largely stillborn: They were fragmented, lacked clear objectives, and had no "controlling mind" at the center. They relied on industry and unions to provide vision and leadership – which neither was interested in doing.

Ironically, British interventionism's very *lack* of energy or strategy limited the harm it could do. The results of this laissez-faire by default were poor nonetheless. Interventionism, mild but ineffective, was incrementally discredited in both parties long before the Thatcher years of the 1980s. But governments were forced by recurrent crises to intervene anyway. The resulting failures instilled an antipathy to picking winners, which then bred a failure to support key industries as globalization intensified.[7]

There were other problems. Britain, no longer a leader in military technology, never reaped the vast benefits the US derived from military spin-offs (see Chapter 26). Nevertheless, delusions of grandeur caused it, for a long time, to overconcentrate governmental support for R&D on defense.[8] It also made defense procurement decisions that wounded strategically important technology companies. Indecision destroyed Britain's civil nuclear and turbine industries. It is the only country to develop the capacity to launch satellites and then just abandon it. It tolerated, even sought, an overvalued currency for decades.

1939–1945: Background

On the eve of World War II, the UK had been losing ground to the US and Germany for two generations but was still the world's leading exporter of manufactures: 22.3 percent of the global market in 1937, compared with 20.1 percent for the US and 19.5 percent for Germany.[9]

During the war, government intervened in industry to an unprecedented degree. It was the prime purchaser of both war materiel and essential civilian goods. It succeeded in devoting a greater percentage of GDP to war production than totalitarian Germany, imposing the most comprehensive direction of the labor force of any combatant save the USSR.[10] Government required labor–management Joint Production Committees in key factories, with pay bargaining in the hands of national union leaders.

But while America's economy grew 70 percent from 1939 to 1945, Britain's grew only 17 percent.[11] The US, unlike Britain, was able to make massive investments in new industrial plants *before* entering the war at scale. Nonetheless, propaganda gave the electorate the impression that the UK had achieved an economic miracle.[12] This contrasted sharply with the economy's performance during the previous Depression decade, when laissez-faire capitalism seemed to have discredited itself.

As victory neared, the idea that wartime planning had vindicated a state-controlled economy took hold. Thus, postwar British economic organization was decided on a bipartisan Labour–Conservative basis while war still raged. The famous Beveridge Report that laid the foundations of the welfare state was published in November 1942. The goal of full employment, passionately desired due to the mass unemployment of the 1930s and expected to be achieved by Keynesian deficit spending, was agreed to by Churchill's Conservative–Labour national unity government in 1944.

1945–1952: Planning Promised and Unfulfilled

A Labour government under Clement Attlee took power in 1945. Its mild, democratic socialism consisted of a comprehensive welfare state plus nationalization of the "commanding heights" of the economy. It favored a mixed economy, then emerging as the European norm, with a powerful but not overwhelming state sector and much private enterprise continuing alongside.

The economic situation was grim. Staple foods were scarce: Rationing did not fully end until 1954. Britain had foreign debts of $145 billion in today's dollars, then the largest in history. Priorities thus were a) to boost exports to earn dollars to pay off these debts, and b) to maintain the international value of the pound in a misguided effort to protect its reserve currency status.

Under these straitened circumstances, in its 1945 manifesto Labour committed itself to economic planning. Industrial policy was supposedly based on four principles:[13]

1. The primacy of Parliament, as opposed to technocrats, in major decisions
2. Economic management through consensual tripartite negotiation between business, labor, and government
3. Promoting efficiency through more technocratic management in larger industrial units
4. Collective bargaining between capital and labor free of state interference

These commitments paved the way in 1947 for Development Councils in key industries. This established, on paper, forums for classic labor-capital-state collaboration.[14] And because of its significance for the balance of payments, government had already taken control of inbound foreign investment.[15] With other new agencies covering financing and the control of monopolies, all the instruments for the most comprehensive system of planning in any Western country seemed to be in place.

But Britain did not put all this machinery to work. For a start, there were huge gaps in the principles it had adopted. Who would actually be *deciding* the industrial plan? The elected government? A stand-alone commission with executive powers? Some mechanism for giving labor a voice? What was the relationship of private industry to planning?

Labour never set any clear industrial policy *goals*, let alone mechanisms to realize them. The greater advantageousness of certain economic activities and industries was not understood, nor why the free market would not realize them on its own. No steps were taken to train a technologically literate bureaucracy. And Attlee's concern to take all major economic decisions to the Cabinet meant that no detailed planning could take place.

The result was paralysis. Collaborative bodies with labor and management representatives were duly set up in key sectors. But government could not decide whether they should be advisory, regulatory (as its Iron and Steel Board would be), or government-led. So they fell between all three stools.[16] The Annual Economic Survey reviewed the allocation of resources to industry, but there was no follow-up.

The Industrial Organisation and Development Act of 1947 might have begun real planning, but forming sectoral Development Councils was left to private-sector players. Only four (cotton, silverware, clothing, and furniture) were established, and all except cotton, which reshaped an existing board, foundered in the face of resistance from employers. So did an attempt to revive the wartime Joint Production committees, which industrialists saw as a move toward workers' control.

In 1945, the Bank of England set up two nominal development banks: the Industrial and Commercial Finance Corporation and the Finance Corporation for Industry. But it did so primarily to ward off pressure for further nationalization, and these two bodies remained under private control, mainly just capitalizing smaller businesses that found existing banks unhelpful.[17] The National Investment Council was formed in 1946, supposedly to coordinate private industrial investment, but was given no priorities by government and was dominated from the outset by private-sector appointees.

The private sector did not supply economic strategy either. Despite being a global financial center, Britain did not have investment banks with the knowledge of industry, the capital, or the leverage over management to drive industrial modernization.[18] Firms like JP Morgan in New York, which proactively shaped entire industries, did not exist. Neither did the universal banks of Germany, with their close, comprehensive ties to the firms they financed. The banking community was snobbish, self-perpetuating, and had little interest in manufacturing, which it considered grubby and provincial. Instead, British industry traditionally raised cash from shareholders – who, atomized, had little capacity to impose strategic direction.

The Nationalization Dead End

Between 1946 and 1948, Parliament nationalized the Bank of England, the railways, coal, gas, electricity, telephones, trucking, and medical care. (Steel and others came later.) This seemed at the time like a decisive step toward a socialist economy, indeed *the* democratic way to achieve socialism without bloody revolution, communist tyranny, or excessive governmental intrusion into sectors, like small retailing, ill suited to public ownership. Owners were paid the value of their holdings, depressed from war and austerity, mostly in government bonds.

The argument over whether the "commanding heights" of the economy should be under private or public ownership was thought to be a central issue of industrial policy. In reality, it was damaging irrelevance that distracted from the real issues facing industry and prevented clear thinking.

Nationalization made much less difference than the socialists expected. Many of its objectives, such as greater income equality, could have been accomplished by taxes or regulation. The step from regulating industry to owning it outright did not necessarily give government more control. But it did make voters hold governments responsible for problems that could previously be blamed on the capitalists. And every dispute formerly kept between workers and owners could now become a political issue.

Governments now had to be expert in pouring steel and hewing coal. The taxpayer, and every competing spending demand, now bore the cost if companies lost money. Absent the complete abolition of the market system, nationalized firms still had to pay markets prices for their inputs, accept market prices for their products, and raise capital at market rates. The tradable sectors of Britain's economy – trade being roughly four times the percentage of GDP as in the US – still had to compete with the mostly nonsocialist outside world.[19]

Nor did the mere fact of nationalization produce better business strategies for the nationalized firms. (Socialist ideology could offer little help on this question.) If their profits were squeezed to raise wages, there would be no retained earnings to finance ongoing investment. If their prices were raised (if they even could be, given import competition), consumers would suffer. There was thus no way to achieve the eternal socialist dream of paying workers more – except greater efficiency, which did not transpire for reasons discussed in what follows.

Coal mines, steel mills, railways and the rest were not, in any case, the commanding heights of the economy. They did not *command* anything, in the sense of exerting strategic control over the rest of the economy. Even the Bank of England was not a development bank like the ones other nations have used to support and control key industries. Labour thought that nationalization per se would give government sufficient control over investment. But it failed to actually direct subsidized capital to rationally chosen strategic industries.

Unbelievably, from the outset there was no link between nationalization and planning.[20] This omission was not deliberate or born of a principled

fear of central planning. It was simply *assumed* that, once nationalized, industries would simply do what was desirable. Each industry was given its own
board, but with little coordination between them. For example, the coal, gas,
and electricity boards did not develop a unified energy policy.[21] The Cabinet in
1948 decided that the nationalized industries should be models of good working conditions and job rationalization, but neither aim was concretely pursued.

Complacency Wins Out

For a few years after World War II, with every other industrial nation
except the US in ruins, British industry appeared to do well. Exports more than
doubled from 1946 to 1950.[22] From 1946 to 1954, shipyards exported a third
of their production, Britain was the world's largest exporter of cars, and other
industries seemed competitive.[23] This apparent success during the postwar
years when economic assumptions were gelling blunted pressure for the structural reforms Britain needed.

Most industrialists saw any governmental initiative to modernize their
sectors as a mere stalking horse for more nationalization.[24] Thus, they opposed
(successfully) a Labour attempt in 1949 to nationalize the huge sugar refiner
Tate & Lyle. More surprising, the unions too saw controls on industry, even by
a Labour government, as a threat to their own freedom of action, especially
their right to strike.[25]

Postwar rising wages and full employment incented neither industry
nor labor to change archaic working arrangements. With governmental passiv-
ity suiting both, Attlee's government did not feel strong enough to intervene.[26]
It also did nothing to reform union structures that promoted militancy, a failure
with vast consequences later.

Short-term balance-of-payments pressures distracted from long-term
economic strategy. Government limited automakers' domestic sales to 25 percent of production to maximize exports to the US. (In 1950, Britain's 398,000
cars and 145,000 commercial vehicles accounted for half of total global auto
exports.)[27]

But beneath the surface of this boom, manufacturers were mostly
maximizing output from existing capacity, not investing in either new products
or production technologies. A golden opportunity to reequip British industry
for postwar competition was also lost with government's response to the
Marshall Plan. As one historian notes:[28]

> Britain actually received more than a third more Marshall Aid than
> West Germany – $2.7 billion as against $1.7 billion. She in fact
> pocketed the largest share of any European nation. The truth is that
> the post-war Labour Government, advised by its resident economic

pundits, freely chose not to make industrial modernisation the central theme in her use of Marshall Aid.

While France directed much of its Marshall Aid toward industrial reequipment and creating modern new capacity in its steel industry, Britain used these scarce dollars to import steel to manufacture currency-earning exports.[29] Slowness in expanding its own steel industry would contribute to shortages into the mid-1950s, as Britain's plants struggled due to ongoing "patch and mend," rather than the new investment public ownership had mistakenly been expected to deliver.

The Productivity Gap

Compared to the US or even Germany, British manufacturers were generally small, undercapitalized, and dependent on skilled workers – not sophisticated machinery – to produce small runs of high-quality goods using obsolete machinery.[30] American-style mass manufacturing for the middle-class consumer market was not their forte. Britain's population in this era was still more working class than middle class, so this was no accident. France's government, facing the exact same problem, deliberately pressed its industry to transition to modern mass production. Britain's did not.

Government noted lagging productivity, but its response was weak. The engineering sector was an obvious place to start. But given no new public investment, shortages of labor and materials, and the export drive, productivity had somehow to be raised *without* additional investment. Sir Stafford Cripps, the president of the Board of Trade, pushed as hard as he could, with the Anglo-American Council on Productivity organizing visits to American plants. Product standardization was a key issue, but employers saw it as a first step toward state control, and while the unions were more supportive, they wanted a plan they had a role in devising.[31] Cripps gave up.

Even when new capacity came online, productivity was substandard. The private Port Talbot steel mill opened in 1951 with three times the workers of an equivalent US plant.[32] Steel production rose by half between 1950 and 1960, but Britain's global market share fell as the unions foiled efforts to reduce featherbedding.[33]

Meanwhile, Britain's rivals were steadily investing. In 1950, the UK invested 9 percent of GNP in industry and infrastructure, versus 19 percent for Germany.[34] Meanwhile, Britain spent 8 percent on defense (more than double what the US spends today), partly on the Korean War but also in doomed efforts to retain the illusion of great power status in Africa, the Middle East, and elsewhere.[35]

1951–1956: The Visible Slide Begins

When Queen Elizabeth II came to the throne in 1952, talk was of a "new Elizabethan age," with Britain reinforcing its still strong position in world industry through its lead in jet aircraft, nuclear power, computers, and other sunrise industries. Yet this was the year when the slide in competitiveness became undeniable.

The Conservatives returned to power in 1951 trumpeting their support for free enterprise. They could have tried to free up markets and work more closely with industry. But they had signed up, through the "Industrial Charter" of 1947, to continuing Labour's policy framework. Their only noticeable change was denationalizing steel and trucking.

Worldwide economic expansion allowed British manufacturers moderate growth in the 1950s. But France, Germany, and Japan were growing almost twice as fast.[36] Auto exports faltered as buyers become more demanding. The Standard Vanguard, for example, lost popularity as motorists found out that its design was shaped "less by market research than the desirability of using the same engine as the Ferguson tractor."[37] Poor quality and inattention to the customer would remain a theme of British industry.

The year 1952 was the turning point for Britain's textile industry, despite a promising postwar start when it turned to synthetic fibers. It began losing out to producers such as Japan and India.

Shipbuilding peaked in 1955, with output 25 percent above 1947, but by 1960, it had lost half the gain.[38] In 1950, British yards had built 38 percent of the world's merchant ships, but management was loathe to invest, having been caught off guard by the slump of the 1930s.[39] Strikes were rife, many the result of disputes between crafts due to the replacement of riveting by welding. Yards failed to adopt modern mass production methods.[40]

As early as 1954, the Cabinet's Economic Policy Committee was told that, if current trends continued, "The relegation of the United Kingdom to the second division in the industrial league would not be far off."[41] But a government that assumed industry should look after itself, and an even more complacent private sector, did nothing.

Britain clung too long to Imperial Preference, a tariff system centered on its former colonies.[42] This hampered access to developed-country markets like the US and continental Europe while giving India, Pakistan, and Hong Kong – too poor to buy much in return – privileged access to its own.

There were a few bright spots. The world's first commercial nuclear power station opened in England in 1956, and more followed over the next decade, sustaining the industry with a regular work stream. But in the long run, questionable technical choices, poor project management, and weak cost control produced uneconomic products that failed to find an export market, and the industry died.[43]

1957–1963: Harold Macmillan

Harold Macmillan's Conservative government took power in 1957. It intervened tentatively in two troubled industries: cotton textiles and shipbuilding. Textile imports from the Commonwealth were capped with (high) import ceilings in 1958, and the 1959 Cotton Industry Act facilitated an orderly shutdown of 50 percent of spinning capacity and 40 percent of weaving. But the surviving firms invested little, so this protection, not combined with other reforms, merely delayed the exposure of the remainder of the industry to the world market and its consequent decline.[44]

Politicization of business decisions took its toll. Faced with the choice of building a subsidized steel-rolling mill in Wales or Scotland, Macmillan approved both locations. Neither plant then ran at full output, crippling their economics.[45] Two new auto plants were directed to Scotland and three to Merseyside in the north of England to alleviate regional unemployment. This appeased local political interests but weakened scale economies and supply chains.[46]

Foreign shipowners started giving their orders to yards with reliable, low-cost delivery and free from Britain's union troubles. In 1960, a government study highlighted managerial weaknesses in shipbuilding, including primitive approaches to production control and poor labor relations. Macmillan's government was shaken but hesitated to intervene. Plans for a capacity reduction scheme were drawn up, then abandoned. Employment plunged anyway, from 78,000 in 1958 to 48,000 by 1963.[47]

Meanwhile, the rest of the world was catching up. West Germany in 1958 overtook Britain as an exporter of manufactured goods.[48]

The Aircraft Industry Exception

The major exception to the incoherence of British industrial policy in this period was aircraft. Real strategies, with plausible economic logic, technological innovation, and some hope of success were pursued. A partnership between industry and the state continued for decades, culminating in nationalization in 1977. But due to a number of mistakes, leadership in the sector was lost regardless.

Aircraft was the one industry for which Attlee's 1945–51 government devised a strategy. At the end of World War II, Germany was barred from producing airplane engines and Britain was ahead of even the US in jet engines, though weaker in airframes. There were 16 different civil aircraft on the drawing boards, plus projects for the military.[49] From 1946, the Ministry of Supply ordered aircraft for the armed services and state-owned airlines. In 1959, the government set out to reduce the 31 aircraft firms to two airframe makers (British Aircraft Corporation (BAC) and Hawker Siddeley) and two engine builders (Rolls-Royce and Bristol).[50]

There were some successes: the Gloster Meteor and Hawker Hunter jet fighters, the Canberra and Vulcan bombers, and the (small) Viscount and (mini) Dove propeller airliners. Government was giving other industries almost no financial support, but in 1957, it introduced launch aid for new civil aircraft: 20–25 percent of development cost, recouped through a levy on sales.[51] (It had already funded De Havilland's Comet, the world's first commercial jet airliner, which first flew in 1949.)

But despite the industry being seen as a driving force for exports, too many aircraft were designed for Britain's forces and airlines without regard to export potential. This led to shorter production runs and lesser scale economies.[52] Commercial debut of the Comet in 1952 was followed by two crashes caused by metal fatigue, not then well understood anywhere. A four-year grounding before it returned to service allowed the Americans to catch up with the much larger Boeing 707 and Douglas DC-8, and British firms thereafter struggled to make up lost ground. Overly optimistic governments encouraged them to compete with the Americans on every front, rather than specializing as viable second-tier players.[53]

In 1962, the supersonic Concorde – a huge diversion of scarce talent and money into a commercial dead end – was thrown into the mix (see Chapter 19). The rationale was partly a desire to technologically leapfrog the Americans, partly delusions of grandeur, and partly a way for Macmillan to please France as he set out to take Britain into the European Common Market. A treaty for BAC and Sud Aviation to develop the plane was signed in November 1962. At the same time, Britain vacillated over joining Airbus: joining in 1967, leaving in 1969, rejoining in 1979 on inferior terms, then seeing the last British participant, BAe, pull out in 2006 with minimal consultation with government.

The National Economic Development Council: 1962–1964

Macmillan's slogan for the 1959 election was, "You've never had it so good." With average income at a record high and GDP growing 4.3 percent in 1959 and 6.3 percent in 1960, his claim was momentarily plausible.[54]

Nowhere did that claim seem more justified than in the auto industry, with a boom in home demand (though exports were declining) and the launch of the iconic Mini and E-type Jaguar. But seeds of trouble were already sown, particularly at the giant British Motor Corporation, an unhappy government-encouraged marriage of Austin and Morris. The antecedent firms largely continued as separate fiefdoms, losing the efficiencies of consolidation. New investment remained minimal and labor unrest was rising, often with groups of workers fighting each other rather than management.

Awareness that industry was losing ground began to spread. The UK was trapped in a cycle of "stop-go," forced to lunge from expansion to recession by the need to hit the monetary brakes every time expansion pulled in too many imports and threatened Britain's fixed exchange rate under the Bretton Woods system (see Chapter 16). Devaluation would have helped, but financial interests and misguided pride in a strong pound prevented it.

An initiative for a more serious industrial policy came from the Federation of British Industries (FBI), which proposed some measure of economic planning in 1960. The Treasury, uninterested in industry and focused on keeping the pound up and public spending down, was lukewarm. But the Trades Union Congress came on board once convinced that the new machinery would not be a vehicle for controls on pay settlements.[55] (Few other countries would have treated organized labor as a partner in industrial policy at a time when the movement's refusal to reform itself was significantly harming industry.)

Thus, in 1962, the National Economic Development Council (NEDC, "Neddy") was launched, chaired initially by the Chancellor of the Exchequer. On paper, it brought together business, unions, and government to set economic strategy. Though it had no prescriptive authority and only a tiny budget, it was supported by a National Economic Development Office (NEDO) with a staff of 75. There would, in time, be 21 "Little Neddies" covering most sectors of industry. Thus Britain apparently embraced the planning structures then successfully being used by France, and NEDO did superficially resemble the Commissariat général du Plan (see Chapter 9).[56]

But Britain *still* did not have a technically informed bureaucracy, faith in the merits of state action, or an economic theory of what interventionism was supposed to do and how. Government *still* would not engage directly in industrial reorganization. NEDO and Neddy were given no actual industrial policy to pursue, beyond a vague idea of setting national targets.[57] Ministers did not even try to set up the machinery to produce a detailed plan. Neddy's committees were dominated by industry and labor, but leadership came from neither. (The unions treated Neddy as a mere extension of collective bargaining.)

NEDC was, in reality, the "complete antithesis to the role of the professional planner as practised under the French system."[58] The lesson London had drawn from French planning was the one it wanted to hear: not that it worked because it was driven by properly thought-out state decision-making and implementing actions, but that planning created a consensus between industry, labor, and government that would encourage business to invest.[59] It was wishful thinking on a grand scale.

The result was the very problem the FBI had wanted to forestall. Neddy set an objective of 4 percent growth to 1966, compared with the 2.5 percent average of the 1950s, but as the economy started to expand, the balance of payments deteriorated. Thus, observes one commentator, "Far from promoting a more stable economic environment, the four percent goal may itself have been destabilizing, since it encouraged the government to stimulate demand in 1963 when a cyclical upturn was already under way. The outcome was another slam on the brakes and a loss of credibility for the new Council."[60]

1964–1972: Technocracy at Last?

In October 1964, Labour returned to power under Harold Wilson, committed to harnessing the "white heat of the scientific revolution" and taking British industry "by the scruff of the neck and dragging it kicking and screaming into the 20th century."[61] Here at last, it seemed, was a government serious about industrial policy.

Wilson's new framework looked bold enough: a Department of Economic Affairs (DEA) to formulate national plans, a Ministry of Technology (MinTech) to foster R&D, an Industrial Reorganisation Corporation (IRC) to facilitate private-sector mergers and modernization, and a Prices and Incomes Board to restrain inflationary wage settlements and encourage productivity agreements between firms and unions. (The already somewhat discredited Neddy continued as a backup.)

Wilson, an academic turned wartime government economist, believed Britain's competitive shortcomings were too deep-seated to be corrected by market forces alone, not only in steel and shipbuilding but also in high-tech industries such as computers. He saw Conservative attempts to modernize and direct the economy as half-hearted and proof that reform could be imposed only from the center left.

MinTech was billed as the central actor in a range of interventions to bring advanced technology and new processes into British industry. But it had no underlying theory of which technologies it should bet on. It made no attempt to "roadmap" the critical relationships between technologies. It did not cover all steps of the innovation process from pure science to saleable product. And it did not realistically assess which industries Britain could succeed in.

MinTech started with an R&D budget of $5.4 billion in today's dollars and supervised machine tools, computers, telecom, and electronics. It worked through the National Research Development Corporation (NRDC) and other institutions. Its leader from 1966, Tony Benn, was a boundless optimist, and it focused on fields British technology had already seeded.

MinTech also aspired, by promoting mergers, to create a "countervailing force" capable of competing with the big US multinationals. But this would have required vastly larger and smarter interventions than it was to deploy. (Britain's size was no bar: France has since done exactly this.)

At the time, all of Europe's computer firms were struggling, and Wilson in 1965 told Frank Cousins, MinTech's first head, that he had "about a month" to save Britain's computer industry.[62] The favored solution was a merger, but the British firms' systems were incompatible. Nevertheless, International Computers Limited (ICL) was formed in 1968, with MinTech taking a stake and government departments being urged to buy from it. Thus began a losing 20-year battle to preserve a national champion in computers. ICL was hopelessly outmatched by IBM, then at its peak, and neither settled for a niche nor scored the technological coup it would have taken to dislodge IBM.[63] (It was out bought by Japan's Fujitsu in 1998.)

The overall results of the DEA were mixed. The government did finally begin to accumulate information about industry. But the Treasury did not want to plan the economy itself and, by hobbling the DEA, made sure nobody else would either. The DEA thus never had the tools or the authority to engage in serious planning. Its National Plan, launched with a fanfare in 1965, was a grab bag of "hastily conceived and wildly ambitious targets for growth, unrelated to the actual trajectories of specific industrial sectors."[64] Those targets were then rendered meaningless by a sterling crisis in the summer of 1966. DEA was formally buried in 1969.

1966–1972: The Industrial Reorganization Corporation

Working in parallel with MinTech was the Industrial Reorganization Corporation (IRC), set up in 1966 with a capital of $3.8 billion in today's dollars. Under the former head of the big textile firm Courtaulds and staffed by young merchant bankers, it was designed to promote mergers. It supported or financed 50 such deals, involving 150 firms, out of 3,400 mergers during this period.[65]

The most successful merger was that of Associated Electrical Industries and English Electric into the General Electric Company (not the same as

America's GE), creating for a generation a near rival to Germany's Siemens. But this success was atypical. A more salient example was IRC's acquiescence to Chrysler's takeover of the small auto maker Rootes, which had been induced by government to expand in Scotland, rather than its home base, to create a nearby customer for the state-owned Ravenscraig steel plant. MinTech secured apparently firm commitments from Chrysler: Expansion plans and higher export targets were confirmed, there was to be a British majority on the Rootes board, and the IRC could nominate a director. But astonishingly, there was no mechanism to actually enforce Chrysler's promises. These were not kept, Rootes did not thrive as Chrysler UK, and the firm was eventually unloaded to Frances's PSA Peugeot Citroën.[66]

Other mergers were questionable, such as the shotgun marriage of several British ball-bearing firms to "protect domestic ownership" after Sweden's SKF tried to take over Pollard, the market leader. (SKF thrives to this day; the merged British firms eventually disappeared into a Japanese takeover.)

IRC engineered shipbuilding's consolidation into regional groups, with the Shipbuilding Industry Board providing financial backing. But this strategy overestimated the advantages of mere size without the integration required for true scale economies. It also underestimated the difficulties of making mergers work and did nothing about underlying inefficiencies, poor product, weak marketing, or labor strife. The industry's slide was not halted, and the best performing yards ended up being those outside the scheme.

And then there was British Leyland (BL). The Austin–Morris merger that produced BMC had not produced rationalization, scale economies, or consolidation of marques. Its design teams were at loggerheads and it was racked by wildcat strikes. Meanwhile, thriving Leyland Motors had added several carmakers to its globally successful truck and bus businesses. In 1966, Tony Benn told IRC to merge Leyland and BMC. The resulting merger did not help reform BMC and damaged Leyland.[67]

Thanks to these blunders and others, from 1961 to 1973, British labor productivity fell steadily behind that of Japan, Germany, and France.[68] Meanwhile, the pound's role as a reserve currency kept successive governments hostage to its overvaluation. They believed that "trust" (read "prestige and the appearance of global power") between London and former colonies holding sterling would be lost if it devalued. The struggle to keep the pound at $4.03 until 1949, then at $2.80 until 1967, led to balance-of-payments crises in 1947, 1949, 1951, 1955, 1957, 1965, 1966, and 1967. Devaluation should have occurred in 1964, but only in 1972 did Edward Heath's Conservatives let the pound (then at $2.40) float, their hand forced by the end of Bretton Woods (see Chapter 16).

Disengagement, U-Turn, and the Neb: 1970-1979

When the Conservatives returned to office in 1970 under Heath, they were committed to a change of course: Industry must experience the stiff breeze of competition, with "lame ducks" going into bankruptcy. During the first year of this policy of "disengagement," the IRC, the Prices and Incomes Board, and the Shipbuilding Industry Board were all disbanded. MinTech was merged with the Board of Trade to form a Department of Trade and Industry. Most of the steel industry (Labour had renationalized the 14 largest firms in 1967) stayed in public ownership, but commitments to expand its capacity were reduced.

Events soon forced government to intervene regardless. IRC had previously identified poor financial controls and managerial weaknesses at Rolls-Royce (until 1973 a maker of both cars and aircraft engines), but the company had refused to change. The Heath government put in $750 million in today's dollars of launch aid for its new RB211 TriStar engine.[69] But in February 1971, because of soaring development costs, bankruptcy loomed. With America's Lockheed desperate for the engine and ministers claiming Rolls-Royce's US rivals were subsidized by Pentagon contracts, Heath nationalized the company. Atypically, its period of public ownership was used constructively to correct the company's managerial weakness, the RB211 proved a success, and RR thrives to this day.[70]

Rolls-Royce proved the start of a complete "U-turn." With unemployment rising, the government bailed out Upper Clyde Shipbuilders. In 1972, Heath pushed through the Industry Act, giving the government sweeping intervention powers, albeit on an ad hoc basis rather than with systematic planning. The Act restored a system of subsidies after an unsuccessful experiment with tax write-offs for investment. But most of the subsidies went either to development grants for lagging regions, or to bail out struggling companies, starting with shipbuilder Cammell Laird. They did not go to helping the industries of the future emerge.

Voluntary restraints on imports (to 11 percent of the market) were negotiated with Japanese carmakers by the industry, with government support.[71] Meanwhile, Henry Ford II was threatening to halt investment in Britain because of strikes. Heath met with him, but could not stop Ford's next plant from going to Belgium. His response was the 1971 Industrial Relations Act, which narrowed unions' legal immunities and established a statutory framework for labor relations. But the unions refused to cooperate. Jailed strikers became martyrs, greeted by jubilant crowds upon release. The Act was dead.[72]

A few aspects of disengagement endured. In 1970, BAC was pressing to develop a new range of airliners to compete with Airbus. The government wisely declined to back it, ending its ambitions in large airliners and leaving it dependent on military orders. Less happily, Britain's once world-leading civilian nuclear program was killed by dithering over what type of reactor to build, which starved the reactor-building industry of orders.

1974–1978: Industrial Policy's Last Hurrah

Harold Wilson returned to power in 1974 with the economy in deep trouble. The 1973–4 oil price shock and the coal miners' strike of 1974 had exposed weaknesses in industry that had been latent for decades. Unemployment was rising, from 600,000 in 1973 to 1.5 million in 1977, as was inflation, peaking at 24.2 percent in 1975.[73] Factories were closing as firms were losing out to foreign competitors, such as the motorcycle maker Triumph, done in by the Japanese.

Union members were in a militant mood after two miners' strikes, one of which had brought down the previous government. From 1975 to 1977, a government committee researched a proposal to induce unions to act more responsibly by implementing "industrial democracy," including worker representation on corporate boards.[74] It was rejected by both management and labor.

Tony Benn again took charge of industrial policy. But his motivation was now left-ideological rather than technocratic. This government was not committed, as Labour had been in 1964, to at least *trying* to implement rationally designed measures to restore industrial competitiveness. It was committed to the extension of state ownership and control as ends in themselves. The new Labour program was thus far more interventionist than that of 1964. But there was *still* no overall economic or technological strategy.

The keystone of the new agenda was the 1975 Industry Act. This gave government authority to prevent any important manufacturing firm from falling under foreign control and established the National Enterprise Board (NEB) intended to foster competitiveness and industrial efficiency by taking active stakes in companies. The government proclaimed a new "Industrial Strategy," creating 39 Sectoral Working Parties (under the still-surviving Neddy and operating by consensus). There would be planning agreements with firms committing to expand in return for government assistance.[75]

But NEB was never even as effective as the IRC of the late 1960s. For a start, there was not much left to merge. There were fewer apparently promising new technologies within Britain's reach. Manufacturing was in even worse shape. Only two planning agreements were ever signed. Most of the NEB's interventions were firefighting responses to crises in individual companies.[76] Over half its original $11 billion in today's dollars went to support Rolls-Royce and BL, and the rest went to the likes of Chrysler, the electrical equipment firm

Ferranti, and the machine tool maker Alfred Herbert, where job losses in its home city would have been politically fraught for Labour.[77] (No real reforms were imposed on Herbert, leading to its ultimate collapse.)

NEB did seek to promote some sunrise industries (notably the semi-conductor firm Inmos), tried to expand ICL after taking a 25 percent stake, and bought shares in 66 firms in all.[78] But little came of all this.

In 1975, BL went into the red. Some of its executives and Parliament's Commons Expenditure Committee warned that it would fail if it stayed in both the volume and specialty car markets. But abandoning mass-market cars would be an immense blow politically and outrage the unions. So government nationalized the firm, putting in $7.4 billion over eight years. But its market share continued to decline and its industrial relations got even worse: 523 walkouts at its main plant alone in three years.[79]

Letting volume cars go would probably have saved the more viable parts of the sprawling firm: Triumph sports cars, Land Rover 4WD vehicles, and once world-leading truck and bus plants. Instead, the firm died piecemeal in a series of incarnations and brand divestments. In 1988, the Thatcher government paid British Aerospace to take it over, and the last credible attempt to run its successor firms ended with BMW unloading it in 2000, with the final collapse five years later. The Minis sold today are built by BMW, albeit in Britain, and Leyland's truck business is now part of the American Paccar. Bus production ended in 1993.

1979–1997: Thatcher Kills Socialism

Inflation, repeated industrial policy failures, worsening labor unrest, and a growing belief that government lost authority the more it interfered in the economy led in the late 1970s to the collapse of Britain's postwar economic consensus.

In 1975, right-wing Margaret Thatcher defeated moderate Edward Heath for the Conservative Party leadership. Her campaign had several themes: Keynesianism was rejected in favor of monetarism, which promised to control inflation by restraining the money supply. Interventionism was rejected in favor of free markets. And socialism was seen as the principal cause of Britain's by then universally acknowledged decline.

Thatcher's instincts were to get government off the back of business, cut regulation, and encourage "enterprise" – a word not much heard since the 1950s. Trade unions would no longer be treated as partners in government, but as an over-mighty and harmful special interest.[80] (Monetarism tacitly rationalized letting unemployment break organized labor to achieve a cooperative labor force.)[81]

In 1979, Mrs. Thatcher led the Conservatives back to power. Labour's industrial policy structures were dismantled. The NEB was disbanded. The last currency controls were abolished. Legislation was passed to ensure genuine competition in business. Subsidies were cut and the support of national champions abandoned. And with the partial exception of defense and aerospace, high-tech industries were no longer privileged.[82] Captains of industry were torn between relief that finally there was a government with a clear sense of direction, not in thrall to the unions, and not bent on interference, and an apprehension that the medicine might kill the patient.

Tight money drove interest rates to 17 percent. Foreign capital flooded in and with no attempt to manage the pound, also pushed up by growing North Sea oil exports, it became overvalued. This put extreme pressure on both exporting and import-competing industries.[83] Many businesses closed, including some of the modern, high-tech factories Thatcher had visited during her 1979 election campaign.[84] Even the mighty chemical firm ICI was reporting losses, cutting its dividend for the first time since 1938.[85] By the end of 1980, even the Confederation of British Industry was voicing concern about manufacturing.

After a deflationary budget in 1981 and with the exchange rate falling back, the economy began to pick up in 1983, though unemployment continued to rise.[86] Thatcherism had cured inflation. When recovery came, service industries were its immediate beneficiaries. For most surviving manufacturers, the recession had stimulated an urgent drive for lower costs and greater efficiency, and a fundamental reassessment of strategy. A long-overdue surge in industrial productivity was the result. Nationalized industries were forced to reform. British Steel closed plants kept on life support by Labour, rationalized industrial relations that had involved 18 separate unions, and, after some automakers started sourcing steel abroad in protest, raised product quality.[87]

The civil service began to take in businessmen on rotation and placed senior officials in companies to see the realities of industry. (Unfortunately, most preferred banks and management consultancies to manufacturers.) Thatcher shrank the unions' legal immunities with the Employment Acts of 1980 and 1982. Secondary picketing was outlawed and strike ballots, instead of the customary show of hands, were made compulsory.[88] Union power was decisively weakened, except in public services such as the railways, and membership declined. A bitter 1984 coal miners' strike resulted in a government victory after Thatcher and the National Coal Board stood firm.

Thatcher's Privatizations

Thatcher won reelection in 1983 mainly because of victory in the Falklands War and a split in the Labour Party, *not* approval of her economic performance, which at that point was still decidedly unvindicated. Privatization began in earnest during her second term. Its motives were not only ideological: It raised substantial sums that could be used for current spending. Most of the firms privatized were utilities: British Telecom, British Gas, electric utilities, British Airways, the British Airports Authority, the international telecom provider Cable & Wireless, the National Bus Company, and the water industry. But state-owned manufacturers were also sold off: British Aerospace (BAe), the medical diagnostics company Amersham, NEB's stakes in ICL and Inmos, the small-plane maker Short Brothers. Improved management enabled Rolls-Royce (in 1987) and British Steel (a year later) to be sold off. Even the car-making side of BL, rebadged as Rover, was temporarily in good enough shape to be handed over to British Aerospace – though BAe was a questionable owner for a car firm and had to be paid a huge "dowry" to take it on.

Other privatizations were less happy. British Shipbuilders's surviving yards were offloaded in 1983 in a race to get merchant shipbuilding out of the public sector before its total collapse.[89]

Privatization did unintended harms. After the National Bus Company was sold off in pieces to its management, its orders for new buses collapsed, which drove yet another nail into the coffin of BL. Privatization of rail under Thatcher's successor John Major did similar damage to the train-building industry. The electric utilities were mostly sold off to French and German utilities, so government later found itself with little say over the country's mix of coal, nuclear, renewables, and other power sources.

Thatcher, despite her image, was not a rigid pro-market ideologue. Her government retained "golden shares" in BAe, partly because it was Britain's main defense contractor, and in Rolls-Royce, a key participant in its nuclear submarine program. In 1983, she upset Washington by authorizing launch aid for the Airbus A320, whose wings were built in Britain.

With fewer state-owned industries to oversee and subsidize, the Department of Trade and Industry (DTI) refocused itself as a booster of enterprise. But businesses were baffled as to what it could actually do to help. Talk of easing regulation broke down because of costly new EU rules, frequently gold-plated by British government departments.

Several of Thatcher's favorite thinkers believed Britain could let its manufacturing go because it had been superseded by services. The "Big Bang" financial deregulation of 1986 triggered a boom in London's financial center that added weight to this argument. But the growth of the financial sector widened the disconnect widened between the needs of manufacturing and a financial market that prioritized short-term gains and saw industrial companies as chips to trade, acquire, or merge.

The Internationalization of British Industry

The early Thatcher years saw imports taking a steadily larger share of the car market, with plant closures correspondingly reducing domestic capacity. In 1982, production bottomed out at 887,969, but then the situation began to improve.[90] In 1985, Ford concluded an agreement with its unions enabling its workers to multitask.[91] Efficiency at Vauxhall, Peugeot, and even BL improved.

But Thatcher felt the industry would have a future only if the Japanese came to Britain. She invested heavy political and diplomatic capital to persuade them to locate their first European assembly plants there, and was rewarded when Nissan opened near Sunderland in 1986, with most of its output exported to Europe. Toyota (Derby) and Honda (Swindon) followed.[92]

Applying Japanese methods to the auto industry was part of a wider attempt to absorb East Asian efficiency by attracting foreign investment. Stepping up a campaign begun by Labour, Britain in 1981–2 spent $10 billion (in today's dollars) on national and regional incentives to foreign investors.[93] In the early 1980s, it was attracting more inward investment than any other member of the EEC, with intense competition between regions to attract firms like LG, Panasonic, Canon, and Lexmark.[94]

Foreign firms were believed to bring better productivity, export performance, technology, and management – which would then supposedly rub off on domestic industry by training staff. But this strategy, although not entirely worthless, had serious flaws. Job gains from new plants often merely offset losses at existing British firms using older technologies. Even in 1995, at the height of the influx of East Asian electronics firms, Britain had roughly the same trade deficit in such products as Germany, France, and Italy, which had received far less such investment.[95]

Most of the new jobs did not last long. Foreign ownership led to key decisions being taken abroad, including plant closures. Hosting foreign firms meant losing the headquarters jobs and many of the technical ones. It also gave up what might have been achieved by strategies that can be imposed only on domestic companies.

The government became more open to foreign companies acquiring British ones. The Monopolies and Mergers Commission waved through a string of big pharmaceutical mergers, starting with SmithKline and Beecham Group in 1989, creating global players no longer based solely in Britain. Meanwhile, any chance of the EU filling the vacuum of industrial strategy in London was systematically blocked. For example, Britain (and Germany, for different reasons) required the EU to *eschew* industrial-policy considerations in competition policy as a condition for accepting its jurisdiction in this domain.[96]

The end of the Cold War opened Eastern Europe to Western firms. Multinationals from Peugeot to Nestlé transferred production from Britain to these new markets. In all this, Whitehall seemed powerless. It also sat by as such British corporate giants as GEC, ICI, and EMI sold off their soundest parts, then imploded.[97]

John Major and Tony Blair

The "nicer," less ideological Conservative John Major replaced Thatcher in 1990, then won reelection in his own right in 1992. He soon hit economic turbulence. British Steel finally closed Ravenscraig (saved during the Thatcher years by ministerial threats to resign) and other major facilities. BAe survived by slashing its workforce 47 percent.[98] British Coal announced more pit closures.

These job losses sparked a revolt by Conservative MPs. Pressure grew for government to step in, and Trade and Industry Secretary Michael Heseltine dramatically pledged to "intervene before breakfast, before lunch, before tea, and before dinner" in support of British industry.[99]

But nothing much changed. Indeed, in some ways Major went further than Thatcher, privatizing what was left of coal and also British Rail. (The latter resulted in a debacle, with ownership of tracks separated from that of trains, a decline in service and safety, renationalization of tracks in 2002, and creeping renationalization of trains ongoing as of 2024.)

In 1997, under Tony Blair, Labour returned to power for the first time in 18 years. This time, repudiating 50 years of Labour ideology, there was no commitment to socialist planning, state ownership, or intervention in industry. Instead, Chancellor Gordon Brown claimed to base his economic policies on "post-neoclassical endogenous growth theory," interpreted wearily by one commentator as, "We have been reading some books and we still want to intervene."[100]

Blair's "pro-business" stance amounted to being starry-eyed about people who made money and allowing Britain's business leaders to make their own mistakes, despite frantic efforts by the DTI to forestall the worst. Labour privatized National Air Traffic Services, the Commonwealth Development Corporation (development finance in Britain's former colonies), and most defense research. Government's attention to industry was concentrated on the strongest remaining British-owned sectors: pharmaceuticals, defense, and aerospace, plus attracting FDI.

Labour came to power with manufacturing apparently in good shape. British Steel had become highly competitive and was Europe's second-ranking producer. After Jaguar was bought by Ford, Rover by BMW, and Rolls-Royce cars by Volkswagen, virtually all of Britain's auto industry was under foreign owners apparently willing to invest.[101] Ford in 1999 announced that its big Dagenham plant was to be expanded from 272,000 to 450,000 cars a year.[102]

Yet the 2000s would see one major British manufacturer after another vanish in the face of governmental misjudgments and powerlessness. Foreign corporate parents decimated car manufacturing: 140,000 out of 870,000 jobs were lost in just four years.[103] As the market for steel weakened, government was reminded that joint ventures with Dutch firms (which British Steel had become, as Corus) have supervisory boards in the Netherlands, with labor representatives, that can close plants outside Holland first.

Technological crown jewel BAe drove home government's impotence when in 2006 it sold off its 20 percent stake in Airbus after only minimal consultation with DTI. This left Airbus plants in Bristol and North Wales vulnerable. (BAe was then, in 2012, frozen out of a proposed merger with Franco-German EADS, owner of Airbus, due to German objections.)

Barring interventionist legislation that Whitehall baulked at lest it upset the EU, nothing much could be done. But from the Treasury, Gordon Brown in 2006 created the Technology Strategy Board, which did set some useful priorities in R&D.

2008–2020: Crash, Brexit, and COVID

Before the financial crash of 2008, Britain enjoyed more than a decade of growth. But it was driven by a boom in financial services, with manufacturing in continuing decline. The crash had its origins in regulatory mistakes in the US, not Britain, but showed how vulnerable to uncontrollable foreign events the economy had become by depending so heavily on its globalized financial sector. Rescued by the government, the banks nevertheless tightened credit, putting manufacturers under further strain.

With the idea that finance could sustain the whole country now discredited, Labour began to realize that manufacturing could not simply be allowed to disappear. (Employment in the sector had nearly halved since 1997, from 4.4 to 2.8 million.)[104] Thus, late in 2008, Business Secretary Peter Mandelson called for a new "market-driven industrial activism."[105] He began piecing together elements of a new industrial strategy under the slogan "New Industry, New Jobs." In 2010, his Cabinet colleague Ed Miliband declared: "We need to rebuild our economy in a different way from the past, with more jobs in real engineering, not just financial engineering."[106] And in 2009, the renamed (again) Department of Business set up a Strategic Investment Fund worth $1.7 billion in 2023 dollars. But this was only 7 *percent* of the equivalent fund set up by the French.

The 2010 election resulted in a government of Conservatives in coalition with the center-left Liberal Democrats and headed by Conservative David Cameron. His Lib Dem business secretary, Vincent Cable, formerly chief economist at Shell, worked up a long-term Industrial Strategy White Paper. This modest document set the following priorities: getting businesses access to finance; supporting (vaguely defined) key sectors; addressing failures in bringing innovative products to market; accelerating work on synthetic biology; fostering smarter government procurement; and strengthening vocational skills.[107] The department's analysis of industry sectors showed a decent *conceptual* understanding of the varying advantageousness of industries, but had little to say about how government could systematically act on this.[108]

After Cameron won a majority in his own right in 2015, his new business secretary tore up the Industrial Strategy, seeing no need. Cameron then launched a charm offensive with Beijing, encouraging China to embark on projects to modernize Britain's infrastructure, starting with its nuclear power stations, and to open factories in Britain.

Conservative Prime Minister Theresa May, in office 2016–19 struggling to implement Brexit, saw a need in this uncertain climate for precisely the sort of industrial strategy her predecessor had discarded. Launched in 2017, hers centered on promoting the construction, AI, auto, and life sciences sectors, with "grand challenges" to business, academia, and civil society to innovate and develop new technologies.[109] But it was far short of what most other developed nations would have recognized as a serious industrial policy.

Boris Johnson, in office 2019–22, campaigned on implementing Brexit and on reviving the "left-behind" areas of the country – mostly Britain's rust belt. He was rewarded with gains in seats that had been Labour's since the 1930s. His "strategy" was the Treasury-driven "Build back better: Our plan for growth," a hodgepodge of COVID recovery, regional "levelling up," education, infrastructure, and environmentalism, with some kind words about innovation.[110] But Johnson was forced from office by scandal before proposing any serious implementation of all this, and was, in any event, notorious for lack of follow-through.

His successor, Liz Truss, represented a deregulating, libertarian faction of the Conservative Party, and was thus ideologically predisposed against proactive industrial policy. But her reckless proposed tax cuts spooked the financial markets, forcing her from office in a record 45 days.

Truss's successor, Rishi Sunak, had abandoned, as Chancellor of the Exchequer, a previous plan for industrial policy, and had a professional background in finance, not industry. *Plus ça change, plus ...*

Strengths

- Political stability and rule of law.
- Good basic science capability.
- Bad decisions have been weakly implemented, limiting the harm done.

Weaknesses

- No systematic understanding of the differing advantageousness of industries, or of how governments should base policy on these distinctions.
- Alternation between nominally laissez-faire and nominally socialist policies, combined with excessive faith in nationalization and privatization per se as solutions.
- The absence, until recently, of a cadre of civil servants knowledgeable about industry.
- Government dominated by an upper class that disdained manufacturing and a labor movement antagonistic to corporations.
- Limited and ineffective efforts to foster the development of technology clusters.
- Domination of the economy by the financial sector, such as misguided attempts to maintain a strong pound and rampant financialization following the Big Bang deregulation in 1986.
- Indiscriminate acceptance of foreign takeovers of British firms.

11 INDIA

Dysfunctional Socialism, Directionless Capitalism

When India won independence in 1947, it was a very poor country, with a per capita GDP of only $1,200 in 2020 dollars.[1] It had inefficient, mostly subsistence agriculture, a low savings rate, and a tiny industrial sector. Partition of the Raj into India and Pakistan had brought disruption of transportation and supply chains, lethal religious strife, an influx of refugees, and war with India's new neighbor.

On the positive side, India was basically untouched by World War II, with a functioning economy, a trade surplus, and healthy currency reserves. It had a rich stock of natural resources (coal, iron, manganese, bauxite), a competent administrative apparatus, a vibrant entrepreneurial class, and a political leadership committed to economic transformation.[2]

Most development economists at the time had higher expectations for India's success than East Asia's.[3] So, with all the preconditions for development apparently in place, the Congress Party (hereinafter "Congress") took power with bold plans for development.

Today, 77 years later, it is fair to say that although advances have been made, the country could have done much better. India underperformed, and continues to underperform, both its own aspirations and what it could plausibly achieve.

The country today has a $3.4 trillion economy, ranking it fifth behind the US, China, Japan, and Germany.[4] It is now classified as a lower-middle-income nation. It has cut poverty by two-thirds since 1980.[5] But China, India's natural comparator, is now, despite being poorer as recently as 1990, three to five times richer per capita, depending on the measure chosen.[6]

The key difference between the two is that China, thanks to its disciplined, proactive industrial policies, has become a global manufacturing leader, while India has not. In the 2015 words of one Indian business journal,

> Currently, India's manufacturing sector contributes about 16% to the GDP, and India's share in world manufacturing is only 1.8%. This is in stark contrast to China; where manufacturing contributes 34% to the GDP and is 13.7% of world manufacturing – up from 2.9% in 1991. India's growth has been on the back of a booming services sector which contributes 62.5% of the GDP. These statistics clearly indicate that while manufacturing has not been the engine of growth for the Indian economy, it now needs to grow at a much faster rate.[7]

Over the past 15 years, manufacturing has actually *fallen* as a percentage of GDP: from 16.9 percent in 2007 to 13.3 percent in 2022.[8] In the same period, Chinese manufacturing also fell, but maintained a much higher level: still 27.7 percent as of 2022.[9] In 2021, China's share of global manufacturing was 31 percent, an *order of magnitude* larger than India's 3 percent.[10]

Since post-socialist economic reforms began in the 1980s, India's growth has taken place mostly in service industries at home and nonmanufacturing high technology for export. Between 1985 and 2010, the GDP share of labor-intensive service exports more than quadrupled, and India is now globally recognized for IT, call centers, and other business process offshoring.[11] But it is not globally competitive in manufacturing outside a few subsectors like generic pharmaceuticals. And even there, despite recent progress, it still depends on China for most active ingredients.[12]

Lacking strength in manufacturing, India has not been able to create rising wages for the bulk of its population on China's scale. Despite the decline in poverty, in 2015 India's rate of extreme poverty (by the global standard of $1.90 per day) was still 13.4 percent, compared to 0.7 percent in China.[13] Thus India's recent economic history, while discrediting socialism, even in the mild, democratic form in which India practiced it, also casts doubt on embracing capitalism without a proactive industrial policy.[14]

As India is comprised of thousands of tribes and ethnic groups large and small, and divided by religion, caste, and language, centrally directed industrialization was always going to be harder to achieve than in the more homogenous East Asian states.[15] Several of the latter also had or still have authoritarian governments that did not have to answer to voters. Indian democracy is chaotic and has been drifting toward Hindu–nationalist authoritarianism in recent years, but for now at least, the country remains democratic. In India's federal system, the central ("Union") government depends on the states to implement many programs, with attendant administrative and political complications.[16]

Historical Background

For most of recorded history, the Indian subcontinent was a multiethnic collection of states accounting for a quarter to a third of the world economy.[17] Its modern economic history begins with the British conquest in the mid-eighteenth century. It is controversial whether Britain held India back economically, modestly advanced it, or merely failed to push forward an economy that had already stagnated.[18] Whatever the cause, during the first 50 years of the twentieth century, per capita income grew at a nugatory 0.2 percent per year.[19]

The economy in 1947 was overwhelmingly agrarian, manufacturing accounting for just 7.5 percent of GDP (up from 3.8 percent in 1913, partly because the British had realized during World War I that a more industrialized India was in their interest).[20] Thus, the country's most important economic task was not even industrialization, but simply raising the agricultural productivity upon which the majority of its population depended. (This eventually happened in the "green revolution" of the 1950s and 1960s.) Only 1,500 of India's 640,000 villages were connected to the electric grid, and just 16 percent of adults were literate.[21]

Colonialism led India's new leaders to associate capitalism with rule by a foreign power. And although India, at the time mainly a subsistence economy, was not as seriously affected by the Great Depression as the industrialized nations, its leaders still saw the global crisis as revealing fundamental defects in capitalism. Thus, as early as 1931, Congress passed its Karachi Resolution declaring, "The state shall own or control key industries and services, mineral resources, railways, waterways, shipping and other means of public transport."[22] And in 1939, it established the National Planning Committee, which vigorously debated the merits of outright state ownership versus state control.[23]

India's private sector responded in 1944 when a small group of leading native industrialists issued their "Bombay Plan" for a state-directed, though not state-owned, economy, with deficit funding of capital investment and the objective of doubling per capita income in 15 years.[24] But this Plan was less a declaration of faith in a mixed economy than an attempt to defuse calls for more radical planning from the Congress Party's socialist faction.[25]

India's postindependence industrial policies divide into four phases. From 1951 to 1965, a state-planned, heavily socialist economy, starting from a very low base, was able to achieve significant progress. There was overall economic growth and some of India's highest rates of manufacturing growth since independence.[26]

From 1966 to 1984, economic policies become more politicized and ideological. There was an intensification of socialism and the economy stagnated. In response, the government, toward the end of 1970s, shifted to more reformist, market-oriented policies.

From 1985 to 1990, successive governments recognized that the existing regime was not working and began piecemeal pro-market reforms. Growth picked up enough to build credibility for later, more aggressive reforms.

From 1991 to the present, aggressively reforming, increasingly nationalist, governments have implemented free-market policies across the board. India has outperformed its socialist past, but has not matched the performance of nations with strong, coherent, rational, proactive industrial policies.

Indian Socialism

India's socialist-era policies were motivated by the belief that the free market would never deliver growth on the scale required to eradicate poverty. Many policies adopted at this time appear irrational in hindsight, but seemed logical in the Indian context and at a historical moment when socialism was on the rise almost everywhere. Furthermore, some policies were imposed for the sake of social cohesion, not economic growth, and so should not be judged by their economic efficiency.

One of Mahatma Gandhi's legacies was a national commitment to "village industries" at the expense of large-scale businesses.[27] Income growth in such industries was expected, in the short and medium term, to be far more beneficial for the majority of the population. Creating mass unemployment by displacing craft production with modern factory production, when the former workers had no place to go, held little appeal. Capital intensive industries were recognized as crucial but being capital, rather than labor, intensive, were not expected to provide many jobs.

Limiting production to small producers ultimately held back many industries such as silk, specialty textiles, soap, leatherworking, blankets, and matches. Because of the desire to create as many jobs as possible, government placed little emphasis on productivity per worker.[28] There was a belief, then common among socialists worldwide, that India needed "socially necessary" goods such as steel, not the "socially useless consumer baubles" that free-market profit seekers would supposedly choose to make. Policies biased in favor of the former then retarded development of modern consumer goods industries.

Though India joined the GATT, World Bank, and IMF, its leaders chose not to fully integrate it into the global economy. They were pessimistic about India's export chances, which meant not counting on imports it would be unable to pay for. And they believed that economic self-sufficiency would help protect India's political independence.

This last idea was not wholly unreasonable, given later attempts by the US to use economic leverage over India for Cold War purposes. During the Cold War, India generally kept its distance from the Western democracies and their capital. Its leaders were often vitriolically anti-American – an antagonism that was sometimes reciprocated, as in Washington's tacit support for Pakistan during some of the Indo-Pakistani wars.

Neither communist nor capitalist, India's leader at independence, Jawaharlal Nehru, positioned his country as a leader of the Non-Aligned Movement. India formed a trading relationship, though not a military alliance, with the USSR, which provided it primitive heavy industrial technologies suited to India's low level of development. India thus relied on globally uncompetitive Soviet products and production technologies for decades.

Setting the Planning Framework

In 1948, Nehru's government issued its first Industrial Policy Resolution. Dividing the economy into four categories, it aimed at a moderate socialism that included some capitalism, both state-directed and otherwise:[29]

1. Armaments, nuclear power, and railroads. These were to be state monopolies.
2. "Basic industries" such as coal, petroleum, steel, iron, shipbuilding, and telecom hardware. The state assumed responsibility for future development, though existing firms were granted 10 years sufferance, after which the state would consider nationalization if they had not delivered.
3. Eighteen other industries, including cars, tractors, machine tools, heavy chemicals, electricity, cotton, and woolen textiles, cement, paper, salt, sugar, airlines, and shipping. These would remain in private hands, but under state and central government regulation.
4. All other industries were left to private initiative, though the state reserved the right to intervene.

The overall theme was self-sufficiency through import substitution. Import-substituting industrialization (ISI) was globally accepted at the time: Even nations such as South Korea that ultimately embraced the far more successful alternative of export-led industrialization (ELI) tried ISI first (see Chapter 6).

In 1951, the relationship between government and business was formalized in the Industries (Development and Regulation) Act, which shifted industrial policy, much of it previously in the hands of the states, to the Union government. Five-year plans for the entire economy were promulgated in an "attempt to hit Soviet-type targets by un-Soviet-type methods," above all without sacrificing democracy.[30] In the words of one American economist:

> Indian planning is an open process. Much of the controversy and the debates that accompany the preparation of the plans are public. The initial aggregate calculations and assumptions are either explicitly stated or readily deducible, and the makers of the plans are not only sensitive but responsive to criticism and suggestions from a wide variety of national and international sources. From original formulation through successive modifications to parliamentary presentation, plan making in India has evolved as a responsive democratic political process ... The political process which leads to the formulation of the final document is undoubtedly an impressive manifestation of the workings of an open society. By its very nature it generates many problems from the point of view of mapping an optimal strategy for economic development.[31]

Nehru wanted to show that socialist planning could work *with* private capital, directing it to national economic goals, rather than either letting it run free or replacing it with Soviet-style state control over everything. India thus aimed to develop state-owned manufacturing capacity in key industries *in addition to* the private sector's capacity.

Business accepted this compromise, as there was a "powerful consensus in the business class in favor of some kind of organized state assistance to industry."[32] A distinctive Indian capitalism thus developed, but generally *despite* the policies of the state, which were often tilted against it. The private sector was regularly required to cover the recurring public sector's production shortfalls – one reason it was tolerated.

The Five-Year Plans

From 1951, a licensing system was imposed, granting permission for particular firms to produce particular goods and specifying output levels and the locations of factories.[33] This was supposed to align private investments with the plans of the national Planning Commission (PC) and, above all, direct scarce resources to strategically important industries. As one scholar explains,

Once the overall targets for the five years had been worked out in aggregate terms for each sector, these would be translated into annual plans and, within each annual plan, they would be set into operation as particular investment projects. These projects in the private sector would be realized through the granting of licenses to applicants who wished to invest in the desired direction of the project. The funding for these projects would come from a portion of the annual budget known as the capital budget.[34]

On paper, creating the PC transferred power to determine economic priorities from politicians to technocrats, and the PC was supposed to be technical, nonpartisan, and insulated from politics. It would become a prominent feature of the Indian state, formulating – and revising after production shortfalls – successive five-year plans.

To make sure that the PC – made up of civil servants, technical experts, and businessmen – drove industrial policy forward, Nehru chaired it himself. By guaranteeing buy-in at the highest levels of authority, his presence should have ensured that its policies were implemented.[35] But this did not happen, thanks to deficiencies in the machinery for implementing its directives.

The First Five-Year Plan, launched in 1951, emphasized agriculture and irrigation. It included many major dam projects, critical infrastructure for the later green revolution that achieved food security. It also boosted investment in manufacturing, with expansion programs for 42 private-sector industries.[36]

Despite all its problems, Indian planning made real progress at first. Large-scale famine was eliminated. The 4 percent-plus growth rate between 1951 and 1965 was a huge improvement over the colonial near-zero rate. Industrial production grew 162 percent, an annual rate of more than 7 percent.[37] Indeed, during its first 15 years of independence, India outperformed the East Asian countries that later surpassed it so dramatically.[38]

Why was the PC successful in this era? The economy was still simple enough that central planning was workable. Its technological level was so low that huge gains could be realized by straightforward mass deployment of mundane technologies such as fertilizer. And India's politics had not yet become so fractious as to complicate every economic decision with ideological antagonisms. (Congress ran the government without significant opposition until the mid-1960s, though it had internal disputes.)

In this era, trade and investment policy were, surprisingly given socialism and the desire for self-sufficiency, relatively liberal.[39] FDI was accepted, especially in sectors not reserved for the state, and Nehru resisted the far left's demands to expel foreign multinationals.[40] It took the Imports (Control) Order of 1955 to require imports to be licensed, and subsequent policies, such as exchange controls, to really clamp down.[41] As late as 1961, the government was issuing lists of industries in which FDI would be welcomed.[42]

Problems of Central Planning

From the start, Indian planning ran into problems, some of which were intrinsic to central planning, some specific to India's implementation. The good results of the first plan were, by Nehru's own admission, "trial and error."[43] Production of locomotives and sewing machines exceeded their targets, but cement, superphosphates (for fertilizer), ethanol, and steel fell short by more than 50 percent. Significantly, as the great Indian economist D. R. Gadgil, a vice-chairman of the PC, observed: "The major achievements of the first Five Year Plan period may, perhaps, be said not to have been planned at all."[44] A good deal of India's industrial development was due to ministries and licensing committees going their own ways, bucking the Plan's priorities.

Fatally, the planners had assumed that the heavy lifting was over once orders had been given.[45] They underestimated the difficulty of monitoring the performance of the industries for which they were planning.[46] Information about what was *already* happening in the economy, let alone about the forward plans of businesses or what could plausibly be planned, was primitive and hoarded by the government departments that generated it.[47] Until the Third Five-Year Plan, there was not even an institutional mechanism for the PC to translate the plans into annual budgets. That was the often-hostile Finance Ministry's job.[48]

The PC lacked the power to either discipline business *or* engage it cooperatively.[49] It even lacked the legal authority to make its decisions binding on other government departments. For example, it lacked full control over jute (handled by the Commerce Ministry), steel and machine tools (the Industry Ministry), coal (the Industry and Supply Ministry), and other key industries.[50] Over time, the initially weak PC grew even weaker as it was ignored with impunity. Reforms such as interministerial committees for purposes of coordination merely produced more talk, as no agency had the authority to impose decisions on any other.[51]

The Plans themselves lacked strategic coherence, especially the crucial factor of coordination between industries that depended upon each other. They were mostly just grab bags of projects from individual ministries. They were decidedly not schemes for systematically developing ever-more-advanced industrial capabilities based on understanding which capabilities had to come first.

The initial lending of the Industrial Finance Corporation of India (IFCI), the country's first development bank, was haphazard. Credit was granted on a "first come, first served" basis to existing industries, mainly in the food and textile sectors, rather than being targeted on building up strategically chosen new industries.[52]

An intrinsic weakness of the system was that if one element fell behind, all the others would suffer. Late completion of a dam due to a shortage of concrete would leave a steelworks without essential water, and nondelivery of its steel would then starve steel-consuming industries. Because a planned economy is necessarily more rigid than a market one, officialdom had difficulty making on-the-fly adjustments to unexpected changes.

Price controls were another problem – for example, textile mills were allowed to increase capacity only if they sold their product at uneconomically low prices. In a democratic country with an impoverished electorate, this was an unavoidable policy temptation. There was no systematic planning for profit levels, so even determining, let alone imposing, reasonable prices was difficult.

The Apogee of Indian Planning

The Second Five-Year Plan (1956–61) was the most comprehensive. Tilting further toward the socialist side of Nehru's vision, it formally gave the state dominance over the economy and primary responsibility for industrialization. Informed in theory by the development model of the brilliant Indian statistician Prasanta Mahalanobis, it aimed to build up heavy industries first. In an economy relatively closed to imports and exports, development of capital goods industries would be, it was not unreasonably thought, the main constraint on growth.

Signs of trouble continued. In 1957, foreign currency reserves fell to a dangerously low level, requiring an IMF bailout. The crisis had been caused in part by a surge in capital goods imports as industrialists with license approvals tooled up.[53] In response, the Finance Ministry imposed foreign exchange budgeting, allowing forex only for the "core" industries of steel, transport, and power. This damaged other industries needing foreign capital goods. In 1957, an urgent review of the Second Five-Year Plan concluded that only two-thirds of it would probably be completed.[54]

The currency crisis left India more protectionist, but also sparked its first attempt at an export strategy to earn more foreign exchange. However, the leadership entrusted matters to process-obsessed bureaucrats, blunting the effort's effectiveness. The state did not help firms with the risks and costs of entering foreign markets, so the initiative evoked little interest from industrialists.[55] Content with secure profits protected from foreign competition by tariffs and from domestic competition by licenses, they had little appetite for competitive foreign markets. Exports of only a few products, such as sewing machines, bicycles, and electric fans, took off.

By the time the Third Five-Year Plan (1961–6) began, the basic pattern for industrial policy was set: determining (supposedly) what products were needed to achieve the targeted growth rate, then investing in plant (supposedly) sufficient to produce them. The Third Plan's targets included 13 million tons of cement, 6.8 million tons of finished steel, 80,000 tons of aluminum, 1,841 locomotives (434 diesel, 232 electric, and 1,175 steam), 5,800 million yards of cotton textiles, 2,000,000 bicycles, 700,000 sewing machines, 100,000 cars, 44,000 tons of electric cable, and 10,000 tractors.[56] (This last item was a tiny number for an agrarian nation the size of India.)

As an alternative to foreign-controlled investment, New Delhi invited foreign firms to help create strategic state-owned industries producing electrical cables, machine tools, steel, penicillin, fertilizer, telephones, locomotives, and many other goods.[57] By 1965, there would be 420 agreements with British firms, 194 with American ones, 149 with West German, 66 with Swiss, and 51 with Japanese.[58]

Planning's Mounting Dysfunction

In the early years, when the Indian economy was still relatively simple, government could make decisions on licenses in a timely fashion. But during the 1960s, the system clogged up. Delays became endemic and bribes to obtain a favorable decision, or just speed up the process, became common.[59]

The licensing committees supposedly based their work on high-level sectoral targets from the PC. But these committees were given little data to develop the plans' details, few criteria to assess firms' compliance, and minimal powers to impose sanctions for failure.[60] The plans' insistence on unrealistic targets made it difficult for the players to take them seriously, undermining the whole idea of a planned economy.

Parts of officialdom were well aware that the system was not working as intended, but could do little about it.[61] The various license-granting bureaucracies, each with its own agenda, frustrated the PC's overall plans. There were de facto vetoes at so many levels that, instead of a centrally directed industrial policy, India had a multitude of disconnected sectoral policies.

Meanwhile, "Made in India" was becoming a watchword in India for shoddy and unreliable products, and a black market in foreign goods developed. Import substitution without the discipline of export requirements kept quality low, prices high, and innovation slow. It made India's private sector more resistant to governmental direction than if the government had required exporting, because firms did not need state support to thrive in tough foreign markets.[62] Subsidies were sometimes paid to import-substituting firms to improve product quality, but many chose to just pocket the subsidy on the usually correct assumption that the bureaucracy would not follow up.[63]

Businesses learned how to game the system. Acquiring a license to produce a product gave an investor a virtual monopoly. Government efforts to prevent India's largest firms from becoming too powerful did not prevent the continued growth of the large family-run conglomerates that predated independence. These families, such as the Tatas and the Birlas, owned many small companies in diverse areas, rather than creating large, focused, strategically coherent firms. Licensing tended to reinforce this commercial oligarchy: From 1956 to 1966, 41 percent of new licensed production capacity would go to the top 20 companies.[64]

Private industry was thus able to frustrate many of the aims of planning.[65] This saved the private sector from being completely stifled, but a) it further undermined any effectiveness the plans might have had, b) it relentlessly corroded the credibility of the economic-policy organs, and c) it opened magnificent opportunities for corruption. Corruption in India has outlived the old planning regime, and by many accounts has gotten worse, as there is now more worth stealing.

Planning created barriers to industry entry and exit, provided indiscriminate and indefinite protection, led to industrial inefficiencies, produced a culture of rent-seeking, fostered misallocation of resources, and undermined domestic and foreign competition.[66] Indians came to call it the "License-Permit-Quota Raj."[67] As early as 1964, Nehru's successor, Lal Bahadur Shastri, began to rein in the PC and make a cautious start at rolling back the scope of state intervention.[68] But the tying of foreign aid to India's importing certain goods from the donor nation, among many other factors, made it hard to cut back on controls such as import licensing.[69]

During its socialist era, India had the ability to produce a wider range of products than most other countries at a comparable level of development.[70] The epitome was its national car, the Hindustan Motors Ambassador. Based on a British design, it was launched in 1957 and, amazingly, produced in updated versions until 2014. It symbolized India's insistence on developing indigenous industries with no regard for their international competitiveness or even domestic attractiveness. Its mid-1950s parameters of cost, quality, features, and performance were obsolete even in 1957. And it stayed that way, due to the reluctance of successive governments to import new foreign technologies, or even to reverse engineer new parts and components. It never became a big export seller.

Indira Gandhi's Lurch to the Left

Shastri died in office in 1966 and Indira Gandhi, Nehru's daughter (no relation to Mahatma Gandhi), became prime minister. She inherited a vacuum in industrial policy due to the general consensus that the Third Five-Year Plan had failed. Due in part to bad weather and war with Pakistan, growth had stalled out. The Plan had aimed for 5.6 percent but delivered only 2.4 percent, barely exceeding population growth.[71]

Gandhi began as an economic reformer, though her reforms concentrated merely on relaxing controls, rather than reforming them to achieve better results.[72] "Plan holidays" were declared (1966–9), during which updates were put on hold, leaving the economy to rely on annual stopgaps.[73] In hindsight, this was a tacit admission that planning was not working, and the holidays were a hiatus from which the planning process never fully recovered.[74]

Then, with the planning system visibly falling apart and a struggle inside the Congress Party about how to respond, Gandhi lurched left, not out of ideological conviction but as a political tactic in her struggle against the party's old guard.[75] She embraced an extreme socialism far beyond Nehru's original vision or the demands of the Indian public.

The constitution was amended to make India officially socialist. The top income tax bracket, applying even to relatively modest incomes, was raised to more than 95 percent. Trade with the Soviet Bloc was expanded, and foreign multinationals were compelled to become Indian-controlled or leave. There was an emphasis on the regions and on keeping economic power out of private hands, and a doubling down on import substitution.[76] Basic industries were prioritized over consumer industries, small firms over large, the public sector over the private. Coal, oil, and copper, plus a large part of textiles, were nationalized.

India turned further away from FDI, blocking investments that could have brought money, technology, and managerial skills.[77] Fourteen banks, containing 85 percent of deposits, were nationalized. Credit was then redirected toward agriculture at the expense of industry. The banks became stagnant and risk-averse, rarely lending to new firms. Manufacturers found themselves short of credit, while banks lent to firms favored by their political masters. This cronyism produced recurring crises of bad loans, followed by government bailouts.

Handicraft production was already favored, and Gandhi extended this bias to small factories with her Small-Scale Industrial Policy, reserving many products for small firms. (Later studies revealed that the benefits to small manufacturers were more than offset by stifling the expansion of larger ones.)[78] These "think small" policies damaged the volume textile industry, which at independence had supplied 76 percent of domestic demand and had been winning export markets.[79] This decline in India's staple export dragged down overall export performance. By 1970, exports touched bottom, at just 4 percent of GDP, compared with the previous peak of 11 percent in 1910, 2.6 percent in 1948, and 18 percent today.[80]

Gandhi also enacted the Monopolies and Restrictive Trade Practices Act, designed to retard the growth of the largest private-sector manufacturers. Many got around the law by dividing themselves and continuing to grow.[81] Many restrictive policies enacted in this period proved politically hard to undo later.[82] For example, legislation was passed requiring firms employing more than 300 workers to get permission from their state government for layoffs. This crude alternative to developing a proper unemployment insurance system prevented economically rational reallocation of resources and discouraged expansions.[83]

Economic Reform Begins

The Fourth Five-Year Plan (1969–74), like the Third, disappointed, delivering only 3.3 percent growth.[84] With the population expanding 2.3 percent per year, this was far too slow to deliver mass relief from poverty.[85] (Poverty in India actually *increased* during the 1960s.)[86] The exasperated self-deprecating phrase "Hindu rate of growth" came into circulation, and the country was increasingly regarded as the world's "most dramatic case of a failed developmental state."[87]

Planning continued, but increasingly as a tool for Gandhi's patronage machine, rather than a national economic agenda. Under the Fifth Five-Year Plan (1974–9), the Union government for the first time acquired powers, previously held by the states, to generate and transmit electricity, and a national highway system was designed and funded. But before the Plan could take effect, failed harvests and the 1973 oil shock led to a severe recession, prompting Gandhi to lurch even *further* left and push import substitution even harder.

Indira Gandhi's economics finally ran aground in 1977 on surging food prices, a massive railway strike, student protests, and a disastrous attempt to nationalize the wheat trade. India's first ever non-Congress government took power. But the center-right coalition headed by Morarji Desai that emerged was even more economically isolationist, doubling down on small-scale and cottage industries and further restricting wholly foreign-owned companies.[88] The Fifth Plan was terminated a year early because it did not conform to the new government's priorities, and a substitute was prepared.

Desai's government, however, proved too weak to lead, and in 1980, a chastened Ms. Gandhi returned to power. During her second term in office

(1980–4), she grudgingly returned to the liberalizing reforms she had begun with.[89] Modest loosening of state controls resumed. Other reforms included raising asset limits on plant and machinery in small-scale enterprises from 1 to 2 million rupees and increasing capacity limits on large-scale manufacturing. Controls on FDI were loosened. Price controls were relaxed, corporate taxes were lowered, and public enterprises were pressured to become more efficient.

The Sixth Five-Year Plan, running to 1985, thus constituted the first significant retreat from socialism since independence. Gandhi tried to win friends in the previously despised business community to compensate for her dwindling mass support.[90] But industrialists outside her charmed circle were beginning to see the licensing system as not only corrupt and inefficient, but also as a barrier to their aspirations.[91] Major players were becoming more ambitious and were no longer prepared just to work around and patch the failings of the public sector. Still, the economy responded favorably to reform: The growth target under the Sixth Plan was 5.2 percent, with the actual coming in at 5.7.[92] New Delhi was clearly doing something right again.

Rajiv Gandhi: Reform Continues

Rajiv Gandhi, Indira's son, succeeded his assassinated mother in 1984 and continued liberalization. He freed the private sector from some constraints on raising capital, importing products, and dealing in consumer goods. The licensing system was loosened and some industries freed from it entirely. The auto, cement, food processing, cotton spinning, and polyester yarn industries began to modernize.[93] Reforms started in 1984 allowed private firms to manufacture telecom equipment.

The Seventh Five-Year Plan (1985–90) cut tariffs and expanded the list of allowable imports. The exposure of Indian industry to foreign competition began to induce technological and managerial modernization and improve productivity. Measures were taken to promote exports, including relaxing foreign exchange constraints on imported inputs and devaluing the rupee. Policies favoring village industry were largely upstaged in 1988 by the designation of 71 geographic "growth centers" to encourage industrialization in backward areas, with power, water, telecommunications, and banking provided.[94]

IT in India began to flourish in the late 1980s, in part because it was not covered by the licensing system.[95] (The sector has since been favored by both the Union government and the individual states through incentives, direct funding, and exemptions from various regulations.)

Rajiv's reforms met resistance from, in the words of one observer, "some of his cabinet and an inward-looking and corrupt civil service, still obsessed with a closed and constrictive relationship with the Soviet Union."[96] Much of Indian industry remained in the grip of a hidebound bureaucracy.

Nonetheless, enough liberalization had occurred that the Seventh Plan's 5 percent growth target was surpassed by actual growth of 6 percent.[97] For the first time, private capital formation in the 1980s exceeded public.[98] And economic growth was now meaningfully outstripping population growth, which was itself slowing as India entered the "demographic transition" most nations experience as they develop.

Systematic Economic Reform

Scandals resulted in Rajiv Gandhi's defeat in 1989 and a short-lived coalition government, under V. P. Singh, a defector from the now declining Congress Party, took power. His government marked the point when India's trickle of reforms turned into a flood.

The economy was already struggling when Iraq's 1990 invasion of Kuwait triggered a rise in oil prices and a decline in remittances from Indians working in the Gulf.[99] The result was sharp fiscal deterioration and a balance-of-payments crisis. With only three weeks' currency reserves remaining, India sought an emergency loan from the IMF. In return, the IMF required a structural adjustment program, including rupee devaluation and partial convertibility, tariff reductions, cuts in industry subsidies, further relaxation of licensing, and privatizations.[100]

Next, the 1991 election, thrown into chaos by the assassination of Rajiv, produced a Congress-led government headed by P. V. Narasimha Rao. For economic leadership he turned to Manmohan Singh, a former governor of the Reserve Bank of India, appointing him finance minister.[101] Singh believed, in his own words, in "getting government out of activities where governments are not very efficient at doing things."[102] His manifesto was the 1991 Industrial Policy Statement, which, despite paying lip service to self-reliance and public-sector industry, announced a 180-degree turn to systematic deregulation, privatization, openness to trade, and foreign investment. It promised that a hatchet would be taken to the "large number of chronically sick public enterprises incurring heavy losses operating in a competitive market and serving little or no public purpose."[103] Entrepreneurs would be permitted to use their own commercial judgment.[104] Government policy would be to assist, not constrain them.

The public-sector monopoly of many sectors was ended. Asset limits on large firms were repealed. FDI was encouraged, with presumptive approval of minority stakes, and majority stakes (up to 51 percent) generally permitted in "high priority industries requiring large investments and advanced technology."[105] Import licensing was abolished except for a handful of intermediate inputs and capital goods. There was a gradual compression of the top tariff rates and a rationalization of the tariff structure. From 1990 to 1995, India cut its average tariff on manufactures from 120 percent to 40 percent, after which it gradually declined to today's 17 percent.[106]

First steps were taken to actively support manufacturing R&D. In 1990, only a quarter of state R&D spending was going to manufacturing (vs. three quarters in Korea), but this began to increase.[107]

In 1995, India joined the WTO. Because WTO rules forbade them, and with the proximate cause being an American WTO dispute from 1997 to 2001, India stopped requiring import licenses for many goods entirely.

Domestic competition intensified, shaking out existing companies and creating new ones. The quality and variety of goods produced improved. Indian firms improved their previously abysmal efficiency. As one economist notes, "Labour intensity in organized Indian manufacturing fell from 1.45 in 1980 to 0.33 in the 2000s."[108]

Because matters were so obviously in flux, the government reverted to annual plans for 1990–1 and 1991–2. The Eighth Five-Year Plan (1992–7) constituted, unsurprisingly, a sharp break. Actual growth of 6.8 percent easily beat the 5.6 percent target.[109]

A Multiparty Reform Consensus

Subsequent governments of all parties continued to liberalize. An improving economy, however, did not save Rao from election defeat in 1996, and a minority government took power, led by the right-wing Hindu nationalist Bharatiya Janata Party (BJP) under Atal Bihari Vajpayee.

This government implemented further reforms in the Ninth Five-Year Plan (1997–2002). The number of products that could be manufactured only by small businesses was cut from 821 to 506.[110] Financial sector liberalization continued. The BJP also further reformed telecoms, privatized more enterprises, expanded primary education, and passed the Fiscal Responsibility and Budget Management Act, an effort to improve slack fiscal discipline.

Under the 10th Five-Year Plan (2002–7), quantitative restrictions on imports were abolished. Power Minister Suresh Prabhu freed firms to trade electricity, first domestically and then with neighboring countries.[111]

By now the straitjacket of central planning had been irreversibly loosened, and the 2004 return of a Congress-led multiparty government under Manmohan Singh seemed to guarantee further liberalization. However, Singh, wrestling with wider political challenges (including an alliance with the communists in his first coalition government), was not able to accomplish all that he wanted. Nevertheless, restrictions on the manufacture of specific items by larger firms were further relaxed. And on the strength of reforms already accomplished, India achieved its highest sustained growth rates since independence.[112]

By the 11th Five-Year Plan (2007–12), New Delhi's approach to industry was largely hands off. India came through the crash of 2007–8 better than most G20 countries, thanks to its limited exposure to Western financial innovations and incomplete currency convertibility. The 10th and 11th Plans delivered 7.6 and 8.0 percent growth, respectively.[113] In 2014, the Planning Commission was abolished and the five-year plans were ended, except for defense.

The 12th and last Five-Year Plan (2012–17) usefully prioritized removing horrendous electricity and transport bottlenecks, which especially hurt manufacturing, and countering trade dumping by East Asian nations, a result of opening up to imports. But the Plan added little substantive pro-manufacturing industrial policy.

In 2021, the government committed to privatizing all remaining public-sector firms outside strategic sectors – "strategic" meaning atomic energy, space, defense, transportation, telecom, electricity, coal, petroleum, minerals, banking, insurance, and financial services – and to consolidation plus *some* privatization even in strategic sectors.[114] But privatization did not always mean a turn to genuinely free markets, as public resources, such as coal, land, and the telecommunications spectrum, were often captured by private monopolies.[115]

Ineffective Support of Manufacturing

By about 2010, India was becoming aware that its manufacturing was lagging. So in 2011, the Singh government announced its National Manufacturing Policy (NMP).[116] Its goals were sector growth of 2–4 percent above GDP growth, an increase in share of GDP to 25 percent by 2025, and the creation of 100 million manufacturing jobs.

Policies included creating National Investment & Manufacturing Zones (NIMZs). These promised quality infrastructure, permissive zoning, and skills development facilities. They also promised to buffer firms against the usual harsh legal consequences of laying off workers or going bankrupt – a clear sign that such laws were retarding investment.[117] Also revealingly, the following industries were targeted: "employment intensive industries, capital goods, industries with strategic significance, industries where India enjoys a competitive advantage, small and medium Enterprises, [and] public sector enterprises."[118] In other words, NMP was less of a strategy than a vague wish list, and its results fell far short.

In 2014, the next government, under the BJP's Narendra Modi, recast NMP as the "Make in India" campaign, targeting 25 mostly manufacturing sectors for job creation and aiming "to transform India into a global design and manufacturing hub." The program aimed to a) increase the sector's growth rate to 12–14 percent per annum, b) create 100 million manufacturing jobs by 2022, and c) increase the sector's contribution to GDP to 25 percent by 2022 (later revised to 2025).[119] But the program, like many of the Modi government, was long on branding and short on implementation, and it failed. In the words of one Indian economist,

> The spate of policy announcements without having the preparedness to implement them is "policy casualness." "Make in India" has been plagued by a large number of under-prepared initiatives . . . First, it set out too ambitious growth rates for the manufacturing sector to achieve. [T]o expect to build capabilities for such a quantum jump is perhaps an enormous overestimation of the implementation capacity of the government. Second, the initiative brought in too many sectors into its fold. This led to a loss of policy focus. Further, it was seen as a policy devoid of any understanding of the comparative advantages of the domestic economy. Third, given the uncertainties of the global economy and ever-rising trade protectionism, the initiative was spectacularly ill-timed.[120]

In 2020, the BJP government created the Production Linked Incentives (PLI) program, paying a bonus to select industries for production exceeding current levels, budgeted at $24 billion over five years.[121] Eligible sectors included electronics, medical devices, active pharmaceutical ingredients, telecom and networking hardware, food products, consumer appliances, photovoltaic modules, autos and auto components, advanced batteries, textiles, and specialty steel. This program has since had some impact in pharmaceuticals, but whether it will help build valuable industries economy-wide, or just subsidize production increases that would have happened anyway, is not yet known.[122] (Given the weakness of its reporting and monitoring provisions, there is a huge risk of the latter.)

Manufacturing as a share of GDP has been stuck at 14–15 percent for two decades.[123] As of 2020, only 27 million people worked in manufacturing, versus 136 million in China, and generally with lower productivity.[124] Firms have been discouraged from expanding by laws that require permission for layoffs, by other complex labor laws at both the national and state levels, and by cumbersome bureaucracy, expensive credit, expensive energy, poor roads, inefficient railways, unreliable electricity, and poor water infrastructure.

R&D spending is still low and linkages between industry and public research institutions are weak. India lacks effective governmental institutions to support the development of new manufacturing technologies and their transmission to firms. The Council of Scientific and Industrial Research, and the Ministry of Micro, Small and Medium Enterprise's Technology Centres, which are supposed to fulfill this role, are regarded as ineffective.[125]

Even India's manufacturing success stories have their flaws. The pharmaceutical industry, for example, is now third in the world by volume – but only fourteenth by value, a clear sign of its focus on the low, generic end of the market.[126] (From around 2010, some Indian firms began developing new drugs, a rare exception to India's generally low level of innovation.) PLI had a big impact on cell phones: In the five years to 2023, the country went from a $3 billion deficit to a $10 billion surplus in this product.[127] But these were built from imported components, making India an even *larger* net importer.[128]

India has pledged $10 billion to encourage chipmaking, but the program has shown few results.[129] In 2023, the government rejected an application for a subsidy from the Indian firm Vedanta Resources, in a joint venture with Taiwan's Hon Hai Precision Industry, to manufacture 28-nanometer chips.[130] The two firms, both cell phone assemblers without chipmaking experience, had been unable to find a partner or licensor for the needed technology.[131] (In addition, the location for the proposed facility in India was isolated, with no supporting infrastructure or industry.) It is unlikely India will be competitive in volume fabrication of advanced semiconductors in the foreseeable future.[132]

India Today and Tomorrow

India today is economically more vibrant than at any time in its history. The cell phone (1 billion by 2016, vs. just 24 million landlines) and satellite TV have revolutionized popular expectations, as have budget airlines for the better off.[133] There is now a middle class of some 200 million people.

But these people are middle class only by Indian standards, as their incomes would not put them in that category in any developed nation.[134] Despite economic growth, the country has not created any net new jobs in the past decade.[135] Nor has it achieved China-scale improvements in mass education, nutrition, sanitation, or infrastructure. Its average educational attainment is where China's was in 1980.[136] Most Indians are still stuck in subsistence agriculture or casual service-sector labor. As of 2018, only 12 percent of India's workforce (vs. 45 percent of China's) even *had* a formal job.[137]

In manufacturing, state-run firms now account for less than 10 percent of output.[138] But those that remain, running the gamut from profitable monopolies to perennial loss-makers, still suffer from politicized management.[139] The economy remains riddled with distorting subsidies and price controls for key inputs such as water, coal, electricity, fertilizer, and rail transport.

China has five times as many companies in the Forbes Global 2000.[140] The median size of India's firms is much lower and the country has too many small, low-productivity companies. In 2014, only 2,300 factories employed more than 500 people.[141] One sign of overdependence on unskilled labor is that China's factories employ more than 20 *times* as many forklifts.[142] Above all, India lacks China's large firms that make products using a lot of unskilled labor. In apparel, even Bangladesh and Sri Lanka are ahead in scale. Too many of India's biggest corporations are still family-dominated conglomerates, not true multinationals.

The vaunted international competitive IT and business process offshoring sectors can only employ a small percentage of the population. Only 8 percent of Indians have college degrees, which generally coincide with the ability to speak English.[143] And some Indian tech firms even outsource to China, Vietnam, and Romania due to poor infrastructure and a limited supply of adequate staff.[144] The IT industry competes mainly on the basis of cheaper labor and has created few globally popular products or technologies. The country now boasts 70 tech "unicorns," but they have produced very few jobs relative to the size of the country, serve mostly domestic consumers, and are not globally competitive.[145]

Officialdom knows the country needs more efficient government. India modernized its bankruptcy laws in 2016 and consolidated and reformed its labor laws four years later. Pro-employer labor reforms have shown positive results.[146] But it still has a tangled system of land laws, with inadequate records of ownership and a history of uncompensated seizures by government and private parties. Land acquisition and permitting delays have forced abandonment of many large industrial and infrastructure projects. In 2015, the Modi government tried to reform the system, but failed.

Corruption remains a huge problem and there have been many corporate scandals. The World Bank in 2019 reported India improving its "Ease of Doing Business" rank by 53 positions in two years, but the country was still only at number 77.[147] In 2020, New Delhi announced a plan to spend $1.5 trillion on infrastructure – roads, trains, ports, airports, telecom – over the next five years.[148] But even this will merely redress the existing dismal state of Indian infrastructure, not raise it to the level of being a competitive advantage.[149]

India's federal structure has enabled some states to draw ahead with better economic policies.[150] Gujarat, Tamil Nadu, and Maharashtra have done better in manufacturing. In states where developers have collaborated with state and local governments to improve living conditions, land-law reform has been more successful.[151]

A Strategically Directionless Capitalism

India today does not have the strategic, coordinated, comprehensive industrial policy it needs. Even if acquires one, it will be difficult for it to become a global industrial hub like the East Asian nations. Cheap labor has little traction against incumbents like China or Vietnam. Earlier industrializers like Japan enjoyed an American market ruled by a government that was largely asleep to the strategies being employed against it, but such "soft targets" are disappearing. In many industries, India simply does not have the needed industrial base or worker skills, and is not making the sustained, systematic effort required to develop them. Seeing policy inconsistency from New Delhi, foreign investors do not yet trust the durability of the country's liberalization.[152]

One of India's strongest cards is simply the size of its domestic market, which is potentially large enough to support many advantageous industries. Sound industrial policy would make full use of this advantage. Precedents include the fact that, behind a 60–100 percent tariff wall, its car industry has flourished.[153] By 2019, Indian and foreign firms were turning out 4 million vehicles a year – 677,000 for export – making India the world's fourth largest producer.[154] This anchored a sizeable industrial commons (see Chapter 3 for this concept) potentially useful for other manufacturing.

Over the decade to 2022, India's dozen largest companies increased their average market capitalization by 386 percent, ushering in an era of concentration.[155] Led by the Adani Group and Reliance Industries, these de facto national champions have been increasingly favored by New Delhi. Although this has enabled accomplishments such as the national rollout of low-cost 4G telephony, other firms have suffered from this favoritism.[156] Unlike Japan's *keiretsus* and Korea's *chaebols*, these conglomerates mainly operate domestically behind tariff walls and lack the discipline of having to export.

The souring view of uncontrolled globalization that hit Europe and the US after 2010 eventually hit India, which had also suffered from a flood of Chinese imports and a chronic trade deficit. Since 2014, pressure from manufacturers has led to an increase in the average industrial tariff from 13 to 18 percent.[157] In 2019, New Delhi walked away from the Regional Comprehensive Economic Partnership, a proposed free trade agreement between the 10 ASEAN states, China, Japan, South Korea, Australia, and New Zealand.

As of 2024, Prime Minister Modi's new watchword was *atmanirbhar*, "self-reliant." This was obviously not the classic Gandhian, home-spinning-wheel version of the concept, but neither was it a step toward a modern, mercantilist industrial policy. At very best, the reforms India is now attempting will lead to a moderately well-regulated mid-level market economy – not to the world-class results of East Asia. Whether New Delhi has the political and bureaucratic capacity to follow in its footsteps is openly debated in the country today.

Strengths

- Huge population and potential internal market that make internally generated growth possible.
- An entrepreneurial culture.

Weaknesses

- Political and bureaucratic corruption. Even honest politics complicated by complexity of the country.
- Historically, central planning crippled ability to respond to market forces, develop new technologies, or engage global opportunities.
- For decades after independence, commitment to village scale industries – with their attendant inefficiencies – and opposition to the large scale enterprise.
- Bureaucracy with poor data to guide policymaking, weak implementation and monitoring, and minimal authority to discipline the private sector.
- Weak social and physical infrastructure: mass education, nutrition, sanitation, and infrastructure other than cellular telephony.
- Lack of good research institutions at any stage of the innovation pipeline.
- Low national R&D spending.
- Little technologically informed strategic targeting of industries for support.
- Little coordinated deployment of the specific industrial policy tools required to support targeted industries.
- Legacy subsidies and price controls for key inputs such as water, coal, electricity, fertilizer, and rail transport.
- Family-owned conglomerates that operate domestically, behind tariff walls, largely avoiding the discipline of competing in global markets.

12 ARGENTINA
A Dual Cautionary Tale

On the eve of World War I, Argentina's living standard was comparable to the world's most advanced nations.[1] But after a century of misgovernment, this spectacularly agriculturally endowed nation is sixty-ninth in per capita GDP and eighty-third in competitiveness.[2] Argentina, Australia, and Canada have comparable population sizes and natural resources. Up to World War II, their income trajectories were similar.[3] Yet Australia and Canada are today developed economies, while Argentina is stalled somewhere between the Third World and the First.

Because Argentina's governments were highly interventionist for much of this period, the country is often viewed as a cautionary tale against economic interventionism per se. But its recurring experiments with deregulation, laissez-faire, free trade, and openness to inbound investment have *also* led to underperformance and recurring crises. Per capita GDP growth during the mostly interventionist years 1943–79 averaged 1.8 percent, the *same* as for the mostly liberalizing years 1984–2009.[4] Argentina's experience demonstrates that neither strategically vacant, tactically incompetent interventionism *nor* reliance on "the magic of the market" suffices to achieve sustained prosperity.

Why did Argentina perform so badly? For a start, unlike the generals who ruled South Korea for much of the post–World War II era (see Chapter 6), or even General Franco's Opus Dei technocrats in Spain, its military rulers had little understanding of, or even interest in, economics, beyond fanatical anti-communism. The civilian economic elite and its wealth had come out of agriculture, so it had little experience in manufacturing or disposition to be elbowed aside by industrialists.[5]

The country thus never had the intellectual or political foundations for planning its industrial development. It had no understanding of climbing the ladder of ever-more-advantageous economic activities.[6] Protectionism became an ideological idée fixe and a political crutch, rather than a strategy. Directed credit, until recently, degenerated into crisis management at best, political favoritism at worst. Other policy tools often simply failed to actually engage with the economy, especially with manufacturing.

Unsurprisingly, the failures of interventionism, obvious to many at the time, triggered recurring repudiations in favor of liberalization. These episodes successfully produced floods of inward investment. But the accompanying reforms, poorly conceived and clumsily implemented, either fizzled out, in which case they accomplished little, or persisted long enough to bring Argentina to the brink of economic success before ending in crashes caused by their flaws. The inflows of capital, technology, foreign firms, and skilled management reversed during these crises.

These crashes, and notably in 1989, 2001, and 2019, undid hard-won gains in GDP, productivity, and manufacturing value added.[7] Several governments saw economic "shock therapy" as the only option, either because of the mess the economy was already in, or because they believed that reform required the most inefficient sectors to be squeezed to the point of bankruptcy. But shock policies such as opening to free trade without a transition period for local firms to adapt simply bankrupted them.

Crudely executed swings of policy were exacerbated by Argentina's polarized politics. Democratic institutions maintained only a fragile grip on deeply oligarchic urges, leading to impulsive and incoherent decision-making. For half a century, the failures of civilian governments allowed the military to present itself as a source of order and leadership. Argentina had six military coups in the twentieth century, rough transitions back to civilian rule, and 14 presidents between 1962 and 1988 alone.[8] General Juan Perón (1895–1974), husband to the legendary Evita, perfected a uniquely counterproductive form of economic populism that complicates the country's politics to this day. Argentina's military governments were more export oriented, and thus devalued its currency, while their civilian counterparts (until Menem in 1989) were more protectionist, producing inflation. The one constant has been the lack of an industrial policy based on pursuing growth by fostering new industries and ever-more-valuable exports.

The Argentine state has generally lacked a competent administrative cadre. Its industrial policy institutions have bogged down in process. A sure sign of administrative dysfunction has been that new presidents, unable to motivate entrenched officials, have often appointed their own parallel bureaucracies – with little success.[9] The failure to create trustworthy government institutions has inhibited entrepreneurial risk-taking.[10] Foreign (and even domestic) investors' confidence has been hampered by weaknesses in the judicial system, including politicized appointment and removal of judges and a perceived lack of fairness. (Argentina is ranked 112th in the world for the quality of its judiciary.)[11] Companies have been controlled by interlocking networks of families, with low standards of managerial professionalism.[12] Corruption has been rampant: Most recent presidents have been prosecuted for it once out of office.

Repeated overvaluation and devaluation of the peso, spurts of hyper-inflation, and two defaults on the country's sovereign debt have added to the disorder. Governments ran up international debts whose interest payments the economy could not afford, then violated agreements with the IMF by allowing the central bank or provincial governments to finance further spending.

History to World War II

Argentina's first industry arose in the nineteenth century as a byproduct of its huge grain and beef exports. During the half-century begin-ning in 1880, per capita GDP grew faster than in the US.[13] By 1920, the country had 47,000 kilometers of railroads, the most in Latin America, and the Rosario grain market was as large as Chicago's.[14] The most sophisticated industry was the mass cold storage of meat for export.

The country's power structure, entrenched well into the late twentieth century, consisted of a cosmopolitan elite of *estancieros* – large-scale landowners – who believed that trying to industrialize a country with such vast agricultural riches was pointless. The quality of the country's governance institutions lagged: Despite having Latin America's most advanced economy, it did not have a central bank until 1935.

Some import substitution had been tried since the 1870s, but Argentina first turned seriously protectionist after the 1929 Wall Street crash, when the military first seized power from an elected government.[15] As the Depression bit, Britain, Argentina's best customer, signed preferential deals within its empire covering beef (from Australia) and grain (from Canada). Argentina secured access to Britain for its beef in 1932, but at the price of letting in Britain's manufactures.[16] Protectionism in other European markets led Argentina to try to protect its deteriorating balance of payments by raising tariffs from an average of 17 percent in 1930 to 29 percent by 1933.[17]

Policy next aimed to encourage domestic manufacturing while impos-ing increasingly severe tariffs, quotas, import licenses, and foreign-exchange rationing. These early attempts at import substitution met with some success, the first stages, focusing on the simplest industries, being the easiest. Annual growth in industrial output accelerated from 5.4 percent in the 1920s to 8.4 percent for 1930 to 1939.[18] Then World War II cut off most imports, which further incentivized domestic manufacturers. Domestically produced textiles, chemicals, metal products, and electrical machinery all increased their market shares.[19]

Uniquely, during this period the government relied on competent, expert policy advice. The military had come to power without a strong economic ideology of its own and therefore deferred to existing specialists.[20] Ministries such as Agriculture and Treasury were conversant in the protectionist thinking common at the time, including in the US. Economist Raúl Prebisch, later a luminary of UN economic institutions, was allowed to build up the central bank.

Although never more powerful than the agribusiness lobby, a coalition of industrialists, organized labor, and the armed forces favoring effective industrialization did haltingly exist just before and after World War II. But it ultimately fragmented due to conflicts between labor and capital.[21] Argentina neither broke its unions with repression (the Korean solution), though it often brutalized them, tamed its unions by bringing them into management (the German solution), or bought them off with high living standards (the American solution), though it tried until it ran out of money. Before and after this period, with agribusiness at best uninterested and militant trade unionism (class-based but not necessarily left-wing) drowning out nuanced decision-making and management, a coherent policy to develop manufacturing had neither champions in government nor strong, mobilized interest-group support.

Juan Perón and Perónism

In 1943, a group of officers with Axis sympathies seized power, with General Juan Perón appointed minister of labor. In this capacity, he enacted prolabor legislation including minimum wages, paid vacations, paid retirement, health benefits, and mandatory bonuses. Then, in the election of February 1946, promising higher pay, social security programs, and in rural areas land, Perón swept to power himself.

Under Perón, unionization tripled as he empowered the Confederación General del Trabajo union federation and created a labor-friendly system of bargaining. From 1946 to 1950, his policies raised the wage share of national income from 37 to 50 percent, firming up his support and expanding the consumer market.[22] Sales of consumer goods burgeoned.

The Perónist unions, per one historian, "abandoned labor's historic anti-capitalist ideologies to embrace [a] capitalism in national hands and responsive to national interests."[23] Largely as a result, socialism has been weak in Argentina compared to peer nations. Perónism even seemed for a while like an idiosyncratic Latin version of the New Deal, a pro-worker but nonsocialist (and fiercely anticommunist) political movement.

Argentina emerged from World War II Latin America's strongest industrial nation and seemingly on the verge of takeoff into developed-nation status. It was in better economic shape than Italy or Spain. In 1945, for the first time, industry accounted for a greater share of GDP than agriculture.[24] The rubber, metallurgy, chemicals, and oil refining sectors were growing fast.[25] The firm SIAM-Di Tella, ranging from gasoline pumps to pasta machines, was Latin America's largest industrial conglomerate.[26]

Yet this surface strength concealed deeper weaknesses. The country's industrial expansion was largely a result of hothouse conditions produced by wartime isolation, and was taking place with almost no foreign competition or exposure to global standards of quality and cost.[27] The small size of the Argentine market – 13 million people in 1944 – limited industry's ability to achieve scale economies. Output growth was not generally accompanied by rising efficiency. A 1946 industrial census showed that the average factory employed just 13 workers, the war having "mainly encouraged the proliferation of small-scale, poorly-capitalized, and technologically backward firms."[28] Production machinery was often secondhand or obsolete, there was a thin base of subcontractors and suppliers, and much of the increase in output was due to longer working hours, not greater efficiency.[29]

The unionists who bought into Perón's "national capitalism" demanded costly social programs, and with Perón fearing postwar unemployment and social unrest, stimulating production to create jobs and fund social programs was his priority.[30] So, he favored light industries, hoping that they would absorb the rural workers streaming into the cities and produce goods his voters could afford.[31] But the state's initially successful understanding with employers to boost both production and demand eventually broke down when union wage demands became unsupportable. And the unfortunate precedent was established, which endured for decades, of pressuring industries to hire more workers than needed.

Perón-Era Policies: 1946–1955

Perón's initial protectionist policies were similar to those in many other countries before and since. Even the World Bank accepted import substitution at the time, and only in the late 1960s did the practice come under serious scrutiny.[32] Having come to power on populist rhetoric that alarmed the business community, he stressed his policies' continuity with the policies of the 1930s, which were perceived as having succeeded.

But Perón soon made protectionism an ideological principle, unmoored from economic logic. In 1947, he issued a bombastic "Declaration of Economic Independence," with industry assigned the role of "liberator for the new

Argentina." This was accompanied by nationalizations of railways and telecommunications, mostly foreign owned at the time.[33] He shifted left, increasing state control of the economy, income redistribution, and spending on social programs.[34]

Perón promulgated a five-year plan supposedly promoting and using tariffs to protect industries, especially those, such as cotton textiles and metalworking, thought vulnerable to a postwar import surge. New import-substituting industries, such as woolen textiles and vegetable oils, were also envisaged.[35] But little beyond protectionism was done to assist the targeted industries, which also included metals, newsprint, plywood, glass, vehicles, and machinery.[36] Few efforts were made to press industry to upgrade technologically, raise quality standards, or secure foreign technology. There was never a plan to systematically move up the value chain.[37]

The regime was also caught in a conundrum of its own making. To maintain its popularity, imports of consumer goods could not be squeezed too much.[38] And locally unavailable raw materials had to be imported to keep factories running. Something had to give, which turned out to be imports of the capital goods needed for long-term growth.[39] For example, Perón let the state oil company YPF atrophy with obsolete equipment while milking its profits.[40]

Despite all these problems, GDP growth during the years of Perón's first presidency averaged 2.9 percent, higher than the 1.8 percent between 1927 and 1943 and only slightly less than the 3.1 percent his supposedly more enlightened successors managed from 1955 to 1965.[41] So Argentina faced no real pressure to confront its underlying problems or learn from its mistakes.

Problems of Perónism

Despite catering to his working-class power base, Perón was too suspicious of communist influence to bring Argentina's unions into a classic tripartite labor-state-capital alliance that *might* have supported coherent pro-growth policies (see Chapter 8 for the German precedent). Instead, he promoted unions personally loyal to him. The ruling coalition of generals, politicians, and bureaucrats kept labor at arm's length, while the agrarian elite tried to ally with the bankers.[42]

Without a strategy to grow productivity, manufactured exports to balance the current account could only be increased by reducing costs, which were mostly wages and therefore politically untouchable. Thanks to protectionism, lax antitrust, and a crony-ridden business culture, manufacturers faced neither foreign nor domestic pressures to excel. This comfortable arrangement favored development of powerful unions, but did not teach them to bargain for a share of the profits while *also* supporting their employers' competitiveness.

Import substitution led Argentina's industrial entrepreneurs to lose their daring, leaving major investments to the state, despite its incompetence, and later to foreign firms.[43]

All this provoked the anti-Perónists as follows:

> They saw Perónism as responsible for declining rates of productivity . . . In their view, overly powerful trade unions had blocked, and indeed reversed, the country's progress. A coddled class of industrialists, locked in an unholy alliance with the trade unions to maintain high levels of domestic consumption and to prevent foreign competition (no matter the ultimate cost to the country's competitiveness in world economy), had showed a galling indifference to the plight of the Argentine people, whom they had burdened with their shoddy, overpriced goods.[44]

Too much investment went into consumer products, too little into credible candidates for high-value import substitution, such as chemicals, machinery, and engineering – which might have then matured into export industries, brought in foreign exchange, and pulled the country up to global standards of technology and productivity.[45]

Potential export industries were handicapped by having to buy inputs from inefficient domestic firms and by being starved of imported capital goods.[46] Perón let makers of consumer goods import machinery, but heavy industries were prevented from obtaining badly needed foreign equipment until the late 1950s.[47] Thus Argentine firms were less automated than their American and European counterparts: Their productivity from 1950 to 1973 correspondingly hovered between 49 and 45 percent of that of their counterparts in the US.[48]

Perónism Sours

Postwar prosperity ended abruptly in 1949 as the small home market in consumer durables saturated. The expansion of exports proved to be a blip, and with priority given to importing raw materials, equipment to create new productive capacity could neither be imported nor produced domestically.[49] From this point on, the lack of exports and resulting depletion of currency reserves held industry back.[50] Public and private investment in industry had grown 67 percent between 1945 and 1949, but was flat from 1950 to 1954.[51] Growth in manufacturing output slowed to a crawl during this period, averaging just 0.4 percent.[52]

Perón responded by doubling down. He banned outright imports of selected consumer goods if domestic substitutes were available.[53] The industries chosen for protection – including metals, newsprint, glass, vehicles, and machinery – were granted lower duties on their imported raw materials and equipment, plus preferential access to credit and foreign exchange.[54] The emphasis switched to heavier industries, and from 1953 the state-owned development bank, Banco Industrial, which had not previously lent strategically, gave credit mainly to the larger import-substituting firms.[55]

In 1952, the second five-year plan, albeit with a welcome attempt to boost agriculture through technological innovation, prioritized developing a steel industry.[56] Thoughtful industrialists regarded this plan as the country's last opportunity to modernize sufficiently to compete with a resurgent Europe. Although it addressed some of their concerns on paper, its implementation was postponed due to a disastrous harvest, which led to deteriorating terms of trade, a bout of austerity, and the extension of import restrictions to capital goods.[57]

Protecting and subsidizing industry while empowering the unions had reduced productivity in most sectors to 1939 levels due to overmanning and inefficient shop-floor practices.[58] So, early in 1955, Perón summoned a Congress of Productivity and Social Welfare.[59] But, refusing to depress consumption, he withdrew the state from union pay negotiations, exasperating employers and disappointing labor militants – who were then brutally suppressed.[60] In September 1955, with strikes paralyzing the country and the immediate spark being Perón's conflicts with the Catholic Church, anti-Perón elements in the military staged an uprising and sent him into exile. The second five-year plan was quietly buried.

After Perón

Perón's overthrow led to a *partial* drift away from his ideology. Argentina began to reengage with the world economy. But the generals had overthrown him to restore stability (starting by outlawing the Perónist movement), not to engineer an economic U-turn. They did not completely break with his policies. Indeed, the military and the civilian presidents it tolerated continued to run the country with Perónist institutions.

Perón had belatedly realized that with Argentina's heavy industries unable to raise enough capital at home, foreign investment was needed. Thus, even before his ouster, he had loosened limits on foreign investment and industry was showing signs of revival. Factories grew larger, less labor intensive, and more productive. Aiming to build on this trend, in 1958 President Arturo Frondizi attempted a number of liberalizing reforms and succeeded in triggering an influx of foreign investment. But he then abandoned key promised reforms, such as slimming the overmanned railroads, and the foreign capital left.[61]

Frondizi then pivoted back toward self-sufficiency, but this time with a strategy of *desarrollismo* (developmentalism). This meant rapidly acquiring foreign technology and concentrating investment in a few capital-intensive and import-substituting sectors. He stepped up Perón's previous encouragement of foreign auto and oil companies to produce in Argentina.[62] Yet *desarrollismo* inevitably sucked in more imports, as it encouraged the expansion of industries that needed foreign capital goods. From the recession of 1962–3 onward, it became obvious that the policy was not bringing sustained development, or even easing pressure on currency reserves. Just 2 percent of industrial output was exported.[63]

The very need for reforms was also questioned, as the economy still seemed adequate without them. As late as 1962, Argentina enjoyed a per capita GDP higher than Spain, Ireland, or Japan.[64] Its industrial structure was at "a level and a complexity comparable to Australia, Canada, and Italy."[65] But on price and quality, it was not internationally competitive.

After 1966, another attempt at liberalization took place under finance minister Adalbert Krieger. Fighting 30 percent inflation, he squeezed the money supply and thus wages, prices, and private sector lending. He privatized some state enterprises and closed others. By 1968, these measures had cut inflation to 10 percent and boosted GDP growth to 5 percent.[66] But in May 1969, just as industrialists began grumbling about the costs of this achievement, he was forced out by a massive civil uprising. The so-called Cordobazo, led by auto workers, showed once again the political risks of reforms that imposed short-term costs on the workers.[67]

The ruling general, Juan Carlos Onganía, was replaced by others, who pledged eventual return to civilian government. Then, between 1971 and 1973, the military government of General Alejandro Lanusse created an economic perfect storm by combining monetary tightening, a surge in public spending, steep wage increases, and a ban on specific imports to counter a rising trade deficit.[68] Amid mounting chaos, including a strike by employers, Lanusse legalized the Perónists, and in June 1973 Perón returned in triumph.

Peron Redux

Perón now took his national capitalist model to its zenith. In exile he had embraced a more leftist, populist agenda, including a commitment to take on the great landowners.[69] He launched a three-year plan embodying a "new model of production, consumption, organization, and technological development," underpinned by *Pacto Social* between business and labor.[70] This plan was, according to one sympathetic historian, "a serious, multifaceted attempt to attack the monopolistic structure and practices of Argentine capitalism and break with the country's reliance on multinational capital without returning to the inflationary policies of the past."[71]

It proved to be too sharp a left turn. Perón's plans also included financing from, and expanded trade with, Cuba and the other Eastern Bloc countries. But these nations had little hard currency or state-of-the art technology to offer, so they would not have been able to help Argentina develop. FDI from the countries that could have done so was discouraged by a law barring foreigners from owning more than 50 percent and blocking foreign investment entirely in sectors such as steel, oil, utilities, banking, and agriculture.[72] On top of this, several American- and Spanish-owned banks were nationalized outright.

In July 1974, Perón died, having dangerously expanded the money supply and failed to heal the increasingly violent fissures in society. His third wife, Isabel, took over, but as the economy went into free fall, she was out of her depth and flailed about with exchange controls and stronger import restrictions. In mid-1975, she appointed her Rasputin, occultist José López Rega, minister of social welfare. He attempted a course correction, seeking to curb 100 percent inflation with unevenly applied wage and price controls.[73] His policies sparked a general strike, followed by 160 percent wage increases acquiesced to by government. The unions then forced Rega out, after which Isabel governed through a coalition of trade unionists and old-school Perónists.

At this point, the country was visibly coming apart, with leftist guerrillas conducting assassinations and army-led death squads battling them. In March 1976, with inflation exceeding 600 percent and the unions resisting controls on wage settlements, the most ruthless of Argentina's military juntas, whose human rights abuses would become infamous, seized power.

Icy Blasts of Liberalization

Ironically, the 1976 coup that installed quasi-fascist General Jorge Rafael Videla was the point at which genuine, sustained attempts to liberalize the domestic economy and foreign trade began. Finance Minister Martínez de Hoz declared the era of import substitution over. Trade barriers were lowered and foreign borrowing was encouraged.

There were some positive results. These policies sparked domestic investment in infrastructure and projects benefiting the military, plus expanded capacity in steel, paper and pulp, and petrochemicals.[74] Foreign investment revived, reaching $837 million in 1981, though most went into oil and finance.[75] But the peso did not fall fast enough to offset high inflation, so exports were uncompetitive. The trade deficit began to grow.[76]

Trade openness subjected domestic industry to sudden import competition, to which it was vulnerable due to long-standing problems such as obsolete technology and featherbedding.[77] SIAM-Di Tella, once Latin America's leading industrial group, stumbled after a failed foray into autos and was eventually nationalized. The state-owned bank supporting it eventually tired of its ballooning loans and let it go bankrupt in 1981. GM pulled out *for the second time* in 1978, not returning until 1994.[78] In 1980, the private Banco de Intercambio Regional, Argentina's largest, failed, having recklessly overlent.[79]

The following year saw the country's worst economic crisis yet of the twentieth century. Recession was accompanied by a huge budget deficit, high inflation, repeated devaluations, and unsustainable external debt. The junta responded by restoring many Perón-era controls. Then, now led by General Leopoldo Galtieri, it attempted in April 1982 to revive its popularity by invading the British-held Falkland Islands, unimportant except as a nationalist symbol.

Argentina lost, a furious public took to the streets, and Galtieri's government fell. The military's claim to be competent rulers never recovered. If they couldn't even win wars, how could they run the country? Defeat was followed by exposure of the various juntas' vast human rights violations and the military (after three failed coups between 1987 and 1990) sullenly acquiesced to civilian rule. Since then, it has stayed in its barracks even in times of political instability.

Civilian Rule and Neoliberalism

The center-left Raúl Alfonsín was elected in 1983, inheriting a highly indebted economy with a far more fragile productive base than in the early 1970s.[80] He attempted reforms. Pain for manufacturers increased as remaining import restrictions were cut from 3,000 products in 1983 to 1,000 by 1988. (Textiles, metal products, machinery, and some chemicals remained protected.)[81] By 1990, industrial output had fallen 25 percent since 1975 and industrial employment 45 percent. Manufacturing's share of GDP declined from 24 percent in 1970 to 17 percent.[82]

With state-owned firms losing large amounts of money and tax collections low due to a sagging economy and tax evasion, the government was desperate for revenue. It printed money, with predictable results: By 1989, hyperinflation reached 3,000 percent. In response to the mounting crisis and despite his Perónist roots, Alfonsín's successor, Carlos Menem, delivered the sharpest liberalizing shocks of all. Facing a budget deficit of 16 percent of GDP and an economy smaller than in 1965, he initiated a program of "major surgery without anesthesia," blaming the country's traditional interventionist policies for Argentina's poor performance.[83]

An end to money printing, imposition of price controls, and credible promises to cut spending halted hyperinflation in weeks. But Alfonsín then had difficulty making his spending cuts stick or stopping a big pay settlement between the main union federation and business. Hyperinflation reignited, peaking at 20,000 percent. Finally, in April 1991, the dam broke. The government announced huge spending cuts, elimination of subsidies, termination of redundant programs, and full convertibility of the currency. It deregulated trade, insurance, financial services, road haulage, and the ports.[84] It pegged the peso to the US dollar and mandated that the central bank back two-thirds of the money it issued with foreign currency reserves, making future money printing impossible.[85]

These radical measures achieved more than any previous stabilization package. Menem then went further. He lifted remaining constraints on inward investment, which induced FDI inflows and external borrowing that alleviated a shortage of domestic financing. He concluded bilateral investment treaties with more than 50 countries and committed Argentina to the Mercosur customs union with Brazil, Paraguay, and Uruguay.[86] Nontariff trade barriers were confined to textiles, basic metals, autos, and paper. Menem privatized almost every business the state still owned.

Privatization, competition, and rationalization had significant benefits. There were dramatic improvements in services such as the telephone system. Industry gained from falling costs, such as a 37 percent fall in wholesale electricity prices and a 73 percent decline in cargo rates at the Port of Buenos Aires.[87] When steel and petrochemical firms were sold off, investment and rationalization followed.

Layoffs were inevitable. Privatization in steel halved the workforce in a still fragmented industry from 32,148 in 1989 to 16,220 in 1994, while output per worker rose from 120 tons per year to 204.[88] With time, however, employment recovered, and GDP grew from 1991 to 1998.[89] Output increased 5 percent per annum and exports, after a slow start, doubled.

Argentina became Latin America's poster child for the "Washington Consensus" of privatization, deregulation, tax reform, import liberalization, price stabilization, and financial reform. In the wake of capitalism's Cold War victory, this was being preached and increasingly attempted globally. It seemed the country had finally turned the corner by embracing the free market.

Collapse of the Washington Consensus

Argentine manufacturing in the 1990s became more efficient. But it was much smaller than and very different from that of the import substitution era. There was even less local innovation, and labor-intensive manufacturing kept losing ground to resource processing, especially of foodstuffs. Capital goods manufacturing also performed poorly, especially after a zero tariff was adopted, as did the few surviving high-tech activities.[90] Import penetration in manufacturing rose from 6 percent in 1990 to 19 percent in 1999.

There were claims that the country had effectively deindustrialized. Times were especially tough for smaller manufacturers, with their obsolete machinery, lack of skills, over-diversified product mixes, lack of export experience, careless quality control, poor marketing, and unprofessional management.[91] Government did not even *try* to help them adapt, and many collapsed or switched to importing.

Menem did seek a smoother transition for the auto industry, with import quotas, local content rules, and preferential tariffs for its inputs. This helped it restructure and improve efficiency: Production, below 100,000 in 1990, quadrupled by 1994. But exemptions for Argentina in Mercosur's automobile rules remained in place, a clear sign of failure to become internationally competitive. (Some were still in place as late as 2020.)[92]

The prosperity of the 1990s was too good to last. By 1999, public spending was rising, government borrowing was surging, and corruption was scaring off foreign investors.[93] In December, Menem, with the economy contracting, made way for Fernando de la Rúa. He, in turn, was forced out in December 2001 amid a corruption scandal that saw five presidents in 12 days, riots, and looting.

Argentina was then engulfed by its worst economic and political crisis since independence.[94] Economists are still debating the precise causes. They included a currency devaluation by key trading partner Brazil combined with an unsustainably high pegged value for the Argentine peso. Thanks in large part to a rapid drying up of investment inflows, the peso slid, causing dollar-denominated debts to balloon in local currency.

The ruling political coalition was already disintegrating under the pressure of its own corruption and was thus unable to take timely, appropriate corrective actions. Within months, firms all across the economy were collapsing. The country defaulted on more than $100 billion of sovereign debt, at the time a world record. Within months, 11 percent of Argentina's companies went under, unemployment neared 20 percent, and half the population was living below the poverty line.[95] By 2002, GDP per capita was 5 percent lower than in 1992 and *11 percent lower than in 1974.*[96]

The gains of four decades were gone.

The End of Neoliberalism: 2003–Present

The crisis discredited neoliberalism and the new president, Nestor Kirchner (elected 2003), signaled a return to a left-inflected version of

Perónism, albeit combined with an uneasy attempt to balance it with concessions to economic realities that the nation had now learned it could not escape.

Kirchner spoke of resuscitating "national capitalism." His solution was "to encourage production, or more specifically the industrial sectors of the economy, at the expense of the financial sector."[97] This meant large public works programs, selective tariffs, promotion of small and medium enterprises (with banks persuaded to provide credit), and encouragement of agricultural exports. But Kirchner *also* embraced sound fiscal policy, low inflation, market-determined prices, freer trade, and foreign investment. He devalued the peso.

Against orthodox advice, Kirchner imposed an expansionary monetary and fiscal policy, plus capital controls to manage the exchange rate. By the end of 2005, contrary to expectations, GDP had recovered its 1998 peak, some labor-intensive industrial sectors were recording large increases in production, and despite export taxes, agricultural production was achieving new records.[98] Real incomes recovered.

By 2007, Kirchner had gone too far stimulating an economy no longer in recession, and inflation was rising so fast (more than 25 percent) that the government pressured the National Institute of Statistics to underreport it. (Global financial agencies then refused to accept its figures.) In 2007, Kirchner was succeeded by his wife, Cristina, who proved even more populist and interventionist than he was. She faced continuing inflation, falling soybean prices, disgruntled creditors, and a global banking crisis. Manufacturing import substitution was back on the agenda, and soybeans, vehicles, and corn were favored for export promotion.

Both Kirchners had sought a compromise between Perónism and the market. But in the words of one observer, "Under their leadership, Argentina grew addicted to fictitious feel-good growth, spending and selling everything it had to keep the positive feelings going, and after a short respite, is ready for its next hit."[99] During their 12-year rule, manufacturing fell inexorably from 22.5 percent of GDP in 2003 to 14.2 in 2015.[100]

Kirchnerismo was ultimately judged by the voters to have failed, and Cristina's intended successor lost the 2015 election. Another attempt at liberalization followed, under construction magnate Mauricio Macri, a political outsider whose SOCMA conglomerate had been Argentina's largest private firm. But his early popularity declined once the costs of cutting public spending and tightening the money supply started to be felt. He had no industrial policy beyond opening to the international marketplace while doing little or nothing to enable Argentina's firms compete there. He failed to control inflation, the country sank into another recession, and there was a near collapse of the peso.

In 2019, the voters returned again to the Perónists, under Alberto Fernández, who promised yet another plan for rebuilding the economy, particularly manufacturing, while fending off yet another debt default. But within weeks, Argentina confronted the coronavirus pandemic, and in 2020, *again* defaulted on its sovereign debt. Then, in late 2023, the country elected as president Javier Milei, a libertarian economics professor. As of 2024, he appears fated to execute the country's next doomed cycle of liberalization.

Here ends our chronology. Let us now look at some recurring themes.

A Weak Financial System

Argentina's capital markets have historically been underdeveloped, and the country has suffered from a weak banking system oriented toward agriculture and prone to crony "gaucho finance."[101] Private banks traditionally were reluctant to lend to manufacturers, favoring agribusiness or the big foreign-owned utilities.[102]

In 1944, the ruling junta created Banco Industrial to supply cheap long-term credit to industry, initially favoring smaller companies in sectors such as food and clothing.[103] Over time, it drifted from its intended function of promoting medium- and long-term investment in manufacturing. So, in the late 1960s, the government relaunched it as the Banco Nacional de Desarrollo (BANADE). For a while, BANADE provided worthwhile state-guaranteed credits that helped the paper, petrochemical, and steel sectors increase capacity. But it too eventually succumbed to strategic drift, with much of its credit going to state suppliers or firms facing bankruptcy.[104] When Perón returned in 1974, its enforced closeness to the Perónist unions earned it a reputation for politicized lending. It was eventually closed in 1992 as nonperforming loans hampered its capacity to lend.

BANADE's successor, Banco de Inversión y de Comercio Exterior, was tasked with helping SMEs and export industries, but initially showed excessive caution by lending at close to market rates and not dealing directly with individual firms.[105] Following a policy shift in 2004, however, it has become more effective, particularly in export-oriented lending. But a number of smaller private banks, which had been lending to SMEs, have since been taken over by foreign institutions with different priorities, reducing that sector's access to needed credit.[106]

It was estimated in 1973 that wealthy Argentines had $10 billion illegally deposited in foreign banks.[107] A further $2 billion flooded out over the next three years as kidnapping and assassinations took their toll, and up to $30 billion more during the crisis years of 1979–82. Potential investment has thus suffered from the export of capital that might have enabled industry to modernize and compete.

State Ownership without Strategy

State ownership was a major policy up to the privatizations of the 1990s, but was never used coherently. It was concentrated in industries where state ownership is the global norm, such as oil and utilities, in military-related products such as iron and steel, shipbuilding and explosives, and in odds and ends such as German firms confiscated after World War II.

Even when government held large ownership positions in many firms, it did not impose strategic direction. Government agencies, on an ad hoc basis, took stakes in and sometimes control of troubled firms or those they thought were strategically important (but without any nationwide concept of what was strategic).[108] In 1958, four of Argentina's top 10 industrial firms were locally and privately owned, 5 were in foreign hands, and the oil company YPF was the only state concern. A decade later, 6 were foreign-owned, and the remaining 4 – YPF, SEGBA (Buenos Aires's electricity), SOMISA (steel), and Gas del Estado – were state-owned.[109]

It was only in 1987 that 13 of the country's largest state-owned industries were brought under unified ownership, with the formation of the Directorate of Public Enterprises.[110] But even this belated attempt to insert some sense of order and priorities proved toothless. With most of its businesses overmanned and losing money, little changed.

The major exception to this lack of deliberate strategy was itself irrational. In 1951, Perón tried to persuade foreign carmakers to resume production in Argentina. When they refused, saying the country lacked the necessary expertise and supply chains, he set up a state-owned company to use the military's aircraft production skills. With a $53 million loan from the state-owned Banco de Crédito Industrial, 10 factories were established, one producing cars and the others products from aircraft engines to parachutes. A second-rate car, reverse engineered from German designs, was manufactured. But it sold poorly and the whole project was abandoned when Perón was overthrown.[111]

Governments from the 1940s to the 1970s also showed a reluctance to foster major private industrial groups, fearing they could become alternative power bases. Thus, the country never developed the conglomerates, such as Japan's *keiretsus*, Korea's *chaebols*, or even neighboring Brazil's *grupos empresarial*, that might have had the scale and skill to impose a strategic coherence of their own.

Stop-and-Go Foreign Direct Investment

Since the 1950s, foreign direct investment, mostly from the US and Europe, has fluctuated in a cycle of invest, disinvest, and reinvest. Many foreign firms have brought secondhand machinery and production processes lagging behind the state-of-the-art methods they used at home. But their techniques and technologies were still better than what Argentina already had, and they often helped transmit sophistication to indigenous firms by bringing them into their supply chains. Between 1958 and 1973, production by affiliates of foreign firms grew at an annual rate of 9 percent, twice that of domestic firms. In 1972, of the country's top 20 industrial exporters, 17 were foreign owned.[112] But foreign firms have never been able to push Argentina's economy onto a sustained upward track. And when crisis came, many just left, stranding their local suppliers.

In 1958, President Frondizi guaranteed multinationals equal treatment with domestic firms and authorized repatriation of earnings. Importation of machinery to reequip domestic industry was liberalized.[113] (Tariffs on capital goods had been between 78 and 130 percent.)[114] By 1963, 200 foreign companies, 60 percent of them American, had built plants and invested $500 million, mainly in chemicals, petroleum, transport, metallurgy, electrical, and engineering.[115] But the failure of Frondizi's domestic reforms eventually soured the foreigners on Argentina.

Argentina's auto policy illustrates its poor FDI strategy. By 1960, it had 21 car plants producing a total of 100,000 vehicles a year – a horrendous diseconomy of scale. With few exported, production exceeded local demand and more than half the plants eventually closed.[116] Ford, for example, spent $6 million launching its German subsidiary's Taunus there in 1974 with 90 percent local content. Engineers spent 300,000 hours adapting the design to the local environment, available raw materials, the idiosyncrasies of the plant (less than one tenth the size of the German original), and the limited capabilities of nearly 400 domestic suppliers. But all this effort did not produce an internationally competitive product.[117]

The sovereign debt defaults of 2001 and 2014 and the financially bumpy period between also discouraged FDI, which plunged from $10.4 billion in 2000 to $1.65 billion in 2003. It did not reach $10 billion again until 2010.[118] Then it fell *again* in 2012 after Cristina Kirchner revoked the privatization of the oil company YPF after accusing Repsol, its Spanish owner, of milking its assets and failing to expand production. The pace of FDI reintensified under Macri, with a spike at the start of his administration and an all-time high at the start of 2019. Then it plunged once more.

Weak R&D and Innovation

With the exception of niche products and techniques, mainly in oil and gas, Argentina has never pulled its weight as an innovator, despite a high literacy rate, a well-established higher education system, and government agencies to support R&D. High technology has struggled across Latin America, but Argentina's performance, considering its advantages, has been the most disappointing. In 2020, the cumulative number of US-registered patents was 104 for Argentina, 539 for Brazil, 13,105 for Taiwan, and 23,705 for Korea.[119]

Perón's isolation of Argentina from the global economy left the country technologically backward by the mid-1950s. As one commentator observes, "Only in the 1920s (under relatively free trade) and in the 1960s (led by multinational corporations) did Argentine industry have good access to techniques at the cutting edge."[120] The results were telling: Between 1980 and 1995, the percentage of manufacturing value-added taking place in high tech rose in Brazil from 30 to 37 percent, and in Mexico from 22 to 26 percent, but in Argentina it *fell* from 24 to 17 percent.[121]

In 1974, the country's manufacturers were spending more than three times as much on importing technologies as on R&D, with the average firm devoting just 0.55 percent of revenue to research.[122] More recent evidence suggests the situation has not improved.[123]

Governmental innovation initiatives have been waylaid by institutional sclerosis. Funds have been authorized but few businesses made aware of them. R&D agencies have been poorly coordinated with each other, inward-looking, and unengaged with industry.

Pharma is a case in point. In the early 1970s, it spent more on R&D than any other industry. Government oversaw vertical integration of national laboratories to produce key starting materials and active ingredients. A serious capability in antibiotic fermentation was developed. Productivity grew and firms began to export.[124] But this success was short-lived. The absence of scale economies started to tell, equipment became unreliable because firms could not afford imported replacements, and because of inadequate connections to universities and other public laboratories, innovation was not sustained.[125]

The Future

It is unlikely that any industrial policy, however technically sound, will deliver in Argentina without fundamental reform of the widespread corruption and incompetence of its state institutions.[126] In 2020, the World Bank ranked Argentina 126th out of 190 countries for ease of doing business, and there are few indications it has improved since.

Argentina today has only one globally competitive industrial product: the steel pipe made by Tenaris. With most of the country's industrial conglomerates losing ground in the turmoil of the late 1970s, only one has since made it into the developing nations' top 50: SOCMA, in auto parts, energy, gas, and construction services. But it would not be among Brazil's top 10 private firms.[127] Today, Argentina hosts just one Forbes Global 2000 corporation: oil producer YPF, in 749th place. Chile has 8, Mexico 13, and Brazil 15.[128]

A few firms, such as the Italian-rooted Techint (the largest steel company) and Arcor (snacks, agribusiness, and packaging) have achieved some success by focusing on core businesses, exporting, and investing abroad.[129] Their leaders are now listened to by government. The country now has Latin America's third-largest auto industry. But Argentina imports roughly 50 percent more cars by value than it exports and the industry depends on protection to survive, with no sign of an export-competitive engine of growth.[130]

The one area where (foreign) technology has had a dramatic impact is agriculture. Argentina's acreage of genetically modified soy crops is the world's third largest after the US and Brazil.[131] Soybeans (Argentina exported $2.7 billion worth in 2021) and wine (more than $800 million) are the country's big export successes.[132] Thus, the country remains essentially the commodity agricultural exporter it was a century ago, and as far away as ever from catching up to the developed countries.

Strengths

- Wealthy agricultural sector could have provided (but did not) capital for industrial development.

Weaknesses

- Lack of a coherent, realistic theory of economic development.
- Volatile, extremist, corrupt political culture created policy instability, weak rule of law, and a poor political foundation for functional institutions.
- Lack of policy discipline, resulting in policies that create short-term gains and long-term failure.
- Lack of a skilled, sophisticated managerial class, with no effective attempts to create one.
- Use of tariffs to pursue autarchy for its own sake, as opposed to as a tool of industrial development.
- Except for commodity agriculture, no attempts to find niches in which it could become internationally competitive.
- State ownership without strategic purpose.
- Government behavior, including stop-and-go liberalizations, that alienated foreign investors.

Part III
The Forgotten History

Part III starts with the Renaissance origins of industrial policy (Chapter 13), documenting its centuries-long record of success. Chapters 14 and 15 describe the largely forgotten economic history of the US, showing that, contrary to prevailing myth, the US was a protectionist nation that used industrial policy for economic development from its founding until World War II. Chapters 16 and 17 explain how America turned away from protectionism after the war, misdiagnosed the economic problems generated by the industrial policies of its East Asian competitors, and unsuccessfully focused on free markets and free trade as the solution. Chapter 18 tells how Obama tried but failed to fix these problems by doubling down on these same policies, and then how Trump broke with the free trade consensus, creating political space for the industrial policy initiatives of the Biden administration.

13 THE RENAISSANCE ORIGINS OF INDUSTRIAL POLICY

Many of the tools of industrial policy go back to the dawn of capitalism 500 years ago.[1] Though their details have evolved over time, many underlying dynamics have remained remarkably consistent.

In the West, industrial policy began during the Renaissance.[2] After the Middle Ages, European thought began to break free of religious concepts like just price theory, enabling economic questions to be considered in their own right, rather than as a branch of religious ethics. Simultaneously, policy slowly escaped from the constraints of feudalism, which had tied economic policies to fixed social relationships, such as that between lord and tenant, and to guild restrictions on prices and production methods. A key intellectual advance was the recognition that wealth is not a zero-sum game, but can be *created* rather than simply taken from someone else.[3] From this, it was a short hop to the idea that economies can – and should – grow. Another major advance was the shift from viewing innovation only as a threat to the status quo to regarding it as a potential source of wealth and human improvement.[4]

Sustained per capita economic growth only arrived toward the end of the period (1500–1800) discussed in this chapter, when the Industrial Revolution finally enabled economies to grow faster than populations. But economic strategies had been developing for centuries before this and, when the Industrial Revolution arrived, such strategies were ready to be applied and refined by industrializing nations. This prehistory of industrial policy is thus key to understanding where later industrial policy came from.

The world of 1500 was poor and technologically primitive by our standards, but the rulers of states and those who lived under them still wanted wealth and had to make decisions about how to get it. Nationalism was emerging at this time on a continent of city-states, dynastic empires, and other nonnational political units, making *national* wealth a meaningful objective. Technological advantage meant something different in an age when high technology might be a mechanical loom, but it was advantage nonetheless. World trade was a lower percentage of economic output, due mainly to primitive transportation technology, but was still important enough for governments to fight wars and build world-spanning empires pursuing it. In fact, the need for enough money to pay for military forces and access to the materiel needed to equip them was a major reason states embraced what we would today call industrial policies, as the alternative was being conquered or becoming a satellite of a great power.

For most of the period 1500–1800, the most important economic ideas were not academic, though scholarly commentary did exist. Instead, they resided in an *organized body of practical policy* understood and implemented by rulers and their officials. These policies are known today collectively as "mercantilism." Mercantilism is often caricatured as a mere obsession with accumulating gold and silver bullion. But it was, in fact, a systematic philosophy of state-backed economic development. Accumulating precious metals was also rational, as these were the only reliable reserves of foreign exchange, a lack of coinage was a common constraint on commerce, and expanding the money supply in a world of metallic currencies necessarily meant "more gold."

Capitalism was thus born as an interventionist undertaking, out of the efforts of rulers to gain wealth by means of deliberate policy, *not* as a coming together of naturally free markets that were only later subjected to political intervention. Despite the claims of ideologues, there is nothing natural, normal, or fundamental about a *free* market.

A Tale of Two Countries

In the sixteenth century, Spain was the most powerful Western nation, with colonies from the Philippines to Cuba. Huge quantities of bullion were flowing in from its mines in the Americas. But starting around 1550, it became clear that this was not causing generalized wealth in Spain. The gold and silver ended up elsewhere, in places, such as Holland and Venice, that produced no precious metals. Instead, they were proactively cultivating their manufacturing – which Spain was not.

Spanish thinkers observed that wealth and purchasing power departed states producing raw materials (even if those raw materials were gold and silver) and accumulated in states that had diversified manufacturing sectors. In the words of an annoyed Luis Ortiz, accountant of the treasury to King Felipe II, in 1558:

From the raw materials from Spain and the West Indies – particularly silk, iron and cochinilla (a red dye) – which cost them only 1 florin, the foreigners produce finished goods which they sell back to Spain for between 10 and 100 florins. Spain is in this way subject to greater humiliations from the rest of Europe than those they themselves impose on the Indians. In exchange for gold and silver the Spaniards offer trinkets of greater or lesser value; but by buying back their own raw materials at an exorbitant price, Spaniards are made the laughing-stock of all Europe.[5]

Spain's colonial plunder, however lucrative in the short run, was a distraction from the far more profitable development of manufacturing.

Spain used tariffs to support not its manufacturing, but its agriculture, such as sheep-raising, olive oil, and wine. Its tax policies favored agricultural estates, not industry.[6] Gold and silver from the Americas caused inflation, which helped make Spanish manufacturing, such as its once internationally respected textile industry, uncompetitive.[7] Spanish economists (though not so called at the time) diagnosed Madrid's policy errors quite accurately.[8] But the vested interests of the day, such as the powerful Council of the Mesta, a sheep-raisers' organization to which the crown owed money, prevailed.[9]

Now consider England. In the late fifteenth century, it was a poor farming nation, heavily indebted to the Italian bankers who financed its government. Its main export was raw wool. But then its government deliberately set out to upgrade its economy by what would today be called moving up the value chain. It proactively pushed its economy out of low-value (what we have called in this book disadvantageous) agricultural activities, such as raising sheep, and into higher-value (advantageous) industrial activities – above all, weaving woolen cloth.

Henry VII, who came to power in 1485, had spent time as a youth in Burgundy, in present-day France, where English wool was woven into cloth. The wealth there contrasted with the poverty he later found in England. But, he observed, the wealth in Burgundy depended upon imported English raw materials: wool and the fuller's earth used to clean it. So, when he came to power, he imposed the classic anti-Ricardian policy, centuries before Ricardo, of not passively accepting a nation's comparative advantage but *proactively shaping it*.[10]

English strategy was gradual. It started with import substitution: In 1489, tariffs on cloth were increased in a classic case of infant-industry protection. Cloth manufacturing was encouraged: The Crown paid for skilled foreign workers to be brought in and businessmen were paid "bounties" (in modern terms, subsidies) for establishing textile manufacturing firms. When sufficient manufacturing capacity had developed to process all domestic wool production, England prohibited its export – which reduced the cost to domestic producers and increased it for foreign ones.[11]

These developments created what has been called "the closest approximation to a businessman's government among the ancien régimes of Europe."[12] The great nineteenth-century German economist Friedrich List, who helped set Germany on its own successful path of protectionist industrialization, wrote, "The principle 'sell manufactures, buy raw material,' was during centuries the English substitute for an (economic) theory."[13]

England's "picking winners" choice of woolen textiles was based on a correct understanding of the technological and economic circumstances of the day. At the time, out of all existing economic activities this was the only large one within reach that was experiencing rapid technological innovation and productivity growth.[14] It could therefore absorb productive (as opposed to mere castle- and cathedral-building) capital, because here large-scale investments could pay back a return. In this industry were major economies of scale to be reaped. It offered opportunities to accumulate technological knowledge that conferred pricing power because not every nation had it. And it taught and financed development of the all-important organizational capabilities that would equip England for success in subsequent industries.

The Elaboration of Mercantilism

During the 1600s and 1700s, mercantilism further developed across Europe as a response to the observed prosperity of nations such as the Dutch Republic, Tudor England, and France under mercantilist minister Jean-Baptiste Colbert (1619–83). Policy was driven not mainly by economic theories, but by seeing what had worked and failed in other nations. Mercantilists were looking at nations much as capitalists managing companies, but instead of maximizing profit, they were maximizing what today would be called national value added or GDP (though these concepts did not yet exist) and employment.

Mercantilism was both state- and nation-building. It was not a rigid ideology, but flexible enough to understand, for example, that prolonging protectionism beyond the point at which a new industry was well established could be counterproductive.[15] And although it privileged manufacturing, it was not simply a pro-manufacturing policy. Manufactures required raw materials, so sourcing these at the lowest possible cost was another key focus. This meant avoiding other nations' monopoly or oligopoly chokeholds and ideally establishing chokeholds of one's own – such as by means of colonialism, especially to obtain products, from spices to tobacco, that did not grow in Europe.

Italian economist Giovanni Botero (1544–1617) offered the first *theories* as to why mercantilist policies were effective. His work is today virtually unknown in the US because contemporary American economics sees his thinking as misguided and economic history, generally, as irrelevant.[16] But his ideas dominated European economic discourse for more than a century and his influence lingered on well into the 1700s. His 1589 work *Della Ragion di Stato* (*About Reason of State*) argued for the superiority of manufacturing because of what would today be called a) its greater synergies than other economic activities, b) its ability to foster greater diversity of economic activities, c) its greater possibilities for innovation, and d) its greater profitability. In the language of this book, manufacturing is *advantageous*.

Italian economist Antonio Serra took the next major step in 1613.[17] He also favored manufacturing over agriculture, but grounded the distinction in increasing and decreasing returns, producing the first coherent statement of this important principle, noted in Chapter 1 as the key to advantageous and disadvantageous industries.[18] He observed how increasing returns, mainly in manufacturing, create barriers to entry, imperfect competition, and pricing power. As a result, he observed, the division of labor is increased, the new manufacturing activities require more skills, new possibilities for technological spillovers are created, competition for labor increases, and new ways of making money raise the general wage level. A high-wage/high-productivity strategy, where increasing wages drive increasing demand, production, and productivity, becomes possible.

Serra was thus the first to describe the virtuous circles of cumulative causation where – protected from the tiny margins of perfect competition – the dynamic increasing returns of manufacturing allow profits, wages, and tax revenue to produce the sustained output growth and rise in the sophistication of production that constitute *economic development*. In his theory, "the number and variety of industrial professions" (i.e., the degree of division of labor), "the quality of the population" (i.e., skill levels), "the presence of a great commerce" (i.e., international trade), and "the regulations of the State" (i.e., good policies), in the presence of manufacturing's increasing returns create a self-reinforcing system where each growth factor supports the others.[19] Serra was thus the first theorist of *uneven development* (that is, of why some nations are richer than others).

Later mercantilist theorists elaborated all of the these ideas, offering the following explanations for mercantilism's successes:

1. Economic development is activity-specific, created by some economic activities (quintessentially, manufacturing) rather than others (quintessentially, agriculture) due to the latter's stagnant productivity, diminishing returns, and lack of synergies.[20] These ideas can be found in writings of Englishman Daniel Defoe in 1728 and Swede Anders Berch in 1747.

2. Tariff protection and other support of manufacturing is beneficial because of manufacturing's:
    a. Ability to create wealth
    b. Ability to create employment
    c. Ability to solve balance-of-payments problems
    d. Ability to accelerate the circulation of money through an economy, increasing the vitality of other sectors

These ideas can be found in the writings of Italians Tommaso Campanella (1602) and Antonio Genovesi (1750s), Englishmen Thomas Mun (1664) and Josiah Child (1668), Spaniard Gerónimo de Uztáriz (1724, 1751), and again, Anders Berch (1747).[21]

3. Starting in the 1700s, great emphasis was put on the *synergies* between manufacturing and agriculture – that is, only where there is manufacturing is there successful agriculture, because:
    a. Manufactured tools and techniques become more readily available to farmers.
    b. Prices for farm goods go up due to higher wages in the local manufacturing sector.
    c. Draining surplus labor off the farm forces per-worker farm productivity to be raised.

These ideas can be found in the writings of Germans Gottfried Leibniz and Johann von Justi,[22] Italian Ferdinando Galiani,[23] and Scotsman David Hume.[24]

English economists came mainly from the ranks of the merchants. German ones, on the other hand, came from the public sector. Economic policymakers known as "cameralists" were usually employed as keepers of the treasury or *Schatzkammer* – hence their name. Like other mercantilists, they generally favored protection of manufacturing.[25]

After 1700, the Enlightenment produced many theories of "good" and "bad" trade. Three bestselling volumes published in 1721 by Englishman Charles King under the title *The British Merchant; or, Commerce Preserv'd* were extremely influential. King gives an elaborate list of "good" and "bad" trade, and one basic message is that exporting manufactures is good trade and importing them is bad trade, as is exporting raw materials to import manufactures.[26]

Scotsman Sir James Steuart (1712–80), author of *An Inquiry into the Principles of Political Economy*, arguably represents the intellectual high point of classic mercantilism. He was the main tacit opponent of his contemporary Adam Smith, whose celebrated *The Wealth of Nations* broached in 1776 an attack on mercantilism that continues to this day.[27] (Contrary to a myth widely believed in the US, Smith did not invent the discipline of economics.)

In Steuart's day, British mercantilism was having a huge impact on Britain's American colonies. Starting with the Navigation Acts of 1651, the

English (British after 1707) government sought to solidify its mercantilist policies. This effort lasted 125 years, increasing in rigor and sophistication over time. The British were playing catch-up to the mercantilism of their Portuguese, Spanish, and Dutch rivals, who had empires of their own. London undertook concerted action to build up its home economy, its merchants, and its investor class, imposing what we would today call industrial policies in shipbuilding, shipping, naval technology, international trade, raw materials, and finished goods. One result was the American events described in the next chapter.

14 US INDUSTRIAL POLICY 1750-1865
Developing a New Nation

The US has been a relatively "lucky" economy, whose circumstances even without government intervention have been favorable to its development. Therefore, the industrial policies it has needed and has used have been less interventionist than those of other economically successful nations. But they have by no means been trivial.

Received opinion tends to view America's first 100 years as an era of laissez-faire, with the government refraining from trying to shape the economy. The implied contrast is with the European governments of this era, which are accurately regarded as more interventionist. But this is a foundation myth, invented retrospectively to justify current thinking. In fact, America was interventionist, with respect to both its domestic economy and foreign trade, from the start.

The 13 colonies were certainly not laissez-faire economies. They and their local governments regulated, for good or ill, aspects of commerce ranging from inns to public transport. Nor did the assumption that economic regulation was an appropriate task for governments disappear after the American Revolution. Per one historian,

> It was not, after all, against colonial governments that the Revolution was waged, but against the British ... There was no question of some mythical "break for freedom" into a world of true laissez faire once the Revolution was won. The ideas of laissez faire were not widely known or espoused in colonial times.[1]

The misapprehension that regulation only appeared later, starting with measures such as the food safety and antitrust laws of the Progressive Era (1896–1916), derives mainly from the fact that federal, as opposed to state and local, regulation did come later, in response to the increasingly national scale of the enterprises being regulated.

The Founders did sometimes talk about the value of "free trade." But their understanding of the term was not the same as today's. They mostly meant not being hindered by regulations such as the Navigation Acts mentioned in the previous chapter. These required Americans to trade only within the British Empire and to ship America's most important crops, such as tobacco and rice, through Britain, rather than directly to buyers elsewhere.

These policies aimed to build up the British economy as a center of manufacturing, shipping, and other high-value economic activities, with the colonies assigned the profitable but still subordinate role of supplying raw materials and captive markets. For Americans at this time, this all made sense. They still thought of themselves as overseas Britons, not as members of a separate nation. The policy conformed to the economic wisdom of the day and all the other European powers (and even Asian nations such as China) regulated their trade.[2]

Britain's policies included privileging production of the most valuable raw materials and crops such as timber, sugar, and indigo. Mercantilists held that this would benefit *all* interests within the empire, including farmers in the colonies, manufacturers in the home country, and merchants in both. Mercantilism was, among other things, a strategy for binding unwieldy empires together by forcing their component parts into mutually profitable relationships that excluded outsiders. Many of the colonies, such as Virginia and New York, had been explicitly founded as commercial ventures, so such thinking seemed reasonable to Americans.

The idea that trade and economic development were part and parcel of geopolitical power came naturally in this era. There was no WTO, or even a pro–free trade naval hegemon like the late nineteenth-century UK or the late twentieth-century US, to enforce trading rights beyond what a nation won by its own military and diplomatic exertions. Without the empire, the colonies would have been defenseless against the other European powers (and probably con-quered into another empire) and would have had difficulty finding markets for their products. Even thinkers of the time such as John Locke, who were liberals in political matters, were mercantilists in economics.[3]

There did exist some opposition to mercantilism but it was not general. Starting in 1696, all laws passed in colonial assemblies were subjected to vetting by the Board of Trade in London – *not* Parliament or the king, a clear sign the motive was economic. Although the Board rejected around 5 percent, general revolt did not emerge until the 1770s.[4] Quantitative estimates today of the costs and benefits of these policies suggest that the result was either favorable on net to the Americans, or at worst not significantly unfavorable.[5]

There was, of course, a catch: These regulations restricted what Americans could do. Laws such as the Hat Act of 1732 and Iron Act of 1750 required colonists to send their raw materials to be manufactured in Britain, rather than manufacturing for themselves. The objective was to shape the colonies into the perfect *complementary* economy for Britain (see Japan and Korea in Chapter 6), providing the resource inputs Britain needed to be a producer in the most advantageous industries, but *not* competing to host those industries themselves. There was therefore also a ban on the export of advanced production machinery to the colonies and on the emigration of skilled workers from Britain.[6]

The British government made no secret of what it was doing, as mercantilism was respectable policy at the time. The Board of Trade thus said of the colonies in 1721, "Having no manufactories of their own, their ... situation will make them always dependent on Great Britain."[7] As the colonies were not sufficiently developed to plausibly aspire to many of the industries they were excluded from, these rules caused little resentment.

British mercantilism was not airtight. Parliament removed a ban on colonial exports of pig and bar iron in 1750, but banned further development of the industry. But the ban was ignored and by 1775, the colonies were producing almost as much iron as Britain itself.[8] The 1733 Molasses Act attempted to force the colonies to buy molasses from British, as opposed to French, islands in the Caribbean, but was so bitterly opposed and evaded by smugglers that London eventually tacitly gave in. Such compromises were part of what made the system work, as was the fact that colonists who objected to mercantilism because it cost them personally generally found smuggling more profitable than political agitation.

Another reason for the low level of American objection was that farming, the activity London pushed the colonists to engage in, was an attractive proposition due to good export opportunities and a ready supply of arable land. Average money incomes in the colonies were similar to the UK itself, while consumption was roughly double due to lower prices.[9] This entailed a living standard approximating one of the more prosperous developing nations of today.[10]

As a result of mercantilist policies and other factors, such as more expensive labor than Britain, a small and scattered population, and a lack of technical skills, there was very little manufacturing in the colonies before the Revolution. It was rarely an attractive option either for investors or people looking for work.[11]

The American Revolution

In time, however, British mercantilism began to chafe. As America's economy become more developed, its enforced status as a supplier of raw materials started to constrain its commercial opportunities.

More importantly, the focus of Britain's taxation of the colonies changed from shaping their economies to bringing in revenue. London was desperate for money after running up huge debts to win the French and Indian War in 1763. Americans had been among the least-taxed people in all of Europe and its colonies, but this made them more rather than less resistant to higher taxes.[12]

The result of this drive for revenue was laws such as the Sugar, Stamp, and Tea Acts, whose unconsented imposition was perceived as illegitimate. As is well known, these laws became catalysts for the Revolution. Thus, while the Revolution was a indeed reaction against certain *aspects* of British mercantilism, few Americans rejected the interventionist assumptions underlying it.[13] Their dispute was over the form and intent of such regulations, and, above all, with the political issue of who – London without the colonists' consent or their colonial legislatures – had the authority to impose them.

One of the patriots' major forms of protest in the years of disruption leading up to the Revolution was so-called nonimportation of British goods. Some Americans who made manufactured goods, known at the time as "mechanics" or "artisans," also supported nonimportation as a means of developing domestic manufacturing. Nonimportation spurred a small industrial boom, with a number of proto-factories, often called manufactories, making goods such as glassware, paper, and textiles.[14]

Tariffs and the New Nation

From 1789, the Constitution provided the federal government with a number of powers that could be used to promote economic development. It created a free trade zone among the states, which under the Articles of Confederation had imposed tariffs on each other. And it received sole authority to impose tariffs on foreign goods.

The states had been unreliable about funding the central government under the Articles, so it was accepted that the new federal government needed revenue sources of its own. A tariff was one of the few practicable options. In a country with a primitive banking system and only the rudiments of bookkeeping, where most transactions were in cash, even barter due to a coin shortage, personal and corporate income taxes were not feasible. But a tariff could be imposed by a relatively small number of inspectors in a few dozen major seaports. A tariff was also more progressive than most alternatives because imports were concentrated in nonnecessities. Alternative taxes, such as on liquor, induced revolts from whiskey-consuming (and producing) frontiersmen several times.

As a result, the pre–Civil War US never really had the option of being for free trade, which consensus economic opinion did not favor anyway. Thus one of the very first laws passed by Congress, in 1789, was a tariff. It was not that protective, despite some protectionist language in its preamble. Dozens of itemized products were assessed specific rates, with the rest at 10 percent or less, except if they were from China or India, in which case 12.5 percent.[15] It set the precedent, which lasted until the Great Depression, that tariffs would be a major instrument of economic policy.

Some 85 percent of federal revenues before the Civil War came from tariffs.[16] They were the single most important economic regulatory device available to the government at the time, and a potent tool for influencing which industries would develop. They also funded the infrastructure, such as roads and ports, that expanded isolated local markets to regional, national, and international scale.

Agriculture, Industry, and Jeffersonianism

The early US was primarily agricultural. Before the Revolution, the major crops were tobacco, rice, and wheat, sold to Europe and the West Indies. After the Revolution, as a result of increased demand from British textile factories and the invention of the cotton gin, the most valuable product became cotton.

Before the late eighteenth century, virtually nothing we would today recognize as a factory – that is, a specialized building with a large number of workers – existed anywhere in the world. Most manufacturing was performed on a craft basis by individual artisans such as blacksmiths, shoemakers, and hatters, working at home or in small workshops. The rare cases of large-scale industry involved trades such as shipbuilding and mining, where the objects worked upon dictated the physical scale, plus a few exceptions such as smelters and sugar refineries, which could employ more than 100 people. The Industrial Revolution, with steam power and large, centralized factories, was only just beginning, and then only in a few industries, such as textiles. It got underway at scale in the US only in the 1830s.

As late as 1810, only 3 percent of Americans worked in manufacturing and 84 percent worked on farms.[17] It seems obvious today that the world's future then was industrial. But at the time, it this still uncertain. None of the great classical economists – Adam Smith, David Ricardo, Thomas Malthus, John Stuart Mill – foresaw the significance of the Industrial Revolution.

America had a serious debate, most famously between Thomas Jefferson and Alexander Hamilton, about whether industrialization made sense for a nation so richly endowed with agricultural land. The Jeffersonian "no" position was based on the fact that in the preindustrial world, the best occupation the average person could hope for was to be a farmer on his own land. Jefferson's dream was that this could become the norm because America had so much land. Jeffersonians believed, based in part on the decline of ancient Rome into decadence and tyranny, that a republic required a citizenry of small independent farmers. They believed that workers dependent upon others for their daily bread could not be true citizens, and that urbanization, the inevitable concomitant of industrialization, would lead to proletarian mob rule.[18]

Hamiltonian Developmentalism

The opposing view was Hamiltonianism, named after the first Treasury secretary. This favored industrial development for reasons of both prosperity and national security, and supported using the powers of the federal government to achieve it. Alexander Hamilton had seen the American army nearly lose the Revolutionary War for want of manufactured supplies such as weapons, uniforms, tents, and blankets. He outlined a multifaceted plan to stimulate manufacturing in his *Report on Manufactures* of 1791, one of a series of economic reports he wrote for Congress. (Another was on the national debt.) His aim was to transform America from a colonial outpost producing raw materials for Europe into a self-sufficient economy.

The first element of Hamilton's policy was protective tariffs, not just for revenue but also for infant-industry purposes. As he put it:

> The superiority antecedently enjoyed by nations, who have pre-occupied and perfected a branch of industry, constitutes a more formidable obstacle, than either of those, which have been mentioned, to the introduction of the same branch into a country, in which it did not before exist. To maintain between the recent establishments of one country and the long-matured establishments of another country, a competition upon equal terms, both as to quality and price, is in most cases impracticable. The disparity in the one, or in the other, or in both, must necessarily be so considerable as to forbid a successful rivalship, without the extraordinary aid and protection of government.[19]

In the language of Gomory and Baumol noted in Chapter 4, industries are *retainable*.

The second element was "internal improvements," which we would call infrastructure: roads, harbors, and river dredging.

The third element was financial, starting with a federally chartered national bank, the Bank of the United States, created in 1791. This was intended to serve as the foundation of an efficient nationwide financial system in place of the existing small, unstable local banks.

Tariff revenue funded the national debt created by federal assumption of the debts the states had run up fighting the Revolution. This new debt consisted of tradable securities, which brought into being a liquid national capital market. Debt repayment could be sped up or slowed down to stabilize the economy in what would today be called Federal Reserve Open Market Operations.

National banking was bitterly controversial, seen by some as today as a tool of plutocratic interests. The tight-money policies the Bank sometimes imposed for financial stability were resented. Hamilton's bank had only a 20-year charter and its successor was abolished by President Andrew Jackson in 1832 in a fit of populism that left the nation's financial infrastructure inefficient and unstable for decades.

Other parts of the Hamiltonian program included state-assisted technology theft and immigration of key skilled personnel, both in violation of British law.[20]

Hamilton's ideas were controversial. In particular, his proposal for bounties (industry subsidies) met with opposition. James Madison (president 1809–1817) claimed they were an unconstitutional attempt to turn the General Welfare clause into a blank check.[21] Hamilton himself, as shown in his *Federalist 35*, understood that a tariff-based development strategy necessarily had costs as well as benefits:

> Suppose, as has been contended for, the federal power of taxation were to be confined to duties on imports, it is evident that the government, for want of being able to command other resources, would frequently be tempted to extend these duties to an injurious excess. There are persons who imagine that they can never be carried to too great a length; since the higher they are, the more it is alleged they will tend to discourage an extravagant consumption, to produce a favorable balance of trade, and to promote domestic manufactures.
>
> But all extremes are pernicious in various ways. Exorbitant duties on imported articles would beget a general spirit of smuggling; which is always prejudicial to the fair trader, and eventually to the revenue itself: they tend to render other classes of the community tributary, in an improper degree, to the manufacturing classes, to whom they give a premature monopoly of the markets; they sometimes force industry out of its more natural channels into others in which it flows with less advantage; and in the last place, they oppress the merchant, who is often obliged to pay them himself without any retribution from the consumer.[22]

The final, least successful, component of Hamiltonianism was subsidized creation of a national manufacturing center. This took place in Paterson, NJ and was known as the Society for Establishing Useful Manufactures (SEUM). Congress refused to fund it, but it got underway as a public-private partnership with over $600,000 in private subscriptions ($20 million in today's money) plus $10,000 in direct aid, tax exemptions, eminent domain, and other privileges from the State of New Jersey.[23] SEUM did not succeed, partly because Hamilton chose a corrupt financier crony to run it, but Paterson eventually became one of the most important early American manufacturing centers.

Manufacturing for Liberty & Security

Hamiltonianism was not just an economic ideology but an alternative view of the social architecture required for a free society. A major reason President Washington chose Hamilton's path was that it did not require slavery.[24]

Congress was divided not so much over whether tariffs were needed, which was almost universally accepted, but over their purpose. Protectionists generally came from proto-industrial regions and wanted tariffs not just for revenue but to keep out foreign competition. Anti-protectionists, usually from agricultural areas, wanted tariffs for revenue only.

Tariff controversies were instrumental in the emergence of America's first political parties. Despite the intention and expectation that the new Constitution would minimize "faction," two very factious parties, the Federalists and the Democratic-Republicans, emerged during Washington's second term.

Initially, Jefferson's Democratic-Republicans, the institutional ancestors of today's Democrats, were skeptical of large-scale manufacturing. But over time they would soften their views, particularly in the Northeast. Their opposition to pro-industrialization policies tended to be an out-of-power luxury, a rhetorical stick to beat the opposition with when no policy consequences would ensue. Once in the White House, their presidents were forced to confront the limitations of their nominally agrarian, small-government ideals.[25] For example, in 1808, Jefferson's Treasury Secretary Albert Gallatin proposed a massive internal improvements bill that would have integrated a number of federal road and canal projects into a coherent national system. (It died in Congress due to conflicting demands of local interests.)[26] Jefferson changed his mind about manufacturing because of the War of 1812. When in Congress, James Madison opposed the first Bank of the United States, but as president in 1816, he signed the legislation creating the second.

The Democratic-Republicans' ideals ran aground on several realities. Small farmers might want to be independent, but they needed the US Army to conquer their land from the Indians, and an army cost money, which meant tariffs. Farmers also didn't *really* want to be fully self-sufficient: They wanted to be able to sell crops in distant urban markets, which meant canals, the nation's first arterial freight system. Thus Madison supported the tariff side in the debate over the so-called Tariff of Abominations in 1828, based on both infant-industry and national-security concerns.[27]

The War of 1812

Thanks to Napoleon and the long aftershocks of the French Revolution, Britain and France, the global superpowers of the day, were at war for most of 1800–1815. These conflicts provided natural protection for American goods by a) interfering with the combatants' seaborne trade and b) making European goods scarcer by weakening the European economies and diverting their production to military needs. Because the US remained neutral, American ships could sell American goods in both French and British ports, albeit with some interference.

The result was an enormously profitable period for American farmers and merchants. This trade was, however, hardly "free." Britain after the Revolution had toyed with a number of alternative trade agreements with the US, including reciprocal openness, but in the end did not agree to anything, being itself still mercantilist. In most European ports, American products were subject to duties. On the high seas, and even in apparently safe ports, the warring nations sometimes seized US ships and goods, despite the accepted doctrine that "free ships make free goods."

To protect American shipping from these hazards, Congress in 1794 funded construction of the first ships of the US Navy at a cost of nearly $700,000 – a huge sum when the entire federal budget was only $7 million.[28] International trade, industrial development, and national security have thus been bound together since America's earliest days. In the 1790s, the Navy worried about its dependence on British copper to sheathe the bottoms of its wooden warships against shipworm. In response, the federal government entered into a public-private partnership with Paul Revere (of the famous midnight ride) to create a domestic source of rolled copper. This partnership, supported by a $10,000 federal loan, established what would eventually become Revere Copper (a company that still exists and is run by a friend of the authors).[29]

Increasing British and French interference with American shipping led Jefferson to sign the Non-importation Act of 1806, the Embargo Act of 1808, and the Non-Intercourse Act of 1809 to punish the two nations by limiting their trade with the US. Excluding European goods stimulated domestic production: Between

1811 and 1815, 111 new manufacturing firms were incorporated in New York state.[30] In Massachusetts, 121 new manufacturing corporations received charters between 1809 and 1815, including 24 textile firms in 1814 alone.[31] The capitalization of the cotton textile industry by the end of this period has been estimated at $800 million in today's money.[32]

The First Protective Tariffs

In 1815, the end of the war halted the creation of new American factories and threatened existing ones. British textiles and other manufactured goods were expected to flood the American market.

Tariffs had been doubled in 1812 when war broke out, but this had been a temporary wartime measure. So, in reaction to the perceived threat of an import surge, Congress in 1816 passed America's first overtly protective tariff, albeit one that would phase down rates over three years.[33] Because of national security concerns and some Anglophobia, Democratic-Republicans such as Andrew Jackson and John C. Calhoun, who would not normally have supported a tariff for anything beyond revenue, supported it. Hamilton was dead, but the influence of his former aide Tench Coxe, acting through Treasury Secretary Albert Gallatin, got the Jefferson administration to issue a new *Report on Manufactures* that largely accepted Hamilton's program.[34]

However, the new tariff provided far less protection than the war had, and America's young manufacturing sector all but collapsed in the Panic of 1819, America's first depression.[35] Some protectionists claimed that Britain had purposely dumped low-priced goods to destroy America's nascent industries, but historians have found little evidence for this.[36] Other contemporaries argued that the Panic of 1819 had been *caused* by the collapse of manufacturing, but this was also not true.

In response to the above events, manufacturers organized the first protectionist lobby groups in America, aiming for tariffs high enough to reserve the domestic market for American producers and thereby make domestic manufacturing viable. They appealed to the public not only on grounds of prosperity, but also of economic independence.

The subsequent decades brought a near-continual struggle between protectionists and their opponents. Congress was inundated with petitions from artisans, manufacturers, and merchants, even wool growers and other farmers. A national protectionist convention in Harrisburg, Pennsylvania in 1827 drew delegates from 13 of the 24 states. Noted editor Hezekiah Niles wrote the convention's address and printed its minutes in his *Niles' Weekly Register*, the leading newsmagazine of the day. Publisher and economist

Mathew Carey was also influential, writing hundreds of letters, publishing books and pamphlets, and working behind the scenes with lobby groups.

Carey, Niles, and their followers were self-styled economic nationalists. They viewed tariffs as one element of a three-part plan to knit the sprawling new nation into a strong, unified economy. First, tariffs would protect the nascent manufacturing sector, centered in the Mid-Atlantic and New England states. Second, a strong national bank would provide credit both to manufacturers and to the agricultural interests of rural America, North and South. Third, federal funding for upgraded roads and waterways would allow farmers to bring their goods to market. Politically, this agenda meant a coalition of the East, which wanted manufacturing protection, with the West, which needed internal improvements and a domestic market. The South, with its export-oriented agriculture, was the odd man out – a fact with vast consequences later.

Clay's American System and Its Collapse

Senator Henry Clay of Kentucky eventually emerged as the leader of the economic nationalists. He had started out as a Jeffersonian, but like many others had been converted by the War of 1812. He had also seen the fickleness and slow growth of America's export markets, and their dependence on a narrow range of crops.[37] His solution was to cultivate America's internal market. His party, the Whigs, labeled their tripartite program the "American System," and by the 1820s, the country seemed to have reached a stable consensus in its favor.[38] The exchange of congressional votes described previously functioned successfully.[39]

However, the System collapsed soon after protection peaked with the 1828 Tariff of Abominations. By 1830, the average tariff on dutiables had reached 62 percent, which overshot the pro-tariff consensus and was the product of political chicanery whose details need not be recounted here.[40] It passed along purely sectional lines, with no support from Southern representatives in Congress, and triggered a crisis remembered today mainly for South Carolina's claim of the right to nullify federal laws.

The fight over this tariff was understood by its participants as being not only about tariffs, but also about the right of the Southern states to national policies that did not threaten their anomalous economy – which was poorly integrated with the rest of the nation, embraced a conflicting economic strategy, and involved slavery. President Jackson, though not generally a supporter of tariffs for any purpose other than revenue, viewed South Carolina's defiance as a threat to both his personal authority and the power of the federal government. He therefore subdued the state with the Force Bill threatening military action while passing the Compromise Tariff of 1833, cutting tariffs over 10 years to a for-revenue-only level. As a policy matter, the South had won, "for revenue only" became accepted, and tariffs generally declined for the next 25 years. In addition, in 1830 Jackson vetoed federal funding for further construction of the National Road, another key part of the American System. And in 1832, he vetoed legislation continuing the Bank of the United States. Clay's American System was dead.

Despite their rhetoric, Jackson's nominally Jacksonian successors such as Martin Van Buren (president 1837–41) were not really interested in ending protectionism outright. And even protectionism's sincere opponents, such as Southern planters, still gained enough from it, and had enough need of political allies in the North, to tolerate it. As a result, tariffs continued throughout the rest of the antebellum period, though at reduced rates.

Setting the Tariffs

Tariff rates in antebellum America were determined, like most things in government then and now, by the jockeying of interest groups within an ideological framework defining what was and was not permissible. Was this corrupt? Yes and no. Special interests certainly got what they wanted often enough. But much of their lobbying was not corrupt, strictly speaking, because modern laws regulating gifts to congressmen and requiring disclosure of lobbying did not exist, so no laws were broken. (Such practices were still criticized, especially by those preferring opposite outcomes.)

Although the tariff system was imperfect, only a few major tariffs were, in retrospect, mistaken as instruments of economic development. (Sugar and raw wool were two.) The main reason was that tariff protection was not something an industry could simply buy with well-funded political pressure. A tariff on any product activated a number of interest groups, pro and con, producers and consumers, upstream and downstream industries – which, taken together, few special interests could overpower. Nakedly corrupt or grossly economically illogical tariffs were thus difficult to pass.

The need for revenue was a constraint, as too high a rate would mean no revenue because no imports, but so would too low a rate. Excessively narrow (on too few products) and excessively broad (on too many) tariffs were also hard to get through Congress.[41] The former failed to attract a large enough supporting coalition, and the latter offended too many consuming interests.

Politics thus kept America's tariff regime in the middle of the road, albeit with a Hamiltonian pro-manufacturing bias. Tariff-making was in large part simply the political process of finding which set of tariffs garnered the most

290/ The Forgotten History

support from the beneficiaries, triggered the least opposition from the victims, and had the best economic arguments for those not directly affected.

Were the tariffs of this era effective policy? Today's academic economics, of course, says no, as it assumes that tariffs have, with only token exceptions, no value as a developmental strategy. Nonetheless, today's estimates of antebellum protectionism's net cost are still low. Free trader Doug Irwin of Dartmouth has estimated this cost as ranging from a maximum of 2.5 percent of GDP in 1828 (under the Tariff of Abominations) to a minimum of 0.2 percent in 1859.[42] Note, crucially, that because tariffs are a tax, and all taxes impose so-called "deadweight" losses on an economy, there may not have been any way these costs could have been avoided, because something else would have had to have been taxed instead.

Fluctuations in the Tariffs

Tariff rates fluctuated for a number of reasons, some unrelated to tariffs. After 1832, lower rates were possible because federal sales of western lands had produced budget surpluses. But by the early 1840s, budget deficits were back and this, combined with a short-lived resurgence of the Whig Party, led to a brief period of higher tariffs. But after the Democrats regained power, they instituted in 1846 the less protectionist Walker Tariff, which lasted for a decade. As the Whig party disintegrated in the early 1850s, its anti-slavery faction created the Republican Party, which would also champion protective tariffs, infrastructure, and a national bank.

The main controversies among protectionists were about the right level of protection, whether it should be permanent, and whether raw materials deserved the same as manufactures. Regarding the latter question, tariffs changed over time. The 1824 tariff, for example, clearly shows the emerging pattern, with lower tariffs on raw materials, higher ones on finished manufactures, and intermediate goods in between.[43] As noted in Chapter 3, such stage-differential tariffs are still used today.

Tariff protection benefitted some industries more than others. It had the greatest impact on infant industries, on products with low elasticities of supply, and on products where much was currently imported.[44] Some of the products estimated to have been the most sensitive to protection, i.e., least likely to survive under free trade, include buttons, cotton bagging, cotton wicks, hardware, augers, saws, sickles, sieves, spades, rolled iron, rifles, shot, refined saltpeter, and medicines – this list giving, in passing, an idea of what America was importing at the time.[45]

The US economy was certainly not mature enough to make infant-industry protection moot. As the US International Trade Commission (ITC) observed in 2017,

> American manufacturers, who remained relatively small in scale in their operations (and largely unincorporated) until the 1870s and 1880s, worried about competition from British manufacturers, who often seemed to be ahead ...[46]

Within particular industries, the strongest firms were often content with a moderate tariff, believing that anything higher would just help their weaker domestic rivals survive.[47]

American Economic Ideology

The leading protectionists were not academics, nor were they always the most systematic thinkers.[48] As a result, they have been of little interest to today's American economists, who tend to regard anything not mathematized as intellectually insubstantial, and who do not have much respect for the thinking of "mere" policymakers, even those of today. And yet figures such as Mathew Carey and Hezekiah Niles were pivotal in setting the policies of what became the world's leading economy by the third quarter of the nineteenth century.[49] These men were the inheritors of the long history of accurate thinking and effective *actual state policy* noted in Chapter 13.

Some commentators have characterized the policymaking of this period as "nonideological." This was not so.[50] Politicians and newspapermen usually addressed the public in the concrete and immediate terms to which it mainly responds, then as now. And some political figures deferred to the consensus of the time or to the views of their political faction. But others, such as Hamilton, were genuine intellectual sophisticates, conversant with the most advanced thinking of the day and holding views of analytical depth comparable to anything one might call "ideology." Pure pragmatism, as opposed to a practical tradition with a *small* theoretical component, is impossible because there is no purely pragmatic way to settle questions of fundamental strategy. The question "Did policy X work?" rarely has an obvious answer, which pure pragmatism would require, because the results take too long to appear and require an analytical framework to connect cause and effect. Hamilton was a longtime associate of George Washington, a "leader of men" type rather than an intellectual, but one who appreciated the talents of his clever young protégé. There was a kind of "food chain of ideas," through which the thinking of the more intellectual participants in the political process filtered down to practical politicians. Note, however, that although actual US policymakers during this period were almost all protectionists, albeit to varying degrees, free trade still enjoyed considerable support among America's then tiny professoriate.[51]

Federal Technology Development

Shortly after independence, the US established a uniquely strong and accessible patent system, then upgraded it starting around 1837. (See Chapter 24 for its current crisis.) The major political figures of this era, including Abraham Lincoln, were acutely aware of technological issues. Lincoln is the only president to hold a patent (No. 6,469, "A device for buoying vessels over shoals"), and his private-sector career had been largely as a lawyer representing railroads, the high-tech big businesses of the day.

The nineteenth-century federal government played a surprisingly large *direct* role in the development of manufacturing technology. The idea of interchangeable machine parts was first applied at scale at the federal armory in Springfield, Massachusetts. This idea, which developed with failures and corruption, was viewed overseas as so distinctly an American phenomenon that the British called it the "American system of manufacturing." Referred to as "armory practice" by Americans, it eventually spread to other industries. For example, Lebbeus Miller, who had worked in the gun industry, introduced it to the manufacturing of sewing machines at Singer.[52]

The US's first engineering schools were military and trained most of America's engineers until the 1850s. The army sent some of its engineers to survey routes for the early railroads.[53]

Slave Labor and Free Trade

The center of political opposition to protectionism was the planter class of the South. Cotton was the boom crop of the era and because American textile manufacturing was still limited, the main market was England, whose fabrics were becoming the world's most important internationally traded manufactured product.

The South was a major factor in the US economy: The larger plantations were among its greatest capital investments, with the largest labor forces and profits. The US at the time grew 80 percent of the world's cotton, which was also America's largest export.[54] Two-thirds of the nation's richest men lived in the South.[55] Planters imported manufactured goods subject to tariffs, which they resented: Doug Irwin has estimated that tariffs reduced their real incomes by about 10 percent.[56]

No physical constraint precluded industrialization of the South. Climate, while a disadvantage, was not an absolute bar, as there were factories in the South, though very few. The main impediment was the plantocracy, which controlled its politics and capital and preferred its existing economic strategy.[57] This elite did not understand manufacturing well enough to venture into it, and feared the upheaval that rival sources of wealth and power would create.[58] This has been a pattern around the world for centuries and continues even today: Reactionary agrarian elites impede industrialization. But from a Southern point of view, their economic strategy was working. Including wealth held as slaves, white Southerners were (controversially) richer than Northerners in 1860, which makes sense with a slave population producing wealth but owning nothing.[59]

Not all Southern planters opposed protection. Growers of hemp in Kentucky and sugar in Louisiana generally supported it. A duty of 2.5 cents per pound (roughly 15 percent) provided the margin that made Louisiana sugar profitable.[60] And some Northern interests, notably importers, opposed tariffs. And despite their general opposition to federal economic development policies, the Southern states used state-level powers for the same purpose.

The pre–Civil War era a saw a number of false starts toward free trade. After Britain adopted free trade unilaterally in 1846–9, it concluded a short-lived free trade agreement with France. With American protectionism in decline after the Compromise of 1832, it appeared for a few years that America would be next and that "tariffs for revenue only" would become the settled consensus worldwide.[61] But this turn toward freer trade turned out to be transient and America's tariffs came back with a vengeance after 1860.

The Civil War

The Civil War was, among other things, a contest between rival economic systems. Antebellum America had essentially two different economies, with a series of political compromises that kept the country together. Then the Kansas–Nebraska Act of 1854 repealed the Missouri Compromise of 1820 and allowed new territories to choose whether they would allow slavery. This made it possible that either a slave or a free system might take over much of the vast area between the Mississippi and the Pacific – which, in turn, would entail dominance over the national government. This threat split and galvanized public opinion, led to the formation of the Republican Party, and eventually to war.

Tariffs were second only to slavery as a flashpoint. It is no accident that the Confederate constitution banned both tariffs and aid to manufacturing, though the Confederacy resorted to state-sponsored industrialization for military goods. It had a considerable disadvantage to redress: The North, with more than twice the South's free population, had 10 times its industrial output.[62]

Antebellum America's tariffs and other developmental policies had been limited by the opposition of Southerners and their Northern allies. But after secession, the Republican majority in Congress, with most Southern votes gone, promptly raised tariff rates with the Morrill Tariff of 1861. Needing more money to pay for the war, Congress raised tariffs even further and made more goods dutiable. Wartime domestic taxes forced tariffs on the same products to be increased to avoid putting domestic producers at a disadvantage. Over the course of the war, the average tariff on dutiable imports rose from 19 to 48 percent, resulting in the highest tariffs of any major nation.[63]

Even while war raged, the Republicans created new programs that built on the earlier American System. The Morrill Land-Grant College Act of 1862 created the first mass federal support of higher education, with an initial focus on agriculture and engineering. Representative Justin Morrill (R-VT) was also the author of the Morrill tariff: These policies were understood to form a package. There are now more than 100 land-grant institutions in the US, and their establishment laid the foundations of America's later technological prowess. And in 1863, the National Academy of Sciences, which still exists and conducted some studies cited in this book, was founded.

The Hatch Act of 1887 provided federal money for agricultural research stations in every state to improve productivity. At the time, much of American agriculture was inefficient. Because each individual farmer produced a tiny percentage of any given crop, individual farmers had limited incentive or money to undertake expensive and time-consuming productivity research. New techniques also had to be transmitted to farmers, hence the Smith–Lever Act of 1914, which funded cooperative extension services teaching agriculture, home economics, and other subjects.[64]

15 US INDUSTRIAL POLICY 1866–1939
The High Point of Protectionism

The defeat of the South discredited its anti-tariff, anti-industrialization policies, resulting in an intensification of America's protectionism and industrialization. The tariff became the centerpiece of Republican economic policy and, with this party occupying the White House for 32 of the 40 years between the start of the war and the turn of the century, the biggest issue in politics. During this period, the golden age of America's tariff-based industrialization, the average tariff on dutiables fluctuated between 40 and 50 percent, though many goods were duty-free.[1]

The Republican Party's overall nationalism was popular, and protectionism was understood to be a part of it, buttressing its electoral appeal. Tariffs continued as a hybrid revenue and protection measure, varying with the ebb and flow of the nation's finances and politics. Congress lowered them when revenues from nontariff sources rose and when Democrats ruled, but they always remained well above antebellum levels. The election of 1888 was framed as referendum on tariff policy and the "revenue-only" – *not* free trade, despite accusations – incumbent Democrat Grover Cleveland lost.

The US was evolving from a raw materials exporter into a leading industrial economy, and the tariff system responded rationally, if imperfectly, to the change. In the words of former USITC chairman Alfred E. Eckes, Jr.:

> In 1872 Congress modified the high tariff system – changing it from one designed to tax *all* imports for revenue to a protective system intended to aid domestic industries and shelter working people from low-wage foreign competition. Accepting a 10 percent horizontal reduction in duties, Congress effectively expunged low-revenue duties, such as for tea and coffee, while retaining protective duties. In effect

the United States moved toward a selective, protective system in which government admitted raw materials and noncompetitive materials duty-free but retained high tariffs on manufactured goods in order to stimulate industry and economic development. Historical statistics record this transition. Customs collections gradually shifted from a sweeping horizontal tariff, covering raw materials, intermediate goods, and manufactured products, to a selective, protective tariff sheltering value-added products.[2]

A third of imports were now duty-free.[3]

Republicans were unable to impose a tariff on manufactured goods only, which would have been the classic mercantilist logic, because political coalition-building required that the Western states, which produced agricultural goods and raw materials, be given something.[4] Hence the tariff, for example, on raw wool, directed mainly against Argentina and Australia.

Partly because of tariffs, the US of this era did not *have* a large volume of imports or exports. Unlike smaller nations before and since, which have needed foreign raw materials, technology, and markets, and therefore pursued export-led growth, the US mainly grew by serving its own market. It was, in fact, the closest thing to an economically successful autarchy in modern history. In 1870, imports were 6.6 percent of GDP, versus 18.5 percent in Germany and 24.4 percent in the UK, and exports were comparable.[5] As steel tycoon Andrew Carnegie put it in 1890, "Even if every port of the United States were blockaded today, and remained so for 10 years, the people of the United States would suffer only some inconveniences."[6]

Even this early, it was understood by some in power, such as President Ulysses S. Grant, that protectionist economic strategy implied an *eventual* opening to free trade.[7] But this moment was generally thought to be far in the future.

The Political Economy of the Tariff

The political economy of the tariff in this era was complex, due to its triple purpose of raising revenue, providing protection, and generating political capital for the Republican Party. Tariffs gave Republicans in Congress the money to meet obligations to key supporters – for example, by paying Union Army veterans' pensions – and won constituencies, such as sugar growers, who might otherwise have supported the Democrats.

As before the war, the specific industries protected, and at what level, was determined almost entirely by political maneuvering, rather than technocratic calculation. The horse-trading took place, however, within a broadly accepted framework of Hamiltonian assumptions, and the tariffs chosen protected approximately the same industries as a hypothetical rational tariff.

Tariff-protected industries were well aware that their fate depended upon coalition-building. They sought agreements among themselves to present a united front to Congress and thus avoid having the key decisions made by politicians.[8]

Some regions, such as the Midwest, were ambivalent about high tariffs because they had strong agricultural and manufacturing interests. So they sometimes supported tariffs in return for votes on other economic issues they cared about more, like railroads, monopolies, or silver money (moderate inflation, as opposed to the deflationary gold standard).[9] Organized labor was so conflicted about tariffs, unable to decide whether they raised wages or consumer prices more, that the leading labor federation declared itself neutral on the issue in 1882.[10]

As before the Civil War, sections of the public opposed high tariffs. Inflation surged in the late 1890s because gold newly discovered in Canada, Australia, and South Africa increased the amount of currency in all countries on the gold standard. Tariffs, however, were falsely blamed for inflation – and falsely also for corporate consolidation, monopolies, and oligopolies.[11] The charge that consumers were net losers from tariffs was common, but is not supported by the detailed analysis of even today's pro-free trade economic historians. In the words of Doug Irwin, "Consumers roughly broke even as a result of protection, paying about 3 percent of GDP to import-competing producers and the government but gaining about 3 percent of GDP at the expense of exporters."[12]

Despite strident accusations at the time, available evidence from the era, notably a congressional investigation of 1913, shows that outright corruption in connection with tariffs, such as bribery, was actually rare. But this should be no surprise, as tariffs were respectable policy that nobody had to conceal their support for, and laws restricting lobbying were looser than today. So there was little incentive to break the law when legal forms of political pressure sufficed.[13]

Setting the Tariffs

For individual congressmen, unless they just deferred to their party leadership or represented districts with firm views, formulating a position on tariffs was often challenging. In the words of economist Andrew Reamer:

> To a large extent, a Congressional member's geographic base determined his priorities, proposals, and concerns about tariffs. Conflict was endemic to tariff-setting … because each member represented

a unique mix of producing and consuming industries . . . Moreover, as each member had multiple values, priorities, and constituencies, it was difficult for him to figure out a set of tariff proposals that appeared to fully satisfy them all. To use a modern term, every member struggled with optimization.[14]

What members really wanted were reliable projections about the likely effects of a tariff of amount X on product Y on jobs, wages, profits, the input costs of downstream industries, and producers' competitiveness against imports.[15] Such information was, however, hard to come by. Because they developed prior to modern econometrics, the economic theories of the protectionists offered only general principles, not formulas for computing the right tariff for each product. The economic statistics such formulas would have required as inputs were only spottily available in this era, anyway.

Not that Congress didn't try. Before the Civil War, it asked a number of government departments to provide trade statistics and estimates of the expected effects of tariffs.[16] In 1865 and 1866, it created in the Treasury Department the Revenue Commission (now the Bureau of Economic Analysis) and the Bureau of Statistics.[17] In 1916, it created the US Tariff Commission (USTC, which eventually became today's US International Trade Commission), which assumed the task of gathering trade statistics.

The USTC was not, contrary to what some had hoped, given any authority to set tariffs. For one thing, Democrats feared that it would simply be stacked with high-tariff men by the Republicans. Furthermore, as even some tariff supporters realized at the time, the "scientific" tariff most often proposed at the time – the equalization of domestic and foreign production costs – was supported by no rational economic theory and was infeasible to implement.[18] Establishing the commission was mainly an effort to mollify populist complaints, not a serious attempt to create a tariff technocracy.

The Later Nineteenth Century

Starting in 1856, the Bessemer process enabled cheap, mass-produced steel. (The shadow of Mars is long: Englishman Henry Bessemer had been trying to make a cannon strong enough to fire new rifled artillery shells.)[19] Just as huge new steamships with steel hulls and high-pressure boilers reduced international shipping costs, America's tariffs were rising to their post–Civil War highs, conveniently compensating for the decline in "natural" protection.

In this era, Great Britain, the world's largest trading nation, was ideologically committed to free trade whether its partners reciprocated or not. As a result, the US, without having to open its own markets, enjoyed free or low-tariff access to those of Britain, much of Britain's vast empire, and other nations under British economic influence at the time, such as Argentina and Brazil.[20] Between 1897 and 1909, the US experimented with a number of reciprocal trade agreements, but protectionists in Congress prevented any significant tariff cuts.[21]

The US made few mistaken choices about which industries deserved protection, mainly because Congress tended to protect products Americans were already consuming and America, being one of the richest and most technologically advanced nations in the world, had strong demand for products of the most advanced industries of the day. Easy industry entry and fierce domestic competition kept the tariff from sheltering inefficient producers, always a danger for tariff-protected economies.

As noted in Chapter 2, economic development is path-dependent, because acquiring each new set of industrial capabilities usually requires that a nation already have certain other industrial capabilities. Because America was already on the *path* of industrialization because of the industry it already had, tariffs in this era were more of an accelerant of industrialization than its cause per se.[22]

From 1870 to 1913, per capita GDP grew at 1.8 percent per year, versus 1.0 percent in free-trading Britain, the world's most advanced economy at the start.[23] Detailed statistics reveal that greater growth in America's non-residential capital stock – that is, its productive industries – was the main cause.[24] Britain was exporting capital all over the world, but increasingly not investing it at home. It was also ceding the technologically emerging industries of the day to Germany and the US. Britain's problems were interrelated: its lack of innovation depressed returns there, as did an increasing fraction of its market having been ceded to foreigners. This then drove British investors to look abroad rather than investing in innovation at home. The US had neither problem.

US exports continued to shift away from raw cotton, grains, and meat products and toward manufactured goods. Manufactures rose from 20 percent of exports in 1890 to 35 percent in 1900 and almost 50 percent in 1913, and the US became a net exporter thereof.[25] Before the Civil War, America's trade had been in deficit for all but a few years, but shortly after the war, it shifted to a consistent surplus which lasted until World War II upended normal trade.[26]

Was the Tariff Effective?

It is not an empty hypothetical that America might have failed to industrialize, or industrialize as much and as fast as it did. The antebellum South makes this clear, as do facts like the US importing 80 percent of its iron rails from the UK before the Civil War.[27] Other New World nations with comparable natural resources, such as Brazil and Argentina, did not industrial-ize (see Chapter 12). One economist has estimated that removing the 20 percent average tariff in 1859 would have lowered industrial production by 17 per-cent.[28] Another has estimated that in the mid nineteenth century, 40 percent of the American iron industry, for example, needed protection to survive.[29]

Consider one of the most important, technologically advanced indus-tries of the day: steel railroad rails. The US began by importing them from Britain in 1862, and Britain had the entire US market until 1866. But the US reached close to 100 percent domestic production by 1877.[30] Econometric reconstruction has estimated that if there had been free trade, the US would have kept importing almost all its steel rails as late as 1905 – a generation later.[31] And as the economist who made this estimate observes, "Protection certainly did not cause stagnation and gross inefficiencies. Furthermore, the duty led to long-run reductions in domestic prices. While the savings to railroad builders were too small and came too late to yield a net gain to consumers, the overall effect on welfare [the economy at large] appears to have been positive."[32] He even concludes that the tariff *reduced* the long-run price of steel rails!

To be fair, less-protected industries also did well in this era, though many were far less advantageous than steel rails.[33] Note also that much of American manufacturing at this time enjoyed "natural" protection due to transport costs, which were high by modern standards. So unprotected indus-tries then were not as exposed to competing imports as they are today.

Remember that the important question is not "Was the tariff effec-tive?" but "Was the tariff *plus all the other related policies* effective?" As noted in Chapter 3, industrial policy tools are rarely effective in isolation, as opposed to in strategic concert. America in this era applied many of these tools, from agricultural research to subsidized railroads. It also enjoyed the good fortune of being the former colony of the nation where the Industrial Revolution began.

Contemplating and Implementing Freer Trade

Starting around the turn of the twentieth century, some leaders of the ruling Republican Party began to consider opening up the economy to more imports. In 1901, President William McKinley said:

> We must not repose in fancied security that we can forever sell every-thing and buy little or nothing . . . We should take from our customers such of their products as we can use without harm to our industries and labor . . . Reciprocity treaties are in harmony with the spirit of the times, measures of retaliation are not. If perchance some of our tariffs are no longer needed, for revenue or to encourage and protect our

industries at home, why should they not be employed [i.e., traded off] to extend and promote our markets abroad?[34]

The devil was in the details. "Without harm to our industries and labor" was well-intentioned, but not a workable criterion for policy, because imports of *any* product produced in America would necessarily harm domestic producers. The appropriate question was whether the benefits that would accrue to the economy as a whole from these imports would exceed that harm – a question whose answer turns on economic theory, data, and strategy far beyond the losses or gains of any one industry.

McKinley's successor, Teddy Roosevelt, had some sympathy for tariff reductions, if reciprocal, but not enough to buck the formidable manufacturing interests that opposed cuts.[35] Consumed with issues he cared about more, such as antitrust, he pragmatically deferred to his party's consensus.[36] When he ran for president on his own Progressive "Bull Moose" Party ticket in 1912, his new party was ambivalent about tariffs.[37]

Democrat Woodrow Wilson was elected in 1912. He was the first president since Jefferson (who changed his mind) with an *ideological* commitment to free trade, as opposed to just being a conventional low-tariff Democrat like most of his party. In his words,

> The experiences of the past among nations have taught us that the attempt by one nation to punish another by exclusive and discriminatory trade agreements has been a prolific breeder of that kind of antagonism which oftentimes results in war, and that if a permanent peace is to be established among nations, every obstacle that has stood in the way of international friendship should be cast aside.[38]

Publicly, however, he hotly denied that the ultimate implication of his position was free trade, an idea still too inflammatory for open advocacy.[39]

Once in office, Wilson called Congress into special session to lower tariffs. The result was the Underwood–Simmons Tariff of 1913, which cut the average tariff from 40 percent to just above 25 percent.[40] He was able to cut tariffs because of revenues from the newly enacted federal income tax, authorized by the Sixteenth Amendment in 1913.

A significant set of US industries were now confident they could compete against imports. They mainly wanted lower tariffs on their imported inputs and better access to foreign markets – which required America to lower its tariffs to induce other nations to lower theirs.[41] These industries included the advanced technologies of the day, such as electrical equipment, telephones, sewing machines, cash registers, printing presses, farm machinery, locomotives, rail steel, structural steel, and automobiles. But they also included lower-technology products where American firms dominated due to superior scale and mechanization, such as cigarettes, milling, meatpacking, petroleum products, and soap.[42] But Wilson never had a chance to gauge the success of his new tariff regime because a year later, Europe plunged into World War I, upending world trade.

The Great Depression and the RTAA Revolution

In 1930, Congress raised America's tariffs with the Smoot–Hawley bill, which had been under consideration before the Crash of 1929. Because America's economy was already tariff protected, this bill had little or no effect, and the canard that it caused the Depression or spread it around the world does not survive scrutiny.[43] The Depression had taken hold before it passed, and it did not affect enough trade or raise the tariff enough to have such a large effect.[44] It applied to only about a third of America's trade, about 1.3 percent of GDP. The average duty on dutiable goods went from 44.6 to 53.2 percent, not a radical change.[45] And tariffs as a percentage of total imports were higher in almost every year from 1821 to 1914.[46]

The alleged death spiral of retaliation by foreign nations is a myth. According to the State Department's official report in 1931: "With the exception of discriminations in France, the extent of discrimination against American commerce is very slight ... By far the largest number of countries do not discriminate against the commerce of the United States in any way."[47] World trade sharply declined, but almost entirely due to the Depression itself, not America's (or any other nation's) tariffs.[48]

Global finance was collapsing and pulling down the world economy with it. Germany had relied on lending by American banks to pay its World War I reparations to France, which serviced its war debts to Britain, which serviced its war debts to the US. The crash interrupted this flow at its source.

Despite the fact that trade policy had basically no connection to the Depression, and this was understood at the time, Secretary of State Cordell Hull, with the acquiescence of FDR, took advantage of the crisis atmosphere to push the Reciprocal Trade Agreements Act (RTAA) through Congress in 1934. It had the following provisions:[49]

- The president was authorized to negotiate tariff cuts with foreign nations by way of "executive agreements" *without* specific congressional approval.
- The president was allowed, without foreign concessions, to raise or lower America's tariff on any given product by up to 50 percent.
- Concessions given would apply to all foreign nations alike, regardless of their tariffs on American goods, unless the president decided otherwise for a particular nation.[50]

FDR said at the time that the reason for the RTAA was that America needed growth in exports to recover from the Depression. But exports, at 6 percent of GDP, were far too small for this to be a plausible motivation.[51] Hull, a progressive former congressman and senator from Tennessee, believed, like Woodrow Wilson, that free trade conduced to world peace – a belief as seductive and as dubious then as now. (To be fair, he was also concerned that foreign nations be able to earn enough dollars to repay their debts to US lenders.)

RTAA was attacked in Congress as surrendering its constitutional (Article 1, Section 8) authority over trade. This argument foundered on the fact that previous delegations of tariff-setting authority by Republican Congresses had been upheld by the Supreme Court.[52] Hull defended the bill on the grounds that it was an emergency measure authorized for only three years.

RTAA was also attacked, presciently, on the grounds that the promised foreign markets would never materialize. A more potent argument inside the administration was that many New Deal programs required protectionism to work. For example, without trade barriers, agricultural price supports would just suck in foreign production rather than raising American farm incomes.

Regardless, Roosevelt had a strong hold over his party in the early years of his term, and that was enough for many members of Congress. Congressional Republicans mostly voted against the RTAA, and ran against it in 1936, but to no avail.

Roosevelt, unlike Hull, favored tariff cuts conditional upon reciprocity. But Hull, who carried the day, insisted on non-conditionality – unless there was a flagrant violation of commitments. The bar proved to be very high: In 1935, despite foreign trade barriers being officially noted by the State Department, every major trade counterparty qualified except Germany, ruled out because the Nazis were now in power.[53]

RTAA marked the start of a fundamental turn toward freer trade that lasted until the Trump administration. Combined with subsequent legislation, it formed the legal basis for the successive tariff reductions that inexorably turned the US into a free trade economy.

The Act transferred tariff-setting from Congress to the president, who is elected by the whole country and therefore less susceptible to special-interest pressures from the industries in any one district. Presidents also have responsibility for America's foreign relations as a whole, where tariff cuts may be swapped for noneconomic concessions or given out to aid foreign nations.

By linking tariff cuts to US access to other nations' markets, RTAA brought America's exporting interests more directly into the tariff-setting process than they had been, tilting the balance of political pressures toward American concessions to win foreign concessions.[54]

RTAA helped set the precedent that nonreciprocal trade concessions were acceptable and could be used to curry political favor with foreign countries. In the run-up to World War II, this happened often, a pattern that grew further with the Cold War.

The Act did not immediately have large effects. The administration concluded trade agreement with 27 countries between 1939 and 1945, but many of these were small, and the average tariff reduction was only 6 percent.[55] Many such agreements were blatantly nonreciprocal, committing the US to real tariff reductions in return for mere pledges to refrain from raising tariffs in the future. And foreign chicanery went unpunished: When Belgium and Switzerland, for example, depreciated their currencies and used quantitative controls to offset their tariff reductions, the State Department did nothing.[56]

The Support of Emerging Industries

Because several important technologies received strong government support during the period covered by this chapter, we turn now to the technological side of industrial policy. The last fundamental technologies developed almost entirely by the private sector were the automobile and the electric grid, both of which flowered in the 20-year period surrounding World War I. These could be privately developed because incremental advances in the technologies were saleable, so the technological ladder could be climbed on a for-profit basis. The underlying science was simple enough that known physical phenomena could be exploited before complete scientific explanations existed.[57]

But in the early twentieth century, America began a new style of innovation that required government support. Despite their poor economic conditions, the 1930s are now estimated to have been the most technologically innovative decade of the twentieth century.[58] The plastics industry, for example, first commercialized many of the products we rely on today, such as nylon, polystyrene, and polyethylene.[59] This multi-industry burst of innovation was due to the fact that much of America's innovation support system was put in place after World War I. Let us now look at some specific industries.

Aviation

After Kitty Hawk in 1903, Europeans instantly grasped the airplane's military significance and seized the technological lead. As late as 1914, only 49 individual aircraft were built in the US.[60] It took the growing likelihood of being drawn into World War I for the federal government to begin supporting the industry.

In 1915, Congress funded the National Advisory Committee on Aeronautics (NACA), the institutional forerunner of NASA. NACA's first accomplishment was the 1917 brokering of a cross-licensing agreement with the newly formed Manufacturers Aircraft Association (MAA). This allowed aircraft, engine, and parts makers to access one another's patents and avoid holdups as a result of patent disputes. Over the next decade, NACA supported civil and military aviation with technological, not just pure science, research at its wind tunnels, engine test stands, and flight-testing facilities. Both private-sector firms and the military used its facilities. For example, the first aluminum alloy adequate for aircraft use, Alclad, was the result of cooperation during the 1920s between NACA and the private firm Alcoa.[61]

By the end of World War I, American companies were producing 21,000 aircraft per year. In 1919, the government formed the American Aviation Mission to report on military and civil aviation in Europe. It reported on flight regulation, the training and licensing of pilots, the building of airports and navigational aids, and aircraft certification. The mission concluded that military aircraft procurement was inextricably linked to and dependent on civil aircraft production. It recommended federal control of all operational aspects of aviation and further funding to support development of commercial aircraft manufacturing.[62]

Almost every panel recommendation eventually became law. The first enacted, in 1925, directed the postmaster general to contract with private airlines to carry airmail.[63] Thus began a deliberate federal effort to create a viable aircraft-manufacturing industry. Washington systematically worked to solve the problem that full-scale, nationwide airlines were impossible without better airplanes, but developing better airplanes required airline demand. Carrying mail was an effective way to *create* demand ahead of the market, because mail did not require the same comforts as passengers and paid more per pound than freight.

It is easy to forget how farsighted this was at the time. One historian records:

> Before 1925, American commercial aviation remained very much in its infancy ... Even in 1940, airplanes presented no serious challenge to long-distance railroads, or even buses ... It was clear that in the 1920s American commercial aviation had little hope of surviving without some form of federal support ... Corporations like Boeing, Douglas, and Beechcraft struggled to find buyers for their products – large orders were still measured in the single digits until well into the latter half of the decade.[64]

In 1920, flying between New York and San Francisco required 15 stops.[65]

The Air Commerce Act of 1926 gave the government responsibility for certifying aircraft, licensing pilots, establishing airways and navigational aids, and building airports. It established the Aeronautics Branch in the Commerce Department and rules for matters such as aircraft altitude separation and exterior markings on aircraft. The Civil Aeronautics Act of 1938 established the Civil Aeronautics Authority (precursor of the Civil Aeronautics Board (CAB)) to regulate the airlines, a framework that remained in place until the end of the 1970s.[66]

The CAB was charged with ensuring that airlines remained profitable, that new entrants were not disruptive, and that service was adequate. It kept short-haul rates low, subsidizing them by permitting higher rates on long-haul routes. Washington deliberately encouraged mergers in a fragmented airline industry full of financially weak firms. Military procurement saved the aircraft manufacturing industry during the Great Depression, when civilian air traffic declined, drying up airline demand.

Thanks to these policies, on the eve of World War II America had the world's largest and most advanced airline network. Passengers could fly from coast to coast in under 24 hours in safety and reasonable comfort, arriving and departing at well-designed airports. The world's largest and most technically sophisticated aircraft manufacturing industry supplied the planes. From the 1920s to the 1960s (when IT took the crown), the industry's productivity growth outpaced all others, averaging 8 percent per year.[67]

Petroleum

During the period covered in this chapter, the transition from coal to oil was a major technological and economic advance in all the advanced nations. Oil production, despite being legendary in the US for robber barons and laissez-faire practices, was in fact substantially assisted by the government. Specifically, much of the regulatory infrastructure that allowed the industry to function efficiently was laid down.

The modern oil industry began with the invention of the kerosene lamp in 1853, creating a mass demand for petroleum. In 1859, Edwin Drake drilled the first successful oil well, near Titusville, Pennsylvania. Following that state's lead, Texas passed its first regulations in 1899, covering protection of ground-water, abandoned wells, and the handling of natural gas, regarded then largely as a nuisance. Other states followed.

Oil drilling's central regulatory problem is that if two adjacent property owners tap the same oil field, they both have an incentive to pump as fast as they can because their neighbor will pump whatever they do not.[68] The so-called law of capture means that whoever brings the oil to the surface, regardless of where it may have flowed from underground, owns it. Thus the normal logic of supply and demand breaks down, because as prices drop, producers lack any incentive to produce less. Worse, pumping a field too fast dissipates its reservoir energy – pressure from natural gas and other causes – that brings the oil to the surface, lowering the amount that can ultimately be extracted.

Transaction costs, particularly holdout bargainers, make it hard for private parties to reach agreements to limit drilling. Without government ownership of oil reserves, the global norm, or private monopoly, the only solution is regulation. This took time to emerge in the US. From 1882, the Standard Oil monopoly was able to enforce a private-sector solution. Through its chokehold on refining, it could regulate the price of oil and discipline producers. But in 1911, the Supreme Court ordered it broken up. Nevertheless, the industry survived happily without regulation for a few years as oil prices remained high because demand was growing faster than supply. But starting in 1924, major field discoveries in the US tilted the demand–supply balance back toward glut, and the industry began to favor regulation. Then, in 1930, the discovery of the East Texas oil field, the largest yet found in the entire world, caused a rapid 90 percent price drop. The Texas Railroad Commission, through a quirk of law, had the authority to regulate production and used it, but enforcement was difficult. (The governor of Texas had to declare martial law in the oil-producing areas in 1931.)

Production was only fully stabilized with the creation of the Interstate Oil Compact Commission in 1935. This agreement between the major oil-producing states was then supported by the federal Connally Hot Oil Act, which banned interstate commerce in oil produced in violation of state laws. Subsequently, in the words of one scholar:

> Led by Arkansas and New Mexico, states began passing comprehensive oil and gas conservation acts that required drilling permits, managed the drilling and location of wells, regulated well spacing and density, permitted exception locations to prevent waste or to protect correlative rights, authorized regulatory forced pooling, and later allowed compulsory unitization [multiple drillers required to share a single reservoir so as to maximize total production]. With respect to drilling, regulations came to include strict permitting, casing, cementing, plugging, and abandonment requirements ... Market-demand prorationing [allocating permissible production quantities among drillers] was effectively used, along with tariffs on imported oil in the 1960s, to manage supply and demand in the United States until the Arab oil embargo in the 1970s. By then, domestic production in the United States had fallen to the point where it had little influence on global oil prices.[69]

Laissez-faire this was not.

The emerging petroleum industry, like many other industries, also benefited from publicly funded research. In 1915, the Department of the Interior's Bureau of Mines established 17 facilities for minerals research around the country. The one for petroleum was in Bartlesville, Oklahoma, where it researched both production and refining. In its first year alone, it studied ways to keep water from polluting oil wells, new methods for producing gasoline and carbon black, and the causes of the loss of "light" hydrocarbons from stored crude. During the 1930s, it researched issues such as reservoir pressure, how fluids behave under different conditions underground, and how to measure the saturation of oil in reservoir sands, all important for maximizing quantity of oil extractable. It studied how flooding oil fields with water could keep aging fields producing. Its research into the use of drilling "muds" to lubricate drill bits saved steel for the World War II war effort. Its research into fire hazards, evaporation losses, and the corrosive effects of water helped improve oil transportation and storage. This facility is widely considered the birthplace of modern petroleum technology.

Telecommunications

From 1913 to 1984, America's telephone system, the best in the world, was owned and operated essentially by one company: American Telephone and Telegraph (AT&T), a government-sanctioned monopoly.

After Alexander Graham Bell's original patents expired in 1894, America's telephone industry fragmented into a free-for-all. Thousands of firms built telephone exchanges, strung wires, and signed up customers. Some were financially sound and technologically innovative, but many were not, resulting in bankruptcies and poorly functioning networks. In cities served by multiple providers, customers often had to subscribe to multiple systems.

Simultaneously, the Bell System, the largest operator, was coming under antitrust scrutiny, with some critics favoring a breakup and others government ownership. In 1910, telecommunications were brought under the supervision of the Interstate Commerce Commission.

The technology of the day would have made a patchwork of separate systems inefficient, and a nationwide system would have the largest possible subscriber base to fund and deploy technological advances. Theodore Vail, the visionary president of AT&T, understood all this and set out to shape AT&T into a firm that could succeed as a regulated monopoly.

He adopted a cooperative attitude toward federal regulatory efforts. In 1913, the federal government made an out-of-court settlement with AT&T, the so-called Kingsbury Commitment, accepting its emerging monopoly in return for agreement on certain rules.[70] AT&T agreed to let other phone companies connect to its long-distance network. Instead of trying to destroy them, AT&T made it attractive for them to connect to its own exchanges and incrementally bought them out. Through these measures, AT&T consolidated its control over the telephone system. The Willis–Graham Act of 1921 made it easier for it to acquire the remaining non-AT&T local systems and by 1924, the ICC had approved its acquisition of 223 of the 234 remaining independents.

AT&T's stable and generous monopoly profits, long planning horizons, and assured ability to deploy innovations at scale allowed the firm to undertake some of the most fundamental scientific and technological research ever performed by a private company. This research, centralized in AT&T's legendary Bell Laboratories in 1925, produced many significant innovations before World War II and even more in its golden age afterwards. Its most important prewar accomplishments were the vacuum-tube amplifiers that made long-distance calls possible and the automatic telephone exchanges that cut the number of human operators and made cheap, universal, frequently used service feasible. Other innovations included high-fidelity sound recording, synchronous-sound motion pictures, stereo radio, the modern microphone, the wearable hearing aid, the quartz clock, transmission of early TV images, radio astronomy, and statistical process control. (This last item forms the mathematical basis for quality control techniques used in almost all manufacturing industries today.) Although these were all fruits of private enterprise, they were most assuredly *not* the results of a free market.

Radio

Governmental support has been key to emerging technologies in other nations too. In 1896, Guglielmo Marconi, the Italian scientist who invented radio, was unable to get support from his own government to further develop his invention. So he moved to England, where the Navy and the Post Office had already been researching "wireless telegraphy." The Post Office, after some initial help, declined to cooperate because it had a legal monopoly on wired telegraphy and Marconi wanted to construct a new proprietary wireless system that might undermine it.[71] But the Navy gave Marconi significant funding and he eventually founded near London a company to exploit radio commercially.

In the years right after World War I, Britain thus dominated long-distance global communications, due to both Marconi's work and its existing network of undersea telegraph cables. Even the dominant radio firm in the US, American Marconi, was partly British-owned. During the war, the US government had used wartime powers to pool the patents of the different American radio producers, no one of which owned all the patents needed to produce a complete, efficient system. But when peace came, the government, especially the Navy, faced the lack of a large, stable, state-of-the-art American producer.[72]

The solution eventually arrived at was for GE to buy American Marconi and then sell part ownership of the new firm, Radio Corporation of America, to major patent holders such as Westinghouse and AT&T. They then cross-licensed their patents to make RCA technologically complete.[73] RCA rapidly became the dominant US electronics and communications manufacturer, remaining so until the late 1970s. Its oligopoly position enabled it to pay for fundamental research that contributed to the development of color television, key types of integrated circuits, liquid-crystal displays, and electron microscopy. And Army Signal Corps Captain Edwin Armstrong invented of the superheterodyne circuit that enabled the use of loudspeakers, laying the foundation for radio as a mass broadcast medium.

Governmental allocation of radio frequencies was a prerequisite for everything from military communications to broadcast television to (decades later) cellular telephony. The Radio Act of 1912 was the first law to regulate frequency usage and require licenses, but proved too weak for the task, as did subsequent efforts through the mid-1920s. Then Congress passed the Radio Act of 1927, which addressed broadcasting specifically for the first time. It created a full regulatory framework, with decision-making vested in an independent agency, the Federal Radio Commission, which eventually became the Federal Communications Commission (FCC). The law established public ownership of the airwaves and a public interest in the content of broadcasts – this last provision dealing with questions that have recently exploded again in social media and other internet communications. The FCC's Fairness Doctrine, which lasted until 1987, required radio and TV stations to provide equal coverage of controversial public issues.

16 US INDUSTRIAL POLICY 1940-1973
The Golden Age of the US Economy

At the end of the 1930s, America was an isolationist nation, regretting its involvement in World War I and reluctant to get entangled in another conflict. Its military was tiny compared to the major European powers. But the Nazi regime posed such an obvious danger that the US began preparing to defend itself.

These preparations included industrial mobilization. In June 1939, Congress passed the Strategic Materials Act to stockpile key materials, and in August, it created a War Resources Board to plan for, but not execute, industrial mobilization.

After Germany overwhelmed Western Europe in 1940, FDR told the nation, "The Nazi masters of Germany have made it clear that they intend ... to enslave the whole of Europe, and then to use the resources of Europe to dominate the rest of the world." In response, America set out to become the arsenal of democracy, beginning the greatest governmental orchestration of its economy before or since.

In June 1940, the federal government, aware that the coming war would be in part a technological contest, compiled the National Roster of Scientific and Specialized Personnel. In August, it created the government-funded Defense Plant Corporation. It then adopted a comprehensive industrial policy to maximize the output of weapons and other war materiel. Covering more than half the country's industrial output, this effort was carried out through government procurement directed by federal agencies and boards, but executed almost entirely by the private sector.

Starting in 1941, the Lend–Lease program allowed the US to export vast amounts of military and other goods to the UK, France, China, and the USSR, despite their inability to pay cash, under the polite fiction of "lending" it.

The US also waged economic warfare against the Axis. Japan, not yet at war with the US but having already invaded China, was hit with an embargo on scrap iron, scrap steel, and oil, the last joined by the British and Dutch Empires. Germany faced a 25 percent punitive US tariff from 1939 on political grounds, then was cut off from seaborne trade by a British blockade.[1]

US defense spending increased from $1.7 billion in 1940, 1.7 percent of GDP, to $83 billion in 1945, 38 percent.[2] GDP grew 70 percent from 1939 to 1945.[3] In 1941, 1942, and 1943, the US had the fastest economic growth in world history: an average of 18 percent per year.[4]

Creating a War Economy

In 1941, President Franklin Roosevelt created the Office of Production Management (OPM), appointing former GM president Bill Knudsen as its director, and the agency began transitioning industry from civilian to military products. The administration set up new agencies to manage the industrial war effort, many having precursors during World War I. The Reconstruction Finance Corporation, created for nonmilitary purposes during the Depression, financed and built arms factories that were then leased to private manufacturers at nominal rents.

In 1942, after the US entered the war, Roosevelt abolished the OPM and put in its place the War Production Board (WPB). The WPB was staffed by private-sector executives from across the industrial economy. Its primary mission was converting firms to war production and managing the resulting supply chains through 12 regional and 8 industry-specific offices. Factories that had made silk garments produced parachutes, automobile factories made aircraft and tanks, and so on. Production of discretionary civilian goods such as automobiles was stopped or curtailed.

The WPB managed the economy at the highest levels by assigning production priorities and rationing key inputs including oil, metals, rubber, paper, and plastics.[5] It presided over vast bureaucratic battles among the military services, other government agencies, and businessmen (who often wanted to continue some civilian manufacturing). A particular flashpoint was scarce materials such as copper, aluminum, and rubber, the last having no domestic sources until synthetic production was ramped up.

Some on the political left wanted a socialized defense sector. But Roosevelt was a pragmatist who knew that government officials could not run the vast industrial effort, so he did not nationalize plants and have bureaucrats or generals run them. Only private-sector executives, working inside or outside government, had the needed skills in organization, procurement, product development, and manufacturing.

The war thus ended Roosevelt's New Deal–era fights with Big Business as class conflict took a back seat to winning the war. Where the private sector did not already have suitable corporations, the government created new state-capitalist ones. Among them were the Defense Plant Corporation, the Metals Reserve Company, the Defense Supplies Corporation, the Rubber Development Corporation, the Petroleum Reserve Corporation, and the US Commercial Company (foreign trade and economic warfare).

Government also intervened in the structure of existing industries. For example, at the beginning of the war the Aluminum Corporation of America (Alcoa) was the monopoly provider of aluminum. To provide competition, reduce Alcoa's pricing power, and increase capacity, the government encouraged the existing Reynolds Metals Company to expand into bauxite mining and aluminum smelting.

Success under Government Management

The federal government was immensely successful at getting American capitalism to produce what was needed without resorting to a command economy. Outproducing the Axis was the Allies' decisive advantage. Thanks to America's large industrial base, its army was fully mechanized, whereas Germany, despite its *blitzkriegs*, only managed to get about 15 percent of its forces beyond traditional horse-and-foot transport.[6] And the US supplied much of the UK's and USSR's military needs as well its own.

Between 1940 and 1945, governmental additions equaled roughly half of all preexisting industrial investment.[7] From 1942 to 1945, Washington oversaw the production of $2.1 trillion (2020 dollars) of armaments – about 40 percent of the world's total. Industries scaled vastly: Military aircraft production rose from 6,000 in 1939 to 85,000 in 1943. By 1944, US war production equaled that of all allies and adversaries combined.[8]

Industrial capacity dictated much of the war's timetable. In 1942, after Germany failed to conquer the USSR, the US considered launching an Anglo-American invasion of Europe in 1943. But a report to the WPB made it clear that 1944 was the earliest that the required materiel would be available, and D-Day was rescheduled accordingly, despite military opposition.[9]

The sudden diversion of production from civilian goods, while spendable income was rising as the last unemployed were being put to work, created inflationary pressure. In response, the government imposed rationing plus price and wage controls. In 1941, it created the Office of Price Administration (OPA). The OPA set price ceilings on all goods except certain agricultural items and rationed scarce products – including automobiles, tires, gasoline, oil, shoes, nylon, sugar, coffee, meat, and other foods. At its height, it controlled almost 90 percent of retail food prices through a vast bureaucracy reaching down to local grocers. Competition for workers would have raised the cost of the war effort and created even more inflation, so there were controls on wages (but not on benefits, leading to a spread of health insurance). To prevent profiteering, there was an excess profits tax.

The Postwar Economy

In 1945, the US constituted 50 percent of the world economy. The war had shown that government spending could induce full employment, increasing the credibility of then new Keynesian economics. Unlike in the Axis nations, the USSR, or the UK, personal consumption had *grown* during the war (by 10 percent) due to wage growth and more people working.[10] As one historian records, "During the war 17 million new civilian jobs were created, industrial productivity increased by 96 percent, and corporate profits after taxes doubled."[11]

Existing economic trends were accelerated. The farm population fell by a fifth.[12] By creating vast new plants in new locations, such as the aviation cluster in Southern California, the war moved the center of America's manufacturing, technology, and wealth away from the Northeast and Midwest.

The war showed that government could deliberately drive productivity gains as wartime pressure for greater output and new technologies forced the pace of innovation. Industrialist Henry J. Kaiser's shipyards, for example, reduced the time needed to build a cargo-carrying Liberty Ship from 230 to 42 days by adapting mass-production techniques from the auto industry.

Key technologies that flowered during the war included jet aircraft, radar, nuclear energy, penicillin, and blood transfusions. The new proximity fuses for antiaircraft shells required breakthroughs in the miniaturization of electronics. Plastics expanded as a miracle material into a vast array of products. And the Manhattan Project that produced the atom bomb laid the foundation for postwar civilian atomic power.[13] Catalytic cracking, a way to produce high-octane gasoline that had been in small-scale use, was improved and widely deployed. Government funding resulted in the US producing synthetic rubber in 1944 at double the rate it had consumed natural rubber in 1940.[14]

Twice as many Americans worked in industrial research labs in 1946 as in 1940.[15] After the war, many of the government-financed defense plants were sold off cheaply to the firms that ran them, adding to the manufacturing base of the postwar expansion.[16] Labor naturally wanted its share of the economy's new potential: More Americans went on strike in 1946 than in any other year.

Regulated Capitalism, American-Style

By the early 1950s, the main components of the large, bureaucratic American state that endures to this day were in place as a result of government expansion during the New Deal, World War II, and the early Cold War. The political consensus supporting it was ideologically liberal but bipartisan. Eisenhower and Nixon were part of it. Liberal Republicanism was at its peak.

New Deal legislation had transformed almost every sector of the economy, bringing the laissez-faire, Wild West capitalism of the Roaring Twenties to heel. The postwar expansion was thus built on a more stable foundation. Recessions became milder and rarer.[17] The Employment Act of 1946, while avoiding explicitly Keynesian language due to Republican pressure, de facto committed the government for the first time to maintaining full employment and stable prices – goals only believed attainable by government action because of the Keynesian revolution in economics.

Critical sectors were now regulated to ensure their smooth functioning. Railroads, trucking, airlines, and telecommunications had price and service controls. Private electric-power conglomerates had been dismantled by the Public Utility Holding Company Act of 1935 and replaced with publicly regulated utility firms or cooperatives. On a foundation of federal and state regulation, an American-led cartel of private domestic and foreign oil producers kept production and prices stable (see Chapter 15).

Much of the economy that was not under regulation consisted of large firms in oligopolistic industries, from televisions to automobiles to chemicals. Innovation was concentrated: As late as 1974, a mere 126 firms did three fourths of America's R&D.[18]

The 1933 Glass–Steagall Act had separated commercial banking (low-risk lending of depositors' money) from investment banking (wheeling and dealing with one's own). Savings accounts now had federal deposit insurance. The Securities Act of 1933 brought discipline and transparency to public offerings of securities and the 1934 Securities Exchange Act did the same for the secondary market. These and other constraints, such as fixed commissions on stock trades and investment banks being required to be partnerships (with unlimited individual liability), prevented the financialization of the economy that later took place (see Chapter 18).

Corporate managers, not financiers, held the balance of power in industry.[19] Executives were well paid, but not grossly overpaid. The defining remark of the era, "What's good for the country is good for General Motors and vice versa," made by GM's president Charlie Wilson, raised eyebrows but was also correctly accepted as basically true.

The "countervailing power" of unions balanced the might of the concentrated corporate sector. Union membership peaked in 1954 at a third of the workforce, and at an even higher percentage of the family breadwinners' manufacturing jobs (as they generally were then) that set the tone for the overall labor market.

Defying the market-fundamentalist view that an economy so far from the free-market ideal must perform poorly, America prospered. From 1947 to 1967, real GDP growth averaged 3.9 percent, versus 3.3 percent for the whole period 1930 to 2023.[20] Recessions were mild and averaged just 11 months; expansions 58.[21] Wage growth tracked productivity growth, a relationship that held until 1973. Median family income doubled between 1940 and that year.[22]

Based on this success, major economists such as John Kenneth Galbraith and Adolf Berle saw a trend by which free markets, even in capitalist economies, were being fruitfully replaced by "planning," be it corporate or governmental.[23] Although it became clear later that they had overstated their case, it is significant that the economy certainly *seemed* to function that way for a time. Similarly, it seemed in the late 1950s and early 1960s that the antagonism between labor and capital that had convulsed the politics of all industrial nations for a century had reached a lasting détente in the US.[24]

National Security Strategy Drives Trade Policy

In its new role as global peacekeeper, the US shifted away from the protectionism that had been the cornerstone of its industrial policy for 150 years (see Chapters 14 and 15). With major rivals either in tatters or broke due to the war, policymakers believed they did not need to protect American industries. Instead, they took the lead in creating an interlocking set of international institutions whose mission was *global* prosperity.

Soon after the war, the US realized that its punitive, deindustrializing treatment of the defeated Axis nations was a mistake. It assisted with the reindustrialization of Germany and Japan because it needed strong economies there and elsewhere to fight Soviet expansionism (see Chapters 5 and 8). Between 1946 and 1953, the US gave foreign countries $375 billion (2023 dollars) of nonmilitary aid.[25] It also took in their exports, protected them militarily, tolerated their currency manipulation and other mercantilist practices, and integrated them into new American-led global financial and trade institutions.

In 1951, Congress passed the Trade Agreements Extension Act, which continued RTAA's delegation of tariff-cutting authority while directing the president to withdraw concessions from communist countries. For three decades, through the early 1970s, the needs of US manufacturers explicitly took a back seat to geopolitics. As the Bureau of the Budget put it in 1950, "Foreign economic policies should not be formulated in terms primarily of economic objectives; they must be subordinated to our politico-security objectives."[26] Such policies included, in the words of historian Judith Stein,

> [T]o make certain that Europe could export, the United States bro-kered a huge continent-wide devaluation in 1949, between 20 and 50 percent ... The United States assisted the European Payments Union, which allowed Western Europeans to trade more with each other, even though this trade came at the expense of America's own commerce. US companies received tax incentives to transfer American technology to foreign corporations, despite the dangers to the nation's economic dominance.[27]

Washington also used access to the American market to keep nations politically aligned with the US. This had started during World War II, when the US had used trade concessions to cement Iceland, Turkey, and several Latin American nations to the Allied side.[28] The risk of this policy inflicting unemployment on American workers was discussed at the highest levels of the Eisenhower administration (Treasury Secretary George Humphrey saw trouble), but the foreign policy payoffs were considered worth the price.[29]

The Defense-Industrial Economy

America had rapidly demobilized in 1945. But events soon forced it to adopt a defense-oriented industrial policy: the USSR sealing off Eastern Europe from the West in 1945–6; the Berlin Blockade of 1948–9; Soviet support for communist parties in France, Italy, and Greece; the Greek civil war of 1946–9; the Soviet atomic bomb in 1949; the fall of China to Mao's communists in 1949; and the invasion of South Korea by North Korea, assisted by Soviet weaponry and Chinese troops, in 1950.

In April 1950, a special committee of Cabinet members sent a controversial report, National Security Council Paper 68, to President Truman recommending a hard line against the USSR. Its recommendations included a massive increase in military and R&D spending to develop the hydrogen bomb and the bombers and missiles to deliver it.[30] Truman was initially reluctant, but signed off after the invasion of South Korea.[31] Global containment of communism replaced the more limited, selective version.

The new danger of nuclear attack was a major impetus to America's choice of a technology-oriented military. The Korean War, fought to a stalemate due to huge numbers of Chinese troops the US and its allies could not match, reinforced the need for a strategy based on superior technology to overcome the manpower disadvantage. This required a defense industrial policy of unprecedented size and complexity.

Sustaining an advanced military-industrial complex required that government support related elements of the *civilian* manufacturing base as well. Although economic benefits were not its motivation, security-motivated industrial policy subsequently had immense, generally positive, effects on civilian technology development and the civilian industrial base.[32] The impact was especially large on semiconductors, aviation, and space technology (see Chapter 26).

The US also aimed to degrade the economy and technological capabilities of the Soviet Union. In 1949, it and its allies set up the Coordinating Committee for Multilateral Export Controls to block Soviet access to military and dual-use technologies. America sought to deter attack with its nuclear arsenal. It also sought to prevent the USSR from ever matching America's economic performance, which would have increased both Soviet military resources and the attractiveness of Marxism–Leninism to other countries. The plan was then to wait for that ideology to fail, which it did in 1989.

Imposing Fixed Exchange Rates

The Roosevelt administration believed that the breakdown in trade before the war had been a major cause of fascism (partly true) and therefore (more dubiously) that global institutions to prevent such breakdowns would promote lasting peace.[33] As the world's largest economy, largest creditor, and holder of the largest gold reserves, America had the leverage to establish the institutions it wanted.

In 1944, the US hosted a conference in Bretton Woods, New Hampshire, attended by representatives from 44 nations, to reconstruct the international monetary system. To forestall the competitive devaluations that had disrupted trade and exacerbated the Depression, a system of fixed but adjustable exchange rates was created. Currencies would be pegged to the dollar, which would be pegged to gold at a fixed rate guaranteed by the US government.

It took more than a decade to get the system fully operational, but in 1958 the last exchange controls were lifted abroad and currencies became freely exchangeable at their fixed rates to buy imports. Gold was fixed at $35 an ounce and nations kept their currencies within 1 percent of parity by having their central banks buy and sell currency on the open market.

Postwar International Trade Agreements: ITO and GATT

The US did not believe it had much to fear from foreign economic competition. As Truman put it: "Our industry dominates world markets ...

American labor can now produce so much more than low-priced foreign labor in a given day's work that our workingmen need no longer fear, as they were justified in fearing in the past, the competition of foreign workers."[34]

Imports during the 1950s averaged only 3 percent of GDP (versus 14 percent in 2023), so trade was not even a major economic or political issue.[35] Even the American Federation of Labor (which merged with the Congress of Industrial Organizations in 1955 to become the AFL–CIO) supported cutting trade barriers, so long as nations committed to fair labor standards and adjustment assistance was provided to displaced American workers.[36] (How such provisions would actually be implemented did not get nearly enough attention.)

There had been an attempt at Bretton Woods to establish an International Trade Organization (ITO) to administer basic rules for trade and conduct tariff reduction negotiations. In 1948, a treaty negotiated in Havana was signed by 53 nations. But the US Senate never ratified it. Big Business was concerned about the treaty's lack of protection for its foreign investments. The US Chamber of Commerce and the National Association of Manufacturers believed (presciently, as the WTO later showed) that it would open the US market to imports while blocking retaliation against foreign trade barriers. The American Bar Association deemed it unconstitutional because of the powers it delegated to a foreign body.[37] The agreement failed to pass multiple times and in 1950, Truman gave up. (In 1955, Eisenhower tried again with an Organization for Trade Cooperation, but also got nowhere.)

During the ITO negotiations, the US had invited 19 countries to meet in Geneva to negotiate tariff reductions. These meetings ultimately produced the General Agreement on Tariffs and Trade (GATT), a far looser agreement that succeeded in becoming the basis of the postwar trading system after the US and 22 other nations ratified it in 1947.

The GATT negotiations were contentious. The UK (still accounting for 25 percent of world trade in manufactures and clinging to its Imperial Preference system favoring its empire) was the largest dissenter. The lead US negotiator, William Clayton, advised Robert Lovett, the undersecretary of state, to walk out. But Lovett convinced Truman that a major break between the US and UK would send the wrong geopolitical signal, especially to the Soviets, and that a weak GATT was better than none at all. So Truman decided to go ahead.[38]

The GATT was based on five principles.

1. Transparency: Each signatory agreed to publicly reveal its trade barriers and negotiate to simplify them.
2. National Treatment: Each signatory agreed that after applicable tariffs had been paid, imported goods would be treated the same as "like" goods produced domestically.

3. Most Favored Nation (MFN) treatment: Each signatory agreed to offer all other GATT countries the lowest tariff on a product it offered any.[39]
4. Tariff Binding and Reduction: Each signatory agreed to freeze its tariffs at current levels and then negotiate to reduce them.
5. Nations were allowed to impose sales and consumption taxes, and safety and other regulations on goods, if (with a few exceptions) they were also applied domestically.

Even today, The GATT is still technically the trade agreement governing tariffs for most imports, though the WTO was created in 1995 and took over its administration.

The GATT was not an agreement to engage in free trade per se, but a framework designed to facilitate nations' reducing their trade barriers. Crucially, in the words of Judith Stein, "Most countries rejected the free trade vision. They did not view the GATT as an instrument to create a liberal international order, but only as a body to provide a civilized common law to govern relationships among mercantilist states."[40]

In the initial negotiations, the US cut its average tariff by 35 percent.[41] With America running a large (3.9 percent of GDP) trade surplus in 1946 and 1947, this was not viewed as problematic.[42]

The GATT had three major "trade remedy" tools for private parties to petition their governments for tariffs. The first two dealt with "unfair" practices: antidumping duties to offset below-normal-value sales injuring the petitioner and countervailing duties to offset export subsidies. Then the safeguard remedy, also known as the escape clause, offered tariffs against import surges that threatened injury even when no bad or unfair actions were involved. In the US, all three remedies required investigations and findings by the federal government.

GATT also offered two broader remedies that only governments could initiate:

1. Balance-of-payments tariff relief, allowing temporary tariffs on all imports to deal with significant trade deficits. (President Nixon briefly invoked this power in 1971.)
2. Tariffs to deal with threats to national security, as defined by the nation imposing them.

Successive GATT Rounds Undermine America's Trade Position

The GATT lowered trade barriers through a series of "rounds" or international negotiating meetings. There were eight prior to 1995: Geneva in 1947; Annecy, France, in 1949; Torquay, England, in 1950–1; Geneva again in

1956 and 1960–2 (the "Dillon" Round); the "Kennedy Round" in 1964–7; the Tokyo Round in 1973–9; and the Uruguay Round in 1986–93.

In every round, the US cut its tariffs more quickly and deeply than its trading partners. And when foreign nations did cut tariffs, they often imposed offsetting import quotas and currency controls. In the 1947 round, with economies still recovering from World War II, it was understandable for the US to tolerate these asymmetries, but this became less justifiable as time went by. Meanwhile, MFN allowed foreign nations to free ride on tariff reductions granted to other nations, depriving the US of leverage.

Barriers to trade other than tariffs (a/k/a nontariff barriers) appeared over time. These included import licensing, foreign-exchange rationing, and cartels excluding foreign producers.[43] Foreign nations also subsidized their exports. Value-added taxes, designed in part to offset tariff reductions, first appeared in France in 1957, then spread.[44] Japan set up a VAT-like consumption tax. (See Chapter 4 for why VAT remains a problem for the US.)

Eisenhower pushed for Japan's inclusion in the GATT in 1955, overriding the opposition of Britain and 14 other nations that remembered its mercantilist behavior in the 1930s.[45] As part of Japan's accession negotiations, the US granted it tariff reductions on $37.2 million worth of imports in return for reductions on a mere $6.4 million.[46] Japan acted with classic mercantilist logic, making concessions on raw materials and agricultural products in return for concessions on manufactured goods.[47]

The European Economic Community (EEC), consisting initially of West Germany, Belgium, France, Italy, Luxembourg, and Holland, was created in 1957 with American encouragement. It was a de facto customs union and thus contested by many nations as violating MFN, but to no avail.[48] As anticipated, preferential trading within the EEC prejudiced America's trade with its members.[49] As intended, the arrangement started to draw in the plants of American multinationals seeking access to the large market inside its tariffs, quotas, and other barriers.[50]

By the end of the 1950s, the first American unions, in the apparel industry, began to question their previous support for trade opening.[51] By this time, the US should have been insisting on full reciprocity, de facto and not just on paper, taking nontariff trade barriers into account and measured by actual trade volumes. It did not.

The Trade Expansion Act of 1962

Between 1932 and 1960, America's average tariff on dutiable goods fell from 60 to 12 percent.[52] As a result, it became the only significant global market truly open to foreign trade.

John F. Kennedy had promised on the campaign trail to help industries threatened by imports.[53] But in office he sought congressional authorization for another GATT round with the Trade Expansion Act (TEA) of 1962. His primary stated motivations were a) propping up the Atlantic alliance, b) strengthening ties with Western Europe, and c) preventing the EEC from closing further against American exports.[54] Additional stated goals were to d) reverse the already visible deterioration in America's trade balance, e) increase economic growth, f) counter communist attempts to garner a larger share of world trade, and g) further integrate Japan into the world economy.[55]

Political objectives thus loomed large, while the economic ones were questionable. The US could achieve equal access to the EEC's market only if it offered something comparable in exchange and actually enforced reciprocity. But American tariffs were already low, so the US had little to bargain with, and it had a poor record of enforcement. Improving the overall trade balance would require obtaining greater concessions than America gave – which had not happened in decades. Overall faster growth was unlikely: The European nations had grown faster as they had opened to each other, but America was not a small economy recovering from a war and achieving continental scale for the first time. Integrating Japan risked being one-sided.

Unlike today, big business was not strongly in favor of trade opening: NAM took no stand on TEA and the US Chamber was only weakly in favor.[56] TEA was more ambitious than any previous trade authorization, granting the president greater authority and flexibility in cutting tariffs.[57] It authorized cutting tariffs by up to half, even eliminating them for some products. For the first time, it authorized not just item-by-item reductions but across-the-board cuts applying to many products.[58] It eliminated the existing "peril point" provision forbidding tariff reductions that would harm the domestic industry, and weakened the escape-clause provision that enabled withdrawal of tariff concessions if such harms appeared later.

In fact, TEA contained no requirement that trade concessions not harm American industries or workers. Instead of trying to protect either, it switched to the "compensate the losers from trade" idea beloved of pro–free trade economists. The resulting Trade Adjustment Assistance (TAA) program (which still reappears for periodic reauthorization alongside congressional authorizations for trade agreements) thus included income support, relocation benefits, training assistance, and other benefits.

TAA helped win union support for TEA. The American Farm Bureau Federation supported TEA because of its promise to win better access to European agricultural markets.[59] Congress was mollified by TEA's establishment of the Special Trade Representative (today's USTR) to get trade out of the hands of the State Department, regarded as too willing to sacrifice economic interests for diplomatic ends.[60]

President Kennedy systematically neutralized other potential opposition: Oil and lumber got promises of help; carpets and glass received escape-clause determinations in their favor that led to tariffs.[61] The textile industry – large, labor-intensive, and highly vulnerable to increased imports – got a seven-point assistance program that included protection.[62] And in 1962, the five-year Long-Term Arrangement Regarding International Trade in Cotton Textiles was concluded with 19 exporting and importing nations, limiting the rate at which cotton textile imports could grow.[63]

The Kennedy Round of 1963–1967

Kennedy added Third World development to the long list of objectives already being sought by opening America's markets.[64] He framed this as not just a geopolitical strategy, but a moral obligation, saying in 1963, "By opening our markets to the developing countries of Africa, Asia, and Latin America, by contributing our capital and our skills, by stabilizing basic prices, we can help assure them of a favorable climate for freedom and growth. This is an Atlantic responsibility."[65] "Atlantic" meant that the European nations would supposedly participate in this effort. But in practice, it was America's vision, not theirs.

Twenty-three countries, including developing-world powerhouses such as South Korea, India, Indonesia, and Brazil, participated in the Kennedy Round under a GATT declaration that less developed countries would be given special treatment.[66] As noted in the official *Economic Report to the President*, "The United States made particular efforts to reduce tariffs on products of special interest to less-developed countries. It granted concessions on more than $900 million of such products without attempting to obtain full reciprocity."[67] Overall, the US made $8.5 billion of concessions.[68] Relying on MFN, Tokyo stood back while the US and the Europeans slugged it out, and continued to protect its economically strategic industries.[69]

Such asymmetries did not go unnoticed. America's chief negotiator, Francis Bator, told President Johnson that the deal was economically unfavorable – but should be signed anyway for political reasons.[70] The Vietnam War was heating up and the US was looking for allies. Johnson was unpopular at home and needed accomplishments to tout. The trade deficit was spiraling out of control and European cooperation was needed to prevent the collapse of Bretton Woods.

Thus the Kennedy round opened the US market more than any previous round. It reduced tariffs applying to a quarter of global trade and nearly two-thirds of America's dutiable imports.[71] The average US reduction was 35 percent, versus only 4 percent in the previous round.[72] In the words of historian and former US International Trade Commission chairman Alfred Eckes,

> Viewed from a historical perspective, the Kennedy Round marked a watershed. In each of the seventy-four years from 1893 to 1967 the United States ran a merchandise trade surplus (exports of goods exceeded imports). During the 1968–72 implementation period for Kennedy Round concessions, the US trade surplus vanished and a sizable deficit emerged.[73]

America's average tariff on dutiables, which had been stable at about 12 percent since the early 1950s, was put on course to reach 6 percent by 1975.[74]

Other factors coming into play at the same time that these tariff cuts took effect (1968 to 1972) then created a perfect storm that wrecked America's trade balance:

- Other nations were increasingly competing in key US industries. From 1950 to 1970, Europe's share of global exports went from 33 to 43 percent, Japan's from 1.4 to 6.1 percent.[75]
- Bretton Woods was starting to show cracks, not least because its fixed rates gave Germany and Japan currencies more undervalued with each passing year.
- Rising inflation in the US de facto cut tariffs because many were set as fixed amounts, as opposed to percentages of price.
- The shipping container revolution reduced the "hidden tariff" of sea transport costs, which have been estimated at 10 percent of the cost of America's imports in 1961.[76]
- Government support for US exports was declining. As one economist notes, "In 1960, about 13 percent of US exports received government financing through loans and grants. By 1977, that figure had shrunk to 1.5 percent."[77]

The first US trade deficit of the twentieth century appeared in 1971, and except for small surpluses in 1973 and 1975, America's trade balance has been negative ever since.[78]

An Attempted Protectionist Revival Fails

The Kennedy Round soon drew congressional fire. Per one historian, "By the end of 1967, no fewer than 729 House bills, and 19 in the Senate, proposed quotas on over 20 imports."[79] The skeptics included future president Gerald Ford, then a Michigan congressman. But with only a few exceptions, President Lyndon Johnson, a traditional Southern free trader, was against protectionism.[80]

The textile industry employed a million Americans in 1967, mostly in the South, and had corresponding political clout.[81] In 1968, Senator Ernest Hollings (D-SC) got 68 cosponsors to attach an amendment protecting the industry to a trade bill. Johnson had House Ways and Means Committee chairman Wilbur Mills kill it.[82]

During the 1968 presidential campaign, Republicans took the tougher stance on trade.[83] In 1970, President Richard Nixon agreed with textile industry leaders to strengthen its protections.[84] When Japan backed out of an apparent deal, the industry turned to Congress, which then added footwear and apparel to the bill.[85] Nixon opposed it, then relented, then watched Congress, under pressure from other industries, add quotas for them, too, which he did not want.[86] The bill passed the House, but the Senate adjourned before it could be considered, and Nixon had planned to veto it.[87]

In 1971, Pete Peterson, assistant to the president for international economic affairs and later secretary of commerce, prepared a secret report tracing America's diminished international economic standing to the trade and industrial policies of its trading partners.[88] It concluded that the US would need to respond with an industrial policy of its own focused on governmental support for technology development and an aggressive defense of America's interests in trade. Commerce Secretary Maurice Stans sympathized, and testified before Congress in favor of creating a single agency to fund technology development.[89] Treasury Secretary John Connally, an instinctive economic nationalist with great sway over Nixon, agreed, especially on trade.[90]

The administration's economists dismissed Peterson's thinking as economically illiterate. But Nixon was sold, albeit largely because he thought a tougher stance against foreigners in defense of American jobs would be a vote getter.[91] He sharply ramped up trade policy actions, using the escape clause, antidumping provisions, countervailing duties, and the TAA.[92] Then, although he was sympathetic to the idea of a national trade and technology strategy, he put these ideas on hold to deal with immediate economic problems, and never returned to them. In August 1971 he imposed wage and price controls against inflation, slapped a 10 percent surcharge on dutiable imports for six months, and ended the dollar's gold convertibility. The moment of opportunity passed.

Organized labor, which had supported the TEA, turned against further trade opening by the end of the 1960s. In 1972, the Burke–Hartke bill was introduced in the House by two Democrats acting at the behest of labor. It would have limited imports, on a country-by-country and product-by-product basis, to the average quantity of 1965–9. This would have cut imports by a third and have been equivalent to raising America's average tariff from 7 to 20 percent.[93] A new agency would have regulated exports of technology and capital to curtail multinationals' ability to move production abroad.[94] These firms would also lose their tax credit for foreign taxes paid and their ability to defer US taxes until foreign profits were repatriated.[95] The bill never made it out of committee.

Protectionist forces in this era thus had a serious opportunity to fix America's trade policy right after it had gone radically off track, but fumbled it. In the words of historian Nitsan Chorev,

> Even in Congress, protectionist industries failed to utilize their poten-
> tial resources. During negotiations over general trade bills in Congress,
> protectionists exerted weak influence because they lacked an umbrella
> association to represent them. Instead, protectionists were divided
> along industrial lines, each promoting its own distinct objectives ...
> The logic of selective protectionism did not encourage industries to
> cooperate with each other, since the chances for congressional support
> increased if protectionist bills were narrowly constructed. In addition,
> protectionist industries did not cooperate with organized labor.[96]

Remedies Sabotaged by Nonenforcement

Many foreign trade practices of the era covered in this chapter could been blunted by vigorous enforcement of existing American laws.[97] The US had had a countervailing duties law requiring a tariff to offset foreign subsidies since 1897.[98] Since 1921, it had had a law against dumping.[99] The Tariff Act of 1930 reiterated both provisions.[100] But these remedies were rarely used, in part due to the steep legal costs they imposed on petitioners.

It was no secret that American industries were being harmed. As noted, starting in the mid-1950s textiles were a flashpoint, as documented in Senate Commerce Committee reports.[101] From 1947 to 1957, employment in the sector dropped from 1.3 to 1 million.[102] The machine tool industry, which had opposed TEA in 1962, lost 40 points of market share between 1968 and 1988, partly due to Japanese dumping.[103] The electronics industry faced rising imports of dumped transistor radios and TVs.[104]

When the US Tariff Commission (USTC) found in favor of safeguard measures, which needed presidential assent to take effect, the State Department often succeeded in blocking them on foreign policy grounds.[105]

Treasury, where most enforcement was lodged because tariffs are a tax, had little interest in enforcement. Sometimes it didn't even collect *existing* duties. It accepted foreign promises to increase prices at face value.[106] And its investigations took forever: A 1968 complaint about milk was not even considered until 1974, and then only after a court order.[107] In 1971, the USTC ruled that Japan was dumping color TVs. Three years later, the Japanese *appeared* to raise their US prices – but in reality were giving kickbacks to American retailers.[108] Treasury declined to impose countervailing duties until ordered to by the US Customs Court.[109] (See Chapter 5 for the larger story of color TVs and how the industry fit into Japan's overall industrial policy.)

Nor did presidents enforce safeguard mechanisms as Congress had intended. So, GATT's escape clause was neutered by US inaction. From 1951 to 1962, USTC investigated 113 complaints and recommended relief in 41. But the president granted relief in only 15.[110] During the Kennedy Round, the Commission, by this time stacked with free traders, *never* recommended relief.[111] From 1962 to 1969, the Labor Department received 25 petitions for TAA but denied them all.[112]

Meanwhile, the US government was actively encouraging offshoring. For example, in 1964 the US changed its rules so that goods made overseas with US components were tariffed only on the value added by assembly.[113] Starting in the late 1960s, American firms started offshoring low-skilled steps of their production processes.[114] American-made components were shipped to Mexico to be assembled into TVs. By 1985, there were 825 such *maquiladora* plants, in many industries.[115]

The Collapse of Bretton Woods

By the late 1960s, America's trade balance was also suffering from the increasing overvaluation of the dollar caused by the failure to adjust exchange rates. In May 1971, Treasury concluded that the dollar was overvalued by 10–15 percent.[116] The surplus nations wanted no part of the burden of rebalancing the system, as they were well aware of the benefits of their undervalued currencies. An obvious solution, expanded capital controls, had no support in the US or abroad. Instead, in August 1971, the Nixon administration made two bold moves:[117]

- It suspended, with a few exceptions, the convertibility of the dollar into gold.
- It imposed a 10 percent tariff surcharge on all imports except those that were duty-free (a third) or under quantitative controls (17 percent).[118]

These unilateral actions brought America's trade counterparties to the bargaining table. The surcharge was eventually dropped as part of the Smithsonian Agreement, a general currency revaluation. Germany agreed to a 14 percent upward revaluation, Japan to 17 percent.[119] All told, the dollar received a trade-weighted devaluation of 12 percent excluding Canada, which presented different issues.[120] But the agreement provided only a temporary respite. Currency speculators dragged the dollar down because they had no confidence the US really had fixed its trade balance, and the US government did not intervene in currency markets to keep the dollar at its new parity.[121] The US devalued again, by 10 percent, in February 1973, but the dollar continued to fall. Shortly thereafter, the other participants permanently gave up trying to maintain their parities, and Bretton Woods was dead.

In the short and medium term, devaluation helped: The US posted trade surpluses in 1973 and 1975. Protectionist pressures in Congress temporarily declined.[122] Longer term, the very problem Bretton Woods had been created to solve reappeared as nations began manipulating their currencies to gain a competitive edge. Of equal importance, the dismantling of international capital controls enabled a vast increase in private-sector capital flows, large enough to independently cause the dollar overvaluation that is a huge problem today (see Chapter 4).

The End of the Golden Age

The long US economic boom that had begun in 1940 ended in 1973. The following decade was marked by instability, unemployment, inflation, high interest rates to fight that inflation, several recessions, and the beginnings of the decline of key manufacturing industries.

The once lockstep climb of wages and productivity broke down. Productivity kept rising, but real hourly earnings for private, nonfarm, production and nonsupervisory workers were virtually *the same* in 2019 as in 1973.[123] Alternative calculations including more affluent earners, medical benefits, and government transfer payments told a happier story, as did adjusting for declining household size and the controversial idea that government statistics overstate inflation.[124] But the income growth Americans had gotten used to had definitely slowed down, even if by how much was debatable, especially for the bottom 80 percent of the workforce.

Manufacturers were hurting too. In the 1950s, they had averaged a before-tax return on capital of more than 15 percent. But in 1974, it bottomed out at 8 percent.[125] For some industries, decline was partly self-inflicted. The travails of the auto industry, for example, are recounted in Chapter 25. American steelmakers were slower to adopt continuous casting and the basic oxygen furnace than the Europeans and Japanese. But the latter were also being subsidized by their governments.[126]

There were several causes for the 1970s slowdown. The industries of Europe and Japan had rebuilt from war, mastered mass production, and were now competing against their American counterparts. The easy growth of extending the postwar paradigm – suburbia, cars, electrification, mass-produced consumer goods – to most Americans had reached its limit. The Arab oil embargo of 1973–4 did not greatly reduce America's physical access to foreign oil, but prices quadrupled because of disruption, uncertainty, and panic.[127] Echoed by a second oil crisis in 1979, it disrupted many industries, not just petroleum. For example, it gave Japan an opening to penetrate the American market with small, fuel-efficient cars.

A new word, "stagflation," was coined to describe the combination of high unemployment and high inflation that Keynesianism had implied was impossible. Keynes's theories were eventually adjusted and survived, but their apparent failure created room for a renaissance of repackaged older ideas such as the monetarism of Milton Friedman – which then helped revive laissez-faire economics generally. From the mid-1960s on, the influence of academic economists on policy grew.[128] Almost all believed that open US markets and increased trade were best, even without reciprocity.

Why didn't America react more effectively to its emerging problems? Early signs of trouble were ignored because the economy was still growing overall. Some issues were too technical to rally the public. Other pressing problems, from civil rights to the Vietnam War, absorbed public attention and complicated attempts to build political coalitions. A new generation of Democratic politicians had less attachment to the New Deal economic model, the trade unions, and lunch-bucket economic concerns.[129]

Most of America's great corporations had surprisingly little experience with international competition. They had grown up in the old tariff-protected US, then in a postwar world in which America was so supreme that their success was assured. Those that had previously gone abroad had done so either in pursuit of natural resources or on the basis of overwhelming technological superiority. Neither schooled them in mercantilism and, although they complained about the outcomes, they did not understand many of the strategies the Japanese and others were using against them.[130]

When America started rolling back its protectionism after World War II, it was so economically dominant at first that it didn't need to think much about economic strategy to succeed. Initial policy moves in the wrong direction were sufficiently moderate that they did not produce the kind of shock that might have induced a reappraisal. Because the US had developed economically almost entirely through internal growth, not exports, its policymakers had no sense of urgency about, or sophisticated knowledge of, trade strategy. One clear sign of America's relative unconcern about trade policy, and an impediment to doing anything about it, was that its formulation and administration was fragmented among Treasury, State, Commerce, Agriculture, the USTR, and other agencies.

Corporate America's interests had begun to diverge from America's.[131] Between 1950 and 1979, US foreign direct investment, deliberately subsidized by the Overseas Private Investment Corporation, the Commodity Credit Corporation, and the Export-Import Bank, grew 16-fold, to $192 billion.[132] Multinationals were now manufacturing at scale in other countries, thereby acquiring an interest in preserving or enhancing those nations' access to the US market. These firms might want tariffs on foreigners selling competing products into the US, but they were now conflicted because they did not want restrictions on their own ability to import goods they had produced abroad. And a new ideology – later labeled globalism – that was openly dismissive of the nation-state as an economic unit of central importance to its citizens, was beginning to emerge.

17 US INDUSTRIAL POLICY 1974–2007
Doubling Down on Free Markets

By the late 1970s, it was becoming clear that all was not right with American industry and the US economy. Defeated World War II adversaries were taking significant shares of the American market, causing large and persistent trade deficits. Inflation spiked twice during the decade, peaking at almost 15 percent in March 1980.[1] Productivity was static from 1973 to 1983, real incomes from 1974 to 1985.[2] Federal bailouts – of the Penn Central Railroad, Lockheed, Chrysler, and New York City – seemed to be accelerating.[3]

The consensus that the New Deal's Keynesian policies could deliver prosperity began to fray. A discussion about what should replace them, possibly including proactive industrial policies, began. But with Republicans outright hostile and ideologically divided Democrats unable to unite behind a clear plan, debate petered out. Instead, America doubled down on free-market policies – deregulation at home and continuance of the GATT model of tariff-reduction negotiations abroad.

Some domestic deregulations, such as railroads, trucking, airlines, telecommunications, oil, and gas, succeeded. Others, notably finance and regional electric grids, were disasters, as was progressively opening America's markets to the rest of the world. Executive and legislative officials did not change course despite constant, well-documented complaints from manufacturers about foreign trade practices, often backed up by US International Trade Commission (USITC) (the former USTC) findings, loss of market share, and surging trade deficits.

Addressing Manufacturing Decline with New Trade Laws

In response to America's 1971 and 1972 deficits, the first since 1893, Congress passed the Trade Act of 1974.[4] Its stated purpose was:

[T]o promote the development of an open, nondiscriminatory, and fair world economic system, to stimulate fair and free competition between the United States and foreign nations, to foster the economic growth of, and full employment in, the United States, and for other purposes.[5]

It authorized participation in GATT's Tokyo Round and updated the domestic trade laws that implement GATT's escape clause. The Act thus granted authority to both conduct liberalizing negotiations *and* counter foreign trade practices.

Trade votes were still mainly bipartisan, without the rancor that developed in the 1980s and 1990s. But a minority in Congress – mainly Democrats and a few Republicans from manufacturing states – doubted that the benefits of freer trade would outweigh its costs. This split was reflected in an early House vote on the 1974 Act: Northern Democrats voted 101–52 against, while Southern Democrats (60–20) and Republicans (160–19) were heavily in favor.[6] But the final vote was 323–36 in the House and 72–4 in the Senate, reflecting the still general acceptance of free trade.[7]

Title II of the Act required USITC to investigate in response to petitions claiming injury or the threat thereof from import surges. It could then recommend to the president a remedy such as tariffs or quotas. For example, such Section 201 petitions were filed in 1980 by Ford and the UAW in response to a surge in Japanese car imports.

The Act also created a new authority, Section 301, for the president to impose tariffs in retaliation for "unreasonable restrictions against U.S. commerce." And it codified the president's authority to impose GATT-authorized retaliatory tariffs, augmenting a vaguer existing authority.

Congress being aware of foreign cheating, the Act required an annual Special 301 Report from USTR to identify trade barriers due to foreign intellectual property laws and practices.[8] As amended in 1984 and 1988, the Act today also mandates the annual National Trade Estimate Report on Foreign Trade Barriers on trade barriers to goods and services, foreign investment, and electronic commerce.[9] The thirty-eighth annual report, issued on March 1, 2023, addressed 14 substantive areas, covered 60-plus countries, ran to 440 pages plus appendices, and documented a large number of issues that remained unresolved despite decades of trade agreements.

Finally, the Act introduced a fast-track process for passing the legislation that amends US law to implement new trade agreements. After the executive negotiates the agreement, Congress cannot filibuster or amend it, only approve or disapprove within 90 days.

Congress passed additional major trade laws in 1979, 1984, and 1988. But despite such constant attempts to fine-tune to cure problems, the main thrust of trade policy from 1974 to 2016 was the relentless quest for a more open and legally codified global trading system. In pursuit thereof, the US negotiated bilateral, regional, and multilateral trade agreements. But all this effort, based on fundamentally misunderstanding the realities of trade, did not spare American industry from the mercantilist trade and industrial policies of other countries.

America Debates Industrial Policy, 1979–1984

Beginning in the late 1970s – provoked largely by the contrast between free-market America's economic troubles and the success of industrially planned Japan – articles exploring proactive industrial policy began to appear.[10] The *Washington Post, The Wall Street Journal, The Chicago Tribune, Foreign Affairs, The Public Interest, National Journal, Commentary, Brookings Review*, the Heritage Foundation, the Cato Institute, and others carried them, pro and con. A June 1980 special issue of *Business Week*, the best-selling in the magazine's history, devoted 80 largely sympathetic pages to the subject.[11] The *New York Times* followed with a five-part series in anticipation of the Carter administration's expected Economic Revitalization Plan (ERP).[12]

In 1979, Ezra Vogel's *Japan as Number One: Lessons for America* explored the reasons for Japan's economic success and potential lessons for the US. In 1980, Robert Müller's book *Revitalizing America* offered industrial policy strategies for an economic comeback. In 1981, Ira Magaziner and Thomas Hout published *Japanese Industrial Policy*. Other books included *Renewing American Industry* by Paul Lawrence and Davis Dyer, *Miracle by Design* by Frank Gibney, and many more, of varying intellectual rigor.

Industrial policy clearly had the attention of academics, journalists, politicians, and policymakers. Even some corporate executives, such as Philip Caldwell of Ford, favored it, motivated in part by the idea that Japan was competing as a country while American firms lacked equivalent backing.[13]

During 1979–80, the Senate Democratic Caucus, under the leadership of Sen. Adlai Stevenson (D–IL), held hearings on science and technology policy and issued a report calling for a national infrastructure bank to invest in new technologies and worker training, plus tax breaks for capital investment.[14] These hearings led to the Stevenson–Wydler Technology Innovation Act of 1980, which required federal labs to proactively try to commercialize their discoveries. This Act, coupled with a 1979 ruling by the Labor Department allowing pension funds to invest in venture capital, was a major enabler of the 1980s boom in tech startups.

President Jimmy Carter, plagued by a dismal economy, considered industrial policy as a means to improve US competitiveness. His ERP was introduced in August 1980. It centered on $27 billion of tax cuts and investment tax credits, mostly for business. It also promised to create a million jobs in two years by spending $3.6 billion on federal R&D, aiding depressed areas, retraining workers, insulating homes, and upgrading transport infrastructure.[15] But despite his Democratic primary rival, Sen. Ted Kennedy (D-MA), speaking in favor of an American Reindustrialization Corporation, Carter did not push his own plan, apparently because his administration was split on industrial policy.[16] Its final *Economic Report of the President*, issued in January 1981 and written by the Council of Economic Advisors led by free-market economist Charles Schultze, stated that industrial policy "went beyond legitimate [economic] needs," and entailed picking winners and losers, which should be left to the market.[17]

Carter lost to Ronald Reagan, who believed that government was the problem, not the solution – a insurmountable barrier to any comprehensive, coherent industrial policy. Nevertheless, the debate continued.[18] In 1982, Chalmers Johnson published *MITI and the Japanese Miracle*, a seminal examination of Japan's political economy that coined the term "developmental state" to describe Tokyo's success at proactively *creating* an advanced industrial economy (see Chapter 5). Two other important industrial policy books appeared that year: *Minding America's Business* by Robert Reich (later Bill Clinton's Secretary of Labor) and Ira Magaziner, and *The Deindustrialization of America* by Barry Bluestone and Bennett Harrison. In 1983, in his bestseller *A New Democracy*, Democratic presidential primary candidate Sen. Gary Hart (D-CO) called for "a national strategy for industrial revitalization."

During the 1983–4 congressional session, Rep. John LaFalce (D-NY), who represented Buffalo, one of the hardest-hit industrial cities, held hearings on US manufacturing and industrial policy. He introduced his Industrial Competitiveness Act in November 1983, garnering 132 Democratic cosponsors and one Republican who later withdrew.[19] It called for a 16-member advisory Council on Industrial Competitiveness, tasked with seeking consensus on how manufacturing industries might restructure to become more competitive, but without spending or directive authority. There would also be a public Bank for Industrial Competitiveness to fund both emerging technology companies and manufacturers in existing industries. The range and prominence of the witnesses at the hearings on the bill showed that industrial policy was receiving serious national consideration. The bill was reported out of the House Banking Committee, but never had enough support for a floor vote.

The First Reagan Administration

Ronald Reagan took office in 1981 believing that American competitiveness could be restored if government would "get off the back of business," especially regarding taxes and regulations. Thus his administration never put forth a comprehensive plan to deal with foreign trade barriers, industrial subsidies, or currency manipulation. Instead, he bet on broad-brush pro-market growth measures: income tax cuts, corporate tax cuts, capital-gains tax reductions, regulatory rollbacks, and R&D tax credits.

Reagan implemented a robust defense industrial policy, which passed ideological muster because it was for national security. This included investments in the B-1 bomber, the B-2 stealth bomber, the MX missile, and the SDI missile defense shield. There was a build-out of existing forces depleted during the Vietnam War, including a 600-ship navy.

Reagan appointed former senator Bill Brock (R-TN) as USTR. Congress had no stomach for further GATT rounds, so Brock pursued bilateral agreements. The first, with Israel, was signed into law in June 1985. The US has since negotiated FTAs (or similar regional agreements) with 19 countries: Australia, Bahrain, Canada, Chile, Colombia, Costa Rica, the Dominican Republic, El Salvador, Guatemala, Honduras, Jordan, Korea, Mexico, Morocco, Nicaragua, Oman, Panama, Peru, and Singapore.

Despite its free-market ideology, the Reagan administration resorted to trade-restricting or other industrial policies in support of automobiles, steel, motorcycles, computers, and semiconductors.[20] It established quotas, tariffs, managed-trade arrangements, and the government-funded semiconductor research consortium Sematech. (See Chapter 25 for autos and Chapter 26 for semiconductors.) But these were all just ad hoc, temporary responses to political pressure or the threat of a major sector collapsing, not attempts at systematic industrial policy.

Under Nixon, Ford, and Carter, on-again-off-again loose monetary policy had let inflation slip out of control, peaking in March 1980 at almost 15 percent.[21] To quash it, Fed Chairman Paul Volcker raised interest rates sharply starting in 1979. The Fed funds rate topped out at 20 percent in 1980–1, causing a deep recession that brought inflation down.[22] But the high interest rates attracted foreign capital, pushing up the dollar. From January 1980 to March 1985, it rose 48 percent against the yen, mark, franc, and pound, and the merchandise trade deficit ballooned from $25.5 billion to $122 billion.[23] Reagan's first Treasury secretary, Donald Regan, a free trade ideologue, did nothing, touting the strong dollar as a mark of confidence in America. Furthermore, he reasoned that a strong dollar, by making imports cheaper, would cut inflation.

The dollar peaked in March 1984, dropped, then rose again later that year and in early 1985.[24] American manufacturing, joined by agricultural and services interests, was roused to action. Lee Morgan, CEO of Caterpillar, testified to a House committee in favor of an end to the hands-off policy.[25] Both the Business Roundtable (Morgan headed its dollar task force) and the National

Association of Manufacturers came out against the overvalued dollar. Farm lobbies and the AFL-CIO joined in. This broad coalition prompted stirrings in Congress against the overvalued dollar and in favor of a torrent of protectionist bills.

James Baker, more pragmatic than Regan, became treasury secretary in February 1985. In large part to preempt trade-restricting legislation, he began the negotiations that led that year to the Plaza Accord signed by the US, Germany, Japan, France, and Britain. The US and France pledged to rein in their budget deficits, Germany and Japan to stimulate domestic demand, and all signatories to intervene in currency markets against the dollar. The dollar did depreciate substantially, though how much this was due to governmental action and how much markets would have pushed it down on their own is not knowable. Although the trade deficit continued to rise through a transition period until 1987, it then fell to a low of $77 billion in 1991.[26]

The Second Reagan Administration

In the summer of 1983, Reagan was gearing up for reelection against either Walter Mondale or Gary Hart, both of whom appeared to favor some form of industrial policy. That large sections of the electorate wanted something done was obvious. Reagan responded with two major proposals.

First, he proposed creating a new Department of International Trade and Industry (DITI) out of the USTR, the International Trade Administration, the Foreign Commercial Service, the Export Administration, the Import Administration, the Export–Import Bank, the Overseas Private Investment Corporation, the Trade and Development Agency, and other agencies.[27]

Second, he announced a Commission on Industrial Competitiveness, composed of industry (but no labor) representatives and headed by John Young, CEO of Hewlett-Packard. The *Washington Post* characterized it thus:

> President Reagan yesterday announced that he is establishing a National Commission on Industrial Competitiveness that aides hope will help counter growing pressure for quotas and other protectionist steps to insulate US businesses from foreign competition. The commission ... also is seen by the administration as a high-profile alternative to calls from Democrats – particularly Democratic presidential candidates – for a national industrial policy.[28]

But despite initial signs of interest, Walter Mondale, the 1984 Democratic nominee, didn't mention industrial policy in his campaign.[29] He thought that proposing an industrial bank (part of the LaFalce legislation) would open Democrats to Reagan's claim that they were a tax-and-spend party.[30] His own plan did not entail a comprehensive government-industry-labor plan, but concentrated on negotiating industry bailouts.[31]

DITI died even before the election, victim of the USTR's unwillingness to be subsumed. An industrial development bank also split entrepreneurial, new-technology Sun Belt Democrats (against) and old-industry-revival-plus-tariffs Rust Belt Democrats (for).[32] Both were reluctant to split the party openly over the issue during an election.[33]

Thus neither party put forth a well-developed industrial policy. Reagan was reelected in a landslide and the debate over industrial policy receded with the recovery. GDP grew 4.6 percent in 1983, 7.2 percent in 1984, and 3.4 percent or better in each remaining year of his presidency.[34] It seemed that his remedies had worked and that industrial policy was not needed.[35] For the next three decades, until the Biden administration, to the extent that it was discussed at all, euphemisms like industrial strategy, manufacturing revitalization, or competitiveness policy were used in place of the now discredited term.

Reagan's Competitiveness Commission issued a thoughtful report in January 1985, but the election was over and the administration ignored it.[36] In September, Reagan announced a cabinet-level trade strike force to look into foreign trade barriers, but it turned into an review of facts already known. His 1987 Trade, Employment, and Productivity Act was mainly an attempt to seize populist high ground.[37] (The bill was eventually incorporated into the Omnibus Trade and Competitiveness Act of 1988.)[38]

The trade deficit grew from $28 billion in 1981 to $160 billion in 1987.[39] Many in Congress, industry, and the unions blamed closed foreign markets, resulting in the 1988 Omnibus Act. A controversial amendment – offered by Rep. Richard Gephardt (D-MO) and passing the House 218 to 214 – would have required that countries running large trade surpluses with the US reduce them or face tariffs.[40] Reagan threatened to veto the whole bill if it contained this amendment, so the bill ultimately passed without it – thus ending one of the few serious attempts to shrink the trade deficit through unilateral US action.[41]

From GATT to WTO

Starting with the 1973–9 Tokyo Round, governments had begun negotiating issues beyond tariffs. This included banning expansion of nontariff barriers and "codes" governing import licensing, customs valuation, government procurement, technical standards, health, safety, subsidies, countervailing duties, anti-dumping duties, civil aircraft, bovine meat, and dairy products.[42] The codes were generally waived for developing countries.

With the 1986–93 Uruguay Round, more than 20 codes were lumped into an all-or-nothing "single undertaking."[43] (The Government Procurement Agreement was the big exception and remains optional to this day.)[44] The Uruguay Round also had a broad mandate to extend GATT rules to areas previously found too difficult to liberalize, such as agriculture, textiles, banking, financial services, foreign investment, and intellectual property. These issues were covered in a 23,000-word all-or-nothing Final Act signed in Marrakesh in 1994.[45] Trade agreements now reached unprecedentedly far into the domestic governance of nations.

The Uruguay Round created the WTO, which came into existence in 1995. Unlike the GATT, it had its own staff, rather than secondees from the UN. Dispute settlement was made more judicial with the creation of its Appellate Body, which could now issue binding precedents rather than GATT's patchy guidance. As with GATT, it had no direct enforcement powers, instead granting winners permission to impose tariffs on losers. It was hoped, and used as an argument to pacify critics, that such a mechanism, open to all nations and enjoying the legitimacy of a treaty commitment, would make the rules stick. In the words of then WTO Director General Renato Ruggiero, "We are writing the constitution of a single global economy."[46]

The first signs of revolt against the new order came quickly. In 1999, the US and its WTO partners tried but failed to launch a new round in Seattle. Its negotiating objectives had included:

1. Further extending agreements on agriculture and the General Agreement on Trade in Services.
2. Sorting out more than 150 proposals from WTO members on tariffs, anti-dumping, subsidies, safeguards, investment regulations, trade facilitation, electronic commerce, competition policy, fisheries, government procurement, technical assistance, and intellectual property.
3. Producing, in the WTO's words, a "special deal to help least-developed countries gain easier access to richer countries' markets" and "technical assistance to least-developed countries under an integrated framework set up by the WTO and a number of other organizations."[47]

The meeting turned into a bureaucratic and public relations disaster. The major trade blocs – the EU, Japan, the US, and the big developing countries such as India and Brazil – could not even agree on an agenda. In the streets of Seattle, 50,000 people protested over labor, environmental, and human rights issues; anti-capitalism; anti-corporatism; national sovereignty; indigenous peoples' rights; and Third World trade concerns. These protests made the American public aware that opposition to trade agreements was widespread and not limited to tariffs, subsidies, and foreign trade practices.[48]

The next WTO round (2001–15) was held in Doha, Qatar, an authoritarian state where demonstrations could be simply forbidden. The primary issues were trade in services, rules of origin, dispute settlement, and "differential treatment" for developing countries. But despite years of ministerial meetings, negotiations stalled in 2008. A split had emerged between developed nations, including the US, Japan, and the members of the EU, and developing ones, led by China, India, and Brazil. The latter were happy with their asymmetrical access to developed markets and saw no need to make further concessions. There was also tension between the Americans and the Europeans over agriculture. After several attempts to resuscitate the talks, the US declared Doha dead in 2015, its failure underscoring the near impossibility of negotiating any more broad-based agreements.[49]

The George H. W. Bush Administration

George H. W. Bush enthusiastically championed free trade. He was a prime architect of the 1980s–90s push for globalization, especially the integration of the North American market. He negotiated most of NAFTA and the Uruguay Round. He began NAFTA negotiations after Mexico's president, seeing the results of the 1988 US–Canada FTA, requested one and Canada joined, afraid to miss out on further concessions. Bush signed NAFTA in December 1992, after losing reelection in a year in which trade was a looming issue, and it became the model for the many FTAs the US signed in the 1990s and 2000s.

NAFTA was opposed by unions, smaller manufacturers, environmentalists, and groups concerned with US sovereignty. Notable among its opponents were paleoconservative Republicans, including Pat Buchanan, who had run against Bush in the 1992 Republican primaries. Opposition also came from Ross Perot – the most successful third-party presidential candidate in decades – who famously predicted a "giant sucking sound" as American jobs moved to Mexico.

Despite sanctioning China after the 1989 Tiananmen Square massacre, Bush sought to cement the economic relationship by secretly sending his national security advisor to reassure Beijing.[50] After the fall of the Soviet Union, he pushed for trade liberalization with Eastern Europe, which led to the opening of new manufacturing plants there, mostly by Western European companies.[51] He even signed a trade agreement with the crumbling Soviet Union in June 1990, extending it normal trade relations.

Bush's free trade ideology led him to reject pleas from US automakers to restrict Japanese car imports. Instead, he invited the Big Three's CEOs to accompany him to Tokyo in 1992, planning to bring them together with

Japanese auto CEOs and get everyone to agree on increased Japanese purchases of American cars and parts. He hoped thereby to avoid a formal managed trade agreement or protectionist action by Congress, but after a tense meeting, the plan fell apart.[52]

Two other examples illustrate Bush's ideological rigidity.

Project Socrates was a CIA–DIA (Defense Intelligence Agency) program established in 1983 by a presidential executive order and led by physicist Michael Sekora. Growing out of efforts to stop American technology from flowing to the Soviet Union, its mission was to determine the causes of America's loss of competitiveness and use that knowledge to design programs to rebuild American industry for both civilian and military benefit. It examined all-source intelligence on global technologies and competitiveness and developed a novel model of technology-centered economic strategy with immense promise. Reagan wanted the program continued, but Bush canceled it, not because it was a failure but because it was considered industrial policy.[53] (The authors propose in the Recommendations chapter that it be revived.)

The Defense Advanced Research Projects Agency (DARPA) had long funded development of key technologies, many with both military and civilian applications. In 1990, Director Craig Fields and Commerce Secretary Robert Mosbacher favored escalating such dual-use programs, the immediate test case being HDTV, then in its infancy.[54] But White House officials, believing non-defense R&D should take place only in the private sector, became concerned that DARPA was poised to pick winners and losers. Mosbacher was called to the White House for a reeducation session and Fields was removed as DARPA's director and reassigned, resigning rather than accept the transfer. The "HDTV massacre" was reportedly led by the Office of Management and Budget's director, Richard Darman, and Michael Boskin, the chairman of the Council of Economic Advisors, who allegedly said, "It doesn't make any difference whether a country makes computer chips or potato chips!"[55] The message was not lost on the rest of the federal bureaucracy.

The US merchandise trade deficit declined during Bush's presidency, but not because of increased US competitiveness or the success of his trade policies. Instead, it fell mainly because of the Plaza Accord and the recession of 1990–1, and began rising again in 1992.

The Clinton Administration

In the years before Bill Clinton's election in 1992, there was a second wave of interest in industrial policy, evidenced by such books as *Trading Places: How We Are Giving Our Future to Japan and How to Reclaim It* by Clyde Prestowitz, *Head to Head: The Coming Economic Battle among Japan,*

Europe, and America by Lester Thurow, and *Agents of Influence* by Pat Choate. A 1991 survey reported that 61 percent of voters favored some kind of government-industry national competitive strategy.[56]

Clinton himself showed interest, saying in a San Diego shipyard in May 1992:

> All these countries we are competing with, they're working in partnership, hand in hand, government, business, labor, education, to stake a position for their workers of the future ... Only the United States is saying we don't have to do that ... We have not had the kind of partnership we need to compete in the global arena.[57]

Clinton won the presidency linking expanded trade to human rights. His campaign phrase – "an America that will never coddle tyrants, from Baghdad to Beijing" – was taken to mean that he might limit their access to US markets.[58]

Once in office, Clinton stuck with free trade orthodoxy. Indeed, it was part of how he defined himself as a New Democrat unbeholden to the party's traditional union constituency.[59] His presidency began with the US as the world's sole military and economic superpower: The Soviet Union had collapsed, Japan appeared to be economically adrift after its financial bubble had burst, Germany was tied up expensively absorbing East Germany, and China was only just beginning to develop a modern economy. The Washington Consensus, with free flows of goods and capital as its lynchpin, was gospel in the US, and the US government was pressuring other nations to adopt it.

Clinton's inner circle was split. There was a "Wall Street group" composed of Robert Rubin, Leon Panetta, Alice Rivlin, Lloyd Bentsen, Larry Summers, and Roger Altman, which favored fiscal discipline to bring down interest rates and free up funds for investment. And there was an "industrial policy group" composed of Robert Reich, Ira Magaziner, Laura Tyson, Alan Blinder, and Joseph Stiglitz, which favored worker training, federal infrastructure investment, and other industrial policy staples that Clinton had promised during his campaign. Clinton chose to go with the Wall Street group, hoping that a lower budget deficit would induce the Fed and bond markets to lower interest rates, stimulating the economy.[60]

The economy did perform well during Clinton's presidency. Productivity grew as the microcomputer revolution spread throughout the economy. The budget deficit declined from 1993 to 1997 and there were surpluses from 1998 to 2000.[61] Trade was the exception: The trade deficit increased from $132 billion in 1993 to $447 billion in 2000.[62]

When Clinton took office, two major trade agreements negotiated by Bush were pending: NAFTA and the agreement creating the WTO. Clinton secured congressional passage of NAFTA after adding weak side letters on labor and the environment to placate industrial-state Democrats. He cut deals with members of Congress from districts whose products – glass, citrus, wine, and others – were expected to be harmed.[63] In the words of Michael Wessel, a staffer to House Minority Leader Richard Gephardt (D-MO), who opposed NAFTA, "The fact of the matter is they won NAFTA because of money, because of gifts, because of special interests, goodies, and everything else. They did not necessarily win the debate."[64]

The final vote was 234–200 in the House and 61–38 in the Senate.[65] Republicans, rather than Clinton's own badly split Democratic Party, supplied the majority of yes votes in both houses.

When the Mexican economy collapsed in December 1994, the supposed gains of NAFTA were undone overnight by a collapse of the peso. Clinton was forced to bail out Mexico with a $20 billion emergency loan, part of a $50 billion IMF loan.

Integration of the primitive Mexican economy with the US and Canada was then undertaken without adequate preparation, unlike the EU's years of assistance before it integrated similarly backward Portugal and Greece. For example, NAFTA required elimination of subsidies to Mexican corn farmers, which, together with a flood of cheap American corn, devastated more than 2 million of its farmers.[66]

Clinton requested renewal of fast-track authority in 1995, 1997, and 1998, but was rebuffed by a Congress that had grown skeptical of FTAs.[67] Members saw that despite ever more trade agreements, the trade deficit, then at $370 billion, kept growing.[68]

Just before leaving office, Clinton guided China's accession to the WTO through a congressional vote, making permanent its most-favored nation (MFN) status with permanent normal trade relations (PNTR). This ended periodic congressional review of its trade status and gave the US business community confidence to invest there. He promised that this move would reduce America's China trade deficit, liberalize China's economy, and democratize its political system.[69] In actuality, PNTR was a major enabler of the "China shock" that destroyed 2 million American jobs after 2000.[70]

The George W. Bush Administration

In January 2001, the new George W. Bush administration requested fast-track authority. In July 2002, it was granted after a political battle that included expansion and consolidation of TAA, workers' rights issues, trade preferences for Andean countries, transshipment issues, and miscellanea. Despite intensive administration lobbying, the bill did not have the votes when brought to the House floor, and the vote had to be held open as administration officials and House Republican leaders pressured recalcitrant representatives.[71] It finally passed at 3:30 a.m., 215 to 212.[72]

Bush then went on a fast-track binge, negotiating FTAs with Singapore, Chile, Australia, Morocco, the Dominican Republic, Central America, Bahrain, Colombia, Peru, Panama, Korea, and Oman. (All went into effect on his watch except for Korea, Colombia, and Panama, which did so under Obama.) USTR Robert Zoellick hoped to create thereby a "fear of missing out" among the BRICS nations (Brazil, Russia, India, China, and South Africa), thereby inducing further concessions from them at Doha.[73] The strategy did not work, and the goods trade deficit continued to grow, doubling from $447 billion in 2000 to $837 billion in 2006.[74]

Steel emerged as a flash point. There was (and is) excess capacity worldwide, mostly due to China dumping excess capacity abroad. In 2001, the American industry, with many firms in bankruptcy, obtained antidumping and countervailing duty orders against China. China then redirected some of its excess production to steel-producing countries *other* than the US, causing them to increase offsetting steel exports to the US. In response, in 2002 Bush levied tariffs ranging from 8 to 30 percent on certain types of steel from all nations other than China, Canada, Mexico, Israel, and Jordan. Continuing negotiations and the formation of an international steel-monitoring organization failed to solve the problem. Bush rescinded the tariffs after 21 months due to international political pressure and threats of retaliation. Reports using skewed models (see "Flawed Trade Models" in Chapter 18) then claimed the tariffs had cost American consumers much more than the value of the protected jobs.[75]

18 US INDUSTRIAL POLICY 2008-PRESENT
The End of the Old Order

Barack Obama was the last president able to maintain the decades-old orthodoxy in favor of free trade. But he was aware early on of festering problems. During his 2008 campaign, like Bill Clinton in 1992, he tried to have it both ways. He wanted to send a populist message to his blue collar base that he was against NAFTA while signaling the opposite to his corporate and finance sector donors and the Democratic economic intelligentsia. He said that there either should be a renegotiation of NAFTA's labor and environmental provisions or it should be scrapped.[1] He deployed the shopworn slogan that free trade must be fair trade. But a Canadian news source revealed that an advisor, economist Austan Goolsbee, had met with Canadian consular officials in Chicago to reassure them that they should not worry about any actual retreat from free trade.[2]

By the time Obama took office, America's China problem, obvious to the unbiased for years, was becoming undeniable even by China's American apologists. Between 2001 and 2008, the trade deficit with China had more than tripled, from $83 to $268 billion.[3] The political and economic promises Beijing had made during its WTO accession, widely accepted at the time by America's national security and foreign policy establishments, were being openly broken. China's apologists had once argued that increased trade would make it more democratic and respectful of human rights. But instead, it was refining and exporting a high-tech authoritarianism with control of the internet, facial recognition software, and social credit scores – plus old-fashioned repression of its Tibetan and Uighur minorities.

Western observers had once predicted that China would evolve into a market economy, but this was not happening. Its state-owned enterprises (SOEs) were not being phased out. While many closures and mergers had occurred, Beijing's goal was not to dismantle its state-run economy but to turn key SOEs into subsidized national champions capable of dominating global markets (see Chapter 7).[4] China was also ignoring or evading many other WTO obligations, notably with state-assisted theft of intellectual property.[5]

Obama's Response

Obama's response was to pursue yet another trade agreement. The Trans-Pacific Strategic Economic Partnership Agreement had originally been signed by Brunei, Chile, New Zealand, and Singapore in 2005.[6] It was expanded in 2008 with Australia, Canada, Japan, Malaysia, Mexico, Peru, Vietnam, and the US. Its scope was broadened, and it was renamed the Trans-Pacific Partnership (TPP).[7] In 2015, Obama sought and obtained fast track authority to help him get it through Congress once signed.

TPP's American advocates often referred to it as "establishing the rules of the road for trade" in the Pacific region.[8] The lengthy and complex agreement covered rules of origin, technical barriers to trade, trade remedies, investor–state dispute settlement, sanitary and phytosanitary (plants) measures, intellectual property, government procurement, trade in services, and competition policy.[9] It also called for a 90 percent reduction of tariffs and the rooting out of nontariff barriers.[10]

TPP's investor–state dispute mechanism, despite similar provisions in existing US trade agreements, proved controversial. It let a panel of trade lawyers, potentially with conflicts of interest, override a nation's domestic laws if they disadvantaged a foreign corporation.[11]

Supporters talked up the growth that would result from the agreement, but according to an 806-page USITC report using a 2017 baseline, if the TPP were fully implemented, by 2032 US income would increase by a paltry 0.2 percent, GDP by 0.15 percent, and employment by 0.07 percent.[12] But if the TPP's motivation was not growth, what was it? Revealingly, the report noted that "TPP would generally establish trade-related disciplines that strengthen and harmonize regulations, increase certainty, and decrease trade costs for firms that trade and invest in the TPP region." Translation: It would make life easier for the multinationals.

Obama touted the pact as a way to curb China's growing economic influence by bringing American rules and values to the region – the same, now discredited, argument that had been used in favor of China's 2001 WTO accession.

Many NGOs and political figures opposed the TPP, including both 2016 presidential candidates, Donald Trump and Hillary Clinton. Obama signed the TPP in February 2016, but it was not ratified by Congress in that election year and Trump abandoned it.

In 2013, Obama began negotiations with the EU on the Transatlantic Trade and Investment Partnership (TTIP). This deal was criticized as a threat to publicly owned physical and social infrastructure such as water systems and Britain's National Health Service, to food and environmental protections, to EU banking regulations, to data privacy, and to unionized, high-wage European jobs.[13] Obama did not complete the deal and it too was abandoned under Trump.

More Free Trade Plus Manufacturing USA

Despite his criticisms of NAFTA on the campaign trail, in office Obama did not scrap or renegotiate it. Instead, he repeated a familiar refrain:

> Trade has helped our country a lot more than it's hurt us. Exports helped lead us out of the recession. Companies that export pay workers higher wages than folks who don't export. And anybody who says that somehow shutting ourselves off from trade is going to bring jobs back, they're just not telling the truth. In fact, most of the manufacturing jobs that we lost over the past decade, they weren't the result of trade deals – they were the result of technology and automation that lets businesses make more stuff with fewer workers.[14]

The automation argument was a misleading half-truth. While automation was indeed costing jobs, it was also creating them, as it had for 250 years. But according to an Economic Policy Institute study, the huge increase in net imports from China between 2001 and 2018 destroyed 3.7 million jobs.[15]

Facing ongoing public complaints, Obama made two attempts beyond new FTAs to solve America's trade problem. Both ignored its real causes, accepted economic orthodoxy, and therefore failed.

During his 2010 State of the Union address, Obama pledged to double exports in five years.[16] His stated premise was that Americans were not doing enough to promote their goods and services abroad.[17] Executive Order 13534 established a National Export Initiative involving 14 cabinet departments and agencies in an Export Promotion Cabinet.[18] Measures included increased export assistance to SMEs, advertising of federal resources available to exporters, more overseas trade missions, increased support for companies seeking to export, increased SME access to Export–Import Bank financing, attempts to reduce barriers to trade, attempts to open new markets, and better enforcement of existing trade agreements.[19] But this just repackaged existing programs, albeit with slightly better coordination. And from 2010 to 2016, exports rose by 19.7 percent, not 100 percent.[20]

Obama's second initiative was announced during the 2012 campaign: a promise to create one million new manufacturing jobs by the end of his second term. The means would include reforming corporate taxes, challenging unfair Chinese trade practices, setting up new community college–employer partnerships, and creating up to 15 manufacturing innovation institutes. With the important exception of these institutes (which became the Manufacturing USA program discussed in Chapter 21), this initiative was another repackaging of existing measures. And between January 2013 and December 2016, only 373,000 net manufacturing jobs were created.[21]

Obama's first deviation from free trade came in 2009 when, in response to a 215 percent surge in imports of Chinese tires, he imposed a 35 percent tariff.[22] This reduced tire imports from China and caused a smaller increase in imports from third countries.[23] A better-designed tariff, addressing both Chinese and third-country tires plus downstream products such as cars and trucks, would have worked much better. Instead, the tariff mainly provoked the usual poorly designed studies falsely claiming inordinately high costs per job saved.[24] It expired in 2012.

In 2012, Obama imposed a tariff on dumped Chinese solar panels. In 2016, he imposed a tariff on dumped Chinese steel and tightened enforcement of an existing ban on goods made with slave labor. The solar tariff caused Chinese producers to relocate production abroad, while the steel tariff caused China to dump into other countries, causing them to flood the US. On anti-subsidy grounds, Obama also imposed or raised tariffs against China on, inter alia, wind towers, steel cylinders, aluminum extrusions, thermal paper, coated paper, lawn trimmers, kitchen shelving, steel sinks, citric acid, magnesia carbon bricks, pressure pipe, line pipe, seamless pipe, steel cylinders, drill pipe, oil country tubular goods, and wire strands.[25] But the volume of trade affected was only about $7 billion a year.[26]

On Obama's watch, the overall trade deficit grew from $395 to $510 billion, the goods deficit from $510 to $799 billion, and the Advanced Technology Products deficit from $56 to $111 billion.[27] it was estimated that the US would have had 3 million more manufacturing jobs in 2014 if its trade had been in balance.[28]

Free Trade Agreements

During the years covered by this chapter, FTAs played a large role in America's trade ideology and practice. They lowered US tariffs and provided legal protections – for example, against expropriation – for American investors. But they also created asymmetries that disadvantaged America's trade. The US

Table 18.1 US trade balances with FTA countries and China in $billions[29]

Country/Year	Goods	Services	Total
Canada (NAFTA)			
1993 (yr. before NAFTA)	−10.8	not avail.	not avail.
2008	−78.3	19.7	−58.6
2022	−88.7	26.6	−62.1
Mexico (NAFTA)			
1993 (yr. before NAFTA)	1.7	not avail.	not avail.
2008	−64.7	7.4	−57.3
2022	−138.4	0.7	−139.1
South Korea			
2011 (yr. before FTA)	−13.2	8.0	−5.2
2015	−28.3	11.7	−16.6
2022	−43.2	7.6	−35.6
China (WTO)			
2001 (yr. before WTO)	−83.1	2.3	−80.8
2011	−295.2	12.6	−282.6
2022	−381.2	14.8	−366.4

mostly honored its market-opening commitments, while many other nations did not, and subsidized their exports. FTAs, despite the fair labor provisions in all 13 negotiated since 2001, encouraged US multinationals to offshore manufacturing for lower wages and laxer health and safety regulations.

All US FTAs with nations of significant size, plus China's admission to the WTO and grant of PNTR status, were followed by increased trade deficits, despite establishment predictions of the opposite. Table 18.1 shows part of this record.

In constant dollars, the overall US trade balance deteriorated from a surplus of $12 billion in 1975 to a deficit of $951 billion in 2022.[30] While services trade was $232 billion in surplus that year, this offset only 19 percent of the overall deficit. The balance in Advanced Technology Products, once a signature American strength, turned negative in 2002 and steadily worsened to a record $243 billion deficit in 2022.[31]

Flawed Trade Models

America signed trade agreements based on computer models projecting that they would expand trade and reduce the trade deficit. These models were inaccurate for several reasons:

1. They assumed full employment before and after implementation of a trade agreement – that is, that an FTA could never increase unemployment.[32]
2. They ignored currency manipulation and private-sector capital inflows that drive up the dollar (see Chapter 4).[33]
3. They ignored flaws in the theory of comparative advantage, including its unjustified assumptions that a) industries lost to exports are always replaced by better ones and b) the costs of shifting capital and employees from lost to gained industries are negligible (see Chapter 4).
4. They ignored the fact that many foreign nations would not live up to market opening commitments.
5. They ignored the long-term effects of losing advantageous industries (see Chapter 2) to foreign nations.[34]

Conversely, when models were used to forecast the supposedly deleterious effects of increases in US tariffs:

1. They ignored the effect of tariffs in stimulating domestic manufacturing investment and employment. (See, for example, the steel tariffs discussed later under "Trump's Tariffs.")[35]
2. They assumed that tariff revenues would be sequestered, thus reducing investment and consumer spending, rather than injected back into the economy as government spending or tax cuts.[36]
3. They assumed that US importers and consumers would bear the full costs of tariffs, ignoring evidence that a significant percentage is often borne by the exporting nations due to a reduction in profit margins.[37]
4. They ignored the long-term value of retaining advantageous industries (see Chapter 2).

The public failures of these models, and their criticism by economists such as Tim Kehoe of the University of Minnesota, eventually prompted minor attempts at a rethink.[38] Thus, while continuing to forecast with flawed models per legislative requirement, the USITC began to also produce more accurate analyses. For example, its 2007 review of the KORUS agreement with South Korea added analyses of specific industries.[39] Here, USITC projected a significant increase in America's net imports of vehicles – which is exactly what happened. However, these industry-specific predictions were largely ignored in the political debate, while the inaccurate forecasts of GDP gains got the attention.[40]

Financialization

This book has not said much about finance because its focus is the real side of the economy. Nonetheless, we now discuss financialization because of its powerful negative effects on the real economy and thus on America's capacity for effective industrial policy.

Financialization is when the financial side of the economy undermines rather than supports the real side.[41] Expanding beyond the point of usefulness, it becomes a destabilizer and a drag. Excess debt, much of it in risky new forms, and real estate speculation crowd out productive investment.

The roots of the 2008 financial crisis lay in the financialization of the US economy that began with the deregulation of finance beginning in the late 1970s. Memories of the Crash of 1929 and the bank failures of the Depression had faded. Post-Depression regulations such as limits on deposit interest rates were rendered unworkable by inflation and not rebuilt after inflation was tamed. In the 1980s and 1990s, other stabilizing rules were dismantled based on two mistaken ideas: first, that systemic financial risk had been conquered, and second and more important, that what was good for Wall Street was good for the economy as a whole. By the time the Depression-era Glass–Steagall Act – which had separated commercial from investment banking, preventing speculation with depositors' money – was repealed in 1999, the old protections had been almost entirely eroded.[42]

Starting in the 1980s, new classes of assets and the rise of shadow banking meant that even when existing rules were not relaxed, they were worked around.[43] Nonbank firms such as money market mutual funds and broker–dealers began to undertake bank-like activities such as borrowing short-term to fund long-term loans.[44] Calls to regulate these new activities were dismissed, as when Alan Greenspan opposed calls to regulate over-the-counter derivatives trading in 2000.[45] Shadow banks were subject to few or no requirements as to leverage, capital, transparency, data reporting, or even fiduciary responsibilities.[46]

As economist Hyman Minsky (1919–96) taught, a financial system regulated to remain stable will inevitably generate pressures to deregulate it, as its stability will be misinterpreted as evidence that markets can take care of themselves.[47] Thus, stability itself is destabilizing, leading to recurring cycles of deregulation, financial expansion, rising debt, crisis, and reregulation.

Overconfidence was exacerbated by the mistaken belief that modern risk management tools had conquered financial risk, especially credit risk, and that federal regulation – for example, to limit leverage by banks – was therefore no longer needed.[48] But hedging techniques that work in normal markets failed during the 2007–8 crisis because it is impossible to hedge the entire highly interconnected financial market against itself.[49] The Fed stepped in to prevent crashes, bailing out banks, investment banks, and other financial institutions, thereby creating the moral hazard of de facto insurance known as the Wall Street Put.

Financial-Sector Hypergrowth

The politics of deregulation, freeing up international capital flows, and unfettered financial growth was bipartisan.[50] The shift began under Carter, not Reagan, and was supported by academic economists, business schools, institutions such as the Business Roundtable, and media such as the *Wall Street Journal*.[51] It had echoes abroad, especially in the UK.

As the US economy financialized, the sector's share of GDP almost doubled, rising from 4 to 5 percent in the 1970s to more than 8 percent in the 2000s.[52] But how did this harm the larger economy? Finance supports the real economy when it:

1. Provides a payments system so households and businesses can buy goods and services.
2. Enables families to save for large expenses such as retirement and college.
3. Provides credit so that families can purchase homes and businesses can make long-term investments.
4. Channels capital into productive investment by allowing firms to raise equity and borrow money.
5. Maintains a liquid market for assets so that stocks, bonds, and other financial and real assets can be monetized.
6. Helps businesses and households reduce risk by providing insurance and forward purchase contracts.
7. Develops new products and processes to make these activities better, cheaper, and more readily available.[53]

Expansion of the financial sector to the size required to perform these functions supports GDP growth, but beyond this, retards it. The most widely cited study draws this line at nonfinancial private sector debt (mortgages plus personal and business loans to nonfinancial companies and households) equal to 100 percent of GDP.[54] In the US, this level was reached in 1990 and kept rising, peaking at 234 percent of GDP in 2008 before dropping to 218 percent in 2022.[55]

The composition of this expansion explains the shift from benefit to harm. It did not take place on the equity side – that is, in the stocks and venture capital that largely do finance investment in the real economy. Nor was it in debt directly owed by real-side firms. Instead, the growth was heavily skewed to household debt, facilitated by a weakening of mortgage standards, and to debt issued *by financial institutions to financial institutions* to purchase, securitize, and resell this debt.[56]

This credit expansion enabled households to increase their buying and selling of existing houses, driving up their prices. This price rise created apparent security for the loans and forced other households to go deeper into debt to buy their own houses, completing the cycle. This did little for production or real-economy innovation, instead feeding the subprime mortgage bubble whose collapse caused the Great Recession of 2007–9. Since real estate is the asset class most widely held by households and nonfinancial businesses, its violent swings as the mortgage market financialized, ballooned, and collapsed did huge damage to the real economy.[57]

As noted, the debt explosion was based in part on loans by financial institutions to other financial institutions. This quadrupled from 24 percent of GDP in 1990 to 105 percent in 2009, and in 2023 stood at 80 percent.[58] The main instruments were mortgage-backed securities, other asset-backed securities (mostly credit-card receivables and auto loans), derivatives of these securities, derivatives of these derivatives, collateralized loan obligations, and credit default swaps.[59] These highly leveraged credit instruments were created by financial institutions to trade for their own accounts and ultimately to sell to individual investors and nonfinancial companies. The systemic fragility that imploded in 2007 built up in these markets.

This credit expansion also damaged the real economy even before its collapse.[60] Debt growth within the financial sector was financed almost entirely with very short-term credit. To do this, firms took advantage of the extraordinarily low amounts of equity permitted under relaxed regulations. One report notes that "The largest [bank holding companies] increased their leverage from 20-to-1 in 2001 to more than 45-to-1 in 2009."[61] In consequence, between 1980 and 2008, financial assets more than doubled as a percentage of GDP, from 180 to 450 percent.[62] And between 1982 and 2002, financial-sector profits rose from 10 to 40 percent of total corporate profits.[63] This shifted income from real-economy companies and working- and middle-class families to a small number of investors and finance professionals – who then mostly reinvested it in more financial instruments.[64]

The Great Recession is estimated to have directly caused lost economic output of between $7 and $14 trillion.[65] In addition, $10 trillion was lost due to human and physical capital obsolescence as investments were postponed or cancelled, careers delayed or abandoned, and worker skills degraded due to unemployment.[66]

Shareholder Primacy and Short Termism

Financialization was legitimized and sustained by "shareholder primacy," the idea that returns to shareholders are the sole appropriate measure of corporate success. This shifted corporate governance away from older norms that also recognized obligations to communities, customers, suppliers, and employees.

Shareholder primacy supported the idea that the best way to align management incentives with shareholder gains was to tie top management's compensation directly to the price of the company's stock. Stock options and grants quickly became the largest part of their remuneration. Shareholder primacy thus legitimized and incented management to take actions that boosted stock prices in the short term regardless of their effects on technological leadership, long-term profits, or even the survival of the enterprise.[67] Such actions included outsourcing manufacturing to foreign countries, reducing spending on R&D and upgraded plant, and stock buybacks.

One 2020 study showed that publicly traded US companies reduced investment when the required holding periods of their executives' equity incentives were shortened.[68] Another showed that public firms – that is, those with traded stock to grant – invested less in their own businesses than similar privately held firms, and that public firms were less responsive to changes in investment opportunities, "especially in industries in which stock prices are the most sensitive to earnings news."[69]

Increased pressure for short-term profitability also came from the changing composition of shareholders. Institutional investors hold most debt and equity securities, and a 2017 study found that the percentage with short-term "transient" strategies, involving high portfolio turnover, as opposed to long-term strategies with low turnover, increased from 20 percent in 1985 to more than 30 percent in 2013.[70]

A rise in stock buybacks and dividends transferred cash from firms to shareholders. From 2003 through 2012, the 449 companies in the S&P 500 index used 54 percent of their earnings – $2.4 trillion – to buy back their own stock. This was *in addition to* dividends that absorbed 37 percent.[71] They ipso facto had to reduce their investments in productive capabilities, fund more of them with debt, or both. A 2020 SEC report confirmed that these share repurchases and dividend payments (jointly "payouts") came at the cost of lower capital expenditures and employment.[72] This growth in payouts more than offset rising corporate debt, thereby reducing funds available for investment. Since 1980, productive real-economy investments by nonfinancial corporations declined, while their financial investments rose substantially.[73] Firm-level studies show a negative correlation between financial asset ownership and capital goods investment.[74] An *American Compass* analysis put the resulting deficit of real-economy investment during 2009–17, compared to 1971–99, at $300 billion per year.[75]

The absence of sound national industrial policy was another cause of short-termism and lower real investment. The government's failure to support commercialization of US-invented technology, to protect American firms from subsidized foreign competition, and to correct the overvaluation of the dollar all reduced opportunities for profitable investments in America's real economy, increasing pressure to boost earnings per share by financial maneuvering. Its absence also forced the Fed to set progressively lower interest rates to sustain employment, consumption, and the financial markets. These ultra-low rates improved the short-term profitability of debt-financed mergers and acquisitions. These mergers transferred money from the real economy to the financial sector in the form of fees and interest on debt but, with some exceptions, did not increase the productivity of the merged companies.[76]

Shareholder primacy and short-termism also produced a tilt toward finance-oriented corporate management. This contributed to the replacement of CEOs who understood their companies' technology and employed strategies based on long-term technological dominance with those more oriented toward finance. General Electric, Intel, Southwest Airlines, and Boeing, among others, paid dearly for this change.[77]

Boeing, for example, once had a deep-rooted culture prioritizing safety, careful engineering, close coordination between R&D and manufacturing, and extensive inspection and testing. It consistently made the large, risky, long-term investments required to develop safe new planes. But after its merger with McDonnell Douglas in 1997, financially oriented management took over.[78] In the words of the 2020 Final Report of the House Committee on Transportation and Infrastructure:

> After the merger, Harry, the Chief Executive Officer (CEO) of McDonnell Douglas became the President and Chief Operating Officer of Boeing. In 2004 he told the *Chicago Tribune*: "When people say I changed the culture of Boeing, that was the intent, so it's run like a business rather than a great engineering firm. It is a great engineering firm, but people invest in a company because they want to make money." Those sentiments, according to many observers and current and former Boeing employees, infected the company. They point to that philosophy, which focused on financial benefit rather than technical solutions and innovation, as setting the stage for many of the issues that ultimately contributed to the crashes of the two 737 MAX aircraft.[79]

For example, Boeing replaced experienced senior engineers with younger, cheaper ones, losing skills and institutional memory. It undertook a costly (and ultimately repudiated) effort to outsource to other companies and foreign nations the manufacturing of major sections of its aircraft.[80] It rushed development and manufacturing of the 787 Dreamliner to meet profit targets, ultimately causing cost overruns, production problems, safety issues, and delivery delays.[81]

We do not offer recommendations as to how to return the financial sector to its critical but limited role of supporting the real economy because an extensive literature on this subject already exists. But the negative effects of an unchecked financial sector on the management and resources of the real economy remain a powerful and independent factor undermining US industrial policy that cannot be siloed and ignored.

We now return to our chronology because starting in 2017, the Trump administration began to address some, though not all, of America's trade problems.

Trump Breaks the Mold

In 2016, Donald Trump was elected on what opponents in both parties dismissed as an economically illiterate nationalist and protectionist platform.[82] Although democratic socialist Senator Bernie Sanders (I-VT) had raised many of the same trade issues in the Democratic primaries, the party apparatus united behind establishment candidate Hillary Clinton. Ironically, even Clinton was forced by public opinion during the campaign to oppose the TPP that she had helped promote as Obama's secretary of state.[83]

In office, Trump broke sharply with the consensus. He said what had been unsaid and unsayable by presidents, senior officials of both parties, and almost all American economists for decades: that US trade policy had failed, that trade deficits were a real problem, and that the "uneducated" view that free trade had made things worse for most Americans was true.

His administration took actions to oppose and reverse existing trade policies. These included a) paralyzing the WTO dispute resolution appeals process by blocking appointment of new judges, b) imposing a wide array of tariffs on China and other countries, c) keeping many of these tariffs in place to the end of his term in office, d) renegotiating a major treaty (NAFTA) under threat of withdrawal, and e) declining to pursue ratification of the TPP negotiated by his predecessor.[84]

But Trump did not articulate, much less implement, an effective or even coherent replacement for existing policy. In fact, his administration did not appear to *have* systematic ideas about, or strategy for, trade economics.[85] Trump himself, despite his valid overall intuitions, had a weak grasp on many basic realities of trade economics. He seems to have believed, for example, that his tariffs were paid entirely by the exporting nations.[86]

A small circle in the administration shared Trump's skepticism about free trade: USTR Robert Lighthizer, Commerce Secretary Wilbur Ross, and Peter Navarro, head of the Office of Manufacturing and Trade Policy (a newly invented office with no staff). Of these officials, Lighthizer was the most systematic thinker, expressing – once out of office and able to speak freely – a far-reaching and coherent view of the trade and industrial policies, including exchange rate management, that the US should adopt.[87] But many of Trump's appointees and preexisting agency staff opposed Trump's views, most prominently Gary Cohn, head of the National Economic Council. Cohn clashed with Navarro, reportedly sometimes in shouting matches in front of the president.[88] Treasury Secretary Robert Mnuchin was also a committed free trader. This lack of shared policy commitment undermined the ability of the administration to design, implement, or even settle upon trade policies.

Trump and Trade Agreements

Soon after his inauguration, Trump, fulfilling a campaign pledge, withdrew the US from the TPP, sending shock waves through the establishment, which claimed that this put in doubt American leadership in the Asia-Pacific.[89] This claim was dubious, given that the US already had FTAs with 6 of the 11 other TPP countries, security treaties with Australia, South Korea, and Japan, and multiple other treaties, organizational memberships, and information-sharing arrangements with nations in the region.[90]

Trump had called NAFTA "the worst trade deal ever," and made its renegotiation a priority. Its replacement, the US-Mexico-Canada Agreement (USMCA), came into force in 2020. It required, inter alia, that a higher percentage of an imported car be made in the three nations and that more of it be made by workers earning at least $16 per hour. It had stronger provisions for enforcement of union rights in Mexico. It had enhanced environmental and dispute resolution provisions. After USMCA's labor provisions were strengthened, it was endorsed by the AFL–CIO, unlike NAFTA. But its changes had limited impact potential, given that America's low tariffs meant that the incentive for corporations to comply with its provisions to qualify for the lower USMCA rate was small. These changes *may* benefit US workers and manufacturers in the future, but as of 2024, few signs of this have appeared. Although exports to Mexico reached their highest level ever in 2022, $324 billion, imports from Mexico were also at a record, resulting in the highest-ever trade deficit with that country.[91] The situation with Canada was analogous.[92]

Trump also renegotiated KORUS. The changes were minor, in areas such as dispute settlement, Korean medicine, Korea's steel exports (a Trump tariff discussed later in this chapter was replaced with a quota), and US auto exports (America's de facto quota was raised from 25,000 to 50,000). No changes to US law were required and the new agreement became effective in January 2019.[93] Nonetheless, by 2022, the trade deficit with Korea had reached a new record of $44 billion.[94]

The US and China had been discussing a possible bilateral investment treaty since 2013. Trump scuttled the idea. Only a limited trade agreement was negotiated with Japan. It eliminated $7 billion in agricultural quotas and tariffs and the US reduced tariffs on industrial products like steam turbines and machine tools. But it did not cover the all-important auto sector.[95] Nor did it win Japan relief from America's national security-related trade actions such as the steel tariff discussed later in this chapter.

Tech War and Export Controls

During Trump's term, technology export controls, long a back-burner issue, moved to the center of the debate on restraining China's technological advances, especially its military exploitation of American technology.[96] For related reasons, Trump cracked down on Chinese FDI in the US, especially in tech firms. Early-stage Chinese minority investments in US startups had not historically triggered review by the Committee on Foreign Investment in the United States (CFIUS), allowing key technologies to be licensed or transferred to China.[97] The Foreign Investment Risk Review Modernization Act of 2018 expanded CFIUS's authority to block such transactions.

In 2018, Trump by executive order prohibited sales of American high technology to Chinese companies suspected of acting as agents of the country's security forces, including products made in allied nations with American components and thus subject to American export controls. The administration placed hundreds of Chinese firms, including its leading semiconductor maker, Semiconductor Manufacturing International Corporation, on the Treasury Department's Entities List, thereby requiring a special license for exports to them.[98] Trump even succeeded in halting exports of non-American technologies over which the US had no direct jurisdiction, such as the world-leading semiconductor manufacturing equipment made by the Dutch company ASML.[99]

The administration targeted electronics and telecommunications giant Huawei, which had been selling 5G infrastructure to the US and other Western countries. This firm, also suspected of planting back doors in its equipment for spying, was indicted for technology theft.[100] Trump issued an emergency order in 2018, extended in 2019 and 2021, barring it and certain other Chinese firms from selling in the US.[101] Britain and Australia joined the US in banning Huawei's 5G technology, though other allies' cooperation varied.[102] Singapore's Broadcomm, suspected of being a stalking horse for China, was blocked from taking over leading American 5G chip producer Qualcomm.

In 2017, the Commerce Department fined Chinese cellphone maker ZTE $1.2 billion for selling its phones, which contained US semiconductors, to nations on the US sanctions list: Iran, Syria, Sudan, North Korea, and Cuba.[103] ZTE promised to discipline its executives, but instead gave them bonuses, so Commerce activated a clause in the settlement and banned sales of American components to ZTE for seven years, collapsing the firm.[104] President Trump then tweeted that he would help ZTE because of the resulting job losses in China, stunning official Washington.[105] Trump, who said Xi Jinping had approached him, may have wanted to tactically cool tensions, but at a minimum he appeared inconsistent and raised concerns that he had diminished the credibility of American law.[106]

Export bans are a double-edged sword, as they can hurt American firms by depriving them of the revenue they need to stay on the cutting edge. They can also induce firms to offshore production beyond US jurisdiction.[107] They inevitably force China to accelerate its efforts to make the products itself. Using these arguments, American chipmakers pushed back in Washington against the bans.[108] But only a very small percentage of exports to China was subjected to licensing, and the approval rate of applications was 94 percent in 2020 and 88 percent in 2021.[109] The Biden administration described this as a "small yard, high fence" policy.

Trump and the WTO

Since the early 2010s, the US had issues with the WTO's dispute resolution process, in particular with its appellate body, centering on the body's judicial activism and infringements of US sovereignty. Despite efforts to mobilize other WTO members for reform, cooperation was not forthcoming until 2018, after Trump's jolt to the entire system.[110] In February 2020, the USTR explained its concerns:

> Specifically, the Appellate Body has added to US obligations and diminished US rights by failing to comply with WTO rules, addressing issues it has no authority to address, taking actions it has no authority to take, and interpreting WTO agreements in ways not envisioned by the WTO members who entered into those agreements. This persistent overreaching is plainly contrary to the Appellate Body's limited mandate, as set out in WTO rules.[111]

The biggest issue was the panel's cuts to the permitted application of America's three main trade remedies: antidumping actions against undervalued goods, countervailing duties against subsidized goods, and safeguard actions against import surges endangering industries. Of the 141 disputes brought against the US between the start of the WTO in 1995 and 2017, two-thirds involved such remedies.[112] The US had fought hard to keep them when negotiating the WTO's charter, but successive administrations had felt that the WTO's judges were not committed to them, indeed were happy to curb or even eliminate them.

In 2018, the Trump administration undertook to render the panel inoperable. With the terms of all but one of its judges having expired and three needed to hear a case, it refused to agree to the appointment or reappointment of any more, bringing the panel to a halt in 2019.[113] As of mid-2024, the panel remains defunct, with the Biden administration continuing to block appointments. Sixteen WTO members had created a voluntary substitute process, the Multi-Party Interim Appeal Arbitration Arrangement.[114]

In 2018, the Trump administration filed a complaint with the WTO accusing China of massive patent and other intellectual-property violations under the Agreement on Trade-Related Aspects of Intellectual Property Rights. Beijing was also charged with massive forced technology transfers, including requiring R&D in China, forced joint ventures with Chinese firms, mandatory disclosure of software source code, and mandatory data localization. These charges were later used to justify Trump's first China tariffs.

Trump's Tariffs

Trump's first tariff, in April 2017, was on Canadian softwood lumber, a long-standing trade irritant. (As of 2024, a tariff remains in effect.)

Because of the antidumping and countervailing duties imposed in 2011, China was not a major source of solar cells and solar modules for the US. But Chinese firms producing in Vietnam, Malaysia, South Korea, and Thailand were, as was Mexico.[115] China also had a chokehold on key inputs, producing most of the world's polysilicon and 99 percent of its silicon ingots and wafers.[116] More than 100 American solar firms had been put out of business, with the loss of $10 billion in investment.[117] In October 2017, the USITC found, under Section 201, that cells and module imports were injuring industry – the first time in more than 15 years this provision had been used. The administration then imposed tariffs on $8.5 billion per year of such imports, starting at 30 percent and declining to 15 percent in their fourth year.[118]

There were dire predictions about sabotaging America's deployment of solar energy, but as the bipartisan Coalition for a Prosperous America (CPA) documented:

> The Section 201 solar tariffs have had no negative impact on the U.S. market for solar energy installations, which grew 43% in 2020. Solar installations are set to be more than 50% greater than they were expected to be prior to the implementation of the 201 tariffs in 2017.

Importantly, several U.S. solar module manufacturers have ramped up production substantially in the last three years under the stimulus of the Section 201 safeguard tariffs on solar module imports, leading US producers to achieve a 10-year high in market share of 19.8% in 2019.[119]

In November 2017, USITC found that imports of washing machines had caused injury to the industry.[120] The following January, Trump imposed a 20 percent tariff on the first 1.2 million units, and 50 percent thereafter, on $1.8 billion worth from all countries except Canada, plus a tariff on their parts. Whirlpool, Samsung, and LG then announced plans to add production capacity in the US, creating 1,800 jobs.[121] Controversy raged about the cost per job (see later in this chapter for the outcome under Biden).[122] Whirlpool so dominated the US industry that it could increase its prices, and thus the cost per job, underscoring the importance of combining tariffs with effective antitrust.[123] In January 2021, just before leaving office, Trump extended these tariffs another two years.[124]

In February 2019, the Commerce Department found that imports of automobiles, SUVs, vans, light trucks, and their parts were a threat to national security under Section 232, recommending tariffs of up to 35 percent. But the industry was unsupportive.[125] Its supply chains were global, with the average US-made car consisting of 40–50 percent imported parts.[126] A large percentage of US-made cars were built by foreign automakers. Trump ignored the legal requirement to make the nonclassified portions of the report public, and attempted to use the threat of these tariffs as leverage over the EU in his attempt to get a trade agreement.[127] But in November, the statutory deadline for imposing a tariff passed without action by the administration.

Steel, Aluminum, and the Turn toward Managed Trade

In February 2018, the Commerce Department found that steel and aluminum imports constituted a threat to national security.[128] In March, Trump announced near-global tariffs of 25 percent on steel and 10 percent on aluminum, covering $48 billion of imports. Thanks to prior antidumping and countervailing duties, only 6 percent were officially from China, with most coming from friendly nations.[129] The EU retaliated in June 2018 with duties on $4.5 billion worth of American goods such as bourbon, motorcycles, and orange juice. It did not wait for a WTO ruling, a clear sign of the organization's diminishing ability to channel global trade conflicts.[130] USITC later estimated that imports were reduced by 24 percent for steel and 31 percent for aluminum.[131]

After these tariffs were imposed, US steel capacity utilization rose above the 80 percent required for the industry's long-term viability. Aluminum capacity utilization rose from 39 to 64 percent, then stabilized near 50 percent.[132] Both the steel (investing $16 billion) and aluminum ($9 billion) industries added significant new US capacity, including greenfield plants.[133] Trump expanded the steel tariffs in 2020 to include downstream products such as wire, tacks, staples, nails, and certain metal automotive castings.[134]

Negotiations for a managed trade regime to handle global overcapacity in these metals began. Argentina, Brazil, and Korea agreed to annual steel quotas in May 2018.[135] Voluntary restraint agreements were reached with Canada and Mexico in May 2019, capping their exports at historic volumes.[136] In 2022, the Biden administration reached tariff rate quota agreements with Europe, Japan, and the UK, letting in specific volumes of steel tariff-free with a 25 percent tariff thereafter.[137]

Models by free-trade economists claimed that the cost per job saved was exorbitant and paid entirely by American consumers.[138] But more accurate studies by CPA and the liberal Economic Policy Institute showed that the tariffs did not significantly increase consumer prices, did increase domestic production, and did induce significant domestic investment.[139] The USITC later backed up these claims, estimating an inflationary impact of only 2.4 percent for steel and 1.6 percent for aluminum.[140]

Trump's China Tariffs and the Phase One Deal

Trump levied tariffs on China in strategically designed stages, pausing, delaying, and raising again to see how Beijing would react. In March 2018, the USTR released a report, related to its WTO complaint, asserting that four Chinese practices justified action under Section 301, which covers unfair foreign trade practices:

1. Forced technology transfer requirements
2. Cyber-enabled actions to steal US IP and trade secrets
3. Discriminatory and nonmarket licensing practices
4. State-funded strategic acquisition of US corporate assets[141]

In June 2018, the US issued a list of products covered by an initial round of 25 percent tariffs, so-called List 1, covering annual trade worth $34 billion. China retaliated against roughly the same value.[142]

In August, the US issued List 2, applying a 25 percent tariff to $16 billion more trade. China retaliated against $34 billion.[143]

In September, the US imposed a 10 percent tariff on $200 billion in imports on List 3. China retaliated against $60 billion. Washington then announced that in January 2019, this tariff would increase to 25 percent.[144] After another round of Chinese retaliation, Trump delayed the increase until March, then indefinitely.[145] But in June, he imposed it, and China retaliated.[146]

In August 2019, the US announced its intention to impose tariffs on *another* $300 billion worth of imports (List 4). In September 2019, it imposed 15 percent tariffs on a subset, List 4a, and China retaliated.[147]

Thus the average tariff on Chinese imports went from 3 percent at the start of 2018 to 4 percent in April, 7 percent in July, 8 percent in August, and 12 percent in September – where it remained for eight months.[148] In June 2019, it rose to 17 percent, then to 21 percent in October.

In December 2019, Trump announced plans for another $160 billion in tariffs, starting December 15.[149] But these were indefinitely postponed when the so-called Phase One managed trade deal was agreed on January 15, 2020. Existing 15 percent tariffs on $110 billion of imports were halved.[150] This reduced the average tariff on China to 19 percent, where it remained until the end of the administration.[151] (As of 2024, it had not significantly changed.)[152]

When the deal was signed, roughly two-thirds of China's exports to the US were subject to tariffs: $335 billion.[153] Average Chinese retaliatory tariffs were similar on paper: 21 percent, covering 58 percent of China's imports from the US. But given China's vastly greater nontariff barriers, they were not equivalent.[154] And China was retaliating against a smaller volume of trade than the US simply because China's imports from the US were so much smaller than the reverse.

The Phase One deal promised to open China's markets to more American products, increase China's American farm and energy imports, and increase protection for American technology and trade secrets. Beijing committed to buying $200 billion more of American goods and services in 2020 and 2021 versus a 2017 baseline: $32 billion more of agricultural goods, $78 billion more of manufactures, and $52 billion more of energy.[155] Finally, America seemed to have made a trade deal tied to actual results.

Two years later, China's American imports were $12.5 billion short in agriculture, $42 billion short in energy, and $86.5 billion short in manufactures.[156] It had purchased only 58 percent of what it had promised to – less than before the trade conflict began.[157] Inexplicably, 27 percent of the products that China *already* regularly imported from the US were not even covered by the deal, eliminating any incentive for China to buy more of them.[158] And there were costs, such as the $23 billion in taxpayer money paid to compensate American farmers who sold less to China due to retaliatory tariffs.[159]

The primary cause of the deal's failure was simply Beijing's refusal to compromise its mercantilist policies. Other factors included COVID, African swine fever's decimation of China's huge American-fed pig population, China's existing commitments to other agricultural exporters, the grounding of the 737-MAX, and the inability of American energy firms to supply the quantities China wanted to buy – this last item reflecting unrealistic goals set by the administration's negotiators.[160]

The Phase One deal confirmed, once and for all, that China was not interested in rebalancing its trade with the US and that negotiating with it to do so was futile. Any solution would therefore have to consist solely of actions the US could take unilaterally. According to a CPA computer model, revoking China's MFN status would create 2 million new jobs and expand the US economy by 1.75 percent.[161]

What Did Trump Accomplish?

Trump imposed tariffs that, compared to other post–World War II tariff episodes, covered more countries, more products, and, with a few exceptions – light trucks, clothing, shoes – remained in place longer. He raised the average tariff on China from 3 to 19 percent and the average on other nations from 2 to 3 percent.[162]

Trump did not prove to be the extremist his free trade opponents had predicted. Nor did he trigger the uncontrollable cycle of tariffs and counter-tariffs, "trade war," that free traders had long warned about. Instead, America acted and its counterparties responded in the measured fashion normal in commercial disputes. Nor was America abandoned by its geopolitical allies, despite decades of scare talk.

Trump thus destroyed myths that had paralyzed America for decades. He broke the momentum of ever more trade agreements. He finished the process, begun by his predecessors, of neutering the WTO Appellate Panel, a significant step toward deactivating the unworkable organization as a whole. Most important, by making it impossible for elected officials, the press, or the public to continue ignoring the damage done by free trade, Trump forced a much more open and in-depth public debate about alternatives, albeit one of limited intellectual rigor and policy ambition.

Trump started the process of decoupling trade and investment from China.[163] By late 2023, imports from China had dropped to their lowest percentage of American imports in two decades, though some of this decrease was offset by a rise in the laundering of Chinese exports by way of shipping through or final assembly in third countries.[164]

Trump failed to reverse, halt, or even slow the growth of the trade deficit, which rose from $479 billion in 2016 to $654 billion in 2020.[165] (To be fair, part of this was due to COVID-19, which hit American exports harder than imports.)[166] Nor did he install or even credibly propose policies that would reduce the deficit going forward. He grasped neither the importance of managing exchange rates nor the need for proactive governmental support of advantageous industries. He thus took no action on currency, tried to defund the Manufacturing Extension Partnership (Chapter 22), and cut funding for Manufacturing USA (Chapter 21), two important pro-manufacturing programs.[167] He failed to induce a boom in industrial investment like the one the Biden administration's industrial policy initiatives later delivered.[168]

Biden's Tariff Actions

President Joe Biden's trade policies were, for his first three years, primarily a holding action by an administration that was sufficiently soured on free trade to leave standing most of Trump's changes but that lacked the theoretical clarity, policy conviction, or political need to move further.

Because of China's failure to honor its Phase One obligations, the tariffs that existed when Phase One went into effect were not removed, and no plan was formulated for a Phase Two. Trump's tariffs on washing machines were initially extended, but expired in February 2023 and Biden did not renew them.[169] They had already caused major changes in the US industry: New factories had been built in Clarksville, Tennessee, and Newberry, South Carolina, and 2,000 jobs had been added.[170] After an initial spike, prices fell and showed no long-term effect.[171]

Trump's tariffs on steel and aluminum were extended, with the US eventually settling into a managed trade regime. Biden continued Trump's negotiations with friendly nations to limit their steel exports and stood down the tariff on European steel after reaching a quota agreement with the EU.[172] Biden settled a long-festering dispute with Brussels over Airbus and Boeing, enabling both sides to remove their tariffs on each other's aircraft (see Chapter 26).

In March 2020, the administration raised the tariff on Russian aluminum to 200 percent in retaliation for the invasion of Ukraine. That same month, it gave Britain a duty-free quota for steel and aluminum, and did the same for the EU in October.[173]

Thanks to Trump's solar tariffs, American solar panel manufacturing capacity had been growing.[174] But Biden then made two troubling decisions. In February 2022, moved by climate change concerns, he nominally renewed Trump's solar tariffs, but de facto gutted them by granting an exemption for "bifacial" panels, which generate electricity on both sides.[175] This had been an immature technology with no US production when Trump imposed the original tariff, but now dominated the market for large, utility-scale projects. The Solar Energy Industries Association, which had supplied flawed economic analysis and misleading jobs claims to justify Biden's move, was later discovered to be fronting for Chinese producers.[176]

In June 2022, Biden issued an emergency declaration suspending for two years tariffs on Chinese solar manufacturers who had been circumventing antidumping and countervailing duties by moving the final stages of production to Thailand, Malaysia, and Vietnam. The administration argued that faster deployment of solar power was more important than the health of the domestic industry. When Congress, disputing the potential slowdown, passed a resolution against the declaration in April 2023, Biden vetoed it.

The *de minimis* rule exploded as a controversy on Biden's watch. This rule exempts imports valued at $800 or less (far more than other nations) from tariffs, taxes, and most other notification and review regulations.[177] It was being used to import huge volumes of goods, mostly via online shopping. A single container might contain more than 5,000 packages and content descriptions were fragmentary or false. In 2022, China alone accounted for $188 billion worth of these imports.[178] The lack of accurate information and the huge volume make screening for undervaluation, narcotics, illegal weapons (including chemical and nuclear materials), counterfeits, and health-and-safety violations virtually impossible.[179] As the issue heated up in 2023, Congress, not the administration, took the lead with hearings and two bipartisan reform bills, but as of 2024, no reform bill had passed.[180]

Embracing Industrial Policy

Biden's greatest improvement to American economic policy was enacting major proactive industrial policies in some industries. After decades of disuse, the term began reentering public discourse, usually with a favorable connotation.[181]

The administration argued early on that the US needed an "industrial strategy" to a) promote innovation, b) ensure competitiveness, c) safeguard national security, d) counter China's ambitions, e) secure supply chains, f) engage with allies, and g) meet the science and engineering workforce needs of key industries.[182] Its thinking was set forth in speeches by officials including Commerce Secretary Gina Raimondo, National Economic Council head Brian Deese, and National Security Advisor Jake Sullivan.[183]

In October 2022, Sullivan, albeit recapitulating America's decades-old national security justification for industrial policy, said, "We are pursuing a modern industrial and innovation strategy to invest in our economic strength and technological edge at home, which is the deepest source of our power in the world."[184] (Military-related industrial policies are discussed in Chapter 26.)

Then, in June 2021, Brian Deese broke new ground, saying,

> Markets on their own will not make investments in technologies and in infrastructure that benefit an entire industry. We know that when the benefits of innovation are broadly shared, no one firm has incentive to invest in the kind of game-changing technologies or the kind of connecting infrastructure that fosters long-term economic competitiveness at the industry, the region, and the nationwide level.[185]

(See Chapters 20 and 21 for federal support of innovation.)

About the same time, the White House National Science and Technology Council released its "National Strategy for Advanced Manufacturing," which zeroed in on advanced manufacturing as a priority, saying, "It is, therefore, imperative for the United States to develop and implement strategies to regain American leadership through investments in advanced manufacturing."[186] (See Chapters 21 and 22.)

Biden's industrial policies were enacted in 2021 and 2022 in a set of loosely coordinated acts of Congress, executive orders, and export controls. At the center were three laws aimed at, inter alia, strengthening the nation's innovation system and manufacturing capabilities:

- The Bipartisan Infrastructure and Jobs Act of 2021 (BIA)
- The CHIPS and Science Act of 2022 (CHIPS)
- The Inflation Reduction Act of 2022 (IRA)

The BIA, which added $550 billion to the baseline budget, looked much like a traditional highways bill. It was administered by DOT ($274 billion), EPA ($67 billion), DOE ($63 billion), Commerce ($51 billion), and Interior ($28 billion).[187] It promised broadband internet for every home and upgrades for highways, bridges, electrical transmission lines, and other infrastructure.[188] (A substantial component addressed hardening infrastructure against climate change.)[189] By October 2022, BIA funding exceeded $185 billion, with 6,900 projects in 4,000 communities in all 50 states.[190]

The BIA included the Build America Buy America Act establishing a domestic-content preference for infrastructure projects.[191] Their iron, steel, manufactured products, and other construction materials had to be made in the US.[192] Foreign products required a waiver that generally could not be obtained unless the item was either not produced in the US or using American materials would increase the project's cost by more than 25 percent.[193] These policies were accurately characterized as protectionist by complaining foreign governments.

The Science part of CHIPS authorized increased funding for applied science research at NSF, NIST, and elsewhere (see Chapter 20). The CHIPS part, in addition to supporting the semiconductor industry (see Chapters 26 and 30), set up an all-agency initiative to support R&D in biomanufacturing and the bioeconomy. In September 2022, this was followed by Executive Order 14081, assigning coordination of such programs jointly to the national security advisor, the assistant to the president for economic policy, and the director of the Office of Science and Technology Policy.[194]

The $369 billion IRA encouraged production and purchases of clean-energy technologies.[195] Tax incentives of $270 billion went to firms and consumers.[196] These included tax credits for renewable electricity, solar and wind facilities in low-income communities, nuclear power, and clean manufacturing. There were also cost recovery mechanisms for clean-energy facilities, property, and storage technologies.[197]

The IRA included $43 billion in incentives to lower the cost to consumers of EVs, other zero-emission vehicles, geothermal heating, energy-efficient appliances, roof solar panels, and home batteries.[198] Consumers could get a tax rebate of up to $7,500 for purchasing an EV, but to be eligible, the manufacturer was required to meet three conditions:

- Final assembly had to take place in North America.
- Fifty percent of battery components had to be manufactured in North America.
- Forty percent of critical minerals by value had to be extracted, processed, or recycled in the US or a country with which the US had an FTA.

These percentages were slated to rise over time. They too were accurately attacked by foreign governments as protectionist.[199]

Biden's industrial policy legislation was reinforced by several executive orders:

- EO 13974: Addressing the Threat from Securities Investments That Finance Certain Companies of the People's Republic of China. This strengthened a Trump EO prohibiting Americans from investing in Chinese firms connected to that nation's military and security apparatus.[200]
- EO 14005: Ensuring the Future Is Made in All of America by All of America's Workers. This directed the US government to buy American whenever legal and practicable.[201]

- EO 14017: America's Supply Chains. This mandated investigation and mitigation of supply chain risks in critical industries.[202]
- EO 14081: Advancing Biotechnology and Biomanufacturing Innovation for a Sustainable, Safe, and Secure American Bioeconomy. This enjoined a "whole-of-government approach to advance biotechnology and biomanufacturing towards innovative solutions in health, climate change, energy, food security, agriculture, supply chain resilience, and national and economic security."[203]
- EO 14083: Ensuring Robust Consideration of Evolving National Security Risks by the Committee on Foreign Investment in the United States. This required CFIUS to consider the effect of transactions on supply chains, technological leadership, foreign investment in industry sectors, cybersecurity, and data privacy.[204]
- EO 14104: Federal Research and Development in Support of Domestic Manufacturing and United States Jobs. This directed that "whenever feasible and consistent with applicable law," products resulting from federally funded research be manufactured in the US.[205]
- EO 14105: Addressing United States Investments in Certain National Security Technologies and Products in Countries of Concern. This directed Treasury to issue regulations identifying transactions involving technologies and products potentially threatening national security, specifically artificial intelligence, quantum computing, semiconductors, and microelectronics.[206]
- EO 14110: Safe, Secure, and Trustworthy Development and Use of Artificial Intelligence. This sought to advance and govern the development and use of AI in accord with eight principles and priorities.[207] It included a requirement that companies developing AI tools advise the government of their activities and safety tests, and mandated development of a National Security Memorandum to direct further actions.

These policies were generally well designed and were a huge step forward. But they were confined to a limited subset of industries connected to public health, national security, or climate change, the last category being new at scale with Biden. They did not cover all American industries needing industrial policies, nor were they designed to *serve economic objectives for economic reasons*. However, they broke the taboo that had ruled out explicit, proactive industrial policy for decades, making future, more ambitious actions more likely. Their initial effect came fast, inducing a quadrupling of construction spending for manufacturing facilities between the beginning of 2022 to June 2023, concentrated in computers, electronics, and electrical goods and not occurring in other advanced economies.[208]

Constraining China's Tech Industry

Although new US VC investments in China had fallen dramatically due to political tensions, China's existing penetration of US capital markets began to draw congressional attention.[209] As of 2022, Chinese securities traded on US exchanges or otherwise held by US investors, including through intermediaries, were estimated at up to $1.1 trillion in equity and $100 billion in debt.[210] Many were included in major emerging markets indices and therefore in the index funds that tracked them. These index funds were widely held by exchange-traded funds (ETFs), mutual funds, endowments, insurance companies, and pension funds, including the $720 billion-plus Thrift Savings Plan for federal employees.

Approximately 2,000 Chinese companies were involved, among them some of China's largest state-owned enterprises (see Chapter 7).[211] The SOEs were under the control of the government and the Chinese Communist Party, while many of the private firms competed with US counterparts in key industries. Some made armaments, ships, vehicles, and other systems for the Chinese military, while others were in dual-use industries, such as semiconductors and AI, that supported military, intelligence, police state, forced labor and ethnic repression operations.

Table 18.2 shows some of these firms and the indices that included them. None complied with the auditing and disclosure standards required of publicly traded American companies. Even for the 250 listed on US exchanges, independent reviews of their audits had not been allowed.[212]

Biden kept Trump's tariffs and export restrictions against Chinese industries directly serving its military or producing advanced dual-use technologies. He prohibited firms funded under the CHIPS Act from manufacturing in China and other "countries of concern," namely Russia, North Korea, and Iran. Using CFIUS, the administration restricted Chinese tech investment in the US and began limiting US semiconductor and other high-tech investments in China.[213]

In October 2022, Treasury's Bureau of Industry and Security (BIS) hit China with tough new export controls on advanced computing and semiconductors, including semiconductor manufacturing equipment.[214] In addition, extending a Trump policy, foreign manufacturers using US-made production equipment were prohibited from supplying high-end semiconductors and equipment. According to BIS, "licenses for facilities owned by PRC entities will face a 'presumption of denial,' and facilities owned by multinationals will be decided on a case-by-case basis."[215] BIS added 36 Chinese companies to its Entities List, broadly limiting their access to certain sensitive US hardware, software, materials, and technologies.[216]

Table 18.2 Select problematic Chinese firms in US capital markets[217]

DEFENSE	AEROSPACE	BIOTECH	SOFTWARE & AI
Inner Mongolia First Machinery Group Co., Ltd. 600967.SS — CSI Small Cap / SSE Composite / SSE A Share	**Guizhou Space Appliance Co., Ltd.** 002025.SZ — China Shenzhen SE A Share Index	**BGI Genomics Co., Ltd.** 300676.SZ — MSCI China / MSCI China IMI / MSCI Emerging Markets	**Inspur Software Co., Ltd.** Class A 600756.SS — MSCI China / FTSE China / MSCI Emerging Markets
Addsino Co., Ltd. 000547.SZ — FTSE All-World Emerging / FTSE All-World x US / MSCI AC World ex USA IMI / FTSE China	AECC Aero-Engine Control 000738.SZ — MSCI China IMI / MSCI Emerging Markets / FTSE All-World Emerging / MSCI China / FTSE China		Sugon (Dawning Information Industry Co., Ltd.) 603019.SS — FTSE China / FTSE All-World / FTSE All-World Emerging / SSE Composite
Asian Star Anchor Chain Co., Ltd. Jiangsu (AsAc) 601890.SS — SSE A Share / SSE Composite	AVIC Electromechanical Systems Co., Ltd. 002013.SZ — MSCI China / MSCI China IMI / MSCI EM / FTSE Chin		ChinaSoft International Ltd. 0354.HK — MSCI ACWI / MSCI Emerging Markets
SURVEILLANCE	**SEMICONDUCTORS**	**CONSTRUCTION**	**GREEN ENERGY**
OFILM Group Co., Ltd. 002456.SZ	Advanced Micro-Fabrication Equipment Inc. (AMEC) 688012.SS	XCMG Construction Machinery Co., Ltd. 000425.SZ	LONGi Green Energy Technology Co., Ltd 601012.SS

MSCI China / MSCI China IMI / FTSE China

FiberHome Telecommunication Technologies Co., Ltd.
600498.SS
MSCI China / MSCI Emerging Markets / FTSE China / FTSE All-World Emerging

Wuhan Guide Infrared Co., Ltd.
002414.SZ
MSCI China / MSCI Emerging Markets / FTSE China / MSCI BRIC

MSCI EM / MSCI China / MSCI China IMI / FTSE China

Ingenic Semiconductor
300223.SZ
MSCI China / MSCI China IMI / FTSE China / MSCI EM (Emerging Markets)

Anji Microelectronics Technology (Shanghai) Co., Ltd.
688019.SS
FTSE China Small Cap / SSE Composite / DJ Global World (All)

Indices: FTSE China / MSCI China / FTSE All-World Emerging / MSCI EM (Emerging Markets) / MSCI China

China Nuclear Engineering & Construction Corporation, Ltd. (CNECC)
601611.SS
SSE A Share / CSI Small Cap 500 / SSE Composite

MSCI China / MSCI China IMI / FTSE China

GCL-Poly Energy Holdings
3800.HK
FTSE All World / FTSE Emerging Markets

Daqo New Energy Corp.
DQ.NYSE
MSCI China / MSCI China IMI / FTSE Small Cap China / MSCI Emerging Markets

A year later, the administration doubled down with new rules requiring more US firms to advise the government and obtain licenses in advance of sales to China. The controls also required licenses for third countries that might transship them to China.[218] In March 2023, Holland, home of ASML, maker of the world's most advanced semiconductor manufacturing equipment, announced it would join with the US in curtailing China's access to it.[219] In April, Japan said it would impose export restrictions on 23 chip manufacturing technologies.[220]

One Washington think tank described the sanctions as a "new US policy of actively strangling large segments of the Chinese technology industry – strangling with an intent to kill."[221] One sign of their potency is that Apple abandoned plans for a collaboration with Yangtze Memory Technologies that would have supplied 40 percent of the chips for iPhones made and sold in China.[222] The controls were intended to hinder not just China's semiconductor industry, but also sectors such as artificial intelligence and supercomputing that depend on advanced chips.[223]

In late 2023, the administration wisely withdrew US support for proposed WTO rules that would have required nations to allow largely unrestricted cross-border data flows, banned national requirements for data localization, and banned export controls on source code.[224] These rules would have made it basically impossible for national governments, including the US, to regulate multinational tech giants such as Google, Amazon, Facebook, and Microsoft for purposes of national security, personal privacy, industrial policy, or antitrust.[225]

Real but Limited Progress

How foreign nations would fit into America's new overall turn toward economic nationalism became a huge open question. Biden's overtures to foreign nations did not include any traditional trade agreements. His new Indo-Pacific Economic Partnership and his Americas Partnership for Economic Prosperity were only "frameworks" for engaging foreign nations, not full-fledged trade agreements.[226] The White House described their objectives as "fair and resilient trade; supply chain resilience infrastructure; clean energy and decarbonization; tax and anti-corruption" – not the usual FTA material. And in November 2023, pressure from liberal Democrats such as Senator Sherrod Brown (D-OH) caused Biden to drop the Partnership's trade component entirely.

In September 2021, in an effort to, inter alia, coordinate trade and technology policies better with allies, President Biden and European Commission president Ursula von der Leyden created the Trade and Technology Council.

Cooperation regarding export controls, investment screening, and trade with nonmarket economies (read "China") was part of its remit.[227]

If there is ever a Phase Two deal with China, always doubtful and now even more so, or a similar deal with another country, it would be structured very differently. In the words of Biden's USTR Katherine Tai:

> [W]e continue to have serious concerns with the PRC that were not addressed in the Phase One deal, specifically related to its state-centered and non-market trade practices including Beijing's non-market policies and practices that distort competition by propping up state-owned enterprises, limiting market access, and other coercive and predatory practices in trade and technology . . . Even as we work to enforce the terms of Phase One, we will raise our broader concerns . . . in coordination with our allies and partners. We will defend American economic interests using the full range of tools we have and by developing new tools as needed.[228]

As of 2024, what these "new tools" would be had not been explained. But Ambassador Tai had successfully deflected pressures to revive the Trans-Pacific Trade Partnership or begin negotiations on new trade agreements using the old Bush–Obama playbook. Her tenure as USTR was proving a success.

Biden's trade policy was far from perfect. In the first three years of his presidency, he did not even seriously *try* to reduce the trade deficit, and in 2022, after trade recovered from COVID-19, it exploded to $948 billion.[229] Above all, his administration did nothing about either currency manipulation or misalignment. It gave no sign of understanding that dollar overvaluation was the single largest cause of the deficit and would be a huge headwind for Biden's ambitious new industrial policies. Even outside the administration, the role of private-sector capital flows in causing this overvaluation independently of government manipulation was not widely recognized. Exchange rate management was not even part of the policy debate.

Most of the Washington establishment kept trying to square the circle, clinging to the mantra of free trade but now favoring support and protection for a few key industries. This cognitive dissonance led to contradictory statements, half measures, and stasis. As of mid-2024, as this book went to press, it was uncertain whether the US would keep moving toward the coherent, comprehensive industrial policy, including management of exchange rates to balance trade overall and the selective use of tariffs to control its composition, that it so badly needed.

Part IV
Innovation as a System

The following chapters show that, although usually not acknowledged as such, the US already has quite a lot of effective industrial policy–supporting innovation and, in certain mission-driven sectors, production. This is evidence for our thesis that the US can design and execute successful industrial policy. Equally important, these chapters highlight deficiencies of America's current innovation system. The programs covered are described in some detail to make clear their scope, diversity, and varying mechanisms, showing how innovation requires institutions tailored to the needs of specific industries and technologies. Chapter 19 challenges the widely held belief that innovation comes from the private sector with striking counterexamples. Chapter 20 describes the most-established existing federal programs. Chapter 21 turns to lesser-known, more controversial institutions that exemplify the path we advocate for the US. Chapter 22 looks at advanced manufacturing programs in critical sectors where international rivalry will be particularly intense. Chapter 23 examines the micro-governance – the organization and management of day-to-day operations – of successful agencies in the US and abroad for innovation and its commercialization. Chapter 24 describes the current crisis of the US patent system, today a major negative for US industrial policy, and how to reform it.

19 GOVERNMENTALLY SUPPORTED INNOVATIONS

Bar-code scanners. Disposable diapers. Closed captioning. Cordless vacuums. Memory foam. Scratch-resistant sunglasses. These are merely humble examples of the vast number of post–World War II innovations attributable to US government support. Many others got similar help on the long, complicated path from pure science to finished product – a path whose logic we will examine in detail in the next two chapters.

The examples that follow illustrate, above all, that government supports innovation in many different ways. Sometimes its contribution is only to the pure science on which a new product is based. Other times it deliberately sets out to achieve a technology, pays for its entire development path, and enables commercialization by buying the end product. Government sometimes pays to develop technologies whose main economic value turns out to be different from what was originally envisioned. Sometimes it nurtures private-sector innovation by providing a market for the product before anyone else will buy it. And sometimes government provides only parts of a complex technological mosaic, making it difficult to apportion credit. The implication is that effective innovation policy cannot be one-size-fits-all, but must be tailored to widely differing technological and economic circumstances.

Nuclear Power

Nuclear power accounts for about 20 percent of America's electricity and about half the carbon-free total.[1] Its origins lie in World War II's Manhattan Project to develop atomic weapons. After the war, research continued on more advanced weapons, including the hydrogen bomb. In 1954, Congress passed the Atomic Energy Act, committing the government to developing nuclear technologies for civilian uses. The following year, the Atomic Energy Commission (AEC), which had assumed control of the vast complex of nuclear-related plants built up during the war, announced its Power Reactor Demonstration Program, a partnership with industry to develop a reactor for electricity generation.

America's first commercial nuclear plant opened in 1958 at Shippingport, Pennsylvania. From 1954 to 1962, the AEC spent $1.3 billion, and industry $500 million, developing civilian reactors.[2] The Los Alamos, Oak Ridge, and Idaho National Laboratories were key participants. Widely touted at the time as "too cheap to meter," nuclear power also benefited from policies such as the Price–Anderson Act of 1957, which capped the liability of utilities in case of an accident, helping them raise capital.

More than 100 nuclear plants were built in the US between 1958 and 1973. Then rising costs and public concerns about safety, especially after the accidents at Three Mile Island in 1979 and Chernobyl in 1986, halted orders for new plants for more than three decades. And in 2011, the industry's hopes for a renaissance were dealt a blow by the Fukushima meltdown in Japan.

Today, there is growing support for constructing new facilities and extending the lives of existing ones. Many environmentalists have come around, as shown by their campaigns in 2022 to keep California's last remaining nuclear plant, Diablo Canyon, open. Both industry and the Department of Energy (DOE) are researching new, safer advanced small-modular reactors, which can be built in a factory and trucked complete to their site.

Jet Engines

The federal government has played a major role in the creation and growth of aviation since World War I, partly by supporting the development of jet engines, the enabling technology for modern aircraft (see Chapters 15 and 26).

Microelectronics

Federal support for the most important element of microelectronics, the microprocessor, is discussed in Chapter 26. But the prerequisite of the microprocessor was the transistor, also a sine qua non of modern electronics in its own right. This was invented, in 1947–8, not in a free-market context but at Bell Labs, the research arm of the government-regulated monopoly AT&T. AT&T's research was supported by monopoly profits, a guaranteed market for the commercial products stemming from that research, and a decades-long time horizon. The transistor is thus a prime example of *indirect* federal technology support. AT&T's transistor work also built on military research on germanium and silicon technology for radar during World War II. Government was an important early buyer of transistors, helping the industry get off the ground: The Defense Department funded pilot production lines at AT&T, General Electric, Raytheon, Sylvania, and RCA.[3]

Federal support for the development of modern computers is discussed in Chapter 26. But the earlier computers that laid their foundation also enjoyed federal support. The first electronic digital computer in the US, the vacuum-tube-based ENIAC, was built in 1945 at the University of Pennsylvania by the Army's Ordnance Ballistic Research Laboratory. In 1951, MIT's Jay Forrester, as part of the Navy's Whirlwind I computer project, created the first random-access memory, a key component of all subsequent computers, using magnetic cores. Whirlwind II, in turn, provided many technological precursors for the Air Force's later Semi-Automatic Ground Environment (SAGE) air defense system. SAGE, the largest computer system in the world in the 1950s, introduced fundamentals including keyboard terminals and communication between separate computers.[4] It accounted for 80 percent of IBM's computer revenues from 1952 to 1955 and helped established the firm's global dominance that it held until the PC revolution of the 1980s.[5]

The Internet, Part I: Underlying Technologies

The internet was made possible by decades of direct and indirect government support – not just for the internet but also for its underlying technologies. There were five distinct phases in its development.

During the first phase (roughly 1960–70) networking was invented. One key innovation was packet switching, which breaks up messages into "packets" that can travel by separate routes for reassembly at their destination. Paul Baran at America's RAND Corporation and Donald Davies at Britain's National Physical Laboratory, funded by their respective governments, invented this concept.[6] The resulting first version of the internet, ARPANET, connecting 61 computers as of the late 1970s, was funded by DOD's Advanced Research Projects Agency (ARPA/DARPA, see Chapter 23).[7]

During the second phase (mid-1970s), more universities and defense research organizations joined the network. A key development was Transmission Control Protocol/Internet Protocol (TCP/IP), used to this day, created by Vint Cerf and Bob Kahn with DARPA funding.[8] (IP finds the address to which data is to be sent; TCP sends it.) During this period, the National Science Foundation (NSF) also funded research on solid-state physics, glass, and related subjects that aided development of the optical fibers that eventually would carry the internet's data.

The third phase (1977–85) saw the internet penetrate the commercial market, driven by the spread of desktop computing. Apple's first computer appeared in 1976 and the IBM PC five years later. In 1978, a Small Business Investment Company supported by the Small Business Administration invested $500,000 in Apple.[9]

During the fourth phase (1985–91) the internet expanded, due largely to three events:

1. In 1985, the NSF adopted TCP/IP for its network of computers at universities and other research institutions.
2. Email, networking's first "killer app," spread, giving corporations, universities, and other institutions reason to expand their networks.
3. The internet developed governance institutions, initially federally sponsored, including the Internet Engineering Task Force (IETF) and the Internet Assigned Numbers Authority. A public–private partnership, the Internet Society, was formed in 1992 to oversee its growth.

Of ongoing importance was the maintenance of *consistent but open* standards, neither under the proprietary control of one company nor fragmented into incompatible private standards.

During the fifth phase (1991–present), the system opened to the public. In 1991, after lobbying by business interests, the NSF abandoned its former policy of banning commercial uses to conserve a then very limited resource. By 1995, operation of the system's main long-distance arteries had been transferred to private firms.[10]

The Internet, Part II: The World Wide Web

The key enabling technologies of the World Wide Web are Hypertext Markup Language, which specifies how its pages are written, and Hypertext Transfer Protocol, which specifies how they are transmitted. Both were developed, with assistance from IETF, by Englishman Tim Berners-Lee, working in Switzerland at the European Organization for Nuclear Research funded by 23 European governments.[11]

Browsers were essential for widespread adoption of the Web. The first commercially available one, Mosaic, was developed by Marc Andreesen, a grad student at the University of Illinois working at its NSF-sponsored National Center for Supercomputing Applications, and Eric Bina.[12] In 1995, Andreessen's firm Netscape implemented Hypertext Transfer Protocol Secure (HTTPS), which, by enabling secure communications, made web commerce viable.

HTTPS is based on public-key encryption, initially invented at Britain's GCHQ spy agency in 1970 but kept secret and not used due to the limited computing power of the day.[13] It was reinvented, and elaborated into a usable technology, in 1977 at MIT by Ronald Rivest, Adi Shamir, and Leonard Adleman.[14] They were not directly supported by government for this specific project, but NSF grants funded their lab–another form of indirect support.[15]

Google was created by Stanford computer science grad students Sergey Brin and Larry Page while working on the Stanford Digital Library Project (SDLP) in 1996. This project, funded mainly by NSF but also by DARPA, NASA, and corporate partners, aimed to develop a universal digital library. Brin and Page developed an algorithm, PageRank, which formed the basis for a search engine, BackRub. They continued to work on their search engine at SDLP using NSF-funded equipment, then obtained private investment to commercialize it.

Smartphones

The smartphones of today were made possible by accumulated decades of federally funded innovations.[16] The resistive touchscreen was invented in 1971 at the University of Kentucky by George Hurst as an accidental byproduct of his work at Oak Ridge National Laboratory.[17] The first screen that could register multiple touches at once was created in 1984 by Bob Boie at Bell Labs, and in 1999 full multi-touch functionality was developed with NSF funding by Wayne Westerman and John Elias at the University of Delaware. Smartphones' Complementary Metal–Oxide–Semiconductor (CMOS) image sensors were invented in 1992 at NASA's Jet Propulsion Laboratory at Caltech during work on cameras for satellites.[18] Their thin-film transistor LCD displays descend in part from work done at Westinghouse in the 1970s with Army funding.[19] Their speech-recognition capability is discussed later under Artificial Intelligence. Their signal processing technology depends upon Fast Fourier Transform algorithms, also discussed later. Their lithium-ion batteries are discussed under Electric Cars and Advanced Batteries. Their GPS is discussed in Chapter 26.

Solar Energy

Bell Labs, which produced the first photovoltaic cells for government satellites, produced the first usable version in 1954. NASA was heavily involved in their later development, including for military satellites.

In 1974, Congress passed the Solar Heating and Cooling Demonstration Act, mandating installation of solar heating and cooling systems (mostly non-photovoltaic) in federal buildings by 1977. It also passed the Solar Energy Research, Development and Demonstration Act, establishing a new federal office, the Solar Energy Research Institute, which became today's National Renewable Energy Laboratory (NREL).

For decades, solar cells' cost per kilowatt was too high for mass use. So, in 2011, the DOE announced its SunShot initiative aiming at a 75 percent reduction by decade's end. This initiative built on previous DOE investments of $1 billion in solar cell R&D, much in collaboration with industry.[20] SunShot met 90 percent of its original goal in only five years, so in 2016 a new initiative, SunShot 2030, was launched, aiming at further 50 percent reduction by 2030.[21] In 2019, a new world record for efficiency – 47 percent – was set by cells developed by NREL.[22]

Wind Turbines

Thanks largely to federal support, the cost of wind-generated electricity fell 90 percent from 1980 to 2000, and it is today cost-competitive in many contexts.[23] By 2021, wind was America's largest source of renewable electricity, accounting for 32 percent of the growth in electricity-generation capacity that year and employing more than 120,000 people.[24]

During the 1980s, government funded a Big Science push by NASA and DOE for large, high-tech wind turbines. It was relatively unsuccessful, in part because it was detached from the private sector's operational experience. But DOE also made another effort, focused on component innovations for smaller turbines and drawing on manufacturers to inform its research agenda. This effort succeeded, producing such key innovations as twisted blades and special-purpose airfoils. In all, government helped fund 7 of the era's 12 major advances.[25]

Tax credits for wind power and the Public Utilities Regulatory Policy Act (PURPA) of 1978 also helped. PURPA required utilities to buy power from renewable electricity producers at "avoided cost" – that is, what they would otherwise have had to spend to generate it. In the 1980s, most of the market was in California, where generous state implementation of PURPA reduced risks for producers by requiring utilities to offer long-term contracts. But state and federal incentives were discontinued at the end of the 1980s, leading to a stagnating market.

In the early 1990s, Washington enacted new policies, including a 1.5 cents per kilowatt-hour tax credit and NREL's Advanced Wind Turbine Program. In 1993, DOE built the National Wind Technology Center near

Boulder, Colorado, now the nation's premier wind energy research facility. By 2015, money from the American Recovery and Reinvestment Act of 2009 had played a significant role in tripling wind and solar electricity generation.[26] Today, America's position in wind turbines is threatened by Chinese competition using stolen intellectual property and huge subsidies that dwarf support provided to US competitors.

Electric Vehicles and Advanced Batteries

High-capacity batteries are the enabling technology of electric cars. They are also required for wind and solar to become dominant sources of power because neither is available 24/7. The federal government has funded vehicle battery R&D since 1976, when Congress passed the Electric and Hybrid Vehicle Research, Development, and Demonstration Act. From 1976 to 2007, 222 patents deriving from DOE-funded research were granted for batteries, ultracapacitor storage devices, and supporting components.[27] The government also funded private organizations such as the US Advanced Battery Consortium and the Council for Automotive Research.

Inventor Stanford Ovshinsky, founder of the Ovonic Battery Company, whose work was partly funded by DOE, created the first practicable nickel-metal hydride (NiMH) battery in 1993.[28] General Motors purchased Ovonic's patents in 1994 and NiMH technology was used in many early electric and hybrid cars.

Lithium-ion batteries, which have largely superseded NiMH, were made possible by the invention of lithium cobalt oxide cathode materials by John Goodenough in 1980 at Oxford, England. Later, at the University of Texas, with funding from NSF and DOE, he discovered less expensive materials, making such batteries practical. The Advanced Photon Source at the DOE's Argonne National Lab then allowed scientists to better understand the reactions that happen in an NiMH battery, enabling a safer, cheaper, higher-capacity, more durable version.[29]

But the resulting products have not been manufactured in the US. As one team of analysts notes:

> U.S. battery companies including Duracell and Energizer opted out of volume manufacturing these new products – not because of domestic labor costs, but because of fears of high upfront investments, long development cycles, and a lack of access to consumers of rechargeable batteries. Countries in East Asia saw an opportunity for job creation and decided to help homegrown firms overcome these hurdles. They provided facilities, loans, and other assistance to establish domestic

manufacturing in the field. It worked. Today, US firms have less than 2% of market share in the multi-billion automotive lithium-ion battery industry.[30]

In 2017, the Pacific Northwest National Laboratory in Washington State played a key role in improving the vanadium redox battery that is well suited to very-large-scale applications, including the electric grid.[31] A US startup, UniEnergy Technologies, then set out to commercialize it. Then, in violation of its own rules, DOE licensed the technology to the Chinese firm Dalian Rongke Power, which then became the dominant worldwide manufacturer of these batteries. UniEnergy went bankrupt in 2021.[32]

Solid-State Lighting

The principal solid-state lighting technologies are light-emitting diodes (LEDs) and organic light-emitting diodes (OLEDs). LEDs were first invented in 1961 by researchers at Texas Instruments – narrowly beating out RCA, GE, IBM, Bell Labs, and MIT's Lincoln Labs – but only in infrared. A year later, Nick Holonyak at GE, working under an Air Force contract, created the first visible-light LED, in red.[33] Yellow and green soon followed. The next key innovation, by Shuji Nakamura at Japan's Nichia Corporation in the early 1990s, was blue, which made white LEDs, and thus lighting applications, possible. A number of firms working on this technology, such as Cree (now Wolfspeed) and GE, have received federal funding. Many continue privately funded research today. In 2003, DOE's Next Generation Lighting Industry Alliance was formed as a partnership of government, industry, academia, and national labs, including Sandia National Laboratories and the Pacific Northwest National Laboratory.

Fracking

Federal support for the initial development of the oil and gas industries is discussed in Chapter 15.

Hydraulic fracturing has been used to extract natural gas from limestone and sandstone since the 1950s.[34] It was long known that shale rock throughout the country contained plentiful, albeit hard to extract, natural gas, and shale was first fracked in 1965.[35] But economically feasible fracking at scale – sufficient to turn the US by 2019 into a net petroleum exporter for the first time in 75 years – was only achieved after decades of public and private research into a *package* of new technologies, including fracking itself, horizontal drilling, micro-seismic imaging, and underground mapping.[36]

During the 1970s, a perceived energy crisis and declining US natural gas output induced interest in increasing domestic petroleum production. Federal efforts included the Energy Research and Development Administration's Eastern Gas Shales Project, begun in 1976, which carried out demonstration projects with universities and gas-drilling companies.[37] DOE's National Energy Technology Laboratory helped develop key fracking technologies, including foam fracturing, oriented coring, fractographic analysis, and large-volume hydraulic fracturing.[38] In 1977, it first successfully demonstrated massive hydraulic fracturing in shale. Working with a private company, Mitchell Energy, it drilled the first horizontal shale well and extracted gas.[39] In 1998, Mitchell's engineers applied an innovative drilling technique, slick water fracturing, which brought costs down to commercial viability.[40]

Fracking was developed in part because DOE's *portfolio* approach funded research on a wide range of possible solutions, not just the most promising. In the words of one report,

> Even experts within the Department of Energy were skeptical that large quantities of oil and gas could ever be extracted economically from shale. After the oil embargo, the vast majority of fossil energy innovation funding spent by the US government was on underground coal gasification and synthetic fuels, either from coal or from oil shales. Even within the niche of unconventional oil and gas exploration, most experts believed that tight sands gas would play a larger role than shale ever would. And yet, in the end, it was the red-headed stepchild that became king.[41]

Key fracking technologies came from outside the petroleum industry. For example, the underground mapping required to find the oil and gas came from unrelated research into geothermal energy.[42]

Biotechnology

Biotechnology is based upon recombinant DNA (rDNA) technology, which enables transplantation of genes from one organism to another. This was first achieved in 1973 by Herbert Boyer at the University of California at San Francisco and Stanley Cohen at Stanford, both supported by NSF and the National Institutes of Health (NIH). In 1976, Boyer founded Genentech, one of the first biotech firms.

By then, NIH was funding 123 biotech projects.[43] Viewing rDNA as likely to yield progress against cancer, by 1987 it had invested more than $100 million.[44] This support spurred academic interest and private-sector investment, enhanced by the Bayh–Dole Act of 1980. This legislation accelerated technology commercialization by allowing researchers working under federal contracts to own their inventions. And the Stevenson–Wydler Technology Innovation Act that same year made it easier for federal labs to transfer their technology to nonfederal entities.

Between 1995 and 2008, NIH's total funding nearly tripled, from $11 to $29 billion, with a dramatic impact on biotech. Thirteen of the 15 American-developed "blockbuster" (more than $1 billion in annual sales) biotech drugs received federal support for their discovery, development, or clinical trials.[45] For 8 of these, the government either funded university research or NIH scientists made the key discoveries. (A state-level effort to nurture the biotech industry is described in Chapter 29.)

Human Genome Sequencing

In the early 1980s, scientists were slowly deciphering the human genetic code. Then two events caused NIH to undertake mapping the entire thing, the "genome."[46] In 1986, at Caltech, Leroy Hood and Lloyd Smith invented the first automated DNA sequencing machine, and that same year DOE allocated $5.3 million to its own effort aimed at understanding how radiation affects the genome.[47] DOE created genome research centers at three of its national laboratories: Lawrence Berkeley, Lawrence Livermore, and Los Alamos.

Launched in 1990 and costing $2.7 billion over 13 years, the Human Genome Project (HGP) was implemented jointly by NIH and DOE. Teams were housed at MIT, the University of Michigan, the University of California at San Francisco, Baylor College of Medicine in Texas, and Washington University School of Medicine in St. Louis. The goal was a complete description of the 3 billion "base pairs" that make up the genome and its 20,000–25,000 genes.

HGP was one of the most important basic research projects in the history of biology. It was a major success, completed two years ahead of schedule and under budget. A competing, lower-cost effort, launched by Celera Genomics and initially aiming to keep portions of its results proprietary, spurred HGP to speed up. In 2003, NIH researchers released their final draft, guaranteeing future researchers free and open access, with incalculable benefits for medicine, biotechnology, and the life sciences.

Other Innovations

In the 1980s and 1990s, NSF-funded research developed important mathematical algorithms, including the so-called reverse auction in which many sellers propose prices to a single buyer. The FCC has since used this technique to repurchase parts of the radio spectrum from television stations in order to resell them to mobile broadband companies.[48] The General Services Administration now has a reverse auction platform for federal agencies to purchase office products, equipment, and services.[49] And private companies such as FreeMarkets Inc. manage reverse auctions for corporate clients.

Another federally funded project focused on matching algorithms to pair producers and consumers of a good or service for which there is no market. Pioneering studies funded by the Office of Naval Research were conducted in 1962 by David Gale at Brown University and Lloyd Shapley at the RAND Corporation and later at UCLA. In the 1980s and 1990s, economist Alvin Roth applied Gale and Shapley's algorithm to several practical situations, notably kidney donation, as under the existing inefficient system, patients unnecessarily died waiting.[50] Roth and Shapely shared the Nobel in Economics for this research in 2012.

Digital devices like smartphones rely upon algorithms known as Fast Fourier Transforms to convert analog radio waves into digital information. The most common such algorithms ultimately derive from work by Princeton mathematician John Tukey on seismic detection of Soviet nuclear tests.[51] DARPA also funded two mathematicians who developed the Fast Multipole Method algorithm, which was first used to identify aircraft by their radar signatures. This algorithm has since been used for computer simulations of blood flow, a good example of the unpredictable cross-pollinations of research.

Magnetic Resonance Imaging (MRI) technology was built on NIH- and NSF-funded research into the underlying physics.[52] Starting in the 1950s, the technology itself was developed with NSF and NIH funding at several universities.[53] Raymond Damadian at Downstate Medical Center in Brooklyn, New York discovered that tissues stimulated by a magnetic field emit different signals and built the first scanner. Paul Lauterbur at Stony Brook University in New York State developed the first NMR image, sharing a 2003 Nobel with Peter Mansfield of the UK, who patented the technology and wrote a seminal paper on image formation. To be fair, Swiss Richard Ernst of the private firm Varian Associates, a 1991 Nobelist, developed Fourier Transform NMR, noise decoupling, and other key techniques.[54]

Artificial Intelligence

Federally funded research played a key role in AI's development. In 1956, Air Force funding of the RAND Corporation enabled Herbert Simon and

Allen Newell to create the first AI computer program, the Logic Theorist, which could prove mathematical theorems. The field took off in 1963, when MIT received $2.2 million from ARPA, which funded most fundamental AI research over the next three decades.[55]

DARPA's Speech Understanding Research program, begun in 1971, produced Carnegie Mellon University's Harpy system, with a vocabulary of 1,000 words.[56] DARPA's ongoing support for speech recognition research drove progress into the 2000s. In 1990, Dragon Dictate, a commercial speech recognition system, was developed by James and Janet Baker, who did their underlying research at Carnegie Mellon with DARPA money. Another initiative, the $150 million Cognitive Assistant that Learns and Organizes, was launched in 2003. The Stanford Research Institute led the effort, resulting in Siri, acquired by Apple in 2010.

DARPA's Strategic Computing Initiative (SCI) was a 10-year, $1 billion project, launched in 1983, that illustrates how technology research can succeed even when it nominally fails. Inspired by Japan's Fifth Generation Computing project (see Chapter 5), SCI set the ambitious goal of humanlike intelligence, including abilities such as driving a car.[57] It failed because its objectives were far in advance of available computing power. But its research significantly advanced many key technologies, laying the foundations for the video cameras, laser scanners, and inertial navigation systems now used in self-driving vehicles. (Specific funding for AI, as opposed to the broader SCI, was modest, totaling only $44 million in 1984, rising to $86 million by 1988.)[58]

Federal AI funding rose dramatically as the technology flowered and became publicly visible in the 2020s. The Biden administration's 2023 National Artificial Intelligence Strategic Plan designated it a key technology.[59] Funding totaled $2.4 billion in 2021, $2.9 billion in 2022, $2.9 billion in 2023, and $3.1 billion (requested) for 2024.[60] Most went to 11 agencies, with 30 percent to DOD, 26 percent to NSF, and 21 percent to NIH.[61] In 2023, Biden issued Executive Order 14110 on Safe, Secure, and Trustworthy Development and Use of Artificial Intelligence, beginning the process of creating the regulatory framework required for this potentially dangerous technology.[62]

The Failures

We look next at some *failures* of governmentally supported technology development. The big lesson here is that the causes of such failures are not mysterious or random, but understandable and thus potentially avoidable.

Supersonic Airliners

The supersonic Anglo-French Concorde was a technological triumph but a commercial failure, kept in service by British Airways and Air France from 1976 to 2003 solely for prestige. But when development began in 1962, it seemed to make sense. Funded by the British and French governments, it was an attempt to seize a commanding position in what was widely expected to be the next generation of airliners. This forecast was sufficiently plausible that even the USSR built a (much inferior) supersonic jetliner, the Tu-144, and in 1961, the FAA's chief administrator, Najeeb Halaby, proclaimed such aircraft inevitable.[63]

In 1963, Pan American Airways announced an order for six Concordes. President Kennedy, fearing that Britain and France would steal an entire generation of airliner sales, was jolted into announcing the very next day that the US government would help fund an American competitor.[64] The FAA projected a market for more than 500 such planes by 1990.[65]

With a production target of 1970, a contest was organized to choose the firm to receive federal support. Major player Douglas Aircraft concluded that the plane would never be viable and declined to participate. Preliminary designs were submitted in 1964. Boeing's 2707 won out over alternatives from Lockheed and North American-Rockwell. Despite the absence of a final design, airline orders started coming in.

Boeing's program went through years of changes in its schedule, technology, and in the declining percentage of its funding that the firm, as opposed to the taxpayer, would provide. Even so, successive studies attempting to demonstrate its economic viability depended on performance assumptions that none of its proposed designs met.[66]

The plane was doomed by its high fuel cost per passenger mile, inevitable for an aircraft whose speed required a narrow fuselage, thus limited seating, and extremely powerful engines. It could not fly over land because of sonic booms and lacked the range to cross the Pacific. Hopes that its high speed would enable more trips per day ran afoul of night-time curfews and customer preferences.

Commercial service began in 1976, but its operators soon discovered that the number of passengers willing to pay more than $7,000 in 2022 dollars to fly from New York to London or Paris was very small. Even at pre-1973 oil prices, it would not have been viable, and when oil prices rose, its economics got even worse.

As early as 1964, the Concorde's commercial viability had been questioned by officials in Britain, and the UK attempted to quit the project. But Anglo-French politics and financial liability under the project's governing treaty intervened, and London stayed in.[67]

In 1963, President Johnson rejected an independent study that had concluded that the 2707 was not viable. Nixon rejected a similar study.[68]

In 1971, after eight years of development, the House killed the program 215 to 204. House Minority Leader Gerald Ford repeated the AFL-CIO's assertion that "If you vote for the SST, you are ensuring 13,000 jobs today plus 50,000 jobs in the second tier, and 150,000 jobs each year over the next 10 years."[69] But the project had lost economic credibility. Boeing's demand for even more government funding was the final nail in its coffin.[70]

The total federal contribution came to $920 million.[71] If the program had respected the criteria set by the FAA at its start, it would have been cancelled in 1968, when Boeing's proposed design fell short of the required range and payload.[72] But, even though it took longer than ideal, Congress did ultimately make the right decision. Nixon objected, calling it "a mortal blow for our aerospace industry for years to come."[73] But the blow never came because the impressive technology had no commercial utility.

Synthetic Fuels

The rise in oil prices after the Arab Oil Boycott of 1973 and the Iranian Revolution of 1979 inspired federal initiatives to develop domestic energy sources. As noted, some, such as photovoltaics, wind power, and fracking eventually made game-changing contributions to America's energy supply. The Synthetic Fuels Corporation (SFC) did not.

Established by Congress in 1980, SFC's goal was to make gas, gasoline, and other products from America's abundant supply of coal. Initially authorized funding of more than $200 billion in 2022 dollars over 12 years, it aimed to replace almost half of America's oil imports by the early 1990s.[74]

Synfuels were credible at the time. The respected business group the Committee for Economic Development issued a report in favor in 1979, and the consensus was that oil would reach $115 per barrel by 1990, making synfuels price competitive.[75] Petroleum from coal was a known technology used by Germany during World War II. For decades, the DOE had researched production methods and built pilot plants to validate them.

But the challenges were considerable. The proposed production scale was 100 times what had ever been done before. Because the massive investments required were judged too risky for the private sector on its own, SFC was slated to engage in joint ventures with industry, offering subsidized loans for plant construction and guaranteed governmental purchases of the output.

During SFC's first two years, cost projections came in above natural equivalents, but close enough for the program to remain credible.[76] But when oil prices fell, the gap became unbridgeable. No plausible technological advance could overcome the fact that breaking down coal was intrinsically more expensive than extracting petroleum already formed by nature. The Corporation thus struggled to find projects meeting funding criteria. Out of about 100 proposals, it funded only 2 before the entire program was cancelled in 1986.[77] It had spent about 5 percent of its initially planned budget.

Looked at one way, this cancellation was a good outcome: The program had been launched when it appeared rational, then terminated when the facts changed. The money wasted on a dead end was not excessive given the huge scale of the problem it aimed to solve. If oil prices had stayed high, SFC might have eventually made a major contribution to the nation's energy supply, and the program's inefficiencies and mistakes would have been remembered as minor irritants.

Still, some experts have argued that it should have been obvious from the start that synfuels would never be economically viable.[78] And certain counterfactuals present themselves. What if SFC's budget had been spent on accelerating development of fracking, the technology that eventually did deliver vast quantities of domestic petroleum? DOE did do some fracking research at the time, but could this technology's emergence have been accelerated by a decade with greater effort? Could fracking have been judged *in 1980* to be more likely to pan out than synthetic fuels? Should we be spending more money not on research itself but on *figuring out which research path to follow?*

The Breeder Reactor

Conventional nuclear power plants extract only about 1 percent of the energy in their fuel. As a result, it was estimated in the 1950s and 1960s that America's domestic uranium reserves would last only a few decades if the nation kept building nuclear plants at its then rapid pace. Unless, that is, it developed the "breeder" reactor, so called because as it runs, it converts the non-fissionable U-238 that makes up most of its fuel into fissionable plutonium. A complete "fuel cycle" based on breeder reactors can, in principle, extract close to 100 percent of the fuel's energy.

The breeder thus appeared an attractive solution. But it is a difficult, expensive technology. Plutonium is more toxic and harder to handle than uranium, and breeder reactors use coolants such as liquid sodium metal rather than water. Beginning in 1969, the federal government spent more than $5 billion, focusing on a demonstration plant at Clinch River, Tennessee. But the program was cancelled by a 56–40 Senate vote in 1983. Several economic factors combined to end it. (A significant noneconomic factor was the nuclear proliferation risks of plutonium.)

First, more uranium reserves were discovered in the US and world-wide, pushing out the projected exhaustion date beyond policymakers' time horizons. These discoveries also pulled down the price of uranium in the short run.[79] Cheap newly mined uranium would price "bred" plutonium out of the market, so a breeder program would not be profitable for decades.

Second, America stopped building new nuclear plants, partly because of slowing growth in electricity consumption and partly because of safety fears after the Three Mile Island accident of 1979. With less need for fuel, uranium exhaustion receded even farther. (In the late 1960s, the AEC projected the US would have 1,000 reactors by 2000. We ended up with 103.)

Third, the program was done in by repeated cost overruns, a problem that has bedeviled *all* types of reactors in the US. Each overrun both antagonized Congress and worsened the projected economics. As commercial viability slipped beyond reach, the program was redefined away from immediate applications and toward more speculative, longer-term research.[80]

The US has not had a working breeder reactor since the National Reactor Testing Station in Idaho was shut down in 1994. Russia has two in commercial operation, and research reactors still exist in countries – Russia, India, Japan, and China – with plans (of varying degrees of seriousness) to develop the technology.[81]

Reading today the reports that led to abandoning the breeder, it is ironic to see the date 2020 repeatedly used as shorthand for so far in the future as to be irrelevant. Was the breeder a missed opportunity to obtain an almost limitless supply of carbon-free energy from a technology already known?[82] Perhaps this need will be filled by other technologies soon enough – or perhaps it will not, illustrating how technology-development policies depend on accurate assessments of the trajectories of *other* technologies. Nearly 40 years after its cancellation, with the urgency of climate change better understood, it looks increasingly like abandoning the breeder was a mistake.[83] The key lessons are not technological, but for how such decisions should be made.

20 FEDERAL SCIENCE AND TECHNOLOGY PROGRAMS

Innovation is required for economic growth and national security. We thus doubly depend on the strength of our *national innovation system*, meaning all the public and private institutions and policies that encourage, facilitate, fund, and execute the development and deployment of technology. Private firms are central players, but federal and state agencies, programs, and labs are key enablers and partners. Technical standards bodies, entrepreneurs, and the science and technology workforce are also important elements. The Silicon Valley startups that many people think of as synonymous with innovation are thus only the tip of a far larger iceberg.

America's national innovation system dates back to the country's founding, developed in earnest in the nineteenth century, and flowered after World War II. It was until recently the best in the world, leading in everything from government-funded universities to corporate research laboratories to venture capital. But in recent decades, it has become less globally competitive because:

1. Technological and economic change made many legacy parts of the system obsolescent.
2. Funding of the governmental parts of the system did not grow proportionately to increasing need.
3. The offshoring of American manufacturing removed much of the foundations of private-sector innovation.
4. Higher standards were set by rivals as other countries improved their innovation systems.

In the post–World War II period, Europe and Japan produced the first national innovation systems rivaling America's, followed by Taiwan, South Korea, and then China.

R&D intensity is R&D as a percentage of GDP. In 2021 – the most recent data available – three nations ranked higher than the US at 3.5 percent: Taiwan at 3.8, South Korea at 4.9, and Israel at 5.6. (China was at 2.4 but rising fast.) The OECD average was 2.7, while Germany and Japan scored 3.1 and 3.3. In absolute dollars, the US led at $710 billion, followed by China at $620 billion, Japan at $172 billion, Germany at $129 billion, South Korea at $110 billion, and the UK at $84 billion.[1]

In continually upgrading its innovation system to keep it internationally competitive, every country faces challenges specific to its circumstances and history. Those the US faces today are:

1. Its system, compared to those of its rivals, is institutionally fragmented, with no single government agency or coordinated group thereof accountable for its overall strategy and health.
2. Because its system mostly developed indirectly to serve noneconomic goals such as national security (see Chapter 26), policymakers and the public only dimly grasp that innovation for economic purposes is a necessary responsibility of government.
3. Because its system remains strong in highly visible areas like biopharma and software, there is a widespread if lessening misperception that the entire system is healthy and that the methods used in these areas are sufficient for the entire system.

Where Does Innovation Come From?

There are five standard models for understanding national innovation systems. None is sufficient on its own but, taken together they provide an analytical framework for sound policy.[2] We will look in detail at the first two in this chapter and the others in the next:

1. The pipeline model
2. The extended pipeline model
3. The induced innovation model
4. Manufacturing-led innovation
5. Innovation organizations

The Pipeline Model

The pipeline model views basic scientific research as the main driver of innovation. It assumes that basic research plus the free market will over time *automatically* cause economically valuable innovations to appear. The steps are illustrated in Figure 20.1.

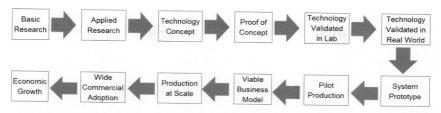

Figure 20.1 The innovation pipeline

"Basic research" in Figure 20.1 refers to investigation into laws of nature with no specific useful application in mind. "Applied research" means such investigation to solve a technological problem. "Pilot production" refers to test manufacturing of the product, generally at small scale and without assembly lines or other methods of mass production.[3]

Reality, of course, is far more complicated, with intermediate stages and arrows sometimes running in reverse. But this model is still a useful first approximation. FDR's science advisor Vannevar Bush, dean of MIT's engineering school and founder of Raytheon, argued for it in his seminal 1945 report, "Science: The Endless Frontier."

> In the nineteenth century, Yankee mechanical ingenuity, building largely upon the basic discoveries of European scientists, could greatly advance the technical arts. Now the situation is different. A nation which depends upon others for its new basic scientific knowledge will be slow in its industrial progress and weak in its competitive position in world trade, regardless of its mechanical skill.[4]

The pipeline model has dominated America's understanding of government's proper role in innovation ever since. It is sometimes referred to as a "technology push" as opposed to a "demand pull" model, because changing technological possibilities created by scientific advances supply its causal impulse. Everything else is assumed to be taken care of by the private sector.

Federal Research Funding

After serving as director of the Office of Scientific Research and Development during World War II, Bush pushed for growth in the federal basic research infrastructure. This led to establishment of the National Science Foundation (NSF) in 1950 and huge federal investment, by way of this and other agencies, in basic research to this day. Federally funded university programs and federally owned research institutions remain the main locations of basic science. This funding has been relatively uncontentious, receiving broad bipartisan support.

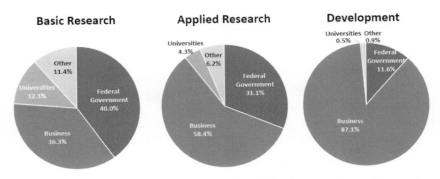

Figure 20.2 Basic research, applied research, and development by funder 2021[5]

Almost half of basic research is conducted by academic institutions. Two thirds of academic R&D goes to basic research, with applied research and then development receiving smaller but growing shares.[6] As shown in Figure 20.3, 1980 was the first year that business funded more R&D ($31 billion) than the federal government ($30 billion), and its share has grown since. As innovations move through the pipeline, the public-sector contribution diminishes and the private-sector contribution increases. In 2021, the federal government funded 40 percent of basic research, 31 percent of applied research, and only 12 percent of development (see Figure 20.2).

The Extended Pipeline Model

The private sector is not always able to translate basic research into usable products, so government must also support later stages of the pipeline. Since World War II, it has often done so, sometimes all the way to creating the initial markets for new products. This is the extended pipeline model.

For 80 years, federal support for *all* the steps of the innovation pipeline has been the major source of technologically radical, economically significant innovations. Above all, it has been the source of innovations that the private sector probably would not have created on its own, would have taken decades longer to deliver, or might have produced in another country, resulting in the resulting industry taking root overseas.

A business model premised on selling a currently unknown product based on a not yet developed technology 20 years in the future is unlikely to attract investors. But government agencies can act on time horizons this long and longer. They can also fund technologies that are hard themselves to

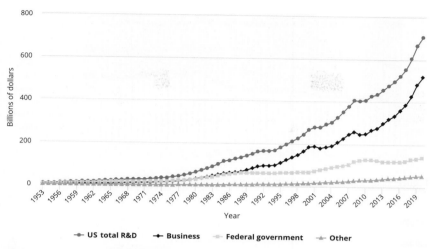

Figure 20.3 US extended pipeline R&D by source of funds 1953–2020[7]

monetize but that serve as enablers or platforms for products or services that can be monetized – the classic example being the internet.

Applied research and subsequent technology development are funded by government through agencies including the Department of Defense (DOD), the National Institutes of Health (NIH), the Department of Energy (DOE), the National Aeronautics and Space Administration (NASA), the Department of Agriculture (USDA), the National Institute of Standards and Technologies (NIST), and the National Science Foundation (NSF). They carry out this work using their own labs plus external contracts with universities, nonprofits, and for-profit firms. The breakdown of extended-pipeline spending by technological field is shown in Figure 20.4. Its distribution by agency in Figure 20.5.

One reason for the extended pipeline's success is that it can include actual production paid for by federal procurement, which totaled $705 billion in 2022.[8] DOD accounts for 62 percent of this and is especially potent because it oversees institutions suited to each stage of the pipeline.[9] The Defense Advanced Research Projects Agency (DARPA) can focus on early-stage breakthroughs while later R&D is led by the individual military services, including their Federally Funded Research and Development Centers (FFRDCs), for engineering, prototyping, demonstration, and testing. The technology is then transferred to a defense contractor and DOD buys the resulting weapons. Other agencies have analogous but more limited capabilities.

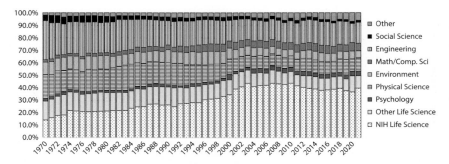

Figure 20.4 Extended pipeline percentage support by discipline 1970–2021[10]

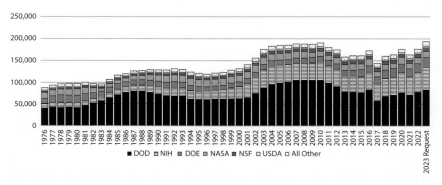

Figure 20.5 Trends in R&D by agency (in billions of constant FY 2022 dollars)[11]

Federal Science and Technology Programs

Federal science and technology agencies differ in their statute-defined missions and in which stages of the pipeline they implement.

NSF and NIH emphasize investigator-initiated, peer-reviewed pure research – though practical applicability is often a funding consideration and these agencies help support application of their discoveries.

Almost all other federal innovation agencies, such as DOD, DOE, and NASA, are "mission oriented." Their research focuses on particular practical objectives, such as defense, space, or energy, though they also fund some fundamental research.

Federal agencies conduct about a quarter of their basic research on an "intramural," in-house basis, using scientists and engineers who are federal employees, though often in government-owned, contractor-operated (GO CO) labs. They also fund "extramural" research by public and private universities, industry labs, and nongovernmental research institutions. The intramural/extramural split varies by agency (see Table 20.1).

Table 20.1 Federal basic R&D by agency and performer 2022 in millions of dollars[12]

Agency	Total	Internal	External		
			Business	Academic	Nonprofit
USDA	1,459	850	15	539	48
DOC	287	268	6	10	3
DOD	2,977	701	510	1,602	103
DOE	5,947	4,875	68	972	8
HHS	21,412	3,517	1,307	12,471	3,499
NASA	4,589	1,680	1,304	965	625
NSF	6,050	321	317	5,113	262
TOTAL	43,791	13,165	3,557	21,373	4,557

Funding Trends

Federal R&D burgeoned with the Cold War and then further with the space program (see Chapters 16 and 26).[13] It peaked at 12 percent of federal spending in 1965 then dropped steadily, reaching 4.4 percent by 1983. There it remained relatively stable until 2010, when it started falling again, reaching 2.4 percent by 2021. With 2022's CHIPS and Science Act, it rose back up to 3 percent in 2022 and a projected 2.9 percent for 2023, but as of mid-2024, it is still unclear how much of the dramatic increases *authorized* by 2022's CHIPS Act will actually be appropriated.[14]

Since the mid-2000s, funding has been volatile due to changing priorities in the White House and Congress. The budget sequester was disruptive, especially to long-term research contracts.[15] The Trump administration proposed major cuts to R&D, though Congress rejected them.[16] The Biden administration then authorized an increase of $170 billion (nearly 50 percent) for 2023 through 2027.[17] Of equal importance, the objectives of many of R&D programs were rewritten to make commercialization of the resulting technologies on American soil a major objective.

In the early 2020s, federal R&D spending, fueled by COVID-19 research, spiked from $167.4 billion in 2020 to $190.1 billion in 2021 and an estimated $189 billion in 2023.[18] But the additional funds were narrowly targeted, with 95 percent going to the Department of Health and Human Services.[19] And from 2022 to 2024 (proposed), total federal R&D funding flatlined.[20]

Let us now look at some specific institutions. The key lesson of the mass of bureaucratic detail is that effective government support of innovation is granular, that is specific to sciences, technologies, institutions, and industries. Unlike with private-sector innovation, government's role is not confined to merely establishing the right incentives (profit), the right legal infrastructure (intellectual and other property rights), and then staying hands-off to let the market do the rest.

The National Science Foundation

NSF primarily, but not exclusively, pursues pure scientific and engineering knowledge. Its original mission encompassed all of science and engineering except medicine, then was amended to include applied research in 1968 and give engineering equal status with science in 1986.[21]

With no labs or researchers of its own, NSF funds other organizations. Most of its money goes to colleges and universities, but it also funds K–12 school systems, businesses, informal science organizations, and other recipients.[22] In 2022, 85 percent of its basic research funds went to higher education, 4 percent to nonprofit organizations, 5 percent to business, and less than 5 percent to federal agencies and laboratories.[23] It makes 12,000 new grants per year, supporting approximately 320,000 scientists, engineers, teachers, and students for an average of three years at a time.[24] Approximately 40,000 volunteer scientific and technical experts review funding applications for their intellectual merit and impact potential.[25]

NSF's 2023 budget was $9.8 billion.[26] In 2022, it provided 14 percent of all governmental support for basic R&D.[27] The CHIPS and Science Act authorized it $81 billion over 2023–7, an increase of $36 billion over its baseline.[28]

NSF has eight science directorates:

1. Biological sciences
2. Environmental research and education
3. Mathematical and physical sciences
4. Geosciences
5. Engineering
6. Computer and information science and engineering
7. Social, behavioral, and economic sciences
8. Technology, innovation, and partnerships (created by the CHIPS and Science Act to foster development and commercialization of new technologies and authorized $20 billion for 2023–7)

The National Science Board (NSB) is the NSF's primary oversight body. By law, its members must be leaders from industry or universities in basic, medical, or social sciences, engineering, agriculture, education, research management, or public affairs. A balance of geographic regions and technical disciplines is required.[29] NSF's director, though presidentially appointed, serves a six-year term and is not expected to resign at the beginning of a new administration, reflecting NSF's deliberate insulation from partisan politics. Program officers come to NSF from around the country to serve for only a year or two, producing a constant flow of new ideas.

NSF does not attempt to calculate the economic impact of its research. As former director Subra Suresh has put it,

> $7.3 billion a year – for a program that has supported 70 percent of all American Nobel Prize winners, that has supported or seeded the ideas for the initial evolution of companies like Qualcomm, Symantec, and Google – is a relatively small amount of money for the impact it has had on the US and global economies. But if the NSF had asked, "What is the return on investment?" as the initial condition for funding, many of these projects would not have been funded. With the best ideas, you don't see an outcome immediately. There is no return on investment from a conventional point of view.[30]

NSF is not, however, indifferent to economic value: The potential usefulness of knowledge is a funding consideration.

In addition to funding scientists directly, NSF has funded the creation of 51 Engineering Research Centers at universities around the country. These focus on particular areas and are expected to become self-supporting within 10 years. It also has an interdisciplinary network of Science and Technology Centers: Integrative Partnerships to conduct research through partnerships among academic institutions, national laboratories, industry, and other organizations.[31] Examples include the Center for Layered Polymeric Systems, the Center for Engineering MechanoBiology, and the Center for Integrated Quantum Materials. In addition, NSF has helped fund the establishment of Industry-University Cooperative Research Centers (IUCRCs) focused on pre-competitive research. Once established, these are primarily funded by their industry members with faculty from universities, nonprofits, and federal, state, and local governments.[32]

NSF sometimes partners with other federal agencies to coordinate funding of applied research. Examples include algorithms for electric power systems (with DOE), military threat detection (with the National Geospatial-Intelligence Agency), computational neuroscience (with NIH), and advanced manufacturing (with NIST).[33]

The National Institutes of Health

With a 2022 budget of $45 billion, NIH is the best funded of all civilian research agencies.[34] In its own words, its interlocking goals are:

1. "To foster fundamental creative discoveries, innovative research strategies, and their applications as a basis to advance significantly the nation's capacity to protect and improve health.
2. To develop, maintain, and renew scientific human and physical resources that will assure the Nation's capability to prevent disease.
3. To expand the knowledge base in medical and associated sciences in order to enhance the nation's economic well-being and ensure a continued high return on the public investment in research."[35]

In pursuit of these goals, it conducts and supports research:

1. "In the causes, diagnosis, prevention, and cure of human diseases.
2. In the processes of human growth and development.
3. In the biological effects of environmental contaminants.
4. In the understanding of mental, addictive, and physical disorders.
5. In directing programs for the collection, dissemination, and exchange of information in medicine and health."[36]

NIH consists of 27 institutes and centers. Institutes are generally focused on particular medical conditions, while the centers address more cross-cutting issues.[37] More than 80 percent of NIH's research is extramural, but it also has its own labs. Each year, it awards more than 60,000 grants to more than 300,000 researchers at more than 2,500 institutions.[38]

NIH is mandated by law to use peer review. Its criteria are: 1) the significance of the project's underlying science or problem being solved, 2) the track record of the applying investigators, 3) the innovativeness of the proposed study approach, and 4) the quality of the research environment – that is, institutional support, available equipment, and other resources. NIH uses reviewers both from its own institutes and centers and from outside. Both groups must recommend a proposal for it to be accepted, though the institute's or center's director has the final say.[39]

NIH's National Center for Advancing Translational Sciences helps pharmaceutical firms translate scientific discoveries into treatments.[40] NIH estimated that in fiscal year 2023, its $38 billion of research funding generated an estimated $93 billion in new economic activity.[41] Not included in this total is the value of the pharmaceuticals and medical devices the research enables, or the improved health, lives saved, improved patient quality of life, or the healthier, more productive workforce caused by these advances.[42]

The National Aeronautics and Space Administration

The story of NASA's creation, largely due to the Cold War, is in Chapter 26. Its 2022 budget was $24 billion, of which $4 billion went for human space flight,

$7.6 billion for science research, $1.1 billion for space technology, $880 million for aeronautics, and $137 million for STEM outreach.[43]

NASA has five mission directorates at its headquarters and 13 laboratories and centers around the country.[44] Its Science Directorate researches earth and planetary science, heliophysics (the sun), astrophysics (the universe), and biological and physical sciences.[45] Each year, it funds 10,000 researchers via 3,000 competitive grants worth $600 million.[46] In addition, it invests $379 million annually in technology development.[47]

NASA's Exploration Systems Development Mission Directorate and its Space Operations Mission Directorate support the agency's crewed space-flight programs. Its Space Technology Mission Directorate focuses on developing and testing advanced technologies on the moon for potential later use in a human mission to Mars. This directorate includes NASA's technology transfer office. Among its activities are an innovation fund to encourage creativity and innovation at NASA centers, plus programs designed to invite the private sector to take on various NASA tasks (see Chapter 26).

NASA's Aeronautics Directorate includes six major research programs:

1. "Safe, Efficient Growth in Global Operations.
2. Innovation in Commercial Supersonic Aircraft.
3. Ultra-Efficient Commercial Vehicles.
4. Safe, Quiet, and Affordable Vertical Lift Air Vehicles.
5. In-Time System-Wide Safety Assurance.
6. Assured Autonomy for Aviation Transformation."[48]
(The last item means safe self-piloting aircraft and drones).

NASA works in partnership with industry, academia, and other government agencies to implement its technologies. As of 2022, it had 2,655 partnership agreements.[49] NASA's extramural Innovative Advanced Concepts Program works to develop radically new ideas in aerospace. In 2022, this included a small radioisotope battery to power lightweight spacecraft, a robot to explore caves on Mars, and a diffractive solar sail to improve heliophysics research and space weather forecasting.[50]

NASA's Space Technology Directorate invests in what it calls "tipping point technologies" – that is, where a demonstration project is likely to significantly advance a technology usable by both NASA and the private sector.[51]

NASA increasingly emphasizes private-sector execution of its goals, specifying *what* should be accomplished and leaving much of *how* to industry.[52] For example, it has sought industry partners for its Orion spacecraft, a human-carrying vehicle ultimately intended for deep space missions.

NASA has thousands of spin-offs: Every US commercial aircraft and control tower uses its technology.[53] Its economic returns are clearly huge, but hard to disaggregate from the larger effects of the defense-and-space complex.[54] Isolating specific products from the agency's annual spin-off report – insulin pumps, vertical farms, cochlear implants – misses entire industries it has spawned, such as satellites and commercial space launch.[55] Still, it reported that in 2021, its activities induced additional private sector economic output of $71.2 billion and 339,600 jobs.[56] It was estimated in 2011 that its funding had a rate of return between 33 and 43 percent and a multiplier effect between 7 and 23.[57]

The National Institute of Standards and Technology

NIST was formed from the old National Bureau of Standards by the Omnibus Trade and Competitiveness Act of 1988. This designated it the lead national laboratory for measurement, calibration, and quality assurance techniques. It also charged the Institute with running technology-transfer centers and public–private partnerships to develop and deploy "generic" technologies – that is, those used in a wide range of applications.[58] For example, NIST does low-profile but crucial work developing the Standard Reference Materials (SRMs) used to calibrate instruments for industrial materials production, environmental analysis, health measurements, and scientific research.[59] It also reports and analyzes technology transfer on a government-wide basis.[60]

NIST has five laboratory programs: 1) communications technology, 2) engineering, 3) information technology, 4) materials measurement, and 5) physical measurement. It has labs in Maryland and Colorado employing 3,400 scientists, engineers, and other staff, plus facilities used by 3,800 outside scientists and engineers annually for their own research.[61] It forms partnerships and research collaborations with companies, universities, and local, state, and federal agencies.[62] These programs provide access to its facilities, make grants, and support transfer of resulting technologies.

NIST manages interagency coordination for a number of federal programs, including the Interagency Working Group for Technology Transfer, and acts as the host agency for the Federal Laboratory Consortium for Technology Transfer. It is the home of the Advanced Manufacturing National Program Office, whose staff are drawn from manufacturing companies, academia, and the various federal agencies (DOD, DOE, NASA, NSF, USDA, Department of Education) that support advanced manufacturing.[63] It is the parent agency for Manufacturing USA (MFG-USA, see Chapter 21) and the Manufacturing Extension Partnership (MEP, see Chapter 22).

In its own words, "NIST evaluates its own work using the concept of Social Rate of Return (SRR). SRR is similar to the net present value metric commonly used to evaluate investments. The difference is that the 'net value' SRR accounts for the benefits and costs that accrue to all who benefit, not just the project investors."[64] NIST has computed SRRs for its own research in approximately 20 industries.[65] For example, test methods developed for semiconductor resistivity led to increased industry productivity and an SRR of 181 percent.[66] Research on electromagnetic interference in communications test methods had an SRR of 266 percent.[67] Research on flat-panel-display measurement standards scored 48 percent.[68] The CHIPS and Science Act authorized $10 billion for NIST for 2023–7, double its baseline.[69]

The Department of Energy

The DOE was established in 1977 in response to the OPEC oil embargo of 1973 and the resulting perception that the US had an energy crisis, merging several existing agencies with the goal of developing and implementing a national energy plan. Its 2023 R&D budget was $8.4 billion, divided among many programs, of which the largest were Energy Efficiency and Renewable Energy ($4.2 billion), Fossil Energy and Carbon Management ($1.6 billion), Nuclear Energy ($1.5 billion), ARPA-E ($470 million), and Clean Energy Demonstration ($217 million).[70]

DOE administers 17 national laboratories: Ames National Laboratory, Argonne National Laboratory, Brookhaven National Laboratory, Fermi National Accelerator Laboratory, Lawrence Berkeley National Laboratory, Oak Ridge National Laboratory, Pacific Northwest National Laboratory, Princeton Plasma Physics Laboratory, SLAC National Accelerator Laboratory, and Thomas Jefferson National Accelerator Facility. DOE's National Nuclear Security Administration runs Lawrence Livermore National Laboratory, Los Alamos National Laboratory, and Sandia National Laboratory. DOE also administers Idaho National Laboratory, National Energy Technology Laboratory, National Renewable Energy Laboratory, and Savannah River National Laboratory.[71]

One example, Ames National Lab in Iowa, with 500 staff, 200 students, and a $54 million 2023 budget, is currently leading DOE's Critical Materials Institute, responding to concerns that there are insufficient rare-earth materials to maintain the nation's energy security.[72] Another, Lawrence Berkeley National Laboratory in California, has 3,700 staff, 500 students, 14,000 facility users, 1,800 visiting scientists, and a $1.1 billion budget (2023).[73] It focuses on advanced biogenic chemicals and materials, machine learning for science, the water–energy nexus, electron microscopy, microbes-to-biomes research, next-generation microelectronics, and quantum information science.[74]

DOE also has 41 Energy Frontier Research Centers.[75] These are collaboration centers for large, multi-team projects, typically located at universities and focusing on high-risk, high-reward fundamental research.

DOE also has Energy Innovation Hubs that focus on combining basic and applied R&D. These multidisciplinary, multi-investigator, multi-institutional facilities focus on challenges such as the computer simulation of nuclear reactors, improving battery technology, and producing fuels directly from sunlight.[76]

DOE has offices for specific technologies. These include the offices of Electricity (OE), Fossil Energy and Carbon Management (FECM), Nuclear Energy (NE), and Energy Efficiency and Renewable Energy (EERE).

OE's mission is a secure and resilient power grid, focusing on grid modernization and the ability to recover from disruptions.[77] It pursues this through a mix of technological and policy solutions in the public and private sectors.[78] For example, it is developing a megawatt-scale grid storage system, increasingly important as the nation relies on variable energy sources like wind and solar.[79] Its 2022 budget was $327 million.[80]

FECM's mission is to ensure that as long as the US uses fossil fuels, they remain as clean, secure, affordable, and environmentally benign as possible. It thus focuses on clean coal, emergency petroleum reserves, responsible development of oil and gas resources, and natural gas regulation, including its import and export. It researches "point-source carbon capture, hydrogen with carbon management, methane emissions reduction, critical mineral production, and carbon dioxide removal to address the accumulated CO_2 emissions in the atmosphere."[81]

NE's mission is to support America's nuclear reactor fleet, including its complete fuel cycle and the security of nuclear materials, while researching better nuclear technologies. It researches 1) small modular reactors, 2) light water reactors, 3) advanced reactors, 4) space power systems, and 5) versatile test reactors. This work is done through universities, industry, and at the Idaho National Lab. Its 2023 budget was $1.8 billion.[82]

EERE's mission is the transition to renewable energy, focusing on technologies for transportation, industry, and buildings. The National Renewable Energy Lab, in Golden, Colorado, centralizes EERE's intramural research, and it also has more than 900 technology partnerships with outside entities. Its 2023 budget was $3.5 billion.[83]

With the existing Defense Advanced Research Projects Agency as a model, ARPA-E ("E" for "Energy") was created in 2009 to focus on energy technologies that are insufficiently developed for private investment but have major impact potential. It does not fund basic research, but instead provides short-term funding focused on overcoming specific technical barriers. (See Chapter 23 for details about both DARPA and ARPA-E.)[84]

DOE does not attempt to calculate the economic impact of its basic science programs because their benefits are too widely dispersed to measure, but it does try to measure its applied programs. For example, its fossil energy R&D programs from 1986 to 2000 cost $4.5 billion and have been estimated to have had returns over that same time period of $7.4 billion. These programs included research on petroleum drilling, atmospheric fluidized bed combustion, western and eastern gas shales, improved enhanced oil recovery, seismic technology, coal-bed methane, and waste management and utilization. But if the shale gas revolution (see Chapter 19), which bore fruit mostly after 2000, is included, the returns become almost incalculably large.[85]

In 2017, EERE commissioned studies on the costs and benefits of its research in home appliances, energy storage, and vehicles – about one-third of its research portfolio. They found that $12 billion of federal investment had resulted in $388 billion in economic benefits.[86] Another study found that three energy efficiency R&D programs, with a total budget of $7 billion over their 22-year lifetime, had resulted in same-period economic benefits of $30 billion.[87]

2022's CHIPS and Science Act authorized $67.9 billion for DOE's R&D programs for 2023–7, an increase of $30.5 billion. Some $16.5 billion was directed to 10 technologies identified by the US Innovation and Competition Act of 2021, including artificial intelligence and machine learning, advanced manufacturing, cybersecurity, biotechnology, high-performance computing, advanced materials, and quantum information science.[88] As of mid-2024, however, actual appropriations have increased only modestly.[89]

The Department of Defense

This book's main discussion of federal defense research and its huge economic impact is in Chapter 26.

DOD funds R&D as part of its Research, Development, Test, and Evaluation (RDT&E) budget. Most of the "R" is divided into basic research (budget category 6.1), applied research (6.2), and advanced technology development (6.3). The rest, categories 6.4–6.6, goes to prototyping, testing, and managing weapons programs. In 2023, funding was $3.0 billion for category 6.1, $7.8 billion for 6.2, and $11.7 billion for 6.3.[90]

Over the past several decades, defense R&D has had peaks and valleys due to the changing preferences of the secretary of defense and Congress, changes in the overall DOD budget, and external events such as 9/11 leading to "raiding" this budget category for other parts of DOD.[91] There has also been a budgetary tug-of-war between basic and applied R&D, and weapons testing.

About 16 percent of DOD's overall research budget, about $2 billion per year, goes to basic research. This is split roughly equally among the Army, Air Force, Navy, DARPA, and other defense agencies. About a quarter of this goes to intramural research, a fifth to industry, the rest to a mix of nonprofits and nonfederal government agencies.[92] Each military service has its own labs, with the undersecretary of defense for research and engineering overseeing all research and engineering operations.[93]

The Army's 2023 science and technology budget was $4.9 billion, of which $635 million went to basic research.[94] The Army Research Lab (ARL) is overseen by Combat Capabilities Development Command (DEV-COM), under Army Futures Command (AFC). ARL, in turn, oversees the Army Research Office, which funds ARL's extramural research. ARL's 11 core research areas include biotech, photonics and electronics, weapons, extreme materials, and cyber and computational sciences.[95]

The Air Force's 2021 science and technology R&D budget was $3.1 billion, of which $536 million went to basic research. Its Office of Scientific Research is part of the Air Force Research Lab (AFRL), which serves US air, space, and cyberspace forces. Based at Wright-Patterson Air Force Base in Ohio, AFRL is home to eight other technical directorates, focused on aerospace, sensors, information, munitions, materials, and manufacturing, directed energy, space vehicles, and human performance.[96]

The Navy's total 2023 science and technology budget was $3.5 billion, of which $689 million went to basic research.[97] The Office of Naval Research (ONR) manages both intramural and extramural programs. ONR Global, in Chile, Brazil, the UK, the Czech Republic, Singapore, and Japan, focuses on international collaboration.[98] ONR oversees the Naval Research Lab, whose remit includes:

- "Advanced radio, optical and infrared sensors
- Autonomous systems
- Computer science, cognitive science, and artificial intelligence
- Directed energy technology
- Electronic electro-optical device technology
- Electronic warfare
- Enhanced maintainability, reliability, and survivability
- Environmental effects on naval systems
- Human–robot interaction
- Imaging research and systems
- Information technology
- Marine geosciences
- Materials
- Meteorology

- Ocean acoustics
- Oceanography
- Space systems and technology
- Surveillance and sensor technology
- Undersea technology."[99]

DARPA's mission is radical technological breakthroughs for purposes of national security (see Chapter 23).

The Independent Research and Development clause in the DOD's Federal Acquisition Regulations allows the defense industry to charge "independent" research as a cost on DOD contracts.[100] The defense industry thereby spends $4 billion annually on research judged to be in DOD's interest.[101]

DOD has several programs to encourage partnerships and interactions between defense R&D institutions, industry, academia, and other federal R&D agencies.

The Defense Innovation Marketplace (DIM) is a forum to connect DOD staff with industry to improve the planning of independent R&D investments and enable DOD to better understand what technologies might result. Within DIM, there are Communities of Interest (CoIs) and technology interchange meetings (TIMs) among DOD agencies. CoIs have formed around topics including advanced electronics; command, control, communications, computers and intelligence (C4I); countering weapons of mass destruction; countering improvised explosive devices; materials and manufacturing processes; sensors; and space weapons technologies.[102]

The DOD's manufacturing technology program (ManTech) has since 1956 developed technologies for the efficient manufacturing of military hardware. It has offices in all the services, in the Defense Logistics Agency (DLA), the Missile Defense Agency (MDA), and in the DOD-wide Manufacturing Science and Technology program. Its activities are coordinated through the Joint Defense Manufacturing Technology Panel as part of DOD's Office for Manufacturing and Industrial Base Policy.[103]

DOD partners with NSF's I-Corps program (see Chapter 21) to provide DOD-funded researchers with training in entrepreneurship.[104] And the Defense Innovation Unit (DIU) launched in 2015 provides financial support to companies to accelerate commercial innovations for national defense challenges.[105]

The CIA and Homeland Security

The CIA's Directorate of Science and Technology (DS&T) develops and applies tools for gathering and analyzing information. For example, the lithium-ion battery was developed during the 1960s by DS&T to power surveillance equipment and reconnaissance satellites.[106]

The Intelligence Advanced Research Projects Agency (IARPA) created in 2006 supports high-risk, high-payoff research and facilitates deployment of the results. It has four main research areas: artificial intelligence, quantum computing, machine learning, and synthetic biology.[107] For example, it has researched tools to differentiate between naturally occurring and deliberately introduced pathogens in food, methods to combat "Trojan horses" in artificial intelligence, and ways to protect biometric technology against attack.[108] Among its successes are photo-refractive materials that increase the brightness, image speed, and energy efficiency of digital displays, and using machine learning to translate high volumes of text and speech in exotic foreign languages. Longer-term research includes work with the Army Research Office on advanced materials and fabrication techniques for quantum computers.[109]

During the late 1990s, the CIA became concerned it could not develop information technology as fast as the commercial sector or recruit top technical talent. In-Q-Tel (IQT) was the result. This independent, nonprofit, private company invests in startups whose products have potential intelligence value. By March 2022, it managed $1 billion in assets in more than 500 companies.[110] None of IQT's investments are in classified work, nor does it produce products, which it leaves to the private sector. It aims to eventually become independent of CIA funding. Google Earth was derived from software it funded.[111]

In-Q-Tel Labs is a partnership between industry, academia, and the intelligence community. Its labs include CosmiQ Works, which develops artificial intelligence for geospatial uses; B.Next, which focuses on rapidly detecting and quenching epidemics; and Cyber Reboot, which targets the post-compromise stage of cyberattacks. By allowing open-source access to their data, computer code, and findings, these labs support private industry.

The Science and Technology Directorate of the Department of Homeland Security (DHS S&T) funds research in support of DHS agencies such as Customs and Border Protection, the Secret Service, the Coast Guard, and the Transportation Security Administration, plus nonfederal first responders and critical infrastructure operators.[112] Its interests include border and maritime security, chemical and biological defense, critical infrastructure, cybersecurity, explosive detection, and unmanned aerial systems.

DHS S&T has partnered with universities to form Centers of Excellence for topics such as infrastructure resilience and explosives detection.[113] It developed a smartphone app for guiding first responders to emergencies.[114] It developed a lightweight air-filtration system to protect firefighters looking for hot spots after a fire.[115] It supports commercial technology developers as part of its Smart City Internet of Things Innovation (SCITI) Labs program by taking a "buy commercial whenever possible" approach to product development, working with companies to develop and field-test new technologies.

The Homeland Security Advanced Research Projects Agency (HSARPA) conducted basic and applied research, technology development, prototype demonstration, testing, and evaluation.[116] For example, it created technologies to help first responders practice responding to an active shooter incident, to screen people and luggage without physical contact, to find people during rescue events, to conduct rapid DNA testing for victim identification, and to identify potential suspects using forensic video analysis.[117] But it lacked a clear mission, the right structure to pursue DARPA-style radical innovations, or solid support from its parent agency, so it was absorbed into DHS S&T in 2019.[118]

Federally Funded Research and Development Centers

Federally Funded Research and Development Centers (FFRDCs) are public–private partnerships run by universities and private firms to conduct R&D for the US government. For example, an agency might fund parallel streams of research in an FFRDC, a university, and an intramural lab. FFRDCs have considerable latitude in working with private industry. They can fund projects quickly, rather than going through the government's standard long and complex grant and contracting procedures. In 2022, federal funding for FFRDC R&D was $26.5 billion.[119]

Thirteen federal agencies sponsor or cosponsor a total of 42 FFRDCs, each sponsored by one or more agencies, including DOE, DOD, NIST, and NSF. FFRDCs include not only the aforementioned national laboratories, but also institutions such as the Center for Advanced Aviation System Development, the Center for Communications and Computing, the Center for Nuclear Waste Regulatory Analyses, the Jet Propulsion Laboratory, the National Defense Research Institute, the Science and Technology Policy Institute, and the Software Engineering Institute.[120]

By law, FFRDCs cannot manufacture products, compete with industry, or work for commercial firms. However, the Stevenson–Wydler Act of 1980 allowed them to enter into Partnership Intermediary Agreements (PIAs). The intermediary, supported by either a state or local government, enables private companies and universities to work with an FFRDC. Examples include NIST's Science and Technology Entrepreneurship Program (N-STEP), established by the State of Maryland to facilitate access to NIST's lab in Gaithersburg, and TechLink, set up initially by Montana State University to work with DOD.[121]

21 FEDERAL PROACTIVE INNOVATION PROGRAMS

The previous chapter discussed the pipeline model of innovation, the extended pipeline model, and the many federal programs implementing them.[1] This chapter will examine three other models:

- Induced innovation
- Manufacturing-led innovation
- Innovation organizations

The induced innovation model describes how innovation occurs in response to market changes, either naturally occurring or deliberately induced by government. This model is characterized by "market pull", as opposed to "technology push", because changes in market demand, rather than available technologies, are its driving force.

The manufacturing-led innovation model describes the role of production itself in driving both product (new goods) and process (new ways of making existing goods) innovation.

The innovation organizations model describes institutions deliberately designed to make innovation happen. We will look at the two major types that have recently been established in the US: *innovation orchards* and *manufacturing institutes*.

Induced Innovation, Part I: The Free Market

The market generates much innovation automatically. Firms see sales opportunities and develop technologies to meet them. This is how most firms innovate most of the time, generally with incremental, not breakthrough, innovations.

Unfortunately, America's former dominance in corporate innovation has broken down. Through the mid-1980s, large, vertically integrated firms such as DuPont, General Electric, Westinghouse, IBM, Xerox, Corning, Dow, Kodak, and AT&T invested massively from one end of the pipeline to the other. They had sufficiently strong market positions to count on selling the ultimate products at a profit, even including the costs of going all the way back to fundamental research. They had sophisticated labs of their own and also funded university researchers.

Today, because of increased foreign competition, deregulation in some industries, a management vogue for eliminating all but "core" activities, and Wall Street pressures for short-term profits, few firms have all the stages of innovation in house anymore. Bell Labs, despite nine Nobel prizes, was sold off after the 1984 court-ordered breakup of AT&T and morphed into an ordinary product-development laboratory, currently owned by the Finnish firm Nokia. From 1975 to 2006, the percentage of key commercial innovations developed by private-sector in-house R&D fell from 47 to 13 percent.[2]

The few exceptions to this pattern, such as SpaceX in rocketry, Boeing in aircraft, and Intel in semiconductors, are revealing. SpaceX and Boeing benefit from the vast military-oriented industrial policies America has for aerospace. SpaceX is technologically supported by NASA and shielded by law from foreign competition for national-security reasons. Intel, outpaced by foreign competitors TSMC and Samsung that were heavily supported by their governments, is only now beginning a possible recovery with the help of the CHIPS Act. (See Chapter 26 about all three industries.)

GE, once centered in Upstate New York, illustrates another problem. Until the firm was upended in 2022 by plans to break it up, it maintained five overseas R&D centers, including in India, China, Germany, and Brazil. As of 2019, US-located firms conducted about 21 percent of their R&D abroad, $104.5 billion, versus $493.0 billion at home.[3] (In 2021, half of all US corporate IT R&D was performed in India, China, Canada, or Israel.)[4] This internationalization diminishes the probability that production resulting from the research will take place in the US. This trend is no accident: China has for decades pushed American firms to perform R&D there in exchange for access to its market, and other nations impose similar, milder, WTO-legal, but still effective policies.

Induced Innovation, Part II: Government Intervention

Inducements to innovate can also come from deliberate governmental interventions. Standards set by the Clean Air Act of 1970 helped spur technologies such as sulfur dioxide scrubbers and electrostatic precipitators.[5]

Department of Energy (DOE) appliance standards have led to more efficient home appliances and a new generation of digital lighting. The 1975 Corporate Average Fuel Economy standards prompted lighter vehicles, more efficient engines, hybrids, and eventually electric cars.[6]

Government regulation is thus not the one-sided enemy of innovation its critics claim. It has been used not only for noneconomic goals like environmental protection, but also to force national industries to upgrade technologically. Japan, for example, imposes extremely high standards on its protected domestic car market to keep the industry at the technological frontier despite the absence of import competition (see Chapters 5 and 25).

Induced-innovation policies often involve the tax code. The Inflation Reduction Act of 2022 included $370 billion in climate-related incentives, of which $270 billion was tax subsidies.[7] America's R&D tax credit is another example, though from 2000 to 2021 it fell from being the tenth most generous in the OECD to thirty-third.[8] And it is of little use to innovative startups that have no taxable income (reforms are proposed in Recommendations).

When the US government designs programs to induce innovation, it should better consider how targeted technologies are likely to evolve in response. It should systematically map out their potential development and commercialization pathways, their performance, and their costs. Tax incentives, R&D, technology demonstrations, pilot projects, and technology launch paths should all be considered and evaluated as a package, not in isolation.

Manufacturing-Led Innovation

The manufacturing process itself is a major source of innovation. Some of the most important innovations are not new products, but new ways of making existing ones. In the US, process innovation has often taken a back seat to product innovation for management and in public perception.[9] But it is frequently easier for firms to monetize, as it often takes the form of trade secrets and processes inside firms that are easier to keep private than new products openly sold. And it is less risky because incremental steps are less expensive than big jumps and the product already has a market.

Process innovation can still be radical. The Ford Model T, launched in 1908, was based both on innovations in the product and on application of the assembly line, already used in simpler industries, to auto production. The result was the first car cheap enough for mass consumption. Decades later, the Toyota Production System, later generalized into Lean Production, enabled the rise of Japan's auto industry at the expense of US car makers (see Chapter 25). There was no single breakthrough, but the systematization of incremental efficiency improvements throughout the production system led to decisively higher quality and lower cost. Today, manufacturing-led innovation can be seen in Chinese manufacturing's famous ability to scale up rapidly, a major competitive advantage.[10]

Optimal process innovation generally requires that production be integrated into the innovation process, playing a role in product development and influencing even earlier stages of R&D. Geographical and corporate separation of R&D and manufacturing can therefore be a problem. In the 1970s and 1980s, American industry transitioned from "innovate here, produce here" to "innovate here, produce there," and in the 1990s and 2000s, to "innovate there, produce there."[11] Between 1998 and 2010, nearly 60,000 American manufacturing establishments, in almost every sector, closed.[12]

Other types of innovation have suffered too, as corporate labs have followed manufacturing offshore. Products whose US production is threatened or already lost include:

- Fine chemicals
- Forgings and castings
- Advanced ceramics
- Consumer-grade advanced composites
- LEDs for lighting
- Advanced LCD displays and smartphones
- Advanced carbon fiber components
- Key starting materials (KSMs) for drugs
- Active pharmaceutical ingredients (APIs) for drugs
- Integrated-circuit packaging (though US firms, incentivized by the CHIPS Act, are attempting to bring it back using new technology)[13]

Offshoring the production step to save money in the short run assumes a unidirectional model of innovation, from research to design to manufacturing, with little knowledge gained during manufacturing flowing back to the earlier steps. *Sometimes* a company can successfully perform all the R&D and then use a contract manufacturer elsewhere to make the product. But, as Harvard Business School's Gary Pisano and Willy Shih note, "It's devilishly difficult to determine when manufacturing is critical to innovation and when it can be safely outsourced to lower costs and reduce capital outlays."[14]

In rapidly developing breakthrough sectors, the link between manufacturing and R&D is especially crucial because the manufacturing methods themselves are still being developed. In some fields, such as new materials, the manufacturing process itself is a major innovation. For example, many of the techniques required to make difficult-to-work titanium a usable technology came not from the lab, but from the factory floor.[15]

Developing manufacturing capabilities and losing them is an asymmetrical process: Capabilities that take years to develop take little time to wipe out.[16] As one observer notes,

> Manufacturing, like a living organism, evolves and learns to improve its processes, or better to say that the engineers and workers who use the equipment evolve and learn as they gain experience. Once the knowledge and experience of industrial traditions is lost, it will have evolved into something else by the time you want to bring it back. Workers with industrial skills will have left the labor force without passing on their knowledge to younger workers, so it is impossible to get new industrial technology set up here, because workers who knew the old technology are no longer accessible to learn the new.[17]

Reversing capability loss is always expensive, sometimes prohibitively so. Given the entrenched, interlocking skill sets and supply chains of many industries, one cannot assume that needed capabilities will spring up spontaneously *in the US* in response to market demand.

Because of these lost manufacturing capabilities, whole sectors are no longer innovating here. Many foreign competitors started as contract manufacturers for American firms but eventually grew to challenge them. Even when foreign companies, such as Taiwan Semiconductor, have stayed in the contracting role, they have created a worrisome dependence by killing off American contract manufacturers. This loss of manufacturing capability has also undermined the skills base America needs to innovate, because deep knowledge about what is manufacturable is part of creating designs at the cutting edge of a technology.

The Role of Venture Capital

America's VC system is important, but its role is more limited than many realize. It generally has neither the assured revenue streams to fund basic research nor the extended time horizons and the large, ongoing capital resources required to bring most breakthrough *manufactured* products all the way to market. It thus focuses on industries and stages of innovation where neither is required. Prior to Industry 4.0 (see below), there was little VC investment even in high-tech manufacturing.

In software and related fields, startups need comparatively little equipment and infrastructure. Development is fast, testing and scale-up are relatively cheap, marginal cost often gets close to zero once the technology is developed, and profit margins can be very large.[18] This pattern suits VC investment horizons of 7 to 10 years, which means that most of the firms in a fund's portfolio have about 5 years to show a return.[19] This time frame is a problem for industries that take longer. Because manufacturing requires physical hardware and factory space, marginal cost does not approach zero once the technology is developed. As a result, ongoing investments are required. Developing a suitably trained technical workforce for new manufacturing equipment and techniques also takes time.[20]

From 1995 to 2016, 25 percent of VC money went to the internet, 14 percent to mobile, 12 percent to software, and 19 percent to healthcare. Electronic hardware got only 4 percent, and the industrial sector a tiny 3 percent.[21] The well-funded sectors benefited from decades of governmentally supported technology development, which created what economist and venture capitalist William Janeway calls "platforms upon which entrepreneurs and VCs would later dance."[22]

The exceptions to this pattern of underinvestment are revealing. Consider Tesla: Elon Musk's initial $100 million investment came from his earnings as a cofounder of PayPal. Furthermore, the industries in which he has since succeeded – space launch, electric cars, solar power – have *all* been the recipients of huge government support. Solar-electric power systems and electric vehicles receive direct and indirect federal subsidies for purchasers, while SpaceX was built upon national-security-motivated protectionism plus decades of NASA research and launch infrastructure. (See Chapter 26.)

The hand of government is similarly visible in another manufacturing industry in which venture capital has long succeeded: biopharmaceuticals. Almost all innovative drugs today derive from NIH-funded research.[23] After initial drug discovery, the next stage can be a VC-funded startup, often with one of the original researchers as a cofounder. These startups typically take the drug through its preclinical stage, then its Phase One and sometimes Phase Two clinical trials. This structured FDA-driven approval process provides uniform benchmarks that create comparability between investments and thereby reduces risk. The startups then generally license their technology to, or sell themselves outright to, the large pharmaceutical companies that have the resources for the expensive Phase Three trials, providing the needed exits.[24]

AI also fits this pattern. Its VC funding doubled in 2021, when generative pretrained transformer (GPT) models finally neared commercial applicability.[25] But this progress was based upon decades of federally funded research into machine learning, mathematics, and computing.[26] From 2020 to early 2023, NSF launched 47 National Artificial Intelligence Research Institutes, spending $360 million at more than 500 institutions in the US and abroad.[27] AI is also unusual in that much basic research can be applied directly to product development.[28] In Google's "Hybrid Research Model" and Meta's "Fundamental AI Research," the line between research and development is blurred, which has led to years of fundamental research with no product on the horizon.[29] Like AT&T with Bell Labs, both firms enjoy monopoly profits and confidence in monetizing the eventual fruits of long-term research. AI systems, once developed, are generally inexpensive to replicate and distribute, which brings them within VC time horizons and profit targets.[30] Google, Meta, and Microsoft buy a lot of startups, providing timely exits.[31]

The digitization of manufacturing (a/k/a Industry 4.0; see Chapter 22) finally drew VC interest to the sector. Targets include advanced materials, composites, non-semiconductor nanotechnology (see Chapter 28), environmentally sustainable manufacturing, continuous-flow drug manufacturing, flexible electronics, biomanufacturing, 3D and additive manufacturing, advanced forming and joining, and industrial robotics (see Chapter 27).[32] From 2017 to 2020, VC investment in industrial technology exceeded $160 billion, about a quarter of all VC funding, yielding 29 unicorns. And 12 percent of this money went to seed funding. This upsurge was driven, in part, by a sharp reduction in the per-unit cost of key manufacturing tools such as industrial robots, 3D printers, and internet-of-things (IoT) devices.[33]

Innovation Organizations Fill the Gaps

Innovation organizations are for-profit, nonprofit, or governmental institutions designed to advance new technologies to the point where they fall within VCs' risk appetites and time horizons. They fall into two categories.

First are *direct innovators*, such as the government agencies described in the previous chapter, which themselves research science and develop technologies. Second are *innovation facilitators*, which help other public and private participants in the innovation process. They provide, among other things, institutional infrastructure for developing prototypes, building test beds, and developing production systems.

Most civilian government agencies do not focus on these crucial early steps. Innovation facilitators focus on impediments to and gaps in the innovation process known collectively as the valley of death.[34] Moving a technology from the controlled conditions of the lab to a functioning prototype can be derailed by the high cost of resolving technical challenges. Without a prototype, attracting venture capital to move forward is difficult. The original researchers may not have the skills needed for the later stages of the path to commercialization. The transition from pilot production to full-scale manufacturing is another common sticking point.

One such facilitator is TechBridge in Cambridge, Massachusetts, a program of Fraunhofer USA, the American branch of a huge German government- and industry-funded technology development institution (see Chapters 8 and 23). Founded in 2010, TechBridge finds industry sponsors with specific innovation needs and matches them with startups developing technologies that match these needs. A validation or demonstration project is then executed.[35] TechBridge's validation can help startups find industry partners and venture capital. By 2021, it had helped form 18 companies, with a survival rate of at least 95 percent, created more than 367 jobs, and raised $186 million in follow-on investments – a record of modest but real success.[36]

Greentown Labs in Somerville, Massachusetts, has a different approach. This clean-energy "incubator" partners with the Massachusetts branch of the federal Manufacturing Extension Partnership (see Chapter 22). Startups emerging from universities typically know their science but are not versed in manufacturing. Greentown aims to fill that gap by connecting local manufacturers with hardware startups that are ready for prototyping or pilot production. It focuses on consultations and workshops to get startups ready to meet with manufacturers, familiarizing the former with manufacturing processes and ensuring that their design is production-ready.

Innovation Facilitators: Innovation Orchards

In 2015, MIT's President Rafael Reif laid out a model for comprehensively supporting innovations that were technologically promising, potentially socially significant, and unjustly neglected by existing funding sources. He proposed "innovation orchards" that would bring together universities, other nonprofits, and startup firms. The orchard would provide space, equipment, and capital to nurture innovations until they were ready for venture capital.[37] This proposal went far beyond existing incubators' focus on mentorship, networking, and VC matchmaking.

MIT's first orchard, The Engine, was announced in 2016. Organized as both a venture capital firm and a public benefit corporation, it began making long-term capital investments in areas such as advanced manufacturing, next-generation semiconductors, clean energy production, energy storage, quantum computing, and synthetic biology.

MIT seeded its first investment fund with $25 million, eventually raising another $175 million from investors. By 2022, its 44 portfolio companies had raised $4.1 billion in equity and convertible debt and their total valuation was $9.4 billion. For every dollar The Engine invested, its portfolio companies raised $14.[38]

One of The Engine's supported firms was Boston Metal, which developed a novel molten oxide electrolysis process to produce iron with reduced carbon emissions. The founder of another portfolio company, Form Energy, which was developing long-term energy storage systems, described his experience: "Our first meeting with [Engine officials] was unique in my experience of pitching to investors. We walked in with a dream to solve a huge problem. To get started, we needed millions of dollars, extremely specialized lab space, and connections to the largest industrial companies in the world. We walked out with all three."[39]

Innovation Facilitators: DOE, NSF, and SBIR

DOE's model for innovation facilitation, specifically for clean energy, is its Lab-Embedded Entrepreneurship Program (LEEP). DOE's national labs are ideally situated between university and industry labs, with strong connections to both. They are well suited to the later stages of research on promising technologies that require complex, multidisciplinary work with experts from other institutions.[40] But they have long been criticized for making little effort to address commercialization.[41]

To overcome this problem, in 2014 DOE created LEEP. Its first program was Cyclotron Road in Berkeley, California, cofounded by the DOE's Advanced Manufacturing Office and Lawrence Berkeley National Laboratory. It selected cohorts of roughly a dozen researchers based on demonstrated talent and proposed technologies. LEEP has since added Chain Reaction Innovations at Argonne National Lab in Illinois, Innovation Crossroads at Oak Ridge National Lab in Tennessee, and West Gate at the National Renewable Energy Lab in Colorado.[42] Researchers receive a small amount of seed funding ($100,000 plus living expenses) and, more importantly, are given access to technology, equipment, and scientists at the lab. Throughout the two-year program, they are proactively connected with corporations, VCs, and other potential funders.

In 2023, Cyclotron Road announced its ninth cohort of scientists. Since 2015, 95 fellows have taken part, creating 74 companies employing nearly 1,000 people.[43] They have attracted more than $1 billion in follow-on funding from public and private sources.[44] Some have received international acclaim, such as Mosaic Materials for the carbon capture materials it developed.[45]

The NSF's Innovation Corps (I-Corps) provides small research teams with six months of intensive entrepreneurship training. This includes customer discovery, business model development, minimum-viable-product development, and real-world interviews with potential customers, partners, and competitors. NSF's objectives for each team are:

1. "A decision on a clear path forward based on an assessment of the business model.
2. Substantial first-hand evidence for or against product-market fit, with the identification of customer segments and corresponding value propositions.
3. A narrative of a technology demonstration for potential partners."[46]

NSF partnered with the nonprofit VentureWell, formerly the National Collegiate Inventors and Innovators Alliance, to implement I-Corps nationwide. The I-Corps model has now spread to federal agencies such as NIH, NASA, and DOE.

For many I-Corps recipients, the next step is often to seek an SBIR grant. This program, coordinated by the Small Business Administration, requires federal agencies to allocate part of their extramural R&D budgets to small companies. SBIR is implemented across 12 federal agencies, with each agency's program adapted to the types of technological advances likely to emerge from that agency's R&D. SBIR's Phase One grants focus on feasibility or proof-of-concept, while its Phase Two grants can be used to develop a commercial prototype (see Chapter 23).

The CHIPS and Science Act created an entirely new structure in NSF – the Technology, Innovation and Partnership Directorate. Authorized at $20 billion over five years, its mandate is to bridge the gap between science and commercialization.

Manufacturing Institutes

Starting in 2011, the concept of manufacturing institutes was developed in three successive White House reports. These broke from previous federal approaches to innovation in a conscious attempt at government-backed, manufacturing-led innovation.[47]

The first report, "Ensuring American Leadership in Advanced Manufacturing," was written by the Council of Advisors on Science and Technology.[48] It discussed the need for R&D on new manufacturing processes supported by industry–university partnerships, cross-government-agency coordination, public–private co-investment, shared infrastructure to help SMMs adopt new manufacturing technologies, and strengthening of workforce skills. The resulting initiative was launched as the Advanced Manufacturing Partnership (AMP), whose creation was the Obama administration's "car czar" Ron Bloom's parting shot as he left government service in 2011.

In 2012, AMP issued the second report, laying out strategy in more detail, with 16 recommendations on "enabling innovation," "securing the talent pipeline," and "improving the business climate."[49] It included a starter list of priority technologies, including:

- Advanced sensing, measurement, and process control
- Advanced materials design, synthesis, and processing
- Visualization, informatics, and digital manufacturing technologies
- Sustainable manufacturing
- Nanomanufacturing
- Flexible electronics manufacturing
- Biomanufacturing
- Bioinformatics
- Additive manufacturing
- Advanced manufacturing and testing equipment
- Industrial robotics
- Advanced forming and joining technologies[50]

The third report, in 2014, called for better coordination of federal investments in advanced manufacturing and a portfolio approach to managing them.[51] It recommended developing processes and standards for a) the interoperability of manufacturing technologies, b) the exchange of materials and manufacturing-process information, and c) the certification of cybersecurity processes. It recommended creating a public–private scale-up investment fund and tax incentives for manufacturing investments. Finally, it called for the creation of a National Network for Manufacturing Innovation (NNMI).

Manufacturing USA

In 2014, NNMI, since renamed Manufacturing USA (MFG-USA), was established as a nationwide network of institutes, along with an interagency Advanced Manufacturing National Program Office (AMNPO) at NIST to oversee it. Moved by urgency and believing that the first institutes would acquit themselves well and thus build support for more, the Obama administration did not wait for Congress to provide funding. Instead, even before the first report was released it used existing legal authority and funding to begin setting up institutes.

DOD had already stood up the first in 2012: America Makes, in Youngstown, Ohio, focusing on 3D printing and additive manufacturing.[52] DOD followed up with the Digital Manufacturing and Design Innovation Institute in Chicago, since renamed Manufacturing times Digital (MxD), specializing in digital tools for manufacturing, and Lightweight Innovations For Tomorrow (LIFT) in Detroit, specializing in lightweight metal technologies. DOE established Power America in Raleigh, North Carolina, focused on wide-bandgap semiconductors.

Each institute focuses on a specific group of related technologies, performing research, building demonstration projects, and training workers. The institutes have facilities and staff for technology development, testing, prototyping, and refinement. They sometimes develop technologies in house, but mostly work by linking industry with researchers at universities, companies, and other sources by way of jointly funded projects and provision of shared infrastructure.

The institutes are deliberately led by industry, not government, to keep them focused on the real needs of firms. Funding comes from the federal government, state and local governments, and the institutes' corporate clients. Each is managed and funded through a multiyear cooperative agreement between its sponsoring federal agency and some nonfederal entity in charge of operations.

The process for selecting research topics is rigorous and includes a wide range of stakeholders. Criteria include:

- Is there a demand by industry or consumers for this technology?
- Does this technology cut across many industry sectors and apply to both large and small manufacturers?
- Would a failure of the US to maintain competence or dominance in this technology threaten national security?
- Would a failure of the US to maintain competence or dominance in this technology threaten American supply chains?
- Does this technology leverage America's existing assets in terms of workforce, education, unique infrastructure, and policies?[53]

The institutes are intentionally crosscutting in nature, employing multiple technologies to avoid the silo thinking of single-technology labs. While each focuses on specific areas, many of their tools and knowledge bases are useful across many manufacturing sectors. Their aim of rebuilding America's manufacturing ecosystem is informed by mapping key technologies and their relationships to each other (see Chapter 3). The institutes did not develop as a coordinated portfolio but ad hoc, based on which agencies were prepared to fund them. (The 16 established before the Biden administration are shown in Table 21.1.)

President Trump did not grasp the value of MFG-USA and did not expand it. Then, under Biden in 2022, DOE announced the Clean Energy Manufacturing Innovation Institute and the Industrial Decarbonization through the Electrification of Process Heating Institute, with up to $70 million in federal

Table 21.1 The Manufacturing USA Institutes[54]

Institute	Organizer	Focus Areas
AFFOA, Advanced Functional Fabrics of America, Cambridge, MA [DOD]	Massachusetts Institute of Technology	Fabrics that act as electronics, such as sensors and communications devices
AIM Photonics, American Institute for Manufacturing Integrated Photonics, Albany, NY [DOD]	Research Foundation for the State University of New York	Photonic integrated circuits, integration of light technology into existing semiconductors
America Makes, The National Additive Manufacturing Innovation Institute, Youngstown, OH [DOD]	National Center for Defense Manufacturing and Machining	Additive manufacturing and 3D printing
ARM, Advanced Robotics for Manufacturing Institute, Pittsburgh, PA [DOD]	Carnegie Mellon University	Advanced robotics for manufacturing
BioFabUSA, Advanced Regenerative Manufacturing Institute, Manchester, NH [DOD]	Advanced Regenerative Manufacturing Institute	Regenerative medicine and large-scale manufacturing of engineered tissues
BioMADE, Biomanufacturing and Design Ecosystem Institute, St. Paul, MN [DOD]	Engineering Biology Research Consortium / University of Minnesota	Sustainable and reliable bioindustrial manufacturing technologies.
MxD, Manufacturing times Digital, Chicago, IL [DOD]	UI Labs, doing business as MxD	Digital manufacturing and design technologies, such as digital models and augmented reality.
LIFT, Lightweight Innovations for Tomorrow, Detroit, MI [DOD.]	America Lightweight Materials Innovation Institute	Lightweight materials manufacturing technologies

Institute	Organization	Description
NEXTFLEX, America's Flexible Hybrid Electronics Manufacturing Institute, San Jose, CA [DOD]	FlexTech Alliance	Flexible hybrid electronics that can bend, stretch, and flex as part of the Internet of Things
CESMII, Clean Energy Smart Manufacturing Innovation Institute, Los Angeles, CA [DOE.]	University of California at Los Angeles	Digital process controls and technologies to improve the energy efficiency and productivity of advanced manufacturing
CYMANII, Cybersecurity Manufacturing Innovation Institute, San Antonio, TX [DOE]	University of Texas at San Antonio	Cybersecurity for manufacturing and supply chains
IACMI, The Institute for Advanced Composites Manufacturing Innovation, Knoxville, TN [DOE]	Collaborative Composite Solutions Corporation/ University of Tennessee Research Foundation	Advanced polymer composites technology
Power America, The Next Generation Power Electronics Manufacturing Innovation Institute, Raleigh, NC [DOE]	North Carolina State University	Wide-bandgap power electronics manufacturing
RAPID, Rapid Advancement in Process Intensification Deployment Institute, New York, NY [DOE]	American Institute of Chemical Engineers	Modular chemical processes for process industries such as chemicals, oil, gas, pulp, and paper.
REMADE Institute, Reducing Embodied-energy And Decreasing Emissions, Rochester, NY [DOE]	Sustainable Manufacturing Innovation Alliance	Technologies to reuse, recycle and remanufacture materials such as metals, fibers, polymers, and electronic waste.
NIIMBL, The National Institute for Innovation in Manufacturing Biopharmaceuticals, Newark, DE [DOC]	University of Delaware	Manufacturing technologies for biopharmaceutical products

funding.[55] The CHIPS and Science Act of 2022 also authorized up to three new institutes related to semiconductors.[56] By March 2024, the Biden administration had established a National Semiconductor Technology Center and taken steps to create a CHIPS Manufacturing USA Institute and a National Advanced Packaging Manufacturing Program.[57]

The Institutes in Action

The accomplishments of the institutes include:[58]

- *PowerAmerica* worked with X-FAB, a semiconductor firm in Lubbock, Texas, to create standardized processes for silicon carbide foundries, eliminating technical and logistical complexities arising from different design processes. X-FAB can now fabricate silicon carbide power devices with economies of scale approaching that of existing less advanced devices.
- *CESMII* developed data analytics, machine learning, and modeling technology to reduce the energy consumption and environmental impact of cement production. A scale model of a rotary cement clinker production kiln was built by the University of Louisville and the cement firm Argos USA, and equipped with sensors and control systems combined with a multiphysics flow and heat transfer predictive model.[59]
- *LIFT* "supported development of an iron-manganese-aluminum alloy for use as armor on military ground vehicles," reducing armor weight by more than 10 percent. It also optimized "processing conditions to produce affordable, high quality armor plate in large volumes."[60]
- *AIM Photonics* developed a way for organizations of any size to use its advanced silicon photonics fabrication facility. Its Multi Project Wafer (MPW) services use standard elements to shorten design time and improve first-run success rates.
- *NIIMBL* brought together nearly 1,000 individuals from 302 organizations across the biopharmaceutical industrial base to collaborate on innovations to strengthen domestic manufacturing for gene therapy, antibody–drug conjugates, bio-specific antibodies, and vaccines.

The institutes vary in their organization and methods, but one will illustrate the basics of how they operate.[61] IACMI focuses on advanced composite materials like carbon fiber and advanced ceramics. Its goals are to cut the cost of composites, use less energy to make them, and recycle them better. Its web platform enables its participating firms to perform simulations of design, product integrity testing, and manufacturing issues.[62]

IACMI's current technology focus areas are composite materials and their manufacture, the use of composite materials for compressed gas storage and wind turbines, and the design, modeling and simulation of various composite uses.[63] It has working groups on infrastructure and construction, recycling and the circular economy, high-rate aerostructures fabrication, simulation and digital twins, future mobility, vehicles technology, and wind energy.[64] The low-cost and energy-efficient techniques it has refined include recyclable discontinuous carbon fiber, and thermoplastic resin for fiber-reinforced polymer composites.[65]

To start IACMI, DOE committed $70 million, and industry and state partners $180 million. It is managed by the Collaborative Composite Solutions Corporation, a nonprofit collaboration between several government agencies, universities, and industry. As of 2021, the consortium had more than 130 members, 1,600 projects, 400 patents, and 270 technologies that had advanced toward commercialization. In addition, 175,000 people had participated in its workforce development programs.[66]

IACMI's partnership with Oak Ridge National Lab's (ORNL) Manufacturing Demonstration Facility illustrates how the institutes makes shared infrastructure useful to industry. ORNL and the metal fabrication equipment firm Cincinnati Incorporated developed the Big Area Additive Manufacturing printer, which is capable of printing parts up to 6' by 12' by 1.5'. (It is one of more than 60 3D printers at the facility.) IACMI also partnered with Local Motors on 3D printing of automobiles.[67]

In 2018, IACMI started developing Vertical Axis Wind Turbines (VAWTs) with thermoplastic composite blades. VAWTs are less powerful and less efficient than horizontal turbines, but can perform at a wider range of wind speeds, are indifferent to wind direction, and are easier to fabricate, transport, and maintain. This project involved the National Renewable Energy Laboratory, Colorado State University, Steelhead Composites, and the high-performance materials firm Arkema, Inc. Using novel infusion and fabrication techniques, it went all the way from theoretical analysis to materials characterization and prototype fabrication.[68]

Is Manufacturing USA Effective?

The institutes help anchor regional manufacturing ecosystems and sustain the industrial commons (see Chapter 3). As of 2021, key indicators of their effectiveness were:[69]

- **Wide Reach into the Innovation Ecosystem.** Of the network's 2,320 institutional members, 63 percent were manufacturers, of which 72 percent had fewer than 500 employees. Academic institutions represented 22 percent. State and local economic development entities, federal laboratories, assorted nonprofits, and others accounted for the remaining 15 percent.[70]

- **Good Leverage of Federal Money.** In 2021, federal funding provided $127 million, 26 percent, of the institutes' money, while $354 million, 74 percent, was from state, emergency pandemic, and private funds. The resulting 2.7-to-1 non-federal-to-federal investment match far exceeded the program's design goal of 1-to-1.[71]
- **Successful Technology Advancement.** In 2021, the institutes and their members collaborated on 708 R&D applied research and development projects. An average of 82 percent of key technical milestones were met.[72]

A 2017 evaluation by the consulting firm Deloitte concluded in MFG-USA's favor: "The public–private partnership institute-based model attracts significant and meaningful participation from industry (including large companies and small enterprises), academia, and local, state, and federal government. Institute members have made substantial joint investments in collaborative approaches to R&D and commercialization of cutting-edge advanced manufacturing technologies."[73]

Three Government Accountability Office (GAO) reports have also given MFG-USA high marks.[74] The last, in 2021, reported that the institutes were making progress toward their goals, which were tracked using technology readiness levels (TRL), a standard metric of technology maturity and risk. And a National Academy of Sciences report in 2021 found that DOD had a meaningful framework for its five-year assessments of its institutes.[75]

The Future of Manufacturing USA

MFG-USA is thus off to a solid start, but still far too small. The Obama administration originally envisioned 45 institutes by 2020. As of mid-2024, there are only 16, with 2 more planned and 3 more authorized, but no concrete plans to establish the rest.[76] Institutes should be established to address cutting-edge fields not currently covered, including:

- Biomass processing and conversion
- Critical materials
- In-space manufacturing
- Digital manufacturing
- Artificial intelligence in manufacturing
- Agricultural robotics
- Cultured meat
- Vertical farming
- Neuromorphic engineering

- Quantum radar
- Fusion electric power
- Three-dimensional integrated circuits
- Optical transistors
- Artificial photosynthesis
- Nuclear batteries
- Ocean energy conversion
- Space-based solar power
- Bioplastics
- Conductive polymers
- Programmable matter
- High-temperature superconductivity
- Graphene (see Chapter 28)
- Microfluidics
- Self-healing materials
- Superalloys
- Nanosensors
- Tissue engineering
- Hypersonic flight
- Fusion rockets
- Plasma propulsion

Other institutes should be established to cover more technologically mature areas. Some should focus on specific industries, such as machine tools, construction, food processing, automobiles, aviation, maritime engineering, and spaceflight. Others should address specific existing technologies such as photovoltaics, wind power, nuclear fission, and energy storage. Still others should focus on technologies with relevance across many industries, such as optics, printing, packaging, nondestructive testing, advanced ceramics, advanced magnets, mechatronics, metal forming, powder metallurgy, and precision machining. Still others should focus on generic technologies such as metrology, materials characterization, industrial mathematics, materials flow, logistics, separation and purification, laser processing, process engineering, industrial engineering, and operations research. Finally, some should focus on specific materials, such as hydrogen, water, polymers, concrete, steel, and wood.

MFG-USA's appropriations remain subject to politically driven fluctuation. The CHIPS Act, despite authorizing new institutes, authorized only $829 million total over 5 years, a *cut* of $4 million per year from the average of the previous 10 years.[77] Germany, with a GDP one-fifth of the US, provides its analogous Fraunhofer Institutes central-government funding of $1 billion per year (see Chapter 8).[78] (The comparison is not exact because Germany is

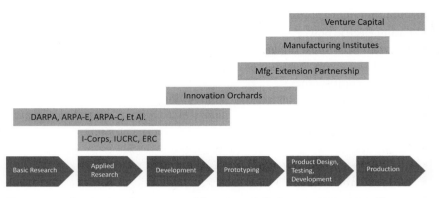

Figure 21.1 Institutional coverage of the steps of the innovation process[79]

behind the US in other institutions.) China says it will create 40 manufacturing institutes by 2025, and as of late 2022, had established 21.[80] Funding for the Chinese program has been estimated at 10 to 200 times (!) the budget of MFG-USA.[81]

The original plan was for each institute to receive federal support for five years, then be self-sustaining. This requirement contradicted the program's core premise that the for-profit sector on its own cannot provide important parts of the manufacturing ecosystem. Many of the manufacturing technologies the institutes are nurturing are at early stages, and will not generate income any time soon. Fortunately, the 2020 National Defense Authorization Act provided for the renewal of institutes' federal support in five-year increments, subject to merit review.[82]

Fitting the Pieces Together

How the various institutions that support innovation fit together is illustrated in Figure 21.1. (The Manufacturing Extension Partnership is discussed in the next chapter.)

22 INDUSTRIAL POLICY FOR ADVANCED MANUFACTURING

Manufacturing worldwide is in the early stages of a technological revolution, one that offers opportunities for the US to regain leadership in many key manufacturing industries. This revolution, by making a wide range of industries more technology and capital, rather than labor, intensive, will reduce America's disadvantage as a high-wage nation. The recent slowdown of US manufacturing's productivity growth can potentially be reversed.[1] But American industry will benefit only if both development and deployment of these technologies receive adequate industrial policy support.

Often referred to as the Fourth Industrial Revolution (4IR) or Industry 4.0, the revolution's root cause is the recent dramatic rise in computing power, digital connectivity, and accessible data, and the sharp decline in their costs. 4IR means digitizing not only functions that are easy to digitize, such as accounting and inventory systems, but basically everything that goes on in manufacturing. This includes, for example, new materials that, with help from AI, will be designed electronically based on computer models of their desired characteristics and molecular structures.[2] Figure 22.1 summarizes these new technologies, sometimes referred to as "cyber-physical systems."

These technologies will have their greatest impact not in isolation, but connected and working in concert in "smart" factories. They will reduce costs, improve quality, speed fulfillment, reduce risk, increase supply chain robustness, and improve environmental performance. 4IR is thus not just an enhancement of existing manufacturing processes and technologies, but a transformation of the entire production process that will take decades to complete.

Considering the technologies in Figure 22.1 in turn:

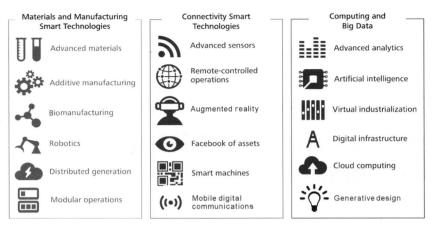

Figure 22.1 After Deloitte, "Industry 4.0: An Introduction"[3]

- **Additive manufacturing,** a/k/a 3D printing, enables rapid, automated production of prototypes and one-off parts. It can produce a wider, more flexible range of parts than conventional methods such as casting. It promises mass customization, smaller inventories, less waste, and some products that cannot otherwise be made at all.
- **Advanced materials** include familiar items such as the carbon composites that have replaced much of the aluminum in the latest airliners. The ultimate goal here is "designer materials" in which molecular modeling enables creation of materials with chosen properties of strength, weight, hardness, flexibility, electrical conductivity, transparency, ease of manufacturing, recyclability, et cetera.
- **Robotics** and factory automation generally have been around for decades. What is new are robots that can handle irregular objects and non-repetitive tasks that previously required humans. Robots designed to safely operate alongside people ("cobots") can raise human productivity at tasks robots cannot yet do entirely on their own (see Chapter 27).
- **Distributed generation** refers to using large numbers of diverse small electricity sources instead of the current system of a small number of huge power plants. This requires a smart grid, including power storage, that can deliver a stable flow of power from fluctuating renewable energy sources.
- **Modularization** refers to building industrial production systems from modular subassemblies. The modules are then combined in different ways for different products and production requirements. Because the individual modules have already been developed and tested, this saves time, reduces costs, and increases flexibility.

- **Advanced sensors** monitor complex systems, such as assembly lines, elevators, and aircraft engines, in real time. This enables precise tracking, optimization, remote control, and preemptive maintenance.
- **Smart machines** can do things like know when one step of a production process is not functioning properly and work around the damage until it is repaired. They can manufacture different products on the same assembly line and make timely parts-restocking requests.
- **Mobile digital communications** include Quick Response (QR) codes, Radio Frequency Identification (RFID) tags, Short-Range Wireless (SRW) systems such as Bluetooth and Wi-Fi, and Ultra-Wideband (UWB) networks. These are crucial when the objects being managed, from trucks to parcels, move around.
- **Remote-controlled operation** is a key way of applying all the information acquired by these technologies. It integrates geographically dispersed supply chains and intervenes in the production process over long distances, sometimes automatically.
- **Advanced analytics** digests the huge amounts of data generated or gathered by these technologies and analyzes it, especially in order to direct real-time production changes. Advanced visualization techniques are often employed to make this data comprehensible and actionable for managers.
- **Artificial intelligence** performs by machine cognitive tasks that previously required a human. Computer vision, for example, enables machines to handle objects and select parts needed for particular tasks. Self-driving trucks will eventually load, move, and deliver freight.
- **Virtual industrialization** uses digital models of factory machines, their buildings, and their components sufficiently detailed to accurately simulate the entire production process. Designs of existing facilities can be automatically captured by laser scanning and digital photography.
- **Digital infrastructure** enables all steps in the value chain, from raw materials to the customer, to be in instantaneous communication, forming an "internet of things" (IoT). This enables production to be tightly attuned to real-time market demand and logistics optimized.
- **Cloud computing** hosts key computing functions over the internet on large server farms, rather than on local machines. It is a key enabler of the increase in computing power required by many 4IR technologies.
- **Augmented reality** includes tools such as head-mounted displays to provide real-time information to frontline workers. It allows hands-free access to documents such as assembly and repair instructions, and is also useful for training workers and documenting production processes.
- **Generative design** uses computer simulations to develop and test product designs. Based on a design brief, an AI algorithm can explore alternative

production methods, materials, and budgets much faster than building physical prototypes or manually iterating through designs and financial projections.

- **Biomanufacturing** uses engineered biological processes to produce biomolecules and biomaterials for pharmaceuticals, foods, beverages, and industrial uses. It can use naturally occurring or genetically engineered cells to produce its output.

What Industry 4.0 Will Change

4IR will affect all industries, not just high-tech ones, and its economic impact is expected to be large. New products and entire industries not yet foreseeable will emerge. (A time-honored way to misunderstand technological revolutions is to assume they will only be applied to existing industries and products.) Many current jobs will be obsoleted and entire new categories of work created.

The impact may be even greater on low-tech industries. Industries like automobiles and consumer electronics are already very automated because the products have stable, firm, regular shapes well suited to past generations of relatively "dumb" robots. Emerging robots, however, with sophisticated tactile and vision capabilities, are potentially suited to industries such as food preparation and garment production that now require human labor because the products have soft, changeable, irregular forms.[4]

When used at the required scale and comprehensiveness, 4IR technologies are disruptive, not mere add-ons that leave existing processes intact. They therefore require restructuring of production processes and corporate organizations. Management techniques must evolve. For example, the ability to see and manipulate processes as they happen contradicts the "arm's length" mentality of much traditional manufacturing management, which developed when real-time information and the ability to act on it were available only on the factory floor. Demand for workers with both technical and soft skills such as creativity, analytical thinking, and complex problem-solving will grow.[5]

A 2022 survey found that 72 percent of smart-factory professionals had now scaled up from proof-of-concept projects and reached actual 4IR implementation: 80 percent in North America, 70 percent in Europe, and 66 percent in the Asia-Pacific.[6] Deployment problems vary by industry. Well-established legacy industries are held back by their sunk-capital costs, established operating procedures, and workforces skilled in older technologies.[7] Startups, while not locked into legacy technologies, often lack the capital to establish new production processes from scratch.[8]

The previous generation of advanced manufacturing technologies, such as conventional robots and computer numerical control (CNC) machine tools, has to date had a larger impact.[9] As IT analyst Rob Atkinson observed in 2021,

> Leaving aside that the best way to sell books and give TED Talks is to exaggerate the pace of technological change, the reality is that these technologies are still in the early part of the "S" curve. They are often costly, with limited performance. This is one reason why few companies are adopting them.[10]

It is uncertain how fast these technologies will deploy at scale. In 2013, McKinsey projected the economic impact of 3D printing by 2025 at $230–550 billion annually.[11] But by 2024, analysts were estimating a mere $25 billion for the next year.[12]

Deploying Advanced Manufacturing Technology

In recent decades, America has been less successful at deploying new technologies at scale than at inventing them. This has partly been because the federal government has offered little support for technology deployment, especially in manufacturing, outside of military and medical goods.[13]

Small and medium manufacturers (SMMs) are a particular problem. In 2022, the US had 239,651 manufacturing firms with fewer than 500 workers, representing 98 percent of manufacturers and employing 5.1 million people.[14] In the auto industry, for example, components average over 60 percent of the cost of a car, and a third of suppliers have fewer than 500 employees.[15]

SMMs today are struggling with the rapid introduction of new technologies, the increasing scope and sophistication of automation, changing technical workforce requirements, and the rising complexity of supply chains. On average, they are only 60 percent as productive as large manufacturers, and often lack the financial, technological, and organizational capacity to embrace new technologies without outside help.[16] But they will have to keep up to remain competitive as similar companies abroad, often the beneficiaries of government support, take on 4IR.

When original equipment manufacturers (OEMs) at Tier 1 of the supply chain adopt advanced technologies, their SMMs must be able to interface with them. For example, most OEMs now require just-in-time delivery, and in the early 2000s forced their suppliers to adopt lean production and participate in product development. SMMs in the big OEM supply chains now use common design for manufacturability and assembly (DFMA) software programs such as AutoCAD and Catia. SMMs that cannot adopt such tools and practices are excluded.

This technological lag will not be resolved by the free market alone. OEMs may resist paying to upgrade their suppliers because doing so also helps competitors supplied by the same firms. Small firms' investments in upgrading must often be customer-specific, making them dependent on these customers. Some foreign nations have corporate structures well suited to solving these problems, such as Japan's *keiretsu* families of companies (see Chapter 5) and the long-term business relationships of *Mittelstand* firms in Germany (Chapter 8). The US mostly does not.

The Manufacturing Extension Partnership

This is where the Hollings Manufacturing Extension Partnership (MEP) comes in. This federal public–private partnership's objective is to improve the productivity and technological performance of SMMs by helping them adopt the best technologies and business practices.

MEP was established as part of the Omnibus Foreign Trade and Competitiveness Act of 1988, a response to the perceived economic challenge from Japan. Its original intent was to facilitate the transfer of technologies developed within NIST, its parent agency, and other federal laboratories to SMMs. But it soon discovered that these firms had greater need for help adopting existing production technologies, plus management systems such as continuous improvement and just-in-time (JIT) parts delivery.[17] By the mid-1990s, MEP had pivoted to addressing these needs.

Today, a nationwide network of MEP centers provides a wide variety of technical and business assistance by using its own staff and by connecting SMMs to state and federal agencies, trade associations, universities, research laboratories, and other institutions. The centers are funded by the federal government, state and local governments, and user fees from their client firms. MEP has more than 1,400 in-house manufacturing experts, and also works with 2,100 outside consultants at 51 MEP centers and 450 service locations. Its 2022 federal funding was $158 million ($117 million less than the Biden administration, which understood and strongly supported the program, requested).[18] In 2022, it reported 33,500 interactions with 9,111 different clients.[19]

MEP's National Program Office in Gaithersburg, Maryland, oversees the centers with 60 staffers. It sets strategy, allocates funding, facilitates development of national-level service programs and tools, and shares best practices. MEP's advisory board, made up of outside experts, meets three times a year to evaluate its performance and give NIST's director advice on activities, plans, strategies, and policies.

Over the 33 years from its establishment to 2021, MEP assisted more than 130,000 companies, leading to an estimated $139 billion in sales,

$26 billion in cost savings, and the creation or retention of 1.45 million jobs.[20] According to one study in 2023, its benefit-to-cost ratio was 18 to 1.[21] Another analysis concluded that, for each federal dollar spent in 2022, MEP produced $40.50 in new client investment and $35.80 in new sales.[22] NIST itself has concluded that MEP creates or retains one manufacturing job for every $1,353 of federal support.[23]

Today, MEP emphasizes helping firms adopt all-important lean manufacturing practices, which it has been instrumental in spreading among SMMs.[24] The centers also help the 35,000–40,000 larger, more sophisticated, managerially proactive SMMs with tasks such as process improvement, capacity expansion, technology and supplier scouting, technology-driven market intelligence, capital access, cybersecurity, and international quality standards such as ISO 9001.[25]

The private sector could not do what MEP does. While more private consulting services are available now than when MEP began, SMMs still report that they cannot afford them and that they often do not provide the same services.

The MEP Centers

MEP centers differ in the scale and complexity of their services. Some are small not-for-profit entities, while others are affiliated with universities or state and regional economic development organizations. They vary according to the focus of local manufacturing, the presence of major research universities, regional startup rates, and the type of nonprofit managing them.

For example, the Ohio Development Services Agency's Office of Small Business and Entrepreneurship oversees the Ohio MEP through six sub-recipient centers. One, MAGNET in Cleveland, serving the state's northeastern industrial corridor, has more than 50 experts and support staff.[26] By contrast, New Mexico's MEP Center is a standalone nonprofit. It has an office in Albuquerque, branches in Farmington, Las Cruces, and Roswell, and a total staff of 10. Many of its clients qualify for financial assistance to attend its training sessions or receive onsite help.

Organizations applying to become an MEP center must demonstrate that they can provide the services their region needs and have a solid source of non-federal funding. Cooperative agreements are competitively awarded and reviewed annually for the first 5 years. If a center is found to be effective, it can receive a 5-year extension. All cooperative agreements are fully recompeted after 10 years.

Projects can be carried out by center staff, a partner organization, or third-party consultants. Here are three case studies from MEP's website:

> Doyle Equipment Manufacturing Company is a leading manufacturer of equipment for blending, conveying, tending, and spreading dry

fertilizers ... In 2016, Doyle consolidated most of its manufacturing and administrative functions in Palmyra, Missouri, where it built a new 220,000 square foot facility near its sister company, Riverview Manufacturing ... Doyle recognized the importance of garnering the knowledge and expertise of long-serving employees who were nearing retirement. Losing the experience of critical employees can dramatically impede operational efficiency and productivity, especially as companies expand and prepare for additional growth. To combat the potential loss of tribal knowledge, Doyle decided to introduce an Enterprise Resource Planning system (ERP) to capture and consolidate "islands of information" into one integrated system. Facing the immense task of properly implementing an ERP, company leaders turned to Missouri Enterprise, part of the MEP National Network, for guidance.[27]

Ingevity Corporation provides specialty chemicals, high-performance carbon materials, and engineered polymers that purify, protect, and enhance the world around us. Specifically, the company's plant in Waynesboro, Georgia, makes a carbon honeycomb filter used to collect automotive gas emissions within a vehicle and reuse them, rather than release them into the atmosphere ... In 2016, after a series of automotive recalls (unrelated to Ingevity), the entire automotive industry worked to improve quality standards. Many automotive OEMs began to require new certifications for companies in their supply chain. Even though Ingevity already had a quality management system in place and was certified to ISO 9001 and its automotive supplement, TS16949, the company needed to certify to the new, more stringent automotive- quality standard, IATF16949:2016, by September 2018, to maintain its customer base ... Chuck Sabo, the company's quality systems manager, quickly realized that his team needed some help and reached out to Elliot Price, Augusta Region Manager, who connected them with a GaMEP project manager and quality management system expert.[28]

A 17-year-old spinout of the Bigelow Laboratory of Ocean Science, Fluid Imaging Technologies is based in Scarborough, Maine with 15 employees. The company manufactures industry-leading particle analysis instrumentation based on digital imaging technology. Its flagship product, the FlowCam, is the first automated particle analysis instrument to use digital imaging for measuring size and shape of microscopic particles in a fluid medium. With applications in oceanographic research, municipal water, biopharmaceutical formulations, chemicals, oil and gas, biofuels and many other markets, Fluid Imaging Technologies leads the way in imaging particle analysis ... The challenge was to create tools and protocols to enable a manageable product development process ... Maine MEP, part of the MEP National Network, worked with the company on a weekly basis to not only design tools and protocols, but also run a test product through the system to provide both training and validation of the system with the staff.[29]

In addition to solutions to specific manufacturing problems, the centers increasingly offer more generalized services such as supply chain optimization, sustainability measures, workforce development, procurement assistance for government contracts, and technology acceleration.[30] SMMs need large firms as their customers, and MEP is well positioned to play matchmaker. Most MEP client companies are tier three firms, and the centers help them connect with the larger tier two firms that supply tier one OEMs. With MEP assistance, tier three SMMs often enter into cooperative arrangements with one another to develop products they can then sell to tier two companies.[31]

Other MEP Initiatives

In 2016, MEP began a pilot program embedding at least one MEP staffer at each of the 14 MFG-USA institutes (see Chapter 21).[32] Although this program ended in 2020, MEP and MFG-USA continue to coordinate activities on joint projects.[33] During 2017–23, MEP engaged in several other initiatives:

- **The MEP-Assisted Technology and Technical Resource Program** connected MEP's clients with technical resources at NIST laboratories. These have capabilities in advanced manufacturing technology, collaborative robotics, additive manufacturing, materials design, nanotechnology, information and communications technology, quantum information, biosciences, and industrial standards.[34]
- **The Competitive Awards Program** supported projects at the centers aimed at solving new or emerging manufacturing problems. These awards required no matching funds from the individual centers. They were made on a peer-reviewed and competitive basis, and could extend up to three years. Only centers with sufficient performance ratings were eligible for the awards, which ranged from $50,000 to $1 million.[35]
- **The Defense Manufacturing Supply Chain Support** program enabled MEP centers to provide technical assistance to small and innovative manufacturers in the defense industrial base. This included assistance in capitalizing on market opportunities associated with DOD's MFG-USA institutes. It also helped DOD's agencies integrate new technologies, best practices, and optimal manufacturing approaches into their suppliers' operations.[36]

- **Helping Manufacturers Source Domestically:** In 2021, President Biden signed E. O. 14005: *Ensuring the Future Is Made in All of America by All of America's Workforce.* This specifically requested that MEP Supplier Scouting and MEP-Assisted Technology and Technical Resource services help government procurement offices connect with domestic manufacturers.[37]
- **Improving Domestic Supply Chains:** In 2023, NIST awarded approximately $400,000 apiece to each of the MEP centers to develop programs to make domestic supply chains more efficient and resilient to geopolitical and pandemic disruptions, including funds for connecting small and medium-sized manufacturers with OEMs.[38]

Improving MEP

Recognition of MEP's value has led to improved funding. The original plan was that the centers would receive federal money for only six years, after which they were expected to become self-supporting, but this time limit was removed in 1998.

MEP's former two-to-one nonfederal-to-federal cost-sharing requirement incentivized its centers to focus on larger clients to maximize revenue.[39] To induce them to serve more smaller ones, the American Innovation and Competitiveness Act of 2017 reduced this ratio to one to one.[40]

Although a genuinely collaborative national manufacturing network had been a goal from the start, MEP centers for many years collaborated only regionally.[41] Thus, in 2017, the MEP National Network was launched.

MEP's budget is small compared to similar foreign programs and not commensurate with the number of SMMs in the US. Its federal funding has often been uncertain. In 2009, President Bush sought to end it, as did President Trump in 2018, 2019, and 2020. Congress nevertheless funded the program with $110 million in 2009, $140 million in both 2018 and 2019, and $155 million in 2020.[42] That last year, MEP also received $50 million from the Coronavirus Aid, Relief, and Economic Security Act.[43]

During the 2020 campaign, Joe Biden proposed *quadrupling* MEP's funding.[44] But his first budget proposed a more modest 50 percent increase, partly because there are limits to how fast MEP can expand.[45] For one thing, expansion requires the nonfederal funding to grow proportionally. Relaxing the cost-matching requirement would enable faster growth and have an especially large impact on MEP's ability to help startups and other young companies without much revenue, as they cannot afford high fees.

The CHIPS Act of 2022 expanded MEP's funding, especially for reshoring, domestic supply chains, critical technologies, and foundational manufacturing capabilities.[46] It authorized $2.3 billion for 2023 to 2027, triple the previous five-year period, though the actual appropriation for 2023 was $175 million, only $17 million higher than the previous year.[47]

23 MICRO-GOVERNANCE OF INDUSTRIAL POLICY

This chapter examines effective industrial policy agencies around the world as case studies of the successful *micro-governance* of industrial policy. "Micro" means their day-to-day operation, as opposed to macro-governance, the higher-level political decision-making that sets their overall objectives and methods and provides the authority to implement policy. To wit:

- The Industrial Technology Research Institute (Taiwan)
- The Fraunhofer-Gesellschaft (Germany)
- The Defense Advanced Projects Research Agency (US)
- The Advanced Research Projects Agency-Energy (US)
- The Small Business Innovation Research Program (US)

The Industrial Technology Research Institute

War-torn and impoverished in 1949, Taiwan's per capita GDP, adjusted for purchasing power, is now 93 percent of America's.[1] The Industrial Technology Research Institute (ITRI) played a key role in this transformation, and it remains one of the world's most successful government agencies at building high-tech industries.[2] Its efforts were critical, for example, to Taiwan Semiconductor Manufacturing Company (TMSC) becoming the world's most advanced chipmaker.

Soon after its formation in 1973, ITRI began laying the foundation for a semiconductor industry – an exceptionally ambitious goal given how technologically backward Taiwan was at the time. The Institute successively mastered semiconductor technologies and spun off companies to exploit them, such as United Microelectronics (1980), TMSC (1987), Winbond Electronics (1987),

Taiwan Mask (1988), and Vanguard International Semiconductor (1994). It simultaneously leveraged Taiwan's growing competencies in semiconductors to launch industries in related fields, including LEDs, photovoltaic cells, integrated circuit design, and thin-film-transistor liquid crystal displays (TFT-LCDs). It eventually pushed into nonelectronic fields such as healthcare and biotech.[3]

ITRI launched entire new industries, deliberately nurturing not only individual technological capabilities but complete supply chains to manufacture and distribute the resulting products worldwide.[4] As the director of its Display Technology Center (DTC), Dr. John Chen, explained, "The biggest strength of ITRI is the multidisciplinary cooperation. We create a complete manufacturing supply chain in its early stages. That is the secret. Then you can scale it up, you can have a complete supply chain for the industry. So, DTC does not just work with display companies, but also materials, supplies, and equipment makers."[5]

In recent decades, ITRI has expanded from being a deployer of existing technologies garnered abroad to a major creator of new technologies. It has developed proprietary technology in fields such as three-dimensional integrated circuits, WIMAX wireless broadband, flexible displays, solar cells, light electric vehicles, and RFID.[6] The Institute was named a Clarivate Analytics Top 100 Global Innovator in 2015, 2018, 2019, 2020, 2021, 2022, and 2023. By 2022, it had accumulated more than 30,000 patents.[7] Its core competencies have traditionally been in hardware, but it is now expanding into software and systems integration.[8]

ITRI's achievements do not, however, negate less legitimate tactics that have contributed to Taiwan's success. The country has a long record of infringing US trade laws and stealing intellectual property.[9]

Driving Taiwan's Technology Base

ITRI has continuously developed and refined methods for adapting foreign innovations and helping Taiwanese industry deploy them. It has operated complete pilot plants for its client firms to use for product and process development, testing of equipment and materials, and pre-commercial test production. Its signal technology acquisition was its purchase of semiconductor IP from America's RCA in 1976 and its establishment, based on that technology, of an entire integrated circuit demonstration plant.[10] ITRI's focus was ruthlessly practical: As Ding-Yuan Yang, an ITRI official who oversaw this project, explains, "If we only transferred these techniques in a lab, we wouldn't have been able to attain industrial production."[11]

Today, ITRI has two types of R&D labs, which undergo continuous reorganization to respond to technological change. Its *Core Laboratories* specialize in specific themes, currently a) electronic and optoelectronic devices, b) measurement and standards, c) advanced materials, d) factory automation, and e) big data. Then its *Technology Integration Centers* draw on the Core Laboratories' work, integrating it into cross-cutting technologies and systems. Current examples include microelectronic machines (MEMS), various information and communications technologies, green energy, and additive manufacturing.[12] These Centers are created and disbanded as the Institute's technology foci evolve over time. ITRI allocates budgets to the Centers, which then contract with the laboratories to develop specific technologies.

Taiwan's economy is dominated by small businesses and the country has fewer large multinationals than competitors such as Japan, Korea, and the US. ITRI therefore proactively provides smaller firms with technological resources and research support that would otherwise be beyond their reach. (Compare Fraunhofer-Gesellschaft, discussed later in this chapter.) It licenses them technologies. It performs applied research under contract. It helps them under a number of other government programs, including Taiwan's Small Business Innovation Research program, which differs from America's version (also discussed below) in not being restricted to research serving government agencies. For startups, ITRI's facilities, expertise, training, support, and connections to early-stage public and private funding help provide a bridge across the valley of death (see Chapter 21 for this concept).

ITRI gives management and marketing advice to both new and established firms.[13] It participates in consortia with Taiwanese firms to jointly develop technologies. It has rationalized entire sectors, effectively assigning specialized roles to individual companies and incorporating them into production networks with the scale and skills to compete globally.[14] Typically, ITRI's innovation networks include at least one public research organization, numerous small and medium-sized enterprises, and at least one multinational company.[15]

ITRI's Industry, Science, and Technology International Strategy Center helps firms develop relationships with foreign companies and research organizations. The maturing of ITRI's technological capabilities has enabled it to collaborate with some of the world's leading public and private research organizations, including Merck (US), Fraunhofer-Gesellschaft, Applied Materials (US), Corning Glass (US), Underwriters Laboratories (US), VTT (Finland), AIST (Japan), IMEC (Belgium), NRC (Canada), LM Ericsson (Sweden), and TNO (Holland).[16] For example, it is collaborating with the British firm Oxford Instruments, the world's leading maker of precision instruments, in fields such as light-emitting diodes (LEDs), high-power components, high-k dielectric materials, and wide-bandgap materials and components.[17]

Taiwanese companies have traditionally been weak in the legal skills needed to defend their intellectual property and have therefore been exposed to patent litigation by foreign firms.[18] Because the best defense is ownership of a *pool* of patents covering *all* elements of a new technology, ITRI in 2005 began auctioning off such pools under exclusive licenses. It defends its own patents in litigation and has built the capacity to assist local firms in overseas patent defense and management. It groups firms into alliances to exert greater leverage in negotiations with foreign multinationals over licensing terms and royalty rates. Its Technology Transfer and Law Center assists in developing IP strategies such as patent portfolio management and patent quality improvement.[19]

ITRI and Taiwan's Talent Base

ITRI employs 6,000 people, many with advanced degrees.[20] Most leave after a few years, with 85 percent moving to industry, where they have a powerful impact. ITRI's staff have an aggressive, can-do outlook and a strong work ethic, manifested in the bold, risky, *and successful* strategic moves made by ITRI and its industrial progeny and collaborators.[21] Its close cooperation and long-term outlook are underpinned by a strong sense of national purpose in this small, threatened, diplomatically isolated nation.

ITRI's founding generation drew heavily on American ideas, institutional models, and scientific, engineering, and business practices. Kuo-Ting Li, who drove the establishment of Hsinchu Science Park (see later in this chapter), consulted with Frederick Terman, the Stanford provost known as the father of Silicon Valley. Morris Chang, the billionaire founder of TSMC who headed ITRI from 1985 to 1987, held a doctorate from Stanford, earned three degrees from MIT, and worked for 25 years at Texas Instruments, where he served for a time as head of its global semiconductor business.[22] Virtually the entire top echelon of Taiwan's early semiconductor industry was formed out of a group called the RCA 37 – 37 young ITRI staffers sent to RCA in the 1970s to learn semiconductor technology.[23] When ITRI decided to launch TSMC as the world's first pure-play foundry – to make but not design chips – it drew on the teachings of Carver Mead, a visionary US scientist and engineer who was arguing that semiconductor manufacturing could be separated from design.[24]

ITRI's ties with Silicon Valley remain strong. In 2004, ITRI and Stanford formed the ITRI–Stanford Platform, which ITRI describes as "the kernel of Silicon Valley's innovation system." This vehicle for the exchange of ideas on innovation, applications, and entrepreneurship has benefited both institutions.[25] More recently, ITRI established a liaison network to the field of artificial intelligence, linking Taiwanese companies and research organizations with the Stanford Artificial Intelligence Laboratory.[26]

Seeding a Supercluster

ITRI's headquarters and main physical site are located in a dense cluster of research universities, high-tech manufacturing companies, and supply-chain firms centered on Hsinchu Science Park (HSP) in Hsinchu, an hour south of Taipei. HSP was established in 1973 by the Ministry of Economic Affairs (MOEA) through a merger of three existing government laboratories.

Most locations in the cluster are within close proximity (see Chapter 3 about clusters). To qualify for space there, companies must spend a certain proportion of their revenues on R&D and a certain proportion of their employees must be scientists or engineers.[27] Firms enjoy tax holidays for their first five years of operation, plus tax breaks for various forms of industrial upgrading.[28]

HSP allows Taiwan's semiconductor industry to achieve economies of scale in R&D, facilitates technology transfer between large firms and the supporting tier of smaller companies, and enhances information exchange between rival firms.[29] ITRI and two excellent technology universities, National Chung Hsing and National Chiao Tung, create a fertile R&D climate.

These universities provide trained, motivated students and locations for cooperative research. Beginning in the early 1980s, the government launched numerous new technology graduate programs, and by 1999, the number of Taiwanese PhDs trained in Taiwan exceeded the number trained in the US.[30] Today, ITRI College provides technical training in major and emerging industries, including an entrepreneurship "boot camp."[31] ITRI has proactively seeded HSP with startups.

HSP exerts a steady pull on the global diaspora of educated, skilled Taiwanese.[32] Knowledge and work experience acquired in world-class firms and labs in the US and elsewhere have come home with them.[33] They have also brought personal connections: As two scholars have observed, "[A]n engineer facing a technical problem in HSP would easily pick up a phone and call a friend in Silicon Valley, which would often result in quick solutions."[34]

ITRI's Lessons

A number of ITRI's attributes are especially relevant to the US:

Close industry ties. ITRI's ties with industry are so extensive and close that the boundaries between ITRI, the private sector, and local universities can be indistinct. Top ITRI engineers serve on the faculty of nearby universities, and between its founding in 1973 and 2008, 13,000 ITRI staff moved to industry.[35]

Relative autonomy. ITRI's overall strategic direction is set by Technology Development Plans developed by MOEA's Department of Industrial Technology after extensive consultation with foreign and domestic experts, including those at ITRI.[36] But ITRI enjoys considerable autonomy thanks to a tradition of political noninterference in economic policy.[37]

Bridging role. ITRI proactively serves as a bridge between Taiwanese industry and international supply chains, helping domestic firms integrate themselves into the latter. It has served as a matchmaker between Taiwanese enterprises and leading multinationals, vouching for the former's bona fides and negotiating favorable terms on their behalf.[38]

Incubator role. ITRI established Taiwan's first tech incubator in 1996, hosting startups less than 18 months old and with less than $2.4 million in capital. Today, new companies remain at the incubator for an average of seven years. More than 270 firms have been incubated, with two dozen reaching IPOs.[39] In 2021, for example, ITRI spawned new firms in water treatment, semiconductor fabrication, and 5G networking.[40]

Venture financing. ITRI's subsidiary the Industrial Technology Investment Corporation (ITIC) invests in its spin-offs. When ITRI wants to spin off a startup, ITIC screens the proposal and works with ITRI's Commercialization and Industry Service Center to assess its commercial potential. Not all candidates receive funding, but the most promising ones receive it early on, with ITIC taking equity.[41]

Advisory support. ITRI has long benefited from sophisticated strategic and technological advice from foreign and domestic leaders in industry and academia.[42] For example, the 1970s decision to create a semiconductor industry was based on recommendations from the government's Technical Advisory Committee, whose members were all "Chinese people overseas who had gained considerable experiential knowledge working in MNCs located in the USA."[43]

Coherence and Coordination. ITRI combines a) an authoritative central coordinating entity, b) autonomy for subunits in implementing its overall strategy, c) intensive continuing consultations and movement between government, industry and academia, and d) proactive organizational change in response to global economic and technological developments.

High-level political backing. ITRI is viewed as crucial to Taiwan's world-leading, prestigious, and highly profitable semiconductor industry. In a clear sign of its importance, the prime minister of Taiwan directly appoints its president and board chairman.[44] It is led by a president and supervised by a board of directors comprised of university leaders, company executives, and government officials.

* * *

The Fraunhofer-Gesellschaft

Founded in 1949, Germany's Fraunhofer-Gesellschaft (FhG) is a nationwide network of 76 research institutes that do applied research for governmental and industrial clients. Named after Joseph von Fraunhofer, a nineteenth-century scientist, engineer, and entrepreneur, it has 30,000 employees and an annual budget of €3 billion, €2.6 billion of which goes to contract research.[45] FhG is the largest applied research organization in Europe, providing firms large and small with capabilities they lack internally: personnel, equipment, and the knowledge of how to use it. FhG has more than 1,000 distinct competencies.[46] Its personnel include students who combine academic study with practical research for industry. It has been so successful that it was the model for America's Manufacturing USA (see Chapter 21).[47]

The Fraunhofer Institutes

Each institute is an elaborately equipped physical site with an average staff of 400 (some have more than 1,000), many with advanced degrees. The institutes specialize in particular technologies. (A list of the institutes is in Figure 23.1.)[48] They develop product prototypes and industrial processes for their clients, demonstrate them, even test them on pilot production lines.[49] They also conduct research at their clients' own facilities.[50] The institutes' work ranges from small one-off projects to multi-project, multi-institute collaborations over many years.

The institutes' specializations often align with local industries and university programs.[51] For example, the Institute for Applied Optics and Precision Engineering supports the optics cluster around Jena, which boasts 170 firms, 14,000 employees, annual revenues of $2.5 billion, and 900 research scientists.[52] The institute in Chemnitz is near the Technische Universität Chemnitz and focuses on machine tools and production systems. The one in Dresden is near the Dresden University of Technology and focuses on mechatronics and medical engineering.

FhG supports both existing and emerging industry clusters.[53] It helps tie companies, universities, other research organizations, and service providers together, and fosters their connections to wider supply chains. In the early 1990s, FhG even began establishing research centers outside Germany to stay abreast of technologies in which other countries led.[54]

Mechatronic Systems Design

Software and Systems Engineering

Algorithms and Scientific Computing

Applied Information Technology

Applied and Integrated Security

Applied Optics and Precision Engineering

Applied Polymer Research

Applied Solid State Physics

Biomedical Engineering

Building Physics

Cell Therapy and Immunology

Ceramic Technologies and Systems

Chemical Technology

Communication, Information Processing and Ergonomics

Computer Graphics Research

Digital Media Technology

Digital Medicine

Electronic Microsystems and Solid-State Technologies

Electronic Nano Systems

Energy Economics and Energy Systems

Environmental, Safety and Energy Technology

Large Structures in Production Engineering

Experimental Software Engineering

Factory Operation and Automation

High-Frequency Physics and Radar

High-Speed Dynamics

Industrial Engineering

Industrial Mathematics

Information Center for Planning and Building

Integrated Circuits

Integrated Systems and Device Technology

Intelligent Analysis and Information Systems

Interfacial Engineering and Biotechnology

International Management and Knowledge Economy

Laser Technology

Energy Infrastructures and Geothermal Systems

Casting, Composites, and Processing

Individualized and Cell-Based Medical Engineering

Organic Electronics, Electron Beam, and Plasma Technology

Machine Tools and Forming Technology

Manufacturing Technology and Advanced Materials

Manufacturing Engineering and Automation

Material and Beam Technology

Material Flow and Logistics

Materials Recycling and Resource Strategy

Mechanics of Materials

Microelectronic Circuits and Systems

Microstructure of Materials and Systems

Microengineering and Microsystems

Molecular Biology and Applied Ecology

Non-Destructive Testing

Optronics, System Technologies, and Image Exploitation

Open Communication Systems

Photonic Microsystems

Physical Measurement Techniques

Process Engineering and Packaging

Production Systems and Design Technology

Production Technology

Reliability and Microintegration

Secure Information Technology

Silicate Research

Silicon Technology

Solar Energy Systems

Structural Durability and System Reliability

Surface Engineering and Thin Films

Systems and Innovation Research

Technological Trend Analysis

Telecommunications

Toxicology and Experimental Medicine

Translational Medicine and Pharmacology

Transportation and Infrastructure Systems

Wind Energy Systems

Wood Research

Cognitive Systems

Battery Cell Production

Figure 23.1 The Fraunhofer Institutes

Much of FhG's work is with large companies, but it provides critical support for Germany's small and medium manufacturers, which generally have no in-house R&D capability.[55] Indeed, FhG is rightly regarded as responsible for much of their exceptional international competitiveness (see Chapter 8).[56] It not only does research for small firms, but also hires them to work on its own projects, exposing them to its technological expertise, intellectual property portfolio, research equipment, and contacts throughout industry and government.

Each institute has an advisory board from the private sector, the science community, and government entities. Although FhG receives most of its revenue from public sources, it is not under strict governmental control. It is under no absolute obligation, for example, to follow the direction of the ministries in Berlin, although its practices generally align well with central government policy. Each operates with great autonomy, choosing its own research fields, specific topics within them, and how to distribute project results. The institutes determine their own internal organization, how they set up their various profit centers, and how they allocate their funding. When an institute has a budget shortfall, its funds can be supplemented by headquarters. Every five years, the institutes are required to review their strategic plans and are audited by headquarters.[57] While the system has been remarkably stable overall, there have been cases of less successful institutes shutting down or being merged with stronger ones.

Fraunhofer-Gesellschaft's Strengths

Dedication to Applied Research. FhG supports applied, not basic, research. Because it derives a third of its revenues from industry, its research is automatically aligned with the needs of companies. Individual projects are expected to achieve commercially relevant results in 6 to 24 months, ruling out transformational projects.

Incremental Innovation. Steady implementation of thousands of incremental projects per year keeps German firms at the technological forefront of *established* industries. This, rather than leadership in new industries, is Germany's forte. FhG is a major foundation of the country's engineering prowess and its success retaining a larger manufacturing sector and more well-paid manufacturing jobs than other developed nations.[58]

Integration of Research and Business. An FhG research contract is carried out by both a research unit that provides the scientific and technical expertise and a business unit that understands the commercial side. These units interact with the corresponding external parties – that is, university and governmental research departments and FhG's industrial clients, respectively.

Major Physical Research Sites. FhG institutes are well staffed and equipped. For example, the Institute for Solar Energy Systems has 1,400 employees and more than 300,000 square feet of lab space.[59] It has machines for photovoltaic manufacturing including a diffusion furnace, wet-chemical equipment, automated deposition equipment, physical vapor deposition equipment, printing and laser processing equipment, inline furnaces with flexible cell testers, and a fully automated screen-printing line.[60]

Close University Ties. Each institute is linked with one or more universities or other institutions of higher learning. Directors of the institutes are usually university faculty and they steer promising students into their institutes. FhG personnel teach and enroll in university courses. Technical problems arising out of FhG's work can be developed into course offerings and dissertations. FhG's research costs industry less than in-house work in part because students make up much of its workforce.

Training Function. Effective technology transfer to firms is ensured by training FhG gives their workers.[61] Each institute also provides hands-on training to its own staff. The majority are PhD candidates and postdocs, working part-time. Most move on to industry, creating a flow of trained personnel to the private sector.[62] They bring not only theoretical, technological, and business knowledge, but also industrial and academic contacts.[63]

Intellectual Property Development. FhG is consistently the leader among German research organizations in annual invention disclosures, annual patent applications, and total patent portfolio.[64] It owns the rights to the generic technologies developed in its research, though its industry partners may receive exclusive licenses for their own specific applications. (It retains the right to license the same technology to other users for different applications.) Its licensing revenues in 2021 were €114 million.[65]

Spin-Off Promotion. FhG's institutes encourage their personnel to start companies, then give them technical, managerial, and operational support. FhG often transfers intellectual property in return for a minority equity stake. Its spin-offs have an exceptional success rate, between 65 and 90 percent, though partly because they emphasize low-risk, incremental advances.[66] FhG also participates in Germany's

High-Tech Gründerfonds (HTG), a public–private partnership that provides seed capital for tech startups.[67]

FhG's Collaborations and Networks

FhG combines its institutes in three ways.

Nine *Groups* focus on broad technology areas. For example, the Group for Microelectronics involves 16 institutes and more than 3,000 employees. Eleven institutes within this group combine with two institutes from Germany's Leibnitz Gesellschaft (nonuniversity research institutes) to form Research Fab Microelectronics Germany.[68]

Six *Clusters of Excellence* focus on narrower technologies requiring the expertise of different institutes. For example, the Programmable Materials Cluster develops materials that can "replace complete systems comprising sensors, controllers and actuators." This cluster is comprised of the institutes for Applied Polymer Research, Building Physics, Chemical Technology, Mechanics of Materials, and Machine Tools and Forming Technology.[69]

Ten *Alliances* coordinate FhG resources relevant to a particular industry, such as automobiles, construction, energy, or food.

FhG understands the competitive benefits of standards-setting (see Chapter 3). It therefore participates in the 5G Automotive Association, AUTOSAR, the CAR 2 CAR Communication Consortium, the European Telecommunications Standards Institute, the Bluetooth Special Interest Group, the Eclipse Foundation, ITS Bavaria, the BroadBand Forum, Bit-Kom e.V., the EAST-ADL Association, and nearly two dozen other standards-setting groups.[70]

A Key Part of the German System

FhG's success is partly due to the milieu in which it operates.[71] As discussed in Chapter 8, Germany is a coordinated market economy (CME) with close cooperation between the state and business. Institutions ranging from banks to labor unions operate differently than in many other developed countries, including the US. Thus, most efforts to replicate FhG outside Germany have failed or have achieved only modest results – including the research centers established abroad by FhG itself. For example, Germany has:

1. A university system deliberately designed to transfer the fruits of scientific discovery to industry
2. A dual system of education that simultaneously teaches both academic learning and practical applications

3. Vocational training that combines publicly funded academic courses with on-the-job training by companies
4. A business culture that values cooperation and collaboration as well as competition

Germany does not suffer from the cultural split – with separate communities and values – that hampers university-industry collaboration in the UK, France, Canada, and many other countries. Its personnel are trained to collaborate and subordinate individual competitive instincts to teamwork and the smooth integration of multiple disciplines.

FhG is headquartered in Munich, not the capital, Berlin, reflecting its relative political independence. It is amply and stably funded, so it can plan and execute long-term strategy, staffing, and research. Since 1975, federal and state funding of scientific research has been governed by a multiparty agreement, and the difficulty of reaching the original agreement makes it equally difficult to modify.[72]

About a third of FhG's money is "core" funding from the federal government and the states (*Länder*). This is not earmarked for specific tasks or projects and can be used by the institutes at their discretion. Another third is from contract research performed for government ministries and other public entities. The remaining third comes from contract research for private companies.

In addition to its operating budget, FhG receives substantial governmental support for capital outlays such as the establishment of new institutes and the upgrading of existing ones.[73] These monies are augmented, directly or indirectly, by various state and federal subsidies for specific purposes, such as green energy, and by EU funding. FhG will play a large collaborative role in implementing Germany's National Industrial Strategy 2030 and Industrie 4.0, two major industrial policy programs (see Chapters 8 and 22).[74]

* * *

The Defense Advanced Research Projects Agency

Created in 1958 in response to the shock of Sputnik, the Defense Advanced Research Projects Agency (DARPA) (originally and also later called the Advanced Research Projects Agency) was founded to ensure that the US would thereafter be the initiator, rather than the victim, of militarily significant technological advances. This remains its primary mission today. ARPA aimed to overcome the then stove-piped military services' procurement programs and bridge the disconnect with US space programs.

DARPA's goal is radically new technologies in defense, space, and dual-use military-civilian products.[75] It develops and demonstrates them, then leaves further development and production to the private sector and the armed services.[76] It has, in the words of the *Harvard Business Review*, "[T]he longest-standing, most consistent track record of radical innovation in history."[77]

DARPA does not have its own labs or perform its own research. Instead, it funds research by companies, universities, federal labs, and nonprofits. It has only 200 employees, but an annual budget of $3.5–4 billion.[78] Its focus has shifted from the space race (1950s) to the Vietnam War (1970s) to the semiconductor industry (1980s) to information technology (1990s) to intelligence gathering for counterterrorism, Iraq, and Afghanistan (2000s). Since 2010, it has focused on AI, quantum computing, and neuro-synaptic processors, which are microprocessors modeled on biological brains.[79]

DARPA has large and stable federal funding, autonomy within the defense bureaucracy, and exemption from civil service rules and many other federal regulations.[80] It also has a well-funded customer, DOD, even if the adoption of its innovations has sometimes been less straightforward than the military's high-tech reputation would imply.

DARPA's Biggest Achievements

This partial list necessarily omits those that are still classified.

The Information Revolution. In the 1960s, ARPA created ARPANET, a computer network of that eventually evolved into the internet. Other projects led to personal computing, voice recognition, touchscreen displays, many key wireless communications technologies, lithium-ion batteries, artificial intelligence, cellular roaming technology, speech recognition, and graphical user interfaces.[81]

Smart Weapons. Battlefields increasingly defined by sophisticated information and communications systems, "smart" precision-strike weapons, stealth aircraft, drones, and soon AI, resulting in the so-called Revolution in Military Affairs.[82]

The Global Positioning System. In the late 1950s, DARPA started working on satellite navigation systems that evolved into today's GPS (see Chapter 26).

Night Vision. DARPA developed this technology based on infrared-detecting sensors. It has helped American soldiers operate in and, until recently, dominate night battlefields.[83]

Stealth Technology. DARPA developed technologies to make aircraft harder to track by radar and infrared. These included new aircraft shapes, radar absorbing surfaces, exhaust cooling, and active radar signal cancelation. The first test plane flew in 1977 and the first operational stealth aircraft, the F-117A fighter, in 1983.

Micro-Electro-Mechanical Systems (MEMS). MEMS include accelerometers, used in vehicle airbags, drone guidance systems, and smartphones. Another example is "lab on a chip" medical diagnostic systems.

The agency continues to evolve. In 2017, it launched its Disruptioneering initiative, which seeks rapid identification and exploration of high-risk ideas that could lead to quantum leaps forward. Program managers are tasked with developing small programs ($5 million or less) that can progress from idea to contract award within 90 days.[84]

Key Features

DARPA is small and flexible. It has only 100 program managers, augmented by a similar number of support personnel, mainly contract managers and consultants. These have been characterized as a shield protecting its leadership and program managers from bureaucratic demands that would sap their energy and attention.[85] It has a flat organizational structure with a director's office, six technical program offices, and three other specialized offices.[86] Its program offices are:

The **Biological Technologies Office** researches bio-related topics such as countermeasures against bioterrorism and support for warfighters' physiological readiness.

The **Information Innovation Office** researches information technologies to support military operations, including cyberwarfare, and seeks to anticipate new modes of warfare in these domains.

The **Microsystems Technology Office** researches microprocessors, microelectromechanical systems, and photonic devices, including phased-array radars, high-energy lasers, and infrared imaging.

The **Tactical Technology Office** researches revolutionary ground, maritime, air, and space system platforms, a/k/a vehicles.[87]

The **Strategic Technology Office** researches increasing military effectiveness, cost leverage, and adaptability.

The **Defense Sciences Office** researches foundational physical and social sciences including mathematics, computational design, sensing, and social systems.

The Defense Sciences Office, sometimes called DARPA's DARPA, enjoys the broadest latitude, with many of its projects starting as "blue sky adventures."[88]

The DARPA director's most important job is recruiting talented program managers.[89] DARPA recruits from universities, government labs, and the private sector. A former director said in 2016 that he looked for a technically strong individual who had project management experience and was "a bit of a dreamer and not constrained by thinking 'this we know to be true.'"[90] DARPA hires a mix of people with theoretical and experimental backgrounds.

Because program managers have nearly absolute power in assembling their research teams, the position attracts ambitious, qualified applicants. Former director Arati Prabhakar told one potential recruit, "You don't want to go to a university, where you'll have graduate students working for you. If you come to DARPA, you'll have professors working for you."[91] Program managers are responsible for creating, and if necessary terminating, projects and programs. They may, but are not required to, use peer review to assess proposals.

Although DARPA's leadership must approve their proposals, program managers have a degree of independence that is unique in the federal bureaucracy. They are expected to remain at the agency no more than three to five years, ensuring a constant inflow of new ideas and preventing institutional ossification. One program manager commented in 2016 that the sense of time ticking is "the heart of the whole thing. It is an impetus to venture into the unknown, to get people to put something forward, to build a prototype, warts and all."[92]

DARPA enjoys budgetary "other transactions" authority, which lets it enter into agreements with outside parties tailored to project needs and not necessarily conforming to the traditional federal formats of grant, contract, or cooperative agreement.[93] It can augment its own staff with temporary assignees from the Defense Department, the military, other federal agencies, and elsewhere. This lets it staff up quickly in a particular area without the burden of sustaining permanent capabilities. These staff then often become advocates for DARPA-developed technologies when they return to their home organizations.[94]

Because DARPA pursues innovations at the edge of the possible, it often faces the possibility, even likelihood, of failure.[95] But unlike most government bureaucracies, where failures can be career-enders, it is tolerant if the potential payoff was large enough.[96] Furthermore, its apparent failures often succeed in their larger consequences. For example, its Strategic Computing Initiative of the 1980s spent billions in a vain attempt to achieve artificial intelligence, which required more computing power than was available at that time. However, as one journalist notes, "this failure laid the foundations for most of the great computing science advances in artificial intelligence ... So, what you call 'success' or 'failure' sometimes just takes time."[97]

How DARPA Operates

DARPA generates its "thrust areas" and individual programs based on DOD's Long-Range Research and Development Planning Program (LRRDPP). DARPA plays a role in developing LRRDPP, which identifies key strategic threats and potential technological countermeasures. DARPA identifies break-through outcomes (e.g., a self-driving car, an unmanned combat aircraft), then organizes portfolios of projects needed to overcome their key technological challenges.

DARPA makes iterative investments to drive technologies from incep-tion through proof-of-concept.[98] While its projects typically last three to five years, major technological themes may entail multiple interconnected projects over a longer period. For example, starting in the 1970s, DARPA sponsored research in stealth technology, standoff precision strike, and intelligence, surveil-lance, and reconnaissance (ISR) technologies. These were combined to create the *systemic* military capabilities demonstrated in Operation Desert Storm in 1991, which allowed the US to change the rules of warfare.[99] Underpinning these systems were capabilities created by other DARPA projects in areas such as microelectronics, networking, computing, and information processing.

DARPA program managers use the following tools to develop new projects:

> **Requests for Information Special Notices** are sent to experts in a field asking about their current work. DARPA guarantees nondisclosure, thereby enabling researchers to freely share confidential information. For program managers, these notices are "a uniquely efficient way to understand what is happening and get a handle on what might be possible."[100]
>
> **Broad Agency Announcements** are solicitations for proposals linked to program-specific areas.[101] They identify technological mile-stones the would-be performers should achieve. These proposals often elicit responses from individuals and institutions not previously asso-ciated with DARPA, and thus serve to irrigate its portfolio with new concepts and approaches.[102]
>
> **Grand Challenges** are competitions in areas such as robotics, response to epidemics, and autonomous vehicles. They are deliberately open to all individuals and institutions to avoid closing off new areas of inquiry by relying only on established experts.
>
> **The Defense Sciences Research Council** convenes leading scientists to brainstorm technological developments that could address military challenges. At its annual conference, leading experts are presented with current problems of concern and asked for solutions.[103]

DARPA Creates Technology Communities

DARPA also catalyzes innovation by seeding research communities in new areas. These often outlive the programs that spawned them and can be as valuable as the technologies the programs developed.[104] For example, DARPA has funded creation of entire new academic departments, computer science in the 1960s being the paradigm case.

DARPA funding helps sustain researchers and research organizations and nudge them toward ambitious, transformational research. Startup firms have historically played a major role in DARPA's work, particularly for technologies with commercial potential.[105]

DARPA often funds projects by several groups pursuing different solutions to the same problem, because for novel technologies the best approach cannot be known at the start. A program manager will often share knowledge from one team with another, but at least initially, he or she is often the only connection between the teams. Farther along, however, DARPA's researchers are required to present to each other.[106]

DARPA enjoys good support from other federal research agencies. In 2016, for example, it announced its Spectrum Collaboration Challenge (SC2) to encourage research on smart systems that collaboratively adapt to the congested, rapidly changing, wireless spectrum. NSF reinforced this effort by funding SC2 research teams that did not win DARPA support.[107]

Challenges of Deploying DARPA's Technology

DARPA's main "customer" is DOD. Defense is largely a legacy sector, based on long-established technologies, infrastructure, and practices. Disruptive capabilities challenge existing bureaucracies and programs.[108] The Air Force, for example, initially resisted drones as a threat to the role of human pilots.[109]

DARPA addresses this challenge in several ways. Its Adaptive Execution Office (AEO) consists of five retired senior military officers, one government civilian, two active-duty officers, plus systems engineering and technical assistance contractors. AEO serves as a matchmaker and liaison, working with program managers throughout their projects to develop strategies for deploying their technologies. It provides operational expertise, sponsors demonstrations and field trials, and tracks transition activity.[110]

DARPA has operational liaisons to each of the services.[111] It uses the service branches as real-world laboratories, and they use DARPA to access experimental technologies.[112] For example, beginning in 2010 it deployed what eventually became a team of more than 100 to Afghanistan to develop and refine Nexus 7, a data-mining and analysis system used for intelligence analysis and event prediction.[113]

Replicating DARPA

DARPA's successes have led to efforts to replicate it elsewhere. There are now six analogous agencies: ARPA-E (DOE, 2009), AG-ARDA (USDA, 2019), ARPA-H (HHS, 2022), BARDA (DHS, 2006), ARPA-C (DOE, 2022), and ARPA-I (DOT, 2022).

The Homeland Security Act of 2002 established the Homeland Security Advanced Research Projects Agency. However, HSARPA did not enjoy DARPA's autonomy and flexibility, and for most of its existence the risk-averse budget and policy bureaucracy at Homeland Security confined its projects to low-risk conventional R&D. The unimpressive results led to its being absorbed into DHS's Science and Technology Directorate in 2019.[114]

Between 1977 and 2000, DOE ran a small organization for novel, high-risk research: the Advanced Energy Project Division. But it was subject to federal civil service rules and embedded in and stifled by the DOE bureaucracy, so it too did not achieve exceptional results.[115] Its failure ultimately led to ARPA-E, a more successful replacement discussed later in this chapter.

The Biomedical Advanced Research and Development Authority (BARDA), part of the Department of Health and Human Services, more closely resembles DARPA. Congress established it in 2006 to protect against chemical, biological, radiological, and nuclear threats, plus pandemic influenza and emerging infectious diseases.

In 2021, the Biden administration announced creation of the Advanced Research Projects Agency-Climate (ARPA-C).[116] The Bipartisan Infrastructure Act of 2021 authorized creation of the Advanced Research Projects Agency-Infrastructure, with a budget in 2023 of $3.2 million.[117]

* * *

The Advanced Research Projects Agency-Energy

ARPA-E was created in 2007 to fund high-risk, high-return research in energy, in particular problems that the private sector was unlikely to undertake. Its budget in 2020 was $390 million, roughly one-ninth of DARPA's.

ARPA-E is an atypical federal agency. Because it funds high-risk, potentially transformational research, it expects a substantial number of its projects to fail. Like DARPA, it is small, nonhierarchical, and informal: It has a three-level organizational structure with a director, deputy director, 3 associate directors, 13 program directors, 13 technology-to-market advisors, 6 fellows, and 19 other professionals in legal, advisory, and administrative roles.[118] ARPA-E's first director, Arun Majumdar, recalls, "We came in with a clean slate. There was no 30-year history to overcome. We have a sense of urgency. We are in fact building the plane while we are flying it."[119]

ARPA-E thus enjoys many (though not all) of DARPA's advantages, including relative autonomy and exemption from many federal rules and regulations. It is authorized by statute to hire up to 120 scientists, engineers, and other professionals unencumbered by normal civil service laws, including pay levels.[120] It has its own contracting process, independent from the DOE bureaucracy, enabling it to enter into contracts and cooperative agreements quickly.[121] Program directors are given wide latitude in creating programs, choosing research themes, selecting researchers, running projects, spotting commercial opportunities and, when necessary, terminating projects.

Key Features of ARPA-E

Pursuit of Unexplored Opportunities. ARPA-E deliberately seeks "off roadmap opportunities that are not the subject of existing private, academic, or government research. It does so knowing that many of its projects will result only in knowledge (including which research pathways are dead ends), rather than commercializable products."[122]

Up-Front Project Funding. ARPA-E funds its projects in their entirety up front from its current year's budget, even though they may run two to three years. This avoids the risks and distractions associated with having to find additional funds mid-project and protects against the political risk of ARPA-E being terminated.[123]

Technology-to-Market (T2M) Expectation. ARPA-E requires a T2M plan, created with the aid of its T2M advisors. Commercialization strategies may involve training, development of business information, or modification of the technology effort itself to better address commercial needs. ARPA-E's T2M program, far more explicit than any previous effort, has been so successful that DARPA hired its T2M director to develop a similar one.[124]

ARPA-E's Projects

Projects fall into two categories. The first is Proof of Concept (under $1 million, 6–18 months) intended to validate new technological ideas. The second is Technology Development ($2–10 million, 36 months), intended to move a technology from concept to prototype.[125]

Most projects develop from ideas pitched by applicants for the position of program director during their interview process. Once hired, they execute "deep dive" studies to identify all relevant existing public and private-sector research programs. They then look for technological "white spaces" that no one is addressing.[126] Next, they convene workshops of experts in the field and engage other DOE offices to identify possible solutions.[127] The project is then subjected to "constructive challenge" – that is, scrutiny, criticism, and debate with other program directors. Using this input, the program director then tries to sell the now fleshed-out program to ARPA-E's director.[128]

If the director approves the program, the agency publicly releases a Funding Opportunity Announcement (FOA). FOAs are open to companies, nonprofits, universities, federal laboratories, and research consortia. There are two types. The first is Focused Announcements, aimed at specific topics and themes whose value is already well understood.[129] For example, one 2014 FOA asked for proposals regarding Micro-scaled Optimized Solar Cell Arrays with Integrated Concentration (MOSAIC) technology, targeting a 50 percent efficiency improvement over conventional cells. The second type is the OPEN FOA, which solicits ideas across an entire field to ensure that the agency doesn't miss opportunities.

FOA applicants submit five-to-seven-page concept papers for initial screening. Proposals are graded according to potential impact (50 percent) and scientific and technical merit (50 percent). ARPA-E's Merit Review Board, an internal body usually chaired by the program director who would manage the project, vets proposals, with its decision subject to approval by ARPA-E's director. Next is review of the full application by the Merit Review Board, program directors, and other staff, including the director and external experts. Applications are scored according to potential impact (30 percent), scientific and technological merit (30 percent), qualifications of the researchers (30 percent), and their management plan (10 percent). But ARPE-E will sometimes choose a low-scoring project if it has transformational potential.[130]

Following project selection, ARPA-E and the researchers negotiate the terms of the award, including a work plan, project milestones, and ownership of any resulting intellectual property. Milestones must be quantifiable, specific, and unambiguous, though they can later be renegotiated.[131] The award can be a grant, a contract, a cooperative agreement, a cash prize, or, occasionally, something else.[132] Recipients of funding are required to provide at least 20 percent of the project's cost themselves. This can be cash or in-kind contributions, including personnel, administrative costs, buildings, equipment, or services.[133]

Ongoing project management includes meetings, quarterly reports, site visits to confirm claimed results, conference calls, written feedback by the agency, and frank exchanges about shortfalls in performance. ARPA-E can intervene in a project, directing and redirecting its technological aspects, changing its milestones, even terminating it. At least 45 percent of projects have more than one milestone change.[134]

ARPA-E has systematically cultivated relationships with outside researchers, government agencies, Congress, and the energy industry. It works with the rest of DOE, primarily its Office of Energy Efficiency and Renewable Energy (EERE), to avoid duplication and identify areas where EERE can help.[135] In return, EERE has studied and adopted many of ARPA-E's methods. ARPA-E hosts a well-attended annual Energy Innovation Summit that that brings together leading individuals in the energy field from academia, government, and industry. Breakthrough achievements by ARPA-E awardees are described, as are promising developments outside the agency.

Is ARPA-E a Success?

Conservatives concerned about governmental overreach and liberals concerned about corporate welfare have argued government should have a very limited, if any, role in funding civilian technology development. Other critics believe that ARPA-E's funding of private entities entails picking winners, a task for the market. Still others question the need to duplicate expertise and capabilities that supposedly already exist elsewhere within DOE, or assert that the agency merely accelerates work that would have been done anyway.[136] The Trump administration tried to zero out ARPA-E's budget several times.[137]

The market for many of ARPA-E's technologies is a conservative legacy sector: utilities and the federal energy bureaucracy. This sector has few incentives to adopt unproven technologies and then ask ratepayers to absorb their cost. Therefore, many ARPA-E projects involve prototyping and demonstrating the potential of new technologies.[138] ARPA-E also faces a vast, disparate array of other users: manufacturers of all kinds, makers of batteries, renewable energy equipment producers, electric vehicle manufacturers, and the almost infinite variety of end users of energy. There is no settled way to reach them all.

The most recent formal evaluation of ARPA-E was by the National Academies of Sciences (NAS) in 2016–17. It concluded that the agency's six years of existence had not been long enough to generate evidence of "widespread deployment of funded technologies." However, it identified "intermediate outcomes" indicating that the agency was making progress. In particular, the study identified three early projects as "successful."[139]

> **Distributed power flow control.** ARPA-E funded the startup Smart Wires, which developed devices that, when clamped onto power transmission lines, control the flow of power more efficiently than existing systems. ARPA-E funded building prototypes and deploying them for

testing in an actual operating environment, thereby enabling Smart Wires to raise the funding to bring its technology to commercial scale.

Slippery liquid-infused porous surfaces (SLIPS). ARPA-E funded a team to develop a proof of concept and launch a company based on slippery-surface technologies derived from the carnivorous pitcher plant. The technology serves as a coating for refrigeration coils – preventing water and ice buildup, reducing defrost cycles, and achieving energy savings. The company was also pursuing applications such as coating ship hulls to prevent buildup of barnacles and other marine life, cutting energy-wasting drag.

Cheaper silicon wafers for solar cells. An ARPA-E-funded firm, 1366 Technologies, halved the cost of solar wafer manufacturing by making wafers directly from molten silicon, rather than slicing them from ingots. In 2011, it was awarded $4 million by ARPA-E, $3 million by EERE, and DOE offered it a $150 million loan guarantee.[140] By 2015, the company had raised $70 million in private financing.[141] But during the Trump administration, negotiations with DOE funding for a plant in New York state bogged down and the firm announced plans to manufacture in Malaysia instead.[142] But in late 2022, CubicPV (as the firm had become after a merger) announced it would complete a plant in the US by 2024, thanks to tax incentives under the Inflation Reduction Act of 2022.[143]

This last example shows how even a capable and well-run innovation organization like ARPA-E depends upon political support at the highest levels. Trump's budget request for 2021 proposed to eliminate the agency, though Congress instead appropriated $427 million. (The CHIPS and Science Act (2022) authorized $1.2 billion for 2023–6.)[144]

* * *

The Small Business Innovation Research Program

The Small Business Administration's (SBA) Small Business Innovation Research (SBIR) program is a single program implemented by multiple agencies. In it, federal agencies with extramural R&D budgets of more than $100 million a year are required to have a certain percentage performed by small businesses.[145]

As of 2020, this set-aside was 3.2 percent, for a total of some $3.3 billion.[146] Five agencies – DOD, HHS, DOE, NSF, and NASA – account for more than 90 percent, and DOD is about half. Figure 23.2 shows the 2019 breakdown by agency.[147] Small Business Technology Transfer (STTR) is a sister program that teams private firms with governmental research agencies to *transfer* technologies from the latter.

SBIR's participating agencies regularly publish solicitations and offer competitive awards to implement their proposals. Applicants must be for-profit US businesses with greater than 50 percent American ownership by individuals. They must be independently operated, employ 500 or fewer workers, and the work must be performed in the US.

SBIR has three phases. Phase I is to establish feasibility, technical merit, and commercial potential. About 15 percent of applicants are selected, with firms generally receiving $50,000 to $250,000 over six months.[148] Next, 30–50 percent of Phase I firms are selected for Phase II (up to $1 million over two years) to develop and demonstrate a prototype.[149] Finally, Phase III is commercialization: This phase is not funded by SBIR, though it can involve follow-on R&D founded by government outside SBIR or government procurement contracts.[150]

In some cases, government needs can be met by the results of Phase I or Phase II. SBIR permits awarding sole-source contracts in Phase III, bypassing the onerous federal regulations otherwise required to purchase new technology through competitive bidding.[151] With DOD especially, this avoids the notoriously complex procedures that effectively bar many innovative firms from the defense supply chain.[152]

Agencies with Both SBIR and STTR Programs	2020 **Budget**
Dept. of Defense*	$1.9700 billion
Dept. of Health & Human Services (HHS), Inc. NIH	$1.2100 billion
Dept. of Energy, Inc. ARPA-E	$0.3200 billion
National Science Foundation	$0.2190 billion
NASA	$0.2190 billion
Agencies with SBIR Programs Only	
Dept. of Agriculture**	$0.0300 billion
Dept. of Homeland Security	$0.0140 billion
Dept. of Transportation	$0.0127 billion
National Oceanic & Atmospheric Administration	$0.0100 billion
Dept. of Education	$0.0077 billion
National Institute of Standards & Technology	$0.0037 billion
Environmental Prortection Agency	$0.0037 billion

* Budgeted Amount; Other Agencies Obligated Amount
** Estimated from Prior Years

Figure 23.2 2020 SBIR and STTR budgets[153]

Why SBIR Is Effective

SBIR has become an integral part of America's innovation ecosystem. From 1992 to 2005, it supported 14,800 small firms with Phase II grants.[154] A series of assessments by the NAS found the program "sound in concept and effective in practice."[155]

SBIR enables the government to, in effect, crowdsource solutions. It can serve as an inexpensive technological probe to explore ideas and rule out dead ends. It introduces into public procurement cheaper and more innovative products and services, plus new entrants to challenge incumbents.

SBIR's competitive review process helps convince potential investors of the merits of the innovations it supports. It is uniquely suited to helping firms overcome the valley of death (see Chapter 21) compared to policies such as the R&D tax credit, which only helps firms that have taxable income or large staffs for which they are paying payroll taxes. Unlike venture capital, SBIR grants require no dilution of existing ownership, and unlike loans, no repayment. Grant recipients retain rights to technologies developed without owing royalties to the government, though the government enjoys royalty-free use for a time.

The chance of significant funding, and the ability to apply without first founding a company, encourage applications from academicians who might not otherwise try to commercialize their discoveries. As of 2004, over half of SBIR firms had university involvement and of these, more than 80 percent had at least one academician founder.[156] SBIR awards also have a demonstration effect, encouraging more researchers to commercialize their work.[157]

SBIR's agency-by-agency funding structure means that there is no single budget line item that can be cut or cancelled. This budgetary stability, along with the relatively lengthy periods over which Congress has authorized (1982) and reauthorized (1991, 2001, 2011, 2022) the program, has allowed the creation of a broad portfolio of SBIR-sponsored companies.

A Different Version for Each Agency

A key factor in SBIR's effectiveness is its ability to adapt to its implementing agencies, to their institutional cultures, to its participating firms, to the technologies developed, and to the pathways needed to commercialize them. Agencies differ in the objectives they assign the program, the management structures they use to run it, their award sizes and durations, their selection processes, their adherence to SBA guidelines, and their evaluation and assessment activities.[158] To select awardees, peer review is widely used, sometimes by staff from outside the agency (NIH), sometimes by internal staff (DOD), and sometimes by both (NSF). Some agencies, such as NIH, use quantitative scoring; others, such as NASA, do not. Some agencies have multiple levels of review, others do not.

Procurement agencies, such as DOD, which develop technology for their own use, generally implement SBIR through contracts, wherein award winners agree to perform certain research and deliver certain outputs. Non-acquisition agencies, such as NIH, operate primarily through grants, which have less closely specified deliverables.

Firms participating in SBIR also vary, approaching the award process at different stages of technology development and with different objectives. Some seek to develop their own ideas, others are contract researchers developing ideas for others, while still others focus on the commercialization end. Some 20–25 percent of firms in the SBIR program are startups, and each year more than a third are new to the program.[159]

Growing Acceptance

When SBIR was created in the early 1980s, many universities objected, seeing it as a competitor for scarce federal R&D funds. But today, they appreciate it as a source of early-stage financial support for ideas from their labs and as an instrument of regional job creation.[160] Similarly, when SBIR began, many government managers resented the loss of control over part of their own funding, but now appreciate the program.

The initial perception in government agencies that SBIR was a tax on "real" research meant that the awards were not always well integrated with existing departmental programs, though this varied by agency. Partly, this reflected the fact that a small award to a small company can take as much management time as a big award to a big company, yet produce smaller results, creating a natural bureaucratic bias in favor of the latter. Selection procedures were often copied from elsewhere in the agency, rather than being designed for small businesses.

Beginning in the late 1990s, recognition of the program's value by senior management at DOD led to greater support from the top. This, and successful initiatives by individual SBIR program managers, began to alter perceptions in many agencies. Over time, the government's large prime contractors developed a greater understanding of the program's value for nurturing the smaller subcontractors that supply them.[161]

SBIR still faces challenges. Finding advocates inside agencies with sufficient power to get new products embraced can be difficult. Choosing the technology of a new and untested SBIR firm over an established prime contractor can be a career risk for procurement officials. In 2022, after some political uncertainty, SBIR and STTR were reauthorized for three years.[162] The funding bill added a requirement that agencies assess the security risks of their applicants and prohibited funding companies with ties to "countries of concern."[163]

Evaluating SBIR

Assessing SBIR is complicated by its diversity and limited data. Its impacts lag its awards by years, are hard to track, and develop over periods that vary by technology. As a result, most agencies do not even try to track the full impacts of their SBIR technologies. Nonetheless, a comprehensive 2008 NAS study concluded that the program was sound and effective, specifically, that it:

1. Stimulated technological innovation in small companies
2. Created knowledge outputs such as scientific publications, analytical models, patents, algorithms, prototypes, data, spin-off firms, and additional human capital
3. Supported transfer of research from universities to public and private markets
4. Increased commercialization of innovation in the private sector
5. Provided additional and alternative technology development strategies for companies
6. Used small businesses to meet R&D needs of the federal government
7. Used small businesses to meet federal procurement needs.[164]

A 2008 NAS report found that about half of SBIR firms commercialized a product.[165] However, most of their financial returns were modest, and there were many failures. But this was precisely what one would expect, given the technological and business risks. There were also companies with very high returns, both financially and in meeting agency mission needs. This skewed distribution of outcomes, which also occurs in private-sector venture capital, implies that SBIR needs a large portfolio of projects and a long program life to succeed on net.[166]

A 2017 assessment for the Small Business Technology Council also evaluated SBIR and STTR favorably, as did NAS studies of the program at DOE and NIH in 2020 and 2022.[167] These NAS assessments underpinned reauthorizations of the program in 2011, 2017, and 2022, and the upward adjustment of award sizes and percentage of agency R&D budgets allocated. Also reflecting the program's credibility, nations such as Sweden, Singapore, the UK, Russia, the Netherlands, Japan, Korea, India, Canada, Australia, and Taiwan have adopted the SBIR concept.

* * *

Lessons

The takeaway from this chapter is that the development and commercialization of technologies that cannot be achieved by the market alone *can* be achieved with the help of properly designed and funded government programs. Specific lessons include:

1. Government is often the only way to concentrate the expertise and resources needed to bring new breakthrough technologies to commercialization. It alone has sufficiently long time horizons and the ability to recoup their costs from the benefits to the entire economy.

2. Government support is especially critical for a) breakthrough, game-changing, new technologies, because of their many high-risk steps and dead ends; b) technologies based on hard sciences, like new materials, which have long development periods; and c) technologies aimed at legacy industries that are slow and cautious adopters.

3. Governmental technology development organizations should be closely integrated into the rest of the public and private sector research community. They should have programs to deliberately engage them with the for-profit firms that commercialize their technologies.

4. Agencies charged with developing breakthrough technologies should be flexible and hierarchically flat, with autonomous, empowered, "best and the brightest" mid-level managers.

5. Breakthrough agencies should reflect the risky nature of their mission by having the capacity to pause, drop, and redirect funding when necessary. A mistaken bet or a dead end should not be treated as a punishable failure.

6. Such agencies should operate outside the hiring, procurement and grant-making procedures of legacy government agencies designed with very different missions in mind. Individual researchers, small teams, and start-ups often do not have the resources to comply with complex bureaucratic processes or survive lengthy delays.

7. Breakthrough agencies should enjoy significant autonomy, *subject to high-level accountability*. This will both free them from political interference and force them to develop coherent strategic plans for what they do.

8. The tenure of program managers at breakthrough agencies should be limited. This creates a sense of urgency, fights ossification, and institutionalizes the flow of talented people and their ideas *from and to* universities, private firms, and other government departments, helping build communities of expertise.

9. Agencies focused on helping private firms adopt existing technologies need organizational structures that allow managers discretion to accommodate a wide range of technologies, industries, firm sizes, and regional resources.

10. Agencies devoted to the development *and deployment* of technologies should be led by people with scientific or engineering expertise, and experience managing teams in either the public or private sector. They should *not* be led by political figures, by people whose primary expertise is in economics, or by people from the finance side of the private sector, although staff with technology-focused venture capital experience are useful.

11. Stable government funding over sustained periods of time enables long-term planning, the acquisition of advanced equipment and other infrastructure, and the ability to credibly commit to partners in industry and academia.

12. Size matters. For example, Manufacturing USA (see Chapter 21) and the Manufacturing Extension Partnership (see Chapter 22) are effective but far too small.

13. The amount and time frame of government support should match the characteristics of the technologies in question.

14. Widely geographically distributed programs and proactive outreach are required to ensure that programs benefit the entire economy, not just its most advantageous industries and major urban centers, and reach deep into US supply chains.

15. For incremental, as opposed to breakthrough, research, industry-led, as opposed to government-led, cooperative research programs will be more attuned to industry's needs and more adaptable to changing technological environments.

16. For new technologies, having a preestablished pipeline to customers at scale is an advantage, and best obtained by institutionalized early cooperation with such customers.

17. Internal and external evaluations can provide valuable feedback to agency management, to Congress, and to the Executive. Methodologies and success criteria must be adapted to the particular goals, processes, and technological time frames of the agency being evaluated.

24 THE CRISIS OF THE AMERICAN PATENT SYSTEM

America's patent system today is in a self-inflicted crisis that endangers our leadership in innovation. Our legal system is *deliberately* weakening patents, instead of nurturing and protecting them. Patent laws and administrative procedures are now both counterproductive and changing unpredictably, lowering investors' returns and increasing their risks. Ironically, it was rogue factions of the patent-using business community that did the damage, illustrating the harm well-funded special interests can do, especially in technically complex areas that are difficult for Congress and the public to understand. To make matters worse, this failure is occurring at a time when nations are competing to have the most effective patent systems, and our rivals are improving theirs.

The Dark Side of the iPhone

There is a dark side to Apple's iconic smartphone and products like it. They have sorely tested our intellectual property system by incenting their producers and others into assaults on the patent system that have ramifications far beyond their own products.

Companies like Apple compete in rapidly evolving markets where products rarely remain at the technological frontier for more than a few years. Time to market has thus become more important than the standard 20-year duration of patents. A single iPhone includes patented components from non-Apple patent holders numbering in the *thousands*. Apple's concern is that any one of these firms could use its patents to interfere with timely market entry or demand eye-watering royalties for critical intellectual property. Therefore, it is more profitable for Apple to use its technology *without* a license and deal with the consequences later. Although this violates the patent holders' rights, it is now standard operating procedure, cynically called "efficient infringement." And this abuse is not limited to Big Tech. Walmart, Lowe's, Home Depot, even Bed Bath and Beyond are all abettors of the practice by selling products they know depend on it. Even Sears has infringed patents for its Craftsman tool line.

However, efficient infringement doesn't mean patents have become irrelevant to Apple and its peers. But for them, their real utility is for purposes far from their intended uses.

The first is in these firms' ongoing battles over market share. When Apple sues Samsung or Google squabbles over a patent with its Asian competitors, they deploy patents *tactically*, as weapons to deter their competitors' market entry or to sabotage its timing. The result is an equilibrium resembling the Cold War's mutual assured destruction (MAD). These firms gather many patents – regardless of whether they intend to use the technologies – and store them in patent "arsenals." Thus, when these companies' patents are challenged by their peers, they can counterattack not only by defending the patents they use, but by attacking those their rivals use in a "best defense is a good attack" maneuver. This warfare is expensive, but the stakes are billions in damages, counter-damages, license fees, and sales. It is a game only the very largest corporations can afford.

The second front of Big Tech's patent warfare is less public: against the patent holders whose technology they need. The efficient infringement model is still vulnerable to lawsuits and damages, so here, the same companies that war with each other publicly over market share have common interests behind the scenes. They *collectively* seek to degrade the patents held by individuals or small entities to weaken their bargaining power. The Big Tech firms thus want to use patents when fighting among themselves, but obstruct their use by less-resourced patent owners. Their de facto goal? Patents only for the companies at the top of the corporate food chain. For everyone else, patents in theory but in reality, an expensive and unreliable system conferring only weak protection.

Big Tech's strategy for achieving this result has been an assault on the patent system as a whole.

What Are Patents?

Patents aim to reward innovation without interfering with related innovations. They provide a limited period of market exclusivity in exchange for public disclosure of the invention. The intent is that protection will enable investors to earn sufficient returns to incentivize and fund inventions. The other purpose of this protection is to make inventors comfortable making public their valuable knowledge, upon which others can build, instead of keeping it a trade secret.

Patents allow additional inventions that build on the disclosed invention, and the system deliberately encourages *designing around* patents – that is, solving the same problem by different means. For example, one could have patented a light bulb with a non-carbon filament, or a non-glass enclosure, despite Thomas Edison's patent on bulbs with carbon filaments and glass enclosures.

A patent does not confer a monopoly, as other inventions may occupy the same market or perform the same function. Patents usually run 20 years from the date of application. They may be practiced, licensed, sold, traded, and asserted against infringers though litigation.

A patent's "subject" must be defined narrowly enough to precisely identify its scope and accurately enough to transmit its "teaching," but *not* defined so broadly as to cover aspects of the invention that are not actually unique.

Patents apply only in their country of origin. In the contemporary globalized economy, an adequate return on investment often requires global sales and thus patent protection in many jurisdictions. Suffice it to say this is complicated.

America's Founding Fathers believed patents should be full-fledged property rights, not mere privileges granted by the state – the design of most foreign patent systems then and now. They said so in in Article I of the Constitution: "to promote the Progress of Science and useful Arts, by securing for limited Times to Authors and Inventors the exclusive Right to their respective Writings and Discoveries." This status of patents as actual property rights is part of what is now under attack.

How Patenting Works

US Patent and Trademark Office (USPTO) examiners specializing in the relevant technology review patent applications for compliance with applicable rules and legal requirements, then grant or deny them. By law, a patent must be a) useful, b) eligible, c) novel, d) nonobvious, and e) enabled. All five criteria have elaborate legally defined meanings:

> *Usefulness* requires the invention to show some benefit and be capable of actual use. Thus, a perpetual motion machine would be unpatentable because it cannot work for its intended purpose and is therefore not useful.
>
> *Eligibility* is complex. It has traditionally been defined generously, with few things being ineligible. Machines, processes, manufacturing

methods, and compositions of matter are eligible by statute. In the past, the Supreme Court has interpreted congressional intent regarding patent eligibility to "include anything under the sun that is made by man."[1] More recent Supreme Court decisions, however, have raised the eligibility hurdle, making it confusing, difficult to predict, and liable to post-grant revision.[2]

Novelty requires that a patent not consist merely in restatement of "prior art" – that is, existing knowledge. This includes everything already patented or published anywhere in the world.[3]

Nonobviousness means that a patent would not be granted for an invention painted red if a patent already existed for the same thing painted blue.[4] But there are situations when a change in color would completely change the device's functioning, so a patent *would* be granted.

Enablement requires that a patent include a description of the thing patented, including the process of making it. The description must be full and clear, such that a practitioner in the field (known in patent law as a person of ordinary skill in the art) would be able to reproduce and use it.

Patents do not enforce themselves. Holders must generally first give notice to the violator, asking either for damages and an agreement to stop, or for licensing on agreed terms. However, the holder is commonly ignored and thus forced to sue. The holder must then convince the court, through often lengthy and expensive litigation, to grant an injunction (a court order to stop infringing) and/or monetary damages.

Patent enforcement thus requires significant financial wherewithal. This is why efficient infringement is so rewarding for the well resourced: They can threaten wars of attrition their victims cannot afford. Small businesses, startups, universities, and other less-resourced patent holders have found it increasingly difficult to protect their patents. And without assurance of this protection, it is difficult or impossible to attract investment for the next phase of their invention's development. This resource differential has become a dividing line between those who favor Big Tech's self-serving version of patent "reform" and those who oppose it.

The Rising Importance of Patents

Forty years ago, three events helped establish the strong patent regime that has since fallen into decay.

The first was a 1979 Labor Department ruling that triggered a boom in venture capital (which had previously been exotic and quantitatively small) that continues to this day. The "prudent man rule" governing acceptable investments by pension funds was changed to include the idea that portfolio diversification was a legitimate consideration. This implied that allocating a small part of a portfolio to venture capital would be legal. The result was that from 1980 to 1994, venture capital rose from $1.7 billion to $30 billion.[5] This increased flow of capital, particularly into high-risk, early-stage innovation, enabled technological invention, development, and commercialization outside of large firms. It made patents more important, because while large firms can defend their inventions using entrenched positions in the production, marketing, and financing needed to commercialize them, small innovators are far more dependent on the patent itself.

The second event was the 1982 centralization of the interpretation of patent law in a new, specialized Court of Appeals for the Federal Circuit (CAFC). CAFC hears appeals on patents and international trade from all the federal district courts and thus sets national standards. Congress's aim was to bring technological expertise and consistent decision-making to rulings. As intended, this reform strengthened the system, as shown by the fact that decisions became more pro patent. As one commentator notes, "Whereas the circuit courts had affirmed 62 percent of district-court findings of patent infringement in the three decades before the creation of the CAFC, the CAFC in its first eight years affirmed 90 percent."[6]

The third event was the Patent and Trademark Law Amendments Act of 1980, commonly known as Bayh–Dole. This law enabled recipients of federal research grants, mainly universities, to patent, own, and commercialize that research. This helped end dependence on federal bureaucrats for commercializing federally funded research, decentralizing American innovation through partnerships between universities and corporations. Previously, the private sector had licensed only about 5 percent of commercially promising federal patents. Some 28,000 sat on shelves gathering dust.[7] Bayh–Dole changed all this: Today many universities have full-time technology transfer offices to facilitate patent commercialization.

How the System Was Corrupted

This legal infrastructure, the best in the world, started to unravel around 2004. The tech titans' efficient-infringement model was in place, but occasionally resulted in expensive damages. The titans reasoned that they could reduce these costs by undermining patent enforcement. As a longer-term bonus, this would also help return the locus of innovation to large firms. So, they coalesced around a sophisticated strategy to hobble enforcement.[8]

Because Congress was not expert in patent law, it was vulnerable to a misleading narrative. Enter the myth of the patent troll, coined at Intel.[9] The troll's technique, allegedly, was to buy a valid patent, assert applicability beyond its true scope, charge innocent firms with infringement, then demand license fees to go away. This was depicted as a hidden tax on innovation, a cause of job loss, and a drag on competitiveness. An extensive public campaign was launched, including recruiting scholars to publish studies claiming to show economic harm. (These studies were later discredited. For example, a widely cited one from Boston University was found to use a biased estimate of litigation costs and to lack an adequate baseline of comparison.)[10]

Troll-like conduct by a few bad actors was taking place. Every part of the legal system has its abuses. But the troll narrative was overblown.

First, patent trolling was not an economically significant phenomenon, as studies eventually revealed.[11] The large, respectable law firms that dominated corporate practice refused to get anywhere near it, leaving it to sleazy small-time operators. And it didn't attract that many smaller firms either, because filing nuisance lawsuits against companies too poor to fight back is intrinsically unprofitable. (Large companies rarely get trolled because they can afford to maintain a reputation for fighting every demand in court.)

Second, since the patents in question were valid (if sometimes poorly drafted) the trolls' conduct *was not illegal*. Damages can be awarded only if the patent owner wins, and those filing truly abusive demand letters had no intention of actually suing. Contrary to myth, trolls were not able to just harass companies out of the blue.

Third, insofar as they did exist to a limited extent, trolls (and the fear of trolls) were performing the valuable service of creating a disincentive to violate other people's patents *even when the victim didn't have the money to defend itself*. Potential infringers were aware that trolls could buy the victim's patent and take over the case.

Many legitimate reforms could have been used to crack down on the small troll nuisance. But these, aimed at so-called abusive demand letters, were deliberately sabotaged in Congress. Among other things, the theory was put out that it was impossible to distinguish trolls from legitimate operators.[12] But if this were true, it would have been impossible to prove the existence of trolls in the first place!

The troll myth demonized so-called nonpracticing entities (NPEs), which own but do not use patents. But many patent holders quite legitimately do not commercialize their own patents. Among their reasons: They are inventors, not businesspeople. They do not want the headaches of running a manufacturing operation. They do not have the appropriate expertise. As in many other areas of the economy, owning and operating assets are different functions performed by different organizations with different skills. But the claim that NPEs were abusive captured enough congressional support to mask Big Tech's real objective.

A Patent Reform Trojan Horse

Because the titans held patents themselves, they could pose as pro patent, forming groups such as the Coalition for Patent Fairness and the High-Tech Inventors Alliance (HTIA). But most of HTIA's funding, a telltale of its real agenda, came from eight major tech firms: Adobe, Amazon, Cisco, Dell, Google, Intel, Oracle, and Salesforce.[13] Firms such as Google also funded nonprofits such as Engine Advocacy and the Electronic Frontier Foundation. These hid their anti-patent agendas among thickets of unrelated issues, some perfectly legitimate, that they used to build reputations they could then deploy against patents.[14]

Although it took more than six years, this campaign succeeded. For all its money and power, Big Tech could not manipulate Congress on its own. It needed a partner to generalize the story to patents economy-wide, as its own concerns were vulnerable to accusations of special-interest pleading. Luckily, at the time, industrial-age multinationals such as Procter and Gamble and 3M were working on their own patent-reform initiative focused on "harmonizing" American and foreign patent law. Despite the fact that our patent system was demonstrably outperforming foreign nations, consistency would be valuable to multinationals patenting in multiple jurisdictions.[15]

The multinationals' reform bill was the perfect Trojan horse for Big Tech, so a marriage between the two groups was effected. Microsoft's lawyer Marshall Phelps explained the "problem" in Senate testimony in 2005:

> While our business and that of a growing number of American companies big and small are global, there is not a global patent system. Inventors who desire protection in a country must seek to obtain protection in that country. A focus on promoting international harmonization and greater cooperation at work sharing among national patent authorities is key to reducing these barriers. It is essential that the US recognize where its system is out of step. As you just heard, the United States is the only country that applies a first-to-invent standard for establishing priority. Every other country awards the patent to the first-inventor-to-file.[16]

All the pieces for a successful lobbying campaign were now in place. But the order in which events unfolded requires that we now turn our attention to the courts.

How the Courts Undermined Our Patent System

Because laws are often vague, do not interpret themselves, and are outrun by new developments, the courts have much to say about what they mean in practice. This has allowed the patent system to be damaged by a succession of unwise court decisions.

Except in rare circumstances, CAFC used to promptly award infringed patent holders permanent injunctions ordering the infringer to stop. In the fast-moving world of technology, this is essential for giving patents real bite. But permanent injunctions are used more sparingly in other areas of federal law, a difference that created the opportunity for a misguided harmonization. In its 2006 *eBay v. MercExchange* decision, the Supreme Court overturned CAFC's practice.[17] Instead, it mandated the traditional four-factor test employed in non-patent cases:

1. The victim has suffered *irreparable* injury.
2. Mere monetary damages would be inadequate.
3. An injunction would not unfairly disrupt the alleged infringer's business, compared to the hardship suffered by the patent holder.
4. The public interest would not be disserved.

The justices' written opinions reveal that their motivation was the troll narrative.

They then went even further, identifying circumstances where mere monetary damages, as opposed to an end to infringement, were all that the patent holder was entitled to. First, where "the patented invention is but a small component of the entire article," and second "where the infringer seeks to sell, or where the patent holder asserts, business method patents that allegedly suffer from potential vagueness and suspect validity." (More on "business method patents" below.)

A more perfect invitation to efficient infringement could not have been devised. Lower courts interpreted the *discretion* over injunctions ordered by the Supreme Court as a green light to make outright denial their *norm* for nonpracticing entities. The court thus de facto eliminated injunctions for NPEs in favor of what money they would hypothetically have received under licensing. The entire secondary market for monetizing the patents of underfunded inventors was stigmatized as abusive.

Other Harmful Court Decisions

After the dust of *eBay* settled, the affected parties fell into roughly three categories:

First were the large tech companies, for whom injunctions were still available because they could afford to slog through the legal thickets now required to obtain them.

Second were patent holders whose lesser but still meaningful resources enabled them to defend their patents to an impaired but nontrivial extent. This included universities, some independent inventors, pure licensors, and other NPEs. Their judicial remedies were, however, now truncated by *eBay*: not what they deserved, but still something.

Third were patent holders who now could not afford any meaningful enforcement. Many of their patents were now virtually worthless. Invention for them was no longer financially viable.

Meanwhile, the market-share war among the tech titans had become even more furious, pulling them beyond their defensive MAD stances into offensive action against each other.[18] Patents originally acquired for defensive purposes were now being used proactively to attack rivals, sabotaging their technology paths and delaying their product introductions. Companies were deliberately avoiding patent searches to avoid treble damages for willful infringement. The previously imaginary crisis of legal harassment by means of patents was becoming a self-fulfilling prophecy.

The America Invents Act and Its Sequelae

Meanwhile, after several abortive attempts, the tech-led congressional leadership was discovering that the alliance between Big Tech and the multinationals was still not enough to pass the patent bill they wanted.

Major industries such as pharmaceuticals, which still cared about patents in their traditional usage and had the lobbying muscle to defend existing patent laws, were in the way. The pharmaceutical industry makes products that are often physically easy to copy, making effective patent protection crucial. Initially skeptical, Big Pharma was eventually won over by the argument that any damage to the patent system would not apply to its well-resourced members.[19]

With Big Pharma on board, the remaining opposition of universities and independent inventors was too weak to prevail. Most members of Congress were unfamiliar with the detailed content of the America Invents Act (AIA) of 2011.[20] They voted as requested by their congressional leadership, by home-state multinationals, and by campaign-cash-laden Big Tech firms. The few who understood fought an unsuccessful rear-guard action. In September, AIA was enacted and signed by President Obama, who had become enthralled by Big Tech when it rescued him from his Obamacare registration snafu. Universities were thrown a few crumbs in the form of an AIA exemption for its first two years. Big Tech had finally converted America's flexible, democratic, creative, bottom-up patent system into a top-down oligopoly maintenance machine.

AIA imposed several big changes. The most significant was from first-to-invent to first-to-file. It also changed what qualified as prior art, which was then used to invalidate patents and prevent them in the first place. It also changed the fee structure for the pursuit and maintenance of patents.

Chaos began soon thereafter. The non-tech multinationals mostly sidelined themselves, protecting their AIA-acquired harmonization by preaching its benefits but otherwise dropping out of the debate. Meanwhile, political and judicial war raged between entrenched, well-resourced component assemblers such as Apple and less-resourced early-stage innovators.

Starting in 2012, Big Tech sought more revisions. With Republicans controlling Congress, the drive to further degrade patent law made heavy use of the "dog whistle" that a new bill, the Innovation Act, with loser-pays provisions, was a step toward "tort reform," a long-sought Republican objective promoted by the insurance industry. Failure to prevail in a patent lawsuit would require the plaintiff to reimburse the alleged infringer for its defense costs, making litigation even more costly and further discouraging less-resourced patent holders.

In 2013, Innovation Act "reform" bills were introduced in the House and Senate. Aided by the House leadership's fast-track scheduling, the House version was hastily passed 325 to 91. Its Senate companion's less onerous content (still including loser-pays) easily cleared the Judiciary Committee. By 2014, however, the likely harms of the bill had become clearer to Congress. It had become too controversial for a floor vote just before an election. So the bill languished without a vote. Big Tech tried again in 2015, but by then, the AIA's accumulating victims were better organized and had been hard at work on the Hill. So again the Innovation Act failed to receive floor consideration.

The Patent Nullification Crisis

The AIA's most significant anti-patent impact was unforeseen even by its proponents. This was its three new post-patent-grant challenge proceedings, touted as ways to reduce litigation and efficiently address trolls:

- Inter Partes Review (IPR)
- Post Grant Review (PGR)
- Covered Business Methods (CBM, since repealed)

Inter Partes Review, or review "between parties," was intended to challenge overly broad patents. It was expected to be invoked sparingly, mainly for electronics. But it has become a staple of the infringer's tool kit for *all* types of patents. Here is what infringers like:

- IPRs are expensive, typically costing patent defenders $500,000.[21] To successfully defend an IPR, then return to district court to continue infringement proceedings, may take eight years and $5,000,000. Because the same patent can be serially attacked by multiple challengers, final resolution may take even longer, by which time the technology may have moved on.

- The burden of proof on the patent challenger is a mere "preponderance" (more than 50 percent) of the evidence. This standard is lower than that in federal district courts, where patent validity can only be defeated by "clear and convincing evidence."
- If even *one* claim of a patent is found to have so much as a "reasonable likelihood" of being nullified, the Patent Trial and Appeal Board (PTAB) allows the IPR to proceed, forcing the owner to defend it.
- "Claim construction," or the interpretation of the patent claim's language, is broader in IPR than in litigation, allowing more prior art to be swept in to invalidate patents as not novel.
- Essentially anyone can file an IPR, whereas standing is required in district court.

IPR denies patent holders due process because it treats patents as mere "public rights," such as the use of a waterway, as opposed to the full-fledged property rights the Constitution stipulates. (The Supreme Court reinforced this error in its 2018 *Oil States* decision, which overturned nearly 200 years of case law and upon which patent supporters had staked great hopes.)[22]

PGR allows more grounds for filing and must be brought within nine months of issuance of a patent, but is otherwise similar to IPR, with similar problems.

IPR and PGR proceedings are presided over by panels consisting of three PTAB administrative patent judges (APJs). APJs, unlike so-called Article III judges (referring to the section of the Constitution authorizing them) are "Article I" judges. Such judges serve in many other executive branch agencies to adjudicate administrative disputes and in many ways their streamlined proceedings are similar to Article III trials – *except* they lack key constitutional protections such as trial by jury.

The very concept of reviewing patents after they have been granted is misguided except in the rarest cases. If a patent is invalid, it should be denied in the first place, not subjected to the uncertainty of being granted and then undone after its owners believe they have a property right and have based business decisions on this assumption. The uncertainty makes all patents, valid and invalid, riskier investments, further discouraging innovators and their funders.

There are no cash winnings from successful PTAB defenses: Inventors just get to keep their patents. As a result, contingency representation (the attorney shares the winnings) has all but disappeared, so most inventors with modest means have little or no access to justice.

The Attack on Patent Eligibility

One of the easiest ways to destroy a patent is to deny that the thing patented was even eligible in the first place. Thus the ongoing attack on eligibility standards is very important. The courts have recently injected considerable uncertainty into what should be a stable, easily anticipated area of law.

The Supreme Court long ago augmented the statutory definition of eligibility by ascribing *non*-eligibility to a) "laws of nature," b) "natural phenomena," and c) "abstract ideas." In 2012, however, the Court began creating an eligibility mess, starting with *Mayo v. Prometheus*. In *Mayo*, it held that a patent on a method for adjusting the dose of a drug merely identified a law of nature corresponding to the drug's proper level. Next, in 2014's *Alice Corp. v. CLS Bank*, it further muddled the law by setting forth a novel two-step test.[23] The first is to see if a patent falls under a), b), or c) above. If so, then a *second* step turns on whether the invention contains "significantly more" – that is, whether it innovatively packages or implements one of these three things.[24] So the underlying mathematics of a new method of cryptography would not be eligible, but a new way of programming a computer to implement it would be.[25] Unfortunately, the Court did not officially define "significantly more," "abstract," or the other key terms. Nor has it done so since.

Mayo and *Alice* muddied the case law coming out of the CAFC and the district courts as they struggled to confer eligibility on important, groundbreaking innovations.[26] The Supreme Court has been unwilling to stabilize the situation, or even provide further guidance, by taking up appeals, despite at least 43 attempts.[27] The CAFC, given no guidance for what qualifies as "significantly more," has produced an inconsistent and unworkable thicket of case law. Even PTAB has ventured into eligibility territory and has begun invalidating patents. By definition, uncertain eligibility has the power to affect just about everything done with patents, and patents are now being invalidated at high rates.[28]

This judicial mess has been particularly harmful in biomedicine, especially in diagnostics. Consider CAFC's 2015 *Ariosa v. Sequeno*. This invalidated a patent on a noninvasive method of determining paternity and other characteristics of a fetus by testing the mother's blood for fetal DNA. Following the precedents of *Mayo* and *Alice*, CAFC invalidated the patent because it "begins and ends with a natural phenomenon" – the existence of fetal DNA in maternal blood – and failed to contain any new invention beyond "conventional techniques" for detecting this DNA. The judge wrote that the "sweeping language" of *Mayo* required him to invalidate.

More than any other misguided new doctrine, eligibility uncertainty has driven patent applications to the EU and China. Between August 2014 and

September 2017, nearly 1,700 applications that were rejected in the US for eligibility reasons led to patent grants in China or the EU.[29]

There is one bright spot for Big Tech. The added unpredictability has further boosted Big Tech's leverage over its component suppliers by making it easier to threaten their patents. Threats to petition PTAB to invalidate patents have now become a staple of bargaining. These harms were then consolidated under Obama appointee Michelle Lee, former head of Google's patent practice, USPTO director from 2015 to 2017.

Summary

In our current patent system:

- Patents are increasingly weaponized, used for threats and counterthreats, not for their intended purposes.
- Infringed patent holders are denied enforcement by insurmountable costs.
- New legal doctrines retroactively nullify eligibility.
- The PTAB imposes delays.
- Court rulings continue to make things unpredictably worse.

The situation is so bad that in 2010, Federal Judge Paul Michel, the chief judge of the CAFC, resigned his lifetime judicial tenure (an almost unheard-of move) in order to speak out. In July 2017, he testified before the House Judiciary Committee:

> Well, in just the past three or four years, the patent world has been turned upside down. The combination of how the Patent and Trademark Office's Patent Trial and Appeal Board shaped and implemented procedures governing the AIA reviews, unintended consequences of a few design features in the AIA itself, continuing, aggressive interventions by the Supreme Court, particularly on eligibility, and rules and practice changes in the lower courts has totally changed perceptions of the current patent system. It is no longer viewed as reliable.[30]

There is evidence that uncertain patentability has undermined venture investment. A 2017 survey of 475 investors at 422 venture capital and private equity firms revealed that reduced eligibility would cause them to significantly reduce funding of technological developments, especially in medical devices, biotech, and pharmaceuticals.[31] Forty percent said that Supreme Court decisions had negatively affected their firm's investment activity. Only 14 percent saw positive effects.[32]

Meanwhile, America's rivals are improving their patent systems. For example, despite violating foreign intellectual patents and stealing trade secrets on a massive scale, China now is also creating its own new technology. Beijing understands that it needs an effective patent system to support and protect its own corporate and individual inventors, and its improving patent regime has been noted by IP experts.[33] The creation of specialized courts and stronger penalties for infringers have shown its seriousness.[34]

Other Attempts at Reform

There have been a number of attempts at real patent reform. For example, there has been action at USPTO on eligibility, especially under Trump appointee Andrei Iancu, the director from 2018 to 2021. In January 2019, it released revised eligibility guidelines improving the patentability of inventions involving practical applications of a law of nature or abstract idea.[35] But there are limits to what USPTO can do on its own. CAFC has subsequently issued several decisions that invalidate the new USPTO guidelines, including one in 2021 declaring that "this [USPTO] guidance is not, itself, the law of patent eligibility, does not carry the force of law, and is not binding on our patent eligibility analysis."[36]

In June 2023, a glimmer of hope came from the Senate's Intellectual Property Subcommittee. Its Democratic chair and ranking Republican jointly introduced the Patent Eligibility Restoration Act of 2023. This would a) eliminate judicially created exceptions such as abstract ideas by abrogating *Alice* and *Mayo*, b) require eligibility to be determined by considering all the parts of an invention together so patents cannot be carved into separate elements deemed ineligible in isolation, c) return eligibility enquiries to the former basic patentability threshold, and d) prevent the creation of new judicial exceptions. If passed, these changes would restore some clarity and predictability. But as of mid-2024, Tech's power over Congress makes a near-term legislative fix for eligibility unlikely.

"Recommendations" discusses other needed reforms.

Part V
Industry Case Studies

These chapters look at the impact of US and foreign industrial policies on several major American industries. Chapter 25 examines the auto industry because it illustrates how poor industrial policy has allowed advantageous US industries to decline. Chapter 26 examines the industrial policy the US has done best since World War II – that related to defense, specifically in semiconductors, aviation, and space. Chapter 27 looks at robotics because the technological powers of the world are racing to deploy the best industrial policies to nurture this crucial industry. Chapter 28 looks at nanotechnology as an example of the emerging technologies for which the US will need industrial policies in the future.

25 AUTOMOBILES
Decline and a Chance at Revival

The American auto industry is a key case study for future US industrial policy. It is large and advantageous, and its well-known, multi-decade travails were caused by a *combination* of self-inflicted wounds, foreign mercantilism, and poor US policy. Untangling these three strands will be crucial to the success of future industrial policy efforts in many industries.

Once the world's largest and most advanced, the American industry has been in decline in fits and starts since the mid-1960s, when it began losing ground to imports. In 1965, the domestic market share of the Big Three exceeded 90 percent.[1] Today, GM, Ford, and Stellantis (which owns Chrysler) have only 43 percent.[2] In 2021, for the first time in 90 years, GM was not number one in the American market – Toyota was.[3] And in 2019, the last year before COVID-induced supplychain shocks distorted the numbers, the US ran a trade deficit in automobiles and parts of $211 billion.[4]

For decades, Washington's policies toward the industry swung between neglect and outright hostility, punctuated by assistance in recurring crises. The federal government failed to respond appropriately to foreign incursions into the American car market. It distorted corporate strategies with vacillating antitrust enforcement. It imposed poorly designed environmental policies. And it failed to manage exchange rates. The net result was that it failed to do its part to preserve a distinct industry owned, managed, and located in America. As a result, car and parts production in this country is increasingly foreign-owned and run, complicating future efforts to support the sector.

However, the auto industry worldwide is undergoing three huge changes, which have created an opening for an American revival *if the right industrial policies are applied.*

First and most important is the transition to vehicles not powered solely by internal combustion engines (ICEs). This includes battery-powered vehicles (BEVs), gasoline/electric plug-in hybrids (PHEVs), and others such as hydrogen fuel cell vehicles (FCEVs). Although Tesla leads in the luxury segment in the US, the US lags Europe and China overall in electric vehicle (EVs = PHEVs + BEVs) production and adoption.[5]

Second, ride sharing and car sharing are reducing personal car ownership, with an impact not yet known. On the one hand, fewer vehicles will be needed because private cars mostly sit parked. On the other, car use is concentrated on commutes, when a large fraction is in active use, and shared cars, wearing out faster due to nearly continual operation, will need more frequent replacement.[6]

Third is self-driving cars. These will one day improve safety, but cannot yet be deployed at scale for safety reasons. (Fully self-driving personal vehicles are unlikely before 2030.)[7] Carmakers and AI firms are investing in-house or through startups, with 6 American and 2 Chinese firms among the top 10.[8] The larger autonomous vehicle market – which includes trucks, busses, vans, and shuttles, including those not fully autonomous – is projected to reach $327 billion by 2030.[9] Longer-term, autonomous cars and trucks *may* prove capable of platooning and driving safely at higher speeds, and thus shrink regional geographies, with huge economic benefits.[10]

As of 2024, there is a race among American, East Asian, and European manufacturers to mass produce electric vehicles of all types. Entrenched carmakers, indeed entire nations with large ICE industries such as Germany, are facing disruption.[11] The legacy automakers are attempting to reinvent themselves, and startups have arisen. Making more cars than any other country, China is, thanks to the EV revolution, finally closing in on the first rank of car producers, although quality and design issues still rank its ICE industry below this level.[12]

Antitrust Policy

The decades-long difficulties of America's carmakers have their roots in the early post–World War II period. The US was overwhelmingly dominant, producing 79 percent of the world's automobiles as late as 1950.[13] Then and for too long thereafter, auto executives and political leaders assumed this dominance would last forever.

During the 1950s and 1960s, GM was roughly half the American industry, Ford half GM's size, and Chrysler half Ford's, with minor players (Studebaker, Nash, Packard, et alia) and a trickle of imports accounting for the rest.[14] GM and Ford were subjected to antitrust investigations, congressional hearings, and proposed laws aimed at breaking them up.[15] The Eisenhower administration announced an antitrust investigation in 1954.[16] Nothing came of it. The Johnson administration ended its own in 1967 without an indictment.[17] It has since been speculated that breaking GM into four and Ford into two – they were big enough for the resultant firms to have been viable – might have made for a more competitive, dynamic industry. George Romney, CEO of the much smaller American Motors, said in 1958, "Where competition is shrinking below adequate minimum levels, even the most efficient company will ultimately lose its competitive drive. Like boxing champions who lack suitable opponents, companies will become soft and flabby. Furthermore, artificial and undesirable restraints on competition develop more easily and even unintentionally."[18] Automotive historians still debate whether such a breakup was feasible, given the integration of the production systems of the divisions with their parent companies.[19]

America thus ended up with the worst of both worlds: The Big Three were not broken up to increase competition, but antitrust worries distorted GM's and Ford's corporate strategies for decades.[20] As auto expert Professor Jim Womack of MIT recounts, "I learned early in my automotive research career that the senior leaders in Detroit thought that GM could not go past 60 percent of the market and that Chrysler had to be kept in the game."[21]

The UAW

Unions had a double effect on the industry in the 1950s. On the one hand, the high wages achieved by the United Auto Workers (UAW), which set the pattern for many other industries, helped pull millions of Americans into the middle class. On the other, union contracts eventually became albatrosses around the necks of the Big Three. The "Treaty of Detroit," a landmark contract between GM and the UAW in 1950, granted healthcare coverage, pensions, and higher wages. In exchange, the union abandoned prior demands for a share in production decisions and accepted a long-term contract that ended annual strikes.

Four contract provisions became problematic over time. The first was the annual improvement factor (AIF) of 2.5 percent annual real wage increases. The second was blue-chip healthcare coverage, including for retirees. The third was defined-benefit pensions. The fourth was inflation-linked cost of living adjustments (COLA).

These provisions made sense when adopted. They did not undermine the firms' competitiveness as they applied to all American carmakers equally and there was little foreign competition. AIF and COLA made contract negotiations less acrimonious, and labor peace was essential for efficient production. Productivity was rising at more than 2.5 percent annually and inflation was low. The industry's work force was young, so pension costs were small and healthcare costs had not yet begun to climb. But these benign circumstances started to change in the mid-to-late 1960s. Productivity improvements slowed, but AIF did not fall to reflect this.[22] Medical costs rose. COLA raised labor costs in lockstep with inflation.

These expenditures did not, however, buy permanent labor peace. As one observer notes, "The industry has been scarred by a succession of unrelenting adversarial contests between labor and management, with the periods between massive strikes punctuated by constant bickering, mutual recriminations and sagging productivity."[23] Blame attaches not only to management: There were instances of sabotage by workers.[24] Contracts with rigid job classifications interfered with flexibility and invited a "check your brains at the door" style of plant operations. Both caused trouble when the Japanese challenged the industry with Lean Production (see later in this chapter).[25]

Still, life under the UAW was good for a while. As one observer describes it,

> There's nothing easy about the job. It can be mind-numbingly repetitive, stressful on the back and shoulders and knees, an eight-hour-long daily grind. No question the work paid extremely well – $27 an hour for an assembler on up to $33 an hour for a skilled tradesman. The benefits were excellent, and after thirty years a worker could retire with a generous pension. What outsiders could not appreciate, though, were the feelings of pride and togetherness and shared history.[26]

As late as 1978, before GM began to really unravel, Flint, Michigan, where more than half the workforce labored for the company, had the second highest average blue-collar wage in the country.[27] GM's US employment peaked in 1979 at 468,000 people, Ford's in 1978 at 261,000.[28] And the industry's multiplier effect – creating jobs in other industries – has been estimated at five to one.[29]

The 1950s and 1960s: Beginnings of Decline

In the 1950s, policymakers and auto executives assumed that foreign carmakers could never achieve the required scale economies in the kinds of cars Americans bought because such vehicles were mostly unsaleable in their home markets. Imports were thus expected to remain confined to niche markets.

American cars tended to be large, with powerful V8 engines, automatic transmissions, and air conditioning, and were designed for comfort over long distances. European and Japanese cars were generally small and urban-oriented, with four-cylinder engines and no A/C. These nations were smaller, had more mass transit, and their cities had narrow streets with limited parking.

Gasoline was (and is) more expensive than in the oil-rich US, and governments imposed high gas taxes to reduce petroleum imports.

Auto imports began in the early 1950s with small numbers of charming but unreliable British sports cars such as Austin-Healey, MG, and Jaguar. The late 1950s saw larger foreign inroads led by Volkswagen with its Microbus and cheap, odd-looking Beetle. [30]

The first Japanese car imports, in the early 1960s, were of low quality, ill suited to the American market, and sold poorly. But Japan's automakers learned fast, improved quality, and began designing cars specifically for the US. Their mid-to-late 1960s second generation, such as the Toyota Corona and Datsun 510, sold much better. Japanese imports, popular first in California, jumped from 25,000 in 1965 to more than 380,000 in 1970. [31]

Contrary to myth, American carmakers did not ignore smaller cars. The popularity of AMC's Nash Rambler (1950) and Rambler American (1958) had demonstrated demand. So, beginning in 1960, the Big Three, AMC, and Studebaker produced American compacts, including the Ford Falcon, Chevy Corvair, Dodge Dart, Plymouth Valiant, and Studebaker Lark. But they had six-cylinder engines and were compacts, not true subcompacts. And despite this promising start, Detroit lost focus and did not continually upgrade them. Even when the firms made US versions of the small cars of their European subsidiaries – the Chevette was based on an Opel from Germany – the results were inferior. [32] Their hearts were not in it, partly because small cars were less profitable, as they sold for less but were not proportionately simpler to make. [33]

The American auto industry also began to draw public criticism, most famously with Ralph Nader's 1965 book *Unsafe at Any Speed*. The firms were charged not only with safety flaws but with "a fascination with overweight, over-chromed, over-powered automobiles," and became the environmental villains to many that they remain to this day. [34]

While some of these criticisms were unwarranted, by the mid-1960s, the Big Three were complacent. They assumed that superficial annual style changes, rather than real engineering innovations, would be enough to keep cars marketable. [35] Top leadership shifted away from design or manufacturing experts and toward executives who had risen in finance or marketing. [36] Dissenting voices such as AMC's Romney and GM's John DeLorean were overridden.

Starting in the late 1960s, labor strife undermined quality as unmotivated workers reciprocated perceived management contempt by becoming indifferent and sloppy. [37] The generation that had lived through the Great Depression and was grateful for any steady work was passing from the scene, and the general militancy of the decade could not be stopped at the factory gates.

The 1970s: Decline Accelerates

By the early 1970s, GM had abandoned the vision of its brilliant founder, Alfred P. Sloan, and centralized decision-making away from its once highly autonomous divisions.[38] Creativity in design was repressed in the name of "rational" management.[39] Brand identities were blurred. The firm formed an Assembly Division in 1970 that took assembly out of the hands of the divisions. (This has been attributed, disputably, to a desire to make it harder to break up the company.) This shift disrupted plant operations, contributed to plummeting quality, and undermined brand loyalty.[40] Ford and Chrysler made mistakes of their own.

By 1970, imports had 15 percent of the market.[41] As they continued to increase, Ford, GM, and AMC introduced their second wave of "import fighters," subcompacts such as the Ford Pinto, Chevy Vega, and AMC Gremlin. (The Pinto and the Vega had four-cylinder engines, but AMC couldn't afford to develop one and used an existing six.) In 1971, Chrysler brought in a rebadged Hillman from its British factories, the Cricket, and a new car, the Dodge Colt, made in Japan by its joint-venture partner Mitsubishi.

Although these cars sold well at first, most were soon beset with problems, lawsuits, and bad publicity. The Cricket was rapidly abandoned due to poor quality and reliability (though the Colt lasted until 1994). The Pinto's gas tank exploded in rear-end collisions. The Vega's aluminum engine was liable to overheating. The Gremlin's odd styling made it the butt of jokes. The Vega and Pinto were basically scaled-down big cars, with cramped interiors due to the transmission hump required by rear-wheel drive, not true designed-from-the-ground-up subcompacts.

Nevertheless, these cars did stop the growth of small European imports such as Fiat and Renault. The only European firm to prosper in the US was VW, at least until its Bug aged out and it opened an unsuccessful plant in Pennsylvania in 1978. But Japanese imports continued to grow, thanks to high quality, good standard (as opposed to optional) features, and ease of maintenance. Consumers were learning to trust, even to like them.

The ongoing deterioration of America's trade in autos had been enabled by a trade policy that assumed the industry was not under threat. During the 1963–7 Kennedy Round of GATT tariff cuts, phased in to 1972, the US cut its auto tariff from 6.5 to 3 percent, while the Europeans maintained an 11 percent tariff and quantitative restrictions (see Chapter 16). Fearing antitrust accusations, US automakers played little role in the negotiations. America's auto market thus became the world's most open.

The First Oil Shock and CAFE Standards

The Arab Oil Embargo of 1973–4 had little effect on physical flows of oil to the US, but prices quadrupled due to disruption, uncertainty, and panic.[42] Federal price controls and gasoline allocations were imposed to shield consumers from higher prices, but, predictably given basic supply and demand, this resulted in shortages – remembered today as gas lines.[43]

Higher gas prices reduced demand for large – which meant American-made – vehicles. By 1975, small cars were 51 percent of the market.[44] The Japanese were well placed to take advantage due to the oil shock, years of better planning, superior technology, and closer attention to consumers. In 1973, they had 5.8 percent of the market. By 1977, they had 9.6 percent.[45]

In 1975, Congress legislated the Corporate Average Fuel Economy (CAFE) scheme, first applied in 1978. Carmakers were required to meet gradually rising standards for the average gas mileage of the cars they produced. Although CAFE cost the economy six times more per gallon of gas saved than just raising the gas tax, the latter was viewed as politically impossible.[46] It was also falsely believed that consumers do not respond rationally to changes in gas prices when buying cars.[47] The industry opposed CAFE but to no avail, as the (in hindsight, ludicrous) belief that the world was running out of oil had taken hold of the public and Congress.[48]

Implementation of fuel efficiency standards and the new safety standards that had started hitting a few years earlier was not always rational. Standards sometimes called for technologies that did not yet exist, and Congress did not fund developing them.[49] Collaborative research was prohibited on antitrust grounds.[50] The Big Three also made poor decisions, such as trying to adapt existing engines to lower their emissions rather than developing new ones.[51]

Demand for larger cars recovered when the embargo ended, and by 1978, Japanese imports were down. But as oil prices fell and consumers reverted to larger vehicles, CAFE hampered the ability of US automakers to respond by producing more of the large cars Americans actually wanted. Instead, they had to produce smaller low-profit or no-profit cars to offset sales of large cars. CAFE had the opposite impact on the Japanese. Because their existing sales base was in small cars, they could easily expand into large ones. And they did: The three largest firms (Toyota, Nissan, and Honda) upsized their product mix, entering the mid-sized and ultimately the luxury markets.

The Roots of Japanese Advantage

Japanese cars continued to improve. In 1976, the pathbreaking Honda Accord reached America: a comfortable, inexpensive, high-mileage car with impressive standard features such as independent suspension, five-speed transmission, radial tires, disc brakes, and an aluminum cylinder head.[52] It seemed Japan could build more than cheap, spartan subcompacts. Datsun, Toyota, Mitsubishi, Isuzu, Mazda, and Subaru were close behind.

Contrary to myth, an increasingly prosperous Japan was not competing mainly on cheap labor. Its advantage in wages was estimated in 1982 at only about $500 per vehicle, and most of this was in productivity – that is, man hours per car, not wage rates.[53] Direct labor only averages about 7–8 percent of the cost of building cars anyway.[54] This period saw a boom in Japanese auto R&D, and the Japanese required only half the engineers and half the time to develop a new car.[55]

And then there was lean manufacturing. Led by Toyota, the Japanese had originally developed this novel approach due to their limited capital, space, and technology. But they eventually realized that it could beat classic American-style production focused on mass production, vertical integration, and economies of scale. That system had been designed to maximize output, which meant keeping assembly lines running and fixing problems later. This produced high defect rates, forcing many buyers to take their new cars back to the dealer multiple times.[56] The low defect rates of the Japanese changed consumer expectations, setting a new standard that the entire industry eventually had to meet worldwide.

"Lean" was eventually generalized to many other industries, even outside manufacturing.[57] It meant, in a nutshell, squeezing out of the production process every last bit of labor, materials, inventory, design, or time that didn't add value to the product. This entailed a rigorous focus on what *did* add value – which is simple in principle but has infinite ramifications all through a manufacturing firm.[58]

Lean entails, for example, greater flexibility on the assembly line, with quick die changes, so that scale economies kick in at lower quantities. Just-in-time (JIT) delivery of parts reduces inventories, saving the capital tied up in the cost of the parts and the storage space to hold them. But with no extra stock of parts to substitute for defective ones, quality control becomes crucial. Lean thus both requires and exerts pressure for greater quality. It also forces the causes of defects to the surface.

The resulting incremental improvement of quality and cost is systematized with "continuous improvement," *kaizen*. The lean approach involves suppliers earlier in product development, shortening time-to-market and delivering the needed quality. But unlike the Japanese, with their long-term *keiretsu* relationships (see Chapter 5), the Big Three were bullying their suppliers for cost reductions and ignoring the long-run implications of poor quality for consumer perceptions, warranty claims, depreciation, and scrappage.[59] For example, the Oldsmobile Cutlass and the Ford Thunderbird were recalled *nine* times from 1977 to 1981 to fix fuel, steering, suspension, and electrical problems.[60]

Japanese auto plants were estimated to be up to 50 percent more productive.[61] One Ford versus Mazda comparison estimated that the Japanese needed *half* the man hours per car.[62] And, contrary to another myth, Japan was not using more advanced production technology or greater capital investment.[63] Nevertheless, GM's response during the 1980s was to plow billions of dollars into robotics (plus some initial fruitless attempts to imitate lean). But its robots were unreliable, cost more in skilled labor to manage than the labor they replaced, and failed to achieve higher productivity.[64] The Big Three's initial attempts at lean grasped only disconnected parts of the philosophy.[65]

Responding to Japan

The 1979 Iranian Revolution, followed the next year by the Iran–Iraq War, again spiked gas prices. The Carter administration again made the problem worse with price and allocation controls.[66] Japan's share of the US light vehicle (cars, pickups, vans) market again grew, from 10 percent in 1975 to 22 percent in 1981 – all imported. Meanwhile, Chrysler owned 25 percent of Mitsubishi, Ford the same amount of Mazda, and GM 38 percent of Isuzu. The Big Three also ran manufacturing joint ventures with the Japanese firms and many of their own-brand cars were, in fact, made there.[67] So while they complained about the Japanese, they were in fact "sleeping with the enemy".

By the late 1970s and early 1980s, the Big Three were playing catch-up with Japan. Between 1970–4 and 1980–4, Ford's and GM's capital spending for physical plant increased by 75 and 120 percent, respectively.[68] The American industry's R&D rose by more than 40 percent.[69] This paid for electronic engine management to meet new mileage standards, downsizing their fleets through new body designs, and catalytic converters to meet pollution rules.[70] Chrysler, struggling to avoid bankruptcy, had trouble keeping up.

But the Big Three rushed their development efforts. GM's much anticipated "J cars," sold as the Chevrolet Cavalier and other models, were pale imitations of what the Japanese had already achieved. They lacked major technological advances and achieved adequate (though not impressive) mileage only at the cost of poor performance.[71] Their styling was dull, their amenities spoiled by cheap design decisions.

In 1984, GM undertook a vast restructuring of its North American operations, aiming to decentralize manufacturing authority and eliminate duplication of functions. The reorganization accomplished neither, but it did considerable damage to existing, often informal, ways of getting things done.[72]

GM's creation of its new small-car Saturn division was an attempt to start from scratch, given the difficulty of fixing the existing divisions' entrenched practices – a tacit confession that it didn't know how to reform itself.[73]

In the late 1980s, the Big Three all diversified into unrelated or weakly related businesses, such as IT, aerospace, and finance, revealing their lack of strategic focus. They agreed to labor contracts based on unrealistic optimism about their own future sales, failing to recognize the deep trouble they were in.[74]

Treasury and the Fed Wound US Auto Firms

Inflation peaked at 13 percent in 1979.[75] To quash it, Fed Chairman Paul Volcker hiked rates sharply, deliberately inducing the 1981–2 recession. The high interest rates attracted foreign capital, pushing the dollar up 25 percent on a trade-weighted basis.[76]

All of US manufacturing suffered from the overpriced dollar, but the automakers were hit by five factors at once:

1. The recession, with the worst unemployment since the Depression, cut sales.
2. High interest rates made auto loans more expensive, worsening #1.
3. High gas prices from the 1979 oil crisis drove consumers to imports.
4. The appreciation of the dollar made imports cheaper.
5. Their labor cost per car was above their foreign competitors'.[77]

Light vehicle sales dropped from 14 million per year in 1980 to under 9 million in 1981.[78] Imports rose from 18 percent of the market in 1978 to 26.5 percent by 1980.[79] By mid-1985, the dollar's trade-weighted value was almost 50 percent higher than before the 1979 oil crisis.[80] The landed-cost advantage for small Japanese cars was estimated at $1,500 to $2,000, making American manufacturers totally uncompetitive in that segment.[81]

US manufacturers also faced foreign rivals whose medical and retirement costs were borne wholly or in part by their governments. In the US, medical costs were rising economy-wide, and with the number of auto workers falling because of rising productivity and falling sales, fewer workers were supporting more retirees. UAW leadership was aware of these problems but constrained by their rank and file from making big enough concessions to make the automakers' obligations sustainable.[82]

The Chrysler Bailout and Voluntary Restraints

In 1979, the collapse in auto sales forced Chrysler to ask Washington for help. Advocates of the proposed bailout emphasized the number of Chrysler's employees and the many communities where its plants were located.

Opponents argued that bad management decisions and its UAW contract were the real problem. With the 1980 election approaching, the advocates won, and the firm was rescued by $1.5 billion in loans guaranteed by the Treasury.

Chrysler ultimately returned to health and repaid its loans early, netting the government a $300 million profit.[83] While its bailout was a single-company, rather than industry-wide, solution, it did trigger a national debate about the failing health of the industry. Imports were an obvious cause, so in 1980, Ford and the UAW filed Section 201 petitions before the US International Trade Commission (USITC) for temporary protection from an injurious import surge.[84] The petitions sought a five-year quota limiting Japanese imports to 8 percent of the market.[85]

These petitions were opposed by academic economists and environmental and safety advocates, with many critics attributing Ford's difficulties to its unwillingness or inability to produce good small cars. Congress was generally unsupportive, with many of its members believing that the UAW should just give Ford a cheaper contract. Most damaging was the lack of support from GM and Chrysler.[86] The USITC, in a split decision, denied the petitions just after the 1980 election on the grounds that the harm had resulted from a poor economy and a shift in consumer preferences toward smaller cars, not from increased imports.[87]

A number of bills to slow the growth of Japanese imports were introduced. Opponents argued that the automakers and the UAW would never become competitive if they were protected. None passed. Meanwhile, auto workers were smashing Japanese cars at rallies.

When Ronald Reagan took office in 1981, he generally favored free trade and was initially reluctant to use protective trade measures for autos. But it soon became clear that auto production was at risk of catastrophic and probably permanent decline if nothing was done. So, in 1981, the administration, wielding the protectionist pressures in Congress as a threat, negotiated a "Voluntary" Restraint Agreement (VRA) with Tokyo to limit Japan's car exports to the US.

The VRA began in May 1981 at 1.68 million cars per year, was raised to 1.85 million in 1984, to 2.3 million in 1985, and ended in 1994.[88] As economic recovery began in the last quarter of 1982, it did slow the erosion of the Big Three's market share, giving them breathing room. But this reprieve masked unresolved problems. By limiting the supply of Japanese cars, the VRA allowed Japanese carmakers to raise prices. Their higher profits then helped fund the development of new, larger models. The VRA also pushed Japan into pricier vehicles, as it limited the number of imported cars, not their value, and after some initial blunders, the Japanese succeeded.

The Transplants

America's debate on Japanese imports was distorted by the mistaken belief that they were competitive due to factors specific to Japan: supposedly cheaper labor, a more cooperative workforce, company-dominated unions, a unique management culture, a different overall type of capitalism (see Chapter 6), and a more supportive government. It was therefore believed that forcing the Japanese to shift production to the US would diminish them as a competitive threat. It was assumed that the UAW would unionize their plants, raising their labor costs to the level of the Americans.[89]

Based on this mistaken premise, the US welcomed Japanese transplants. Honda opened in Marysville, Ohio, in 1982 (a plant visited by one of the authors during the writing of this book), Nissan in Smyrna, Tennessee, in 1983, and Mazda in Flat Rock, Michigan, in 1987. Others followed, setting up plants and entering into joint ventures with US auto manufacturers.[90]

Despite the firms' initial, ultimately disproved, fears about the quality of American workers, these plants proved viable. The Japanese, backed by their *keiretsu* corporate "families" and their government, were able to transfer their efficient production systems to the US, including much of their supplier base. By locating mostly in right-to-work states, they were able to avoid unionization. Japan-specific factors turned out not to matter very much.[91]

The transplants initially only assembled cars from imported parts, so many supply chain jobs were lost. American firms could hypothetically have produced many of the imported parts, but *keiretsu* ties excluded them. Even when parts production was eventually onshored, it tended to go to Japanese firms in the US, a problem the Japanese also created in Europe.[92] President Bush pressed Japan on this issue in 1992, but with little result.[93] Meanwhile, Japan kept its home market closed to American cars and parts. And although Europe was not *as* closed, it still had formal and informal barriers limiting both American and Japanese imports.

Japan's share of the American car market, counting both imports and onshore production, continued to grow. In the early 1990s, Korean firms took advantage of the rise of the yen to penetrate the lower end of the market.[94] Eventually they and even the Germans opened plants in America. (For a discussion of Japan's strategy in automobiles from its own point of view, see Chapter 5, for Korea's, see Chapter 6.)

Simultaneously, as Pulitzer-Prize-winning auto journalist Paul Ingrassia notes,

> Between 1984 and 1989 General Motors, Ford, and Chrysler spent some $20 billion on acquisitions, most of them outside the car business, The acquisitions came on top of dividend increases, stock splits,

and share-buyback programs, all generated by that ultimate enabler of corporate spending-copious amounts of free cash flow. The diversification moves were intended to outflank the Japanese, who were busy in the boring business of building more automobile factories in America. The real question was, who was outflanking whom?[95]

All the growth in sales by foreign firms from American plants came at the expense of the Detroit Three, as the Big Three were increasingly known due to their diminished status. For every transplant that opened between 1979 and 1991, one of their plants closed.[96] The result was that America's auto industry became increasingly foreign-owned and foreign-managed, while no net additional jobs or production capacity were created. Over time, nonunion foreign competition helped force the UAW into a two-tier contract system with new hires paid roughly 50 percent less than existing workers. Since the early 1990s, the parts situation has improved somewhat, but the US still runs a $69 billion trade deficit in auto parts.[97]

Clinton, Japan, and NAFTA

Starting in 1993, the Clinton administration tried to take a hard line against Japan on autos. It threatened 100 percent tariffs on 13 luxury models unless Japan opened its market to US cars and parts and Japanese producers in the US increased purchases from American parts suppliers.[98] Tokyo agreed in principle but refused even "voluntary" plans to increase purchases of US parts or any target for the number of dealers selling American cars in Japan.

A trade war was expected, but was avoided when both sides realized that the other was serious. Japan threatened to stop purchasing American debt if the US imposed higher tariffs, and interest rates on Treasuries jumped.[99] Treasury Secretary Robert Rubin interceded with Clinton and persuaded him that higher interest rates threatened his reelection hopes, so the president asked the US Trade Representative (USTR) to reach a compromise. The resulting agreement included plans for, inter alia, increased vehicle and component production in the US, increased local content for Japanese vehicles produced in the US, and increased imports of US auto parts by Japan. Most of these commitments had previously been agreed to, so little was new, but the agreement allowed both sides to claim victory.

To address the competitiveness challenges of all US manufacturers, including the auto sector, the administration in 1993 completed the North American Free Trade Agreement (NAFTA) that the Bush administration had begun and got Congress to ratify it. The thinking was that automakers would unite American know-how with inexpensive Mexican labor to produce cars that would be competitive with the Japanese.

But NAFTA did not help. As should have been foreseen, foreign automakers took advantage of it by setting up plants in Mexico, and today 76 percent of Mexico's auto output is exported to the US.[100] The hope that low-end activities would be allocated to Mexico, with high-value, high-wage activities remaining in the US, did not pan out.[101] GM reports that its productivity and quality in Mexico are as good as in the US, all for $7 per hour in wages and benefits.[102] For the Detroit Three, NAFTA was always primarily a way to get around the UAW. Their market share continued to decline, from more than 70 percent when NAFTA went into effect in 1994 to a historic low of 41 percent in 2021.[103]

Starting in 2017, the Trump administration renegotiated NAFTA with stricter rules of origin (where goods must be made to qualify for a lower tariff) and provisions favoring employment of US and Canadian workers. But the impact was small because the non-NAFTA tariff on cars is only 2.5 percent, making the incentive to qualify for the zero USMCA (as NAFTA was renamed) rate minimal.[104]

Trucks, SUVs, and Minivans

For decades there has been one major exception to America's open vehicle market. During the "chicken war" of 1961–4, President Johnson responded to tariffs placed by the Common Market (predecessor of the EU) on imports of US chicken with a 25 percent tariff on brandy, dextrin, potato starch, and light trucks. The vehicle tariff remains in place, covering pickups, cargo vans, and two-seat SUVs.[105]

American carmakers saw that, given the tariff and lower CAFE standards for SUVs and pickups, they could prosper in this segment. They set out to migrate customers to these vehicles and eventually succeeded. The SUV revolution began with the 1986 Jeep Cherokee and went mainstream with the 1991 Ford Explorer, and light trucks became the Detroit Three's most profitable products.[106] Sales rose from 2.2 million in 1980 to 11.6 million in 2021.[107] Their sales of cars correspondingly dropped, between 1986 and 2022, from 11.4 to 2.9 million.[108]

By 2022, vans and full-size pickups were 14 percent of the light-vehicle market, and the Detroit Three sold 94 percent of them.[109] To be fair, tariffs are not the only reason they held on to market share.[110] Pickup buyers are more brand loyal. The firms' truck divisions made fewer management mistakes. Domestic brands had good quality, durability, and innovation – contrary to the claim of free-trade ideologues that protected markets preclude excellence. (The all-electric 2022 Ford F-150 Lightning is the latest standard setter in this class.)

Thanks to the SUV boom, America's auto industry in the late 1990s was on an upswing, and the Japanese automakers' miss in this category reduced their share of the US market from 26 percent in 1991 to 23 percent in 1993.[111] The Americans made record profits. But their response, once again, was complacency, strategic drift, and disinvestment. GM tweaked its accounting to increase apparent earnings.[112] In 1999 and 2000, Ford went on an acquisition spree, picking up smaller carmakers with questionable futures (Sweden's Volvo, Britain's Land Rover) and several firms that didn't even make cars.[113]

To be fair, there were some good management decisions in this era. One was the Detroit Three's adoption, starting in 1994, of the QS9000 quality standard that they developed together, which improved their products and helped their suppliers achieve the 50-per-million defect rate required for JIT operations.[114]

Financial Crisis and Industry Collapse

From January 2002 to August 2006, oil rose from $16 to $67 a barrel due to 9/11, recovery from recession, and the invasion of Iraq.[115] American consumers once again shifted toward smaller cars. Once again, this increased the foreigners' market share, especially as the Detroit Three were no longer making much effort in the segment. And although they had made design and manufacturing improvements, they had not made enough.[116] By the first half of 2006, foreign brands, some built in the US, had 53 percent of the market – the first time the Americans had had less than half.[117]

GM's last profitable year was 2004 and then it, Chrysler, and Ford began sliding toward bankruptcy. By 2006, GM's market share was *half* its 1962 peak.[118] By the end of that year, GM's and Ford's unfunded liabilities for retiree benefits had reached $47 billion and $26 billion respectively, which left the firms extremely vulnerable to a downturn.[119] By 2007, even GM's finance arm, sucked into the mortgage bubble, was losing money.[120] But headquarters was still denying that the firm was headed for bankruptcy.[121] That same year, the UAW agreed to its first two-tier contract, with lower wages for new hires, because *it* understood how bad the situation was.

When the 2007–8 financial crisis hit, credit dried up. This made it harder to obtain auto loans, and between 2006 and 2009, GM's US sales fell by nearly half.[122] It and Chrysler were about to collapse. Ford was spared only because of a $24 billion line of credit it had negotiated in 2007, essentially mortgaging the entire firm to survive.[123]

Federal bailouts were proposed. But elected representatives from states with transplants were unenthusiastic. The *Wall Street Journal* favored letting the firms die. Republican presidential candidate Mitt Romney was opposed, as were 55 percent of the public.[124] The congressional testimony of the firms' executives, arriving in Washington in private jets, did not help. In the words of Obama administration "Car Czar" Steve Rattner,

> From [CEO] Wagoner on down, GM seemed to be living in a fantasy that, despite the evidence of decades of decline, it was still the greatest carmaker on earth, in a class by itself . . . The overall concept seemed to be to trim only what was easily achieved and absolutely necessary, and use taxpayer dollars to ride out the recession.[125]

What proved decisive was not just the number of jobs – including employment at suppliers, about 3 million – but also the fear of pulling down the entire industry as supplier firms collapsed.[126] For each assembly-plant job, there were an estimated 10 others supporting it in parts, logistics, and services.[127] Because all the auto companies shared suppliers, even the transplants would be harmed.

Thus the federal government gave GM and Chrysler emergency loans so they could continue paying their bills, then put them through structured, expedited bankruptcies. The US and Canadian governments, plus the province of Ontario, eventually extended the firms a rescue package totaling $US96 billion – $US82 billion from Washington and $US14 billion from Ottawa and Toronto.[128]

Bailout and Recovery

The condition of the bailouts was that the firms be completely restructured. This allowed them to shed debt and excess dealerships, drop brands and product lines, and renegotiate union contracts.[129] There was no alternative to bankruptcy: It was the only way to force shared concessions by the many stakeholders. Even Ford used the threat of bankruptcy to win concessions.

Reorganizing the firms was difficult. GM's financial systems were so decrepit that they could not properly support decision-making.[130] Its corporate culture, despite decades of on-and-off crisis, was conformist, hierarchy-bound, and unresponsive to bad news.[131]

On the bright side, some of the Detroit Three's historic problems had been corrected. GM had learned from working with Toyota, and their productivities in man-hours per car were now almost equal. So were their labor costs per hour and, by some measures, their quality.[132] Ford's quality now even *surpassed* Toyota, which had suffered from its own too rapid expansion.[133] GM's labor relations had improved since a damaging strike in 1998, and pride had returned to its once demoralized workforce.[134]

Thus the US government became the main owner of GM and the UAW and Italy's Fiat (since merged into Stellantis) the main owners of Chrysler. In 2010, GM's first year as a reformed company, it made its highest net income since 1999. Its revenues, helped by a higher average price per car, were even 25 percent higher than the government had anticipated.[135] It went public, enabling the government to gradually sell off its stake.

The bailouts cost the taxpayer $9.3 billion.[136] Given the social and economic costs avoided and the future tax revenues preserved, they were a success. Since then, of the Detroit Three, only Chrysler, the smallest, has regained its pre-crisis sales volume. But all have restructured their operating economics. For example, GM can now make money in a US car market of 11.5 million units a year, as opposed to losing money in a 17.5-million-plus market.[137] But it withdrew from Europe in 2017, giving up its aspiration to be a global producer. Ford stayed in Europe but withdrew from the fast-growing Indian market in 2021.

Nor has America's trade deficit in cars been fixed. The US runs a 75:1 deficit in cars with Japan, 22:1 with Mexico, 10:1 with Korea, and 3:1 with Europe.[138] In 2019, foreign automakers had US production of 4.9 million, versus 5.7 million for the Detroit Three plus Tesla. Thus almost half of US-located auto manufacturing is now foreign owned and operated.[139]

The electric car, however, is now changing the game for everyone.

New Technologies

The federal government has been reckoning with the limits of the internal combustion engine (ICE) for some time. In 1993, it launched the Partnership for a New Generation of Vehicles (PNGV), which aimed to develop cars with up to 80 mpg by 2003. PNGV involved eight federal agencies, universities, national labs, plus DaimlerChrysler, Ford, and GM. The Clinton administration won the industry's cooperation by agreeing not to raise CAFE standards.[140]

By 2001, having spent more than $1 billion taxpayer dollars, PNGV was on track to meet its targets using diesel-electric hybrid propulsion and lightweight aluminum and thermoplastic bodies. GM had developed the 80 mpg Precept, Ford the 72 mpg Prodigy, Chrysler the 72 mpg ESX-3. But these were only concept cars, not production models, would have cost 50 percent more than normal vehicles, and would have required subsidies.

At the request of the carmakers, President Bush cancelled PNGV in 2001. Its replacement, the FreedomCAR program, pivoted to hydrogen. In principle, this had the advantage of emitting no greenhouse gasses, but the program raised the same suspicion as PNGV that it was a diversion to avoid immediate action.[141] As of 2024, Hydrogen vehicles are not yet a success, and their inefficient underlying physics makes them an outside bet at best.[142]

The Japanese, ironically, treated PNGV as a serious competitive threat. The result was the first generation of hybrids, the 1997 Toyota Prius and 1999 Honda Insight. The Detroit Three then had to again play catch-up, with Ford licensing technology from Toyota in 2004 to build its Fusion Hybrid. By 2007, 350,000 hybrids were being sold in the US each year.[143]

America's Catch-Up Effort in Electric Cars

In 2012, only 120,000 EVs were sold globally, but by 2021, that many were sold every week: 10 percent of the market.[144] That year, the Detroit Three pledged that by 2030, 40 to 50 percent of their sales would be EVs, FCEVs, or hybrids, and they committed to invest $100 billion in North American EV production.[145] By 2024, two dozen manufacturers from around the world were selling BEVs in the US. They were now inexorably replacing ICE vehicles worldwide – though with a 15-year average lifespan, the last ICE vehicles are unlikely to leave the road until 2050.

GM announced that by 2035, it would sell only zero-emissions vehicles.[146] It projected a $35 billion investment by 2025 in 30 different models.[147] Stellantis, owner of Chrysler, Dodge, Ram, and Jeep, also announced it would spend $35 billion by that year, much of it on these brands.[148] Ford said in 2022 that it would separate its ICE and EV businesses and increase spending on the latter to $50 billion between 2022 and 2026.[149] GM planned to produce 1 million EVs a year by 2025, Ford 2 million by 2026, and Tesla (overoptimistically) 20 million by 2030.[150]

But the American BEV market cooled in 2023, causing the industry to delay these investments. Tesla said it might postpone a $1 billion plant in Mexico, GM put off production of EV versions of its Sierra and Silverado pickups, and Ford delayed $12 billion of a planned $15 billion investment in EVs and related technologies.[151] Stellantis, however, a latecomer to EVs, said it would proceed with its planned investments in a bid to catch up.[152]

Even before the slowdown, North America was lagging in the new technology, with only 1.1 million sold in 2022, versus 2.7 million in Europe and 6.2 million in China.[153] Thanks to less maintenance, lower fueling costs, and government rebates, the total cost of BEV ownership was similar to ICE vehicles. But as of 2023, their average US purchase price was still considerably higher. GM and others predicted that the price premium would eventually disappear, but until then, subsidies would be required.[154]

China and Europe Lead in Electric Cars

As of 2024, China was the largest EV producer, accounting for roughly half of world production. The price premium there, was down to 10 percent.[155] Prices started around $10,000, but many of the cheaper models weren't exportable due to safety regulations, though Chinese manufacturers were improving. (In the US, they also faced a 25 percent tariff imposed by President Trump and ineligibility for purchaser subsidies.)

China's success was the result of its proactive industrial policies. Around 2011, its indigenous ICE carmakers were struggling to catch up with the Japanese, Korean, German, and American brands producing there. The country was also facing a huge oil import bill. Therefore, it began a technological leapfrogging effort, pouring an estimated $57 billion into EVs from 2016 to 2022.[156] Beijing subsidized the entire supply chain: mining, refining, batteries, auto parts, auto assembly, battery recycling, and charging stations. By 2019, the industry had 500 car firms. Four years later, this had fallen to 100 and consolidation was ongoing.[157]

By 2024, China's EV progress was so impressive that Toyota, straining to catch up, was jointly developing its subcompact crossover bZ3X with China's BYD and imitating its technology. This privately owned firm, rather than state-owned SAIC or First Automotive, was thus poised to become China's first world-class carmaker. In 2023, it surpassed Tesla to become the best-selling EV, although it had not yet penetrated the US.[158] Meanwhile, Swedish-headquartered but Chinese-made and -owned Polestar had begun US deliveries in 2021.

Europe, number two in electric cars, had also gotten there through deliberate industrial policy. EV adoption was supported by the EU itself, by 26 of its 27 national governments, and by many provincial and local governments.[159] They subsidized consumers, manufacturers, and charging infrastructure. Incentives included purchase grants, tariff exemptions, toll exemptions, congestion pricing exemptions, registration fee waivers, and waivers of annual ownership charges. By 2019, the EU 27 were exporting €8.2 billion worth of EVs (and importing €7.1 billion).[160] By 2022, 12 percent of sales were BEVs and 9 percent were PHEVs. Incrementally rising standards for CO_2, reaching zero in 2035, forced the hands of the carmakers.[161]

Biden Administration Policies

The Biden administration's first move in support of EVs was to restore then strengthen CAFE standards weakened under Trump. It then set a target that 50 percent of vehicle sales be zero emissions by 2030.[162]

In 2022, the Inflation Reduction Act (IRA) extended and changed the existing $7,500 purchaser tax credit covering BEVs, some plug-in hybrids, and hydrogen vehicles. It extended the subsidy – up to $4,000 – to used cars and eliminated the limit of 200,000 cars per manufacturer.[163]

The IRA also allocated $10 billion to a tax credit for establishing or expanding manufacturing plants for many green technologies, including EVs.[164] It built on the Bipartisan Infrastructure Act (BIA) passed nine months earlier, which had included $5 billion over five years to establish a national EV charging network.[165]

In defiance of America's WTO obligations, the IRA's subsidies were limited to vehicles made in North America. Final assembly had to take place there and 40 percent of key battery minerals had to come from the US or one of the 20 countries with which it has an FTA. This percentage was slated to rise to 50 percent in 2024, 60 percent in 2025, 70 percent in 2026, and 80 percent in 2027.[166] Geopolitical adversaries – for example, China, Russia, Cuba, and North Korea – were excluded outright, while Korea and the EU duly (and accurately) complained about "protectionism."

The IRA was one of America's most ambitious pieces of civilian industrial policy in decades, with its triple aim of a) decarbonizing, b) de-China-izing and c) democratizing EV ownership. It was accused of deliberately driving up the cost of ICE vehicles to push consumers into EVs.[167] It was even argued that the legal basis for regulating gas mileage *prohibited* considering electric vehicles: Trade groups and some states sued under the Major Questions Doctrine, which the Supreme Court had used in 2022 to curtail the EPA's authority to close coal power plants.[168]

The Minerals Crunch

As of 2022, world EV production was projected to reach 40 million per year by 2030, but there was no guarantee that supplies of critical minerals, such as nickel, cobalt, lithium, and manganese, would grow enough to meet this schedule. Lithium, for example, was geologically abundant, but its production was concentrated: in Chile, Australia, Argentina, and to a lesser extent, China. As of late 2023, Bolivia, with the largest reserves, had no active mining, largely for political reasons.[169] New lithium sources – mines or brine-harvesting operations – cannot be accessed quickly by just investing more money. The US in 2023 had only one working mine, in Nevada, though there were plans for a new mine in Nevada and for geothermal lithium-brine plants at California's Salton Sea. Mines were also planned in Tennessee, North Carolina, Quebec, and Alberta.[170] Then, in 2023, the world's largest deposit, 120 million tons, was discovered at the McDermitt Caldera on the border of Oregon and Nevada, with game-changing potential (see later in this chapter).[171]

As of 2024, China has secured rights to critical minerals in Africa, Australia, and South America. The Democratic Republic of the Congo produces 70 percent of the world's cobalt, and Chinese firms now control 15 of its 19 major cobalt mines.[172] The US once proactively sought to block Soviet access, but the last major American firm there, Freeport-McMoRan, sold its rights to a Chinese company in 2016, and the Obama administration did nothing. The Trump administration was no better: In 2020, Freeport put an undeveloped cobalt mining site up for sale, but again Washington failed to act, and a Chinese company bought it.[173]

Refining was another potential choke point: China refined 70 percent of the world's lithium and 60 percent of its graphite.[174] It had a near monopoly in rare earths, needed for many EV's motors (which provoked Tesla to announce plans in 2023 to develop a new motor not requiring them).

American EV makers were thus almost entirely dependent on Chinese minerals, even when their batteries were produced by Japanese or Korean firms (as most were). With the battery representing 30 to 40 percent of the price of an EV, even US-assembled EVs thus resulted in substantial transfers of wealth to foreign nations if they had imported batteries.[175] If the whole supply chain is counted, it is a myth that EVs require less total labor to build, but the battery accounts for 8 percent of that work.

The Biden administration was the first to take these issues seriously. In 2022, the Department of Energy (DOE) released a supply chain strategy for green energy technologies from wind to nuclear to electric cars.[176] DOE announced projects to expand domestic lithium production and EV battery manufacturing, awarding $2.8 billion to 20 companies in 12 states: Alabama, Georgia, Kentucky, Louisiana, Missouri, Nevada, New York, North Carolina, North Dakota, Ohio, Tennessee, and Washington.[177] In March 2024, the owner of the McDermitt Caldera, Lithium Americas, reported a conditional commitment from the DOE for a $2.3 billion loan to construct processing facilities.[178] In 2023, the US signed an agreement with Japan that weakened the Inflation Reduction Act's made-in-America requirements in return for cooperation in strengthening China-free battery minerals' supply chains.[179] And in March 2023, American officials started negotiating a similar agreement with the EU.[180]

In May 2024, Biden imposed a 100 percent tariff on Chinese electric cars. Policies still needed, but not yet imposed, to achieve a coherent all-of-government-and-industry EV strategy include additional selective tariffs, an end to dollar overvaluation, and an upgrade of the inadequate electric grid to support the projected number of EVs.

26 SEMICONDUCTORS, AVIATION, AND SPACE

The Military Developmental State

America's greatest industrial policy successes since World War II have been in industries and technologies related to defense. A comprehensive national industrial policy would have integrated policies for the defense industrial base with a broader vision of science, technology, industry, and trade, and aimed at *both* national security and economic prosperity. Instead, the US pursued a de facto industrial policy aiming only at the former, one that has been called its "hidden developmental state," a disjointed but potent set of policies that profoundly influenced both defense and nondefense industries.

Starting in the late 1950s, defense-oriented industrial policies nurtured new industries, and many of America's most advanced industries today derive from defense R&D, or were supported by defense procurement before commercial markets existed. Jet aircraft, nuclear power, satellites, microwaves, lasers, integrated circuits, microprocessors, computers, the internet, digital photography, GPS, and many other technologies fall into this category (see Chapter 19). This support continues today, most visibly in the CHIPS Act of 2022, which was largely motivated by national security concerns.

Because these industries emerged and thrived without the aid of economically motivated policies, many US policymakers and business leaders came to believe that – except for government sponsorship of pure science – technological progress was an *automatic* consequence of the interaction of pure science with free markets. This belief then hampered the nation's ability to design and implement civilian industrial policies for decades.

Defense Is Different

Defense industrial policy is shaped by the profound differences between the defense sector and the civilian economy. Defense for a superpower necessarily prioritizes superior performance in battle almost regardless of cost, while hopefully minimizing dependence on foreign sources. DOD imposes uniquely extreme specifications, performance standards, and auditing requirements on military manufacturing and technology development. Most companies outside the sector are unable or unwilling to conform to its highly bureaucratic, rule-bound processes. So the Pentagon works with a relatively small group of contractors that understand and live by its rules. But for these, it offers virtually unlimited funds, pays to develop technologies unavailable in the commercial sector, and funds cost overruns when performance requirements are changed midstream. Once a contract has been awarded, there is often basically no competition and DOD has to tolerate delays and cost overruns. Free-market forces play only a small role in the sector because a single buyer is purchasing its major systems from an oligopoly of "prime" contractors. Through the exercise of this monopsony power, DOD has created a highly regulated industry.

Origins of the Defense Industrial Base

After World War II, the US rapidly demobilized and converted its defense industries to civilian production. It had emerged from the war the politically and economically dominant nation and its leaders saw little reason to retain huge, expensive standing forces. But following the Soviet consolidation of power in Eastern Europe by 1948, the Chinese Communist Revolution in 1949, the Soviet atom bomb test in 1949, and the Korean War of 1950–3, Washington reversed course. The new Cold War appeared likely to go on indefinitely, requiring a robust, permanent defense industrial base capable of producing the most advanced weapons and having surge capacity in the event of war.

For the first time, the US, caught unprepared by both world wars and the Korean War, committed to building a large peacetime military and a defense industrial base sufficient to defeat any likely adversary. In both world wars, the US had harnessed its civilian manufacturing sector, converting existing plants and adding new ones for military production, but the new defense industrial base was different. It was (and is) comprised of tens of thousands of companies operating under contract to DOD and its prime contractors. US military strategy was based on countering the Communist Bloc's superiority in manpower and materiel with better technology. To this end, the Pentagon developed many leading-edge technologies and helped stand up industries to produce them at scale. Later and to a lesser extent, NASA played a similar role.

The Contemporary Defense Industrial Sector

The defense industrial base today has three parts: military contractors, R&D institutions, and the military–civilian-dual use sectors of the economy.

In 2022, the Pentagon obligated $424 billion in contracts to the major primes and their subcontractors. The industry is highly concentrated, with the top five accounting for 30 percent: Lockheed Martin ($45.7 billion), Raytheon ($25.4 billion), General Dynamics ($21.2 billion), Pfizer ($16.7 billion), and Boeing ($14.7 billion), with the next 25 making up another 20 percent.[1] Some are US subsidiaries of foreign firms: BAE Systems – a UK-based international defense, aerospace, and security company – was the ninth largest in 2022, at $5.1 billion.[2] Most large primes have one foot in defense and the other in the civilian economy: as of 2022, an average of 24 percent of their business.[3] The primes subcontract to smaller companies, which in turn subcontract further. As funds percolate down the supply chain, the percentage of products sourced from civilian industry increases. America's primes concentrate on systems integration, where the US leads the world, but often delegate development and production of subsystems and components to lower-tier contractors.

The second part of the defense industrial base is its R&D institutions. These include DOD-operated labs, DOD-affiliated research centers, DOD-funded university labs, and DOD-funded industry labs. Many, such as the Naval Research Laboratory, operate within or under contract to a single service branch. Several other defense agencies, including the Defense Health Agency and Missile Defense Agency, have labs of their own (see Chapter 20).

Defense R&D is also carried out by parts of NASA, Federally Financed Research and Development Centers, University Affiliated Research Centers, and by several of the Department of Energy's National Laboratories.[4] Many research facilities in universities and private industry are funded under the Pentagon's Research, Development, Test, and Evaluation (RDT&E) budget category. DARPA, which contracts out its research, has played a major role in the development of technologies such as semiconductors, the internet, advanced materials, and robotics (see Chapter 23).

The third element of the defense industrial base is the dual-use sectors of the economy: the laboratories, companies, industries, and personnel that develop technologies and manufacture products used for *both* military and civilian purposes. Due to the wide scope of military requirements, this includes a huge swath of the manufacturing and technology economy.

The Military Fraction of Technology Development

In 2022, DOD accounted for 46 percent ($85 billion of $187 billion) of federal R&D, and 2023 and proposed 2024 numbers showed an even larger fraction of an even larger total.[5] Since the late 1950s, two trends have been key.

The first is the growth of *all* kinds of R&D, both in real terms and as a percentage of GDP. While federally funded R&D has steadily declined as a percentage of GDP since the early 1960s, business R&D has continued to grow. As shown in Figure 26.1, between 1960 and 2019, they grew in absolute terms by factors of 2.3 and 15.2, respectively.

The second trend, shown in Figures 26.2 and 26.3, is that while federal defense R&D was 36 percent of global R&D in 1960, by 2019, that number had fallen to 3 percent. Meanwhile, non-US R&D increased from 31 percent of the total to 70 percent of a much larger total.[6]

These trends have weakened America's defense industrial base. First, the Defense Department has much less sway in determining the direction and pace of technology development than it once had. Most innovation today is in the civilian sectors of the US and global economies. Second, DOD is now under pressure to buy many products abroad simply because that is where the technologies are being researched, developed, and manufactured.

The US defense industrial base, once nearly self-sufficient, is now significantly dependent on foreign firms and technologies. Some of these are located abroad, while some are US subsidiaries of foreign companies. Six of the world's 25 largest defense companies in have major US subsidiaries: BAE (UK),

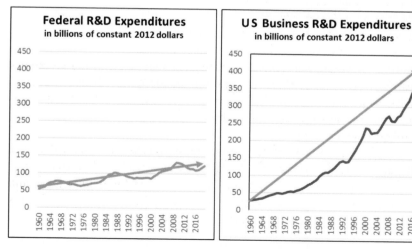

Figure 26.1 Growth in federal and US business R&D expenditures 1960–2019[7]

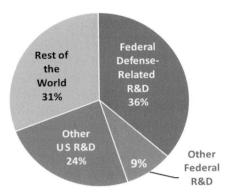

Figure 26.2 Global R&D expenditures 1960[8]

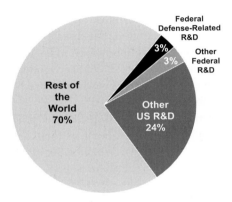

Figure 26.3 Global R&D expenditures 2019[9]

Leonardo (Italy), Airbus (several European nations led by France), Thales (France), Dassault (France), and Mitsubishi (Japan).[10] In addition, many foreign defense companies have subsidiaries that subcontract to the big US primes.

In welcoming these foreign firms, the Pentagon has tried to make a virtue of necessity, adopting a global perspective to obtain cheaper and better products. Thus, in 2012, three prominent commentators, including a former undersecretary of defense for acquisition, wrote,

> [T]oday, technology development and production are globally dispersed. As a result, the United States depends on offshore sources for defense-related technologies (especially in critical, lower tier component areas). Increasing reliance on foreign sources for production has allowed the DoD to achieve higher performance, while reducing costs

(thus increasing the number of units produced), and to improve deployment times (Moran, 1990). The use of foreign sources has also allowed for greater competition among firms, realizing cost savings for the DoD.[11]

At its best, international procurement enables greater scale economies, global price competition, exploitation of differing comparative advantages among nations, interoperability of weapon systems with allies, and improvements in foreign relations.[12] Its downsides are discussed in the next section.

The Problem of Defense Dependence

There is disturbingly little DOD oversight over the US military's dependence on foreign manufacturers. It generally does not even know exactly what its primes are doing. As a 1994 General Accounting Office report concluded, "DOD officials have little awareness of the extent of foreign sourcing or dependency in their weapon systems ... officials are not required, and take no special action, to maintain visibility into foreign sourcing/dependency."[13] DOD lags in component tracking, despite the availability of suitable civilian supply-chain-management technologies.[14] Malicious actors can implant faulty or altered parts or code into weapons or communications systems at any stage from design to production to deployment. A 2010 Commerce Department study found that counterfeit parts and software had already made significant inroads into US defense systems, specifically electronic components.[15]

In the past, the Pentagon has relied on specially designated trusted semiconductor foundries, microelectronics assemblers, and software companies. But the efficacy of this model was challenged by a 2017 Defense Science Board study, which concluded DOD lacks adequate mechanisms to discover hidden vulnerabilities.[16] It also concluded that the cost of operating a dedicated semiconductor foundry to supply DOD alone was prohibitive and that due to the international character of the semiconductor industry, foreign parts and software were inevitable.[17]

Many defense-related products and technologies are no longer made, or made to state-of-the-art standards, in the US. A 2012 report by the National Technology Council listed these: "aircraft landing gear; railcar components; large rotor disks for turbines; rocket engine parts; missile launch systems; unmanned aerial and ground vehicles; nuclear power components; aircraft fuselages; orbital vehicles; network routing and switching; optical data transport; advanced power electronics; low-cost composites; and transmission conductors."[18]

Key raw materials are also at risk. From the 1960s through the 1980s, the US led in production of rare earth elements (REEs) such as neodymium and samarium, which are irreplaceable in high-tech applications such as optics, displays, lasers, alloys, and magnets. But starting in the 1990s, China took the lead in mining and refining REEs.[19] From 2017 to 2021, 78 percent of REE imports came from China, followed by Estonia, Malaysia, and Japan.[20] Beijing is well aware of its ability to weaponize this dependence: A 2019 editorial in Xinhua, China's official press agency, said that "by waging a trade war against China, the United States risks losing the supply of materials that are vital to sustaining its technological strength."[21] In July 2023, Beijing imposed export restrictions on eight gallium and six germanium products.[22]

A 2020 DOD report to Congress recommended that the US "reshore our defense industrial base and supply chains to the United States and to allies, starting with microelectronics."[23] But legislative initiatives to create sufficient domestic mining, processing, and refining capabilities of rare earths floundered until the US started funding new domestic mining operations under the Inflation Reduction Act of 2022.[24] That year, DOD prepared a report on increasing domestic REE production and collaborating with allies and other friendly nations to secure defense supply chains.[25] The Biden administration undertook additional measures, including a $35 million contract for the firm MP Materials to begin developing a processing and separation facility for REEs, an equally important part of their supply chain.[26]

The Military Roots of Integrated Circuits

Integrated circuits (ICs) are critical to modern information-intensive weapons, enabling radical improvements in the size, weight, speed, and processing power of electronics. Whole categories of military and civilian device are inconceivable without them. DOD was centrally involved in their early development.

The IC was invented in 1958 in multi-chip form by Jack Kilby at Texas Instruments and in 1959 in its mature single-chip "monolithic" form by Robert Noyce at Fairchild Semiconductor. Their inventions were based on the work of Fairchild's Jean Hoerni, who created the crucial planar process derived from work at Bell Labs.[27] Initial invention thus took place in the private sector, albeit with help from Bell Labs, a government-regulated monopoly.

But the crucial next steps took place under contract to the Defense Department.[28] The Air Force had already been working on microelectronics and immediately grasped the value of ICs, especially for missiles, so it funded the R&D needed to develop them further. In 1959, DOD awarded Texas Instruments a contract worth $12 million in 2023 dollars for this purpose, followed by another in 1960 to develop larger-scale production processes.[29]

The Air Force designed ICs into the guidance system of the Minuteman II intercontinental ballistic missile (ICBM), creating market pull. This was the first large-scale use of ICs, accounting in 1962 for 100 percent of monolithic IC production. ICs would soon be infused into many other information-intensive weapon systems in all three services. DOD continually funded their improvement. NASA also played a role: By 1964, as the Apollo program got underway, it was spending one-third as much as DOD to develop ICs.[30]

This procurement advanced the technology to the point of technological and economic feasibility for civilian use. Civilian IC applications began in the mid-1960s and by the end of the decade, civilian and military demand were roughly equal.[31] Civilian demand skyrocketed in 1970s, and by 1978, total annual shipments of ICs had reached $8 billion in 2020 dollars and the defense share was down to 10 percent.[32]

From Spin-Off to Spin-On

The civilian IC industry continually engaged in process innovation, made massive investments in research and fabrication facilities, and reaped economies of scale orders of magnitude beyond those available to manufacturers of specialized military ICs. By the mid-1980s, it was a decade ahead of the military sector technologically. As a result, technology transfer changed from spin-off to spin-*on*, *from* the commercial sector *to* the defense sector, and the Pentagon's leverage over the direction and pace of technological advances plummeted.[33]

DOD leadership understood what was happening and sought to make a virtue of necessity. First, it tried to bridge the civilian–military technology gap by increasing its use of commercial components and technologies.[34] Its Commercial-Off-The-Shelf (COTS) initiative aimed to obtain the most advanced technology and address the cost overruns and inefficiency common in defense procurement.

Second, it launched several large-scale initiatives aimed at improving government-industry R&D collaboration. Most defense R&D focuses on specific weapon systems, but these, listed in Table 26.1, concentrated on generic technologies.

These initiatives employed DOD and industry specialists working in collaboration, included management teams from all three services, and received multiyear funding. They reached beyond existing primes to smaller, more entrepreneurial companies, including those at the forefront of civilian-led technologies.

Successful and Unsuccessful Programs: VHSIC and VLSI

The Very High-Speed Integrated Circuit (VHSIC) program in Table 26.1 had several goals, but its main technical objective was to develop

Table 26.1 DOD R&D initiatives of the 1980s in 2023 dollars[35]

1978 – Very-Large-Scale Integration (VLSI) program ($340 million)[36]

1980 – Very-High-Speed Integrated Circuit (VHSIC) program ($2.8 billion)

1983 – Strategic Computing Initiative to develop next generation computer hardware and artificial intelligence ($1.5 billion)

1984 – Strategic Software Initiative to design advanced computer software ($730 million)

1987 – Monolithic Microwave Integrated Circuit (MMIC) program to develop radiation-hardened Gallium Arsenide semiconductors ($400 million)

1987 – Superconductivity Initiative to develop advanced materials with no resistance to electrical current ($1.3 billion)

1987 – Sematech to develop competitive semiconductor manufacturing technologies ($1.3 billion)

---

better processes to design and fabricate ICs for defense, leapfrogging generations of manufacturing technology.[37] It sought to encourage civilian firms to develop capabilities to meet military needs and to bring designers of military systems into closer contact with the larger IC community.[38]

The program included civilian semiconductor firms such as Honeywell, Hughes, IBM, Texas Instruments, TRW, and Westinghouse.[39] It was intended to last six years and cost $750 million (2023 dollars). In fact, it lasted 10 years, cost $2.8 billion, and failed to meet its objectives. There was no generation-skipping progress.[40] A RAND Corporation study found that "little coordination appears to have taken place between government-funded R&D and developments underway in commercial markets."[41] Two lessons were learned: First, DOD projects in semiconductors designed to *overtake* civilian industry were unlikely to succeed, and second, if DOD wanted state-of-the-art integrated circuits, it would have to source them commercially.

DARPA's 1978–82 Very Large-Scale Integration (VLSI) Circuit program had a very different result. This highly successful program demonstrated that a DOD-sponsored program could lead the way not just for the defense side, but for the whole industry. It made research grants to universities including Berkeley, Stanford, MIT, Caltech, and Carnegie Mellon. DARPA program managers took a hands-off approach, encouraging grantees to define their own research paths after defining general target areas.[42]

The program led to major advances. One was reduced instruction set computing (RISC), rapidly adopted by civilian industry. Another was the Metal Oxide Silicon Implementation System (MOSIS), which enabled designers to make small batches of custom chips more efficiently. Other advances included parallel computing and computerized tools for designing ICs. The program also spawned the Stanford University Network (SUN), and subsequently Sun

Microsystems, which in 1981 demonstrated its first workstation for technical and scientific applications.

One reason for VLSI's success is that DARPA did not insist that the research be classified. The project's biggest contribution was what came to be known as the Mead–Conway revolution: Carver Mead was an engineering professor at Caltech, Lynn Conway a computer scientist at Xerox's Palo Alto Research Center.[43] They established standard rules and approaches that enabled the separation of IC design and fabrication.[44] Their research was widely disseminated throughout civilian industry, partly through their text-book, *Introduction to VLSI Systems*, adopted for university courses worldwide.[45] In time, their idea generated whole new sectors: "fabless" (design without manufacturing) and "foundry" (manufacturing without design) semi-conductor firms.[46]

Foreign Dependence

Starting in the late 1970s, as the European and East Asian countries became more prosperous and technologically sophisticated, there was a general technological leveling among the advanced nations.[47] IC production diffused to many parts of the developed world, aided by exports of US know-how; growing foreign direct investment; and international joint ventures, mergers, and acqui-sitions. Civilian US IC firms increasingly offshored their manufacturing.

The result was increasing DOD dependence on foreign-made parts and supplies. US semiconductor firms started by offshoring simpler, more labor-intensive tasks in the 1960s, then added more advanced processes in the 1970s and 1980s. The latter included assembly, testing, wafer fabrication, and even some R&D, design, and software development.[48] This trend was partly driven by demand growth in Asia, which eventually became the largest semiconductor market.[49] Also, the US industry had been penetrated by foreign firms more inclined to offshore production. Between 1975 and 1991, of the 41 major investments made in US semiconductor companies, 21 were made by US-based companies and 20 by foreign firms.[50]

By the early 1980s, the Pentagon's ability to keep semiconductor and electronics supply chains in the US was severely compromised. There was concern that technology produced abroad could be withheld in a crisis and that distant supply chains could be disrupted by wars, trade disputes, natural disasters, pandemics, or diplomatic conflicts. The Pentagon tried funding and promoting domestic production, but American corporations kept exporting technology and offshoring manufacturing.[51] And although defense contractors maintained their national orientations longer than other firms, they were not immune to the forces driving globalization.

Congress and the Executive were aware of the problem but did nothing. A 1986 National Defense University study reviewed 12 reports and concluded that "foreign dependencies in weapon systems have not been dealt with in any systematic or effective way by DOD."[52] The idea of limiting DOD acquisition to American-made products made garnered lip service, but won little real support because it would have conflicted with free trade and required the time-consuming, expensive building out of the needed production capabilities, greatly raising costs.

The Semiconductor Crisis

There was, however, a major policy response in one critical area: the dynamic random-access memory (DRAM) chips that are ubiquitous in electronic devices. In 1975, US producers had 90 percent of the global market, but 10 years later, due mainly to massive Japanese investment in production capacity, prices had collapsed. By 1986, US companies had only 5 percent, with the rest held mainly by the Japanese but also by East Asian and European firms.[53] And DRAMs were the flashpoint for the larger concern that Japan seemed to be taking an overall lead in semiconductors: in market share, quality, and production efficiency. Figure 26.4 shows worldwide "merchant" semiconductor market shares by country.[54]

Japan deployed a full range of industrial policies to grow its semiconductor industry, including subsidies for research, low- or no-interest loans, dumping, currency manipulation, and administrative guidance from its Ministry of International Trade and Industry (MITI). It kept foreign products out of its home market, financed trading companies with global reach, and orchestrated fierce domestic competition to drive excellence. (See Chapter 5.)

US firms faced huge losses and their capacity utilization and employment crashed. Only two civilian producers remained: Texas Instruments and Micron. Profit margins in DRAMs are slim, favoring agile companies with deep pockets. US-based companies had a higher cost of capital than their Japanese rivals, which benefited from a financial system deliberately structured to favor long-term investment and who could obtain loans from banks associated with their *keiretsu* corporate groups.

The US responded when its semiconductor industry was at risk of collapse. Reacting to a lobbying blitz by the Semiconductor Industry Association and its members, the Reagan administration in 1986 negotiated the US–Japan Semiconductor Agreement. Tokyo agreed to end dumping DRAMs and other semiconductors below production cost and to help foreign producers achieve a 20 percent share of the Japanese market within five years.

But the agreement did not revive US production. The Japanese had invested more in plant and equipment and had superior design and

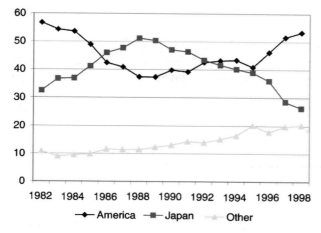

Figure 26.4 Merchant semiconductor market shares[55]

manufacturing processes, beating US firms in time-to-market and achieving lower defect rates. They appeared to have superior management and a quality philosophy their US competitors could not match.[56] When Japan failed to prevent its companies from dumping DRAMs into third countries in 1987, violating the terms of the deal, the US imposed a 100 percent tariff on $300 million of Japanese electronic goods, many containing DRAMs.[57]

Sematech

In this dire context, the Defense Science Board (DSB) released its "Semiconductor Dependency" report.[58] It said that although DOD dependence on foreign-made semiconductors was still "modest," it would get worse if no action was taken.[59] The report proposed a consortium of semiconductor companies to upgrade US research, development, and manufacturing.[60] In an unprecedented move, DSB recommended funding of $200 million a year for five years.[61]

The resulting organization, established that same year, was Sematech (or SEMATECH), short for Semiconductor Manufacturing Technology. It was funded through DARPA at $100 million per year for its first five years, plus an equal amount from 14 US companies. Membership was limited to US-owned firms: American subsidiaries of foreign companies were excluded.[62] Sematech developed cutting-edge manufacturing technology, transferred it to 142 affiliated US semiconductor equipment makers, and coordinated R&D among its corporate sponsors.[63]

Sematech's purposes were intentionally mainly civilian, with an explicitly indirect relationship to national security: It would bolster US military strength by bolstering the overall industry.[64] Congress intended that Sematech be led by industry, so DARPA was not given full oversight, due to concerns that it might steer Sematech toward defense-specific applications.[65] Instead, its involvement was limited to attending meetings of Sematech's board of directors, its technical advisory boards, and its special training sessions.[66]

To preserve competition and avoid giving its members reason to withhold technological advances, Sematech's remit was to develop only generic, precompetitive technologies – that is, nothing product-specific or less than 18 months away from the market. Per its advisory council, its goal was: "High yield, factory-scale application of 0.35-micron production technology in Sematech's own fabricating facility ("fab") by 1993 – an estimated six to twelve months ahead of leading foreign chipmakers, and three years ahead of most US merchant firms (without SEMATECH)."[67] This acknowledgment – that without Sematech most US companies would have been three years behind the state of the art by 1993 – was stunning, because a three-year advantage in this fast-moving industry would be almost impossible to overcome.

The US government's total financial contribution to Sematech between 1988 and 1996 was approximately $2 billion in 2023 dollars.[68] It did help the industry rebound: In 1993, Sematech announced that it had achieved one of its primary technical goals, 0.35-micron manufacturing using only US-made equipment.[69] Another indicator of Sematech's effectiveness is that its corporate members continued to fund it after the government's contribution ended.[70] They had learned that a consortium could address technical challenges too complex and costly for any single firm. The General Accounting Office reported to Congress that Sematech worked because it was led by its private-sector members.[71]

To be sure, other policies contributed to the revival of the US semiconductor industry. The 1985 Plaza Accord, the Semiconductor Agreement of 1986, and the tariff on Japanese electronics in 1987 all did their part. Together with Sematech, these policies constituted a rare instance of broadly coordinated US industrial policy.[72]

Two years after its last government grant in 1996, Sematech opened to foreign firms – including Hyundai (South Korea), Philips (Netherlands), SGS-Thomson (France and Italy), Siemens (Germany), and TSMC (Taiwan). The American industry now saw itself as part of a global industry, engaging in alliances with foreign firms and building plants abroad. When asked about admitting foreign companies, Sematech's CEO responded, "We are a global industry. Not one of our members doesn't have facilities around the world. Why wouldn't you have a global consortium?"[73] Similarly, in 1998, SIA published its first "International" Technology Roadmap for Semiconductors (ITRS). Unlike the 1992 edition, it was created with foreign participation.

The Industry Today

Global semiconductor sales – more than 90 percent of them ICs – rose from $139 billion in 2001 to a forecasted $602 billion in 2024.[74] By 2020, Asia had 80 percent of such sales, with China, Japan, and the rest of the region accounting for 58, 7, and 15 percent, respectively.[75]

Despite electronics becoming ever more important to DOD, and with AI poised to further increase its importance, purpose-built military ICs long ago dwindled to an insignificant fraction of the market: by 2003, 0.3 percent.[76] It has long since become impossible for the primes to fabricate limited-run chips at state-of-the-art standards. Indeed, it has become difficult for DOD to get civilian firms to meet its requirements, and some even decline to work with it. Semiconductor problems have created major delays in weapons programs. By 2017, due to the rapid evolution of technology, on average 70 percent of the electronics in US weapons systems were obsolete or no longer being produced by the time the systems were fielded.[77]

In 2021, DOD experienced major supply chain disruptions due to COVID. In response, it developed a plan to address foreign dependency in four areas: kinetic capabilities (physical weapons like bullets and missiles), energy storage and batteries, castings and forgings, and microelectronics.[78] The 2022 CHIPS Act included $500 million for DOD to work with other nations on trustworthy telecom networks and on diversifying the semiconductor supply chain away from problem countries.[79] If the Act succeeds in restoring civilian US semiconductor manufacturing and its supply chains, DOD will be a major beneficiary (see Chapters 18 and 30).

Space and Aviation, Military and Civilian

Rockets, satellites, and tracking systems are inherently dual use, simply because similar technologies launch satellites and ICBMs. The military and civilian space industrial bases thus developed in tandem and remain deeply integrated. The Pentagon has also made deliberate efforts to nurture the civilian side, and NASA has made concerted efforts to stand up a private-sector space industry.

The US government's huge role in nurturing America's civilian aircraft industry before World War II is discussed in Chapter 15. It helped fund increases in the speed, passenger capacity, reliability, all-weather operability, navigation, fuel economy, and speed of aircraft to the point where a nationwide airline network became feasible. Since then, the US has enjoyed, primarily due to the military importance of aircraft, an incomplete, usually lacking in economic objectives, but still highly effective, industrial policy in aviation.

Origins of American Rocketry

In 1945, 1,600 German scientists and technicians were brought to the US, including Wernher von Braun, developer of the first ballistic missile, World War II Germany's V-2. Installed at the Army's Redstone Arsenal in Alabama, von Braun became technical director of the Guided Missile Development Group in 1950.[80] In 1956, Redstone became the home of the Army's Ballistic Missile Agency. Within two years, the Redstone team had developed the first stage of the four-stage rocket used for the *Explorer 1* satellite, America's response to *Sputnik I* and *II* launched by the USSR in 1957.

In 1957, the Air Force engaged the Convair Division of General Dynamics to build the SM-65 Atlas rocket, which would become the nation's first operational ICBM. Although created for military purposes, the Atlas family have since been primarily used as launch vehicles for space projects. Over the 60 years since, more than 600 Atlas rockets have flown.[81]

In 1958, Senate Majority Leader Lyndon Johnson proposed a comprehensive plan to win what he called the "race for survival." His plan included moving the nascent space program from the military to the National Aeronautics and Space Agency, a new civilian agency.[82] NASA initially worked with the defense contractors already building rockets, missiles, satellites, and tracking equipment for DOD. Over time, it built up a closely related space industrial base. The Pentagon constantly transferred experts and technology between the military and NASA. In 1965, NASA employed 411,000 people, 92 percent of them at external contractors.[83]

During its first half-century, NASA developed, inter alia, rockets, launch infrastructure, tracking systems, spacecraft, satellites, capsules, landers, robots, orbiters, telescopes, space stations, and stellar observatories. From 1960 to 2022, its budget averaged $20 billion per year in 2022 dollars.[84] In the heat of the contest with the USSR to put a man on the moon, its funding peaked in 1966 at 4.5 percent of the federal budget. By 1975, it had fallen to 1 percent, and by 2021, 0.5 percent ($23 billion).[85] Table 26.2 lists some of its major programs.

Table 26.2 Sample of major NASA programs 1958–2022 (M = $Million, B = $Billion)

Date	Spacecraft	Purpose	Cost (Then-Year Dollars)
1958	*Explorer 1*	First US satellite into space	200 M
1961	*Freedom 7*	First American in space	400 M
1960–73	*Apollo*	Lunar exploration	283 B[86]
1972–89	*Voyager*	Deep space probe	865 M[87]
1981–2011	Space Shuttle	Reusable spacecraft	263 B[88]
1978–93	Hubble Telescope	Orbiting telescope	2.5 B[89]
1993–7	Int'l Space Station	Sustained presence in space	150 B[90]
	Mars Pathfinder	Robotic exploration of Mars	440 M[91]
1999	Chandra X-ray	Orbital Observatory	3 B[92]
2011	Juno Spacecraft	Study Jupiter	1.1B[93]
2011–	Commercial Crew	Shuttle to the ISS	6.7 B[94]
2018	Mars Science Lab	Explore Mars	2.53B[95]
2016–22	DART spacecraft	Crash on asteroid to relay data	324.5 M[96]
2022	SLS launch	Artemis mission to moon	20 B + 2B/flight[97]

NASA, the Private Sector, and the Military

Starting in the late 1950s, Washington deliberately supported development of a commercial space industry. NASA encouraged private companies to enter the whole arena except for space launch itself, where the technology was too immature and the infrastructure too expensive.[98] From 1963 to 1982, all rockets for US launches were produced under contract to NASA or DOD, and private companies had to contract with NASA to launch payloads.

In 1962, Congress passed the Communications Satellite Act, establishing a private company, the Communications Satellite Corporation (Comsat), to create a commercial communications satellite system.[99] Comsat then helped create the International Telecommunications Satellite Consortium (Intelsat). In 1963, Comsat launched its first satellite, *Intelsat I*, the first geosynchronous satellite for commercial communications.[100] Built by Hughes Aircraft and launched and tracked by NASA, it provided telecommunications and broadcasting services between Europe and North America.[101] In time, Comsat would provide communications worldwide.[102]

From the outset, NASA cooperated in secret military and surveillance missions with the Defense Department and the CIA.[103] For example, Comsat was designed to also carry secure US military traffic. Over the next 20 years, military dependence on satellites deepened – for communications, reconnaissance, surveillance, and intelligence.[104]

Today's Global Positioning System (GPS) is a spin-off from the military. Based on 24 to 32 satellites, it was created by, and is still operated by, the Air Force.[105] Its technical specifications were initially set forth in a 1966 Air Force study.[106] Its first prototype satellite was launched in 1978 as part of a military-only system known as NAVSTAR.[107] It was opened to the public in 1983 with less accuracy than for military users, and in 2000 civilian users were granted the same 10-meter accuracy.

Commercial Launch Services

The first commercial launch company was the French-led Arianespace, founded in 1980. The US phased out expendable rockets in favor of the (clumsily) reusable Space Shuttle in the early 1980s. Although NASA heavily subsidized the expensive Shuttle, whose reusability had been intended to deliver low costs, demand for launches outpaced what NASA could provide. Thus in 1983 President Reagan issued National Security Decision Directive (NSDD) 94, which said, "The US government fully endorses and will facilitate the commercialization of US expendable launch vehicles [ELVs]. The US Government will license, supervise, and/or regulate US commercial ELV operations only to the extent required to meet its national and international obligations and to ensure public safety."[108]

This directive and its supporting legislation, the 1984 Commercial Space Launch Act, established the statutory framework and regulatory basis for commercial space activities. Among other things, it established an indemnification regime to limit liability for firms conducting space launches. But because of the Shuttle's subsidized prices, no private sector providers arose.

After the 1986 explosion of *Challenger* effectively ended the shuttle's commercial use, Reagan issued NSDD 254, "US Space Launch Strategy." This directive limited NASA's commercial space launches to those requiring the Shuttle's unique capabilities.[109] "NASA will no longer be in the business of launching private satellites," it said. "NASA will keep America on the leading edge of change. The private sector will take over from there."[110]

Next came the Commercial Space Launch Amendments Act of 1988, the Land Remote Sensing Policy Act of 1992, the Commercial Space Act of 1998, and the Commercial Space Transportation Competitiveness Act of 2000.[111] Together, these created a sufficiently comprehensive legal and policy framework for the emergence of private-sector launch. Space Services Inc. executed the first American commercial launch – a suborbital scientific payload – in March 1989.[112] That year, McDonnell Douglas performed the first commercial orbital launch, using a Delta I rocket whose design originated with NASA and the Air Force.[113]

But the industry struggled and cost-to-orbit remained high. By 1992, the three US manufacturers of large orbital launch vehicles were General Dynamics, Martin Marietta, and McDonnell Douglas, with some smaller firms focusing on suborbital rockets. This oligopoly's technologies stagnated, largely because their launch business was predominantly government contracts, with cost-plus structures that did not incentivize innovative technologies or cost reductions. US providers were losing the global commercial market: China's Long March rockets earned 43 percent of their revenues, and Arianespace 77 percent, from commercial launches.[114] In 1994, General Dynamics sold its Space Systems division to Martin Marietta, leaving only two major players.[115]

New Policies Revitalize Private-Sector Space

The shuttles were grounded again after the 2003 *Columbia* disaster, making the US dependent on Russia to ferry astronauts to the International Space Station (ISS) and Russian rockets the low-cost choice for putting satellites in orbit. The need for new launch systems became undisputable. But it took additional regulatory and institutional reform and well-funded new players for private-sector space launch to succeed.

President Bush's 2004 vision for space policy called for a reinvigorated private sector and was followed by the Commercial Space Launch Amendments Act of 2004.[116] In 2005, Congress gave NASA $500 million to investigate commercial means to supply the ISS with crews and cargo. This program came to be known as Commercial Orbital Transportation Services (COTS). It had roots in 1990s efforts to build "faster, better, cheaper" spacecraft by having NASA partner with, instead of managing, private firms.[117] The agency solicited proposals from private companies to provide various capabilities, with fixed payments for achieving specified milestones.[118]

Given only 3 percent of NASA's budget, COTS was very cost-effective. In 2006, a contract was signed promising $278 million to SpaceX (founded 2002) for reaching certain milestones. Rocketplane Kistler got a similar contract for $206 million.[119] But Kistler failed to raise sufficient outside funding and missed financial milestones, freeing up $170 million for a similar contract with Orbital Sciences.[120] With the retirement of the Shuttle in 2010, Congress gave COTS a further $300 million.[121] Both firms eventually delivered cargo to the ISS: SpaceX in 2012 and Orbital Sciences in 2013. COTS thus delivered two working launch systems for $850 million.[122]

This compared favorably to more than $13 billion for United Launch Alliance's (ULA) NASA-designed cost-plus Space Launch System (SLS), a super-heavy expendable rocket derived from Space Shuttle technology. This project was started about the same time as COTS and arrived six years behind schedule.[123] ULA was a government-brokered 2006 merger between Boeing and Lockheed Martin's launch businesses. These firms had had a near monopoly on high-end launches for the military with their Delta IV and Atlas V rockets, but were in financial trouble. Despite concerns that the merger would end competition, Washington decided that it would be cheaper to consolidate their management and manufacturing than to prop up two firms.

ULA's military launch monopoly ended in 2012, when SpaceX won two USAF contracts. The Air Force reported in 2020 that, through competitive bidding and buying in bulk, its National Security Space Launch program had saved $22 billion compared to 2013 costs.[124] In 2020, new fixed-price military contracts were negotiated, 60 percent with ULA and 40 percent with SpaceX, for launches from 2020 to 2024.[125]

In 2012, following the COTS model, NASA set up its Commercial Crew Integrated Capability program, allocating $1.1 billion over 21 months for private efforts to bring crews to the ISS. Boeing got $460 million, SpaceX $440 million, and Sierra Nevada Corporation $212 million.[126] The goal was to eliminate reliance on Russia by 2017. This deadline was missed, but in 2020, SpaceX made history with the first private orbital launch of a crewed rocket. By mid-2023, it had executed 237 launches, 198 landings, and 171 flights of previously used rockets.[127] Boeing had planned a crewed mission of its Starliner for July 2023, but it was delayed due to technical problems and rescheduled several times, eventually launching in June 2024.[128]

The Space Industry Today

Today, private American firms have capabilities and scale far beyond those of NASA. The agency's role has changed: It can now articulate high-level requirements and rely on the private sector to fulfill them, as opposed to managing the entire process. Cost-plus contracts are largely a thing of the past, with project risks instead shared with a private sector that is technologically mature and financially robust enough to bear them.[129]

For example, in NASA's Artemis project for a sustainable presence on the Moon in preparation for a mission to Mars, key systems have been farmed out to the private sector. And in 2021, NASA contracted with SpaceX for

$2.9 billion to build a lunar landing system to ferry astronauts in lunar orbit to and from a lunar base station.[130]

By building first partly and then fully reusable rockets, SpaceX has reduced cost-per-pound to orbit by almost a factor of 10.[131] Its existing Falcon Nine and Falcon Heavy rockets are cost-competitive for their payload classes, and the fully reusable super-heavy Starship, if fully successful, may be 10 to 100 times cheaper yet.[132]

One report counted $362 billion in revenue for the commercial space industry globally in 2022, compared to $102 billion in government expenditures, including NASA's budget of $24 billion.[133] The biggest end markets were satellite communications ($144 billion) and satellite navigation ($228 billion).[134]

Annual global private investment flowing into the space sector now roughly equals NASA's entire budget.[135] From 2013 through 2023, VCs invested $272 billion in 1,746 space startups.[136] An analysis by Merrill Lynch put the value of the space launch market at $339 billion in 2018 and predicted it would reach $2.7 trillion by 2045.[137] Another by Morgan Stanley estimated space sales at $350 billion in 2016, predicting over $1 trillion annually by 2040.[138]

The US has a dominant position but, given Chinese, European, and Russian competitors, not a monopoly.[139] American firms include SpaceX (Elon Musk, 2002), Blue Origin (Jeff Bezos, 2000), Virgin Galactic (Richard Branson, 2004), Breakthrough Starshot (Mark Zuckerberg, 2016), Stratolaunch (Paul Allen, 2011), ConsenSys Space (James Cameron, Larry Page, and Eric Schmidt, 2009), and Moon Express (Naveen Jain, 2010).[140] Hundreds of smaller firms design and construct cargo and crew vehicles, suborbital launch platforms, landers, rovers, obiters, research craft, technology demonstrators, and propulsion equipment.

Going forward, private firms are likely to enter space manufacturing (to take advantage of zero gravity), space station construction, and other activities. The most ambitious ultimately aim at distant goals such as space tourism, asteroid mining, colonization of the moon and Mars, and building extraterrestrial human habitats. The Commercial Space Launch Competitiveness Act of 2015 acknowledges these possibilities, explicitly authorizing private firms to "engage in the commercial exploration and exploitation of space resources."[141]

The US space industry is unique in that national security laws protect it from foreign competition, above all from China. It is basically forbidden to work with that country or offshore production.[142] The US government's International Traffic in Arms Regulations (ITAR) regime has kept its supply chain free of Chinese parts. After a 1990s scandal in which Loral Corporation transferred missile guidance technology to China (CEO Bernard Schwartz, a major Democratic donor, avoided punishment), technology transfers have been avoided. CFIUS has kept China from buying up companies in the sector to extract their knowhow or move them to China. Despite the cliché that high technology requires global sourcing, the industry outcompetes foreign rivals.

Although Chinese rockets, mostly manufactured by massive state-owned enterprises, executed more launches than the US as recently as 2021, SpaceX single-handedly returned America to the number one spot the following year.[143] In addition to launching thousands of satellites for its own Starlink satellite internet system, it now leads the global launch market. China's Great Wall Industry Corporation struggles to sell its launch services abroad. Most Chinese launches are for domestic customers, largely the military and state-owned enterprises.

The Cold War Origins of Modern Aviation

By 1944, due to war production, the US aircraft industry was the single largest industry in the entire world: Its $17 billion output was more than 10 percent of GDP.[144] And the government was already planning for a successful civil industry after the war.[145]

Military spending on aviation R&D grew more than tenfold between 1951 and 1967.[146] Government controlled 65 percent of the assets used in aerospace manufacturing, paid for 20 percent of all new factories built, and paid for more than 80 percent of new production equipment during the Korean War.[147] As late as the early 1960s, despite the growth of civilian aerospace markets, the Pentagon still owned more than 50 percent of the sector's productive assets.[148] Throughout the 1950s, it accounted for more than 80 percent of aircraft sales, almost always on long-term, cost-plus contracts that provided a guaranteed income flow.[149] Military specifications dominated R&D, and military planners and technicians determined not just what should be built, but how.

Military production yielded manufacturing technologies, plants, and test facilities later used for civilian purposes. Only in 1979 did the civilian aircraft market exceed the military one in size. The federal government paid to develop many key aviation technologies for military use that spun off to the civilian side. Of the 38 major innovations in aviation from 1941 to 1972, 29 came from the military, 6 from civilian government programs, and only 2 from the private sector acting alone.[150]

Defense contracts maintained firms' financial strength and risk tolerance, enabling them to make the risky bets required to develop and launch new civilian aircraft. During its first 20 years, Boeing ran losses on its civilian operations, as did its subsidized European rival Airbus during its first 20 years. The US government has been unwilling to let major aerospace defense contractors collapse. At key junctures, military business sustained otherwise unviable firms.[151] Federal loan guarantees and antitrust acquiescence enabled the 1967 "arranged marriage" between the McDonnell and Douglas companies. And in 1971, a $250 million loan guarantee rescued Lockheed.

A succession of agencies, currently the Defense Security Cooperation Agency, has proactively supported military aviation exports. Security concerns, congressional pork-barrel interests, and (for decades) the Buy American Act of 1933 blocked much foreign sourcing.[152] These constraints were loosened somewhat after the end of the Cold War, though they will probably be retightened if the emerging Cold War with China endures and the product import and technology export controls already applied to semiconductors are extended to aviation.

The Aircraft

The world's first jet airliner was the British de Havilland Comet, introduced in 1952. But a series of crashes due to metal fatigue, a problem poorly understood at the time, blunted its commercial momentum. Although the Comet did sell after its flaws were fixed, it did not confer first-mover advantage on its manufacturer or on Britain's aircraft industry, the free world's second largest at the time.

Meanwhile, Boeing had gained crucial experience building the world's first large jet plane, the B-47 bomber, and then the giant, nuclear-armed, B-52 that debuted in 1955 and remains in service today. Airlines began asking Boeing for a comparable passenger jet. Around the same time, the Air Force was seeking a new jet-powered flying tanker to service its new jet fighters. Boeing built a prototype, the 367-80, with both uses in mind, and the civilian 707 and the military KC-135 tanker were both derived from it.

The 707 first flew in 1957. When Boeing began developing it in 1952, turboprops were still considered more promising because of better fuel economy, and it was not obvious that the industry would soon transition to jets. As the CEO of American Airlines later explained: "I don't think anybody could have anticipated, at the time I made all the speeches about fuel consumption, that we'd get the problem cured as readily as we did. And we would not have gotten it cured had it not been a military necessity, because the military necessity brought about a tremendous expenditure of funds for that purpose."[153]

Douglas Aircraft, before World War II the dominant aircraft builder on the strength of its legendary DC-3, decided in 1953 not to develop a jet airliner – a decision that ultimately resulted in Boeing's enduring dominance (and 1997 takeover of McDonnell Douglas).

The 707's first engines were the same J57s that powered the B-52.[154] Its flight controls derived from those of the B-47 and B-52.[155] Its autopilot and, in later models, inertial navigational system were also based on military hardware, as were half its navigation systems.[156]

The 707 revolutionized civil aviation worldwide. Flying rapidly replaced ocean liners and long-distance trains. It and the related 720 outsold its latecomer rival, the Douglas DC-8, 1,010 units to 556. And because development costs were fixed regardless of the number of planes sold, the difference in profitability was even larger.

On the strength of the profits and technical knowledge from the 707, Boeing subsequently developed a whole family of aircraft of different sizes and ranges. This included the 747, for three decades the world's largest passenger plane. Its military origins were not as direct as the 707's, but it incorporated technologies Boeing had developed for the CX-HLS, its losing entry in the Air Force competition for a large, long-range transport that was won by Lockheed's C-5, which is still in service today.

Jet Engines

The jet engine's first version, the turbojet, was invented before World War II by Hans von Ohain in Germany and Frank Whittle in England. During the war, the US Army Air Force arranged transfer of the British technology to General Electric. Several firms, including GE, Westinghouse, Pratt and Whitney, and Lockheed, received federal funding to develop their own turbojets.[157] The first American model, the I-A, was developed 1942 by GE, followed by the J33.[158] In 1950, Pratt and Whitney introduced the J57, the first with 10,000 pounds of thrust.

The next crucial innovation was the turbofan. The first was built in 1956 by Pratt and Whitney using components from the military J-57 and J-75.[159] Powerful, fuel-efficient *high-bypass* turbofans, without which widebody jetliners would not be possible, came next, initially developed for the military C-5.[160] The Air Force spent more than $30 million on the Pratt and Whitney JTF-14, from which developed the JT-9D used on the 747.[161] Smaller GE engines for regional jets derived from engines built for the S-3 Viking and A-10 warplanes.[162]

Many engine components are used in both military and civil aviation. For example, the Auxiliary Power Unit (for when the main engines are off) of the B-2 bomber is the same as on the Boeing 737NG and even the Airbus A320. Engine cores are frequently designed for both military and civilian uses and engine controls are often identical. Many key innovations, such as now ubiquitous thrust reversers, were initially developed for the military.

Today, the Versatile Affordable Advanced Turbine Engines program is a joint technology research effort of DOD, NASA, DOE, academia, and private industry. Fuel economy concerns are bringing back the unducted fan researched by NASA in the 1970s and 1980s, which is potentially more efficient than jets but was previously tried and rejected in its 7J7 program.[163] Work is now being done in this area by GE Aerospace and Rolls Royce Ultrafan, with NASA collaborating with GE under its Environmentally Responsible Aviation Project and Subsonic Fixed Wing Project.[164]

Aerospace Materials

Modern aircraft are mostly aluminum and composites. The latter consist of high-strength fibers, such as carbon, graphite, or boron, in a matrix of metal or plastic resin. Thanks to their high strength and stiffness-to-weight ratios, composites were first used in military aircraft. Carbon fiber was developed at the military Royal Aircraft Establishment in Britain and at America's Union Carbide with support from the Air Force Materials Laboratory.[165]

Composites' first in-flight test was in 1969, when a boron composite rudder was installed on an F-4 fighter.[166] Composites have since enabled major weight reductions in the airframes and engines of military planes including the F-4, F-14, F-15, and B-2. The Boeing 787, which entered service in 2011, was the first airliner to be mostly made of composites, a fact noticeable to passengers mainly in its large windows and higher, more comfortable, cabin pressure.

Adhesives for gluing aluminum airframes reduce assembly costs and weight. These were first developed for the military and by 1942 were being used in the B-26 bomber and P-40 fighter.[167] Decades later, they were used in the Boeing 707, 737, and 747.

Between 1947 and 1961, DOD invested huge sums to establish the titanium industry and funded development of vacuum melted superalloys.[168] Together, these materials underpin high-performance military and civilian jet engines.[169]

Navigation and Avionics

Instrument landing capability is necessary for all-weather operation and thus for scheduled airline service. Experiments were conducted by the airlines, the Army, the Navy, and the federal Bureau of Air Commerce between 1937 and 1941. This resulted in creation of the SCS-51 Instrument Landing System by the Army Air

Corps, which became the standard for both civilian and military aviation. Modified versions of the SCS-51 are still in use.[170]

Or consider the following group of technologies, as described in a US government report:

> Airborne radar was first developed in the US for use in navigation and bombing during World War II. In 1944, MIT developed the radar-assisted Norden Bombsight, which resulted in improved bombing accuracy. In 1949, the first airborne Doppler navigation radar was delivered to the Air Force by General Precision Laboratory for flight testing. A vast improvement over earlier radars ... [t]he first operational military Doppler radar was installed in the F-101 aircraft in about 1954, and, in 1955, Bendix fabricated a doppler radar navigation system for use in commercial aircraft ...
>
> Air Force interest in a non-radiating, self-contained navigation capability to satisfy military mission needs resulted in the development of the Space Position Inertial Reference Equipment (SPIRE) system by MIT in 1953. Then, in the years that followed, the military sponsored development of the Litton series of medium accuracy, small, light-weight inertial navigation systems for the E-l, A-6, P-3, and F/RF-4C aircraft. [A direct descendant of these systems was installed] in the 707 aircraft as an additional navigation aid ...
>
> The inertial navigation system is highly dependent upon its associated computer. In 1957, the first general purpose airborne digital computer was developed as part of the Hughes fire control system for the F-106. The same year also marked the beginning of the development of the Autonetics solid-state computer and digital differential analyzer for the Hound Dog missile, as well as the first Librascope solid state general purpose digital computer for airborne use. This computer was tested on C-131s and became operational on the C-141. The first commercial use of an airborne digital computer was in conjunction with the inertial navigation equipment described above.[171]

Fly-by-wire controls use digital electrical signals, rather than tensioned cables or hydraulic lines, to connect the cockpit with the plane's control surfaces. In 1967–70, the Air Force tested a single-axis system in a B-47 and then a C-141.[172] It next demonstrated a quadruple-redundant three-axis system in a YF-4E.[173] Fly-by-wire was introduced to airliners with the Airbus A-320 in 1984 and is now standard on new aircraft other than the 737 Max (except for its extended spoilers).

The End of Aviation Spin-Offs

Beginning in the 1960s, further advances in military aviation, with the exception of composites and a few others, became less useful to the civilian sector. Supersonic airliners were a commercial failure (see Chapter 19). Vertical take-off and landing technology has found no significant civil application, though civilian short take-off and landing aircraft exist. Civilian use of stealth technology would be absurd. The extreme performance embodied in, say, an F-22 fighter is useless to airlines and cargo carriers. As are the secret technologies used to harden aircraft against the electromagnetic effects of a nuclear blast.

Military technology outrunning civil is the reverse of what happened in semiconductors, where civilian industry ran so far ahead that the military had to resort to civilian inputs. But there have still been spin-ons from the civil to the military sector. Decades ago, airliners used off-the-shelf military engines with only minimal adaptions, while today, at least for military transports, the situation has reversed, as with the C-17 and the replacement engines for the C-5M.[174]

Foreign Competition

Japan was forbidden to manufacture aircraft for seven years after World War II, critical years for the transition from propellers to jets. It later attempted to break into airliners with the Mitsubishi SpaceJet regional jet, but the firm gave up in 2020 after problems getting its FAA safety certification. The country is strong, however, in aircraft components ranging from avionics to entire wings: 35 percent of the airframe of the Boeing 787 is made there today, thanks to unwise outsourcing decisions which Boeing is now trying to reverse.[175] Germany's aircraft industry, which produced world-leading aircraft as late as World War II, including the world's first jet fighters, was devastated by the war. The country has since returned as a major partner in the French-led Airbus consortium.

Even before the war, the US had the world's most advanced civilian airliners and airline network (see Chapter 15). When jets appeared, this large home market gave US aircraft makers a scale advantage over European firms. European recognition of this problem led to creation of the Airbus consortium in 1967, which eventually included France, Germany, Britain, Holland, and Spain, with all of Europe as its home market.

Unlike the US, Europe has pursued an aviation policy with explicitly commercial goals, though sometimes justified by the need to preserve its military industrial base. Airbus has been supported with equity infusions, subsidized loans, loan guarantees, debt forgiveness, tax breaks, exchange-rate hedges, government contracts, and bailouts. Each firm in the consortium is or has been government owned. In the decade to 1992, it received subsidies of $25 billion, which covered 100 percent of the launch costs of the A300 and 75 percent of those of the A320.[176] Government ownership of Airbus has also given it the preferred patronage of many of Europe's major airlines.

Including their engines and avionics, the first Airbus planes had up to 40 percent American content.[177] Starting in 1974, GE was forced to share its jet engine technology, by way of a joint venture, with France's SNECMA as a condition of supplying Airbus.[178] Airbus's first plane, The A300, filling a niche between the Boeing 737 and 747 for a medium-sized twin-engine airliner, was introduced in 1972. It was a pedestrian craft, based on existing technologies, but sold well enough to drive America's Lockheed out of civil aircraft.

Starting with the A320 in 1984, Airbus began to innovate, introducing new technologies such as composites, variable camber wings, fly-by-wire, active controls (tactile feedback for pilots), digital flight systems, and side-mounted joysticks.[179] In the late 1990s, it overtook Boeing as the largest plane maker, though it and Boeing have since traded the number one spot several times.

US–EU Aviation Trade Conflict

Airbus's subsidized success eventually provoked a US response. In 1978, it attempted to break into the American market by offering aircraft to Eastern Airlines on highly favorable terms. US aircraft manufacturers complained about "predatory export financing" and countervailing duties (CVDs) were proposed.

But the interests of US aircraft producers and their customers differed. Eastern lobbied Treasury against imposing duties. Aircraft producers feared retaliation against their European sales, so they lobbied for continuance or expansion of existing policies, such as R&D support and tax credits, and for the Export–Import Bank to match Airbus's financing terms.[180] And they called for an industry-specific GATT agreement to restrain subsidies.

Washington wanted free trade and no subsidies. In the resulting 1979 Agreement on Trade in Civil Aircraft, it got the former, as the pact eliminated many trade barriers, including tariffs, quotas, technical standards, mandatory subcontracting, procurement rules, and formal export subsidies. This increased international component sourcing and subcontracting. Exports of aircraft parts and components grew by 36 percent annually from 1977 to 1982.[181]

But the Europeans would not agree to effective limits on development aid. Because their subsidies were structured as loans repayable (with interest) by a levy on each aircraft sold, the Europeans argued that they were GATT-compliant. They agreed only to anti-subsidy rules that were limited in scope, vague in content, and weakly enforceable. They were so committed to Airbus that they could probably only have been stopped by American retaliation more aggressive than what was plausible between friendly, economically intertwined nations. The US wanted a no-subsidies regime that would preserve its dominance. The Europeans wanted "managed competitive balance" – enough subsidies to make Airbus competitive, though not enough to wipe out the Americans.

Thus matters stood until 1984, when Airbus announced it would launch the A320 with subsidies. In 1985, the Reagan administration accused Airbus of violating Article 6 of the 1979 Agreement, which required that prices reflect a reasonable recovery of costs. Boeing asked Washington to negotiate, but from fear of retaliation did not ask the administration to initiate a Section 301 investigation against unfair foreign trade practices.[182]

The administration was divided. Some took the traditional free-trader's position that a foreign subsidy was simply a gift to American buyers. Others argued that Boeing should file an antidumping complaint.[183] For geopolitical reasons, the State Department opposed doing anything. Reagan convened a strike force in the fall of 1985, but it did not recommend any actions. In 1987, the US and the EC began intermittent talks in hopes of solving the problem by modifying the 1979 agreement, but agreed only to foster a more favorable environment for trade in civil aircraft and reduce trade tensions.[184]

Aviation Trade Détente

By 1991, the dispute was heating up again. Although Washington had resigned itself to Airbus's development and launch subsidies, *ongoing* subsidies to take market share from Boeing and McDonnell Douglas were another matter. Trade war loomed. Then, in April 1992, to general surprise, the US and Europe reached the Agreement on Trade in Large Civil Aircraft (TLCA). Both had recognized that some degree of subsidy was inevitable, but wished to avoid an arms race of subsidy and counter-subsidy that would only end up benefiting aircraft buyers, including in third countries.

The pact put limits on the quantity and types of development subsidies, including a cap of 33 percent of development costs.[185] It required that such support take the form of royalty-based loans, be repaid within 17 years, and carry an interest rate no less than the subsidizing government's own cost of borrowing. It limited indirect support, such as that provided in the US by NASA and DOD, to 3 percent of the country's annual large civil aircraft sales. Information about subsidies would henceforth be openly published, with semiannual meetings to monitor compliance.

The agreement successfully defused tensions until 2004. Conveniently for Airbus, the pact only applied going forward and imposed no penalty for past subsidies. It was now successful enough that it could survive without many of them.

McDonnell Douglas

Meanwhile, McDonnell Douglas (MD) was collapsing. It had been weakened by competition between its DC-10 and Lockheed's L-1011 during the 1970s and 1980s, and was now up against the vastly stronger Boeing and Airbus. Its MD-11 update of the DC-10 was not proving successful enough to make up for the decline of its military contracts with the end of the Cold War.[186]

In 1991, Taiwan Aerospace offered to buy 40 percent of the firm, which would have financed developing the new MD-12 that MD needed to survive. But it would also have enabled the wholesale transfer of production and technologies abroad, supposedly to Taiwan. Then it was discovered that the Taiwanese firm was a corporate shell, a stalking horse for a consortium of Japan's Kawasaki, Fuji, and Mitsubishi.[187] (See Chapter 5 for Japan's other efforts in aerospace.)

The threat of Japan using MD's technology base to break into airliners set off congressional alarms.[188] The plan fell through after 30 senators asked President Bush to block the transaction under the Exon–Florio Amendment to the 1988 Omnibus Trade Bill. In retrospect, this was the correct decision. (MD did not last much longer and was bought by Boeing in 1997).

Trade Clash with Europe, 2005–2022

In 2003, Airbus announced plans for its A350, which would compete with Boeing's pending 787, and its A380, which would displace the 747 as the world's largest airliner. The Europeans announced their intention to provide launch aid and the US cried foul once again. Negotiations in 2004 to update the TLCA failed, and the US withdrew from the pact and filed a complaint with the WTO.[189]

The EU retaliated with a similar WTO complaint against the US. It claimed Boeing was subsidized by military R&D, by overly generous military contracts, by tax breaks from states where Boeing had major plants, and by federal tax provisions such as Foreign Sales Corporations and the Extraterritorial Income Exclusion Act. The issue was further complicated by Boeing's huge offshoring to Japan, because Japan had subsidies of its own.[190]

In 2010 and 2011, the WTO ruled both complaints valid. A complex series of appeals, attempts to comply with judgments, and counterclaims followed. Finally, in 2019 the WTO authorized the US to impose tariffs on $7.5 billion per year of European imports. The next year, it authorized the EU to tariff $4.0 billion of US imports. The US and EU both then imposed tariffs on products chosen to maximize political impact.

In 2021, the US and EU reached a truce, each suspending its tariffs for five years. Among other causes, they had been pushed together by the rise of China. Since 2001, Beijing's five-year plans had targeted the industry. Comac, its leading large aircraft firm, was nearing completion of the C919, intended to rival the 737 Max and the A320neo, with first deliveries (to Chinese airlines) scheduled for 2022.

Bombardier (Canada) and Embraer (Brazil), builders of smaller regional jets, had their own long, parallel trade war. Bombardier was even set to step into Boeing's turf with a larger passenger jet, the C-series, but Boeing in 2017 won a preliminary 300 percent tariff at the Commerce Department after Delta placed an order. Although the USITC ultimately did not go through with the tariff, it was the nail in the coffin for Bombardier, which even before the final ruling gave up and sold its jet business to Airbus for a dollar. In 2018, Boeing made arrangements to acquire Embraer's jet operations, but backed out in 2020 due to the COVID air travel shutdown and cancellation of orders for its discredited 737 Max. (Embraer dragged it into arbitration for backing out.)

Counterfactuals

Could America have played its aviation hand better? Perhaps. But Washington was constrained by the very strength of America's aircraft industry, as its large foreign sales made it vulnerable to retaliation against any American protectionist measures. With American sales in Europe larger than the reverse, America's industry would have been harmed more by tit-for-tat retaliation. Boeing also historically opposed direct countervailing subsidies, which would have been outside America's policy consensus and would have risked a subsidy race.

Still, unlike in many industries, the US government did, intermittently, seek and enforce trade pacts to keep the American industry viable. It consistently funded keeping the industry at the technological cutting edge. It wisely blocked the Japanese from buying McDonnell Douglas, albeit by tacit political means and without a formal prohibition. However, it failed to stop Boeing from offshoring key technologies and production to Japan.[191] Boeing now admits this was a mistake, but so much expertise is now lodged in Japan that it will take much time and expense to reverse.[192]

Future US industrial policy should aim at keeping America's technological crown jewels at home, as Airbus has done better. China required Boeing to start producing there as a condition of selling there. Beijing's leverage came from the threat to buy from Airbus instead, which suggests that the US and EU should form a common front to avoid being played off against each other.[193]

27 ROBOTICS
A Global Industrial Policy Competition

Robotics is a critical technology for the automation of many kinds of work, for the smart factories of the future, for national security, and for social issues ranging from education to unemployment to aging. Robots have already transformed many manufacturing industries, such as semiconductors, electronics, aviation, automobiles, chemicals, plastics, and metal products. They are now poised to penetrate industries, such as clothing, from which they have mostly hitherto been absent.[1]

Robots will reduce the number of dull, dirty, and dangerous jobs, address skills shortfalls, and reduce or even eliminate the current disadvantage of high-wage nations in tradable industries. They will revolutionize service industries such as transportation, medicine, nursing, policing, elder care, and others – often in ways not yet foreseen.

But utopian or apocalyptic speculations about robots' social implications are not our subject here. We only note in passing two facts. First, developed nations with *more* robots than the US have, for now at least, a lower, not higher, proportion of low-wage jobs.[2] Second, robots will not necessarily have the same positive effect on wages as earlier technological advances. Unlike them, robots will eventually duplicate basically all, not just some, human capabilities – though the rate at which their capabilities will grow and be deployed at scale is not yet known.

Our concern here is with the global race to develop and deploy robots in the short and medium term. Whatever robots' longer-term consequences, the nations that do this most effectively will be best positioned to capture their ultimate benefits and manage their ultimate costs. Robots even today are an essential competitive tool, especially in manufacturing. Having a strong position in industrial robotics will help America stay competitive in other advantageous industries.

Industrial Robots

This chapter is mostly about *industrial* robots: programmable, automated machines that work in component assembly, materials handling, fastening, inspection, and quality control. This is the type that is now having and will have the greatest impact on manufacturing. Service-industry robots, another rapidly developing use, technologically overlap them in vision systems, path-planning, and multi-robot cooperation technologies.

The distinctions between industrial *robots* and non-robotic production equipment, which can be very sophisticated without being robotic, include adaptability and programmability. The classic industrial robot is the robotic arm, for decades now a fixture in auto plants and other factories. These can be mounted to fixed points or movable gantries, and are capable of grabbing and manipulating parts of various shapes and sizes. They have multiple axes of movement, and their advanced sensors and control algorithms enable responsive, extremely fine control.

Another common type of robot is the "enterprise" robots used in warehousing, logistics, retail, consumer services, and agriculture. Autonomous mobile robots (AMRs) independently navigate their surroundings, plan efficient routes, find objects, and deliver them where needed while avoiding obstacles. Still other robots include airborne drones and autonomous cars, trucks, ships, and submarines. These are currently improving rapidly, with huge military implications already visible in the Russo-Ukrainian war.

In 2022 (the latest available data), 553,000 new industrial robots were installed globally, bringing the total to 3.9 million.[3] Firms in North America installed 56,000, those in Europe 84,000, and those in Asia 405,000.[4] In 2021, Jeff Bernstein, the president of the Association for Advancing Automation (A3), explained the increase thus: "Ongoing labor shortages, easier-to-use robotic solutions, and new industries embracing robotics, such as restaurants, retail, construction and even agriculture, have led to record units sold."[5]

The US lags. In 2022, it ranked *tenth* in robot density (robots per 10,000 workers) at 285. The leaders were South Korea, Singapore, Germany, Japan, and China, at 1,012, 730, 415, 397, and 392, respectively.[6] Only 1 of the world's 10 largest industrial robot firms is American: Adept Technology of Pleasanton, California.[7] And in 2015, Japan's Omron acquired Adept for $200 million, so even this is foreign-owned.[8] While some foreign firms have offices and even production facilities in the US, they are headquartered in Europe or East Asia and do most of their R&D and new product introductions there.

The basic robot arm has changed little in 60 years, so current advances center on software, which increasingly means AI. The battle for the future of robotics concerns smart, intelligent, collaborative robots that will use AI to operate in the irregular, unpredictable, human-filled environments from which they have mostly been excluded. Thanks to its relatively strong position in AI, the US has an opportunity here to regain a strong position, but only if it imposes the needed industrial policies – which it is not now doing.

Competitors' Robot Promotion Policies

America's lagging position in robotics is no accident. Although the US spends more money on robotics research than any other country, this mostly goes for military and space exploration uses, not commercial applications.

By contrast, our major rivals all have serious national *commercial* robotics strategies, with spending to match. They have embedded these policies in multi-policy, economy-wide industrial policies designed to advance their manufacturing sectors. They support R&D in the technologies on which robotics depends, such as machine learning, neural networks, cloud computing, AI, actuators, sensors, miniaturization, digitization, and 5G. And they support R&D in the fields that robotics enables, such as additive manufacturing, the internet of things, and cyber-physical systems (see Chapter 22).

In Germany, for example, robotics policy is part of Plattform Industrie 4.0, a government program designed around the idea that the world is transitioning to a fourth industrial revolution (4IR) (see Chapters 8 and 22). The EU has had the European Clearing House for Open Robotics Development, SPARC: The Partnership for Robotics in Europe, and parts of a larger high-tech industrial policy program, Horizon 2020.[9] Japan's policy, as set forth in its New Robot Strategy (2016–20), envisages a Robot Revolution.[10] Singapore's program is called Manufacturing 2030. In Korea, the 3rd Basic Plan on Intelligent Robots is pushing to develop robotics as part of 4IR, with $172.2 million in 2022 funding for its Implementation Plan for Intelligent Robots.[11] In Taiwan, robotics is a major part of the government competitiveness program Productivity 4.0.[12]

Robotics Policy Comparisons

Table 27.1 shows robotics programs in the leading robot-producing nations.[13] It makes clear how the US generously funds military and space robotics R&D, but devotes comparatively little to commercial robotics. In recent years, the Defense Department has funded autonomous military systems at about $4.5 billion a year, and NASA funds robotics, mainly for lunar and Mars exploration, at about $8 billion annually. But most of this research is classified, extremely application-specific, or both, and thus neither available to, nor especially useful for, civilian firms. The spin-off dynamic of semiconductors or aerospace is absent (see Chapter 26).

Table 27.1 Government funding for robotics R&D

Country	Robotics R&D Program	$ Millions
CHINA[14]		
2016–20	Development Plan for Robot Industry	577
2020	Key Special Program on Intelligent Robots	9
2021–5	14th Five-Year Plan for Robot Industry Development	unknown
2022	Key Special Program on Intelligent Robots	44
Total		~630
JAPAN		
2014–18	imPACT	484
2014–18	Strategic Innovation Promotion Program	463
2016–20	New Robot Strategy	842
2016	Robot Related Budget	259
2014–18	Strategic Innovation Promotion Program	440
2018–22	Strategic Innovation Promotion Program	574
2019	Robot Related Budget	333
2020	Support to Robotics Industry	1,234
2021	NEDO COVID robot R&D	80
2022	NEDO COVID robot R&D	68
2022	Projects in the Robotics and Industrial Automation Fields	67
2020–5	Moonshot robotics R&D Program[15]	440
2022	Japanese government robotics R&D funding[16]	931
Total		6,215
GERMANY[17]		
2009–14	AUTONOMIK (14 robotics programs)	43
2013–17	AUTONOMIK für Industrie 4.0 (16 projects)	43
2016–20	PAiCE program (industry 56 projects, govt. 55)	49
2019–20	Follow-up to New Directions report	19
2020	HTS 2025 ("Together through Innovation")	69
2019–21	Development of Digital Technologies	165
2022–6	High-Tech Strategy 2025 (HTS)	345
Total		733
EUROPEAN UNION		
2007–13	FP7 ECHORD (130 projects)	529
2007–13	Other robotics-related projects under FP7	68
2014–15	ICT Work Program (36 projects)	155
2016–17	ICT R&D projects	120
2018–20	ICT digitization of industry through robotics	154
2014–20	Factories of the Future (> 200 projects)[18]	1,115
2014–20	SPARC: The Partnership for Robotics in Europe[19]	3,900

Table 27.1 (cont.)

Country	Robotics R&D Program	$ Millions
2020	Horizon 2020 ICT Robotics Work Program	780
2018–20	Development of Digital Technologies (36 projects)	175
2021–2	FP9 Horizon Europe Work Programme	199
Total		**7,195**
KOREA		
2002–7	Government R&D	349
2009–13	First Intelligent Robot Basic Plan	363
2008–13	Fund to train 100,000 students in robotics[20]	1,000
2914–18	Second Basic Plan for Intelligent Robots	497
2018	Implementation Plan for Intelligent Robots	150
2022	Implementation Plan for Intelligent Robots	172
2019	Third Basic Plan on Intelligent Robots	113
2020–23	Third Basic Plan on Intelligent Robots	126
2020	Full Cycle Medical Device Development Project	83
2021–5	Full Cycle Medical Device Development Project	1,000
2022–4	Test bed for special-purpose aerial vehicles	7
Total		**3,860**
UNITED STATES		
NASA Robotic Space Exploration[21]		
2018	NASA Robotics Budget	6,245
2019	NASA Robotics Budget	6,450
2020	NASA Robotics Budget	6,789
2021	NASA Robotics Budget	6,981
2022	NASA Robotics Budget	7,212
2023	NASA Robotics Budget	7,672
Subtotal		**41,349**

DOD (Both autonomous and unmanned systems, and including testing and evaluation)

2019	Autonomous & Unmanned Systems Technology (AUST)[22]	5,333
2020	AUST[23]	4,630
2021	AUST[24]	4,213
2022	AUST[25] (est.)	4,600
Subtotal		**18,776**

NSF Robotics & Manufacturing USA

2012–22	National Robotics Initiative (NRI)[26]	250
2021– ongoing	Foundational Research in Robotics (FRR)[27]	75
2017	Manufacturing USA (ARM Institute)[28]	101

Table 27.1 (cont.)

Country	Robotics R&D Program	$ Millions
Subtotal		426
US Military & Space Total		60,125
US Commercial Total		426

The 2022 CHIPS and Science Act began to redress America's deficit in civilian robotics R&D funding. It greatly expanded funding for the National Science Foundation (NSF), and because robotics is a deeply interdisciplinary field, advances in a wide range of engineering and computer science capabilities will drive it forward. NSF is also expanding its Foundational Research in Robotics (FRR) program, which has made $77 million in grants to more than 150 universities since 2020.[29] While CHIPS did not earmark major new money specifically for robotics, it did list "Robotics, automation, and advanced manufacturing" as number 4 of 10 items on its Initial List of Key Technology Focus Areas, which will hopefully have an effect on other federal programs over time.[30]

Let us now look at robotics policies by country.

Japan

Japan is the world's largest manufacturer and exporter of industrial robots, shipping 136,069 in 2020, 45 percent of global sales.[31] (It imports only 2 percent of its robots.) Leading firms include FANUC, Kawasaki, Epson, Mitsubishi, Yaskawa, Nachi-Fujikoshi, and Omron.

Robots are deployed throughout industry, with 34 percent in the electronics industry, 32 percent in the auto industry, and 13 percent in the metal and machinery industry.[32] Installations of new manufacturing robots in Japan climbed steadily from 25,000 in 2013 to 55,000 in 2018, fell to 39,000 in 2020 during COVID, then rebounded to 50,400 in 2022.[33]

In 2004, the Ministry of Economy, Trade, and Industry (METI) adopted a strategy to increase the country's global market share in industrial robots. By 2007, policymakers also saw robots as the answer to major social problems confronting Japan, such as an aging and shrinking population, a rising dependency ratio of retirees and workers, and an aging skilled industrial workforce. METI therefore refocused its efforts on service and interactive robots, underwriting 50 percent of companies' R&D for robots designed to interact with humans.[34] Once METI's policy was set, other Japanese ministries reinforced its effort in their own areas of expertise, as shown in Table 27.2.

Table 27.2 Responsibility for robot R&D among Japanese agencies[35]

Organization	R&D Focus
Ministry of Internal Affairs and Communications	Robot network technology
Fire and Disaster Management Agency	Robots to assist during fires and disasters
Ministry of Education, Culture, Sports, Science & Technology	Cognitive computers and rescue robots
Ministry of Agriculture, Forestry, and Fisheries	Robotic pickers for fruit and vegetables
Ministry of Land Infrastructure and Transport	IT-controlled systems

Since 2014, Japan has invested $6.2 billion in robotics R&D. (Its individual programs are listed in Table 27.1.) In 2015, it released a set of industrial policy guidelines, Japan's Robot Strategy: Vision, Strategy, and Action Plan.[36] This laid out a grand vision of a robotics-infused industrial base and a society with robots deployed in all areas of life. It addressed regulatory reform, standards setting, systems integration, and key performance indicators in a variety of fields.[37]

The guidelines noted that Japan lost more than ¥20 trillion ($150 billion) in manufacturing value-added between 1995 and 2015, and aimed to grow the robotics sector as a remedy.[38] It noted that Japan supplied more than 90 percent of essential robotics components globally, including precision reduction gears, servomotors, and force sensors. These capabilities, it said, would enable Japan to enhance its position as a "robotics superpower."[39] The plan set three targets for 2020: 1) double Japan's global market share for industrial robots, 2) increase 20 fold the nonindustrial Japanese robot market, including service robots, and 3) expand the domestic market for surgical robots to $450 million.[40]

Japan has since maintained its dominance in industrial robots, but the massive expansion of service robots envisioned has yet to materialize there or anywhere else.[41] The tasks and environments of many service-sector applications are less controlled than in manufacturing, and the dispersed nature of many service operations makes it hard to support the on-site repair personnel required to keep robots running smoothly.[42]

Germany

Germany is the leading robotics power in Europe.[43] In 2022, it added 25,636 industrial robots, bringing its installed total to 260,636.[44] The country's global sales in robotics and automation reached €14.3 billion in 2022, with

€15.7 billion forecast for 2023.[45] The country produces state-of-the-art, globally competitive robots and parts across all sectors of the industry, notably in machine vision and human–robot interaction.

Germany's robotics policy is a part of a comprehensive industrial policy designed to keep it at the cutting edge of manufacturing and prepare its workforce for an increasingly high-tech manufacturing environment. The country launched its High-Tech Strategy (HTS) in 2006 to advance manufacturing competitiveness, foster more-advantageous industries, deepen scientific and engineering collaboration between universities and industry, and improve the innovation ecosystem.[46] HTS explicitly included robotics funding and established the overall framework for robotics industrial policy. Four years later, the government broadened and updated the plan, now called High-Tech Germany.[47] Total government funding for robotics from 2009 to 2026 is estimated to be $733 million. (Its specific programs are listed in Table 27.1.)

The European Union

The EU's and Germany's industrial policies for robotics are similar and mutually reinforcing. Between 1984 and 2027, the EU funded nine Framework Programmes (FPs) for Research and Technological Development: FP1 (1984–7, €3.3 billion) through FP9 (2021–7, €95.5 billion).[48]

From 2006 to 2013, the EU operated the European Clearing House for Open Robotics Development (ECHORD), funded under FP7 and involving 53 universities and 80 companies.[49] FP8 (a/k/a Horizon 2020) then went further, sponsoring 130 robotics projects at 500 companies and institutions with $529 million.[50] The robotics budget of Horizon 2020 was €700 million and it was expected to generate additional private investment of around €2 billion.[51]

In 2013, a second public–private partnership, SPARC: The Partnership for Robotics in Europe, was launched as the world's largest civilian robotics program.[52] SPARC built on ECHORD with expanded funding: $3.9 billion from 2014 through 2020, one quarter from government and the rest from industry.[53] It focused on next-generation intelligent robots, including service and other human-interacting robots, with the goal of capturing 42 percent of global robot production by 2020.[54] (As of 2014, Europe had 32 percent of the market for industrial robots and 63 percent of nonmilitary service robots.)[55]

SPARC was closely coordinated with the EU's broader high-tech industrial policies.[56] Starting in 2020, the EU funded its Factories of the Future 2020 public–private partnership, a €1.15 billion program to stimulate advanced manufacturing by infusing robotics, which funded more than 200 industrial projects with the participation of over 1,000 organizations.[57]

Korea

Korean companies have designed and built robots since the mid-1970s, but it was only in 2003 that the government officially designated robotics an engine of economic growth.[58] Like Tokyo, Seoul sees robotics as helping replace a declining industrial workforce, not as a threat to jobs. Its number of industrial robots grew from 156,000 in 2013 to more than 300,000 in 2018, though growth in new installations leveled off in 2020 and 2021.[59] Korean companies, including global leaders like Doosan, sold approximately 7,000 robots per year from 2000 to 2007, and by 2018, that figure had risen to 30,000, most of them industrial.[60]

The rise of Korea as a robotics powerhouse has been driven by its Intelligent Robots Development and Distribution Promotion Act of 2008. This Act requires that the government issue a basic plan to develop and distribute intelligent robots every five years.[61] The plan has since been amended more than a dozen times to keep pace with advances in the technology and its intended uses. Implementation is overseen by the Ministry of Trade, Industry and Energy (MOTIE), the country's main industrial policy agency.

Beginning in 2008, Seoul invested $3.5 billion to support and expand the robot industry, funding not only the top *chaebol*, including LG, Samsung, and Hyundai, but also small- and medium-sized manufacturers (SMMs).[62] Between 2008 and 2012, Korea achieved success, creating a $1.9 billion industry with $600 million in exports. By 2016, it had 2,127 robotics firms, of which 96 percent were SMMs.[63]

From 2008 to 2013, the government funded a $1 billion program to train 100,000 graduate students in robotics and mechatronics.[64] Today, it also provides grants to robotics R&D centers at the nation's premier technical universities.[65] These centers initially concentrated on industrial robotics, but increasingly research diverse areas, such as surgical, household, and maritime robots, and the world's first microscopic nanobots to detect and treat cancer from inside the body.[66]

To boost the robotics industrial base, in 2018, MOTIE established an $84 million fund in partnership with Samsung to help 2,500 SMMs transition to smart manufacturing, in part to remedy Korea's reliance on imported advanced manufacturing equipment and software.[67] Over the decade to 2024, MOTIE focused on expanding demand for robots by creating markets and building infrastructure.[68] For example, in 2014, the government made a $660 million investment in Robot Land, a conglomeration of robot companies, robot-training universities, and a theme park designed to promote public acceptance of robots located on 1.15 million square meters near Seoul.[69]

In 2019, MOTIE announced the Intelligent Robot Action Plan to finance 7,560 robots to replace workers in textile, food, and beverage production, aiming to make Korea the world's fourth largest robot producer by 2023.[70] (It reached number four in new installations of industrial robots in 2022.)[71] The government is also encouraging the transition to smart manufacturing by developing robot-utilization models for specific industries such as aerospace, shipbuilding, and chemicals.[72] The Seoul Metropolitan Government in 2023 declared itself a "robot-friendly city," with a $160 million four-year plan including a fund for development and commercialization, an industry cluster hub, deployment of robots in eldercare and childcare, and a robotics museum.[73]

China

Robotics has been a major part of China's larger high-tech industrial policy framework of the past three decades. This has included the 863 Program (1986), the Eighth Five-Year Plan (1991–5), and every Five-Year Plan thereafter, all of which designated robotics a key technology. Today, Beijing's main goal is to increase its robotics industry's share of its enormous and expanding home market. As described in its Made in China 2025 program (see Chapter 7), it aims to become a top-tier robotics manufacturer by 2025 and has established a far-ranging set of policies to achieve this.[74]

China became the world's largest market for industrial robots in 2013 and has led the world in number installed since 2016. In 2016, Beijing announced its Robot Industry Development Plan (2016–20).[75] This focused on arc-welding robots, vacuum-cleaning robots, intelligent industrial robots, cobots (robots that work with humans), dual-armed robots, automatic guided vehicles, firefighting and rescue robots, surgical robots, public service robots such as for policing and mail, and nursing robots.[76] It sought to expand robot production, strengthen innovation capacity, and improve integration of robot subsystems.[77] The plan set a 2020 target robot density of 100, up from 68 in 2016, and an annual production goal of 100,000.[78] Both goals were surpassed: Output increased from 72,000 in 2016 to 212,000 in 2020, and by 2021, China's robot density reached 322, overtaking the US.[79]

But China was still importing its most advanced robots and key parts, including actuators, servos, reducers, joints, and cabling, mainly from Japan and Germany.[80] From 2017 to 2020, only 22–27 percent of new installations were sourced domestically.[81] A subsequent plan, Declaration Guidelines for the "Key Special Program on Intelligent Robots" of 2019, had much deeper technical specificity than previous Chinese robotics policies. It described 33 specific programs in four major topic areas:

1. Basic cutting-edge theory (3 programs)
2. Common technology (6 programs)

3. Key technologies and equipment (16 programs)
4. Application demonstration (8 programs)

Thirty-two robot types were described in detail, as was the proposed R&D to advance them.[82]

Chinese robotics companies have pursued robotics technology through state-subsidized acquisitions of foreign firms.[83] In the two years after 2015, they made numerous high-profile acquisitions of US and European firms, including the acquisition of Germany's largest robotics company, Kuka, for $5 billion in 2016. Germany responded in 2020 with a new law making it harder for non-EU firms to acquire strategic companies (see Chapter 8).[84]

Like the US, China is making significant investments in autonomous military systems, and it is believed to be conducting research on military AI on a par with the US.[85] However, the official US-China Economic and Security Review Commission was unable to locate an authoritative comparison between American and Chinese robotic military R&D because the research is classified in both countries.[86]

Comparing National Policies

Table 27.3 compares the major elements of foreign nations' robotics policies with those of the US. The policies in question are:

China	Robot Industry Development Plan – 2016–20
Germany	Industry 4.0 – 2011–30
Japan	New Robot Strategy – 2016–20
Korea	Basic Plans for Intelligent Robots – 2009–20
USA	NSF National Robotics Initiative – 2013–21

Weak US Support for Commercial Robotics

America's limited governmental support for commercial robotics R&D has been channeled through three programs:

1. Manufacturing USA's Advanced Robotics in Manufacturing (ARM) Institute ($80 million)
2. NSF's National Robotics Initiative (NRI) ($169 million) (2012–22)
3. NSF's Foundational Research in Robotics (FFR) program (2020–present)

NRI ran from 2012 to 2022 and was a funding vehicle for the integration of robots with people, focusing on AI, mobility, safety, and other

Table 27.3 National robotics industrial and innovation policies

	China	Germany	Japan	Korea	US
Goal	Increase competitiveness in 10 robot product areas; increase domestic market share	Expand factory digitization through robotics	Deploy robotics throughout industry and society	Promote science-based R&D and infrastructure for intelligent robots	Develop cobots that can work safely with humans in the same space without barriers
Stated Objectives	Produce 100,000 industrial robots annually by 2020; replace parts imports	Transform business, especially SMMs, through deployment of cyber-physical systems	Drastic growth of robotics sector; establish Japan as global robot innovation hub	Support deployment of robots first in manufacturing and then in service industries	Support basic and applied research on cobots (safety and independence)
Developmental Focus	Enable Chinese industry to supply internal market	Digital integration across entire manufacturing value chain	Service and interactive robots	Improve weakest areas: robotics software and services	Link science, engineering, technology development to use of robots and cobots
Employment Strategy	Counter rising cost of manufacturing labor with robots	Counter decline in skilled manufacturing workforce with robots	Counter decline in skilled manufacturing workforce with robots	Counter decline in skilled manufacturing workforce with robots	Concern about robotics displacing jobs and workers

Larger Policy Context	Embedded in larger industrial policy programs beginning with the Seventh Five-Year Plan in 1986	Embedded in Germany's ongoing High-Tech Strategy since 2006	Large enhancement of existing policy: Japan as robotics superpower	Three five-year plans under 2008 national robotics legislation	Robotics designated as one of several key high-tech industries
Scope of Government Effort	All of government	Federal Ministry of Education & Federal Ministry of Economics and Energy	All of government	All of government	Voluntary participation of three or four agencies
Educational Component	Coordination of public vocational training for workers	Training, continuing education, and employment benefits for workers	Primary, secondary, advanced, and vocational education society-wide	Grants for robotics R&D to top tech centers; $1 billion to educate 100,000 grad students in robotics	R&D grants to universities, some of which fund graduate student education
Infrastructure and markets	Expand industrial scale in robotics; improve systems integration	Interconnection of products, value chains, IoT, and business models	Build infrastructure to make Japan world's top robot innovation hub	Expand demand base by building infrastructure and market creation	No coordination with infrastructure and markets

capabilities.[87] It supported collaborative R&D among academic, industry, nonprofit, and other organizations.

NRI grants were, and FRR grants are, made to university research groups, providing $100,000 to $500,000 per year for relatively small science and engineering research projects undertaken by a primary investigator (a professor) and some graduate students or postdoctoral fellows. This funding structure is very limiting, as it will neither fund large and risky exploratory projects nor bridge the gap from lab-proven prototypes to commercialization.

After NRI ended, NSF directed applicants seeking robotics funding to either FRR or a number of ongoing robot-related programs such as Cyber-Physical Systems or Dynamics, Control and Systems Diagnostics.[88] FRR continues, but with little funding: as of 2022, only $15–20 million per year (see Table 27.1). It emphasizes basic research on "intelligence, computation, and embodiment, ambitiously seeking to "enable transformative new robot functionality."[89] Various other federal agencies and offices fund mission-specific robotics projects within NSF, but this provides only intermittent funding as agencies enter and exit the program.

Other US programs are closer to the commercialization end of the innovation pipeline. ARM was created in 2017 as part of the Manufacturing USA program described in Chapter 21. Its explicit mission is "to accelerate the use of industrial robots to drive growth in the US manufacturing sector." Carnegie Mellon University got $80 million from DOD to start it and then attracted $173 million from corporate and nonprofit partners.[90] Virtually all the major non-Chinese suppliers of robots in the US are members, while Chinese firms are excluded because ARM is sponsored by DOD.

As of 2024, ARM was a standalone nonprofit with 415 member organizations and had trained 25,000 people in the previous three years.[91] Since its founding, it has attracted another $21 million from DOD, $10 million from other federal sources, and $980 million from academia and industry.[92] However, ARM remains at the mercy of congressional politics and its other funding sources, which makes it difficult to achieve a sustained focus on manufacturing needs and technological opportunities – let alone an overall national robotics strategy.

NSF's and ARM's robotics programs are not based on a formally defined vision of industry or society suffused with robots, nor on a mandate to improve US manufacturing automation or the competitiveness of America's robot industry. They do not offer major funding to help US robotics companies thrive in global markets. They tacitly assume that R&D conducted under grant programs will eventually migrate into and benefit the commercial industry. (See Chapter 20 for why this is a mistaken model.) The world's top nine academic robotics programs – CMU, MIT, Penn, Michigan, Georgia Tech,

Stanford, Columbia, Harvard, and Cornell – are in the US, but all have weak links to commercialization by foreign standards.[93]

China, Germany, Japan, and South Korea view robotics as a way to offset the aging of their workforces, while China sees it as a means to address the rising cost of its manufacturing labor. But the US has no explicit policy at all on robot versus human employment dynamics, except for the lingering fear of job displacement. These foreign nations promote continuing and vocational education to help workers adapt to the increasing robotic presence in their workplaces. Despite America's lack of a strong system of vocational education for advanced manufacturing as a whole, it actually has an abundance of vocational robotics training programs, but their lack of consistent criteria, promotion, and recognition by employers undermines their efficacy.[94]

28 NANOTECHNOLOGY
Is America Losing the Future?

Nanotechnology is the manipulation of matter at scales from a fraction of a nanometer to a few hundred nanometers – sizes between individual atoms and small single-celled organisms – at which it has radically different properties. Nanotech is already significant in many industries. Integrated circuits are a form of nanotech (see Chapter 26). Other nanotech provides the light, strong composites in aircraft and space vehicles (see Chapter 26). Still other nanotech powers the solid-state lasers used to transmit information through the internet and the light-emitting diodes in LED light bulbs and flat-screen TVs. Nanotech also makes possible solar cells, the batteries in electric cars, and medical technologies such as vaccines. It is thus the unifying thread of many of today's most advanced technologies. Unfortunately, America is falling behind.

In the future, nanotech-based quantum computing and communications will lead to more powerful computers, transforming national security and internet commerce by making currently secret communications insecure. Medical nanotechnologies will permit targeted interventions at the cellular level, providing new weapons against diseases, biological weapons, and defenses against them. China is known to be working on these.[1]

Much of the science underpinning these advances was developed at firms and universities in the US. But the huge manufacturing industries built on it are mostly overseas. For example, the organic light-emitting diode (OLED) technology Kodak created didn't save that firm from going bankrupt in 2012. But it did enable lucrative businesses for Korea's Samsung, to whom Kodak licensed the technology, and LG, which bought Kodak's entire OLED business in 2009. Today, American firms like Nanosys and Universal Display develop important nanotechnologies, but do not actually manufacture the end products and are thus relatively small.

How did the US get itself into this situation? A major government program, the National Nanotechnology Initiative (NNI), has been funded since 2001, but Washington failed to appreciate the importance of having both a technology *and* a manufacturing strategy. The prevailing wisdom was that if the academic science was supported, mass manufacturing would follow automatically. (See Chapter 20 for why this is a poor model of innovation.) By contrast, successful rival nations in nanotech have focused on *making these technologies manufacturable at scale*, employing every policy tool from R&D subsidies to cheap capital to tariffs. A 2020 National Academies review of the NNI urged that the US recognize that "the recent, focused, and in some cases novel commercialization approaches of other nations may be yielding better societal outcomes."[2]

Nanotechnology Emerges

Today's nanotech emerged from many scientific disciplines, including chemistry, physics, and materials science, and from existing electronic, chemical, and biomedical technologies. Many of its pivotal advances were made in private-sector laboratories. For example, the scanning tunneling microscope was invented at IBM in 1986, and a few years later, a similar device was used to arrange individual atoms to spell out the letters "IBM." This tool was the first of a whole new series of nanotools: A related device, the atomic force microscope, is today in even wider use in labs around the world.

By the late 1990s, after the revolution in IT and biotechnology, there were hopes that nanotech would soon produce a similar wave of innovative spin-offs and startups. But outside of aerospace and medicine, commercializing underlying nanotech discoveries has turned out to be more difficult than expected.

President Clinton announced NNI in 2000, citing the success of Sematech (see Chapter 26) as a precedent.[3] By 2003, its budget exceeded $1 billion a year, and by 2024 (requested), $2.2 billion. Today, about two-fifths of its money goes to the National Institutes of Health, a quarter goes to the Department of Energy, and the rest mainly to the Defense Department and National Science Foundation.[4] Cumulative funding for NNI and its predecessors since 2001, including its 2024 budget request, exceeds $43 billion.[5]

NNI does fund some programs designed to transfer technology to industry. For example, starting in 2018, the Presidential Management Agenda's Lab-to-Market Cross-Agency Priority Goal has sought to improve the transfer of technology from federally funded R&D to the private sector.[6] But outside biotech and aerospace, NNI, unlike the programs of America's rivals, has not financially supported big companies with the resources to develop and deploy nanotech at scale.

Nanotechnology requires costly facilities with high operational expenses and specialized staff. Capital costs include clean rooms, nanofabrication equipment, advanced microscopes, and other equipment to characterize the properties of nanomaterials. Only the largest corporations can afford this hardware, so startups need shared, government-supported facilities. The National Nanotechnology Infrastructure Network, established in 2001 to meet this need, has since evolved into the National Nanotechnology Coordinated Infrastructure (NNCI), which in 2024, reported its scope thus:

> The 16 NNCI sites and their 13 partners (universities, colleges, national labs, and non-profit foundations) provide access to more than 2,200 tools located in 71 distinct facilities. As will be detailed later in this report, these tools have been accessed during Year 8 by more than 13,000 users including nearly 3,600 external users, representing more than 220 US academic institutions, nearly 800 small and large companies, 47 government and non-profit institutions, as well as nearly 40 foreign entities. Overall, these users have amassed more than 1 million tool hours.[7]

Total NNCI funding since its inception in 2014 has been $165 million.[8]

There are other major government initiatives. DOD funds MIT's Institute for Soldier Nanotechnologies, which concentrates on enhancing military protection and survivability through nanotech-based body armor, specialized clothing, battlefield wound management, detection, evasion, and communication. NIH has its Cancer Nanotechnology Plan.[9] Organizations such as the University of California's Center for the Environmental Implications of Nanotechnology research the dangers of nanoparticle toxicity, while NIST, the FDA, and the EPA develop the corresponding regulatory policy. This precautionary and preemptive research and regulation are essential to maintaining public confidence in nanotech, which otherwise risks the fate of nuclear energy, a valuable technology curtailed due to overblown fears.

A Global Policy Race

About the same time as NNI was launched, major initiatives were getting underway in the EU, in its member states, in Korea, in Japan, and later in China.

The EU's initial program allocated $1.9 billion from 2001 to 2006, with this roughly doubled for the next five-year period.[10] Japan's 2006 Third Science and Technology Basic Plan set nanotech as one of four priority areas. Korea's stated goal in its 2006 Nanotechnology Development Plan was to be in the top three in the world for nanotechnology and nanomaterials. China's Thirteenth Five-Year Plan for Science and Technology Innovation, covering 2016–20, cited nanotechnology as the first of 13 Major Strategic and Forward-Looking Scientific Issues.[11]

The scientific achievements of these national programs are often measured by number of papers published. By raw count, the EU had always produced more than the US, but it was displaced from the top spot by China in 2014. If one adjusts for quality by taking only the top 10 percent most cited papers, America's performance looks somewhat better.[12]

Governmental support for commercialization has been less in the EU, where state aid rules limit large-scale corporate subsidies, than in the East Asian countries.[13] The EU and its member states have instead emphasized basic science, shared facilities, and supporting spin-offs through grants and government contracts. In addition, the EU has programs to nurture startups, including its Start-up Scale-up Initiative and its Innovation Radar Initiative, which are not specific to nanotech but include it.

Europe has had some nanotech successes, but also spectacular failures. In the first category is the Interuniversity Microelectronics Centre (IMEC) in Leuven, Belgium. IMEC's $896 million yearly budget comes from the Flemish regional government, EU grants, and contract research for industry. Its Advanced Patterning Center, a joint research center with the Dutch company ASML, has helped secure ASML's global monopoly of the extreme ultraviolet lithography tools needed to make the world's most advanced computer chips.[14]

One UK effort, on the other hand, is an example of how *not* to support nanotech. This 2003 initiative, funded at $63 million a year from 2003 to 2009, set up a network of 24 micro- and nanotechnology centers across the country.[15] But funding and other resources were spread far too thin, so the centers never achieved critical mass. They were not well connected with the academic researchers generating new science or with the industries that were supposed to commercialize it. Nor were they equipped to recognize market opportunities. Most disappeared without a trace and with no public accountability.

Germany is Europe's leader in nanotech research and applications. The Fraunhofer Institutes' (see Chapter 23) Nanotechnology Alliance conducts practical research for industrial applications. The Helmholtz Association, Germany's largest public scientific organization ($6.5 billion annual budget, 70 percent from government) works to integrate nano- and micro-systems. The pure-science-oriented Max Planck Society ($2.3 billion budget) works on nano-materials, supramolecular (multi-molecule) systems, and characterization methods. The Leibniz Association, a 97-member group of nonuniversity research entities ($2.4 billion), has achieved significant results in nanomaterials, surfaces, and opto- and nano-electric properties.

In nanotech, China for a long time followed the development model practiced in the rest of East Asia for decades – that is, commercializing technologies developed elsewhere. But in recent years, according to its latest Five-Year Plan, it has begun aiming to generate original research as well.[16] Nanotech is a central element in its "Made in China 2025" plan (see Chapter 7) to achieve dominant positions in all of high-tech manufacturing.[17]

* * *

The following nanotech applications are of the greatest international interest and thus subject to the most intense competition.

Current Nanotech: Batteries

When matter is finely divided, it has more surface area because every time a particle is split in two, more surface is created. A pound of sugar with grains half a millimeter big has a surface area of less than a square yard. But if the grains are 50 nanometers (nm), their surface is about 15 *acres*. As a result, any process that depends on what happens at a surface will work faster and better with a nanoscale material, including catalysts that accelerate chemical reactions, membranes that filter contaminants from water, and the electrodes in batteries.

In a lithium-ion (Li-ion) battery, the cathode is made of nanoscale layers of a lithium compound that ions enter and leave as the battery charges and discharges. Although the technology was invented in the US, the manufacturing is mostly in East Asia. Japanese and Korean companies have the most advanced technologies, though Chinese firms have the advantage in cost and scale. But Li-ion batteries are still expensive and have relatively short lifespans. Next-generation batteries will require new nano-structured materials for their electrodes, electrolytes, and separators, creating opportunities for innovation that *may* allow the US to leapfrog current technologies and regain a leading position in the industry.

New types of nano-engineered batteries may resolve some mineral scarcity issues. Lithium-iron-phosphate (LFP) batteries need no cobalt, nickel, or manganese (though they need more lithium). They are cheaper than Li-ion batteries, were also originally developed in the US, and are already widely used in China. There are many R&D efforts worldwide both to improve lithium-ion and LFP batteries and to find new alternatives, such as lithium-sulfur, aluminum-ion, and sodium-ion.

Current Nanotech: Fibers

Dividing matter more finely can also make it stronger. Nanoscale forms of carbon, such as carbon nanotubes, are among the strongest materials by weight known. Their strength is an expression of the strength of the carbon–carbon chemical bond, which is maximized at the nanoscale because the strength of a solid is controlled by its weakest link. In a superthin fiber, there can be no scratch deeper than the thickness of the fiber, so the thinner the fiber, the stronger it will be.

Carbon fiber composites have long been used in military aircraft to make lighter airframes with the strength and stiffness of metals. For the military, the big benefits are higher performance and larger payloads. For commercial aircraft, such as the Boeing 787, fuel efficiency is the major gain, with improvements of 20–30 percent. Spacecraft benefit, too: The suborbital spacecraft *SpaceShipOne*, built by Scaled Composites, won the Ansari X Prize for the first private manned spaceflight in 2004 and today, carbon fiber composites enable the high performance of SpaceX's rockets.

Composites made using carbon nanotubes and graphene could be stronger yet. In graphene, carbon atoms are joined together in linked hexagons in a single sheet just one atom thick. A nanotube is a strip of this material rolled up into a tube. Nanotube and graphene composites are just beginning to come onto the market. Aerospace is their major market now, but longer term, the greatest potential applications will be in space. Nanocomp Technologies of New Hampshire has developed carbon nanotube materials for NASA's Juno space probe to Jupiter, following earlier funding by the Air Force.

Air Force aircraft and drones contain nanomaterials as part of their stealth technology, but the classified details are kept out of the open literature. The next generation of military nanomaterials will aim at functionality such as integrated sensors and the ability to change their shape and other properties on command or in response to the environment. For example, plastics that repair small cracks in themselves were pioneered by Scott White at the University of Illinois with Air Force support. More advanced versions will eventually give sixth-generation fighter aircraft skin that will be able to close battle damage holes automatically.

Current Nanotech: Displays and Lighting

At nanoscale, quantum-mechanical effects become more important. For example, for very fine particles of an electron-containing material, the smaller the particles, the higher the energy of the electrons. Fluorescent materials emit light when excited by ultraviolet and because their color depends on their electron energy, different colors can be generated by controlling particle size. These "quantum dots" are already used in flat-screen TVs, many of them using materials developed by the American firm Nanosys based on technologies from the Department of Energy's (DOE) Lawrence Berkeley National Laboratory in California.[18]

The range of semiconductors that can be readily made today is limited: Silicon does most of the work, with a few simple compounds like gallium arsenide fulfilling specialized roles. But this narrow palette of materials, with their limited range of properties, limits what the resulting devices can accomplish. That palette could be massively increased by creating artificial nanostructures: alternating layers, each only a few atoms thick, of different materials with different properties. Early versions of this technology are already in some LEDs and the solid-state lasers in supermarket checkouts and laser pointers.

The blue LEDs that enable solid-state lighting were invented in 1993 by Shuji Nakamura at Japan's Nichia Corporation, but today the world's largest LED lighting manufacturer is the Chinese firm MLS. China's dominance began with its Twelfth Five-Year Plan in 2010, which drove major investments in R&D and began building manufacturing capacity. (Technical expertise was added by MLS's 2016 acquisition of the German lighting and semiconductor company Osram.) The Chinese government proactively created a massive market for the products by phasing in a ban on incandescent bulbs beginning in 2011. (In 2019, the Trump administration *rolled back* regulatory actions favoring low-energy lighting, prolonging the life of an obsolescent technology; President Biden later reversed this decision.)[19]

Organic light-emitting diodes (OLEDs) are used in the displays of high-end mobile phones and elsewhere. Key early work was done by Americans Alan Heeger and Stephen Forrest, the latter receiving substantial support from the Air Force.[20] But by 2017, although a US company retained key intellectual property and sold some nanomaterials, 97 percent of its licensing revenues were from foreign companies – mostly Chinese, Japanese, and Korean.[21] The industry did not develop in the US largely because America had previously lost its predecessor technology, LCDs, also invented in the US but mass-produced in Asia. When LCD manufacturing took root there, a cluster of firms with skilled personnel and the supporting infrastructure for R&D developed, and this cluster quickly adapted to producing OLEDs.[22] (For the concept of an industrial commons, see Chapter 3.)

Current Nanotech: Solar Cells

Nanotechnology also promises cheaper and more efficient solar cells. Existing cells have two problems. The first is the theoretical limit to their efficiency, the Shockley–Queisser limit, about 26 percent for silicon.[23] This leaves little room for improvement from current best values of around 24 percent. The second problem is that manufacturing them is complex, expensive, and hard to scale.

One approach to the cost problem came from the aforementioned Alan Heeger, who in 2005, invented a plastic solar cell made from thin films of a blend of semiconducting polymer and buckminsterfullerene, a type of nano-scale carbon in the form of hollow sphere invented by America's Robert Curl and Richard Smalley and the UK's Harry Kroto.[24] The new cells were not as efficient as silicon ones, but their potentially much lower cost had game-changing potential.

A startup, Konarka, formed to commercialize this new technology, was spun off from the University of Massachusetts at Lowell. It obtained initial R&D support from the US Army's nearby Natick Soldier Research, Engineering and Development Center. By 2007, it had received nearly $100 million in venture capital funding, plus nearly $10 million in research funding from government agencies including the US Army, US Air Force, NIST, and NSF.[25]

But in 2012, the firm filed for bankruptcy, with some of its assets being acquired by the German solar company Belectric. Konarka's technology had not been perfect, but there was a bigger problem: China's massive, subsidized push into silicon solar cell manufacturing, which dragged down prices. In 2010 alone, five Chinese companies received more than $30 billion in subsidized loans. The effect on the US industry was devastating. By 2019, China's share of the world market had grown to 66 percent, with the rest of Asia at 18 percent. North America's share was just 4 percent. (See Chapter 18 for details of the Trump and Biden administrations' tariff actions in response.)

Konarka was not the only company to fail for this reason. California-based solar cell maker Solyndra had filed for bankruptcy the year before. Market fundamentalists cited these bankruptcies as evidence against all state support for civilian technology commercialization, but DOE's solar power loan program had been profitable overall.[26] The price of solar cells has fallen further in recent years, but because of process improvements and scale economies due to increased production, not fundamental technological advances.

Looking ahead, there are two major promising technologies in solar nanotech. In 2012, Henry Snaith at Oxford discovered that efficient solar cells could be made, using simple processes like spraying and printing, from hybrid organic/inorganic materials called perovskites. By 2019, Snaith's spin-off, Oxford PVI, had raised $90 million in funding and set up a factory in Germany. In 2023, its commercial-size perovskite-on-silicon tandem cell set a efficiency world record of 26.8 percent, and it claimed to have a clear road map to surpass 30 percent.[27] As of late 2023, at least a dozen other companies around the world were also pursuing the technology.[28] Three American firms were serious players: Cubic PV, Frontier Energy Solutions, and Energy Materials.[29] (Cubic is the result of a merger between Hunt Perovskite Technologies and 1366 Technologies, both DOE funded.)

The other major new technology involves cells that absorb more wavelengths of light by using layers of different semiconductors. The underlying technology is similar to solid-state lasers, and one of these "tandem" cells currently holds the world efficiency record: 45 percent. Tandem cells were developed by Germany's Fraunhofer Institute for Solar Energy Systems (see chapters 8 and 23).[30] They are still expensive, though there are uses, such as on satellites, where their efficiency is worth their cost.

Current Nanotech: COVID Vaccines

The COVID vaccine developed by the American firm Moderna in 2020 was a spectacular success for US nanotechnology. In contrast to the usual multiyear process of vaccine development, it took just 10 months to move from the first trials to mass deployment. By December 2020, the US government had spent $4.1 billion on it, including development, clinical trials, and manufacturing.[31]

This achievement was not an accident. Its foundations were laid by many years of government investment in the underlying science. For example, the vaccine contains a lipid nanoparticle that encloses the tiny strand of messenger RNA that makes it work. This nanoparticle protects the mRNA from the body's defense mechanisms, allowing it to reach the target cells. This technique was developed at MIT by Robert Langer, Moderna's founder. The world-leading cluster of biotechnology companies in the Boston area provided a fertile environment for the company to thrive (see Chapter 29).

The National Institutes of Health's (NIH) National Institute of Allergy and Infectious Diseases played a key role in turning Langer's science into a usable vaccine. Pfizer, the maker of the other mRNA COVID vaccine, also relied on NIH-funded research. Although it did not receive subsidies for development and testing, its development risk was backstopped by advance governmental orders. The vaccine it manufactured was developed by the German firm BioNTech, showing the strength of European bioscience.

America is strong in bionanotech for three reasons. The first is government-funded basic and proof-of-concept research, mainly managed by NIH, a competent, respected agency insulated from politics (see Chapter 20). Second is large pharmaceutical firms such as Pfizer – that is, research-based companies with multiple revenue streams, oligopoly pricing power, and the ability to scale up quickly. Third is a thriving sector of biotech startups backed by an experienced, technologically sophisticated, capital-rich VC sector. Creating all three elements at once by deliberate policy would be difficult – though other nations have shown that with multipronged, long-term, coordinated industrial policy, it is not impossible.

Future Nanotech: Bionanotechnology

In the future, bionanotechnology will be used to intervene in the human body at the cellular level with great precision. For example, the technology the COVID vaccines used to deliver engineered molecules to targeted cells will have other applications. It will be possible to seek out cancer cells and kill them with minimum damage to nearby healthy cells, or use mRNA to stimulate the immune system to destroy the cancer cells itself. And whatever the most promising mechanism for fighting degenerative diseases such as Alzheimer's and Parkinson's turns out to be, the solutions will almost certainly be delivered using similar technology.[32]

Other emerging therapies also use nucleic acids like the mRNA in COVID vaccines. One type of gene therapy, for example, delivers nucleic acids into a patient's cells to treat genetic diseases. This therapy exploits the recently discovered phenomenon of RNA interference, which can be used to silence specific genes linked to disease. The promise is huge, as RNAi allows, in principle, the disabling of any gene in any cell type – not only genes that cause inherited diseases but also the mutated genes that cause cells to turn cancerous, and genes introduced by viruses. The first RNAi-based drug to receive FDA approval, in 2018, was Onpattro, for hereditary amyloidosis.[33] Its delivery system is a lipid nanoparticle. Its producer, Alnylam, was founded in 2002, and it took 16 years and $2 billion in R&D to bring it to commercial viability.

Future Nanotech: Nanobots and Molecular Machines

In his 1986 bestseller *Engines of Creation*, K. Eric Drexler popularized the idea of building nanomachines at the molecular level. He imagined atomic-scale cogs and gears, conveyor belts, and robot arms. But this fascinating vision is either impossible or a long way off, precisely because physics operates differently at nanoscale. A bloodstream nanobot, for example, will be in an environment where everything is shaken around, buffeted by the random collisions of surrounding atoms, and in which even the stiffest and hardest materials bend and flex. It would be like making a clock from rubber and throwing it into a running washing machine.

Progress toward such devices has been slow. American Fraser Stoddart won the 2016 chemistry Nobel for his work making molecules that were physically, not chemically, connected with each other. Molecular rods thread molecular rings, and a change in their chemical conditions makes them move like a piston through a cylinder. Scientists have even built molecules that walk along tracks and carry cargoes. But these are basically toys to demonstrate capabilities. The key to making a true nano-robot will be achieving a meaningful degree of autonomy: The nanobot will need to sense its environment, process that information, and make decisions such as going in one direction or another.

Will it ever be possible to build *useful* molecular machines? Biology certainly offers precedents. Consider ATP-synthase, the rotary motor that converts the energy in the fuel molecule ATP into motion. Every muscle movement humans make uses similar molecular "motors," and ATP-synthase's conversion of energy into motion is almost 100 percent efficient. Understanding how such natural nanotech works and trying to imitate it will be a key future research theme. One approach that has already started to bear fruit is, instead of directly fabricating nanodevices, to induce naturally occurring cells to *grow* themselves into the desired shapes.[34]

Although nanobot technology is unlikely to lead to applications any time soon, speculative research is being funded. The EU's seven-year Horizon 2020 program distinguishes "Excellent Science" from "Industrial Leadership" and "Societal Challenges," and provides $1.5 billion for nanotech research in the first category.[35] In the US, the NSF has prime responsibility for funding such long-term speculative nanotech research, but other agencies, such as NIH and DOE, also make substantial contributions. In 2024 (requested), NSF funded nanotechnology "foundational research" with $259 million out of its total NNI funding of $428 million.[36]

Future Nanotech: Faster Computers

Moore's law – that the number of transistors on a chip doubles roughly every two years – has underpinned growth in the capabilities of digital devices for 60 years. Unfortunately, the current paradigm for microelectronics, complementary metal-oxide-semiconductor (CMOS), has run up against constraints in its underlying physics, and ongoing performance increases stem from advances other than increased transistor density. But there is no reason electronics cannot be made even smaller with a new engineering paradigm. It could also gain in energy efficiency, a key constraint on increasing the power of microprocessors.

For example, what if components weren't microprinted onto silicon wafers but built up from individual molecules into circuits? This is the dream of molecular electronics. The technology has been proven in principle, with demonstrations of individual molecules being used as circuit elements. The problem is scale: So far, most of these experiments have been done with individual molecules, and the technology to assemble the millions of such elements a microprocessor would need does not exist.

In the near and medium term, progress will more likely come from combining existing electronics technologies with new nanoscale elements.

Plausible candidates include semiconductor nanowires, carbon nanotubes, and ribbons of graphene and other materials in sheets one atom thick. Graphene, in particular, has attracted huge attention since its 2004 discovery. The EU is making a big bet on it through its Graphene Flagship, a $1.4 billion collaborative project between industry and academia.

Nanowires have attracted China's interest, and also provided some insight into China's methods. Harvard chemist Charles Lieber, a pioneering researcher in multiple areas of bionanotechnology and molecular electronics, was convicted in 2021 of secretly setting up a parallel research group at the Wuhan Institute of Technology in violation of disclosure laws.[37] His is not an isolated case. Beijing also offers substantial incentives to Chinese scientists and graduate students working in the US to return, bringing back knowledge, materials, and intellectual property developed with US taxpayer funding.[38]

Future Nanotech: Quantum Computers

Nanotech is the basis of quantum computing. Conventional "classical" computing encodes information in ones and zeros known as bits, which are, like switches, either on or off. But quantum bits ("qubits") can, paradoxically, be both on and off at the same time – until a measurement is made and they are forced into one state or the other. Furthermore, in a classical computer, there is no intrinsic correlation between different bits, which are independent. But in a quantum computer, different qubits can be correlated through so-called entanglement. So if someone looks at the first qubit and finds it to be a "one," they know that the second must be a "zero," even if it is miles away. Strangely, *the act of looking itself* forces the second qubit into a definite state. This property, for reasons too complex to relate here, makes quantum computers much faster than classical computers for some important calculations.

Quantum computers will not replace the chips in smartphones. (For one thing, they need ultra-low, liquid helium temperatures.) Instead, they will be used in cloud computing for specialized purposes such as ultrafast database searches and especially cryptography. National security agencies around the world have taken a deep interest because it may become possible to decipher currently unbreakable codes. Cryptography is also important for cryptocurrencies and for protecting financial transactions through the internet.

Competition in quantum research is global and accelerating. As of 2023, 29 nations and political entities had coordinated quantum development strategies, with 9 allocating more than $1 billion for R&D. The US National Quantum Initiative ranked second, at approximately $3.75 billion, surpassed only by China at $15 billion and followed by Germany ($3.3 billion), South

Korea ($2.4 billion), France ($2.2 billion), Russia ($1.5 billion), Canada ($1.1 billion), and the European Quantum Flagship ($1.1 billion).[39]
Here is a list of such initiatives:

South Africa	$3M	Thailand	$6M	Qatar	$10M
Switzerland	$11M	Hungary	$11M	Brazil	$12M
Philippines	$17M	Finland	$27M	Spain	$67M
Austria	$127M	Singapore	$138M	Australia	$155M
Sweden	$160M	Taiwan	$282M	Israel	$390M
Denmark	$406M	Japan	$700M	India	$735M
Netherlands	$904M	EU	$1.1B	Canada	$1.1B
Russia	$1.45B	France	$2.2B	S. Korea	$2.35B
Germany	$3.3B	US	$3.75B	UK	$4.3B
China	$15B	NZ	$37M		

US Quantum Information Science (QIS) research was initially authorized under the National Quantum Initiative Act of 2018 and funded at $855 million in 2021 and $918 million in 2022.[40] Three agencies were involved: NIST, NSF, and DOE. DOE established research centers at five national labs. Private American companies – IBM, Microsoft, Intel, Applied Materials, and Lockheed Martin – contributed $340 million.[41] In 2023, QIS funding was raised to $3.75 billion and expanded to seven principal agencies: NIST, NSF, DOE, DOD, NASA, NSA, and IARPA (the Intelligence Advanced Research Projects Agency). QIS activities were placed under the supervision of the National Quantum Coordination Office, housed under the Office of Science and Technology Policy in the Executive Office of the President.[42]

China's program has received the personal endorsement of President Xi.[43] Beijing aspires to create a fully indigenous quantum technology system, from basic research to applied research to technology development and deployment at scale. These efforts are bearing fruit: One Chinese research group, led by physicist Pan Jian-Wei, achieved "quantum supremacy" in 2020, executing a calculation on a quantum computer that would be impossible on a classical computer,[44] less than year after Google and NASA announced a similar breakthrough.[45]

China has aggressively invested in and acquired American startups to capture quantum technologies developed in the US. CFIUS has the authority to block such foreign acquisitions, and the Biden administration expanded its brief to include economically strategic assets, in addition to its existing review of those directly affecting national security. Nanotech falls into both categories.

Part VI
Cluster Case Studies

As discussed in Chapter 3, industry clusters are powerful but hard-to-establish tools of industrial policy. These chapters look at two in the US. Chapter 29 is about the Massachusetts life sciences cluster, a state-level industrial policy success story and a good illustration of how to tailor policies to the specific needs of the supported industry. Chapter 30 covers the Upstate New York semiconductor cluster, showing how state-level industrial policies require many different players to work cooperatively. It also demonstrates that gaining and holding technological and manufacturing leadership in fast-moving, capital-intensive, advanced technology industries requires federal financial and policy support.

29 THE MASSACHUSETTS LIFE SCIENCES CLUSTER

Nurturing industry clusters has been an effective industrial policy all over the world. Because clusters are geographically specific, they often coincide with political jurisdictions trying to improve their economies. And because clusters work largely because of non-free-market dynamics, they are tractable to government policy interventions. One example is the life sciences cluster in Greater Boston nurtured by the Massachusetts Life Sciences Center (MLSC).[1] This program grew so successfully an existing cluster of the biotechnology, pharmaceutical, and medical equipment industries that metropolitan Boston now has the world's largest conglomeration of life science companies.[2]

Massachusetts has been through several cycles of economic reinvention. Its agriculture declined, along with the rest of rocky-soiled New England, when the Midwestern states joined the Union. It was the nation's textile manufacturing hub until Southern states captured this industry in the early twentieth century. By the 1950s, it, along with the rest of New England, was regarded as a structurally declining region. But in the 1970s and 1980s, the state became a leader, second only to California, in the development of computers. Large firms such as Digital Equipment, Data General, Prime, and Wang clustered around Boston, and the "Route 128" region was spoken of as a peer to Silicon Valley. Democratic governor Michael Dukakis based part of his 1988 bid for the presidency on the so-called Massachusetts Miracle of economic resurgence.

But by the 1990s, Massachusetts was losing out to Silicon Valley as microcomputers replaced the minicomputer. The region had been strong in minicomputers at their peak, but it had a less creative and flexible innovation ecosystem than Silicon Valley – with more large firms rather than startups – and thus transitioned less well to the next generation of technology. (This

Table 29.1 Industries of the Massachusetts life sciences cluster[3]

Medicinal and Botanical Manufacturing
Pharmaceutical Preparation Manufacturing
In-Vitro Diagnostic Substance Manufacturing
Biological Product (except Diagnostic) Manufacturing
Electromedical and Electrotherapeutic Apparatus Manufacturing
Analytical Laboratory Instrument Manufacturing
Irradiation Apparatus Manufacturing
Surgical & Medical Instrument Manufacturing
Surgical Appliance & Supplies Manufacturing
Dental Equipment & Supplies Manufacturing
Medical, Dental & Hospital Equipment & Supplies Wholesalers
Drugs & Druggists' Sundries Merchant Wholesalers
Research & Development in Biotechnology
Research & Development in Physical, Engineering & Life Sciences (non-Biotech)
Testing Laboratories
Medical Laboratories

experience points to the need for nations to have not just advantageous *industries* but also economic *ecosystems* that can adapt to ongoing technological and economic change.)

Since the decline of its computer industry, the life sciences have emerged as a major new cluster in the state. The cluster consists of the 16 related industries listed in Table 29.1.

The cluster includes 2 R&D industries, 2 laboratory industries, 2 distribution industries, and 10 manufacturing industries.[4] It also includes the universities and medical centers where basic research is conducted.[5] Of the 758 life sciences firms in the Massachusetts Biotechnology Council as of 2023, 59 percent specialized in drug development, 18 percent did contract research and manufacturing, 8 percent made research products and instrumentation, 5 percent produced agricultural and industrial biotechnology, 3 percent made medical devices, and the rest fell into other categories.[6]

The Massachusetts Life Sciences Center

Well before this account begins, Greater Boston's universities and research hospitals had already created the academic core of the cluster. In 2003, the state set out to strengthen and expand it, aiming to capture both existing life science jobs from other locations and the new jobs that scientific advances were expected to generate.

Harvard Business School professor Michael Porter, one of the leading academic authorities on industry clusters, convened a conference, cohosted by Harvard and MIT, to strategize. MLSC, a public–private agency, was the result. The push to create it, led by Democratic governor Deval Patrick, quickly gained support from the legislature, industry, the academic community, and local officials.

To support the MLSC's mission, in May 2007, Patrick announced an ambitious 10-year, $1 billion public investment program. Its mandate was broad:

- To fund the translational research that converts new science into marketable products and services
- To invest in promising new technologies
- To ensure that the state's workforce's skills aligned with the needs of the life sciences industries
- To create new scientific infrastructure with shared resources to accelerate innovation
- To build partnerships between the local and international life sciences communities[7]

MLSC was equipped with a wide array of policy tools, from corporate tax credits to higher education funding. Its main thrust was to systematically improve the innovation capacity of its industries at *all* stages of their innovation pipelines (see Chapters 20 and 21 for this concept): not just research but also subsequent steps to ultimate commercialization.

Massachusetts was not new to tax incentives or corporate subsidies. It already provided subsidized capital for redeveloping industrial brownfields. MassDevelopment offered trade finance, loans for new equipment, and working capital. This agency's Emerging Technology Fund made loans of up to $2.5 million for working capital, equipment, expansion, and facilities.[8] The state provided mortgage guarantees for certain real estate ventures and working capital loan guarantees for manufacturers.[9] But it was not clear that benefits of these scattered expenditures exceeded their $345 per capita annual cost.[10]

MLSC was designed to break from this unfocused set of policies. Instead, it a) targeted an industry cluster, neither the whole state economy nor a single industry; b) had a "whole cluster" strategy, not limited to particular types of public institutions or firms; c) deployed multiple policy tools; d) targeted an already existing cluster; and e) had enough funding to make a difference. The hope, from the state government's perspective, was that the additional growth generated by MLSC would produce tax revenues exceeding the program's cost.

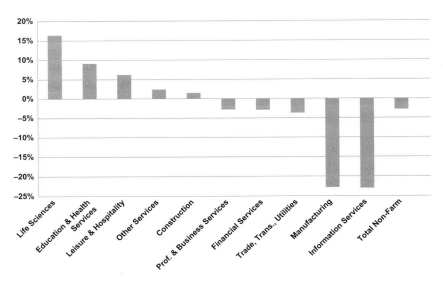

Figure 29.1 Massachusetts employment growth by industry sector 2001–2006[11]

The life sciences were also targeted because they were seen as having good potential for medium- and long-term growth. Between 2001 and 2006, their employment had increased by 11,300 (15 percent), faster than any other major sector in a period when total employment in the state was declining. (See Figure 29.1.) The state's other major industries, such as financial services and defense manufacturing, were already well capitalized, either by private investors or by federal funding, and were not expected to benefit much from additional state support. Because of the large number of possible points for policy interventions, the life sciences were also perceived as the area in which state policies could make the biggest difference.

MLSC Strategy

During its first years, the MLSC set up the following programs:

Cooperative Research Grants. These supported industry-sponsored university research with up to $250,000 per year for up to two years in a one-to-one match with a private sector pharmaceutical or medical device firm. Between 2008 and 2017, the MLSC provided 80 such grants totaling $27 million.

The Internship Challenge. To grow the talent pipeline, this program provided up to $8,160 per college intern per year at small biotech firms, defined as fewer than 100 employees in the state and 250 globally. (One sign of success: 20 percent of interns were hired by the companies they interned with.) MLSC also offered summer internships for high school students.

New Investigator Grants. Scientists need help starting their postgraduate careers, an often difficult transition essential to maintaining an ongoing supply of talent. These grants helped support emerging researchers at the state's universities, providing up to $100,000 per year for up to three years.

The Accelerator Loan Program. This program provided loans of up to $1 million to early-stage companies, helping them leverage other sources of capital. Examples included $750,000 to Allurion for a device to induce weight loss, $750,000 to Alcyone for a microcatheter for neurological problems, and $245,000 to Strohl Medical for a device for stroke victims.

The Small Business Matching Grant Program. This offered up to $500,000 to help firms commercialize new technologies emerging from Phase II or post–Phase II federal Small Business Innovation Research awards or Small Business Technology Transfer grants (see Chapter 23), complementing HIH, NSF, and DOD funding.

The Capital Projects Fund. This paid for equipment and supplies at vocational and technical high schools, community colleges, business incubators, research institutions, and universities. Examples include $10 million for the Dana Farber Cancer Institute's Molecular Cancer Imaging Facility, $14.6 million for UMass Dartmouth's Biomanufacturing Center, and $10 million for UMass Lowell's Emerging Technologies and Innovation Center. A more unusual example is $14.3 million to help the town of Framingham improve its wastewater-treatment system to allow local bioscience manufacturing.[12]

The Life Sciences Tax Incentive Program. This included:

- A tax credit for research conducted in the state
- A tax credit of 10 percent of the cost of qualifying investments in facilities, equipment, and other items
- A tax credit for the fees the FDA charges companies whose drugs and medical devices it evaluates for approval
- An extension of the carryover period for net operating losses from 5 to 15 years, allowing losses accumulated while a firm develops a product to offset later profits
- A deduction for clinical testing of "orphan" drugs: those that will never be profitable due to the small number of people with the condition they treat

- Exemption from the Sales Factor Throwback provision, which requires that revenue from sales in states that do not tax it be taxed as if generated in Massachusetts
- An exemption from state sales taxes for qualifying purchases
- A tax exemption for construction costs

Over time, MLSC added other programs to fill gaps in its approach:

The Milestone Achievement Program. This targeted the Valley of Death (see Chapter 21), aiding early-stage firms with grants for reaching specific technical milestones. It provided up to $200,000 in non-dilutive funding – that is, financing that did not reduce existing investors' ownership percentages. Milestones included market analysis, competitive evaluation, technology assessment, prototyping, manufacturing process testing, clinical trials, and regulatory-strategy design.

The Massachusetts Ramp-Up Program. This supported commercialization by firms with federal SBIR or STTR Phase I awards or federal contracts. Targeting a later phase of development than the existing Small Business Matching Grant Program, the money could be used to pay for staff salaries, clinical trials, consultants, subcontractors, materials, supplies, or equipment.

The Massachusetts Transition and Growth Program. This was designed to cover companies that did not qualify for any of the MLSC's other programs but could credibly promise to bring at least 50 new jobs to the state.

These grants were not automatic. Firms competed for them based on their hiring goals, technical and commercial credibility, and ability to add specific needed competencies to the state's innovation ecosystem.

Through its battery of programs, as of 2023, the MLSC was annually investing or committing the sums listed in Table 29.2.

Seeding Collaborative Research

MLSC seeds and administers collaborative research institutions designed to generate technological advances that firms will not invest in on their own because the advances would be hard for any one firm to monetize.

For example, the Massachusetts Neuroscience Consortium helps firms collaborate in funding and sharing pre-competitive academic research. Initial sponsors included Biogen Idec, Abbott Labs, Janssen R&D, EMD Serono, Merck, Sunovion, and Pfizer. Each pledged $250,000 and MLSC was charged

Table 29.2 MLSC 2023 program expenditures[13]

Program	Count	Amount
Capital Infrastructure & Research Equipment	197	$576,000,000
Tax Incentives	436	$203,000,000
Other Grants	194	$51,000,000
Internships & Apprenticeships	6,400	$45,000,000
Company Grants & Loans	126	$40,000,000
STEM Equipment & Supplies	281	$25,000,000
Workforce Capital	35	$23,000,000
Women's Health	43	$16,000,000
STEM Professional Development for Teachers	100	$1,500,000
TOTAL	7,071	$980,000,000

with supervising the program.[14] Without MLSC support, there would likely have been no consortium: In the words of one company executive, "Our legal department would likely not have taken on the work to understand how to form such agreements across the industry participants and with the researchers, and that alone would have made this a non-starter."[15] This is a good example of how, even if something is potentially profitable to firms, it often will not happen without a noncommercial organization to supply its institutional framework.

Similarly, in June 2011, Pfizer opened the Boston Centers for Therapeutic Innovation (CTI), a set of partnerships with academic medical centers in the region. The Boston CTI then established partnerships in New York City and San Francisco, helping connect the Massachusetts cluster to innovations elsewhere.

Both institutions regularly exchanged nonproprietary information and data in both formal and informal meetings. And Sanofi-Aventis used MLSC as an intermediary between the firm and institutions such as the University of Massachusetts Medical Complex in Worcester and the Tufts Veterinary School. When the resulting new drugs were ready for production, Sanofi built a plant in Framingham, MA.[16]

Measuring Success

A 2011 report by real estate developer Jones Lang LaSalle concluded that Massachusetts's life sciences cluster was succeeding. Five years after the start of MLSC, Greater Boston had become the number one region in the nation for biosciences, measured by its research, hospital, and medical employment; its number of science and engineering grad students; its levels of NIH and venture capital funding; life sciences R&D as a percentage of regional GDP; and the square footage of its academic and other nonprofit research facilities.[17] Boston was followed by New York/northern New Jersey at number two, the San Francisco Bay Area, and metro Los Angeles.[18]

By 2019, the state as a whole ranked second in life sciences employees, and the industry continued to expand.[19] (In 2003, Massachusetts had been *sixth*.[20]) By 2020, 32 percent of all US-based biotech IPOs were by Massachusetts-based firms, raising a record $5.8 billion, nearly double 2019's total.[21] In 2022, Boston was rated the number one life sciences hub in the US by the life sciences consulting firm Astrix.[22] Jones Lang's 2022 follow-up report showed that Boston had held onto its ranking despite intense efforts by other regions.[23]

By 2011, 42 states were offering assistance to life science industries.[24] Washington, for example, earmarked $350 million from its portion of the federal tobacco settlement for its Life Sciences Discovery Fund. Pennsylvania created its Life Sciences Greenhouse Initiative in 2001, allocating $100 million to early-stage companies. Michigan created its 21st Century Jobs Fund, a 10-year initiative with twice MLSC's budget. But nearly $800 million of Michigan's unfocused $2 billion effort was going to a variety of industries, including life sciences, alternative energy, homeland security, and advanced automotive materials and manufacturing.[25]

By 2018, all the major drug companies in America had their headquarters, R&D, or manufacturing in Massachusetts. Pfizer, Novartis, Takeda, Sanofi, AstraZeneca, AbbVie, Merck, Biogen, and Bristol-Myers Squibb were all there.[26] (See Figure 29.2.) One firm, Alexion Pharmaceuticals, a rare-disease drug maker, even moved its headquarters from New Haven, CT.[27] Pfizer moved

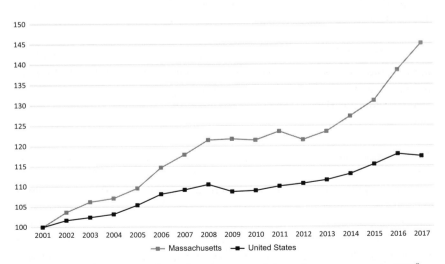

Figure 29.2 Life sciences jobs, indexed to 2001, Massachusetts versus the US[28]

operations to Massachusetts from other locations specifically to participate in the cluster.[29] In 2010, it announced that Cambridge would become one of its worldwide research and development hubs, with half of its current Biotherapeutics R&D employees relocating there. A year later, it announced plans to move another two existing research units, Cardiovascular Medicine and Neuroscience, from Groton, Connecticut, to Cambridge. Takeda, a large Japanese drug maker, announced in 2018 that it would move its US headquarters, with nearly 1,000 employees, from suburban Chicago to Lexington[30]

Moderna, based in Cambridge, MA, is a standout. Beginning in March 2020, it grew from 830 to about 1,500 people to work on its eponymous COVID vaccine. In June 2021, it received a state tax incentive based on its commitment to hire an additional 155 full-time-equivalent employees in 2021 and retain them through 2025.[31]

Did MLSC Make a Difference?

Two questions must be asked. First, did the cluster in the state do better than those in other states, given that these industries were growing nationwide? Yes. It outpaced other states over MLSC's first five years (2007–11), and after 2011, it expanded so rapidly that by 2017, employment was 45 percent higher than in 2001 – growth 2.5 times faster than nationwide. Massachusetts pulled ahead of all of its key rivals: New York, New Jersey, California, Florida, and Texas. New Jersey and California actually *lost* jobs in the sector between 2010 and 2016. Some of these states still had more total jobs, but adjusted for its population (one-fifth that of California, which had biotech clusters in San Francisco, Los Angeles, and San Diego), Massachusetts was ahead.[32]

The second question is more hypothetical: Given its preexisting advantages, would the cluster have been just as successful *without* MLSC? Although, like all counterfactuals, there is no definitive answer, the weight of the evidence strongly indicates that MLSC played a large and critical role in the cluster's success.

In 2013, Northeastern University in Boston was asked by MLSC and the Boston Foundation, a local philanthropy, to conduct an independent evaluation.[33] As of 2012, tax incentives had totaled $57 million. The study's estimate was that these incentives had created just over 2,500 jobs, and given their average $105,000 salary, they were projected to pay $266 million in salaries over the next five years. The study projected that these employees would pay more than $93 million in state income and sales taxes during this period. Assuming the jobs lasted this long, every dollar of tax incentive would thus repay $1.66 to state coffers. Even if one dials back this estimate to reflect the fact that these jobs may not have been 100 percent due to the incentives, the rate of return was still high. And this did not include the multiplier effect of spending by these jobholders at other businesses, or the taxes these businesses and their employees would then pay.

Since the 2012 evaluation, even more jobs have been created: As of 2022, total job commitments by firms receiving tax incentives exceeded 10,000.[34] By 2023, approximately 132,000 people were employed.[35] In several cases, firms have exceeded their hiring targets by factors of four or more. Within the cluster, job growth has varied across industries. For example, from 2001 to 2017, jobs in research, testing, and medical laboratories increased by more than 50 percent, nearly twice as fast as the cluster as a whole.

Were these jobs out of reach for most residents of the state, a concern that has been raised? No. Contrary to their reputation, science-based industries are *not* economically elitist. Life sciences firms, for example, hire at a wide range of skill levels. In addition to PhDs, they hire middle managers, lab technicians, secretaries, manufacturing technicians, and other less educated employees. As of 2022, 43 percent of their staff had an MA, a professional degree, or a PhD. But 41 percent had no more than a BA or BS, and 16 percent had less than a BA.[36] Sixty-five percent worked in scientific roles, while 35 percent were in administrative, business-side, or other positions.[37]

Nationwide, the average salary for life sciences research professionals grew 79 percent from 2001 to 2021, compared to 8 percent for all occupations.[38] As of June 2023, there were approximately 545,000 life science researchers nationwide, with average pay of $124,000.[39] At least two-thirds were paid more than $100,000 a year, and 32 percent were paid more than $150,000.[40]

Survey Evidence

Northeastern University's researchers interviewed industry executives, trade association leaders, and industry scientists.[41] To obtain candid assessments, confidentiality was guaranteed. Each interviewee was asked: Would the life sciences in Massachusetts be much different today if the MLSC had never been created and given long-term funding?

Responses differed by firm size. Leaders of large firms said that due to their wide, largely self-sufficient operations, the MLSC had played at best a minor direct role in their success. But they reported that it had played an immense indirect role: It had been instrumental, as intended, in bringing together an *interactive community* of life sciences institutions. The Center had been critical in helping build a "platform" for the sector and to cultivate a "collaborative gene" among its disparate parts. One Pfizer executive observed that while his company had not received any direct funding from MLSC, the Center had created a "mentality" about the life sciences that had reached even the local level – for example, speeding up local permitting and rezoning.

But the most important lesson from the interviews was an insight into the unique growth pattern of the industry. For mature industries such as autos, jet engines, or financial services, a cluster takes root in a region after a large "anchor" firm opens there. Once it is established, smaller firms are then attracted to serve in its supply chain. For example, once Detroit became home to the Big Three's huge assembly facilities, hundreds of small parts plants and specialized service providers opened nearby. The same was true for jet engines in New England, an industry dominated by Pratt & Whitney in East Hartford, CT, and General Electric in Lynn, MA.[42]

For the life sciences, the reverse is true: The large firms prosper by being close to many small ones. Despite their huge research budgets, even the largest firms do not have the resources to generate more than a handful of major innovations. In an industry that needs a continual pipeline of new innovations to replace expiring patents, large firms therefore monitor fundamental science in university laboratories and translational research in small startups. Then they acquire the startups that are developing potential blockbuster drugs or medical devices. The secret to success is having a "front-row seat" – that is, being plugged in to the local network of small firms.

The key to having this rich supply of small firms is supporting them at *every* stage of their development, not just basic research or final product commercialization, because the binding constraint on their emergence is the Valley of Death (see Chapter 21). In Massachusetts today, small firms emerging from research universities and medical centers can, at the appropriate time, turn to MLSC. The support MLSC provides also helps keep recipient companies in the state. In several cases, when small firms were being lured with tax incentives to relocate elsewhere, MLSC quickly moved to narrow the cost differential and retain them.

MLSC Governance

Governance is critical to MLSC's success. Its board of directors includes state officials, industry CEOs, leaders from academia and medical centers, bioscience researchers, and other nongovernmental leaders with life sciences experience. Funding applications are reviewed by a panel that draws from more than 200 experts, who send their recommendations to the Center's Scientific Advisory Board (SAB), itself dominated by academic researchers, industry scientists, and private-sector venture capital experts.[43]

MLSC insists on specific job creation pledges, and retains the power to claw back tax incentives and other investments if the pledges are not met.

Every year, companies that fail to achieve their job targets are investigated, and the Center notifies the Massachusetts Department of Revenue to recover the value of any award. If a company has met at least 70 percent of its goals, MLSC may allow it another year.[44] MLSC has successfully recouped incentives in the few cases where firms have failed, a precedent that exerts pressure for realistic job creation promises by award seekers.

MLSC's Accelerator Loans appear to have been well targeted: their default rate has been low. During the first years of the program, six firms paid them off *before* they were due, enabling MLSC to create a revolving fund, further expanding its resources.

Having scientists, venture capitalists, and engineers decide which firms to fund, coupled with the clawback provision, has allowed MLSC to insulate itself from corruption and political manipulation. Its application review process resembles those at NSF and NIH: competitive, transparent, and scientifically rigorous. The Pew Center on the States has singled it out as an example of good policy.[45]

MLSC was scheduled to sunset in 2018, but because of its success the state legislature voted to continue it, authorizing it to invest up to $623 million in bond proceeds and tax credits through 2024.[46] Since its 2013 evaluation, it has reorganized its existing programs and added more. Going forward, its credibility and excellent financial results will likely allow it to attract more corporate funding to supplement what it receives from the state.

Other states have created similar initiatives, some with less integrity. In 2013, for example, the Texas legislature temporarily defunded the state's Cancer Prevention and Research Institute following the resignation of its chief scientific officer and many of its grant reviewers in protest of the corruption of independent peer review by political pressure.[47]

Lessons

The key takeaways from the MLSC experience are:

- Regional tax incentives and loan guarantees work best when focused on an industry cluster – that is, neither an entire economy nor a single industry (let alone a single firm) – because this approach nurtures the industry ecosystem that generates growth.
- A portfolio approach, with investments spread out over many companies, is the right way to assist the private sector, as no one company will be certain to succeed.
- A wide range of mutually supporting policies is required to make an industry ecosystem viable. Clusters need everything from skilled labor to smart capital, so deploying only one or two policies is insufficient.

- In science-based industries, expert scientific panels should have major input into granting tax credits, underwriting loans, and awarding grants.
- Job creation is an appropriate, unfakeable metric of results. The concomitant use of clawback provisions is an important motivational tool and a safeguard that preserves legislators' and taxpayers' confidence in the program.
- Incentives should focus on stages in the industry's development process that are *not* adequately supported by either the private sector or existing public-sector institutions. In the life sciences, this largely means crossing the Valley of Death (see Chapter 21).
- When a cluster is healthy, it creates a virtuous cycle of discovery, innovation, investment, and employment. Firms spin off new firms, each discovery becomes the foundation for the next, and experience raises workers' skill levels, attracting still more companies.
- Because clusters are location-specific, having a significant part of their funding at the state level ensures that the citizens reaping the benefits are also bearing the costs. A purely federal approach would tempt states and localities to say yes to projects with poor prospects because "it's free money."
- Results will vary for different segments of a cluster. For example, employment in medical device companies grew only slightly in Massachusetts. Compared to pharma companies, their regulatory hurdles are fewer and less costly, so MLSC's programs did not make as big a difference.
- Advantages gained by programs like MLSC do not endure forever. The Center's 2018 report declared that "competitor states are catching up," and recorded that Massachusetts had failed to match its exceptionally strong 2003–9 outperformance versus other states, though it still outpaced the nation as a whole.[48]
- Workforce development helps assure a pipeline of skilled workers. This attracts new employers to the region, especially if the region's job opportunities and quality of life induce graduates to stay.

The MLSC model described in this chapter is not universally applicable. Industries differ, as do their clusters and growth dynamics. However, analyzing the dynamics of other industries is likely to suggest policies that differ from those of the MLSC but respond to a corresponding set of basic needs.

30 THE UPSTATE NEW YORK SEMICONDUCTOR CLUSTER

"Tech Valley" is a cluster of semiconductor-related companies in Upstate New York, 170 miles north of New York City. The region runs along a north–south belt from Saratoga Springs to the Albany-Schenectady-Troy area, with a penumbra extending south to Westchester County and west to Rochester. Over the past three decades, the region has emerged, due in significant part to proactive state-level policies, as a significant center of the industry's research and manufacturing.

Tech Valley today has an extensive production and innovation ecosystem: chip-making firms, their supply chains and supporting services, skilled workers, universities doing research and training employees, and government agencies. It has major manufacturing plants, such as GlobalFoundries (GF) at Luther Forest and the former IBM plant at East Fishkill now run by ON Semiconductor. It includes the State University of New York at Albany (SUNYA); SUNY Polytechnic, colocated in Oneida County and Albany, especially its College of Nanoscale Science and Engineering (CNSE); and the private Rensselaer Polytechnic Institute (RPI) in Troy.

Since about 1990, Tech Valley has enjoyed remarkable multi-decade, bipartisan state-level policy support, focused on university research programs and incentives for private investments in research and production. Today, firms are attracted by the region's technology ecosystem, by state-level subsidies, and by county and municipal incentives such as tax abatements. Leading multinationals such as IBM and GE have been induced to stay, and new firms such as GF, Wolfspeed, and Micron have come. As a 2020 history observes,

> [W]ith almost all metro areas [in NY state] experiencing double-digit percentage declines decade after decade ... in the 5-year period from 2010 to 2014, during the worst recession since the Great Depression,

the Albany/Troy/Schenectady metro area saw a surge in manufacturing employment of nearly 21%, the only increase of such magnitude recorded by any of the upstate metro areas in nearly half a century.[1]

Tech Valley has created large numbers of high-paying jobs. As of 2015, the average salary for the 3,500 employees at GF was $91,235, and the firm's total annual payroll was around $350 million.[2] ON Semiconductor's payroll was $160 million and, conservatively assuming a $40,000 average salary, the region's academic research complex paid out $160 million.[3] These dollars cycled through local economies, creating a jobs- and tax-revenue multiplier effect that benefited local residents outside the industry.

From 2011 to 2016, GF paid more than $77 million in taxes to the towns of Malta and Stillwater, combined population 23,000.[4] Under an in-lieu-of-taxes agreement, more than $49 million went to the Malta and Ballston Spa School Districts, plus money for their fire departments, their libraries, and other uses.[5] Communities around Luther Forest have also benefited from improvements to highways, water systems, sewage systems, the electricity grid, and natural gas supply made to support the GF plant.

Tech Valley thus shows what state-level, innovation-based industrial policies can accomplish. Unfortunately, large-scale, systematic support of its foreign competitors by their national governments, compared to decades of patchy federal assistance, today places its achievements at risk. The 2022 CHIPS Act was a major step toward ending this policy deficit, but the outcome is not yet known.

The Starting Point

The region has been a technology center since the nineteenth century. RPI was then the country's leading engineering school and the region hosted firms such as Gurley Precision Instruments, Burden Iron Works, and the huge federal Watervliet Arsenal that still makes high-tech artillery today. It thus made sense for General Electric to move its headquarters (since relocated elsewhere, though leaving important facilities behind) to Schenectady in 1892, eventually employing 45,000 in the region.

But RPI never developed the graduate programs and externally funded research that built up rivals like Caltech and MIT. While MIT got more than $100 million in federal contracts during World War II, RPI got a mere $200,000 and failed to blossom into a major research center after the war.[6]

In the postwar era, the region hosted several large technology-based firms, including IBM, GE, and Kodak. From 1963 to 2015, IBM, headquartered in a suburb of New York City, made semiconductors at East Fishkill, and maintained major research facilities in the southern part of the region.

But GE moved its headquarters out of the region in 1974. And by the 1990s, major firms such as Xerox, Bausch & Lomb, Kodak, and IBM were cutting jobs all over the state, including in Tech Valley. Like the rest of the Rustbelt, the region was losing jobs to the Sunbelt. Technological evolution had eroded its economic base: Kodak had failed to adapt to digital photography, IBM missed the PC revolution, and Xerox failed in small copiers and gave away pathbreaking research in computers. In 2014, IBM almost moved all its manufacturing out of the state.

With jobs increasingly scarce, young people were voting with their feet. Between 1995 and 1997 alone, Upstate New York lost nearly 170,000 people.[7] Employers were complaining that its public education systems were producing students without satisfactory business or manufacturing skills.[8] Fewer than a third of RPI's graduates remained in the state, let alone the region. The longer the region's decline continued, the less attractive it would be to investors, with a deteriorating quality of life, weakening business infrastructure, and taxes rising as its economic base shrank.

On the other hand, legacy firms such as IBM and GE were powerful advocates for improvements to education in the region and provided state policymakers with valuable advice about the competition the state faced in attracting high-tech employers.[9] The region was strategically located, with good access to NYC, Boston, and Montreal, good highway, rail and river transportation, and a recently renovated airport. Unlike coastal tech centers such as Silicon Valley and Greater Boston, it had affordable housing for potential employees. For people who didn't mind cold winters, it had a high quality of life. And New York was one of the wealthiest states, allowing it to offer sizable inducements for companies and nonprofit institutions.

The Proactive Cluster Strategy

Organized industrial policy to build the cluster began in the early 1960s when an Advisory Council for the Advancement of Industrial Research and Development was appointed by Republican governor Nelson Rockefeller. The Council sought direction from Stanford's visionary provost and pioneer of Stanford Industrial Park, Frederick E. Terman. Terman had elevated Stanford's electrical engineering department to world-class status and forged the academic, industrial, and government ties that launched Silicon Valley. The Terman meetings sought to assess whether this model could be replicated in New York.[10] Once the governor was convinced that it could, state investments in academic research infrastructure followed. Despite opposition from private institutions, Rockefeller began to build SUNY into a major research complex with an economic development mandate. Through a series of steps begun in

1962, SUNY Albany was upgraded from a small teachers' college to a full-fledged research university.

RPI's 1976–84 president, George Low, former manager of NASA's Apollo Spacecraft Program Office, had a vision of making RPI a second Stanford, linking high-tech businesses with its research. RPI opened a Center for Interactive Computer Graphics, a Center for Manufacturing Productivity and Technology Transfer, and a Center for Integrated Electronics, all intended to develop technology in cooperation with private firms.[11] In 1980, RPI set up a business incubator, a relatively new idea at the time, providing management assistance and skills training to small firms and startups. In 1981, Low founded Rensselaer Technology Park.[12] Working with GE's CEO Jack Welch and other business leaders, he also developed a Center for Industrial Innovation that opened in 1987. The state's Urban Development Corporation helped fund its facilities.

The initial results were disappointing. In 1983, RPI lost its bid to host the Microelectronics and Computer Technology Corporation, a major industry research consortium, to Austin, Texas. Four years later, it also lost (again to Austin) its bid to host the research consortium Sematech (Chapter 26). RPI's technology park struggled. By 1989, it had only 35 companies, employing about 1,000 people, better than nothing but not a nascent Silicon Valley.[13]

But the region's leaders did not give up. In 1986, New York State launched its Empire Zone program, which, although not specifically aimed at the chip companies, gave them significant tax credits and other benefits during Tech Valley's formative years.[14] In 1988, the Semiconductor Research Corporation and Sematech designated RPI as a Center of Excellence, with SUNYA as a specialist affiliate. RPI then collaborated with SUNYA on thin film materials and process technologies.[15]

By the late 1980s, SUNYA was becoming a player in semiconductor research. In 1993, Democratic governor Mario Cuomo directed funding of $1 million a year for 10 years toward creation of a Center for Advanced Thin Film Technology at SUNYA.[16] The Center soon attracted $7 million a year in grants and equipment from industry. New corporate deals were struck after it developed a process for depositing high-purity metals on silicon wafers.[17] By 1995, SUNYA was ready to launch its Center for Environmental Sciences and Technology Management (CESTM). Its mission was to develop technology, commercialize it, and help companies with their manufacturing.[18]

RPI's contributions to the region continued, especially under the leadership of President Shirley Ann Jackson beginning in 1999. In RPI's own words, "Among other accomplishments, President Jackson championed The

Rensselaer Plan and The Rensselaer Plan 2024 to increase investments in research, faculty, facilities, and student life; oversaw the hiring of more than 450 new faculty members; strengthened the endowment, which has reached a record of more than $1 billion."[19] In 2001, she secured an anonymous $360 million donation, expanded RPI's faculty, and launched a Center for Nanotech Studies supported by IBM, Kodak, Philip Morris, local composites maker Albany International, and several federal agencies.[20] In 2006, RPI established its Computational Center for Nanotechnology Innovations (now the Center for Computational Innovations) featuring IBM's $100 million "Blue Gene" supercomputer, then the most powerful at any university. The cost was shared by IBM, NY State, RPI, and other industry partners.[21]

State and Federal Investments

As late as 2000, Tech Valley did not seem a success. Commentators were even writing its obituary as a cautionary tale of failed regional industrial policy.[22] Even firms with strong roots in the region like IBM and GE were expanding their R&D elsewhere.[23] But clusters take a long time to create, and the foundations were being laid.

Political issues arose. For the state government, even geographically defining the cluster was controversial. Regional resentments were a given, with Rochester, 200 miles to the west and already a center for optics and electronics, feeling left out. There was pushback in the legislature about funding the private RPI as opposed to a public institution. As a compromise to resolve diverse political tensions, the state *also* supported biotech at SUNY Stony Brook on Long Island, optics at the (private) University of Rochester, and telecom at Brooklyn's (public) Polytechnic University.

Over 11 crucial years between 1995 and 2006, the region's development policy was driven by a bipartisan alliance between Republican governor George Pataki (in office 1995–2006), Republican State Senate Majority Leader Joseph Bruno (1994–2008), and Democratic Assembly Speaker Sheldon Silver (1994–2015).[24] They and other state political leaders consistently supported innovation-based economic development. There were also efforts by regional development institutions, such as the Capital Region Chamber of Commerce, the Saratoga Economic Development Corporation, and the Rensselaer County Regional Chamber of Commerce, to win local support for high-tech manufacturing.

Making Tech Valley a success required huge public and private investments. In 2013, New York State's public Empire State Development Corporation estimated that the state's total investment of $1.3 billion had attracted $20 billion in private investment.[25] Municipalities made tax concessions to attract facilities. Nonprofits such as the Saratoga County Prosperity Partnership (now defunct) worked with the public and private sectors to create shovel-ready sites for semiconductor fabs. The federal government did not target Tech Valley specifically, but its numerous programs supporting science and technology research funded much of the work that took place there.[26]

Growing Technical Sophistication

In 2001, a pilot production line designed to test production processes for 300mm semiconductor wafers was established at CESTM. The 300mm size, larger than the prevailing 200mm, significantly reduced production costs, and establishing a 150mm production line at Sematech's facility in Austin a decade before had brought that city spectacular economic growth. SUNYA argued that the $150 million facility would closely support IBM's manufacturing and enable SUNYA to compete with universities such as MIT and Stanford. In April 2001, IBM announced it would commit $100 million to the project, and New York State added $50 million.[27]

Because it reduced the risks and costs of new product development, this pilot production line was SUNYA's trump card for developing closer ties with semiconductor manufacturers.[28] Running a production batch on a pilot line can reveal defects in a chip's design or production process, allowing retooling before production at scale.[29] SUNYA had the world's *only* 300 mm fab available for collaborative applied research. It had equipment that would be extremely expensive for any one firm to buy: One cutting-edge lithography tool, for example, cost $65 million.[30]

In his 2004 State of the State Address, Governor Pataki announced the formation of the College of Nanoscale Sciences and Engineering (CNSE) at SUNY Polytechnic. CNSE was designed to be a neutral "research Switzerland" where companies could work together on precompetitive research, sharing the costs and the results.[31] In 2005, the Center for Semiconductor Research, a multiphase cooperative program, was established at CNSE, hailed as the "world's only university-based R&D center which integrates device design, fabrication, modeling, testing, and pilot manufacturing."[32] It was one part of a $2.7 billion research operation involving IBM, Sony, AMD, Infineon (Germany), Samsung, Chartered Semiconductor (Singapore), and Toshiba. New York gave the project $225 million for equipment.

CNSE has since fostered university–industry collaborations extraordinary for their scale, including world-class firms such as IBM, Tokyo Electron, Applied Materials, ASML, AMD, and GlobalFoundries. In 2008, CNSE and IBM reached a $1.6 billion agreement that included creation of a 675-employee facility for R&D on semiconductor packaging that CNSE would own and operate.[33]

In 2005, the Dutch firm ASML, the *sole* supplier of the world's most advanced semiconductor manufacturing equipment, invested $325 million at Albany NanoTech to establish with IBM its first R&D center outside Europe.[34] IBM, Applied Materials, and Tokyo Electron were given access to new clean rooms at the complex to conduct research on 32 and 22nm semiconductors.[35] ASML had itself been aided by regional cluster strategy, namely the Interuniversity Microelectronics Centre (IMEC), a research center in Leuven, Belgium, whose $896 million annual budget comes from its regional government, EU grants, and contract research for industry.

The Semiconductor Industry Embraces Tech Valley

In 2001, Sematech unveiled plans for a $400 million facility next to SUNYA's pilot fab. Its function was to research extreme ultraviolet light (EUV) lithography, the next step in etching ever-smaller circuits.[36] By 2006, it was the world's leading facility for this purpose.[37] This marked the beginning of a phased move by Sematech, which in 2006 announced that it would relocate its headquarters from Austin to Albany. It directly created 450 jobs, invested $300 million in cash and in-kind contributions, and added two board members from New York, one from SUNY Albany and the other from CNSE's facilities management corporation.[38] New York State contributed $300 million.[39] Sematech's complex soon housed more than 1,600 people, and in 2010 the bulk of its remaining operations were moved there. As its CEO Dan Armbrust explained, "There are enough entities investing here that we have to be here too."[40]

In 2006, the Semiconductor Industry Association and the Semiconductor Research Corporation (a consortium of more than 25 private firms and government agencies) launched two nanotechnology institutes. One was in Silicon Valley and the other was in Albany and managed by CNSE. This Institute for Nanoelectronics Discovery and Exploration (INDEX) focused on developing nanomaterials, fabrication technologies, nanochip designs, and architectural integration schemes for future designs. INDEX partnered with researchers from Harvard, Yale, RPI, MIT, Georgia Tech, and Purdue – plus IBM, AMD, Intel, Texas Instruments, Micron, and Freescale. New York State contributed $80 million of the $435 million cost.[41]

When the global recession of 2008 triggered a worldwide slump in the semiconductor business, Democratic governor David Paterson committed $140 million to keep IBM in the state, avert layoffs, and create 1,000 new jobs. IBM spent $1 billion upgrading its East Fishkill plant, put $375 million into expanding its Albany NanoTech research, and created 675 jobs at a new R&D center nearby for the semiconductor packaging that surrounds and protects the delicate chips.[42]

But the state's efforts had not yet earned the big prize that could anchor the entire cluster: a major plant using technology at or close to the global state of the art. The state made several attempts. In 2003, Texas Instruments was sufficiently impressed to consider a site at Luther Forest, but ultimately chose Texas. In 2005, Intel announced that a $3 billion facility New York had courted would go to Arizona. In 2006, Samsung, despite serious efforts, went to Austin, where it already had a plant. That same year, AMD announced that a $2.5 billion facility for which New York had bid would go to Dresden, Germany.[43]

GlobalFoundries Joins Tech Valley

Beginning in 2003, AMD, for years leader Intel's main American rival in microprocessors, had collaborated with IBM on semiconductor design at East Fishkill, and had plans to use RPI's supercomputer. It moved staff to Tech Valley from Dresden in 2005.[44] As of early 2006, it was booming, with its profits rising and its market share expanding. So the firm announced plans for a new 300 mm fab – at a site yet to be determined. Governor Pataki, joined by the entire state and regional economic development machine, offered the firm inducements totaling $1.2 billion. The package consisted of $650 million in tax credits and Empire Zone incentives, a $500 million subsidy for buildings and equipment, and $150 million for R&D – all subject to clawback if the firm did not keep its end of the bargain.

Unfortunately, AMD ran into the financial volatility that semiconductor manufacturing, with its high capital costs, evolving technology, and sharp competition, suffers from. In the fourth quarter of 2007, it reported a loss of $574 million due to a price war with Intel and AMD's expensive takeover of graphics-processor manufacturer ATI. its stock fell by 60 percent and rumors of a takeover were rife.[45] Although the firm was borrowing heavily to finance an upgrade to its Dresden facilities, when its CEO was asked in July 2007 whether the Luther Forest project might have to be abandoned, he replied, "Not at all."[46]

But after a second-quarter loss of $1.2 billion in 2008, AMD reversed itself and sold its entire manufacturing division, ultimately under the name of GlobalFoundries (GF), to the sovereign wealth fund of Abu Dhabi, an emirate of the United Arab Emirates. (For sovereign wealth funds, see Chapter 3.) GF's acquirer committed to investing $8.1 billion to upgrade two of its existing fabs in Dresden and build a new $4.2 billion fab at Luther Forest.[47] Luther Forest – the largest single private industrial investment in the history of New York State – was moving forward, but with a company owned and controlled by an Arab potentate.[48]

Luther Forest's 2009 groundbreaking was followed by site clearance, building construction, and installation of the production machinery. This final step was extremely complex, due to the precision of the manufacturing process and the need for dust-free clean rooms. In mid-2010, GF contracted the German firm M+W to install more than $3 billion worth of hardware from Germany, Israel, Japan, the Netherlands, and the US.

The new fab brought an influx of suppliers, with locally stocked spare parts and engineers on call. The leading semiconductor manufacturing equipment maker Tokyo Electron took space nearby. Its American rivals Axcelis Technologies and Applied Materials also came. The Swiss logistics firm Panalpina opened a facility. KLA-Tencor, a developer of process-control systems, arrived, later forming a manufacturing partnership with the RPI startup PBC Tech. Vacuum pump supplier Sumitomo Cryogenic arrived, as did Beard Integrated Systems, a Texas firm providing specialized piping. PeroxyChem, which was shipping in three truckloads of hydrogen peroxide a day from Texas, set up a $30 million plant.

GlobalFoundries Thrives at Luther Forest

At first, GF thrived at Luther Forest, producing its first chips for IBM (at 32nm) in December 2011 even though the plant was not fully complete. By the end of the next year it was serving multiple customers and preparing to manufacture 20nm and 14nm chips for smartphones and tablets.[49] In 2010, GF applied to the Town of Malta to expand its clean room from 210,000 to 300,000 square feet, bringing its total investment to more than $6 billion. The firm then unveiled plans for another building, adjacent to its fab, to be the administrative hub for a second fab at least as large as the first. This would double employment at the site to 3,000.[50] In 2012, GF submitted plans for a $2 billion Technology Development Center the size of two city blocks. This would be used for testing and perfecting the products of its research with IBM at CNSE. The plan was swiftly approved by the municipality and construction, starting with a 12-foot-thick concrete foundation to dampen vibrations, began in early 2013.

In 2014, GF bought IBM's old plant at East Fishkill, and in 2019 sold it to ON Semiconductor. It remains a going concern today. If GF had not already been in the region, it probably would have closed, a major loss.

GF's use of its Luther Forest complex evolved with its strategies. In 2015, it decided to use the complex more for manufacturing and less for research.[51] But its research investments elsewhere in the region continued to grow. In 2016, GF and CNSE allocated $500 million over five years to create an Advanced Patterning and Productivity Center.[52] This was intended to speed the introduction of next-generation EUV lithography into its manufacturing and support eventual production of 7nm chips there.[53]

In 2016, GF announced billions in investment to develop the technology for manufacturing at 7nm; in 2017, it announced that it had perfected same.[54] That same year, an alliance of SUNY Poly, GF, and Samsung reported a breakthrough in *5nm* technology, with production slated for mid-2018.[55] GF also increased its 14nm production capacity at Luther Forest, Dresden, Singapore, and Chengdu, China. Tech Valley thus appeared to be on track to host one of the world's most advanced semiconductor plants – in fact one of the most sophisticated manufacturing facilities of any kind ever built.

GlobalFoundries Stumbles

In 2018, GF unexpectedly announced that it was putting its 7nm plans on indefinite hold.[56] The firm had been on track for production in the fourth quarter and its CTO stressed that the decision was not based on technical problems but on "careful consideration of business opportunities the company had with its [7nm] platform as well as financial concerns."[57] GF's CEO said that most of its customers did not plan to buy 7nm chips in 2018 and that "when we look out to 2022, two-thirds of the foundry market will be in nodes at 12nm and above, so it's not like we are conceding a big part of this market."[58]

Before its decision to drop 7nm, GF had made a sustained effort to secure support from Washington, notably from the Defense Department, to make going ahead viable. Although there was growing recognition at DOD of the need for US-located semiconductor manufacturing, it did not offer help, even though it had once worked to keep American chip manufacturing at the leading edge (see Chapter 26).

GF's pivot was a setback to its reputation for cutting-edge technology. The cancellation undermined SUNY Poly's research efforts, because 7nm would have been the first class of chips using the EUV lithography on which CNSE's researchers had expended so much effort. Success would have been a huge technological and economic vindication. IBM, which had paid GF $1.5 billion in 2015 to take over its loss-making chip business and become its sole chip supplier, sued GF for abandoning its plans.[59]

Short-term job losses – only about 500 – were not the problem. GF retained significant vacant floor space in its current fab to expand production at the larger nodes. The firm has since secured the permits required to build a second fab at 14nm and 12nm. And in 2021, it announced the relocation of its headquarters to Malta from Santa Clara, California. But GF's commitment to staying on the cutting edge was gone.

Tech Valley's Future

In 2022, Wolfspeed, maker of *two-thirds* of the world's silicon carbide chips for power electronics and EVs, opened a $1 billion plant in Utica.[60] Incented by the CHIPS Act, Micron that year announced a $100 billion investment over 20 years for a megafab to make leading edge memory chips in Clay, outcompeting Austin.[61] Academic institutions involved in this project included Syracuse University, the University of Rochester, Rochester Institute of Technology, and Clarkson University. (Both locations were outside Tech Valley proper but nearby.) In 2024, GF announced it would indeed build its second fab nearby, adding to its existing workforce, now more than 3,000.[62]

In late 2023, Senate Majority Leader Charles Schumer (D-NY) and Democratic governor Kathy Hochul announced that TTM Technologies would invest up to $130 million in Dewitt New York to make circuit boards for military and security purposes.[63] Senator Schumer also obtained from Korean president Yoon Suk Yeol a commitment for an R&D partnership between the Korean Institute for Advanced Science and Technology (see Chapter 6) and the New York Center for Research, Economic Advancement, Technology, Engineering, and Science at the Albany NanoTech Complex.[64]

In December 2023, New York State announced a $1 billion investment to expand NanoTech, including a $500 million state-of-the-art clean room. IBM, Micron Technology, Applied Materials, and Tokyo Electron said they would put in $9 billion. The money would also be used to purchase next-generation semiconductor manufacturing equipment from ASML. These investments helped induce the Defense Department to designate the region one of its eight regional Microelectronics Commons Hubs, winning $40 million for a group of universities and tech firms named the Northeast Regional Defense Technology Hub.[65]

But Tech Valley still faces significant challenges. It has not yet developed a full-fledged ecosystem that generates the startups required to sustain growth. Although some have emerged from SUNY Poly and RPI, the region has retained only a limited number of new firms. Some of the most promising have left for regions with even stronger tech clusters.

The region remains dependent upon a few firms, above all GF. The cluster's industry faces subsidized foreign competitors, rapid shifts in demand and supply, upheavals due to corporate decisions, and relentless and extremely capital-intensive technological change. Other electronics clusters, such as Silicon Glen in Scotland, which at one time built 30 percent of Europe's PCs, have bloomed and then faded as technology and markets shifted.[66] Tech Valley still lacks the deep bench of truly exceptional talent that draws firms to places like Silicon Valley.

CNSE is today considered one of the world's foremost centers of semi-conductor nanotechnology, turning out highly regarded graduates.[67] It continues to add facilities and expertise. As of 2024, Albany was a leading contender for the National Semiconductor Technology Center funded by the CHIPS Act.[68] But despite its excellence, CNSE is a relatively small, narrowly specialized anchor for an entire regional cluster. It is not even remotely comparable to full-scale technology universities such as Stanford and MIT that excel in multiple disciplines and their underlying science. RPI has not managed to become a top engineering school, ranking only fifty-first nationally as of 2023.[69] (Such institution-building is not impossible: Since 1970, Georgia Tech has risen from obscurity to eighth.)

Above all, a region that depends on incentives to attract firms lacks the accumulated, interlocking advantages that define a true cluster. As two analysts have put it, "[T]he key question is what will happen not if, but when, another jurisdiction offers a combination of major incentives, including a more stable and predictable public policy and infrastructural environment. In that case, the question arises as to whether GlobalFoundries would build its next fab in New York at all."[70]

On the positive side, state-level political commitment has survived political turnover. In 2016, Governor Andrew Cuomo moved quickly to reinforce CNSE following a management scandal in which SUNY Poly's president Alain Kaloyeros was sent to prison for three and a half years for alleged bid rigging. (His conviction, the product of overreach by a politically ambitious prosecutor, was later overturned by the US Supreme Court.) The Empire State Development Corporation, the umbrella organization for the state's two main economic development public-benefit corporations, continues to provide significant incentives for new investment.

Foreign Support for the Chip Industry

Between Sematech in the 1980s and the CHIPS Act of 2022, the federal government provided little direct support for American semiconductor manufacturing. But without it, US makers of leading-edge chips cannot compete with foreign national champions supported by all-of-government industrial policies, including huge financial support. State-level assistance, even the large amounts New York provides to GF, cannot match either the scale of potential federal support or its ability to deploy other policy tools, such as tariffs.

A 2020 analysis by the Boston Consulting Group and the Semiconductor Industry Association compared foreign and American support for semiconductor fabrication over a fab's first 10 years of operation. The US ranked *last* behind China, Israel, Taiwan, South Korea, Singapore, and Japan.[71] The study estimated total cost of ownership of a new fab to be about 30 percent more than in Singapore, South Korea, and Taiwan, and 37–50 percent more than in China. Subsidies and other incentives were major factors, as were America's lengthy periods for permitting and environmental compliance.[72] A Commerce Department report later seconded these estimates.[73]

Other nations have taken the industry's value and needs far more seriously. For example, Taiwan proactively nurtured its semiconductor industry for decades (see Chapter 23). Today, it subsidizes new fabs up to 50 percent of their land costs, 45 percent of their construction costs, and 25 percent of their equipment costs.[74] In 2020, it pledged $335 million over seven years to subsidize up to *half* the cost to foreign companies of opening chip R&D facilities in Taiwan.[75] And in 2022 it raised its R&D tax credit from 15 to 25 percent.[76]

In 2021, South Korea announced semiconductor investments totaling $451 billion over the coming decade. These included direct government support, tax incentives, and private sector investments.[77] Samsung plans to begin fabricating 2nm chips in South Korea in 2025 and progress to the 1.4nm (!) node in 2027 (see Chapter 6 for more on Korean industrial policy).[78]

From 2014 to 2020, China invested an estimated $179 billion in its chip industry. As of 2022, it was readying another $143 billion, but the fund was later put on hold due to concerns about ineffective and corrupt investments (See Chapter 7).[79]

Even Europe, traditionally a laggard in semiconductors, has been getting serious. Brussels in 2023 approved an EU-wide Chips Act, promising $47 billion to increase semiconductor production and aiming to raise the EU's share of global output from 10 to 20 percent by 2030.[80]

These foreign incentives have taken their toll: America's share of global chip production fell from 37 percent in 1990 to 12 percent in 2021.[81] While the US-*owned* share was 47 percent in 2019, far more than any other country, 58 percent of the production of US-headquartered firms was overseas.[82] Seventy-five percent of global semiconductor fabrication now takes place in East Asia.[83] As of 2024, only Korea's Samsung and Taiwan's TSMC can make the most advanced chips, at 7nm, 5nm, and 3nm.

Hopes for an American Revival

After GF abandoned 7nm, Intel was the only American company making chips at that node, which it called 10nm.[84] And it was in trouble. Once the unquestioned global leader, it had prioritized short-term profit for years. As a result, it had fallen behind technologically, lost market share to

AMD, and lost Apple's Mac business to the M-series chips Apple designed for itself and had manufactured by TSMC.[85] Intel was not even in the competition to reach 3nm or 2nm. Highlighting how far behind it was, Intel in 2021 began testing a 3nm chip design *for manufacturing by TSMC*.[86]

But in 2021, Intel replaced CEO Bob Swan with Pat Gelsinger. Swan was an MBA who had come up through the finance side of the company; Gelsinger's roots were in engineering. This signaled a return to a technology-driven, as opposed to a finance-driven, corporate strategy. After overcoming management and technical challenges, Intel finally brought its "Ice Lake" 10nm CPU to market in 2021, several years late. It was designed in Haifa, Israel and manufactured at Kiryat Gat, Israel and Chandler, Arizona. Gelsinger then announced that the firm would rededicate itself to leading-edge production and build two new fabs on its Arizona campus. It also announced plans to go into the foundry business making chips for other firms. While onshore capacity at the most advanced nodes was welcomed by chip design firms, there was skepticism whether they would entrust their designs to a competitor, as Intel was also in the design space.

State-of-the-art semiconductor manufacturing may return to the US due to investments by American and foreign-based companies induced by the CHIPS Act. In 2024, despite ongoing budget disputes, the Biden administration announced $8.5 billion in grants and $11 billion in loans for Intel to build a new fab and expand others. The White House claimed this funding had also motivated Intel to invest an additional $100 billion in facilities in Ohio, New Mexico, and Oregon.[87]

The Act is a major advance, but the aid it provides, while sizeable, is dwarfed by that provided by Taiwan, Korea, and China. Going forward, for the US to succeed, Washington will have to deal with not only these foreign subsidies, but also with the headwinds created by dollar overvaluation and the mercantilist trade policies of these countries. (See Chapter 4 about the dollar and their respective country chapters about the mercantilism.)

RECOMMENDATIONS
An Industrial Policy for the United States

America has begun its return to industrial policy. The Bipartisan Infrastructure Act, the Inflation Reduction Act, and the CHIPS and Science Act, passed in late 2021 and 2022, with their related executive orders, were together the largest civilian industrial policy initiative since the Depression. Equally important is that they were explicitly described *as* industrial policy by the Biden administration and their supporters in both parties.

But these valuable first steps are not enough. The need now is to make industrial policy comprehensive, coherent, institutionalized, and a fixture of America's policy consensus. It will need to be flexible enough to adapt to changing technologies, markets, and competitor country policies. The US needs not just new laws, but new standing authorities with the ability to maneuver and shift gears when needed. And advocates of industrial policy must be prepared to fight off the pressures to abandon it that will inevitably appear when the first project failure occurs, or when early success dispels the sense of crisis that jolted the country out of its laissez-faire illusions.

America's industrial policy should seek to establish or retain leading positions in almost all *advantageous* industries, as we defined this term in Chapters 1 and 2. This means positions of scale, technological sophistication, and sustained profitability matching or exceeding those of the best foreign competitors. America has sufficiently large markets, reserves of capital, science and technology skills, and business capabilities for this to be a realistic goal.

The US needs oligopoly, not monopoly, positions in these industries, so there will be room in them for friends and allies. America should, so far as practical, decouple its economy from that of China and other problematic nations in advantageous and otherwise economically, technologically, or militarily critical industries. Our goal should be to stay ahead of geopolitical adversaries in industries important to national security, at least equal in others, and to have reliable supply chains in both.

The industrial policies America needs fall into three broad categories: *trade, technology development*, and *manufacturing at scale*. The US should use tools such as tariffs and capital controls to protect key industries and balance its overall trade (see Chapter 4). It should fund basic and applied R&D at a percentage of GDP equal to or higher than rivals (see Chapter 20). And it should support innovation through *all* the steps from basic science to production at scale (see Chapters 21 and 22).

Fitting America's Political System

Every nation's industrial policy must work within and exploit the advantages of its political culture and institutions (see Chapters 5 to 9). In the US, political power is widely dispersed between the president, the courts, and Congress, within Congress itself, and between the states and the federal government. Social solidarity is weak due to regional, cultural, ethnic, and political diversity. There are few limits on lobbying by interest groups, and thus on their influence on policy. Compared to most nations, we place few legal or social constraints on the freedom of individuals and firms to act in their own self-interest without regard to the effects on society at large.

America's industrial policymaking and its implementation will thus never be as smooth as, say, Japan's, with its powerful drive for consensus, strong social solidarity, and deference to elite government bureaucrats (see Chapter 5). There will never be a single official, agency, or committee, no matter how well qualified or broadly representative, able to prescribe an overall US industrial policy. Policies will therefore not come from top-down fiat – although strong, consistent presidential support will be a sine qua non for success. Instead, policies from trade to technology to education will need to be developed through our existing multiplayer political process. This book is therefore emphatically *not* a call for the creation of a centrally directed and prescriptive US industrial policy, for Tokyo-on-the-Potomac.

That said, a corps of civil servants dedicated to industrial policy will be needed for day-to-day administration. It will also be needed to maintain institutional memory and to track ongoing changes in technologies, US and foreign supply chains, the strategies of other governments, and the competitive positions of US and foreign companies. As institutional design scholar Ganesh Sitaraman has said, "This is not work that can be done on an occasional basis by politically appointed advisors who serve for a couple of years before their next gig."[1] Industrial policy is no different in this respect from other major governmental missions such as defense, environmental protection, transportation, or energy.

Ideally, to ensure that the disparate elements of industrial policy work in concert, these civil servants should work in a single agency. Accordingly, while America does not need an industrial policy "czar," it should consolidate many of the existing offices whose functions will require coordination. Success otherwise would require the White House to continuously enforce coordination among agencies now structured to pursue their missions independently. This will be inevitable during the early stages of America's embrace of comprehensive industrial policy, but over time, for industrial policy to have staying power and efficiency, it should be institutionalized through structural reforms like those discussed in this chapter.

Industrial policy will require a shift of mentality at the federal, state, and local levels. The required consensus will – and should – be broad, leaving room for partisan differences, debate about specifics, and enough skepticism to force industrial policy's advocates to give valid arguments and enable the rejection of bad ideas. But it should be grounded in a shared understanding of why proactive industrial policy is desirable, what its major elements and tools are, and why they should be coordinated.

America's industrial policy will not need to be perfect. This is no different from any other area of policymaking or business. Some incoherence and failure are unavoidable in a complex, uncertain, politicized world, but *tolerable if the benefits outweigh the costs.*

General Guidelines for Industrial Policy

- Industries should be supported not only by economy-wide policies, but also by policies tailored to their specific needs. For example, hard-science-intensive manufacturing, such as new materials, advanced semiconductors, renewable energy systems, and large aircraft, requires more capital than software development. (See Chapters 25 to 28.)
- Programs should be lodged at the appropriate levels (sometimes more than one) of government. For example, nurturing internationally competitive industry clusters requires the money and policy authority of a national government.
- Programs should be assigned to agencies with the technical skill, underlying inclination, and statutory missions to execute them. (See Chapter 23 for examples.)
- To ensure buy-in and commitment, funding responsibility should be split among the parties benefiting from the program whenever possible. Often these parties will be the federal government, private industry, a state, and a region or municipality. State and local commitment should be important criteria for determining where place-specific federally funded programs are sited.

- Programs should be held accountable for their performance at the aggregate level, but insulated from political interference at the detail level. Some projects of even the best programs will fail, so programs should be judged by the success of their overall portfolios. (E.g., the 2011 uproar over Solyndra's failure was a mistake.)
- Time scales should be appropriate. Regional clusters take decades to become self-sustaining and internationally competitive. Development projects applying existing technologies to specific commercial uses sometimes take only weeks. A sense of urgency has helped agencies like DARPA (see Chapter 23), but a long-term view is essential for agencies like NSF (see Chapter 20).
- There should be involvement of and codirection by the private sector for projects involving technologies close to or already at the stage of commercialization (see Chapters 29 and 30). The private sector has the expertise and the right incentives; the government generally does not.
- Programs should have structured protocols with consistent, albeit evolving criteria for selecting, modifying, and continuing projects. For pure science and science-intensive technology development (i.e., not existing-technology deployment), peer review should be used. Programs should draw on business and technical experts from both inside and outside government.
- Which initially promising technologies will pan out is inherently uncertain for radical innovations, so multiple options should be supported. This process should be disciplined by tools, such as required performance levels, to enable early culling of failing approaches.
- The "eternal life" problem of government programs should be preempted by building in termination dates or periodic reauthorization reviews. But these reviews should not be so frequent as to deprive programs of the stability needed for long-term investments and credible commitments from the private sector. There should be funding for effectiveness assessments at reauthorization.
- There should be mechanisms for terminating failing programs. For programs (like the supersonic airliner in Chapter 19) where correct criteria of success were established at the outset, government should stick to them. Conversely, programs (the breeder reactor in the same chapter) should *not* be terminated on inappropriate grounds such as a failure of precompetitive technologies to turn a profit, a failure to hit budgetary estimates in the face of innate scientific and technological uncertainty, or a failure to consider indirect benefits such as environmental protection.
- Audit and oversight to reduce both hard and soft corruption should be well funded because the close collaboration between government and business required for many industrial policies to work increases the risk of political capture by the industries involved.

What the President Should Do

Effective industrial policy will require coordination of many executive branch agencies and the congressional committees overseeing them. The only government official with the electoral mandate, legal authority, and broad purview to lead this effort is the president. Strong, consistent presidential commitment will thus be essential.

All relevant White House staff, cabinet secretaries, agency heads, and members of the Council of Economic Advisors should be chosen, in part, for their commitment to industrial policy as a core part of the administration's economic program, and have the skills and experience to contribute.

The president should establish the following structures and policies:

- A White House Industrial Policy Council (IPC) with direct access to the president, modeled on and with status equal to the National Security Council (NSC) and the National Economic Council (NEC). It would coordinate the work of the executive branch agencies while consulting with congressional leaders of both parties.
- High-level participation in the IPC by the White House Office of Science and Technology Policy, the Council of Economic Advisors, and the Council on Environmental Quality, to ensure that all relevant administration voices are heard and that the IPC's policy choices are understood and accepted.
- The IPC's membership should include the secretaries of the Treasury, Commerce, Defense, Energy, Labor, and Education; the US Trade Representative; the directors of National Intelligence, the National Science Foundation, the National Institutes of Health, the National Institute of Standards and Technologies (NIST), and the White House Office of Science and Technology Policy (who is often also the assistant to the president for science and technology); and the chairs of the Council on Environmental Quality and the Council of Economic Advisors.
- IPC staff should have experience and expertise in the diverse policy areas that require coordination, including manufacturing, commercial lending, and venture capital. But to reduce the risk of capture by private-sector interests, the IPC's director should *not* come from the business community.
- Industrial policy offices should be established in each department and agency whose head sits on the IPC. The chiefs of these offices should report directly to the departmental secretary or agency head and liaise with the senior staff of the IPC.
- To support coordination with the NSC and NEC, select staff from these councils could serve jointly on the IPC. Other staff structures are possible so long as they include a) institutionalized cross-disciplinary expertise and b) leadership with direct access to the president.

What the Industrial Policy Council Should Do

The IPC should produce an *indicative* multiyear industrial policy for the US. "Indicative" means that it is not intended as an exhaustive description of US industrial policy and is not designed for adoption as a single comprehensive bill. Instead, it would be analogous to the existing National Defense Strategy drawn up by the Defense Department, laying out fundamental realities, objectives, and means of achieving them.

This document would provide a shared vision and a division of responsibilities for the agencies involved. It would offer a coherent baseline for congressional oversight. And it would communicate the US government's intentions to key audiences at home and abroad. It should look something like this:

- A list of advantageous and otherwise economically and militarily critical industries. For an illustrative subset of the technologies these industries produce, see the "Critical and Emerging Technologies List Update" compiled by the National Science and Technology Council and the section "The Future of Manufacturing USA" in Chapter 21.[2]
- An assessment of where the US stands in each of these industries, including the percentage of its domestic market held by imports, including supply chains.
- An assessment of the same for major competitor nations.
- An assessment of the national security impact of America's competitive positions in these industries.
- Trade balances in these industries by sector, product, and counterparty nation, and their effects on US employment and manufacturing capacity.
- Statistics by counterparty nation on public and private inbound and outbound investment in these industries, including debt and equity financing in US capital markets by companies from problematic nations.
- An assessment of the policy tools being used by major competitor nations in these industries, with evaluations of their effectiveness and effects on the US.
- An assessment of the policy tools being used by the US in these industries, with evaluations of their effectiveness.
- A report on currency manipulation by economically significant trade counterparties.
- A report on the volume and composition of gross and net debt and equity capital inflows into the US and their impact on the value of the dollar.[3]
- An estimate of the dollar valuation that would bring overall US trade into balance within five years.[4]
- Proposals for new or changed policies and programs to meet the needs identified by the foregoing analyses.

The president could direct the production of this document by executive order, but it would have more impact if authorized by and delivered to

Congress. The process of developing it will be at least as important as its recommendations. The interagency consultations required will sharpen awareness of the interconnectedness of and trade-offs between different elements of industrial policy and help establish channels of communication and protocols for coordination.

In support of the IPC's mission, NIST should establish an office to monitor and analyze American and foreign innovation capabilities in key industries. Its output should include a detailed digital map of the technological capabilities of companies, universities, and government labs around the world, including current and potential supply chains. This "techspace map," an early version of which was developed during the Reagan administration as Project Socrates, would then be used by American firms, universities, and government agencies to develop better competitive strategies, including trade and manufacturing policies. (See the section "Technology Mapping" in Chapter 3.)

What Congress Should Do

Congress should develop its own nonpartisan capacity for industrial policy analysis. Using the US–China Economic and Security Review Commission as a model, it should establish an Industrial Policy Commission with members from the private sector appointed by the majority and minority leaders of the House and Senate. The Commission should be supported by a small permanent staff with the capability to model the economic effects of existing and proposed technology, trade, and exchange rate policies.

Expert staff focused on industrial policy issues should be added to all relevant congressional committees and should liaise with the IPC. The Congressional Research Service should add staff experts in industrial policy. The Congressional Office of Technology Assessment abolished in 1995 should be reactivated.[5]

The House Ways & Means Committee and the Senate Finance Committee control tax and trade policy and are thus deeply involved in developing and enacting industrial policy legislation, so they should have staff with an understanding of and commitment to industrial policy.

Agency Reforms and Consolidations

Despite agency turf-guarding and Congress's resistance to government reorganizations that threaten committee fiefdoms, large-scale governmental restructurings have taken place after major crises, most recently 9/11. Thus, when the political stars align, many of the agencies and functions that should be coordinated for a maximally effective industrial policy should be consolidated.

With its many existing industrial policy-related agencies, the Commerce Department is the most suitable location. It should take on the Small Business Administration (SBA), the Trade Adjustment Assistance program, the State Department's several trade bureaus, the Trade and Development Agency, the Export–Import Bank, the US International Development Finance Corporation, and the Office of Foreign Assets Control. It should have an Office of Policy Planning that, like the State Department's equivalent, reports to and advises the secretary. The US Trade Representative should also become part of Commerce, but with the USTR retaining his or her cabinet position.

A new Economic Security Agency in Commerce should assume the US government's existing fragmented controls over sensitive exports, technology transfers, and outbound investments.[6] It should take on CFIUS, State's Directorate of Defense Trade Controls, and Commerce's Bureau of Industry and Security.

Training Industrial Policy Professionals

As noted, a corps of specialists should be developed. These high-level permanent civil servants would be a significant bulwark against capture by special interests. As would legislation prohibiting companies from hiring industrial policy officials with jurisdiction over their industries for seven years after they leave office.

The government should fund academic specializations in industrial policy. This should include a) college scholarships followed by b) internships in federal or state agencies followed by c) the promise of a job. The National Security Education Program and the Presidential Management Fellows Program are precedents.

Restructuring the Commerce Department and creating the Industrial Policy Council would accelerate development of this corps. The Department would gain higher status, creating a series of cascade effects. In the words of Ganesh Sitaraman, "Think-tank experts will spend more time working on industrial policy-related issues; academics will have much fodder for research, creating a pipeline of scholars who study industrial policy and a body of literature on what works and what doesn't; and civil servants who develop expertise in these currently sleepy areas will have a path to greater influence and prominence."[7] Commerce's new Policy Planning Office in particular would become a career goal for ambitious and talented individuals, as would the IPC.

Supporting Innovation and Manufacturing in Advantageous Industries

- Manufacturing USA's funding should grow by an order of magnitude and at least 30 new institutes should be established. What their foci should be is discussed in the section "The Future of Manufacturing USA" of Chapter 21.

- The Manufacturing Extension Partnership (see Chapter 22) needs more staff expert in helping small and medium manufacturers (SMMs) implement continuous innovation. For MEP to plan and execute the needed multiyear engagements, funding for this should be appropriated for at least five years. Since it will take time to raise the increased matching funds from the states and client firms, the current one-to-one match should be temporarily reduced.

- Funding of Small Business Innovation Research and Small Business Technology Transfer should increase (see Chapter 23). Currently, SBIR receives $3.5 billion a year and STTR $485 million; both should be doubled. Increases in the budgets of participating agencies authorized by the CHIPS and Science Act will automatically add $2 billion.[8] The percentages of their budgets allocated to SBIR and STTR should be raised to generate the rest.[9]

- Civilian robotics R&D should be better funded (see Chapter 27). Funding for the ARM Institute should be increased to $800 million over five years and NSF's funding for civilian robotics R&D to $1 billion annually. The focus of both programs should be broadened to include, inter alia, Manufacturing 4.0 applications plus interactive, service, and healthcare robots.

- Equity financing to bridge the Valley of Death. To help advanced manufacturing startups and SMMs cross the Valley of Death (see the section "Innovation Organizations fill the Gaps" in Chapter 21), the SBA should provide equity or equity-like financing. This could take the form of loans with repayment from a share of earnings, instead of interest and principal.[10] Another option would be for the small business investment company (SBIC) administering the investment to take nonvoting common stock, providing the government with the upside without the power to meddle. To discourage recipients of SBA money from offshoring production, the profit share payable to the SBA should, with limited exceptions, be raised to prohibitive levels when that occurs.

- Scale-up loans for advanced manufacturing SMMs. To help them scale up capital-intensive production, SBA should directly make advanced manufacturing growth loans.[11] The maximum amount should be $50,000,000, the maximum term 15 years, and SBA should guarantee up to 80 percent.[12] To ensure accountability, these loans should be disbursed in tranches conditioned on meeting growth benchmarks. A large percentage of the loan – for example, 75 percent – should be spent only on capital equipment located in the US. SBA should be authorized to charge fees sufficient to ensure that the program breaks even.

- Expansion loans for SMMs: To scale and grow, many SMMs need longer-term and lower-interest loans than commercial banks provide. SBA should therefore be authorized to issue a 15-year discounted debenture that does not require interest or principal payment for the first 5 years to finance the purchase of capital equipment for manufacturing SMMs. The SBA guarantee on these loans should be up to 90 percent and the maximum loan size increased from the current $5.5 million to $10 million.

- Purchase order financing: US and foreign OEMs delay payments to SMM suppliers as much as 180 days.[13] Private financing to cover this is expensive. Many foreign SMMs enjoy government-subsidized financing for this purpose, giving them a price advantage.[14] SBA, working with MEP, should establish a program to finance SMM purchase orders at below-market rates.

- Expedite critical SMM contracting: The SBA and Defense Department should establish an expedited process for issuing contracts to SMMs in sectors of the defense industrial base that DOD identifies as at risk in its existing annual Industrial Capabilities Report.

- Guardrails: The CHIPS Act prohibits funding semiconductor companies from "countries of concern" and bars companies it funds from manufacturing advanced semiconductors in those countries for 10 years. But nothing in the Inflation Reduction Act or Bipartisan Infrastructure Act prevents such countries' firms from setting up shop in the US and claiming their tax credits and applying for their grants. Companies owned or controlled by these nations should therefore be made ineligible.[15]

R&D Expensing and Tax Credits

America's R&D tax credit is smaller than in all other developed nations, so it should be reformed.[16]

- Although SMMs may now take the credit against payroll as well as income taxes, many do not have enough of either to benefit. Therefore, the credit should be made refundable for SMMs.

- The credit is currently only for spending above what the firm would supposedly otherwise have spent, requiring a contentious calculation. Instead, it should apply to all costs above the highest of the three previous years, with the percentage of costs recoverable reduced to keep the total tax expenditure constant.

- The percentage of eligible costs recoverable should be doubled for manufacturing R&D.

- Products whose development costs have been reduced by the tax credit and that are sold into US market should, with limited exceptions, be required to be manufactured in the US for a number of years, with violators made ineligible for further tax credits.
- Collaborative research is generally basic, exploratory, and precompetitive. Because the resulting knowledge is shared by all collaborating firms, often made public, and thus inappropriable, firms do less of it than is optimal for the economy. Congress should therefore expand from just energy research the current tax credit for pre-competitive research collaboration among businesses and university or federal labs, and increase it from 20 to 40 percent.[17]
- In 2017, Congress changed the law to require that R&D be amortized over five years, rather than expensed as incurred. This policy is burdensome to SMMs and should be reversed.[18]

Patent Reform

See Chapter 24 for a discussion of the crisis of the US patent system. When real reform becomes politically feasible:

- The Supreme Court's *Oil States* decision should be overturned to restore the idea that patents are actual property rights.
- The injunctive remedy eliminated by the Supreme Court's *eBay* decision should be restored.
- The bipartisan STRONGER Patents Act should become law.[19] This would restore injunctive relief, eliminate multiple challenges to the same patent, and make bad-faith demand letters punishable by the Federal Trade Commission.
- The bipartisan Patent Eligibility Restoration Act of 2022 should become law.[20] This would a) eliminate judicially created eligibility exceptions by abrogating the Supreme Court's decisions in *Alice* and *Mayo*; b) require eligibility be determined by considering all the parts of an invention together, so patents cannot be carved into separate elements deemed ineligible in isolation; c) return eligibility enquiries to the basic patentability threshold they used to employ; and d) prevent judicial creation of new exceptions.

These four steps would do much to restore the patent system. Furthermore:

- Eligibility review should be less adversarial and expensive. It should revert to being conducted by the Patent Office alone without involvement of an adversary seeking to invalidate a patent.[21]

- Patent challenges should be rare, and used mainly to deal with changes in applicable law during a patent's term. To prevent repeated challenges, if a patent's validity is challenged, other potential challengers should be put on notice in the *Federal Register* and required to join the petition or forever keep their peace.
- The Patent Trial and Appeal Board diverts scarce Patent Office resources from where they belong, when patents are first granted, so it should eventually be abolished. Better initial examinations would do more good than draining their funding and trying to clean up the mess later.
- "First to file" should be changed back to "first to invent." First to file advantages wealthy organizations with armies of lawyers, as opposed to actual inventors. It creates a scientifically unjustifiable pressure to rush to the patent office and discourages inventors from sharing information about work in progress.
- Congressional financial oversight of the USPTO is necessary, but depriving the Office of a portion of its fees subjects it to budget constraints inappropriate for an independent and self-supporting agency. Patent applications are regularly delayed for three years or more because of inadequate staffing.
- Deliberate efficient infringement should be punished with treble damages, as it used to be.

Trade

The GATT–WTO rule book that has shackled US trade policy since 1947 should be discarded. Instead, trade policy should aim to a) ensure that America's trade is balanced overall and b) protect and support advantageous (as defined in Chapters 1 and 2) and other militarily and economically critical industries.

Exchange Rate Management and Tariffs for Overall Balance

Because a lower dollar will make *all* imports more expensive here and *all* US exports cheaper abroad, ending its overvaluation is the single most potent tool for balancing our overall trade.[22] Ending its overvaluation will also remove a very large headwind to almost all US industrial policies. (See Chapter 4 for details.)

To accomplish this, the US should enact the Market Access Charge (MAC), a system of controls on inbound capital flows proposed in the Senate in 2019 in the Competitive Dollar for Jobs and Prosperity Act (see Chapter 4).[23] The MAC would impose a small tax on incoming capital, reducing the net return on foreign investments into the US and thus reducing the inbound capital flows – including those attracted by Federal Reserve interest rate increases to combat inflation – that drive up the dollar. This charge would be adjusted to bring the dollar down to a trade-balancing level within five years.

A permanent MAC would require amending the charter of the Federal Reserve to add balanced trade to its mission. Because this would take years, the MAC should be implemented on an interim basis by executive order under the International Emergency Economic Powers Act of 1977.

Even after America's trade is balanced overall, the US should neutralize currency manipulation, such as the undervaluation of the Taiwan dollar and the Korean won that undermines America's attempts to reenter high-end chip fabrication (see Chapter 30). Washington can do this with countervailing currency intervention (CCI) – that is, buying the currency of the offending country (see Chapter 4).[24] Another option is a balance-of-payments tariff on all imports from the offending country, appropriate for Eurozone countries such as Germany, where CCI would affect nontarget countries.[25]

The US should not seek overall trade balance by exporting more commodities while continuing to lose ground in advantageous industries. It should instead proactively manage the composition of American trade to maintain a positive trade balance in such industries. Because tariffs and quotas can target specific industries and products, they are indispensable here.

The first set of recommendations that follow can be taken within America's existing WTO commitments. The second is designed to implement the needed post-WTO system of managed trade.

Before Leaving the WTO

- Subject to very limited exceptions discussed in the next section, enter into no additional free trade agreements. (See Chapter 18 for their poor record.)
- Raise or eliminate US maximum ("bound") tariff rates. The US has the world's lowest, averaging 3.4 percent.[26] Higher rates, or no commitments at all to keep tariffs below a certain level, will give us greater leverage in bilateral tariff negotiations.
- Revoke Trade Promotion Authority, including Fast Track. Trade agreements should be negotiated, debated, and voted upon by Congress in the regular order. TPA limits America's authority to use domestic laws for trade and industrial policy purposes, including tariffs and (through its implementing legislation or executive orders) rules of origin, customs rules, and food safety.
- Maintain the tariffs on China that were in place as of 2024. The Section 301 tariffs that were suspended in January 2021 as part of Trump's Phase I deal

with Beijing should be reimposed and no similar agreements with China should be concluded.

- Implement more Section 232 tariffs on imports that the president finds threaten national security.
- Free US industry from the burden of petitioning for antidumping and anti-subsidy countervailing duty orders. This is costly and often provokes retaliation against complaining firms by the offending country. Instead, the International Trade Administration should self-initiate such investigations.
- Implement more Section 301 tariffs against foreign subsidies and dumping. These tariffs provide broader relief than antidumping and countervailing duties, whose narrow scope leads to endless "whack-a-mole."
- Use Section 122 of the Trade Act of 1974, which authorizes the president to impose quotas, and tariffs of up to 15 percent, for up to 150 days to offset "serious United States balance-of-payments deficits."[27]
- Each year, the USTR publishes a list of significant foreign trade barriers. It should automatically launch Section 301 investigations and, if a positive finding is made, impose countervailing duties.
- Leave the WTO's Agreement on Government Procurement, which opens procurement to foreign bidders on the same terms as domestic suppliers and has been consistently violated. (The Biden administration's "Buy America" rules are a good start.)
- America's General System of Preferences grants the poorest countries lower tariffs to foster their development. It has not accomplished its mission, has been inappropriately extended to middle-income countries such as Brazil and Thailand, and has been widely abused. Its authorization expired in 2020 and it should not be renewed.[28]

Policies for Managed Trade in the Post-WTO Era

- It is easier for American firms to take back their home markets than to penetrate those of other countries. Therefore, retaking US markets should be the primary focus of trade policy. Prying open foreign markets, while important, should take second place in funding, political capital, and executive branch focus.
- Almost all trade matters should be handled by domestic US laws or executive orders defining the conditions, including tariffs, under which foreign goods and services may be sold here. These conditions may be negotiated with counterparty nations, but the US should reserve the right to decide whether said conditions are being met and to change them.
- To support its industries in advantageous and otherwise critical sectors, the US should reserve enough of its own markets for US firms and their supply

chains to attain internationally competitive scale, including profits sufficient to fund ongoing R&D.

- When the US lacks sufficient capacity to supply domestic needs, tariff rate quotas (no tariff up to a certain quantity and a tariff thereafter) should be used to give domestic producers certainty while also allowing supply and price stability.[29] (Except in these and a few other circumstances, quotas are inferior to tariffs because less favorable to the American taxpayer and a license for foreign price-fixing.)
- Tariff rate quotas and tariffs phased in over time should be used to nurture industries the US is attempting to develop, is in danger of losing, or is trying to regain. For example, the federal government's current $54 billion effort to rebuild US capability in semiconductors should be supported by a staged tariff and quota policy. Said policy should track along with and protect development of American production capacity, but *not* prematurely burden US users of advanced chips that domestic manufacturers are not yet capable of making.
- When the US imposes a tariff, it should impose proportional tariffs on downstream goods containing the tariffed product to avoid handicapping domestic producers.
- Industries protected by tariffs should be subject to rigorous antitrust scrutiny to ensure strong domestic competition. But this scrutiny should not be allowed to disrupt technologically dynamic oligopolies subject to effective competition from abroad. (See the section "Imposing Competitive Industry Structure" in Chapter 3.)
- No economically significant industries, even the less advantageous, should be left at the mercy of other countries' industrial policies.[30] The US should not allow them to be moved offshore because of subsidies, below-cost pricing, or lower environmental standards.
- Free trade agreements should have a very limited role in US policy (see Chapter 18 for their poor record). They are hard to withdraw from and should be used only in narrowly defined situations requiring major long-term financial commitments to achieve a common goal. Possible examples include an EU–US agreement to each concentrate on different sectors of rare earth refining.

Other Needed Trade Reforms

- Increase funding for US Customs and Border Protection. Its Commercial Customs Operations Advisory Committee, captured by importers, should be disbanded.
- Expand country-of-origin labeling. Existing exemptions, mostly for agricultural goods, established by Treasury should be revoked. Manufactured goods, processed foods, and the like should disclose origins of their

significant inputs, as cars do. E-commerce platforms should disclose the country marking on a product if it has one.

- The *de minimis* exemption in US customs law should be abolished. Exempting imports of $800 or less from tariffs, taxes, and most notifications and reviews, it is used to import $130 billion of small parcel shipments per year tariff-free and with little or no inspection (see Chapter 18).[31]
- The Justice Department should be authorized to grant companies antitrust exemptions to coordinate in resisting foreign government pressures, such as China pressing US companies to transfer technology by playing them off against each other.
- Corporate income should be taxed based on sales factor apportionment. Current laws incent US corporations to manufacture in and shift profits to low-tax foreign jurisdictions. SFA would solve this by allocating a corporation's taxable income to each country in proportion to its sales there.
- To provide sound guidance to policymakers, the flawed computer models that have incorrectly projected lower deficits from every major trade agreement and net economic harm from every tariff should be reformed. (See the section "Flawed Trade Models" in Chapter 18.)
- The US should set a higher bar for using trade concessions as bargaining chips for geopolitical or other noneconomic objectives. Such concessions should be based on realistic, historically grounded analysis of their economic costs and the likelihood that the concessions will cause the desired outcome. For example, Japan's fear of China will likely cause it to increase its military strength and coordinate with the US to strengthen critical minerals supply chains without new trade concessions or technology transfers.[32]
- The US should establish a "reverse CFIUS" to screen *outbound* investments in the development and production of militarily important products, including dual-use technologies, by geopolitical adversaries.[33] To avoid unnecessary administrative expense and uncertainty for investors, this screening should be narrowly focused on high-tech choke points. The US should urge friends and allies to adopt similar measures.[34]
- Chinese companies, including SOEs, in advantageous and otherwise critical industries, especially military and dual-use technologies, should be barred from raising funds in US capital markets (see Chapter 18).[35] Such investments help China advance these industries and create hostages Beijing can leverage to soften US policy, both directly and by increasing Wall Street's incentive to lobby Washington on its behalf.
- Foreign lobbying on US trade and industrial policies should be curtailed. Direct and indirect support by foreign governments and corporations for US think tanks, universities, other nonprofits, and persons testifying before Congress should be publicly disclosed, and support from geopolitical

adversaries prohibited outright. Former members of Congress and senior executive branch officials should be barred from representing adversary nations or corporations based in or controlled by them. Consideration should be given to amending the Foreign Agents Registration Act to apply to American entities with foreign assets or profits above a certain threshold.

Allies and Friends

America's 2023 trade deficit in goods with China was the largest with any single country. But other nations, mostly allies and friends, accounted for 75 percent of our $1.4 trillion total gross bilateral deficits, the appropriate metric.[36] Virtually all US allies and friends maintain tariff and/or nontariff trade barriers.

The US should acknowledge every country's right to provide special protection and support to particular industries. Support of advantageous industries is the core of the industrial policy that America needs, so this acknowledgment is the only honest response to criticism of the US for exercising this right itself.

Subject to this right for the US and foreign nations, America should condition the privilege of foreign direct investment (FDI) in the US on trade and investment reciprocity. Considerations should include counterparty nations letting American firms sell into and make direct investments into their economies, and their not manipulating their currency or subsidizing exports to the US.

FDI policy should be more restrictive in advantageous industries so that it does not displace American firms. But in advantageous industries in which the US needs foreign technology from FDI, this requirement should be relaxed, subject to conditions. For example, the CHIPS Act's support for new US-located TSMC and Samsung fabs should be conditioned on these companies agreeing to a) manufacture their most advanced products in the US soon after doing so in their home countries, b) colocate cutting edge research here, and c) hire, train and, promote US citizens to senior levels in their US operations.

America's general policy should be to have domestic design and manufacturing capacity in all advantageous and otherwise militarily or economically critical technologies. But there may be exceptions where the technology is controlled by a reliable ally that is not in harm's way and catching up is overly expensive and uncertain. One example would be the Dutch company ASML's EUV lithography machines. These are incredibly complex – with 457,329 components from a worldwide supply chain – and cost more than $350 million.[37] Establishing a US-made alternative would require not only duplicating the current machine and its supply chain, but also chasing a moving target as ASML continues to improve. Under these circumstances, the US should continue to rely on this company while a) inducing it with rewards and pressures to make some of these machines in the US, and b) funding American R&D aimed at new technologies that could eventually leapfrog EUV entirely.

ACKNOWLEDGMENTS

We owe so much to so many. Thanks to Robert Dreesen, our editor at Cambridge University Press, for believing in this project and accepting our argument that its subject required that the book be comprehensive. Andrew Stuart, our literary agent, found just the right home for it. Our tireless senior editors – Oberon Dixon-Luinenburg, Kevin Kearns, William Keller, and Joel Yudken – worked with our specialist contributors and edited their drafts. Our specialist contributors and reviewers, including: Marie Anchordoguy, Andrea Boltho, Atul Kohli, Hironori Sasada, Walter Skya, Yves Tiberghien (Japan); Dong Wook Huh, John Lie, Wonhyuk Lim, Karl Moskowitz, Stewart Paterson, Jitendra Uttam (Korea); Thomas Hout, Ernest Liu, Seung-Youn Oh, Erik Wernberg-Tougaard (China); Tilman Altenburg, Volker Berghahn, Alexander Ebner, James Foreman-Peck, Robert Hancké, Jeffrey Hart, Gary Herrigel, Stephen Silvia, Andrew Weaver (Germany); Elie Cohen, Jean Comte, Robert Hancké, John Zysman (France); Nicholas Comfort, Michael Hobday, Geoffrey Hodgson (Britain); Shobha Ahuja, Premachandra Athukorala, Aniruddha Bagchi, A. K. Bhattacharya, Utpal De, Saibal Kar, Rajendra Kondepati, Alok Kumar, Rishabh Kumar, Sumit Majumdar, Nitya Nanda, Badri Narayanan, M. Parameswaran, Lydia Powell (India); Ted Kahn (Argentina); Erik Reinert (the Renaissance); Kevin Kearns, Lawrence Peskin (US history); Steve Brachman, Hannah Cohen, Chris Gallagher, Randy Landrenau, Josh Malone, Richard McCormack (patents); Barry Bluestone (MA life sciences); Sujai Shivakumar, Deborah Stine (US science and technology programs); David Bourne, Ira Moskowitz (robotics); John Hansen (exchange rates); Richard Jones (nanotech); Andrew Graves, Mustafa Mohaterem, John Voelcker, Michael Ward (automobiles); Justin Bernier (Chinese securities); Frank Gayle, Phillip Singerman, Carol Thomas (MEP, MFG-USA); Alan Fletcher (semiconductors); Dan DiMicco (steel); Doug Berger (4IR); Ganesh Sitaraman, Robert Wade (policy); Stan Sorscher (aviation); Charles Wessner (micro-governance, NY semiconductors); Greg Tassey (technology strategy); Dirk Bezemer (financialization); Steve Cohen, Jeff Faux, Adam Kolasinski, Richard Nelson, Richard Sandbrook (other). Our thanks also to Mark Fortier, Kailey Tse-Harlow, Jessica Pellien, and the rest of the Fortier team for creating the promotional campaign; to the Coalition for a Prosperous America's Nick Iacovella, Michael Stumo, and Jon Toomey for helping us bring the book to the attention of policymakers of both parties; and to Charles Benoit, Jeff Ferry, and Robby Saunders for answering many questions and reviewing drafts. Thanks to friends who provided encouragement and support: Daniel Alpert, Jeanine Chirlin, Ignacio Contreras, Alan Engbrecht, Rana Foroohar, Ronald Frohne, Jock Gilliland, Malcolm Handley, Stefanie Magda, Ken Miller, and Michael Waldman. To the thinkers who laid the theoretical foundations for this book: William Baumol, Ha-Joon Chang, Ralph Gomory, Michael Pettis, and Erik Reinert. Finally, we are immeasurably grateful to our wives: Anne G. Fredericks, for enthusiastic-ally supporting Marc's work on this project through the distractions and ups and downs of its eight years of gestation; and Abby T. Mohan, for her devotion despite the book's hold on Ian's time and attention. Without all of the above, we could not have written this book. The errors, however, are ours alone.

NOTES

Introduction

1. Since then, just over 1 million have been regained. "Employment, Hours, and Earnings from the Current Employment Statistics Survey (National): All Employees, Thousands, Manufacturing, Seasonally Adjusted," US Bureau of Labor Statistics, data.bls.gov/timeseries/CES3000000001.

2. Stephen J. Rose, "Do Not Blame Trade for the Decline in Manufacturing Jobs," Center for Strategic and International Studies, October 4, 2021. (Note that different job loss numbers reported in this book may be inconsistent because these are econometric estimates, not data, and different analysts legitimately make different assumptions and use different calculation methods.)

3. Lawrence Mishel, "Yes, Manufacturing Still Provides a Pay Advantage, but Staffing Firm Outsourcing Is Eroding It," Economic Policy Institute, March 12, 2018. See also Jeff Ferry, "Manufacturing Jobs and Income Decline," Coalition for a Prosperous America, August 15, 2019. Earnings: Some metrics, including more affluent earners, medical benefits, and government transfer payments, show some increase, as does adjusting for declining household size and the controversial idea that US government statistics overstate inflation. See chart for wages of production and non-supervisory workers in: "Americans' Paychecks Are Bigger than 40 Years Ago, but Their Purchasing Power Has Hardly Budged," Pew Research Center, August 7, 2018. For criticisms, see Scott Lincicome, "The Annoying Persistence of the Income Stagnation Myth," Cato Institute, October 9, 2020.

4. "Exhibit 16: Trade in Advanced Technology Products," in "US International Trade in Goods and Services, April 2023," Release Number: CB 23-84, BEA 23-22, US Census Bureau, June 7, 2023. The Advanced Technology Products (ATP) deficit number would be somewhat lower if the tax avoidance strategies of multinationals such as the transfer of intellectual property to subsidiaries in low-tax jurisdictions were taken into account, but the point still stands. This deficit has been rising quickly and steadily, a trend that even a significant percentage discount due to tax avoidance would not reverse. Furthermore, ATP is a category in which the US should be running large, consistent surpluses.

5. "US Trade in Goods and Services: Balance of Payments (BOP) Basis," Census Bureau, census.gov/foreign-trade/statistics/historical/gands.pdf.

6. Debtor in the sense of having the world's most negative net international investment position – that is, including all foreign holdings, not just bonds and bank debt. See "US International Investment Position: Fourth Quarter and Year 2021," US Bureau of Economic Analysis (BEA), bea.gov/sites/default/files/2022-03/intinv421.pdf.

7. "US International Investment Position: Fourth Quarter and Year 2021," BEA.

8. William Bahr, *The Economic Consequences of Blind Faith in Free Trade* (Draft), chapter 5. In 2004, William A. Lovett estimated that "with stronger, reciprocity-based trade policy, U.S. GDP could have been 10 to 20 percent higher," in William Anthony Lovett, Alfred E. Eckes, and Richard L. Brinkman, *U.S. Trade Policy: History, Theory and the WTO* (Armonk, NY: M. E. Sharpe & Company, 1999), 130. Another estimate of the size of the problem, by economist Charles McMillion of MBG Information Services, notes that in the 25 years leading up to 1980, our real GDP grew at an average of 3.8 per year. But in the 25 years afterward, as our trade deficit ballooned, it grew at only 3.1 percent. Charles McMillion, "Guest Editorial: Forever in Their Debt," *Manufacturing & Technology News*, October 25, 2006, 5.

9. "US Trade in Goods and Services: Balance of Payments (BOP) Basis," Census Bureau, census.gov/foreign-trade/statistics/historical/gands.pdf.

10. Q2 number. "US Domestic Market Share Index Hits All-Time Low," Coalition for a Prosperous America, October 17, 2022.

11. Robert Atkinson, "US Manufacturing Productivity Is Falling, and It's Cause for Alarm," *Industry Week*, July 12, 2021.

12. Also, counting each doubling of computer capacity is like producing twice as many units. See Susan Houseman, "Is American Manufacturing in Decline?" W. E. Upjohn Institute for Employment Research, October 2016.

13. On the limited supply of US-made hardware, see Sascha Segan, "Silicon, USA: Technology That's Actually Made in America," *PC Magazine*, September 2, 2021. There is some US production of servers and desktop computers, and of chips, but no mass production of laptops beyond one tiny Lenovo plant. There are some custom US-domiciled fabricators of PCs and laptops, such as Falcon Northwest.

14. Andrew Heritage, "Pro-growth Tariffs: Modified Economic Model Shows Domestic Growth," Coalition for a Prosperous America, June 29, 2023.

15. In retrospect, some of their problems were self-created and so did not deserve help, but others were not.

16. "Appeared to" is the appropriate qualifier because Chrysler, for example, was in large part a victim of Japan's subsidies to its auto industry.

17. "Purported" is the appropriate term because it is legitimately controversial whether these particular projects were failures on their own account or rendered useless by changes in the larger policy and economic environment for which policymakers were not responsible.

18. This is not to hold these countries out as models for the US to imitate per se, or to claim that their economic performance is better than ours. (A more complicated question than one might imagine: GDP per hour worked is more suitable than per capita.) It is merely to suggest they may know things we don't, and one can learn from anybody.

19. Manufacturing is 19 percent of GDP in Germany and 20 percent in Japan, versus 11 percent in the US (2021 data). See "Manufacturing, Value Added (% of GDP): Japan, Germany, United States," World Bank, data.worldbank.org/indicator/NV.IND.MANF.ZS?+start=1960&end=2021&locations=JP-DE-US.

20. Liberals tend to be more comfortable with its interventionist aspect, conservatives with its economic-performance and national security implications. Senators who

have spoken in favor of systematic, proactive industrial policy include Chris Coons (D-DE), Jeff Merkley (D-OR), and Todd Young (R-IN).

21. Marco Rubio, "Made in China 2025 and the Future of American Industry," February 12, 2019.

22. Elizabeth Warren, "A Plan for Economic Patriotism," *Medium*, June 4, 2019.

23. Christian Gonzales et al, "How state and local governments win at attracting companies," McKinsey & Company, September 13, 2019, mckinsey.com/industries/public-sector/our-insights/how-state-and-local-governments-win-at-attracting-companies.

24. "GDP Growth (Annual %): China," World Bank, data.worldbank.org/indicator/NY.GDP.MKTP.KD.ZG?locations=CN.

25. Or to be more precise, the model we mistakenly think our economy implements, because the reality is far more complicated than just free markets.

26. See "Assessing and Strengthening the Manufacturing and Defense Industrial Base and Supply Chain Resiliency of the United States: Report to President Donald J. Trump by the Interagency Task Force in Fulfillment of Executive Order 13806," US Department of Defense, September 2018, especially pages 36–7.

27. See, for example, Michael Porter, "Why America Needs an Economic Strategy," *Bloomberg Businessweek*, October 29, 2008.

28. The net cost of the auto bailout was $9.3 billion. Given the avoided social and economic costs of not doing it and the tax revenue protected by keeping automakers viable, this may credibly be described as a success. See Brent Snavely, "Final Tally: Taxpayers Auto Bailout Loss $9.3B," *Detroit Free Press*, December 30, 2014.

29. "Bipartisan Infrastructure Investment and Jobs Act Summary: A Road to Stronger Economic Growth," Senate, September 2022, 2.

30. "CHIPS and Science Act of 2022," Office of US Senator Chris Van Hollen, July 27, 2022, 5, 1.

31. "Fact Sheet: Treasury, IRS Open Public Comment on Implementing the Inflation Reduction Act's Clean Energy Tax Incentives," US Department of the Treasury, October 5, 2022.

32. "CHIPS and Science Act of 2022," Sen. Van Hollen, 2.

33. Prominent economists constituting exceptions included John Kenneth Galbraith of Harvard, Nobelist Wassily Leontief, Lester Thurow of MIT, and Robert Heilbroner of the New School for Social Research.

34. As the senior staff economist of the President's Council of Economic Advisors, his important work in this respect was Paul R. Krugman, "Targeted Industrial Policies: Theory and Evidence," in *Industrial Change and Public Policy: A Symposium Sponsored by the Federal Reserve Bank of Kansas City* (Kansas City, MO: Federal Reserve Bank of Kansas City (August 1983), 123–69.

35. Paul R. Krugman, "The Current Case for Industrial Policy," in *Protectionism and World Welfare*, ed. Dominick Salvatore (Cambridge: Cambridge University Press, 1993), 160.

36. John Maynard Keynes, *The General Theory of Employment, Interest, and Money* (New York: First Harvest/Harcourt, 1964), 383–4.

37. The math itself may be true, in the sense that the equations employed are internally consistent, but the choice of *what* gets modeled and how is made on the basis of judgments that are not themselves mathematical. For a discussion of the abuse of mathematics in economics, see Paul M. Romer, "Mathiness in the Theory of Economic Growth," *American Economic Review: Papers and Proceedings* 105, no. 5 (2015): 89–93. The economics profession tends to reward cleverness over practical relevance, and math also gives the *illusion* of precision and control. This

criticism has been made by at least two Nobelists in economics: Wassily Leontief, "Academic Economics," *Science*, July 9, 1982, 104–107, and James Heckman and R. Robb, "Alternative Methods for Solving the Problem of Selection Bias in Evaluating the Impact of Treatments on Outcomes," *Drawing Inference from Self Selected Samples, ed.* Howard Wainer (Springer-Verlag, 1986), 63–107. Criticism of the potential for excessive mathematization to distort economics goes back to a warning by Italian mathematician Ignazio Radicati in 1752. See Erik S. Reinert, *How Rich Countries Got Rich and Why Poor Countries Stay Poor* (London: Constable, 2007), 45.

38. In 2008, for example, misplaced confidence in computer modeling of financial risk led to costly inaction by government regulators. By "deliberate inaction," we refer to choices like the refusal to regulate off-exchange derivatives and other components of the shadow banking system because of the publicly stated belief that markets are basically self-stabilizing and any interference would reduce the financial sector's productivity.

39. This book also draws upon the older, once respectable "institutionalist" tradition in American economics, consisting of such thinkers as Thorstein Veblen, Simon Patten, John Commons, Wesley Mitchell, Charles Van Hise, Rexford Tugwell, and John Kenneth Galbraith.

40. Foreword by Kenneth J. Arrow to Brian Arthur, *Increasing Returns and Path Dependence in the Economy* (Ann Arbor: University of Michigan Press, 1994), ix.

41. The phrase "market imperfections" is used here only loosely, and in a sense not necessarily identical with all other uses of the phrase in the discipline of economics. Exactly what is meant is explained in the rest of this book.

42. Strictly speaking, true or "economic" profits – that is, profits in excess of the cost of capital.

43. In the words of Erik Reinert, "Typically, present economic thinking – having internalized the standard assumptions of neo-classical theory – focuses exclusively on the interests of man-the-consumer, which only under perfect competition are identical to those of man-the-wage-earner." See Erik S. Reinert, "Competitiveness and Its Predecessors: A 500-Year Cross-National Perspective," *Studies in Technology, Innovation and Economic Policy* 6, no. 1 (March 1995): 23–42. Mainstream economics does take seriously producer welfare (producer surplus), but this is not the same thing as producer productivity.

44. Creating a single master agency is not an empty hypothetical. A number of observers have argued for one. See, for example, Barry Bluestone and Bennett Harrison, *The Deindustrialization of America: Plant Closings, Community Abandonment, and the Dismantling of Basic Industry* (New York: Basic Books, 1982), and Ira Magaziner and Robert Reich, *Minding America's Business: The Decline and Rise of the American Economy* (New York: Harcourt Brace Jovanovich, 1982).

45. Granted, there are complexities to which sectors are traded and which are not, like medical tourism or, as with China's Belt and Road Initiative, the practice of nations sending workers overseas to build real estate and infrastructure. But these generalizations are true enough to be valid for most analytical purposes, especially in America's case.

46. Much economic activity that was formerly assumed to be non-tradable is now tradable through offshoring.

47. For example, a national banking system, which was lacking in early America for several decades, requires a regulatory framework. Even privately built toll roads, such as the turnpikes of early America, depend on the state for eminent domain.

1. Why the Free Market Can't Do Everything

1. The authors do not use the phrase "markets fail" here in the technical sense of market failure. As Cimoli, Dosi, and Stiglitz observe,

   A misleading point of departure: market failures. Conventionally, one would start from the very general question, when are public policies required from the point of view of the theory? And, as known, the standard answer would be, when there are market failures of some kind. However, albeit quite common the "market failure" language tends to be quite misleading in that, in order to evaluate the necessity and efficacy of any policy, it takes as a yardstick those conditions under which standard normative ("welfare") theorems hold. The problem with such a framework is not that market failures are not relevant ... In a profound sense, when judged with standard canons, the whole world can be seen as a huge market failure (Mario Cimoli et al., "Institutions and Policies Shaping Industrial Development," in *Industrial Policy and Development: The Political Economy of Capabilities Accumulation*, ed. Mario Cimoli, Giovanni Dosi, and Joseph E. Stiglitz (Oxford: Oxford University Press, 2009), 19–38, at 20.

2. This and subsequent chapters adapted from Marc Fasteau and Ian Fletcher, "The Economic Foundations of Industrial Policy," *Palladium*, June 15, 2020, palladium mag.com/2020/06/15/the-economic-foundations-of-industrial-policy.

3. The authors are not claiming that all government interventions are successful, nor embracing naïveté about how difficult they can be to get right.

4. See Edwin Mansfield, "Social Returns from R&D: Findings, Methods, and Limitations," *Research Technology Management* 34, no. 6 (1991): 24–7; Charles Jones and John Williams, "Measuring the Social Return to R&D," *Quarterly Journal of Economics* 113, no. 4 (1998): 1119–35.

5. William Nordhaus, "Schumpeterian Profits and the Alchemist Fallacy," Yale Economic Applications and Policy Discussion Paper No. 6, Yale University, April 2005.

6. Naturally, some capitalists do, but enough do not that this can be a problem.

7. Michael Porter, *The Competitive Advantage of Nations* (New York: Free Press, 1990), 89.

8. Some changes, such as inducing a greater percentage of the population to work or increasing the length of the workweek, can also have this effect, but are not relevant to the present argument.

9. The majority of growth by far comes from innovation, not adding more capital at the same level of technology. One study is "The Innovation Index: Measuring the UK's Investment in Innovation and Its Effects," National Endowment for Science, Technology and the Arts, November 2009, 4.

10. Peter Klenow and Andrés Rodríguez-Clare, "The Neoclassical Revival in Growth Economics: Has It Gone Too Far?" In *NBER Macroeconomics Annual 1997, Volume 12*, ed. Ben S. Bernanke and Julio J. Rotemberg (Cambridge, MA: MIT Press, 1997), 73–114.

11. Innovation doesn't only mean technology. Consider mail-order catalogs, stock exchanges, or retail franchises: all these innovations in business *technique* unlocked new opportunities for growth. But technology is the main event. This is also not to say that innovation itself is the *only* bottleneck of possible growth.

12. Ignoring for now all the issues raised at Google's antitrust trial that began in 2023.

13. For a similar analysis, see W. Brian Arthur, "Increasing Returns and the New World of Business," *Harvard Business Review* (July–August 1996), 101–9.

14. Erik Reinert, *How Rich Countries Got Rich and Why Poor Countries Stay Poor* (London: Constable, 2007), 161. The point was first made in modern economics in Hans Singer, "The Distribution of Gains between Investing and Borrowing Countries," *American Economic Review* (May 1950): 473–85, at 478.

15. Porter, *Competitive Advantage of Nations,* 50.

16. The classic theoretical statement is in W. Brian Arthur's *Increasing Returns and Path Dependence in the Economy* (Ann Arbor: University of Michigan Press, 1994).

17. In technical terms, "Nonconvexities, such as increasing returns to scale in production, are common in reality. If they are allowed into the theory, then the existence of an equilibrium is no longer certain, and a Pareto optimum need not be a market equilibrium," from Frank Ackerman, "Still Dead after All These Years: Interpreting the Failure of General Equilibrium Theory." In *The Flawed Foundations of General Equilibrium: Critical Essays on Economic Theory*, ed. Frank Ackerman and Alejandro Nadal (New York: Routledge, 2004), 14–32, at 15. These topics were given more of the attention they deserved prior to World War II. See, for example, Allyn A. Young, "Increasing Returns and Economic Progress," *The Economic Journal* 38, no. 152 (December 1928).

18. Porter, *Competitive Advantage of Nations,* 36.

19. Reinert, *How Rich Countries Got Rich and Why Poor Countries Stay Poor.*

20. There are, of course, other important causes, like the oligopoly pricing power of the multinationals who sell them their inputs, such as fertilizer and seed, and buy their outputs, squeezing the farmers in between, that do not concern us here.

21. Erik S. Reinert, "Diminishing Returns and Economic Sustainability: The Dilemma of Resource-Based Economies under a Free Trade Regime," in *International Trade Regulation, National Development Strategies and the Environment: Towards Sustainable Development?* ed. Stein Hansen, Jan Hesselberg, and Helge Hveem (Oslo: University of Oslo Centre for Development and the Environment, 1996), 119–50.

22. Justin Yifu Lin, *New Structural Economics: A Framework for Rethinking Development and Policy* (Washington, DC: World Bank Publications, 2012), 350.

2. The Dynamics of Advantageous Industries

1. This material was adapted from Marc Fasteau and Ian Fletcher, "The Economic Foundations of Industrial Policy," *Palladium*, June 15, 2020, palladiummag.com/2020/06/15/the-economic-foundations-of-industrial-policy.

2. Note the use of the word "often." The authors are not claiming that zero major technological advances come from the unaided private sector.

3. Erik S. Reinert, *How Rich Countries Got Rich and Why Poor Countries Stay Poor* (London: Constable, 2007), 317. Also see Allan Dahl Andersen, Björn Johnson, Erik Reinert et al., "Institutions, Innovation and Development: Collected Contributions from Workshop," working paper series, Department of Business Studies, Aalborg University, 2009, 39.

4. The authors wish to acknowledge their indebtedness to Erik Reinert both for his help writing this book and for the underlying intellectual breakthroughs without which it would not have been possible.

5. Typically, at the start many small firms compete to gain a foothold and get their product designs accepted. Many get selected out, a few establish a dominant design, then they increasingly compete on process innovation and cost/price, which involves

heavy capital expenditures. At this stage, it is much harder to enter the industry, especially for newcomers. This is the standard Utterback and Abernathy story of product-process innovation, as in William J. Abernathy and James M. Utterback, "Patterns of Industrial Innovation," *Technology Review* 80, no. 7 (June/July 1978): 41–7.

6. "Jobs Lost, Jobs Gained: Workforce Transitions in a Time of Automation," McKinsey Global Institute, December 2017, 4.

7. "Table 2.11: Employment and Output by Industry ('Computer and Peripheral Equipment Manufacturing, Excluding Digital Camera Manufacturing')," in "Employment Projections," US Bureau of Labor Statistics (BLS), June 21, 2022.

8. Douglas A. Irwin, *Clashing over Commerce: A History of US Trade Policy* (Chicago, IL: University of Chicago Press, 2017), 534.

9. "Businesses Spent over a Half Trillion Dollars for R&D Performance in the United States during 2020, a 9.1% Increase over 2019," National Center for Science and Engineering Statistics, ncses.nsf.gov/pubs/nsf22343.

10. Reinert, *How Rich*, 132.

11. Austan Goolsbee and Chad Syverson, "The Strange and Awful Path of Productivity in the US Construction Sector," working paper 30845, National Bureau of Economic Research, revised February 2023, 2.

12. According to the Economic Research Institute, German barbers make an annual salary of €36,206, or $34,647 USD, and average annual barber salaries in the Philippines are ₱216,386 ($3,992 USD). Salary Database, Economic Research Institute, June 21, 2022.

13. Tab "Data," Rows 1043–80 in "World KLEMS Data," World KLEMS, worldklems.org/data/basic/usa_WK_apr_2013.xlsx.

14. In 1950, steel production man-hours per ton in the US was 15.1. See Keun Lee and Ji-hoon Ki, "Rise of Latecomers and Catch-Up Cycles in the World Steel Industry," *Research Policy* 46, no. 2 (2017). In 2022, it was 1.9. See "Profile of the American Iron and Steel Institute," American Iron and Steel Institute, 2022, 9.

15. With the possible exception of the healthcare sector, but that is outside our remit here.

16. "Value Added by Industry: Manufacturing As a Percentage of GDP," Federal Reserve Bank of St. Louis, fred.stlouisfed.org/series/VAPGDPMA; "Employment by Major Industry Sector," BLS, bls.gov/emp/tables/employment-by-major-industry-sector.htm.

17. Robert E. Scott, "The Manufacturing Footprint and the Importance of US Manufacturing Jobs," Economic Policy Institute, January 22, 2015, 7.

18. Authors' calculation based on column "Value-Added & Imports" in "How Important Is US Manufacturing Today?" MAPI Foundation, June 2021.

19. "How Important Is US Manufacturing Today?" MAPI Foundation.

20. "How Important Is US Manufacturing Today?" MAPI Foundation.

21. Note that our economic statistics do not capture the number of workers in sectors classified as services who are actually supporting manufacturing activities. See Marc Levinson, "Job Creation in the Manufacturing Revival," Congressional Research Service, July 19, 2019.

22. Table 2, column "Value-Added & Imports" in "How Important Is US Manufacturing Today?" MAPI Foundation.

23. Susan Helper, Timothy Krueger, and Howard Wial, "Why Does Manufacturing Matter? Which Manufacturing Matters? A Policy Framework," Brookings Institution, February 2012.

24. William B. Bonvillian, "Reinventing American Manufacturing: The Role of Innovation," *Innovations: Technology, Governance, Globalization* 7, no. 3 (Summer 2012): 97–125.
25. For this concept, see Gary Pisano and Willy Shih, "Restoring American Competitiveness," *Harvard Business Review*, July–August 2009.
26. YiLi Chen and Paul Morris, "Is US Manufacturing Really Declining?" Federal Reserve Bank of St. Louis, April 11, 2017, 2.
27. Let alone asset-based sectors such as finance or real estate, where bubbles and zoning restrictions can drive up prices with little connection to actual value. Manufacturing also inflates more slowly than services because it is more tradable, and hence cheap foreign labor does more to keep its price down.
28. Chen and Morris, "Is US Manufacturing Really Declining?"
29. See for example: Louis Jacobson, Robert J. LaLonde, and Daniel G. Sullivan, *Earnings Losses of Displaced Workers*, staff working paper no. 92–11, W. E. Upjohn Institute for Employment Research, February 1992; David H. Autor, David Dorn, and Gordon H. Hanson, "The China Shock: Learning from Labor-Market Adjustment to Large Changes in Trade," *Annual Review of Economics* 8 (October 2016): 205–40.
30. Note, however, that the across-the-board manufacturing wage premium that once existed is now gone: Manufacturing jobs per se do not pay more than comparable nonmanufacturing jobs. But this does not invalidate our argument, which does not turn upon this former fact and is precisely what one would expect in a fungible labor market. See Kimberly Bayard, Tomaz Cajner, Vivi Gregorich, and Maria D. Tito, "Are Manufacturing Jobs Still 'Good' Jobs? An Exploration of the Manufacturing Wage Premium," Federal Reserve Board, March 4, 2022.
31. "Exhibit 15: US Trade in Advanced Technology Products," in "US International Trade in Goods and Services, Annual Revision Release," Number: CB 23–90, BEA 23–23, US Census, June 7, 2023.
32. "International Comparisons of Hourly Compensation Costs in Manufacturing, 2012," BLS, August 9, 2013; "Manufacturing, Value Added (% of GDP)," World Bank, data.worldbank.org/indicator/NV.IND.MANF.ZS.
33. "Production Account Tables, 1987–2018," US Bureau of Economic Analysis, bea .gov/data/special-topics/integrated-industry-level-production-account-klems.
34. Susan Houseman, "Is American Manufacturing in Decline?" W. E. Upjohn Institute for Employment Research, October 2016. The rapid growth reported by statistical agencies in computer manufacturing reflects highly questionable quantifications of the value of increased product quality, not straightforward observations of increased output per se.
35. Susan Houseman, Christopher Kurz, Paul Lengermann, and Benjamin Mandel, "Offshoring Bias in US Manufacturing: Implications for Productivity and Value Added," Board of Governors of the Federal Reserve System, September 2010.

3. The Industrial Policy Tool Kit

1. Granted, some nations, like South Korea, have had successful industrial policy in the face of high inflation, but this must still be accounted a negative factor, a problem struggled with.
2. Granted, some countries do not tax certain things, but this just means they tax other things. And some forms of tax competition are indeed harmful, though this is a topic outside the scope of this book.

3. Consider Henry Clay's schemes for "internal improvements," as infrastructure was called in the nineteenth-century US, or Andrew Jackson's controversial abolition of the second Bank of the United States.

4. Richard G. Lipsey and Kenneth I. Carlaw, "Industrial Policies: Common Not Rare," Discussion Paper 20–11, Department of Economics, Simon Fraser University, September 2020.

5. Singapore did have some protectionism early on in its development, which was abandoned in favor of other strategies because it was not effective. And earlier in economic history, when the optimal scale in most industries was smaller, countries that would not be classified as large today, such as the UK, were protectionist.

6. Some industries, like the Japanese car industry, probably could survive the removal of protection, but continue to receive it. Whether this is good for Japan depends on whether this subsidy serves other valid purposes.

7. This is not an apologia for authoritarianism. Most right-wing and military governments in Latin America, for example, were tightly tied to their nations' economic oligarchies and had no ability to discipline business interests when this was needed.

8. "Local Content Requirements Impact the Global Economy," Organisation for Economic Co-operation and Development (OECD), 2018.

9. "World Tariff Profiles," World Trade Organization, 2019.

10. Jeonghoi Kim, "Recent Trends in Export Restrictions on Raw Materials," in *The Economic Impact of Export Restrictions on Raw Materials* (Paris: OECD Publishing, 2010), 15.

11. 2011 Report to Congress of the US-China Economic and Security Review Commission, November 2011, 72, uscc.gov/sites/default/files/annual_reports/annual_report_full_11.pdf.

12. "World Tariff Profiles," World Trade Organization, 2019.

13. Technically, this is only partly an example of import substitution, as the jet was intended from its inception for global markets, but the larger point still stands.

14. "Trade and Development Report, 1997," United Nations Conference on Trade and Development, September 1997, 180–2.

15. See Michael Hobday, "Export-Led Technology Development in the Four Dragons: The Case of Electronics," *Development and Change* 25 (1994): 333–61.

16. See Wontack Hong, "Export-Oriented Growth and Trade Patterns of Korea," in *Trade and Structural Change in Pacific Asia*, ed. C. I. Bradford and W. H. Branson (Chicago, IL: University of Chicago Press, 1987), 273–305.

17. Indian Ministry of Commerce and Industry, "Remission of Duties and Taxes on Exported Products (RoDTEP) Scheme Gets Extended to Chemicals, Pharmaceuticals and Articles of Iron & Steel from 15.12.2022," December 7, 2022, pib.gov.in/PressReleasePage.aspx? PRID=1881602; "India Subsidies, Export Promo," India Filings, February 26, 2020, indiafilings.com/learn/export-oriented-units-scheme; "EPCG Scheme Relaxed for Sectors Affected by COVID-19 Pandemic," Indian Ministry of Commerce and Industry, January 20, 2021, pib.gov.in/PressReleaseIframePage.aspx? PRID=1892586; "India – Country Commercial Guide," US International Trade Administration, trade.gov/country-commercial-guides/india-import-requirements-and-documentation.

18. This includes only large firms. This estimate is obtained by merging two datasets: the annual survey of Chinese manufacturing firms by China's National Bureau of Statistics and transaction-level customs data from the Chinese General Administration of Customs. See Fabrice Defever and Alejandro Riaño, "Subsidies with Export Share Requirements in China," *Journal of Development Economics* 126 (May 2017): 33–51.

19. Adapted from Martin Murray, "Export Processing Zones (EPZ)," The Balance Small Business, liveabout.com/export-processing-zones-epz-2221273, June 1, 2019.

20. Douglas Zhihua Zeng, "Global Experiences with Special Economic Zones, With a Focus on China and Africa," World Bank, February 2015, 4.

21. Jesus Cañas, Roberto Coronado, and Robert W. Gilmer, "Texas Border: Employment and Maquiladora Growth," Federal Reserve Bank of Dallas, October 2005, 28; "The IMMEX Maquiladora Sector of the Mexican Economy Is a Main Economic Driver," Tecma, June 9, 2015.

22. GDP per capita, 1990: US $39.304, Mexico $7,461, 2019: US $60,687, Mexico $9,820; Mexico as a percentage of US 1990: 19 percent, 2019: 16 percent, "GDP per Capita (Constant 2015 US$)," World Bank. OECD data show that the share of domestic value added in Mexican manufacturing exports did not increase significantly from 2005 to 2016 (from 50.3 percent to 54.1 percent). And in 2016, it was still among the lowest across OECD countries and lower compared to China (82.5 percent), for example. Even in industrial sectors where maquiladoras played a larger role (transport equipment, apparel, electrical machinery, and computer and electronics), shares of domestic value added in exports are not much higher. See Stacy Frederick and Gary Gereffi, "Upgrading and Restructuring in the Global Apparel Value Chain: Why China and Asia Are Outperforming Mexico and Central America," *International Journal of Technological Learning, Innovation and Development* 4, nos. 1–3 (August 2011): 67–95. See also Juan Blyde, "The Participation of Mexico in Global Supply Chains: The Challenge of Adding Mexican Value," Technical Note No. IDB-TN-596, Inter-American Development Bank, September 2013. And see Juan Carlos Castillo and Gaaitzen de Vries, "The Domestic Content of Mexico's Maquiladora Exports: A Long-Run Perspective," *Journal of International Trade & Economic Development* 27, no. 2 (2018): 200–19.

23. See Kristine Farla, Francesca Guadagno, and Bart Verspagen, "Industrial Policy in the European Union," in *Development and Modern Industrial Policy in Practice: Issues and Country Experiences*, ed. Jesus Felipe (Cheltenham: Edward Elgar, 2015), 346–95.

24. "Guarantees," Bpifrance, bpifrance.com/products/guarantees.

25. "Competitiveness and Innovation Framework Programme (2007–2013)," Eur-Lex, eur-lex.europa.eu/EN/legal-content/summary/competitiveness-and-innovation-framework-programme-cip-2007–2013.html.

26. "Banking on Research, Banking for Research, Risk-Sharing Finance Facility (RSFF)," European Commission, 2008.

27. Tacit approval must, of course, give off *some* evidence, or else nobody but the government engaging in it will know it is occurring. The usual sign is when a certain practice is observably known to that government, and that government has the legal and political means to stop it, but does not do so.

28. "China: National Accounts," CEIC Data, 2021.

29. "Shares of Gross Domestic Product: Personal Consumption Expenditures," Federal Reserve Bank of St. Louis, fred.stlouisfed.org/series/DPCERE1Q156NBEA.

30. Robert E. Hall and Charles I. Jones, "Why Do Some Countries Produce So Much More Output Per Worker Than Others?" *Quarterly Journal of Economics* 114, no. 1 (February 1999): 83–116.

31. "Rankings by Total Assets," Sovereign Wealth Fund Institute, swfinstitute.org/fund-rankings/sovereign-wealth-fund.

32. Anna Zakrzewski et al., "Standing Still Is Not an Option: Global Wealth 2022," Boston Consulting Group, June 2022, 3.

33. "Our Portfolio," Temasek, temasek.com.sg/en/our-investments/our-portfolio#sector. Also, "Temasek Review," temasek.com.sg/en/our-financials/library/temasek-review.
34. "State Capital Optimization Gets Impetus," State-Owned Assets Supervision and Administration Commission of the State Council, February 2021, en.sasac.gov.cn/2021/02/24/c_6685.htm. Note that this size estimate indicates a range of supervision, not a unified entity. (A total nearing $40 trillion is reported in a number of sources, but this implies an implausibly high average of $400 billion in assets per company.) Note also that SASAC exercises a range of supervision over firms, not total control over all. SOEs also have many subsidiaries, listed and not listed, and wholly owned versus partly owned, so asset totals depend on what is counted.
35. "Total Market Value of US Stock Market," Siblis Research, December 31, 2021.
36. "About DSM," DSM, dsm.com/engineering-materials/en_US/connect.html.
37. Department of Pharmaceuticals, "Annual Report 2022–23," Government of India, March 23, 2023.
38. Joe Leahy, Peggy Hollinger, and Patti Waldmeir, "Boeing Strikes Deal for Control of Embraer Regional Jet Operations," *Financial Times*, July 5, 2018.
39. Andrea Goldstein, "Embraer: From National Champion to Global Player," *Cepal Review* 77 (August 2002): 97–115; "Investor Relations: Golden Share of the Brazilian Federal Government," Embraer, ri.embraer.com.br/en/governance/golden-share.
40. Artificial "mergers of equals" are especially prone to failure to establish clear overall authority, and failure to impose painful reforms like shutting down duplicative plants and product lines.
41. Airbus was organized at first by France, Germany, and, briefly, the UK, then joined by Spain in 1971 and later by the Netherlands. Exact market share figures vary by segment.
42. There were, for example, four automakers and three shipbuilders. Email from Stewart Paterson, author of *China, Trade, and Power: Why the West's Economic Engagement Has Failed* (London: London Publishing Partnership, 2018).
43. Andy Medici, "CHIPS Act's $500M Tech Hubs Program Has Launched," *The Playbook*, May 12, 2023, commerce.gov/sites/default/files/2023-05/Grant%20program%20for%20tech%20hubs%20launches%20-%20The%20Business%20Journals.pdf.
44. Gary Pisano and Willy Shih, "Restoring American Competitiveness," *Harvard Business Review*, July–August 2009.
45. Pisano and Shih, "Restoring American Competitiveness." Also, Prof. Willy Shih, email to author Ian Fletcher, April 11, 2022.
46. William D. Nordhaus, "Schumpeterian Profits and the Alchemist Fallacy" Yale Economic Applications and Policy Discussion Paper No. 6, Yale University Department of Economics, 2005.
47. Gary Guenther, "Research Tax Credit: Current Law and Policy Issues for the 114th Congress," Congressional Research Service, March 13, 2015.
48. R&D expenditure for SMEs and large enterprises in OECD, EU, and other major economies. See "OECD R&D Tax Incentives Database, 2022 edition," OECD, June 15, 2023.
49. Fraunhofer Society: "Finances," Fraunhofer, fraunhofer.de/en/about-fraunhofer/profile-structure/facts-and-figures/finances.html. National Institute of Advanced Science and Technology: "Collaborative Research," AIST, aist.go.jp/aist_e/collab/collabresearch/index.html.
50. "MEP International Network," National Institute of Standards and Technology (NIST), nist.gov/mep/mep-national-network.

51. "FY 2022 NIST MEP Economic Impact," NIST, Manufacturing Extension Partnership, January 2023.
52. See "Figure RD-3: Ratio of US R&D to Gross Domestic Product, by Roles of Federal, Business, and Other Funding for R&D: 1953–2020," in Mark Boroush and Ledia Guci, "Recent Trends in US R&D Performance," National Science Board, April 2022.
53. Sridhar Kota, Justin Talbot-Zorn, and Tom Mahoney, "How the US Can Rebuild Its Capacity to Innovate," *Harvard Business Review*, October 23, 2018.
54. Gregory Tassey, *The Technology Imperative* (Northampton, MA: Edward Elgar, 2007), 213.
55. "Exhibit 3: US Exports of Services by Major Category" and "Exhibit 4: US Imports of Services by Major Category," in "US International Trade in Goods and Services, December and Annual 2022," US Bureau of Economic Analysis, February 7, 2023.
56. "The Theft of American Intellectual Property: Reassessments of the Challenge and United States Policy," The Commission on the Theft of American Intellectual Property at the National Bureau of Asian Research, 2017.
57. Atsuko Kamiike, "The TRIPS Agreement and the Pharmaceutical Industry in India," *Journal of Interdisciplinary Economics* 32, no. 1, January 2020.
58. Sun Xiaohua, "3G Trouble for China Mobile?" *China Daily*, January 5, 2009.
59. "Project Socrates," projectsocrates.us/index.html.
60. NSF, "Assessing and Predicting Technology Outcomes (APTO)," NSF 23–600, 2023, nsf. gov/pubs/2023/nsf23600/nsf23600.htm.

4. Trade, Currencies, and Industrial Policy

1. Granted, there are, of course, some benefits to the American consumer of being able to buy foreign goods more cheaply because they have been subsidized. But this is definitely no longer a free-market situation.
2. Production: "After the Personal Computer: Companies Built on PCs Are Adapting to a Changed World," *Economist*, July 6, 2013; "Decline in Global Market Share Dampened Greater China Notebook PC Shipments in 2Q 2013, Says MIC," Market Intelligence & Consulting Institute, Taipei, September 6, 2013. Market: Authors' estimate based on percentage of world GDP.
3. This material adapted with permission from Ian Fletcher, *Free Trade Doesn't Work: What Should Replace It and Why* (Washington, DC: US Business and Industry Council, 2010).
4. The idea that all voluntary exchanges must be mutually beneficial is misleading anyway, because it says nothing about the context of relative bargaining power in which exchanges take place. It may be mutually beneficial for a starving man to sell his shoes!
5. Programs such as Trade Adjustment Assistance (TAA), which try to "compensate the losers" of freer trade, are far too small and suffer intrinsic limits to what they can do.
6. Dani Rodrik, *Has Globalization Gone Too Far?* (Washington, DC: Institute for International Economics, 1997), 30.
7. Louis S. Jacobson, Robert J. LaLonde, and Daniel G. Sullivan, "Earnings Losses of Displaced Workers," staff working paper no. 92–11, W. E. Upjohn Institute for Employment Research, February 1992.
8. See, for example, Jacobson et al., "Earnings Losses of Displaced Workers." Also, David H. Autor, David Dorn, and Gordon H. Hanson, "The China Shock: Learning

from Labor-Market Adjustment to Large Changes in Trade," *Annual Review of Economics* 8, no. 2 (October 2016): 205–40.

9. A 2001 study found that equipment from shuttered aerospace factories was sold at an average market value of 28 cents per dollar value of replacement cost. See Valerie Ramey and Matthew Shapiro, "Displaced Capital: A Study of Aerospace Plant Closings," *Journal of Political Economy* 109, no. 5 (October 2001): 958–92, at 978.

10. As he put it, "The difference in this respect, between a single country and many, is easily accounted for, by considering the difficulty with which capital moves from one country to another, to seek a more profitable employment, and the activity with which it invariably passes from one province to another of the same country." Ricardo then elaborates, using his favorite example of the trade in English cloth for Portuguese wine: "It would undoubtedly be advantageous to the capitalists of England, and to the consumers in both countries, that under such circumstances the wine and the cloth should both be made in Portugal, and therefore that the capital and labor of England employed in making cloth should be removed to Portugal for that purpose." But he does *not* say it would be advantageous to the workers of England! Given that consumers and workers are ultimately the same people, this means they may lose more as workers than they gain as consumers. Having observed that capital mobility would undo his theory, Ricardo then argues why capital will not, in fact, be mobile – as he knew he had to prove for his theory to hold water: "Experience, however, shows that the fancied or real insecurity of capital, when not under the immediate control of its owner, together with the natural disinclination which every man has to quit the country of his birth and connections, and entrust himself, with all his habits fixed, to a strange government and new laws, check the emigration of capital." David Ricardo, *The Principles of Political Economy and Taxation* (Mineola, NY: Dover, 2004), 83.

11. Working Group on Human Capital Accounting Disclosure, letter to Vanessa A. Countryman, Secretary, Securities and Exchange Commission, June 7, 2022.

12. Causation goes both directions here, of course, as a rise in productivity will make a particular industry in a particular nation more export competitive.

13. See Paul A. Samuelson, "Where Ricardo and Mill Rebut and Confirm Arguments of Mainstream Economists Supporting Globalization," *Journal of Economic Perspectives* 18, no. 3 (Summer 2004): 135–46. See also Ralph E. Gomory and William J. Baumol, *Global Trade and Conflicting National Interests* (Cambridge, MA: MIT Press, 2000); Harry G. Johnson, "The Possibility of Income Losses from Increased Efficiency of Factor Accumulation in the Presence of Tariffs," *Economic Journal* 77, no. 305 (March 1967): 151–4.

14. For a detailed formal treatment, see Thomas I. Palley, "Rethinking Trade and Trade Policy: Gomory, Baumol, and Samuelson on Comparative Advantage," Levy Economics Institute of Bard College, October 2006. This point is also noted in Stephen S. Cohen and J. Bradford DeLong, *Concrete Economics* (Boston, MA: Harvard Business Review Press, 2016), 18.

15. Granted, things could play out with merely our production declining and theirs rising, but the logic is the same.

16. This point is noted in Cohen and DeLong, *Concrete Economics*, 19.

17. Samuelson, "Where Ricardo and Mill Rebut and Confirm Arguments," 135–46. See also Timothy R. Gulden, "Agent-Based Modeling As a Tool for Trade and Development Theory," *Journal of Artificial Societies and Social Simulation* 16, no. 2 (March 2013): 1 for a computer model confirming this result.

18. Naturally, overall prosperity is a matter of productivity in traded and non-traded sectors both, so strictly speaking, we are not talking about prosperity, but trade's contribution to a nation's prosperity.

19. For a precise Ricardian analysis of this problem, see Frank D. Graham, "Some Aspects of Protection Further Considered," *Quarterly Journal of Economics* 37, no. 2 (February 1923).

20. The first published work of this type of multiple-equilibrium trade theory was Ralph E. Gomory, "A Ricardo Model with Economies of Scale," *Proceedings of the National Academy of Sciences* 88, no. 18 (September 1991): 8267–71. The book setting forth the complete theory is Ralph Gomory and William Baumol's *Global Trade and Conflicting National Interests*. Gomory and Baumol were not the first economists to identify the value of winning retainable industries, or to establish firm theoretical grounds for the possibility that government intervention might help a nation win them. Credit for rediscovering this ancient truth and putting it into the theoretical framework of modern economics goes to James Brander and Barbara Spencer of the University of British Columbia, who developed a theory of so-called strategic trade around 1983. Their point, elaborated without Gomory and Baumol's multiple-equilibrium approach, was that in monopoly industries, a well-timed government subsidy could potentially hand a "winner take all" industry to one nation or another.

21. The classic statement of the concept of retainable industries is in Gomory and Baumol, *Global Trade and Conflicting National Interests*.

22. Do not misunderstand this as meaning that the so-called first mover advantage is everything. A whole host of other things need to happen for a producer to hang on to said advantage once seized. But focusing on this one dynamic for now will still give us the right answer to the immediate set of questions we are asking here, even if it would be an oversimplification in other contexts.

23. Indeed, freer trade can bring about the so-called Vanek–Reinert effect, in which freer trade kills off the more advantageous (in the sense we have used the term in this book) sectors of the more primitive economy. See Erik Reinert, "International Trade and the Economic Mechanisms of Underdevelopment" (PhD diss., Cornell University, May 1980).

24. The framers of the GATT worked in the context of the Bretton Woods system of fixed exchange rates, which at least prevented currency manipulation.

25. This material adapted with permission from Fletcher, *Free Trade Doesn't Work*.

26. These are gross, not net, jobs. The workers who would have been employed building aircraft will presumably (*pace* cyclical and frictional unemployment) find jobs doing *something*.

27. See, for example, Martin Feldstein, "Inconvenient Truths about the US Trade Deficit," Project Syndicate, April 25, 2017.

28. The technical way of saying this is that free-market economics treats the time discount on consumption as an exogenous preference.

29. This is done indirectly, by way of ordinary Chinese commercial banks, which are required to turn over the dollars to the People's Bank of China.

30. "Preliminary Report on Foreign Holdings of US Securities at End–June 2022," US Department of the Treasury, February 28, 2023, Table B, includes Hong Kong.

31. Article IV, revised, which went into effect in 1978. See "Article IV of the Fund's Articles of Agreement: An Overview of the Legal Framework," International Monetary Fund, June 28, 2006.

32. Jeff Ferry, "Currency Misalignment Monitor, October 2023," prosperousamerica .org/currency-misalignment-monitor-october-2023.

33. Robert E. Scott, "Testimony before the US Department of Commerce on Causes of Significant Trade Deficits for 2016," Economic Policy Institute, May 18, 2017. (This estimate and the one in the previous sentence do not agree exactly, but still confirm the approximate range.)

34. Atish R. Ghosh and Mahvash S. Qureshi, "What's in a Name? That Which We Call Capital Controls," working paper, International Monetary Fund, February 2016.

35. S. 2357 (116th Congress). The proposal is derived from work done by John Hansen, former World Bank economist and a member of the Advisory Board of the Coalition for a Prosperous America, to whom the authors would like to express their thanks for helping them understand this issue.

36. Jeff Ferry, "Fix the Dollar to Build Back Better," Coalition for a Prosperous America, November 2021, prosperousamerica.org/wp-content/uploads/2023/04/211101-CPA-Fix-Dollar-to-Build-Back-Better-Nov-2021.pdf.

37. "Indirect Tax Rates Table," KPMG, kpmg.com/it/it/home/services/tax/tax-tools-and-resources/tax-rates-online/indirect-tax-rates-table.html; Cristina Enache, "2022 VAT Rates in Europe," Tax Foundation, January 25, 2022.

38. The exceptions are state and local sales taxes that are imposed upon sale to the user of a final product. These taxes are not charged on exports and are charged on imports when they are sold in the US. To the extent that they are substitutes for taxes that *do* burden exports and are not charged on imports: these taxes function like VATs. However, the level of sales taxes varies widely and are virtually all much lower than the VATs of the major US trade counterparties.

39. Emmanuel Farhi, Gita Gopinath, and Oleg Itskhoki, "Fiscal Devaluations," *Review of Economic Studies* 81, no. 2 (April 2014): 725–60.

40. See the chapter "The Natural Strategic Tariff" in Fletcher, *Free Trade Doesn't Work* for details.

41. Jeff Ferry and Amanda Mayoral, "Pro-growth Tariffs: Estimates from CPA's New Trade Model," Coalition for a Prosperous America, September 2022.

42. Andrew Heritage, "Model Shows That Universal 10% Tariff Would Improve Incomes, Output and Jobs," Coalition for a Prosperous America, September 18, 2023, prosperousamerica.org/model-shows-that-universal-10-tariff-would-improve-incomes-output-and-jobs.

5. Japan: The First Asian Miracle

1. "GDP (Current US$): Japan, United States, United Kingdom, France, Germany, China," World Bank, data.worldbank.org/indicator/NY.GDP.MKTP.CD?end=2021&locations=JP-US-GB-FR-DE-CN&start=1960&view=chart.

2. For example, the Competitiveness Policy Council, an independent federal advisory committee chartered in 1988. (Its 1992 report was largely ignored and it ceased operations in 1997.) This organization is not to be confused with the Council on Competitiveness, a private group founded in 1986 by John Young, CEO of Hewlett-Packard and Chairman of President Reagan's Commission on Industrial Competitiveness.

3. Bureau of Industry and Security, "US Trade with Japan: 2020," US Department of Commerce, 2020, 2.

4. Shoya Okinaga, "Japan Fights for Lead in Advanced Chip and EV Materials," Nikkei Asia, September 21, 2021.

5. Antonio Varas, Raj Varadarajan, Jimmy Goodrich, and Falan Yinug, "Government Incentives and US Competitiveness in Semiconductor Manufacturing," Boston Consulting Group and the Semiconductor Industry Association, September 2020, 7.

6. Observatory of Economic Complexity, cars: oec.world/en/profile/hs92/cars; ships: oec.world/en/visualize/tree_map/hs92/export/show/all/178901/2020.

7. "Driving ROI through AI," ESI ThoughtLab, October 2020, 13.

8. "2018 BSA Global Cloud Computing Scorecard," The Software Alliance, 2018, 12.

9. William W. Lewis, *The Power of Productivity: Wealth, Poverty, and the Threat to Global Stability* (Chicago, IL: University of Chicago Press, 2004), xvi–xvii, 25.

10. Bai Gao, *Economic Ideology and Japanese Industrial Policy: Developmentalism from 1931 to 1965* (Cambridge: Cambridge University Press, 1997), 47.

11. "Gini Index: United States, China, Japan, Germany, United Kingdom," World Bank, data.worldbank.org/indicator/SI.POV.GINI?end=2019&locations=US-CN-JP-DE-GB&name_desc=false&start=2000.

12. Giovanni Dosi, Laura D'Andrea Tyson, and John Zysman, "Trade, Technologies, and Development: A Framework for Discussing Japan," in *Politics and Productivity: How Japan's Development Strategy Works*, ed. Chalmers Johnson, Laura D'Andrea Tyson, and John Zysman (Cambridge, MA: Ballinger, 1989), 3–38.

13. Dosi et al., "Trade, Technologies."

14. Myohei Shinohara, *Industrial Growth, Trade and Dynamic Patterns in the Japanese Economy* (Tokyo: University of Tokyo Press, 1982), 29.

15. Eric Helleiner, *The Neomercantilists: A Global Intellectual History* (Ithaca, NY: Cornell University Press, 2021), 202.

16. Gao, *Economic Ideology*, 18–120; James Fallows, *Looking at the Sun: The Rise of the New East Asian Economic and Political System* (New York: Pantheon, 1994), 177–216.

17. Anton Chaitkin, "Japan and America Banish Feudalism," The Schiller Institute, July 27–August 2, 2014.

18. Marie Anchordoguy, *Reprogramming Japan: The High Tech Crisis under Communitarian Capitalism* (Ithaca, NY: Cornell University Press, 2005), 67–8. Also see Chalmers Johnson, *MITI and the Japanese Miracle: The Growth of Industrial Policy, 1925–1975* (Stanford, CA: Stanford University Press, 1982), 23.

19. Chalmers Johnson, "The Japanese 'Miracle,'" in *The Japanese Economy: Part 2*, ed. Peter Drysdale and Luke Gower (Abingdon: Routledge, 1999), 20.

20. Tetsuji Okazaki and Masahiro Okuno-Fujiwara, eds., *The Japanese Economic System and Its Historical Origins* (New York: Oxford University Press, 1999).

21. Professor Walter Skya, University of Alaska–Fairbanks, by email to author Ian Fletcher.

22. Noguchi Yukio, *1940-nen Taisei [The 1940 System]* (Tokyo: Toyokeizai Shimposha, 1995).

23. Noguchi, *1940-nen Taisei*; Gao, *Economic Ideology*, 18–120.

24. Johnson, *MITI and the Japanese Miracle*, 83–115; Gao, *Economic Ideology*, 18–120; Yasusuke Murakami, *An Anticlassical Political–Economic Analysis: A Vision for the Next Century*, trans. Kozo Yamamura (Stanford, CA: Stanford University Press, 1997); Fallows, *Looking at the Sun*, 177–216.

25. See, for example, K. K. Kawakami, "Britain's Trade War with Japan," *Foreign Affairs*, April 1934.

26. David Flath, "The Japanese Economy" (4th ed.), Chapter 4: Economic History, Part 3: Postwar Recovery (1945–1964), June 2022, academic.oup.com/book/44167/chapter-abstract/372364328?redirectedFrom=fulltext&login=false.

27. David A. C. Addicott, "The Rise and Fall of the Zaibatsu: Japan's Industrial and Economic Modernization," *Global Tides* 11 (2017): 11.

28. Nakamura Takafusa, *The Postwar Japanese Economy: Its Development and Structure*, trans. Jacqueline Kaminski (Tokyo: Tokyo University Press, 1981), 44.

29. Nakamura, *Postwar Japanese*, 44.

30. Johnson, *MITI and the Japanese Miracle*, 210–11.

31. Eamonn Fingleton, *Blindside: Why Japan Is Still on Track to Overtake the US by the Year 2000* (New York: Houghton Mifflin Buttonwood Press, 1995), 202.

32. Eamonn Fingleton, "The Long Arm of Japanese Industrial Policy: Northern Ireland's Experience," blog post, *Sandcastle Empire*, October 14, 2020, fingleton.net/the-long-arm-of-japanese-industrial-policy-northern-irelands-experience.

33. Nakamura, *Postwar Japanese*, 45.

34. Merton J. Peck and Shuji Tamura, "Technology," in *Asia's New Giant*, ed. Hugh Patrick and Henry Rosovsky (Washington, DC: Brookings Institution, 1976), 553.

35. They are thus naturally understandable as solutions to Prof. Fred Block's problem of "network failure."

36. Today, the main bank still has a voice on the board, but there are also outside directors and insiders not from the main bank. Thus, main banks still are involved in corporate governance, but they do not lead it. Also, the MOF is no longer involved.

37. Anchordoguy, *Reprogramming Japan*, 47.

38. Judith Stein, *Pivotal Decade: How the United States Traded Factories for Finance in the 1970s* (New Haven, CT: Yale University Press, 2010), 163–4.

39. Robert H. Hayes, "Why Japanese Factories Work," *Harvard Business Review*, July 1981.

40. David J. Teece, "Profiting from Technological Innovation: Implications for Integration, Collaboration, Licensing, and Public Policy," *Research Policy* 15, no. 6 (1986): 285–305.

41. Anchordoguy, *Reprogramming Japan*, 47–54.

42. Japan had significant leftist political movements, enough so that there were huge demonstrations in 1959–60 against the new US–Japan security treaty – which had to be forced through the Diet by tactics so problematic that Prime Minister Kishi ultimately had to resign over them.

43. For the full details, see Pat Choate, *Agents of Influence* (New York: Knopf, 1990).

44. Stephen Cooney and Brent D. Yacobucci, *US Automotive Industry: Policy Overview and Recent History* (New York: Novinka Books, 2007), 84–5.

45. Motoshige Ito and Kazuharu Kiyono, "Foreign Trade and Direct Investment," in *Industrial Policy of Japan*, ed. Ryutaro Komiya, Masahiro Okuno, and Kotaro Suzumura (Tokyo: Academic Press, 1988), 161.

46. Patricia A. O'Brien, "Coordinating Market Forces: The Anatomy of Investment Decisions in the Japanese Steel Industry, 1945–1975" (PhD diss., Harvard Business School, 1986), 42.

47. Ira C. Magaziner and Thomas M. Hout, *Japanese Industrial Policy* (London: Policy Studies Institute, 1980), 62–3.

48. See Leonard L. Lynn, *How Japan Innovates: A Comparison with the US in the Case of Oxygen Steelmaking* (Boulder, CO: Westview Press, 1982), 1–2; Kiyoshi Kawahito, *The Japanese Steel Industry* (New York: Praeger, 1972), 44–6.

49. Lynn, *How Japan Innovates*, 97.

50. Lynn, *How Japan Innovates*, 83–5.

51. Kawahito, *The Japanese Steel Industry*, 48.

52. Paul R. Krugman, "Targeted Industrial Policies: Theory and Evidence," in *The New Protectionist Threat to World Welfare*, ed. Dominick Salvatore (New York: Elsevier Science Publishing, 1987), 283–8.

53. This information on protectionism all comes from Phyllis A. Genther, *A History of Japan's Government–Business Relationship: The Passenger Car Industry* (Ann Arbor: University of Michigan Press, 1990), 85–7.

54. C. S. Chang, *The Japanese Auto Industry and the US Market* (New York: Praeger, 1981), 47.

55. Genther, *A History of Japan's*, 43–63.

56. Genther, *A History of Japan's*, 87–9.

57. Genther, *A History of Japan's*, 69–73.

58. Hiroya Ueno and Hiromichi Muto, "The Automobile Industry of Japan," *Japanese Economic Studies* 3, no. 1 (Fall 1974): 12–13.

59. Magaziner and Hout, "Japanese Industrial Policy," 69–70.

60. The Basic Policy for the Introduction of Foreign Investment into Japan's Passenger Car Industry. See Genther, *A History of Japan's*, 80, 85–7.

61. Genther, *A History of Japan's*, 80, 85–7.

62. Michael Cusumano, *The Japanese Automobile Industry: Technology and Management at Nissan and Toyota* (Cambridge, MA: Harvard University Press, 1985), xix.

63. Komiya Ryutaro, Takeuchi Hiroshi, and Kitahara Masao, "Kaden Denki," in *Nihon no Sangyo Soshiki Ron Vol. I*, ed. Kumagai Hisao (Tokyo: Chuo Koron Sha, 1973), 73.

64. Komiya, Takeuchi, and Kitahara, "Kaden Denki."

65. Komiya, Takeuchi, and Kitahara, "Kaden Denki."

66. Merit E. Janow, "Whither the Future of Japanese Industrial Development Policies?" *Michigan Journal of International Law* 6, no. 1 (1984): 121–2.

67. This overview of the color TV case draws heavily on Kozo Yamamura and Jan Vandenberg, "Japan's Rapid-Growth Policy on Trial: The Television Case," in *Law and Trade Issues of the Japanese Economy*, ed. Gary Saxonhouse and Kozo Yamamura (Seattle: University of Washington Press, 1986), 238–3.

68. Komiya, Takeuchi, and Kitahara, "Kaden Denki," 28. Also, *Denshi Kogyo Nenkan [Electronics Industry Yearbook]*, 1973, 752.

69. *Toyokeizai*, January 23, 1971, 12; Komiya, Takeuchi, and Kitahara, "Kaden Denki," 66–7.

70. Ishida Hideto and John O'Haley, "Anticompetitive Practices in the Distribution of Goods and Services in Japan: The Problem of Distribution Keiretsu," *Journal of Japanese Studies* 9, no. 2 (Summer 1983): 319–34.

71. James E. Millstein, "Decline in an Expanding Industry: Japanese Competition in Color Television," in *American Industry in International Competition: Government Policies and Corporate Strategies*, ed. John Zysman and Laura Tyson (Ithaca, NY: Cornell University Press, 1983), 106–41.

72. Alfred E. Eckes Jr., *Opening America's Market: Foreign Trade since 1776* (Chapel Hill: University of North Carolina Press, 1995), 272.

73. David Yoffie, "Zenith and the Color Television Fight," case no. 383–070, Harvard Business School, 1982, 7; David Schwartzman, *The Japanese Television Cartel: A Study Based on Matsushita v. Zenith* (Ann Arbor: University of Michigan Press, 1993), 117.

74. Yamamura and Vandenberg, "Japan's Rapid-Growth Policy on Trial," 261; *Toyokeizai (The Oriental Economist)*, January 26, 1980, 84; "Scandals: Kickbacks in Living Color," *Time*, June 13, 1977, 63.

75. Yoffie, "Zenith and the Color Television Fight," 1–17; Schwartzman, *The Japanese Television Cartel*, 117–28; Millstein, "Decline in an Expanding Industry," 132–3.
76. Millstein, "Decline in an Expanding Industry," 129–35.
77. Barnaby J. Feder, "Last TV Maker Will Sell Control to Koreans," *New York Times*, July 18, 1995.
78. Feder, "Last TV Maker."
79. See, for example, Gary R. Saxonhouse, "Why Japan Is Winning," *Issues in Science and Technology* 2, no. 3 (Spring 1986): 72–80; Edward J. Lincoln, *Japan's Industrial Policies* (Washington, DC: Japan Economic Institute of America, 1984), 34–6; Paul R. Krugman, "Targeted Industrial Policies: Theory and Evidence," Economic Policy Symposium–Jackson Hole, Federal Reserve Bank of Kansas City, August 24–26, 1983, 123–55, 289–94. Also, Michael G. Borrus, *Competing for Control: America's Stake in Microelectronics* (Cambridge, MA: Ballinger, 1988) and Michael Borrus, Laura D'Andrea Tyson, and John Zysman, "Creating Advantage: How Government Policies Shape International Trade in the Semiconductor Industry," in *Strategic Trade Policy and the New International Economics*, ed. Paul R. Krugman (Cambridge, MA: MIT Press, 1986), 91–113.
80. *Toyokeizai (The Oriental Economist)*, October 22, 1966, 26, cited in Anchordoguy, *Reprogramming Japan*, 179.
81. *Denshi Kogyo 30 Nenshi [Thirty-Year History of the Electronics Industry]* (Tokyo: Nihon Denshi Kikai Kogyokai, 1979), 101–3; Yasuzo Nakagawa, *Nihon no Handotai Kaihatsu [The Development of Japan's Semiconductor Industry]* (Tokyo: Daiyamondosha, 1981), 154–8, cited in Anchordoguy, *Reprogramming Japan*, 179.
82. *Toyokeizai (The Oriental Economist)*, October 22, 1966, 26, cited in Anchordoguy, *Reprogramming Japan*, 179.
83. *Asahi Shimbun [Asahi Newspaper]*, April 27, 1967, 7; Nihon Choki Shinyo Ginko, *Chogin Chosa Geppo [Industrial Bank of Japan Monthly Survey]*, May 1966, 55.
84. *Denshi Kogyo Nenkan [Electronics Industry Yearbook]* (Tokyo: Dempa Shimbun), 1970–1, 634; *Nihon Keizai Shimbun [Japan Economic Newspaper]*, April 17, 1967, 12; *Toyokeizai (The Oriental Economist)*, special first issue of 1967, 142–3; *Japan Economic Journal*, November 22, 1966, 3.
85. *Nihon Keizai Shimbun [Japan Economic Newspaper]*, July 26, 1967, 5, cited in Anchordoguy, *Reprogramming Japan*, 180.
86. Interview of former MITI official involved in the negotiations, April 11, 1989, cited in Marie Anchordoguy, "A Challenge to Free Trade? Japanese Industrial Targeting in the Computer and Semiconductor Industries," in *Japan's Economic Structure: Should It Change?* ed. Kozo Yamamura (Seattle, WA: Society for Japanese Studies, 1990), 309.
87. *Toyokeizai*, June 10, 1972, 81; and February 26, 1972, 81, cited in Anchordoguy, *Reprogramming Japan*, 180.
88. *Nihon Keizai Shimbun*, September 26, 1971, cited in Anchordoguy, *Reprogramming Japan*, 181.
89. *Toyokeizai*, June 10, 1972, 81, cited in Anchordoguy, *Reprogramming Japan*, 182.
90. *Toyokeizai*, June 10, 1972, 82, cited in Anchordoguy, *Reprogramming Japan*, 182.
91. Anchordoguy, *Reprogramming Japan*, 88.
92. Anchordoguy, *Reprogramming Japan*, 81. A Fujitsu official once explicitly said that his firm used profits from NTT to enter and survive in the computer industry. See Anchordoguy, *Reprogramming Japan*, footnote 49, 89.

93. Yasuzo Nakagawa, *NTT Gijutsu Suimyaku [NTT's Technological Veins]*, 119, 138; NTT, *Denden 10 Nen no Ayumi [NTT's First 10 Years]*, (Tokyo: Tōyō Keizai Shinpōsha, 1990), 78; Interview of former top-level NTT official, November 14, 1996, cited in Anchordoguy, *Reprogramming Japan* (Tokyo: NTT, 1962), footnote 36, 77.

94. Kenneth Flamm, *Mismanaged Trade? Strategic Policy and the Semiconductor Industry* (Washington, DC: Brookings Institution Press, 1996); Borrus, *Competing for Control*.

95. Robert D. Hof, "Lessons from Sematech," *MIT Technology Review*, July 25, 2011.

96. Laura D'Andrea Tyson and David Yoffie, "Semiconductors: From Manipulated to Managed Trade," working paper no. 47, Berkeley Roundtable on the International Economy, August 1991, 26.

97. Tyson and Yoffie, "Semiconductors," 33–4.

98. Electronics Industry Association of Japan, *A Look at 50 Years of the Japanese Electronics Industry* (Tokyo: Electronics Industry Association of Japan, 1998), 81–2; Wataru Nakayama, William Boulton, and Michael Pecht, *The Japanese Electronics Industry* (New York: Chapman and Hall/CRC Press, 1999), 47–8; Flamm, *Mismanaged Trade?* 227–304; Tyson and Yoffie, "Semiconductors."

99. Antonio Varas et al., "Government Incentives and US Competitiveness in Semiconductor Manufacturing," Boston Consulting Group and Semiconductor Industry Association, September 2020, 7.

100. Brandon Gaille, "Japan Semiconductor Industry Statistics, Trends and Analysis," *BrandonGaille*, December 3, 2018, brandongaille.com/14-japan-semiconductor-industry-statistics-trends-analysis.

101. Marie Anchordoguy, Computers Inc.: Japan's Challenge to IBM (Cambridge, MA: Council on East Asian Studies, Harvard University, 1989), 34–5.

102. Anchordoguy, *Computers, Inc.*, 22.

103. Marie Anchordoguy, "Mastering the Market: Japanese Government Targeting of the Computer Industry," *International Organization* 42, no. 3 (Summer 1988): 516.

104. Chalmers Johnson, *Japan's Public Policy Companies* (Stanford, CA: American Enterprise Institute–Hoover Policy Studies, 1977).

105. Anchordoguy, *Reprogramming Japan*, 131.

106. Flamm, *Mismanaged Trade?* 60.

107. Tarui Yasuo, "Japan Seeks Its Own Route to Improved IC Techniques," *Electronics*, December 13, 1965, 90–1, cited in Marie Anchordoguy, *Reprogramming Japan*, 179.

108. One exception to this was Matsushita, which entered the industry but dropped out soon after.

109. Anchordoguy, *Reprogramming Japan*, footnote 25, 135.

110. Anchordoguy, *Reprogramming Japan*, 132.

111. Anchordoguy, *Reprogramming Japan*, 132.

112. Anchordoguy, *Reprogramming Japan*, 136.

113. Anchordoguy, *Reprogramming Japan*, 136.

114. Anchordoguy, *Reprogramming Japan*, 160–1.

115. Anchordoguy, *Reprogramming Japan*, 160–1.

116. Robert P. Merges, "A Comparative Look at Intellectual Property Rights and the Software Industry," in *The International Computer Software Industry*, ed. David Mowery (New York: Oxford University Press, 1996), 272–303; Telegram

from US Embassy Tokyo to Department of Commerce Undersecretary Lionel Olmer, record #79620, January 20, 1984.

117. Amakasa Keisuke, *Denshi Rikkoku Nippon [The Establishment of Japan As an Electronics Nation]* (Tokyo: Shashoku Shobo, 1991), cited in Anchordoguy, *Reprogramming Japan*, 162.

118. Much of this draws on Anchordoguy, *Computers, Inc.*, and Marie Anchordoguy, "Japan's Software Industry: A Failure of Institutions?" *Research Policy* 29, no. 3 (2000): 391–408.

119. Andrew Pollack, "'Fifth Generation' Became Japan's Lost Generation," *New York Times*, June 5, 1992.

120. "Embedded System Market by Product (Software and Hardware), Functionality (Real-Time Embedded System, Network Embedded System, Standalone Embedded System and Mobile Embedded System), System Size, End-Users, Region, Global Industry Analysis, Market Size, Share, Growth, Trends, and Forecast 2020 to 2027," report no. 418045, Fior Markets, May 2020.

121. "Market Share Analysis: Microcontrollers, Worldwide, 2019," Gartner Research, April 2020, 2.

122. "Made with Japan: A Partnership on the Frontiers of Aerospace," Boeing Japan, November 2012, 6.

123. Fiona Harrigan, "Integrating Theories of Boundary Choice: A Case from the Global Aircraft Industry," paper prepared for the International Conference on Coordination and Cooperation across Organisational Boundaries, Università Cattolica del Sacro Cuore, Milan, April 20–21, 2006.

124. Richard J. Samuels, *"Rich Nation, Strong Army": National Security and Technological Transformation of Japan* (Ithaca, NY: Cornell University Press, 1994), 232.

125. For examples of Japan alarmism (of varying degrees of rationality), see Herman Kahn and Thomas Pepper, *The Japanese Challenge: The Success and Failure of Economic Success* (New York: Thomas Y. Crowell, 1979); Daniel Burstein and Herman Kahn, *Yen! Japan's New Financial Empire and Its Threat to America* (New York: Simon & Schuster, 1988); George Friedman and Meredith LeBard, *The Coming War with Japan* (New York: St. Martin's Press, 1991); Lester Thurow, *Head to Head: The Coming Economic Battle among Japan, Europe, and America* (New York: William Morrow, 1992); Marvin J. Wolf, *The Japanese Conspiracy: The Plot to Dominate Industry World-Wide and How to Deal with It* (New York: Empire Books, 1983); Jeffrey E. Garten, *A Cold Peace: America, Japan, Germany and the Struggle for Supremacy* (New York: Times Books, 1992); Clyde V. Prestowitz et al., *Powernomics: Economics and Strategy after the Cold War* (Chicago, IL: Madison Books, 1991); Eamonn Fingleton, *Blindside: Why Japan Is Still on Track to Overtake the US by the Year 2000* (New York: Houghton Mifflin, 1995).

126. "Working Better with Age: Japan," Organisation for Economic Co-operation and Development (OECD), 2018, 13. Calculation from "Working Age Population: Aged 15–64: All Persons for Japan," Federal Reserve Bank of St. Louis, fred.stlouisfed.org/series/LFWA64TTJPM647S.

127. "Hours Worked: Japan and United States," OECD, 2021.

128. Reported in Paul Krugman, "What Happened to Japan?" newsletter, *New York Times*, July 25, 2023, with sources fred.stlouisfed.org, OECD, BEA, Japanese Cabinet Office.

129. Steven K. Vogel, "The Rise and Fall of the Japanese Bureaucracy," in *The Oxford Handbook of Japanese Politics*, ed. Robert J. Pekkanen and Saadia M. Pekkanen (New York: Oxford University Press, 2021), 101–16.

130. William W. Grimes, *Unmaking the Japanese Miracle: Macroeconomic Politics, 1985–2000* (Ithaca, NY, Cornell University Press, 2001), xviii.

131. "Japan Share Ownership: Foreigners," CEIC data, ceicdata.com/en/japan/all-stock-exchange-percentage-of-shareownership-by-investors/share-ownership-foreigners.

132. Anchordoguy, *Reprogramming Japan*, 50–4.

133. Katsuki Aoki and Thomas Taro Lennerfors, "The New, Improved Keiretsu," *Harvard Business Review*, September 2013.

134. See Yves Tiberghien, *Entrepreneurial States: Reforming Corporate Governance in France, Japan, and Korea* (Ithaca, NY: Cornell University Press, 2007).

135. Mori Hamada and Matsumo Shintaro Okawa, "The Overview of the Economic Security Promotion Bill and Its Impact on Business," Center for Information on Security Trades Control, February 28, 2022.

6. Korea: Development despite Turbulence

1. "GDP per Capita Growth (Annual %)," World Bank, data, worldbank.org/indicator/NY.GDP.PCAP.KD.ZG.

2. "GDP per Capita, PPP (Current International $)," World Bank, data.worldbank.org/indicator/NY.GDP.PCAP.PP.CD?locations=JP-KR-US.

3. Most recent available data from "Gini Index: Korea, Rep., United States," data.worldbank.org/indicator/SI.POV.GINI?locations=KR-US.

4. Ha-Joon Chang, "The Political Economy of Industrial Policy in Korea," *Cambridge Journal of Economics* 17, no. 2 (June 1993): 131–57.

5. Byung-Kook Kim and Ezra F. Vogel, eds., *The Park Chung Hee Era: The Transformation of South Korea* (Cambridge, MA: Harvard University Press, 2011), 86.

6. "Korean Corruption," GlobalSecurity.org, globalsecurity.org/military/world/rok/corruption.htm.

7. David C. Kang, *Crony Capitalism: Corruption and Development in South Korea and the Philippines* (New York: Cambridge University Press, 2002), 96–121.

8. Atul Kohli, "Where Do High Growth Political Economies Come From? The Japanese Lineage of Korea's 'Developmental State,'" *World Development* 22, no. 9 (September 1994): 1269–93.

9. Korean GDP per capita in 1953 was $65.70 in 2015 dollars, according to Statistics Korea, kosis.kr/eng. US GDP per capita in 1953 was $16,906 in 2012 dollars, according to the US Bureau of Economic Analysis, fred.stlouisfed.org/series/A939RX0Q048SBEA. Converted to 2023 dollars, Korea's per capita GDP was $83.73 and the US's was $22,405.51, which puts Korea's per capita GDP at 0.4 percent of that of the US. As for Korea's literacy rate, see Kim Shinil, "Adult Learning and Education in Korea," UNESCO, Keynote Address, Sixth International Conference on Adult Education, Belem, Brazil, 2009.

10. Alice H. Amsden, *Asia's Next Giant: South Korea and Late Industrialization* (New York: Oxford University Press, 1989), 68.

11. Ki Hyuk Pak, "Outcome of Land Reform in the Republic of Korea," *Journal of Farm Economics* 38, no. 4 (November 1956): 1015–23; In-Joung Whang, "Administration of Land Reform in Korea," working paper no. 8301, Korea Development Institute, December 1982, 1–2.

12. Joe Studwell, *How Asia Works: Success and Failure in the World's Most Dynamic Region* (New York: Grove Press, 2013), 20–63.

13. Early in the US military administration, US policymakers were not sure whether they were occupying an enemy or a future self-governing nation-state, and there were many missteps.

14. David C. Cole and Yung Chul Park, *Financial Development in Korea, 1945–1978* (Cambridge, MA: Harvard University Press, 1983), 52.

15. Stephan Haggard, Byung-Kook Kim, and Chung-in Moon, "The Transition to Export-Led Growth in South Korea: 1954–1966," *Journal of Asian Studies* 50, no. 4 (November 1991): 850–73, here 855.

16. Haggard et al., "Transition to Export-Led Growth," 854. Also, Kim and Vogel, *Park Chung Hee*, 273.

17. John Lie, *Han Unbound: The Political Economy of South Korea* (Stanford, CA: Stanford University Press, 1998).

18. Douglas A. Irwin, "From Hermit Kingdom to Miracle on the Han: Policy Decisions That Transformed South Korea into an Export Powerhouse," NBER Working Paper No. 29299, National Bureau of Economic Research, September 2021, 10.

19. Lee Hyun-hee, Park Sung-soo, and Yoon Nae-hyun, *New History of Korea* (Seoul: Jimoondang, 2005), 593–5.

20. Haggard et al., "Transition to Export-Led Growth," 857–8.

21. Edward M. Graham, *Reforming Korea's Industrial Conglomerates* (Washington, DC: Institute for International Economics, 2003), 23.

22. Haggard et al., "Transition to Export-Led Growth," 860.

23. Hwasook Nam, "Progressives and Labor under Park Chung Hee: A Forgotten Alliance in 1960s South Korea," *Journal of Asian Studies* 72, no. 4 (November 2013): 887–8.

24. Nam, "Progressives and Labor," 887–8.

25. Haggard et al., "Transition to Export-Led Growth," 858.

26. Martin Hart-Landsberg, *The Rush to Development: Economic Change and Political Struggle in South Korea* (New York: Monthly Review Press, 1993), 140–4.

27. Hart-Landsberg, *Rush to Development*, 147–8.

28. Kim Hyung-A, *Korea's Development under Park Chung Hee: Rapid Industrialization, 1961–79* (London: Routledge Curzon, 2004), 140.

29. Amsden, *Asia's Next Giant*, 147.

30. Haggard et al., "Transition to Export-Led Growth," 861.

31. Kim and Vogel, *Park Chung Hee*, 203.

32. This pressure was not just from the party in charge in Korea. The administrators of US aid, which was a huge mission at the time, played a major role in defining priorities.

33. Haggard et al., "Transition to Export-Led Growth," 864.

34. Whang In-Joung, "Korea's Economic Management for Structural Adjustment in the 1980s," working paper no. 8606, Korea Development Institute, December 1986, 5–9.

35. "Ho-Am Byung-chul Lee," Ho-Am Foundation, hoamfoundation.org/eng/hoam/hoam_intro.asp.

36. Karl Moskowitz, ed., *From Patron to Partner: The Development of US–Korean Business and Trade Relations* (Lexington, MA: Lexington Books, 1984), 166–9.

37. Haggard et al., "Transition to Export-Led Growth," 866. Also see Kim and Vogel, *Park Chung Hee*, 151.

38. Kim and Vogel, *Park Chung Hee*, 117–18.

39. Korea and Japan did have a modest economic relationship already, but normalization enabled its expansion.

40. Hart-Landsberg, *Rush to Development*, 145.

41. For analyses of the concept of complementary economies, please see Ian Fletcher, *Free Trade Doesn't Work: What Should Replace It and Why* (Washington, DC: US Business and Industry Council, 2010), 224; Ralph E. Gomory and William J. Baumol, *Global Trade and Conflicting National Interests* (Cambridge, MA: Massachusetts Institute of Technology, 2000), 56.

42. Hart-Landsberg, *Rush to Development*, 150.

43. Atul Kohli, *State-Directed Development: Political Power and Industrialization in the Global Periphery* (New York: Cambridge University Press, 2004), 111.

44. Amsden, *Asia's Next Giant*, 66–70.

45. Amsden, *Asia's Next Giant*, 67.

46. "Exports of Goods and Services (% of GDP): Korea, Rep.," World Bank, data .worldbank.org/indicator/NE.EXP.GNFS.ZS?locations=KR.

47. As explained in Chapter 4, trade deficits incurred to import capital goods and other inputs for advantageous industries can – unlike trade deficits incurred by purchasing consumption goods – boost long-term economic growth.

48. Hart-Landsberg, "Rush to Development," 153–4.

49. Kim and Vogel, *Park Chung Hee*, 267.

50. Kim and Vogel, *Park Chung Hee*, 304–5.

51. Kim and Vogel, *Park Chung Hee*, 212.

52. From 1971 to 1980, the won fell from about 250 against the dollar to 500 while the yen rose from 350 to 225. By 1990, the won had fallen further to about 675 against the dollar and the yen had risen to about 145.

53. Suk-Jun Lim, "Politics of Industrialization: Formation of Divergent Industrial Orders in Korea and Taiwan" (PhD diss., University of Chicago, 1997), 111.

54. Wonhyuk Lim, "The Development of Korea's Electronics Industry during Its Formative Years (1966–1979)," KDI School of Public Policy and Management, 2016, 114.

55. Running life insurance companies was used as a substitute by Samsung; others used property or casualty insurance.

56. Kim and Vogel, *Park Chung Hee*, 214–15, 268–9.

57. Young-Iob Chung, *South Korea in the Fast Lane: Economic Development and Capital Formation* (New York: Oxford University Press, 2007), 309.

58. Daniel Tudor, *Korea: The Impossible Country* (North Clarendon, VT: Tuttle, 2012), 265.

59. Chung, *South Korea*, 349.

60. Chung, *South Korea*, 349.

61. Chung, *South Korea*, 214.

62. Jeffrey D. Sachs and Susan M. Collins, eds., *Developing Country Debt and Economic Performance, Volume 3: Country Studies – Indonesia, Korea, Philippines, Turkey* (Chicago: University of Chicago Press, 1989), 171.

63. Chung, *South Korea*, 131.

64. Chung, *South Korea*, 129–36.

65. Kim and Vogel, *Park Chung Hee*, 226.

66. Jung-en Woo, *Race to the Swift: State and Finance in Korean Industrialization* (New York: Columbia University Press, 1991), 168.

67. Kim and Vogel, *Park Chung Hee*, 162.

68. Takatoshi Ito and Anne O. Krueger, eds., *Growth Theories in Light of the East Asian Experience* (Chicago, IL: University of Chicago Press, 1995), 192–3.

69. Woo, *Race to the Swift*, 128–9.

70. Edward M. Graham, *Reforming Korea's Industrial Conglomerates* (Washington, DC: Peterson Institute for International Economics, 2003), 40.

71. Kim and Vogel, *Park Chung Hee*, 632.

72. Kim and Vogel, *Park Chung Hee*, 397.

73. Ha-Joon Chang and Peter Evans, "The Role of Institutions in Economic Change," presentation to meeting of the Other Canon, Venice, Italy, January 2000, 26.

74. George Lodge and Ezra Vogel, eds., *Ideology and National Competitiveness: An Analysis of Nine Countries* (Boston, MA: Harvard Business School Press, 1987), 235–6.

75. Kim and Vogel, *Park Chung Hee*, 634–7.

76. Anne O. Krueger and Junho Yoo, "Chaebol Capitalism and the Currency–Financial Crisis in Korea," in *Preventing Currency Crises in Emerging Markets*, ed. Sebastian Edwards and Jeffrey A. Frankel (Chicago, IL: University of Chicago Press, 2002), 601–61, here 622.

77. Krueger and Yoo, "Chaebol Capitalism," 631–7.

78. Krueger and Yoo, "Chaebol Capitalism," 654.

79. Kim and Vogel, *Park Chung Hee*, 635.

80. Lodge and Vogel, *Ideology and National Competitiveness*, 235.

81. Hyeong-ki Kwon, "Changes by Competition: Evolution of the Korean Developmental State," Seoul National University, Department of Political Science and International Relations, February 2021, 153.

82. Kang, *Crony Capitalism*, 153–4.

83. Krueger and Yoo, "Chaebol Capitalism," 631–2.

84. Kim and Vogel, *Park Chung Hee*, 636.

85. Chung H. Lee, Keun Lee, and Kangkook Lee, "Chaebols, Financial Liberalization, and Economic Crisis: Transformation of Quasi-Internal Organizations in Korea," *Asian Economic Journal*, 16, no. 1 (December 2002).

86. Krueger and Yoo, "Chaebol Capitalism," 628.

87. Ralf J. Leiteritz, "Capital Account Policy in South Korea: The Informal Residues of the Developmental State," *Colombia Internacional*, no. 83 (January–April 2015): 235–65.

88. Krueger and Yoo, "Chaebol Capitalism," 631.

89. Robert C. Feenstra, Gary H. Hamilton, Eun Mie Lim, "Chaebols and Catastrophe: A New View of the Korean Business Groups and Their Role in the Financial Crisis," Asian Economic Policy Conference, Seoul, South Korea (October 25–26, 2001), 75.

90. Hyun-Hoon Lee, "The IMF Rescue Program in Korea: What Went Wrong?" *Journal of the Korean Economy* 2, no. 1 (Spring 2001): 73.

91. Lee, "IMF Rescue," 73.

92. Lee, "IMF Rescue," 73–5.

93. Krueger and Yoo, "Chaebol Capitalism," 655.

94. Keun Lee, "Corporate Governance and Growth in the Korean Chaebols: A Microeconomic Foundation for the 1997 Crisis," Working Paper Series Vol. 2000–01, Seoul National University, February 2000, table 8, 19.

95. John Malcolm Dowling, *Future Perspectives on the Economic Development of Asia* (Singapore: World Scientific, 2008), 305.

96. "Trade Summary for Korea, Rep, 1997," World Bank, wits.worldbank.org/CountryProfile/en/Country/KOR/Year/1997/Summary; "Trade Summary for Korea, Rep, 1999," World Bank, wits.worldbank.org/CountryProfile/en/Country/KOR/Year/1999/Summary.

97. Feenstra et al., "Chaebols and Catastrophe," 45.

98. Jung Suk-yee, "Cross Shareholding Is Becoming a Thing of the Past," *Business Korea*, April 25, 2018. Some of this undoubtedly reflects nominal changes to meet

new regulations rather than real changes in control structure, but the efforts to reduce cross-shareholding have nevertheless been sustained and forceful.

99. Chikako Baba and Annamaria Kokenyne, "Effectiveness of Capital Controls in Selected Emerging Markets in the 2000s," working paper, International Monetary Fund, December 2011, 11.

100. Amsden, *Asia's Next Giant*, 65.

101. Amsden, *Asia's Next Giant*, 55–78.

102. Y. B. Kim, "The Growth and Structural Change of the Textile Industry," in *Essays on the Korean Economy. Volume III: Macroeconomic and Industrial Development in Korea*, ed. C. K. Park (Seoul: Korea Development Institute, 1980), 232.

103. Authors' calculation from Amsden, *Asia's Next Giant*, 67, table 3.4.

104. Amsden, *Asia's Next Giant*, 66–9.

105. Amsden, *Asia's Next Giant*, 249.

106. Amsden, *Asia's Next Giant*, 249.

107. Amsden, *Asia's Next Giant*, 252–5.

108. Amsden, *Asia's Next Giant*, 257–9.

109. Amsden, *Asia's Next Giant*, 293.

110. Amsden, *Asia's Next Giant*, 293–6.

111. Amsden, *Asia's Next Giant*, 291.

112. Woo, *Race to the Swift*, 134.

113. Studwell, *How Asia Works*, 93.

114. Amsden, *Asia's Next Giant*, 297.

115. Amsden, *Asia's Next Giant*, 302.

116. Amsden, *Asia's Next Giant*, 293, 303.

117. Amsden, *Asia's Next Giant*, 297.

118. Amsden, *Asia's Next Giant*, 301.

119. Amsden, *Asia's Next Giant*, 303–4.

120. Amsden, *Asia's Next Giant*, 317.

121. Amsden, *Asia's Next Giant*, 275.

122. Amsden, *Asia's Next Giant*, 269–89.

123. "Peer Review of the Korean Shipbuilding Industry and Related Government Policies," OECD Council Working Party on Shipbuilding, 2014, 63.

124. Woo, *Race to the Swift*, 136–7.

125. Woo, *Race to the Swift*, 136–7.

126. HMMC ran into numerous problems, and a lot of other Korean shipping companies have gone bankrupt over the years.

127. Donatien Loret, "The Shipbuilding Industry in Korea, 1945–1990," *Entreprises et Histoire* 32, no. 1 (April 2003): 102.

128. Amsden, *Asia's Next Giant*, 279.

129. Loret, "The Shipbuilding Industry," 102.

130. Amsden, *Asia's Next Giant*, 290.

131. Chuel Cho, Kyungyou Kim, and Minji Kim, "Korea's Automotive Industry," Korea Institute for Industrial Economics and Trade, 2014, 90.

132. Kim and Vogel, *Park Chung Hee*, 302.

133. Kim and Vogel, *Park Chung Hee*, 304.

134. Kim and Vogel, *Park Chung Hee*, 305.

135. Kim and Vogel, *Park Chung Hee*, 306. Toyota had pulled out due to a new Chinese policy preventing Japanese companies from doing business in China if they had a presence in South Korea.

136. Cho et al., "Korea's Automotive Industry," 99.

137. "Hyundai Excel Sales Figures," Car Sales Base, carsalesbase.com/us-hyundai-excel.

138. "Production Statistics," International Organization of Motor Vehicle Manufacturers (OICA), oica.net/production-statistics.

139. Yonhap, "Auto Exports Hit 7-Year High in 2021," *Korea Herald*, January 27, 2022.

140. Lim, "Korea's Electronics," 51.

141. Lim, "Korea's Electronics," 59–63.

142. Wonhyuk Lim, "The Development of Korea's Electronics Industry during Its Formative Years (1966–1979)," Ministry of Strategy and Finance (MOSF), Republic of Korea, 2016, 78.

143. Amsden, *Asia's Next Giant*, 82.

144. "The History of Samsung Electronics (1): Paving a New Path (1968–1970)," Samsung Newsroom, news.samsung.com/global/the-history-of-samsung-electronics-1-paving-a-new-path-19681970.

145. Nargess Kayhani, "Foreign Direct Investment and Exports of Manufacturing: The Case of South Korea's Electronics," *Journal of International Economic Integration* 3, no. I (Spring 1988), table 1, 117.

146. Lim, "Korea's Electronics," 100–10.

147. Yonhap, "S. Korea's ICT Exports Hit Record High of $227b in 2021," *Korea Herald*, January 12, 2022.

148. Jang-Sup Shin, "Dynamic Catch-Up Strategy, Capability Expansion and Changing Windows of Opportunity in the Memory Industry," GPN Working Paper Series, National University of Singapore, May 2015, 17.

149. Amsden, *Asia's Next Giant*, 83.

150. Shin, "Dynamic Catch-Up," 13–19.

151. Ji-Hoon Lee, Sin-Young Park, and Eui-Jin Jeong, "Korea Exports Hit Record to Top $640 Bn in 2021," *Korea Economic Daily*, December 14, 2021.

152. Samuel K. Moore, "South Korea's $450-Billion Investment Latest in Chip Making Push," *IEEE Spectrum*, May 22, 2021.

153. Kim Byung-Koo, *Nuclear Silk Road: The "Koreanization" of Nuclear Power Technology* (Scotts Valley, CA: CreateSpace Independent Publishing Platform, 2011), 4.

154. Kim and Vogel, *Park Chung Hee*, 487–8.

155. Kim, *Nuclear Silk Road*, 145–57.

156. "Country Nuclear Power Profiles: Republic of Korea," International Atomic Energy Agency, 2022; Max S. Kim, "How Greed and Corruption Blew Up South Korea's Nuclear Industry," *MIT Technology Review*, April 22, 2019.

157. Philip Andrews-Speed, "South Korea's Nuclear Power Industry: Recovering from Scandal," *Journal of World Energy Law and Business* 13, no. 1 (March 2020): 47–57.

158. Kim, "How Greed and Corruption."

159. Andrews-Speed, "South Korea's Nuclear Power."

160. Kim, "How Greed and Corruption."

161. Jhoo Dong-chan, "Korea's Nuclear Reactor Certified by Europe," *Korea Times*, October 9, 2017. Also see "Advanced Power Reactor 1400 (APR1400) Design Certification," Nuclear Regulatory Commission, May 22, 2019. The NRC granted design approval, not an operating license: necessary but not sufficient for building plants in the US.

162. "Country Nuclear Power Profiles: United Arab Emirates," International Atomic Energy Agency, 2022.

163. Jessie Yeung and Gawon Bae, "South Korea Bets on Nuclear Power, Restarting Construction on Two Reactors," CNN, July 6, 2022.

164. Celia Becherel and Stephen Thomsen, "Championing Trade Openness and Investment," OECD, October 25, 2021.

165. In the WTO's list of cases since 1995, Korea has 19 against it, compared with 16 for Japan, 15 for Indonesia, 103 for the European Union, and 170 for the United States, as of July 2023. See "Disputes by Respondent," World Trade Organization, wto.org/english/tratop_e/dispu_e/dispu_by_country_e.htm#respondent.

166. "Trade in Goods with Korea, South," United States Census Bureau, census.gov/foreign-trade/balance/c5800.html.

167. "Korea-Trade Barriers," Privacy Shield Framework, privacyshield.gov/article?id=Korea-Trade-Barriers.

168. "South Korea: Country Commercial Guide," International Trade Administration (2022), trade.gov/country-commercial-guides/south-korea-import-requirements-and-documentation.

169. Korea does not meet the official US Treasury standards for currency manipulation, but these standards are, for reasons too complex to dispute here, far too tolerant.

170. "South Korea: Sales of Domestic Make (2022)," MarkLines Automotive Industry Portal, marklines.com/en/statistics/flash_sales/automotive-sales-in-korea-by-month-2022.

171. US Congress, Senate, Subcommittee on Interstate Commerce, Trade, and Tourism, *Imbalance in Korea Automobile Trade*, 110th Cong., 2nd sess., September 24, 2008.

172. "Samsung Phone Market Share in South Korea Fell below 60% for the First Time," SamNews24, October 4, 2022.

173. Leiteritz, "Capital Account Policy in South Korea," 258–9.

174. Jihoon Lee, "South Korea Seeks to Improve Foreign Access to Its Markets," Reuters, January 12, 2023.

7. China: Pursuing Economic Hegemony through Mercantilism

1. The US's average manufacturing wage in 2018: $21.40. "United States Average Hourly Wages in Manufacturing," Trading Economics, tradingeconomics.com/united-states/wages-in-manufacturing. China's average manufacturing labor cost in 2018: $5.51. "Manufacturing Labor Costs per Hour for China, Vietnam, Mexico from 2016 to 2020," Statista, statista.com/statistics/744071/manufacturing-labor-costs-per-hour-china-vietnam-mexico.

2. 2020 data. China: authors' calculation from Table 4–1: "Number of Employed Persons" in "China Statistical Yearbook 2021," National Bureau of Statistics of China, stats.gov.cn/sj/ndsj/2022/indexeh.htm; percentage in manufacturing: Lin Xiaozhao, "Almost 20% of China's Workforce Is in Manufacturing, Study Shows," Yicai Global, July 22, 2023. US: "All Employees, Manufacturing," Federal Reserve Bank of St. Louis, fred.stlouisfed.org/series/MANEMP.

3. Adam Lysenko, Mark Witzke, Thilo Hanemann, and Daniel H. Rosen, "US–China Financial Investment: Current Scope and Future Potential," Rhodium Group, January 26, 2021.

4. China's percentage of our gross bilateral trade deficit – that is, the sum of all our individual deficits with nations with which we have a negative trade balance – is the appropriate measure, not the more-often-quoted China's percentage of our total trade deficit. The latter does not sum to 100 percent for any nation that, like the US, also runs bilateral trade surpluses with some nations. It thus overstates the deficit

contribution of any one deficit nation. Use of the percentage of gross bilateral trade deficit measure does not, of course, imply that eliminating the US gross trade deficit or deficits with all countries is either possible or desirable. It is not. The gross measure simply more accurately tracks the relative contributions of different countries to the total US trade deficit. Data from "US International Trade in Goods and Services, December and Annual 2022," US Bureau of Economic Analysis, February 7, 2023, bea.gov/news/2023/us-international-trade-goods-and-services-december-and-annual-2022.

5. Daron Acemoglu et al., "Import Competition and the Great US Employment Sag of the 2000s," *Journal of Labor Economics* 34, no. S1, part 2 (January 2016): S95–S139. Jobs that were moved to Mexico and elsewhere to match Chinese labor costs should be added to these totals.

6. David Autor et al., "On the Persistence of the China Shock," Brookings Papers on Economic Activity, September 8, 2021. See also Andrew Heritage, "Post PNTR: 3.8 Million Jobs Lost Due to China," Coalition for a Prosperous America, May 4, 2023. (Note that different job loss numbers reported in this book may be inconsistent because these are econometric estimates, not data, and different analysts legitimately make different assumptions and use different calculation methods.)

7. Angus Maddison, "Chinese Economic Performance in the Long Run," Development Centre of the Organisation for Economic Co-operation and Development, 1998, 39.

8. Note, however, that China, although historically one of the world's greatest civilizations for thousands of years, was never a global power, unlike much smaller nations such as Spain, France, Britain, Holland, and Portugal. The CCP's contemporary geopolitical aspirations are thus without precedent.

9. Chong-en Bai, Chang-Tai Hsieh, and Zheng Song, "Special Deals with Chinese Characteristics," in *Macroeconomics Annual: 2019*, ed. Martin S. Eichenbaum et al. (Chicago, IL: University of Chicago Press, 2020), 342.

10. Wei Xiong, "The Mandarin Model of Growth," working paper no. 25296, National Bureau of Economic Research, November 2018.

11. Cheng Li, "The Powerful Factions among China's Rulers," BBC News, November 6, 2012.

12. Yasheng Huang, "Chinese Exceptionalism Just Won't Die," *Foreign Policy*, March 2, 2024.

13. "2017 Report to Congress on China's WTO Compliance," US Trade Representative, January 2018, Executive Summary, 2. Also, Stephen Ezell, "False Promises II: The Continuing Gap between China's WTO Commitments and Its Practices," Information Technology and Innovation Foundation, July 26, 2021.

14. "State Capital Optimization Gets Impetus," State-Owned Assets Supervision and Administration Commission of the State Council, en.sasac.gov.cn/2021/02/24/c6685.htm. Note that this "size" estimate for SASAC indicates a range of supervision, not a unified entity. A total nearing $40 trillion is reported in a number of sources, but this implies an implausibly high average of $400 billion assets per company. Note also that this "size" of SASAC indicates a range of supervision of firms, not a monolithic entity. SOEs also have many subsidiaries, listed and not listed, and wholly owned versus partly owned, so asset counts depend on what is counted. "Directory," State-Owned Assets Supervision and Administration Commission of the State Council, en.sasac.gov.cn/directorynames.html.

15. "GDP per Capita (Current US$): China, United States," World Bank, data.worldbank.org/indicator/NY.GDP.PCAP.CD?locations=CN-US. "Population, Total: China, United States," World Bank, data.worldbank.org/indicator/SP.POP.TOTL?locations=CN-U.

16. "Trade (% of GDP)," World Bank, data.worldbank.org/indicator/NE.TRD.GNFS.ZS?locations=CN.

17. "Evolution of the World's 25 Top Trading Nations," United Nations Conference on Trade and Development, unctad.org/topic/trade-analysis/chart-10-may-2021.

18. This section draws materially on the US Trade Representative's 2016 and 2017 "Report to Congress on China's WTO Compliance." Also, Advant Nctm's 2016 report "Does China Respect Its WTO Commitments?" James McGregor, *No Ancient Wisdom, No Followers* (Westport, CT: Prospecta Press, 2012); and Thomas Hout and Pankaj Ghemawat, "China vs. the World: Whose Technology Is It?" *Harvard Business Review*, December 2010.

19. Hearing on "Evaluating China's Past and Future Role in the World Trade Organization," US–China Economic and Security Review Commission, June 9, 2010.

20. Mike Moore, "The WTO and the New Economy," speech before the National Foreign Trade Council, May 22, 2000.

21. "Tariff Rate, Applied, Weighted Mean, All Products (%): China," World Bank, data.worldbank.org/indicator/TM.TAX.MRCH.WM.AR.ZS?locations=CN.

22. G. E. Anderson, *Designated Drivers: How China Plans to Dominate the Global Auto Industry* (Singapore: John Wiley & Sons Singapore), 6.

23. Daniel Zipser and Felix Poh, eds., "Understanding Chinese Consumers: Growth Engine of the World," China Consumer Report 2021, McKinsey & Company, November 2020, 30.

24. The US's average manufacturing wage in 2018: $21.40. "United States Average Hourly Wages in Manufacturing," Trading Economics, tradingeconomics.com/united-states/wages-in-manufacturing. China's average manufacturing labor cost in 2018: $5.51. "Manufacturing Labor Costs per Hour for China, Vietnam, Mexico from 2016 to 2020," Statista, statista.com/statistics/744071/manufacturing-labor-costs-per-hour-china-vietnam-mexico.

25. Thomas Hout, "A New Approach to Rebalancing the US–China Trade Deficit," *Harvard Business Review*, December 2021.

26. "Chinese Yuan Renminbi to US Dollar Spot Exchange Rate," Federal Reserve Bank of St. Louis, last updated March 31, 2023, fred.stlouisfed.org/series/DEXCHUS.

27. Other things being equal.

28. Prof. Thomas Hout, Middlebury Institute of International Studies, by email to author Ian Fletcher, September 14, 2022.

29. Hout, by email to author.

30. Hout, by email to author.

31. Hout, by email to author.

32. "State-Owned Enterprises in China: Reviewing the Evidence," OECD Working Group on Privatisation and Corporate Governance of State-Owned Assets, January 26, 2009, 6–7; Hout, by email to author; Nicolas Borst, "Has China Given Up on State-Owned Enterprise Reform?" Lowly Institute, April 15, 2021; Amir Guluzade, "How Reform Has Made China's State-Owned Enterprises Stronger," World Economic Forum, May 21, 2020; Clay Chandler, "Chinese Corporations Now Dominate the Fortune Global 500 List of Biggest Companies by Revenue: But They Are Far Less Profitable Than Their Rivals," *Fortune*, August 18, 2022.

33. Paolo Confino, "Here Are the 20 Biggest Companies in Mainland China," *Fortune*, August 10, 2022. List extracted from the 2021 Fortune Global 500 list.

34. Margit Molnar and Jiangyuan Lu, "State-Owned Firms behind China's Corporate Debt," Economics Department Working Papers No. 1536, OECD, February 7, 2019, 19.

35. Authors' calculation from "Country and Product Trade Data: Product Detail and Partner Country: Country by 5-Digit End-Use Code, Annual Totals, 2012–Present," US Census Bureau, census.gov/foreign-trade/statistics/product/enduse/exports/endu se_exports.xlsx.

36. Toshiba sold its stake in Westinghouse in 2018.

37. Areva was restructured in 2017 and the nuclear component operating in China is now called Orano.

38. The comparable 2018 US figures are $43 billion in payments and $115 billion in receipts, so China runs a big deficit and the US a big surplus. See "Charges for the Use of Intellectual Property, Receipts (BoP, Current US$)," data.worldbank.org/indica tor/BM.GSR.ROYL.CD; and "Charges for the Use of Intellectual Property, Payments (BoP, Current US$)," data.worldbank.org/indicator/BM.GSR .ROYL.CD.

39. Kenneth Jarrett and Amy Wendholt, "Transferring Technology to Transform China: Is It Worth It?" *China Business Review*, March 1, 2020.

40. Nigel Cory, "Heading Off Track: The Impact of China's Mercantilist Policies on Global High-Speed Rail Innovation," ITIF, April 26, 2021, itif.org/publications/ 2021/04/26/heading-track-impact-chinas-mercantilist-policies-global-high-speed-rail.

41. Hout and Ghemawat, "China vs. the World."

42. "Findings of the Investigation into China's Acts, Policies, and Practices related to Technology Transfer, Intellectual Property, and Innovation under Section 301 of the Trade Act of 1974," US Trade Representative, March 22, 2018, 9.

43. Ian Clay and Robert D. Atkinson, "Wake Up, America: China Is Overtaking the United States in Innovation Capacity," Information Technology and Innovation Foundation, January 23, 2023, 17.

44. Clay and Atkinson, "Wake Up, America," 14–15.

45. Hout and Ghemawat, "China vs. the World," 6.

46. Evan Zimmerman, "Germany Is Losing the Electric Vehicle Transition," *Palladium*, February 9, 2023.

47. Frank Greve, "Boeing Called a Target of French Spy Effort," *Seattle Post-Intelligencer*, April 18, 1993. Also see Imre Karacs, "France Spied on Commercial Rivals," *Independent*, January 11, 1996.

48. "Investigative Report on the US National Security Issues Posed by Chinese Telecommunications Companies Huawei and ZTE: A Report by Chairman Mike Rogers and Ranking Member C. A. Dutch Ruppersberger of the Permanent Select Committee on Intelligence," US House of Representatives, October 8, 2012, 11–42.

49. Jeff Ferry, "Top Five Cases of Huawei IP Theft and Patent Infringement," Coalition for a Prosperous America, December 13, 2018.

50. Michael Stumo, "Huawei's Employee Bonus Program for Stealing Technology," Coalition for a Prosperous America, January 30, 2019.

51. Mengqi Sun, "Chinese National Sentenced to Prison in $1 Billion Trade Secret Theft Case," *Wall Street Journal*, February 27, 2020.

52. Julie Zhu et al., "Insight: China Quietly Recruits Overseas Chip Talent as US Tightens Curbs," August 24, 2023, reuters.com/technology/china-quietly-recruits-overseas-chip-talent-us-tightens-curbs-2023-08-24.

53. Eric Rosenbaum, "1 in 5 Corporations Say China Has Stolen Their IP within the Last Year: CNBC CFO Survey," CNBC, March 1, 2019.

54. "Harvard University Professor and Two Chinese Nationals Charged in Three Separate China Related Cases," US Department of Justice, January 28, 2020.
55. Anderson, *Designated Drivers*, 5.
56. "US Charges Four Chinese Military Hackers in 2017 Equifax Breach," Reuters, February 10, 2020.
57. Jeff Ferry, "Currency Misalignment Monitor, June 2023," Coalition for a Prosperous America.
58. "Final Consumption Expenditure (% of GDP): China," World Bank, data.worldbank.org/indicator/NE.CON.TOTL.ZS?locations=CN.
59. "Gross Capital Formation (% of GDP): China," World Bank, data.worldbank.org/indicator/NE.GDI.TOTL.ZS?end=2021&locations=CN&start=1960&view=chart.
60. Rough estimate based on Michael Berlemann and Jan-Erik Wesselhöft, "Aggregate Capital Stock Estimations for 122 Countries: An Update," *Review of Economics* 68, no. 2 (August 2017), 75–92.
61. "Exports of Goods and Services (% of GDP): China," World Bank, data.worldbank.org/indicator/NE.EXP.GNFS.ZS?locations=CN.
62. Marco Rubio , "Made in China 2025 and the Future of American Industry," Project for Strong Labor Markets and National Development, February 12, 2019, 18, web.archive.org/web/20210409000438/https://www.rubio.senate.gov/public/files/Rubio-China-2025-Report.pdf.
63. "China Power: How Dominant Are Chinese Companies Globally?" CSIS, n.d., chinapower.csis.org/chinese-companies-global-500.
64. Kyle Stock, "Why Can't Americans Buy Cheap Chinese EVs?" Bloomberg, September 22, 2023, bloomberg.com/news/articles/2023%9609%9622/why-can-t-americans-buy-cheap-chinese-evs.
65. Mo Hong, "Total Number of Chinese Companies on Fortune Global 500 List Drops First Time in 15 Years," August 3, 2023.
66. Rubio, "Made in China 2025," 21. Based on "4-digit HS line in chapters 82 through 90, excluding aircraft, weighted by 2017 global export value."
67. Kenji Kawase, "'Made in China 2025' Thrives with Subsidies for Tech, EV Makers," Nikkei Asia, July 22, 2022.
68. Kawase, "'Made in China 2025' Thrives."
69. Xinmei Shen, "China Added 74 Unicorns in 2022, Maintaining Steady Pace of Growth Despite Fundraising Crunch," *South China Morning Post*, February 3, 2023.
70. Justinas Baltrusaitis, "Revealed: The US Has Twice as Many Unicorns as China and India Combined," Finbold, December 5, 2022.
71. "Global Innovation Index's Global Science and Technology Clusters: East Asia Dominates Top Ranking," World Intellectual Property Organization, Geneva, September 14, 2022.
72. "US Access to China's Consumer Market," Hearing before the United States–China Economic and Security Review Commission, 115th Cong., 1st sess., June 22, 2017, 21–54, uscc.gov/sites/default/files/transcripts/June%2022%20Transcript.pdf.
73. "How Restrictions to Trade with China Could End US Leadership in Semiconductors," Boston Consulting Group, March 2020, 22.
74. "China Has Limited Options to Counter US-Led Chip Export Curb," Economist Intelligence Unit, December 20, 2022.
75. "China Has Limited Options," Economist Intelligence Unit.
76. Noah Berman, Lindsay Maizland, and Andrew Chatzky, "Is China's Huawei a Threat to U.S. National Security?" February 8, 2023, cfr.org/backgrounder/chinas-huawei-threat-us-national-security.

77. Edward Graham, "FCC Bans Sale of New Devices from Chinese Companies Huawei, ZTE and Others," NextGov, November 28, 2022, nextgov.com/emerging-tech/2022/11/fcc-bans-sale-new-devices-chinese-companies-huawei-zte-and-others/380214.

78. "Protecting against National Security Threats to the Communications Supply Chain through the Equipment Authorization Program, ET Docket 21–232," Federal Communications Commission, November 11, 2022.

79. Karen M. Sutter, "China's New Semiconductor Policies: Issues for Congress," Congressional Research Service, April 20, 2021, 3.

80. Sutter, "China's New Semiconductor Policies," 4; Julie Zhu, "Exclusive: China Readying $143 Billion Package for Its Chip Firms in Face of U.S. Curbs," Reuters, December 13, 2022.

81. "Battered by Covid, China Hits Pause on Giant Chip Spending Aimed at Rivaling US," January 3, 2023, Bloomberg News.

82. "US–China Investment Ties: Overview," Congressional Research Service, January 15, 2021, 2.

8. Germany: The Art of Relationship Capitalism

1. Peter A. Hall and David Soskice, "An Introduction to Varieties of Capitalism," in *Varieties of Capitalism: The Institutional Foundations of Comparative Advantage*, ed. Peter A. Hall and David Soskice (Oxford: Oxford University Press, 2001), 1–68, at 21–7.

2. Peter J. Katzenstein, "Between Power and Plenty: Foreign Economic Policies of Advanced Industrial States," *International Organization* 31, no. 4 (1977): 900; Werner Abelshauser et al., *Wirtschaftspolitik in Deutschland 1917–1990* (Berlin: De Gruyter, 2016), 12–14.

3. Alexander Ebner, "Varieties of Capitalism and the Limits of Entrepreneurship Policy: Institutional Reform in Germany's Coordinated Market Economy," *Journal of Industry, Competition and Trade* 10, no. 3–4 (July 2010): 319–41, at 332.

4. "SMEs Are Driving Economic Success: Facts and Figures about German SMEs," German Federal Ministry for Economic Affairs and Energy, January 30, 2018.

5. 2021 data. "Manufacturing, Value Added (% of GDP)," World Bank, accessed April 12, 2023, data.worldbank.org/indicator/NV.IND.MANF.ZS?end=2021&start=1960.

6. "GDP Per Capita, PPP (Constant 2017 International $): France, Germany, Italy, United Kingdom, Japan, Korea, Rep., Canada, Spain, Poland, United States," World Bank, accessed June 13, 2023, data.worldbank.org/indicator/NY.GDP.PCAP.PP.KD?end=2022&locations=FR-DE-IT-GB-JP-KR-CA-ES-PL-US&start=2006.

7. "Exports of Goods and Services (% of GDP)," World Bank, accessed April 12, 2023, data.worldbank.org/indicator/NE.EXP.GNFS.ZS?end=2021&start=1960.

8. Authors' calculation based on "Exports of Goods and Services (BoP, Current US$)," World Bank, accessed April 12, 2023, data.worldbank.org/indicator/BX.GSR.GNFS.CD.

9. Ebner, "Varieties of Capitalism," 336–7.

10. William Wilkes and Jana Randow, "Europe's Economic Engine Is Breaking Down," BNN Bloomberg, May 25, 2023.

11. Evan Zimmerman, "Germany Is Losing the Electric Vehicle Transition," *Palladium*, February 9, 2023.

12. "Post-crisis Changes in Global Bank Business Models: A New Taxonomy," Monetary and Capital Markets Department Working Paper, International Monetary Fund, December 2019, 14.

13. Mark Lehrer and Sokol Celo, "German Family Capitalism in the 21st Century: Patient Capital between Bifurcation and Symbiosis," *Socio-Economic Review* 14, no. 12 (October 2016): 729–50.

14. "Three Lessons from the German 'Mittelstand,'" IDB Invest, accessed July 14, 2023, idbinvest.org/en/blog/three-lessons-german-mittelstand.

15. John Zysman, *Governments, Markets and Growth: Financial Systems and the Politics of Industrial Change* (Ithaca, NY: Cornell University Press, 1983).

16. David B. Audretsch and Erik E. Lehmann, "The Neuer Markt as an Institution of Creation and Destruction," *International Entrepreneurship and Management Journal* 4 (2008): 419–29.

17. Richard Deeg, *Finance Capitalism Unveiled: Banks and the German Political Economy* (Ann Arbor: University of Michigan Press, 1999), 19–20.

18. Deeg, *Finance Capitalism*, 17–23, 117–18. See also Sigurt Vitols, "German Industrial Policy: An Overview," *Industry and Innovation* 4, no. 1 (1997): 15–36.

19. "Inside the Savings Banks Finance Group," Deutscher Sparkassen-und Giroverband, December 2020.

20. "Financial Report 2022," KFW, March 30, 2023.

21. Term translated from *Industrie-und- Handelskammertag*. Eberhard Sasse and Andre Habisch, eds., *The German Chambers of Commerce and Industry* (New York: Springer, 2021), 34–5.

22. "Nutzen für die Wirtschaft," Deutsche Institut für Normung (in German), accessed April 24, 2023, din.de/de/ueber-normen-und-standards/nutzen-fuer-die-wirt schaft/nutzen-fuer-die-wirtschaft-69368.

23. "China Overtakes USA in Robot Density, according to World Robotics 2022 Report," International Federation of Robotics, December 5, 2022.

24. German Federal Ministry of Education and Research, "Federal Report on Research and Innovation 2022, short version," bundesbericht-forschung-innovation.de/ files/ BMBF_BuFI-2022_Short-version.pdf.

25. Statistisches Bundesamt (Destatis), "Research and Development: Expenditure on Research and Development by Sector," 2024, destatis.de/EN/Themes/Society-Environment/Education-Research-Culture/Research-Development/Tables/research-development-sectors.html.

26. About 30 percent of German higher education institutions, as of 2020, were state approved but privately operated. Most are universities of applied science. See "The Right University," German Academic Exchange Services, accessed May 2, 2023, daad.de/en/study-and-research-in-germany/plan-your-studies/the-right-university.

27. "Universities of Applied Sciences (UAS) in Germany," My German University, November 18, 2020.

28. "Bundesbericht Forschung und Innovation 2022," German Federal Ministry of Education and Research (Bundesministerium für Bildung und Forschung), 35.

29. Alexander Ebner and Florian Täube, "Dynamics and Challenges of Innovation in Germany," in *The Innovation for Development Report 2009–2010: Strengthening Innovation for the Prosperity of Nations*, ed. Augusto López-Claros (London: Palgrave-MacMillan, 2010), 183–98.

30. European Commission, "Digital Economy and Society Index (DESI) 2022, Germany," 2022, pp. 3–4, DESI_2022__Germany__eng_jLtWXlDS8j4ptxpiRJDQExt70s _88702.pdf.

31. Kurt H. Becker, "Young and Innovative Entrepreneurs Are Pushing into the Market in the US and Germany Alike. How Do the Start-Up Scenes in the Two Countries Differ?" German Centers for Research and Innovation Annual Report, 2017, 35–6.

32. "Shortage of Later Stage Venture Capital in Germany: More Acute Due to Corona Crisis," Dealroom.co, March 2020, 10.

33. Lifelong Learning Program, "An Introduction to the Dual VET System: The Secret behind the Success of Germany and Austria," European Commission, accessed June 8, 2023, dualvet.eu/docs/productos/1_The%20Dual%20VET%20system.pdf, 7, 10.

34. "Youth Unemployment Rate in the European Union as of October 2022, by Country," Statista, February 28, 2023.

35. Eric A. Hanushek, "German-Style Apprenticeships Can't Be Easily Replicated," Wall Street Journal, June 18, 2017.

36. Kathleen Thelen, How Institutions Evolve: The Political Economy of Skills in Germany, Britain, the United States, and Japan (Cambridge: Cambridge University Press, 2004).

37. Ewan McGaughey, "The Codetermination Bargains: The History of German Corporate and Labour Law," Law, Society and Economy Working Papers No. 10/2015, London School of Economics and Political Science, 2015.

38. Germany: "Education at a Glance 2022: Germany Country Note," OECD, 2022. US: "Education at a Glance 2022: United States Country Note," OECD, 2022.

39. "Trade Union Dataset, Trade Union Density," OECD, accessed April 23, 2023, stats.oecd.org/index.aspx?DataSetCode=CBC.

40. "Trade Union Dataset, Collective Bargaining Coverage," OECD, accessed April 23, 2023, stats.oecd.org/index.aspx?DataSetCode=CBC.

41. See Stephen J. Silvia, Holding the Shop Together (Ithaca, NY: Cornell University Press, 2013).

42. "Besser mit Betriebsrat: Zahlen und Fakten," IG Metall, igmetall.de/im-betrieb/betriebsrat/besser-mit-betriebsrat-zahlen-und-fakten.

43. Carol D. Rasnic, "Germany's Statutory Works Councils and Employee Codetermination: A Model for the United States," Loyola of Los Angeles International and Comparative Law Review 13, no. 2 (1992): 278.

44. "Offshoring and the Internalization of Employment: A Challenge for a Fair Globalization?" International Labour Organization, 2005, 183.

45. Thorsten Schulten and Reinhard Bispinck, "Varieties of Decentralisation in German Collective Bargaining," in Multi-employer Bargaining under Pressure: Decentralisation Trends in Five European Countries, ed. Salvo Leonardi and Roberto Pedersini (Brussels: European Trade Union Institute, 2018), 5.

46. Jordi Franch Parella and Gemma Carmona Hernandez, "The German Business Model: The Role of the Mittelstand," Journal of Management Policies and Practices 6, no. 1 (June 2018): 14; Ravi Kumar, "Understanding the German Mittelstand's Contribution towards Making Germany a Manufacturing World Leader," Product, Platforms, Business & Innovation in Industry 4.0/IIoT, March 23, 2019.

47. Christian Homburg, ed., Structure and Dynamics of the German Mittelstand (Heidelberg: Physica, 1999).

48. Bernd Venohr and Klaus E. Meyer, "The German Miracle Keeps Running: How Germany's Hidden Champions Stay Ahead in the Global Economy," working paper no. 30, Berlin School of Economics Institute of Management, May 2007, 6.

49. David Audretsch and Erik Lehmann, *The Seven Secrets of Germany: Economic Resilience in an Era of Global Turbulence* (Oxford: Oxford University Press, 2015), 16–30.

50. Hermann Simon, "The German Mittelstand in Globalia," German Asia–Pacific Business Association, accessed July 14, 2023, oav.de/iap-32016/artikel-210.html.

51. "German Mittelstand: Engine of the German Economy," German Federal Ministry of Economics and Technology, 2013.

52. German turnover: Parella and Hernandez, "German Business Model," 11. US turnover: "Ageing and Employment Policies: Retaining Talent at All Ages," OECD, 2023, 24. Skills investment: "What Is Wrong with the German Economy? The Case for Openness to Technology and Human Capital," European Centre for International Political Economy, 2021, 7.

53. Alfredo De Massis et al., "Innovation with Limited Resources: Management Lessons from the German Mittelstand," *Journal of Product Innovation Management* 35, no. 1 (2017): 125–46.

54. Jefferson Chase, "Bundestag Passes Controversial Inheritance Tax Reform," Deutsche Welle, September 29, 2016.

55. "Global Startup Ecosystem Index 2022," StartupBlink, 2022.

56. Ebner, "Varieties of Capitalism," 319–20.

57. "EXIST: University-Based Business Start-Ups," Federal Ministry for Economic Affairs and Climate Action, accessed September 15, 2022, exist.de/EXIST/Navigation/EN/About_EXIST/about_exist.html.

58. "Departmental Budget 09: Federal Ministry for Economic Affairs and Climate Action," Federal Ministry for Economic Affairs and Climate Action, accessed September 15, 2022, bmwk.de/Redaktion/EN/Artikel/Ministry/budget-2019.html.

59. "Seed Investor for High-Tech Start-Ups," High-Tech Gründerfonds, htgf.de/en/about-us/fund-investors.

60. "Seed Investor for High-Tech Start-Ups," High-Tech Gründerfonds, accessed May 1, 2023, htgf.de/en.

61. "Departmental Budget 09: Federal Ministry for Economic Affairs and Climate Action," Federal Ministry for Economic Affairs and Climate Action, accessed May 2, 2023, bmwk.de/Redaktion/EN/Artikel/Ministry/budget-2019.html; "The High-Tech Gründerfonds," High-Tech Gründerfonds, accessed May 1, 2023, htgf.de/en/about-us.

62. Michael Rothgang et al, "Cluster Policy: Insights from the Germany Leading Edge Cluster Competition," *Journal of Open Innovation: Technology, Market, and Complexity* 3, no. 3 (September 2017): 1–20.

63. "Leading-Edge Cluster Competition," Cool Silicon, accessed September 15, 2022, cool-silicon.de/en/leading-edge-cluster/leading-edge-cluster-competition.

64. German Federal Ministry of Education and Research, "Clusters4Future Initiative: Next Generation Innovation Networks," 2024, bmbf.de/bmbf/en/research/hightech-and-innovation/future-research-and-innovation-strategy/cluster4future/cluster4future_node.html.

65. Mark Elam, "National Imaginations and Systems of Innovation," in *Systems of Innovation: Technologies, Institutions and Organizations*, ed. Charles Edquist (London: Pinter, 1997), 157–73.

66. David Levi-Faur, "Friedrich List and the Political Economy of the Nation-State," *Review of International Political Economy* 4, no. 1 (Spring 1997), 154–78.

67. Elam, "National Imaginations."

68. Jana Heinz and Georg Jochum, "The Emergence and Development of the German Dual Vocational System: Between Crises and Praises," Technische Universität München School of Education, 2014, 13.

69. Kathleen Thelen, *How Institutions Evolve: The Political Economy of Skills in Germany, Britain, the United States, and Japan* (Cambridge: Cambridge University Press, 2008), 44–5.

70. Paul Bairoch, "Free Trade and European Economic Development in the 19th Century," *European Economic Review* 3, no. 3 (1972).

71. Adam Klug, "Why Chamberlain Failed and Bismarck Succeeded: The Political Economy of Tariffs in British and German Elections," *European Review of Economic History* 5, no. 2 (August 2001): 219–20.

72. Steven B. Webb, "Cartels and Business Cycles in Germany, 1880 to 1914," *Journal of Institutional Theoretical Economics* 138. no. 2 (June 1982): 208–12.

73. Translated from *Allgemeiner Deutscher Arbeiterverein*.

74. "Anti-socialist Law (October 21, 1878)," German History in Documents and Images (GHDI), accessed June 8, 2023, ghdi.ghi-dc.org/sub_document.cfm?document_id=1843.

75. Caroline Fohlin, "The History of Corporate Ownership and Control in Germany," in *A History of Corporate Governance around the World: Family Business Groups to Professional Managers*, ed. Randall K. Morck (Chicago, IL: University of Chicago Press, 2005), 223–9.

76. Patrick Behr and Reinhard H. Schmidt, "The German Banking System: Characteristics and Challenges," Safe White Paper No. 32, Goethe University Frankfurt, 2015.

77. Webb, "Cartels and Business," 208–12.

78. Otto Keck, "The National System for Technical Innovation in Germany," in *National Innovation Systems: A Comparative Analysis*, ed. Richard R. Nelson (New York: Oxford University Press, 1993), 115.

79. Johann Peter Murmann, *Knowledge and Competitive Advantage: The Coevolution of Firms, Technology, and National Institutions* (Cambridge: Cambridge University Press, 2003).

80. Frank Pfetsch, "Scientific Organisation and Science Policy in Imperial Germany, 1871–1914: The Foundation of the Imperial Institute of Physics and Technology," *Minerva* 8 (1970): 562–3.

81. Translated from *Physikalisch-Technische Reichsanstalt*.

82. Keck, "The National System," 118–23; Correlli Barnett, *The Collapse of British Power* (New York: William Morrow, 1972), 101.

83. "All Nobel Prizes," The Nobel Prize, data.nobelprize.org. Data based on years 1901–33 in the categories of "Physics," "Chemistry," and "Physiology or Medicine."

84. Keith Pavitt and Luc Soete, "International Differences in Economic Growth and the International Location of Innovation," in *Emerging Technologies: Consequences for Economic Growth, Structural Change, and Employment*, ed. Herbert Giersch (Tubingen: J. C. B. Mohr, 1982), 109.

85. Harold James, *Krupp: A History of the Legendary German Firm* (Princeton, NJ: Princeton University Press, 2012), 58–9.

86. Keck, "National System," 126–7.

87. Alfred D. Chandler, *Shaping the Industrial Century: The Remarkable Story of the Evolution of the Modern Chemical and Pharmaceutical Industries* (Cambridge, MA: Harvard Studies in Business History, 2004), 481.

88. Keck, "National System," 127, 129.

89. Hans-Joachim Braun, *The German Economy in the Twentieth Century: The German Reich and the Federal Republic* (London: Routledge, 1990), 19–22.
90. William O. Henderson, "Walther Rathenau: A Pioneer of the Planned Economy," *Economic History Review* 4, no. 1 (1951): 98–108.
91. This name was changed in 1926 and, most recently, in 1975. See "Timeline," Deutsches Institut für Normung, accessed July 23, 2023, din.de/en/din-and-our-partners/100/timeline.
92. C. E. Noyes, "Economic Controls in Nazi Germany," *Editorial Research Reports* 2, no. 17 (November 1, 1940).
93. Werner Abelshauser, *The Dynamics of German Industry: Germany's Path toward the New Economy and the American Challenge* (Oxford: Berghahn Books, 2005).
94. Keck, "National System," 131–2.
95. Christoph Buchheim and Jonas Scherner, "The Role of Private Property in the Nazi Economy," *Journal of Economic History* 66, no. 2 (June 2006): 390–416.
96. Jonas Scherner, "The Beginnings of Nazi Autarky Policy: The 'National Pulp Programme' and the Origin of Regional Staple Fibre Plants," *Economic History Review* 61, no. 4 (November 2008): 1.
97. Noyes, "Economic Controls."
98. Robin Havers, *The Second World War: Europe, 1939–1943* (London: Bloomsbury, 2002), 71–7.
99. Adam Tooze, *The Wages of Destruction: The Making and Breaking of the Nazi Economy* (London: Penguin, 2006), 99–165.
100. Manfred Knapp et al., "Reconstruction and West-Integration: The Impact of the Marshall Plan on Germany," *Journal of Institutional and Theoretical Economics* 137, no. 3 (September 1981): 424.
101. John H. Backer, *Priming the German Economy: American Occupational Policies, 1945–1948* (Durham, NC: Duke University Press, 1971).
102. Braun, *German Economy*, 152–4.
103. Braun, *German Economy*, 179.
104. "Kreditanstalt für Wiederaufbau," Encyclopedia.com, accessed September 13, 2022, encyclopedia.com/books/politics-and-business-magazines/kreditanstalt-fur-wiederaufbau.
105. John P. Windmuller, "German Codetermination Laws," *Industrial and Labor Relations Review* 6, no. 3 (April 1953): 399–416.
106. Robert Brenner, *The Economics of Global Turbulence* (London: Verso, 2006), 73.
107. Herbert Giersch, Karl-Heinz Paqué, and Holger Schmieding, *The Fading Miracle: Four Decades of Market Economy in Germany* (Cambridge: Cambridge University Press, 1992), 7–15.
108. Giersch et al., *Fading Miracle*, 3–4.
109. Giersch et al., *Fading Miracle*, 5–7.
110. Giersch et al., *The Fading Miracle*, 7–8.
111. Giersch et al., *Fading Miracle*, 68–73.
112. Brenner, *Economics of Global*, 72.
113. Braun, *German Economy*, 180–1.
114. Judith Stein, *Pivotal Decade: How the United States Traded Factories for Finance in the 1970s* (New Haven, CT: Yale University Press, 2011), 162. Statistics from *Statistische Jahrbucher der Bundesrepublik Deutschland*, Statistiches Bibliothek, accessed July 14, 2023, statistischebibliothek.de/mir/receive/DESerie_mods_00006972, 1951–76.
115. James Foreman-Peck, "European Industrial Policies in the Post-war Boom: Planning the Economic Miracle," in *Industrial Policy in Europe after 1945: Wealth, Power*

and Economic Development in the Cold War, ed. Christian Grabas and Alexander Nützenadel (London: Palgrave Macmillan, 2014), 36.

116. Caroline Fohlin, "The History of Corporate Ownership and Control in Germany," in *A History of Corporate Governance around the World: Family Business Groups to Professional Managers*, ed. Randall K. Morck (National Bureau of Economic Research, 2005). See also Ulrich Wengenroth, "The Rise and Fall of State-Owned Enterprise in Germany," in *The Rise and Fall of State-Owned Enterprise in the Western World*, ed. Pier Angelo Toninelli (Cambridge: Cambridge University Press, 2000), 12–125.

117. Braun, *German Economy*, 249–50.

118. Giersch et al., *Fading Miracle*, 10–11, 14.

119. Folker Fröbel, Jürgen Heinrichs, and Otto Kreye, *The New International Division of Labour: Structural Unemployment in Industrialised Countries and Industrialisation in Developing Countries* (Cambridge: Cambridge University Press, 1980), 106–31.

120. Silvia, *Holding the Shop Together*, 119.

121. Paolo Guerrieri, "Technological and Trade Competition: The Changing Positions of the United States, Japan, and Germany," in *Linking Trade and Technology Policies: An International Comparison of the Policies of Industrialized Nations*, ed. Martha C. Harris and Gordon E. Moore (Washington, DC: National Academy Press), 34–40.

122. Merged in 1994 with the Ministry for Education and Science. Keck, "National System," 142–7.

123. Gert-Jan Hospers, "Restructuring Europe's Rustbelt: The Case of the German *Ruhrgebiet*," *Intereconomics* 39, no. 3 (May/June 2004): 150.

124. Alexander Ebner, "The Transition to a Low-Carbon Economy in Germany's Coordinated Capitalism," in *National Pathways to Low Carbon Emission Economies: Innovation Policies for Decarbonizing and Unlocking*, ed. Kurt Hübner (New York: Routledge, 2019), 114–46.

125. Ferdinand Protzman, "Germans in Accord on a 'Unity Fund,'" *New York Times*, May 17, 1990. "The Agreement on the Solidarity Pact," GHDI, accessed September 14, 2022, ghdi.ghi-dc.org/sub_document.cfm?document_id=3105.

126. Stefan Locke, "The Solidarity Pact That Provided Cash and Financial Stability to the Eastern German States Following Reunification Is about to Expire," *German Times*, October 2019.

127. George A. Akerlof et al., "East Germany in from the Cold: The Economic Aftermath of Currency Union," *Brookings Papers on Economic Activity* 1991, no. 1 (1991).

128. Hans-Werner Sinn, "Germany's Economic Unification: An Assessment after Ten Years," working paper no. 7586, National Bureau of Economic Research, March 2000; "Gross Domestic Product in Current Prices Per Capita, Eastern Germany as a Percentage of Western Germany," in "Annual Report of the Federal Government on the Status of German Unity 2019," Federal Ministry for Economic Affairs and Energy, 2019, 97.

129. Ferdi De Ville, "Domestic Institutions and Global Value Chains: Offshoring in Germany's Core Industrial Sectors," *Global Policy* 9, no. 52 (October 2018): 12–20.

130. Eike Ahlers, Fikret Öz, and Astrid Ziegler, *Standortverlagerung in Deutschland: Einige empirische und politische Befunde* (Dusseldorf: Hans-Böckler-Stiftung, 2007).

131. John Cody, "How Labor Manages Productivity Advances and Crisis Response: A Comparative Study of Automotive Manufacturing in Germany and the US," Global Labour University Working Paper No. 32, International Labour Organization, 2015.

132. Holger Görg and Aoife Hanley, "Globalization: Implications for Firms in Germany," Arbeitspapier 04/2017, Sachverständigenrat zur Begutachtung der gesamtwirtschaftlichen Entwicklung, 2017. See also Ludger Schuknecht, "The Empire Strikes Back," *The International Economy* (Fall 2014): 50–4.

133. "2021 Forecast," Avision Young, accessed May 25, 2023, avison-young.foleon .com/2021-forecast/germany-real-estate-trends/industrial.

134. Christopher S. Allen, "Ideas, Institutions and Organized Capitalism: The German Model of Political Economy Twenty Years after Unification," *German Politics and Society* 28, no. 2 (Summer 2010): 130–50. See also Directorate General for Economic and Financial Affairs, "Germany's Growth Performance in the 1990s," European Economy Economic Papers No. 170, European Commission, May 2002, 1.

135. Christian Dustmann et al., "From Sick Man of Europe to Economic Superstar: Germany's Resurgent Economy," *Journal of Economic Perspectives* 28, no. 1 (Winter 2014): 167–88.

136. Valentina Romei, "Germany: From 'Sick Man' of Europe to Engine of Growth," *Financial Times*, August 14, 2017.

137. Dustmann et al., "From Sick Man," 183–5.

138. "The High-Tech Strategy 2025 Progress Report," Federal Ministry of Education and Research, September 2019, 2, 7. The [German] Federal Government, "The New High-Tech Strategy Innovations for Germany," August 2014, ec.europa.eu/ futurium/en/system/files/ged/hts_broschuere_engl_bf_1.pdf; The [German] Federal Government, "The High-Tech Strategy 2025 Progress Report," n.d., 3, congreso .es/docu/docum/ddocum/dosieres/sleg/legislatura_14/spl_36/pdfs/44.pdf.

139. "Germany: Industrie 4.0," 3, Digital Transformation Monitor, European Commission, January 2017, ati.ec.europa.eu/sites/default/files/2020-06/ DTM_Industrie%204.0_DE.pdf.

140. "Industrie 4.0," German Federal Ministry for Economic Affairs and Climate Action, Accessed December 30, 2023, bmwk.de/Redaktion/EN/Dossier/industrie-40.html.

141. "Manufacturing Research in the SME Sector: The Federal Ministry of Education and Research (BMBF) Research Programme 'Innovation for the Manufacturing, Services and Work of Tomorrow,'" German Federal Ministry for Economic Affairs and Climate Action, accessed September 16, 2022, plattform-i40.de/IP/Redaktion/EN/Standardartikel/areas-of-action-research-and-innovation.html.

142. "Industrie 4.0: Revolutionizing the Hidden Champions of Germany," Germany Works, 2018.

143. "Germany Smart Manufacturing Industry to Grow at a CAGR 17.9% from 2021 to 2027," Global Newswire, Markets and Markets, May 12, 2023, globenewswire .com/en/news-release/2023/05/12/2667549/0/en/Germany-Smart-Manufacturing-Industry-to-Grow-at-a-CAGR-17-9-from-2021-to-2027.html.

144. "Smart Factories Set to Boost Global Economy by $1.5 Trillion by 2023," Press release, Capgemini Research Institute, November.

145. "Top 10 Smart Factories," Manufacturing Digital, Helen Sydney Adams, July 26, 2023, manufacturingdigital.com/smart-manufacturing/top-10-smart-factories#.

146. "Partner and Systemic Competitor: How Do We Deal with China's State-Controlled Economy?" Federation of German Industries (BDI), January 2019.

147. Georgina Prodham and Irene Preisinger, "Kuka's Robotics Boss See Benefits of Chinese Ownership," Reuters, June 22, 2016; "Chinese-Owned Robot Maker Is Gunning for No. 1 in Booming Market," Bloomberg News, March 8, 2017.

148. Björn Alexander Düben, "Are the Gloves Coming Off in China–Germany Economic Relations?" *Diplomat*, May 3, 2019.

149. Julian Germann, "Global Rivalries, Corporate Interests, and Germany's 'National Industrial Strategy 2030,'" *Review of International Political Economy* 30, no. 5, 1749–75, published online October 14, 2022.

150. *National Industrial Strategy 2030: Strategic Guidelines for a German and European Industrial Policy* (Berlin: Federal Ministry for Economic Affairs and Energy, February 2019).

151. Germann, "Global Rivalries, Corporate Interests."

152. Germann, "Global Rivalries, Corporate Interests."

153. Germann, "Global Rivalries, Corporate Interests."

154. Andreas Rinke, "Germany Blocks Chinese Stake in Two Chipmakers of Security Concerns," Reuters, November 9, 2022.

155. Government of the Federal Republic of Germany, "Strategy on China," Federal Foreign Office, July 13, 2023.

156. "A Europe That Protects, Transforms and Projects: Industrial Policy the European Way. Speech by Commissioner Thierry Breton at the Bruegel Annual Meeting," European Commission, September 6, 2023, ec.europa.eu/commission/presscorner/detail/ en/speech_23_4369.

157. Council of the European Union, "Chips Act: Council Gives Its Final Approval," July 25, 2023.

158. "A Europe That Protects."

159. European Commission, "Political Agreement on New Anti-Coercion Instrument to Better Defend EU Interests on Global Stage," June 6, 2023, ec.europa.eu/commission/presscorner/detail/en/ip_23_3046. In the Commission's words, "There are many types of coercive practices. For example, an EU trading partner may try to shape future legislative initiatives of the EU or dissuade the EU from putting in place a measure altogether by, for example, introducing (or threatening to introduce) extra, discriminatory import duties, intentional delays or refusing (or threatening to refuse) authorisation needed to do business. They might also impose discriminatory selective border or safety checks on goods from a given EU Member State or organise state-sponsored boycotts against goods or investors from that country," from "What Is the Anti-Coercion Instrument (ACI)?" European Commission, policy. trade.ec.europa.eu/enforcement-and-protection/protecting-against-coercion/qa-political-agreement-anti-coercion-instrument_en.

160. Germann, "Global Rivalries, Corporate Interests."

9. France: The Triumph and Failures of the State

1. Augusta Cadars and Annie Badower, *La France Industries Services Depuis 1945* (Paris: Sirey, 1991), 2; "A Millennium of Macroeconomic Data," spreadsheet, *Quarterly Bulletin* (London: Bank of England, 2010). UK figure is for 1948.

2. Luis Miotti and Frédérique Sachwald, "Growth in France, 1950–2030: The Innovation Challenge" (Paris: Institut Français des Relations Internationales, 2004), 12, 13.

3. Authors' calculation based on "Maddison Project Database 2020," spreadsheet, rug.nl/ggdc/historicaldevelopment/maddison/data/mpd2020.xlsx.

4. The OECD reported 10.8 percent unionization in 2016, the latest year available. See "Trade Union Dataset," OECD, stats.oecd.org/Index.aspx?DataSetCode= TUD.

5. France has indirectly devalued, making its exports cheaper by implementing value-added taxes (VATs) that are refunded on exports and commensurately reducing taxes, like corporate income tax, that are not so refunded.

6. Andrew Shonfield, *Modern Capitalism: The Changing Balance of Public and Private Power* (London: Oxford University Press, 1965), 71–2, 123.

7. Alice H. Amsden, *The Rise of "the Rest": Challenges to the West from Late Industrializing Economies* (New York: Oxford University Press, 2001), 33.

8. Peter A. Hall, *Governing the Economy: The Politics of State Intervention in Britain and France* (New York: Oxford University Press, 1986), 139.

9. *The Industrial Policy of France* (Paris: Organisation for Economic Co-operation and Development, 1974), 9.

10. Jean-Pierre Dormois, *The French Economy in the Twentieth Century* (Cambridge: Cambridge University Press, 2004), 17.

11. Dormois, *French Economy*, 58.

12. Richard F. Kuisel, *Capitalism and the State in Modern France: Renovation and Economic Management in the Twentieth Century* (Cambridge: Cambridge University Press, 1981), 128.

13. Shonfield, *Modern Capitalism*, 171.

14. Hall, *Governing*, 141.

15. Shonfield, *Modern Capitalism*, 73.

16. Dormois, *French Economy*, 67.

17. *Industrial Policy of France*, 33.

18. Vivek Chibber, *Locked in Place: State-Building and Late Industrialization in India* (Princeton, NJ: Princeton University Press, 2003), 240.

19. Shonfield, *Modern Capitalism*, 159.

20. Hall, *Governing*, 139–40.

21. Dormois, *French Economy*, 69.

22. Chibber, *Locked*, 229.

23. Henri Aujac, "An Introduction to French Industrial Policy," in *French Industrial Policy*, ed. William James Adams and Christian Stoffaës (Washington, DC: Brookings Institution, 1986), 14.

24. Noel Whiteside and Robert Salais, eds., *Governance, Industry and Labour Markets in Britain and France: The Modernizing State in the Mid-Twentieth Century* (New York: Routledge, 1998), 87.

25. *Industrial Policy of France*, 33.

26. *Industrial Policy of France*, 33.

27. Dormois, *French Economy*, 17–18.

28. Hall, *Governing*, 152.

29. Dormois, *French Economy*, 19.

30. Dormois, *French Economy*, 28.

31. Bela Balassa, "Selective versus General Economic Policy in Postwar France," in *French Industrial Policy*, 97.

32. Shonfield, *Modern Capitalism*, 86.

33. Shonfield, *Modern Capitalism*, 137.

34. Shonfield, *Modern Capitalism*, 129.

35. "Figure 3: Évolution du PIB de 1950 à 2017" (in French) Institut national de la statistique et des études économiques, December 7, 2023, insee.fr/fr/statistiques/3676727?sommaire=3696937#tableau-figure3.

36. Shonfield, *Modern Capitalism*, 143.

37. Shonfield, *Modern Capitalism*, 126–7.

38. Shonfield, *Modern Capitalism*, 130.

39. Shonfield, *Modern Capitalism*, 74.

40. Cadars and Badower, *La France Industries*, 12.

41. Shonfield, *Modern Capitalism*, 140–1.

42. Aujac, "Introduction to French Industrial Policy," 14–15.

43. Hall, *Governing*, 150.

44. Hall, *Governing*, 168.

45. Dormois, *French Economy*, 29.

46. Christian Stoffaës, "Industrial Policy in the High-Tech Industries," in *French Industrial*, 41–2.

47. Dormois, *French Economy*, 68.

48. John Zysman, "Comments," in *French Industrial*, 105.

49. John Fayerweather, ed., *Host National Attitudes toward Multinational Corporations* (New York: Praeger, 1982).

50. David Bailey, George Harte, and Roger Sugden, *Transnationals and Governments: Recent Policies in Japan, France, Germany, the United States and Britain* (London: Routledge, 1994), 50.

51. Bailey et al., *Transnationals*, 60.

52. Bailey et al., *Transnationals*, 50–1.

53. Bailey et al., *Transnationals*, 57.

54. Dormois, *French Economy*, 42.

55. Stoffaës, "Industrial Policy in the High-Tech Industries," 51.

56. Stoffaës, "Industrial Policy in the High-Tech Industries," 40.

57. Stoffaës, "Industrial Policy in the High-Tech Industries," 47.

58. Stoffaës, "Industrial Policy in the High-Tech Industries," 47.

59. Authors' calculation based on "GDP Growth (Annual %): France, United Kingdom, Japan, Spain, Germany, Italy, Canada, United States," World Bank, data.worldbank.org/indicator/NY.GDP.MKTP.KD.ZG?end=1973&locations=FR-GB-JP-ES-DE-IT-CA-US&start=1961.

60. "GDP per Capita (Current US$): France, United Kingdom," World Bank, data.worldbank.org/indicator/NY.GDP.PCAP.CD?end=1966&locations=FR-GB&start=1960.

61. Robert W. Crandall and Kenneth Flamm, eds., *Changing the Rules: Technological Change, International Competition, and Regulation in Communications* (Washington, DC: Brookings Institution, 1989), 285.

62. Bailey et al., *Transnationals*, 50–1.

63. Stoffaës, "Industrial Policy in the High-Tech Industries," 57.

64. Stoffaës, "Industrial Policy in the High-Tech Industries," 60.

65. Dormois, *French Economy*, 120.

66. Hall, *Governing*, 145.

67. Aujac, "Introduction to French Industrial Policy," 15–16.

68. Raymond Lévy, "Industrial Policy and the Steel Industry," in *French Industrial*, 66–7.

69. Lévy, "Industrial Policy and the Steel Industry," 69; Hall, *Governing*, 181.

70. Lévy, "Industrial Policy and the Steel Industry," 69.

71. Lévy, "Industrial Policy and the Steel Industry," 70.

72. Dormois, *French Economy*, 59.
73. Hall, *Governing*, 187.
74. Hall, *Governing*, 185–6.
75. Aujac, "Introduction to French Industrial Policy," 16.
76. Aujac, "Introduction to French Industrial Policy," 16.
77. Figures for fiscal year 1978: Hall, *Governing*, 189–90, converted at 4.7 FF to 1 USD.
78. François Perrin-Pelletier, "Industrial Policy and the Automobile Industry," in *French Industrial Policy*, 75.
79. Judith Stein, *Pivotal Decade: How America Traded Factories for Finance in the 1970s* (New Haven, CT: Yale University Press, 2010), 255.
80. Stoffaës, "Industrial Policy in the High-Tech Industries," 44.
81. Hall, *Governing*, 196–7.
82. Hall, *Governing*, 192–3.
83. Hall, *Governing*, 213–14.
84. Hall, *Governing*, 145, 195.
85. Hall, *Governing*, 194.
86. Dormois, *French Economy*, 64.
87. Ministère de la Recherche et de l'Industrie, *Une Politique Industrielle pour la France: Actes des Journées de Travail des 15 et 16 novembre 1982* (Paris: La Documentation Française, 1982), 387.
88. Hall, *Governing*, 211.
89. Aujac, "Introduction to French Industrial Policy," 18.
90. Richard Holton, "*Industrial Politics in France: Nationalisation under Mitterrand,*" *West European Politics* 9 no. 1 (1986): 71–7; and Aujac, "Introduction to French Industrial Policy," 28–9.
91. Hall, *Governing*, 203–4.
92. Hall, *Governing*, 205.
93. Hall, *Governing*, 205.
94. Philippe Herzog, "Public Enterprises Should Promote Efficiency," in *French Industrial Policy*, 127.
95. Hall, *Governing*, 208–9.
96. Hall, *Governing*, 199.
97. Hall, *Governing*, 202–3.
98. Stoffaës, "Industrial Policy in the High-Tech Industries," 206.
99. Hall, *Governing*, 211–12.
100. Vivien A. Schmidt, *From State to Market? The Transformation of French Business and Government* (Cambridge: Cambridge University Press, 1996), 121.
101. Aujac, "Introduction to French Industrial Policy," 33.
102. Dormois, *French Economy*, 129.
103. Dormois reckons it took until around 2004 for this message to impact the French psyche. See Dormois, *French Economy*, 64.
104. Dormois, *French Economy*, 24–6.
105. Francois Morin, "A Transformation in the French Model of Shareholding and Management," *Economy and Society* 29, no. 1 (2000): 36–53.
106. Nicholas Comfort, conversation in 1992 with Sir Leon Brittan, reported by email to author Ian Fletcher, 2022.
107. This number has been consecrated in the public debate since it appeared in 2001 in a yearly academic book published on French economy and society (*L'Etat de la France: 2001–2002* [Paris: La Découverte, 2001]). Some economists suggest lower figures – Jean-Marc Daniel says 65 billion in *Le Gâchis Français: 40 Ans de*

Mensonges Économiques (Paris: Tallandier, 2015), and Pierre Favier says 70 billion in *La Décennie Mitterrand* (Paris: Points, 1991).

108. Dormois, *French Economy*, 24–6.
109. Dormois, *French Economy*, 129.
110. Jean-Louis Beffa, "Pour une Nouvelle Politique Industrielle," January 1, 2005.
111. "Developing UK Industrial Policy: Lessons from France," Trades Union Congress, December 2009, 5–6.
112. "Grand Emprunt: Les Choix de M. Sarkozy," *Le Monde*, December 14, 2009, converted at 1.5EUR:1USD.
113. David Jolly, "Peugeot Wins Promise of State Aid and Announces Pact with G.M.," *New York Times*, October 24, 2012.
114. Louis Gallois, "Pacte pour la Compétitivité de l'Industrie Française," November 5, 2012, vie-publique.fr/rapport/32798-pacte-pour-la-competitivite-de-industrie-francaise.
115. Gallois, "Pacte pour la Compétitivité de l'Industrie Française."
116. "Clarivate Analytics Names 2016 Top 100 Global Innovators," Clarivate, January 10, 2017.
117. "La French Tech Heads to the CES," Business France, 2018, businessfrance.fr/presse-dp-ces-2018-anglais.
118. Elke Asen, "Tax Subsidies for R&D Expenditures in Europe," Tax Foundation, February 6, 2020.
119. "Second Annual Report on the Screening of Foreign Direct Investments into the Union," European Commission, January 9, 2022, passim,ec.europa.eu/transparency/documents-register/detail?ref=COM(2022)433&lang=en.
120. For example, "Making Europe's Businesses Future-Ready: A New Industrial Strategy for a Globally Competitive, Green and Digital Europe," European Commission, March 10, 2020.
121. European Parliament, "EU Strategic Autonomy 2013–2023: From Concept to Capacity," EU Strategic Autonomy Monitor, July 2022, 1, europarl.europa.eu/RegData/etudes/BRIE/2022/733589/EPRS_BRI(2022)733589_EN.pdf.

10. Britain: No Theory and Little Execution

1. Felix Richter, "China Is the World's Manufacturing Superpower," Statista, May 4, 2021.
2. Nicholas Comfort, *Surrender: How British Industry Gave Up the Ghost, 1952–2012* (London: Biteback, 2012), 1.
3. John Burn-Murdoch, "Britain and the US Are Poor Societies with Some Very Rich People," *Financial Times*, September 15, 2002.
4. Peter Hall, *Governing the Economy: The Politics of State Intervention in Britain and France* (New York: Oxford University Press, 1986), 61.
5. Comfort, *Surrender*, 70.
6. Hall, *Governing*, 52; Andrew Shonfield, *Modern Capitalism: The Changing Balance of Public and Private Power* (New York: Oxford University Press, 1965), 437.
7. "Developing UK Industrial Policy: Lessons from France," Trades Union Congress (TUC), December 2009, 20.
8. Hall, *Governing*, 52–3.
9. R. C. O. Matthews, C. H. Feinstein, and J. C. Odling-Smee, *British Economic Growth 1856–1973* (Stanford, CA: Stanford University Press, 1982), 435.

10. Robin Havers, *The Second World War: Europe, 1939–1943* (London: Bloomsbury, 2002), 71–7.
11. Mark Harrison, ed., *The Economics of World War II: Six Great Powers in International Comparison* (Cambridge: Cambridge University Press, 1998), 10.
12. Correlli Barnett, *The Audit of War: The Illusion and Reality of Britain as a Great Nation* (London: Macmillan, 1986), 6.
13. Noel Whiteside and Robert Salais, eds., *Governance, Industry and Labour Markets in Britain and France: The Modernizing State in the Mid-Twentieth Century* (New York: Routledge, 1998), 9.
14. Marvin Frankel, "Joint Industrial Planning in Great Britain," *Industrial & Labor Relations Review* 11, no. 3 (April 1958): 429–45.
15. Tim Rooth and Peter Scott, "British Public Policy and Multinationals during the 'Dollar Gap' Era, 1945–1960," *Enterprise & Society* 3, no. 1 (March 2002): 135.
16. Shonfield, *Modern Capitalism*, 99.
17. Hall, *Governing*, 73.
18. Hall, *Governing*, 59–60.
19. Matthew Ward, "UK Trade, 1948–2019: Statistics," Briefing Paper, House of Commons Library, December 10, 2020, 7; "Shares of Gross Domestic Product: Exports of Goods and Services, Imports of Goods and Services, 1947–2022," Federal Reserve Bank of St. Louis, fred.stlouisfed.org/series/B020REIQ156NBEA.
20. Geoffrey Owen, *From Empire to Europe: The Decline and Revival of British Industry since the Second World War* (London: HarperCollins, 2000), 48.
21. Shonfield, *Modern Capitalism*, 88–91.
22. 1946: £978 million, 1950: £2,293 million. "Table 1: UK Trade in Goods, 1946–2011," in Grahame Allen, "UK Trade Statistics," House of Commons Library, October 8, 2012, 11.
23. F. T. Willey, *Plan for Shipbuilding*, Fabian Tract 299 (London: Fabian Society, 1956), 11.
24. Shonfield, *Modern Capitalism*, 98.
25. Unions also opposed formal compensation for layoffs, lest it institutionalize laying workers off and hamper their ability to prevent it through strikes. With Labour governments, from the 1940s through the 1970s, the unions feared that if firms cooperated with government too closely, "free collective bargaining" would be undermined. Shonfield, *Modern Capitalism*, 114n, 160; also Nick Comfort email exchange with author Ian Fletcher, August 2, 2023.
26. Owen, *From Empire*, 48–9.
27. New York Times, "British Auto Exports Up," February 6, 1951.
28. Correlli Barnett, "The Wasting of Britain's Marshall Aid," BBC, March 3, 2011, bbc.co.uk/history/british/modern/marshall_01.shtml.
29. See Matthias Kipping, "Competing for Dollars and Technology: The United States and the Modernization of the French and German Steel Industries after World War II," *Business and Economic History* 23, no. 1 (Fall 1994): 229–40. Also, Whiteside and Salais, *Governance, Industry and Labour Markets*, 7–8.
30. Whiteside and Salais, *Governance, Industry and Labour Markets*, 6–7, 12–13.
31. Jonathan Zeitlin, "Americanisation and Its Limits: The Reconstruction of Britain's Engineering Industries, 1945–1955," in Whiteside and Salais, *Governance, Industry and Labour Markets*, 103–7.
32. Comfort, *Surrender*, 45.
33. Owen, *From Empire*, 132–3.
34. Barnett, "The Wasting of Britain's Marshall Aid."
35. Barnett, "The Wasting."

36. Hall, *Governing*, 25.
37. Zeitlin, "Americanisation," 109–10.
38. Roy Mankelow and Frank Wilkinson, "Industrial Relations in Iron and Steel, Shipbuilding and the Docks, 1930–1960," in Whiteside and Salais, *Governance, Industry and Labour*, 232.
39. Owen, *From Empire*, 99.
40. Mankelow and Wilkinson, "Industrial Relations in Iron and Steel."
41. "The Role of Government in Promoting Higher Industrial Productivity," Productivity and Conditional Aid Committee, March 11, 1954.
42. The UK did not take part in the GATT bilaterals at Annecy. It did at Torquay in 1950–51, but only to cover its trading relations with some European countries. Imperial preference continued a little longer.
43. Comfort, *Surrender*, 17, 102, 145.
44. Owen, *From Empire*, 67.
45. Jim Love and Jim Stevens, "The Scottish Lobby: Ravenscraig and Hunterston," *Quarterly Economic Commentary* 8, no. 4 (May 1983): 34.
46. Owen, *From Empire*, 128.
47. Owen, *From Empire*, 103–4.
48. Robert Saunders, *Yes to Europe! The 1975 Referendum and Seventies Britain* (Cambridge: Cambridge University Press, 2018), 47–8.
49. Owen, *From Empire*, 304–5.
50. Owen, *From Empire*, 307.
51. Owen, *From Empire*, 307.
52. Owen, *From Empire*, 310.
53. Owen, *From Empire*, 325–6.
54. "Gross Domestic Product: Year on Year Growth: CVM SA %," Office for National Statistics, ons.gov.uk/economy/grossdomesticproductgdp/timeseries/ihyp/pn2.
55. Hall, *Governing*, 86–7.
56. Shonfield, *Modern Capitalism*, 151.
57. Shonfield, *Modern Capitalism*, 102–5.
58. Shonfield, *Modern Capitalism*, 156.
59. Owen, *From Empire*, 451.
60. Owen, *From Empire*, 451.
61. Hall, *Governing*, 87, 89.
62. Harold Wilson, *The Labour Government 1964–1970* (London: Weidenfeld and Nicolson and Michael Joseph, 1971), 8.
63. Owen, *From Empire*, 264–5.
64. Hall, *Governing*, 88.
65. Hall, *Governing*, 88.
66. David Bailey, George Harte, and Roger Sugden, *Transnationals and Governments: Recent Policies in Japan, France, Germany, the United States and Britain* (London: Routledge, 1994), 157.
67. Owen, *From Empire*, 250.
68. Defining the UK's productivity level at 100 for both 1960 and 1973, Japan increased from 47 to 74, Germany from 96 to 119, and France from 95 to 116. Mary O'Mahony, *Britain's Productivity Performance 1950–1996: An International Perspective* (London: National Institute for Economic and Social Research, 1999), 16.
69. "Rolls-Royce (Launching Aid)," UK Parliament Hansard, November 1970.
70. Owen, *From Empire*, 314–17, 325.

71. Judith Stein, *Pivotal Decade: How America Traded Factories for Finance in the Seventies* (New Haven, CT: Yale University Press, 2011), 255.
72. Stein, *Pivotal*, 435.
73. Unemployment: James Denman and Paul McDonald, "Unemployment Statistics from 1881 to the Present Day," Labour Market Statistics Group Central Statistical Office, January 1996, 7.
74. Roy Lewis and Jon Clark, "The Bullock Report," *Modern Law Review*, May 1977: 323.
75. Hall, *Governing*, 90.
76. Owen, *From Empire*, 453-4.
77. Hall, *Governing*, 90.
78. Hall, *Governing*, 90.
79. Comfort, *Surrender*, 68.
80. Owen, *From Empire*, 455.
81. Hall, *Governing*, 96-7.
82. Owen, *From Empire*, 456.
83. Owen, *From Empire*, 78.
84. Comfort, *Surrender*, 112.
85. Hall, *Governing*, 105.
86. Hall, *Governing*, 106.
87. Owen, *From Empire*, 138-9.
88. Hall, *Governing*, 109.
89. Comfort, *Surrender*, 125.
90. Comfort, *Surrender*, 116.
91. Owen, *From Empire*, 246.
92. Comfort, *Surrender*, 134.
93. Bailey et al., *Transnationals and Governments*, 171.
94. Bailey et al., *Transnationals*, 170.
95. $5.7 billion, compared with $7.3 billion for Germany, $3.6 billion for France, and $6.2 billion for Italy. Owen, *From Empire*, 289.
96. Hubert Buch-Hansen and Angela Wigger, *The Politics of European Competition Regulation: A Critical Political Economy Perspective* (New York: Routledge, 2011).
97. Comfort, *Surrender*, 177-81.
98. Comfort, *Surrender*, 144.
99. Comfort, *Surrender*, 260.
100. Gordon Brown, conference on "New Policies for a Global Economy," London, September 26, 1994; James Bartholomew, "The Chancellor of Gobbledygook," *Daily Mail*, September 28, 1994.
101. Owen, *From Empire*, 2.
102. "Ford Forks Out on Dagenham," BBC News, May 6, 1999; Owen, *From Empire*, 247.
103. Comfort, *Surrender*, 232.
104. "Employment by Economic Activity: Manufacturing: All Persons for the United Kingdom," Federal Reserve Bank of St. Louis, fred.stlouisfed.org/series/LFEAMNTTGBQ647S.
105. Allegra Stratton, "Mandelson Calls for 'Industrial Activism' to Revitalise Britain after the Recession," *Guardian*, December 2, 2008.
106. Ed Miliband, "Labour Can Still Win the Battle of Ideas," *Guardian*, January 9, 2010.

107. Vince Cable, "Industrial Strategy: Cable Outlines Vision for Future of British industry," Imperial College, London, September 11, 2012.
108. Department for Business, Innovation, and Skills, "Industrial Strategy: UK Sector Analysis," HM Government, September 2012.
109. Department for Business, Energy, and Industrial Strategy, "Forging Our Future. Industrial Strategy: The Story So Far," HM Government, December 2018.
110. "Build Back Better: Our Plan for Growth," HM Treasury, March 3, 2021.

11. India: Dysfunctional Socialism, Directionless Capitalism

1. Authors' adjustment to 2020 GDP based on Angus Maddison's "Historical Statistics of the World Economy: 1–2008 AD," rug.nl/ggdc/historicaldevelop ment/maddison/releases/maddison-project-database-2020.
2. Vivek Chibber, *Locked in Place: State-Building and Late Industrialization in India* (Princeton, NJ: Princeton University Press, 2003), 3.
3. Chibber, *Locked*, 3. Also Arvind Panagariya, *India: The Emerging Giant* (Oxford: Oxford University Press, 2008), xiii.
4. "Gross Domestic Product 2022," World Bank, databank.worldbank.org/data/download/GDP.pdf.
5. Measured by India's own poverty standard. See Gaurav Datt, Martin Ravallion, and Rinku Murgai, "Growth, Urbanization and Poverty Reduction in India," working paper no. 21983, National Bureau of Economic Research (NBER), February 2016, 43.
6. For 1990: "GDP per Capita (Current US$)," World Bank, databank.worldbank.org/reports.aspx?source=world-development-indicators. Supporting the five times estimate for 2020: "2020 Data. GDP (Current US$) – India," World Bank, data bank.worldbank.org/reports.aspx?source=world-development-indicators.
7. "Enhanced Maintenance Practices Leads [*sic*] to Increase in Productivity: Indian Maintenance Scenario," *Industrial Business MART* 12, no. 5, September 2015.
8. "India Manufacturing Output 1960–2023," Macrotrends, 2023, macrotrends.net/countries/IND/india/manufacturing-output.
9. "China Manufacturing Output 2004–2023," Macrotrends, 2023, macrotrends.net/countries/CHN/china/manufacturing-output.
10. "China's share of global manufacturing was 31% in 2021, according to the United Nations, up from 26% in 2017. India's was 3%," from "Countries Compete to Lure Manufacturers from China," *Wall Street Journal*, March 23, 2023.
11. Manmohan Agarwal and John Whalley, "The 1991 Reforms, Indian Economic Growth, and Social Progress," working paper no. 19024, NBER, May 2013, 18.
12. "29 Out of 43 'Critical' APIs Now Locally Produced," *Times of India*, February 22, 2023.
13. "Poverty and Equity Brief, South Asia, India, April 2020," World Bank; and "Poverty and Equity Brief, East Asia & Pacific, China, April 2019," World Bank.
14. The meaning of the term "socialist" is, of course, debatable. Writing in 1958, eminent economist John Kenneth Galbraith, who would become US ambassador to India in 1961, said that reference to socialism contributed greatly to the failure to understand India. Galbraith noted that in the US, supposedly a free-market capitalist country, the state constituted 20 percent of GDP, while in supposedly socialist India it was less than 10 percent. John Kenneth Galbraith, "Rival Economic Theories in India," *Foreign Affairs* 36, no. 4 (July 1958): 587–96.
15. India has 22 official languages, plus English is an unofficial lingua franca and an official language in some Indian states.

16. Article 246 and the Seventh Schedule of the Indian Constitution play a crucial role in defining the dynamics between the central and state governments. Legislative subjects are organized into three categories: the Union List (List I), the State List (List II), and the Concurrent List (List III). Some important industrial policy issues fall under the states.

17. Shashi Tharoor, *Inglorious Empire: What the British Did to India* (London: C. Hurst & Company, 2017), 2.

18. For a start, it is impossible to know the counterfactual to the existence of the Raj. The political development of the different Indian polities and their economic policies could have taken a vast variety of paths. For the mildly positive case, see Tirthankar Roy, "The Economic Legacies of Colonial Rule in India: Another Look," *Economic and Political Weekly* 50, no. 15 (April 11, 2015): 51–9. For the strongly negative case, see Tharoor, *Inglorious Empire*. For the case that India's economy had already stagnated before the Raj, see Aniruddha Bagchi, "Why Did the Indian Economy Stagnate under the Colonial Rule?" Ideas for India, September 16, 2013.

19. Vijay Joshi, *India's Long Road: The Search for Prosperity* (Oxford: Oxford University Press, 2017), 15.

20. Tharoor, *Inglorious Empire*, 2–3.

21. Tharoor, *Inglorious*, 217, 183, 217.

22. A. H. Hanson, *The Process of Planning: A Study of India's Five-Year Plans 1950–1964* (London: Oxford University Press, 1966), 28.

23. Chibber, *Locked*, 89–90.

24. Amal Sanyal, "The Curious Case of the Bombay Plan," *Contemporary Issues and Ideas in Social Sciences* 6, no. 1 (June 2010): 10.

25. Chibber, *Locked*, 103.

26. Pulapre Balakrishnan, Mausumi Das, and M. Parameswaran, "The Internal Dynamic of Indian Economic Growth," *Journal of Asian Economics* 50 (2017): 46–61.

27. As Swedish economist Gunnar Myrdal put it, "Commingling revolutionary views on economic and social questions with the solicitude for the vested interests of the Indian upper classes was one of Gandhi's (and India's) more subtle ideological achievements." See Gunnar Myrdal, *Asian Drama: An Inquiry into the Poverty of Nations. Volume I* (New York: Twentieth Century Fund, 1968), 260.

28. Alice H. Amsden, *The Rise of "The Rest": Challenges to the West from Late Industrializing Economies* (New York: Oxford University Press, 2001), 157.

29. Panagariya, *India*, 32.

30. Hanson, *Process*, 535.

31. Richard Eckaus, "Planning in India," in *National Economic Planning*, NBER, 1967, 305–6.

32. Chibber, *Locked*, 129.

33. Jesus Felipe, Utsav Kumar, and Arnelyn Abdon, "Exports, Capabilities, and Industrial Policy in India," working paper no. 638, Levy Economics Institute of Bard College, November 2010, 5.

34. Chibber, *Locked*, 179.

35. Hanson, *Process*, 72.

36. Hanson, *Process*, 455.

37. Authors' calculation, based on *Reserve Bank of India Bulletin*, November 1960, June 1961, June 1970, December 1972, and December 1973; as reported by Jagdish N. Bhagwati and T. N. Srinivasan, "Foreign Trade Regimes and Economic Development: India," NBER, January 1975, 17.

38. Pulapre Balakrishnan, "The Recovery of India: Economic Growth in the Nehru Era," *Economic and Political Weekly* 42, no. 45/46 (November 10–23, 2007): 52–66.

39. Panagariya, *India*, 23.

40. Arvind Panagariya, *New India: Reclaiming the Lost Glory* (Oxford: Oxford University Press, 2020), 26, xvii.

41. Sumit Majumdar, *Lost Glory: India's Capitalism Story* (Oxford: Oxford University Press, 2018), 82.

42. Panagariya, *India*, 31.

43. S. Gopal, ed., *Selected Works of Jawaharlal Nehru, Second Series. Volume 20: 19 October 1952–31 December 1952* (New Delhi: Jawaharlal Nehru Memorial Fund, 1997), 60.

44. D. R. Gadgil, "Prospects for the Second Five-Year Plan Period," *India Quarterly* 13, no. 1 (January–March 1957): 5–23.

45. Chibber, *Locked*, 18.

46. Chibber, *Locked*, 21.

47. Chibber, *Locked*, 179.

48. Chibber, *Locked*, 180.

49. Chibber, *Locked*, 7.

50. Chibber, *Locked*, 157.

51. Chibber, *Locked*, 181.

52. Amsden, *Rise*, 314.

53. Chibber, *Locked*, 197.

54. Hanson, *Process*, 155.

55. Chibber, *Locked*, 235, 40–1.

56. Hanson, *Process*, 208–9.

57. Hanson, *Process*, 47.

58. Chibber, *Locked*, 203.

59. Panagariya, *India*, 40.

60. Chibber, *Locked*, 186–7.

61. Chibber, *Locked*, 45.

62. Chibber, *Locked*, 37.

63. Chibber, *Locked*, 37.

64. Chibber, *Locked*, 191.

65. Chibber, *Locked*, 190.

66. Felipe et al., "Exports, Capabilities," 5.

67. Majumdar, *Lost Glory*, 84.

68. Chibber, *Locked*, 214.

69. Majumdar, *Lost Glory*, 83.

70. Felipe et al., "Exports, Capabilities," 3, 12.

71. L. N. Dash, *World Bank and Economic Development of India* (New Delhi: A. P. H., 2000), 114.

72. Chibber, *Locked*, 206.

73. The plan holidays were called for several reasons: 1) Crop failures for two years, leading to inflation, 2) wars with China and with Pakistan diverted resources away from investments, 3) the US cutting off foreign aid, and 4) currency devaluation.

74. Chibber, *Locked*, 171.

75. Mihir S. Sharma, "The Day India's Banks Died because of Political Priorities of a Populist PM," *Business Standard*, December 16, 2019.

76. Amsden, *Rise*, 139.

77. Kartar Lalvani, *The Making of India: The Untold Story of British Enterprise* (London: Bloomsbury, 2016), 38.

78. Rakesh Mohan, "Small-Scale Industrial Policy in India: A Critical Evaluation," in *Economic Policy Reforms and the Indian Economy*, ed. Anne O. Kruger (Chicago, IL: University of Chicago Press, 2002).

79. Tharoor, *Inglorious*, 8.

80. Figures excepting 1948: Amsden, *Rise*, 164. Figure for 1948: Jagdish N. Bhagwati and T. N. Srinivasan, *Foreign Trade Regimes and Economic Development: India* (Washington, DC: National Bureau of Economic Research, 1975), 19.

81. Amsden, *Rise*, 233.

82. Panagariya, *India*, xvii.

83. Felipe et al., "Exports, Capabilities," 6.

84. Dash, *World Bank*, 114.

85. Panagariya, *India*, xvii.

86. Datt et al., "Growth," 43.

87. Ronald J. Herring, "Embedded, Particularism: India's Failed Developmental State," in *The Developmental State*, ed. Meredith Woo-Cummings (Ithaca, NY: Cornell University Press), 306.

88. Narendra Jadhav, "Indian Industrial Policy since 1956," drnarendrajadhav.info/ drjadhav-data_files/Published%20papers/Indian%20Industrial%20Policy% 20Since%201956.pdf.

89. Panagariya, *India*, 79.

90. Chibber, *Locked*, 250.

91. Chibber, *Locked*, 254.

92. Dash, *World Bank*, 114.

93. Jadhav, "Indian Industrial," 6.

94. Jadhav, "Indian Industrial," 6.

95. Felipe et al., "Exports, Capabilities," 2.

96. Lalvani, *Making of India*, 44.

97. Ministry of Statistics and Programme Implementation, "Chapter 7: Five-Year Plans," in *Statistical Year Book of India 2022*, Government of India, 2, mospi .gov.in/statistical-year-book-india/2022.

98. Kunal Sen, "Why Did the Elephant Start to Trot? India's Growth Acceleration Re-examined," *Economic and Political Weekly* 42, no. 43 (October 27–November 2, 2007): 37–47.

99. John Farndon, *India Booms: The Breathtaking Development and Influence of Modern India* (London: Virgin Books, 2008), 13.

100. Ava Lillian Samuel, "Structural Adjustment in India: Economic Crisis and Policy Choice" (master's thesis, University of British Columbia, 1994), 48.

101. There are still debates in India whether the bulk of the credit should go to Singh as finance minister or to Rao as prime minister.

102. Farndon, *India Booms*, 55.

103. Ministry of Industry, "Statement of Industrial Policy," Government of India, July 4, 1991, paragraph 34.

104. "Statement of Industrial Policy," paragraph 21.

105. "Statement of Industrial Policy," paragraph 25.

106. Deb Kusum Das, "Trade Policy and Manufacturing Performance: Exploring the Level of Trade Openness in India's Organized Manufacturing in the Period 1990–2010," Reserve Bank of India, January 29, 2016, figure 4.3.

107. Amsden, *Rise*, 278–9.

108. Bibhas Saha, Kunal Sen, and Dibyendu Maiti, "Trade Openness, Labour Institutions and Flexibilisation: Theory and Evidence from India," *Labour Economics* 24, issue C (October 2013): 180–95.
109. "Five-Year Plans," in *Statistical Year Book of India 2022*.
110. Jadhav, "Indian Industrial," 9.
111. Adam Roberts, *Superfast Primetime Ultimate Nation* (London: Profile Books, 2017), 17.
112. Growth 1947–60: Deb Kusum Das, Abdul Azeez Erumban and Jagannath Mallick, "Economic Growth in India during 1950–2015," table 1: "GDP and Per Capita GDP Growth and Per Capita Income Levels in India, 1900–2016," *Journal of Economic Surveys* 35, no. 3 (July 2021): 927. Growth since 1961: "GDP Growth (Annual %) – India," World Bank, data.worldbank.org/indicator/NY.GDP.MKTP.KD.ZG?locations=IN.
113. "Five-Year Plans," in *Statistical Year Book of India 2022*.
114. Press Information Bureau, "Policy of Strategic Disinvestment Announced: Clear Roadmap for Strategic and Non-strategic Sectors," Government of India, February 1, 2021.
115. Arvind Subramanian and Josh Felman, "India's Stalled Rise," *Foreign Affairs*, January/February 2022.
116. Ministry of Commerce and Industry, "Press Note No. 2 (2011 Series), Subject: National Manufacturing Policy," November 4, 2011, Government of India, 4.
117. "Press Note No. 2," 11–12.
118. "Press Note No. 2," 4–5.
119. M. Suresh Babu, "Why 'Make in India' Has Failed," *Hindu*, January 20, 2020.
120. Suresh Babu, "Why 'Make in India' Has Failed."
121. National Investment Promotion and Facilitation Agency, "Production Linked Incentive (PLI) Schemes in India," Government of India, March 2020. Budget: Press Information Bureau, "Commitment of Financial Outlay of Rs 1.97 Lakh Crore in the Next 5 Years Starting FY 2021–22 for PLI Schemes in 13 Sectors," Government of India, February 1, 2021.
122. "29 Out of 43 'Critical' APIs Now Locally Produced," *Times of India*, February 22, 2023.
123. R. Nagaraj, "Make in India: Why Didn't the Lion Roar?" India Forum, April 8, 2019.
124. India: Ankur Bhardwaj, "CEDA–CMIE Bulletin: Manufacturing Employment Halves in 5 Years," Centre for Economic Data & Analysis, Ashoka University, May 2021. China: Authors' calculation from "China Statistical Yearbook 2021," table 4-1: "Employment," National Bureau of Statistics of China. Percentage in manufacturing: Lin Xiaozhao, "Almost 20% of China's Workforce Is in Manufacturing, Study Shows," YiCai Global, July 22, 2023.
125. India has its Council of Scientific and Industrial Research (CSIR) and Ministry of Micro, Small and Medium Enterprises (MSME) Technology Centres, but these are not considered very effective.
126. "Indian Pharmaceutical Industry," India Brand Equity Foundation, July 19, 2023, ibef.org/industry/pharmaceutical-india.
127. Andy Mukherjee, "Modi's $24 Billion Manufacturing Push Is Stuck on the Assembly Line," Bloomberg, June 1, 2023.
128. Mukherjee, "Modi's $24 Billion."
129. Mukherjee, "Modi's $24 Billion."
130. Sankalp Phartiyal and Sudhi Ranjan Sen, "Billionaire's Chip Dreams Stymied as India Set to Deny Funding," Bloomberg, May 30, 2023.

131. Phartiyal and Sen, "Billionaire's Chip Dreams Stymied."
132. Alex Travelli, "Modi Wants to Make India a Chip-Making Superpower. Can He?" *New York Times*, September 13, 2023.
133. Roberts, *Superfast*, 9.
134. Estimates of the size of India's middle class vary so much by definition and by estimator that no definitive reference can be given, 200 million being an approximate median of such estimates.
135. Ashoka Mody, "India's Boom Is a Dangerous Myth," *Project Syndicate*, March 29, 2023.
136. Joshi, *India's Long Road*, 53.
137. Most recent available data. Source: *Women and Men in the Informal Economy: A Statistical Picture* (Geneva: International Labour Organization, 2018), 88.
138. Roberts, *Superfast*, 62.
139. Joshi, *India's Long Road*, 114.
140. China: 302, India: 55. Source: Andrea Murphy and Hank Tucker, "The Global 2000," *Forbes*, June 8, 2023.
141. Sharmila Kantha, "Indian Manufacturing Isn't Creating Enough Jobs," The Wire, January 2, 2017.
142. Roberts, *Superfast*, 58.
143. S. Rukmini, "Only 8.15% of Indians are Graduates, Census Data Show," *Hindu*, August 4, 2015.
144. Farndon, *India Booms*, 161.
145. Subramanian and Felman, "India's Stalled Rise."
146. Philippe Aghion, Robin Burgess, Stephen J. Redding, and Fabrizio Zilibotti, "The Unequal Effects of Liberalization: Evidence from Dismantling the License Raj in India," *American Economic Review*, September 2008, 1397–1412.
147. "Doing Business 2019," World Bank, 5, worldbank.org/content/dam/doingBusiness/media/Annual-Reports/English/DB2019-report_web-version.pdf. "Doing Business 2017," World Bank, 213, 2023, archive.doingbusiness.org/content/dam/doingBusiness/media/Annual-Reports/English/DB17-Report.pdf.
148. Vrishti Beniwa, "India Plans $1.5 Trillion Infrastructure Spending to Spur Growth," December 31, 2020, Bloomberg News, bnnbloomberg.ca/india-plans-1-5-trillion-infrastructure-spending-to-spur-growth-1.1367910.
149. "India's Eye-Watering 1.7 pc Spend on Transport Upgrade to Set Stage for $5 Trillion Economy," *Economic Times*, March 21, 2023, economictimes.indiatimes.com/news/economy/indicators/indias-eye-watering-1-7-pc-spend-on-transport-upgrade-to-set-stage-for-5-trillion-economy/articleshow/98862248.cms.
150. Rahul Mukherji, "Special Economic Zones in India," Institute of South Asian Studies Working Paper 30. Singapore, Institute of South Asian Studies, 2008, 4–10.
151. Rahul Mukherji, "The State, Economic Growth, and Development in India," *India Review* 8, no. 1 (2009): 81–106, https://doi.org/10.1080/14736480802665238.
152. Subramanian and Felman, "India's Stalled Rise."
153. "Import Duty on Cars in India," SBI General Insurance, September 3, 2022.
154. Ministry of Road Transport and Highways, "Road Transport Year Book (2017–18 and 2018–19)," Government of India, 49, 51.
155. Niharika Mandhana and Newley Purnell, "Modi's Vision for India Rests on Six Giant Companies: Conglomerates Are Executing Projects with a Scale and Speed That Have Eluded India in the Past," *Wall Street Journal*, June 21, 2023, wsj.com/articles/modi-india-economy-reliance-industries-adani-group-tata-d2c4f89e.
156. Subramanian and Felman, "India's Stalled Rise."

157. Asit Ranjan Mishra, "Wary of FTAs, India May Be Turning Trade Protectionist," *Mint*, December 16, 2020.

12. ARGENTINA: A Dual Cautionary Tale

1. Gerardo della Paolera and Alan M. Taylor, eds., *A New Economic History of Argentina* (Cambridge: Cambridge University Press, 2003), 5.
2. 2023 data: "World Economic Outlook Database," International Monetary Fund, April 2023; 2019 data: Klaus Schwab, "The Global Competitiveness Report 2019," World Economic Forum, 2019, xiii. (Rankings were paused in 2019 due to COVID-19.)
3. Della Paolera and Taylor, *New Economic History*, 239.
4. "Maddison Project Database 2020," University of Groningen, last modified May 23, 2022, rug.nl/ggdc/historicaldevelopment/maddison/?lang=en. Naturally, these numbers are sensitive to the endpoints chosen, due to the economic cycle and how one classifies policies. But the larger point survives choice of endpoints.
5. Carlos F. Díaz Alejandro, *Essays on the Economic History of the Argentine Republic* (New Haven, CT: Yale University Press, 1970), 217.
6. Alice H. Amsden, *The Rise of "The Rest": Challenges to the West from Late-Industrializing Economies* (Oxford: Oxford University Press, 2001), 83.
7. GDP: "GDP per Capita (Constant LCU) – Argentina," World Bank, data.world bank.org/indicator/NY.GDP.PCAP.KN?locations=AR. Value-added in manufacturing: "Manufacturing, Value Added (Constant LCU) – Argentina," World Bank, data.worldbank.org/indicator/NV.IND.MANF.KN?locations=AR. Productivity: "Total Factor Productivity at Constant National Prices for Argentina," Federal Reserve Bank of St. Louis, fred.stlouisfed.org/series/RTFPNAARA632NRUG.
8. "Military Coups in Argentina," Wikipedia, en.wikipedia.org/wiki/Military_coups_in_Argentina#Coup_of_28_June_1966; "Anexo: Presidentes de la Nación Argentina," Wikipedia, es.wikipedia.org/wiki/Anexo:Presidentesde_la_Naci%C3%B3n_Argentina.
9. Daniel Chudnovsky and Andrés López, *The Elusive Quest for Growth in Argentina* (New York: Palgrave Macmillan, 2007), 26.
10. James P. Brennan and Marcelo Rougier, *The Politics of National Capitalism: Perónism and the Argentine Bourgeoisie, 1946–1976* (University Park: Pennsylvania State University Press, 2009), 201.
11. Mac Margolis, "Argentina's Good Behavior Won't Deliver It from Economic Pain," Bloomberg, June 3, 2020.
12. As late as the early 1990s, a survey of 271 large enterprises found that 117 had no managerial structure whatever. See Amsden, *Rise*, 244.
13. Yair Mundlak and Marcelo Regúnaga, "Agriculture," in Della Paolera and Taylor, *New Economic History*, 235; Paul H. Lewis, *The Crisis of Argentine Capitalism* (Chapel Hill: University of North Carolina Press, 1990), xiii.
14. Keith Barrow, "Argentina's Roadmap to a Rail Revival," *International Railway Journal*, November 29, 2016; Mundlak and Regúnaga, "Agriculture," 237.
15. Chudnovsky and López, *Elusive Quest*, 34.
16. Lewis, *Argentine Capitalism*, 38.
17. "A Century of Decline," *Economist*, February 17, 2014.
18. Maria Inés Barbero and Fernando Rocchi, "Industry and Industrialization in Argentina in the Long Run: From Its Origins to the 1970s," in Della Paolera and Taylor, *New Economic History*, 265.
19. Lewis, *Argentine Capitalism*, 95.

20. Díaz Alejandro, *Essays*, 103.
21. Della Paolera and Taylor, *New Economic History*, 288.
22. Brennan and Rougier, *Politics*, 3.
23. Brennan and Rougier, *Politics*, xxii.
24. Javier Villanueva, "El Origen de la Industrialización Argentina," *Desarrollo Económico* 12, no. 47 (October–December, 1972): 450.
25. Julio Berlinski, "International Trade and Commercial Policy," in Della Paolera and Taylor, *New Economic History*, 213.
26. Brennan and Rougier, *Politics*, 64.
27. Brennan and Rougier, *Politics*, 64–5.
28. Lewis, *Argentine Capitalism*, 45, 118.
29. Barbero and Rocchi, "Industry," 277–9.
30. Díaz Alejandro, *Essays*, 107.
31. Díaz Alejandro, *Essays*, 270.
32. Chudnovsky and López, *Elusive Quest*, 2.
33. Della Paolera and Taylor, *New Economic History*, 193.
34. Harold F. Peterson, *Argentina and the United States 1810–1960* (New York: University Publishers, 1964), 464.
35. Brennan and Rougier, *Politics*, 47–8.
36. Della Paolera and Taylor, *New Economic History*, 213.
37. Lewis, *Argentine Capitalism*, 135.
38. Alan M. Taylor, "Tres Fases del Crecimiento Económico Argentino," *Revista de Historia Económica* 12, no. 3 (December 1994): 649–83.
39. Della Paolera and Taylor, *New Economic History*, 193.
40. Lewis, *Argentine Capitalism*, 187.
41. Díaz Alejandro, *Essays*, 70.
42. Vivek Chibber, *Locked in Place: State-Building and Late Industrialization in India* (Princeton, NJ: Princeton University Press, 2003), 240.
43. Lewis, *Argentine Capitalism*, 329; Díaz Alejandro, *Essays*, 271.
44. Brennan and Rougier, *Politics*, xiii.
45. Diaz Alejandro, *Essays*, 119.
46. Díaz Alejandro, *Essays*, 136.
47. Díaz Alejandro, *Essays*, 119, 248–50.
48. Chudnovsky and López, *Elusive Quest*, 20.
49. Díaz Alejandro, *Essays*, 114.
50. Barbero and Rocchi, "Industry," 280.
51. Barbero and Rocchi, "Industry," 279.
52. Barbero and Rocchi, "Industry," 279.
53. Berlinski, "International Trade," 213.
54. Berlinski, "International Trade," 213.
55. Sebastian Galiani and Pablo Gerchunoff, "The Labor Market," in Della Paolera and Taylor, *New Economic History*, 132; Brennan and Rougier, *Politics*, 6; Díaz Alejandro, *Essays*, 262.
56. Díaz Alejandro, *Essays*, 231.
57. Brennan and Rougier, *Politics*, 58, 73–6.
58. Díaz Alejandro, *Essays*, 240–1.
59. Brennan and Rougier, *Politics*, 55.
60. Brennan and Rougier, *Politics*, 83–4.
61. Lewis, *Argentine Capitalism*, 305.
62. Lewis, *Argentine Capitalism*, 303.
63. Barbero and Rocchi, "Industry," 284.

64. "Maddison Project Database 2020."
65. Della Paolera and Taylor, *New Economic History*, 285–6.
66. Inflation: "Inflation, GDP Deflator (Annual %) – Argentina," World Bank, data .worldbank.org/indicator/NY.GDP.DEFL.KD.ZG?locations=AR. GDP: "GDP Growth (Annual %) – Argentina," World Bank, data.worldbank.org/indicator/ NY.GDP.MKTP.KD.ZG?locations=AR.
67. Brennan and Rougier, *Politics*, 157.
68. Brennan and Rougier, *Politics*, 158.
69. Brennan and Rougier, *Politics*, 14–15.
70. Brennan and Rougier, *Politics*, 159.
71. Brennan and Rougier, *Politics*, 183.
72. Lewis, *Argentine Capitalism*, 421–2.
73. Berlinski, "International Trade," 212.
74. Chudnovsky and López, *Elusive Quest*, 56.
75. "Foreign Direct Investment, Net Inflows (BoP, Current US$) – Argentina," World Bank, data.worldbank.org/indicator/BX.KLT.DINV.CD.WD?end=1983&locations= AR&start=1970; Edward Schumacher, "Argentina's Instability Slows Inflow of Foreign Investment," *New York Times*, October 26, 1981.
76. Jeff Frieden, "Classes, Sectors, and Foreign Debt in Latin America," *Comparative Politics* 21, no. 1 (October 1988): 15.
77. Barbero and Rocchi, "Industry," 290.
78. "General Motors de Argentina," Wikipedia, wikipedia.org/wiki/General_Motors_ de_Argentina.
79. Lewis, *Argentine Capitalism*, 466–8.
80. Juan E. Santarcángelo, Daniel Schteingart, and Fernando Porta, "Industrial Policy in Argentina, Brazil, Chile and Mexico: A Comparative Approach," *Revue Interventions Économiques* 59 (January 2018): 3.
81. Berlinski, "International Trade," 217–18.
82. Chudnovsky and López, *Elusive Quest*, 58.
83. J. Onno de Beaufort Wijnholds, "The Argentine Drama: A View from the IMF Board," in *The Crisis That Was Not Prevented: Lessons for Argentina, the IMF, and Globalisation*, ed. Jan Joost Teunissen and Age Akkerman (The Hague: FONDAD, January 2003), 104; Chudnovsky and López, *Elusive Quest*, 19, 74–5.
84. Mundlak and Regúnaga, "Agriculture," 254.
85. Gerardo della Paolera, Maria Alejandra Irigoin, and Carlos G. Bozzolli, "Passing the Buck: Monetary and Fiscal Policies," in Della Paolera and Taylor, *New Economic History*, 63.
86. "Information on Argentina," Organization of American States Foreign Trade Information System, sice.oas.org/ctyindex/ARG/ARGagreements_e.asp; "Legal Framework of the Common Market of the Southern Cone," Organization of American States Foreign Trade Information System, sice.oas.org/mercosur/ instmt_e.asp.
87. Electricity: John E. Besant-Jones, "Reforming Power Markets in Developing Countries: What Have We Learned?" World Bank, 2006, 32. Cargo: Antonio Estache and José Carbajo, "Competing Private Ports: Lessons from Argentina," World Bank, 1996, 1.
88. Chudnovsky and López, *Elusive Quest*, 67, 191.
89. Mundlak and Regúnaga, "Agriculture," 255; Chudnovsky and López, *Elusive Quest*, 10.
90. Chudnovsky and López, *Elusive Quest*, 164.
91. Chudnovsky and Lopez, *Elusive Quest*, 112.

92. Legislación y Avisos Oficiales, "Nomenclatura Común del Mercosur, Decreto 1064/2020," *Boletín Oficial de la República Argentina*, November 4, 2022.

93. "Chronology: Argentina's Turbulent History of Economic Crises," Reuters, July 30, 2014.

94. "La Cronología: Del Default de Argentina en 2001 a la Ultima Oferta de Canje," *Economista*, March 16, 2010.

95. "Unemployment, Total (% of Total Labor Force) (National Estimate): Argentina," World Bank, data.worldbank.org/indicator/SL.UEM.TOTL.NE.ZS? locations=AR; Carlos G. Fernández Valdovinos, "Growth, Poverty, and Social Equity in Argentina," *En Breve* no. 82 (November 2005): 3; "Desempleo en Argentina," Wikipedia, es.wikipedia.org/wiki/Desempleo_en_Argentina.

96. "GDP per Capita (Constant LCU) – Argentina," World Bank, data.worldbank .org/indicator/NY.GDP.PCAP.KN?locations=AR.

97. Jonathan Wylde, "Argentina, Kirchnerismo and Neodesarrollismo: Argentine Political Economy under the Administration of Nestor Kirchner 2003–2007," Facultad Latinoamericana de las Ciencias Sociales, April 2010, 2–4.

98. Chudnovsky and López, *Elusive Quest*, 154–5, 157.

99. Joseph Wornom, "Peronism and the Kirchners: The Addiction Argentina Can't Quit," *Harvard International Review*, November 9, 2019.

100. "Manufacturing, Value Added (% of GDP): Argentina," World Bank, data.world bank.org/indicator/NV.IND.MANF.ZS?locations=AR.

101. Della Paolera and Taylor, *New Economic History*, 373.

102. Lewis, *Argentine Capitalism*, 66.

103. Díaz Alejandro, *Essays*, 262.

104. Chudnovsky and López, *Elusive Quest*, 48.

105. Chudnovsky and López, *Elusive Quest*, 82.

106. Chudnovsky and López, *Elusive Quest*, 91.

107. Lewis, *Argentine Capitalism*, 362.

108. Brennan and Rougier, *Politics*, 12–13.

109. Lewis, *Argentine Capitalism*, 300–1.

110. Lewis, *Argentine Capitalism*, 490–1.

111. IAME survived after Perón by producing pickup trucks, and then gradually broadened its range to include motorcycles, tractors, and other products, but was closed in 1980.

112. Lewis, *Argentine Capitalism*, 313.

113. Alberto Petrecolla, "Unbalanced Development, 1958–62," in *The Political Economy of Argentina, 1946–83*, ed. Guido di Tella and Rudiger Dornbusc (Pittsburgh, PA: University of Pittsburgh Press, 1989), 112.

114. Díaz Alejandro, *Essays*, 327.

115. Barbero and Rocchi, "Industry," 284.

116. Chudnovsky and López, *Elusive Quest*, 48.

117. Mario Cimoli and Jorge Katz, "Structural Reform, Technological Gaps and Economic Development: A Latin American Perspective," *Industrial and Corporate Change* 12, no. 2 (April 2003): 387–411.

118. "Foreign Direct Investment, Net Inflows (BoP, Current US$) – Argentina," World Bank, data.worldbank.org/indicator/BX.KLT.DINV.CD.WD?locations=AR.

119. "Granted Patents: Total Patents Originating in Argentina," Federal Reserve Bank of St. Louis, fred.stlouisfed.org/series/PATENT4NARTOTAL; "Granted Patents: Total Patents Originating in Brazil," Federal Reserve Bank of St. Louis, fred .stlouisfed.org/series/PATENT4NBRTOTAL; "Granted Patents: Total Patents Originating in South Korea," Federal Reserve Bank of St. Louis, fred.stlouisfed

.org/series/PATENT4NKRTOTAL; "Granted Patents: Total Patents Originating in Taiwan," Federal Reserve Bank of St. Louis, fred.stlouisfed.org/series/PATENT4NTWTOTAL.

120. Barbero and Rocchi, "Industry," 288.

121. Amsden, *Rise*, 223.

122. Chudnovsky and López, *Elusive Quest*, 43.

123. Hugo A. Carignano and Juan P. Jaworski, "Argentina's Subpar Investment in Science," *Science* 363, no. 6428 (February 15, 2019): 702.

124. Chudnovsky and López, *Elusive Quest*, 182–3.

125. Chudnovsky and López, *Elusive Quest*, 183.

126. Chudnovsky and Lopez, *Elusive Quest*, 177.

127. As of SOCMA's appearance on the list in 1993: Amsden, *Rise*, 227–30.

128. "The Global 2000," *Forbes*, last modified May 5, 2023, forbes.com/global2000./#7977813a4aa2.

129. Chudnovsky and López, *Elusive Quest*, 111.

130. Mathilde Carlier, "Imports and Exports of the Automotive Industry in Argentina from 2009 to 2021 (in Billion US Dollars)," *Statista*, October 7, 2022.

131. M. Shahbandeh, "Global Genetically Modified Crops by Countries 2019, Based on Acreage," *Statista*, December 16, 2022.

132. Daniel Workman, "Soya Bean Exports by Country Plus Average Prices," *World Top Exports*, worldstopexports.com/soya-beans-exports-country; "2021 Was Record Year for Argentine Wine Exports, Says Foreign Ministry," *Buenos Aires Times*, January 23, 2022.

13. The Renaissance Origins of Industrial Policy

1. This chapter is adapted with permission from a number of works by Erik Reinert, to whom the authors are profoundly grateful for his collaboration.

2. Fragments of these ideas and policies can, of course, be found in other civilizations and earlier epochs. For East Asia, see Eric Helleiner, *The Neomercantilists* (Ithaca, NY: Cornell University Press, 2021).

3. Erik Reinert, *How Rich Countries Got Rich and Why Poor Countries Stay Poor* (London: Constable, 2007), 72.

4. Reinert, *How Rich*, 74.

5. Luis Ortiz, "Memorandum to the King to Prevent Money from Leaving the Kingdom," Madrid, 1558, quoted in Earl Hamilton, "Spanish Mercantilism before 1700," in Edwin Frances Gay, *Facts and Factors in Economic History: Articles by Former Students* (Cambridge, MA: Harvard University Press, 1932), 214–39, here 237.

6. Reinert, *How Rich*, 84–5.

7. Bernard Moses, "The Economic Conditions of Spain in the Sixteenth Century," *Journal of Political Economy* 1, no. 4 (September 1893): 513–34, here 527.

8. A US observer, historian Earl Hamilton (1932), argued that hardly ever had so much good economic advice gone unheeded as in sixteenth-century Spain. See Earl J. Hamilton, "Spanish Mercantilism before 1700," in *Facts and Factors in Economic History: Articles by Former Students of Edwin Francis Gay* (Cambridge, MA: Harvard University Press, 1932), 237.

9. Reinert, *How Rich*, 85.

10. Reinert, *How Rich*, 79.

11. Daniel Defoe, the polymath historian best known as the author of *Robinson Crusoe*, described the English strategy years later in his 1728 book *A Plan of the English Commerce*.

12. Patrick O'Brien and Roland Quinault, eds., *The Industrial Revolution and British Society* (Cambridge: Cambridge University Press, 1993), 125.

13. Erik Reinert, "Catching Up from Way Behind: A Third World Perspective on First World History," in *The Dynamics of Technology, Trade and Growth*, ed. Jan Fagerberg, Bart Verspagen, and G. N. von Tunzelmann (Cheltenham: Edward Elgar, 1994), 9.

14. Reinert, "Catching Up from Way Behind," 9.

15. Reinert, *How Rich*, 81.

16. Ninety percent of American PhD programs in economics have no economic history requirement, per "The Economic History Requirement: Past, Present, Future," PowerPoint presentation, Robert Margo, Boston University and NBER, ASSA 2019, Atlanta GA, aeaweb.org/conference/2019/preliminary/powerpoint/Z3tzEk8B.

17. Reinert, *How Rich*, 7.

18. The first *mention* of increasing returns is in the ancient Greek Xenophon's *Oeconomicus*, published in the fourth century BC, which gave economics its name. See Reinert, *How Rich*, 37.

19. Erik Reinert, "The Role of the State in Economic Growth," *Journal of Economic Studies* 26, no. 4/5 (August 1999): 268–326.

20. Agricultural productivity often *was* stagnant in this era. In our own time it is not, but for reasons examined in Chapter 1, this does not help farm incomes or make farming a viable source of a large number of good jobs.

21. Reinert, *How Rich*, 86.

22. Stephan Waldhoff, "Proposals for Administrative, Economic, and Social Reform," in *The Oxford Handbook of Leibniz*, ed. Maria Rosa Antognazza (Oxford: Oxford University Press, 2018), 684–98, here 694; and Ulrich Adam, *The Political Economy of J. H. G. Justi* (Bern: Peter Lang AG, 2006), 187.

23. Ferdinando Galiani, *Dialogues sur le Commerce des Bleds* (London, 1770).

24. David Hume, *History of England*, vol. 3 (London: A. Millar, 1773), 430. "Promoting husbandry . . . is never more effectually encouraged than by the increase of manufactures."

25. A key cameralist book, a few decades after Mun and Child in England, was German Philipp Wilhelm von Hornigk's *Austria Supreme (If It So Wishes)*, published in 1684.

26. Charles King, *The British Merchant; or, Commerce Preserv'd* (London: John Darby, 1721), 1–4.

27. Gary M. Anderson and Robert D. Tollison, "Sir James Steuart As the Apotheosis of Mercantilism and His Relation to Adam Smith," *Southern Economic Journal* 51, no. 2 (October 1984): 456–8.

14. US Industrial Policy 1750–1865: Developing a New Nation

1. Jonathan Hughes and Louis P. Cain, *American Economic History*, 5th ed. (Reading, MA: Addison-Wesley, 1998), 121.

2. Japan went to the extreme of essentially cutting itself off from the outside world.

3. Michael Lind, *Land of Promise: An Economic History of the United States* (New York: HarperCollins, 2012), 23.

4. Hughes and Cain, *American Economic History*, 71–2.

5. Robert Paul Thomas, "A Quantitative Approach to the Study of the Effects of British Imperial Policy on Colonial Welfare," *Journal of Economic History* 25, no. 4 (December 1965): 616. Also, Douglas A. Irwin, *Clashing over Commerce: A History of US Trade Policy* (Chicago, IL: University of Chicago Press, 2017), 36.

6. Lind, *Land*, 25.

7. David Bertelson, *The Lazy South* (New York: Oxford University Press, 1967), 86.

8. Lind, *Land*, 24.

9. Peter H. Lindert and Jeffrey G. Williamson, "American Colonial Incomes, 1650–1774," working paper no. 19861, National Bureau of Economic Research, January 2014.

10. Hughes and Cain, *American Economic History*, 48.

11. There were, of course, some complexities to this picture. The colonies were allowed, for example, to make and export pig iron. See Samuel Eliot Morison and Henry Steele Commager, *The Growth of the American Republic*, vol. 1 (New York: Oxford University Press, 1942), 102–3.

12. Hughes and Caine, *American Economic History*, 71–3.

13. One clear sign that mercantilism was a minor issue is that of the 27 specific grievances listed in the Declaration of Independence, only one – "cutting off our Trade with all parts of the world" – refers to it, and only to one aspect.

14. Hughes and Cain, *American Economic History*, 48–9.

15. "Tariff of 1789," in *Encyclopedia of Tariffs and Trade in US History*, ed. Cynthia Clark Northrup and Elaine C. Prange Turney (Westport, CT: Greenwood Press, 2003): 356–7.

16. Lind, *Land*, 107.

17. Stanley Lebergott, "Labor Force and Employment, 1800–1960," in *Output, Employment, and Productivity in the United States after 1800*, ed. Dorothy S. Brady (New York: National Bureau of Economic Research, 1966), table 1.

18. Stephen S. Cohen and J. Bradford DeLong, *Concrete Economics: The Hamiltonian Approach to Economic Growth and Policy* (Boston, MA: Harvard Business Review Press, 2016), 36.

19. Alexander Hamilton, *Papers on Public Credit, Commerce and Finance* (Indianapolis, IN: Bobbs-Merrill, 1957), 204–5.

20. Doron Ben-Atar, "Alexander Hamilton's Alternative: Technology Piracy and the Report on Manufactures," *William and Mary Quarterly* 52, no. 3 (July 1995): 389–414.

21. Irwin, *Clashing*, 83.

22. Library of Congress, Federalist Papers: Primary Documents in American History, Federalist No. 35.

23. Because Hamilton had required that these subscriptions be in government securities, the project retained some implicit federal support.

24. James Thomas Flexner, *Washington, the Indispensable Man* (New York: Little, Brown and Company, 1969), 387.

25. Cohen and DeLong, *Concrete Economics*, 8.

26. Lee W. Formwalt, "Benjamin Henry Latrobe and the Revival of the Gallatin Plan of 1808," *Pennsylvania History: A Journal of Mid-Atlantic Studies* 48, no. 2 (April 1981): 123.

27. Lind, *Land*, 45.

28. Maury Baker, "Cost Overrun, an Early Naval Precedent: Building the First US Warships, 1794–98," *Maryland Historical Magazine* 72, no. 3 (Fall 1977): 361–2. Also, "Federal 1794 Government Spending," US Spending, usgovernmentspending .com/fed_spending_1794USmn.

29. Robert Martello, *Midnight Ride, Industrial Dawn: Paul Revere and the Growth of American Enterprise* (Baltimore, MD: Johns Hopkins University Press, 2010), 204–44.

30. Lawrence A. Peskin, *Manufacturing Revolution: The Intellectual Origins of Early American History* (Baltimore, MD: Johns Hopkins University Press, 2003), 185.

31. Peskin, *Manufacturing Revolution*, 185.

32. Clark Northrup and Prange Turney, *Encyclopedia of Tariffs and Trade*, 538. Adjusted from 1815 to 2023 dollars per CPI Inflation Calculator, officialdata.org/us/inflation/1815?Amount=40000000.

33. Irwin, *Clashing*, 126, 131.

34. Lind, *Land*, 44.

35. Harry Ammon, *James Monroe: The Quest for National Identity* (Charlottesville: University Press of Virginia, 1990), 463–4. The key book written about this at the time was Matthew Carey's 1820 volume *The New Olive Branch, or, An Attempt to Establish an Identity of Interest between Agriculture, Manufactures, and Commerce* (Philadelphia, PA: M. Carey and Son, 1820), 88, 129.

36. Irwin, *Clashing*, 126.

37. C. Donald Johnson, *The Wealth of a Nation: A History of Trade Politics in America* (New York: Oxford University Press, 2018), 57.

38. Lind, *Land*, 106–8.

39. Douglas A. Irwin, "Historical Aspects of US Trade Policy," *NBER Reporter* 3 (Summer 2006): 17.

40. Irwin, *Clashing*, 154; Johnson, *Wealth*, 67.

41. Jonathan J. Pincus, *Pressure Groups and Politics in Antebellum Tariffs* (New York: Columbia University Press, 1977), 175.

42. Irwin, *Clashing*, 194.

43. Pincus, *Pressure*, 92–3.

44. Irwin, *Clashing*, 193–9, 245–54.

45. Pincus, *Pressure*, 95.

46. W. Elliot Brownlee, "The Creation of the US Tariff Commission," in *A Centennial History of the USITC*, ed. Paul R. Bardos (Washington, DC: United States International Trade Commission, 2017), 74.

47. Daniel Peart, *Lobbyists and the Making of US Tariff Policy, 1816–1861* (Baltimore, MD: Johns Hopkins University Press, 2018), 24.

48. Regarding free-trade American academicians of this era: Irwin, *Clashing*, 248.

49. Kenneth W. Rowe, *Mathew Carey: A Study in American Economic Development* (Baltimore, MD: Johns Hopkins University Press, 1933), 112.

50. See, for example, Cohen and DeLong, *Concrete Economics*, 1.

51. Michael Hudson, *America's Protectionist Takeoff 1815–1914: The Neglected American School of Political Economy* (Dresden: ISLET: 2020), 1.

52. Lind, *Land*, 97.

53. Lind, *Land*, 95.

54. Irwin, "Historical Aspects," 17.

55. Burton J. Hendrick, *Bulwark of the Republic: A Biography of the Constitution* (Boston, MA: Little, Brown, and Company, 1937), 221.

56. Irwin, *Clashing*, 194.

57. Fred Bateman and Thomas Weiss, *A Deplorable Scarcity: The Failure of Industrialization in the Slave Economy* (Chapel Hill: University of North Carolina Press, 1981), 160.

58. Lind, *Land*, 103.
59. The upper bound, twice as rich, is in Lee Soltow, *Men and Wealth in the United States, 1850–1870* (New Haven, CT: Yale University Press, 1975), 65. For a review of the controversy, see William Cawthorn, "Was the South Poor before the War?" Abbeville Institute, May 26, 2017, abbevilleinstitute.org/was-the-south-poor-before-the-war.
60. Richard Follett et al., *Plantation Kingdom: The American South and Its Global Commodities* (Baltimore, MD: Johns Hopkins University Press, 2016), 67.
61. Irwin, *Clashing*, 203.
62. "1860 Census: Population of the United States," US Census Bureau, 1864, census .gov/library/publications/1864/dec/1860a.html; Benjamin T. Arrington, "Industry and Economy during the Civil War," National Park Service, nps.gov/articles/indus try-and-economy-during-the-civil-war.htm.
63. Irwin, *Clashing*, 211, 213.
64. Louis Ferleger and William Lazonick, "The Managerial Revolution and the Developmental State: The Case of US Agriculture," *Business and Economic History* 22, no. 2 (Winter 1993): 73.

15. US Industrial Policy 1866–1939: The High Point of Protectionism

1. Paul Bairoch, *Economics and World History Myths and Paradoxes* (Chicago, IL: University of Chicago Press, 1993), 35.
2. Alfred E. Eckes Jr., *Opening America's Market: US Foreign Trade Since 1776* (Chapel Hill: University of North Carolina Press, 1995), 46.
3. Douglas A. Irwin, *Clashing over Commerce: A History of US Trade Policy* (Chicago, IL: University of Chicago Press, 2017), 249.
4. Irwin, *Clashing*, 240.
5. Angus Maddison, "Growth and Fluctuation in the World Economy 1870–1960," *Banca Nazionale del Lavoro Quarterly Review* 15, no. 61 (1962): 138.
6. Irwin, *Clashing*, 285.
7. "For centuries England has relied on protection, has carried it to extremes and has obtained satisfactory results from it. There is no doubt that it is to this system that it owes its present strength. After two centuries, England has found it convenient to adopt free trade because it thinks that protection can no longer offer it anything. Very well then, Gentlemen, my knowledge of our country leads me to believe that within 200 years, when America has gotten out of protection all that it can offer, it too will adopt free trade." Ulysses S. Grant, cited in A. G. Frank, *Capitalism and Underdevelopment in Latin America* (New York: Monthly Review Press, 1967), 164.
8. Irwin, *Clashing*, 241.
9. Irwin, *Clashing*, 242.
10. Robert D. Leiter, "Organized Labor and the Tariff," *Southern Economic Journal* 28, no. 1 (July 1961): 56.
11. Irwin, *Clashing*, 314.
12. Irwin, *Clashing*, 252.
13. Irwin, *Clashing*, 337. Special interests could, of course, want an even higher tariff than what legal lobbying could obtain, but as noted earlier, pushing for excessively high tariffs mobilized significant opposition, so there were limits to what bribery could buy.
14. Andrew Reamer, "Before the US Tariff Commission: Congressional Efforts to Obtain Statistics and Analysis for Tariff-Setting 1789–1916," in *A Centennial*

History of the USITC, ed. Paul R. Bardos (Washington, DC: United States International Trade Commission, 2017), 38.

15. Reamer, "Before," 39.
16. Reamer, "Before," 40.
17. Reamer, "Before," 55.
18. For a few decades later, President Coolidge, see C. Donald Johnson, *The Wealth of a Nation: A History of Trade Politics in America* (New York: Oxford University Press, 2018), 183. Also see Irwin, *Clashing*, 341, and Joseph F. Kenkel, *Progressives and Protection: The Search for a Tariff Policy, 1866–1936* (Lanham, MD: University Press of America, 1983), 28–9. As late as 1932, FDR announced his support for what he called a "competitive" tariff, defined as equalizing foreign and domestic production costs, though this may have been just campaign rhetoric, as he never attempted to implement anything like this in office. Source: *The Public Papers and Addresses of Franklin D. Roosevelt*, Vol. 1 (New York: Random House, 1938), 766.
19. Henry Bessemer, *Sir Henry Bessemer, F.R.S.: An Autobiography* (London: The Institute of Metals, 1989), 135.
20. David A. Lake, *Power, Protection and Free Trade: International Sources of US Commercial Strategy, 1887–1939* (Ithaca, NY: Cornell University Press, 1988), 91–118. Tariffs in Britain's colonies did vary, with those with a greater degree of self-government, such as Canada and Australia, being more protectionist. But essentially all Britain's colonies had tariff schedules that did not discriminate in favor of Britain versus other nations, including the US Imperial Preference that came later.
21. W. Elliot Brownlee, "The Creation of the US Tariff Commission," in *A Centennial History of the USITC*, ed. Paul R. Bardos (Washington, DC: United States International Trade Commission, 2017), 78.
22. Irwin, *Clashing*, 284.
23. Irwin, *Clashing*, 278. Free trade versus protectionism was not, of course, the only difference between the American and British economies at the time, and hence not the only explanation for the difference in their growth rates.
24. Irwin, *Clashing*, 278.
25. Douglas A. Irwin, "Explaining America's Surge in Manufactured Exports, 1880–1913," *Review of Economics and Statistics* 85, no. 2 (May 2003): 364.
26. Brian Reinbold and Yi Wen, "How Industrialization Shaped America's Trade Balance," Federal Reserve Bank of St. Louis, February 6, 2020, figure 1.
27. Nathan Rosenberg, *Technology and American Economic Growth* (New York: Harper & Row, 1972), 73.
28. C. Knick Harley, "The Antebellum American Tariff: Food Exports and Manufacturing," *Explorations in Economic History* 29, no. 4 (October 1992): 375–400.
29. Irwin, *Clashing*, 199.
30. Keith Head, "Infant Industry Protection in the Steel Rail Industry," *Journal of International Economics* 37, no. 3–4 (November 1994): 143.
31. Head, "Infant Industry," 156.
32. Head, "Infant Industry," 163.
33. Kanda Naknoi, "Tariffs and the Expansion of the American Pig Iron Industry, 1870–1940," paper no. 1214, Institute for Research in the Behavioral, Economic, and Management Sciences (September 2008). Also see Lawrence A. Peskin and Edmund F. Wehrle, *America and the World: Culture, Commerce, Conflict* (Baltimore, MD: Johns Hopkins University Press, 2012), 106.

34. President William McKinley, speech in Buffalo, New York, September 5, 1901: UVA Miller Center, Presidential Speeches, millercenter.org/the-presidency/presidential-speeches/september-5–1901-speech-buffalo-new-york.

35. Irwin, *Clashing*, 317.

36. Irwin, *Clashing*, 317.

37. Irwin, *Clashing*, 333.

38. Irwin, *Clashing*, 345.

39. Irwin, *Clashing*, 345.

40. Irwin, *Clashing*, 338.

41. Brownlee, "Creation," 77.

42. Ronald Rogowski, *Commerce and Coalitions: How Trade Affects Domestic Political Alignments* (Princeton, NJ: Princeton University Press, 1989), 48.

43. This section adapted with permission from Ian Fletcher, *Free Trade Doesn't Work: What Should Replace It and Why* (Washington, DC: US Business and Industry Council, 2010).

44. William J. Bernstein, *A Splendid Exchange: How Trade Shaped the World* (New York: Atlantic Monthly Press, 2008), 354.

45. Comparison between trade under the Fordney–McCumber tariff in 1930 and to trade under the Smoot–Hawley tariff in 1931 from Eckes, *Opening*, 107. The effects of Smoot-Hawley were also blunted by currency depreciation in America's major trade counterparties.

46. Eckes, *Opening*, 106.

47. Alfred Eckes Jr., quoted in Sherrod Brown, *Myths of Free Trade: Why America's Trade Policies Have Failed* (New York: New Press, 2004), 180.

48. Gertrud M. Fremling, "Did the United States Transmit the Great Depression to the Rest of the World?" *American Economic Review*, 75, no. 5 (December 1985): 1181–5.

49. Douglas A. Irwin, "From Smoot–Hawley to Reciprocal Trade Agreements: Changing the Course of US Trade Policy in the 1930s," in *The Defining Moment: The Great Depression and the American Economy in the Twentieth Century*, ed. Michael D. Bordo, Claudia Goldin, and Eugene N. White (Chicago, IL: National Bureau of Economic Research with the University of Chicago Press, 1998), 341.

50. Unconditional MFN had first been adopted by the US in 1923, but in the protectionist context of its adoption, had minimal effects. Its opposite is *conditional* MFN, in which trade concessions offered to one nation are only extended to other nations if they make concessions of value equivalent to those of the first foreign nation.

51. C. Donald Johnson, *The Wealth of a Nation: A History of Trade Politics in America* (New York: Oxford University Press, 2018), 260.

52. Karen E. Schnietz, "The Institutional Foundation of US Trade Policy: Revisiting Explanations for the 1934 Reciprocal Trade Agreement Act," *Journal of Policy History* 12, no. 4 (October 2000): 427, 442.

53. Eckes, *Opening*, 144–6.

54. Irwin, *Clashing*, 432.

55. Irwin, *Clashing*, 441.

56. Eckes, *Opening*, 145, 147.

57. "The first Industrial Revolution – and most technological developments preceding it – had little or no scientific base. It created a chemical industry with no chemistry, an iron industry without metallurgy, power machinery without thermodynamics.

Engineering, medical technology, and agriculture until 1850 were pragmatic bodies of applied knowledge in which things were known to work, but rarely was it understood why they worked." Joel Mokyr, "The Second Industrial Revolution, 1870–1914," Northwestern University, August 1998.

58. Valerie A. Ramey, "Secular Stagnation of Technological Lull," University of California, San Diego and NBER, May 2020, 10–11.

59. Robert J. Gordon, *The Rise and Fall of American Growth* (Princeton, NJ: Princeton University Press, 2016), 561.

60. "Aerospace Industry," encyclopedia entry, Encyclopedia Britannica, britannica .com/technology/aerospace-industry.

61. E. H. Dix Jr., "Alclad, A New Corrosion Resistant Aluminum Product," technical note no. 259, National Advisory Committee for Aeronautics, August 1927.

62. David Allan Tretler, "Opportunity Missed: Congressional Reorganization of the Army Air Service, 1917–1920" (master's thesis, Rice University, 1978), 70.

63. Airmail was previously carried by the Post Office itself, first with military pilots then with the Post Office's own.

64. McMillan Houston Johnson V, "Taking Off: The Politics and Culture of American Aviation, 1920–1939" (PhD diss., University of Tennessee, Knoxville, 2011), 12, 17, 42, 47.

65. Julie Summers Walker, "US Air Mail Centennial: Four Days to Retrace History," Aircraft Owners and Pilots Association, September 1, 2020.

66. In 1940, the CAA split into the Civil Aeronautics Administration and the CAB: "A Brief History of the FAA," Federal Aviation Administration, faa.gov/about/history/ brief_history.

67. Vernon Ruttan, *Is War Necessary for Economic Growth?* (New York: Oxford University Press, 2006), 33.

68. Subject to certain constraints, such as storage capacity, which do not solve the underlying problem.

69. Owen L. Anderson, "The Evolution of Oil and Gas Conservation Law and the Rise of Unconventional Hydrocarbon Production," *Arkansas Law Review* 68, no. 2 (2015), 241.

70. Paul R. Lawrence and Davis Dyer, *Renewing American Industry: Organizing for Efficiency and Innovation* (New York: Free Press, 1983), 212–15. The Department of Justice did not actually sue AT&T, but the threat to do so was understood by all.

71. Elizabeth Mary Bruton, "Beyond Marconi: The Roles of the Admiralty, the Post Office, and the Institution of Electrical Engineers in the Invention and Development of Wireless Communication Up to 1908" (PhD diss., University of Leeds, 2012), 82.

72. Gleason L. Archer, *History of Radio to 1926* (New York: American Historical Society, 1938), 168.

73. Regrettably, Congress after the war failed to honor some obligations arising from the creation of RCA, and the firm's subsequent legal history, as in the case of patents for color TV, was not unproblematic.

16. US Industrial Policy 1940–1973: The Golden Age of the US Economy

1. Tariff: Adam Tooze, *The Wages of Destruction: The Making and Breaking of the Nazi Economy* (London: Penguin, 2008), 30.

2. Office of Management and Budget, *Historical Tables: Budget of the US Government, Fiscal Year 2010* (Washington, DC: Government Printing Office, 2009), 47, govinfo.gov/content/pkg/BUDGET-2010-TAB/pdf/BUDGET-2010-TAB.pdf.

3. Mark Harrison, ed., *The Economics of World War II: Six Great Powers in International Comparison* (Cambridge: Cambridge University Press, 1998), 10.

4. For any nation-state of meaningful size for which credible figures are available. Authors' calculation from US Bureau of Economic Analysis, "National Income and Product Accounts," tables 1.1.5 and 1.16, December 2021, apps.bea.gov/iTable/?reqid=19&step=2&isuri=1&1921=survey; and "Maddison Historical Statistics," University of Groningen Growth and Development Centre, rug.nl/ggdc/historical development/maddison/?lang=en.

5. Thomas Zimmerman, "Strategic Decisions to Key World War II Victory," US Army War College, October 1, 2008.

6. Spencer C. Tucker, ed., *A Global Chronology of Conflict: From the Ancient World to the Modern Middle East, Volume 5* (Santa Barbara, CA: ABC–CLIO, 2010), 1885.

7. Michael Lind, *Land of Promise: An Economic History of the United States* (New York: HarperCollins, 2012), 317.

8. Alain L. Gropman, "Mobilizing US Industry in WWII: Myth and Reality," McNair Paper 50, Institute for National Strategic Studies, August 1996, 1–2.

9. Lind, *Land*, 311.

10. J. W. Mason and Andrew Bossie, "Public Spending as an Engine of Growth and Equality: Lessons from World War II," Roosevelt Institute, September 2020, 9.

11. Doris Goodwin, "The Way We Won: America's Economic Breakthrough during World War II," *The American Prospect*, December 19, 2001.

12. Harold G. Vatter, *The US Economy in World War II* (New York: Columbia University Press, 1985), 114.

13. David Mindell, "The Science and Technology of World War II," National World War II Museum, 2009.

14. Charles C. Price, "Synthetic Rubber," *Science Teacher* 10, no. 1 (February 1943): 13.

15. "Industrial Research Laboratories of the United States, Including Consulting Research Laboratories," *Bulletin of the National Research Council* no. 113 (July 1946): iii.

16. Goodwin, "The Way We Won."

17. "US Business Cycle Expansions and Contractions," National Bureau of Economic Research, updated March 14, 2023, nber.org/research/data/us-business-cycle-expansions-and-contractions.

18. John Kenneth Galbraith, *The New Industrial State: Fourth Edition* (Boston, MA: Houghton Mifflin, 1985), 78.

19. Lind, *Land*, 349.

20. Alfred E. Eckes Jr., *Opening America's Market: Foreign Trade since 1776* (Chapel Hill: University of North Carolina Press, 1995), 179.

21. Dan Burrows, "What Is a Recession? 10 Facts You Need to Know," Kiplinger, November 22, 2022.

22. Chad Stone et al., "A Guide to Statistics on Historical Trends in Income Inequality," Center for Budget and Policy Priorities, January 13, 2020, 8.

23. See Galbraith's *The New Industrial State* and Adolf A. Berle's *The American Economic Republic* (New York: Harcourt, Brace & World, 1963).

24. Judith Stein, *Pivotal Decade: How the United States Traded Factories for Finance in the Seventies* (New Haven, CT: Yale University Press, 2011), 13.

25. Authors' calculation from Eckes, *Opening*, 157 and "Report to the President and the Congress," Commission on Foreign Economic Policy, January 23, 1954, 3, 6.

26. Melvyn P. Leffler, *A Preponderance of Power: National Security, the Truman Administration, and the Cold War* (Stanford, CA: Stanford University Press, 1992), 317.
27. Stein, *Pivotal*, 7.
28. Eckes, *Opening*, 154.
29. Lind, *Land*, 369–70.
30. "A Report to the National Security Council by the Executive Secretary on United States Objectives and Programs for National Security," National Security Council Paper NSC-68, April 14, 1950, 60.
31. Jeffrey A. Larsen and Robert M. Shelala II, *Rearming at the Dawn of the Cold War: Louis Johnson, George Marshall, and Robert Lovett, 1949–1952* (Washington, DC: National Defense University Press, 2012), 16.
32. For the opposing case that defense-oriented industrial policy *harmed* the civilian industrial base, see a number of works by Seymour Melman, such as *American Capitalism in Decline* (New York: Simon and Schuster, 1975).
33. Greatly liberalized European trade from 1870 to 1914 had failed to prevent World War I or authoritarian governments such as Germany's. Benito Mussolini took power in Italy in 1922, years before the Depression hit. Liberalization of trade after the end of the Cold War similarly failed to induce political liberalization in China or defuse geopolitical antagonisms with that nation. Many nations around the world experienced the shocks of the Depression, but only a few turned fascist. In any case, trade between nations and *free* trade are different things.
34. William A. Lovett, Alfred E. Eckes Jr., and Richard L. Brinkman, *Trade Policy: History, Theory, and the WTO* (Armonk, NY: M.E. Sharpe, 2004), 62.
35. Douglas A. Irwin, *Clashing over Commerce: A History of US Trade Policy* (Chicago, IL: University of Chicago Press, 2017), 590; "Shares of Gross Domestic Product: Imports of Goods and Services (Annual)," Federal Reserve Bank of St. Louis, fred.stlouisfed.org/series/B021RE1Q156NBEA.
36. Irwin, *Clashing*, 590–1.
37. William Diebold Jr., "The End of the I.T.O.," *Essays in International Finance* no. 16 (October 1952): 15–23.
38. Thomas W. Zeiler, "GATT Fifty Years Ago: Trade Policy and Imperial Tariff Preferences," *Business and Economic History* 26, no. 2 (Winter 1997): 714.
39. With an exception for "frontier" countries, who could be extended preferential rates to facilitate customs unions.
40. Stein, *Pivotal*, 7.
41. Douglas A. Irwin, "The GATT's Contribution to Economic Recovery in Post-War Western Europe," International Finance Discussion Papers, no. 442, Board of Governors of the Federal Reserve System, March 1993, 10.
42. Trade surplus: E. A. Brett, *The World Economy since the War* (Santa Barbara, CA: Praeger, 1985), 106. GDP: "Gross Domestic Product: Seasonally Adjusted, Annual Average," Federal Reserve Bank of St. Louis, fred.stlouisfed.org/series/GDP.
43. Eckes, *Opening*, 188.
44. William J. Scott, "Would Europe's Value Added Tax Work for the United States?" *Florida Journal of International Law* 2, no.1 (January 1986): 15.
45. David Flath, "A Perspective on Japanese Trade Policy and Japan-US Trade Friction," North Carolina State University Department of Economics, October 1998, 2.
46. Eckes, *Opening*, 173.
47. Eckes, *Opening*, 173.

48. Étienne Deschamps, "The Customs Union and the GATT," Centre Virtuel de la Connaissance sur l'Europe, last updated July 8, 2016, cvce.eu/obj/the_customs_union_and_the_gatt-en-b0e31fb4-bbfa-4edf-b656-8b13c4a1b6c5.html.

49. Stein, *Pivotal*, 57.

50. Stein, *Pivotal*, 11.

51. Irwin, *Clashing*, 620.

52. Eckes, *Opening*, 140.

53. Irwin, *Clashing*, 627.

54. Irwin, *Clashing*, 625.

55. Irwin, *Clashing*, 625.

56. Edward Alden, *Failure to Adjust: How Americans Got Left Behind in the Global Economy* (Washington, DC: Rowman & Littlefield, 2016), 80.

57. Eckes, *Opening*, 189.

58. Irwin, *Clashing*, 523.

59. Irwin, *Clashing*, 627.

60. Donald Johnson, *The Wealth of a Nation: A History of Trade Politics in America* (Oxford: Oxford University Press, 2021), 458.

61. Tom Wicker, "President Orders Tariff Increases for Two Imports," *New York Times*, March 20, 1962, 1.

62. Irwin, *Clashing*, 627.

63. WTO, "Long-Term Arrangement Regarding International Trade in Cotton Textiles," October 1, 1962, wto.org/gatt_docs/English/SULPDF/90100029.pdf.

64. Eckes, *Opening*, 179.

65. John F. Kennedy, "Address in the Assembly Hall at the Paulskirche in Frankfurt," June 25, 1963.

66. Committee on Trade and Development, "Past Discussions on the Concept of Non-reciprocity," General Agreement on Tariffs and Trade (GATT), October 14, 1968, 5–7.

67. *Economic Report of the President 1968* (Washington, DC: United States Government Printing Office, 1968), 187.

68. *Economic Report of the President 1968*, 187.

69. Eckes, *Opening*, 200; Stein, *Pivotal*, 10.

70. Eckes, *Opening*, 195–6; Stein, *Pivotal*, 10.

71. Eckes, *Opening*, 197.

72. Eckes, *Opening*, 197; Irwin, *Clashing*, 624; "Analysis of the Rate-Reducing Authority in the Trade Reform Act of 1973," Staff Papers Provided by the Tariff Commission for the Committee on Finance, United States Senate, July 1974, 5.

73. Eckes, *Opening*, 202–3.

74. T. Norman van Cott and Larry J. Wipf, "Tariff Reduction via Inflation: Specific Tariffs, 1972–79," *Weltwirtschaftliches Archiv* 119 (1983): 724–33.

75. Eckes, *Opening*, 180.

76. Irwin, *Clashing*, 534. Cost from Marc Levinson, *The Box: How the Shipping Container Made the World Smaller and the World Economy Bigger* (Princeton, NJ: Princeton University Press, 2008), 9.

77. Irwin, *Clashing*, 641.

78. "U.S. International Trade in Goods and Services," US Census Bureau, December 6, 2023, bea.gov/sites/default/files/2023-11/trad-time-series-0923.xlsx.

79. Thomas W. Zeiler, *American Trade and Power in the 1960s* (New York: Columbia University Press, 1992), 240.

80. Johnson's biggest protectionist action was 1964's tariff on light trucks, which exists to this day and is called the "chicken tax" because it was imposed in

retaliation for European barriers to American chicken. His free-trade Southern roots: Steve Dryden, *Trade Warriors: USTR and the American Crusade for Free Trade* (Oxford: Oxford University Press, 1995), 79.

81. US Bureau of Labor Statistics, "Labor in the Textile and Apparel Industries," Bulletin No. 1635, US Department of Labor, August 1969.
82. Irwin, *Clashing*, 518.
83. Irwin, *Clashing*, 531.
84. Office of the Historian, "Memorandum from President's Assistant for Congressional Relations (Timmons) and the President's Special Counsel (Dent) to Nixon," US Department of State Archive, June 4, 1970.
85. "Textiles and Politics," Memo of Conversation, Department of State, Bureau of East Asian and Pacific Affairs, Office of Japanese Affairs, October 23, 1969; Stein, *Pivotal*, 33–6.
86. Stein, *Pivotal*, 34–5.
87. Irwin, *Clashing*, 533.
88. Allen J. Matusow, *Nixon's Economy: Booms, Busts, Dollars, and Votes* (Lawrence: University Press of Kansas, 1998), 131–7.
89. US Congress, House, Subcommittee on Science, Research, and Development, "Statement of Hon. Maurice H. Stans, Secretary of Commerce of the United States," 92nd Cong., 1st sess., July 27, 1971.
90. Matusow, *Nixon's Economy*, 141, 145.
91. Matusow, *Nixon's Economy*, 137–8; Dryden, *Trade Warriors*, 147; Eckes, *Opening*, 211; Stein, *Pivotal*, 467.
92. Eckes, *Opening*, 211; Stein, *Pivotal*, 33.
93. Irwin, *Clashing*, 647.
94. Alden, *Failure*, 89.
95. Johnson, *Wealth*, 469.
96. Nitsan Chorev, *Remaking US Trade Policy: From Protection to Globalization* (Ithaca, NY: Cornell University Press, 2007), 89.
97. Eckes, *Opening*, 272.
98. Stein, *Pivotal*, 38.
99. Stein, *Pivotal*, 38. There had previously been the Anti-Dumping Act of 1916, which made dumping a criminal offense, but it was not enforced well.
100. "Antidumping and Countervailing Duty Laws under the Tariff Act of 1930," US International Trade Commission, usitc.gov/press_room/usad.htm.
101. Eckes, *Opening*, 183.
102. Eckes, *Opening*, 183.
103. Eckes, *Opening*, 187; Clyde Prestowitz, *Trading Places: How We Are Giving Our Future to Japan & How to Reclaim It* (New York: Basic Books, 1990), 380.
104. Transistor radios: Kenneth Flamm and Peter C. Reiss, "Semiconductor Dependency and Strategic Trade Policy," *Brookings Papers on Economic Activity, Microeconomics 1993*, no. 1 (1993): 254; David Yoffie, "*Zenith* and the Color Television Fight," Harvard Business School Case No. 383–070, December 1982.
105. Eckes, *Opening*, 229.
106. Chorev, *Remaking*, 97.
107. Chorev, *Remaking*, 97.
108. Yoffie, "*Zenith*," 7; David Schwartzman, *The Japanese Television Cartel: A Study Based on* Matsushita v. Zenith (Ann Arbor: University of Michigan Press, 1993), 117; Kozo Yamamura and Jan Vandenberg, "Japan's Rapid-Growth Policy on Trial: The Television Case," in *Law and Trade Issues of the Japanese Economy*, ed.

Gary R. Saxonhouse and Kozo Yamamura (Seattle: University of Washington Press, 1986), 261; "Scandals: Kickbacks in Living Color," *Time*, June 13, 1977.

109. Yoffie, "*Zenith*," 1–17; Schwartzman, *Japanese Television*, 117–28; James E. Millstein, "Decline in an Expanding Industry: Japanese Competition in Color Television," in *American Industry in International Competition*, ed. John Zysman and Laura Tyson (Ithaca, NY: Cornell University Press, 1983), 132–3.

110. Christopher W. Derrick, "The Evolution of the Escape Clause: The United States' Quest for Effective Relief from Fairly Traded Imports," *North Carolina Journal of International Law* 13, no. 2 (Spring 1988): 353.

111. Will E. Leonard and F. David Foster, "The Substantive and Institutional Evolution of the US Tariff Commission/International Trade Commission (1917–2016)," in *A Centennial History of the United States Trade Commission*, 129–30.

112. Alden, *Failure*, 14.

113. J. F. Hornbeck, "US Trade Policy and the Caribbean: From Trade Preferences to Free Trade Agreements," Congressional Research Service, January 6, 2011, 3.

114. Irwin, *Clashing*, 648.

115. Stein, *Pivotal*, 12, footnote 48.

116. Irwin, *Clashing*, 543.

117. Christopher A. Casey, "The International Emergency Economic Powers Act (IEEPA) and Tariffs: Historical Background and Key Issues," Congressional Research Service, February 20, 2020.

118. Irwin, *Clashing*, 654.

119. Irwin, *Clashing*, 654.

120. Irwin, *Clashing*, 654.

121. Stein, *Pivotal*, 46.

122. Irwin, *Clashing*, 655.

123. Drew DeSilver, "For Most Workers, Real Wages Have Barely Budged in Decades," Pew Research Center, August 7, 2018.

124. Scott Lincicome, "The Annoying Persistence of the Income Stagnation Myth," Cato Institute, October 9, 2020.

125. Daniel M. Holland and Stewart C. Myers, "Profitability and Capital Costs for Manufacturing Corporations and All Nonfinancial Corporations," *American Economic Review* 70, no. 2 (May 1980): table 1.

126. William R. Nester, *American Industrial Policy: Free or Managed Markets?* (London: Palgrave Macmillan, 1997), 25–6.

127. Daniel Yergin, *The Prize: The Epic Quest for Oil, Money & Power* (New York: Simon & Schuster, 1991), 615.

128. See Binyamin Appelbaum, *The Economists' Hour: False Prophets, Free Markets, and the Fracture of Society* (Boston, MA: Little, Brown and Company, 2019).

129. Stein, *Pivotal*, xi.

130. Eamonn Fingleton, *Blindside: Why Japan Is Still on Track to Overtake the US by the Year 2000* (Boston, MA: Houghton Mifflin Harcourt, 1995), 16, 45–6, 50, 59–60, 77–8, 85, 123, 210, 237, 267–9, 271, 313, 319, 322; Frank Gibney, *Miracle by Design: The Real Reasons behind Japan's Economic Success* (New York: Times Books, 1982), xiii, 11, 54, 70, 84, 129, 166–70; Prestowitz, *Trading Places*, 348, 351, 370; James Fallows, *Looking at the Sun* (New York: Vintage, 1995), 144, 209–10; Ronald Dore, *Taking Japan Seriously: A Confucian Perspective on Leading Economic Issues* (London: Bloomsbury Academic, 1987), 237; Thomas McCraw, ed., *America versus Japan* (Boston, MA: Harvard Business School Press, 1986), 19.

131. Patrick Buchanan, *The Great Betrayal: How American Sovereignty and Social Justice Are Being Sacrificed to the Gods of the Global Economy* (Boston, MA: Little, Brown and Company, 1998), 98–105.

132. Barry Bluestone and Bennett Harrison, *The Deindustrialization of America* (New York: Basic Books, 1984), 42, 132.

17. US Industrial Policy 1974–2007: Doubling Down on Free Markets

1. "The Great Inflation," Federal Reserve History, Federal Reserve Bank of St. Louis, federalreservehistory.org/essays/great-inflation.

2. "The Great Inflation," Federal Reserve Bank of St. Louis; "Real Median Personal Income in the United States," Federal Reserve Bank of St. Louis, fred.stlouisfed.org/series/MEPAINUSA672N.

3. Jesse Nankin and Krista Kjellman Schmidt, "History of US Gov't Bailouts," *ProPublica*, April 15, 2009, propublica.org/article/government-bailouts.

4. "US Trade in Goods and Services: Balance of Payments (BOP) Basis," US Census Bureau, census.gov/foreign-trade/statistics/historical/gands.pdf.

5. US Congress, House, *An Act to Promote the Development of an Open, Nondiscriminatory, and Fair World Economic System, to Stimulate Fair and Free Competition between the United States and Foreign Nations, to Foster and Economic Growth of, and Full Employment in, the United States, and for Other Purposes*, HR 10710, 93rd Cong., 2d sess., introduced in House October 3, 1973.

6. Douglas A. Irwin, *Clashing over Commerce: A History of US Trade Policy* (Chicago, IL: University of Chicago Press, 2017), 550–2.

7. Keigh E. Hammond, "Major Votes on Free Trade Agreements and Trade Promotion Authority," Congressional Research Service, updated June 29, 2023, CRS-12, sgp.fas.org/crs/row/R45846.pdf.

8. "Fact Sheet: 'Special 301' on Intellectual Property," US Trade Representative, May 25, 1989.

9. US Congress, House, Omnibus Tariff and Trade Act of 1984, HR 3398, 98th Cong., introduced in House on June 23, 1983.

10. See also Otis Graham Jr., *Losing Time: The Industrial Policy Debate* (Cambridge, MA: Harvard University Press, 1992), 19–25.

11. Seymour Zucker et al., *The Reindustrialization of America* (New York: McGraw Hill, 1982), 1.

12. Clyde H. Farnsworth, "US Industry Seeking to Restore Competitive Vitality to Products," *New York Times*, August 18, 1980; Agis Salpukas, "Depressed Industrial Heartland Stressing Urgent Need for Help," *New York Times*, August 19, 1980; Peter J. Schuyten, "Amid Stagnation, High Technology Lights a Path," *New York Times*, August 20, 1980; Henry Scott Stokes, "Can Japan's Aid to Its Industry Guide US?" *New York Times*, August 21, 1980; Edward Cowan, "Carter's Economic Renewal Plan," *New York Times*, August 22, 1980.

13. Graham, *Losing Time*, 48.

14. Graham, *Losing Time*, 51.

15. Lee Lescaze, "President Introduces Economic Revival Plan," *Washington Post*, August 29, 1980.

16. T. R. Reid, "Kennedy: 'Reindustrialize' the US," *Washington Post*, May 21, 1980; Lescaze, "President."

17. Graham, *Losing Time*, 39, 51–2.

18. Graham, *Losing Time*, 82.

19. US Congress, House, Industrial Competitiveness Act, HR 4360, 98th Cong., introduced in House on November 10, 1983.
20. Alan Tonelson, "Beating Back Predatory Trade," *Foreign Affairs*, July 1, 1994.
21. "The Great Inflation," Federal Reserve Bank of St. Louis.
22. Kimberly Amadeo, "Fed Funds Rate History: Its Highs, Lows, and Charts," *The Balance*, December 14, 2022.
23. "US Trade in Goods and Services: Balance of Payments (BoP) Basis," US Census Bureau.
24. "US Dollar Index: 43 Year Historical Chart," Macrotrends, macrotrends.net/1329/us-dollar-index-historical-chart.
25. Tom Mangan, "Ex-Caterpillar CEO Lee Morgan Dead at 89," Cat Stock Blog, January 22, 2009, catstockblog.com/tag/obituaries; Peter F. Kilborn, "Reagan's New Dollar Strategy," *New York Times*, March 3, 1985.
26. Dick K. Nanto and Thomas Lum, "US International Trade: Data and Forecasts," Congressional Research Service, May 16, 2005, CRS-9.
27. Kevin P. Phillips, "US Industrial Policy: Inevitable and Ineffective," *Harvard Business Review*, July–August 1992, 84.
28. Juan Williams and Michael Schrage, "Reagan Names Commission on Industrial Competition," *Washington Post*, August 5, 1983.
29. James Lardner, "Selling America on the Reich Stuff," *Washington Post*, July 6, 1983; Graham, *Losing Time*, 69, 164.
30. Graham, *Losing Time*, 161.
31. Graham, *Losing Time*, 165.
32. Graham, *Losing Time*, 160–5.
33. Graham, *Losing Time*, 160–1.
34. "US GDP 1960–2023," Macrotrends, macrotrends.net/countries/USA/united-states/gdp-gross-domestic-product.
35. Kevin L. Kearns, "Meanwhile, the Meltdown in Motor City," *Washington Post*, June 16, 1991.
36. President's Commission on Industrial Competitiveness, *Volume I: Global Competition, The New Reality*, 1985; US Congress, Senate, Committee on Finance, *Review of Findings of the President's Commission on Industrial Competitiveness*, 99th Cong., 1st sess., March 29, 1985.
37. Robert D. Hershey, "Reagan Selects Trade 'Strike Force,'" *New York Times*, October 3, 1985; Peter T. Kilborn, "Reagan Call: Productivity; Economic Woes Laid to Society's Failings," *New York Times*, January 29, 1987.
38. US Congress, House, Trade, Employment, and Productivity Act of 1987, HR 1155, 100th Cong., introduced in House August 23, 1988.
39. "US Trade in Goods and Services: Balance of Payments (BOP) Basis," US Census Bureau.
40. Gephardt Trade Amendment Voted: Measure Requiring Sanctions Squeaks by House 218 to 214," *Los Angeles Times*, April 29, 1987.
41. Stuart Auerbach, "Senators Strike Gephardt Amendment," *Washington Post*, March 15, 1988; Ronald Reagan, "Message to the House of Representatives Returning without Approval the Omnibus Trade and Competitiveness Act of 1988," Ronald Reagan Presidential Library & Museum, May 24, 1988.
42. "The Tokyo Round Codes," World Trade Organization, wto.org/english/thewto_e/minist_e/min98_e/slide_e/tokyo.htm.
43. Debra Steger, "Strengthening the WTO Rulemaking Function," Center for International Governance Innovation, May 11, 2020, cigionline.org/articles/strengthening-wto-rulemaking function.

44. "Revised Agreement on Government Procurement," World Trade Organization, n.d., wto.org/english/tratop_e/gproc_e/gp_revised_gpa_e.htm.

45. "One Signature per Country Covering 23,000 Pages," World Trade Organization, wto.org/english/thewto_e/minist_e/min98_e/slide_e/slide016.htm.

46. Renato Ruggiero, "The High Stakes of World Trade," *Wall Street Journal*, February 28, 1997.

47. "The Seattle 'Ministerial,'" World Trade Organization, wto.org/english/thewto_e/minist_e/min99_e/english/about_e/03bgd_e.htm.

48. Gene Johnson, "WTO Protests in Seattle 20 Years Ago Helped Change Progressive Politics," *Los Angeles Times*, November 29, 2019.

49. The Editorial Board, "Global Trade after the Failure of the Doha Round," *New York Times*, January 1, 2016.

50. Maureen Dowd, "2 US Officials Went to Beijing Secretly in July," *New York Times*, December 19, 1989.

51. Svetlana Savranskaya and Thomas Blanton, "The Washington/Camp David Summit 1990: From the Secret Soviet, American and German Files," National Security Archive Electronic Briefing Book No. 320, posted June 13, 2010, nsarchive2.gwu.edu/NSAEBB/NSAEBB320/index.htm.

52. David E. Sanger, "A Trade Mission Ends in Tensions As the 'Big Eight' of Autos Meet," *New York Times*, January 10, 1992.

53. Tom Wicker, "The High-Tech Future," *New York Times*, May 24, 1990.

54. Graham, *Losing Time*, 231; George C. Lodge, *Perestroika for America: Restructuring US Business–Government Relations for Competitiveness in the World Economy* (Boston, MA: Harvard Business School Press, 1990), 70.

55. John Markoff, "Pentagon's Technology Chief Is Out," *New York Times*, April 21, 1990.

56. Phillips, "US Industrial Policy."

57. Ronald Brownstein, "Clinton Revives Debate over Industrial Policy, Economy: He Says Government Should Take a More Active Role in Supporting Business," *Los Angeles Times*, May 20, 1992.

58. Nicholas D. Kristof, "China Worried by Clinton's Linking of Trade to Human Rights," *New York Times*, October 9, 1992.

59. Nelson Lichtenstein, "A Fabulous Failure: Clinton's 1990s and the Origin of Our Times," *American Prospect*, January 29, 2018.

60. Lichtenstein, "Fabulous Failure."

61. "Largest Surplus in History on Track," The Clinton/Gore Administration Government Archive, September 27, 2000.

62. "US Trade in Goods and Services: Balance of Payments (BOP) Basis," US Census Bureau.

63. Lichtenstein, "Fabulous Failure."

64. Michael Wessel, quoted in John R. MacArthur, The Selling of Free Trade: NAFTA, Washington, and the Subversion of American Democracy (New York: Hill and Wang, 2000), 274.

65. "Final House Vote on NAFTA," Public Citizen, citizen.org/article/final-house-vote-on-nafta; US Senate, "Roll Call Vote on Passage of the Bill (H.R. 3450)," 103 Cong., 1st sess., November 20, 1993.

66. "NAFTA's Legacy for Mexico: Economic Displacement, Lower Wage for Most, Increased Migration," Public Citizen, March 2018, citizen.org/wp-content/uploads/migration/nafta_factsheet_mexico_legacy_march_2018_final.pdf.

67. John Sweeney, "Clinton's Last Chance on Fast-Track Trade," The Heritage Foundation, August 17, 1998.

68. "US Trade in Goods and Services: Balance of Payments (BOP) Basis," US Census Bureau.

69. Matthew Vita, "Senate Approves Normalized Trade with China, 83–15," *Washington Post*, September 20, 2000.

70. Bob Davis and Jon Hilsenrath, "How the China Shock, Deep and Swift, Spurred the Rise of Trump," *Wall Street Journal*, August 11, 2016.

71. US Congress, House, Trade Act of 2002, HR 3009, 107th Cong., introduced in House October 3, 2001.

72. Clerk, "Roll Call 370, Bill Number: H.R. 3009," US House of Representatives, July 27, 2002.

73. Daniel W. Drezner, "The Path to Free Trade," *Foreign Policy*, December 12, 2002, available at foreignpolicy.com/2002/12/12/the-path-to-free-trade.

74. "US Trade in Goods and Services: Balance of Payments (BOP) Basis," US Census Bureau.

75. Jeff Ferry, "Steel and Aluminum Tariffs Produce Minimal Impact on Jobs, GDP," Coalition for a Prosperous America, March 20, 2018.

18. US Industrial Policy 2008–Present: The End of the Old Order

1. Doug Palmer, "Clinton, Obama Threat to End NAFTA Alarms Business," Reuters, February 27, 2008.

2. Jennifer Parker et al., "Obama Campaign Denies Duplicity on Trade," ABC News, March 3, 2008.

3. "Trade in Goods with China," US Census Bureau, census.gov/foreign-trade/balance/c5700.html#2008.

4. Fan Gang et al., "Labour Market Aspects of State Enterprise Reform in China," OECD Development Centre, October 1998.

5. "2008 Report to Congress on China's WTO Compliance," US Trade Representative, December 2008.

6. Ministry of Foreign Affairs and Trade "Trans-Pacific Strategic Economic Partnership," Government of New Zealand, mfat.govt.nz/en/trade/free-trade-agreements/free-trade-agreements-in-force/trans-pacific-strategic-economic-partnership-p4.

7. James McBride et al., "What's Next for the Trans-Pacific Partnership (TPP)?" Council on Foreign Relations, September 20, 2021.

8. Ian F. Fergusson and Brock R. Williams, "The Trans-Pacific Partnership (TPP): Key Provisions and Issues for Congress," Congressional Research Service, June 14, 2016.

9. "Summary of the Trans-Pacific Partnership Agreement," Office of the US Trade Representative, October 4, 2015.

10. Alyson Cuervo, "The Trans-Pacific Partnership: Opportunities for International Trade and Internal Growth," National Center for Policy Analysis, December 4, 2014.

11. Jane Kelsey and Lori Wallach, "'Investor–State' Disputes in Trade Pacts Threaten Fundamental Principles of National Judicial Systems," Public Citizen, April 2012.

12. "USITC Releases Report Concerning the Likely Impact of the Trans-Pacific Partnership," US International Trade Commission, May 18, 2016.

13. Lee Williams, "What Is TTIP? And Six Reasons Why the Answer Should Scare You," *Independent*, October 6, 2015.

14. Office of the Press Secretary, "Remarks by the President on the Economy," The White House of President Barack Obama, June 1, 2016.

15. Robert E. Scott and Zane Mokhiber, "Growing China Trade Deficit Cost 3.7 Million American Jobs between 2001 and 2018," January 30, 2020, epi.org/publication/growing-china-trade-deficits-costs-us-jobs.

16. Office of the Press Secretary, "Remarks by the President in State of the Union Address," The White House of President Barack Obama, January 27, 2010.

17. Henry J. Pulizzi, "Obama Details Effort to Double Exports over Five Years," *Wall Street Journal*, March 11, 2010.

18. "Fact Sheet: National Export Initiative," US Department of Commerce, May 24, 2013.

19. Office of the Press Secretary, "Executive Order 13534: National Export Initiative," The White House, March 11, 2020.

20. "US Trade in Goods and Services: Balance of Payments (BOP) Basis," US Census Bureau, 1960–2022, census.gov/foreign-trade/statistics/historical/gands.pdf.

21. Katelynn Harris, "Forty Years of Falling Manufacturing Employment," US Bureau of Labor Statistics, November 2020.

22. Edmund L. Andrews, "US Adds Tariffs on Chinese Tires," *New York Times*, September 11, 2009; Susan Cornwell, "Chinese Imports Harming the US Tire Market," Reuters, June 18, 2009.

23. Sunghoon Chung et al., "Did China Tire Safeguard Save US Workers?" Munich Personal RePEc Archive, June 2014, 17–21.

24. Mark J. Perry, "2009 Tire Tariffs Cost US Consumers $926K per Job Saved and Led to the Loss of 3 Retail Jobs per Factory Job Saved," American Enterprise Institute, January 25, 2017.

25. "AD/CVD Orders in Place," spreadsheet, US International Trade Commission, usitc.gov/trade_remedy/documents/historical_orders_data.xls, tab "orders."

26. Tom Miles, "China Partially Wins WTO Case over Obama-era US Tariffs," Reuters, March 21, 2018.

27. "US Trade in Goods and Services, 1960–Present," US Bureau of Economic Analysis, bea.gov/data/intl-trade-investment/international-trade-goods-and-services; "Trade in Goods with Advanced Technology Products, 1989–2023," US Census Bureau, census.gov/foreign-trade/balance/c0007.html#2009.

28. Edward Alden, *Failure to Adjust: How Americans Got Left Behind in the Global Economy* (Lanham, MD: Rowman & Littlefield, 2016), 30.

29. "Exhibit 20a. US Trade in Goods by Selected Countries and Areas – BOP Basis," in "US International Trade in Goods and Services, April 2023," Release Number: CB 23–84, BEA 23–22, US Census Bureau and the US Bureau of Economic Analysis, June 7, 2023, 25; "Trade in Goods with Canada," US Census Bureau, census.gov/foreign-trade/balance/c1220.html#1993; "Trade in Goods with Mexico," US Census Bureau, census.gov/foreign-trade/balance/c2010.html#1993; "Trade in Goods with Korea, South" US Census Bureau, census.gov/foreign-trade/balance/c5800.html#2011; "Trade in Goods with China," US Census Bureau, census.gov/foreign-trade/balance/c5700.html#2022; "Table 2.2. US Trade in Services, by Type of Service and by Country or Affiliation," in "International Data, International Transactions, International Services, and International Investment Position Tables," US Bureau of Economic Analysis, July 7, 2022.

30. "US Trade in Goods and Services: Balance of Payments (BOP) Basis," US Census Bureau.

31. "Trade in Goods with Advanced Technology Products," US Census Bureau, census.gov/foreign-trade/balance/c0007.html#2021.

32. Or no change in unemployment. See Jeff Ferry and Steven Byers, "CPA Briefing Paper: Why Economic Forecasts of the Effects of Trade Action Are Consistently Wrong," Coalition for a Prosperous America, June 2019.

33. Robert E. Scott, "Trans-Pacific Partnership Agreement," Economic Policy Institute, January 13, 2016; Lance Taylor and Rudiger von Arnim, "Modelling the Impact of Trade Liberalisation," Research Report, Oxfam International, July 2006, 41.

34. Jeff Ferry and Steven Byers, Why Economic Forecasts.

35. Ferry and Byers, "Why Economic Forecasts."

36. Roberta Piermartini and Robert Teh, "Demystifying Modelling Methods for Trade Policy," Discussion Papers, World Trade Organization, 2005, 6.

37. Stephen Tokarick, "What Do We Know about Tariff Incidence?" working paper no. WP/04/182, International Monetary Fund, September 2004, 19–20.

38. Timothy J. Kehoe, "An Evaluation of the Performance of Applied General Equilibrium Models of the Impact of NAFTA," in Frontiers in Applied General Equilibrium Modeling: Essays in Honor of Herbert Scarf, ed. Timothy J. Kehoe, T. N. Srinivasan, and John Whalley (Cambridge: Cambridge University Press, 2005), 341–77.

39. "US–Korea Free Trade Agreement: Potential Economy-Wide and Selected Sectoral Effects," US International Trade Commission, September 2007.

40. For example, see Mauricio Cárdenas and Joshua Meltzer, "Korea, Colombia, Panama: Pending Trade Accords Offer Economic and Strategic Gains for the United States," Brookings Institution, July 27, 2011.

41. See Rana Foroohar, Makers and Takers: The Rise of Finance and the Fall of American Business (New York: Crown Business, 2016), 153–5, 163–6, for an excellent nonspecialist treatment of the financialization of GE. For an industry-specific example, see Bob Lutz's insider account of the US car industry, Car Guys vs. Bean Counters: The Battle for the Soul of American Business (New York: Portfolio books, 2011).

42. Oonagh McDonald, "The Repeal of the Glass–Steagall Act: Myth and Reality," CATO Institute, November 16, 2016.

43. Shadow banks issue their own liabilities (for instance, bond repurchase contracts, or repos) issued as means of payments between financial institution. Zoltan Pozsar et al., "Shadow Banking," Economic Policy Review 19, no. 2 (December 2013). This creates additional liquidity, pushing up asset prices. During the real estate and financial asset price boom of 2002–8, outstanding amounts of repo in the US markets exploded from $75 trillion to $175 trillion, then collapsed to $85 trillion within one year. See "Repo Market Functioning," CGFS Papers No. 59, Committee on the Global Financial System, April 2017, 8.

44. Tanju Yorulmazer, "Literature Review on the Stability of Funding Models," Economic Policy Review 20, no. 1 (February 2014).

45. "Greenspan Urges Congress to Exempt OTC Derivatives from US Regulation," Wall Street Journal, February 11, 2000.

46. Laura E. Kodres, "What Is Shadow Banking?" Finance & Development 50, no. 2 (June 2013).

47. Hyman Minsky, Stabilizing an Unstable Economy (New York: McGraw-Hill, 1986).

48. Minsky, Stabilizing, 77–106; "Risk Management Lessons from the Global Banking Crisis of 2008," US Securities and Exchange Commission, October 21, 2009.

49. This is described in detail in Markus Brunnermeier, "Deciphering the Liquidity and Credit Crunch 2007–2008," *Journal of Economic Perspectives* 23, no. 1 (Winter 2009): 77–100.

50. Deregulation was started under Carter and gathered pace during the Reagan administration. See Douglas Evanoff, "Financial Industry Deregulation in the 1980s," *Economic Perspectives* 9 (September/October 1985). See also Judith Stein, *Pivotal Decade: How America Traded Factories for Finance in the Seventies* (New Haven, CT: Yale University Press, 2010), 251–2. Deregulation was embraced by Bill Clinton, who presided over the 1999 Financial Services Modernization Act of 1999 that repealed the Glass–Steagall Act. While the Obama administration started in the immediate aftermath of the crisis in 2009 with promises of regulating the financial industry, this was watered down during the rest of his presidency. The Trump presidency was characterized by yet more deregulation. For example, the 2018 Economic Growth, Regulatory Relief, and Consumer Protection Act raised the primary asset threshold for application of enhanced prudential standards for banks and other financial institutions from $50 billion to $250 billion in total consolidated assets, leaving fewer entities subject to these standards. See "President Trump Signs First Major Financial Deregulation Law in a Decade," *Jones Day*, 2018.

51. See, for example, N. Craig Smith and David Rönnegard, "Shareholder Primary, Corporate Social Responsibility, and the Role of Business Schools," *Journal of Business Ethics* 134, no. 3 (March 2016): 463–78.

52. See figure 1 in Robin Greenwood and David Scharfstein, "The Growth of Finance," *Journal of Economic Perspectives* 27, no. 2 (Spring 2013): 3–28.

53. Adapted from Gerald Epstein and Juan Antonio Montecino, "Overcharged: The High Cost of High Finance," Roosevelt Institute, 2016, 6.

54. Jean Louis Arcand, Enrico Berkes and Ugo Panizza, "Too Much Finance?" *Journal of Economic Growth* 20, no. 2 (June 2015): 105–48. The authors use data on bank loans as a proxy measure for all debt (bank loans, bonds, and other debt). For most countries, this is a good proxy measure, since bank loans constitute the major share of nonfinancial sector debt in most countries. But in the US, bank loans are an unusually small share of total nonfinancial debt, so total debt numbers are reported in the text. This article is a cross-country study giving the average effect for dozens of countries, and applying it to any single country must account for that country's specifics. Because the US is a highly developed economy with long and sophisticated production chains needing intensive financing, and because New York is the financial center of the world and the dollar the global currency, one would expect it to have deeper than average financial markets. For these reasons, nonfinancial debt exceeding 100 percent of GDP need not be as harmful to the US as it would be to many other countries. Still, the current 220 percent is so far above 100 percent that justifiable concerns remain.

55. 1990 data from "Financial Accounts of the United States – Z.1," Statistical Release, Federal Reserve, September 9, 2022: Households and the nonfinancial firms that make up the productive sector held debt equal to 63 percent and 36 percent of GDP, respectively, for a total of 100 percent. For 2008 and 2022 data see "United States Private Debt to GDP," Trading Economics, tradingeconomics.com/united-states/private-debt-to-gdp.

56. "Final Report of the National Commission on the Causes of the Financial and Economic Crisis in the United States," Financial Crisis Inquiry Commission, February 25, 2011, xvii, xx, 68.

57. Total US real estate at market values, expressed as percentage of GDP, rose from a trough of 204 percent in 1996 to 297 percent in 2007, then dropped to 224 percent by 2012, before starting to climb again. The swings in land values devastated many balance sheets. See "Total Real Estate at Market Values," in "Financial Accounts of the United States – Z.1," Federal Reserve, account B104 line 6. Structures (residential and nonresidential) on current cost basis is Z.1, account B104, lines 39 and 40.

58. Data from "Financial Accounts of the United States – Z.1," Federal Reserve.

59. For example, the volume of outstanding asset-backed securities (ABS), a financial innovation product, exploded in the run-up to the 2007 crisis from $650 billion outstanding debt in 2004 to $1,200 billion in 2007. Then it collapsed back to $700 billion by early 2009 (Brunnermeier, "Deciphering the Liquidity and Credit Crunch 2007–2008," 84). Mortgage-backed securities, the most prevalent type of ABS, were instrumental in the rise and fall of the housing market, discussed in more detail below.

60. For instance, the mortgage-backed securities (MBS, a type of ABS) market allowed American banks to initiate and sell mortgages at a profit to investors like hedge funds and pension funds. As a consequence, mortgages were given out recklessly. US household mortgage debt exploded from $7 trillion in 2001 to $15 trillion in 2008. "Value of Mortgage Debt Outstanding in the United States from 2001 to 2022," Statista, May 15, 2023. This was the last phase of the long US real estate boom that began in 1990, during which US homeownership rates increased from 63 percent to 69 percent in the summer of 2006 just before the housing market turned. See "Homeownership Rate in the United States from 1990 to 2022," Statista, February 6, 2023.

61. Epstein and Montecino, "Overcharged," 13.

62. Epstein and Montecino, "Overcharged," 7, figure 1.

63. Epstein and Montecino, "Overcharged," 7, figure 2.

64. Epstein and Montecino, "Overcharged," 18.

65. Epstein and Montecino, "Overcharged," 24–5.

66. Epstein and Montecino, "Overcharged," 25.

67. This section draws on J. W. Mason, "Understanding Short-Termism: Questions and Consequences," Roosevelt Institute, November 6, 2015.

68. Tomislav Ladika and Zacharias Sautner, "Managerial Short-Termism and Investment: Evidence from Accelerated Option Vesting," *Review of Finance* 24, no. 2 (March 2020): 305–44. This studied 4,486 publicly traded US firms and found that firms cut investment when their executives' equity incentives became more short-term. Under an accounting rule that went into effect in 2005, executives were allowed to exercise options earlier and thus profit from boosting short-term performance, and based on this change, the study reported that "CEOs cut investment and reported higher short-term earnings after option acceleration," and then increased their equity sales.

69. John Asker, Joan Farre-Mensa, and Alexander Ljungqvist, "Corporate Investment and Stock Market Listing: A Puzzle?" *Review of Financial Studies* 28, no. 2 (February 2015): 342–90.

70. Paul Borochin and Jie Yang, "The Effects of Institutional Investor Objectives on Firm Valuation and Governance," *Journal of Financial Economics* 126, no. 1 (October 2017): 171–99. Note that critics of the claim that US companies are overly short-term oriented typically evaluate this claim using financial-market performance indicators, or business profits. For example, a 2018 paper "considers

the implications of sustained short-termism for corporate profits, venture capital investments and returns, private equity investments and returns, and corporate valuations." It "finds little long-term evidence that is consistent with the predictions of the short-term critics." However, the short-termism concerns are not about corporate profits, venture capital investments and returns, private equity investments and returns, or corporate valuations. They are about investment, productivity, and employment – indicators not analyzed in the paper. See Steven Kaplan, "Are US Companies Too Short-Term Oriented? Some Thoughts," National Bureau of Economic Research (NBER), June 2017.

71. William Lazonick, "Profits without Prosperity," *Harvard Business Review*, September 2014.

72. "Response to Congress: Negative Net Equity Issuance," Securities and Exchange Commission, December 23, 2020, 26, figure 7C. A Securities and Exchange Commission report shows that for reporting companies, capital expenditure (as percentage of market value) was higher in firms that did not repurchase their shares than in firms that *did* repurchase their shares, in every year from 1983 to 2016 except 1999. Another study, of 385,488 firms between 1988 and 2010, found that share repurchases made to increase earnings per share were followed by reduced employment and capital investment: Heitor Almeida, Vyacheslav Fos, and Mathias Kronlund, "The Real Effects of Share Repurchases," *Journal of Financial Economics* 119, no. 1 (2016): 168–85. A common counterargument is that increased corporate payouts are positive for the economy because they move capital from mature enterprises to more innovative faster-growing firms. But this is not supported by the data: In 2014, total shareholder payouts in the forms of dividend and share buybacks were more than $1.2 trillion, but investors put less than $200 billion into the productive economy via IPOs and venture capital. See Mason, "Understanding Short-Termism," 18. Other economists, such as Jesse Fried and Charles Wang, have taken aim at the argument by William Lazonick that high levels of payouts amount to real value destruction at the cost of financial value creation (Lazonick, "Profits without Prosperity.") Whereas Lazonick reports payouts as percentage of profit, Fried and Wang consider equity issuance (and net debt issuance) by US public firms over 2007–16 as inflows that balance payout outflows, resulting in much lower (net) payout ratios than Lazonick reports. See Jesse Fried and Charles Wang, "Short Termism and Capital Flows," *Review of Corporate Finance Studies* 8, no. 1 (March 2019): 207–33. But this is precisely what critics of financialization lament: nonfinancials using their credit and their ability to raise equity for payout, not for real investment and real value creation. Besides, Fried and Wang actually find that for S&P 500 firms for the decade 2007–16, payouts were $7 trillion while equity issuances totaled approximately $3.3 trillion. So *net* shareholder payouts were only about $3.7 trillion. They present this as reassuring – but with payouts double the size of equity raised, how was the other half of the payouts financed? Surely at the cost of a combination of more debt, lower wages, and lower investment – as the studies cited in the main text testify.

73. For a large sample of nonfinancial US firms across industries, financial assets increased from 28 percent of sales in 1980 to 45 percent of sales in 2014, while the volume of capital goods declined from 23 percent of sales to 18 percent during the same period. Also, the same study found that financial assets and capital goods moved in tandem until 1980, but this correlation disappeared thereafter. See Leila Davis, "Identifying the 'Financialization' of the Nonfinancial Corporation in the US Economy: A Decomposition of Firm-

Level Balance Sheets," *Journal of Post Keynesian Economics* 39, no. 1 (2016): 115–41, figure 1.

74. Two mechanisms for the observed negative relationship between real investment and financialization have been identified. First, "increased financial investment and increased financial profit opportunities crowd out real investment." Second, increased payments connected to financial obligations (e.g., on bonds and stocks) have impeded real investment by decreasing available internal funds, shortening the planning horizons of the firm management and increasing uncertainty. See Özgür Orhangazi, "Financialization and Capital Accumulation in the Non-financial Corporate Sector: A Theoretical and Empirical Investigation on the US Economy: 1973–2003," *Cambridge Journal of Economics* 32, no. 6 (November 2008): 863–86.

75. "[N]et nonresidential investment for the economy as a whole [fell] from an average of 4.3% of GDP during 1971–85 and 3.8% of GDP during 1971–99 to an average of 2.3% during 2009–17." Epstein and Montecino, "Overcharged," 25. Had the net nonresidential investment rate remained at the level of 3.8 percent of GDP that prevailed during 1971–99, investment over 2009–17 would have been $640 billion per year on average, instead of the actual $341 billion per year. On these numbers, the loss in investment due to the lower rate in 2009–17 compared to 1971–99 comes to $300 billion per year on average over 2009–17.

76. A study covering the entire US manufacturing sector from 1997 to 2007 showed that on average mergers and acquisitions boosted market values of the surviving companies, but had no statistically significant effect on productivity. See Bruce A. Blonigen and Justin R. Pierce, "Evidence for the Effects of Mergers on Market Power and Efficiency," NBER, October 2016.

77. GE: See Rana Foroohar, *Makers and Takers: The Rise of Finance and the Fall of American Business* (New York: Crown Business, 2016), 163–5 for a succinct account of CEO Jack Welch's financialization of GE and its consequences. Intel: Chris Miller, *Chip War: The Fight for the World's Most Critical Technology* (New York: Simon & Schuster, 2022), 191–6. Southwest: Zeynep Tufekci, "The Shameful Open Secret behind Southwest's Failure," *New York Times*, December 31, 2022.

78. Natasha Frost, "The 1997 Merger That Paved the Way for the Boeing 737 Max Crisis," *Quartz*, January 3, 2020.

79. US Congress, House, Committee on Transportation and Infrastructure, *Final Committee Report: The Design, Development and Certification of the Boeing 737 Max*, 116th Cong., 2nd sess., September 2020, 36.

80. L. J. Hart-Smith, "Out-Sourced Profits: The Cornerstone of Successful Subcontracting," Third Annual Technical Excellence Symposium, Boeing, February 14–15, 2001.

81. Marshall Auerback, "Boeing Might Represent the Greatest Indictment of 21st-Century Capitalism," Salon, April 27, 2019; Natalie Kitroeff and David Gelles, "Claims of Shoddy Production Draw Scrutiny to a Second Boeing Jet," *New York Times*, April 20, 2019.

82. James G. McGann, "Why Donald Trump Won the Election and Does It Mean the End to Think Tanks and Policy Advice as We Know It?" Think Tanks and Civil Societies Program, University of Pennsylvania, 2016.

83. Doug Palmer, "Clinton Raved about Trans-Pacific Partnership before She Rejected It," *Politico*, October 8, 2016.

84. Stephanie Nebehay, "US Seals Demise of WTO Appeals Bench – Trade Officials," Reuters, December 9, 2019; Chad P. Bown and Melinda Kolb, "Trump's Trade War Timeline: An Up-to-Date Guide," Peterson Institute for International Economics, March 24, 2023; "United States–Mexico–Canada Agreement," Office of the US Trade Representative, July 1, 2020; McBride et al., "What's Next for the Trans-Pacific Partnership (TPP)?"

85. Jim Zarroli, "On Trade, Trump Administration Likes to Leave Other Countries Guessing," NPR, June 1, 2018.

86. Twitter statement by Trump: "Billions of Dollars are pouring into the coffers of the U.S.A. because of the Tariffs being charged to China, and there is a long way to go. If companies don't want to pay Tariffs, build in the U.S.A. Otherwise, let's just make our Country richer than ever before!" President Donald Trump, November 29, 2018, twitter.com/realdonaldtrump/status/1068120444279103488.

87. Cathalijne Adams, "Former USTR Robert Lighthizer Tells Congress the CCP 'May Be the Most Perilous Adversary We've Ever Had,'" Alliance for American Manufacturing, May 19, 2023; Robert Lighthizer, No Trade Is Free: Changing Course, Taking on China, and Helping America's Workers (New York: Broadside Books, 2023).

88. Greg Robb, "Meet Peter Navarro, the Man Who Pushed Gary Cohn out of the White House," Market Watch, March 8, 2018; Jill Colvin, "Views of Trump's Trade Adviser Carry the Day at White House," AP News, March 8, 2018.

89. "Why Trump's Withdrawal from the TPP Is a Boon for China," South China Morning Post, January 24, 2017.

90. "Treaties in Force: A List of Treaties and Other International Agreements of the United States in Force on January 1, 2020," US Department of State, January 1, 2020.

91. "Trade in Goods with Mexico," US Census Bureau.

92. "Trade in Goods with Canada," US Census Bureau.

93. Simon Lester, Inu Manak, and Kyounghwa Kim, "Trump's First Trade Deal: The Slightly Revised Korea-US Free Trade Agreement," CATO Institute, June 13, 2019.

94. "Trade in Goods with Korea, South," US Census Bureau.

95. Matthew P. Goodman et al, "The U.S.–Japan Trade Deal," Center for Strategic & International Studies, September 25, 2019, csis.org/analysis/us-japan-trade-deal; USTR, "FACT SHEET on U.S.-Japan Trade Agreement," September 2019, ustr .gov/about-us/policy-offices/press-office/fact-sheets/2019/september/fact-sheet-us-japan-trade-agreement.

96. Kate O'Keeffe, "US Approves Nearly All Tech Exports to China, Data Shows," Wall Street Journal, August 16, 2022.

97. One example is the venture fund Haiyan Capital, funded by the Everbright Group, a state-owned financial conglomerate founded by an arm of the State Council, the highest body of the Chinese government.

98. Bureau of Industry and Security, "Commerce Adds Seven Chinese Entities to Entity List Supporting China's Military Modernization Efforts," US Chamber of Commerce, August 23, 2022.

99. Alexandra Alper, Toby Sterling, and Stephen Nellis, "Trump Administration Pressed Dutch Hard to Cancel China Chip-Equipment Sale: Sources," Reuters, January 6, 2020.

100. Dan Strumpf and Patricia Kowsmann, "US Prosecutors Probe Huawei on New Allegations of Technology Theft," Wall Street Journal, August 29, 2019.

101. David Shepardson and Karen Freifeld, "Trump Extends US Telecom Supply Chain Order Aimed at Huawei, ZTE," Reuters, May 13, 2020.

102. Stephen Fidler and Max Colchester, "UK to Ban Huawei from Its 5G Networks Amid China–US Tensions," *Wall Street Journal*, July 14, 2020; Jordan Fabian, "Trump Extends Order That Curbs Huawei's Access to US Markets," Bloomberg News, May 14, 2020.

103. James Vincent, "ZTE Receives Record $1.2 Billion Fine for Breaking US Sanctions," *The Verge*, March 8, 2017, theverge.com/2017/3/8/14852182/zte-embargo-iran-north-korea-record-fine.

104. Paul Mozur, "All about ZTE, the Chinese Sanctions Breaker That Trump Wants to Help," *New York Times*, May 14, 2018.

105. Chris Tognotti, "Trump Promises to Help Chinese Telecom ZTE – and the Internet Can't Believe It," *Daily Dot*, May 13, 2018.

106. Henry Farrell, "Bolton Alleges That Trump Helped Out China's Leader on ZTE. What's ZTE?" *Washington Post*, January 28, 2020.

107. Farrell, "Bolton Alleges."

108. Ian King and Jenny Leonard, "Chip CEOs Urge US to Study Impact of China Curbs and Take Pause," Bloomberg, July 21, 2023.

109. O'Keeffe, "US Approves."

110. Marianne Schneider-Petsinger, "Reforming the World Trade Organization: Prospects for Transatlantic Cooperation and the Global Trade System," Chatham House, September 2020, 18.

111. "Report on the Appellate Body of the World Trade Organization," US Trade Representative, February 2020.

112. Chad P. Bown and Soumaya Keynes, "Why Trump Shot the Sheriffs: The End of WTO Dispute Settlement 1.0," Peterson Institute for International Economics, March 2020.

113. Nebehay, "US Seals."

114. "Multi-Party Interim Appeals Arbitration Arrangement (MPIA)," Geneva Trade Platform, wtoplurilaterals.info/plural_initiative/the-mpia.

115. Michaela D. Platzer, "Domestic Solar Manufacturing and New US Tariffs," Congressional Research Service, February 2, 2018.

116. Jeff Ferry, "Reclaiming the US Solar Supply Chain from China," Coalition for a Prosperous America, March 10, 2021.

117. Ferry, "Reclaiming."

118. Bown and Kolb, "Trump's Trade."

119. Ferry, "Reclaiming."

120. Bown and Kolb, "Trump's Trade."

121. Tori K. Smith, "Washing Machine Tariffs Are Still Putting Consumers through the Wringers," Heritage Foundation, July 17, 2019.

122. Justin Sink and Shawn Donnan, "Trump Touts Whirlpool Job Gains from Tariffs That Hit Consumers," Bloomberg, August 6, 2020.

123. Jim Tankersley, "Trump's Washing Machine Tariffs Stung Consumers While Lifting Corporate Profits," *New York Times*, April 21, 2019.

124. Bown and Kolb, "Trump's Trade."

125. Ana Swanson, "On Trump's Car Tariffs, Companies Are United in Dissent," *New York Times*, July 19, 2018.

126. Michael Schultz et al., "US Consumer and Economic Impacts of US Automotive Trade Policies," Center for Automotive Research, February 2019, 4.

127. "Trump: Car Tariffs Hinge on EU Trade Talks," Deutsche Welle, February 21, 2019.

128. Bureau of Industry and Security Office of Technology Evaluation, "The Effect of Imports of Steel on the National Security: An Investigation Conducted under Section 232 of the Trade Expansion Act of 1962, As Amended," US Department of Commerce, January 11, 2018.

129. Bown and Kolb, "Trump's Trade."

130. "EU tariffs on US goods come into force," June 22, 2018, BBC News, bbc.com/news/business-44567636.

131. "Economic Impact of Section 232 and 301 Tariffs on U.S. Industries," US International Trade Commission, May 2023, pp. 21–2, usitc.gov/publications/332/pub5405.pdf.

132. Chad P. Bown and Katheryn Russ, "Biden and Europe Remove Trump's Steel and Aluminum Tariffs, but It's Not Free Trade," Peterson Institute for International Economics, November 11, 2021; Bureau of Industry and Security Office of Technology Evaluation, "The Effect of Imports on Aluminum on the National Security: An Investigation Conducted Under Section 232 of the Trade Expansion Act of 1962, As Amended," US Department of Commerce, January 17, 2018.

133. Steel: "US Steel Industry: A Look back at 2021 and a Look ahead to 2022," SteelOrbis, December 30, 2021; Aluminum: "US Aluminum Drives Modern Manufacturing with $9+ Billion Invested," The Aluminum Association, aluminum.org/investment.

134. Joe Deaux, "Trump Expands Aluminum, Steel Tariffs to Some Imported Products," Bloomberg, January 24, 2020.

135. Presidential Proclamation 9740 (April 30, 2018) for Korea, and Proclamation 9759 for Argentina and Brazil.

136. Joint Statements here: ustr.gov/about-us/policy-offices/press-office/press-releases/2019/may/united-states-announces-deal-canada-and.

137. Presidential Proclamations 10327 and 10328 implementing the aluminum and steel tariff rate quotas, respectively, for Europe. See Proclamations 10356 (March 31, 2022) and 10406 (May 31, 2022) implementing steel tariff rate quotas for Japan and the UK respectively.

138. Heather Long, "Trump's Steel Tariffs Cost US Consumers $900,000 for Every Job Created, Experts Say," Washington Post, May 7, 2019.

139. "US Steel Industry," SteelOrbis; "US Aluminum Drives Modern Manufacturing with $9+ Billion Invested," The Aluminum Association; Andrew Heritage, "Tariff Incidence in the Real World: Why Consumers (Mostly) Didn't Pay the Steel Tariffs," Coalition for a Prosperous America, October 20, 2021; David Lawder, "Trump Era Aluminum Tariffs Have Revived the US Industry – Think-Tank," Reuters, May 25, 2021.

140. "Economic Impact of Section 232 and 301 Tariffs on U.S. Industries," US International Trade Commission, May 2023, pp. 21–2, usitc.gov/publications/332/pub5405.pdf.

141. Karen M. Sutter, "US-China Phase One Trade Deal," Congressional Research Service, December 16, 2022.

142. Chad P. Bown, "US China Trade War Tariffs: An Up-to-Date Chart," Peterson Institute for International Economics, last modified April 6, 2023, piie.com/research/piie-charts/us-china-trade-war-tariffs-date-chart.

143. Bown, "US China Trade."

144. Bown, "US China Trade."

145. March: Office of the United States Trade Representative, notice of modification of action, "China's Acts, Policies, and Practices Related to Technology Transfer,

Intellectual Property, and Innovation," *Federal Register* 83, no. 243 (December 19, 2018): 65198. Indefinitely: Office of the United States Trade Representative, notice of modification of action, "China's Acts, Policies, and Practices Related to Technology Transfer, Intellectual Property, and Innovation," *Federal Register* 84, no. 43 (March 5, 2019): 7966.

146. Bown, "US China Trade."

147. Bown, "US China Trade."

148. Bown, "US China Trade."

149. Bown, "US China Trade."

150. Erica York, "Tracking the Economic Impact of US Tariffs and Retaliatory Actions," Tax Foundation, April 1, 2022; Andrew Mullen, "US-China Trade War: Was the Phase-One Trade Deal a 'Historic Failure,' and What's Next?" *South China Morning Post*, February 27, 2022.

151. Bown, "US China Trade."

152. Lori Ann LaRocco, "As Biden and Xi Meet, Asian Manufacturing Slowdown Returns to a 2020 Low, Led by a Softer China," CNBC, November 15, 2023, cnbc.com/2023/11/15/asia-manufacturing-slowdown-returns-to-2020-low-led-by-softer-china.html.

153. Bown, "US China Trade."

154. Bown, "US China Trade."

155. Bown, "US China Trade."

156. Bown, "US China Trade."

157. Chad P. Bown, "China Bought None of the Extra $200 Billion of US Exports in Trump's Trade Deal," Peterson Institute for International Economics, July 19, 2022.

158. Chad P. Bown, "Anatomy of a Flop: Why Trump's US-China Phase One Trade Deal Fell Short." *Peterson Institute for International Economics*, February 8, 2021.

159. Phil Levy, "The Verdict on Trump Trade Policy, part 2: Challenging China," *Forbes*, August 10, 2020.

160. Chad P. Bown, Euijin Jung, and Eva Zhang, "Trump Has Gotten China to Lower Its Tariffs. Just Toward Everyone Else," Peterson Institute for International Economics, June 12, 2019; Bown, "Anatomy."

161. Andrew Heritage, "Removing China's MFN Status Would Create 2 Million Jobs, Grow U.S. Economy by 1.75%," Coalition for a Prosperous America, September 26, 2023, prosperousamerica.org/removing-chinas-mfn-status-would-create-2-million-jobs-grow-u-s-economy-by-1-75.

162. Bown, "US China Trade."

163. Bryce Baschuk, "DHL Digs into Trade Data to Track US-China Decoupling," Bloomberg, March 15, 2023. See also Noah Smith, "Stop Saying 'There Is No Decoupling.' There is!" and Thomas Gatley, "The Truth about Trade Decoupling," and Andrew Heritage, "Section 301 Tariffs Reduced US Dependence on China, Decoupling Has Begun," Coalition for a Prosperous America, June 28, 2023.

164. Anthony DeBarros and Yuka Hayashi, "How US and China Are Breaking Up, in Charts," *Wall Street Journal*, August 12, 2023. Kyo Kitazume et al., "Chinese Goods Navigate Alternate Trade Routes to US Shores: Data Shows Increased Flows via Vietnam and Mexico with Origin Disguised," Nikkei Asia, June 1, 2019, asia.nikkei.com/Spotlight/Datawatch/Chinese-goods-navigate-alternate-trade-routes-to-US-shores; Chuin-Wei Yap, "American Tariffs on China Are Being Blunted by

Trade Cheats," *Wall Street Journal*, June 26, 2019, wsj.com/articles/american-tariffs-on-china-are-being-blunted-by-trade-cheats-11561546806; Keith Bradsher, "Tariff Dodgers Stand to Profit Off U.S.-China Trade Dispute," *New York Times*, April 22, 2018, nytimes.com/2018/04/22/business/china-trade-tariffs-transshipment.html; HKTDC Research, "CBP Outlines Efforts to Tackle Illegal Transshipment Practices," October 27, 2020, research.hktdc.com/en/article/NTcoODAzODIx.

165. "US Trade in Goods and Services – Balance of Payments (BOP) Basis," US Census Bureau.

166. Fernando Leibovici and Ana Maria Santacreu, "The Dynamics of the US Trade Deficit during COVID-19: The Role of Essential Medical Goods," Federal Reserve Bank of St. Louis, September 16, 2020.

167. "Trump Budget Proposal Undermines US Innovation and Competitiveness," Information Technology and Innovation Foundation, May 23, 2017. The Trump 2017 budget attempted to eliminate the Manufacturing Extension Partnership and the Economic Development Administration at the Commerce Department. See Niv Elis, "Here Are the 66 Programs Eliminated in Trump's Budget," *Hill*, March 23, 2017. The budget also constituted a broad-based attack on federal R&D programs. See Henry Fountain and John Schwartz, "Scientists Bristle at Trump Budget's Cuts to Research," *New York Times*, March 16, 2007. Trump's budget cuts also attacked innovation and manufacturing programs. See Clare Foran, "Trump's Budget Could Hurt Manufacturing and Innovation," *Atlantic*, March 16, 2017.

168. "Real Private Fixed Investment: Nonresidential: Structures: Manufacturing," Federal Reserve Bank of St. Louis, fred.stlouisfed.org/series/C307RX1Q020SBEA.

169. Bown and Kolb, "Trump's Trade."

170. Jeff Ferry, "Washing Machine Tariffs Come Out Clean, Sparkling for US Manufacturing," Coalition for a Prosperous America, January 16, 2024, prosperousamerica.org/washing-machine-tariffs-come-out-clean-sparkling-for-us-manufacturing.

171. Ferry, "Washing Machine Tariffs."

172. Bown and Russ, "Biden and Europe."

173. "Section 232 Tariffs on Steel & Aluminum," Sandler, Travis & Rosenberg, P.A., strtrade.com/trade-news-resources/tariff-actions-resources/section-232-tariffs-on-steel-aluminum.

174. Jeff Ferry, "Tariffs and Tax Credits Driving a New Manufacturing Boom," Coalition for a Prosperous America, April 25, 2023.

175. Jarrett Renshaw, "Biden Admin Eases Trump-Era Solar Tariffs but Doesn't End Them," Reuters, February 4, 2022.

176. David Dayen, "Trade Group Driving Solar Controversy Includes Slave-Labor Companies," *American Prospect*, May 12, 2022.

177. "Overview of De Minimis Value Regimes World-Wide" Global Express Association, November 4, 2021.

178. Jeff Ferry, "US De Minimis China Imports Hit $188 Billion Last Year," Coalition for a Prosperous America, May 15, 2023. For the history and a more technical analysis of the de minimis rule, see: Michael Stumo, CEO of the Coalition for a Prosperous America, "Written Testimony before the House Ways and Means Subcommittee on Trade: Modernizing Customs Policies to Protect American Workers and Secure Supply Chains," Coalition for a Prosperous America, May 25, 2023.

179. "Privacy Impact Assessment for the E-Commerce, 'Section 321' Data Pilot," DHS/CBP/PIA-059, US Department of Homeland Security, September 26, 2019, 2.

180. Jordyn Holman, "Bipartisan Proposals Would Hit E-Commerce Like Fast Fashion," *New York Times*, June 15, 2023.

181. The *New Yorker* magazine described the Biden strategy as "an ambitious industrial policy designed to strengthen manufacturing, hasten a green energy transformation, create well-paid jobs, and insure American technological leadership over China." John Cassidy, "Joe Biden's Innovative Attempt to Reshape the American Economy," *New Yorker*, February 7, 2023.

182. Brian Deese, "Brian Deese on Biden's Vision for 'A Twenty-First-Century American Industrial Strategy,'" Atlantic Council, June 23, 2021.

183. Gina M. Raimondo, "Remarks by US Secretary of Commerce Gina Raimondo: The CHIPS Act and a Long-Term Vision for America's Technological Leadership," US Department of Commerce, February 23, 2023.

184. Jake Sullivan, "Remarks by National Security Advisor Jake Sullivan on the Biden-Harris Administration's National Security Strategy," The White House, October 12, 2022.

185. Brian Deese, "Biden's Vision."

186. National Science and Technology Council, "National Strategy for Advanced Manufacturing," The White House, October 2022, 1.

187. Justin Badlam et al., "The US Bipartisan Infrastructure Law: Breaking it down," McKinsey & Company, November 12, 2021.

188. "Fact Sheet: The Bipartisan Infrastructure Deal," The White House, November 6, 2021.

189. Federal Highway Administration, "Bipartisan Infrastructure Law: Climate/Resilience," US Department of Transportation, fhwa.dot.gov/bipartisan-infrastructure-law/climate.cfm.

190. "Understanding the Components of the US Bipartisan Infrastructure Law," Union Pacific, February 14, 2023.

191. "Title IX – Build America, Buy America," Department of Housing and Urban Development, hud.gov/sites/dfiles/GC/documents/Build%20America,%20Buy%20America%20Act%20Provisions.pdf.

192. Office of Acquisition Management, "Build America Buy America," US Department of Commerce, commerce.gov/oam/build-america-buy-america.

193. Office of Acquisition Management, "Build America Buy America."

194. "Executive Order on Advancing Biotechnology and Biomanufacturing Innovation for a Sustainable, Safe, and Secure American Bioeconomy," The White House, September 12, 2022.

195. Kelsey Simpkins, "What Does the Inflation Reduction Act Do to Address Climate Change?" University of Colorado Boulder, August 17, 2022.

196. "Fact Sheet: Treasury, IRS Open Public Comment on Implementing the Inflation Reduction Act's Clean Energy Tax Incentives," US Department of Treasury, October 5, 2022.

197. "Building a Clean Energy Economy: A Guidebook to the Inflation Reduction Act's Investment in Clean Energy and Climate Action, Version 2," The White House, January 2023, 9–11.

198. Justin Badlam et al., "Inflation Reduction," McKinsey & Company, October 24, 2022.

199. Owen Minott and Helen Nguyen, "IRA EV Tax Credits: Requirements for Domestic Manufacturing," Bipartisan Policy Center, February 24, 2023.

200. "Executive Order on Addressing the Threat from Securities Investments that Finance Certain Companies of the People's Republic of China," The White House, June 3, 2021.

201. "Executive Order on Ensuring the Future Is Made in All of America by All of America's Workers," The White House, January 25, 2021.

202. Executive Office of the President, "Executive Order 14017: America's Supply Chains," Federal Register, February 24, 2021.

203. "Executive Order on Advancing Biotechnology and Biomanufacturing Innovation for a Sustainable, Safe, and Secure American Bioeconomy," The White House, September 12, 2022.

204. Executive Office of the President, "Executive Order 14083: Ensuring Robust Consideration of Evolving National Security Risks by the Committee on Foreign Investment in the United States," Federal Register, September 15, 2022.

205. "Federal Research and Development in Support of Domestic Manufacturing and United States Jobs," Federal Register, July 28, 2023.

206. "Addressing United States Investments in Certain National Security Technologies and Products in Countries of Concern," The White House, August 9, 2023.

207. The White House, "Executive Order on Safe, Secure, and Trustworthy Development and Use of Artificial Intelligence," October 30, 2023, whitehouse .gov/briefing-room/presidential-actions/2023/10/30/executive-order-on-the-safe-secure-and-trustworthy-development-and-use-of-artificial-intelligence.

208. "Unpacking the Boom in US Construction of Manufacturing Facilities," US Department of the Treasury, Eric Van Nostrand, Tara Sinclair, and Samarth Gupta, June 27, 2023, home.treasury.gov/news/featured-stories/unpacking-the-boom-in-us-construction-of-manufacturing-facilities.

209. Chris Metinko, "US Investment in China Tech Scene Falls as Political Headwinds Strengthen," Crunchbase News, May 11, 2023. And see for example, "Written Testimony of Roger W. Robinson Jr., Chairman, Prague Security Studies Institute and former Chairman of the Congressional US-China Economic and Security Review Commission before the House Select Committee on the Strategic Competition Between the United States and the Chinese Communist Party, Hearing Entitled 'Leveling the Playing Field: How to Counter the CCP's Economic Aggression,'" Coalition for a Prosperous America, May 17, 2023.

210. Adam Lysenko et al., "US-China Financial Investment: Current Scope and Future Potential," The Rhodium Group, January 6, 2021. Also see Sayad Baronyan, "Comfort with China Exceeds $1 Trillion," EPFR, January 30, 2023, epfr.com/insights/quants-corner/comfort-with-china-exceeds-usd-1-trillion-emerging-mar kets-fund-flows-allocations-etfs-apac-alibaba.

211. The Vanguard FTS Emerging Markets ETF (VWO), the largest US emerging markets fund, held approximately this number of Chinese companies as of May 31, 2023. The authors wish to thank Justin Bernier, founder of the National Security Index, for a spreadsheet with this data.

212. Of the total, only about 250 are listed on US exchanges. "Chinese Companies Listed on Major US Stock Exchanges," United States-China Economic and Security Review Com-mission, uscc.gov/sites/default/files/2023–01/Chinese_Companies_Listed_ on_US_Stock_Exchanges_01_2023.pdf; Claudius B. Modesti, et al., "Navigating the Holding Foreign Companies Accountable Act – The Road to Delisting or Redemption for China-Based Companies," Akin Gump, May 16, 2022; "CPA Letter to PCAOB and SEC Regarding Chinese Companies' Compliance with US Securities Laws," Coalition for a Prosperous America, December 22, 2022.

213. Ana Swanson and Lauren Hirsch, "US Aims to Curtail Technology Investment in China," *New York Times*, February 9, 2023.

214. Bureau of Industry and Security, "Commerce Implements New Export Controls on Advanced Computing and Semiconductor Manufacturing Items to the People's Republic of China (PRC)," US Department of Commerce, October 7, 2022.

215. Bureau of Industry and Security "Commerce Implements."

216. Bureau of Industry and Security, "Commerce Adds 36 to Entity List for Supporting the People's Republic of China's Military Modernization, Violations of Human Rights, and Risk of Diversion," US Department of Commerce, December 15, 2022.

217. Robby Stephany Saunders, Vice President of National Security Policy and Strategy, Coalition for a Prosperous America, email to Marc Fasteau, June 13, 2023.

218. Anna Swanson, "U.S. Tightens China's Access to Advanced Chips for Artificial Intelligence," *New York Times*, October 17, 2023, nytimes.com/2023/10/17/business/economy/ai-chips-china-restrictions.html?smid=nytcore-ios-share&referringSource=articleShare.

219. "Dutch to Restrict Semiconductor Tech Exports to China, Joining US Effort," March 8, 2023, Reuters.

220. "China Dissatisfied with Japan's Chip Export Restrictions – Spokesperson," Reuters, April 3, 2023.

221. Gregory C. Allen, "Choking Off China's Access to the Future of AI," October 2022, Center for Strategic and International Studies.

222. Cheng Ting-Fang, Lauly Li, and Yifan Yu, "Apple Freezes Plan to Use China's YMTC Chips amid Political Pressure," Nikkei Asia, October 17, 2022.

223. Michael Schuman, "Why Biden's Block on Chips to China Is a Big Deal," *Atlantic*, October 25, 2022.

224. David Lawder, "US drops digital trade demands at WTO to allow room for stronger tech regulation," Reuters, October 25, 2023, reuters.com/world/us/us-drops-digital-trade-demands-wto-allow-room-stronger-tech-regulation-2023–10-25.

225. Kenneth Rapoza, "Big Tech Companies Still Mad With USTR Decision on Global Data Storage," November 27, 2023, prosperousamerica.org/big-tech-mad-ustr-decision-on-data-wto; Farah Stockman, "How the Biden Administration Took the Pen Away from Meta, Google and Amazon," *New York Times*, November 27, 2023, nytimes.com/2023/11/27/opinion/google-facebook-ai-trade.html.

226. "On-the-Record Press Call on the Launch of the Indo-Pacific Economic Framework," The White House, May 23, 2022; Steven Overly, "Biden's 'Ambitious' Economic Plan for Latin America Offers a 'Social Contract,' Not Trade Agreements," *Politico*, June 7, 2022.

227. Chad P. Bown and Cecilia Malmstrom, "What is the US-EU Trade and Technology Council? Five Things You Need to Know," Peterson Institute for International Economics, September 24, 2021.

228. "Fact Sheet: The Biden-Harris Administration's New Approach to the US-China Trade Relationship," US Trade Representative, October 4, 2021.

229. "US Trade in Goods and Services – Balance of Payments (BOP) Basis," US Census Bureau.

19. Governmentally Supported Innovations

1. David Roberts, "How to Save the Failing Nuclear Power Plants That Generate Half of America's Clean Electricity," *Vox*, May 11, 2018; Office of Nuclear Energy, "5 Fast Facts about Nuclear Energy," US Department of Energy, March 23, 2021.

2. Glenn T. Seaborg, "Civilian Nuclear Power: A Report to the President, 1962," US Atomic Energy Commission, 1962, 8.

3. Rebecca M. Henderson and Richard G. Newell, eds., *Accelerating Energy Innovation: Insights from Multiple Sectors* (Chicago, IL: University of Chicago Press, 2011), 163.

4. "SAGE: The First National Air Defense Network," IBM, ibm.com/ibm/history/ibm100/us/en/icons/sage; Vernon W. Ruttan, *Is War Necessary for Economic Growth? Military Procurement and Technology Development* (New York: Oxford University Press, 2006), 98.

5. "SAGE: The First National Air Defense Network."

6. "Paul Baran and the Origins of the Internet," RAND, rand.org/about/history/baran.html; "Scientist Who Transformed the Internet," *Irish Times*, June 24, 2000.

7. 1975: The ARPANET geographical map now shows 61 nodes. "Internet History of the 1970s," Computer History Museum, computerhistory.org/internethistory/1970s.

8. Peter High, "The Father of the Internet, Vint Cerf, Continues to Influence Its Growth," *Forbes*, March 26, 2018.

9. Deborah Sweeney, "Not Just for Small Businesses: How the SBA Helped Grow 3 Major Companies," *Forbes*, September 4, 2018.

10. Office of the Manager, "Internet/PSN Interconnectivity and Vulnerability Report," National Communications Systems, December 1996.

11. Elizabeth Nix, The World's First Web Site, History.com, August 30, 2018, history.com/news/the-worlds-first-web-site.

12. David Hart, "Mosaic Launches an Internet Revolution," National Science Foundation, April 8, 2004; "Marc Andreesen and Eric Bina Internet Browser Technology," Lemelson-MIT, lemelson.mit.edu/resources/marc-andreesen-and-eric-bina.

13. Except for sharing it with America's National Security Agency. "Clifford Cocks, James Ellis, and Malcolm Williamson," National Security Agency/Central Security Service, 2021.

14. Ronald Rivest, email included in correspondence between John Young and Vin McLellan, May 28, 1998, cryptome.org/jya/pk-royal.htm.

15. Ronald Rivest, email.

16. For a critique of some exaggerated commentary on this topic, see José Luis Ricón, "The Entrepreneurial State: The Case of the iPhone (II)," Nintil, August 21, 2015.

17. "Touching the Future," *Economist*, September 6, 2008; Florence Ion, "From Touch Displays to the Surface: A Brief History of Touchscreen Technology," Ars Technica, April 4, 2013.

18. Eric R. Fossum, "The Invention of CMOS Image Sensors: A Camera in Every Pocket," IEEE Xplore, April 9, 2020.

19. Jeffrey Hart and Michael Borrus, "Display's the Thing: The Real Stakes in the Conflict Over High-Resolution Displays," *Journal of Policy Analysis and Management* 13, no. 1 (Winter, 1994): 21–54.

20. Solar Technologies Office, "DOE Pursues SunShot Initiative to Achieve Cost Competitive Solar Energy by 2020," US Department of Energy (DOE), February 4, 2011.

21. "Energy Department Announces More than 90% Achievement of 2020 SunShot Goal, Sets Sights on 2030 Affordability Targets," DOE, November 14, 2016.

22. "News Release: NREL Six-Junction Solar Cell Sets Two World Records for Efficiency," NREL, April 13, 2020.

23. Paul Dvorak, "Where the Wind Industry and Renewables Are Headed in the Near Future," *Windpower Engineering & Development*, October 10, 2016.

24. "DOE Finds Record Production and Job Growth in US Wind Power Sector," US Department of Energy, August 16, 2022.

25. Vicki Norberg-Bohm, "Creating Incentives for Environmentally Enhancing Technological Change: Lessons from 30 Years of US Energy Technology Policy," *Technological Forecasting and Social Change* 65, no. 2 (October 2000): 125–48.

26. Will Mathis, Ryan Beene, and Josh Saul, "Wind Power's 'Colossal Market Failure' Threatens Climate Fight," Bloomberg, April 25, 2022.

27. Rosalie Ruegg and Patrick Thomas, "Linkages of DOE's Energy Storage R&D to Batteries and Ultracapacitors for Hybrid, Plug-In Hybrid, and Electric Vehicles," US Department of Energy Office of Energy Efficiency and Renewable Energy, February 2008, x.

28. Margot Hornblower, "Listen, Detroit, You'll Get a Charge Out of This," *Time*, February 22, 1999; Rachael Lallensack, "Stanford Ovshinsky Might Be the Most Prolific Inventor You've Never Heard Of," *Smithsonian*, October 15, 2018.

29. Dr. Paul Kearns, Interim Laboratory Director, Argonne National Laboratory, "Report: Senate Hearing 115–484," US Government Publishing Office, September 12, 2017.

30. Sridhar Kota, Justin Zorn, and Tom Mahoney, "How the US Can Rebuild Its Capacity to Innovate," *Harvard Business Review*, October 23, 2018.

31. Pacific Northwest National Laboratory, "Battery Based on PNNL Tech Given EPA Green Chemistry Award," DOE, June 12, 2017.

32. Mary Louise Kelly, "How the US Gave Away Cutting-Edge Technology to China," NPR, August 9, 2022.

33. Peter L. Singer, "Federally Supported Innovations," Information Technology and Innovation Foundation, February 2014, 19–20.

34. Mason Inman, "How the Prophet of Peak Oil Explained Fracking in the 1950s: An Excerpt from Mason Inman's *The Oracle of Oil*," *Scientific American*, April 8, 2016.

35. David E. Pierce, "Developing a Common Law of Hydraulic Fracturing," *University of Pittsburgh Law Review* 72, no. 4 (2011).

36. Javier Blas, "The US Just Became a Net Oil Exporter for the First Time in 75 Years," Bloomberg, December 6, 2018; Michael Shellenberger and Ted Nordhaus, "A Boom in Shale Gas? Credit the Feds," *Washington Post*, December 16, 2011; Singer, "Federally Supported Innovations," 17–20.

37. Michael Shellenberger et al., "Where the Shale Gas Revolution Came From: Government's Role in the Development of Hydraulic Fracturing in Shale," Breakthrough Institute, May 23, 2012; Shellenberger and Nordhaus, "A Boom."

38. National Energy Technology Laboratory, "Shale Gas: Applying Technology to Solve America's Energy Challenges," DOE, March 2011, 5.

39. Shellenberger and Nordhaus, "A Boom."

40. Gregory Zuckerman, "Breakthrough: The Accidental Discovery That Revolutionized American Energy," *Atlantic*, November 6, 2013.

41. Loren King, Ted Nordhaus, and Michael Shellenberger, "Lessons from the Shale Revolution: A Report on the Conference Proceedings," Breakthrough Institute, April 2015.

42. Justin Ong and Ron Munson, "Hydraulic Fracturing: A Public–Private R&D Success Story," ClearPath and Cogentiv Solutions, January 2019.

43. Steven P. Vallas, Daniel Lee Kleinman, and Dina Biscotti, "Political Structures and the Making of US Biotechnology," in *State of Innovation: the US Government's Role in Technology Development*, ed. Fred Black and Matthew R. Keller (New York: Routledge, 2011), 62.

44. Vallas et al., "Political Structures," 62.

45. Nicolas Rasmussen, *Gene Jockeys: Life Science and the Rise of Biotech Enterprise* (Baltimore, MD: Johns Hopkins University Press, 2014).

46. W. Henry Lambright, "Managing 'Big Science': A Case Study of the Human Genome Project," in *Leaders*, ed. Mark A. Abramson and Kevin Bacon (Lanham, MD: Rowman & Littlefield, 2001), 19–20.

47. The Energy Department, superficially a curious location for genetics research, was involved because it had long been tasked, as a byproduct of its nuclear energy research, with understanding the dangers of genetic mutations caused by radiation. See "Human Genome Project Information Archive," DOE, March 26, 2019.

48. "How It Works: The Incentive Auction Explained," Federal Communications Commission, February 3, 2017.

49. Singer, "Federally Supported Innovations," 25.

50. Singer, "Federally Supported Innovations," 26.

51. David Brillinger, "John W. Tukey: His Life and Professional Contributions," *Annals of Statistics* 30, no. 6 (2002): 1552.

52. Specifically, MRI resulted from federally funded research (NSF and NIH) by faculty members at Columbia, Stanford, and Harvard Universities on nuclear magnetic resonance (NMR). Stanford's Felix Bloch and Harvard's Edward Purcell jointly discovered NMR, which describes the phenomenon where nuclei absorb and then readmit electromagnetic energy. See "MRI: Magnetic Resonance Imaging – Nifty 50," National Science Foundation, April 2000; Amar Bhidé, Srikant M. Datar, and Katherine Stebbins, "Case Histories of Significant Medical Advances: Magnetic Resonance Imaging," working paper no. 20–001, Harvard Business School, July 2019; Singer, "Federally Supported Innovations," 20–1.

53. Tal Geva, "Magnetic Resonance Imaging: Historical Perspective," *Journal of Cardiovascular Magnetic Resonance* 8, no. 4 (2006): 573–80.

54. Prime credit for MR imaging, evidenced by their receiving the Nobel Prize, attaches to Mansfield and Lauterbur. Damadian, nonetheless, deserves recognition for his own innovations, and especially for construction of the first full-body MRI.

55. Jon Guice, "Controversy and the State: Lord ARPA and Intelligent Computing," *Social Studies of Science* 28, no. 1 (February 1998): 120.

56. Raj Reddy, "Words into Action II: A Task-Oriented System: Harpy Is an Experimental, Continuous-Speech Recognition System That Exploits a Low-Cost Minicomputer," *IEEE Spectrum* 17, no. 6 (June 1980): 26–8.

57. Alex Roland and Philip Shiman, *Strategic Computing: DARPA and the Quest for Machine Intelligence, 1983–1993* (Cambridge, MA: The MIT Press, 2002).

58. "Table 9.1 Total Federal Funding for Artificial Intelligence Research (in millions of dollars), 1984–1988," in *National Research Council, 1999. Funding a Revolution: Government Support for Computing Research* (Washington, DC: National Academies Press, 1999), 215, doi.org/10.17226/6323.

59. "National Artificial Intelligence Strategic Plan 2023 Update," May 2023, vii, white house.gov/wp-content/uploads/2023/05/National-Artificial-Intelligence-Research-and-Development-Strategic-Plan-2023-Update.pdf; The White House, "Remarks by National Security Advisor Jake Sullivan at the National Security Commission on Artificial Intelligence Global Emerging Technology Summit," July 13, 2021, whitehouse.gov/nsc/briefing-room/2021/07/13/remarks-by-national-security-advisor-jake-sullivan-at-the-national-security-commission-on-artificial-intelligence-global-emerging-technology-summit.

60. "Artificial Intelligence R&D Investments Fiscal Year 2018: Fiscal Year 2023," Networking and Information Technology Research and Development (NITRD) Program, 2, nitrd.gov/apps/itdashboard/ai-rd-investments.

61. "Artificial Intelligence R&D Investments Fiscal Year 2018."

62. The White House, "Executive Order on Safe, Secure, and Trustworthy Development and Use of Artificial Intelligence," October 30, 2023, whitehouse.gov/briefing-room/presidential-actions/2023/10/30/executive-order-on-the-safe-secure-and-trustworthy-development-and-use-of-artificial-intelligence.

63. Linda R. Cohen and Roger G. Noll, *The Technology Pork Barrel* (Washington, DC: Brookings Institution, 1991), 98–9.

64. Cohen and Noll, *The Technology Pork Barrel*, 99.

65. Congress, House, *Department of Transportation and Related Agencies Appropriations for 1968*, 293.

66. Cohen and Noll, *The Technology Pork Barrel*, 119.

67. Keith McLoughlin, "Concorde's First British Test Flight, 50 Years On," GOV.UK History of Government blog, April 9, 2019, history.blog.gov.uk/2019/04/09/concordes-first-british-test-flight-50-years-on.

68. Cohen and Noll, *The Technology Pork Barrel*, 101, 103.

69. "Showdown on the SST," *Time*, March 29, 1971.

70. Cohen and Noll, *The Technology Pork Barrel*, 107–8.

71. Cohen and Noll, *The Technology Pork Barrel*, 97.

72. Cohen and Noll, *The Technology Pork Barrel*, 135.

73. Cohen and Noll, *The Technology Pork Barrel*, 107.

74. SFC also researched alcohol fuels, solar power, and production of fuel from urban waste.

75. Research and Policy Committee of the Committee for Economic Development, *Helping Insure Our Energy Future: A Program for Developing Synthetic Fuel Plants Now* (New York: Kearny Press, 1979), ix; Milton R. Copulos, "Salvaging the Synthetic Fuels Corporation," Heritage Foundation, April 12, 1985, 3.

76. Cohen and Noll, *The Technology Pork Barrel*, 270.

77. The Cool Water coal gasification plant in California, and Dow Syngas in Louisiana. See Cohen and Noll, *The Technology Pork Barrel*, 295. There were other synfuel pilot plants supported by the DOE through other programs.

78. Cohen and Noll, *The Technology Pork Barrel*, 297.

79. "Running out" is, as with most (though not all) nonrenewable natural resources, strictly speaking a misnomer. The commodity never literally ceases to be available, but becomes too expensive for practical use.

80. Cohen and Noll, *The Technology Pork Barrel*, 240.

81. "Breeder reactor," Wikipedia, en.wikipedia.org/w/index.php?title=Breeder_reactor&oldid=1009576953.

82. Especially given that technology for extracting uranium from seawater is known to work, though currently twice the price of mined uranium. Spiro D. Alexandratos

and Stephen Kung, "Preface to the Special Issue: Uranium in Seawater," *Industrial & Engineering Chemistry Research* 55, no. 15 (April 20, 2016).

83. For the case in favor of the breeder, see Nick Touran, "Nuclear Fuel Will Last Us for 4 Billion Years," WhatIsNuclear.com, whatisnuclear.com/nuclear-sustainability .html.

20. Federal Science and Technology Programs

1. OECD Data, "Gross Domestic Spending on R&D, Total, % of GDP, 2022, data .oecd.org/rd/gross-domestic-spending-on-r-d.htm.
2. These concepts are developed in detail in William B. Bonvillian and Charles Weiss, *Technological Innovation in Legacy Sectors* (New York: Oxford University Press, 2015), 9–10.
3. Benoit Godin, "The Linear Model of Innovation: The Historical Construction of an Analytical Framework," *Science, Technology, and Human Values* 31 no. 6 (November 2006): 659–60.
4. Vannevar Bush, *Science – The Endless Frontier: A Report to the President* (Washington, DC: US Government Printing Office, July 1945), 14.
5. Mark Boroush and Ledia Guci, "Research and Development: US Trends and International Comparisons," National Science Board (NCSES), NSB and NSF, Figure RD-1, "US R&D, by Performing Sector and Source of Funds: 1953–2020," ncses.nsf.gov/pubs/nsb20225/recent-trends-in-u-s-r-d-performance, April 28, 2022.
6. Josh Trapani, "Science and Engineering Indicators 2022: Academic Research and Development (NSB-2021–3)," NSB and NSF, September 14, 2021, 7.
7. Boroush and Guci, "Research and Development."
8. "BGOV 200: Federal Industry Leaders 2022," *Bloomberg Government*, 2023, 1, assets.bbhub.io/bna/sites/3/2023/06/2023-BGOV200-Annual-Report-Rankings_0621.pdf.
9. "BGOV 200: Federal Industry Leaders 2022," 2.
10. "Historical Trends in Federal R&D," American Association for the Advancement of Science (AAAS), aaas.org/programs/r-d-budget-and-policy/historical-trends-fed eral-rd.
11. "Historical Trends in Federal R&D," AAAS.
12. National Center for Science and Engineering Statistics | NSF 24-309, TABLE 27, "Preliminary Federal Obligations for Basic Research, by Agency and Performer: FY 2022." Numbers in Table 20.1 are rounded to the nearest $1 million. Basic R&D expenditures are excluded for the following agencies – Education, DHS, Interior, Justice, State, Treasury, and the Smithsonian – because added together they amount to less than $400 million or less than 1 percent of the total for all agencies. Basic R&D payments to state and local governments as well as payments to non-US performers are excluded because taken together, they account for only 1.8 percent of total federal spending for basic R&D.
13. The Comptroller General of the United States, "NASA Report May Overstate the Economic Benefits of Research and Development Spending," US Government Accountability Office, October 18, 1977.
14. "Historical Trends in Federal R&D: Defense, Nondefense, and Total R&D, 1976–2023," AAAS, updated September 2022, aaas.org/programs/r-d-budget-and-pol icy/historical-trends-federal-rd.
15. Jessie Ellman and Kaitlyn Johnson, "Federal Research and Development Contract Trends and the Supporting Industrial Base, 2000–2015," Center for Strategic and International Studies, September 2016, 13–17.

16. "Trump, Congress Approve Largest US Research Spending Increase in a Decade," *Science*, March 23, 2018.
17. "CHIPS and Science Act of 2022," Office of US Senator Chris van Hollen, July 27, 2022, 5.
18. "Federal Obligations for R&D Increased Nearly 14% in FY 2021, Supported by COVID-19 Pandemic-Related Funding," NSF, National Center for Science and Engineering Statistics, ncses.nsf.gov/pubs/nsf23352#utm_medium=email& utm_source=govdelivery.
19. "In FY 2021, HHS accounted for 94.5% ($33.7 billion) of all [COVID-related] stimulus funds for R&D … Within HHS, the Biomedical Advanced Research and Development Authority (BARDA) alone accounted for 98.6% of the entire department's stimulus funds for R&D," NSF, National Center for Science and Engineering Statistics, ncses.nsf.gov/pubs/nsf23352.
20. NCSES, "Federal R&D Funding, by Budget Function: FYs 2022–24," p. 1, ncses .nsf.gov/pubs/ncses24204.
21. "The NSF Mission," NSF, nsf.gov/pubs/1995/nsf9524/mission.htm.
22. "FY 2020 Agency Financial Report," NSF, November 16, 2020, 4–7.
23. "Federal Obligations for R&D and R&D Plant, by Agency, Performer, and Type of R&D: FY 2020."
24. "About NSF: What We Support," NSF, new.nsf.gov/about#what-we-support-b2a.
25. "About NSF: How We Work," NSF, new.nsf.gov/about#how-we-work-58d.
26. US National Science Foundation, "Fiscal Year 2023 Appropriations," nsf.gov/ about/budget/fy2023/appropriations.
27. "FY 2021 Budget Request to Congress," NSF, February 10, 2020. (Most recent data available.)
28. "CHIPS and Science Act of 2022," Office of Senator Chris van Hollen, July 27, 2022, 5. (Most recent data available.)
29. "About the NSB," NSF, nsf.gov/nsb/about/index.jsp; US Congress, Senate, National Science Foundation Act of 1950, as amended Public Law 81–507, S 247, 81st Cong., adopted May 10, 1950.
30. Subra Suresh, "Research Universities, Innovation, and Growth," *Research-Technology Management* 58, no. 6 (November 1, 2015): 19–23.
31. "Science and Technology Centers (STCs): Integrative Partnerships," NSF, nsf.gov/ od/oia/programs/stc.
32. "About the IUCRC Program," National Science Foundation, iucrc.nsf.gov/about# strategic-engagements.
33. "NSF Collaborations with Federal Agencies and Others," NSF, nsf.gov/about/ partners/fedagencies.jsp.
34. "What We Do: Budget," National Institutes of Health, last modified August 18, 2022, nih.gov/about-nih/what-we-do/budget.
35. "What We Do: Mission and Goals," NIH, last modified July 27, 2017, nih.gov/ about-nih/what-we-do/mission-goals.
36. "What We Do: Mission and Goals," NIH.
37. "Institutes at NIH," National Institutes of Health, nih.gov/institutes-nih.
38. "Impact of NIH Research: Direct Economic Contributions," NIH, March 1, 2023, nih.gov/about-nih/what-we-do/impact-nih-research/serving-society/direct-eco nomic-contributions.
39. "Grants and Funding: Peer Review," NIH, last modified October 24, 2021, grants.nih.gov/grants/peer-review.htm#Overview.
40. "Report on NIH Collaborations with Other HHS Agencies for Fiscal Year 2020," NIH.

41. "2024 Update: NIH's Role in Sustaining the U.S. Economy FY 2023, United for Medical Research.

42. "The Impact of NIH Research," NIH, March 1, 2023, nih.gov/about-nih/what-we-do/impact-nih-research/serving-society/direct-economic-contributions.

43. "FY 2024 President's Budget Request Summary," NASA, 2023, 3–7.

44. "NASA Organizational Chart," NASA, last modified June 5, 2023, nasa.gov/about/org_index.html.

45. "NASA's Science Vision," NASA, science.nasa.gov/about-us/smd-vision; "Science by the Numbers," NASA, science.nasa.gov/about-us.

46. "Science by the Numbers," NASA.

47. "Science by the Numbers," NASA.

48. "Aeronautics Research: ARMD Programs," NASA, nasa.gov/aeroresearch/programs.

49. "NASA's Economic Benefit Reaches All 50 States," NASA, October 27, 2022, nasa.gov/press-release/nasa-s-economic-benefit-reaches-all-50-states.

50. "NIAC 2019 Phase I, Phase II and Phase III Selections" NASA, last modified June 11, 2019, nasa.gov/directorates/spacetech/niac/2019_Phase_I_Phase_II; "NIAC 2022 Phase I and Phase II Selections," NASA, last modified June 13, 2022, nasa.gov/directorates/spacetech/niac/2022; "Prototype Spacecraft Power System for Deep Space Secures $600K NASA Grant," Aerospace Corporation, March 31, 2022.

51. "Space Tech Industry Partnerships," NASA, last modified April 26, 2023, nasa.gov/directorates/spacetech/solicitations/tipping_points.

52. Michael Sheetz, "How NASA Is Evolving through Partnerships with Private Space Companies," CNBC, November 30, 2019.

53. "NASA Spinoff," NASA, spinoff.nasa.gov.

54. National Research Council, *Pathways to Exploration: Rationales and Approaches for a US Program of Human Space Exploration* (Washington, DC: National Academies Press, 2014).

55. See NASA, "Spinoff," 2022, spinoff.nasa.gov/sites/default/files/2022-01/Spinoff.2022.pdf.

56. NASA, "Economic Impact Report," October 2022, 3, nasa.gov/wp-content/uploads/2022/10/nasa_fy21_economic_impact_report_brochure.pdf.

57. Douglas Comstock, Daniel Lockney, and Coleman Glass, "A Sustainable Method for Quantifying the Benefits of NASA Technology Transfer," AIAA Space 2011 Conference and Exposition, September 27–29, 2011.

58. US Congress, House, Omnibus Trade and Competitiveness Act of 1988, HR 4848, 100th Cong., introduced in House June 16, 1988.

59. "NIST General Information," NIST, last modified March 9, 2022, nist.gov/director/pao/nist-general-information.

60. "About the NIST Office of Advanced Manufacturing and Institutes," NIST, last modified February 14, 2017, nist.gov/oam/about-us.

61. "NIST General Information," NIST, last modified March 9, 2022, nist.gov/director/pao/nist-general-information.

62. "Partnerships," NIST, last modified February 11, 2021, nist.gov/tpo/partnerships.

63. "Partnerships," NIST.

64. NIST, "Summary of NIST Impact Study Results," August 23, 2023, nist.gov/tpo/summary-nist-impact-study-results.

65. See "Summary of NIST Impact Study Results," NIST, June 27, 2018: "The BCR is the ratio of the net present value of benefits to the net present value of costs. A positive BCR value indicates the number of dollars in benefits that have resulted

from the technology transfer activity for each of the dollars invested, adjusted for inflation.".

66. "Outputs and Outcomes of NIST Laboratory Research," NIST, June 20, 2021.

67. "Outputs and Outcomes of NIST Laboratory Research."

68. "Summary of NIST Impact Study Results," NIST.

69. "CHIPS and Science Act of 2022," Office of US Senator Chris van Hollen, 5.

70. NCSES, NSF 24-310, Table 10, Federal Budget Authority for Energy (270) R&D and R&D plant: FYs 2022–4: FYs 2022–4, ncses.nsf.gov/data-collections/federal-budget-function/2022–2024#data.

71. "The DOE Laboratory System," Office of Science National Laboratories, Department of Energy, n.d., energy.gov/science/office-science-national-laboratories.

72. "Laboratory Table Summary Report," DOE, FY 2024, 4; Ames National Laboratory, "Critical Materials Institute," DOE, ameslab.gov/cmi.

73. Lawrence Berkeley National Laboratory, "Berkeley Lab by the Numbers," DOE, lbl.gov/about; "Laboratory Table Summary Report," DOE, 38.

74. Lawrence Berkeley National Laboratory, "Our Research," DOE, lbl.gov/research.

75. Energy Frontier Research Center, Homepage, DOE, energyfrontier.us.

76. "Hubs," DOE, energy.gov/science-innovation/innovation/hubs.

77. Office of Electricity, "About the Office of Electricity: Our Mission," DOE, energy.gov/oe/about-office-electricity.

78. Office of Electricity, "Technology Development," DOE, energy.gov/oe/activities/technology-development.

79. Office of Electricity, "About the Office of Electricity: Our Priorities," DOE, energy.gov/oe/about-office-electricity.

80. Office of Chief Financial Officer, "FY 2022 Congressional Budget Request: Budget in Brief," DOE, June 2021, 5.

81. Office of Fossil Energy and Carbon Management, "Mission," DOE, energy.gov/fecm/mission.

82. Office of Nuclear Energy, "Nuclear Reactor Technologies," DOE, energy.gov/ne/nuclear-reactor-technologies; Idaho National Library, Home-page, DOE, inl.gov; "FY 2024 Budget in Brief," DOE, March 2023, 41.

83. Office of Energy Efficiency & Renewable Energy, "Mission," DOE, energy.gov/eere/mission; National Renewable Energy Laboratory, Homepage, DOE, nrel.gov/index.html; "The State of the DOE National Laboratories: 2020 Edition," DOE, 2020, 72; "FY 2024 Budget in Brief," DOE, 31.

84. "ARPA-E History," Advanced Research Projects Agency-Energy (ARPA-E), arpa-e.energy.gov/about/arpa-e-history; "Budget Requests," ARPA-E, arpa-e.energy.gov/about/budget-requests.

85. See "Table ES-2: Fossil Energy Technology Case Studies Slotted in the Matrix Cells That Are Most Relevant Today," in National Research Council, *Energy Research at DOE: Was It Worth It? Energy Efficiency and Fossil Energy Research 1978 to 2000* (Washington, DC: National Academies Press, 2001), 5, 6.

86. Gross economic benefits (undiscounted) less EERE investment costs (undiscounted). Jeff Dowd, "Aggregate Economic Return on Investment in the Office of Energy Efficiency and Renewable Energy," DOE, October 2017, 2.

87. National Research Council, *Energy Research at DOE*, 6.

88. "CHIPS and Science Act of 2022," Office of US Sen. Chris van Hollen, 5.

89. NCSES, NSF 24-310, Table 10, Federal Budget Authority for Energy (270) R&D and R&D plant: FYs 2022–4: FYs 2022–4, ncses.nsf.gov/data-collections/federal-budget-function/2022-2024#data.

90. "Department of Defense Research, Development, Test, and Evaluation (RDT&E): Appropriations Structure," Congressional Research Service, October 7, 2020, 1–5. Since 2018, the Office of Management and Budget no longer counts certain Department of Defense (DOD) funding (budget activities 6.6, 6.7, and 6.8) as a part of total federal R&D; "FY 2024 R&D Appropriations Dashboard," AAAS.

91. National Research Council, *Review of the Future of the US Aerospace Infrastructure and Aerospace Engineering Disciplines to Meet the Needs of the Air Force and the Department of Defense* (Washington, DC: National Academies Press, 2001), 4.

92. John F. Sargent Jr., "Defense Science and Technology Funding: Summary," Congressional Research Service, February 21, 2018, 9–10.

93. Until 2018, this position was called the undersecretary of defense for acquisition, technology, and logistics.

94. "FY 2024 R&D Appropriations Dashboard," AAAS.

95. "Who We Are: DEVCOM ARL Directorates," US Army, arl.army.mil/who-we-are; "Foundational Research," US Army, arl.army.mil/what-we-do/ #competencies.

96. "FY 2024 R&D Appropriations Dashboard," AAAS; Air Force Research Lab (AFRL), "Structure and Locations," US Air Force, afresearchlab.com/about.

97. "FY 2024 R&D Appropriations Dashboard," AAAS.

98. Office of Naval Research, "About ONR Global," Navy, onr.navy.mil/Science-Technology/ONR-Global/About-ONR-Global; Office of Naval Research, "FY2021 ONR Global International Science Prospectus," US Navy, nre.navy .mil/organization/onr-global/about-onr-global.

99. Office of Naval Research, "Naval Research and Development Framework," Navy, 2018.

100. Jacques S. Gansler and William Lucyshyn, "Independent Research and Development (IR&D): The Challenges Continue," Naval Postgraduate School, October 2015, 13.

101. Gansler and Lucyshyn, "Independent Research," 1.

102. "About: Defense Innovation Marketplace," DOD, defenseinnovationmarketplace .dtic.mil/about; "Defense Innovation Marketplace: Communities of Interest," Department of Defense, defenseinnovationmarketplace.dtic.mil/communities-of-interest.

103. "Report to Congress: Fiscal Year 2017, Annual Industrial Capabilities," DOD, March 2018, 35–6.

104. "I-Corps @ DoD Funding Announcement," DOD, April 11, 2018.

105. Aaron Mehta, "Defense Innovation Unit Chief on Keeping the Office Relevant," *Defense News*, January 11, 2021.

106. "About CIA's Impact on Technology," Central Intelligence Agency (CIA), cia.gov/ legacy/museum/exhibit/cias-impact-on-technology; "Important CIA Contributions to Modern Technology over the Last 75 Years," CIA, September 14, 2022.

107. Intelligence Advanced Research Projects Activity (IARPA), "About IARPA," Office of the Director of National Intelligence, iarpa.gov/who-we-are/about-us.

108. IARPA, "IARPA in the News 2019," Office of the Director of National Intelligence, iarpa.gov/index.php/newsroom/iarpa-in-the-news/2019?Start=10.

109. "Army, Air Force Fund Research to Support Multi-domain Operations Superiority," US Army, March 16, 2021.

110. IN-Q-TEL INC: Form 990, ProPublica Nonprofit Explorer, projects. Propublica .org/nonprofits/organizations/522149962/202330459349300808/full; "How We Work," In-Q-Tel, iqt.org/how-we-work.

111. Leanna Garfield, "The CIA's EarthViewer Was Basically the Original Google Earth," *Business Insider*, December 30, 2015.

112. "Our Work," Department of Homeland Security (DHS), dhs.gov/science-and-technology/our-work.

113. "Welcome to the Centers of Excellence," DHS, dhs.gov/science-and-technology/centers-excellence.

114. Science and Technology Directorate, "Snapshot: New App Provides Emergency Response Vehicles with the Fastest, Safest Path to Incident Scenes," DHS, June 4, 2019.

115. Science and Technology Directorate, "Snapshot: Fire Is Out. However, There Is Still Work to Be Done," DHS, May 28, 2019.

116. Science and Technology Directorate, "About S&T," DHS, dhs.gov/science-and-technology/about-st.

117. "S&T Impact: Mobilizing Innovation Critical Incidents," DHS, dhs.gov/science-and-technology/st-impact-mobilizing-innovation-critical-incidents.

118. Nate Bruggeman and Ben Rohrbaugh, "Closing Critical Gaps That Hinder Homeland Security Technology Innovation," Harvard Kennedy School Belfer Center, April 2020.

119. Michael T. Gibbons, "Federally Funded R&D Centers Spent $26.5 Billion on R&D in FY 2022," NSF, National Center for Science and Engineering Statistics, September 6, 2023, ncses.nsf.gov/pubs/nsf23348; "Federal Research and Development (R&D) Funding: FY2024, Congressional Research Service, May 19, 2023, sgp.fas.org/crs/misc/R47564.pdf.

120. Marcy E. Gallo, "Federally Funded Research and Development Centers (FFRDCs): Background and Issues for Congress," Congressional Research Service, April 3, 2020, 20–2.

121. Brett Heinz, "Partnership Intermediary Agreements: A Policy Option for Innovation Orchards," MIT Washington Office, April 2016, 5, 7–9.

21. Federal Proactive Innovation Programs

1. These concepts are developed in detail in William B. Bonvillian and Charles Weiss, *Technological Innovation in Legacy Sectors* (New York: Oxford University Press, 2015), 9–10.

2. Fred Block, "Swimming against the Current: The Rise of a Hidden Developmental State in the United States," *Politics & Society* 36, no. 2 (June 2008): 169–206.

3. Francisco Moris, "Foreign R&D Reported by IT-Related Industries Account for about Half or More of US-Owned R&D Performed in India, China, Canada, and Israel," National Science Foundation National Center for Science and Engineering Statistics, April 28, 2022.

4. Moris, "Foreign R&D."

5. Jody Foster and Rob Brenner, "Clean Air and Technology Innovation: Working Concepts for Promoting Clean Technology Innovation under the Clean Air Act," Duke University Nicholas Institute for Environmental Policy Solutions, June 2013, 3.

6. "Corporate Average Fuel Economy (CAFE) Standards," US Department of Transportation, August 11, 2014.

7. "Tax Credit and Grant Opportunities in the Inflation Reduction Act," Brownstein Client Alert, January 10, 2023, bhfs.com/insights/alerts-articles/2023/tax-credit-and-grant-opportunities-in-the-inflation-reduction-act.

8. J. Silvia Appelt, "OECD R&D Tax Incentives Database, 2021 Edition," Organisation for Economic Co-Operation and Development, February 23, 2022, 18, Panel A.

9. Simon Korwin Milewski, Kiran Jude Fernandes, and Matthew Paul Mount, "Exploring Technological Process Innovation from a Lifecycle Perspective," *International Journal of Operations and Production Management* 35, no. 9 (September 7, 2015): 1312–13.

10. Jonas Nahm and Edward S. Steinfeld, "Scale-Up Nation: China's Specialization in Innovative Manufacturing," *World Development* 54 (February 2014): 288–300.

11. Bonvillian and Weiss, *Technological Innovation*, 53.

12. Joel S. Yudken, *Manufacturing Insecurity: America's Manufacturing Crisis and the Erosion of the US Defense Industrial Base*, High Road Strategies, September 2010, 93. Since the second quarter of 2013, when the US reached a record low of 334,186, that number has risen steadily. Since then, the US has gained 51,327 new factories, to 385,513 through the fourth quarter of 2023. "Establishments," in "Industries at a Glance: Manufacturing: NAICS 31–33," US Bureau of Labor Statistics, bls.gov/iag/tgs/iag31-33.htm.

13. Integrated-Circuit Packaging: Willy Shih, "American Semiconductor Is Taking a Step towards US Domestic Chip Packaging," *Forbes*, January 9, 2022. New Technology: Don Clark, "US Focuses on Invigorating 'Chiplets' to Stay Cutting-Edge in Tech," *New York Times*, May 11, 2023. Advanced Composites: Gary P. Pisano and Willy C. Shih, "Restoring American Competitiveness," *Harvard Business Review*, July–August 2009; Willy Shih, by email, April 11, 2022.

14. Gary P. Pisano and Willy C. Shih, "Does America Really Need Manufacturing?" *Harvard Business Review*, March 2012.

15. Brian Potter, "The Story of Titanium," blog post, July 7, 2003, construction-phys ics.com/p/the-story-of-titanium.

16. Pisano and Shih, "Does America."

17. Comment of unidentified reader on John Keilman, "Why America's Largest Tool Company Couldn't Make a Wrench in America," *Wall Street Journal*, July 22, 2023.

18. Peter L. Singer and William B. Bonvillian, "'Innovation Orchards': Helping Tech Start-ups Scale," Information Technology and Innovation Foundation, March 27, 2017, 9.

19. Bob Zider, "How Venture Capital Works," *Harvard Business Review*, November–December 1998, 131.

20. See Singer and Bonvillian, "Innovation Orchards."

21. "Investments by Sector Q1 1995–Q1 2017," in "*MoneyTree Report*," PricewaterhouseCoopers and CB Insights, 2017.

22. William H. Janey, "The Making of the Digital Revolution," Project Syndicate, February 21, 2020.

23. Marcia Angell and Arnold Seymour Relman, "Patents, Profits and American Medicine: Conflicts of Interest in the Testing and Marketing of New Drugs," *Daedalus*, Spring 2002.

24. Singer and Bonvillian, "Innovation Orchards," 10–11.

25. "Annual Private Investment in Artificial Intelligence," Our World in Data, [Data source: NetBase Quid via AI Index Report, 2023], ourworldindata.org/grapher/private-investment-in-artificial-intelligence; Jeffrey Dastin, "From Meta to Microsoft, AI's Big Moment Is Here," February 3, 2023, reuters.com/technology/

meta-microsoft-ais-big-moment-is-here-2023–02–03; and Krystal Hu, "Exclusive: Google in Talks to Invest in AI Startup Character.AI," November 10, 2023, reuters .com/technology/google-talks-invest-ai-startup-characterai-sources-2023–11–10.

26. Diana Cheung, "Demystifying Generative AI: Introducing the Underlying Technologies & Models of Generative AI," August 30, 2023, codesmith.io/blog/ demystifying-generative-ai-introducing-the-underlying-technologies-models-of-gen erative-ai.

27. "Artificial Intelligence," National Science Foundation, n.d., new.nsf.gov/focus-areas/artificial-intelligence.

28. Nur Ahmed, Muntasir Wahed, and Neil C. Thompson, "The Growing Influence of Industry in AI Research: Industry Is Gaining Control over the Technology's Future," *Science* 379, no. 6635 (March 2, 2023): 884–6, science.org/doi/10.1126/science .ade2420.

29. Alfred Spector, Peter Norvig, and Slav Petrov, "Google's Hybrid Approach to Research," n.d., 2, static.googleusercontent.com/media/research.google.com/en// pubs/archive/38149.pdf; see also, Ashish Vaswani et al., "Attention Is All You Need," 31st Conference on Neural Information Processing Systems (NIPS 2017), Long Beach, CA, 2017, a paper that introduced the transformer to AI after years of incubation at Google, arxiv.org/pdf/1706.03762.pdf; Meta, "FAIR Turns Five: What We've Accomplished and Where We're Headed," December 5, 2018, ai .meta.com/blog/fair-turns-five-what-weve-accomplished-and-where-were-headed; and Meta, "Research: Innovating with the Freedom to Explore, Discover and Apply AI at Scale," n.d., ai.meta.com/research.

30. Ahmed, Wahed, and Thompson, "The Growing Influence of Industry in AI Research."

31. Dastin, "From Meta to Microsoft"; Hu, "Exclusive."

32. Trond Arne Undheim, "The Top 40 Investors in Industrial Tech: How Investments in Transformative Solutions Using AI, Cloud, and Edge Act Like Probiotics for Manufacturing," *Forbes*, April 21, 2022.

33. "Sector Overview: Industrial Technology," White Star Capital, H2 2020, slideshare .net/rozetaa/explore-the-2020-industrial-technology-sector.

34. Lewis M. Branscomb and Philip E. Auerswald, "Between Invention and Innovation: An Analysis of Funding for Early-Stage Technology Development," National Institute of Standards and Technology, November 2002, 35.

35. Singer and Bonvillian, "'Innovation Orchards,'" 22–4.

36. "The Fraunhofer TechBridge Program," Fraunhofer USA, 2, cmi.fraunhofer.org/ techbridge.

37. L. Rafael Reif, "A Better Way to Deliver Innovation to the World," *Washington Post*, May 22, 2015.

38. The Engine, "The Engine Report 2021 and 2022," Massachusetts Institute of Technology, December 15, 2022, 18–19.

39. The Engine, "The Engine Report: 2016–2018," Massachusetts Institute of Technology, April 5, 2019, 18.

40. "Securing America's Future: Realizing the Potential of the Department of Energy's National Laboratories, Volume 1: Executive Report (Prepublication Copy)," Commission to Review the Effectiveness of the National Energy Laboratories, October 23, 2015, 6–7.

41. Scott Andes, Mark Muro, and Matthew Stepp, "Going Local: Connecting the National Labs to their Regions for Innovation and Growth," Brookings/ITIF/ CCEI Advanced Industries Series, September 2014, 5–6.

42. See Office of Energy Efficiency and Renewable Energy, "Lab-Embedded Entrepreneurship Program," DOE, energy.gov/eere/technology-to-market/lab-embedded-entrepreneurship-program.

43. "Cyclotron Road Announces 2023 Cohort of Entrepreneurial Fellow," News from Berkeley Lab, June 22, 2023, newscenter.lbl.gov/2023/06/22/cyclotron-road-announces-2023-cohort-of-entrepreneurial-fellows.

44. "Cyclotron Road Fellows Surpass $1 Billion in Follow-on Funding," Cyclotron Road press release, June 26, 2023, cyclotronroad.lbl.gov/news/cyclotron-road-fellows-surpass-1.

45. Katherine Bourzac et al., "Mosaic Materials: Capitalizing on Carbon Capture," *Nature* 545 (May 18, 2017): S15–S20.

46. "Innovation Corps – National Innovation Network Teams Program: Program Solicitation, NSF 21–552," National Science Foundation, 2021.

47. Singer and Bonvillian, "Innovation Orchards."

48. Office of Science and Technology Policy, "Report to the President on Ensuring American Leadership in Advanced Manufacturing," President's Council of Advisors on Science and Technology, June 2011.

49. President's Council of Advisors on Science and Technology, "Report to the President on Capturing Domestic Competitive Advantage in Advanced Manufacturing," Executive Office of the President, ix.

50. "Report to the President on Capturing Domestic Competitive Advantage in Advanced Manufacturing," 18–20.

51. President's Council of Advisors on Science and Technology, "Report to the President: Accelerating US Advanced Manufacturing," Executive Office of the President, October 2014, 3, 17.

52. Jamison Cocklin, "$70M Youngstown Hub to Spur Manufacturing across US," *Vindicator* (Youngstown, OH), August 17, 2012.

53. "Report to the President: Accelerating US Advanced Manufacturing," 59–60.

54. "Manufacturing USA Highlights Report: A Summary of 2020 Accomplishments and Impacts," National Institute of Standards and Technology, November 2021; "Report to Congress FY 2020," Manufacturing USA, June 2021.

55. Industrial Efficiency & Decarbonization Office, "US Department of Energy Announces 7th Clean Energy Manufacturing Institute," US Department of Energy, June 23, 2022.

56. Section 103, 136, STAT.1389 of the CHIPS and Science Act includes an authorization to create "not more than three" new semiconductor-related institutes. Section 10751 refers to creating the "Low-Emission Steel Manufacturing Research Program," under "Additional Coordination." See US Congress, House, *Chips and Science Act*, HR 4346, 117th Cong., introduced in House July 1, 2021.

57. NIST, "Fact Sheet: Biden–Harris Administration Announces over $5 Billion for the CHIPS and Science Act for Research, Development, and Workforce," February 9, 2024, nist.gov/system/files/documents/2024/02/09/Consortium%20Signing%20Fact%20Sheet.pdf; and NIST, CHIPS Manufacturing USA Institute," 2024, nist.gov/chips/research-development-programs/chips-manufacturing-usa-institute.

58. "Report to Congress FY 2020," Manufacturing USA, June 2021, manufacturingusa.com/reports/mfg-usa-report-congress-fiscal-year-2020.

59. See "Smart Manufacturing of Cement," CESMII: The Smart Manufacturing Institute, cesmii.org/project/sopo-238. [RM]

60. "Report to Congress FY 2020," Manufacturing USA, June 2021, 24.

61. This section draws with permission on the IACMI case study in William B. Bonvillian and Peter L. Singer, "The Advanced Manufacturing Innovation

Institute Model," in *Advanced Manufacturing: The New American Innovation Policies* (Cambridge: The MIT Press, 2017).

62. "Online resource provides free tools, simulations for composite materials," *Perdue University Research Park News*, October 2, 2014.

63. "Project Reports," Institute for Advanced Composites Manufacturing Innovation, iacmi.org/innovation/project-reports.

64. "Working Groups," Institute for Advanced Composites Manufacturing Innovation, iacmi.org/innovation/working-groups.

65. Robert Bedsole et al., "Big Area Additive Manufacturing (BAAM) Materials Development and Reinforcement with Advanced Composites," Final Technical Report to the Department of Energy, IACMI/0015–2017/3.6, 2018, iacmi.org/wp-content/uploads/2021/08/Project-3.6-Local-Motors-Final-Report.pdf.

66. "State of the Institute 2021," Institute for Advanced Composites Manufacturing Innovation, September 24, 2021.

67. Ginger Gardiner, "Additive Manufacturing: Can You Print a Car?" *Composites World*, March 2, 2015.

68. Robert Bedsole et al., "Vertical Axis Wind Turbine (VAWT) with Thermoplastic Composite Blades," Final Technical Report to the Department of Energy, IACMI/R0001-2019/4.5, IACMI, 2019, iacmi.org/wp-content/uploads/2021/08/IACMI-4.5-Final-Project-Report-Approved.pdf.

69. "Report to Congress FY 2021," Manufacturing USA, August 2022, 7.

70. Manufacturing USA, "2022 Manufacturing USA Highlights Report," October 20, 2022, manufacturingusa.com/reports/2022-manufacturing-usa-highlights-report.

71. "2022 Manufacturing USA Highlights."

72. "2022 Manufacturing USA Highlights."

73. "Manufacturing USA: A Third-Party Evaluation of Program Design and Progress," Deloitte, January 2017.

74. "Advanced Manufacturing: Commerce Could Strengthen Collaboration with Other Agencies on Innovation Institutes," US Government Accountability Office, April 2017; "Advanced Manufacturing Innovation Institutes Have Demonstrated Initial Accomplishments, but Challenges Remain in Measuring Performance and Ensuring Sustainability," May 2019; "Advanced Manufacturing: Innovation Institutes Report Technology Progress and Members Report Satisfaction with Their Involvement," December 2021.

75. National Academies of Sciences, *DoD Engagement with Its Manufacturing Innovation Institutes: Phase 2 Study Final Report* (Washington, DC: National Academies Press, 2021), 2.

76. National Science and Technology Council, "A National Strategic Plan for Advanced Manufacturing," Executive Office of the President, February 2012, 11; Advanced Manufacturing National Program Office, "National Network for Manufacturing Innovation Program Strategic Plan," National Science and Technology Council of the Executive Office of the President, February 2016, 8; "Manufacturing USA: An Update on Program Status, Congressional Reauthorization and Key 2020 Initiatives," National Institute of Standards and Technology, February 12, 2020.

77. Over the 10 annual budgets from its founding in 2012 to 2021, MFG-USA (formerly the National Network for Manufacturing Innovation) received federal funding averaging $170 million per year. Source: US Government Accountability Office (GAO), "Advanced Manufacturing: Innovation Institutes Report Technology Progress and Members Report Satisfaction with Their Involvement," Accessible Version, GAO-22–103979, December 2021, 4. The CHIPS Act authorizes (but does not appropriate) $829M over five years, or $166M per year. Source: House

Committee on Science, Space, and Technology, "CHIPS and Science Act of 2022," 1, vanhollen.senate.gov/imo/media/doc/CHIPS%20and%20Science%20Act%20of%202022%20Summary.pdf, 5. It is likely that the money, if Congress appropriates it, will run through existing budget lines in the three agencies and will replace, not supplement, existing funds. It is impossible to know if these funds will materialize because they are only authorized, not appropriated, and will require separate annual legislative vehicles to fund them in the out years.

78. The Fraunhofer employs more than 30,000 technical staff in its 76 Institutes. See "Income Statement for the Financial Year 2021" in "Annual Report 2021: Knowledge and Prosperity: Impact and Innovation," Fraunhofer, January 2022, 126. Even if, for full apples-to-apples comparison to the Fraunhofer Institutes that service SMMs as well as larger companies, the MEP's annual $460 million is added to M-USA's $166 million, Germany's spending for these purposes as a percentage of GDP and per capita still dwarfs that of the US.

79. For a more complete diagram of the various federal programs and the technology readiness levels covered by each program, see National Academies of Sciences, Engineering, and Medicine, *A New Vision for Center-Based Engineering Research* (Washington, DC: National Academies Press, 2017), 14.

80. John F. Sargent Jr., "Manufacturing USA: Advanced Manufacturing Institutes and Network," Congressional Research Service, October 3, 2022, 25.

81. Sargent, "Manufacturing USA," 25.

82. These concerns were raised in a number of reports, such as: "Manufacturing USA: A Third-Party Evaluation of Program Design and Progress," Deloitte; National Academies of Sciences, Engineering, and Medicine, *Revisiting the Manufacturing USA Institutes: Proceedings of a Workshop* (Washington, DC: National Academies Press, 2019); National Academies of Sciences, Engineering, and Medicine, *Strategic Long-Term Participation by DoD in Its Manufacturing USA Institutes* (Washington, DC: National Academies Press, 2019).

22. Industrial Policy for Advanced Manufacturing

1. "Manufacturing Sector: Multifactor Productivity," Federal Reserve Bank of St. Louis, fred.stlouisfed.org/series/MPU9900013#0.

2. "From Atoms to Materials: Algorithmic Breakthrough Unlocks Path to Sustainable Technologies," University of Liverpool, July 5, 2023.

3. "Industry 4.0: An Introduction," Deloitte, 2015. "Mobile Digital Communications," Augmented reality, and Generative design do not appear in original.

4. Timothy Aeppel, "Robots Set Their Sights on a New Job: Sewing Blue Jeans," Reuters, December 12, 2022.

5. Centre for the New Economy and Society, "The Future of Jobs Report 2018," World Economic Forum, September 17, 2018, ix. William B. Bonvillian and Peter L. Singer, "Workforce Education and Advanced Manufacturing," in *Advanced Manufacturing: The New American Innovation Policies* (Cambridge, MA: MIT Press, 2017).

6. Microsoft, Intel, and IoT Analytics, "IoT Signals Manufacturing Spotlight," August 2022, pp. 3 and 14, info.microsoft.com/ww-landing-IoT-signals-manufacturing-spotlight.html.

7. William Bonvillian and Charles Weiss, *Technological Innovation in Legacy Sectors* (New York: Oxford University Press, 2015).

8. See Bonvillian and Singer, "Advanced Manufacturing Emerges at the Federal Level," in *Advanced Manufacturing*.

9. Harry Moser, Reshoring Initiative, email to coauthor Ian Fletcher, 2018.
10. Robert Atkinson, "US Manufacturing Productivity Is Falling, and It's Cause for Alarm," *IndustryWeek*, July 12, 2021.
11. "Disruptive Technologies: Advances That Will Transform Life, Business, and the Global Economy," McKinsey Global Institute, May 2013, 105.
12. SmarTech Quarterly Data Service, cited in Michael Molitch-Hou, "3D Printing Industry Worth $13.5B, Will Reach $25B by 2025," 3DPrint.com, March 21, 2023.
13. It has done somewhat better in sectors such as IT, healthcare, the military, and greentech.
14. Office of Advocacy, "2022 Small Business Profile," US Small Business Administration, August 2022, 4.
15. Paul Eisenstein, "As Trump Stresses Manufacturing Jobs, How Important Are Labor Costs for Automakers?" NBC News, February 6, 2017. Susan Helper, Kyoung Won Park, Jennifer Kuan, et al., "The US Auto Supply Chain at a Crossroads," Case Western Reserve University, August 18, 2011, 4.
16. "Supply Chain Innovation: Strengthening America's Small Manufacturers," Executive Office of the President and US Department of Commerce, March 2015, 2.
17. GAO, "Federal Efforts to Enhance the Competitiveness of Small Manufacturers," Report to the Ranking Minority Member, Committee on Small Business, US Senate, November 1991, 3.
18. MEP, "FY 2022 NIST MEP Economic Impact," 3 (Note 3); John F. Sargent Jr., "Federal Research and Development (R&D) Funding: FY2022," Congressional Research Service, January 19, 2022.
19. MEP, "FY 2022 NIST MEP Economic Impact."
20. MEP, "Annual Report 2021," NIST, January 2022, 6.
21. Brian Pittelko, Iryna Lendel, Kassim Mbwana, and Kami Ehrich, "The National-Level Economic Impact of the Manufacturing Extension Partnership (MEP): Estimates for Fiscal Year 2022," W. E. Upjohn Institute, March 13, 2023, 2.
22. MEP, "FY 2022 NIST MEP Economic Impact."
23. MEP, "FY 2022 NIST MEP Economic Impact."
24. National Research Council, *21st Century Manufacturing: The Role of the Manufacturing Extension Partnership Program* (Washington, DC: National Academies Press, 2013), 45.
25. MEP, "FY 2022 NIST MEP Economic Impact," NIST, January 2023; MEP, "ISO and Quality Management," NIST, nist.gov/mep/iso-and-quality-management; GAO, "Manufacturing Extension Partnership: Most Federal Spending Directly Supports Work with Manufacturers, but Distribution Could Be Improved," Report to Congressional Committees, March 2014, 2.
26. "Your Manufacturing Growth Partners," MAGNET, manufacturingsuccess.org/meet-the-team.
27. Missouri Enterprise, "ERP Implementation Helps Farm Equipment Manufacturer Support Future Growth," NIST, May 11, 2018.
28. "Automotive Supplier Achieves IATF 16949:2016 Certification and Expands Business," NIST, August 4, 2022.
29. "Product Development System Design and Implementation," NIST, June 2, 2020.
30. John F. Sargent Jr., "The Manufacturing Extension Partnership Program," Congressional Research Service, August 10, 2018, 4; National Research Council, *21st Century Manufacturing*, 103–6.
31. "Supplier Scouring," MEP National Network, nist.gov/system/files/documents/2020/04/13/MEPNN%20Supplier%20Scouting%202020–508.pdf.
32. Sargent, "Manufacturing Extension," 16.

33. Mike Simpson, "Strengthening US Manufacturing: Manufacturing USA and the Manufacturing Extension Partnership," NIST, March 24, 2022; "About Us," Manufacturing USA, manufacturingusa.com/about-us.
34. Sargent, "Manufacturing Extension;" MEP, "MEP-Assisted Technology and Technical Resource (MATTR)," NIST, nist.gov/mep/matter.
35. MEP, "Annual Report 2020," 37; Sargent, "Manufacturing Extension," 13–14; MEP, "NIST MEP Competitive Awards Program (CAP)," NIST, nist.gov/mep/nist-mep-competitive-awards-program-cap.
36. MEP, "Annual Report 2020," 28; MEP, "The Defense Manufacturing Supply Chain: Critical to the US Economy and National Security," NIST, nist.gov/mep/manufacturing-infographics/defense-manufacturing-supply-chain.
37. MEP, Annual Report 2021, 22.
38. "Biden–Harris Administration Awards $20 Million to Make Domestic Supply Chains More Resilient," NIST News, June 9, 2023.
39. GAO, "Manufacturing Enterprise Partnership: Centers Cite Benefits from Funding Change, but Impacts Hard to Distinguish from Other Factors," Report to Congressional Committees, 2019, 6.
40. US Congress, House, Coronavirus Aid, Relief, and Economic Security Act, HR 748, 116th Congress, introduced in House, January 24, 2019.
41. Sargent, "Manufacturing Extension," 3.
42. Sargent, "Manufacturing Extension," Summary and 1.
43. MEP, "Annual Report 2020," 1.
44. Petra Mitchell, "Looking Ahead to Biden Administration Manufacturing Policies," Pittsburgh Technology Council, February 3, 2021.
45. Office of Management and Budget, "Summary of the President's Discretionary Funding Request," Executive Office of the President, April 9, 2021, 3.
46. Stephen Ezell and Stefan Koester, "Three Cheers for the CHIPS and Science Act of 2022! Now, Let's Get Back to Work," Information Technology and Innovation Foundation, July 29, 2022.
47. Ezell and Koester, "Three Cheers." House Committee on Appropriations, "Consolidated Appropriations Act, 2023: Summary of Appropriations Provisions by Subcommittee," US House, December 2022, 4.

23. Micro-governance of Industrial Policy

1. 2021 IMF data. Wikipedia, "List of Countries by GDP (PPP) per Capita," accessed 2022, en.wikipedia.org/wiki/List_of_countries_by_GDP_(PPP)_per_capita.
2. Allen Hsu, "ITRI Pushes Technology Sector to New Frontier of Innovation," Taiwan Today, October 18, 2007, taiwantoday.tw/news.php?unit=23,45&post=68185.
3. Tim Kastelle, Mei-Chih Hu, and Mark Dodgson, "Innovation in Taiwan: What Is Next?" Innovation: Management, Policy and Practice 14, no. 4 (December 2013): 397.
4. Interview with Lee Chong Chou, Director, STAG Biotechnology Program, cited in Tommy Shih, "Scrutinizing a Policy Ambition to Make Business Out of Science: Lessons from Taiwan," Uppsala University Department of Business Studies, 2009, 4.
5. National Research Council, 21st Century Manufacturing: The Role of the Manufacturing Extension Partnership Program (Washington, DC: National Academies Press, 2013), 297.
6. Patarapong Intarakumnerd and Akira Goto, "Role of Public Research Institutes in National Innovation Systems in Industrialized Countries: The Cases of Fraunhofer,

NIST, CSIRO, AIST, and ITRI," Research Institute of Economy, Trade and Industry, March 2016, 29–30.

7. Top 100 Global Innovators 2023," Clarivate, February 2023, 13; Frank Shiu, "The Present and the Future of TW-EU Cooperation," Industrial Technology Research Institute, 2022, 5. Clarivate's Top 100 Global Innovators are selected for excellence based on volume of patents, influence, success, globalization, and technical distinctiveness. Other prize-winning innovators in 2023 included Qualcomm and Siemens.

8. Hsu, "ITRI Pushes." ITRI has 12 R&D campuses located in Taiwan, each of which specializes in specific research themes linked to local industrial activities and competencies. Chan-Yuan Wong, Mei-Chih Hu, and Jyh-Wen Shiu, "Collaboration between Public Research Institutes and Universities: A Study of Industrial Technology Research Institute, Taiwan," *Science, Technology and Society* 20, no. 2 (July 2015): 162.

9. Taiwan only began to reform its lax intellectual property laws and approach the standards of developed countries in 1983, and then only under intense pressure from the US. Ten years later in 1993, the US Trade Representative added Taiwan to its "priority watch list" of countries that failed to protect US intellectual property rights. In 2020, a major Taiwanese semiconductor company, United Microelectronics Corporation, pleaded guilty to criminal theft of trade secrets. See US Attorney's Office, Northern District of California, "Taiwan Company Pleads Guilty to Trade Secret Theft in Criminal Case Involving PRC State-Owned Company," US Department of Justice, October 28, 2020. See also Y. Kurt Chang, "Special 301 and Taiwan: A Case Study of Protecting United States Intellectual Property in Foreign Countries," *Northwestern Journal of International Law and Business* 15, no. 1 (1994): 217.

10. Ling-Fei Lin, "Taiwanese IT Pioneers: Robert H. C. Tsao," Computer History Museum, February 17, 2011.

11. Ling-Fei Lin, "Taiwanese IT Pioneers: D. Y. (Ding-Yuan) Yang," Computer History Museum, February 23, 2011.

12. "Innovations and Applications," Industrial Technology Research Institute, accessed 2023, itri.org.tw/english/ListStyle.aspx?DisplayStyle=01&SiteID=1&MmmID=1037333526356626457.

13. Intarakumnerd and Goto, "Role of Public," 19, 31.

14. "ITRI Established Industry, Science and Technology International Strategy Center," Industrial Technology Research Institute, July 27, 2018.

15. Kastelle, Hu and Dodgson, "Innovation in Taiwan."

16. Wong, Hu, and Shiu, "Collaboration," Industrial Technology Research Institute, accessed 2022, itri.org.tw/english/ListStyle.aspx?DisplayStyle=04&SiteID=1&MmmID=1037333533642360150; "Media Center," Industrial Technology Research Institute, accessed 2022, itri.org.tw/english/ListStyle.aspx?DisplayStyle=06&SiteID=1&MmmID=617731531241750114.

17. Industrial Technology Research Institute, "R&D Cooperation with Oxford Instruments," *ITRI Today* 96 (Spring 2019).

18. P. L., "World Patent War 1.0," *Economist*, December 19, 2011.

19. "Technology Transfer and Law Center," Industrial Technology Research Institute, accessed 2022, itri.org.tw/english/Technology-Transfer-and-Law-Center?CRWP=620145305652171365.

20. In ITRI's Biomedical Technology and Device Research Laboratories, for example, nearly 90 percent of the scientists, engineers and staff hold advanced degrees, including more than 100 PhDs. See "ITRI Overview," Industrial Technology Research Institute,

accessed 2022, itri.org.tw/english/ListStyle.aspx?DisplayStyle=20&SiteID=1& MmmID=617731521661672477; "Biomedical Technology and Device Research Laboratories," Industrial Technology Research Institute, accessed 2022, itri.org.tw/ english/Biomedical-Technology-and-Device-Research-Laboratries?CRWP= 617753101734067544#.

21. Barry Lam, who served as president of Kinpo Electronics, asserted in a 2011 interview that "This was the fundamental competitive edge of Taiwan. The foundation was strong. How should I put it? Employees are extremely loyal to companies they work for due to the profound Confucian influence on Taiwanese people. We had tremendous motivation. We could accomplish anything we set our hearts on." See Ling-Fei Lin, "Taiwanese IT Pioneers: Barry (Pak-Lee) Lam," Computer History Museum, March 2, 2011.

22. Alan Patterson, "Oral History of Morris Chang," Computer History Museum, August 24, 2007; Tekla S. Perry, "Morris Chang: Foundry Father," *IEEE Spectrum*, April 19, 2011.

23. John A. Mathews, "The Hsinchu Model: Collective Efficiency, Increasing Returns and Higher-Order Capabilities in the Hsinchu Science-Based Industry Park, Taiwan," 20th Anniversary Conference, Tsinghua University, Hsinchu, Taiwan, Chinese Society for Management of Technology, December 10, 2010.

24. Readers of Mead's work included Morris Chang, the founder of TSMC, who cited his influence. See Patterson, "Oral History of Morris Chang."

25. See Industrial Technology Research Institute, "ITRI-Stanford Platform Fosters Innovation and Entrepreneurship," *ITRI Today* 96 (Fall 2019).

26. "ITRI Annual Report 2018," Industrial Technology Research Institute, 2019, 2.

27. Chang-Yuan Liu, "Government's Role in Developing a High-Tech Industry: The Case of Taiwan's Semiconductor Industry," *Technovation* 13, no. 5 (July 1993): 306.

28. Wong, Hu, and Shiu, "Collaboration," 163.

29. A. C. Tung, "Taiwan's Semiconductor Industry: What the State Did and Did Not," *Review of Development Economics* 5, no. 2 (June 2001): 279.

30. Yeo Lin and Rajah Rasiah, "Human Capital Flows in Taiwan's Technological Catch Up in Integrated Circuit Manufacturing," *Journal of Contemporary Asia* 44, no. 1 (January 2014): 77.

31. See "College: Main Courses," Industrial Technology Research Institute, accessed 2022, college.itri.org.tw/en.

32. Lin, "D. Y. (Ding-Yuan) Yang."

33. Lin and Rasiah, "Human Capital," 72.

34. Lin and Rasiah, "Human Capital," 75.

35. Mark Dodgson et al., "The Evolving Nature of Taiwan's National Innovation System: The Case of Biotechnology Innovation Networks," *Research Policy* 37, no. 3 (April 2008): 435.

36. The TDPs identify and draw up plans to promote new technologies and seek to coordinate public and private research resources to achieve their objectives. See Shih, "Scrutinizing a Policy Ambition to Make Business Out of Science," 82.

37. Robert Wade, *Governing the Market: Economic Theory and the Role of Government in East Asian Economic Development* (Princeton, NJ: Princeton University Press, 1990), 247.

38. Wade, *Governing*, 98.

39. Industrial Technology Research Institute, "ITRI Celebrates Its 46th Anniversary," *ITRI Today* 98 (Fall 2019). Also, Intarakumnerd and Goto, "Role of Public," 31.

40. "ITRI Annual Report 2021," Industrial Technology Research Institute, 2022, 14.

41. National Research Council, *21st Century Manufacturing*, 299–300.
42. "Taiwan's Technology Success Underappreciated: Canadian Scientist," *Focus Taiwan*, July 24, 2010.
43. Lin and Rasiah, "Human Capital," 70.
44. Otto Chui Chau Lin, *Innovation and Entrepreneurship: Choice and Challenge* (Singapore: World Scientific, 2018), 147.
45. "About Fraunhofer," Fraunhofer-Gesellschaft, accessed June 20, 2023, fraunhofer.de/en/about-fraunhofer.html.
46. "Annual Report 2021," Fraunhofer-Gesellschaft, 2022, 31.
47. In 2011, in a report that eventually led to the creation of Manufacturing USA, the President's Council of Advisors on Science and Technology (PCAST) stated, "Germany's Fraunhofer Program offers a potential model for shared infrastructure facilities and resources." President's Council of Advisors on Science and Technology, "Report to the President on Ensuring American Leadership in Advanced Manufacturing," Executive Office of the President, June 2011.
48. "Institutes and Research Establishments in Germany," Fraunhofer-Gesellschaft, fraunhofer.de/en/institutes/institutes-and-research-establishments-in-germany.
49. National Research Council, *21st Century Manufacturing*, 247–8.
50. In 2005, the FhG entered into a public–private partnership with Advanced Micro Devices and Infineon, establishing a new research center, the Center for Nanoelectronic Technologies (CNT) in Dresden, with the companies operating the center. "Germany Opens Nanoelectronics Center in Dresden," Deutsche Presse-Agentur, May 31, 2005.
51. Oliver Mauroner, "Innovation Clusters and Public Policy: The Case of a Research-Driven Cluster in Germany," *American Journal of Industrial and Business Management* 5, no. 12 (December 2015).
52. Mauroner, "Innovation Clusters."
53. "Tomorrow's Technologies. Today," Fraunhofer Institute for Production Systems and Design Technology IPK, aprimin.cl/site/wp-content/uploads/2015/06/Fraunhofer-IPK-Profile.pdf.
54. Office of Technology Policy, "The Fraunhofer Society: A Unique German Contract Research Organization Comes to America," US Department of Commerce, October 1998, 11–12, 17.
55. Jordi Franch Parella and Gemma Carmona Hernández, "The German Business Model: The Role of the Mittelstand," *Journal of Management Policies and Practices* 6, no. 1 (June 2018): 10–16.
56. William Brown, "Focus: Britain's Plan to Revitalise Its Industry with Bright Ideas Was Inspired by a German Concept. But the Second-Hand Version Is a Poor Copy of the Original – German Innovation, British Imitation," *New Scientist*, November 21, 1992.
57. National Research Council, *21st Century Manufacturing*, 241.
58. "Manufacturing, Value Added (% of GDP)," World Bank, accessed December 27, 2022, data.worldbank.org/indicator/NV.IND.MANF.ZS.
59. "Data and Facts," Fraunhofer Institute for Solar Energy Systems ISE, accessed June 20, 2023, ise.fraunhofer.de/en/about-us/data-and-facts.html.
60. "About Fraunhofer ISE," Fraunhofer Institute for Solar Energy Systems ISE, accessed December 27, 2022, ise.fraunhofer.de/en/about-us.html; "PV-TEC – Photovoltaic Technology Evaluation Center," Fraunhofer Institute for Solar Energy Systems ISE, accessed December 27, 2022, ise.fraunhofer.de/en/rd-infrastructure/tecs/pv-tec.html.

61. "Annual Report 2017/2018," Fraunhofer Institute for Manufacturing Technology and Advanced Materials IFAM, 2, 8, accessed December 27, 2022, ifam.fraun hofer.de/en/Publications/Annual_Reports.html.
62. National Research Council, *21st Century Manufacturing*, 224.
63. National Research Council, *21st Century Manufacturing*, 257–9.
64. See "Patents/Licenses," Fraunhofer-Gesellschaft, accessed December 27, 2022, fraunhofer.de/en/about-fraunhofer/profile-structure/facts-and-figures/patents-lcenses.html.
65. "Annual Report 2021," Fraunhofer-Gesellschaft, 125. Subsequent annual reports lack detailed data.
66. National Research Council, *21st Century Manufacturing*, 262–3.
67. "Annual Report 2017/2018," Fraunhofer-Gesellschaft, 16.
68. "Fraunhofer Group for Microelectronics," Fraunhofer-Gesellschaft, accessed December 27, 2022, fraunhofer.de/en/institutes/institutes-and-research-estab lishments-in-germany/fraunhofer-groups/microelectronics.html; "Research Fab Microelectronics Germany (FMD)," Fraunhofer-Gesellschaft, accessed December 27, 2022, fraunhofer.de/en/institutes/cooperation/research-fab-microelectronics-ger many.html.
69. "Fraunhofer Cluster of Excellence," Fraunhofer-Gesellschaft, accessed December 27, 2022, fraunhofer.de/en/institutes/institutes-and-research-establishments-in-ger many/cluster-of-excellence.html; "Fraunhofer Cluster of Excellence Programmable Materials," Fraunhofer-Gesellschaft, accessed 2022, fraunhofer.de/en/institutes/ institutes-and-research-establishments-in-germany/cluster-of-excellence/program mable-materials.html.
70. "Annual Report 2016/2017," Fraunhofer Institute for Embedded Systems and Communication Technologies ESK, 2018, 23.
71. Hermann Hauser, "The Current and Future Role of Technology and Innovation Centres in the UK," a report for Lord Mandelson, Secretary of State, Department for Business Innovation and Skills, 2010, 9–10.
72. Markus Winnes and Uwe Schimank, "National Report: Federal Republic of Germany," Max Planck Society, 1999, 14. Any changes to the status quo can be vetoed by adversely affected *Länder* governments.
73. Some of the FhG's capital outlays for infrastructure are reported separately from its operating results. See "Annual Report 2011," Fraunhofer-Gesellschaft, 19–20.
74. "A Modern Industrial Policy," German Federal Ministry for Economic Affairs and Climate Action, accessed June 21, 2023, bmwk.de/Redaktion/EN/Dossier/modern-industry-policy.html.
75. US Congress, House, Committee on Science, Should Congress Establish "ARPA-E," the Advanced Research Projects Agency-Energy? 109th Cong., 2nd sess., March 9, 2006, 52–9.
76. "Innovation at DARPA," Defense Advanced Research Projects Agency (DARPA), July 2016, 1.
77. Regina E. Dugan and Kaigham J. Gabriel, "'Special Forces' Innovation: How DARPA Attacks Problems," *Harvard Business Review*, October 2013.
78. William Thomas, "DOD Budget: FY22 Outcomes and FY23 Request," American Institute of Physics, June 15, 2022; Marcy E. Gallo, "Defense Advanced Research Projects Agency: Overview and Issues for Congress," Congressional Research Service, August 19, 2021.
79. Sharon Weinberger, *The Imagineers of War: The Untold Story of DARPA, the Pentagon Agency That Changed the World* (New York: Alfred A. Knopf, 2017).

80. Title V of the Federal Acquisition Streamlining Act of 1994 establishes numerous strictures with respect to hiring and management of federal employees. Among other things, it requires applicants to undergo a competition with other applicants pursuant to a merit system administered by the Office of Personnel Management.

81. "Breakthrough Technologies for National Security," DARPA, March 2015, 32.

82. "Breakthrough Technologies," DARPA, March 2015, 20.

83. "Breakthrough Technologies," DARPA, 28–9.

84. "Disruptioneering: Streamlining the Process of Scientific Discovery," DARPA, August 11, 2017.

85. William Chappell in "Innovation at DARPA," DARPA, July 2016, 22–3.

86. Gallo, "Defense Advanced Research Projects Agency," 3–4; "DARPA Offices," DARPA, accessed June 19, 2023, darpa.mil/about-us/offices.

87. "Tactical Technology Office (TTO)," DARPA, accessed 2022, darpa.mil/about-us/offices/tto.

88. Jeffrey Mervis, "What Makes DARPA Tick?" *Science* 351, no. 6273 (February 5, 2016).

89. William B. Bonvillian, "The Connected Science Model for Innovation: The DARPA Role," in *21st Century Innovation Systems for Japan and the United States: Lessons from a Decade of Change: Report of a Symposium*, Sadao Nagaoka et al., eds. (Washington, DC: National Academies Press, 2009), 224.

90. Nils Sandell quoted in "Innovation at DARPA," DARPA, July 2016, 9.

91. Jane Alexander quoted in Mervis, "What Makes DARPA Tick?"

92. Mike Walker in "Innovation at DARPA," DARPA, July 2016, 2.

93. Congress granted DARPA OT authority in 1989. US Congress, House, *National Defense Authorization Act for Fiscal Years 1992 and 1993*, HR 2100, 102nd Cong., introduced in House April 25, 1991.

94. Tony Tether, "Statement before the Subcommittee on Terrorism, Unconventional Threats and Capabilities, House Armed Services Committee, US House of Representatives," DARPA, March 13, 2008, 1–2.

95. "Innovation at DARPA," 9.

96. Tether, "Statement before the Subcommittee," 3.

97. Kristin Suleng, "DARPA's Failures Are the Ones That Did Not Leave a Foundation of Good Research," Conec, June 21, 2017.

98. Richard H. van Atta and Michael J. Lippitz et al., "Transformation and Transition: DARPA's Role in Fostering an Emerging Revolution in Military Affairs, Volume I – Overall Assessment," Institute for Defense Analyses, April 2003.

99. Van Atta and Lippitz, "Transformation and Transition," S-1.

100. John Main in "Innovation at DARPA," DARPA, July 2016, 12.

101. For examples of current BAAs, see "Office-Wide Broad Agency Announcements," DAR-PA, accessed December 27, 2022, darpa.mil/work-with-us/office-wide-broad-agency-announcements.

102. William Regli, "Innovation at DARPA," DARPA, July 2016, 12.

103. Erica R. H. Fuchs, "Rethinking the Role of the State in Technology Development: DARPA and the Case for Embedded Network Governance," *Research Policy* 39 (June 2010): 1140.

104. "[T]he community, energized and inspired by DARPA work, may ultimately produce innovations that go well beyond the ambitious but limited agency programs." "Innovation at DARPA," 15.

105. Van Atta and Lippitz, "Transformation and Transition," 2.

106. Fuchs, "Rethinking," 1140–1.

107. Jim Kurose, "Dear Colleague Letter: NSF Support for DARPA Spectrum Collaboration Challenge (SC2) Participants," National Science Foundation, July 21, 2006.

108. Van Atta and Lippitz, "Transformation and Transition," S-1, VII-19; Richard H. van Atta, "DARPA: The Innovation Icon at 60," in *DARPA: Defense Advanced Research Projects Agency:1958–2018*, ed. Ivan Amato et al. (Tampa, FL: Faircount Media Group, 2018), 18.

109. Having convinced senior DOD officials of the value of DARPA-developed technologies, those officials "pushed the US Air Force to adopt both stealth aircraft and unmanned aerial vehicles, which DARPA programs had developed and demonstrated." See Van Atta, "DARPA: The Innovation Icon at 60," 18.

110. Tom Masiello, "DARPA/AEO Overview," NDIA Air Armament Symposium, November 1, 2017, 7.

111. "Military Operational Liaisons," DARPA, accessed June 20, 2023, darpa.mil/work-with-us/for-government-and-military/liasons.

112. Tether, "Statement before the Subcommittee," 5.

113. Weinberger, *The Imagineers of War*, 353–7.

114. US Congress, House, Subcommittee on Energy and Environment, *Establishing the Advanced Research Projects Agency-Energy*, 110th Cong., 1st sess., April 26, 2007, 21–8.

115. In the mid-1990s, AEP had a budget of around $10 million. In 1995, it was incorporated in DOE's Computational and Technology Research Program. Beginning in 1998, DOE starved the office for funding, requesting only $3 million in its FY 1999 budged. DOE ordered the cancellation of several projects and prohibited the initiation of "new novel energy-related concepts." National Academies of Sciences, Engineering, and Medicine, *An Assessment of ARPA-E* (Washington, DC: National Academies Press, 2017), 23.

116. "Biden–Harris Administration Launches American Innovation Effort to Create Jobs and Tackle the Climate Crisis," The White House, February 11, 2021.

117. Chris Atkinson, "Advanced Research Projects Agency-Infrastructure (ARPA-I)," US Department of Transportation (DOE), January 2023, 7.

118. "Team Directory," Advanced Research Projects Agency – Energy (ARPA-E), accessed January 2, 2023, arpa-e.energy.gov/about/team-directory.

119. Paul R. Lawrence and Mark A. Abramson, *What Government Does: How Political Executives Manage* (Lanham, MD: Rowman & Littlefield, 2014), 139.

120. Pay levels may be set by the director up to Level II of the Office of Personnel Management; Executive Schedule (Ex-11). Additional payments can be made, subject to limitation formula. *Advanced Research Project Agency – Energy*, § 16538, (g)(3)(A)(ii) and (iii). See National Academies of Sciences, *An Assessment of ARPA-E*, 2–4.

121. National Academies of Sciences, *An Assessment of ARPA-E*, 32.

122. National Academies of Sciences, *An Assessment of ARPA-E*, 9.

123. National Academies of Sciences, *An Assessment of ARPA-E*, 42.

124. William Bonvillian, "DARPA and Its ARPA-E and IARPA Clones: A Unique Innovation Organization Model," *Industrial and Corporate Change* 27, no. 5 (October 2018): 908–9. T2M advisors are recruited from private companies active in the energy field and from consultancies advising such companies. See "Tech-to-Market," ARPA-E, accessed January 2, 2023, arpa-e.energy.gov/?q=about/arpa-e-team/tech-to-market-team.

125. National Academies of Sciences, *An Assessment of ARPA-E*, 37–40.

126. Response of ARPA-E to question from Dr. Paul Broun, Chairman. US Congress, House, Committee on Science, Space and Technology, *Investigations and Oversight Subcommittee* Hearing – *A Review of the Advanced Research Projects Agency – Energy,* 112th Cong., 2nd sess., January 24, 2012.
127. National Academies of Sciences, *An Assessment of ARPA-E,* 34.
128. National Academies of Sciences, *An Assessment of ARPA-E,* 34.
129. National Academies of Sciences, *An Assessment of ARPA-E,* 34–6.
130. National Academies of Sciences, *An Assessment of ARPA-E,* 42.
131. National Academies of Sciences, *An Assessment of ARPA-E,* 41.
132. *Advanced Research Project Agency – Energy,* § 16538, (f).
133. National Academies of Sciences, *An Assessment of ARPA-E,* 41.
134. National Academies of Sciences, *An Assessment of ARPA-E,* 68.
135. A 2011 assessment of ARPA-E concluded that the agency had met with success in forging a working alliance with EERE, a much larger $1.5–2 billion a year applied agency. See William Bonvillian and Richard Van Atta, "ARPA-E and DARPA: Applying the DARPA Model to Energy Innovation," *Journal of Technology Transfer* 36, no. 5 (October 2011): 491.
136. US Congress, House, Committee on Science, Space and Technology, A Review of the Advanced Research Projects Agency – Energy.
137. Megan Geuss, "Trump Really Wants to Kill Arpa-E; Federal Agency Says That's Folly," Ars Technica, March 14, 2018.
138. Varun Mehra, "ARPA-E Is Here to Stay," *Science Progress,* January 22, 2013.
139. National Academies of Sciences, *An Assessment of ARPA-E,* 116–19.
140. $4 million: "Federal Investment in Research and Development Spurs U.S. Competitiveness," Pew Charitable Trusts, February 2015, 12, pewtrusts.org/-/media/assets/2015/02/cleanenergy_combined_fact_sheets.pdf. $3M: Eric Wesoff, "DOE's Chu and SunPower's Swanson on the SunShot Initiative," GreenTechMedia, February 4, 2011, greentechmedia.com/articles/read/does-chu-and-sunpowers-swanson-on-the-27m-sunshine-initiative. $150 million: Ucilia Wang, "DOE Loves Solar, Offers $150 Million Loan Guarantee to 1366 Technologies," *Forbes,* June 17, 2011.
141. Peter Kelly-Detwiller, "1366 Technologies Aims to Slash Solar Wafer Costs 50% And Make Solar Cheaper Than Coal," *Forbes,* November 23, 2015.
142. Peter Behr, "What Solar Pioneer's Turbulent Path Means for Biden," E&E News, May 7, 2021, eenews.net/articles/what-solar-pioneers-turbulent-path-means-for-biden.
143. "CubicPV Receives First Stage of $103M in Equity Financing to Support U.S. Factory Plans and Tandem Development," *Businesswire,* June 13, 2023, businesswire.com/news/home/20230613280901/en/CubicPV-Receives-First-Stage-of-103M-in-Equity-Financing-to-Support-U.S.-Factory-Plans-and-Tandem-Development.
144. Section 10771(o)(7) in US Congress, House, *Chips and Science Act,* HR 4346, 117th Cong., introduced in House July 1, 2021.
145. "Small Business Innovation Research Program (SBIR)," US Department of Education, last modified April 25, 2022, ed.gov/programs/sbir/legislation.html.
146. SBA, "Leveraging America's Seed Fund," March 2020, sbir.gov/sites/default/files/SBA_SBIR_Overview_March2020.pdf.
147. SBA, "Leveraging America's Seed Fund."
148. "Introduction to the SBIR Program," University Lab Partners, last modified September 8, 2021, universitylabpartners.org/blog/introduction-to-the-sbir-pro

gram; "About," Small Business Innovation Research, accessed June 21, 2023, sbir.gov/about.

149. "SBIR/STTR Frequently Asked Questions," Arkansas Small Business and Technology Development Center, accessed June 21, 2023, asbtdc.org/sbir-sttr-frequently-asked-questions; "About," Small Business Innovation Research.

150. "The Three Phases of SBIR/STTR," Small Business Innovation Research (SBIR) and Small Business Technology Transfer (STTR), accessed June 20, 2023, sbir.gov/about.

151. Small Business Innovation Research, "Tutorial 4: What Makes Phase III So Valuable?" *Course 9: SBIR Data Rights*, accessed 2023, sbir.gov/tutorials/data-rights/tutorial-4.

152. A "sole source" procurement can be defined as any contract entered into without a competitive process, based on a justification that only one known source exists or that only one single supplier can fulfill the requirements. See "Non-competitive /Sole Source Procurement: Seven Questions," National Association of State Procurement Officials, January 2015.

153. Small Business Innovation Research (SBIR) and Small Business Technology Transfer (STTR), "Leveraging America's Seed Fund," 8. Figures rounded.

154. National Research Council, *An Assessment of the SBIR Program* (Washington, DC: National Academies Press, 2008) 3–6, doi.org/10.17226/11989.

155. National Research Council, *Assessment of the SBIR Program*, 3.

156. National Research Council, *Assessment of the SBIR Program*, 42.

157. David B. Audretsch, Juergen Weigand, and Claudia Weigand, "The Impact of the SBIR on Creating Entrepreneurial Behavior," *Economic Development Quarterly* 16, no. 1 (February 2002): 32–8.

158. Office of Investment and Innovation, "Small Business Innovation Research (SBIR) and Small Business Technology Transfer (STTR) Program: Policy Directive, Effective: May 2, 2019," US Small Business Administration, 2019.

159. National Research Council, *Assessment of the SBIR Program*, 6.

160. Jack Miner, "Encouraging University Spin-Outs," National Academies of Sciences Workshop on SBIR-STTR and the Commercialization Challenge, April 12, 2016.

161. National Research Council, *Assessment of the SBIR Program*.

162. Summary S.4900 – 117th Congress (2021–2022), "Public Law No: 117–183 (09/30/2022): SBIR and STTR Extension Act of 2022," congress.gov/bill/117th-congress/senate-bill/4900?s=1&r=7.

163. "Required Disclosures of Foreign Affiliations or Relationships," SBIR/STTR website, n.d., sbir.gov/foreign_disclosures.

164. National Research Council, *Assessment of the SBIR Program,* 3–6.

165. National Research Council, *Assessment of the SBIR Program*, 116, figure 4.1.

166. National Research Council, *Assessment of the SBIR Program*, 47, 56, 156, 168, 220.

167. Robin Gaster, "Impacts of the SBIR/STTR Programs: Summary and Analysis," Small Business Technology Council, May 2017. National Academies of Sciences, Engineering, and Medicine, *Review of the SBIR and STTR Programs at the Department of Energy* (Washington, DC: National Academies Press, 2020); National Academies of Sciences, Engineering, and Medicine, *Assessment of the SBIR and STTR Programs at the National Institutes of Health* (Washington, DC: National Academies Press, 2022).

24. The Crisis of the American Patent System

1. *Diamond v. Chakrabarty*, 447 US 303, 308–9 (1980).
2. Kevin J. Hickey, "Patent-Eligible Subject Matter Reform in the 116th Congress," Congressional Research Service, September 17, 2019.
3. Except for a one-year grace period preceding the filing of a patent application. See Hickey, "Patent-Eligible Subject," 5.
4. Hickey, "Patent-Eligible Subject," 6.
5. Jerry Feigen, "Potential Exiting through ADRs (and/or GDRs?) for International Private Equity Investors," *American University International Law Review* 13, no. 1 (1999): 109–24, at 117.
6. Adam B. Jaffe and Josh Lerner, *Innovation and Its Discontents* (Princeton, NJ: Princeton University Press, 2004), 104.
7. Lila Feisee, "Anything under the Sun Made by Man," Biotechnology Innovation Organization, archive.bio.org/advocacy/letters/anything-under-sun-made-man.
8. Rana Foroohar, "Big Tech vs Big Pharma: The Battle over US Patent Protection," *Financial Times*, October 16, 2017.
9. Ronald S. Katz, Shawn G. Hansen, and Omair Farooqui, "Patent Trolls: A Selective Etymology," Law360, March 20, 2008, manatt.com/uploadedFiles/News_and_Events/Articles_By_Us/patentroll.pdf.
10. See David L. Schwartz and Jay Kesan, "Analyzing the Role of Non-practicing Entities in the Patent System," *Cornell Law Review* 99, no. 2 (January 2014): 431–3.
11. Schwartz and Kesan, "Analyzing the Role."
12. Joe Mullin, "New Anti-Patent-Troll Bill Advances, but Some Say It Hurts More than It Helps," Ars Technica, July 11, 2014; Gene Quinn, "Myths about Patent Trolls Prevent Honest Discussion about US Patent System," IPWatchdog, June 22, 2017.
13. Steve Brachmann, "The High Tech Inventors Alliance: The Newest Institution of the Efficient Infringer Lobby in DC," IPWatchdog, July 16, 2017.
14. "The Lobbyist in the Garage," Campaign for Accountability, May 2018.
15. Robert H. Rines, "America's *Different* Patent System: The Reason the US Outperforms the World, a Report to the 107th Congress," May 9, 2002.
16. US Congress, Senate, Subcommittee on Intellectual Property of the Committee on the Judiciary, *Perspective on Patents: Harmonization and Other Matters*, 109th Cong., 1st sess., July 26, 2005.
17. *eBay Inc. v. MercExchange*, L.L.C., 547 US 388 (2006).
18. Stuart Dredge, "Mobile Patent Warfare: Who's Suing Who and Why," CNET, August 21, 2011.
19. "Intellectual Property," Pharmaceutical Research and Manufacturers of America, phrma.org/policy-issues/Intellectual-Property.
20. For details of the act, see "Leahy–Smith America Invents Act Index," BitLaw, September 16, 2011.
21. "2017 Report of the Economic Survey," American Intellectual Property Law Association, August 2017, aipla.org/detail/journal-issue/economic-survey-2017.
22. Brief of 27 Law Professors As Amici Curiae in Support of Petitioner, *Oil States Energy Services, LLC, v. Greene's Energy Group*, LLC, 548 U.S. (2018).
23. *Alice Corporation v. CLS Bank International*, 573 US 208 (2014).
24. Robert Merges, "Symposium: Go ask *Alice* – What Can You after *Alice v. CLS Bank*?" SCOTUSblog, June 20, 2014.

25. For example, Ronald L Rivest et al., Cryptographic Communications System and Method, US Patent 4405829, filed 14 December 1977, and issued September 20, 1983.
26. Hickey, "Patent-Eligible Subject."
27. Burman York (Bud) Mathis III, "Supreme Court Denies 43rd Petition for Cert on 101 Grounds in *Vellena v. Iancu*," IPWatchdog, June 16, 2019. For example, in May 2023, the Supreme Court denied certiorari petitions in two cases (*Interactive Wearables LLC v. Polar Electro Oy* and *Tropp, David A. v. Travel Sentry, Inc., et al.*) in which the Justice Department had filed an amicus brief asking for "much-needed clarification," noting "significant confusion" in the Circuit 101 decisions and that the PTO "has also struggled to apply this Court's Section 101 precedent in a consistent manner." In 2022, the government filed a similar amicus brief in support of another 101 certiorari petition – *American Axle & Manufacturing, Inc. v. Neapco Holdings LLC* – which was also denied by SCOTUS. This confusion has frustrated everyone, including Federal Circuit judges. On July 3, 2019, the Federal Circuit issued an *en banc* decision in *Athena Diagnostics, Inc. v. Mayo Collaborative Services, LLC.* In that decision, they considered whether they should rehear an appeal of a patent regarding a medical diagnostic invention, which a three-judge panel had earlier held to be ineligible for patent protection pursuant to the precedent of the Supreme Court. The decision included the majority opinion, three concurring opinions, and four dissenting opinions. Each of the eight opinions requested that the Supreme Court or Congress do something to clarify the confusion.
28. Orin Herskowitz, "Washington Threatens NYC's Burgeoning Tech Economy," *Crain's New York Business*, July 27, 2016.
29. Kevin Madigan and Adam Mossoff, "Turning Gold to Lead: How Patent Eligibility Doctrine Is Undermining US Leadership in innovation," *George Mason Law Review* 24, no. 4 (Summer 2017): 939–60, here 956.
30. Paul R. Michel, "The Impact of Bad Patents on American Business," Statement before the US House Subcommittee on Courts, Intellectual Property, and the Internet, July 13, 2017, 1.
31. David O. Taylor, "Patent Eligibility and Investment," *Cardozo Law Review* 41, no. 5 (June 2020): 2019–2116.
32. Taylor, "Patent Eligibility."
33. Kevin Madigan, "As Investment Moves Overseas, the US Must Restore Its Gold-Standard Patent System," George Mason University Center for Intellectual Property x Innovation Policy, June 22, 2017.
34. Adam Houldsworth, "Charting China's Changing Pharma Patent Landscape," IAM, March 31, 2019.
35. US Patent and Trademark Office, "2019 Revised Patent Subject Matter Eligibility Guidance," *Federal Register*, January 7, 2019, 50–7.
36. *CxLoyalty, Inc. v. Maritz Holdings Inc.*, 986 F.3d 1367, 1380 (Fed. Cir. 2021).

25. Automobiles: Decline and a Chance at Revival

1. Mark J. Perry, "Animated Chart of the Day: Market Shares of US Auto Sales, 1961 to 2018," American Enterprise Institute, June 28, 2019.
2. Mathilde Carlier, "Selected Automakers' US YTD Market Share in 2022, by Key Manufacturer," Statista, March 29, 2023.

3. Bart Demandt, "US Car Sales Analysis 2021," CarSalesBase, 2022. GM did regain the lead the following year, but the fact is still telling. See Todd Lassa, "US Auto Sales Hit Coronavirus Nadir, Down 8% to 13.9 Million Units in 2022," *Autoweek*, January 5, 2023.

4. The 2019 data are used due to COVID-19 distortions in subsequent years. International Trade Administration, "New Vehicle Trade Data Visualization," US Department of Commerce, trade.gov/data-visualization/new-vehicle-trade-data-visualization; International Trade Administration, "Automotive Parts Trade Data Visualization," US Department of Commerce, trade.gov/data-visualization/automotive-parts-trade-data-visualization.

5. Eric Stafford, "Tesla Was the Bestselling Luxury Brand in 2022," *Car and Driver*, February 16, 2023.

6. Anthony Hughes, "The Effect of Ride-Sharing on the Auto Industry," Moody's Analytics, July 2017.

7. John Voelcker, auto industry expert, email exchange with the author, September 3, 2022.

8. Nicu Calcea, "Revealed: The Automotive Companies Leading the Way in Autonomous Vehicles," *Just Auto*, November 16, 2021.

9. "Global Autonomous Vehicle Market 2020–2030 by Offering, Automation Level, Vehicle Type, Power, ADAS Feature, Ownership, and Region: Trend Outlook and Growth Opportunity," GMD Research, December 2021.

10. Brian Wang, "Self-Driving Trucks Will Create a Megaregion Economic Boom," blog post, NextBigFuture, March 17, 2021.

11. Evan Zimmerman, "Germany Is Losing the Electric Vehicle Transition," *Palladium*, February 9, 2023.

12. "China New-Vehicle Quality Decreases as Design-Related Problems Increase, J. D. Power Finds," J. D. Power, September 1, 2022.

13. Brock Yates, *The Decline and Fall of the American Auto Industry* (New York: Empire Books, 1983), 15.

14. Perry, "Market Shares."

15. Harry First and Peter Carstensen, "Too Big and Failing: The Missed Chance to Break Up GM," Bloomberg, June 19, 2008.

16. "Anti-trust Study of Auto Industry Is Started by US," *New York Times*, April 29, 1954.

17. First and Carstensen, "Too Big."

18. Tom Mahoney, *The Story of George Romney* (New York: Harper & Brothers, 1960), 220.

19. "What If GM and Ford Were Broken Up in the 1960s?" Indie Auto, March 26, 2021.

20. James Womack, Daniel T. Jones, and Daniel Roos, *The Machine That Changed the World: The Story of Lean Production* (New York: Harper Perennial, 1990), 128.

21. Professor James Womack, MIT, draft markup, October 30, 2022.

22. Robert J. Flanagan, "Wage Concessions and Long-Term Union Wage Flexibility," Brookings Institution and Stanford University, 1984, 183.

23. Yates, *Decline*, 244.

24. Paul Ingrassia, *Crash Course: The American Automobile Industry's Road from Glory to Disaster* (New York: Random House, 2010), 53.

25. The firms and the UAW did eventually adapt, but it took time.

26. Bill Vlasic, *Once Upon a Car* (New York: William Morrow, 2011), 106.

27. Yates, *Decline*, 100.

28. General Motors, Form 10-K 1979, Detroit, MI: General Motors, 1979; Frank Swoboda, "GM's Deep Cuts Signal the End of a Work Force Era," *Washington Post*, December 20, 1991; Ford Motor Company, Form 10-K 1978, Dearborn, MI: Ford Motor Company, 1978; "UAW Officials Hint Ford Motor Co. Might Be Strike Target," United Press International, March 15, 1987.

29. Kim Hill et al., "Contribution of the Automotive Industry to the Economies of All Fifty States and the United States," Center for Automotive Research, January 2015, 2.

30. 3% and 11%: US Congress, Joint Economic Committee, *US Trade and Investment Policy: Imports and the Future of the American Automobile Industry: Hearing before the Joint Economic Committee*, 96th Cong., 2nd sess., March 19, 1980, 4. 6.5%: Kenneth Thomas, "Capital Mobility and Trade Policy: The Case of the Canada-US Auto Pact," *Review of International Political Economy* 4, no. 1 (Spring 1997): 146.

31. "Automotive Trade Statistics: 1964–1980," US International Trade Commission, August 1981, 2.

32. Yates, *Decline*, 31.

33. Yates, *Decline*, 34.

34. Yates, *Decline*, 15.

35. Yates, *Decline*, 190.

36. Yates, *Decline*, 29; Maryann Keller, *Collision: GM, Toyota, Volkswagen, and the Race to Own the 21st Century* (New York: Currency Doubleday, 1993), 29, 179.

37. Yates, *Decline*, 241–2; Keller, *Collision*, 154, 182.

38. Yates, *Decline*, 183.

39. Bob Lutz, *Car Guys vs. Bean Counters* (New York: Portfolio, 2011), 17.

40. It can be argued that the problem was poor execution rather than an unworkable concept, as most auto companies today have a unified assembly division making a number of brands on the same lines. However, changes in auto production since 50 years ago, such as the rapid die changes that make it easier to produce different models on a single assembly line, make the situations somewhat different.

41. Thomas Klier, "From Tail Fins to Hybrids: How Detroit Lost Its Dominance of the US Auto Market," *Economic Perspectives* 33, no. 2 (May 2009): 5.

42. Daniel Yergin, *The Prize: The Epic Quest for Oil, Money & Power* (New York: Simon and Schuster, 1991), 615.

43. Yergin, *The Prize*, 617; Jerry Taylor and Peter van Doren, "Time to Lay the 1973 Oil Embargo to Rest," Cato Institute, October 17, 2003.

44. "US Industrial Outlook for 200 Industries with Projections for 1986," US Department of Commerce, January 1982, 243.

45. "Top Vehicles Manufacturers in the US Market: 1961–2016," Knoema, May 21, 2020.

46. Valerie J. Karplus et al., "Should a Vehicle Fuel Economy Standard Be Combined with an Economy-Wide Greenhouse Gas Emissions Constraint? Implications for Energy and Climate Policy in the United States," *Energy Economics* 36 (March 2013): 322–33.

47. Which, in fact, they do. See James M. Sallee, Sara E. West, and Wei Fan, "Do Consumers Recognize the Value of Fuel Economy? Evidence from Used Car Prices and Gasoline Price Fluctuations," *Journal of Public Economics* 135 (March 2016): 61–73; Molly Espey, "Do Consumers Value Fuel Economy?" *Regulation* 28, no. 4 (Winter 2005): 8–13.

48. The world does not have now, and did not have then, too little petroleum in the ground. It has, in fact, far too much – that is, a quantity exceeding what can safely

be consumed, given climate change. If fracking at scale had developed decades earlier, the US would never have experienced supply disruptions deriving from Middle East politics, and the idea of running out would likely never have become popular.

49. William R. Nester, *A Short History of American Industrial Policies* (New York: MacMillan Press, 1998), 187.

50. Yates, *Decline*, 260.

51. Yates, *Decline*, 261.

52. Yates, *Decline*, 38.

53. Yates, *Decline*, 173, 238.

54. Steven Rattner, *Overhaul: An Insider's Account of the Obama Administration's Emergency Rescue of the Auto Industry* (Boston, MA: Mariner Books, 2011), 322.

55. James P. Womack, Daniel T. Jones, and Daniel Roos, "How Lean Production Can Change the World," *New York Times*, September 23, 1990.

56. The decision to keep the lines running not only led to rework at the dealers, but ultimately undermined plant efficiency too. "When I visited Cadillac's assembly plant in 1979, the number of workers in the rework building (about 2,500) was the same as the number of workers in the assembly building, and yet the vehicles were still reaching the dealers with high levels of defects." Womack, email exchange with the author, January 29, 2023.

57. John F. Krafcik, "Triumph of the Lean Production System," *MIT Sloan Management Review* 30, no. 1 (Fall 1988): 41–52.

58. Michael A. Cusumano, "Manufacturing Innovation: Lessons from the Japanese Auto Industry," *MIT Sloan Management Review* 30, no. 1 (Fall 1988): 29–39.

59. Yates, *Decline*, 241–2; Keller, *Collision*, 150.

60. Yates, *Decline*, 233.

61. National Research Council, *The Competitive Status of the US Auto Industry: A Study of the Influences of Technology in Determining International Industrial Competitive Advantage* (Washington, DC: National Academies Press, 1982), 5.

62. Yates, *Decline*, 239.

63. National Research Council, *Competitive Status*, 5.

64. Lutz, *Car Guys*, 50; Paul Ingrassia and Joseph B. White, *Comeback: The Fall and Rise of the American Automobile Industry* (New York: Simon & Schuster, 1995), 97; Keller, *Collision*, 169.

65. Keller, *Collision*, 157, 171.

66. Samantha Gross, "What Iran's 1979 Revolution Meant for US and Global Oil Markets," Brookings Institution, March 5, 2019.

67. Ingrassia and White, *Comeback*, 252.

68. Comptroller General of the United States, "Producing More Fuel-Efficient Automobiles: A Costly Proposition," Report to the Chairman Committee on Energy and Commerce, January 19, 1982, 18.

69. Womack, Jones, and Roos, *The Machine*, 135.

70. "US Light-Duty: Fuel Economy and GHG," TransportPolicy.net, 2018.

71. Yates, *Decline*, 22–3.

72. Rattner, *Overhaul*, 15; Ingrassia, *Crash Course*, 87; Keller, *Collision*, 32.

73. Keller, *Collision*, 32.

74. Keller, *Collision*, 32.

75. Inflation: Kimberly Amadeo, "US Inflation Rate by Year From 1929 to 2023," The Balance, thebalancemoney.com/u-s-inflation-rate-history-by-year-and-forecast-

3306093. Unemployment: "US Unemployment Rate by Year," multpl.com/unemployment/table/by-year.

76. "United States: Nominal Major Currencies US Dollar Index (Goods Only)," Federal Re-serve Bank, tradingeconomics.com/united-states/trade-weighted-exchange-index-major-currencies-index-mar-1973-100-m-na-fed-data.html.

77. John Holusha, "G.M. and Ford Press U.A.W. on Labor Costs," *New York Times*, June 3, 1981.

78. US Bureau of Economic Analysis, "Light Weight Vehicles Sales: Autos and Light Trucks," Federal Reserve Bank of St. Louis, fred.stlouisfed.org/series/ALTSALES.

79. Klier, "From Tail Fins to Hybrids," 3.

80. "United States: Nominal Major Currencies US Dollar Index (Goods Only)," Federal Reserve Bank.

81. Jim McElroy et al., "A Review of Recent Developments in the US Automobile Industry Including an Assessment of the Japanese Restraint Agreements," US International Trade Commission, February 1985, 12.

82. Lutz, *Car Guys*, 31; Ingrassia, *Crash Course*, 57.

83. Peter Behr, "When the Taxpayers Saved Lee Iacocca's Bacon, What Did They Get Out of It?" *Washington Post*, May 13, 1984.

84. Keller, *Collision*, 122–3; Peter D. Ehrenhaft and Karen I. Ward, "United States: International Trade Commission Determination on Lack of Injury to Domestic Injuries by the Importation of Japanese Auto Imports," *International Legal Materials* 20, no. 1 (January 1981): 186–222.

85. "Top Vehicles Manufacturers in the US Market: 1961–2016," Knoema.

86. Douglas A. Irwin, *Clashing over Commerce: A History of US Trade Policy* (Chicago, IL: University of Chicago Press, 2017), 575. GM expected consumers to return to large cars once interest rates came down, and worried about being accused of anticompetitive tactics. Chrysler had already told the country that its problems were due to recession and its own management problems, not imports, and didn't want to change its story.

87. Clyde H. Farnsworth, "US Rejects Limits on Japanese Autos," *New York Times*, November 11, 1980.

88. Daniel Benjamin, "Voluntary Export Restraints on Automobiles," PERC, September 1, 1999.

89. Keller, *Collision*, 202.

90. Mike Arnholt and Tim Keenan, "Foreign Invasion: Imports, Transplants Change Auto Industry Forever," Wards Auto, May 01, 1996.

91. Ingrassia and White, *Comeback*, 353; Keller, *Collision*, 24, 221.

92. Richard G. Newman, "The Second Wave Arrives: Japanese Strategy in the US Auto Parts Market," *Business Horizons* 33, no. 4 (July/August 1990): 24–30. Europe: Keller, *Collision*, 17.

93. Keller, *Collision*, 19.

94. Steven Brull and Kevin Murphy, "Five-Day Surge Is Mixed Blessing for Exporters and Importers," *New York Times*, March 9, 1995; Mai Fujita, "Industrial Policies and Trade Liberalization: The Automotive Industry in Thailand and Malaysia," Institute of Developing Economics, 1998, 154.

95. Ingrassia, *Crash Course*, 90.

96. Lorraine Eden and Maureen Appel Molot, "Made in America? The US Auto Industry, 1955–95," *The International Executive* 38, no. 4 (July/August 1996): 512.

97. The 2019 data are used in order to avoid distorting effects of the pandemic. See International Trade Administration, "Automotive Parts Trade Data

Visualization;" Joel Cutcher-Gershenfeld, Dan Brooks, and Martin Mulloy, "The Decline and Resurgence of the US Auto Industry," Economic Policy Institute, May 6, 2015.

98. James Gerstenzang, "Clinton Advisers Back Punitive Japan Tariffs," *Los Angeles Times*, May 7, 1995.

99. "Treasury Market Suffers Steepest Loss in 9 Months," Associated Press, June 10, 1995.

100. International Trade Administration, "Mexico-Country Commercial Guide: Automotive Industry," US Department of Commerce, September 23, 2022; "Important Facts," Canadian Vehicle Manufacturers' Association, cvma.ca/industry/facts.

101. Greg Gardner and Brent Snavely, "Ford Shifting all US Small-Car Production to Mexico," *Detroit Free Press*, September 14, 2016.

102. Rattner, *Overhaul*, 322.

103. Paul Niedermeyer, "Chartside Classics: US Market Share by Manufacturers: 1961–2016," Curbside Classic, April 10, 2018; Demandt, "US Car Sales Analysis: 2021."

104. Bill Canis, M. Angeles Villareal, and Vivian C. Jones, "NAFTA and Motor Vehicle Trade," Congressional Research Service, July 28, 2017, 15.

105. Julia Kagan, "Chicken Tax: What It Is, How It Got the Name," Investopedia, August 14, 2022; Robert Longley, "The Chicken Tax and Its Influence on the US Auto Industry," ThoughtCo, September 2, 2019.

106. Ian Thibodeau, "As US Carmakers Quit Sedans, Others Cash In," *Detroit News*, January 14, 2019; Daniel Griswold, "Why Are Pickups So Expensive? Blame the Chicken Tax," *Dallas Morning News*, March 13, 2022.

107. "US Light Truck Retail Sales from 1980 to 2022," Statista, May 11, 2023.

108. "US Light Truck Retail Sales from 1980 to 2022," Statista; "Light Vehicle Retail Sales in the United States from 1976 to 2022," Statista, March 10, 2023.

109. "Light Vehicle Retail Sales," Statista; Andre Smirnov, "Full-Size Truck US Sales Report for 2022: GM Is Still on Top, Ram Slides Down–Here Is What Happened," The Fast Lane Truck, January 5, 2023.

110. Lutz, *Car Guys*, 172.

111. Ingrassia, *Crash Course*, 107.

112. Ingrassia, *Crash Course*, 93.

113. Ingrassia, *Crash Course*, 146.

114. Max E. Zent, "QS-9000: An Executive Overview," *Quality Digest*, May 1997.

115. US Energy Information Administration, "US Crude Oil First Purchase Price," US Department of Energy (DOE), last modified June 1, 2023, eia.gov/dnav/pet/hist/LeafHandler.ashx?n=pet&s=f000000__3&f=m.

116. Ingrassia, *Crash Course*, 78.

117. Vlasic, *Once Upon*, 128.

118. "Detroit 3 (Domestic Brands): US Market Share History," *Automotive News*, June 1, 2009.

119. Kevin Krolicki, "Ford, GM Propose Health Care Fund to Union: Sources," Reuters, August 24, 2007.

120. General Motors, Form 10-K 2007, Detroit, MI: General Motors, 2007, 9.

121. Ingrassia, *Crash Course*, 193.

122. "General Motors Annual Sales and Market Share," GoodCarBadCar, goodcarbadcar.net/general-motors-us-sales-figures.

123. Bill Vlasic, "Choosing Its Own Path, Ford Stayed Independent," *New York Times*, April 8, 2009.

124. G. E. Anderson, *Designated Drivers: How China Plans to Dominate the Global Auto Industry* (Singapore: John Wiley and Sons Singapore, 2012), 11.

125. Rattner, *Overhaul*, 86.

126. Vlasic, *Once Upon*, 306.

127. This figure differs from the 5:1 multiplier mentioned earlier because the former is for the entire industry's jobs count, not just assembly-line jobs. See Hill et al., "Contribution," 31.

128. US figure: Maria Shao, "Steven Rattner: The 2009 US Auto Bailout Was Necessary," *Insights by Stanford Business*, March 1, 2011. Canadian figure: Mark Milke, "Crunching the Numbers on the 2009 Auto Bailout," Fraser Institute, 2019.

129. Bill Canis and Brent D. Yacobucci, "The US Motor Vehicle Industry: Confronting a New Dynamic in the Global Economy," Congressional Research Service, March 26, 2010.

130. Rattner, *Overhaul*, 184, 196.

131. Rattner, *Overhaul*, 185–6, 191.

132. Rattner, *Overhaul*, 74–5.

133. Ingrassia, *Crash Course*, 261.

134. Rattner, *Overhaul*, 190–3.

135. Rattner, *Overhaul*, 297–8.

136. See Brent Snavely, "Final Tally: Taxpayers Auto Bailout Loss $9.3B," *Detroit Free Press*, December 30, 2014.

137. "US Car Sales Data by Brand," CarSalesBase, carsalesbase.com/car-sales-us-home-main/car-sales-by-brand-us; Lutz, *Car Guys*, 193.

138. International Trade Administration, "New Vehicle Trade Data Visualization," US Department of Commerce, trade.gov/data-visualization/new-vehicle-trade-data-visualization.

139. These figures only include autos manufactured in the US, not autos imported to the US or produced by US automobile companies abroad. See American International Automobile Dealers Association, "International Automakers and Dealers in America 2020," 2020, 7.

140. Tom McCarthy, *Auto Mania: Cars, Consumers, and the Environment* (New Haven, CT: Yale University Press, 2007), 244.

141. Amanda Little, "What Can We Learn from Bush's FreedomCar Plan?" *Grist*, February 26, 2003.

142. Leigh Collins, "Liebrich: 'Oil Sector Is Lobbying for Inefficient Hydrogen Cars Because It Wants to Delay Electrification,'" Recharge, June 30, 2021.

143. Stacy C. Davis and Robert G. Boundy, *Transportation Energy Data Book: Edition 40*, DOE Oak Ridge National Laboratory, February 2022, table 6.2.

144. "Global EV Outlook 2022," International Energy Agency, May 2022, 4.

145. David Shepardson, "US Automakers to Say They Aspire to Up to 50% of EV Sales by 2030: Sources," Reuters, August 4, 2021; David Welch and Bloomberg, "Carmakers Are Struggling to Make Electric Vehicles Affordable for Pinched Consumers – and Rethinking Their Investments amid Sagging Demand," *Fortune*, November 4, 2023, fortune.com/2023/11/04/carmakers-rethink-electric-vehicle-investments-demand-inflation-interest-rates.

146. Neal E. Boudette and Coral Davenport, "G.M. Will Sell Only Zero-Emission Vehicles by 2025," *New York Times*, January 28, 2021.

147. "GM Will Boost EV and AV Investments to $35 Billion through 2025," General Motors, June 16, 2021.

148. Michael Wayland, "Electric Dodge Muscle Car and Ram Pickup Part of Stellantis' $35.5 Billion EV Plans," CNBC, July 8, 2021.

149. Michael Wayland, "Ford Will Split EVs and Legacy Autos into Separate Units as It Spends $50 Billion on Electric Vehicles," CNBC, March 2, 2022.

150. "GM Signs Agreements with Suppliers, on Course to Reach 1 Million EV Capacity by 2025," Reuters, July 26, 2022; Michael Wayland, "Ford Plans to Produce 2 Million EVs Annually, Generate 10% Operating Profit by 2026," CNBC, March 3, 2022; Matt Pressman, "Tesla's Goal: 20 Million Annual Car Sales by 2030," CleanTechnica, October 8, 2021.

151. Welch and Bloomberg, "Carmakers Are Struggling."

152. Breana Noble, "Stellantis EVs Could Arrive at Right Time as Industry Pulls Back," *Detroit News*, November 1, 2023, gmtoday.com/autos/stellantis-evs-could-arrive-at-right-time-as-industry-pulls-back/article_2f1c1ea8-792f-11ee-8097-3bed956dd6f5.html.

153. Roland Erie, "Global EV Sales for 2022," Electric Vehicle World Sales Database, ev-volumes.com/country/total-world-plug-in-vehicle-volumes.

154. Tom Taylor and Josh Rosenberg, "Total Cost of Ownership Analysis," Atlas Public Policy, February 2022; Renee Valdes, "Electric Car FAQ: Your Questions Answered," Kelley Blue Book, October 31, 2022; Deivis Centeno, "GM Estimates That EVs Will Soon Cost the Same as ICE Vehicles," GM Authority, October 20, 2022.

155. Mathilde Carlier, "Projected Production of Electric Vehicles and Plug-In Hybrid Electric Vehicles in Selected Countries between 2018 and 2023," Statista, September 30, 2022. First 11 months of 2022: see Mark Kane, "China: Plug-In Car Sales Increased by 50% in November 2022," InsideEVs, January 2, 2023; "Global EV Outlook 2022," International Energy Agency, 4; Daisuke Wakabayashi and Claire Fu, "For China's Auto Market, Electric Isn't the Future. It's the Present," *New York Times*, September 26, 2022.

156. Anderson, *Designated Drivers*, 75; "Western firms are quaking as China's electric-car industry speeds up," *The Economist*, January 11, 2024.

157. "China's Cutthroat EV Market Is Squeezing Out Smaller Players," Bloomberg, June 26, 2923, bloomberg.com/news/features/2023-06-26/china-s-electric-vehicle-bubble-is-starting-to-deflate.

158. Meaghan Tobin and Lyric Li, "Chinese EV Giant BYD Overtakes Tesla, but Can It Crack the U.S. Market?" June 14, 2023, washingtonpost.com/world/2023/06/13/china-byd-electric-vehicle-tesla-rival; Aaron Gold, "BYD Dolphin First Drive: Could This $31,000 Chinese EV Swim in the U.S. Market?" *Motortrend*, July 24, 2023, motortrend.com/reviews/2023-byd-dolphin-first-drive-review.

159. "Overview – Electric Vehicles: Tax Benefits and Purchase Incentives in the European Union (2022)," European Automobile Manufacturers' Association, September 21, 2022.

160. "Fuel Types of New Cars: Battery Electric 12.1%, Hybrid 22.6%, and Petrol 36.4% Market Share Full-Year 2022," European Automobile Manufacturers' Association, February 1, 2023; "Electric Cars: EU Trade Surplus of €1.1 Billion," Eurostat, August 4, 2020.

161. Kate Abnett, "EU Countries Approve 2035 Phaseout of CO_2-Emitting Cars," Reuters, March 29, 2023; "EU Gives Final Approval to 2035 Ban on Sales of New Fossil Fuel Cars," France 24, February 14, 2023.

162. Ari Sillman, "A New Automotive Era? Promoting Electric Vehicles in the Biden Administration," Harvard University Environmental & Energy Law Program, March 3, 2021; "Fact Sheet: President Biden Announces Steps to Drive American Leadership Forward on Clean Cars and Trucks," The White House, August 5, 2021.

163. Sarah O'Brien, "Buying a Car and Want to Go Electric? Inflation Reduction Act Extends $7,500 Tax Credit – But with Price, Income Caps," CNBC, August 10, 2022.

164. "Inflation Reduction Act (IRA) Summary: Energy and Climate Provisions," Bipartisan Policy Center, August 4, 2022.

165. US Department of Transportation, "President Biden, USDOT and USDOE Announce $5 Billion over Five Years for National EV Charging Network, Made Possible by Bipartisan Infrastructure Law," February 10, 2022, highways.dot.gov/newsroom/president-biden-usdot-and-usdoe-announce-5-billion-over-five-years-national-ev-charging.

166. US Congress, House, Inflation Reduction Act of 2022, HR 5376, 117th Cong., introduced in House September 27, 2021; "Credits for New Clean Vehicles Purchased in 2023 or After," Internal Revenue Service, last modified June 22, 2023, irs.gov/credits-deductions/credits-for-new-clean-vehicles-purchased-in-2023-or-after.

167. Derrick Morgan, "We Don't Need a Costly, Mandated Detour to Electric Cars," Heritage Foundation, June 16, 2022.

168. Editorial Board, "Biden's EPA Remakes the Auto Industry," *Wall Street Journal*, April 12, 2023.

169. Ivan Castano, "Can Lithium Save Bolivia's Economy?" *Forbes*, May 1, 2023; Mario Orospe Hernández, "Bolivia Is Sitting on a Goldmine of Lithium but It's Setting Up an Ideological Collision between Modern Society and Indigenous Religious Views," *Fortune*, April 21, 2023. As of this writing, a $1 billion deal with three Chinese firms to begin mining lithium had been established, but active mining had not yet begun.

170. Hannah Northey and Timothy Cama, "'Silicon Valley of Lithium': Nevada Mine Breaks Ground," *E&E News*, March 3, 2023. [BK]; Ivan Penn and Eric Lipton, "The Lithium Gold Rush: Inside the Race to Power Electric Vehicles," *New York Times*, May 6, 2021; "About Us," E3 Lithium, e3lithium.ca/corporate/about-us; Gowri Abhinanda, "Lithium Mining Company Pushes for Permit Approval in NC despite Local Opposition," *Daily Tar Heel*, March 21, 2023; "Projects," Piedmont Lithium, piedmontlithium.com/projects.

171. Anthony King, "Lithium Discovery in US Volcano Could Be the Biggest Deposit Ever Found," *Chemistry World*, September 6, 2023, chemistryworld.com/news/lithium-discovery-in-us-volcano-could-be-biggest-deposit-ever-found/4018032.article.

172. John D. Graham et al., "How China Beat the US in Electric Vehicle Manufacturing," *Issues in Science and Technology* 37, no. 2 (Winter 2021): 72–9; Jason Mitchell, "Kinshasa Is Already Africa's Biggest City: Could Cobalt Make It the Richest?" Mining Technology, February 15, 2022; Cade Ahlijian, "Congo's Cobalt Controversy," GlobalEdge, April 20, 2022.

173. Eric Lipton and Dionne Searcey, "How the US Lost Ground to China in the Contest for Clean Energy," *New York Times*, November 21, 2021.

174. Lithium: "China Controls 70% of Global Lithium Production: That's a Worry for the World," *Meghalayan*, February 25, 2023. Graphite: John Xie, "How China Dominates Global Battery Supply Chain," VOA News, September 1, 2020.

175. "Electric Vehicle Battery Costs Soar," Institute for Energy Research, April 25, 2022.
176. "America's Strategic to Secure the Supply Chain for a Robust Clean Energy Transition," Response to Executive Order 14017, DOE, February 24, 2022.
177. "Fact Sheet: Biden–Harris Administration Driving US Battery Manufacturing and Good-Paying Jobs," The White House, October 12, 2022.
178. "Lithium Americas Receives Conditional Commitment for $2.26 Billion ATVM Loan from the U.S. DOE for Construction of Thacker Pass," Lithium Americas press release, March 14, 2024.
179. US–Japan Critical Materials Agreement, March 28, 2023, ustr.gov/sites/default/files/2023–03/US%20Japan%20Critical%20Minerals%20Agreement%202023%2003%2028.pdf.
180. Philip Blenkinsop, "U.S. Optimistic It Will Reach Critical Minerals Deal with EU," Reuters, October 2, 2023, reuters.com/markets/commodities/us-optimistic-it-will-reach-critical-minerals-deal-with-eu-2023–10–02.

26. Semiconductors, Aviation, and Space: The Military Developmental State

1. Forecast International, "Top 100 Defense Contractors 2022," *Defense & Security Monitor*, February 22, 2023.
2. Forecast International, "Top 100 Defense Contractors 2022."
3. "Top 100 Defense Companies for 2022," *Defense News*, people.defensenews.com/top-100.
4. The funding arrangements and categorization of the labs can so complex that there is at least the possibility of overlap. For example, an FFRDC could host a lab that was on its premises but which was funded under separate contract with the AFOSR.
5. Most recent data available. Mark Boroush and Ledia Guci, "Research and Development: US Trends and International Comparisons," National Science Board and National Science Foundation Science and Engineering Indicators 2022, April 28, 2022, table RD-15, 56.
6. Sargent and Gallo, "Global Research," 4.
7. CRS analysis of data from National Science Foundation, *National Patterns of R&D Resources: 2018-19 Data Update*, April 9, 2021, in John F. Sargent Jr. and Marcy E. Gallo, "The Global Research and Development Landscape and Implication for the Department of Defense," Congressional Research Service, June 28, 2021, 4.
8. CRS analysis of data from US Department of Commerce, Office of Technology Policy, *The Global Context for U.S. Technology Policy*, Summer 1997, in Sargent and Gallo, "Global Research," 3.
9. CRS analysis of US data from National Science Foundation, *National Patterns of R&D Resources: 2018–19 Data Update*, April 9, 2021. Rest of the world share from CRS analysis of OECD data, in Sargent and Gallo, "Global Research," 3.
10. "Top 100 Defense Companies for 2022," *Defense News*.
11. Jacques S. Gansler, William Lucyshyn, and John Rigilano, "The Impact of Globalization on the US Defense Industrial Base," Center for Public Policy and Private Enterprise, October 2013, 6. The Moran source referenced in the quotation is Theodore Moran, "The Globalization of America's Defense Industries," *International Security* 15, no. 1: 57–99.
12. Gansler, Lucyshyn, and Rigilano, "The Impact," viii.

13. US General Accountability Office (GAO), "Industrial Base: Assessing the Risk of DOD's Foreign Dependence," *Report to the Chairman, Subcommittee on Technology and National Security, Joint Economic Committee*, January 1991, 1.

14. Beth Stackpole, "5 Supply Chain Technologies that Deliver Competitive Advantage," MIT Management Sloan School, February 14, 2020.

15. Office of Technology Evaluation, "Defense Industrial Base Assessment: Counterfeit Electronics," US Department of Commerce, January 2010, i.

16. Defense Science Board, "Report of the Defense Science Board Task Force on Cyber Supply Chain," February 2017, Office of the Under Secretary of Defense for Acquisition, Technology, and Logistics.

17. Defense Science Board, "DSB Task Force on Cyber Supply Chain," US Department of Defense (DOD), April 2017, 4–5. The DOD Office of Industrial Policy subsequently confirmed and augmented the DSB's analysis. See Office of Industrial Policy, "Fiscal Year 2019 Industrial Capabilities: Report to Congress," DOD, June 23, 2020.

18. National Science and Technology Council, "A National Strategic Plan for Advanced Manufacturing," Executive Office of the President, February 2012, 6.

19. Valerie Bailey Grasso, "Rare Earth Elements in National Defense: Background, Oversight Issues, and Options for Congress," Congressional Research Service, December 23, 2013.

20. US Geological Survey, "Rare Earths," *Mineral Commodity Summaries*, January 2022.

21. Wayne M. Morrison, "Trade Dispute with China and Rare Earth Elements," Congressional Research Service, June 28, 2019, 2.

22. "China Gallium, Germanium Export Curbs Kick In; Wait for Permits Starts," Reuters, August 1, 2023.

23. OSD A&S Industrial Policy, "Fiscal Year 2020 Industrial Capabilities Report to Congress," DOD, January 2021, 8.

24. Oscar Serpell, "Impacts of the Inflation Reduction Act on Rare Earth Elements," Kleinman Center for Energy Policy, September 24, 2022.

25. "Executive Order on America's Supply Chains," The White House, February 24, 2021; "Securing Defense-Critical Supply Chains: An Action Plan Developed in Response to President Biden's Executive Order 14017," DOD, February 2022.

26. "DoD Awards $35 Million to MP Materials to Build US Heavy Rare Earth Separation Capacity," DOD, February 22, 2022.

27. "Jean Hoerni's 'planar' process improved transistor reliability by creating a flat surface structure protected with an insulating silicon dioxide layer. Robert Noyce then proposed interconnecting transistors on the wafer by depositing aluminum 'wires' on top. Following Noyce's lead, Jay Last's team built the first planar IC in 1960, spawning the modern computer chip industry." From "Fairchild's Approach: The Planar Process," Computer History Museum, computerhistory.org/revolution/digital-logic/12/329.

28. Norman J. Asher and Leland D. Strom, "The Role of the Department of Defense in the Development of Integrated Circuits," Institute for Defense Analysis, May 1977, 2.

29. Asher and Strom, "The Role," 4. The two contracts together were worth $32.7 million in 2022 dollars.

30. Asher and Strom, "The Role," 5, S-2.

31. David C. Mowery, "Federal Policy and the Development of Semiconductors, Computer Hardware, and Computer Software: A Policy Model for Climate Change R&D?" in *Accelerating Energy Innovation: Insights from Multiple*

Sectors, ed. Rebecca M. Henderson and Richard G. Newell (Chicago, IL: University of Chicago Press, 2011), 169.

32. Mowery, "Federal Policy," 166–8.
33. Mowery, "Federal Policy," 169.
34. William J. Perry, "A New Way of Doing Business: A Memorandum by William J. Perry," June 29, 1994.
35. Table adapted from Glenn R. Fong, "The Future of Pentagon-Industry Collaboration in Technology Development," in *The Political Economy of Defense: Issues and Perspectives*, ed. Andrew L. Ross (Westport, CT: Greenwood Press, 1991).
36. According to the National Research Council, "DARPA was by far the largest federal supporter of VLSI research. Its funding for the VLSI program grew from less than $15 million in 1979 to over $93 million in 1982." National Research Council, *Funding a Revolution: Government Support for Computing Research* (Washington, DC: National Academies Press, 1999), 122.
37. Anna Slomovic, "An Analysis of Military and Commercial Microelectronics: Has DOD's R&D Funding Had the Desired Effect?" RAND, 1991, v.
38. Office of Technology Assessment, "Microelectronics Research and Development: A Background Paper," US Congress, March 1986, 21.
39. Office of Technology Assessment, "Microelectronics Research," 21.
40. Slomovic, "An Analysis," 161.
41. Slomovic, "An Analysis," vi.
42. National Research Council, *Funding a Revolution*, 117.
43. National Research Council, *Funding a Revolution*, 116.
44. National Research Council, *Funding a Revolution*, 115.
45. National Research Council, *Funding a Revolution*, 116.
46. Marco Casale-Rossi et al., "The Heritage of Mead & Conway: What Has Remained the Same, What Was Missed, What Has Changed, What Lies Ahead," Design, Automation and Test in Europe Conference & Exhibition, March 2013.
47. According to a report by the Office of Technology Assessment, "Over the past 25 years, technology differences have steadily decreased among competing firms of different nations. The technological superiority of an IBM, AT&T, or Boeing has been offset by the rise of capable competitors worldwide. The traditional US advantages of privileged access to broad, deep, and liquid capital markets, as well as large economies of scale and scope, have similarly leveled off." Office of Technology Assessment, "Multinationals and the National Interest: Playing by Different Rules," US Congress, September 1993.
48. "Offshoring: US Semiconductor and Software Industries Increasingly Produce in China and India," GAO, September 2006, 1.
49. Chad Bown, "How the United States Marched the Semiconductor Industry into Its Trade War with China," *East Asian Economic Review* 24, no. 4 (December 2020): 349–388, 365.
50. David B. Yoffie, "Foreign Direct Investment in Semiconductors," in *Foreign Direct Investment*, ed. Kenneth A. Froot (Chicago, IL: University of Chicago Press, 1993), table 7.4, 206–207.
51. Office of Technology Assessment, "Global Arms Trade: Commerce in Advanced Military Technology and Weapons," US Congress, June 1991, 37–8.
52. Roderick L. Vawter, "US Industrial Base Dependence/Vulnerability, Phase I: Survey of Literature," National Defense University Mobilization Concepts Development Center, December 1986, iv.

53. Dorinda G. Dallmeyer, "The United States–Japan Semiconductor Accord of 1986: the Shortcomings of High-Tech Protectionism," *Maryland Journal of International Law* 13, no. 2 (1989): 180.
54. A captive semiconductor company makes chips for its own use, a merchant semiconductor company makes chips to sell to other companies, and a semiconductor foundry fabricates chips from designs provided by its customers.
55. Richard Langlois and W. Edward Steinmueller, "Strategy and Circumstance: The Response of American Firms to Japanese Competition in Semiconductors, 1980–1995," *Strategic Management Journal* 21, no. 10 (October 2000): 1163.
56. Office of Technology Assessment, "The Big Picture: HDTV and High-Resolution Systems," US Congress, June 1990, Appendix C, 95–7.
57. James Gerstenzang, "100% Tariff Put on Some Japan Goods: Reagan Move to Halt Chip Dumping Could Double TV, Computer Prices," *Los Angeles Times*, April 18, 1987.
58. Defense Science Board, "Report of the Defense Science Board Task Force on Defense Semiconductor Dependency," DOD, February 1987.
59. Defense Science Board, "Report of the Defense Science Board," Charles A. Fowler memorandum.
60. Defense Science Board, "Report of the Defense Science Board," Norman R. Augustine memorandum.
61. Defense Science Board, "Report of the Defense Science Board."
62. Sematech could, however, enter into joint ventures with foreign firms. Douglas A. Irwin and Peter J. Klenow, "Sematech: Purpose and Performance," *Proceedings of the National Academy of Sciences of the United States of America (PNAS)* 93, no. 23 (November 12, 1996): 12739–40.
63. "Federal Research: Sematech's Efforts to Strengthen the US Semiconductor Industry," GAO, September 1990, 2.
64. "Sematech: Progress and Prospects," Report of the Advisory Council on Federal Participation in Sematech, May 1989, ES-2, 34
65. "Federal Research: Lessons Learned from Sematech," GAO, September 1992, 6; "Sematech: Progress and Prospects," 27–8.
66. "Memorandum of Understanding Sematech," DOD, May 12, 1988, 8.
67. "Sematech: Progress and Prospects," ES-1.
68. Michaela D. Platzer, John F. Sargent Jr., and Karen M. Sutter, "Semiconductors: US Industry, Global Competition, and Federal Policy," Congressional Research Service, October 26, 2020, 48.
69. National Research Council, *Securing the Future: Regional and National Programs to Support the Semiconductor Industry* (Washington, DC: National Academies Press, 2003), 39.
70. National Research Council, *Securing the Future*, 43, 50.
71. "Federal Research: Lessons Learned from Sematech," GAO, September 1992, 2.
72. National Research Council, *Securing the Future*, 87.
73. Jeff Dorsch, "Sematech Goes Fully International," EDN, July 12, 1999.
74. "2023 Factbook," Semiconductor Industry Association, May 5, 2023, 2.
75. Thomas Alsop, "Distribution of Semiconductor Sales Worldwide from 2015 to 2020, by Region," Statista, December 2, 2021.
76. The Industrial College of the Armed Forces, "Electronics Industry Study Report: Semiconductors and the Defense Electronics," National Defense University, 2003, 7.
77. Defense Science Board, "Cyber Supply Chain," DOD, April 2017, 5.
78. "Securing Defense-Critical Supply Chains," DOD, 2–3.

79. "The US Department of State International Technology Security and Innovation Fund," n.d., state.gov/the-u-s-department-of-state-international-technology-security-and-innovation-fund.

80. Sandra Bearden, "Redstone Arsenal," Encyclopedia of Alabama, December 8, 2002; Piers Bizony, "Wernher von Braun: Director of the Marshall Space Flight Center/Saturn V Chief Architect," *BBC Science Focus*, July 11, 2019.

81. "Atlas Rockets Overview," Historic Spacecraft, historicspacecraft.com/Rockets_Atlas.html.

82. Jeff Shesol, "Lyndon Johnsons Unsung Role in Sending Americans to the Moon," *New Yorker*, July 20, 2019.

83. Van Nimmen and Bruno, *NASA Historical Data Book Volume 1*, 119.

84. Thomas C. Roberts, "History of the NASA Budget," Center for Strategic and International Affairs, September 1, 2022.

85. Andrew Chatzky, Anshu Siripurapu, and Steven J. Markovich, "Space Exploration and US Competitiveness," Council on Foreign Relations, September 23, 2021.

86. "How Much Did the Apollo Program Cost?" The Planetary Society, planetary.org/space-policy/cost-of-apollo.

87. Jet Propulsion Laboratory, "Voyager: Did You Know?" California Institute of Technology, voyager.jpl.nasa.gov/mission/did-you-know.

88. Adjusted for inflation. The cost in 2010 dollars was $209 billion. See Mike Wall, "NASA's Shuttle Program Cost $209 Billion: Was It Worth It?" Space.com, July 5, 2011.

89. Jamie Carter, "Is This the End for the Hubble Space Telescope? Its Computer Has a Memory Problem, Says NASA," *Forbes*, June 21, 2021.

90. Michael Sheetz, "NASA Wants Companies to Develop and Build New Space Stations, with Up to $400 Million Up for Grabs," CNBC, March 27, 2018.

91. "Mars Pathfinder Rover," NASA Space Science Data Coordinated Archive, nssdc.gsfc.nasa.gov/nmc/spacecraft/display.action?id=MESURPR.

92. Mike Wall, "NASA's Chandra X-Ray Space Telescope Celebrates 15 Years of Discoveries," Space.com, July 13, 2014.

93. Jet Propulsion Laboratory, "Juno Spacecraft: Quick Facts," California Institute of Technology, jpl.nasa.gov/news/press_kits/juno/facts.

94. Casey Dreier, "NASA's Commercial Crew Program Is a Fantastic Deal," The Planetary Society, May 19, 2020.

95. "Cost of MSL Curiosity," The Planetary Society, planetary.org/space-policy/cost-of-msl-curiosity.

96. "Cost of the Double Asteroid Redirection Test (DART) Mission," The Planetary Society, planetary.org/space-policy/cost-of-dart.

97. Eric Berger, "NASA Has Begun a Study of the SLS Rocket's Affordability," Ars Technica, March 15, 2021.

98. Daniel R. Glover, "NASA Experimental Communications Satellites, 1958–1995," in *Beyond the Ionosphere: Fifty Years of Satellite Communication*, ed. Andrew J. Butrica (Washington, DC: US Government Printing Office, 1997).

99. Legal Information Institute, "47 US Code, Chapter 6: Communications Satellite System," Cornell Law School, law.cornell.edu/uscode/text/47/chapter-6.

100. "This Week in NASA History – Intelsat I: The 'Early Bird' of Satellites,'" NASA/APPEL Knowledge Services, February 25, 2010; "Meet Intelsat 1," Intelsat, intelsat.com/meet-intelsat-1.

101. "Satellite Communications: Development of Satellite Communication," Encyclopedia Britannica, britannica.com/technology/satellite-communication/Development-of-satellite-communication# ref52603.

102. "Comsat Corporation," Reference for Business, referenceforbusiness.com/history2/70/Comsat-Corporation.html.

103. James E. David, "NASA's Secret Relationships with US Defense and Intelligence Agencies," National Security Archive, April 10, 2015.

104. Richard A. Morgan, "Military Use of Commercial Communication Satellites: A New Look at the Outer Space Treaty and 'Peaceful Purposes,'" *Journal of Air Law and Commerce* 60, no. 1 (1994): 239–325.

105. "Global Positioning System," Space Operations Command, March 22, 2017.

106. Bradford W. Parkinson et al., "Part 2: The Origins of GPS, Fighting to Survive," *GPS World*, June 2010.

107. Ailsa Harvey and Mike Wall, "Everything You Need to Know about the Space-Based Technology Keeping Us on Track," Space.com, December 6, 2022.

108. "Origins of the Commercial Space Industry," Federal Aviation Administration (FAA), faa.gov/about/history/milestones/media/commercial_space_industry.pdf.

109. "Origins of the Commercial Space Industry," FAA.

110. Philip M. Boffey, "Commercial Lunching by NASA Ordered Shifted to Private Sector," *New York Times*, August 16, 1986.

111. Cody Knipfer, "Congress and Commerce in the Final Frontier (Part 1)," *The Space Review*, December 10, 2018.

112. William J. Broad, "Private Rocket Industry in Giant Step Skyward," *New York Times*, March 30, 1989.

113. "Origins of the Commercial Space Industry," FAA.

114. Craig R. Reed, "Factors Affecting US Commercial Space Launch Industry Competitiveness," *Business and Economic History* 27, no. 1 (1998): 226.

115. Mike Gerow, "End of an Era: Exit General Dynamics, Enter Lockheed Martin and ULA," San Diego Air and Space Museum, sandiegoairandspace.org/exhibits/online-exhibit-page/end-of-an-era-exit-general-dynamics-enter-lockheed-martin-and-ula; "Company News; Martin Marietta to Buy General Dynamics Unit," *New York Times,* December 23, 1993.

116. President's Commission on Implementation of United States Space Exploration Policy, "A Journey to Inspire, Innovate, and Discover," NASA, June 2004.

117. "Commercial Orbital Transportation Services: A New Era in Spaceflight," NASA, 5

118. "Commercial Orbital," 12.

119. "Commercial Orbital," 5, 37.

120. "Commercial Orbital," 5, 37.

121. "Commercial Orbital," 36–8.

122. "Commercial Orbital," 100.

123. "NASA Chief Acknowledges More Trouble with SLS Rocket," CGTN, March 14, 2019; Andrew Jones, "NASA's Artemis Moon Rocket Will Cost $6 Billion More than Planned: Report," Space.com, May 26, 2023.

124. "Space Force Awards National Security Space Launch Phase 2 Launch Service Contracts to ULA, SpaceX," US Air Force, August 7, 2020.

125. "Space Force Awards," US Air Force.

126. Erik Seedhouse, *SpaceX: Starship to Mars, the First 20 Years* (London: Springer Nature, 2022), 111–29.

127. "Launches," SpaceX, spacex.com/launches.

128. Russell Lewis, "Boeing Finds New Problems with Starliner Space Capsule and Delays First Crewed Launch," NPR, June 1, 2023; Mike Wall, "Boeing Delays 1st Starliner Astronaut Launch for NASA to March 2024 (at the Earliest), *Space*, August 7, 2023, space.com/boeing-starliner-launch-delay-march-2024.

129. Gary Martin, "New Space: The 'Emerging' Commercial Space Industry," NASA Ames Research Center, 2014, 23.

130. Matthew S. Schwartz, "SpaceX Wins $2.9 Billion Contract for Next Lunar Lander," NPR, April 17, 2021.

131. NASA's space shuttle cost about $30,000 (2021 dollars) per pound when it was retired in 2011, expendable launch vehicle providers Rocket Lab (US/New Zealand) and Roscosmos (Russia) cost about $10,000 and $8,000 per pound respectively as of a 2021 report, and SpaceX cost about $1200 per pound. See Denise Chow, "To Cheaply Go: How Falling Launch Costs Fueled a Thriving Economy in Orbit," NBC News, April 8, 2022; "Falcon 9," SpaceX, spacex.com/vehicles/falcon-9.

132. SpaceX has suggested costs to orbit as low as $10 per kilogram once Starship development is complete, and anything within even an order of magnitude would be extraordinary. Conversely, NASA's SLS system has been projected by auditors to cost $60,000 per kilogram. See Sarah Scoles, "Prime Mover: Starship Will Be the Biggest Rocket Ever. Are Space Scientists Ready to Take Advantage of It?" *Science*, August 11, 2022.

133. "Space Economy Report 2022, 9th Edition (Extract)," Euroconsult, January 2023, 8; "NASA's FY 2022 Budget," The Planetary Society, planetary.org/space-policy/nasas-fy-2022-budget.

134. "Space Economy Report 2022, 9th Edition (Extract)," Euroconsult, 11.

135. "Space Investment Quarterly Q4 2022," Space Capital, January 2023.

136. "Space Investment Quarterly: Q1 2023," Space Capital, April 2023.

137. Anthony Mirhaydari, "Elon Musk, Jeff Bezos and the New Race for Space," PitchBook, March 27, 2018.

138. "A New Space Economy on the Edge of Liftoff," Morgan Stanley, February 17, 2021.

139. "Arianespace at Europe's Spaceport," The European Space Agency, esa.int/Enabling_Support/Space_Transportation/Europe_s_Spaceport/Arianespace_at_Europe_s_Spaceport; Neel V. Patel, "China's Surging Private Space Industry Is Out to Challenge the US," *MIT Technology Review*, January 21, 2021; "Creation of International Launch Services," International Launch Services, June 10, 1995.

140. Svetla Ben-Itzhak, "Companies Are Commercializing Outer Space. Do Government Programs Still Matter?" *Washington Post*, January 11, 2022; Jake Parks, "Breakthrough Starshot: A Voyage to the Stars within Our Lifetimes," *Astronomy*, June 17, 2021; "Planetary Resources Intellectual Property Pledge," ConsenSys Space, consensys.space/pr; Loren Grush, "To Mine the Moon, Private Company Moon Express Plans to Build a Fleet of Robotic Landers," The Verge, July 12, 2017.

141. K.G. Orphanides, "American Companies Could Soon Mine Asteroids for Profit," *Wired*, November 12, 2015.

142. Office of Space Commerce and Federal Aviation Administration Office of Commercial Space Transportation, "US Export Controls for the Commercial Space Industry," US Department of Commerce, 2017; "Export Controlled or

Embargoed Countries, Entities and Persons," University of California, Berkeley Research, vcresearch.berkeley.edu/export-controls/export-controlled-or-embar goed-countries-entities-and-persons; Jeff Foust, "One Nation, Over Regulated: Is ITAR Stalling the New Space Race?" *Ad Astra* 17, no. 3 (Winter 2005).

143. Deng Xiaoci and Fan Anqi, "China Scored 55 Orbital Launches in Super 2021, Topping US to Become 1st in the World," *Global Times,* December 31, 2021; Alexandra Witze, "2022 Was a Record Year for Space Launches," *Nature* 613, no. 7944 (January 19, 2023).

144. John G. Paulisick et al., "Research and Development Contributions to Aviation Progress (RADCAP), Volume I, Summary Report," Department of the Air Force, August 1972, III-12.

145. Donald M. Pattillo, *Pushing the Envelope: The American Aircraft Industry* (Ann Arbor: University of Michigan Press, 1998), 149.

146. Charles D. Bright, *The Jet Makers: The Aerospace Industry from 1945 to 1972* (Lawrence: Regents Press of Kansas, 1978), 114.

147. Herman O. Stekler, *The Structure and Performance of the Aerospace Industry* (Berkeley: University of California Press, 1965), 16.

148. Stekler, *The Structure.*

149. Gregory Hooks, "The Rise of the Pentagon and US State Building: The Defense Program as Industrial Policy," *American Journal of Sociology* 96, no. 2 (September 1990): 358–404.

150. Pattillo, *Pushing the Envelope,* 324.

151. For example, during the early 1980s, the Air Force bought from McDonnell Douglas 60 KC-10 flying tankers, almost identical to the DC-10 except for their refueling equipment. This sale enabled the firm to keep its DC-10 production line running until the civilian market improved sufficiently for development of the derivative MD-11 later in the decade.

152. Pattillo, *Pushing the Envelope,* 250.

153. C.R. Smith cited in John B. Rae, *Climb to Greatness: The American Aircraft Industry, 1920–1960* (Cambridge, MA: The MIT Press, 1968), 207.

154. Paulisick, "Contributions to Aviation Progress," III-23.

155. Paulisick, "Contributions to Aviation Progress," V-4.

156. Paulisick, "Contributions to Aviation Progress," V-6.

157. Obaid Younossi et al., "Military Jet Engine Acquisition: Technology Basics and Cost-Estimating Methodology," RAND, 2002, 101.

158. Younossi et al., "Military Jet Engine Acquisition," 101–2.

159. Paulisick, "Contributions to Aviation Progress," III-23.

160. Paulisick, "Contributions to Aviation Progress," III-32, V-10.

161. Paulisick, "Contributions to Aviation Progress," III-32.

162. "Aviation History," GE Aerospace, 2023, geaerospace.com/company/aviation-history.

163. "Full Scale Technology Demonstration of a Modern Counterrotating Unducted Fan Engine Concept. Design Report, Document ID, 19900000732, December 1, 1987, ntrs.nasa.gov/citations/19900000732.

164. S. Arif Khalid, David Lurie, et al., "Open Rotor Engine Aeroacoustic Technology Final Report," FAA, May 2013.

165. "High Performance Carbon Fibers," American Chemical Society, September 17, 2003.

166. E. B. Birchfield and R. Kollmansberger, "Develop Fabrication/Processing Techniques for High Temperature Advanced Composites for Use in Aircraft Structures," McDonnell Aircraft Company, July 1972.

167. D. L. Grimes, "Plastic Adhesives and Aircraft Construction," *Army Air Force Technical Data Digest*, October 1944, 56.

168. Paulisick, "Contributions to Aviation Progress," III-17.

169. Art Kracke, "Superalloys, the Most Successful Alloy System of Modern Times: Past, Present and Future," The Minerals, Metals & Materials Society, 2010, 21.

170. "Ground-Based Navigation: Instrument Landing System (ILS)," Federal Aviation Administration, February 8, 2023, faa.gov/about/office_org/headquarters_offices/ato/service_units/techops/navservices/gbng/ils.

171. Paulisick, "Contributions to Aviation Progress," III-18, III-26.

172. Paulisick, "Contributions to Aviation Progress," III-18, III-33.

173. Paulisick, "Contributions to Aviation Progress," III-18, III-33.

174. C-17: "C-17 Globemaster III," US Air Force, n.d., af.mil/About-Us/Fact-Sheets/Display/Article/1529726/c-17-globemaster-iii; C-5M: "C-5 A/B/C Galaxy and C-5M Super Galaxy," US Air Force, af.mil/About-Us/Fact-Sheets/Display/Article/1529718/c-5-abc-galaxy-and-c-5m-super-galaxy.

175. "Made with Japan: A Partnership on the Frontiers of Aerospace," Boeing Japan, November 2012, 4. Confirmed by Stan Sorscher, former staffer, SPEEA, IFPTE Local 2001, April 6, 2022. See also Kevin Michaels, *AeroDynamic: Inside the High-Stakes Global Jetliner Ecosystem* (Reston, VA: American Institute of Aeronautics and Astronautics, 2018), 193.

176. Statement of J. Michael Farren, Undersecretary of International Trade Administration, US Department of Commerce, US Congress, Joint Economic Committee, *The Aerospace Industry: Hearings before the Subcommittee on Technology and National Security of the Joint Economic Committee*, 102nd Cong., 2nd sess., February 27, 1992, 170; Laura D'Andrea Tyson, *Who's Bashing Whom? Trade Conflict in High-Technology Industries*. Peterson Institute for International Economics 86 (Washington, DC: Peterson Institute Press, 1992).

177. Brian Rowe and Martin Ducheny, *The Power to Fly: An Engineer's Life* (Reston, VA: American Institute of Aeronautics and Astronautics), 54.

178. Rowe and Ducheny, *The Power to Fly*, 69.

179. Rosita Mickeviciute, "Airbus A320: A Game-Changer in Commercial Aviation," June 16, 2023, Aerotime Hub, aerotime.aero/articles/a320-a-game-changer-in-commercial-aviation.

180. Tyson, *Who's Bashing Whom?* 198.

181. David C. Mowery and Nathan Rosenberg, *Technology and the Pursuit of Economic Growth* (New York: Cambridge University Press, 1989), 196.

182. Tyson, *Who's Bashing Whom?* 203–4.

183. Tyson, *Who's Bashing Whom?* 204.

184. "EC and US Agree on Principles and Objectives for Future Negotiations on Trade in Civil Aircraft," EC Press Release, October 28, 1987, aei.pitt.edu/view/eusubjects/HOnatranreltrade.default.html.

185. "EU–US Agreement on Large Civil Aircraft 1992: Key Facts and Figures," European Commission, October 6, 2004.

186. Laura D'Andrea Tyson and Pei-Hsiung Chin, "McDonnell Douglas and Taiwan Aerospace: A Strategic Perspective on the National Interest in the Commercial Aircraft Industry," *Journal of Policy Analysis and Management*, 11, no. 4 (Autumn, 1992): 697–701.

187. Ervin Ackman, *President Reagan's Program to Secure US Leadership Indefinitely: Project Socrates: How All Americans Can Participate and Reap the Benefits* (Austin, TX: Ervin Ackman, 2013), 210.

188. Ackman, *President Reagan's Program*, 213.

189. Stephan Wittig, "Transatlantic Trade Dispute: Solution for Airbus-Boeing under Biden?" *Intereconomics* 56, no. 1 (2021): 23–31.

190. "EU–US Agreement on Large Civil Aircraft 1992: Key Facts and Figures," European Commission, October 6, 2004.

191. Louis Uchitelle, "A Japanese Strategy for Boeing," *New York Times*, November. 3, 1989.

192. Michaels, *AeroDynamic*, 195.

193. Michaels, *AeroDynamic*, 200.

27. Robotics: A Global Industrial Policy Competition

1. While spinning, weaving, knitting, and dying lend themselves well to mass production and economies of scale with relatively simple equipment, many steps in the handling of fabrics require fine dexterity. It is only with new advancements in "soft grippers" and control systems that the use of industrial robots has become feasible for these tasks. This is in contrast with, for example, electronics assembly, many steps of which are easier to handle with robots. See "The Textile (R)evolution: KUKA Small Robotics Automates the Textile Industry," YouTube video, KUKA – Robots and Automation, January 23, 2019, www.youtube.com/watch?v=2JjUnKpsJRM.

2. Japan, South Korea, and Germany have more robots per worker than the US, but a lower fraction of their workers making low wages, per the OECD definition as under two-thirds of the median wage, per Peter Morici, "Opinion: Don't Tax Robots!" MarketWatch, January 13, 2023.

3. International Federation of Robots, "World Robotics 2023 Report": Asia Ahead of Europe and the Americas," ifr.org/ifr-press-releases/news/world-robotics-2023-report-asia-ahead-of-europe-and-the-americas.

4. International Federation of Robots, "World Robotics 2023 Report."

5. Brianna Wessling, "Robot Sales on Track to Hit a New High in 2022," *Robot Report*, December 21, 2022.

6. International Federation of Robots, "Global Robotics Race: Korea, Singapore and Germany in the Lead Robot Density Data by International Federation of Robotics reveal, January 10, 2024, ifr.org/ifr-press-releases/news/global-robotics-race-korea-singapore-and-germany-in-the-lead.

7. Sudeep Chakravarty, "World's Top 10 Industrial Robot Manufacturers," Market Research Reports, May 8, 2019.

8. "Omron to Acquire US based Adept Technology," Omron, September 16, 2015.

9. ECHORD: "Robotics 2020: Strategic Research Agenda for Robotics in Europe," Draft 0v42, European Commission and euRobotics, October 11, 2013, 20. Horizon: "The total budget [for Horizon 2020] in current prices is nearly €80 billion and in constant prices €70.2 billion." "Factsheet: Horizon 2020 Budget," European Commission, November 25, 2013; "Work Programme 2014–2015," Horizon 2020, European Commission, April 17, 2015. SPARC: "Robotics 2020 Multi-annual Roadmap for Robotics in Europe," Initial Release B, euRobotics, January 15, 2014.

10. "New Robot Strategy: Japan's Robot Strategy – Vision, Strategy, Action Plan," Headquarters for Japan's Economic Revitalization, October 2, 2015.

11. "Robotics Research: How Asia, Europe and America Invest – Global Report 2023 by IFR," International Federation of Robots, January 12, 2021.

12. Ya-Ping Lee, "Executive Yuan Yuan Promoted 'Productivity 4.0' to Boost Global Competitiveness," Science & Technology Law Institute, September 2016.

13. Data are compiled in part from "World Robotics R&D Programs: Information Paper," International Federation of Robotics, ifr.org/r-and-d. Some US data are from "Accelerating US Robotics for American Prosperity and Security," American Society of Mechanical Engineers, January 2019, 2–4.

14. Chinese government funding for robotics R&D is almost certainly understated "due to difficulty in accessing governmental materials." See "World Robotics R&D Programs," International Federation of Robotics, December 2022, 5. In addition, the National Bureau of Statistics of China put China's national R&D funding at $441.38 billion for 2021. See "China's R&D Expenditure Reached 2.79 Trillion Yuan in 2021," National Bureau of Statistics of China, January 27, 2022.

15. The word "moonshot" is a metaphor and is not related to space exploration.

16. These funds are targeted to manufacturing ($77.8 million), nursing/medical ($55 million), infrastructure ($643.2 million), and agriculture ($66.2 million). "Report: How Asia, Europe and America Invest in Robotics," Automation.com, January 17, 2023, automation.com/en-us/articles/january-2023/report-how-asia-europe-america-invest-robotics.

17. German firms and research institutions receive a large but unspecified percentage of European Union robotics R&D funding. That increment is not included in the German total on this table.

18. "Factories of the Future," European Factories of the Future Research Association (EFFRA), effra.eu/factories-future#How%20It%20Works; "Progress Monitoring Report for 2017," EFFRA, 2018, 2; "Factories of the Future: Multi-annual Roadmap for the Contractual PPP under Horizon 2020," EFFRA, 2013, 9.

19. Pablo Valerio, "Robotics: EU Launches $3.9 Billion Initiative," EE Times, June 5, 2014.

20. John Edwards, "The Quiet Giant of Asian Robotics: Korea," Robotics Business Review, May 8, 2014.

21. Authors' calculations from "Table 1. NASA Budget Authority, FY2018–FY2023," in "NASA Appropriations and Authorizations: A Fact Sheet," Congressional Research Service, 2. The numbers are derived by multiplying the total budget authority by 0.30. According to the Planetary Society, while funding varies from year to year, about 30 percent is spent "on robotic missions and scientific research." See "Your Guide to NASA's Budget," The Planetary Society, planetary.org/space-policy/nasa-budget.

22. Authors' calculation based on "World Robotics R&D Programs," International Federation of Robotics, December 2022, 15.

23. Authors' calculation based on "World Robotics R&D Programs."

24. David Klein, "2021 Defense Budget for Unmanned Systems and Robotics," Association for Unmanned Vehicle Systems International, 2021, 24.

25. Authors' estimate based on "World Robotics R&D Programs," 15.

26. "Robotics at NSF," n.d., nsf.gov/eng/robotics.jsp.

27. This number is based on the sum of all the awards made by the FRR program, found at nsf.gov/awardsearch/advancedSearchResult?ProgEleCode=144Y&BooleanElement=Any&BooleanRef=Any&ActiveAwards=true#results.

28. Initial funding from DOD to start the institute, plus subsequent DOD funding.

29. Individual grants to universities can be examined at nsf.gov/awardsearch/advancedSearchResult?ProgEleCode=144Y&BooleanElement=Any&BooleanRef=Any&ActiveAwards=true#results.

30. See Section 10387(c)(4) in US Congress, House, Chips and Science Act, HR 4346, 117th Cong., introduced in House July 1, 2021.

31. "Operational Stock of Robots – Japan," International Federation of Robotics, ifr.org/news/japan-is-worlds-number-one-robot-maker.

32. "Robot Race: The World's Top 10 Automated Countries," International Federation of Robotics, July 27, 2021.

33. "Robotics 2/47, "World Robotics Report 2023 Shows Ongoing Global Growth in Installations, Finds IFR," September 26, 2023, robotics247.com/article/ world_robotics_report_2023_shows_ongoing_global_growth_installations_finds_ifr.

34. "Trends in the Japanese Robotics Industry," *JETRO Japan Economic Monthly*, March 2006, 3.

35. "Trends in the Japanese Robotics Industry," 14.

36. "New Robot Strategy," Headquarters for Japan's Economic Revitalization, kantei .go.jp/jp/singi/keizaisaisei/pdf/robot_honbun_150210EN.pdf.

37. Japan's Regulatory Reform Council sought both to "establish new rules for collaboration of human and robots ... while abolishing unnecessary [robot] regulations." See "New Robot Strategy," Headquarters for Japan's Economic Revitalization, 15.

38. "New Robot Strategy," 3.

39. "New Robot Strategy," 1.

40. "Japan Revitalization Strategy: Japan's Challenge for the Future," Prime Minister's Office of Japan, June 24, 2014, 23, 81; "New Robot Strategy," Headquarters for Japan's Economic Revitalization, 65.

41. Samo Burja, "China Tests Our Dream of an Automated Future," Bismarck Analysis, June 1, 2022.

42. An example of the dynamics at play can be found here: Raden Agoeng Bhimasta and Pei-Yi Kuo, "What Causes the Adoption Failure of Service Robots? A Case of Henna Hotel in Japan," 2019 ACM International Joint Conference on Pervasive and Ubiquitous Computing, September 2019.

43. "China Overtakes USA in Robot Density," International Federation of Robotics.

44. IFR, "World Robotics 2023 Report: The Number of Robots in German Industry Is Increasing," Newscast, n.d., newcast.com/en/Media_News/News/IFR_ "World_Robotics_2023_Report"_-_The_number_of_robots_in_German_industry_ is_increasing.

45. Brianna Wessling, "Robotics and Automation Germany," *Robot Report*, March 29, 2023.

46. "Germany: Industrie 4.0," Digital Transformation Monitor, European Commission, January 2017, 3, ati.ec.europa.eu/sites/default/files/2020–06/ DTM_Industrie%204.0_DE.pdf.

47. "New High-Tech Strategy: Innovation for Germany," Federal Ministry for Economic Affairs and Climate Action, 2022. The 2010 report outlining the plan is called "High-Tech Strategy 2020 for Germany," but the plan itself is called the "High-Tech Strategy." A 2014 update also referred to it as the "High-Tech Strategy."

48. FP1: Michael Artis and F. Nixson, eds., *The Economics of the European Union: Policy and Analysis* (Oxford: Oxford University Press, 2001) 162, table 7.3. FP9: "Horizon Europe," European Commission, research-and-innovation.ec.europa.eu/ funding/funding-opportunities/funding-programmes-and-open-calls/horizon-europe_en.

49. "Robotics PPP: The Next Generation of Intelligent Robots to Keep EU Manufacturing Competitive," European Commission, 2013.

50. "Robotics 2020: Strategic Research Agenda for Robotics in Europe," European Commission and euRobotics, 20.
51. "Robotics PPP," European Commission.
52. European Commission press release, "EU Launches World's Largest Civilian Robotics Programme: 240,000 New Jobs Expected," June 3, 2014, ec.europa.eu/commission/presscorner/detail/en/IP_14_619.
53. Valerio, "Robotics."
54. "Official Launch of SPARC, the PPP in Robotics, with the European Commission at AUTOMATICA 2014 Opening," SPARC, Press Release, March 6, 2014.
55. "Robotics 2020: Strategic Research Agenda for Robotics in Europe," euRobotics aisbl, November 10, 2013, 25.
56. "The total budget [for Horizon 2020] in current prices is nearly €80 billion and in constant prices €70.2 billion." See "Factsheet: Horizon 2020 Budget" and "Work Programme 2014–2015," Horizon 2020, European Commission.
57. See "Factories of the Future," EFFRA; "Progress Monitoring Report for 2017," EFFRA, 2; "Factories of the Future: Multi-annual Roadmap for the Contractual PPP under Horizon 2020," EFFRA, 9.
58. Edwards, "The Quiet Giant of Asian Robotics."
59. Mai Tao, "South Korea Reaches New Record of 300,000 Industrial Robots in Operation," Robotics & Automation News, February 3, 2020; "Executive Summary World Robotics 2022 Industrial Robots," International Federation of Robotics, 2022, 13.
60. "The Robots Are Rising Faster in Korea than Elsewhere," *Korea JoongAng Daily*, January 27, 2021.
61. "Article 5" in "Intelligent Robots Development and Distribution Promotion Act," Korea Law Translation Center, enacted March 28, 2008, last amended January 6, 2016.
62. Doug Lee, "South Korea Gets Ambitious, Invest Billions in Next-Gen Industrial Robotisation," *World Industrial Reporter*, July 28, 2014.
63. Kim Sang-mo, "Policy Directions for S. Korea's Robot Industry," *BusinessKorea*, August 17, 2018.
64. Mechatronics is defined as technology combining electronics and mechanical engineering. Edwards, "The Quiet Giant of Asian Robotics."
65. Edwards, "The Quiet Giant of Asian Robotics."
66. Michelle Starr, "Scientists Unveil World's First Cancer-Fighting Nanobot," CNET, December 17, 2013.
67. Sam Kim, "South Korea's Robots Are Both Friends and Job Killers," Bloomberg, November 10, 2019.
68. Kim, "Policy Directions."
69. Sarah Dougherty, "South Korea's Robot Land: Theme Park or Training Ground for Robot Armies?" *The World*, January 22, 2014, theworld.org/stories/2014–01–22/south-koreas-robot-land-theme-park-or-training-ground-robot-armies.
70. "S. Korea Aims to Become No. 4 Robotics Player by 2023," *Korea Herald*, March 22, 2019, koreaherald.com/common/newsprint.php?ud=20190322000576.
71. Felix Richter, "China Leads Growth of Global Industrial Robot Stock," Statista, November 27, 2023, statista.com/chart/31337/new-installations-of-industrial-robots-by-country.
72. "Robotics Industry Expected to Become a Game Changer," Invest Korea, June 7, 2022, investkorea.org/ik-en/bbs/i-308/detail.do?ntt_sn=490769.

73. "Development and Utilization of Robotic Services to Assist Care Facilities," Seoul Metropolitan Government, July 28, 2023, english.seoul.go.kr/development-and-utilization-of-robotic-services-to-assist-care-facilities.

74. "China Aims to Be Hub of Global Robotics Industry," State Council of the People's Republic of China, December 29, 2021.

75. The Development Plan of the Robot Industry (2016–10) is characterized and published in English as an appendix in "World Robotics R&D Programs," International Federation of Robotics, 77–84.

76. "World Robotics R&D Programs," International Federation of Robotics, 6; Jonathan Ray et al., "China's Industrial and Military Robotics Development," US-China Economic and Security Review Commission, October 2016, 10.

77. He Huifeng, "China's Five-Year Plan to Transform Its Robotics Industry," *South China Morning Post*, April 6, 2016.

78. "Robot Density Rises Globally," International Federation of Robotics, February 7, 2018. Andrew Zaleski, "China's Blueprint to Crush the US Robotics Industry," CNBC, September 6, 2017.

79. "China's Booming Robotics Industry Shapes Intelligent Future," Xinhuanet, September 13, 2021.; "China Overtakes USA in Robot Density," International Federation of Robotics; "World Robotics R&D Programs," International Federation of Robotics, 18; "World Robotics R&D Programs: Executive Summary," International Federation of Robotics, April 2021.

80. "Under the Hood: China's Robot Parts Industry: China Challenges the Foreign Robot Parts Monopoly's 75% Market Share," *Asian Robotics Review*, 2021.

81. "China Aims for Global Leadership in Robotics with New 5-Year Plan," IFR Press Room, International Federation of Robotics, January 20, 2022. ifr.org/ifr-press-releases/news/china-aims-for-global-leadership-in-robotics.

82. "Declaration Guidelines for the 'Key Special Program on Intelligent Robots' of 2019," in "World Robotics R&D Programs," International Federation of Robotics, 85–99.

83. Shin Watanabe, "China's Robot Makers Gobble Up Global Rivals, with Help from State," *Nikkei Asia*, November 26, 2019.

84. Germany amended its Foreign Trade and Payments Act to tighten controls over foreign investments in "critical technologies such as artificial intelligence, robotics and semiconductors." See "Foreign Direct Investment Regimes 2021," International Comparative Legal Guides, November 5, 2020.

85. Graham Allison, "Is China Beating America to AI Supremacy?" *The National Interest*, December 22, 2019.

86. Ray et al., "China's Industrial and Military Robotics Development," 10.

87. "National Robotics Initiative 3.0: Innovations in Integration of Robotics (NRI-3.0)," National Science Foundation, manufacturing.gov/programs/national-robotics-initiative.

88. "Robotics at NSF," National Science Foundation, nsf.gov/eng/robotics.jsp.

89. "Sunsetting of NRI: Guidance for Researchers," National Science Foundation, June 2, 2022; "Foundational Research in Robotics," National Science Foundation, February 11, 2020.

90. "Institute Snapshot," Department of Defense Manufacturing Technology Program, dodmantech.mil/About-Us/Manufacturing-Innovation-Institutes-MIIs/ARM-Institute; "$250 Million to Support Advanced Robotics Venture Led by CMU," Carnegie Melon University, January 13, 2017.

91. "ARM: Advanced Robotics for Manufacturing Institute," Department of Defense Manufacturing Technology Program, dodmantech.mil/About-Us/Manufacturing-Innovation-Institutes-MIIs/ARM-Institute.

92. "Institute Snapshot," Department of Defense Manufacturing Technology Program, dodmantech.mil/About-Us/Manufacturing-Innovation-Institutes-MIIs/ARM-Institute.

93. This material adapted from a December 21, 2023 email from Ira Moskowitz, CEO, Advanced Robotics for Manufacturing (ARM) Institute, to author Ian Fletcher.

94. Email from Ira Moskowitz, December 21, 2023.

28. Nanotechnology: Is America Losing the Future?

1. L. J. Eads, Ryan Clarke, and Xiaoxu Sean Lin, "In the Shadows of Science: Unravelling China's Invisible Arsenals of Nanoweapons," CCP Biothreats Initiative, August 2023.

2. National Academies of Sciences, Engineering, and Medicine, *A Quadrennial Review of the National Nanotechnology Initiative: Nanoscience, Applications, and Commercialization* (Washington, DC: National Academies Press, 2020).

3. See "Preface," in *National Research Council, Small Wonders, Endless Frontiers: A Review of the National Nanotechnology Initiative* (Washington, DC: National Academies Press, 2002), 22.

4. National Nanotechnology Coordination Office, "NNI Supplement to the President's 2024 Budget," March 5, 2024, 6.

5. "NNI Supplement to the President's 2024 Budget," vi.

6. "President's Management Agenda," White House Archives of President Donald Trump, March 2018, 47.

7. National Nanotechnology Coordinated Infrastructure, "NNCI Coordinating Office Annual Report (Year 8) April 1, 2023–March 31, 2024," February 12, 2024, 6.

8. "NNCI Coordinating Office Annual Report (Year 8)," 5.

9. See National Cancer Institute, "Cancer Nanotechnology Plan," National Institutes of Health, cancer.gov/sites/nano/research/plan.

10. Figure based on end-of-period exchange rate.

11. English Translation of PRC State Council, "State Council Notice on the Publication of the National 13th Five-Year Plan for S&T Innovation," Central People's Government of the People's Republic of China, January 8, 2020.

12. Suresh K. Chauhan, "Nanotechnology Research Output: Bibliometric Analysis with Special Reference to India," *Journal of Nanoparticle Research*, September 20, 2020, 278.

13. EU member states can, get around EU rules, to some extent, if they make a serious strategic effort to do so. Some cheat by either disregarding the rules and getting a slap on the wrist from the EU (France consistently does so), or they disguise the funding through a multitude of federal and state agencies/institutions and various banking system ploys (as in Germany).

14. "How ASML Became Chipmaking's Biggest Monopoly," *Economist*, February 27, 2020; "ASML and Imec Launch Advanced Patterning Center," *Silicon Semiconductor*, October 18, 2013.

15. "UK to Promote Nanotechnologies," Cordis, August 24, 2004.

16. English Translation of PRC State Council, "State Council Notice on the Publication of the National 13th Five-Year Plan for S&T Innovation," Central People's Government of the People's Republic of China.

17. See Jost Wübbeke et al., "Made in China 2025: The Making of a High-Tech Superpower and Consequences for Industrial Countries," Mercator Institute of China Studies (MERICS), August 12, 2016.

18. Julie Chao, "From the Lab to Your Digital Device, Quantum Dots Have Made Quantum Leaps," Berkeley Lab, January 8, 2015.

19. John Schwartz, "White House to Relax Energy Efficiency Rules for Light Bulbs," *New York Times*, September 4, 2019.

20. Office of the Dean of the Faculty, "Stephen Ross Forrest," Princeton University, dof .princeton.edu/people/stephen-ross-forrest; Steven Schultz, "New Technique Could Lead to Widespread Use of Solar Power," *Princeton Weekly Bulletin* 93, no. 17 (February 23, 2004).

21. Universal Display Corporation, Form 10-K 2017, Ewing, NJ: Universal Display Corporation, 2017, F-31.

22. The term "industrial commons" was coined by Pisano and Shih in Gary P. Pisano and Willy C. Shih, "Restoring American Competitiveness," *Harvard Business Review*, July–August 2009, 114–25.

23. The theoretical Shockley–Queisser is actually closer to 30 percent, but practical considerations mean that the actual practical upper limit is now thought to be closer to 26 percent.

24. Wanli Ma, Cuiying Yang, Xiong Gong, Kwanghee Lee, and Alan J. Heeger, "Thermally Stable, Efficient Polymer Solar Cells with Nanoscale Control of the Interpenetrating Network Morphology," *Advanced Functional Materials*, October 2005.

25. "Our History," Konarka Technologies, archived September 28, 2010, web.archive .org/web/20100928083056/konarka.com/index.php/company/our-history.

26. Nichola Groom, "Exclusive: Controversial US Energy Loan Program Has Wiped Out Losses," Reuters, November 13, 2014.

27. oxfordpv.com/perovskite-pv-transform-global-solar-market.

28. Andy Extance, "The Reality behind Solar Power's Next Star Material," *Nature*, June 25, 2019.

29. "Top 10 Perovskite Solar Cell Manufacturers Setting the New Standard for Renewable Energy," Verified Market Research, May 2023.

30. "Tandem Photovoltaics Enables New Heights in Solar Cell Efficiencies: 35.9% for III-V//Silicon Solar Cell," Fraunhofer, April 23, 2021.

31. Sydney Lupkin, "How Will Moderna Meet the Demand for Its COVID-19 Vaccine?" *All Things Considered*, National Public Radio, December 17, 2020.

32. Michael Fossel, "A Unified Model of Dementias and Age-Related Neurodegeneration," *Alzheimer's & Dementia* 16, no. 2 (February 2020): 245–384.

33. "FDA Approves First-of-Its Kind Targeted RNA-Based Therapy to Treat a Rare Disease," Food and Drug Administration, August 10, 2018.

34. G. Gumuskaya, P. Srivastava, B. G. Cooper, H. Lesser, B. Semegran, S. Garnier, and M. Levin, "Motile Living Biobots Self-Construct from Adult Human Somatic Progenitor Seed Cells." *Advanced Science* 2023, 2303575.

35. See "NanoData Landscape Compilation: Update Report 2017," European Commission, 2018, 17–20.

36. "FY 2021 Budget Request to Congress," National Science Foundation, February 10, 2020, 53–5.

37. "Harvard University Professor and Two Chinese Nationals Charged in Three Separate China Related Cases," Department of Justice, January 28, 2020.

38. US Congress, Senate, Permanent Subcommittee on Investigations, Committee on Homeland Security and Governmental Affairs, *Threats to the US Research*

Enterprise: China's Talent Recruitment Plans, 116th Cong., 1st sess., November 2019.

39. "Overview of Quantum Initiatives Worldwide 2023," Qureca, July 19, 2023, qureca.com/overview-of-quantum-initiatives-worldwide-2023.

40. "National Quantum Initiative Supplement to the President's FY 2023 Budget," Subcommittee on Quantum Information Science, Committee on Science of the National Science and Technology Council, January 2023, 3.

41. Stephen Shankland, "US Begins $1 Billion Quantum Computing Plan to Get Ahead of 'Adversaries,'" CNET, August 26, 2020, cnet.com/tech/computing/us-begins-1-billion-quantum-computing-plan-to-get-ahead-of-adversaries.

42. "National Quantum Initiative Supplement to the President's FY 2023 Budget: A Report by the Subcommittee on Quantum Information Science, Committee on Science of the National Science & Technology Council, January 2023, ii and 10–13, quantum.gov/wp-content/uploads/2023/01/NQI-Annual-Report-FY2023.pdf.

43. English translation of Pan Jianwei, "To Seize the Opportunity of a New Round of Quantum Revolution, We Must Give Full Play to the Advantages of the New Nationwide System," *Sina Technology Comprehensive*, October 19, 2020.

44. Han-Sen Zhong et al., "Quantum Computational Advantage Using Photons," *Science* 370, no. 6523 (March 2020): 1460–3.

45. Frank Tavares, NASA, "Google and NASA Achieve Quantum Supremacy," October 23, 2019, nasa.gov/technology/computing/google-and-nasa-achieve-quantum-supremacy.

29. The Massachusetts Life Sciences Cluster

1. This chapter is based in large part, with permission, on Barry Bluestone and Alan Clayton-Matthews, "Life Sciences Innovation as a Catalyst for Economic Development: The Role of the Massachusetts Life Sciences Center," The Kitty and Michael Dukakis Center for Urban and Regional Policy, Northeastern University, 2013.

2. "Boston Is Now the Largest Biotech Hub in the World," EPM Scientific, February 2023.

3. The specific life sciences industry sectors used in this report are based on the nonagricultural six-digit NAICS (North American Industry Classification System) as reported in "Battelle/Bio State Bioscience Industry Development 2012," the Battelle Institute, the Biotechnology Industry Organization (BIO), and MPM Public Affairs Consulting, Inc., June 2012.

4. This set of NAICS industries omits perhaps 50 percent of the growth in life sciences jobs in Massachusetts because it omits life sciences in research in hospitals and universities. These jobs are not counted in the Battelle report because the NAICS industrial coding system cannot distinguish between research jobs in hospitals and other jobs in hospitals such as physicians and nurses, and life sciences research jobs in universities and other jobs such as English and social science professors.

5. This research could not break out faculty, staff, and students involved in the life sciences departments and research institutes from all others employed at universities and hospitals. As a result, this report does not include an analysis of the educational attainment, earnings, and occupations for those working in these institutions. If this

had been possible, these estimates of the number of those employed in the life sciences in Massachusetts would be much greater.

6. See "Member Directory," MassBio, massbio.org/members. Institutions in the Life Sciences category: 758. Of those 758: 59% (450) drug development; 18% (134) contract research and manufacturing; 8% (60) research products and instrumentation; 3% (24) make medical devices; 5% (35) produce agricultural and industrial biotechnology.

7. Bluestone and Clayton-Matthews, "Life Sciences Innovation," 5.

8. "Emerging Technology Fund," MassDevelopment, 1, massdevelopment.com/assets/what-we-offer/etf-download.pdf.

9. See "Massachusetts Incentives and Workforce Development Guide," Business Facilities, December 9, 2014.

10. Bluestone and Clayton-Matthews, "Life Sciences Innovation," 19.

11. Bluestone and Clayton-Matthews, "Life Sciences Innovation," figure 4: Massachusetts Employment Growth by Industry Sector, 33.

12. See "Funding Programs," Massachusetts Life Sciences Center, masslifesciences.com/funding-programs.

13. "Massachusetts Life Sciences Center Annual Report Fiscal Year 2023," Massachusetts Life Sciences Center, 2023, 3.

14. See D. C. Denison, "Drugmakers, Mass. Form Consortium," *Boston Globe*, June 20, 2012.

15. TEConomy Partners, LLC and Mass Economics, "Public–Private Partnerships in Action: The Statewide Impact of the Massachusetts Life Sciences Center on the Life Sciences Ecosystem," The Massachusetts Life Sciences Center, 2018, 20.

16. See Jeanne Whalen and Mimosa Spencer, "Sanofi Wins Long-Sought Biotech Deal," *Wall Street Journal*, February 17, 2011.

17. "Life Sciences Cluster Report: Global 2011," Jones Lang LaSalle, November 30, 2011, 3, 16.

18. "Life Sciences Cluster Report: Global 2011," Jones Lang LaSalle, 16. Boston ranked number one on each component of the composite score with the exception of venture capital funding, where it ranked number two.

19. Tom Acitelli, "The Boston Area's Booming Life Sciences Industry and Why It Matters for Real Estate," Curbed Boston, January 13, 2020.

20. TEConomy Partners, LLC and Mass Economics, "Public–Private Partnerships in Action."

21. "The Biotech IPO Boom," BDO United States, February 2021; Jonathan Saltzman, "Massachusetts Biopharma Firms Raised a Record $5.8 Billion in Venture Capital Last Year," *Boston Globe*, March 4, 2021.

22. "The Top Ten Life Science Hubs in the US," Astrix, October 27, 2022, astrixinc.com/the-top-ten-life-science-hubs-in-the-us; and "2022 Industry Snapshot," MassBio, August 30, 2022, massbio.org/Industry-Snapshot.

23. Amber Schiada and Travis McCready, "2022 Life Sciences Research Outlook and Cluster Rankings," Jones Lang LaSalle, September 28, 2022.

24. Lee Dunham, Mark Ahn, and Anne S. York, "Building a Bioeconomy in the Heartland: Bridging the Gap between Resources and Perceptions," *Journal of Enterprising Communities: People and Places in the Global Economy* 6, no. 1 (2012): 84–100.

25. Peter M. Pellerito and George Goodno, "Successful State Initiatives That Encourage Bioscience Industry," Biotechnology Industry Organization (BIO), 2012.

26. "2019 Industry Snapshot," MassBio, August 2019, 6.

27. Jonathan Saltzman, "Boston Newcomer Alexion Strikes Second Deal in Less Than a Month," *Boston Globe*, October 25, 2018.
28. Barry Bluestone analysis from the US Bureau of Labor Statistics, Quarterly Census of Employment and Wages.
29. "Pfizer Signs Agreement with MIT for Future Cambridge Research Center," Pfizer, September 1, 2011.
30. Jonathan Saltzman, "Takeda Signs $50 Million Deal with French Biotech Enterome," *Boston Globe*, October 24, 2018.
31. "Moderna Reaffirms Commitment to Job Creation in Massachusetts," BusinessWire, June 18, 2021.
32. As previously noted, job creation figures here are known to be understated because they do not include certain occupations in hospitals and universities whose statistics are not separately available in government data. And salary results may, for similar reasons, be incomplete.
33. See Bluestone and Clayton-Matthews, "Life Sciences Innovation," 44.
34. "FY 2022 Annual Report," Massachusetts Life Sciences Center, 5.
35. "Massachusetts Life Sciences Employment Outlook, 2023," Massachusetts Biotechnology Education Foundation, May 2023, 3.
36. "2022 Massachusetts Life Sciences Workforce Analysis Report," Massachusetts Biotechnology Council, figure 5: Employee Educational Attainment, 17.
37. "2022 Massachusetts Life Sciences Workforce Analysis Report," Massachusetts Biotechnology Council, figure 6: Employee Roles, 17.
38. "Life Sciences Research Talent 2022," CBRE Research, June 13, 2022, 1.
39. "Life Sciences Salaries," Glassdoor, glassdoor.com/Salaries/life-scientist-salary-SRCH_KO0,14.htm.
40. "2022 Massachusetts Life Sciences Workforce Analysis Report," Massachusetts Biotechnology Council, 2022, 18.
41. Bluestone and Clayton-Matthews, "Life Sciences Innovation."
42. See Barry Bluestone, Peter Jordan, and Mark Sullivan, *Aircraft Industry Dynamics: An Analysis of Competition, Capital, and Labor* (Boston, MA: Auburn House, 1981).
43. Office of the State Auditor, "Audit of the Massachusetts Life Sciences Center Objectives, Scope and Methodology," Commonwealth of Massachusetts, February 14, 2018.
44. "Office of Performance Management and Oversight Fiscal 2014 Annual Report Guidance," MLSC, no date, mass.gov/doc/malife-science-centerfy14/download, 23.
45. "Avoiding Blank Checks: Creating Fiscally Sound State Tax Incentives," Pew Center on the States, December 2012, 5, table 1: Tools to Avoid Blank Checks Not Used Consistently; Windham-Bannister, Memo to Jay Gonzalez, 14.
46. RSM US LLP, "Financial Statements and Reports Required for Audits Performed in Accordance with Government Auditing Standards, June 30, 2019, and 2018," Massachusetts Life Sciences Center, September 30, 2019, 3.
47. Monya Baker, "Texas Cancer Institute Gets No Funds for New Grants in Proposed Budget," Nature.com, January 16, 2013.
48. Bluestone and Clayton-Matthews, "Life Sciences Innovation," 16, 37.

30. The Upstate New York Semiconductor Cluster

1. Charles W. Wessner and Thomas R. Howell, *Regional Renaissance: How New York's Capital Region Became a Nanotechnology Powerhouse* (Cham: Springer, 2020), 3–4.

2. Wessner and Howell, *Regional Renaissance*, 203, 213.

3. Wessner and Howell, *Regional Renaissance*, 202–3.

4. Wessner and Howell, *Regional Renaissance*, 211.

5. Wessner and Howell, *Regional Renaissance*, 210.

6. MIT: Carroll W. Pursell Jr., ed., *The Military Industrial Complex* (New York: Harper & Row, 1972), 242. RPI: Thomas Phelan, D. Michael Ross, and Carl Westerdahl, *Rensselaer: Where Imagination Achieves the Impossible* (Troy, NY: Rensselaer Polytechnic Institute, 1995), 123–4.

7. Charles W. Wessner, ed., *Best Practices in State and Regional Innovation Initiatives: Competing in the 21st Century* (Washington, DC: National Academies Press, 2013), 144.

8. Wessner and Howell, *Regional Renaissance*, 217–25.

9. Wessner and Howell, *Regional Renaissance*, 24–5.

10. Stuart W. Leslie and Robert H. Kargon, "Selling Silicon Valley: Frederick Terman's Model for Regional Advantage," *Business History Review* 70, no. 4 (Winter 1996): 435–72.

11. Stuart W. Leslie, "Regional Disadvantage: Replicating Silicon Valley in New York's Capital Region," *Technology and Culture* 42, no. 2 (April 2001): 236–64.

12. Wessner and Howell, *Regional Renaissance*, 33, 240.

13. Leslie, "Regional Disadvantage," 258.

14. Wessner and Howell, *Regional Renaissance*, 118.

15. Wessner and Howell, *Regional Renaissance*, 51.

16. Wessner and Howell, *Regional Renaissance*, 52.

17. Wessner and Howell, *Regional Renaissance*, 52.

18. Wessner and Howell, *Regional Renaissance*, 53.

19. "Rensselaer President Shirley Ann Jackson to Step Down in 2022, Concluding Historic Tenure," Rensselaer Polytechnic Institute, Press Release, June 25, 2021.

20. Wessner and Howell, *Regional Renaissance*, 27, 237.

21. Wessner and Howell, *Regional Renaissance*, 73, citing Eric Anderson, "A Magical Moment for Tech Valley," *Times Union* (Albany), May 12, 2006.

22. See, for example, Leslie, "Regional Disadvantage."

23. Leslie, "Regional Disadvantage," 261.

24. Wessner and Howell, *Regional Renaissance*, xix, 27.

25. Wessner and Howell, *Regional Renaissance*, 69.

26. "There hasn't been much federal investment in GlobalFoundries. The infrastructure here has all been New York State. There has been no federal money, no foundation money. It's all state money." Interview with Mike Russo, Director of Government Relations, GlobalFoundries, Malta, New York, April 3, 2013, quoted in Wessner, *Best Practices*, 156.

27. Richard Pérez-Peña, "SUNY Albany Gets $150 Million for Development of Microchips," April 24, 2001, nytimes.com/2001/04/24/nyregion/suny-albany-gets-150-million-for-development-of-microchips.html.

28. Michael A. Fury and Alain E. Kaloyeros, "Metallization for Microelectronics Program at the University at Albany: Leveraging a Long-Term Mentor Relationship," in *Proceedings of the Tenth Biennial University/Government/Industry Microelectronics Symposium, May 18–19, 1993, Research Triangle Park, North Carolina* (New York: Institute of Electrical and Electronics Engineers, 1993), 63.

29. Michael Tittnich et al., "A Year in the Life of Immersion Lithography Alpha Tool at Albany NanoTech," in *Proceedings Volume 6151: Emerging Lithographic*

Technologies X, ed. Michael J. Lercel (Bellingham, WA: SPIE–The International Society for Optical Engineering, 2006), 1–3.

30. Wessner and Howell, *Regional Renaissance*, 59.
31. Wessner and Howell, *Regional Renaissance*, 79.
32. Wessner and Howell, *Regional Renaissance*, 79–80.
33. Larry Rulison, "Region Wins in $1.6B IBM Pact," *Times Union* (Albany), July 16, 2008.
34. Wessner and Howell, *Regional Renaissance*, 71.
35. Wessner and Howell, *Regional Renaissance*, 81.
36. Wessner and Howell, *Regional Renaissance*, 65.
37. Tittnich et al., "A Year in the Life," 2. Also, Vibhu Jindal et al., "Getting Up to Speed with Roadmap Requirements for Extreme-UV Lithography," SPIE, April 19, 2011.
38. Wessner and Howell, *Regional Renaissance*, 66.
39. Good Jobs First Subsidy Tracker: Sematech, New York, 2008, goodjobsfirst.org/megadeals-largest-economic-development-subsidy-packages-ever-awarded-state-and-local-go.
40. Robin K. Cooper, "Sematech Moving Operations, 100 Jobs to Albany," *Albany Business Review*, October 12, 2010; James M. Odato, "Details of Agreement Emerge in Contract Documents," *Times Union* (Albany), May 11, 2007; "International Sematech Move Expected to Transform Albany Economy," *Austin Business Journal*, May 10, 2007.
41. "New York Gets Nanotech Institute," *Austin Business Journal*, January 3, 2006; "Albany Leads in Tiny Realm," *Times Union* (Albany), January 6, 2006.
42. Jack Lyne, "IBM's Big New York Compute: $1.5B Investment, 1,000 Jobs," *Site Selection*, August 2008.
43. Wessner and Howell, *Regional Renaissance*, 115.
44. Wessner and Howell, *Regional Renaissance*, 119.
45. Wessner and Howell, *Regional Renaissance*, 122.
46. Wessner and Howell, *Regional Renaissance*, 122.
47. Wessner and Howell, *Regional Renaissance*, 127.
48. "History of the Luther Forest," Luther Forest Technology Campus, web.archive.org/web/20220328133220/lutherforest.org/about_concept.php. Also, "The Saratoga Economic Development Corporation," saratogaspringsrebirth.com/index.php/articles/the-saratoga-economic-development-corporation.
49. Wessner and Howell, *Regional Renaissance*, 171.
50. Wessner and Howell, *Regional Renaissance*, 170.
51. Wessner and Howell, *Regional Renaissance*, 172.
52. "SUNY Poly and GlobalFoundries Announce New $500M R&D Program in Albany to Accelerate Next Generation Chip Technology," SUNY Polytechnic Institute, February 9, 2016.
53. "SUNY Poly and GlobalFoundries Announce," SUNY Polytechnic Institute, February 9, 2016.
54. Robin K. Cooper, "GlobalFoundries Will Invest Billions of Dollars to Develop Next Generation of Chips," *Albany Business Review*, September 15, 2016.
55. "IBM News Release: IBM Research Alliance Builds New Transistor for 5nm Technology," SUNY Polytechnic Institute, June 5, 2017.
56. Mark LaPedus, "GF Puts 7nm on Hold," *Semiconductor Engineering*, August 27, 2018.
57. Anton Shilov and Ian Cutress, "GlobalFoundries Stops All 7nm Development: Opts to Focus on Specialized Processes," AnandTech, August 27, 2018.
58. Rick Merritt, "GlobalFoundries Halts 7nm Work," *EE Times*, August 27, 2018.

59. Sebastian Moss, "IBM Sues GlobalFoundries over Dropping 7nm, Demands $2.5Bn," Data Center Dynamics, June 11, 2021.

60. Steve Howe, "What to Know about Wolfspeed and Its $1B Facility in Upstate New York," Observer-Dispatch (Utica), May 2, 2022.

61. Steve Lohr, "Micron Pledges Up to $100 Billion for Semiconductor Factory in New York," New York Times, October 4, 2022.

62. Luther Forest Business Park digital brochure, 2024, lfbusinesspark.com.

63. New York State Press Release, November 1, 2023, governor.ny.gov/news/governor-hochul-and-majority-leader-schumer-unveil-ttm-technologies-plans-invest-130-million. In 2020, TTM divested itself of four manufacturing plants in China. See "TTM Technologies, Inc. to Sell Four China Manufacturing Plants Comprising Its Mobility Business Unit," TTM Technologies press release, January 22, 2020.

64. Press Release, "Schumer Secures Commitment from South Korea," Office of Senator Charles Schumer, October 13, 2023, schumer.senate.gov/newsroom/press-releases/schumer-secures-commitment-from-south-korea-president-yoon-for-korea-to-partner-with-ny-creates-albany-nanotech-complex-for-advanced-semiconductor-research-and-development.

65. Jaspreet Gill, "CHIPS Are Down: DoD Awards $240M to Build 8 Tech Hubs, Official Warns Shutdown Would Be 'Crushing,'" Breaking Defense, September 20, 2023, breakingdefense.com/2023/09/chips-are-down-dod-awards-240m-to-build-8-tech-hubs-official-warns-shutdown-would-be-crushing.

66. "Mapping the Electronics and Electrical Equipment Sector in Scotland," AP Benson, January 1, 2012.

67. Wessner, Best Practices, 153.

68. Larry Rulison, "Feds Release Plans for National Chip Lab Being Pitched for Albany Nanotech," The Times-Union, April 25, 2023.

69. "2023–2024 Best Engineering Schools," US News & World Report.

70. Wessner and Howell, Regional Renaissance, 355.

71. Antonio Varas et al., "Government Incentives and US Competitiveness in Semiconductor Manufacturing," Semiconductor Industry Association and Boston Consulting Group, September 2020, 19.

72. Varas et al., "Government Incentives," 1.

73. "Building Resilient Supply Chains, Revitalizing American Manufacturing, and Fostering Broad-Based Growth: 100-Day Reviews under Executive Order 14017," The White House, June 2021, 11.

74. "Building Resilient Supply Chains," The White House, June 2021, 11.

75. "Taiwan Dangles US$335 Million to Woo Foreign Chip Makers," South China Morning Post, June 3, 2020.

76. Debby Wu, "Taiwan Passes Its Chips Act, Offers Tax Credits to Chipmakers," Bloomberg, January 8, 2023.

77. Sebastian Moss, "South Korea to Spend $451 Billion on Becoming a Semiconductor Manufacturing Giant," Data Center Dynamics, May 14, 2021.

78. Arjun Kharpal, "Samsung Aims to Make the World's Most Advanced Chips in 5 Years, as It Plays Catch Up with TSMC," CNBC, October 4, 2022.

79. Karen M. Sutter, "China's New Semiconductor Policies: Issues for Congress," Congressional Research Service, April 20, 2021, 4; Julie Zhu, "Exclusive: China Readying $143 Billion Package for Its Chip Firms in Face of U.S. Curbs," Reuters, December 13, 2022; "Battered by Covid, China Hits Pause on Giant Chip Spending Aimed at Rivaling US," Bloomberg News, January 3, 2023.

80. "Chips Act: Council Gives Its Final Approval," Council of the EU, July 25, 2023.

81. "2022 Fact Book," Semiconductor Industry Association.

82. "2020 Fact Book," Semiconductor Industry Association, 5, 7.
83. US Congress, Senate, "The Facilitating American-Built Semiconductors (FABS) Act," 117th Cong., 1st sess., introduced in Senate June 17, 2021, finance.senate .gov/imo/media/doc/FABS%20Act%20-%20One%20Pager.pdf.
84. Anton Shilov and Ian Cutress, "GlobalFoundries Stops"; Ian Cutress, "Intel's Process Roadmap to 2025: With 4nm, 3nm, 20A and 18A?!" AnandTech, July 26, 2021.
85. Chris Miller, *Chip War: The Fight for the World's Most Critical Technology* (New York: Scribner, 2022), 191–6.
86. Cheng Ting-Fang and Lauly Li, "Apple and Intel Become the First to Adopt TSMC's Latest Chip Tech," Nikkei Asia, July 2, 2021.
87. White House, Fact Sheet: President Biden Announces Up to $8.5 Billion Preliminary Agreement with Intel under the CHIPS & Science Act, March 20, 2024, whitehouse .gov/briefing-room/statements-releases/2024/03/20/fact-sheet-president-biden-announces-up-to-8-5-billion-preliminary-agreement-with-intel-under-the-chips-sci ence-act.

Recommendations: An Industrial Policy for the United States

1. Ganesh Sitaraman, "On Agency Structure," American Compass, June 10, 2020.
2. Fast Track Action Subcommittee on Critical and Emerging Technologies of the National Science and Technology Council, "Critical and Emerging Technologies List Update," Executive Office of the President of the United States, February 2022.
3. For an analysis of how these large, continuing inflows push the value of the dollar above the trade balancing level, see Jeff Ferry, "Fix the Dollar to Build Back Better," Coalition for a Prosperous America, November 2021.
4. For an example of this calculation, see Jeff Ferry, "New Study: Global Currency Misalignment Challenges US Reindustrialization Efforts," Coalition for a Prosperous America, February 7, 2022. For current levels of global currency misalignment, see "Currency Misalignment Monitor," "Coalition for a Prosperous America," prosperousamerica.org/currency-misalignment-monitor-july-2024.
5. The Government Accountability Office has a Science, Technology Assessment, and Analytics team. While this team makes a valuable contribution, technology assessment is just one of its four mandates, and it does not have staff specializing in this task. The Congressional Research Service also prepares reports on technology for Congress, but does not maintain a technology assessment capability.
6. For an early recommendation along similar lines, see "Remarks by Secretary Gates to the Business Executives for National Security on the US Export Control System," Department of Defense, April 20, 2010, sgp.fas.org/news/2010/04/gates-export .html.
7. Sitaraman, "On Agency Structure," 2.
8. The CHIPS Act increased the aggregate extramural research budgets of the participating agencies by approximately 50 percent, thus increasing the current aggregate SBIR/STTR funding of $4 billion by approximately the same percentage.
9. On average this will require that the current percentage allocations be increased by approximately one-third. Since the current allocation percentage applied to the enlarged aggregate research budget base will generate $6 billion for SBIR and STTR, a one-third increase in these percentages will generate the additional $2 billion.

10. This and a number of the following ideas involving the SBA are drawn from and more fully explained in the Committee on Small Business and Entrepreneurship's "SBA Reauthorization and Improvement Act of 2019, Section-by-Section Analysis," accessed February 4, 2023, rubio.senate.gov/wp-content/uploads/cache/files/7484023b-dc28-49b1-a251-383478d332ee/6E65795BC3306E93F868AF3F20054CE8.reauthorization-section-by-section-master-final.7.18.19.pdf. Some are also included in a 2021 bill cosponsored by Senator Rubio and Jim Risch (R-ID), the American Innovation and Manufacturing Act, rubio.senate.gov/public/index.cfm/2021/3/rubio-risch-introduce-bill-to-support-small-business-manufacturing-and-innovation.

11. "Directly" because, even with the SBA guarantee, the banks lending to SBICs have difficulty accepting newly developed manufacturing equipment for which there is no secondary market as collateral for loans. Email correspondence with Carroll Thomas, former acting associate director of innovation and industry services, NIST, and director of the Manufacturing Extension Partnership (MEP), including the MEP National Network.

12. Elizabeth B. Reynolds and Hiram Samel, "Manufacturing Startups," *Mechanical Engineering* 135, no. 11 (November 2013): 36–41.

13. Email correspondence with Zachary Mottl, president, Atlas Tool Works, Lyons, IL, and Carroll Thomas, former National Institute of Standards and Technology's acting associate director of innovation and industry services and director of the Manufacturing Extension Partnership (MEP), including the NIST MEP National Network.

14. See, for example, the Business Development Bank of Canada's Purchase Order Financing program, bdc.ca/en/financing/purchase-order-loan.

15. Jeff Ferry, "Chinese Manufacturers Could Earn Up to $125 Billion in US Renewable Energy Tax Credits," Coalition for a Prosperous America, April 18, 2023.

16. "R&D Tax Incentives: United States, 2021," Organisation for Economic Co-operation and Development (OECD), accessed February 12, 2023, oecd.org/sti/rd-tax-stats-united-states.pdf.

17. See Matthew Stepp and Robert T. Atkinson, "Creating a Collaborative R&D Tax Credit," Information Technology and Innovation Foundation, June 2011.

18. "Congress in its 2017 tax bill put in place a revenue raising provision (intended to be a placeholder) requiring R&D costs be amortized (over 5 years) and no longer expensed. This change in law requiring amortization – effective date January 1, 2022 – has placed a major tax burden on businesses." From Dean Zerbe, "R&D Tax Credit: An Update on a Lifeline for Small and Medium Business," *Forbes*, April 24, 2023, forbes.com/sites/deanzerbe/2023/04/24/rd-tax-credit–an-update-on-a-lifeline-for-small-and-medium-business/?sh=6558ca4944f7. As of this writing, the issue of amortization had not been addressed. See Cady Stanton, "House Republicans Urge Johnson to Move on Business Provisions," Tax Notes, November 30, 2023, taxnotes.com/featured-news/house-republicans-urge-johnson-move-business-provisions/2023/11/29/7hlp2.

19. US Congress, Senate, Stronger Patents Act of 2019, S. 2082, 116th Congress (2019–20), congress.gov/bill/116th-congress/senate-bill/2082.

20. See US Congress, Senate, Patent Eligibility Restoration Act of 2022, S. 4734, 117th Cong., 2d sess., introduced in Senate August 2, 2022, congress.gov/117/bills/s4734/BILLS-117s4734is.pdf.

21. Such reexaminations could formerly be petitioned by adversaries but did not involve them after that point.

22. The dollar would have to fall by approximately 17 percent while the Chinese yuan would have to rise against the dollar by approximately 22 percent, the Japanese yen by 40 percent, the euro by 27 percent, and the Korean won by 31 percent. The exact size of these adjustments will necessarily vary over time, but the study clearly demonstrates their order of magnitude and direction. No treaty obligations, including the IMF, forbid action to lower the value of the dollar when the trade balance is consistently negative. See Jeff Ferry, "New Study: Global Currency Misalignment Challenges US Reindustrialization Efforts," February 7, 2022.

23. S. 2357 (116th Congress). The proposal is derived from work done by John Hansen, a former World Bank economist and a member of the advisory board of the Coalition for a Prosperous America.

24. In fact, as CCI succeeds, the currency or securities of the manipulating country that it buys will appreciate and generate more dollars than they cost if and when the US decides to sell them. Some of the USD CCI injects into the forex market will be used to purchase US assets, goods and services. Any inflationary pressures created by such purchases would be offset through a) sales of bonds by the Treasury Department and/or the Federal Reserve from its large portfolio as well as b) Federal Reserve action to raise domestic interest rates. The tendency of these measures to draw more foreign private sector capital into the US and thus strengthen the USD would be effectively countered by increasing the MAC charge.

25. Economy-wide import quotas are another option, with a much higher certainty of result. However, such quotas would have to be set product by product (or at least industry by industry), a politically fraught and complex task, and would generate no revenue for the US government.

26. Under the GATT's Article XXVIII, which defines the WTO's procedure on this matter, the US can just inform other WTO countries that it is going to raise its tariffs and is free to then do so. The penalty is that the affected counterparties then have WTO permission to raise their own tariffs in response.

27. Per GATT Art. XII.

28. Michael Stumo, "Tariff Relief Hasn't Helped America's Poorest Trading Partners," Coalition for a Prosperous America, September 7, 2023, prosperousamerica.org/tariff-relief-hasnt-helped-americas-poorest-trading-partners. See also Charles Benoit, "General System of Preferences Renewal Would Delight China," Coalition for a Prosperous America, September 15, 2023, Parts III and IV, prosperousamerica.org/generalized-system-of-preferences-renewal-would-delight-china.

29. Tariff rate quotas permit a specified quantity of imported merchandise to be entered at a reduced rate of duty during the quota period. Once the tariff-rate quota limit is reached, goods may still enter, but at a higher rate of duty.

30. SMMs in these industries should be assisted in identifying and adopting the best available technology and business practices to improve productivity. Ideas for such assistance are presented in this chapter under "Support for Startups and Small Firms".

31. Because these imports are not counted in official trade totals, the actual trade deficit in 2021 was $128 billion (15 percent) higher than official figures show, causing the loss of an estimated 768,000 high-quality jobs. See Jeff Ferry, "Trade Deficit Is Worse Than We Thought: De Minimis Hides $128 Billion of US Imports," January 26, 2022, Coalition for a Prosperous America, and Charles Benoit, "Falsehoods and Facts: The Truth about De Minimis," August 14, 2023, Coalition for a Prosperous America. For an example of such reform, see a bipartisan bill introduced in 2023: the De Minimis Reciprocity Act of 2023,

accessed June 16, 2023, cassidy.senate.gov/imo/media/doc/de_minimis_bill.pdf and the accompanying press release, "Cassidy, Baldwin Introduce Bill to Stop China from Taking Advantage of Lax US Trade Laws," June 14, 2023, Bill Cassidy, MD, US Senator for Louisiana, cassidy.senate.gov/newsroom/press-releases/cassidy-baldwin-introduce-bill-to-stop-china-from-taking-advantage-of-lax-us-trade-laws.

32. In 2023, the US signed a Critical Materials Agreement with Japan that weakened the IRA's made-in-America requirements for EVs in return for coordination in strengthening critical battery minerals supply chains. See US–Japan Critical Materials Agreement, March 28, 2023, ustr.gov/sites/default/files/2023-03/US%20Japan%20Critical%20Minerals%20Agreement%202023%2003%2028.pdf.

33. Although transfers per se of such technologies are prohibited by export controls strengthened in 2022 and 2023, the active involvement of sophisticated US venture capitalists and multinational corporations can greatly accelerate foreign efforts to design, manufacture and market them at scale. Sarah Bauerle Danzman, "Testimony before the Senate Committee on Banking, Housing, and Urban Affairs Hearing on 'Examining Outbound Investment' toward a Balanced Outbound Investment Screening Regime," US Senate, September 29, 2022, banking.senate.gov/imo/media/doc/Danzman%20Testimony%209-29-22.pdf.

34. On August 9, 2023, President Biden issued an executive order directing the Treasury Department to issue regulations that will prohibit US venture capital and private equity firms, corporations, and others from making active investments in Chinese companies developing or manufacturing three technologies critical to advanced military, intelligence, surveillance, and cyber-enabled capabilities: semiconductors and microelectronics; quantum information technologies; and certain artificial intelligence systems. If effectively enforced, this rule will be an important step forward, but not a substitute for a reverse CFIUS with a mandate to screen investments in a broader although still limited set of technologies that are economically strategic but not directly related to the military, intelligence, and cyber-enabled capabilities covered by the order. See "Fact Sheet: President Biden Issues Executive Order Addressing United States Investments in Certain National Security Technologies and Products in Countries of Concern; Treasury Department Issues Advance Notice of Proposed Rulemaking to Enhance Transparency and Clarity and Solicit Comments on Scope of New Program," US Department of the Treasury, August 9, 2023.

35. With reserves of treasuries and other US securities in excess of $3 trillion, China is not short of hard currency. And, although it still has only about 10 percent of the accumulated capital per capita as developed nations, it has an effective system of suppressing consumption to generate capital for investment in favored industries. So stopping US investment is unlikely to prevent it from funneling large amounts of capital and other forms of support to these companies. But there is no reason the savings of US citizens, including those of our government employees and military, should make it easier for these enterprises to compete with American companies or contribute to the development of Chinese military and intelligence capabilities.

36. Authors' calculations from "U.S. Trade in Goods and Services by Selected Countries and Areas, 1999–present," Bureau of Economic Analysis, bea.gov/sites/default/files/2024-03/trad-geo-time-series-0124_0.xlsx, Table 3. China's percentage of our gross bilateral trade deficit – that is, the sum of all our individual deficits with nations with which we have a negative trade balance – is the appropriate measure, not the more-often-quoted China's percentage of our total trade deficit. The latter does not sum to 100 percent for any nation that, like the US, also runs surpluses with some nations. It

thus overstates the deficit contribution of any one deficit nation. Use of this metric does not imply that eliminating deficits with all countries is desirable; it simply more accurately tracks the relative contributions of different nations.

37. Chris Miller, *Chip War: The Fight for the World's Most Critical Technology* (New York: Scribner, 2022), 225–9.

SELECT BIBLIOGRAPHY

Abelshauser, Werner. *The Dynamics of German Industry: Germany's Path toward the New Economy and the American Challenge.* Oxford: Berghahn, 2005.

Abernathy, William J., and James M. Utterback. "Patterns of Industrial Innovation." *Technology Review* 80, no. 7 (June/July 1978): 41–7.

Acemoglu, Daron, David Autor, David Dorn, Gordon H. Hanson, and Brendan Price. "Import Competition and the Great US Employment Sag of the 2000s." *Journal of Labor Economics* 36, no. S1 (Part 2, no. 1) (January 2016): S141–S198.

Advanced Research Projects Agency – Energy (ARPA-E). "An Assessment of ARPA-E."

Agarwal, Manmohan, and John Whalley. "The 1991 Reforms, Indian Economic Growth, and Social Progress." Working Paper, National Bureau of Economic Research, May 2013.

Akhtar, Shayerah I., and Ian F. Fergusson. "The Trans-Pacific Partnership (TPP): Key Provisions and Issues for Congress." Congressional Research Service, June 14, 2016.

Alejandro, Carlos F. Díaz. *Essays on the Economic History of the Argentine Republic.* New Haven, CT: Yale University Press, 1970.

Allen, Christopher S. "Ideas, Institutions and Organized Capitalism: The German Model of Political Economy Twenty Years after Unification." *German Politics and Society* 28, no. 2 (Summer 2010): 130–50.

American Association for the Advancement of Science (AAAS). "Historical Trends in Federal R&D." 2023.

Amsden, Alice H. *Asia's Next Giant: South Korea and Late Industrialization.* New York: Oxford University Press, 1989.

Amsden, Alice H. *The Rise of "The Rest": Challenges to the West from Late-Industrializing Economies*. Oxford: Oxford University Press, 2001.

Anchordoguy, Marie. *Reprogramming Japan: The High Tech Crisis under Communitarian Capitalism*. Ithaca, NY: Cornell University Press, 2005.

Anderson, G. E. *Designated Drivers: How China Plans to Dominate the Global Auto Industry*. Singapore: John Wiley and Sons Singapore, 2012.

Arcand, Jean Louis, Enrico Berkes, and Ugo Panizza. "Too Much Finance?" *Journal of Economic Growth* 20, no. 2 (June 2015): 105–48.

Arnold, Zachary, Jesse Jenkins, and Ashley Lin. "Case Studies in American Innovation: A New Look at Government Involvement in Technological Development." Breakthrough Institute, April 2009.

Arthur, Brian. *Increasing Returns and Path Dependence in the Economy*. Foreword by Kenneth J. Arrow. Ann Arbor: University of Michigan Press, 1994.

Asker, John, Joan Farre-Mensa, and Alexander Ljungqvist. "Corporate Investment and Stock Market Listing: A Puzzle?" *Review of Financial Studies* 28, no. 2 (February 2015): 342–90.

Atkinson, Robert. "US Manufacturing Productivity Is Falling, and It's Cause for Alarm." *Industry Week*, July 12, 2021. bit.ly/4ejkgXU.

Atul, Kohli. "Where Do High Growth Political Economies Come From? The Japanese Lineage of Korea's 'Developmental State.'" *World Development* 22, no. 9 (1994): 1271–81.

Aujac, Henri. "An Introduction to French Industrial Policy." In *French Industrial Policy*, edited by William James Adams and Christopher Stoffaes. Washington, DC: Brookings Institution, 1986, 13–35.

Autor, David H., David Dorn, and Gordon H. Hanson. "The China Shock: Learning from Labor-Market Adjustment to Large Changes in Trade." *Annual Review of Economics* 8, no. 1 (January 2016): 205–40.

Autor, David H., David Dorn, and Gordon H. Hanson. "On the Persistence of the China Shock." Brookings Papers on Economic Activity, September 8, 2021.

Backer, John H. *Priming the German Economy: American Occupational Policies, 1945–1948*. Durham, NC: Duke University Press, 1971.

Badlam, Justin, Jared Cox, Adi Kumar, Nehal Mehta, Sara O'Rourke, and Julia Silvis. *The Inflation Reduction Act: Here's What's in It*. McKinsey & Company, October 24, 2022.

Badlam, Justin, Tony D'Emidio, Rob Dunn, Adi Kumar, and Sara O'Rourke. *The US Bipartisan Infrastructure Law: Breaking It Down*. McKinsey & Company, November 12, 2021.

Bailey, David, George Harte, and Roger Sugden. *Transnationals and Governments: Recent Policies in Japan, France, Germany, the United States and Britain*. London: Routledge, 1994.

Bairoch, Paul. *Economics and World History: Myths and Paradoxes.* Chicago, IL: University of Chicago Press, 1993.

Barnett, Correlli. *The Collapse of British Power.* New York: William Morrow, 1972.

Barnett, Correlli. *The Audit of War: The Illusion and Reality of Britain as a Great Nation.* London: Macmillan, 1986.

Bateman, Fred, and Thomas Weiss. *A Deplorable Scarcity: The Failure of Industrialization in the Slave Economy.* Chapel Hill: University of North Carolina Press, 1981.

Beffa, Jean-Louis. "Pour une Nouvelle Politique Industrielle." *République Française*, January 1, 2005. bit.ly/3Kukj5f.

Berle, Adolf A. *The American Economic Republic.* New York: Harcourt, Brace & World, 1963.

Bernstein, William J. *A Splendid Exchange: How Trade Shaped the World.* New York: Atlantic Monthly Press, 2008.

Black, Fred, and Matthew R. Keller, eds. *State of Innovation: The US Government's Role in Technology Development.* New York: Routledge, 2011.

Bluestone, Barry. *Life Sciences Innovation as a Catalyst for Economic Development.* Kitty and Michael Dukakis Center for Urban and Regional Policy at Northeastern University, 2013.

Bluestone, Barry, and Bennett Harrison. *The Deindustrialization of America: Plant Closings, Community Abandonment, and the Dismantling of Basic Industry.* New York: Basic Books, 1982.

Bluestone, Barry, Peter Jordan, and Mark Sullivan. *Aircraft Industry Dynamics: An Analysis of Competition, Capital, and Labor.* Boston, MA: Auburn House, 1981.

Boeing Japan. *Made with Japan: A Partnership on the Frontiers of Aerospace.* Tokyo: Boeing Japan, 2012.

Bonvillian, William. "DARPA and Its ARPA-E and IARPA Clones: A Unique Innovation Organization Model." *Industrial and Corporate Change* 27, no. 5 (October 2018): 908–9.

Bonvillian, William, and Peter L. Singer. *Advanced Manufacturing: The New American Innovation Policies.* Cambridge, MA: MIT Press, 2017.

Bonvillian, William, and Richard Van Atta. "ARPA-E and DARPA: Applying the DARPA Model to Energy Innovation." *Journal of Technology Transfer* 36, no. 5 (October 2011): 469–513.

Bonvillian, William B., and Charles Weiss. *Technological Innovation in Legacy Sectors.* New York: Oxford University Press, 2015.

Borrus, Michael. *Competing for Control: America's Stake in Microelectronics.* Cambridge, MA: Ballinger, 1988.

Borrus, Michael, Laura D'Andrea Tyson, and John Zysman. "Creating Advantage: How Government Policies Shape International Trade in the Semiconductor Industry." In *Strategic Trade Policy and the New International Economics*, edited by Paul R. Krugman. Cambridge, MA: MIT Press, 1986, 91–113.

Bown, Chad P. "Anatomy of a Flop: Why Trump's US–China Phase One Trade Deal Fell Short." Peterson Institute for International Economics, February 8, 2021.

Bown, Chad P., and Melina Kolb. "Trump's Trade War Timeline: An Up-to-Date Guide." Peterson Institute for International Economics, March 24, 2023. piie.com/blogs/trade-and-investment-policy-watch/trumps-trade-war-timeline-date-guide.

Brady, Dorothy S., ed. *Output, Employment, and Productivity in the United States after 1800*. New York: National Bureau of Economic Research, 1966.

Branscomb, Lewis M., and Philip E. Auerswald. "Between Invention and Innovation: An Analysis of Funding for Early-Stage Technology Development." National Institute of Standards and Technology, November 2002.

Braun, Hans-Joachim. *The German Economy in the Twentieth Century: The German Reich and the Federal Republic*. London: Routledge, 1990.

Brennan, James P., and Marcelo Rougier. *The Politics of National Capitalism: Perónism and the Argentine Bourgeoisie, 1946–1976*. University Park: Pennsylvania State University Press, 2009.

Brett, E. A. *The World Economy since the War*. Santa Barbara, CA: Praeger, 1985.

Bright, Charles D. *The Jet Makers: The Aerospace Industry from 1945 to 1972*. Lawrence: Regents Press of Kansas, 1978.

Brown, Sherrod. *Myths of Free Trade: Why America's Trade Policies Have Failed*. New York: New Press, 2004.

Brownlee, W. Elliot. "The Creation of the US Tariff Commission." In *A Centennial History of the United States Tariff Commission*, edited by Paul R. Bardos. Washington, DC: US International Trade Commission, 2017.

Burja, Samo. "China Tests Our Dream of an Automated Future." *Bismarck Brief*, Bismarck Analysis, June 1, 2022. brief.bismarckanalysis.com/p/china-tests-our-dream-of-an-automated.

Bush, Vannevar. *Science – The Endless Frontier: A Report to the President*. Washington, DC: US Government Printing Office, July 1945.

BusinessWeek Team. *The Reindustrialization of America*. New York: McGraw Hill, 1982.

Buxton, Martin, Steve Hanney, and Teri Jones. "Estimating the Economic Value to Societies of the Impact of Health Research: A Critical Review." *Bulletin of the World Health Organization* 82, no. 10 (October 2004): 733–9.

Cadars, Augusta, and Annie Badower. *La France Industries Services Depuis 1945*. Paris: Sirey, 1991.

Canis, Bill, and Brent D. Yacobucci. "The US Motor Vehicle Industry: Confronting a New Dynamic in the Global Economy." Congressional Research Service, March 26, 2010.

Capgemini. "Smart Factories: How Can Manufacturers Realize the Potential of Digital Industrial Revolution?" Digital Transformation Institute, May 15, 2017.

Chang, C. S. *The Japanese Auto Industry and the US Market*. New York: Praeger, 1981.

Chang, Ha-Joon. "The Political Economy of Industrial Policy in Korea." *Cambridge Journal of Economics* 17 (1993): 131–57.

Chatterjee, Anusuya, and Ross DeVol. "Estimating Long-Term Economic Returns of NIH Funding on Output in the Biosciences." Milken Institute, August 2012.

Chen, YiLi, and Paul Morris. "Is US Manufacturing Really Declining?" Federal Reserve Bank of St. Louis, April 11, 2017.

Chibber, Vivek. *Locked in Place: State-Building and Late Industrialization in India*. Princeton, NJ: Princeton University Press, 2003.

Chorev, Nitsan. *Remaking U.S. Trade Policy: From Protectionism to Globalization*. Ithaca, NY: Cornell University Press, 2007.

Chudnovsky, Daniel, and Andrés López. *The Elusive Quest for Growth in Argentina*. New York: Palgrave Macmillan, 2007.

Chung, Young-Iob. *South Korea in the Fast Lane: Economic Development and Capital Formation*. New York: Oxford University Press, 2007.

Cimoli, Mario, Giovanni Dosi, and Joseph E. Stiglitz, eds. *Industrial Policy and Development: The Political Economy of Capabilities Accumulation*. Oxford: Oxford University Press, 2009.

Cohen, Linda R., and Roger G. Noll. *The Technology Pork Barrel*. Washington, DC: Brookings Institution, 1991.

Cohen, Stephen S., and J. Bradford Delong. *Concrete Economics: The Hamilton Approach to Economic Growth and Policy*. Boston, MA: Harvard Business Review Press, 2016.

Cole, David C., and Yung Chul Park. *Financial Development in Korea, 1945–1978*. Boston, MA: Harvard University Press, 1983.

Comfort, Nicholas. *Surrender: How British Industry Gave Up the Ghost, 1952–2012*. London: Biteback, 2012.

Congressional Research Service. "Semiconductors: US Industry, Global Competition, and Federal Policy." October 26, 2020.

Congressional Research Service. "Manufacturing USA: Advanced Manufacturing Institutes and Network." March 3, 2021. sgp.fas.org/crs/misc/R46703.pdf.

Congressional Research Service. "The Buy American Act and Other Federal Procurement Domestic Content Restrictions." March 31, 2021.

Congressional Research Service. "China's New Semiconductor Policies: Issues for Congress." April 20, 2021. crsreports.congress.gov/product/pdf/R/R46767.

Congressional Research Service. "Federal Research and Development (R&D) Funding: FY2022, R46869." Updated January 19, 2022. crsreports.congress.gov/product/pdf/R/R46869.

Cooney, Stephen, and Brent D. Yacobucci. *US Automotive Industry: Policy Overview and Recent History*. New York: Novinka Books, 2007.

Cowan, Edward. "Carter's Economic Renewal Plan." *New York Times*, August 22, 1980.

Crandall, Robert W., and Kenneth Flamm. *Changing the Rules: Technological Change, International Competition, and Regulation in Communications*. Washington, DC: Brookings Institution Press, 1989.

Cusumano, Michael A. *The Japanese Automobile Industry: Technology and Management at Nissan and Toyota*. Cambridge, MA: Harvard University Press, 1985.

Cusumano, Michael A. "Manufacturing Innovation: Lessons from the Japanese Auto Industry." *MIT Sloan Management Review* 30, no. 1 (Fall 1988): 29–39.

Dallmeyer, Dorinda G. "The United States–Japan Semiconductor Accord of 1986: The Shortcomings of High-Tech Protectionism." *Maryland Journal of International Law* 13, no. 2 (1989): 180.

Dash, L. N. *World Bank and Economic Development of India*. New Delhi: A.P.H., 2000.

Davis, Leila. "Identifying the 'Financialization' of the Nonfinancial Corporation in the U.S. Economy: A Decomposition of Firm-Level Balance Sheets." *Journal of Post Keynesian Economics* 39, no. 1 (2016): 115–41.

Deeg, Richard. *Finance Capitalism Unveiled: Banks and the German Political Economy*. Ann Arbor: University of Michigan Press, 1999.

Defense Science Board. "Report of the Defense Science Board Task Force on Defense Semiconductor Dependency." February 1987.

Deloitte. "Manufacturing USA: A Third-Party Evaluation of Program Design and Progress." January 2017.

Díaz, Alejandro. *Economic History of the Argentine Republic*. First edition. A publication of the Economic Growth Center, Yale University. New Haven, CT: Yale University Press, 1970.

Dormois, Jean-Pierre. *The French Economy in the Twentieth Century*. Cambridge: Cambridge University Press, 2004.

Dosi, Giovanni, Laura D'Andrea Tyson, and John Zysman. "Trade, Technologies, and Development: A Framework for Discussing Japan." In Chalmers Johnson, *Politics and Productivity: The Real Story of Why Japan Works*. Cambridge, MA: Ballinger, 1989, 3–38.

Dowling, John Malcolm. *Future Perspectives on the Economic Development of Asia*. Advanced Research in Asian Economic Studies. World Scientific Illustrated edition. Singapore: World Scientific, 2008.

Dustmann Christian, Bernd Fitzenberger, Uta Schönberg, and Alexandra Spitz-Oener. "From Sick Man of Europe to Economic Superstar: Germany's Resurgent Economy." *Journal of Economic Perspectives* 28, no. 1 (Winter 2014): 167–88.

Ebner, Alexander. "Varieties of Capitalism and the Limits of Entrepreneurship Policy: Institutional Reform in Germany's Coordinated Market Economy." *Journal of Industry, Competition and Trade* 10, no. 3–4 (July 2010): 319–41.

ECHORD. "Robotics 2020: Strategic Research Agenda for Robotics in Europe." ECHORD: European Commission and euRobotics, Draft Ov42, November 10, 2013. bit.ly/4aMgtPJ.

Eckaus, Richard. "Planning in India." In *National Economic Planning*, edited by Max F. Millikan. Washington, DC: National Bureau of Economic Research, 1967.

Eckes, Jr., Alfred E. *Opening America's Market: U.S. Foreign Trade since 1776*. Chapel Hill: University of North Carolina Press, 1995.

Brown, Sherrod. *Myths of Free Trade: Why America's Trade Policies Have Failed*. New York: New Press, 2004, 180.

Eckes, Jr., Alfred E. "The Tariff Commission in Transition, 1917–74." In *A Centennial History of the United States Tariff Commission*, edited by Paul R. Bardos. Washington, DC: US International Trade Commission, 2017, 221.

Edquist, Charles, ed. *Systems of Innovation: Technologies, Institutions and Organization*. London: Pinter, 1997.

Ekonomisuto Editorial Board, ed. *Sengo Sangyo Shi e no Shogen (Interviews toward a History of Postwar Industry)*. Tokyo: Mainichi Shimbunsha, 1977.

Electronics Industry Association of Japan. *A Look at 50 Years of the Japanese Electronics Industry*. Tokyo: Electronics Industry Association of Japan, 1998.

Epstein, Gerald, and Juan Antonio Montecino. "Overcharged: The High Cost of High Finance." Roosevelt Institute, 2016.

European Commission. "EU–US Agreement on Large Civil Aircraft 1992: Key Facts and Figures." October 6, 2004.

Executive Office of the President, National Science and Technology Council, Advanced Manufacturing National Program Office. *National Network for Manufacturing Innovation Program Strategic Plan*. Scotts Valley, CA: CreateSpace Independent Publishing Platform, September 2016.

Fallows, James. *Looking at the Sun: The Rise of the New East Asian Economic and Political System*. New York: Pantheon Books, 1994.

Farndon, John. *India Booms: The Breathtaking Development and Influence of Modern India*. London: Virgin Books, 2007.

Federal Ministry for Economic Affairs and Energy. "National Industrial Strategy 2030: Strategic Guidelines for a German and European Industrial Policy." February 2019.

Federal Ministry of Economics. "The High-Tech Gründerfonds." htgf.de/en/about-us.

Federal Ministry of Education and Research. "Federal Government Report on the High-Tech Strategy 2025." Berlin, Germany. bit.ly/4e9j7Sv.

Federal Reserve. "Financial Accounts of the United States – Z.1." Federal Reserve Statistical Release, September 9, 2022.

Feldenkirchen, Wilfried. "Germany: The Invention of Interventionism." In *European Industrial Policy: The Twentieth Century Experience*, edited by James Foreman-Peck and Giovanni Federico. Oxford: Oxford University Press, 1999.

Felipe, Jesus, ed. *Development and Modern Industrial Policy in Practice: Issues and Country Experiences*. Cheltenham: Edward Elgar, 2015.

Ferleger, Louis, and William Lazonick. "The Managerial Revolution and the Developmental State: The Case of US Agriculture." *Business and Economic History*, 22, no. 2 (Winter 1993): 67–98.

Ferry, Jeff. "New Study: Global Currency Misalignment Challenges US Reindustrialization Efforts." Coalition for a Prosperous America, February 7, 2022.

Ferry, Jeff, and Steven Byers. "CPA Briefing Paper: Why Economic Forecasts of the Effects of Trade Action Are Consistently Wrong." Coalition for a Prosperous America, June 2019.

Fingleton, Eamonn. *Blindside: Why Japan Is Still on Track to Overtake the US by the Year 2000*. New York: Houghton Mifflin Buttonwood Press, 1995.

Flamm, Kenneth. *Mismanaged Trade? Strategic Policy and the Semiconductor Industry*. Washington, DC: Brookings Institution Press, 1996.

Flath, David. "A Perspective on Japanese Trade Policy and Japan–US Trade Friction." Department of Economics, North Carolina State University, October 1998.

Fletcher, Ian. *Free Trade Doesn't Work: What Should Replace It and Why*. Washington, DC: US Business and Industry Council, 2010.

Fong, Glenn R. "The Future of Pentagon–Industry Collaboration in Technology Development." In *The Political Economy of Defense: Issues and Perspectives*, edited by Andrew L. Ross. Westport, CT: Greenwood Press, 1991.

Foroohar, Rana. *Makers and Takers: The Rise of Finance and the Fall of American Business*. New York: Crown Business, 2016.

Frederick, Stacy, and Gary Gereffi. "Upgrading and Restructuring in the Global Apparel Value Chain: Why China and Asia Are Outperforming Mexico and Central America." *International Journal of Technological Learning, Innovation and Development* 4, nos. 1–3 (August 2011): 67–95.

Fried, Jesse, and Charles Wang. "Short Termism and Capital Flows." *Review of Corporate Finance Studies* 8, no. 1 (March 2019): 207–33.

Fröbel, Folker, Jürgen Heinrichs, and Otto Kreye. *The New International Division of Labour: Structural Unemployment in Industrialised Countries and Industrialisation in Developing Countries.* Cambridge: Cambridge University Press, 1980.

Fuchs, Erica R. H. "Rethinking the Role of the State in Technology Development." *Research Policy* 39, no. 9 (November 2010): 1133–47.

Gaddy, Benjamin, Varun Sivaram, and Francis O'Sullivan. "Venture Capital and Cleantech: The Wrong Model for Clean Energy Innovation." MIT Energy Initiative Working Paper, July 2016. energy.mit.edu/publication/venture-capital-cleantech.

Gallo, Marcy E. "Defense Advanced Research Projects Agency: Overview and Issues for Congress." Defense Advanced Research Projects Agency, Congressional Research Service, August 19, 2021. darpa.mil/about-us/offices.

Gallois, Louis. "Pacte pour la Compétitivité de l'industrie Française." *République Française* 5 November 5, 2012.

Gansler, Jacques S., and William Lucyshyn. "Independent Research and Development (IR&D): The Challenges Continue." Naval Postgraduate School, October 2015.

Gansler, Jacques S., William Lucyshyn, and John Rigilano. "The Impact of Globalization on the US Defense Industrial Base." Center for Public Policy and Private Enterprise, October 2013.

Gao, Bai. *Economic Ideology and Japanese Industrial Policy: Developmentalism from 1931 to 1965.* Cambridge: Cambridge University Press, 1997.

Garten, Jeffrey E. *A Cold Peace: America, Japan, Germany and the Struggle for Supremacy.* New York: New York Times Books, 1992.

Genther, Phyllis A. *A History of Japan's Government–Business Relationship: The Passenger Car Industry.* Ann Arbor: University of Michigan Press, 1990.

German Federal Ministry for Economic Affairs and Climate Action. "A Modern Industrial Policy." bmwk.de/Redaktion/EN/Dossier/modern-industry-policy.html.

Germann, Julian. "Global Rivalries, Corporate Interests, and Germany's 'National Industrial Strategy 2030.'" *Review of International Political Economy* 2022. doi.org/10.1080/09692290.2022.2130958.

Germany Works. "Industrie 4.0: Revolutionizing the Hidden Champions of Germany." germanyworks.com/news/industrie-40-revolutionising-thehidden-champions-of-germany.

Giersch, Herbert, ed. *Emerging Technologies: Consequences for Economic Growth, Structural Change, and Employment.* Tubingen: J. C. B. Mohr, 1982.

Godin, Benoit. "The Linear Model of Innovation: The Historical Construction of an Analytical Framework." *Science, Technology, and Human Values* 31 no. 6 (November 2006): 659–60.

Gomory, Ralph E. "A Ricardo Model with Economies of Scale." *Proceedings of the National Academy of Sciences*, 88, no. 18 (September 1991): 8267–71.

Gomory, Ralph E., and William J. Baumol. *Global Trade and Conflicting National Interests*. Cambridge, MA: MIT Press, 2000.

Goodwin, Doris. "The Way We Won: America's Economic Breakthrough during World War II." *The American Prospect*, December 19, 2001.

Goolsbee, Austan, and Chad Syverson. "The Strange and Awful Path of Productivity in the US Construction Sector." Working Paper 30845, National Bureau of Economic Research, revised February 2023.

Gordon, Robert J. *The Rise and Fall of American Growth*. Princeton, NJ: Princeton University Press, 2016.

Görg, Holger, and Aoife Hanley. "Globalization: Implications for Firms in Germany." Working Papers 04/2017, German Council of Economic Experts/ Sachverständigenrat zur Begutachtung der gesamtwirtschaftlichen Entwicklung, 2017.

Government of India, Department of Pharmaceuticals. "Annual Report 2022–23." bit.ly/3Vt7z5e. June 20, 2023.

Government of India, Ministry of Commerce & Industry, Department of Industrial Policy & Promotion. "National Manufacturing Policy." November 4, 2011.

Government of India, Ministry of Finance. "Policy of Strategic Disinvestment Announced: Clear Roadmap for Strategic and Non-strategic Sectors." February 1, 2021.

Government of India, Ministry of Industry. "Statement of Industrial Policy." July 4, 1991.

Government of India, Planning Commission. "The Manufacturing Plan: Strategies for Accelerating Growth of Manufacturing in India in the 12th Five Year Plan and Beyond." New Delhi, 2011.

Graham, Edward M. *Reforming Korea's Industrial Conglomerates*. Washington, DC: Peterson Institute for International Economics, 2003.

Graham, Frank D. "Some Aspects of Protection Further Considered." *Quarterly Journal of Economics* 37, no.2 (February 1923).

Graham Jr., Otis L. *Losing Time: The Industrial Policy Debate*. Cambridge, MA: Harvard University Press, 1992.

Greenwood, Robin, and David Scharfstein. "The Growth of Finance." *Journal of Economic Perspectives* 27, no. 2 (Spring 2013).

Grimes, William W. *Unmaking the Japanese Miracle, Macroeconomic Politics, 1985–2000*. Ithaca, NY: Cornell University Press, 2001.

Hall, Peter A. *Governing the Economy: The Politics of State Intervention in Britain and France*. New York: Oxford University Press, 1986.

Hall, Peter A., and David Soskice, eds. *Varieties of Capitalism: The Institutional Foundations of Comparative Advantage*. Oxford: Oxford University Press, 2001.

Hamada Mori, and Matsumo Shintaro Okawa. "The Overview of the Economic Security Promotion Bill and Its Impact on Business." Center for Information on Security Trades Control, February 28, 2022. cistec.or.jp/service/zdata_gai-tame_kaisei2019/20220228-eng.pdf.

Hamilton, Alexander. *Papers on Public Credit, Commerce and Finance*. Indianapolis, IN: Bobbs-Merrill, 1957.

Hanson, A. H. *The Process of Planning: A Study of India's Five-Year Plans 1950–1964*. London: Oxford University Press, 1966.

Harrison, Mark, ed. *The Economics of World War II: Six Great Powers in International Comparison*. Cambridge: Cambridge University Press, 1998.

Hart-Landsberg, Martin. *The Rush to Development*. New York: Monthly Review Press, 1993.

Hart-Smith, Dr. L. J. "Out-Sourced Profits: The Cornerstone of Successful Subcontracting." Third Annual Technical Excellence Symposium, February 14–15, 2001.

Head, Keith. "Infant Industry Protection in the Steel Rail Industry." *Journal of International Economics* 37 (November 1994): 141–165.

Helleiner, Eric. *The Neomercantilists: A Global Intellectual History*. Ithaca, NY: Cornell University Press, 2021.

Helper, Susan, Timothy Krueger, and Howard Wial. "Why Does Manufacturing Matter? Which Manufacturing Matters? A Policy Framework." Brookings Institution, February 2012.

Henderson, Dan Fenno. *Foreign Enterprise in Japan: Laws and Policies*. Chapel Hill: University of North Caroline Press, 1973.

Henderson, Rebecca M., and Richard G. Newell, eds. *Accelerating Energy Innovation: Insights from Multiple Sectors*. Chicago, IL: University of Chicago Press, 2011.

Heritage, Andrew. "Tariff Incidence in the Real World: Why Consumers (Mostly) Didn't Pay the Steel Tariffs." Coalition for a Prosperous America, October 20, 2021.

Hirschman, Albert O. *The Strategy of Economic Development*. New Haven, CT: Yale University Press, 1958.

Hisao, Kumagai, ed. *Nihon no Sangyo Soshiki Ron Vol. I*. Tokyo: Chuo Koron Sha, 1973.

Hobday, Michael. "Export-Led Technology Development in the Four Dragons: The Case of Electronics." *Development and Change* 25, no. 2 (1994): 333–61.

Hof, Robert D. "Lessons from Sematech." *MIT Technology Review*, July 25, 2011.

Homburg, Christian, ed. *Structure and Dynamics of the German Mittelstand.* Heidelberg: Physica, 1999.

Houseman, Susan. "Is American Manufacturing in Decline?" W. E. Upjohn Institute for Employment Research, October 2016.

Houseman, Susan, Christopher Kurz, Paul Lengermann, and Benjamin Mandel. "Offshoring Bias in US Manufacturing: Implications for Productivity and Value Added." Board of Governors of the Federal Reserve System, September 2010.

Hsu, Allen. "ITRI Pushes Technology Sector to New Frontier of Innovation." *Taiwan Today*, October 18, 2007.

Hughes, Jonathan, and Louis P. Cain. *American Economic History*. Fifth edition. Reading, MA: Addison-Wesley, 1998.

Hull, Callie, comp. "Industrial Research Laboratories of the United States, including Consulting Research Laboratories." Bulletin no. 118. Washington, DC: National Academy of Sciences, National Research Council, July 1946.

Hyun-hee, Lee, Sung-soo Park, and Yoon Nae-hyun. *New History of Korea*. Seoul: Jimoondang, 2005.

Hyung-A, Kim. *Korea's Development under Park Chung Hee: Rapid Industrialization, 1961–1979*. London: Routledge Curzon, 2004.

Industrial Technology Research Institute. *ITRI Annual Report 2021*. Hsinchu, Taiwan: Industrial Technology Research Institute, 2022.

Ingrassia, Paul. *Crash Course: The American Automobile Industry's Road from Glory to Disaster*. New York: Random House, 2010.

Institute for Security & Development Policy. *Made in China 2025*. Washington, DC: Institute for Security & Development Policy, 2018.

Intarakumnerd, Patarapong, and Akira Goto. "Role of Public Research Institutes in National Innovation Systems in Industrialized Countries." *Research Policy* 47, no. 7 (September 2018): 1309–20.

International Federation of Robotics. "World Robotics R&D Programs." Executive Summary, April 2021. bit.ly/4bWu08q.

Irwin, Douglas A. "The GATT's Contribution to Economic Recovery in Post-war Western Europe." International Finance Discussion Papers, no. 442, Board of Governors of the Federal Reserve System, March 1993.

Irwin, Douglas A. "The US–Japan Semiconductor Trade Conflict." In *The Political Economy of Trade Protection*, edited by Anne O. Krueger. Chicago, IL: University of Chicago Press, 1996.

Irwin, Douglas A. "Historical Aspects of US Trade Policy." NBER Reporter (Summer 2006): 17. nber.org/sites/default/files/2021-08/summer06.pdf.

Irwin, Douglas A. *Clashing over Commerce: A History of U.S. Trade Policy*. Chicago, IL: University of Chicago Press, 2017.

Irwin, Douglas A. "From Hermit Kingdom to Miracle on the Han: Policy Decisions That Transformed South Korea into an Export Powerhouse." NBER Working Paper No. 29299, National Bureau of Economic Research, September 2021.

Jaffe, Adam B., and Josh Lerner. *Innovation and Its Discontents*. Princeton, NJ: Princeton University Press, 2004.

Japan Cabinet Office. "Moonshot Research and Development Program." cao.go.jp/cstp/english/moonshot/top.html.

Johnson, C. Donald. *The Wealth of a Nation: A History of Trade Politics in America*. New York: Oxford University Press, 2018.

Johnson, Chalmers. *Japan's Public Policy Companies*. Washington, DC: American Enterprise Institute–Hoover Policy Studies, 1977.

Johnson, Chalmers. *MITI and the Japanese Miracle: The Growth of Industrial Policy, 1925–1975*. Stanford, CA: Stanford University Press, 1982.

Joshi, Vijay. *India's Long Road*. Oxford: Oxford University Press, 2017.

Kahn, Herman, and Thomas Pepper. *The Japanese Challenge: The Success and Failure of Economic Success*. New York: Thomas Y. Crowell, 1979.

Kang, David C. *Crony Capitalism: Corruption and Development in South Korea and the Philippines*. New York: Cambridge University Press, 2002.

Kaplan, Steven. "Are US Companies Too Short-Term Oriented? Some Thoughts." National Bureau of Economic Research, June 2017.

Kawahito, Kiyoshi. *The Japanese Steel Industry*. New York: Praeger, 1972.

Keck, Otto. "The National System for Technical Innovation in Germany." In *National Innovation Systems: A Comparative Analysis*, edited by Richard R. Nelson. New York: Oxford University Press, 1993, 142–7.

Kehoe, Timothy J., T. N. Srinivasan, and John Whalley, eds. *Frontiers in Applied General Equilibrium Modeling: Essays in Honor of Herbert Scarf*. Cambridge: Cambridge University Press, 2005.

Keisuke, Amakasa. *Denshi Rikkoku Nippon (The Establishment of Japan as an Electronics Nation)*. Tokyo: Shashoku Shobo, 1991.

Keller, Maryann. *Collision: GM, Toyota, Volkswagen, and the Race to Own the 21st Century*. New York: Currency Doubleday, 1993.

Keller, William W. *Arm in Arm: The Political Economy of the Global Arms Trade*. New York: Basic Books, 1995.

Keynes, John Maynard. *The General Theory of Employment, Interest, and Money*. New York: First Harvest/Harcourt, 1964.

Kim, Byung-Kook, and Ezra F. Vogel, eds. *The Park Chung Hee Era: The Transformation of South Korea*. Cambridge, MA: Harvard University Press, 2011.

Klier, Thomas. "From Tail Fins to Hybrids: How Detroit Lost Its Dominance of the US Auto Market." *Economic Perspectives* 33, no. 2 (May 2009): 2–17.

Klug, Adam. "Why Chamberlain Failed and Bismarck Succeeded: The Political Economy of Tariffs in British and German Elections." *European Review of Economic History* (August 2001).

Kodres, Laura E. "What Is Shadow Banking?" *Finance & Development* 50, no. 2 (June 2013).

Kogyo, Denshi. *30 Nenshi (Thirty-Year History of the Electronics Industry)*. Tokyo: Nihon Denshi Kikai Kogyokai, 1979.

Kohli, Atul. *State-Directed Development: Political Power and Industrialization in the Global Periphery*. New York: Cambridge University Press.

Komiya, Ryutaro, Masahiro Okuno, and Kotaro Suzumura, eds. *Industrial Policy of Japan*. Tokyo: Academic Press, 1988.

Koopmann, Georg. "German Foreign Economic Policy in the Age of Globalisation." HWWA-Diskussionspapier No. 56. Hamburg: HWWA-Institut für Wirtschaftsforschung, 1998.

Kota, Sridhar, Justin Talbot-Zorn, and Tom Mahoney. "How the US Can Rebuild Its Capacity to Innovate." *Harvard Business Review*, October 23, 2018.

Krafcik, John F. "Triumph of the Lean Production System." *Sloan Management Review* 30, no. 1 (Fall 1988).

Kruger, A. O., ed. *Economic Policy Reforms and the Indian Economy*. Chicago, IL: University of Chicago Press, 2002.

Krugman, Paul R. "Targeted Industrial Policies: Theory and Evidence." Economic Policy Symposium-Jackson Hole, Federal Reserve Bank of Kansas City (1983): 123–76.

Kuisel, Richard F. *Capitalism and the State in Modern France: Renovation and Economic Management in the Twentieth Century*. Cambridge: Cambridge University Press, 1981.

Kumar, Ravi. "Understanding the German Mittelstand's Contribution towards Making Germany a Manufacturing World Leader." *Medium*, Product, Platforms, Business & Innovation in Industry 4.0/IIoT, March 23, 2019.

Ladika, Tomislav, and Zacharias Sautner. "Managerial Short-Termism and Investment: Evidence from Accelerated Option Vesting." *Review of Finance* 24, no. 2 (2020): 305–44.

Lake, David A. *Power, Protection and Free Trade: International Sources of US Commercial Strategy, 1887–1939*. Ithaca, NY: Cornell University Press, 1988.

Lalvani, Kartar. *The Making of India: The Untold Story of British Enterprise*. London: Bloomsbury, 2016.

Lambright, W. Henry. "'Managing 'Big Science': A Case Study of the Human Genome Project." In *Leaders*, edited by Mark A. Abramson and Kevin Bacon. Lanham, MD: Rowman & Littlefield, 2001.

Larsen, Jeffrey A., and Robert M. Shelala II. *Rearming at the Dawn of the Cold War: Louis Johnson, George Marshall, and Robert Lovett, 1949–1952*. Washington, DC: National Defense University Press, 2012.

LaSalle, Jones Lang. *Life Sciences Cluster Report: Global 2011*. Northeastern University and Boston Foundation, November 30, 2011.

Lawrence, Paul R., and Mark A. Abramson. *What Government Does: How Political Executives Manage*. Lanham, MD: Rowman & Littlefield, 2014.

Lawrence, Paul, and Davis Dwyer. *Renewing American Industry*. New York: Free Press, 1983.

Lazonick, William. "Profits without Prosperity." *Harvard Business Review*. September 2014.

Leffler, Melvyn P. *A Preponderance of Power: National Security, the Truman Administration, and the Cold War*. Stanford, CA: Stanford University Press, 1992.

Leonard, Will E., and F. David Foster. "The Substantive and Institutional Evolution of the U.S. Tariff Commission/U.S. International Trade Commission (1917–2016)." In *A Centennial History of the United States Tariff Commission*, edited by Paul R. Bardos. Washington, DC: US International Trade Commission, 2017, 129–30.

Leslie, Stuart W. "Regional Disadvantage: Replicating Silicon Valley in New York's Capital Region." *Technology and Culture* 42, no. 2 (April 2001): 236–64.

Leslie, Stuart W., and Robert H. Kargon. "Selling Silicon Valley: Frederick Terman's Model for Regional Advantage." *Business History Review* 70, no. 4 (Winter 1996): 435–72.

Levi-Faur, David. "Friedrich List and the Political Economy of the Nation-State." *Review of International Political Economy*, 4, no. 1 (Spring 1997): 154–78.

Lewis, Paul. H. *The Crisis of Argentine Capitalism*. Chapel Hill: University of North Carolina Press, 1990.

Lewis, William W. *The Power of Productivity: Wealth, Poverty, and the Threat to Global Stability*. Chicago, IL: University of Chicago Press, 2004.

Li, Cheng. "The Powerful Factions among China's Rulers." *BBC News*, November 6, 2012.

Lie, John. *Han Unbound: The Political Economy of South Korea*. Stanford, CA: Stanford University Press, 1998.

Lim, Suk-Jun. "Politics of Industrialization: Formation of Divergent Industrial Orders in Korea and Taiwan." PhD dissertation, University of Chicago, 1997.

Lim, Wonhyuk. "The Development of Korea's Electronics Industry during Its Formative Years (1966–1979)." KDI School of Public Policy and Management, 2016.

Lin, Otto Chui Chau. *Innovation and Entrepreneurship: Choice and Challenge*. Singapore: World Scientific, 2018.

Lincoln, Edward J. *Japan's Industrial Policies*. Washington, DC: Japan Economic Institute of America, 1984.

Lind, Michael. *Land of Promise: An Economic History of the United States*. New York: HarperCollins, 2012.

Lipsey, Richard G., and Kenneth I. Carlaw. "Industrial Policies: Common Not Rare." *Social Science Research Network*, September 2020. doi:10.2139/ssrn.3854149.

Liu, Chang-Yuan. "Government's Role in Developing a High-Tech Industry: The Case of Taiwan's Semiconductor Industry." *Technovation* 13, no. 5 (July 1993): 306.

Lodge, George C., and Ezra F. Vogel. *Ideology and National Competitiveness: An Analysis of Nine Countries*. Cambridge, MA: Harvard Business School Press, 1987.

López-Claros, Augusto, ed. *The Innovation for Development Report 2009–2010: Strengthening Innovation for the Prosperity of Nations*. London: Palgrave MacMillan, 2010.

Lovett, William A., Alfred E. Eckes Jr., and Richard L. Brinkman. *U.S. Trade Policy: History, Theory, and the WTO*. Armonk, NY: M. E. Sharpe, 2004.

Luther Forest Technology Campus. "History of the Luther Forest." web.archive .org/web/20220328133220/lutherforest.org/about_concept.php.

Lutz, Robert A. *Car Guys vs. Bean Counters: The Battle for the Soul of American Business*. New York: Portfolio Books, 2011.

Lynn, Leonard L. *How Japan Innovates: A Comparison with the US in the Case of Oxygen Steelmaking*. Boulder, CO: Westview Press, 1982.

Maddison, A. *Chinese Economic Performance in the Long Run*. Development Centre Studies. Paris: Organisation for Economic Co-operation and Development, 1998.

Magaziner, Ira C., and Thomas M. Hout. *Japanese Industrial Policy*. London: Policy Studies Institute, 1980.

Magaziner, Ira, and Robert Reich. *Minding America's Business: The Decline and Rise of the American Economy*. New York: Harcourt Brace Jovanovich, 1982.

Mair, Stefan, Friedolin Strack, and Ferdinand Schaff, eds. *Partner and Systemic Competitor: How Do We Deal with China's State-Controlled Economy?* Berlin: Federation of German Industries (BDI), January 2019.

Majumdar, Sumit. *Lost Glory: India's Capitalism Story*. Oxford: Oxford University Press, 2018.

MAPI Foundation. "How Important Is US Manufacturing Today?" bit.ly/ 3Ks8Djo.

Martello, Robert. *Midnight Ride, Industrial Dawn: Paul Revere and the Growth of American Enterprise*. Baltimore, MD: Johns Hopkins University Press, 2010.

Mason, J. W. "Understanding Short-Termism: Questions and Consequences." Roosevelt Institute, November 6, 2015.

Massachusetts Life Sciences Center, TEConomy Partners, LLC and Mass Economics. "Public–Private Partnerships in Action: The Statewide Impact of the Massachusetts Life Sciences Center on the Life Sciences Ecosystem." 2018.

Matthews, R. C. O., C. H. Feinstein, and J. C. Odling-Smee. *British Economic Growth 1856–1973*. Stanford, CA: Stanford University Press, 1982.

McDonald, Oonagh. "The Repeal of the Glass–Steagall Act: Myth and Reality." CATO Institute, November 16, 2016.

McGaughey, Ewan. "The Codetermination Bargains: The History of German Corporate and Labour Law." LSE Law, Society and Economy Working Papers, No. 10/2015, London School of Economics and Political Science, 2015.

McGregor, James. "China's Drive for 'Indigenous Innovation': A Web of Industrial Policies." US Chamber of Commerce, July 2010.

McGregor, James L. *No Ancient Wisdom, No Followers*. Westport, CT: Prospecta Press, 2012.

McKinsey & Company. "The Inflation Reduction Act: Here's What's in It." October 24, 2022. mck.co/4bLW9PF.

McKinsey Global Institute. *Jobs Lost, Jobs Gained: Workforce Transitions in a Time of Automation*. McKinsey & Company, December 2017.

McMillan, Houston Johnson V. "Taking Off: The Politics and Culture of American Aviation, 1920–1939." PhD diss., University of Tennessee, Knoxville, May 2011.

Michaels, Kevin. *AeroDynamic: Inside the High-Stakes Global Jetliner Ecosystem*. Reston, VA: American Institute of Aeronautics and Astronautics, 2018.

Milewski, Simon Korwin, Kiran Jude Fernandes, and Matthew Paul Mount. "Exploring Technological Process Innovation from a Lifecycle Perspective." *International Journal of Operations and Production Management* 35, no. 9 (September 7, 2015): 1312–31.

Miller, Chris. *Chip War: The Fight for the World's Most Critical Technology*. New York: Simon & Schuster, 2022.

Millstein, James E. "Decline in an Expanding Industry: Japanese Competition in Color Television." In *American Industry in International Competition*, edited by John Zysman and Laura Tyson. Ithaca, NY: Cornell University Press, 1983, 106–141.

Ministère de la Recherche et de l'Industrie. *Une Politique Industrielle pour la France: Actes des Journées de Travail des 15 et 16 novembre 1982*. Paris: La Documentation Française, 1982.

Minsky, Hyman. *Stabilizing an Unstable Economy*. New York: McGraw-Hill, 1986.

Miotti, Luis, and Frederique Sachwald. "Growth in France: 1950–2030: The Innovation Challenge." Institut Français des Relations Internationales, November 2004.

Moskowitz, Karl. *From Patron to Partner: The Development of US–Korean Business and Trade Relations.* Lanham, MD: Lexington Books, 1984.

Mowery, David C. "Federal Policy and the Development of Semiconductors, Computer Hardware, and Computer Software: A Policy Model for Climate Change R&D?" In *Accelerating Energy Innovation: Insights from Multiple Sectors,* edited by Rebecca M. Henderson and Richard G. Newell. Chicago, IL: University of Chicago Press, 2011.

Mowery, David, ed. *The International Computer Software Industry.* New York: Oxford University Press, 1996.

Mowery, David C., and Nathan Rosenberg. *Technology and the Pursuit of Economic Growth.* New York: Cambridge University Press, 1989.

Murmann, Johann Peter. *Knowledge and Competitive Advantage: The Coevolution of Firms, Technology, and National Institutions.* Cambridge: Cambridge University Press, 2003.

Nakagawa, Yasuzō. "NTT gijutsu suimyaku: Kyodai jitsuyōka kenkyūjo ni kaketa otokotachi (NTT's Technological Veins)." *Tōyō Keizai Shinpōsha* (January 1, 1990): 119, 138.

Nakayama, Wataru, William Boulton, and Michael Pecht. *The Japanese Electronics Industry.* New York: Chapman and Hall/CRC Press, 1999.

Nam, Hwasook. *Building Ships, Building a Nation: Korea's Democratic Unionism under Park Chung Hee.* Seattle: University of Washington Press, 2009.

National Academies of Sciences. *DoD Engagement with Its Manufacturing Innovation Institutes: Phase 2 Study Final Report.* Washington, DC: National Academies Press, 2021.

National Academies of Sciences, Engineering, and Medicine. "An Assessment of ARPA-E." Congressional Research Service. Washington, DC: National Academies Press, 2017. https://doi.org/10.17226/24778.

National Academies of Sciences, Engineering, and Medicine. "Revisiting the Manufacturing USA Institutes: Proceedings of a Workshop." Congressional Research Service. Washington, DC: National Academies Press, 2019. doi.org/10.17226/25420.

National Academies of Sciences, Engineering, and Medicine. "Strategic Long-Term Participation by DoD in Its Manufacturing USA Institutes." Congressional Research Service. Washington, DC: National Academies Press, 2019. doi.org/10.17226/25417.

National Academies of Sciences, Engineering, and Medicine. *A Quadrennial Review of the National Nanotechnology Initiative.* Washington, DC: National Academies Press, 2020.

National Defense University, Industrial College of the Armed Forces. "Electronics Industry Study Report: Semiconductors and the Defense Electronics." 2003.

National Nanotechnology Coordinated Infrastructure (NNCI). *NNCI Coordinating Office Annual Report: Year 2*. National Nanotechnology Coordinated Infrastructure, NSF Award 1626153. February 14, 2018.

National Research Council. *Energy Research at DOE: Was It Worth It? Energy Efficiency and Fossil Energy Research 1978 to 2000*. Washington, DC: National Academies Press, 2001.

National Research Council. *An Assessment of the SBIR Program, National Research Council*. Washington, DC: National Academies Press, 2008.

National Research Council. *21st Century Manufacturing: The Role of the Manufacturing Extension Partnership Program*. Washington, DC: National Academies Press, 2013.

National Research Council and Charles W. Wessner. *New York's Nanotechnology Model: Building the Innovation Economy*. Washington, DC: National Academies Press, 2013.

National Science and Technology Council. "A National Strategic Plan for Advanced Manufacturing." Executive Office of the President, February 2012.

National Science and Technology Council. "National Strategy for Advanced Manufacturing." White House, October 2022.

National Science and Technology Council, Committee on Science of the National Science, Subcommittee on Advanced Manufacturing. *National Strategy for Advanced Manufacturing*. Washington, DC: National Science and Technology Council, 2022.

National Science Board and National Science Foundation. "Academic Research and Development: NSB-2021-3." Science and Engineering Indicators 2022, September 14, 2021.

National Science Foundation. "Research and Development: U.S. Trends and International Comparisons." April 2022. ncses.nsf.gov/pubs/nsb20225/cross-national-comparisons-of-r-d-performance.

Nelson, Richard R., ed. *National Innovation Systems: A Comparative Analysis*. New York: Oxford University Press, 1993.

"Nihon Choki Shinyo Ginko, Chogin Chosa Geppo (Industrial Bank of Japan Monthly Survey)." May 1966.

Northrup, Cynthia, Turney Clark, and Elaine C. Prange, eds. *Encyclopedia of Tariffs and Trade in US History*. Westport, CT: Greenwood Press, 2003.

Nutzenadel, A., and C. Grabas. *Industrial Policy in Europe after 1945: Wealth, Power, and Economic Development in the Cold War*. Basingstoke: Palgrave Macmillan, 2014.

O'Brien, Patrick, and Roland Quinault, eds. *The Industrial Revolution and British Society*. Cambridge: Cambridge University Press, 1993.

Office of the Under Secretary of Defense for Research and Engineering. "Report of the Defense Science Board 1980 Summer Study Panel on Industrial Responsiveness." January 1981.

Office of the US Trade Representative. "Fact Check: 'Special 301' on Intellectual Property." Washington, DC: Office of the US Trade Representative, May 25, 1989.

Office of the US Trade Representative. "Findings of the Investigation into China's Acts, Policies, and Practices related to Technology Transfer, Intellectual Property, and Innovation Under Section 301 of the Trade Act of 1974." Washington, DC: Executive Office of the President, Office of the United States Trade Representative, March 22, 2018, 9.

Ohanian, Lee E. "The Macroeconomic Effects of War Finance in the United States: World War II and the Korean War." *American Economic Review* 87, no. 1 (March 1997): 25.

Okazaki, Tetsuji, and Masahiro Okuno-Fujiwara, eds. *The Japanese Economic System and Its Historical Origins.* New York: Oxford University Press, 1999.

O'Mahony, Mary. *Britain's Productivity Performance 1950–1996: An International Perspective.* London: National Institute for Economic & Social Research, 1999.

Organisation for Economic Co-operation and Development (OECD), Council Working Party on Shipbuilding. *Peer Review of the Korean Shipbuilding Industry and Related Government Policies.* Paris: Organisation for Economic Co-operation and Development, 2014.

Orhangazi, Özgür. "Financialization and Capital Accumulation in the Non-financial Corporate Sector: A Theoretical and Empirical Investigation on the U.S. Economy: 1973–2003." *Cambridge Journal of Economics* 32, no. 6 (November 2008): 863–86.

Owen, Geoffrey. *From Empire to Europe: The Decline and Revival of British Industry since the Second World War.* London: HarperCollins, 2000.

Palley, Thomas I. "Rethinking Trade and Trade Policy: Gomory, Baumol, and Samuelson on Comparative Advantage." Levy Economics Institute of Bard College, Public Policy Brief No. 86, October 2006.

Panagariya, Arvind. *India: The Emerging Giant.* Oxford: Oxford University Press, 2008.

Panagariya, Arvind. *New India: Reclaiming the Lost Glory.* Oxford: Oxford University Press, 2020.

Paolera, Gerardo Della, and Alan M. Taylor, eds. *A New Economic History of Argentina.* Cambridge: Cambridge University Press, 2003.

Patrick, Hugh, and Henry Rosovsky, eds. *Asia's New Giant.* Washington, DC: Brookings Institution, 1976.

Pattillo, Donald M. *Pushing the Envelope: The American Aircraft Industry.* Ann Arbor: University of Michigan Press, 1998.

Peart, Daniel. *Lobbyists and the Making of US Tariff Policy, 1816–1861.* Baltimore, MD: Johns Hopkins University Press, 2018.

Pekkanen, Robert J., and Saadia M. Pekkanen, eds. *The Oxford Handbook of Japanese Politics.* New York: Oxford University Press, 2021.

Peskin, Lawrence A. *Manufacturing Revolution: The Intellectual Origins of Early American History.* Baltimore, MD: Johns Hopkins University Press, 2003.

Peskin, Lawrence A., and Edmund F. Wehrle. *America and the World: Culture, Commerce, Conflict.* Baltimore, MD: Johns Hopkins University Press, 2012.

Phillips, Kevin P. "US Industrial Policy: Inevitable and Ineffective." *Harvard Business Review* (July–August 1992).

Pincus, Jonathan J. *Pressure Groups and Politics in Antebellum Tariffs.* New York: Columbia University Press, 1977.

Pisano, Gary P., and Willy C. Shih. "Does America Really Need Manufacturing?" *Harvard Business Review*, March 2012.

Pisano, Gary P., and Willy C. Shih. "Restoring American Competitiveness." *Harvard Business Review* 87, no. 7–8 (2009): 114–25.

Porter, Michael E. *The Competitive Advantage of Nations.* New York: Free Press, 1990.

Porter, Michael. "Why America Needs an Economic Strategy." *Bloomberg Business Week*, October 29, 2008.

President's Council of Advisors on Science and Technology. "Report to the President on Capturing Domestic Competitive Advantage in Advanced Manufacturing." July 2012.

President's Council of Advisors on Science and Technology. "Report to the President: Accelerating US Advanced Manufacturing." October 2014.

President's Council of Advisors on Science and Technology, Office of Science and Technology Policy. "Report to the President on Ensuring American Leadership in Advanced Manufacturing." June 2011.

Prestowitz, Clyde V., Ronald A. Morse, and Alan Tonelson. *Powernomics: Economics and Strategy after the Cold War.* Washington, DC: Madison Books, 1991.

Pursell Jr., Carroll W., ed. *The Military Industrial Complex.* New York: Harper & Row, 1972.

Rattner, Steven. *Overhaul: An Insider's Account of the Obama Administration's Emergency Rescue of the Auto Industry.* Boston, MA: Mariner Books, 2011.

Reinert, Erik. "International Trade and the Economic Mechanisms of Underdevelopment." PhD Thesis, Cornell University, May 1980.

Reinert, Erik. "Catching Up from Way Behind: A Third World Perspective on First World History." In *The Dynamics of Technology, Trade and Growth*, edited by Jan Fagerberg, Bart Verspagen, and G. N. von Tunzelmann. Cheltenham: Edward Elgar, 1994, 168–97.

Reinert, Erik S. "Competitiveness and Its Predecessors: A 500-Year Cross-National Perspective." *Studies in Technology, Innovation and Economic Policy* 12 (1994).

Reinert, Erik. "The Role of the State in Economic Growth." *Journal of Economic Studies* 26, no. 4/5 (August 1999): 268–326.

Reinert, Erik. *How Rich Countries Got Rich and Why Poor Countries Stay Poor.* London: Constable, 2007.

Ricardo, David. *The Principles of Political Economy and Taxation.* Mineola, NY: Dover, 2004.

Roberts, Adam. *Superfast Primetime Ultimate Nation* London: Profile Books, 2017.

Rodrik, Dani. *Has Globalization Gone Too Far?* Washington, DC: Institute for International Economics, 1997.

Rogowski, Ronald. *Commerce and Coalitions: How Trade Affects Domestic Political Alignments.* Princeton, NJ: Princeton University Press, 1989.

Roland, Alex, and Philip Shiman. *Strategic Computing: DARPA and the Quest for Machine Intelligence, 1983–1993.* Cambridge, MA: MIT Press, 2002.

Rosenberg, Nathan. *Technology and American Economic Growth.* New York: Harper and Row, 1972.

Rosenstein-Rodan, N. "Problems of Industrialisation of Eastern and South-Eastern Europe." *Economic Journal* (June–September 1943): 202–11.

Ross, Andrew L., ed. *The Political Economy of Defense: Issues and Perspectives.* Westport, CT: Greenwood Press, 1991.

Rowe, Brian, and Martin Ducheny. "The Power to Fly: An Engineer's Life." American Institute of Aeronautics and Astronautics, Reston, VA, November 1, 2004.

Rowe, Kenneth W. *Mathew Carey: A Study in American Economic Development.* Baltimore, MD: Johns Hopkins University Press, 1933.

Ruttan, Vernon W. *Is War Necessary for Economic Growth? Military Procurement and Technology Development.* New York: Oxford University Press, 2006.

Salvatore, Dominick, ed. *The New Protectionist Threat to World Welfare.* New York: Elsevier Science, 1987.

Salvatore, Dominick, ed. *Protection and World Welfare.* Cambridge: Cambridge University Press, 1993.

Samuels, Richard J. *"Rich Nation, Strong Army": National Security and Technological Transformation of Japan.* Ithaca, NY: Cornell University Press, 1994.

Samuelson, Paul A. "Where Ricardo and Mill Rebut and Confirm Arguments of Mainstream Economists Supporting Globalization." *Journal of Economic Perspectives*, 18, no. 3 (Summer 2004): 135–46.

Santarcángelo, Juan E., Daniel Schteingart, and Fernando Porta. "Industrial Policy in Argentina, Brazil, Chile and Mexico: A Comparative Approach." *Revue Interventions Économiques* 59 (January 2018): 1–42.

Sasse, Eberhard, and Andre Habisch, eds. *The German Chambers of Commerce and Industry*. Berlin: Springer, 2021.

Saxonhouse, Gary, and Kozo Yamamura, eds. *Law and Trade Issues of the Japanese Economy*. Seattle: University of Washington Press, 1986.

Schaede, Ulrike. *Choose and Focus: Japanese Business Strategies for the 21st Century*. Ithaca, NY: Cornell University Press, 2008.

Schmidt, Vivien A. *From State to Market? The Transformation of French Business and Government*. Cambridge: Cambridge University Press, 1996.

Schnietz, Karen E. "The Institutional Foundation of US Trade Policy: Revisiting Explanations for the 1934 Reciprocal Trade Agreement Act." *Journal of Policy History* 12, no. 4 (October 2000): 417–444.

Scott, Robert E. "The Manufacturing Footprint and the Importance of US Manufacturing Jobs." Economic Policy Institute, January 22, 2015.

Scott, Robert E. "Growth in US–China Trade Deficit between 2001 and 2015 Cost 3.4 Million Jobs." Economic Policy Institute, January 31, 2017.

Sen, Kunal. "Why Did the Elephant Start to Trot? India's Growth Acceleration Re-examined." *Economic and Political Weekly* 42, no. 43 (2007): 37–47.

Senior Supervisor's Group. "Risk Management Lessons from the Global Banking Crisis of 2008." US Securities & Exchange Commission, October 21, 2009.

Shinohara, Myohei. *Industrial Growth, Trade and Dynamic Patterns in the Japanese Economy*. Tokyo: University of Tokyo Press, 1982.

Shiu, Frank. "The Present and the Future of TW–EU Cooperation." Industrial Technology Research Institute, December 9, 2022.

Shonfield, Andrew. *Modern Capitalism: The Changing Balance of Public and Private Power*. London: Oxford University Press, 1965.

Simpson, Mike. "Strengthening US Manufacturing: Manufacturing USA and the Manufacturing Extension Partnership." National Institute of Standards and Technology, March 24, 2022.

Singer, Peter L. "Federally Supported Innovations." Information Technology & Innovation Foundation (ITIF), February 2014.

Singer, Peter L., and William B. Bonvillian. "'Innovation Orchards': Helping Tech Start-Ups Scale." Information Technology & Innovation Foundation, March 27, 2017.

Smith, N. Craig, and David Rönnegard. "Shareholder Primary, Corporate Social Responsibility, and the Role of Business Schools." *Journal of Business Ethics* 134, no. 3 (March 2016): 463–78.

Solow, Robert M. "Science and Ideology in Economics." *The Public Interest* 21 (Fall 1970): 94–107.

Stein, Judith. *Pivotal Decade: How the United States Traded Factories for Finance in the 1970s*. New Haven, CT: Yale University Press, 2010.

Stoffaës, Christian. "Industrial Policy in the High-Tech Industries." In *French Industrial Policy*, edited by William James Adams and Christian Stoffaës. Washington, DC: Brookings Institution, 1986.

Studwell, Joe. *How Asia Works: Success and Failure in the World's Most Dynamic Region*. New York: Grove Press, 2013.

Subramanian, Arvind, and Josh Felman. "India's Stalled Rise." *Foreign Affairs*, January/February 2022.

Takafusa, Nakamura. *The Postwar Japanese Economy: Its Development and Structure*, translated by Jacqueline Kaminski. Tokyo: Tokyo University Press, 1981.

Tankersley, Jim. "Trump's Washing Machine Tariffs Stung Consumers While Lifting Corporate Profits." *New York Times*, April 21, 2019.

Tassey, Gregory. *The Technology Imperative*. Northampton, MA: Edward Elgar, 2007.

Teunissen, Jan Joost, and Age Akkerman, eds. *The Crisis That Was Not Prevented: Lessons for Argentina, the IMF, and Globalisation*. The Hague: FONDAD, 2003.

Thelen, Kathleen. *How Institutions Evolve: The Political Economy of Skills in Germany, Britain, the United States, and Japan*. Cambridge: Cambridge University Press, 2004.

Thurow, Lester. *Head to Head: The Coming Economic Battle among Japan, Europe, and America*. New York: William Morrow, 1992.

Tiberghien, Yves. *Entrepreneurial States: Reforming Corporate Governance in France, Japan, and Korea* Ithaca, NY: Cornell University Press, 2007.

Tilly, Richard, and Paul J. J. Welfens, eds. *European Economic Integration as a Challenge to Industry and Government: Contemporary and Historical Perspectives on International Economic Dynamics*. Berlin: Springer, 1996.

Tudor, Daniel. *Korea: The Impossible Country*. North Clarendon, VT : Tuttle, 2012.

Tung, An-Chi. "Taiwan's Semiconductor Industry: What the State Did and Did Not." *Review of Development Economics* 5, no. 2 (June 2001).

Tyson, Laura D'Andrea. *Who's Bashing Whom? Trade Conflict in High-Technology Industries*. Washington, DC: Institute for International Economics, 1993.

Tyson, Laura D'Andrea, and Pei-Hsiung Chin. "McDonnell Douglas and Taiwan Aerospace: A Strategic Perspective on the National Interest in the Commercial Aircraft Industry." *Journal of Policy Analysis and Management* 11, no. 4 (Autumn 1992): 697–701.

Tyson, Laura D'Andrea, and David Yoffie. "Semiconductors: From Manipulated to Managed Trade." Berkeley Roundtable on the International Economy, working paper 47 (August 1991).

Ueno, Hiroya, and Hiromichi Muto. "The Automobile Industry of Japan." *Japanese Economic Studies* 3, no. 1 (Fall 1974).

US Department of Defense. "Assessing and Strengthening the Manufacturing and Defense Industrial Base and Supply Chain Resiliency of the United States: Report to President Donald J. Trump by the Interagency Task Force in Fulfillment of Executive Order 13806." September 2018.

US Government Accountability Office. "Federal Research: Lessons Learned from Sematech." September 28, 1992.

US House Select Committee on the CCP. Hearing on the Strategic Competition between the United States and the Chinese Communist Party entitled "Leveling the Playing Field: How to Counter the CCP's Economic Aggression." May 17, 2023.

US Office of Management and Budget. *Historical Tables: Budget of the U.S. Government, Fiscal Year 2010*. Washington, DC: US Government Printing Office, 2009.

US Office of the President, National Science and Technology Council. "Critical and Emerging Technologies List Update." February 2022.

US Office of Technology Assessment. *Competing Economies: America, Europe, and the Pacific Rim*. Washington, DC: US Government Printing Office, 1991.

Van Atta, Richard, Alethia CookIvars Gutmanis, Michael J. Lippitz, Jasper Lupo, Rob Mahoney, and Jack H. Nunn. *Transformation and Transition: DARPA's Role in Fostering an Emerging Revolution in Military Affairs. Volume 2*. Alexandria, VA: Institute for Defense Analyses, 2003.

Varas, Antonio, and Raj Varadarajan. "How Restrictions to Trade with China Could End US Leadership in Semiconductors." Boston Consulting Group, March 2020.

Varas, Antonio, Raj Varadarajan, Jimmy Goodrich, and Falan Yinug. "Government Incentives and US Competitiveness in Semiconductor Manufacturing." Semiconductor Industry Association and Boston Consulting Group, September 2020.

Vatter, Harold G. *The U.S. Economy in World War II*. New York: Columbia University Press, 1985.

Wade, Robert. *Governing the Market: Economic Theory and the Role of Government in East Asian Economic Development*. Princeton, NJ: Princeton University Press, 1990.

Warren, Elizabeth. "A Plan for Economic Patriotism." *Medium*, June 4, 2019.

Weinberger, Sharon. *The Imagineers of War: The Untold Story of DARPA, the Pentagon Agency That Changed the World.* New York: Alfred A. Knopf, 2017.

Wessner, Charles W. *21st Century Manufacturing: The Role of the Manufacturing Extension Partnership Program.* Washington, DC: National Academies Press, 2013.

Wessner, Charles W., ed. *Securing the Future: Regional and National Programs to Support the Semiconductor Industry.* Washington, DC: National Academies Press, 2003.

Wessner, Charles W., ed. *Best Practices in State and Regional Innovation Initiatives: Competing in the 21st Century.* Washington, DC: National Academies Press, 2013.

Wessner, Charles W., and Thomas R. Howell. *Regional Renaissance: How New York's Capital Region Became a Nanotechnology Powerhouse.* Berlin: Springer Nature Switzerland AG, 2020.

Whiteside, Noel, and Robert Salais, eds. *Governance, Industry and Labour Markets in Britain and France: The Modernizing State in the Mid-Twentieth Century.* New York: Routledge, 1998.

Wolf, Marvin J. *The Japanese Conspiracy: The Plot to Dominate Industry World-Wide and How to Deal with It.* New York: Empire Books, 1983.

Womack, James P., Daniel T. Jones, and Daniel Roos. *The Machine That Changed the World.* London: Simon & Schuster UK, 2007.

Woo, Jung-en. *Race to the Swift: State and Finance in Korean Industrialization.* New York: Columbia University Press 1991.

Woo-Cummings, Meredith, ed. *The Developmental State.* First edition. Ithaca, NY: Cornell University Press, 1999.

Wübbeke, Jost, Mirjam Meissner, Max J. Zenglein, Jaqueline Ives, and Björn Conrad. "Made in China 2025: The Making of a High-Tech Superpower and Consequences for Industrial Countries." *MERICS*, August 12, 2016.

Yamamura, Kozo. *A Challenge to Free Trade? Japanese Industrial Targeting in the Computer and Semiconductor Industries.* Society for Japanese Studies, 1990.

Yates, Brock W. *The Decline and Fall of the American Automobile Industry.* New York: Empire Books, 1983.

Yergin, Daniel. *The Prize: The Epic Quest for Oil, Money & Power.* New York: Simon & Schuster, 1991.

You-il, Lee, and Kyung Tae Lee. "Economic Nationalism and Globalization in South Korea: A Critical Insight." *Asian Perspective* 39, no. 1 (January–March 2015): 125–51.

Young, John A. *Global Competition, The New Reality, Results of the President's Commission on Industrial Competitiveness, Volume I: 1985*. Washington, DC: National Academies Press, 1986.

Zysman, John. *Governments, Markets and Growth: Financial Systems and the Politics of Industrial Change*. Ithaca, NY: Cornell University Press, 1983.

Zysman, John, and Laura Tyson. *American Industry in International Competition: Government Policies and Corporate Strategies*. Ithaca, NY: Cornell University Press, 1983, 106–41.

INDEX